INTERNATIONAL DICTIONARY OF

UNIVERSITY HISTORIES

INTERNATIONAL DICTIONARY OF
UNIVERSITY HISTORIES

Edited by

CAROL SUMMERFIELD

and

MARY ELIZABETH DEVINE

FITZROY DEARBORN PUBLISHERS
CHICAGO AND LONDON

Copyright © 1998 by
FITZROY DEARBORN PUBLISHERS

FITZROY DEARBORN PUBLISHERS
70 East Walton Street
Chicago, Illinois 60611
USA

or

11 Rathbone Place
London W1P 1DE
England

**British Library Cataloguing in Publication Data
and Library of Congress Cataloging in Publication Data is available.**

ISBN 1884964230

First published in the USA and UK 1998
Typeset by Print Means Inc., New York, New York
Printed by Braun-Brumfield Inc., Ann Arbor, Michigan
Cover Design by Peter Aristedes, Chicago Advertising and Design, Chicago, Illinois

CONTENTS

EDITOR'S NOTE

Fitzroy Dearborn's *International Dictionary of University Histories* provides detailed and accurate information on selected universities, colleges, and research centers from many nations around the world. Although there are more than 200 institutions represented, this book does not intend to provide a comprehensive listing of universities of the world. Rather, the institutions presented here have been selected as representatives of educational institutions that have arisen to fulfill different educational needs, regional demands, and philosophical goals. Whether political, religious, ideological, or communal in foundation, however, these universities work toward one common goal—increasing knowledge and expertise.

The *International Dictionary of University Histories* covers universities that have been in operation for 1,000 years, such as Al-Azhar in Cairo, Egypt, founded in 972, and much newer institutions, such as the New School for Social Research in New York City, founded in 1919. There are schools that provide education to a broad base of students who are interested in a wide range of studies, such as the many U.S. universities produced by the Morrill Act of 1862, which granted 30,000 acres to 70 institutions that became the foundation of the nation's state university system. Others arose to meet the needs of under-represented groups. Mount Holyoke became the first women's college in the United States in 1837. Atlanta University, now part of the Atlanta University Center in Georgia, was founded in 1865 to educate the newly freed black slaves. Gallaudet, in Washington D.C., centers its educational needs on the deaf community. Laval University in Canada provides the largest higher-education francophone institution outside of Europe. Brandeis provided educational opportunities to Jewish students when options at other American universities were limited.

Each entry in the *International Dictionary of University Histories* outlines the history of the institution, providing descriptive and contact information at the beginning of each entry, and an essay that unfolds chronologically, emphasizing the particular importance of the institution and the role it has historically strived to fill as well as the role it continues to fill for its community. The essays provide the origins of the institutions, with the original names and founders, and cover the shifting focus of the universities, and education in general, over time. The entries end with an annotated list, when available, of books published in English on the history of the university or aspects that relate to that history.

Our contributors and editors have made extensive efforts to ensure the accuracy of the information presented here: sources include the offices of the universities, published books, primary documents, and web sites for various institutions. The universities have been particularly generous with publications, brochures, photos (many of which are included here), and personal assistance. Without their contributions, this publication would have been much more difficult to execute. Many individuals, too many to name here, provided help above and beyond the call of their jobs.

CONTRIBUTORS

Bob Adams
Robin F. Bachin
Andrés Bernasconi
Marla G. Bosworth
Jeanne Munn Bracken
Phyllis Brandano
Justine H. Carson
Richard Allen Chapman
Ron Joseph Chepesiuk
Sharmishtha Roy Chowdhury
Kathleen M. Conley
Bill Coyle
Mary Elizabeth Devine
Diana D'India
Sina Dubovoy
Junelle Dupee
Stephen Ellingson
Theodore A. Emery
Christine Farrow
Christopher D. Felker
Genevieve Cora Fraser
José María García Garduno
Judith B. Gerber
Sandra Gladfelter
Vera-Jane Goodin
Lin Grensing-Pophal
Patrick Heenan
Pam Hollister
Wolfgang Holtkamp
Marcia R. Horowitz
Christopher Hoyt
Christopher Hudson
Mary Jane Isles
Sybil Jack
Frank M. Jossi
Patrice M. Kane
Manon Lamontagne

Monique Lamontagne
Sherry Crane LaRue
Joseph Edward Lee
A.H.T. Levi
Claudia Levi
Daniel C. Levy
Darlene Maciuba-Koppel
Christine Margerum
Edward S. Margerum
Mary McNulty
Cindy Mertz
Marcela Mollis
Michael Mundt
Sharon Messinger Nery
Robert S. Newman
Bette Noble
Cynthia L. Ogorek
Antonella D. Olson
April A. Oswald
Anne C. Paterson
Michael D. Phillips
Michele Picozzi
Ruth Pittman
Karen Price
Warren D. Rees
Beth A. Rillema
Jan Rogozinski
Udo Sautter
Robert P. Schoenberg
Fran Shonfeld Sherman
Carol Shilakowsky
Jan Bitsch Steffensen
Susan R. Stone
Charlene Strickland
James Sullivan
Rosemarie Cardillicchio Sultan
Laura Sutliff

Elizabeth Taggart
Jeffrey M. Tegge
J. Cameron Tew
Alexander Urbiel
Celeste A. Voyer
Tim J. Watts

Lawrence William White
Carol Whitney
Joan Wilder
Melanie Wilson
Wendy Sowder Wippel

PREFATORY ESSAY: THE UNIVERSITY MOVEMENT

As it is now used, the term *university* derives from the Latin abbreviation of the phrase *universitas magistrorum et scholarium* (university of masters and students), which denoted the corporate aspect of a community of teachers and scholars, shortened to the simple *universitas* by the late fourteenth century. The Latin term *universitas* succeeded the term *studium generale,* used in the thirteenth century for a group of teachers and students who had come together, normally from different places, and who were usually claiming the sort of protection and exemptions often afforded in medieval towns to guilds of immigrant craftsmen practicing the same trade and to other communities of foreigners, often businessmen.

The earliest "universities" were national associations of foreign students attending the law schools at Bologna in the late twelfth century, forerunners of the "nations" into which student bodies were divided in late medieval universities. At Vercelli, for instance, there were Italian, English, Provençal, and German groups, and at Paris a French "nation," which included Spaniards, Italians, and Greeks; the Picard nation, which included students from the Low Countries; the Norman nation; and the English nation, which included German-speakers. The teaching body consisted of those on whom membership had been conferred by the grant, normally from ecclesiastical authority, of a license to teach. Any recognized teaching corporation possessed the right to award its own degrees, a privilege that is still regarded as constitutive of university status.

Naturally, the bestowal of guild privileges on any group of scholars, or scholars and teachers, depended on recognition by civil authorities. Since the *studia* overwhelmingly consisted of clerical communities, they were also often licensed by ecclesiastical authority, which could reasonably wish to control the teaching of theology and the subjects (such as astronomy) that bore on it. Much in the early history of the universities is illustrated by the fact that the Paris masters put themselves under papal protection, ultimately finding themselves exempt from the jurisdiction of the bishop of Paris and the chancellor of Notre Dame but bound from 1246 to a considerable measure of papal control. At Oxford, on the other hand, where the university did not grow out of a cluster of monastic and cathedral schools, the ultimate authority was retained by the king.

Oxford quickly developed a freer, more empirical tradition that Paris, more clearly oriented toward scientific and mathematical pursuits.

Both Paris and Oxford were founded as universities by approximately 1200, although each can date its foundation to a variety of years, depending on the dates at which different corporate privileges were bestowed on the community of teachers and scholars. Oxford may well have been established by the return of English scholars from Paris, already at the center of theological teaching, after political relationships deteriorated in 1167. At Paris, in particular, some continuity can be traced between the *studium* recognized in the early thirteenth century and the seven or eight monastic and cathedral schools of the early twelfth century, although the curriculum changed. The practical arts of the *quadrivium* (arithmetic, music, geometry, and astronomy) were jettisoned in statutes promulgated in 1215, and in the trivium the role of rhetoric was reduced in favor of the other two disciplines—logic and grammar.

By the twelfth century there had been, alongside the monastic and cathedral schools, itinerant teachers, such as Peter Abelard, whose activities involved setting up short-lived "schools" as near Paris as possible, but outside the reach of authorities. We know the names of a number of itinerant teachers in or near Paris in the early twelfth century, and their existence influenced the terms of the license of subsequent masters, who were endowed with the *facultas obique docendi* (license to teach anywhere), allowing them to teach at whichever center they pleased. By the end of the thirteenth century, when there were already 22 universities, 5 on the Iberian peninsula, 2 in England, 5 in France, and 10 on the Italian peninsula, the power of conferring the right to teach anywhere was considered by the jurists constitutive of the *studium generale*. In 1233 Gregory IX issued a bull specifically adding that power to the privileges granted to Toulouse in 1229.

The monastic and then the cathedral school had catered, no doubt more or less adequately, to the need (as perceived by civil and ecclesiastical sovereigns) for trained doctors, lawyers, administrators, and a literate clergy. As early as the ninth century, there had been disputes in the monasteries about the propriety of taking pupils not destined to become monks. Medicine was being taught in a separate specialist institution in Saloon. About the same time, a growing tension between the rival claims of military and spiritual sovereignties in Europe was sparking a revival of interest in legal studies.

Demands for professional training were being created that the monastic and cathedral schools were no longer able to meet, and by 1200, with the emergence of the early universities, the arts were already separating from the study of theology and the other professional disciplines (medicine and civil law, to which canon law soon formed the counterweight). In the late medieval universities, the arts course was generally taught by students in one of the four graduate disciplines of theology, medicine, canon law, and civil law. By the mid-twelfth century, Paris had become the most important center of teaching and study north of the Alps. A vortex was generated in which Paris, offering the largest audiences to masters, also increasingly offered the greatest concentration of the best masters and potential patrons to students. Virtually every one of the great scholastic theologians of the thirteenth century either taught or studied at Paris.

Not only did the masters take pupils into residence, forming the ground plan of what would become, as at Oxford and Cambridge, a collegiate university, but more importantly for the growth of the university, they attracted the newly founded religious orders. The Dominicans and Franciscans established their own *studia generalia* in Paris, at first simply reinforcing the institutional development, although soon creating rivalries within it. By 1200 there were probably between 3,000 and 4,000 students in Paris, perhaps a tenth of the total population, with probably about 150 masters, of whom 100 taught in the arts faculty, 20 each in law and medicine, and 8 in theology.

Trouble broke out in Paris in 1270 and in both Paris and Oxford in 1277 when various series of propositions, in which it was stated or implied that human reason reached conclusions incompatible with religiously revealed truth, were condemned. By that date the discipline of logic or dialectic had broken off from theology and gained autonomy to become a fundamental determinant in the subsequent development of the late medieval university system. During the fourteenth and fifteenth centuries, the proliferation of universities reflected political efforts to establish national or ecclesiastical authority.

Such early twelfth and thirteenth-century Italian universities as Reggio, Modena, Vicenza, Padua, and Vercelli appear to have arisen independently of any original action of civil or ecclesiastical authority, but Orléans, Poitiers, and Bourges all profited from the banning of civil law at Paris, where there was political hostility to the loose federation of towns and states that the Holy Roman Empire had fallen into. There was understandably no enthusiasm in the administration for promoting the authority of later imperial Roman legislation. Naples was founded by the emperor Frederick II in 1225 to provide adequate instruction in the arts, theology, jurisprudence, and medicine on his own territory, although he suppressed medicine at Naples in favor of Salerno in 1231. Cologne (1388) and Heidelberg (1389) were universities sponsored by the Roman popes on the German-speaking territory of the disintegrating remnants of the empire to reduce the advantages enjoyed by the Avignon popes at Paris. Poitiers (1431) and Caen (1432) were by-products of the English occupation of northern France, intended to tighten a cultural stranglehold.

When in 1533 the continental theological faculties were invited to pronounce on the validity of the marriage between Henry VIII and Catherine of Aragon, whom the king wished to repudiate, the faculties without exception decided in accordance with the reigning monarch's political interests. To no one's surprise, in the imperial territories, Spain and the Netherlands (notably at Louvain),

Naples, Salamanca, Alcala, and Granada, the arguments opposing the nullity were found stronger, as they were by Luther and most German-speaking canonists on the emperor's territory. Henry's case was just as naturally held to be the weightier by Oxford, Cambridge, Paris (in accordance with the policy of François I), Orléans, Angers, Bourges, Toulouse, Bologna, Siena, Pavia, and Padua, all politically hostile to the emperor Charles V.

Universities, although centers of instruction, were also being founded for political purposes and could normally be expected to respond to the political constraints occasioned locally during Europe's late medieval and Renaissance power struggles. The funding of teaching posts was achieved decreasingly from fees and increasingly through benefices, which were turned into a financial instrument by which excessive ecclesiastical revenues were diverted to the sovereign, whether monarch or pope, to be used for secular and sometimes educational purposes throughout Europe. In particular they were used to support the chancelleries of the new nation states by the device of bestowing ecclesiastical appointments to be held *in commendam* by civil administrators, sometimes clerics only in name. The revenues accruing to abbacies, priories, canonries, and other benefices were attributed, often in plurality, to these administrators and, in their wake, to holders of university offices, who were not expected to reside in the priories or abbeys from which their revenues were drawn. Many universities also benefited from substantial municipal and private patronage, but most were ultimately funded, and therefore controlled, by the territorial sovereign or by ecclesiastical patronage.

Bologna had arisen without a charter, as did Reggio, Modena, Vicenza (the result of a migration from Bologna in 1204), Padua (the result of a similar migration in 1222), and, much later, Siena, which was granted a charter by the emperor Charles IV on a petition from the citizens. The charter was confirmed by Pope Gregory XII in 1408. In 1228 the town of Vercelli appears to have guaranteed the students of Padua the right to rent no less than 500 lodging houses for a fixed rent for eight years, but by the late fourteenth century, the university there had ceased to operate. The first university anywhere constituted by papal charter was that of Toulouse, founded in 1233 by Gregory IX as part of an attempt to extirpate Albigensianism.

The emperor Charles IV bestowed a charter on Arezzo in 1355, after an influx of jurists from Bologna had settled there in 1215, and established Pavia as a university in 1361. In 1398 Pavia was amalgamated with Piacenza (chartered in 1240) by the Visconti rulers of Milan; then the independent existence of Piacenza university ceased. The university of Rome, which continued through the Avignon papacy, was founded by Boniface VIII in 1303, although in 1318 John XXII limited its power of conferring degrees to civil and canon law. From the early fourteenth century, the growth, development, peregrinations, and extinction of the Italian centers of learning were governed by the incidence of plague, the interplay of municipal and regional political interests dominated by the grand families, and the rivalry between popes and emperors.

Early in the thirteenth century, Cambridge had been founded by a group of scholars fleeing the hostility of the Oxford townspeople in 1208–9, and its numbers were subsequently augmented by an influx from Paris in 1228. By 1225 it was certainly a university in the sense that the bishop of Ely was treating it as a separate canonical society. In 1231 the king granted it substantial privileges at the same time as they were granted to Oxford, and by 1233 Gregory IX could issue a bull addressed to the chancellor and university, confining jurisdiction over the *studium* to their own chancellor, or to the bishop. The constitutional model was Paris, not yet removed from local jurisdiction, but the student hostels at Cambridge were fewer and larger than at Oxford. The first college, Peterhouse (1284), was modeled on Oxford's Merton College. Although three universities were established in Scotland during the fifteenth century (St. Andrews, Glasgow, and Aberdeen), the monopoly of university education in England was confined to Oxford and Cambridge until the nineteenth century, no doubt to the detriment of the country's educational system.

A medical school was opened to all qualified teachers at Montpellier, to which was added a school of jurisprudence before the end of the twelfth century. Petrarch was sent to study law there, and the institution, now including a school of arts, was raised to the rank of *studium generale* by Nicholas IV in 1289. There is some evidence that theology was also being taught there by 1289, although the theology faculty was not formally recognized until 1421. The term *generale* applied to *studium* began to refer to the spread of disciplines. Universities came finally to be distinguished from unidisciplinary schools of professional training, such as that devoted to medicine at Salerno.

Orléans was functioning as a university soon after Toulouse in the early thirteenth century but was given corporation status by Clement V only in 1305. After Orléans came Angers (also catering to the civil law excluded from Paris), and Avignon and Cahors, especially favored by John XXII. They were granted immunity from taxation by Edward III of England, acting as duke of Aquitaine. Grenoble received a charter from Benedict XII in 1339. There were also short-lived institutions, as at Perpignan, Orange, and Valence, which failed to achieve critical mass or attract foreign students in adequate numbers.

Like the Inquisition, many Iberian universities, such as Lisbon-Coimbra (1309) were established by civil rather than by ecclesiastical authority. As in France, some failed, but Valladolid, which received a charter from Clement VI in 1346, a celebrated institution by the end of the fourteenth century, became a *studium generale* and a *universitas theologiae* under Martin V in 1418. It served with Salamanca as model and springboard for the new foundation by Cisneros at Alcala in its renaissance form very early in the sixteenth century.

On imperial territory east of the Rhine, the earliest university was Prague, founded by the emperor Charles IV, at whose request Clement VI authorized the institution of a *studium generale* in 1347. The constitutions are largely borrowed from Naples and Salerno. The Jagiellonian University in Kracow was founded in 1364 by the king, Casimir the Great, with the formal permission of Urban V who refused, however, to allow the establishment of a theological faculty for the Vienna *studium* founded by Rudolph IV in 1364. Kracow in Poland, with Buda (1389) and Pecs (Fünfkirchen, 1367) in Hungary, remained the most easterly of the successful European university foundations before 1500. Meanwhile Heidelberg had received its charter in 1385 from Urban VI at the request of the elector of palatine, with degrees to be conferred by the provost of the cathedral at Worms.

Like Vienna, Prague, and Heidelberg, the initiative for the foundation of Cologne was ecclesiastical rather than imperial. The Dominicans had had a *studium* there since the thirteenth century and were the prime movers in seeking, through the city council, the 1388 charter from Urban VI. The sympathies of Cologne remained papal until as late as the sixteenth century. The Erfurt charter was obtained at the instigation of the Franciscans, at first from the antipope Clement VII in 1379, and then from Urban VI in 1389. The university's openness to new ideas, its school of jurisprudence, and its position as the forum for discussions between nominalists and realists enabled it to become the largest university of German-speaking territory in the fifteenth century. The situation was, however, fundamentally changing as the new civic foundations generally required the annexation of prebends for their maintenance. It was the annexation of prebends rather than the desire to control theological teaching that made the issue of papal bulls necessary and increasingly brought the foundation of universities under papal supervision. Imperial approbation became diminishingly important and was solicited only in Greifwald, Freiburg, and Tübingen.

Further European university foundations and suppressions reflected political and religious alignments and powerful relationships, although they also mirrored the growing wealth of commercial communities, such as Louvain, and the need for better educational standards, largely to meet the growing demand for administrators. King's College chapel's heraldic ornamentation became an ostentatious display of Tudor power, stridently proclaiming the defeat of the college's founder, Henry VI, in 1461, and of a size disproportionate to its ostensible purpose, which was to provide a building suitable for the corporate worship of a relatively small foundation. It was built more as a cathedral than as a chapel, but there was already a diocesan cathedral at Ely, so a chapel it has remained.

When Poitiers was instituted by Charles VII in 1431 to counterbalance the pro-English stance of Paris, the pope Eugenius IV restricted its privileges to those already possessed by Toulouse. Charles then unilaterally augmented the privileges of Poitiers to include all those possessed by Toulouse, Paris,

Montpellier, Angers, and Orléans. He placed the new university under his own special protection. Caen was then founded as the pro-English antithesis of Poitiers. The bishop of Bayeux was made its chancellor, and Eugenius IV included in its charter of 1437 the requirement that those graduating should take a vow of fidelity to the see of Rome. The rejoinder from the French king was the celebrated pragmatic sanction of 1438.

Universities that established publishing presses gave themselves a powerful advantage in the late fifteenth and early sixteenth centuries, when the peak demand for text and tracts drew the principal scholars to the important printing centers. At the same time those universities that were committed to defending the old Latin Vulgate translation of the Bible (and therefore opposed the publication of new texts and translations, and indeed opposed the cultivation of the antique Latin, Greek, and Hebrew studies on which a new educational program was becoming based) found that the new "tri-lingual" studies simply bypassed them. Oxford and Cambridge absorbed the new educational outlook, in which the arts course now emphasized philosophy and rhetoric in place of logic and dialectic, with colleges at each founded to further it, while at Paris, Cologne, Louvain, and elsewhere, tri-lingual colleges were projected outside the established university system. The Collège de France today is the result of the establishment of royal lecturerships under François I in a Paris whose university was resolutely hostile to the new studies.

Foundations were made in many towns of considerable commercial or administrative importance (although not at Lyons, which had no university before 1808), and included in the second half of the fifteenth century the universities at Bordeaux, Valence, Nantes, Bourges, Basel, and Ingolstadt, all of which received papal charters at the instigation of secular princes or municipal authorities. Trier, Mainz, Uppsala, and Copenhagen followed before the end of the century, and in 1502 so did Wittenberg, the first university on German-speaking territory to be founded by imperial rather than papal decree. The charter, issued on July 6, 1502, by Maximilian I followed, however, the provisions and phraseology of earlier papal charters. The last German territory to receive its university was Brandenburg, in which Frankfurt-an-der-Oder was founded in 1506 by Pope Julius II. It was given an imperial charter seven months later.

The system as it developed in Europe was characterized by certain important features, such as the interchangeability of teaching posts, as masters, teaching in Latin, moved from one teaching position to another irrespective of nationality and geographical location, and by a very loose discipline among student bodies. After the mid-sixteenth century and the foundation of counter-reformatory Jesuit universities, the religious schism dominated the system until the revolution in France uprooted the French universities, putting higher education in France into administrative abeyance in 1793, pending its restructuring under Napoléon in

1808. Many German universities also disappeared between 1789 and 1816, although some have subsequently been refounded.

The early nineteenth century provides a convenient watershed for any overview of the emergence of what we can now regard as historic universities. The Spanish system was being redesigned from 1857 with a minister responsible for ten university districts, and the French and German systems were being wholly reorganized. In England new universities were founded at London and Durham, then at Manchester, Newcastle, Liverpool, Leeds, Birmingham, and Sheffield; new universities were also founded in Scotland and Wales. The system had spread within Europe to Ireland (where Trinity College dates its foundation to 1591), throughout the Low Countries and to the Scandinavian and Balkan countries, Switzerland, and Russia. In England, legislation promoted in 1877 much loosened the association of the universities with the established church. Colleges in what was then the British Empire became affiliated with British universities, notably Cambridge, before becoming independent universities in their own right. Almost everywhere the development of the university system was primarily promoted by the need to produce doctors, lawyers, and administrators, but decreasingly to produce religious leaders, whose training was increasingly relegated to seminaries for spiritual as well as theological formation. Only of secondary importance in the development of universities was the desire to produce an educated population with an enhanced quality of life.

When in 1852 the foundation of a specifically Catholic university for Ireland was being considered and John Henry Newman published *The Idea of a University,* he no doubt reflected the view of the English-speaking world by insisting that the function of a university was to teach the whole spectrum of disciplines. It was, it must be remembered, the age of the great encyclopedias, catalogs, and dictionaries, of the multivolumed series such as Migne's Latin and Greek patrologies, of the *Encyclopaedia Britannica* and the *Oxford English Dictionary,* in which it was considered possible to encapsulate in printed form vast and exhaustive collections of whole spectrums of what was knowable.

Newman was highly sensitive to the reproach that the university, as he conceived it, would simply create a "gentleman . . . with brilliant general views about all things whatever," but he was adamant in his exclusion of research at the university; for him research was the proper field of activity of non-teaching academies. He no doubt takes his case to its extreme, but it was once commonly pressed and has seldom been so forcefully stated. What was to be expected of a university education according to Newman was "the culture of the intellect, . . . the force, the steadiness, the comprehensiveness and the versatility of the intellect, the command over our own powers, the instinctive just estimate of things as they pass before us." Whatever the culture of the intellect may do for an individual, "In all it will be a faculty of entering with comparative ease into any subject of thought, and of taking up with aptitude any science or profession."

The first step is always to inculcate "the idea of science, method, order, principle, and system; of rule and exception, the richness and harmony."

This was the philosophy of higher education that radiated from Britain to the rest of the Anglo-Saxon world in the mid-nineteenth century, that largely informed the attitudes adopted at that date by Oxford and Cambridge, and that cannot be said subsequently to have been completely abandoned. It was at the opposite pole from the philosophy governing the provision of instruction for lawyers, physicians, clerics, and administrators that had informed the teaching of the medieval schools beyond elementary education. It led to a real if temporary separation of university education not only from research activities but also from provision for professional and vocational training, and even more from the formation required by future practitioners in the performing arts. It is probably the case that scientific research would have continued, even had it not been at all depended on the teaching activities of the universities. It would no doubt have been fueled by the pressure for improved health care and political needs to achieve and maintain superiority in armaments, if not from the simple expectancy of the economic reward. It seems certain that research work in the liberal arts and the more theoretical aspects of the social sciences would have languished if it had been cut off from the motivation provided by the teaching institutions.

As in medieval Europe, in the United States of America, the modern universities (especially the state institutions, often modeled on Jefferson's University of Virginia) had at first little interest in research. They grew largely out of the provision of training in practical skills, as, for instance, in the agricultural colleges, where the cultivation of technical understanding preceded greater emphasis on liberal studies and scientific inquiry. Professional training, even outside the high-demand areas of law, medicine, and, until very recently, religious leadership, was the motivation behind the early western-style universities both in eastern Europe and in the far east.

Except in a purely administrative sense, the British universities were never close models even for the great private colleges of the east coast of the United States, if only because the earlier U.S. universities were set up in a generally poorer society not so stratified by class origins and generally with a more strongly moral or religious educational component than was evident in nineteenth-century Britain. Harvard, Yale, Princeton, Rutgers, Columbia, and Brown all had religious origins. Only the second wave of foundations—Michigan, Wisconsin, Minnesota, and California—strove for freedom from religious control, while North and South Carolina, Georgia, and Maryland followed Virginia's lead in affording extensive state support to higher education. A third wave is constituted by the universities such as Cornell, Johns Hopkins, and Chicago, which grew out of private benefactions with little or no state support or religious affiliation.

The foundations of U.S. universities and colleges can be divided into four periods, of which only the first three are of importance in the context of the present volume. The first period lasted from 1636, the year of Harvard's foundation, to 1776, when Hampden-Sydney was the 15th college to be established. Originally intended primarily for the education of the clergy, these colleges were not at first universities in the continental European sense, although the curriculum invariably adapted from that of the English religious colleges, remained broad. Alongside divinity and the scriptural languages, it included classical literature and history, logic, rhetoric, and mathematics. The admissions of these early colleges were, however, never confined exclusively to those training for the ministry or even to those with the relevant denominational affiliation.

The second period, from 1776 to 1862, saw the foundation of scores of further institutions of higher education, of which 29 had already been established by 1820, with curriculums now more attuned to the production of qualified professionals with practical skills. The older educational institutions were reluctant to adapt, and many of the new ones became separately organized professional schools, including a variety of seminaries, Rensselaer Polytechnic Institute (which offered agriculture), and the U.S. Military Academy, the first institution to offer a program in engineering. Schools of applied science multiplied in the 1850s. State schools of agriculture were founded in Maryland, Pennsylvania, and Michigan, and the established colleges then instituted scientific programs: Harvard in 1847 and Yale in 1851. The Massachusetts Institute of Technology was founded in 1861.

At the time, the Morrill Act of 1862 (commonly called the land-grant act) had the effect of promoting the integration of professional engineering and agricultural training into what had become the U.S. university system. The system also absorbed teacher training, although teacher training colleges continued to develop separately to keep pace with the growing demand for secondary education. The first three state institutions of higher education had been charted by 1800, and by 1819 Virginia had introduced the system of elective courses. During this period, too, the first municipal colleges appeared. At Louisville the college was a creation of the city council in 1837, becoming a university in 1846. The first women's college, Mount Holyoke, appeared during the second quarter of the nineteenth century, and in 1833 Oberlin was the first university to admit both men and women.

It was during the third period of foundation, from 1862 to 1900, that the land-grant act made mandatory the establishment of state colleges for instruction in agriculture and the mechanical arts, and that universities, granting postgraduate degrees (beginning in 1876 at Johns Hopkins), began to develop. The best of the liberal arts colleges became universities, from the independent as well as the state sectors, and nineteenth-century industrial magnates such as Vanderbilt and

Rockefeller began to found university institutions, such as those of Stanford and Chicago. Attempts to import the German tendency to separate research from teaching institutions nearly led to the hiving off of graduate schools, to be devoted primarily to the advancement rather than the transmission of learning. In fact the same institutions did keep undergraduate teaching and graduate research functions together, although nearly insulated from one another, a specifically American compromise between the German and British solutions.

The evolution of the Australian and New Zealand universities is analogous to that of the U.S. institutions. The general administrative pattern was British, and Sydney was incorporated by an act of the colonial legislature that received the royal assent in December 1851. The royal charter dates from 1858. By an act of 1884, denominational halls and colleges were to be affiliated to a strictly interdenominational central institution. Melbourne, Adelaide, and Hobart followed before the end of the century. The university of New Zealand was founded in 1870 with affiliated colleges as far apart as Auckland in the north and Dunedin in the south. In Canada, too, development was similar, although along more stringently denominational lines. McGill College had been instituted in Montreal by royal charter in 1821 as a Protestant nondenominational foundation. The University of Toronto, later split into University College, the principal teaching institution, and Trinity College, the church of England college erected to replace the suppressed theology faculty, was founded in 1827, and the Catholic, French-speaking university of Laval at Quebec was founded in 1852.

The University of Athens (founded 1837) was modeled on the north German system. The universities of Iasi (1860) and Bucharest (1864), both in present Romania, were founded as state institutions, with representation in the senate and training grounds for a professional elite with gratuitous instruction and examination for students. Further east, the Japanese universities of Tokyo (1868) and Kyoto (1897), both amalgamations of previously existing institutions, were similarly established for the provision of professional training in medicine, science, law, and engineering. Sofia (1888) in Bulgaria extended its faculties to include history and philology but chiefly in order to produce competent teachers at the secondary level.

Throughout the history of the development of universities as we know them, there have been three major variables, related to one another in different ways at different times and places. The relative importance in universities attached to professional training and to generalist intellectual formation has clearly varied, as has the relative emphasis given within university institutions to the instruction in available knowledge, the advancement of the boundaries of knowledge by research, the perception of the continuity between research and teaching, and their interdependence within the same institution. Perhaps historically of the greatest importance of all, however, has been the varying relationship between secular education and religious formation.

The development of the theological *studia generalia* in later medieval Europe was no doubt gestated by the need for competent administrative officials alongside priests and physicians to conduct the internal government and external relationships of the new powerful political units that coalesced in the late fifteenth century. It is not surprising that they were at first drawn almost exclusively from the ranks of the clergy, the only source for the recruitment of first literate and then elegantly educated administrators. It is indeed also not surprising that they continued to be recompensed from the same sources of revenue as previously. It is in any case clear that society's need for competent professionals, whether in medicine, engineering, the technologies, administration, agriculture, or any other field, did in fact provide the impetus for the development of what we now regard as university institutions.

With regard to the relationship between teaching and research, the desirable balance is still the subject of considerable debate, with Newman's view that the activities demand separate institutions no longer finding much favor. The real question now centers much more on the nature of the relationship between the teaching and research functions of the same scholars and institutions.

The most important point to be made by any such brief survey as this of the history of the university system must surely be how sensitively it has always responded and still responds to the perceived needs of the society it serves. As the essays in this volume demonstrate, throughout history the world's universities both reflect and influence the societies in which they are created.

A.H.T. LEVI

INTERNATIONAL DICTIONARY OF

UNIVERSITY HISTORIES

AALBORG UNIVERSITY
(Aalborg, Denmark)

Location: South Tranders in Aalborg, Denmark, the northern part of Jutland, a 250 km drive from Copenhagen.

Description: A state university enrolling approximately 9,500 students.

Information: Informationskontoret
Aalborg University
Frederik Bajersvej 5
P.O. Box 159
DK-9100 Aalborg
Denmark
(98) 158522
Fax (98) 159067

Aalborg University is the youngest of the five Danish universities, opening on September 1, 1974. Originally called Aalborg University Center (AUC), it was based on the fundamental idea of integrating a large number of existing disciplines into one institution. In this and other respects, the basic principles of AUC broke with the teaching and research traditions maintained at the "old" universities: Copenhagen (founded 1479), Aarhus (founded 1928), and, to a lesser degree, Odense (founded 1964). Aalborg University Center introduced project-organized studies for student groups and research teams, with interdisciplinary studies as part of the pedagogy. Less course-time was structured as lectures, and a lot of the teaching took place in self-organized student groups, working on a problem defined by the students themselves.

In the beginning of the 1960s, Denmark experienced an educational boom; at the end of the 1960s it became obvious that the universities of Copenhagen, Aarhus, and Odense could no longer keep up with the demand for higher education. This was part of the argument for Aalborg University Center, but the first initiatives towards the foundation of a university in Northern Jutland were taken before this, in the late fifties and early sixties in Aalborg.

In 1959 C. Willum Hansen, headmaster at a local high school, stressed the necessity for a local university. The local paper polled a number of citizens to test the idea, and the opinions were mixed. The idea of a university in Northern Jutland got support primarily from local consultants, who wished for medical education in Aalborg. Others, opposing the idea, stressed the necessity for solving other educational problems. During the first half of the sixties, the idea of a local university gained more sup-

port from the Northern Jutlandic businesses and industries, the local labor movement, and the city council.

In 1961, the Northern Jutlandic Commission for Institutions of Higher Education started more systematic work to create a basis for the university. During the next five years, the commission worked out detailed plans for a university. At a public meeting in 1964 it was concluded "that the size of the population in Northern Jutland, the cultural and educational environment of the province, the size of Aalborg, and the growth in number of college graduates spoke significantly for the location of the fourth Danish university—or part of it—in Aalborg." In 1965, the commission developed more specific plans for a university, including a larger degree of interdisciplinary education, and a certain softening of traditional university structures and teaching principles. The commission also suggested that, along with the implementation of a department of medicine and a department of social science, there ought to be a department of science, building on a close collaboration with the new field of engineering. In order to promote the development of an institute for fishing and biology the commission also argued for the implementation of a program for geographical studies.

During the first half of the sixties similar plans for the expansion of Danish universities developed at the national political level in the Ministry of Education. In May 1964, the Danish parliament passed a bill for expanding Odense University; during the final debate the idea of three additional Danish universities grew. In continuation of this idea, the Planning Commission for the Higher Educations was appointed in December 1964 to start preliminary work on the bill for more centers of higher education. This bill was promoted by the Social-demokratic Minister of Education K.B. Andersen in 1966 and 1967, but was not accepted by parliament. In 1968, the Liberal Minister of Education Helge Larsen promoted a bill for the expansion of existing universities in Copenhagen, Aarhus and Odense.

The Danish Student Council (DSF) intervened in favor of a new university in Aalborg. They argued that "in Aalborg the preparations for a center of education have gone far, and the construction therefore can progress more peacefully than at the other locations." The push for a local university was intensified by the creation of The Northern Jutlandic University Association in 1969.

In November 1969, Minister of Education Larsen passed a new bill proposing a new university in Roskilde, but also promoted the university in Aalborg. A demonstration in Copenhagen in December 1969 drew more than 1,000 people from Northern Jutland, and former Minister of Education, K.B. Andersen, emphasized this massive popular support. May 28, 1970, the Danish parliament passed a bill to start a new university in Aalborg in 1974–75.

Collaboration with DSF continued, and the city council in Aalborg offered 10,000 square meters of existing building space, at no charge to the Ministry of Education. Furthermore the council suggested a more permanent location on unbuilt land in Sdr. Tranders. In 1974 AUC started in the offered buildings. Later, surrounding buildings were integrated into AUC's campus. In 1975 the first part of the new campus in South Tranders was completed, and has been expanded ever since, but has not been able to match the requirements of the growing number of students.

The Planning Commission started its work in 1970 with four tasks: (1) to analyze the possibilities of coordination with existing educational institutions and put forward proposals to promote such a coordination; (2) to put forward proposals for new educational programs; (3) to consider and put forward proposals on the implementation of these programs and the order of establishment of the programs; (4) to put forward proposals, in cooperation with the Building Administration, for the physical setting of the center, covering both short-term as well as long-term needs. In June 1971, Jan Schrøder was appointed administrative leader of Aalborg University Center, and the first office was established in Gug, close to the location of AUC. Schrøder later became a crucial member of the provincial vice-chancellorship.

One of the first tasks was to establish contact with local educational institutions to analyze possibilities for collaboration. The first one, Aalborg Technical College, agreed to integration with the new university center. Later, several other educational institutions were integrated, including programs for social workers, and students from the local branch of The School of Economics and Business Administration.

In 1971 the Liberal government was replaced by a Socialdemokratic one with Knud Heinesen as Minister of Education. He resisted some of his fellow Socialdemokrats and turned down a proposal to quash the university at Aalborg in favor of Roskilde. He gave the Planning Commission a more specific task that committed the commission, among other things, to put forward proposals to integrate education for engineers, to develop basic study programs within the social sciences and the humanities, in order to relieve the pressure on the university in Aarhus, and to possibly integrate the educational programs for primary school teachers. The Planning Commission delivered a report in 1972, proposing four departments. The commission also suggested the concept of a common first part (called the basic-study program) succeeded by separated study programs. This proposal formed the basis of the educational system at AUC.

The first Vice Chancellor of AUC was appointed on December 5, 1972. Jörgen Weibull, a Swedish professor, was appointed head of the provisional vice-chancellorship. His main task was to prepare proposals for educational programs for primary school teachers as well as for studies within the social sciences, technical professions, science, and computer science. The provisional vice-chancellorship had six members, including the later Vice Chancellor Sven Caspersen and two representatives from the Danish Student Council. All were later attached to the university as administrators and professors.

One important field was missing from this list: medical education. The Ministry of Education mentioned that "the foundation of an entire medical education in Aalborg is not part of the ministerial plans." The idea of medical education at Aalborg was defeated, and later suggestions have not been considered with any substantial seriousness.

The provisional vice-chancellorship suggested the matriculation of 950 new students in 1974. Seven hundred thirty students would be transferred from existing institutions. The Ministry of Education reduced the figure of new enrollees to 750, which meant that the university center would start with 1,480 students. The number of new students was later cut back even further to 450 by the new Liberal Minister of Education, Tove Nielsen. The Liberal government was far more critical of the new university centers, and there was strong opposition to integrating programs for primary school teachers at AUC.

When it came to the founding principles at AUC, the provincial vice-chancellorship was divided into two opposing parties. The majority wanted a one-year basic-study program divided into six different entrance possibilities; the minority wanted a two-year basic-study program and divided into only three entrance possibilities. The two groups also had conflicting views on the organization of the studies, the organization of the institutes, and the admission requirements. The conflicts prompted discussion in the local media, and there was substantial local support for the point of view of the minority. When both proposals were presented to the Planning Commission a strong majority showed for the proposals put forward by the majority-held views of the provincial vice-chancellorship. Knud Heinesen supported the decision to go with the majority-held proposal. The students and the local unions protested, stressing the need for a university structured in agreement with public wishes. Subsequently, the unions demanded influence on the organization of AUC.

A new Liberal government was appointed in 1973, and March 15, 1974, Tove Nielsen introduced the bill allowing Aalborg University Center to open its doors in September 1974. Students in the new educational programs for social workers and engineers, students transferring from the School of Business Economics, were the first at AUC. The primary school teachers' program was stopped by Nielsen, although the program was not definitively rejected until later. Eventually, the education of registered land surveyors was moved to AUC. The education of librarians at the local branch of The Royal School of Librarianship was not integrated into AUC, but it was located in the same buildings. In September 1974, 45 percent of the student body came from Northern Jutland. In 1995 a substantial number of new students still come from Northern Jutland.

Sven Caspersen became Vice Chancellor in 1975, and he played a crucial part in building AUC from its tender start in 1974 to the modern, international university it has become. In 20 years, the university introduced a number of new disciplines, adjusted to changing demands from the business world, and added new, interdisciplinary research. Aalborg University Center utilized the educational principles laid down by the provincial vice-chancellorship and the Planning Commission to create a special university profile, which has helped recruit students and professors. Most important of these principles has been stressing and maintaining interdisciplinary teaching and research. Graduates from Aalborg University Center have obtained qualifications in some ways quite different from graduates of other universities in Denmark. Primarily, they have been trained to cooperate with colleagues, solve communication problems, and deal with unfamiliar and unknown situations by applying learned methodology.

In 1994 Aalborg University Center changed its name to Aalborg University (still abbreviated AUC to distinguish it from Aarhus University) to end confusion concerning the status of AUC.

—Jan Bitsch Steffensen

AARHUS UNIVERSITY
(Aarhus, Jutland, Denmark)

Location: Aarhus, Jutland, Denmark, approximately 400 km west of Copenhagen. Set on rolling moraine, the 37-acre University Park is located on the north side of the city within sight of the copper roof and red brick walls of Domkirke, Aarhus's landmark thirteenth-century church—the largest in Scandinavia.

Description: A state university enrolling approximately 18,000 students in undergraduate, graduate, and professional schools.

Information: Studiekontoret (Registry)
Ndr. Ringgade 1
DK-8000 Aarhus C
Denmark
(89) 42 10 25
Fax (86) 13 09 57

Note: Rules of Admission for foreign students can be found on school's website at:
http://www.aau.dk/uk/adm/registra/rules-1.htm

Visiting: To arrange a tour, contact a specific department of the External Relations Office, University of Aarhus, c/o Science Park Aarhus, Gustav Wieds Vej 10C/ DK-8000 Aarhus C.

An outstanding example of Scandinavian architecture, the University of Aarhus is also well-known academically for industrial and scientific research and is a thriving center for the arts and culture of Denmark. The city of Aarhus is located on the eastern coast of the Jutland peninsula, the only part of Denmark attached to the continent of Europe. One of several well-developed industrial centers in Jutland, Aarhus is a bustling seaport. It was a Viking settlement a thousand years ago, and is now Denmark's second largest city with a population of 270,000. Since Jutland is separated from Copenhagen and the 406 islands which make up the rest of Denmark by the Great Belt, many business firms maintain offices in both cities and the business community of Aarhus has always played an important role in the development of the university.

The idea for a university in Jutland had first been discussed in the eighteenth century when the archdeacon of Viborg spoke in favor of building a university there as a supplement to the one in Copenhagen which had shortly before burned down. Denmark was temporarily without a school of higher education and the archdeacon argued against remaining vulnerable to one sole institution's health.

The government in Copenhagen did not move on building a second university, though, until 1925, when a ministry-level committee finally looked into the feasibility of a university in Jutland and found in favor of it. The real initiative, however, came from a group of private citizens and business leaders who called themselves the "University Association." They had campaigned for Aarhus as the site for the new university as early as 1921, and eventually convinced the state to permit a three-year trial period beginning in 1928.

Seventy-eight students attended lectures that year in space rented from the Aarhus Technical School. The teaching staff consisted of a professor of philosophy and four associate professors of Danish, English, German, and French. Soon thereafter, generous financial support from the Aarhus business community allowed the University Association to purchase a former clinic and transform it into the first residence hall. A wealthy businessman endowed a trust that distributed monetary grants to 50 students annually. Such private interest convinced the state of the school's viability and it began to take a more active role in its development. In 1931, the Danish legislature passed a law that provided for the restructuring of university teaching at Aarhus into a true university.

With this official approval and impetus came the need for more buildings, especially one that could house the medical faculty (now known as the Faculty of Health Sciences) and its laboratories for physics and chemistry.

A design competition was held and one winner, architect C.F. Møller, began his lifelong attachment to the university. He died in November 1988, but his firm was still responsible for university construction, including the Science Park and the Steno Museum. Møller and his colleagues, Kay Fisker and Povl Stegmann, designed the first buildings to take advantage of the gap in the moraine landscape. Instead of filling it in, they placed the buildings on the slopes in view of a meandering stream, ensuring a distinguished landscape and architectural design. Landscape architect Carl Theodor Sørensen planted oak trees throughout the campus, making University Park one of the largest oak-clad parklands in Denmark.

The cornerstone of the first building was laid on August 30, 1932. Its classrooms were ready for occupancy in September of the following year when the faculty of arts was moved over from Aarhus Technical School. The formal opening took place under a large marquee where the chairman of the board of the university and the mayor of Aar-

Aarhus University

hus welcomed the Danish royal family, the prime minister, the minister of education and 1,000 spectators. King Christian X then proclaimed, "With a wish that the scientific research that will take place here will do so in a sense of spirit and truth, I hereby declare the University of Aarhus open." Following this auspicious occasion, a number of residence halls were built and the area began to acquire the look of a park in the city.

Late in the thirties, construction began on the Main Hall. Also designed by the Møller firm, it is based on traditional Danish forms. So while the Main Hall is public and monumental, as are all the buildings on the campus, it is also reminiscent of classic Danish architecture. Its concrete frame construction is clad with the traditional yellow brick, laid in ornamental patterns, and the roof is tiled. The interior, meanwhile, is composed of exposed concrete ribs and a window opens up the entire end wall, its top forming the gable-end of the roof. Main Hall is considered one of the finest interiors of mid-twentieth century Danish architecture.

Although construction on the Main Hall continued throughout German occupation during World War II, Møller put off completion for fear that the Germans would confiscate the building. His fears were well-founded when, on August 29, 1943, four professors were seized as hostages. In October, the Gestapo took over all five residence halls and as students hastily moved into private homes, the Germans surrounded University Park with machine gun nests and barbed wire to fend off Resistance forces.

Since the Gestapo's archives were now located on University property and the buildings were also used to interrogate captured Resistance fighters, the Danish Royal Air Force, with the encouragement of the Jutland Resistance movement, decided to bomb the university. On the morning of October 31, 1944, 33 aircraft took off on a course towards Aarhus. Flying very low over the city, they attacked in several waves of precision bombing which killed between 50 and 100 people. The majority of the casualties were Germans and their collaborators, but ten Danish construction workers were also hit.

As soon as possible after the war, repairs were made and the Main Hall was completed and opened in 1946. It housed the faculties of the arts, economics, and law (now the social sciences), and theology, while the medical faculty carried on in the 1933 building, holding biochemistry and physiology labs elsewhere. A fourth faculty, business, which had long been the dream of the managing director of the Aarhus Oliefabrik and the University Association, had been established in 1936, followed by theology in 1942.

In those early years, the University Association depended solely on private sources to fund the university. They solicited from individuals, from local councils, from groups within industrial firms and from the firms themselves. In many cases the donations were in kind, for instance, a load of yellow bricks from a brick factory or lumber from a lumber mill. In the post-war period the generous donations continued. The Cheminova Company, for instance, transferred to the University the entire share capital of the company in 1944. Since then, the dividends have been assigned by the Aarhus University Research Foundation for use in research at the university. In 1954, Ellen Dahl (née Dinesen) presented the Sandbjerg estate in the south of Jutland to the university for scientific conferences, courses, and other similar events. Dahl was the widow of Attorney Knud Dahl and sister of Karen Blixen, the author known as Isak Dinesen. The Dahls had previously donated land for the University's Mols Laboratory. In 1970, the university ceased to be a private foundation and came under the supervision of the Ministry of Education, as do all other Danish universities.

By the mid-fifties, the number of students had increased 25 times and the number of professors and associate professors had increased about ten times. In addition, there was an even larger group of instructors, junior lecturers, and teaching consultants. This latter group was the result of collaboration between the Faculty of Medicine and the hospitals of Aarhus. The university celebrated these and other achievements during its 25th anniversary in 1953 with a festival of concerts and lectures and a fair. The anniversary was an opportune time to launch a new fundraising campaign for the construction of a student union building to be completed in 1964.

In the tradition of European universities, Aarhus took its place among the great European schools in 1953–54 with the full establishment of its fifth faculty, science. Chemistry and physics, which had previously been taught in conjunction with medicine, were now established as separate disciplines and the school was able to focus its energies to a greater degree on cutting-edge research.

The rebellious events of the 1960s did not bypass Aarhus. In the early sixties, those among the teaching staff who did not have professor status—the majority in terms of numbers—began to express their discontent. In the late sixties, they were joined by the students in a nationwide movement of rebellion. The government reacted with a new statute in 1970 which unseated older professors from their positions of power and gave the younger staff and the students greater influence on university administration.

As the student body grew to about 15,000 in the sixties and seventies, so did the breadth of academic instruction and extracurricular activities. This demanded more space. As vacated military and hospital buildings became available, they were acquired by the university. Five professors' houses were torn down and the arts faculty found itself housed partially in a former factory complex in the Trojberg neighborhood, while psychology was taught in the Risskov district. Many other activities were located throughout the city. Growth finally stabilized in the eighties and it was during this decade that the Møller firm completed Forskerparken, the Science Park of Aarhus. A private foundation, Forskerparken provides research facilities for the university and other bodies of higher education who collaborate with the business community in the development of new products.

The most recent addition to University Park is the Danish Museum for the History of Science and Medicine. Also known as the Steno Museum, it is another Møller building located in the southernmost part of the University Park. It houses a planetarium, a medical history museum and a physical sciences collection.

Other museums attached to the university are the Natural History, the Collection of Ancient Art, and the Museum of Prehistory which is located in a former manor house at Moesgaard, south of Aarhus. The famous "bog people"—mummified bodies found in nearby bogs—are displayed at the Moesgaard. Behind the museum is the Prehistoric Trail that leads hikers through mock woodland and bog settings down to the real sand beach. Students of prehistoric archaeology, medieval archaeology, ethnography, and social anthropology find the museum to be a useful resource.

With such a wealth of historical, cultural, and scientific opportunities, the University of Aarhus has become the cultural and scientific center of Jutland, handsomely, if not exactly, fulfilling the hopes of the archdeacon of Viborg.

Further Reading: The bulk of the information about the University of Aarhus in English is to be found through the External Relations office of the University (c/o Science Park Aarhus, Gustav Wieds Vej 10C, DK-8000 Aarhus C). Commentary about its architecture and descriptions of Jutland can be found in any of the standard travel guides. *The Scandinavians* by Donald S. Connery (New York: Simon and Schuster, and London: Eyre and Spottiswoode, 1966) offers general commentary on education in Denmark as well as descriptions of culture and daily life.

—Cynthia Ogorek

AL-AZHAR UNIVERSITY
(Cairo, Egypt)

Location: In the old section of central Cairo; university branches located worldwide.

Description: One of the most influential universities in the Muslim world. A government-run university enrolling approximately 90,000 students in undergraduate, graduate, and professional schools.

Information: Al-Azhar University
Cairo
Egypt
904051

Al-Azhar University is the oldest and most prestigious university in the Muslim world. Situated in the heart of Cairo, its history is rooted in the city's past. Despite its 1,000 existence, Al-Azhar's designation as a university is quite recent, and there was resistance among faculty and students in the early twentieth century to the change in status from a mosque college to what seemed a more secular identity. The appellation "university," in fact, was not officially adopted until 1961.

For 900 years, Al-Azhar was a mosque school geared primarily, though not exclusively, to the study of Islam and the *sharia,* or Islamic law. The highest authority on Islamic law in Egypt (as in other Muslim countries), called the *ulama,* was filled generation after generation by jurists and legal scholars who were graduates or professors from Al-Azhar. This still holds true, despite the fact that, as a university, Al-Azhar has undergone radical changes, including opening its doors to women. Though state run, Al-Azhar is the most distinctively religious institution of higher learning in Egypt, grappling with modernization and secularization on the one hand, and with the phenomenon of Islamic fundamentalism on the other.

The history of this unusual institution began in the tenth century, when most of the population of Upper and Lower Egypt had converted to Sunni Islam and adopted Arabic as their spoken and written language. Shi'ite Islam, however, was winning converts in the Muslim world, becoming the state religion in Persia, and almost overtaking Sunnism in Mesopotamia. The Shi'ite Fatimid dynasty, which came to power first in neighboring Tunisia and then conquered Egypt in 969, was anxious to declare its independence from the caliphate in Baghdad and to establish Shi'ism as the state religion.

The Fatimid general Jawhar, who led the invasion of Egypt, set about establishing a fort outside the city limits of "Al-Qahirah," or Cairo. Surrounding this enclosure were a thick wall and moat. This area would serve as the new capital of the Fatimid dynasty, complete with an elaborate palace and an impressive new mosque, called Al-Azhar, or the "Most Shining," perhaps because the mosque was brilliantly illuminated on feast days.

When completed in 972, the mosque served as the official headquarters for the teaching of Shi'ism. Both the general and the Fatimid caliph used Al-Azhar to make public pronouncements, usually during the Friday prayers, and court sessions were held here during the week. Soon the city markets encroached on the walls of the mosque, and the homeless often sought refuge within the mosque's courtyard.

The original mosque building was rectangular, 280 feet long and 227 feet wide, with a courtyard in the center. Al-Azhar did not develop a reputation as a center of Muslim learning until several decades after its founding, when two great Islamic jurists, ibn-Killis (a Jew converted to Islam) and ibn-Numan were invited to Al-Azhar in the late 900s. Many young men flocked to Al-Azhar to learn from these renowned Islamic scholars. The earliest recorded student dormitory at Al-Azhar was constructed in 988; in addition, upon the request of ibn-Killis, the students received government stipends. The professors themselves, called *shaykhs,* also received a stipend from the government. There were neither formal courses of study nor classrooms nor degrees, as at medieval European universities. There were no entrance requirements, although it was understood that students coming to Al-Azhar would be literate and have memorized the Koran (which most Muslim boys did at an early age). "Graduates" of Al-Azhar (some professors provided written certificates of accomplishment) were ready to become prayer leaders at mosques, local (Koranic) school teachers, lawyers, and civil servants.

In the Fatimid theocracy, the Shi'ite beliefs in the *imamate,* or the caliph's divine right to rule and his infallibility in doctrinal matters, were central to the teachings of the *shaykhs* of Al-Azhar. Consequently, the mosque never lacked patronage in the form of gifts, and it was well maintained and often embellished. Al-Azhar obtained most of its income in the Middle Ages from the profits of nearby buildings and shops, which were earmarked as endowments for the mosque. Although Al-Azhar had no library, in 1005 the Fatimid caliph founded a research library there with thousands of valuable manuscripts that scholars in Cairo could use. Paper, pens, and ink were provided to them free of charge.

By the 1160s, the increasingly corrupt, arbitrary Fatimid dynasty had grown intensely unpopular in Egypt and soon collapsed. For the next several hundred years, Al-Azhar sank into relative obscurity, even in Egypt. This was especially the case during the reign of the famous Crusader-fighter Saladin, a fervent Sunni Muslim who distrusted Al-Azhar because of its reputation as a Shi'ite stronghold. This distrust characterized the dynasty he founded, which lasted until 1252. The government ceased subsidizing students or paying the *shaykhs.* Those students who could afford to stayed on and paid their professors privately; poor students, lacking financial support, were forced to leave. Saladin, however, made a lasting contribution to higher education in Egypt by introducing the college system, which Al-Azhar eventually adopted. Colleges were separate institutions within a mosque compound, containing classrooms, a library, and dormitories. In a theocracy such as Egypt, colleges were similar to monasteries—with required prayer five times a day, no women allowed, and an emphasis on asceticism.

Al-Azhar did not remain obscure. It was still the seat of the Egyptian *ulama,* and the most important center in the Muslim world for the study of Arabic—a fact of major significance because the Koran was written in Arabic, the prophet's language. When the long reign of the Mamluks superseded Saladin's dynasty in the 1260s, Al-Azhar was rescued from its obscurity. The Mamluks originally were Sunni Muslim non-Arab mercenaries from central Asia. Under their chaotic rule in Egypt, which lasted until the Ottoman Turks established their empire in the sixteenth century, they revitalized Al-Azhar, restored stipends for students and salaries for the *shaykhs,* and heavily endowed the mosque college. A college was built adjacent to the mosque and completed in 1340. Blind young boys were given stipends and encouraged to study the Koran (and possibly pursue higher studies), in the belief that they could earn their living afterward as chanters of the Koran on feast days, and even as teachers. Al-Azhar developed into the preeminent institution for the higher study of Islam, Islamic law, and Arabic, and young men throughout the Islamic world flocked to it. In the late 1400s, a generous caliph completely renovated the rectangular mosque and built new dormitories for the students.

By that time, Al-Azhar was already venerable. Senior scholars taught there, while many of the students were older men who had come there to engage in research. Al-Azhar had no counterpart in Europe. It possessed no central library (the library that had existed during the Fatimid period had been largely destroyed in the vicissitudes of wars and political instability that followed the collapse of Fatimid rule). If a student desired to learn a language such as Hebrew or Greek, or to study medicine, he had to go elsewhere in Cairo. In the absence of a printing press, texts were few. Students memorized their *shaykh's* lectures and notes, and texts, if there were any, were summaries of great works, rather than the works themselves.

Al-Azhar's fortune continued after the Ottoman Turks conquered the Mamluks and annexed Egypt to their empire in 1517. Murder and mayhem characterized the Turkish takeover of Cairo, yet the Turks pardoned the fugitives taking refuge in Al-Azhar. Once installed, the Turks treated the institution with great deference, apparently in awe of the venerable mosque college that attracted the greatest Koranic and Arabic scholars. It was also politic to favor an institution that was the pride of Egyptians, who resented the Turks. The scholars of Al-Azhar continued to uphold the *sharia,* and rigidly opposed any deviation from Islamic orthodoxy. When an Egyptian reformer, Wa'iz al-Rum, came to Al-Azhar in 1711 criticizing the corruptions in Islam and attacking certain customs and traditions, the *shaykhs* had him silenced and driven out of their institution.

On the eve of the French conquest of Egypt in 1799, Al-Azhar, still the most prestigious mosque college in Egypt, remained opposed to the study of science, foreign languages, and modern history. In 1748, the Turkish pasha in Cairo learned that neither astronomy nor mathematics was taught at Al-Azhar, and he presented the mosque college with a sundial in the hope of stimulating an interest in those subjects.

Al-Azhar remained loosely administered and organized. There was no college library, no examinations, no formal program of education leading to a degree, and no formal teaching qualifications. A rector, usually the leading jurist teaching there, supervised the mosque college and oversaw its finances. There were rules governing student behavior, and students belonged to *riwaqs,* loose fraternities within Al-Azhar organized according to nationality and the branch of Islamic law the student studied (there were four), if law was his specialty. A *shaykh* took responsibility for a particular *riwaq.* Meanwhile, Al-Azhar Mosque served the religious needs of the public, who freely wandered in and out, swarming there during feast days, while the homeless poor were never discouraged from seeking refuge within Al-Azhar's walls. In many respects, Al-Azhar little resembled an institution of higher learning.

Yet higher education was its purpose, and in the absence of academic degrees, it was the responsibility of the *shaykh,* or professor, to determine if a student was sufficiently prepared to leave Al-Azhar to enter a profession. The average length of study was six years with the academic year lasting seven months. To become a professor or a high civil servant required a longer stay. So while the institution lacked a bureaucratic infrastructure, academic training could be rigorous and prolonged. Al-Azhar also had a special commitment to blind students, who would be trained to qualify for membership in the guild of Koran readers (or reciters).

In July 1798, Napoléon Bonaparte and his forces conquered Egypt, wresting it from the control of the decrepit Ottoman Empire. They governed Egypt for

Al-Azhar University

nearly three years, although Napoléon returned to France a year later. The French takeover sent shock waves throughout Egyptian society, which had not been ruled by non-Muslims in over a thousand years. Everywhere anti-French rebellions took place. Napoléon attempted without success to woo the *shaykhs* at Al-Azhar, an institution hitherto unknown to him and his entourage, which included French scholars. It did not help that French soldiers were sent to occupy the mosque college; they closed it down for a year because of its anti-French sentiment. Nonetheless, French influence on Al-Azhar was nothing less than revolutionary. Not all the *shaykhs* were resistant. In fact, the rector of Al-Azhar from 1830 to 1834, long after the French had departed, took it upon himself to learn French and impart his understanding of European culture to his students at Al-Azhar. The French introduced the printing press to Egypt, an event which had far-reaching effects

on higher education in Al-Azhar; henceforth, students could buy original works instead of relying solely on memorization and condensed texts.

Even after the French departed and another despot sat on the pasha's throne, the old ways never returned. The new ruler, the local governor (nominally subject to the Ottoman porte) Muhammad 'Ali Pasha, favored scientific knowledge and the establishment of secular schools. For the first time in its history, math, modern science, and history found their way into Al-Azhar's curriculum. It remained one of few schools in Egypt that offered courses in theology and Arabic during Ottoman rule.

In 1872, Al-Azhar implemented a formal system of hiring professors. At the same time, Al-Azhar owed a great deal to the influence of an important man of letters, Al-Afghani, who taught there from 1871 to 1878. A liberal Muslim who taught European philosophy at Al-Azhar, he also sought to prove that the Koran did not oppose modern science, and that reason and faith were not incompatible. Al-Afghani finally was pressured to leave because his views were still far ahead of the times at Al-Azhar; nonetheless, his influence was felt there for decades to come.

When the British occupied Egypt in 1882 (remaining until the end of World War I), in large part because of Great Britain's desire to control the newly constructed Suez Canal, Egyptians could no longer ignore the pressure to modernize and westernize. Conservative Al-Azhar changed more rapidly in the next few decades than it had in its entire thousand-year history. In the late 1890s, such major steps were taken as the planning of a central college library and the establishment of a modern clinic and infirmary to oversee the health of its 9,000 students. The rector ordered over 18,000 books and manuscripts owned by the mosque college to be collected as an initial step in establishing a central library. For the first time, hygiene became important and attempts were made to prevent the spread of disease by improving the overall sanitation of the college; traditionally, the indigent, either sick or healthy, slept in the open, and open-air cooking was commonplace. These changes were accompanied by a complete refurbishing and renovation of the mosque and college buildings.

In 1889, Egypt's Grand Mufti Muhammad 'Abduh, a *shaykh* at Al-Azhar who was more highly placed than the rector of the college, happened to be a disciple of the disgraced Al-Afghani. Until his death in 1905, 'Abduh was the leader in introducing reforms at Al-Azhar. This included instituting a regular system of examinations and required courses as a step in reducing the haphazard organization of the college.

Over the years, several important educational statutes followed to strengthen these reforms and introduce new ones. The educational statutes of 1885, 1908, 1911, and 1916 at last created a formal administrative infrastructure for the mosque college and an organizational framework for the student body, which was divided into major academic schools (such as "religious sciences," and "Arabic language"), that carried their own requirements and encompassed a formal course of study. By placing other mosque colleges in Egypt under its administration, the reform statute of 1885 raised Al-Azhar's status to a university. There was so much resistance to changing the name to "University of Al-Azhar," that the matter was dropped.

Independence from Great Britain came to Egypt after World War I, though with numerous conditions, primarily because of the strategic importance of the Suez Canal. World War I had placed Cairo at center stage, as the headquarters of the allied war effort against the Ottoman Empire. With the presence of allied troops throughout the war, Egypt was subjected to western influence as never before in its modern history. Though formally independent with its own monarchy, Egypt could no more resist the tide of westernization than it could the annual flooding of the Nile.

Even as Al-Azhar was swept along in this tide of change, it remained a beacon of conservatism. In 1923, a *shaykh* was censured for being too critical of Al-Azhar's slowness to change: yet change was inevitable. In that particular year, a formal postgraduate degree program was inaugurated in certain disciplines, new courses were introduced, such as foreign languages, and in 1930, Al-Azhar even acquired its own printing press. In 1936, its formal designation as a university took place at last.

During World War II, Egypt once again found itself in the middle of the allied war effort against the forces of Hitler and Mussolini, the country flooded with foreign troops, spies, and movie stars. Western powers still controlled the Suez Canal, while Egypt was still too underdeveloped to assert itself as a sovereign state. The growing and powerful Muslim Brotherhood, established in 1928, reacted against westernization and opposed the Islamic conservatism embodied in the *ulama* and in such institutions as Al-Azhar, since they were impervious to Islamic fundamentalism. At the end of the war, fundamentalism appealed to a growing lower class, and lower-middle-class segment of Egyptian society, rather than to intellectuals and students. The reach of the hardcore fundamentalists within the Muslim Brotherhood (which had its own ideological divisions ranging from moderate to extreme fundamentalism) was inadvertently extended when the Brotherhood threw its support on the side of the forces of Gamal Abdel Nasser and his clique of army officers, who staged a successful coup in 1952. They abolished the monarchy and in 1956 seized control of the Suez Canal.

Al-Azhar University had displayed signs of favoring freedom of thought, symbolized in its foreign-exchange program inaugurated in 1945, but this promising indicator was short-lived. The Nasser government turned out to be pro-Soviet, its economy was quasi-socialistic, and Al-Azhar was put under government control in the same year that Nasser staged his coup. Al-Azhar's nearly 5,000 foreign students were all drawn from nonwestern countries. The Muslim Brotherhood, alarmed at the spread of Soviet-style atheism and secularization, went underground.

Despite the establishment of other universities in Egypt, Al-Azhar remained the largest (currently with more than 90,000 students) and most prestigious. In the 1958–59 academic year, Al-Azhar celebrated its millennium as an institution of higher learning. It boasted new administration buildings, an assembly hall, a large modern university library, and an efficient administration. The rector is president of the university, and the major administrative organ of the university is the supreme council. The old mosque, little changed since its renovation in the early twentieth century, serves as a university mosque.

The educational statute of 1961, Law 103, brought perhaps the most dramatic change to Al-Azhar: the admission of women. To be sure, the "College for Girls" (as it is called to this day) segregates women into their own classrooms and laboratories, and it is headed by a male dean. Nonetheless, deciding that women had a right to a higher education was revolutionary for an Islamic society.

Al-Azhar University has taken upon itself the task of steering a middle course between the tides of westernization on the one hand and strident fundamentalism on the other, and it has antagonized both sides. Fundamentalists criticize the *ulama* (i.e., the law faculty of Al-Azhar) for its rigid orthodoxy and for its 1990s denunciation of the invasion of Kuwait by Iraqi forces, while the Brotherhood sought to reduce the number of female university students overall. The government of Hosni Mubarak was dissatisfied, on the other hand, with the *ulama*'s retraction of its earlier support of family planning and its denunciation of the United Nations' population conference held in Cairo in 1994. What the outcome of its unpopular middle course will be remains to be seen; however, Al-Azhar has prevailed for over 1,000 years, despite both political and social vicissitudes.

Further Reading: Despite the fact that Al-Azhar University is regarded as the premiere university in the Arab world, surprisingly little has been written about it in any western language, although there are many sources in Arabic. The fullest account still is Bayard Dodge's out-of-print *Al-Azhar: A Millennium of Muslim Learning* (Washington, D.C.: Middle East Institute, 1961), which ends, however, before coeducation was inaugurated in 1961.

—Sina Dubovoy

ALBERT LUDWIGS UNIVERSITY
(Freiburg, Germany)

Location: In central Freiburg, a city of approximately 175,000, 80 miles from Stuttgart, in the state of Baden-Württemberg, Germany.

Description: A state university enrolling about 23,000 students in undergraduate and graduate schools.

Information: Albert-Ludwigs-Universität Freiburg
International Office
Werthmannsplatz
Postfach
79085 Freiburg im Breisgau
Germany
(761) 203 437

The Albert Ludwigs University is located in the heart of the town of Freiburg (30 kilometers from the French border and 70 kilometers from Basel, Switzerland) and shares with it more than 535 years of history. With approximately 12,000 employees—out of which 7,000 work in the medical branch—it has become the largest employer in Southern Baden. But in the late fifteenth century, the university started on a much smaller scale and nearly faced extinction in the early nineteenth century. Today, 64 subjects are offered in 14 faculties leading to various degrees. A 15th faculty for applied sciences, with the departments of computer science and microsystem technology, is also being developed.

The Albert Ludwigs University is one of Germany's oldest universities. Archduke Albert VI of Upper Austria founded the university in 1457, but the driving force in setting up the school was his wife Mechthild, who had grown up under educated humanists in the Palatinate. Three years later, academic teaching began in the faculties of theology, law, medicine, and the arts. Albert was very much concerned about educating legal recruits for the state administration as well as theological recruits for the Catholic Church. Therefore, the University of Freiburg was designed to become a bastion of Catholicism.

In the first term 234 students were enrolled. At that time, the average age of the students was between 13 and 16, although the university register books also list students who were ten, nine, and even five years old. Students either lived in private homes with their professors or in residential homes, the so-called Bursen. Because of the difficult social situation of many stu-dents, some respectable citizens donated study houses in which teachers and students lived together. Teaching also took place in these houses since the university did not own lecture halls until the middle of the sixteenth century.

One of the most important houses was the Collegium Sapientiae (House of Wisdom), donated by the Augsburg suffragan bishop, Johannes Kehrer, in 1496. Kehrer not only provided the financial foundation but also determined the social life in the house by formulating 88 rules. Students who lived there were selected by a commission of 12 and received a grant which was to be paid back after they had finished their studies. The daily routine was laid out in the form of monastic rules that determined, for example, when to get up during winter and summer times. Conversation was only permitted in Latin and students were forbidden to gamble and sing indecent songs. Violations were punished by exclusion from the house or by the withdrawal of wine at the meals. For a long time professors received their wages not in money but in wine.

The educational background of students in the later middle ages was very poor. Although a precondition to study was the knowledge of Latin, the language of science, only a few had acquired the necessary language skills in one of the municipal or conventual Latin schools. During a compulsory basic study in the artistic faculty, one could gain the knowledge needed for advancing to the three higher faculties of theology, law, and medicine. In lectures professors would only read aloud from a textbook that had been selected by the faculty. Rhetorical skills of students were developed in disputations that were part of the curriculum.

The term lasted from mid-November to August. Yet in the eighteenth century only 90 out of the 300 days of the academic year were good for study because of the number of days set aside for recreation. Thursdays were off as a matter of principle, and Tuesdays were half-days. In addition, the university took part in some 15 religious processions in Freiburg and the surrounding areas.

In the sixteenth century, some of the most important scholars of the time taught in Freiburg. Among them was Gregor Reisch, who wrote an encyclopedia of 12 volumes that became one of the most important manuals of the time. Martin Waldseemuller, one of his students, created together with Mathias Ringmann the famous world map of 1507. In the accompanying introduction (*Cosmographiae Introductio*) Waldseemuller made a mistake of grave consequence. He supposed that Amerigo Ves-

Albert Ludwigs University

pucci, the Portuguese seaman who had discovered the mouth of the Amazon, was also the discoverer of the new continent. Hence, Waldseemuller called the continent "America." All later attempts to correct the mistake were unsuccessful. The name "America," an invention of two former students from the University of Freiburg, has remained to this day.

Erasmus of Rotterdam also stayed in Freiburg, but although he was asked to deliver lectures, he never did. Another famous scholar, Ulrich Zasius, was an important member of the law faculty. He wrote the new city law in 1520 and was the pathmaker for the reception of the Roman law and, hence, today's basics of law.

The beginning of the Reformation meant for the university the beginning of an unlucky time. Freiburg and its university became a center of Catholic orthodoxy. The theological faculty was asked to work out a report against

Luther and his supporters. At the same time, the university was engaged in a fierce struggle to win its autonomy from the provincial government. The sixteenth century also saw the spread of the plague. Freiburg was afflicted more than 15 times, during which times the university sought shelter in other towns, among them Konstanz. In order to take care of their sick, the university administration bought a house that they turned into a hospital. On the property, a botanical garden was established which still exists today at a different location as the fifth oldest garden in Germany.

In the seventeenth century, the University of Freiburg was the only Catholic university in southwestern Germany. It was surrounded by a ring of Protestant universities in Tübingen, Zurich, Basel, Strasbourg, and Heidelberg. The school's sense of separation was only increased with the entrance of the Jesuits in 1620. While they increased the number of university buildings, they also restricted scholarly teaching. The university was closed to the ideas of the Enlightenment until the middle of the eighteenth century. Students still gained their knowledge by disputations and not by empirical observations or experimental research. Because no fundamental university reform took place, registration at the university dwindled, at times to as few as 50 students.

An opening for new branches of scholarship arose with the university reforms of Empress Maria Theresa. Through these reforms the state gained control of the university, which by then had lost much of its autonomy. The senate was replaced by a consortium of four members, and the faculties were headed by a director chosen by the state. Only the state government could appoint professors in the future. In all faculties, new subjects and chairs were introduced. From then on German was the language in which teaching was conducted. The professors were asked not to read out of a textbook but to introduce and interpret different research results in their lectures. Experimental teaching became part of the academic education at the University of Freiburg.

In 1805 Freiburg became a town in the small state of Baden that already had a Protestant university in Heidelberg. Karl von Rotteck, a famous political scientist at the university, successfully underlined in a memorandum the importance of the denominational difference of the two universities in the state. In 1818 Grand Duke Ludwig assured the survival of the University of Freiburg. As a sign of gratitude, the name of the university was changed to Albert Ludwigs University.

Between 1815 and the March Revolution of 1848, Freiburg's students and professors were involved in the political controversies of the time. At one point the Badian government even ordered the school closed. But the town of Freiburg supported its university and achieved a reopening.

The foundation of the German Empire caused an increase in student enrollment. From 1870 to 1885 the number of students increased from approximately 200 to 1,000. Upon reaching that number, all of Freiburg celebrated, as it did in 1898 and in 1904 when enrollment reached 1,500 and 2,000 students, respectively. The 3,000th student in 1911 was also a cause for celebration and was even offered free lunch for one term by the owner of a local restaurant. When the enrollment reached 4,000 students, during the period of the world economic crisis of 1929, the town stopped celebrating. Although there had been no public celebrations, the first five female students at the university began their studies of medicine in the winter term of 1899–1900.

National Socialism affected the university deeply. Thirty-eight Jewish professors (about 19 percent of the staff) were dismissed by 1935. One hundred thirty-five scholars from Freiburg likewise had their title of doctor withdrawn when the government revoked their German citizenship. "Study of Race" became a compulsory sub-

ject. The opposition to these changes at the university was weak and mostly Christian-oriented, but the majority of the university teachers was passive.

During an air raid in World War II, 3,000 people died and 80 percent of the buildings in the old part of town were destroyed, along with the university church and hospital. Also destroyed were 80 percent of all university buildings. The rebuilding of the university began in 1949. Due to the acquisition of land, which came in part from a generous land exchange with the town, the university complexes were eventually redeveloped.

The humanities and the university library are located in the center of town, the natural sciences are assembled in the institute quarter in the north, and the large hospital is in the west of the Old Town. The university also has gained property for future developments.

Today, 15 faculties are classified in the areas of theology, law, economics, medicine, the arts, mathematics, physics, biology, chemistry and pharmacy, geology, and forestry. Traditionally, the humanities have played an important role at the university. Many outstanding performances in philosophy, in the philology of various European languages, and in historical research are connected with the name of the university. In the economics faculty the main emphasis of teaching is on political economy; among its prominent members are Walter Eucken, founder of the ordoliberal "Freiburg School" and Friedrich August von Hayek, who shared the Nobel Prize in economics in 1974. In the mathematics faculty the whole spectrum of mathematical sciences is covered. The focus in physics is on nuclear, high-energy, and particle physics. Freiberg is a leading center of interdisciplinary polymer research. Hermann Staudinger, who was awarded the Nobel Prize in chemistry in 1953, did research that formed the basis for the development of plastics. In biology, the research of such world-famous biologists as August Weismann and Hans Spemann led to modern genetic studies. Research in geology puts emphasis on the understanding and evaluation of natural resources, their exploitation by humans, and the preservation of raw materials and the environment. In forestry the research is concentrated on the causes and effects of forest diseases. The faculty of medicine enjoys a high international reputation with its large body of experimental and clinical research.

The university has also opened two centers: the France Center, which offers research as well as an extension study course to acquire competence in matters relating to France; and the Freiburg Material Research Center, which conducts application-related basis research.

The university library, built in 1978, holds more than 2 million books. The *studium generale* offers lecture series with scientists and artists and is intended for students and citizens alike. More than 1,800 students come from abroad to study in Freiburg. In recent years students from the south of Europe have outnumbered those from America. Since 1911 Freiburg has been offering international summer courses in July and August. The magnificent landscape around Freiburg certainly supports its popularity within Germany and abroad.

Looking ahead to the future, the university, as a member of the European Confederation of the Universities on the Upper Rhine (EUCOR), has stimulated European integration together with the universities of Basel, Strasbourg, Mulhouse, and Karlsruhe.

—Wolfgang Holtkamp

ALIGARH MUSLIM UNIVERSITY
(Aligarh, Uttar Pradesh, India)

Location:
Aligarh Muslim University lies just outside the town of Aligarh or Koil in the northern state of Uttar Pradesh in India. The city is an agricultural and manufacturing center in the region. Aligarh is known for its lock-making industry and sells most of its products domestically.

Description:
With 12,000 residential students, about 9,000 commuter students, 73 departments, and an annual budget of 10 million rupees, Aligarh Muslim University is the largest residential university in India. AMU is one of the select 12 central universities which gets funds directly from the Indian federal government.

Information:
Aligarh Muslim University
Aligarh
Uttar Pradesh 202002
India
(571) 23994, (517) 23173

Visiting:
Write to the Office of Registrar at the address mentioned above for further information.

Located in the northern Indian town of Aligarh, Aligarh Muslim University (AMU) represents both an institution and a style of politics. Aligarh Muslim University's size and location make it a mini-township unto itself, enclosing both students' residence halls and faculty residences. Among its many important facilities and institutes is an engineering college; the Maulana Azad Library, with over a million books and rare manuscripts; and a college of traditional Unani medicine. Yet the importance of AMU lies above and beyond these statistics of scholarly activities. The most significant image of AMU is connected to the activities of its students and administrators between 1875 and 1947, when South Asia moved from colonial rule to independence and partition. The university has had a decisive impact not only on the social education of Indian middle class elites, but also on the political doctrines that shaped the destinies of present-day India and Pakistan.

Aligarh Muslim University's history goes back to 1875 when the reformist leader, Sir Syed Admed Khen (1817–98), laid the foundation of the Mohammedan Anglo–Oriental College (MAO) that in 1920 became Aligarh Muslim University. In the late nineteenth century, Sir Syed wanted to improve the social conditions of the Indian Muslim community through education, which he felt was essential to

pulling the community out of isolation. This sense of collective marginalization was a consequence of the abortive but bloody Indian uprising of 1857. The shock of the uprising and the accompanying popular violence had a profound impact on British policy in India. The prevalent feeling in administrative circles was that the Indian Muslims were responsible for the unrest. Direct encouragement of Muslim participation in the military and government ceased thereafter, for about two decades. When Sir Syed started the Mohammedan Anglo–Oriental College in 1877, he firmly believed that the institution would play a stellar role in the rejuvenation of Indian Muslim fortunes. According to him, the aims of the college were "to dispel those misty traditions of the past which have hindered our progress" and to "reconcile oriental learning with western literature and science." He felt that Indian Muslims were marginalized because they lagged behind the times and neglected the study of modern science. A stay in England in 1869 crystallized his beliefs along the same lines. Therefore, the college curriculum blended the wisdom of the East and the West, to guarantee the interests of the Muslim community in particular and India in general.

The MAO College quickly became the exemplar of liberal education in northern India. Funded through a mix of government and private funds, it was a blend of the average English public school, and Oxford and Cambridge Universities. At the same time it had a distinctively Islamic flavor with regular breaks for prayer where attendance was mandatory. The ruling families of the princely states of Hyderabad and Bhopal were major contributors to the college. The college also received the support and encouragement of high profile members of the administration, such as the Viceroy Lord Lytton and Sir John Strachey. This was a remarkable achievement at a time when a conservative Muslim opinion was harshly critical of all attempts to break away from the traditional educational pattern, centered around theology. Sir Syed faced strong opposition to his plans for Muslim education, and, indicative of the power of his personality, he succeeded in the teeth of opposition from clerics and religious leaders, many of whom declared him an apostate.

Aligarh Muslim University has a mixed style of architecture; buildings range in style and age from late-nineteenth-century imperial to contemporary. Named after Sir Syed's supporter and then Lieutenant-Governor of the United Provinces Sir Strachey, Strachey Hall was the center of the MAO College's daily activities in the nineteenth century. Architecturally, it is a spacious facility with a gable roof, built with the red brick and red sandstone that was used liberally in campus construction. It stood in the center of a quadrangle that housed the most important buildings of the college. The plan both replicated traditional Indian patterns where all rooms opened onto a central courtyard, and extended this to a larger student community who, the founders hoped, would come together and form close bonds with each other. Meetings and assemblies took place in its many large rooms.

The residential nature of the campus fostered the development of a culture unique to the college. In the nineteenth century, cultural activities on campus followed the British pattern, and some upper-class Indian ones. In 1884 the Siddons Union Club (now the Students' Union), modeled after the debating club at Cambridge began its activities in Strachey Hall. Sports such as cricket, with its emphasis on team spirit and cooperation, were also high on the agenda. Students were encouraged to develop the all-round abilities of the English public-school graduate. Rather than focusing narrowly on examinations, Aligarh teachers interpreted education broadly. The purpose of the college was to equip young men for public life as articulate managers, organizers, and administrators. They were to be the leaders of the new Muslim community that Sir Syed had envisioned. Leaving their families, bound together through their common experiences at the college, they were to be remade into a new brotherhood of distinguished men. Without a doubt, the college had a success disproportionate to its size in this mission. Among graduates of MAO College are Liaquat Ali Khan, the former prime minister of Pakistan; Zakir Hussain, a former president of India; and the nationalist leaders, Muhammad Ali, Shaukat Ali, and Rafi Ahmed Kidwai. The prominent educators A.R. Kidwai, Moonis Raza, and Nurul Hasan were AMU graduates. To this day, the residential nature of AMU and its campus culture have a powerful effect on its students. Many look back on their days at AMU as formative years both socially and culturally.

In its early years the MAO college administration picked a succession of Englishmen as principals, starting with Henry Siddons in January 1877. However, the most influential principal in the history of the college was Theodore Beck, a graduate of Cambridge University, who came to Aligarh in 1883. Under his guidance, the college detached itself from Calcutta University in 1887 and affiliated itself to the closer center, the Allahabad University. Beck, whose personal style was warm and affable, had a close personal relationship with the founder, Sir Syed, and was outspoken in what he considered were Muslim causes. He was only 40 years old when he died in 1899, just a year after his friend, Sir Syed, a victim of the immense stress of running a pioneer institution. His successor, Theodore Morison, carried on the tradition of intervening in issues close to Indian Islam, and he was closely involved in the Muslim Educational Conference, the organization that Sir Syed had founded in order to keep Muslim energies focused on educational innovation modeled on the Aligarh pattern.

In the early twentieth century, women's education became a cause for concern within middle-class Muslim circles. Shaikh Abdullah (a former student of the college, active in the Old Boys' Association and the Muslim Educational Conference) and his wife, Wahid Jahan, started the Aligarh Girl's School in 1906. The school moved to a mango grove not far from the Aligarh college and began classes as a residential school in 1914. Despite opposition from conservative circles, and from the fretful principal of the MAO College (W.A.J. Archbold), who worried about the effects on his male students of a girls' school so near, the school succeeded in creating a fashion for educating Muslim girls outside the home. To a certain extent, the Abdullahs had to make this radical idea acceptable to their middle-class constituency by keeping the general curriculum and culture of the institution conservative. By 1937 the school had established its success, thanks in no small part to the energy of Begum Abdullah, and it began offering college-level classes. The present day Aligarh Women's College, located at the same site, is the heir to this enterprise and is an active center for women's education in the city.

The history of AMU is also inseparable from the political history of modern India. Many scholars feel that the overly loyalist sentiments fostered at the college by Sir Syed and Beck contributed to the rift between Muslims and Hindus in modern India and created the grounds for the politics of separatism among Indian Muslims. It is true that Sir Syed criticized the Indian National Congress that held its first session in 1885. However, it is erroneous to suggest that he is the founding father of Muslim separatism in India. Sir Syed disapproved of any organization that embraced agitational politics. It was for this reason that he asked MAO College students to stay away from the newly created National Muhammadan Association in 1877 which was a political group in Calcutta. Besides, from the beginning, the MAO College was open to non-Muslim students as well.

Aligarh Muslim University is associated with the creation of Pakistan, the Muslim-majority country to the northwest of India. In October 1906, a group of activists, mostly from the Aligarh college, went in a deputation to Simla, the summer capital, urging the Viceroy, Lord Minto, to consider the Muslims a separate electorate from the Hindus with separate representation, in the forthcoming imperial reforms. That same year the Muslim Educational Conference transformed itself into the Muslim League, an explicitly political organization. The dreams of Sir Syed to keep the Muslim community aloof from politics receded. After all, the college had been founded on a political relationship—between the Muslim middle classes and the British rulers.

The hopes and dreams of the college administration, of instilling total loyalism, were not always realized. There was another powerful tradition of dissent that developed among students on campus. This manifested itself in student strikes against the administration, the most serious one being in 1907 when students refused to attend classes, protesting against the high-handedness of the faculty in general and the European faculty in particular. Muhammad Ali and Shaukat Ali, brothers and both former students and active members of the Old Boys' Association, criticized the overzealous loyalism of the college administration. They were actively involved in the pan-Islamic movement and formed an alliance with Mahatma Gandhi in his first Non-Cooperation Movement in 1920. Gandhi spoke to college students at a hugely attended rally in October 1920 and urged them to transform their institution into a truly national institution. On October 29, 1920, at a crowded rally at the College mosque, Muhammad Ali announced the inauguration of a new institution, the Jamia Millia (now the Jamia Millia Islamia University in New Delhi) which was to mark a departure from the government-funded and loyalist Aligarh college. Significantly, all the participants in and supporters of this action were graduates of the MAO College. Thus, MAO College gave to the Muslim community not only leaders who preached loyalism and later separatism, but also talented intellectual activists such as Rafi Ahmed Kidwai and the Ali brothers who participated in the anticolonial movement.

In December 1920, after the momentous incidents on the campus, the college was formally renamed a university, which had the power to grant degrees in its own name. Its social and cultural clout diminished after India and Pakistan gained independence separately on August 15, 1947. Many of its leading intellectuals, including the poet Iqbal left for Pakistan, leaving the university rudderless. However, as a symbol of community activity and solidarity, AMU remained unsurpassed. Jawaharlal Nehru, the first prime minister of independent India visited it in 1955, and in 1960, the Ford Foundation donated 2 million rupees toward the building of the Kennedy House on the campus. Aligarh Muslim University is still a major center of higher education in north India and is likely to maintain its status as such.

Further Reading: Aligarh Muslim University is always mentioned in any book about the partition of India and Pakistan in August 1947. *Struggle for Pakistan: Tragedy of the Triumph of Muslim Communalism in India, 1906–1947* by Lal Bahadur (New Delhi: Sterling Publishers, 1988) and *Modern Muslim India and the Birth of Pakistan, 1858–1951* by Sheikh Mohammad Ikram (Lahore: Sheikh Muhammad Ashraf, 1970) present the opposing arguments on the subject of partition. *Separatism Among Indian Muslims: The Politics of the United Providences' Muslims, 1860–1923* by Francis Robinson (London; New York: Cambridge University Press, 1974) also studies this theme. Books specifically on AMU are few and tend to concentrate on the earlier history of the institution. The standard text on the Mohammedan Anglo–Oriental College is *History of M.A.O. College,* by S.K. Bhatnagar (Aligarh: Asia Publishing House, 1969). For a more analytical treatment of the college, there is *Aligarh's First Generation: Muslim Solidarity in British India* by David Lelyveld (Princeton, New Jersey: Princeton University Press, 1978). The history of Aligarh's Women's College is taken up in "Shaikh Abdullah, Begum Abdullah and *Sharif* Education for Girls at Aligarh" by Gail Minault, in *Modernization and Social Change Among Muslims in India* edited by Imitiaz Ahmad (New Delhi: Manohar, 1983).

—Sharmishtha Roy Chowdhury

AMHERST COLLEGE
(Amherst, Massachusetts, U.S.A.)

Location: In Amherst, 100 miles west of Boston.

Description: A private college enrolling approximately 1,570 undergraduate students.

Information: Office of Admissions
P.O. 5000
Amherst, MA 01002-5000
U.S.A.
(413) 542-2328

Visiting: Regularly scheduled during the school year, four times daily: 10 A.M., 12 noon, 2 P.M., and 4 P.M.

Amherst College came into being almost by accident. The very idea of establishing a college was born of a fundraising effort that missed. Amherst Academy had been open for three years in 1817 when the school's trustees decided to reach for a higher goal and train "indigent pious young men for the ministry." To do that, they reasoned, the school needed a professorship of languages. Colonel Rufus Graves, the trustee chair, went to Boston and the surrounding area to solicit funds for the new position. However, after several months, the funds were not realized.

As one of the trustees, the illustrious Noah Webster, compiler of *An American Dictionary of the English Language,* stated: "the establishment of a single professorship was too limited an object to induce men to subscribe. To engage public patronage, it was found necessary to form a plan for the education for the ministry on a more extensive scale." The trustees thus decided to seek funds for an entirely new institution.

Ironically, Lord Jeffrey Amherst, after whom the town and college were named, never visited. A British soldier who seized Louisburg on Cape Breton Island from the French in 1758, Amherst became a colonial hero and was appointed commander-in-chief of English forces in North America. (Today's Amherst College varsity team players are called Lord Jeffs and Lady Jeffs.)

In 1818, a permanent charity fund of $50,000 was established. Five-sixths of the interest was earmarked for scholarships, with the remaining one-sixth added to the principal for perpetual increase. No money was provided for construction, so students from Amherst Academy dug building foundations, and area residents contributed teams, ox carts, and building supplies. Construction was halted several items when material such as bricks and lime ran out, and contributions had to be sought from churches and individuals.

Four buildings were constructed in seven years. The first, South College, was completed in August 1820. It housed laboratories, recitation halls, and sleeping space for students, but no actual bedrooms. Large, square rooms served as both dormitories and study halls. On the day the cornerstone was laid, Webster was named president of the board of trustees. A popular figure in the town, Webster was often seen farming and conversing with other farmers. In May 1821, Zephaniah Swift Moore, a former president of Williams College, was elected to serve as the institution's first president. Classes began that September. Moore was a popular president and his death at the age of 53, just before the school's second commencement, was devastating to the graduating seniors. Within a month, the board of trustees elected one of its own, Herman Humphrey, to succeed Moore. A graduate of Yale and a pastor by profession, Humphrey subscribed to a strict religious orthodoxy and abstinence from tobacco, traits that did not endear him to the student body. Nevertheless, he served as president for 22 years, stepping down in 1844 over budgetary disputes.

The first two requests for a state charter, brought before the 1824 state legislative hearings held in Amherst's Boltwood Tavern, were denied. Although the college was supported by students, faculty, and most of the town's residents, heavy opposition was voiced by Harvard and Williams Colleges, which viewed Amherst as unwelcome competition. Some wanted to move Williams College to Northampton, seven miles west of Amherst, a move that would have prevented the establishment of a new college. A public debate ensued with newspapers in Boston and New York taking sides on the issue. Ultimately, the legislature bowed to growing support for Amherst and granted the institution a charter in 1825. Although the school's founders were primarily orthodox Calvinists and a close affiliation existed between the college and the First Congregational Church in town, the charter did not tie the college to any creed.

Bachelor of arts degrees were conferred on previous graduates and on the class of 1825, with President Humphrey declaring the seniors "the first legitimate sons of the college," a statement that inevitably resulted in protests from previous students whenever it was repeated. In truth, the first Amherst student to receive a bachelor's degree received it from Union College in New York even though he studied at Amherst. It was 1823, Amherst was not yet chartered, and David O. Allen, a member of the

Amherst College

second graduating class, was teaching in Leominster, Massachusetts, during the winter break of his senior year. He received an appointment as principal of Groton Academy, but a Groton bylaw stipulated that the principal must be the graduate of a college. Since Amherst was prevented from granting degrees, then-President Moore arranged with the president of Union College to administer that school's senior examination to Allen, who passed

it and returned to Amherst, diploma in hand, to complete his studies.

Edward Hitchcock, third president and a professor of chemistry and natural science, was mostly self-taught. Eye trouble prevented him from attending Harvard, but he studied science on his own and later attended Yale for one year to study geology. His efforts gave the school a permanent endowment, a balanced budget, three buildings, and a higher reputation for scholarship and sound finance. During his nine years as president, Hitchcock was critical of the founder for his architectural judgment and for constructing dormitories. The architecture of Woods Cabinet, or Octagon, built in 1848 for the departments of astronomy and geology and today the home of the Black Student Union, was more to his liking. Hitchcock would have preferred no dormitories because he believed that in a rural place such as Amherst, students should find comfortable rooms with residents of "good Christian homes." To counter the effects of dormitory living, he invited freshmen to meet the families of the faculty and of others in the village. Hitchcock's wife Orra received undergraduates at the president's house every two weeks and opened the house on Monday evenings for prayer meetings.

Religion was a factor in William A. Stearns' decision to become the fourth president at Amherst. He left his life in the eastern part of the state in 1854 because he felt it was God's will. Once in Amherst, he considered the students "rough strong scholars" and lamented that the ministry had become "vulgarized." Nevertheless, Stearns saw the college through the tumultuous Civil War period. During his tenure, the college's first gymnasium was built and a department of hygiene and physical education was formed.

Stearns' successor was the mild-mannered Julius H. Seelye, a professor of philosophy. Famous for his "question box," a weekly one-hour meeting with seniors, Seelye encouraged the students to be independent and self-governing. In fact, he expanded the powers of the student senate.

However, his most significant achievement was likely his appointment of Amherst graduate Charles Edward Garman to the position of associate professor of moral philosophy and metaphysics. The stories of Garman's years at Amherst have reached mythical proportions. He was admired and sought after for his innovative teaching methods. Many students of the period, including Calvin Coolidge, an 1895 graduate, cited Garman as a driving influence in their lives.

Coolidge's time was also known for a marked conflict between freshmen and sophomores. The latter were a threat to any freshmen group activity, even one so innocent as having a group photograph taken. Sophomores carried canes, but did not permit freshmen to do so. By the 1890s, the cane conflict had escalated into a sort of sporting event at the beginning of each term, at night under torchlight. The "cane" was now a long broom handle and students competed to see which class had the most hands on it after an eight-minute brawl.

Amherst's sixth president, Merrill E. Gates, was not so well-loved. One student wrote home: "The religious life of the college is carried on . . . fully a quarter of a century behind the times." Gates, a former president of Rutgers College, was orthodox and evangelical. He often sponsored religious revivals, but they were not so successful as the revivals sponsored by President Humphrey had been. Students and some professors soon considered him little more than a name-dropper and an actor. As one alumnus put it, "The truth is that beneath President Gates' rather showy exterior were only a shallow intellect and shallow character. When this opinion became widespread, Gates was doomed."

Student contempt for President Gates was mixed with pride in their school, as evidenced by the alumni yell of the class of 1894, heard day and night: "Hi, Prexy, Hi / We know you're a sham / But we don't give a Damn / We're alumni-i, Ninety-Four." In the evening, students shouted this in front of the president's door and then ran to avoid possible expulsion.

That Gates treated the students like children was a common complaint. When students in his class on ethics did not memorize long definitions, he had them recite in unison. Perhaps his view of the students as schoolboys contributed to his quarrel with the college senate. In the autumn of 1893, when Gates suspended a student for cutting classes, the student senate protested that its rights had been usurped and requested that the student be reinstated so that the senate could consider the matter. Because the president refused to yield, the faculty was forced to oppose the student senate. Newspapers reported the disagreement, alumni took sides, and the student senate resigned. Student self-government, which had been called the "Amherst System," was no more.

For several years the college catalog featured blank spaces in place of the names of student senators, with an explanation that senators had not been elected by press time, and eventually the catalog omitted any mention of the senate. More than 20 years later, alumni asked trustees to grant a degree to the student who had been suspended on grounds that he had been wronged, and trustees agreed. (Today's students govern themselves through an active student government organization.) After the clash with the student senate, President Gates requested a leave of absence "on account of impaired health" and a triumvirate ruled until he resigned three months later.

Any discussion of Amherst College would be incomplete without mention of the Dickinson family. Edward Dickinson, father of poet Emily Dickinson, was the college's treasurer from 1833 to 1873. His son, William Austin, succeeded him. Austin Dickinson, as he was called, was known as an eccentric. As a young man he was often seen wearing a yellow hunting coat, and in his later years he sported a green wig. However, most of the talk centered around his 13-year affair with Mabel Loomis Todd, the editor of Emily Dickinson's first book of poems and the wife of an Amherst astronomy professor. After Austin's death in 1895, a bitter legal battle ensued as Mabel attempted to claim a parcel of land that Austin had left to her. An audit of Austin's office also brought to light an employee's use of $5,500 in school funds for stock speculation. Although the former treasurer was not implicated, he had been lax in collecting student bills, causing the school to operate at a deficit. In spite of the upheaval he caused, the townspeople were fond of Austin Dickinson and his passing was officially mourned for three days.

In spite of Edward S. Dwight's 1803 description of Amherst as "one of the most impressive and delightful objects which can be seen in this country," the land was considered irreclaimable from alluvial bottoms and marshes. Today, the campus is comprised of 964 acres, which include a wildlife sanctuary, a forest, an observatory, and a planetarium.

The college's liberal arts curriculum is designed to guide students toward intellectual competence rather than train them for particular professions. Students study in 28 academic departments with an open curriculum and no distribution requirements. The only required course is "Introduction to Liberal Studies" for first-year students.

Since 1976 Amherst has been fully coeducational. Students represent every state in the union and many countries. In 1984 the college, which had already purchased fraternity property, abolished fraternities. The buildings are now dormitories, reserved mostly for upper-class students, and theme houses such as a language house, a food cooperative, and a house devoted to African-American culture.

Amherst College's contributions include the nation's first college department of hygiene and physical education, the first undergraduate neuroscience program in the country (1973), the "Amherst System" of student self-government, and the "Amherst Idea." The latter resulted when the class of 1885 celebrated its 25th anniversary by presenting a memorial to the college, with the stipulation that entrance be by compulsory examination, that teachers' salaries be increased, that the number of students be limited, and that the bachelor of science degree be eliminated. As one professor at the time put it, the scientific course of study was one "whereby a man could get in, through, and out with the minimum of cerebration." Today, Amherst offers only the bachelor of arts degree.

The college trustees govern the Folger Shakespeare Library, established in Washington, D.C., by Henry Clay Folger, class of 1879, and his wife, Emily Jordan Folger. The Robert Frost Library on campus is named after the poet, who taught at the college for four different periods, from 1917 until his death in 1963, when the new building was dedicated, with President John F. Kennedy in attendance.

Amherst participates in a five-college consortium with Hampshire, Mount Holyoke, Smith College, and the University of Massachusetts. Students have access to courses and other resources at all five schools. Amherst students may also study in exchange programs, including one in Japan, through a special relationship with Doshisha University, founded by Joseph Hardy Neesima, class of 1870, the first Japanese to graduate from a western institution of higher education.

Further Reading: Hendrik Booraem's *The Provincial: Calvin Coolidge and His World* (Lewisburg, Pennsylvania: Bucknell University Press, and London: Associated University Presses, 1994) includes colorful descriptions of college life in the late 1890s. Claude Moore Fuess' *Amherst, The Story of a New England College* (Boston: Little Brown, 1935) takes the story through 1934 and includes several illustrations of the school and its faculty. *"The Consecrated Eminence": The Story of the Campus and Buildings of Amherst College"* by Stanley King, Amherst's president from 1932 to 1946 (Amherst, Massachusetts: Amherst College, 1952) details the growth of the college's campus and buildings. Polly Longsworth's *Austin and Mabel* (New York: Farrar Straus, 1984) relates the love affair between Austin Dickinson and Mabel Todd, with narration from the author and love letters between the two. W.S. Tyler's *History of Amherst College during Its First Half Century, 1821–1871* (Springfield, Massachusetts: Clark W. Bryan, 1873) covers the college's first 50 years.

—Diana D'India

ANTIOCH UNIVERSITY
(Yellow Springs, Ohio, U.S.A.)

Location: Yellow Springs, Ohio, 18 miles east of Dayton, Ohio. Other campuses are at Keene, New Hampshire; Seattle, Washington; Los Angeles and Santa Barbara, California.

Description: A private, coeducational institution of higher learning, which requires that undergraduate students at the Antioch Campus participate in a program alternating work and study. Students at New England and California campuses are adults from 23 to 70 years old. Antioch Seattle offers programs leading to B.A., M.A., and M.S. degrees.

Information: Public Relations Office
795 Livermore
Yellow Springs, OH 45387
U.S.A.
(513) 767-6382

Visiting: Call the school's admission office at (513) 767-6400 for details of visitors' weekends or to arrange for individual tours.

In the twilight of his remarkable career, the educator, social reformer, and abolitionist Horace Mann declined an invitation to run for governor of his native Massachusetts to become president of a new college, Antioch in Yellow Springs, Ohio. In 1850, members of the Christian Church (hereafter referred to as Christians), a Protestant sect, meeting at Marion, New York, had voted to establish that college and to raise $100,000 with which to endow it. The Christians were a loosely bound coalition of Protestant groups assembled from several states. Their liberal religious platform afforded latitude for differing doctrinal views but doubtless weakened the ties among its members. It did, however, attract favorable attention from Unitarians.

The committee charged with planning for this institution—meeting on October 5, 1850—agreed that the college would be located in the state that donated the most money for the endowment and the one that was both the most healthful and most accessible to travelers. Founding members further specified that two-thirds of the trustees and a majority of the faculty of the new school would at all times belong to the Christian group, and that the college would afford equal privileges to students of both sexes. The convention was silent on the subject of admitting African Americans. Meeting in Ohio, a subcommit-

tee of Christians recommended that the proposed college should be known as Antioch College. The group listened to presentations by delegations from various areas in Ohio, each promoting its community as the site for the new college. William Mills, a member of one of the leading families in Yellow Springs, offered 20,000 acres for a campus and $30,000 for the establishment of the college. A bonus offered by Yellow Springs was that the railroad ran through the community and that the station was, in fact, directly across from the acreage donated by Mills.

While the founders of Antioch favored coeducation, an idea that had begun at Oberlin College 20 years earlier and was generally popular, they didn't intend their college to be nonsectarian. Few, if any, nonsectarian colleges existed anywhere at that time, and none in the Ohio Valley. Despite the Marion Convention's clear intention, members of the subcommittee decided that the new school would, indeed, have no sectarian platform. Hence, the denominational tension between the two factions grew. The struggle to make Antioch a Christian school continued for more than 40 years, notwithstanding clear evidence that the Christians could neither fund the school nor provide enough students to warrant placing the college in their hands.

Preparing for 1,000 students, the planners voted to erect three buildings as the heart of the new campus. The buildings were much larger than was needed, since—from 1853 to 1859—enrollment exceeded 500 only once, in 1857, and wouldn't do so again until the early 1920s. Hence, the cost of repairs grew burdensome. Nonetheless, the original buildings still stand.

Mann, a staunch Unitarian, was persuaded to take the presidency because he believed that the college would be liberally endowed, coeducational, and nonsectarian. Indeed, the school was coeducational, but it was far from well endowed, and strife over sectarianism would continue for years. Mann believed Antioch's mission to be to educate young people to contribute to the development of industry and commerce in the vast area surrounding the school.

The first college catalog was issued in March 1853. Its prologue stressed the importance of good health habits, supported cooperation and human brotherhood, and called for the teaching of sound ethical and moral principles, rather than the indoctrination of dogmas. The curriculum consisted of Latin and Greek, mathematics, English, history, philosophy, and science. Since demand for teachers in the vast region far outstripped supply, courses in teaching methods were added.

In his inaugural address, delivered at noon on October 5, 1853—exactly three years after the Marion Convention

Antioch University

resolved to establish a college—Mann spoke for more than two hours. He commented on the wonders of astronomical space and time, on the state of human knowledge of physical and chemical laws, and on the Greek precept of a sound mind in a sound body.

Within a few months of his ascendancy, however, Mann's plan to present features of all religions was termed a "dark plot" that would "Unitarianize" the school and put it on a thoroughly liberal basis. Within just a few months, both faculty and trustees were split into pro- and anti-Mann factions. The biggest salvo to be aimed against Mann was fired by the Reverend Ira W. Allen, a professor of mathematics who was subsequently dismissed and went on to write a vicious account of campus affairs that was circulated among the Christian churches. Mann bore up and pressed on.

His trials were many, but money overshadowed them all. In actuality, the school was bankrupt before it ever opened. By the time the first class was graduated, Antioch's principal supporter had been wiped out in the panic of 1857. Two years later, the college went under the auctioneer's hammer. Mann and some friends bought it, but the luster was gone. They struggled on, however. During the final three years of Mann's presidency, the college showed a deficit of $5,000 each year in a budget of $13,000.

All the trials proved to be too much for Mann, who died late in the summer of 1859. His wife called him a martyr, and Ralph Waldo Emerson lamented his passing, writing that Mann had wasted his talents in trying to salvage Antioch. A later historian of liberal arts colleges, Ernest Earnest, would write that Mann "had been crucified by crusading sectarians."

The financial hardships of the early days continued almost unabated for 60 years. To keep the school afloat, the Christians raised funds through a joint control agreement with Edward Everett Hale and his fellow Unitarians. In 1865 that group at last raised an endowment of $100,000. In effect, the Christians and Unitarians became joint sponsors and owners. That joint sponsorship, however, was only partly successful. The dissension it engendered diverted funds and energy from management of the school. Hale, who served almost 35 years as a trustee, reported that his hopes for the college were realized only to a small degree.

Mann was succeeded by the Reverend Thomas Hill of Waltham, Massachusetts, considered one of Harvard's most brilliant graduates. Hill was reluctant to accept the post as Antioch's president because of the school's unsound financial condition, but he was finally persuaded to do so on condition that operating expenses and faculty salaries be guaranteed. However, even the guarantee didn't completely solve the school's problems. Hill received only part of his salary and had to borrow and call on friends to meet his own expenses and to keep the school operating.

Hill could not long tolerate such conditions and resigned after three years; his successor survived but four years. Between its opening and 1920, a span of 67 years, the school was headed by ten presidents and seven acting presidents, and from 1902 to 1906 a dean performed the duties of president. Furthermore, the college was dormant during the Civil War and closed in 1881–82. During these troubled years graduating classes were very small. Indeed, 34 of the graduating classes included five students or fewer; in five years no students were graduated at all. College enrollment was typically small, often with most students doing preparatory work.

In June 1881, Antioch's financial condition once again reached the critical stage. Trustees voted to suspend the college for three years or until income amassed from the endowment would justify reopening. An article in the January 14, 1882, issue of the *Cincinnati Gazette,* commenting on the school's closing, blamed it on Mann's prickly personality, even though he had been dead for more than 20 years. Blame was also attributed to unfavorable religious doctrine and social surroundings. The author of the article, quoting the Christians, declared that Antioch had been blighted by aggressive radicalism since the Unitarians took over and, hence, had lost its constituency. Clearly religious bias was still rampant.

Christians of southwest Ohio, the Yellow Springs area, were disturbed by the school's closing and, in May 1882, calling themselves the Christian Education Society, developed a plan. Their first proposal, that control of the college be turned over to Christians who would promise to raise another $100,000 endowment and bring about a significant increase in enrollment, was firmly rejected by trustees.

The second proposal was more modest, asking that the Society name the president and faculty, who would have to be confirmed by the trustees. In addition, income from the endowment (about $6,000 a year) would continue to be applied to the school's expenses. When the trustees agreed to this proposal, they appointed a managing committee to work with the Society. Antioch reopened in September 1882, though financial problems continued to plague the school.

At the 1919 annual meeting of the board of trustees, Arthur E. Morgan, of Dayton, Ohio, assumed a vacant place. A Unitarian, Morgan was placed on the board at the behest of Charles W. Eliot, president emeritus of Harvard University. Morgan for years had formulated educational designs in his mind and had been seeking a school at which to put them to use. Recognizing that his fellow board members had no plans for improvement and that Antioch was a school in danger of collapse, Morgan took control. Within just a few months, Morgan presented to the board a "Plan of Practical Industrial Education." Impressed, the board endorsed the plan and authorized him to carry out his plans for Antioch along the lines he proposed. In effect, Morgan became head of the college, with Professor W.M. Dawson as titular president.

In April 1920, at a meeting of the trustees' executive committee, Morgan reported on his plans: the college would remain coeducational, would maintain high standards, and would continue to accept African Americans, as it had since 1863. It would be reorganized to accommodate about 500 students who would be on a cooperative plan of alternate work and study; it would aim to develop well-rounded students, rather than those with highly developed specialties. An early advocate of small business, Morgan planned to include technical industries in the academic community. On July 6, 1920, Morgan was elected president of Antioch by unanimous vote of the trustees. His reorganization was successful, and Antioch reopened in September 1921, under the cooperative plan.

The new board of trustees was vastly different from the old. While the former trustees were mostly from Ohio, elderly, and, for the most part, ministers, Morgan's new board of 20 trustees included four from New York, two from Massachusetts, and one from Michigan. None was a minister. They were industrialists, men of prominence with an interest in education. Thus the new governing body had names, resources, and business acumen.

The major problem Morgan faced in hiring new faculty was finding men whose personal qualities fit his utopian ideals while still meeting the usual standard of academic competence. He kept only five of the inherited 13 staff members, then went looking for men with practical experience and broad interests, who would commit themselves to the adventure of working out a new philosophy at Antioch. The task was not an easy one, since finding qualified industrialists with at least a bachelor's degree, who would accept the lower salaries Antioch could offer was next to impossible. But Morgan persisted and eventually fielded a faculty of 25 in 1922 and then, a year later, 43.

Typical of the type of teacher Morgan sought was Basil H. Pillard, who joined the faculty in 1928. While Pillard had earned only a bachelor's degree from Yale, his experience included a year of teaching and eight years in business. Those years included one as a copywriter and account executive in an advertising agency. At a traditional liberal arts college, such a curriculum vitae wouldn't qualify a man for the faculty, but it was no barrier at Antioch. Pillard arrived as a teacher of business administration, then moved on to English literature, and later became dean of students.

Morgan's commitments to social planning was a part of his pursuit of utopia, a critical element in his revision of the college. Work, education, and the rest of life should have close ties if men are to develop good character, he believed. He also believed that the small community offered the best potential for living and working together.

The college acquired a reputation as one of the most distinctive and academically challenging colleges in the country. In the first year of the new order, enrollment multiplied five-fold, and similar growth continued for several years. In the early 1930s it reached a plateau of about 650 students. By that time, fewer than one student in five was from Ohio.

As successful as he was in transforming Antioch from a tiny, provincial liberal arts college to a challenging, progressive, and growing one, Morgan wasn't entirely successful at eliminating the school's persistent financial problems. Failing to raise the half million dollars authorized by himself and the board of trustees, Morgan was forced to turn to one of the new trustees, Charles F. Kettering, a Dayton industrialist. That benefactor loaned the strapped institution $300,000 and Morgan undertook the raising of funds for annual operating expenses, by now in excess of $100,000 a year. He hoped that college-controlled small industries would contribute to the school's coffers, but they did not.

The Great Depression exacerbated financial woes, forcing the school to rely ever more heavily on tuition. Such a reliance has become a permanent feature of Antioch. While many schools cover less than half their expenses with tuition fees, Antioch finances about three-quarters. Such a practice is feasible because of the work-study nature of the school's program. Students alternate weeks of study with weeks of off-campus work, thus raising money to fund their educations and doubling the number of persons who can utilize the campus.

Although Morgan felt that his dreams had been somewhat diluted, the school had changed significantly during his tenure, and generally for the better. That change didn't stop with Morgan's departure. Antioch became a home for liberal Quakers and Unitarians and, by the advent of World War II, had an unusual educational program built around work, classroom, and campus participation. Student self-government was practiced to an extent all but unknown in most schools in the United States.

With this reputation for educational innovation and progress, it's no surprise that Antioch directors wanted to take the lead in extending educational opportunity to adults, minorities, and the poor. Thus, in the mid-1960s the administration decided to expand beyond the boundaries of Yellow Springs, Ohio.

Outreach centers were created in Putney, Vermont; Philadelphia, Pennsylvania; and Columbia, Maryland. A law school that had been part of George Washington University in Washington, D.C., was adopted by the college in 1972. Some of these centers accomplished the aim of spreading educational opportunity and innovation. With 33 centers operating in the nation and abroad, the school's name was changed to Antioch University in 1978.

Expansion finances were not well managed, however, and placed a huge drain on Antioch's resources. The North Central Association of Colleges and Secondary Schools (NCA), responsible for the school's accreditation, found the president's office located in New York City, even though no academic programs existed there. The NCA found, too, poor long-range planning and academic quality control, as well as problems that had plagued the school since its inception: debt and deficits.

By 1983 the grim picture had brightened somewhat. Most of the centers had been closed and planning had improved. But the fortunes of the college continued to decline; enrollment dropped from a high of 2,500 in 1972 to 1,600 in 1975 and 600 in 1981. By 1985 the situation was perilous: full-time enrollment was down to 420, finances were in disarray, and huge deficits had led to severe cuts in faculty and staff.

In March 1985, Alan Guskin, Chancellor of the University of Wisconsin at Parkside for ten years, was named president. At the same time, the board of trustees moved the administrative offices back to Yellow Springs. The new president and the board were determined to rebuild the reputation of Antioch University.

Antioch School of Law in Washington, D.C., was closed; strict fiscal spending policies were introduced; effective long-range planning became a major management tool. The adult education campuses were asked to contribute funds to rebuild the college, creating a continuing endowment that would provide the school with stable finances. At last Antioch would be able to plan for the future. When NCA surveyed the school in 1988, it found some problems still existing, but acknowledged they were being successfully addressed.

In final steps to adjust the school's programs, the School for Adult and Experiential Learning—now the McGregor School—was formed in 1988. Campuses at Philadelphia and San Francisco were closed in 1989, and the London Centre was closed in 1990. Antioch is finally fulfilling Arthur Morgan's dream: "While we are learning to be effective, we should also be learning what it is most worthwhile to be effective about."

Further Reading: Burton R. Clark's *The Distinctive College: Antioch, Reed and Swarthmore* (Chicago: Aldine, 1970) defines the story of Antioch far better than many longer treatises. Robert L. Straker's *Brief Sketch of Antioch College (1853–1921)* (Yellow Springs, Ohio: Antioch College, 1954) does an excellent job of illustrating the school's early days, as does Ernest Earnest's *Academic Procession: An Informal History of the American College, 1636 to 1953* (Indianapolis, Indiana: Bobbs-Merrill, 1953).

—Ruth Pittman

ATLANTA UNIVERSITY CENTER
(Atlanta, Georgia, U.S.A.)

Location: Numerous locations in Atlanta.

Description: The Center consists of six colleges and universities: Atlanta University, Clark College, Morehouse College, Spelman College, Morris Brown College, and the Interdenominational Theological Center. It is the largest complex of predominantly African-American institutions of higher learning in the United States.

Information: Atlanta University Center
Office of University Relations
223 James P. Brawley Drive, SW
Atlanta, GA 30314
U.S.A.
(404) 880-8094

It would be difficult to speak of African American higher education without mentioning collectively the institutions that form the Atlanta University Center: Atlanta University, Clark College, Morehouse College, Spelman College, Morris Brown College, and the Interdenominational Theological Center. Today these institutions make the Atlanta University Center the largest complex of predominantly black colleges and universities in the country and one of the most significant.

Atlanta University, the hub of the center, was founded in the aftermath of the Civil War and the devastation of Atlanta wrecked by General William Tecumseh Sherman's Union army. In the fall of 1865, missionaries Reverend Frederick Ayers and his wife arrived in Atlanta from Belle Prairie, Minnesota, under the auspices of the American Missionary Association (AMA), and immediately took an interest in the education of Atlanta's African-American community. They began to conduct classes for blacks in a railway box car, providing primary and secondary schooling, but Frederick Ayers envisioned the establishment of a university that could help the newly freed slaves fulfill their role as responsible citizens. The AMA liked and endorsed Ayers' idea, and two years later the state of Georgia provided a charter for a university department. However, there were not enough black students until 1872 to warrant the opening of the university department. Four years later, Atlanta University awarded its first bachelor of arts degrees to six male students.

Clark College's classes were first held in 1869 in a small room in Clark Chapel Methodist Episcopal Church in Atlanta's Summerhill District. The school was under the

direction of Bishop Gilbert Haven, who wanted Clark to "set the tone" for all of the country's black Methodist educational institutions. During its early years, Clark's location changed many times before the school bought 450 acres in south Atlanta in 1877. By then, the college's curriculum had become more specialized, changing in function from a college offering the basics of learning to one that emphasized the training of ministers and teachers. By 1883, Clark was offering college degrees. That same year, Clark established the Gammon School of Theology as a department within the college. Five years later the Gammon school became an independent theological seminary.

During the latter part of the nineteenth century, both Clark and Atlanta University grew slowly. By 1900, Atlanta University had an enrollment of only 296 students, 104 males and 192 females, and a budget of just $40,000. The university, in fact, had no endowment and had to raise $25,000 of its annual budget through gifts. Atlanta University, however, was beginning to distinguish itself through its graduates, many of whom continued their education to become doctors, ministers, teachers, businessmen; through its conferences and published proceedings, which discussed, studied, and analyzed social problems affecting African Americans; and through its faculty, which included several prominent African-American scholars. W.E.B. DuBois, an African-American intellectual who had studied at Fisk, Berlin, and Harvard, came to Atlanta University in 1897 as a professor of history and economics. While a member of the faculty, DuBois completed his classic book *The Souls of Black Folk*, and founded the Niagara Movement in 1906 to promote black freedom.

In 1907, Edward Twitchell Ward, the son of Atlanta University's founders, succeeded Horace Bumstead as president of Atlanta University. During Ware's administration, Atlanta University began to develop increasingly closer ties with Clark, as well as Morehouse College, Spelman College, and Morris Brown College. Meetings were held between the various representatives of the black Atlanta colleges and universities to discuss how they could coordinate their efforts to educate African Americans. Mergers were even proposed. In 1912, Atlanta University joined Clark, Morehouse, Spelman, Morris Brown, and Gammon Theological Seminary to organize the "Atlanta Federation of Schools for the Improvement of Negro Country Life." The following year, Atlanta University and Morehouse worked together on a project that was supported by the Phelps–Stokes Fund and involved a study of crime in Atlanta. In 1914, Atlanta University and Morehouse offered their first joint

Morris Brown College, Atlanta University Center

course in business law and ethics, alternating location of the classes between the two schools.

Morehouse was founded as the Augusta (Georgia) Institute in the basement of the Springfield Baptist Church before the school moved to Atlanta in 1879 and changed its name to Atlanta Baptist Seminary. Started as an institution to prepare black men for the ministry and teaching, Morehouse, in its formative years, had a course of study similar to a high school, but the institution began to grow when John Hope became the college's first black president in 1906. President Hope attracted a number of talented faculty and administrators and expanded the curriculum. During Hope's tenure the college's name was changed to Morehouse College in honor of Henry Lyman Morehouse, the corresponding secretary of the Atlanta Baptist Home Mission Society. Many famous African Americans (Dr. Martin Luther King Jr., Julian Bond, Lerone Bennett, and Spike Lee, to name a few) would graduate from Morehouse College.

Spelman was founded in 1881 by Sophia Packard and Harriet Giles, two white women from New England, in the basement of Friendship Baptist Church in Atlanta.

The school had $100 in capital and 11 students. Originally named the Atlanta Baptist Female Seminary, Spelman had as its objective the training of young black women for careers such as teaching and nursing. In 1884, the school was named Spelman Seminary in honor of Laura Spelman Rockefeller, wife of oil magnate John Davison Rockefeller. The institution awarded its first college degree in 1901 and in 1924 changed its name to Spelman College. One of only two remaining colleges for African-American women, Spelman was buoyed by a gift of $20 million from entertainer Bill Cosby.

The African Methodist Episcopal Church founded Morris Brown College in 1881 after the adoption of a resolution at the denomination's North Georgia Annual Conference meeting calling for the "Christian education of Negro boys and girls" in Atlanta. Four years later, the institution received a charter from the state of Georgia and opened with nine teachers and 115 students. The college grew slowly, adding first a liberal arts college in 1894 and then a theology department for the training of ministers.

Atlanta University and the other black institutions of higher learning in Atlanta played a prominent role in

World War I. About 100 Atlanta University and Morehouse students were put through basic training as part of a student army training camp, which opened on the Atlanta University campus under a contract with the U.S. government. The university also trained two detachments of 243 soldiers in an army school for mechanics.

During the 1920s, cooperation accelerated in several areas. By the 1928–29 term, for example, all upper-level courses at Spelman and Morehouse were open to students at either college and at least three faculty members held joint appointments.

In 1928, the trustees of Atlanta University learned that "the General Education Board would be interested in helping Atlanta's [black] institutions if among themselves they could come to some type of cooperative arrangement which would result in less competition among the institutions, reduce operating expenses, and place the combined resources of the institution behind the education of the students." In February 1929, at a series of meetings, the Board of Trustees of Atlanta University, Spelman, and Morehouse worked out a general plan of affiliation that paved the way for the signing of an agreement, which became known as the "Atlanta University Affiliation."

On April 1, 1929, the presidents of the three institutions signed the "Contract of Affiliation," and John Hope was invited to become president of the university as of July 1, 1929. After discussing the offer with his family, Hope accepted, provided he could remain president of Morehouse until its endowment was raised so that it would be on a sound financial basis.

Under the terms of the agreement, Morehouse and Spelman would continue to be undergraduate colleges, while Atlanta University would concentrate on graduate education. Each institution would have its own trustees, but each would nominate three members of the university board, which, in turn, was authorized to elect five additional members.

Initially, the affiliation didn't sit well with alumni, faculty, and students. Students at Atlanta University said that, if their parents approved, they would complete their undergraduate education elsewhere rather than transfer to Morehouse and Spelman. Meanwhile, many faculty worried about their futures and their pensions. Clark University and Morris Brown College worried about their future, too, since they were not asked to participate in the discussions leading to the affiliation.

But the general education board looked favorably upon the affiliation and gave money for the construction and endowment of a new library, which would be centrally located to serve all institutions of higher learning for blacks in Atlanta. Later, the general education board provided more funds to Atlanta University for the construction of a physical plant and for restricted endowments for both Atlanta University and Morehouse College. In 1930, the general education board entered into an agreement with philanthropist Edward Harkness, matching his gift

of one million dollars toward the endowment and the construction of new buildings. The Harkness and general education board grants were the largest ever received by Atlanta University from any individual or foundation in its history. The Harkness gift made possible an administration building, two dormitories, a dining hall for graduate students, and a new residence for the president.

In 1931, Atlanta University awarded Joseph A. Bailey the first master's degree under the reorganization, and in recognition of the historic event, the institution held a special commencement. Among the requirements: all students were required to pass an examination in English fundamentals and composition, as well as a reading examination in German and French.

During the 1930s and early 1940s, Atlanta University increased its cooperation with Spelman and Morehouse and made a number of gifts of property to the institutions, helping to put them closer together in one geographic area. During World War II, Atlanta University trained numerous people in science, engineering, and war management programs and through a special program for the administrative section of the United States Army Air Forces. Meanwhile, Atlanta University, as well as Clark, Spelman, and Morehouse, provided living accommodations and classroom facilities for the army.

By 1950, Atlanta University had opened several graduate schools: library science (1941), education (1944), business administration (1946), and social work (1947). Enrollment in the graduate school during the regular academic term ran between 450 and 500 students, with another 1,500 to 2,000 registered for summer school. Atlanta University was on a solid financial and educational footing. The endowment had increased from $300,000 in 1929 to a little over $5 million in 1950, and during the same period, the budget jumped annually from $70,000 to $700,000. By 1950, Atlanta University was graduating one-third of all African Americans who earned master's and doctoral degrees from American universities.

Rufus Clement formulated a program he hoped would prepare black students for the post–World War II world. Clement proposed establishing four graduate schools: law, education, business, and fine arts. The university's educational council, which operated under the leadership of the Committee on Post-War Planning, approved the schools of education and business administration and proposed the expansion of library holdings. Another significant step in the historic mission of Atlanta University occurred in 1960 when the board of the university approved a petition for the establishment of a doctoral program in three fields: biology, education, and mathematics.

Atlanta University's affiliation with Atlanta's black institutions of higher learning was expanded in 1958 to include the newly created Interdenominational Theological Seminary (ITS), a cooperative project of four religious institutions, including Gammon School of Theology. The consortium was later expanded to include three more members. In 1964, the state of Georgia issued a charter to the Atlanta University Center. To ensure that the consortium would be a viable entity, the consortium members hired Dr. Prince E. Wilson from Central State University in Ohio to become the executive secretary of the Atlanta University Center. The center grew from an institution with a modest budget of $50,000 and one project in 1960, to one that had a $2.3 million budget and 22 ongoing projects in 1973.

In 1972, a "Plan of Reorganization," developed by the consortium's six presidents and the executive secretary, called for a more centrally coordinated operation and attempted to increase academic and administrative effectiveness. In 1988, the Center experienced one of the biggest developments in its history when Atlanta University and Clark College were consolidated into one university. The merger involved two distinguished institutions of higher learning with rich historical traditions that had begun after the Civil War. Another era in the history of the Atlanta University Center had begun.

Further Reading: For a detailed history of Atlanta University, read Clarence A. Bacote, *The Story of Atlanta University: A Century of Service, 1865–1965* (Atlanta, Georgia: Atlanta University, 1969).

—Ron Chepesiuk

BARNARD COLLEGE
(New York, New York, U.S.A.)

Location: In Morningside Heights, upper Manhattan.

Description: A private liberal arts college for women, enrolling approximately 2,200 students, affiliated with Columbia University.

Information: Office of Admissions
Barnard College
3009 Broadway
New York, NY 10027-6598
U.S.A.
(212) 854-2014

Barnard College, the first college to admit women in New York City, was founded in 1899. Its origins, however, go back to 1879, when Dr. Frederick A.P. Barnard, the tenth president of Columbia University, wrote a report to the trustees discussing plans for admitting women to the university. Barnard, widely respected today for his writings on the development of the American university, was an earnest and public advocate of equal educational opportunities for women. He was an influential proponent of many reforms which had far-ranging effects on American education and which helped shape much of what Barnard has become. An advocate of a uniform system of evaluating college applicants, Barnard also lobbied for student self-government, the elective system, the professionalization of teaching, and graduate education.

In his 1879 report to the trustees, Barnard discussed for the first time the possibility of allowing women to study at Columbia. His report was supported by two petitions generated by Sorosis, an active women's club in New York City. Barnard was a supporter of coeducation, and in his report of 1880 he proposed that, for economic and administrative simplicity, women be educated with men in the same Columbia classrooms. He noted that Columbia could become coeducational more easily than existing finishing schools or relatively new women's colleges could hope to equal men's colleges in quality. He also mentioned the success of women at the University of London, and at Chiron College of Cambridge University.

Although he received no immediate response from the trustees, Barnard included arguments for opening Columbia to women in his reports for the next five years. In 1883, his report was accompanied by a petition with over 1,000 signatures. This petition was the result of an 1882 meeting at the influential Union League Club. At that meeting, presided over by Parke Godwin, editor of the *Evening Post,* proponents of women's education came into dispute with antagonists such as Reverend Morgan Dix, the rector of Trinity Church. Trinity was the richest and most powerful church in New York, and had given Columbia (then Kings College) its first property in the eighteenth century. Dix argued that higher education for women tended to the "fantastic proceedings of female suffrage."

Despite this negative response, Columbia's trustees, in a mood of compromise, agreed to a collegiate course for women in 1883. This program was to prove a complete failure, largely because it did not provide any actual instruction. The name "course" was misleading, because in fact women were only allowed to take examinations leading to a degree—they were not permitted to sit in classes with the male students and had to do all their studying independently. In the collegiate course's four years of existence, only 30 women applied. One of these women was Annie Nathan (later Annie Nathan Meyer), who was to become a major catalyst for the creation of Barnard College. After pursuing the collegiate course for several months, she determined that it was inadequate: Women needed a genuine college education. At Meyer's urging, an advocacy group, the Friends of Higher Education for Women, was formed, and for the next six years they worked to promote the idea of a women's college at Columbia.

In fact, the idea of institutionalized higher education for American women was relatively new. In the mid-nineteenth century, many people felt that advanced education for women was too rigorous for their delicate constitutions; others argued that, while women were capable of the intellectual rigor required for advanced education, the social dangers posed by coeducational classrooms were to be avoided at all costs. New York City had no institution of higher learning for women; although the Normal School (now Hunter College) offered training for women teachers, its curriculum and requirements were not comparable to those of Columbia, for example, and it offered no degree. However, women had been attending colleges in the Midwest and East for several decades. Oberlin College, founded in 1834, was the first coeducational college, and in the 1870s the University of Michigan, Boston University, and Cornell University began to admit women. In addition to these coeducational opportunities for women, several women's colleges had been founded: Vassar in 1865, Wellesley in 1875, and Bryn Mawr in 1885. In 1879, Harvard opened the Harvard Annex (now Radcliffe) to allow women to attend separate courses.

Barnard College

In 1888, after six years of little success, Meyer discovered that Dix was opposed to coeducation rather than to women's education; he also disclosed to her that in 1883 the trustees had approved, in principle, the idea of a separately financed college for women but had chosen not to publicize the fact. The Columbia Review Committee, in its unfavorable report on the collegiate course, indicated that Columbia would recognize and provide faculty for a women's college under the proper circumstances. However, opponents to the idea of a women's college cited the low enrollment and eventual failure of the collegiate course as evidence that women did not really want a college education. In response to this misconception, Meyer wrote an article for the *Nation* in 1888, arguing that the failure of the collegiate course was due to its essential inadequacy rather than to a lack of interest from women. Meyer and the Friends of Higher Education for Women were in fact lobbying for a college on the Harvard Annex model, with separate classes for women but access to all the resources of Columbia. By this time, their advocacy of a women's college linked with Columbia was aided by the positive impression being made by the growing num-

ber of female college graduates and the impressive opening of Bryn Mawr College in Pennsylvania in 1885.

Many conservative Columbia trustees remained reluctant to admit women, for financial as well as for ideological reasons. Some believed that the addition of women would present additional administrative problems and strain limited resources. Although coeducation had been Barnard's goal, its achievement was inhibited by internal disputes among advocates of equal education. In addition to antagonists of higher education for women, Barnard, and, later, Meyer had to deal with three active factions: those who demanded coeducation, those who felt that an "annex" (like the Harvard Annex, Radcliffe) was acceptable, and those who were opposed to an annex because it put men and women in close proximity (this group preferred a separate women's college). Not until 1889, after a decade of fierce campaigning, did the trustees accept the compromise plan proposed by Meyer and an advocacy group led by the Friends of Higher Education for Women. This plan provided for separate classrooms and classes for women, off the Columbia campus (on-campus housing for female students was not part of the original plan). However, the new college would be under the auspices of Columbia, and its students would receive a baccalaureate degree from Columbia. Professors would use both Columbia curricula and tests, and its trustees' activities would be approved by Columbia trustees. The education for women would be separate but strive to be equal.

In 1889, Barnard College, named after the man who had been working for its creation for ten years, opened its doors. Housed in a rented brownstone at 343 Madison Avenue, the first class consisted of 14 students enrolled in the School of Arts and 22 "special students" (non-degree candidates) enrolled in a science program. In 1890, Barnard was incorporated into Columbia University under the unique relationship underlined in the agreement of the previous year. Governed by its own trustees, it shared instructors and a library with Columbia; Barnard was administered under the president of Columbia, but had no dean of its own. While the initial budget provided funds for a "Lady Principal," no one ever took on that rather derogatory title. Instead, Ella Weed, a Vassar graduate recruited by Meyer as president of the Academic Committee, performed all the duties of a college dean during the school's first four years. Weed set strict entrance and academic standards to assure that the quality of the Barnard education equaled that of the men's college. In 1890, Emily L. Gregory, a botanist, became Barnard's first faculty member, and after the premature death of Ella Weed, Emily James Smith, a Bryn Mawr graduate, became the college's first dean. During her tenure, Smith emphasized intellectual discipline, high quality in instruction, and graduate opportunities.

Barnard's present campus, between 116th and 120th Streets on Broadway, is due in part to the generosity of three women, who donated funds for much of the four-acre campus. In 1896, three women offered land and buildings: Mrs. Van Wyck Brinckerhoff donated $100,000, which bought a theater and classrooms; Elizabeth Milbank Anderson gave $170,000 to finance a second classroom building; Mrs. Josiah M. Fiske financed Fiske Hall. Anderson had originally retained the architect Charles A. Rich to design a building for Roosevelt Hospital. When her gift to the hospital was not accepted, she donated a building to Barnard instead. As a result of this gift, Rich was the architect of all three original buildings on campus: Milbank, Brinckerhoff, and Fiske. Unlike Radcliffe, where the architecture of the women's college was purposely unobtrusive to avoid drawing attention away from Harvard, Barnard's original buildings were intended to assert the existence and expected permanence of the school. At the same time as Barnard was being built, Columbia's campus was being designed by Charles Follen McKim using Beaux Arts concepts in college architecture for the first time. While Yale and Bryn Mawr used Oxford and Cambridge as models, separating areas from each other and from the town by using walls, the Beaux Arts design called for massing, symmetry, axial

planning, and key focal points. Barnard shares materials, scale, and decorative treatment with Columbia, but axial planning and focal points were not used to a large degree.

From the beginning, Barnard's policy was to treat its students as responsible adults, consistent with Dr. Barnard's philosophy and the practice at Columbia. This was also made possible because Barnard was not a residential college, and there was less need to act in loco parentis than for other schools with on-campus dormitories. Unlike Radcliffe, Barnard seemed both to emphasize its relationship with the urban environment and simultaneously to develop aspects of campus and collegiate life found at suburban women's colleges.

The first class formed a sorority in 1894, and students also formed social relationships with male Columbia students, meeting them at teas and dances. In order to achieve status comparable to other women's colleges and to attract refined students, Dean Virginia Gildersleeve gave greater emphasis to college life. She began to pattern Barnard's campus life on that of the more rural Vassar and Smith and to downplay Barnard's uniqueness as an urban institution. A wide array of student organizations were fostered, with the residence hall offering an adequate setting for college activities. However, Barnard remained unique in that it did not attempt to protect its students by adopting finishing school attitudes or governing their morals and behavior. Under Gildersleeve, Barnard valued individual independence. Students and faculty were allowed to be politically engaged, and both groups were active in the ongoing battle for the woman's right to vote. Barnard even had an active socialist league in the 1910s.

Because Barnard's student body was more urban than that of most other women's colleges, the tension between the desire to be perceived as an elite women's college and the fact that Barnard served the needs of a cosmopolitan urban community eventually became an obvious problem. Barnard's student body was much more heterogeneous than that of Vassar or Smith, for example; many women of modest means mingled with a large group of wealthy society women from New York's social elite, who preferred to spend their debutante years in New York society rather than at some remote rural campus. This social inequality was a contributor to the sorority controversy. Because (as was typical at the time) sororities were restricted to the wealthy and the Protestant, by 1912 only one quarter of the student body belonged to Greek-letter sororities. In that year, the *Barnard Bear,* a student paper, published an article condemning sororities as useless and reactionary, undemocratic, snobbish, and destructive to school harmony. The discord over sororities reached such a peak that Gildersleeve appointed an ad hoc committee of students, faculty, and alumnae to review the issue. The committee ultimately voted to prohibit sororities permanently.

In addition to sororities, the Christian Association also dominated student life. Any Barnard student could join, but—despite the fact that Jewish students made up an ever-growing part of the student body—Jews and Catholics could only be associate members. The Christian Association permeated campus life: It welcomed new students, advised students on campus activities, gave weekly teas, and presumed to represent the views and desires of the entire student body. In 1908, Catholic students broke with the Christian Association, forming the Catholic-only Craigie Club. In 1912, the Christian Association agreed to affiliate itself with the national YWCA. This new partnership required all members to pledge themselves to Jesus Christ, which clearly forced Jews out of the organization. In response to this, Barnard created an umbrella organization, Religious and Social Organizations. In this group were the Newman Club for Catholics, the YWCA, and ultimately the Menorah Club for Jews.

This initial marginalization of the sizeable Jewish population foreshadowed what came to be known as the "Jewish Problem" of the 1920s. In 1914, Barnard charged only $150 for tuition, compared to $450 at Mount Holyoke, for example. This low tuition, coupled with the great influx of Eastern European Jews into New York City, meant that Barnard admitted many relatively poor Jewish women at the same time that other women's colleges reported only one or two Jews in attendance. Since the newly arrived Eastern European Jews were more ethnically conscious, poorer, and were considered socially inferior to established New York Jews, their increased presence created a social tension which became increasingly evident. Gildersleeve wrote to Meyer (herself a Jew), "Many of our Jewish students have been charming and cultivated human beings. On the other hand, as you know, the intense ambition of the Jews for education has brought college girls from a lower social level than that of most of the non-Jewish students. Such girls have compared unfavorably in many instances with the bulk of the undergraduates."

Although Barnard did not establish a Jewish quota (as did other colleges at this time), Gildersleeve pursued several more oblique strategies to minimize the number of Eastern European Jews at Barnard. Among the most important was the deliberate project Barnard embarked upon to attract Protestant students from across the country; another major project was the building of residence halls to encourage out-of-town (non-Jewish) students and to mitigate the particularly New York, urban nature of the student body. Both these efforts were largely successful, as the student body today includes students from 42 states and 40 countries.

The building of the dormitory Hewitt Hall in 1925 solidified Barnard's identity as one of the elite women's colleges. The hall, designed by McKim, Mead, and White, the architects of Columbia, made it possible for one-third of the students to live on campus (today more than 90 percent of Barnard students live in residence halls). In 1926, Gildersleeve further solidified Barnard's position as an elite women's college by helping to organize the Seven College Conference. Out of this conference of the presidents of east coast women's colleges (Barnard, Bryn Mawr, Mount Holyoke, Radcliffe, Smith, Vassar, and Wellesley) was created a united appeal for seeking donors to ensure support for women's colleges. The conference also gave rise to the name the "Seven Sisters" to describe these schools, a name which has come to signify social and academic prestige.

Barnard has continued to find new ways to provide an excellent education for women. In 1971, the Barnard Center for Research on Women, a research institute and resource center, was established. In 1988, Barnard College and Columbia University renewed and restructured their relationship. Barnard remains an independent college for women with its own curriculum, faculty, admissions standards, graduation requirements, trustees, endowment, and campus. However, Barnard and Columbia allow their students open access to courses, facilities, and libraries at both schools. Barnard has also developed working relationships and joint programs with other educational institutions in the neighborhood such as the Manhattan School of Music, the Jewish Theological Seminary, the Juilliard School, and Teachers College.

Among Barnard's more distinguished alumnae are the anthropologist Margaret Mead (1923), the former U.S. Ambassador to the United Nations Jeane J. Kirkpatrick (1948), choreographer Twyla Tharp (1963), and writers Zora Neale Hurston (1927) and Erica Jong (1963).

Further Reading: Alice Duer Miller and Susan Myers' *Barnard College: The First Fifty Years* (New York: Columbia University Press, 1939) and Marian Churchill White's *A History of Barnard College* (New York: Columbia University Press, 1954) provide detailed histories of Barnard's founding and early history. *Alma Mater: Design and Experience in the Women's Colleges from Their Nineteenth-Century Beginnings to the 1930s* (New York: Knopf, 1984) by Helen Lefkowitz Horowitz discusses Barnard in relationship to other women's colleges. Historical background is also supplied by Frederick Paul Keppel's *Columbia* (New York: Oxford University Press, 1914) and by a collection of the Annual Reports of Frederick A.P. Barnard, edited by William F. Russell, in volume 1 of *The Later Days of Old Columbia College, The Rise of a University* (New York: Columbia University Press, 1937).

—J.H. Carson

BEIJING UNIVERSITY
(Beijing, China)

Location: Beijing University has been located since 1952 in the northeast of the Haidian District, in western suburban Beijing, near the Yuan Ming Gardens and the Summer Palace.

Description: With 29 colleges and departments and 82 research institutes, the university enrolls approximately 18,600 students, employs more than 2,000 faculty, and has a library that holds 4.3 million volumes.

Information: Beijing University
Office of Information
1 Loudouqiao
Hai Dian
Beijing 100871
People's Republic of China
62554002
Fax 62564095

The founding of the Imperial University in June 1898 marked the introduction of modern education to China. The prevailing poor economic climate in the country and recent humiliating losses in the Sino-Japanese War of 1894 boosted reformers in their quest to introduce a modern, western-style educational system. This trend was represented by a move directed by Kang Youwei, Liang Qichao, and others, who were convinced that basic reforms in political, social, and economic systems, not just new technology, were really needed in order to enrich and strengthen their country. They attempted to reform the traditional Civil Service Examination System and the educational system in general based on western and Japanese models. The reform as envisioned by Liang Qichao, and expressed in a memorial by Li Dunfen, consisted of a network of schools set up at county, prefectural, and provincial levels to culminate at a university in Beijing. Initially, China's governing body agreed to the university only. What we now know as Beijing University, then, is essentially a manifestation of the advent of modernization resulting from the push by the Hundred Days' Reform Movement of 1898. It was the only reform to survive the reactionary coup by the Empress Dowager in September of the same year.

The university was initially located just east of the walls of the Forbidden City, in a quarter of Beijing known as *Ma shen miao* (The Temple of the God of Horses). Just as the name of the university would change, the site would change, several times. Since its founding, the uni-

versity experienced a number of rebirths, the first of which came in 1902, when the university reopened after closing following the ransacking of Beijing in the Boxer Uprising of 1900. When it reopened, it subsumed what was left of the old Interpreters' College or *Tongwen guan* into its School of Foreign Language, thereby adding five foreign language programs as well as basic sciences to the existing curriculum. Zhang Baixi was appointed minister of education and president of the Imperial University in January 1902. In order to supply necessary personnel promptly, a School of Officials and a Normal School were attached to the university for retraining currently employed government officials and degree-holders.

With the end of the Qing dynasty and the imperial system in 1911 came the new China and a new name for the University in Beijing. It was not until 1916, when Cai Yuanpei was appointed president, that Beijing University (Beida) initiated an identifiable educational program and set out to build a faculty of distinguished scholars. Inheriting an institution which had, at that time, a reputation as "The Gambler's Den," with faculty and students collectively known as "the Brothel Brigade," Cai demanded that the students achieve more than had been expected of them in the past. In his 1917 inaugural address he reminded the students of the "nature" of the university as a place to seek learning, not to get rich or pursue a bureaucratic appointment.

Cai became one of a number of intellectual leaders with a distinct revolutionary history. He earned the distinguished *jinshi* degree in 1890 and was a member of Hanlin Academy. He served as an education official in his native Zhejiang, then as a teacher and sponsor of radical schools and anti-Qing societies. He also joined the Revolutionary Alliance. He studied philosophy in Germany for three years and lived in France, where he established a work-study program for Chinese students. In 1912 he returned to China and was appointed the Chinese Minister of Education under Sun Yat-sen and Yuan Shikai. In that capacity he convened a National Provisional Educational Conference at which the delegates from all the provinces charted new policies and regulations in educational reform. They recognized the need for China to establish a well-articulated educational system that would reach all parts of the country and that would be brought up to modern standards.

As chancellor of Beijing University, Cai set to appointing faculty based not on political leaning but on intellectual excellence and academic achievement. Cai oversaw the introduction of graduate study in the humanities, sciences, social science, and law, beginning in 1918. Among the faculty hired at this time was Chen Hengzhe (Sophia H. Chen Zen) who joined the history faculty in 1920, mak-

Beijing University

ing Beida the first Chinese university to appoint a woman to a professorship. In the same year, Beida was first in admitting women to a previously all-male campus. Cai staunchly defended the right of the faculty and students to speak their beliefs, and in the wake of the protest which was the central activity of the May 4 Movement in 1919, he in turn protested the arrest of his students by resigning as chancellor of the university. He was reappointed later that year and remained chancellor until 1922.

In its formative thinking and revolutionary influences, Beijing University was critical in galvanizing the country, especially through students, in the May 4 Movement. The protest in Tiananmen Square by 3,000 university students from 13 area colleges and universities was in direct response to the results at the Versailles conference of the settlement of Germany's Shandong rights to Japan. The protest resulted in China's not signing the treaty. The organizers of the movement settled on a series of resolutions to draw attention to the poor treatment of China by Japan and the west. In addition to the protest, another resolution passed by the students called for the implementation of a Peking Student Union that included women,

which influenced similar organizations at other major institutions and ultimately resulted in a Student Union of the Republic of China.

The environment of intellectual and institutional challenge that has characterized Beijing University since 1916 explains how it came to be at the heart of what has become known as the New Culture Movement. May 4 subsequently became the anniversary date for the celebration of the founding of Beida in yet another of the university's rebirths. In 1927 Chiang Kai-shek attempted to rally the forces in the country to emerge from the political chaos of the previous decades with a relatively unified state. Part of his vision included a unified, nationalized higher education system, with the universities following a required national curriculum under the supervision of the Ministry of Education. Beijing University's tumultuous first decades were followed in the early 1930s by a period of relative calm and focused learning.

Wen Xin Ye wrote about student life and the austere sensibility that separated the students at Beida from those of other universities. The construction of a four-story dormitory and the controversy it provoked was described in

Ye; the new dorm had 8 separate entrances and 30 self-contained single rooms, and it was the first housing unit with modern sanitary facilities and hot running water. Ye writes, "As a metaphor for its social place in the university, this modern construction stood alone in an open area at some remove from the rest of the buildings." The senior class, which was granted priority housing, strongly objected that the student body would likely fund those nonessential modern conveniences. One senior named Li Ji, Ye reports, was a self-styled "poor scholar" who later became known as a socialist thinker. He insisted that the extra expenses for the modern facilities of the new dorm would completely upset his precariously balanced budget.

The Japanese, whose presence had been steadily growing larger and ever more overbearing, finally declared war on China in 1937. This forced the issue of whether the students would serve the country better by joining the military to defend the country or continuing their studies to better prepare an already economically endangered country to rebound after the devastation of war. By that time the academic community had resolved that continuing to build education for the country was essential to China's future. Many of the leading institutions chose to relocate to the interior. In his article "The Growth of the Academic Community 1912–1949," Et-tu Zen Sun refers to the overwhelming complexities required in this action, including various planning stages for the move, negotiating for quarters in the new location, the financing and logistics of moving faculty, students, staff, books, and equipment. All of it was accomplished within the first year of the war, simultaneously introducing modern education into more remote areas of the country. Beijing University, together with Nankai and Qinghua Universities, formed first the temporary university of Changsha, Hunan, then from late 1938, the National South-West Associated University in Kunming, Yunnan. Sun describes the arduous trek from the temporary quarters at Changsha to Kunming in the autumn of 1938: "Some 300 students, accompanied by a few professors, had marched overland in two months from Changsha, a distance of about 1,000 miles, while a much larger contingent arrived by ship and rail through Hong Kong and the Yunnan–Indo-China Railway."

Civil unrest and uncertainty returned once again when the Nationalists (the Kuomintang or KMT) and the Chinese Communist Party, who had united forces against Japan, returned to their own conflict immediately after the end of the war of resistance. By 1946, the universities returned to their original locations and began to reopen. The academic community, especially at Beida, had always remained some distance from the political world. But the intellectual leaders among students and faculty alike were grounded and experienced in revolution and protest. This, coupled with the popularity of Marxism at the university, boosted the support of the Communist Party in its campaign to overthrow the KMT.

A key political event was the rape of a Beida female student by two American Marines. The incident became a cause célèbre involving issues of perceived western domination engendered by the United States and the association of the KMT with the United States, which had become a formidable presence in China. In *China and the Christian Colleges, 1850–1950,* Jessie Gregory Lutz relates that editorials in China's newspapers of the time reveal that the United States was in one way or another responsible for a variety of thoughtless accidents and injuries, such as jeeps running down pedestrians or rickshaw men and brawls involving drunken servicemen. Lutz believes this event reveals the power of the students to make themselves and their outrage heard.

The National Student Union of China and its regional federations, especially the North China Student Union and the union encompassing the Shanghai, Nanjing, Hangzhou, and Souzhou area were part of an extremely powerful network of student associations, however illegal. Lutz describes the power they yielded in controlling all extracurricular activities at many universities, especially the largest: "according to one report on Beida, the drama clubs, glee clubs, wall newspaper societies, and other organizations were expected to coordinate their actions with those of the student government associations and contribute their talents and energies to protest demonstrations." All energies at this time focused on a campaign of protests all over the country in the spring of 1948. Strikingly similar manifestos were passed by students in a variety of major cities on May 4. The major issue was United States aid to Japan, which, Lutz believes really represented an attack on the U.S.-supported Kuomintang government.

In 1949 the Communist Party assumed control of the Chinese government. The process of nationalization of higher education begun by Chiang Kai-shek in 1927 was substantially strengthened with the birth of the People's Republic of China. Institutional reorganization, beginning in earnest with the start of the first Five-Year Plan in 1952, illustrated the new government's interest in promoting the development of experts in the technical fields. The economic crisis in China required a campaign of national reconstruction that called for the training of a vast labor force with scientific and technical skills, which would focus on the importance of serving the people and would work to attain a high cultural level within the Marxian ideology. The reorganized universities curricula consisted of short-term courses; highly specialized and narrowly defined majors; scientific and technical programs; and texts, scientific theories, and pedagogical techniques from the USSR that displaced western models. The universities were completely reorganized. Beida experienced still another move: its new home was the property of Yenching University, which was completely dissolved and some of its departments distributed among other local universities. Beijing National University became the comprehensive university in Beijing. Qinghua's colleges of arts, science, and law and Yenching's liberal arts program were absorbed by Beida. Beida's engineering college, along with the science and engineering schools of Yenching, moved to Qinghua University, which became an advanced polytechnic school.

The Soviet Union remained the undisputed model in higher education through the mid-1950s. Soviet advisers and educational materials equipped the educational institutions that were revamped in an effort to duplicate the Soviet educational system. Then, in 1957, in response to the call by Lu Dingyi, the director of the Bureau of Propaganda, to "let a hundred flowers bloom . . . and a hundred schools of thought contend," the Hundred Flowers campaign was launched. Intellectuals accepted encouragement by Mao Zedong and the (however reluctant) Chinese Communist Party to air their grievances, which they did with a forcefulness that surprised and dismayed the Party. On May 19, 1957, a group at Beijing University put up a "Democratic Wall" plastered with "big character" (*dazi bao*) statements attacking the Party's control and mistreatment of the intellectuals. Other complaints included the slavish following of the Soviet model for education, the poor quality of life in the country, and corruption among party cadres. The disgruntled party secretaries began their retaliation in June 1957. By the end of the year, over 300,000 intellectuals were branded "rightists," which effectively ruined their careers in China. Many were sent to labor camps or to jail, others to the countryside for an education in working the land, an education that in some cases turned into a lifetime exile.

Immediately following the backlash of the Hundred Flowers campaign was the Great Leap Forward. This was Mao's intensive nationalization effort to strictly rally and promote the productivity and capability of China's masses. This effort prescribed a massive reorganization of the population into communes and collectives, with the intention of involving every single citizen. Part of the Great Leap Educational Revolution was intended to democratize the university enrollment policy. Universities and colleges were attacked by Mao as elitist and irrelevant to national needs. Education was to be combined with productive labor, administration was decentralized, and students were selected not only on the basis of their examination results but on preferential treatment according to the class line. Ruth Hayhoe tell us in *Contemporary Chinese Education* that Mao "did not succeed in a long-lasting revolution in education, and from 1961 those political factions favoring traditional academic standards got the upper hand in organizing teaching and research and, most importantly, the enrollment system in favor of 'academic achievement' at the expense of 'political commitment.'" An initial impact of the start of the Cultural Revolution on universities was that the originally intended half-year delay in enrollment of students in 1966 to implement the "Reform of Entrance Examinations and Enrollment in Higher Educational Institutions," stretched into five years before the universities were prepared to resume enrollment.

When universities were once again prepared to admit students, the process was drastically different. The entrance examination system was replaced by a program of work group quotas. Slots were filled based on nominations by peasant and worker committees based on an individual candidate's political enthusiasm and the individual's family background of revolutionary experience. The resulting system was often corrupt—students entering by the "back door"—and the overall quality of student ability was poor.

In March 1978 at the National Science Conference in Beijing, Deng Xiaoping unveiled a modernization plan that would include a "crash training program" to achieve development in the specialized areas of science and technology. This led to the design of the system of 88 "key universities" with admission only by rigorous competitive examinations.

True to its self-proclaimed "glorious revolutionary tradition," Beida's students headed the movement that led to the massive protest and standoff in Tiananmen Square in June 1989. The 1989 protest was the culmination of long-standing student dissatisfaction with political and academic control and Communist Party-imposed limitations on the students. The restrictions included clamping down on Beijing University students' use of the Democracy Wall. First used to criticize the ruling KMT party in the Republican years, the Democracy Wall was a device that seemed to enjoy covert government support until the appearance, beginning in the late 1970s, of a more threatening student movement that criticized Marxism and the Communist Party and called for greater democracy and human rights. The government summarily silenced and imprisoned the leaders of the movement. Students were repeatedly prohibited from taking part in local people's elections. Through the 1980s all over China, students demonstrated in protest of various grievances. In addition to their complaint about party intervention in elections and in university activites, students demonstrated against the presence of military and industrial units, and against poor food, housing, and academic conditions. The occurrence and force of the protests escalated, becoming ever more politically based, with nationwide student demonstrations in 1985, 1986–87, and finally, coming together in 1989.

Further Reading: General information on Chinese universities in English is hard to come by, and writings on specific universities are even rarer. Ruth Hayhoe's work, *China's Universities, 1895–1995: A Century of Cultural Conflict* (New York: Garland, 1996), *Contemporary Chinese Education* (Armonk, New York.: M.E. Sharpe, 1984), and other works are good overviews of Chinese higher education.

—April Oswald

BOSTON UNIVERSITY
(Boston, Massachusetts, U.S.A.)

Location: In the Back Bay area of Boston.

Description: One of the largest independent universities in the country with 28,600 students in undergraduate, graduate, and professional programs.

Information: Office of Admission
121 Bay State Road
Boston, MA 02215
U.S.A.
(617) 353-2318

Visiting: Guided tours are available year-round. For more information, call the phone number above.

When the institution known today as Boston University was founded as a Methodist school of theology in 1839, it was neither a university nor located in Boston. It was not even in Massachusetts. The idea of an institution to train clergymen conflicted with a popular image of a minister being a man of God chosen to the calling rather than formally schooled. Yet John Wesley, founder of Methodism, was a graduate of Oxford University and saw his mission as one of education as well as of the study of theology.

Perhaps with that in mind, three Bostonian members of the Methodist Episcopal Church (Lee Clafflin, Isaac Rich, and Jacob Sleeper) called a convocation at the Bromfield Street Methodist Church to explore ways to improve theological education at the centennial of English and American Methodism.

Preferring a rural location for the new school, the founders chose to share the Newbury (Vermont) Seminary building as the first home for their Newbury Biblical Institute. Newbury Seminary had been accepting women (including a black woman) as students, setting an example that was embraced by its new neighbor. Another precedent, established at the beginning and carried through for the institution's first century, was the adaptive reuse of existing buildings rather than relying on new construction.

Within a decade, the original building was overcrowded and the Newbury Biblical Institute was moved in 1847 to a former Congregational church building in Concord, New Hampshire—where it was renamed the Methodist General Biblical Institute. As in Vermont, the students cut firewood and did other farm work in their spare time to help defray their expenses. The school body

had grown considerably by the time of the Civil War and was able to endure through that conflict, although in reduced circumstances. Moving to Boston in 1866, the school was renamed Boston Theological Seminary, bought land in Brookline for a campus, and rented buildings on Beacon Hill—meant to provide temporary quarters but was to be used for nearly a century.

The school's rapid expansion was supported by the three businessmen/philanthropists: Clafflin, Rich, and Sleeper. Although all three were Methodists, they insisted that the original charter provide an assurance of nonsectarian admission (excepting the school of theology).

Boston University was born in 1869 with a petition to the Massachusetts legislature for the incorporation of a European-style university, with undergraduate, graduate, and professional schools under the same administration. From its earliest days, the university followed a nonsexist, nonracist policy. Men and women were admitted on an equal basis. Boston University was the first institution in Massachusetts to grant degrees to women, and it awarded the first Massachusetts woman with a Ph.D. The first woman to pass the Massachusetts bar was a BU graduate.

Early BU students were likely to be working their way through college. There were no dormitories and most students lived with their families, although some did stay in boardinghouses. With students reaching classes by horse-drawn trams, trains, and later electric cars from the far suburbs and beyond, BU was a commuter school for much of its history. Boston was an industrial city—textiles, leather, shoes, shipping—filled with working-class citizens for whom Harvard was out of reach. But the transplanted school on Beacon Hill was not.

Only two American institutions in the wake of the Civil War provided all four regular university faculties (liberal arts, divinity, law, and medicine): Harvard and Yale. The evolving Boston University was the third.

Although it had found its permanent location in Boston, the university was not to have its own campus until the middle of the twentieth century. The university used classrooms that had been vacated by Massachusetts Institute of Technology and other existing schools.

Except for a quirk of fate, BU would have had its own home much sooner. Founder Isaac Rich died in 1872, leaving most of his fortune to the university. (There was some thought of naming the university after him, but it was feared that the name "Rich University" would put off later donors.) The estate was comprised mostly of prime Boston real estate valued at $1 million. At that time, Rich's legacy was the largest ever given by one American

Boston University

for higher education. Rich's gift stipulated that the funds be placed in trust for ten years before disbursement. But all went up in smoke—literally—a few months after Rich's death, in the great Boston fire of November 1872. With a subsequent depression, the property had fallen in value by half by the time BU was able to claim the principle in 1882. The new campus had to wait once more.

The university stayed in its second-hand buildings on Beacon Hill and elsewhere in Boston. The research that went on there, however, was far from second rate. To Boston University came a Scottish immigrant who taught the deaf to communicate. He had some other ideas he wanted to pursue, so BU's first president, William Fairfield Warren granted the young teacher not only the time off to research but also paid him a year's salary in advance—a practice virtually unknown of in those days.

Thus was Alexander Graham Bell freed to work on his invention and it was from his BU laboratory that the first voice transmission over telephone wires took place in 1876. Although Bell was not a faculty member for a long period of time, he afterward said it was BU's generosity that made his invention possible.

Borden Parker Bowne was BU's most famous professor in the late 1800s, well known as the developer of the philosophical school called Personalism (a doctrine which holds that ultimate reality consists of a plurality of spiritual beings or independent persons). His influence extended over half a century, when Professor Edgar Brightman became the leading Personalist in the era between the two world wars.

In branching out to medical education, BU was at first affiliated with the homeopathic New England Female

Medical College, which had graduated the first African-American physician, Rebecca Lee, in 1864. When the Female Medical College went bankrupt in 1871, the Boston University School of Medicine (BUSM) took over the institution in the city's South End, where the campus remains today. Boston University School of Medicine was the first university in the United States to provide a three-year medical curriculum with lectures, laboratory, and clinical work. Again, men and women were admitted equally. In 1897, Dr. Solomon Carter Fuller was graduated, the first African-American psychiatrist in the country.

The College of Liberal Arts (CLA) was launched at BU in 1873, still in "recycled" buildings on Beacon Hill. With Rich's legacy, half of the student body received full tuition scholarships—equally divided between men and women. The CLA chose as their colors red and white, symbolizing equality between the sexes, colors eventually adopted for the entire university.

By 1906 most of the CLA students were women in teacher training; nearly 85 percent of the student body was female. Some other schools, fearing that men would not enroll in a predominately women's college, limited the female population. Instead of limiting women, Boston University increased the number of male students with the "More Men Movement" of 1910. The advent of the College of Business Administration (thought to be a "male" school), as well as evening courses and weekend classes, all made possible the matriculation of additional male students. The College of Liberal Arts, though, remained heavily female until after World War I.

In 1921 the first women's dormitories were opened along Bay State Road at the site of what became the Boston University campus. Still, most students were commuters—an ethnically diverse group that saw a waning of Methodist influence with increasing numbers of Catholics, Jews, and others.

The unified campus, planned for decades, was still no closer to reality than it had been in the ashes of Boston half a century before. The university dreamed of a Charles River campus, like those of its neighbors Harvard and MIT on the opposite bank of the Charles in Cambridge. In 1920 BU bought almost all the land between Commonwealth Avenue and Bay State Road along the banks of the Charles River. In the late 1920s, the riverbank portion of the proposed campus was taken by eminent domain for the construction of Storrow Drive. Boston University was forever after cut off from the riverbank by a busy highway—turning its back on the water and toward the trolleys that brought its students to class.

Enrollment dropped during the Great Depression at BU as elsewhere, but some students continued to work their way through college as doormen, models, restaurant staff, elevator operators, and such. Faculty salaries were cut nearly 20 percent over the course of the 1930s, but the university was still able to start an aeronautical engineer-ing department to train engineers and pilots using facilities at Logan Airport.

In the late 1930s BU was forced out of its College of Business Administration building when it was sold; despite the troubled economy, it was forced to embark on a year-long campaign to raise money for the Charles River campus. With lowered property values, BU was able to purchase the Weld mansion at 147 Bay State Road, former home to wealthy surgeon William Weld, whose art collection is now in the Museum of Fine Arts in Boston. The mansion has gone through several uses over the years and is now the president's office.

World War II brought to Boston University an Army Specialized Training Program for GIs who studied academic and military topics in a grueling program. Of the non-military students, fewer worked part-time during the war, preferring to take advantage of accelerated programs to finish their studies more quickly. When the war ended, returning men and women veterans eligible for the GI Bill created an influx of students. The Depression had begun to swing BU away from being a commuter school to a university with a larger resident population. In the postwar era, GIs who had had a taste of travel did not want to stay at home for college. Boston University began to acquire residences to meet the needs of these men and women.

In the postwar era the General College was created to accommodate students who were unable to meet the normal entrance requirements but who showed potential for college work after remediation. Public relations, nursing, engineering, and technology (including aerospace and optics) were all fields that were enhanced after the war.

Boston University's traditional nondiscriminatory policy brought more ethnic minorities as the Civil Rights movement began. With one of the earliest interdisciplinary African studies programs in the United States, and with the rising population of foreign students, BU was becoming a melting pot. Popular African-American preacher Howard Thurman was lured to BU to head Marsh Chapel, revitalizing the congregation and increasing the racial diversity. Barbara Jordan, later congresswoman from Texas, was a regular worshipper at Marsh Chapel while a student at the law school in the late 1950s. Martin Luther King Jr. was drawn to Boston University by the philosophy of Personalism in which King found confirmation of his long-held beliefs.

In the late 1940s Sarah Caldwell, who had directed BU opera workshops, became the first woman to conduct the Metropolitan Opera. In 1957 she founded the Opera Group of Boston, now the Opera Company of Boston. She remained on the BU faculty until 1960. Boston Pops conductor Arthur Fiedler and eminent Boston theater critic Eliot Norton were also on the faculty.

It was a rare college campus that was tranquil in the turbulent 1960s, and Boston University was no stranger to turmoil. Students were very politically active in the second half of that decade, often abetted by BU newspaper editor Raymond Mungo, who was a national leader in the move to impeach President Lyndon Johnson. Other popular protest causes in that era were the Vietnam War in general, Civil Rights, campus ROTC, and military-related research. Boston University was dubbed "Berkeley East" as drug and alcohol use rose. Campus unrest marred the centennial celebrations in 1969 with walkouts, sit-ins, and other protests.

Boston University struggled to cope with student unrest, the drop in the number of commuter students (a result of the low tuition at the new Boston campus of the University of Massachusetts and the growth of community colleges), an inadequate endowment, and a growing annual deficit. With BU on the brink of bankruptcy, President Arland Christ-Janer abruptly resigned and the search was on, as one writer suggested, for a "silver unicorn" to head the institution.

John Silber, the fired College of Liberal Arts dean from the University of Texas at Austin, was hired to shake up BU. When he arrived in Boston, Silber realized how precarious the financial situation was. Instituting a strong core curriculum that flew in the face of the trend away from course requirements, Silber hired several renowned faculty members from MIT, Harvard, the London School of Economics, and other star institutions. With a strong (some would say autocratic) style, Silber weeded out the faculty at BU, urging some he perceived as weaker to switch to schools where they would be able to shine more brightly. Within five years, BU was in the black, with doubled grants from government and corporations. Silber's confrontational style led to clashes with faculty and students, while he balanced the budget, increased the endowment enormously, successfully fought an attempt to unionize the faculty, and continued to expand the university.

In the mid-1980s Silber engineered the takeover of the Chelsea, Massachusetts public schools by BU for a ten-year period in an attempt to reform the struggling system. Teaching ethics and character along with the traditional curriculum, the experiment's first years saw some improvements, but Chelsea's schools were not fully revitalized.

Part of the basis for the improved financial situation came through commercially successful research, including gene study, that led to scandal and an investigation of grants and bonuses paid to Silber (later returned) and to other faculty. However, according to the regulators, no laws were broken.

Another controversy revolved around Martin Luther King Jr.'s donation of his personal papers to BU. After his assassination, his widow asked for the return of the papers in order to deposit them at the King Memorial Center in Atlanta. In a protracted lawsuit the university won the right to keep the papers, which are deposited in the Mugar Library.

The Mugar Library's Twentieth Century Archives is the repository of some of the papers of some 1,600 luminaries from all walks of life. A small sampling: from the world of music, Sir Rudolf Bing and Ella Fitzgerald; from theater and film Fred Astaire, Douglas Fairbanks Jr., Angela Lansbury, Robert Redford, Edward G. Robinson, George Bernard Shaw, and Orson Welles; from the world of letters, Sylvia Ashton-Warner, Isaac Asimov, Peter Benchley, Nathaniel Benchley, Robert Benchley, James T. Farrell, Rumer Godden, Sue Grafton, David Halberstam, Reginald Hill, Langston Hughes, D.H. Lawrence, Mary Renault, May Sarton, Siegfried Sassoon, H.G. Wells, and Elie Wiesel; media figures Alistair Cooke and Dan Rather; and Cardinal Richard Cushing and former Speaker of the House John W. McCormack.

So high was the visibility of BU by the year of its sesquicentennial, 1989, that several world leaders participated in the celebration. King Hussein of Jordan appeared in April to speak and receive an honorary degree. At the May commencement, both François Mitterand, president of France, and George Bush, president of the United States, spoke and received honorary degrees. Chancellor Helmut Kohl of Germany accepted an honorary degree in his own country.

Boston University in the 1990s is a strong educational institution, with a faculty that includes Nobelist Elie Wiesel and Derek Walcott; Pulitzer Prize-winner Robert V. Bruce (history); National Book Award biographer Roger Shattuck; and opera diva Phyllis Curtin. Among the long-term faculty at the BUSM was the late Isaac Asimov, prolific author and winner of several science fiction and literary awards. For three decades BU has spearheaded the seminal Framingham Heart Study of lifestyle effects and risk factors on cardiovascular health.

Further Reading: Kathleen Kilgore's *Transformations: A History of Boston University* (Boston: Boston University, 1991) is a lively, readable history published just after the university's 150th anniversary. Edward Ray Speare's *Interesting Happenings in Boston University's History, 1839 to 1951* (Boston: Boston University Press, 1957) is an uncritical paean by the son of an associate founder who, with his father, was connected with BU for most of its first century. Speare focuses on events and leadership up to the 1950s. *American University Education in the Birth-Year of Boston University* (Boston: Boston University, 1913) by first BU president William Fairfield Warren compares the birth of BU to the origins of existing colleges such as Yale and neighboring Harvard.

—Jeanne Munn Bracken

BRANDEIS UNIVERSITY
(Waltham, Massachusetts, U.S.A.)

Location: In suburban Boston, nine miles west of downtown. The university occupies 95 buildings on a wooded 235 acres. It is accessible by commuter train from Boston and Cambridge, by the MBTA subway system, and by automobile from the intersection of Routes 128 and 95.

Description: Brandeis is a private, nonsectarian, coeducational university. Combining the flavor of a small liberal-arts center with the facilities of a major research university, it has 3,000 undergraduates and 1,000 graduate students.

Information: Brandeis University
P.O. Box 9110
415 South Street
Waltham, MA 02254
U.S.A.
(617) 736-3500
(800) 622-0622

Visiting: Student guides lead tours Monday through Friday at 10:00 A.M., 11:00 A.M., 1:00 P.M., and 3:00 P.M. when classes are in session. For more information, contact the Office of Admissions at the above address.

Since the mid-nineteenth century, Jewish leaders had debated the merits of a Jewish-sponsored university in America. Their vision revealed a desire by the Jewish community to add a "Jewish cultural expression" to American society, but it also was a practical response to prevalent anti-Semitism in American higher education. Agitation for such an institution increased after World War I, but financial and logistical roadblocks hampered the concept's fruition until early 1946, when the opportunity to fulfill this "aspiration of a century" materialized in unexpected fashion.

Middlesex University, a small college in Waltham, Massachusetts, boasted a student body that was 75 percent Jewish, a result of its rare quota-free admissions policy. Always struggling, the school ran into financial hardship after the death of its founder in 1944. Two years later, bankruptcy loomed. Middlesex's president, cognizant of some Jewish leaders' increasing desire to initiate a university, contacted Dr. Israel Goldstein. An influential New York rabbi, Goldstein had been actively exploring the idea of establishing a Jewish-sponsored college for several years. Middlesex's president offered to transfer title for the university to a committee Goldstein had named. This committee of prominent New York Jews assumed Middlesex's financial obligations, established a board of directors, and set up a charter. The reality of a Jewish-sponsored university had begun.

Goldstein's committee immediately left its mark on the school by changing its name to honor the late U.S. Supreme Court Justice Louis D. Brandeis. The first Jewish justice, Brandeis was known as a peoples' lawyer, whose advocacy of social causes was well known. Goldstein's committee agreed that Louis Brandeis, a minority voice philosophically, was a worthy namesake for this endeavor and a powerful expression of Jewish pride.

Many Jewish leaders initially endorsed the project and, through donations, many in the Jewish community expressed their enthusiasm for the school after its long theoretical gestation. Albert Einstein lent his name to fundraising efforts and boasted that Brandeis University "will satisfy a real need." But fundraising quickly dried up as well-publicized personal differences enveloped Goldstein's board. By the fall of 1946, the project faltered as Goldstein and his committee resigned, and Einstein withdrew his support for Brandeis University.

Boston lawyer George Alpert stabilized the project by organizing a new committee. While financial and moral support from prominent members of the Jewish community had evaporated, this group of Boston entrepreneurs finally secured sufficient financing to rescue the school in December 1947.

With funding stable, the new committee then sought to avoid crippling interpersonal debates by actively recruiting Abram Sachar to be Brandeis University's first president. Sachar was the Hillel Foundation's first national director, a post which he held for 20 years. Sachar understood the needs of the Jewish community and was eager to participate in the debate over a Jewish-sponsored university. To the trustees, almost all of whom were inexperienced in college administration, Sachar represented an organizing force; the board gave him a free hand in the school's academic operations.

Sachar saw special symbolic significance in a Jewish-sponsored university. By making this commitment to American society, American Jews could contribute to the nation's welfare, thus fulfilling what many Jews regarded as their duty. These lofty aspirations compelled Sachar to carefully consider the university's organization. To heighten its symbolic significance, Brandeis University should be nonsectarian. Sachar—

Brandeis University

like many other American Jewish scholars—believed the university should not function as a haven for Jews excluded from American higher education. Thus, students of all faiths should be admitted on a merit basis. Nonetheless, Brandeis University was destined to have a close relationship with the American Jewish community, and Sachar thought the school's curriculum should reflect this unusual position in American higher education. Accordingly, Sachar specified that Brandeis include Judaic studies in its curriculum and, where possible, commit resources to address the nation's social problems.

Sachar and the trustees faced the challenge of developing a curriculum, selecting a faculty, and drastically renovating the existing campus. These tasks would have to be completed without the substantial endowments on which established universities relied and with the prospect of contributions from financially successful alumni nearly two decades away. The financial challenges presented by an absence of tradition were overcome by aggressive fundraising. In Brandeis's first years, the economic support of upper-class Jews was still withheld. But the response was substantial. Indeed, many of Brandeis's early needs were met by amassing extremely small donations.

Brandeis had started classes with a faculty of 13 but rapidly built its faculty by aggressively recruiting young academics selected for their potential scholarly contributions. Sachar balanced these youths—many were only in their twenties—by convincing a few accomplished professors to leave retirement. Sachar also personally recruited noted European academics, especially those displaced by World War II. By the early 1950s the school's increasing reputation and funding prompted prominent scholars in all fields to join the faculty. An endowment by a Jewish organization allowed the recruitment of noted ivy-league visiting professors, thus further bolstering the young school's reputation.

Sachar recruited the crème de la crème of scholars. Among the music department's earliest offerings was a course in modern music given by Leonard Bernstein. French scholar Albert Guerard, novelist Ludwig Lewisohn, and psychologist Abraham Maslow were also among the university's earliest professors. Visiting scholars included Eleanor Roosevelt and social critic Max Lerner. Continuing that tradition in recent years, visiting scholars, lecturers, and professors included Sumner Redstone, CEO of Viacom International; composer Marvin Hamlisch; authors Geoffrey Wolff, Toni Morrison, and Jayne Ann Philips; Israeli parliament member and former refusenik Natan Sharansky; and Nobel laureates Bert Sakmann and Roald Hoffman.

Many Jews who had shied away amid the controversy of Brandeis's first years gradually returned with financial assistance by 1950. Their support increased throughout the 1950s, and grew to substantial proportions in the next decade. Also, by the mid-1950s fund-

raising efforts successfully expanded outside the Jewish community. Nonetheless, Brandeis remained hampered by the lack of a substantial endowment enjoyed by established universities.

This funding spurred the school's rapid growth in the two decades after its founding. The university completed a costly architectural master plan within one decade. Simultaneously, Brandeis purchased adjacent acreage and initiated a campus beautification project. By 1968 Brandeis University had been completely transformed; its campus encompassed over 90 buildings on 235 acres, representing an investment of over $70 million. Usen castle is all that remains of the old Middlesex school, and it still hosts the campus coffeehouse as well as dormitory rooms. Most of the rest of the campus buildings are modern in style. There are nine residential quadrangles, and all of the residential halls are networked into the university computer system. The master plan of the campus was designed by architect Eero Saarinen. The Catholic, Protestant, and Jewish chapels were designed in such a way that the shadow of one would never fall on another, symbolizing religious freedom and tolerance.

Before Brandeis's charter class of 107 students matriculated in the fall of 1948, Sachar had faced a challenge in starting a curriculum from scratch, although this lack of tradition allowed conceptual flexibility. Sachar, wanting to keep the nascent program as manageable as possible, decided to concentrate on liberal arts and limit the size of the student body. Sachar acknowledged the "formative influence" of Brandeis's first curriculum was the innovative Harvard Plan of 1946. This concept recommended a core curriculum in humanities and social and natural sciences through a student's first two years. Then, the student would choose a concentration. Brandeis required all students to take fine arts, subjects shunned by most major universities at the time. Also, Brandeis University emphasized the social utility of its curriculum.

Brandeis strove to combine the intimacy of a small liberal arts college with the facilities, faculty, and depth of a world-class research institution. Undergraduates always had access to a faculty of renowned scholars, and were often invited to participate in ground-breaking research. Interdisciplinary studies were encouraged from the onset. Examples of these fields included journalism, film studies, legal studies, and medieval studies, among others. Many students work as interns in a variety of fields in the Boston area. In addition to filling requirements for a concentration, all undergraduates take one university seminar in humanistic inquiry as well as three cluster courses. The clusters are groups of courses from different departments and schools that explore one theme or period. A cluster on conflict and cooperation, for example, could include courses from anthropology, politics, and English literature departments. A cluster on the Baroque could include courses from departments including music, history, theater, fine arts, and comparative literature.

The university's noted faculty and sound academic program earned the school accreditation by the New England Association of Colleges at the earliest opportunity in 1953. The school's academic reputation continued to grow in the 1950s and 1960s as many of its graduates entered the nation's best graduate and professional schools in disproportionate numbers. Phi Beta Kappa accreditation was conferred in a record 13 years in 1961.

Even before its first class graduated, Brandeis began making a significant contribution in the arts. Brandeis hosted annual classical, jazz, dance, art, film, and poetry festivals and recruited notable faculty, such as Bernstein and Aaron Copland. By 1954 Brandeis had developed a series of endowments encouraging the arts. Not surprisingly, the school's first graduate program was in music. In 1980 Brandeis hired a string quartet in residence. The Lydian String Quartet invigorated the music department. Members of the quartet taught private lessons, gave regular concerts on campus, and led a summer chamber music workshop for musicians, both professional and fine amateurs, from around the country. The quartet performed often in Boston and the surrounding area and participated in a variety of summer music festivals. They were the winners of a Naumburg award in chamber music performance.

In a similar time frame, Brandeis stimulated interest in communal service. In 1959, the university established the centerpiece of this effort, the Florence Heller Graduate School for Advanced Studies in Social Welfare. A professional school for the human services field, the Heller School has grown into a national center for the research of health and welfare issues. In 1964, Brandeis founded the Lemberg Institute for the Study of Violence. This institute explored the social and economic causes of escalating violence in 1960s America.

Brandeis's emphasis on Judaic studies also sprung from its sponsorship. The Jewish studies department began with three highly accomplished European scholars. In 1966 the American Jewish Historical Society relocated its headquarters to Brandeis, beginning a 30-year relationship with the university. The society's archives comprise the world's largest collection of American Judaica. The Lown School of Near Eastern and Judaic Studies remains one of the most significant centers for Judaic research outside Israel.

By the early 1950s, Brandeis had broadened its early emphasis on liberal arts to stress scientific inquiry. The school quickly grew into a significant research university. A 1990 Science Watch study listed Brandeis as the nation's seventh most significant research school in the biological sciences. Volen National Center for Complex Systems was dedicated in the early 1990s. The center connected five of the existing science buildings, and brought faculty together from seven scientific programs: biology, biochemistry, chemistry, computer science, psychology, linguistics and cognitive science, and physics.

The goal of the center was to examine large complex systems, such as the brain and intelligence. The center enabled professors and students from different fields to combine their efforts to create ground-breaking discoveries about the brain, language development, and such ailments as schizophrenia and Alzheimer's disease. New graduate students were drawn to the university because of the center, and a new interdisciplinary major in neuroscience was established. An acclaimed 1997 study on research universities named Brandeis the nation's top rising private research university. Noting Brandeis's youth, the study's author observed, "There's been no institution like it, for its size, that was almost an instant, powerful research institution."

Interestingly, Brandeis's glowing start and its accomplishments were interrupted by a period of decline. Abram Sachar retired in 1968, and a quick succession of presidents proved unable to sustain Sachar's vision or cope with the school's new problems. Many of the school's original faculty had retired by 1970; those remaining expressed discontent over the school's academic decline. Hostility between the faculty and the school's presidents increased. Additionally, the school's financial situation, never strong, worsened, as donations decreased, and Brandeis's lack of a substantial endowment continued to haunt the school. By 1980, the university was running a deficit of $2 million; administrators predicted this figure would sextuple in just five years.

In the 1980s President Evelyn E. Handler initiated a "Blueprint for Renewal" to arrest the school's financial decline. Her blueprint called for an increase in the number of undergraduates, a slight decrease in the number of faculty, and a broadening of the university by adding undergraduate programs and a graduate school of business. Simultaneously, Handler attempted to diversify the student body in an effort to attract greater funding, a strategy reflecting prevailing trends in American higher education.

Many faculty, administrators, and students viewed Handler's efforts as an assault on the school's traditional identity as a small, research university. Causing particular furor were Handler's attempts to secularize Brandeis. Her critics, including Sachar, lambasted Handler's "de-Judaization" of the university. Although Handler improved Brandeis's physical plant and initiated a capital campaign which pulled in over $170 million, she was pressured to resign in 1991.

After her departure, Handler's opponents reasserted their contention that nothing was fundamentally wrong with Brandeis; the school merely needed to reassert its unique niche in American higher education by building on the strengths it had defined in its brief, somewhat turbulent, history. The first step on Brandeis's road to recovery was the inauguration in 1991 of a new president. Dr. Samuel O. Thier became the university's sixth president and the driving force behind Brandeis's re-emergence as an up-and-coming university. Thier was a former professor at Havard

Medical School and the Yale University School of Medicine. He spent several years as president of the Institute of Medicine of the National Academy of Sciences in Washington. There he established his reputation as a fine fundraiser. He reached out to the potential donors and extolled the virtues of Brandeis, focusing on the extraordinary caliber of the faculty. Thier was credited with the renewed enthusiasm that pervaded the university and improved its reputation in the early 1990s. He resigned in 1994 to take the presidency of Massachusetts General Hospital.

Thier's successor was a groundbreaker in a new sense. Jehuda Reinharz became the first Brandeis president who was also an alumnus of the university. At the time he was chosen to be Brandeis's seventh president, Reinharz was a 49-year-old professor of modern Jewish history at Brandeis, and his wife, Shulamit Reinharz, was a professor of sociology and the director of the Women's Studies Program. Reinharz was also the author of the most respected biography of Chaim Weizmann, who was the first president of Israel and a former president of Hebrew University on Mount Scopus in Jerusalem. Reinharz was also welcomed warmly, and he set about to increase the university's endowment while ensuring continued excellence in undergraduate education. He acknowledged that Brandeis faculty members were often payed less than their counterparts at other universities, and he hoped to be able to attract the best of faculty and students and keep both.

In the late 1990s, Brandeis embarked on a new project together with the Jerusalem Foundation. Headquartered at the university and at a new campus to be built in Jerusalem is the International Center for Ethics, Justice, and Public Life. The goal of the center is to address moral issues affecting people around the world by bringing students, scholars, and professionals together. They examine such broad-based issues as coexistence and envisioning a just society. An outreach program for professionals and corporations called Brandeis Seminars was thriving toward the end of the century. These day-long seminars began at the university in 1981 as the Humanities and the Professions Program. The program expanded and was taught by Brandeis scholars to peer groups such as teachers, judges, or physicians and to organizations such as companies. Through the analysis of literary texts and the relation of those texts to the group members' lives, participants addressed issues including leadership, communication, and morality. The seminars were partially funded by the National Endowment for the Humanities and the Exxon Foundation.

The pride of Brandeis University is its faculty. A high proportion of faculty members are members of the National Academy of Science. The faculty/student ratio for undergraduates is 10:1. Of 354 full-time faculty, and 159 part-time faculty, 97 percent hold Ph.D. or equivalent degrees. The university offers degrees including Bachelor of Arts, Master of Arts, Master of Science, Master of Fine Arts, and Doctor of Philosophy. Bachelor of Arts degrees are offered in 32 fields of concentration, and graduate degrees are offered in 29 major fields of study. Specialized academic programs include independent study, honors program, double majors, five-year combined B.A./M.A. programs, and cross-registration with nearby universities.

Students are from highly diverse backgrounds and come to the university from all 50 states and from 65 foreign countries. More than 90 percent of Brandeis students live on campus, which has led to a strong sense of community. Many students take advantage of opportunities to study and intern abroad. Overall, enrollment in the graduate programs at Brandeis increased 75 percent from the late 1980s to the late 1990s.

Brandeis was among the more expensive private universities in the 1990s, with tuition and fees well above $20,000 annually. Many Brandeis students received some form of financial assistance, since the university adhered to a need-blind admissions policy. The university awarded more than $25 million dollars in grant funds to undergraduates in 1995–96.

Brandeis's overall standing among all private research universities was improving toward the end of the century. In humanities, Brandeis was ranked third, ahead of Brown, Harvard, Columbia, and Chicago, and in sciences Brandeis ranked 12th, ahead of the University of Pennsylvania and Duke. In the social science index Brandeis ranked 18th.

Further Reading: For a personal look at the history of Brandeis University the best source is *A Host at Last,* by university founder Abram L. Sachar (Boston: Little Brown, 1976). John A. Gliedman's "Brandeis University: Reflections at Middle Age," in *American Jewish History* 78:4 (1989), covers the controversies of the 1980s. Also, Brandeis has an accessible and attractive web site at http://www.brandeis.edu.

—Michael Mundt and Fran Schonfeld Sherman

BRIGHAM YOUNG UNIVERSITY
(Provo, Utah, U.S.A.)

Location: The 638-acre campus of Brigham Young University is located in Provo, Utah, 45 miles south of Salt Lake City. Provo, a city of 98,000, sits in the Utah Valley, at the western base of the Wasatch Mountains. Provo is nestled between this branch of the Rocky Mountains and by Utah Lake to the west, stretching both north and south of the city.

Description: Brigham Young University, sponsored by The Church of Jesus Christ of Latter-day Saints (the LDS Church), enrolls over 30,000 students in both graduate and undergraduate programs. This school, founded by members of the LDS Church in 1875 as Brigham Young Academy, provides a comprehensive education in an atmosphere which stresses the virtues of academic study and the Mormon way of life. Primarily an undergraduate school, Brigham Young University receives recognition for its law school and business program, and for its nationally ranked athletic teams.

Information: Admissions Office
P.O. Box 21110
Provo, UT 84602-1110
U.S.A.
(801) 378-2507

Visiting: Visits may be scheduled through the Office of School Relations-Campus Visits, P.O. Box 23201, Provo, UT 84602, (801) 378-4431.

Brigham Young University, founded in 1875 as Brigham Young Academy, integrates the teaching of religious doctrine with the pursuit of academic excellence. Established under a deed of trust by Brigham Young, then president of The Church of Jesus Christ of Latter-day Saints, the school struggled for nearly 50 years to remain in operation. In the financial boom of the post–World War II years, the university expanded exponentially in the number and quality of students and faculty, curriculum offerings, library holdings, and campus facilities. Throughout university history, its members have upheld the commandments of the church while pursuing academic integrity in the eyes of the larger American learning establishment. One of the largest private universities in the United States in 1997, Brigham Young is the only church-sponsored institution which refuses to adopt the popular academic attitude of moral rel-ativism. The university operates successfully under an academic code which forbids the teaching or publication of any views against the church as an institution or against church doctrine.

Members of The Church of Jesus Christ of Latter-day Saints (LDS), commonly known as Mormons, settled Provo in 1849. This Mormon settlement was one of many founded in the Salt Lake Valley area during the 1840s and 1850s as Mormons fled religious persecution and mob violence in Illinois and Missouri. Joseph Smith, founder of the Mormon Church, was murdered on June 27, 1844, in Carthage, Illinois, and within a year, mobs surrounded the nearby Mormon settlement and threatened to take the city by force unless the Mormons agreed to evacuate by spring of 1846. Despite the fact that Mormonism embraced the teachings of the Bible, the predominant Christian denominations in the United States found the Mormon practice of polygamy to be blasphemous and took legal and physical action against them. Brigham Young, Smith's successor as president of the Mormon church, saw that the church's survival depended upon evacuation and organized groups of settlers to journey to the Rocky Mountains. Selecting the valleys of Provo and Salt Lake, Mormon wagon trains moved slowly westward toward an agriculturally barren haven in which to practice their religion.

Upon settlement, Mormons moved quickly to secure schooling for their children. They viewed formal education as an essential part of becoming a responsible member of Mormon society; small frontier schools taught rudimentary reading, writing, and arithmetic, and emphasized the teachings of the Bible and the Book of Mormon. Students acquired the skills necessary to study the teachings of God and practiced the values taught by the Mormon community. Brigham Young University grew out of this tradition; established on October 16, 1875, under a deed of trust from church president Brigham Young, Brigham Young Academy taught reading, penmanship, orthography, grammar, geography, and math, inculcating the doctrines of the Old and New Testaments, the Book of Mormon, and the Book of Doctrine and Covenants.

The Academy struggled, as did other Mormon schools, to survive financially during the late nineteenth and early twentieth centuries. Although Brigham Young Academy had the verbal support of both Brigham Young and the church, The Church of Jesus Christ of Latter-day Saints provided little financial support until the school's official incorporation by the church in 1896. For 21 years, the Academy depended upon the small contributions of students and of local Mormon families and received its larg-

Brigham Young University

est support from a small number of wealthy members of the Mormon Church. Abraham O. Smoot—banker, colonizer, financier, legislator, merchant, delegate to territorial conventions, large-scale cattle and sheep man, mayor of Provo, and president of the Utah Stake of the Mormon Church—served on the BYA board of trustees and became the principal benefactor of Brigham Young Academy. When the school's quarters were destroyed by fire in 1884, Smoot enabled the school's survival, initially by acquiring temporary accommodations for the school and secondly by negotiating and underwriting the necessary loans to erect a new school building. Despite financial limitations, the resulting Academy Building was constructed neither of modest material nor of subtle design. Dedicated in 1892, the Academy Building rose two-and-a-half stories against the backdrop of the Wasatch Mountains jutting suddenly into the sky. Constructed of stone and reminiscent of the architecture of Oxford University in England, the Academy Building meant more than a new educational facility; it represented the dedication and hope of BYA officials and trustees to build an influential Mormon Church university. Although no longer a part of Brigham Young University campus, the building still stands on University Avenue in Provo and attests to the fulfillment of early BYA dreams.

Lack of internal funding was only one factor which threatened the development of the university. Throughout its early years and continuing until Utah achieved statehood in 1896, United States' policies endangered the existence of all Mormon schools. The movement toward non-denominational, secular schooling threatened Mormons with the double burden of supporting both secular schools and Mormon schools. Because Utah was a territory, and not a state of the Union, Mormons faced the imposition of laws created by a minority of non-Mormon residents and by the greater United States government. Growing popular antagonism over the Mormon practice of taking plural wives reached critical conditions in 1896, when the United States prepared to physically enforce their laws outlawing polygamy. Young decided to sacrifice the Mormon tradition of plural wives and to accept the laws of the United States, thereby removing the significant point of contention between the Mormons and the U.S. government. When Utah applied for statehood later in the year, the U.S. granted their request, allowing Mormons their right to local and state self-representation. This proved positive both for the continued survival of the Mormon Church and for the dozens of Mormon schools in Utah.

Benjamin Cluff Jr., president of Brigham Young Academy from 1892 to 1904, witnessed the alleviation of the major external and internal threats to BYA survival. The year 1896 not only marked the acquisition of U.S. citizenship for the Utah Mormon population, it also marked the year that the LDS Church agreed to incorporate Brigham Young Academy. Church support had been intermittent in previous years and continued to fall short of Academy requests, especially in times of national depression; but, after incorporation, the church provided for the barest of survival even in times of church poverty. The efforts of Benjamin Cluff account largely for the church's incorporation of the school. In previous years, the church had refused to take the school under its financial wing, even at the request of church dignitary Smoot. During Cluff's administration, church appropriations rose from $2,000 to $30,000 per year.

Cluff worked hard to create an institution of service to the church. In the early years, Brigham Young Academy trained Mormon teachers to fulfill both its own needs for additional teachers and for the needs of surrounding Mormon schools. Continued growth of public and private schools in Utah and the surrounding territory increased demand for teachers and fostered the growth of BYA's normal school for teacher training. A specialized curriculum was also developed to train Mormon missionaries. The LDS Church placed considerable emphasis upon missionary teaching, both in the United States and abroad, and called members to service, sending them on assignments for months or years. The normal and theological departments, developed during the Academy's early years under the principalship of Karl G. Maeser (1876–92), prepared Mormon youth to serve the LDS Church. Under Cluff's administration, the normal school flourished and awarded its first degree, bachelor of pedagogy, in 1897. Twenty years later, the LDS Church named BYU its official church teachers' college.

Cluff began his principalship with one primary goal: to transform Brigham Young Academy into a great Mormon university. Cluff strengthened both the high school and college curricula, creating a number of separate schools, including a kindergarten department, a preparatory department, a missionary department, a high school, a normal school, a commercial school, a music school, and a collegiate department. For years the church had been contemplating the establishment of a university to be the center of LDS education; Cluff and BYA trustees pushed to have Brigham Young Academy chosen for this honor. The church was unprepared to name BYU its official university

in 1903 but recognized the school's growth by authorizing the name change to Brigham Young University.

When Cluff resigned in 1904, Brigham Young University remained unaccredited by U.S. accrediting agencies. President George H. Brimhall strengthened collegiate course work and hired higher-credentialed faculty in his efforts to make BYU worthy of academic accreditation. During the Brimhall years, a variety of new courses were added to the curriculum, including literature and composition, horticulture, medicine, nursing, nutrition, and sex education. During the initial years of the Brimhall administration, BYU enrolled about 100 college-level students. Although most students left before earning a degree, BYU awarded its first bachelor of arts in 1906; some students also continued their education at such U.S. institutions as the University of Chicago, Stanford, Harvard, and Yale. Brigham Young University enrollment doubled in 1909, and the university expanded its campus with the Maeser Memorial Building built on Temple Hill and dedicated in 1911. Although offering new courses, attracting greater numbers of students, and awarding more advanced degrees elevated the school in the eyes of accreditors, the key to accreditation lay in the acquisition of higher qualified faculty.

Because BYU degrees did not confer status in the larger world of learning, Brimhall hired a number of non-BYU faculty with higher degrees. At this time, the greater academic world had largely accepted the theory of evolution; new faculty members who had been introduced to the possibilities of a history of the world far different from that described in the Bible brought their ideas to the attention of both students and faculty. Joseph and Henry Peterson, brothers who had both received undergraduate degrees from the University of Chicago and graduate degrees from Harvard, joined BYU in the fall of 1907. Joseph Peterson was the first Ph.D. to be employed at BYU. Along with other new faculty, they began teaching courses such as "Ecclesiastical Sociology," "The Course of Human Progress," and "The Psychology of Religion," which emphasized scientific principles and the relationship between scientific philosophy and Mormon doctrine. Their efforts to rationalize the teachings of the Bible with the theory of evolution suggested the possibility that some of the basic tenets of the past teachings of the school and the church were either over-simplified or in error. The resulting controversy seemed to indicate the incompatibility of Mormonism and modern standards of higher learning. The campus overall was sympathetic with the new views, and the church became concerned that students were losing their faith as a result of the new teachings. In 1911, the church discharged three faculty members, including Joseph and Henry Peterson, and within the next two years 22 of 60 total faculty members left BYU due both to the pressures of the academic policy and because of low salaries. The university did not receive accreditation during Brimhall's presidency; during the following decade, BYU struggled through the World War I, a flu epidemic which closed the school during the fall term of 1918, and school indebtedness which resulted in the 1918 LDS purchase both of BYU's assets and debts.

Franklin Stewart Harris (1921–45) secured BYU accreditation following a seven-year period of school reorganization and development. He upgraded class requirements and academic regulations, prohibited high school students from enrolling in college courses without special permission, separated upper and lower division university classes, enforced stricter college entrance and graduation requirements, and standardized the university grading system. He created five colleges in three years: the College of Education, the College of Commerce and Business Administration, the College of Applied Science, the College of Fine Arts, and the College of Arts and Sciences. He also created a number of divisions for areas of specialized study, including a research division in 1921 and a graduate division in 1922. Harris strengthened library holdings and upgraded the quality of faculty, not simply by hiring new teachers, but by providing sabbatical leaves for existing BYU faculty to go back to school and receive higher degrees. In 1928, the Association of American Universities put BYU on its approved list of colleges.

On October 24, 1929, the stock market crashed and the resulting nationwide depression significantly depleted LDS Church funds. The church considered closing BYU, but the transference of a number of church junior colleges allowed BYU to remain in operation. In 1935 the church regained its financial footing and provided more aid to BYU. During the next ten years, BYU grew slowly. With the beginning of U.S. involvement in World War II in 1941, BYU's enrollment dropped and women dominated the campus. The return of U.S. veterans in 1945 transformed the school; enrollment doubled, returning to the pre-war numbers of nearly 3,000, and continued to increase during the presidencies of Howard S. McDonald (1945–49) and Christen Jensen (1949–51). BYU's greatest period of physical growth began with the national post-war financial boom during these presidencies and continued during the presidency of Ernest L. Wilkinson (1951–71). Wilkinson executed a massive expansion program, receiving nearly $10 million from the board of trustees in 1953, which resulted in the construction of nearly 250 new academic buildings by 1971. Purchasing land adjacent to the Maeser Memorial Building on Temple Hill, the campus moved entirely to this location. Wilkinson provided substantial increases in faculty salaries; by 1971 the number of full-time faculty had quadrupled to 932, over 500 with doctorates. At the end of Wilkinson's presidency, BYU included 13 undergraduate colleges with 71 departments, offering associate degrees in 20 areas, bachelors degrees in 70 areas, and masters degrees in 40 areas. Library holdings increased from 170,000 available books to 1 million. In 1967, the BYU University Press began publishing books, monographs, and periodicals. Student enrollment grew by 500 percent, to a total of 25,000 in 1971, and included students from all 50 states, from 106 foreign countries, and 8,900 returned missionaries. Church approval and financial prosperity allowed for this astronomical growth; and, although accrediting agencies criticized the fact that 95 percent of faculty were members of the LDS Church, approval could not be withheld in light of the vast and varied academic and research offerings.

During the period of rapid growth under the Wilkinson administration, BYU retained its focus upon a religiously centered education. When it became apparent that lower percentages of students were actively involved in church activities, Wilkinson established campus stakes and wards which paralleled the stake and ward divisions of the church as a whole, increasing the opportunities for student involvement. This effectively increased the percentage of students participating in church activities. A school honor code, still in effect today, required that students follow certain dress and appearance requirements; forbade the use of tea, coffee, tobacco, alcohol, and other drugs; prohibited non-marital sex and abortion; and required that students obey, honor, and sustain the laws of both the church and the United States. During the 1960s, when American campuses became the sites of student riots and demonstrations, BYU's campus remained calm and unaffected, reflecting the strength of the Mormon honor code. Brigham Young University asked both students and faculty to do their utmost to strengthen their commitment to Mormonism. Although faculty were allowed to apply for temporary federal research grants, BYU policy forbade the acceptance of direct federal aid. The LDS Church required, and continues to require, the contribution of one-tenth of personal income from its members. Because membership has grown steadily, church support of BYU has also grown, keeping tuition to one-fourth the tuition of Yale, Princeton, Notre Dame, and other private universities. With church support so strong, BYU has not been forced to accept federal aid and has retained its religious focus.

The Provo campus of BYU stopped growing in the 1970s when undergraduate enrollment was fixed at 25,000 and graduate enrollment at 2,000. Presidents Dallen H. Oaks (1971–80), Jeffrey R. Holland (1980–89), and Rex E. Lee (1989–96) consolidated and streamlined university programs, policies, and procedures in order to maximize the school's academic potential. The church has increasingly utilized BYU to facilitate their work in other areas; the BYU system now includes a campus in Laie, Hawaii (previously the Church College of Hawaii), the LDS Business College in Salt Lake City, and elementary or secondary schools in countries such as Mexico, Fiji, Indonesia, New Zealand, Tonga, and Western Samoa. The BYU Language Research Center works on projects designed to aid the church in its worldwide missions, preparing and updating an intercultural data bank to aid in the translation of words, ideas, and concepts from one culture to another. The Religious Studies Center, founded by Dean Jeffrey R. Holland in 1975, researches church-related historical and doctrinal topics. Topics funded for the 1995–96 academic year included: the Mormon Battalion, the growth of the church in Brazil, and the history of the Book of Abraham.

Over the years, the school never lost sight of its central purpose; the university's mission over a century after its founding remains to teach the gospel of Jesus Christ and to pursue all truths through the arts, letters, and sciences. Brigham Young University has received repeated criticism throughout the years for its tenacious hold on religious tradition, yet academic accrediting agencies have praised both the institution's general undergraduate program and its business and law schools. For, while the singular ideological focus of BYU precludes the university's ability to develop respected graduate programs in the sciences, Mormon dedication to the law has fostered the growth of the J. Reuben Clark Law School, established in the fall of 1973. While most American religious universi-

ties have either compromised their views to gain federal funding or remained satisfied with a secondary role in American higher learning, Brigham Young University has chosen to place emphasis on the fields of learning encouraged by their religious views. The university continues to grow in stature and its current president, Merrill J. Bateman (1996–), announced a $250-million capital campaign designed to secure the university's position well into the twenty-first century.

Further Reading: Good histories of Brigham Young University may be found in *Brigham Young University: A School of Destiny*, edited by Ernest L. Wilkinson and W. Cleon Skousen (Provo, Utah: Brigham Young University Press, 1976), and in *Brigham Young University: The First One-Hundred Years*, edited by Ernest L. Wilkinson (Provo, Utah: Brigham Young University Press, 1975–76).

—Beth Rillema

BROWN UNIVERSITY
(Providence, Rhode Island, U.S.A.)

Location: In central Providence, a half mile from the Providence River and City Hall.

Description: A private university enrolling approximately 6,800 students in undergraduate, graduate, and professional schools.

Information: Admission Office—The College
Brown University
Box 1876
Providence, RI 02912
U.S.A.
(401) 863-2378

Visiting: Guide tours of the campus are available. For more information, please contact the admissions office at (401) 863-2378.

Brown University was founded in 1764 by the Baptists of America. The late eighteenth century was a period ripe with interest in education. As the colonies became more settled and agriculture and commerce flourished, interest turned from day-to-day survival to the more lofty concerns of expansion of the colonies' various religious denominations. The expansion of religious pursuits in the New World was to be achieved primarily by each denomination educating its young men for the ministry. In fact, the first eight colleges founded in America were controlled by religious bodies. Brown University was the seventh college to be founded in America and the third in New England.

The charter of Brown University (then known as Rhode Island College) was one of the most liberal of its kind at the time. While there was a desire to perpetuate an educated ministry, the charter outlined the purpose of the college as "preserving in the Community a Succession of Men duly qualify'd for Discharging the Offices of Life with usefulness and reputation." With an outlook unusually farsighted for the time, the Charter required "that Public teaching shall in general respect the Sciences," which based the university principles on the same premises of religious liberty with which Roger Williams founded Rhode Island.

When Brown University began its life as Rhode Island College in the small village of Warren, Rhode Island, in 1765, it had one student, William Rogers, and one faculty member, the college's first president, James Manning. The university soon grew to an enrollment of

ten. The first commencement exercises were held in 1769, at which time it was determined that the college would be moved. One of the many criteria suggested for choosing among the towns was the presence in the community of scientific books and apparatus and men who knew how to use them. With these criteria, the likely choice was Newport; however, Providence was championed by the mercantile family of the Browns, who pledged slightly more of the cost for the building of a college edifice. The move to what is now known as "College Hill" took place in 1770.

As the young college had just begun to grow, key political changes were occurring in the colonies, with increased rebellion and unrest culminating in the American Revolution. On December 14, 1776, President Manning published a notice in the *Providence Gazette* that "attendance on College Orders is dispensed with until the End of next Spring Vacation." He issued a further notice the following May that "Prosecution of Studies here is utterly impractical, especially while this continues to be a garrisoned Town." The college remained closed from 1776 to 1782, during which time the campus was used by the American and French troops as a barracks and hospital.

After the revolution, the university found itself in a shambles physically and financially. In 1782 the infant government of the United States was presented with a bill for just over £1,309 for damages to the campus. Interest was added as of December 1792, increasing the total due to £2,300 or approximately $7,667.00. The only payment the university received from the government came eight years later in the amount of $2,779.13. The college's financial difficulty drove President Manning to seek funds from numerous sources. Manning sought out prospects ranging from alumni to the king of France. However, numerous attempts to improve the financial situation of the college yielded few donations. The help the college did receive came from a humbler but surer source, an increase in the number of students, with a small advance in the price for tuition. In the fall of 1783, Mr. John Brown offered the college assistance in improving its facilities for instruction. He offered to pay half the amount needed to purchase a "compleat Philosophical Apparatus & Library" if the college could raise the balance. After only a few days £700 was secured for this purpose.

The college also began to increase the size of its faculty. Joseph Brown, a member of the Brown mercantile family, and Benjamin Waterhouse were appointed to it in 1784. They were soon joined by other faculty and tutors.

Brown University

The steadily growing student enrollment allowed for and necessitated the increases in the size of the teaching body. Though Joseph Brown died in 1785, the Brown family's involvement in the college that would bear their name was just beginning. In 1804 Nicholas Brown, a member of the class of 1786, and then treasurer of the college, made a large monetary gift. The name of the college was then changed to Brown University. As a result of Brown's generosity, Hope College, Manning Hall, and the Library Fund came into existence. The John Carter Brown Library, named for Nicholas Brown's son, is the choicest material possession of the university.

Under the third president of Brown University, Asa Messer, the college saw its first major innovation. A medical school was established in 1811 with the appointment of three professors. The standard of medical education in the United States at that time was so poor that even the scantily equipped new Brown University medical program was tolerated. After receiving criticism from a Brown alumnus over the inadequacies of the medical school, additional medical faculty were appointed to begin giving credibility to the fledgling program. Eighty-seven students were graduated from Brown University Medical School between 1804 and 1828. Many of the graduates moved on to become well known members of the medical profession. Jerome V.C. Smith was editor of the Boston *Medical and Surgical Journal* for 28 years. Alden March founded the Albany Medical College and was president of the American Medical Association. Other graduates held positions in the Rhode Island Medical Society, and many went on to professorships at such prestigious schools as Dartmouth and the College of Physicians and Surgeons in New York.

A new young president was appointed in March 1827. The personality of Francis Wayland would change Brown and its educational process. Wayland ruled that no instructor or student could bring a textbook into the classroom. He felt that both student and teacher would thus be forced to be completely familiar with the lessons and would be encouraged to engage in open discussion. He became one of the best known college presidents of his time, and, toward the end of his long administration, he attracted attention in educational circles by introducing his New System at Brown. This was a new curriculum—radical for the era—that emphasized applied science and engineering and gave the students some choice in the selection of courses. Walter C. Bronson commented that by adopting the New System and bringing in new "unconventional" faculty "that the college had evoked a spirit of freedom which flew straight in the teeth of old restrictions." Wayland ended his long administration at Brown in 1855. He stated that the formulation of the New System proved very laborious and worrisome and that he "would not, for any earthly consideration, go through the same work again."

Once again Brown University found itself involved in the political upheaval of war. Barnas Sears, Wayland's successor, conducted most of his tenure during the Civil War. Of the 278 men who were graduated during the war, 132 enlisted for service. The college did not grow in enrollment or equipment during this period, when most energy and efforts were directed to the war. After the end of the war—and after President Sears' resignation—the college enrollment regained its previous vigor.

The college saw great changes over the next 25 years. Athletics were organized and Brown was represented in several intercollegiate sports. The campus grew through increased donations and increased enrollment (as well as higher tuition and board rates). The University Extension was also a new creation just before the turn of the century. Its purpose was to bring the benefit of advanced studies to people other than matriculating students. By 1892 the extension offered 35 courses which were attended by 1,500 persons in 16 towns and cities. Another major change during this time was the creation of Pembroke College, an undergraduate college for women, in 1891. Its first class numbered seven but enrollment quickly increased to 157 by 1896. Elisha Benjamin Andrews, college president at the time, was slowly creating the modern Brown University. New departments were created, enrollment and faculty increased rapidly, and graduate study was encouraged. Brown awarded its first master of arts degree in 1888, followed the next year by its first doctorate. Brown was preparing itself for entry into the next century.

The next president, William Herbert Perry Faunce (a Brown graduate, class of 1880) began the longest administration in the history of the university. He held his position from 1899 to 1929. During these 30 years the college saw major increases in the size of its physical plant, made possible by the ninefold increase in its endowment. The college not only increased its physical presence, it also increased its presence in the American academic community. Entrance requirements were raised, the curriculum was broadened, and graduate studies were formally recognized by the creation of the graduate school.

Henry Merritt Wriston became Brown's 11th president in 1937. His impact on the university was enormous, maybe even greater than that of President Faunce, who had served for three decades. Dr. Wriston moved Brown from a college of only regional renown to a stature that ranked among the outstanding universities of the country. His changes in curriculum and his employment of renowned faculty account for much of what Brown is today. The last changes Wriston made were through an ambitious building program, the chief feature of which is the quadrangle that now bears his name. Andrews Hall at Pembroke was also built during his administration, and he made a start on the West Quadrangle (renamed Keeney Quadrangle in 1982).

Two major innovations in curriculum took place during the mid-1960s. The first was the creation of a flexible approach to course selection and requirements for a bachelor of arts degree. The second was the creation of a six-year course of studies leading to a degree of master of medical science. The growing demand by students for involvement and responsibility in their own college life was only partially answered by these changes. This trend to greater student responsibility was reflected in the major curriculum reform, still widely referred to as the "New Curriculum," adopted in the spring of 1969, which introduced student choice and flexibility in programs.

Dr. Donald F. Hornig was elected as Brown's 14th president in the spring of 1970. Two major accomplishments during his years as president were the merger of the undergraduate college with Pembroke College into a completely coeducational undergraduate institution, and the establishment in 1972 of a full M.D. In October 1991, the program's name was changed to the Brown University School of Medicine. This program became one of the first in the United States to utilize a group of local hospitals for clinical training. Brown's medical program became fully accredited in 1975.

Dr. Hornig resigned in 1976, and the 15th president, Howard Robert Swearer, was named in *Time* magazine "Portfolio of 200 young American leaders." During Swearer's administration, Brown became one of the most sought after universities in the country, evident by major increases in applications for admission. The operating budget was balanced for the first time in a decade. The Campaign for Brown, a major annual fundraising effort begun in 1979, saw annual contributions increase sevenfold. Major construction projects totaling over $40 million were completed during the late 1970s and early 1980s.

The college was again changing physically, but it maintained a philosophical base of integrated learning. In 1980 the Francis Wayland Collegium for Liberal Learning was established to provide a setting in which faculty were encouraged to develop courses that crossed departmental boundaries and to encourage interdisciplinary discussions.

In 1983 the university began a program to link the entire campus via computer network. The goal of having 10,000 work stations in use was accomplished by the end of Swearer's administration in 1988. Swearer's successor, Vartin Gregorian, took office in the spring of 1989 and continued to maintain Brown as a university of Ivy League stature.

Gregorian resigned in 1997. The Boston Globe reported that the retiring president was "widely credited with enhancing Brown's reputation and strengthening its financial base, which had become the weakest in the Ivy League."

Along with doubling the university's endowment, Gregorian developed the Annenberg Institute for School Reform, which distributed $500 million in grants to American public schools.

Brown continues to improve its ability to encourage student involvement in the educational process within Brown, and in the community around Brown. The university has maintained its high number of applicants, making admissions quite competitive.

Further Reading: Janet M. Phillips's *Brown University, Short History* (Providence, Rhode Island: Brown University, 1992) provides the best brief, but thorough, account of the growth of the college from colonial times through the early 1980s. A detailed account of the early college is found in Walter C. Bronson's *The History of Brown University, 1764–1914* (Providence, Rhode Island: Brown University, 1914). Bronson's history was written to commemorate the 150-year celebration of the college founding. *Science and Technology in Providence, 1760–1914* (Providence, Rhode Island: Brown University, 1952) by Donald Fleming, also written as a commemoration, focuses on Brown's role in the development of modern technology in Rhode Island and surrounding communities.

—Celeste A. Voyer

BRYN MAWR COLLEGE
(Bryn Mawr, Pennsylvania, U.S.A.)

Location: Approximately 13 miles from the city center of Philadelphia.

Description: A private women's university enrolling approximately 1,650 students in undergraduate and graduate programs.

Information: Office of Admissions
Ely House
Bryn Mawr College
101 N. Merion Avenue
Bryn Mawr, PA 19010
U.S.A.
(610) 526-5152

Bryn Mawr College, located in Bryn Mawr, Pennsylvania, was formally established in 1880 to extend to women the opportunity for rigorous academic training (including the study of Greek, mathematics, and philosophy) that was then available only to men. When Bryn Mawr opened its doors in 1885, it offered the A.B., M.A., and Ph.D. degrees, making it the first women's college in the United States to develop graduate instruction leading to the doctorate. Today, Bryn Mawr remains a women's college at the undergraduate level, and coeducational in its two graduate schools—arts and sciences, and social work and social research.

Bryn Mawr College was founded by Joseph Wright Taylor in 1877. Taylor, born on March 1, 1810, in a farmhouse in New Jersey, was the youngest child in a large family that belonged to the Society of Friends (the Quakers). Taylor first studied to be an apothecary and later turned to the study of medicine. He became a doctor when he was only 20 years old.

Taylor eventually left the field of medicine and ended up working toward increased educational opportunities for women. He became a member of the Board of Managers of Haverford College (a Quaker institution near Philadelphia). He was one of a few Quakers who believed that the education of Quaker women was necessary and important. He believed that because the Quakers were proud of the fact that women were given the right of leadership as ministers, there should be a formal way to prepare women for this opportunity. Taylor thought that conditions required that the teaching profession include women. One of his reasons was the fact that fewer men were available because of the Civil War; furthermore, men were seeking the growing commercial and industrial opportunities.

At this time, the issue of women's education was being considered at the many new colleges which were opening throughout the United States. Such women's colleges as Vassar, Wellesley, and Smith had opened; a few institutions, such as Cornell, which had formerly admitted only males, began admitting women. Universities in the western United States were beginning to admit women but, overall, those schools had small enrollments.

Taylor, actively involved in both the planning and building of Bryn Mawr, came every day to survey the progress of the work at the site just outside Bryn Mawr, chosen because of its close proximity to Haverford and the wide country landscape that meant so much to Taylor.

On August 4, 1879, ground was broken for Taylor Hall, the administration building. Taylor did not live to see the completion of the college. However, he had included the plan for the college in his will, along with specific instructions as to its completion and organization. Taylor's will specified that future trustees were always to be chosen from among the orthodox branch of the Society of Friends and that they were to be a self-perpetuating body, filling vacancies as they occurred.

Although his successors were puzzled by many of Taylor's goals, one singular purpose has remained clear. According to Cornelia Meigs in her history of the college, "His main purpose was unfalteringly clear, for he never wavered in his intention to give young women a liberalizing education, one that would enlarge their lives and make them more responsive members of society. And, in the process, he wanted them to have the very best that could be given them."

In 1884, James E. Rhoads was elected first president, and Martha Carey Thomas was elected first dean. She had hoped to be Bryn Mawr's first president but was happy to accept the position as Rhoads' assistant. "I feel that in the future it will be constant pleasure to be able to work with thee in promoting its [Bryn Mawr's] success," she wrote. Rhoads' first ten years were consumed by the planning, building, and launching of the college. He was president of the new college for 15 years, during which time, his contributions to Bryn Mawr included opening the college and setting its high faculty and academic standards. In 1893, two years before Rhoads' death, Bryn Mawr's trustees decided to broaden Taylor's mission by declaring that Bryn Mawr would be non-denominational. They did ensure, however, that the college would remain committed to the belief in freedom of conscience.

It is unclear when it was decided that Bryn Mawr, unlike any other women's college already in existence, would offer graduate study. According to Thomas, "A col-

Bryn Mawr College

lege without graduate students . . . never occurred to us."

Bryn Mawr's first dean and second president, Martha Carey Thomas, spent her life promoting the education of women. When only 13 she wrote in her diary, "How unjust—how narrow-minded—how utterly incomprehensible to deny that women ought to be educated and worse than all to deny that they have equal power of mind." She was president from 1894 through 1922. Bryn Mawr credits Thomas with giving "Bryn Mawr its special identity as a college determined to prove that women could successfully complete a curriculum as rigorous as any offered to men in the best universities." She was driven to make Bryn Mawr the best, due largely in part to her competitive spirit. In her biography of Thomas, Helen Lefkowitz Horowitz wrote, "If James Rhoads could not do something, she could. She would learn it all. From faculty and curriculum to entrance standards and furnaces, Bryn Mawr would set the standard."

Cornelia Meigs summarized Thomas's tenure: "Through all the years of her presidency she had a central and often repeated statement of intention 'to raise the standard of the College.' It was not enough to set the pattern and hold it; there must be steady advance along every line, through the oral language examinations, through the

'merit law' by which a student must maintain a certain level of good work, through the constant survey of the quality of teaching."

Thomas faced a great struggle, however, as she had different ambitions from those of the trustees. She felt that the Bryn Mawr of the 1890s was only the beginning, not the end. Thomas had used Taylor's endowment to create a secular and cosmopolitan college, believing that the college should be as large in size as in talent. The trustees, on the other hand, felt that both Rhoads and Thomas had ambitions for Bryn Mawr that far exceeded Taylor's endowment. As a result, initially, they blocked its growth, hoping Bryn Mawr would remain small, as Taylor had desired.

Thomas began work toward the growth of Bryn Mawr. One of her main goals was the construction of a library. In 1901, John D. Rockefeller agreed to give $250,000 to build a dormitory and a new power plant for heating and lighting the college, if the college could raise the same amount to build the library.

During the period of raising money for the library, the alumnae had given great assistance in raising funds. (Formed after Bryn Mawr graduated its first class, the alumnae association soon commissioned renowned artist

John Singer Sargent to paint a portrait of Thomas.) Bryn Mawr's library opened in 1906; at the opening ceremony Thomas declared that the new library not only provided space for books and professors' offices, but would also begin a new era of teaching at Bryn Mawr because teachers would have proper places to confer with students.

Thomas developed the school of education so that Bryn Mawr could study and practice the increasingly popular, newer methods of teaching young children. The school opened in 1913 and enjoyed great success. The founding in 1910 of the Carola Woerishoffer Graduate Department of Social Economy and Social Research was Bryn Mawr's first "professional school." Although called a graduate department, it had its own M.A. and Ph.D. and its own certificate of completion. As testimony to Thomas's understanding of the needs of the time, Bryn Mawr's school devoted to social service studies was followed by the opening within the next few years of similar schools and departments at Northwestern, Johns Hopkins, Harvard, the University of Chicago, and the University of Missouri.

In the later years of her administration, Thomas gave increasing attention to public affairs, as she and Bryn Mawr had become internationally known and respected. Considered the leading authority on women's education in the early twentieth century, Thomas retired in June 1922. She continues to be one of the legends in the history of Bryn Mawr College.

Marion Edwards Park, Bryn Mawr's third president (1922–42), was the first alumna to be president. Park found herself having to guide the college during the Depression. Among the challenges facing her was the issue of whether Bryn Mawr should continue to offer a graduate program. A committee was organized (headed by another active alumna, Eunice Schenk) to decide the issue; it found that providing graduate study was valuable to both the students and the college. As a result, in 1929, Park formally established the graduate school. The school now had a full organization of its own as well as a dean. Reorganization of the graduate school continued throughout the twenties and thirties with studies liberalized and with greater emphasis on independent study and research from primary sources. In the 1930s, men were first admitted to the college's two graduate schools.

Major changes marked Park's presidency. Many new buildings were constructed including a new library, Rhoads Hall, and the science building. In addition, there were important curriculum changes; one was the introduction of honors work, resulting in the offering of the status of "graduation with honors." Foremost among the changes was the introduction in 1937 of the comprehensive examination, officially designated as the Final Examination during which students were required to demonstrate extensive knowledge of their major subject, with one field of special concentration and one of a related area.

Perhaps Park's greatest legacy was the move away from isolation that had previously distinguished Bryn Mawr. It was Park's innovation to form the three-college cooperation between Bryn Mawr, Haverford, and Swarthmore. Although the idea had existed for some time, it was Park's special effort that made it into a reality. The colleges' cooperation led to such practical measures as pooling library resources and allowing students to enroll in courses at the other colleges.

The college's fourth president, Katherine Elizabeth McBride, 1942–70, presided over the college during a time of great change and tremendous growth. The size in the student body increased from 500 in 1940 to 750 in 1970. This growth required the expansion and addition of new facilities. After World War II, the G.I. Bill of Rights provided thousands with the opportunity to go to college. President McBride found herself with the task of deciding whether Bryn Mawr should allow male veterans to be admitted. Men of course were already allowed under the three-college cooperative agreement. "Outside" men were permitted during this time as day-students in order to accommodate the overflowing numbers trying to get into men's and coeducational schools.

Long before the issue of admitting men arose, Bryn Mawr had solved a problem many colleges found thorny—student governance. Bryn Mawr students have one of the oldest systems of self-government in the United States. Today, of the roughly 35,000 colleges and universities in the United States, only about 30 campuses have such a code. Bryn Mawr's self-government system (Self Government Association or SGA) was founded by one of the students—Susan Walker, class of 1893. The campus community functions under a student administered academic and social honor system. The honor code applies to both residential life and academic work, from original research activities to self-scheduled examinations. Today, the SGA, which consists of 124 elected positions, acts as a liaison between Bryn Mawr undergraduates, officers, faculty, and alumnae.

Bryn Mawr College has acquired a reputation for attracting both distinguished students and professors. Woodrow Wilson, who served as president of the United States from 1913 to 1920, joined the faculty of Bryn Mawr as an assistant professor when the college was opened in 1885. Emily Green Balch, class of 1889, was the recipient of the first Bryn Mawr European Fellowship. The fellowship took her to the Sorbonne in Paris, on the first step of a distinguished career as an economist, social reformer, and peace worker. In 1946, Balch received the Nobel Peace Prize for her work in the furthering of peace.

As of 1994, Bryn Mawr was the only women's college and one of five liberal arts colleges among the top ten institutions in the nation with the highest percentage of winners of the National Science Foundation Graduate Fellowships. The college is also proud of the fact that the percentage of graduates earning degrees in the physical sciences is five times higher than the national average overall, and nine times the average of degrees earned by women.

Notable Bryn Mawr alumnae include Marianne Moore, poet; Katherine Hepburn, actress; Alice Rivlin, deputy director of the White House Office of Management and Budget in the administration of President Bill Clinton; Anna Kisselgoff, chief dance critic for *The New York Times*; Katharine White, co-founder of *The New Yorker*; Candace Pert, psychoimmunologist. Bryn Mawr also graduated the co-founder of the League of Women Voters (Edna Fischel Gelhorn), the first woman lawyer to argue a case before the United States Supreme Court (Susan Brandeis Gilbert), the first director of the Congressional Budget Office (Alice Rivlin), and the first woman president of the State Bar of California (Margaret Morrow).

Further Reading: Helen Lefkowitz Horowitz's *The Power and Passion of M. Carey Thomas* (New York: Knopf, 1994) is a very detailed biographical account of both the public and private life of Bryn Mawr's first dean. An extensive historical account of the first 70 years of Bryn Mawr College is contained in Cornelia Meigs' *What Makes A College? A History of Bryn Mawr* (New York: Macmillan, 1956).

—Judi Gerber

CALIFORNIA INSTITUTE OF TECHNOLOGY
(Pasadena, California, U.S.A.)

Location: In Pasadena, 25 miles inland from the Pacific Ocean, and ten miles from the Los Angeles Civic Center.

Description: A university that specializes in science and engineering disciplines for a student body of approximately 900 undergraduates and 1,100 graduate students.

Information: Office of Admissions
California Institute of Technology
Pasadena, CA 91125
U.S.A.
(818) 395-6216

The California Institute of Technology's physical appearance is deceiving. The small and independent university is set in a lush 124-acre California campus, and housed in one-story traditional buildings of stucco. Yet the institute is a "hotbed" of high technology and pioneering science that has changed the course of history. With the additions of such famous off-campus facilities as the Jet Propulsion Laboratory, Palomar Observatory, and the W.M. Keck Observatory, professors and students alike have attained scientific wonders for over 50 years. The university, most often called Caltech, has employed 22 Nobel Prize recipients. Thirty-seven alumni and faculty members also have received prestigious awards for scientific achievements.

In 1891 the Honorable Amos G. Throop founded a local school of arts and crafts in Pasadena. Although it was initially known as the Throop University, the trustees would later rename the university Throop Polytechnic Institute. For almost 20 years, Throop served the Pasadena community, offering a curriculum that led to a bachelor's degree. The campus also hosted an academy that emphasized vocational training, a high school, and an elementary school.

The school quickly became overcrowded. Through the generosity of Arthur H. Fleming and his daughter Marjorie, the Throop Polytechnic Institute moved from its quarters in the center of Pasadena to a new 22-acre site on the southeast edge of town. President James A.B. Scherer opened the school doors to 21 students and a teaching staff of 16 in 1910.

On March 21, 1911, Theodore Roosevelt visited Throop and told the students and faculty during an assembly:

I want to see institutions like Throop turn out perhaps 99 of every 100 students as men who are to do given pieces of industrial work better than any one else can do them; I want to see those men do the kind of work that is now being done on the Panama Canal and on the great irrigation projects in the interior of this country—and the one-hundredth man I want to see with the kind of cultural scientific training that will make him and his fellows the matrix out of which you can occasionally develop a man like your great astronomer, George Ellery Hale.

Roosevelt never dreamed that Hale had even greater ambitions for Throop. Hale, a well-known astronomer and first director of the Mount Wilson Observatory, envisioned Throop as a distinguished institute of engineering and scientific research. Under his inspiration, the institution's evolution began. Hale understood the necessity of modern, well-equipped laboratories. He never forgot, however, that the purpose of technology was to uplift humanity, not simply to develop machines. He said, "We must not forget that the greatest engineer is not the man who is trained merely to understand machines and apply formulas, but it is the man who, while knowing these things, has not failed to develop his breadth of view and the highest qualities of his imagination."

Two other scientists shared his vision. Along with Hale, chemist Arthur A. Noyes and physicist Robert A. Millikan set the school firmly on a new course, with instruction in engineering and the fundamentals of mathematics, physics, and chemistry. They enriched the technological curriculum with coursework in humanities. Noyes would become Throop's director of chemical research in 1919. Millikan became administrative head of the institute as well as director of the Norman Bridge Laboratory in 1921, a year after the university received its present name, the California Institute of Technology. Two years later, Millikan was awarded the Nobel Prize for physics. Because of Millikan's prestige, scientists such as Charles Galton Darwin, Paul Epstein, and Richard C. Tolman also came to Caltech.

The new curriculum meant specialization. The trustees had already decided in 1907 to discontinue the elementary, business, and high schools. Their action left only a college of technology and sciences that granted bachelor of science degrees in civil, electrical, and mechanical engineering. Hale, Noyes, and Millikan embarked on the Institute's renaissance. The three were celebrated

California Institute of Technology

research scientists, were well-respected in their fields, and enjoyed reputations that lured graduate students to the school.

Caltech's 1920 enrollment lists 9 graduate students and 359 undergraduates, with a teaching staff of 60. A decade later, there were 138 graduate students, 510 undergraduates, and a faculty of 180. Presently, there are approximately 1,100 graduate students, 900 undergraduates, and 1,000 faculty members.

Individuals, corporations, and foundations began to keep close watch on the institute's projects. Southern California Edison Company donated a high-voltage laboratory, with a million-volt Sorensen transformer. Foundations such as Carnegie, Rockefeller, and Guggenheim provided economic assistance for new enterprises.

These achievements made it necessary for the university to expand once again. The institute could not continue as simply an instructional and research center in engineering, physics, and chemistry. A gift of $25,000 from the Carnegie Corporation of New York made exten-

sion studies possible. The board of trustees then approved a department of geological instruction and research, and a new seismology laboratory. The disciplines of economics, history, and literature were then added to the undergraduate curriculum in 1925. Thomas Hunt Morgan, who would receive the Nobel Prize in physiology or medicine in 1933, became the first chairman of the new division of biology in 1928. Under Morgan's guidance, Caltech's biology research advanced rapidly, especially in the areas of genetics and biology.

The institute also moved forward in the discipline of aeronautics. For years, Professors Harry Bateman and P.S. Epstein had taught courses in theoretical aerodynamics. In 1917, creators of a wind tunnel at the Throop Institute claimed that it could sustain velocities of 4 to 40 miles an hour. In 1926, the Guggenheim Graduate School of Aerodynamics was established. A related laboratory was completed in 1929. The new program, called GALCIT (Graduate Aeronautical Laboratories at the California Institute of Technology) under the tutelage of

Theodore von Karman, soon became the world-famous research center in aeronautics.

Meanwhile, George Hale and his Mount Wilson Observatory associates were busy in 1928, writing a proposal for a 200-inch telescope. They persuaded the General Education Board to donate $6 million for the project's development. Caltech erected the huge instrument, known as the Hale Telescope, on Mount Palomar. It is still recognized as one of the largest and most powerful optical telescopes in the western world. Scientists and engineers conducted significant astronomical discoveries for 40 years with this mechanism.

Another milestone in Caltech's history occurred in 1930 when Linus Pauling ascertained the nature of the chemical bond—how atoms link up to form molecules in both living and non-living systems. Until then, chemistry had been controlled as much by serendipity as by science. Major advances in chemistry and molecular biology and the development of hundreds of synthetic products evolved from Pauling's discovery. Pauling received the Nobel Prize twice: in 1954 for chemistry and in 1962 for the Nobel Peace Prize.

In 1934, Caltech physicist Carl Anderson discovered a form of antimatter called the positron, the first particle of antimatter known to man. The antiparticle to the electron, the positron is a negatively charged particle that opened up new areas of subatomic physics. Physicists smash positrons and electrons together to investigate the fundamental forces that govern the universe. Anderson was awarded the Nobel Prize for physics in 1936.

From the 1930s to the 1960s, a group of Caltech biologists focused on molecular biology. These pioneers included Thomas Hunt Morgan, whose studies of the relationship of chromosomes to heredity would be the first chapter of modern genetics. In addition, George Beadle (Nobel laureate in physiology or medicine, 1958) made important discoveries about the chemical activity of genes. The third in this triumvirate, Max Delbruck (Nobel Prize for physiology or medicine, 1969) did significant studies about the nature of viruses and viral diseases.

Caltech is known throughout the world as the birthplace of modern earthquake science. Three institute scientists played a crucial part in developing seismology into an international technology of earthquake detection, study, and measurement. Harry Wood, a Caltech geologist, invented the first seismograph able to record distant quakes. Mathematician Beno Gutenberg and physicist Charles Richter devised the Richter Scale, used to this day by seismologists to measure the strength of a quake. During the 1970s, Hiro Kanomori of Caltech developed a new magnitude scale of quakes, able to measure accurately the strongest movements. Presently, the Lawrence Livermore National Laboratory and Caltech's Seismological Laboratory combine forces to understand earthquakes. A network of seismometers throughout Southern California connects

to Caltech over a variety of dedicated communications networks and computers. Caltech, the U.S. Geological Survey (USGS), and Pacific Bell announced in 1995 an 18-month monitoring system that would speed location data of earthquakes. The test not only searches for quake epicenters for all tremors over a magnitude of five, but also areas of highest shaking intensity.

During World War II, a large portion of Caltech's personnel and facilities were denoted to the war effort, through instructional programs and weapons research. Nonprofit contracts from the Office of Scientific Research and Development enabled Caltech scientists and technologists to develop systems essential to the nation's defense during this time. Rockets, jet propulsion, and antisubmarine warfare became the chief priorities of the day. Today, the National Aeronautics and Space Administration (NASA) is beneficiary of a large-scale program controlled by the Institute's Jet Propulsion Laboratory (JPL).

Caltech's JPL program began with four inventors, known affectionately by students and faculty as the "suicide squad," who would hide in trenches with sandbags piled in front of them. The researchers then would test rocket motors in the Arroyo Seco, about three miles above the Rose Bowl. The "suicide squad" researchers helped to transform Southern California into the aircraft capital of the world. From a shaky beginning with the "suicide squad," grew a multi-million dollar, 165-acre, government-owned development facility operated by Caltech to serve NASA. *The Daily News* of Los Angeles described some of JP's achievements:

> JPL . . . is responsible for America's first successful earth satellite; first space probe; first lunar impact; first exploration of Mars, Venus, Mercury, Saturn, Jupiter and Uranus; the operation of Deep Space Network for tracking all U.S. space shots; and innovations and applications of space science to medicine, computers, communications and transportation.

Carl Sagan, the well-known astronomer, wrote in his book *The Cosmos,* "This is time when humans have begun to sail the sea of space." Sagan was at Caltech to assist in the launching of the spacecrafts Voyager 1 and 2. The vessels left earth in 1977, and were able to record images of Jupiter in 1979, Saturn in 1980, and Uranus in 1986.

The Gallileo spacecraft, en route to a December 1995 destination on Jupiter, flew by asteroid Ida in August 1993. Later, scientists were able to release a picture of one of Ida's natural satellites, thus proving moons of asteroids do exist. Meanwhile, NASA and JPL directed the Voyager 1 and 2 space vessels to leave our solar system on a quest to reach the point where the sun's effect ends, and interstellar space begins. Almost one-third of all JPL's work today is related to national defense, computerized communications, and weather reporting systems.

Engineers, technicians, and scientists have pioneered in astrophysics for three decades in Caltech's Kellogg Laboratory. There, a team led by the late Charles Lauritsen proved that nearly all elements in the universe and in our bodies come from the stars. Kellogg physicist William Fowler shared the 1983 Nobel Prize with Subramanyan Chadrasekhar for that research, which further explained the chemical and physical processes between the stars and the universe. Yet Fowler never lost his sense of wonder at science, no matter how complex his discoveries. He once remarked, "It is a remarkable fact that humans, on the basis of experiments, and measurements carried out in the lab, are able to understand the universe in the early stages of its evolution, even during the first three minutes of its existence."

In 1953, Caltech geologist Clair Patterson conducted studies of the decay rate of lead isotopes in the Earth's oldest rocks, and determined that the Earth was 4.6 billion years old. Patterson then switched from analyzing lead in rocks to examining lead pollution in the oceans and atmosphere. He conducted comprehensive tests which proved that lead pollution from automobile exhaust had reached dangerously toxic levels in the environment. His experiments were a determinant in the federal government's decision to establish pollution control in the auto industry.

Robert A. Millikan retired as chairman of Caltech's executive council in 1945. Dr. Lee A. DuBridge became president on September 1, 1946. DuBridge arrived at Caltech after five years as serving as war-time director of the MIT Radiation Laboratory, and remained at Caltech for 22 years. He adhered to the belief in a small, select institution that offered excellence in education. During his administration, however, Caltech did expand. The 30-acre campus grew to 80 acres. The total of endowment increased from $17 million to more than $100 million. The faculty of 250 became 550. The number of campus buildings increased from 20 to 64, and the budget developed from a little less than $8 million to $30 million.

Nonetheless, DuBridge succeeded in keeping his concept of a small institution. Enrollment remained relatively stable. In 1946 the total number of students, graduate and undergraduate, was 1,391. When DuBridge left in 1968, the number was 1,492. Dr. Harold Brown became Caltech's president in 1969. A physicist who received his Ph.D. from Columbia, he had served as President Lyndon Johnson's Secretary of the Air Force in 1965. He arrived at the university after finishing his tenure in that position. Under Brown's management, six new campus buildings were dedicated. A major development campaign for $130 million was in motion when he resigned in 1977 to become Secretary of Defense under President Jimmy Carter.

Appointed president by the board of trustees in 1978, Dr. Marvin L. Goldberger came to Caltech after finishing an assignment at Princeton University, where he was the Joseph Henry Professor of Physics. Under the Goldberger administration, the institute added three new laboratories and received a $70 million grant for construction of the W.M. Keck Observatory to house the Hale telescope, and a $50 million pledge which would establish the Beckman Institute.

Meanwhile, distinguished psychobiologist Roger Sperry formed an important hypothesis about the left and right hemispheres of the brain. His studies led him to the conclusion that nature meant each area for different use. He reasoned that humans use the left side for analytical thinking and language, while they employ the right side for spatial-visual thought. Sperr's successful conclusions had immense impact on such fields as education, behavioral psychology, and neurophysiology. Sperry was awarded the Nobel Prize for physiology or medicine in 1981.

In 1986, scientists at Caltech created a computerized device called a Sequenator, which would become a primary tool for analysis of DNA (a group of nucleic acids, usually the basis of heredity). Commercialized by licensee Applied Biosystems in Foster City, California, the device's accuracy was reportedly close to 99 percent per single strand of DNA. When both strands are sequenced, the error rate is lowered from 1 percent to .01 percent. The Sequenator's price tag of $90,000 caused Applied Biosystems to concoct a greater amount of gel that would allow 16 samples to be tested at once. Two years later, chemists, engineers, and computer programmers would team up with biologist Leroy Hood to successfully decode the structure of DNA molecules.

Another 1986 event was the honor accorded John Whitney Sr. by the Academy of Motion Pictures Arts and Sciences for "cinematic pioneering." Whitney developed some of the fundamental techniques for state-of-the-art digital graphics. He also shared his methods with eager Caltech students, while working on an IBM research grant at the Institute in the 1960s and 1970s.

Thomas E. Everhart came to Caltech in 1987 from his post as chancellor at the University of Illinois. Everhart won recognition for his work in the development of electron microscopy and his research on electron beams as applied to the analysis and fabrication of semiconductors.

In an effort to lift the field of medicine to greater heights, a Caltech team of scientists, led by Joel Burdick, created a five-meter metallic snake. Excitement spread through the medical world in 1994 about Burdick's vision of an eight mm version of this worm which would work its way through a patient's small intestine in search of cancer.

By staying true to DuBridge's vision, Caltech has managed to stay small and selective. Prospective and established scientists find it hard to resist the combination of a palm-bordered campus, celebrated strides in technology and science, plus a certain "nerdy playfulness."

Moreover, because of its productivity and prestige, the institute has harvested a steady flow of gifts for buildings, endowments, and current operations. Caltech has its pick of teachers and scholars. Today, the California Institute of Technology claims that more of its graduates will earn Ph.D.s in engineering and science than those from any other college in the country.

Further Reading: Although there are no histories of the institute, the environment in which it was created is portrayed in *The Letters of Theodore Roosevelt* (Cambridge, Massachusetts: Harvard University Press, 1951); Roosevelt's letters show the accelerated industrial movement in the United States during the early 1900s and the consequent need for advanced technology. *Voyage to Jupiter* by David Morrison and Jane Samz (Washington, D.C.: Scientific and Technical Information Branch, NASA, 1980) provides a detailed account of the space program at Caltech's Jet Propulsion Laboratory.

—Laura Sutliff

CASE WESTERN RESERVE UNIVERSITY
(Cleveland, Ohio, U.S.A.)

Location: In Cleveland's University Circle, about four miles east of the downtown area.

Description: A private liberal arts university with approximately 9,500 students in graduate and undergraduate schools.

Information: Case Western Reserve University
Office of University Communication
10900 Euclid Avenue
Cleveland, OH 44106-7017
U.S.A.
(216) 368-4441

The history of Case Western Reserve University is actually the history of two separate schools that joined in 1967, now centered in the 500-acre park and cultural area of Cleveland known as University Circle. Before federation, the two schools, though adjacent geographically, had different educational focuses; Case Institute of Technology was primarily an engineering and science school, and Western Reserve University was a liberal arts and professional school.

Western Reserve College opened in the fall of 1826 with one tutor and three students in Tallmadge, Ohio, ten miles south of Hudson, where the school's first building was under construction. The following year in Hudson, another tutor undertook the instruction of the three returning students, two new freshmen, and seventeen others in the preparatory school. Because there were no public high schools at that time, preparatory schools ensured a number of freshmen for the college.

Western Reserve College awarded degrees to its first graduating class in August 1830. By then, the faculty had grown to include four professors and one tutor, and three buildings. Later the same year, Charles Backus Storrs became the school's first president.

Under Storrs, Western Reserve College became known as a major center of abolitionism, and several African-American students were accepted at both the preparatory school and college from the 1830s. Students and faculty frequently debated abolition versus colonization instead of scheduled lessons. Professors often absented themselves to give talks in neighboring towns; when they were on campus, professors lectured on abolition rather than their assigned courses. Students neglected their studies in favor of the crusade, many of them also lecturing in favor of abolition. This clearly affected the educational role of the college, leading to a crisis between the faculty and board of trustees. After Storrs died (from consumption caught reportedly during an anti-slavery meeting) in 1834, he was considered a martyr by many, in spite of the damage to the college under his leadership. The Quaker poet John Greenleaf Whittier wrote a poem calling Storrs the "first martyr of abolition."

George Edmond Pierce, a former instructor at Yale, became the new president in March 1834. During the 21 years of his administration, the quality as well as quantity of faculty and students increased dramatically. Most importantly, Pierce developed a new emphasis on science in a curriculum superior to any western college of the time.

The school's reputation greatly improved under Pierce's tenure, but its financial situation grew worse. A temporary solution was found in 1843; the newly formed Society for the Promotion of Collegiate and Theological Education in the West gave Western Reserve College a $6,000 grant and annual supplements lasting until 1849, when the society prematurely pronounced the school able to get along without further aid. Tuition and donations failed to meet the operating expenses of the expanding college.

Financial problems continued, though by the mid-1840s, the college had a good academic reputation. In 1850, Pierce was accused of misusing funds of Western Reserve's endowment. Years earlier trustees had allowed repeated borrowing from permanent funds to pay faculty salaries; now the faculty was in an uproar because Pierce had borrowed to repay a loan from an eastern creditor. The ensuing crisis eventually led to his resignation.

Pierce's successor was Henry Lawrence Hitchcock, a native of Western Reserve, who served for 16 years, from 1855 to 1871. During Hitchcock's tenure as president, new trustees appointed to the board were wealthy men prominent in city churches and metropolitan business centers. Hitchcock also worked to recover more than $43,000 in outstanding subscriptions. Within three years the persistent president had decreased outstanding pledges to just $8,000. Much of the promised subscriptions was in rural land that either was sold for cash or used for rental income.

Nine years after Hitchcock became president, in 1864, the school's debt was cleared for the first time. In addition, he succeeded in adding science to the school's curricula, even though a Bachelor of Science degree program, which granted its first degree in 1857, had failed. To implement the instruction in science, Hitchcock persuaded Charles Augustus Young and Edward Williams Morley to join

Case Western Reserve University

Western Reserve's faculty. Both were brilliant scholars who had left the ministry for science and who ultimately achieved international renown in their fields.

During the Civil War only a few students volunteered, but students and some faculty members formed a company under the tutelage of an army officer. In 1863, the company at Western Reserve served as guards in a prison for Confederate soldiers for four months.

In 1870, following Hitchcock's resignation, Carroll Cutler became acting president. A dedicated professor from the school's own faculty, he agreed to accept the post for a short period during the search for a new president. At the end of four years, he resigned, only to be persuaded by trustees to stay on, when they could find no suitable candidate.

Cutler maintained a good faculty and liberalized the curriculum, emphasizing modern languages, science, and mathematics. He supported the admission of African Americans and women to the college. However, he was not adept in dealing with financial matters and Western Reserve again was confronted with a deficit and the inability to pay the faculty on time.

Western Reserve had been the only college in northern Ohio for years. Competition from other schools for both students and money soon increased around the Hudson area. By 1872 attendance at Western Reserve was down significantly and the school again suffered financial problems. Moving the school to Cleveland seemed a viable option; not only would such a move join the existing undergraduate college with the medical department in Cleveland, but the growing city had only one other college, the Case School of Applied Science, which would not compete with the liberal arts program offered at Western Reserve.

Funding for the move came from Amasa Stone, a millionaire and friend of Abraham Lincoln and Cornelius Vanderbilt. He donated $500,000 at the time of the move and in his will left another $100,000 to the school. Strings were attached to his gifts, however. Stone dictated that the new campus be located close to the Case School of Applied Science and that he be allowed to name 11 trustees for the new school. He insisted that the trustees name it Adelbert College (in honor of his dead son).

After the move to Cleveland, President Cutler continued to be an enthusiastic supporter of the right of women to be educated at Adelbert College, an extremely unpopular position. In his inaugural address in 1872, Cutler said, "If any woman thirsting for knowledge should seek it at this fountain, she should not be refused merely because she was a woman." Women, he decided, would be admitted to the college under the same conditions as men. During the 1870s, about four percent of the student body in Hudson was female; by the 1880s women represented more than 30 percent of the school's enrollment in Cleveland.

In 1884 a confrontation erupted between Cutler and the faculty over Cutler's policy. His plea to the trustees won over enough of them so that women remained part of the college, renamed Western Reserve University in 1882. But he had lost a great deal of popular support and, in 1886, resigned.

Hiram Collins Haydn served as president from 1887 to 1890. He was the first to be chosen directly from the board of trustees, of which he had been a member for 39 years. It was a temporary presidency and all concerned knew it. Haydn's brief tenure would be mainly remembered as the period during which the first gymnasium for men was built and the admission of women at the college ended abruptly, two months after his inauguration.

In 1888, Haydn presided over the opening of the College for Women, with 14 students and 10 members of the university's faculty (who received no additional pay for these duties). Funded in part by the wife of Amasa Stone, the school was located in a farmhouse at Euclid and Adelbert roads (now the site of the Allen Memorial Library). The most generous early supporters of the new school for women were Flora Stone Mather and Mrs. James F. Clark. Thanks to their efforts, the College for Women continued to grow; its enrollment over the years actually was greater at times than that of its male counterpoint. Often, professors at Western Reserve allowed women into their classes. (By the middle of the twentieth century, only physical education classes were divided by gender.)

In 1890, Charles Franklin Thwing became president of Western Reserve, serving for 31 years. When he took office, the university had 246 students and 37 faculty members; when he resigned in 1921, students numbered more than 2,000 and faculty 415. The physical site of the university increased from 4 buildings to 22, and the annual budget from $100,000 to $700,000. He accomplished all of this on a tight budget, refusing to operate at a deficit.

In spite of his popularity with students and his skillful fiscal management, Thwing was pressured into resigning in 1921. During the last years of his tenure, his stature had been diminished by a number of issues, including conflicts over faculty salaries, his insistence on a strict classical curriculum, and a suspect appointment to the newly endowed chair of professor of religious education.

Thwing's successor, Robert Ernest Vinson of South Carolina held the post for ten years, beginning in 1923; his tenure was most notable for the creation of Cleveland College, an undergraduate school of management offering both credit and non-credit courses to adults. It opened in the fall of 1925, using laboratories of both Case and Western Reserve during evening hours and relying on members of both faculties. Newton D. Baker, one of the new school's founders, persuaded Ellen Scripps—a journalist and philanthropist from California—to donate $25,000 to endow the school. On her death, she bequeathed another $50,000 to Cleveland College.

In 1933 Winfred George Leutner succeeded Vinson as Reserve's president. He continued the austerity measures of Vinson, thereby managing to keep Reserve itself afloat through the Depression. During World War II, Reserve provided training for various branches of the service, including the Army Air Corps and the Provost General's office. Sums paid by the government for all this military training were substantial, allowing the school to show a small surplus from 1941 through 1945. The influx of veterans on the G.I. Bill extended the period of prosperity for the entire university system through 1947.

During both the Great Depression and World War II, student enrollment was down considerably and the college suffered financially. It was almost closed at one point, and its success rate continued and fluctuated over the years. From 1946 to 1947, more than 12,000 students attended the school, over 5,000 of them veterans on the G.I. Bill and 3,000 full time. At the time, Cleveland College was Western Reserve's largest school in terms of enrollment, course offerings, and faculty.

When veterans began to disappear from Cleveland College, its glory days ended. Deficits increased once again and the student body shrank dramatically. Competition further depleted dwindling enrollment. By the 1950s, many schools offered similar adult-education programs, often at lower tuition. In 1953, Cleveland College President John Millis, convinced that the school was a losing proposition, suggested that the school move to University Circle, with several smaller extension centers based in the city's high schools. Opposition to the move was intensive and the school continued to decline in enrollment and importance. In 1973 Cleveland College was closed.

At the same time that Western Reserve was establishing itself as a liberal arts university, the Case School of Applied Science developed as a technological institution. In 1877, Leonard Case Jr. donated property in the center of Cleveland. In the deed for the new school, Case stipulated the teaching of "mathematics, physics, engineering mechanical and civil, chemistry, economic geology, mining and metallurgy, natural history, drawing, and modern languages." The school opened in the red-brick building in which the Case family had lived since 1856.

John Nelson Stockwell, a Western Reserve professor who had been engaged to teach mathematics and astronomy, acted as unofficial president, formulating a curriculum, buying equipment, establishing laboratories, and hiring a small faculty. One member of that group, Albert Abraham Michelson, hired to teach physics, went on to renown for his studies of the properties of light. In 1887 Michelson worked with Edward Williams Morley of Western Reserve in an experiment regarding the speed of light. Their findings were significant enough that some claimed that modern physics developed in University Circle in 1887.

In the 80 years between its founding and the union with Western Reserve, Case had four presidents. Cady Staley, a professor of civil engineering, was the first president, from 1886 to 1902. Case previously had outgrown its downtown facility and in 1882 moved to what would become University Circle. The first classes were held in the new building in September 1885, even though construction was still underway. Soon after Staley had assumed his post, fire gutted the new building. Classes quickly resumed in Western Reserve classrooms, a temporary union of the two schools which lasted for two years. The first two floors of the burned building were restored by 1888, but it was not until 1892 that all construction was completed.

During Staley's presidency the school's population increased from 7 teachers and 44 students to a faculty of 21 and 353 students. The civil engineering program grew to include mechanical, electrical, and mining engineering, plus labs for chemistry.

Staley's successor, Charles Sumner Howe, who had been a professor at Case for 13 years, became president in 1902. He guided the school through the years of World War I, when it served as a base for the Student Army Training Corps. That program benefited Case's finances enormously, but was an academic failure, largely because of the scholastic ineptitude of the officers in charge.

Even though a fence separated the two campuses from the time of Western Reserve's move to Cleveland, a spirit of friendly cooperation existed between them. Over the years, however, each viewed the other with disdain, and confrontations between student bodies were not unheard of. Nonetheless, a commission was appointed to study the possibility of uniting the two schools. Its report was published in 1925, recommending formation of a "Greater University." Committees met, letters flew back and forth, but little came of all the discussion.

During Howe's long tenure at Case, faculty development, student enrollment, and new buildings increased the institute's stature. Howe was able to convince several wealthy men to donate buildings, one to endow a physics chair, and even persuaded John D. Rockefeller, a Cleveland resident, to put up the money for buildings to house schools of physics and metallurgy and mining.

After Howe retired, William Elgin Wickenden became president in 1930. One of his first acts was to propose a union of Case and Western. For several months rumors flew about the pending merger. However, the Great Depression scuttled these hopes, as the schools had to scale back rather than grow. Wickenden did manage, however, to introduce a program of graduate studies, upgrade the educational background of the faculty, and emphasize the importance of the humanities in engineering training. He continually worked toward his belief that engineers must be aware of how their work would affect humankind.

During World War II, Case was chosen as the setting for training naval officers, called the V-12 program, the only one in Ohio. It also became the site of study programs to train women to work for the U.S. Army Signal Corps in the aircraft radio laboratory. A few women entered as undergraduates, too, but that opportunity ended soon after the war. (In 1959 acting president Kent Smith announced that Case Institute would open its doors to undergraduate women. The need for the United States to keep pace with Russia's space accomplishments was seen as the reason for this change of an 80-year tradition.)

By judicious management, Wickenden was able to keep Case operating on a balanced budget until the end of World War II, when G.I.s flooded the school. Wickenden retired in 1947, but not before he had succeeded in changing the name of the institution to Case Institute of Technology.

Thomas Keith Glennan was president of Case from 1948 to 1966, when talk of federation with Western Reserve arose once again. John S. Millis was then president of Western Reserve. Millis and Glennan became collaborators; in 1950 the two schools shared one health service and by 1957 they shared athletic facilities. Reserve students began to study astronomy at Case, while Case students took geology at Reserve. Similar trading of instruction began for foreign languages and several sciences. Grants from the Carnegie Corporation, the National Institutes of Health, and the U.S. Public Health Service funded still more cooperative programs.

In 1965, the two presidents agreed that it was time for their colleges to unite. A special commission was formed—funded by the Carnegie Corporation—to study the feasibility of the union. In 1966, after a year of investigation, the commission recommended that the trustees of both institutions create a federated Case Western Reserve University with one board and one president. Rivalry between the two schools was high and opposition to the union was strong. Nonetheless, the trustees approved the union and on July 1, 1967, the merged school came to life under a board of trustees comprising 15 members from each institution.

Just before the federation was completed, Glennan retired, leaving Robert Warren Morse to take over as president of Case; subsequently, he became the first president of Case Western Reserve University. Like so many others before him, Morse had to cope with operating deficits, which by 1971 totaled more than $4 million a year. He resigned because of unresolved differences over the deficits with the trustees.

Louis Adelbert Toepfer stepped in to fill the post until a permanent president could be found. In the spring of 1971 he agreed to accept the permanent post. He attacked the university's problems—including the budget—immediately, overseeing reduction in expenditures and increased fundraising. By 1973 he had the institution operating within its budget.

Through its history, Case Western Reserve University has tried several ways to educate undergraduate men and women. In 1971 it became coeducational once again. Indeed, the first woman to be appointed a federal judge, Florence E. Allen, was educated at Western Reserve.

Over the years, Case Western Reserve University has developed a wide range of traditions that celebrate life in the institution. The annual address by the president on the state of the university is one; others include the faculty-staff talent show and the Hudson Relays, a 26-mile relay between undergraduate classes to commemorate Western Reserve's move from Hudson to the present campus.

Further Reading: C.H. Cramer's *Case Western Reserve: A History of the University, 1826–1976* (Boston: Little Brown, 1976) presents a detailed account of the first 150 years. The school publication *Case Western Reserve University, Institutional Profile* is also helpful and informative.

—Ruth Pittman

CHARLES UNIVERSITY
(Prague, Czech Republic)

Location: In Prague, capital of the Czech Republic in Central Europe. Faculty buildings, schools, and institutions of the university are located in various areas of greater Prague, around the "Carolinum" in the Old Town.

Description: The earliest institution of higher learning in Central Europe, founded in 1348. Today the coeducational Czech-run university enrolls 30,000 students in 13 faculties or schools with a teaching staff of 3,000, and offers absolvent, graduate, and doctoral degrees.

Information: Note that English speakers may be difficult to reach.
Univerzita Karlova (Charles University)
116 36 Prague 1
Ovocny trh 5
Czech Republic
(2) 228-441/8

Charles University was founded April 7, 1348, by Charles IV, then Holy Roman Emperor and king of Bohemia, as part of his plan to make Prague (Praha) a center for culture and a formidable capital of the Holy Roman Empire. Born in Prague in 1316, Charles was raised in Paris at the court of his uncle, the king of France, where he changed his Czech first name from "Vaclav" (Wenceslas) to the more easily pronounced "Charles" (after his hero, Charlemagne). Well-educated, according to the French *studium generale,* Charles studied with Pierre Roger, the future Pope Clement VI. This alliance would be both important and fateful for the history of Prague and the university. (A note about the university's name. At its inception it was *Pragensis studii,* a *studium generale,* as were Paris and Bologna. Since it was located in Bohemia, it would have had a Slavic name, *Univerzitas Praha,* but, out of respect for its founder, it would also have been referred to as *Univerzitas Karlovy.* Today it is officially *Univerzita Karlova,* Charles University.)

As early as 1344, while his father, John of Luxembourg, was off fighting his many crusades, Charles, as temporary ruler of Bohemia, persuaded the pope to elevate the bishopric of Prague to an archbishopric. Through Charles' influence, Ernest of Padubic, a friend and member of a noble old Bohemian family, was chosen the first archbishop of Prague; Charles then appointed Ernest first chancellor of the new University of Prague.

The university began as an institution of the Catholic Church. Charles ordered Czech-language Bibles, produced by copyists at the archbishop's residence, and distributed them to convents throughout the country. Latin legends and meditations were also translated into Czech. The university, according to decree, was to bring Bohemia "the fruits of learning set out on its own table."

At a meeting of the Bohemian Estates (nobles) at Prague in 1348, Charles declared:

> One of our greatest endeavors is that Bohemia . . . should, through our action, be adorned by a great number of learned men; thus will the faithful inhabitants . . . who incessantly thirst for the fruits of learning, be no longer obliged to beg for foreign alms . . . thus will the natural sagacity of their minds move them to become cultured by the possession of knowledge.

Modeling his new university on the University of Paris, Charles intended that it serve the entire continent, not simply Prague. A papal bull confirming the founding of the university states that it shall be "for all inhabitants of the Kingdom and the surrounding countries, and for the students of all nations." Pope Clement VI agreed that it should be, as in Bologna and in Paris, a *studium generale* with a renowned faculty. Law professors were given incentives to come from Bologna, and art professors came from Paris. Bachelor candidates were required to study at Paris and Oxford for long semesters, to take note of what learned scholars taught there.

Charles built a fortified "new city" (*Nové Mesto*) on the right bank of the Vltava River (also called the Moldau) to accommodate the influx of students and new citizens, and endowed the university with all privileges granted older European universities in "royal" cities. Students were divided into "nations" according to their nationality: Bohemian (including Germans living in Bohemia and Hungarians), Polish, Bavarian, and Saxon, each electing members to the general council of the university. The *universitas* of *magisters, baccalaurei,* and students elected the rector.

No special buildings were erected for the university. Many professors lectured in their own apartments; the five professors of the theological faculty taught in religious buildings (one professor at St. Vitus's Cathedral, and four monks at their own monasteries). With the scholarly language of instruction being Latin, the university was, at first, a classical university, without a German or Czech character.

Charles University

Benes of Weitmil, an early historian, wrote:

The University (studium) became so great that nothing equal to it existed in all Germany; students came from . . . England, France, Lombardy, Poland, and all the surrounding countries, sons of nobles and princes, and prelates of the Church from all parts of the world.

More than a thousand students enrolled in the first few years, ushering in Prague's "golden age." Charles was active and interested in the university and often attended "disputations" (debates) which, according to medieval custom, took place there. He bought "the house of the Jew, Lazarus," in the Old Town (*Staré Mesto*), to serve as a dormitory and as classrooms for 12 professors; he also gifted them with a library. After his death, this institution was transferred to the Carolinum, which his son Wenceslas VI bought for the university from the Rotlev family. All that remains of the original Gothic Carolinum is an arbor and the oriel window created by the Parler school. Official ceremonies are still held there.

Events leading to the Hussite movement can be traced to the university; disputations at the Carolinum galvanized the Czech people, the "Pragers," certain clergymen, and students against the practices of the established Catholic Church.

In 1401, an army led by the Margrave of Meissen entered and devastated much of Bohemia and then entered Prague. The citizens (some German-born Czechs), who had not known war for more than a 100 years (spared the 100 Years' War of western Europe), were terrified and incredulous at the German cruelties. It was then that a young preacher, Jan Hus, later rector of the university, first spoke to his countrymen at a sermon in the Bethlehem Chapel. Hus told Bohemians they were "more wretched than dogs or snakes, for a dog defends the couch on which he lies, and if another dog tries to drive him away, he fights with him, and a snake does the same; but us the Germans oppress without resistance."

Hus's fortunes became entwined with those of one of the university's masters. Wenceslas IV (his forebear was Wenceslas I, the sainted "Good King Wenceslas") became unable to control his violent temper in later years; according to legend, he ordered priest John of Nepomuk, a master at the University of Prague and the queen's confessor, to divulge her confessions. Nepomuk refused, and, even though tortured by Wenceslas's henchmen in a dungeon, would not betray his calling. Nepomuk has been revered as a martyr and saint throughout Czech history. The "truer" story might be that Nepomuk represented the archbishop in a dispute against the king who was tolerant of (or apathetic to) the emerging Hussites. Most sources agree that Nepomuk became a saint and legend due to the Counter-Reformation Church's attempt to neutralize the martyrdom of the Czechs' "heretic saint"—Jan Hus, the first Czech rector of the University of Prague, whose execution aroused nationalistic passions, and caused the country 20 years of civil war.

Hus, born in 1369 or 1371, studied at a local school in Husenic in southern Bohemia, went on to Charles University from which he was graduated in 1396 with a master of liberal arts degree, and where he was appointed *ordinus* professor in 1398. He became dean of the faculty of arts at the age of 33, and was ordained in 1400. He then became rector of the university. Preaching from the simple Bethlehem Chapel and teaching at the university, Hus was in accord with the ideas of English reformer John Wycliffe against the excesses of the clergy, ideas brought into Prague through Wenceslas's association with the court of England. (His sister Anne had married English king Richard II.)

Others had laid the nationalistic groundwork by preaching in the native language of Bohemia; Hus went further, writing his sermons on the walls of Bethlehem Chapel, educating the common people to spell and read the Czech language, which he helped to modernize and elevate. At first Hus worked within the established church, seeking internal reform. The first disputes between Hus and his ecclesiastical superiors occurred in May 1403 at a meeting of the university at the Carolinum. Forty-five articles taken from the writings of Wycliffe were declared heretical by the church; they forbade members of the university to circulate them. Hus, a superior debater, proved that some statements as interpreted by the church were not in Wycliffe's writings. A new archbishop, Zbynek Zajic, seemed to bring peace among the clergy for a time. Hus called priests who took money for church functions heretics; he insisted, in letters to his superiors, that priests should be left to preach a simpler, purer Christianity. In addition, he doubted the infallibility of the pope. Hus was excommunicated for his beliefs.

Hus also made the citizens wary of the Germanizing influence of the church. At first, Wenceslas took Hus's side. In January 1409 he issued the Decrees of Kutna Hora (Kuttenberg) which secured supremacy of the Bohemian Nation at the university; 5,000 German students and professors, who were in the majority, left the university in protest, although some German-speaking theologians supported Hus. The Czech citizens were happy to see the German students leave.

Nationalism was aroused; Wycliffe's books were burned in the courtyard of Archbishop Zbynek's palace on July 15, 1410; the university was summoned to a meeting at the Carolinum to debate the issue of paying for the pope's crusade against the king of Naples with indulgence money extracted from "the faithful." Hus argued defiantly against this use of church funds. By 1412, Hus was forced to leave Prague, banned from the university by the church. He preached in the countryside and published his *De ecclesia*—reflections of his doctrines—although excommunicated.

Sigismund (Wenceslas's brother) was elected emperor in 1411. Sigismund offered Hus "safe passage" to the Council of Constance in November 1414, where he could "come unmolested to Constance, there have free audience, and return unharmed, should he not submit to the authority of the council." Hus was imprisoned when he arrived, did not renounce his doctrines, and was burned at the stake as a heretic on July 6, 1415. A civil war known as the Hussite Wars erupted and lasted for 30 years.

The Estates (Nobles) of Bohemia and Moravia addressing the Council of Constance by letter declared Hus their spiritual mentor, pledging themselves to religious liberty, and obedience to the pope and the bishops of Bohemia so long as they adhered to scripture; they further recognized the University of Prague as authority on all matters of doctrine—giving the university the important position of arbiter of doctrine during the Hussite War.

After many skirmishes between religious factions, citizens and Hussite university members gathered on April 3, 1420, at which time the Utraquist faith (both wine and bread at communion: *sub utraque specie* for everyone, not only priests) was fervently adopted. The protest went against the established Catholic Church, which followers felt incited the German race against the Slavs.

Counter-Reformation attacks plagued Bohemia; the university all but ceased to exist. Even after leadership passed to Ferdinand von Hapsbourg, who became Holy Roman Emperor in 1556, Catholicism remained the minority religion, despite Ferdinand's policy of religious tolerance and his founding of another Catholic university (the Clementium) in Prague, when Jesuits returned to teach there.

Two Catholic nobles were thrown from the window of Prague Castle in 1618, precipitating the Thirty Years War and further internal hostility. Soon after the ultimate defeat of the Bohemian Estate, Hussite leaders, including Jessenius, the rector of the University of Prague, and important townsmen were arrested. Ferdinand decreed the confiscation of the Estates' property; of the 27 death penalties called for, 24 people were to be decapitated, 3 hanged. The tongue of Jessenius was cut out before his execution on June 21, 1621. The heads of the nobles were impaled on the bridge towers. This terror, and the consequences of the Thirty Years War, resulted in the re-Catholicization of Bohemia and the University of Prague. Under the Jesuits, the arts faculty—the only remaining one of Charles' original university after the Hussite wars—and the Jesuit Clementinium academy were integrated into a single university: Charles-Ferdinand University.

By the end of the eighteenth century, German education, government, literature, and society in general superseded the Czech; that language and culture all but disappeared.

Non-Catholics were allowed to enter the university under the "enlightened" Joseph II, son of Maria Theresa of Austria, with the expulsion of the Jesuits in 1773.

Joseph also allowed German Calvinism and Lutheranism into Bohemia, using the German language to centralize and strengthen the empire. Hussitism was not allowed to resurface, a precaution against the resurgence of Czech nationalism.

After Joseph II's death in 1791, a chair of Czech language and literature was established at the university. The children of farmers and artisans, with increasing education, brought their language, legends, and national consciousness to the bourgeois class; the German-speaking Bohemian nobles, on the other hand, had allegiances to the German aristocracy and government through marriage and power.

A new national sense erupted, not led by the nobles, but by the people, and nationalism throughout the nineteenth and twentieth centuries was a democratic movement based strongly on language revival. Philologists Josef Dubrovsky and Josef Jungmann were the most prominent in this linguistic renaissance. They wrote Czech-language histories and the first Czech dictionary. Fratisek Palacky, a Protestant Moravian, wrote the first history of the Czech nation, first in German, then in Czech.

In 1848, the year of several European revolutions, the university was in the midst of national, democratic, revolutionary upheaval; democratic students were repressed under Minister Bach after an incident which broke out at the pan-Slavic Conference, causing a week of violent street fights.

The second half of the nineteenth century, with its upsurge in Czech national life, forced the Vienna government in 1882 to divide the university into two separate institutions, one German, one Czech. Each university had its own faculties, libraries, clinics, and observatories. The Germans had inherited astronomical instruments once used by Johannes Kepler; the Czechs got the equipment of Dutch astronomer Tycho Brahe. Both men had lived at Hradcany Castle during the reign of Rudolph II. Joseph Wechsberg writes of his days in Prague during the 1920s: "As a student of the German University, I didn't know for over a year where the Czech University was." The two universities existed separately in Prague until 1939.

Franz Kafka, born in Prague, studied law at the German University, graduating in 1906 at the Gothic chapel of the Carolinum. The Kinsky Palais, built between 1755 and 1765, housed the German school Kafka attended, in the shadow of the Orloj, the astronomical clock tower finished by Hanus Ruze, an Utraquist professor at Charles University in 1480. Kafka, although largely unknown to the Czech people in his youth, lived in the large Jewish ghetto and, though he wrote in perfect German, he captured the soul of Prague. His classmates were philosopher Emil Utitz and Hugo Berman, later rector of the University of Jerusalem.

During the days of the First Czechoslovak Republic (1918), Charles University was represented by the leaders of the new state: Presidents Thomas Garrigue Masaryk and Eduard Benes were on the pre-war faculty. Thus, the intelligensia were involved in the people's government.

On November 17, 1939, Charles University was forcibly closed by the invading Nazi military. After demonstrations, many students were executed and teachers persecuted. Jewish students and professors were interned in the Terezin (Theresienstadt) concentration camp after the arrival of SS officer Reinhard Heydrich in 1941; more were interned after his assassination by the resistance in June 1942. Acts of resistance by students and citizens were paralyzed until 1945.

Czechoslovakia (Czech and Slovak people united by Masaryk's government) was liberated by Russia on May 9, 1945. The German University of the Reich was abolished, and the university developed as a Soviet institution, where the study of sociology became a non-subject. The last philosophy lectures during that period were delivered in 1949 and 1950; the course was replaced by one in Marxist "historical materialism." By 1956, and after Polish influence, the interest in re-introducing sociology to the curriculum was gradually broached. In 1964, professor of philosophy L. Svoboda initiated a sociological section of the Philosophy Department at Charles University with irregular lectures. Regular courses began in 1965.

After student riots in 1968 (called the Prague Spring), Communist Party leader Alexander Dubcek sought "socialism with a human face," as students tried to hold back Russian tanks in protest and university student Jan Palack set himself on fire in Wenceslas Square in an ultimate protest. After the strikes, protests, and ousting of the Soviet government (called the Velvet Revolution, in which university students again played a leading role) in 1989, the Czech Republic elected Vaclav Havel, a playwright, as its president, and Charles University entered another state of flux within an uncertain national future.

Further Reading: Joseph Wechsberg's *Prague: The Mystical City* (New York: Macmillan, 1971) provides a wealth of detail about the history of early Prague, the university, and the author's reminiscences as a student of Prague's German University in the 1920s. Remarkable accounts of the university and its historical and social importance in Prague and in Europe—prior to this century—can be found in the illustrated copies of Count Lützow's *The Story of Prague* (1902), and in R.H. Vickers's *History of Bohemia* (1894). For later historical facts about the university, Samuel Harrison Thomson's *Czechoslovakia in European History* (Princeton, New Jersey: Princeton University Press, 1943), and Vladimir V. Kusin's *The Intellectual Origins of Prague Spring* (Cambridge: Cambridge University Press, 1971) are helpful, as are *Insight Guides: Czech and Slovak Republics* by Alfred Horn (Hong Kong: APA, 1993) and Rob Humphrey's *Rough Guide* Series: *The Czech and Slovak Republics*, 2nd edition (London: Rough Guides, 1993).

—Carol Shilakowsky

CHINESE UNIVERSITY OF HONG KONG
(New Territories, Hong Kong)

Location: The New Territories region of Hong Kong.

Description: Incorporated in 1963, the Chinese University of Hong Kong is a bilingual (Chinese and English) and bicultural institution of higher learning.

Information: Admissions Section
The Chinese University of Hong Kong
Shatin, New Territories
Hong Kong
2609 8947 and 2609 8951

Since its inception in 1963, the Chinese University of Hong Kong has grown from a struggling institution to one with more than 11,000 students and 3,500 staff members. Today, as an institution offering instruction in two languages, Chinese and English, the Chinese University is a self-governing corporation that, through its academic services and research activities, has played a key role in Hong Kong's recent development. The university has its origins in the 1940s when three post-secondary colleges—New Asia, Chung Chi, and United—were founded as private colleges to handle the flood of refugees fleeing mainland China after the Communists gained control of the country. The refugees included a number of scholars who took on the responsibility to educate the exiled young. The so-called refugee colleges (more than 30 were established) were primitive in design, poor in resources, and dependent upon rented facilities for their operation. Most offered short courses of instruction, ranging from two months to two years in duration; none offered four-year programs in arts and commerce.

New Asia College was founded in 1949 by noted scholars Chi'ien Mu and Tsui Shu-chin as a means to preserve traditional Chinese culture while balancing it with western learning. Initially, the college offered evening classes in Chinese history, economics, literature, philosophy, and political science. From the beginning, the institution faced serious financial difficulty and instability. Tsui Shu-chin left Hong Kong for Taipai, and a major financial supporter, Arthur C. Wang, an architect from Shanghai who founded a construction company in Hong Kong, declared bankruptcy. The situation became so desperate, in fact, that the college's teachers could not depend upon a regular salary and were forced to find additional work, primarily freelancing for local newspapers and magazines, to supplement their income. Furthermore, the government gave no grants for tuition to New Asia College students, so many students, unable to afford an education, had to withdraw from the college, a development that accounts for the struggling institution's small enrollment in its early years.

Chung Chi, which literally means "Reverence for Christ," was founded in 1951, also by refugee educators and scholars from the mainland, who wanted to continue their educational work in Hong Kong. Unlike New Asia College, the path to the establishment for Chung Chi was less difficult. The institution received the support of various Christian churches and missionary organizations, which wanted an institution of higher learning that would be Christian and Chinese, and that could also serve as a university for secondary school students who were not admitted to Hong Kong University. The supporting organizations included the Anglican Church, the United Kingdom-based Association of Chinese Christian Universities, and the U.S.-based Lingnan University Foundation. Key figures in the college's founding included the Reverend R.O. Hall, bishop of the Hong Kong Anglican Church; Lu Ying-lin, former president of Lingnan University; and Au Wei-Kuo (David W.K. Au), the former council chairman of St. John's University of Shanghai.

Initially, Chung Chi College offered only evening classes, but in 1952 the college instituted a four-year program. A year later, the college had four departments: foreign languages, Chinese language, economics and business administration, and sociology and education.

The period from 1953 to 1956 was a difficult one for Chung Chi and New Asia College, involving a constant struggle for funds. Fortunately, support from a number of international organizations allowed the colleges to survive. After numerous requests by Chung Chi College to be made a part of the Hong Kong education system were turned away, Bishop Hall took the matter directly to the Hong Kong governor, Sir Alexander Grantham. Hall's persistence paid off, and in June 1953 Chung Chi was accepted into the Hong Kong educational system as a post-secondary college. By 1956 Chung Chi's fortunes began to change. The college moved onto the Ma Liu Shui campus, and the student body grew to more than 300 students, with 26 full-time and 34 part-time instructors.

New Asia College attracted the attention of the Yale-In-China-Association, which had left mainland China after the Communist takeover in 1949 and had since been looking for an Asian institution that could cooperate with its educational and medical work. Dr. Harry Rudin, an association representative, came to Hong Kong in 1953

Chinese University of Hong Kong

for a visit to the New Asia College campus. He was impressed after talking with administrators, including Chi'ien Mu, as well as faculty and students. Three decades after his visit, Rudin remembered

> the reputation of Chi'ien Mu, his greater interest in education than in making money, the spirit of the students as it became apparent at the graduation ceremonies I attended, and the admiration and affection that the faculty had for their leader, a loyalty of which I was made aware at a luncheon which was to acquaint me with the men working for Chi'ien Mu.

The final agreement signed between New Asia College and the Yale-In-China Association provided for a $25,000 subsidy for the college and the promise that the association would help the institution find other sources of revenue for its building fund. The association's strong support, as well as the money received from other international organizations such as the Asia Foundation and the Harvard-Yenching Institute, helped end the college's

difficult financial period and put it on a stable course.

In 1956 five colleges—Wen Hua, Wah Kiu, Canton Overseas, Ping Jing, and Kwang Hsia—amalgamated into United College. Wen Hua and Kwang Hsia had their origins on mainland China as private universities that had established branch campuses in Hong Kong in the 1930s. Ping Jing and Wah Kiu began in Hong Kong.

The idea for the amalgamation came from Grayson Kirk, the president of Columbia University in New York City and an executive committee member of both the Asia Foundation and the Ford Foundation. When Kirk visited Hong Kong in 1956, representatives from the five colleges approached him to ask for financial assistance. Kirk suggested that the colleges would have a better chance of developing if they amalgamated and pooled their resources and efforts. The merger was officially announced in June 1956 and classes officially began the following October. The curriculum was practical, emphasizing courses such as accounting, journalism, banking, and sociology. There were 27 full-time and 59 part-time teachers and an enrollment of 70 students.

United College's early years were also marked by financial difficulty, for it had to depend upon tuition fees for support—a formidable challenge since many of the students came from poor refugee families. The Mencius Foundation Scholarship and the Taiwan-based Sun Scholarship provided some financial support, but faculty salaries remained low and the facilities were substandard.

Chung Chi, New Asia, and United faced a double-barreled problem in their relationships with the Hong Kong government. Hong Kong refused to recognize the colleges' graduation certificates while forcing them to adhere to the Education Ordinance of 1952, which was intended for the regulation of primary and secondary schools. In the late 1950s, the three colleges aggressively sought stronger support from the Hong Kong government. On August 16, 1956, Charles Long, the Yale-In-China representative at New Asia and a trustee of the college, sent a memorandum to D.J.S. Crozier, the Hong Kong government's director of education, recommending that the government provide support for the three colleges. The establishment of the Chinese Colleges Joint Council in February 1957 further strengthened the colleges' efforts to secure government support and recognition.

In 1959 the Hong Kong government announced its plan to set up a new university with Chinese as the primary language of instruction. The plan was put into play when money was made available that year for developing the curricula of United, Chung Chi, and New Asia colleges to the university level. The following year, the Hong Kong government stipulated post-secondary college ordinance and grants regulations that were designed to give financial support for the three colleges. Another step forward was taken in 1962 when the Hong Kong government established a commission under J.S. Fulton to study and consider how a Chinese university could be created. The following year, the Fulton Commission recommended the establishment of the Chinese University of Hong Kong. The government adopted the recommendations of the Fulton Commission and established a provisional council to oversee the university. Dr. Choh Ming Li was appointed the university's first vice chancellor.

Once founded, the university grew quickly. In 1964 it conferred the bachelor's degree for the first time. The following year, the university library and the school of education were established. Other major developments during the first decade of the university's existence include the establishment of the graduate school (1966), the Institute of Chinese Studies (1967), and the faculty of business administration (1974).

In 1975 the government of Hong Kong and the university chancellor appointed another commission to advise on the further development of the Chinese University. The following year, the commission published its report, recommending that the university be reorganized. The boards of governors or trustees of the three founding colleges were dissolved, and a new, wholly integrated board was created from the combined teaching and administrative ranks.

During the next decade, the university continued to carry out curricular and administrative reforms. Among the important developments were the establishment of the department of anthropology in 1979, the faculty of medicine in 1981, and the department of psychology in 1982 and the offering, beginning in 1981, of a part-time degree program in the evenings for those students working full time. In January 1986, Sir Run Run Shaw, a long-time supporter and friend of the Chinese University, gave a gift of $100 million (Hong Kong) to the institution, which it used to establish a fourth college, Shaw College. In 1988, Shaw College admitted its first students.

Today, more than three decades after its founding, the Chinese University of Hong Kong is a well-established institution whose students pursue a wide range of programs leading to bachelor and post-graduate degrees. There are seven faculties and 59 departments, and the university library has impressive holdings of more than 1.1 million volumes. The university has an international focus, maintaining faculty and student exchange programs with universities and centers of learning all over the world.

Even though the Chinese University has reflected the great change that Hong Kong has experienced in recent times, the university, says Alice N.H. Lun, author of a history of the institution, "has not forgotten its unique educational mission" because it has insisted on "the blending of Chinese and Western cultures, the blending of general educational and professional education, and the blending of teaching and research." As for the future, the historian predicts,

the Chinese University will continue to enkindle the spirit of blending Chinese and Western cultures, as well as keeping abreast with the times in order to continue serving Hong Kong, and encouraging the pursuit of learning so that greater developments can be hoped for in the future.

Further Reading: Alice N.H. Lun's *The Quest For Excellence: A History of the Chinese University of Hong Kong from 1963 to 1993* (Hong Kong: Chinese University Press, 1994) provides a comprehensive and interesting overview of the university's history and development from its origins to the present.

—Ron Chepesiuk

THE CITADEL: THE MILITARY COLLEGE OF SOUTH CAROLINA
(Charleston, South Carolina, U.S.A.)

Location: In northern Charleston, west of Interstate 26.

Description: A state-supported, comprehensive liberal arts college. Undergraduate enrollment of approximately 2,000 men and a small number of women, since the school became coeducational in 1996. Also a coeducational College of Graduate and Professional Studies with an enrollment of approximately 2,200.

Information: The Citadel
171 Moultrie Street
Charleston, SC 29409
U.S.A.
(803) 792-7842

Visiting: Visitors may arrange to tour the campus by calling the above number. The Citadel Museum is also open from 2 to 5 P.M. Sunday through Friday and 9 A.M. to 5 P.M. on Saturday.

The ritual for 150 years has been that every Friday afternoon, at precisely 3:45 P.M., a drumroll sounds on Summerall Field in Charleston, South Carolina. Soon after, to the sound of 21 bagpipes, the 2,000 Citadel Corps cadets file in. The traditional Citadel tartan—blue with stripes of red and gold—lends a splash of color to the "Long Gray Line" of dress uniforms. Military pomp is worshipped here; silver sabers gleam, uniform trousers are sharply creased, shoes are brilliantly polished. Precision weapons drills are followed by the lowering of the American flag while "The Star-Spangled Banner" is rendered by the Citadel Military Band. The elite four-member Salute Gun Battery then carries the flag off the field.

Thus ends the weekly ceremony which brings together the city of Charleston and the Citadel, otherwise known as the Military College of South Carolina. One early Charlestonian explained the southerners' unique fervor for military ceremony: "The nature of our institutions of domestic slavery and its exposure of us to hostile machinations . . . render it doubly incumbent on us . . . to cherish a military spirit and to diffuse military science among our people." Indeed, Pat Conroy, a noted writer of fiction and the Citadel's most forthcoming alumnus, expressed the common sentiment that "a Southern man is incomplete without a tenure under military rule."

The Citadel is a unique place, and its history indelibly intertwined with the history and flavor of Charleston itself—the most southern of southern cities. Walter Fraser, a historian and a former professor at the Citadel, has said that more than any other institution, the Citadel reflects the cultural values of the Old South. Conroy observed in *The Lords of Discipline*—a very thinly veiled account of Citadel life—that it is difficult to imagine the Citadel existing in any other city; Charleston and the school have symbiotically shaped each other. Although officially chartered by the state legislature in 1842, the Citadel had its physical origins much earlier, when in 1780 the citizens of Charles Town erected a fortification or "rampart" around the city to protect against British invasion. Its philosophical origins, however, date from the early nineteenth century. In 1820 almost 60 percent of the Charleston population was black, mostly slaves, although there was a contingent of free blacks who clashed repeatedly with the Charleston city council. Abolitionist sympathies were increasing in the North, and rumors were rampant that the black A.M.E. churches in Charleston had been built with money from the North. Another belief was that, in direct opposition to existing state laws, northern abolitionists had come to Charleston to instruct the slaves in reading and writing.

The climate of suspicion and unrest came to a head in May 1822. A slave named Peter Desverneys told his master of hearing of a plot to overturn white rule. According to Desverneys, the slaves, assisted by the freed blacks, planned to rise up on the night of June 16 and kill their white owners en masse. Other blacks were brought in for questioning; they implicated still others. By the night of June 16, the militia had been called out, guards had been posted, and the city was in a virtual state of hysteria. Few white slaveowners slept, and a volunteer patrol of 2,500 mounted and armed men rode up and down Charleston streets. Nothing happened. Although there was considerable room for skepticism regarding the validity of the rumor and the guilt of the implicated conspirators, when it was all over 35 blacks had been hanged, and a bunker mentality had been firmly established in Charleston. In December 1822 the residents of Charleston petitioned the state legislature for the establishment of an arsenal, "to protect and preserve the public property . . . and safety." They stockpiled their own arsenal in the meantime, in a tobacco inspection warehouse at the site of the earlier rampart, and ensured its safety with a 150-member guard. In 1825 approval of state funds permitted the construction

The Citadel

of a permanent facility near the tobacco warehouse (and also near the gallows where the supposed conspirators were hung). A municipal guard was established to oversee the care and distribution of the weapons and ammunition stored within.

In December 1842 the state legislature approved the formation of the South Carolina Military Academy at the weapons arsenal, which had come to be known simply as "the citadel." Its purpose was to train a corps of young men, like those who acted as the municipal guard, in a "broad and practical" education. Having a group of trained and armed young men drilling and parading on the grounds was thought to be "conducive to public order." A massive, turreted stone building, of Spanish-Moorish architecture, was constructed within the city block bounded by King, Meeting, Boundary, and Inspection streets. In March 1843, 20 young men reported and the Citadel Academy, named after the original building, was officially in operation.

Seventeen years later, the Citadel found itself at the center of national upheaval, and the college still regards the ensuing events as among its finest moments. The election of Abraham Lincoln to the presidency in November 1860 was considered by slaveholding southerners as tantamount to a declaration of war. Scarcely a month later, on December 20, 1860, South Carolina voted to secede from the union. Unfortunately, federal troops were stationed at Fort Sumter, barely three miles off Charleston's coast at the mouth of Charleston Harbor. The South Carolina militia and Citadel cadets occupied the abandoned Fort Moultrie, on the north promontory of the harbor, and prepared for conflict. James Buchanan, who remained president until Lincoln's inauguration in March 1861, was reluctant to antagonize the South any further, and so decided to dispatch reinforcements of men and supplies to Fort Sumter on a merchant ship (the *Star of the West*), rather than the armed battleship *Brooklyn* as was originally planned. Buchanan discovered after sending the

Star of the West that fortifications had been made on Morris Island (off the south promontory of the harbor), making it extremely hazardous for a ship to approach Fort Sumter or Charleston. Buchanan hurriedly dispatched the *Brooklyn* to escort the merchant ship, but, unfortunately, the battleship never caught up. To make matters worse, the War Department had notified Major Anderson, the commander at Fort Sumter, of the impending reinforcements by regular mail, apparently not anticipating that the South Carolina authorities might intercept letters to Fort Sumter, which of course they did. Thus it was that Major Anderson was probably the only person in Charleston who was not waiting for the *Star of the West* when it steamed into Charleston Harbor on January 9, 1861. The Citadel Corps of Cadets had stationed themselves along the battery on Morris Island. Citadel cadet George Haynesworth touched off the first cannon, thereby effectively ushering the United States into the Civil War. The Citadel's cadets received this assignment because they were the best-trained men in Charleston in firing the 24-pound siege guns.

The Civil War forced the Citadel to close temporarily as the cadets took their places in the Confederate ranks, although an encampment of Confederate troops occupied the Citadel's green for the duration of the hostilities. Perhaps the worst moment in Citadel history came on February 18, 1865. The bulk of Charleston's population had already fled the advancing Union troops. Lieutenant Colonel Augustus G. Bennett and about 25 other Union soldiers entered the city, accepted a token of surrender from Charleston's mayor, and occupied the Citadel as their headquarters. Bennett's first action was to order the Stars and Stripes raised over the Citadel and all other public buildings. The South, Charleston, and the Citadel had been defeated.

The federal government returned control of the Citadel to the state in 1882, and the Citadel resumed operation; although the cadets no longer served as arsenal guards, the military tradition continued. In 1918 the city of Charleston donated to the state more than 100 acres of high ground and salt marsh along the Ashley River (two miles north of the original rampart) to be used for a new and bigger Citadel. The building, to which the academy moved in 1922, was modeled on the old Citadel. The campus today boasts 24 buildings surrounding Summerall Field, the parade grounds where the Friday afternoon display of the Citadel Corps is held. The Citadel in the twentieth century has faced problems that relate directly to the unique aspects of the college's military model, its reverence for tradition, and the "holistic" educational philosophy embraced by the military command structure of the school. To understand the Citadel in the modern era, it is vital to understand the Citadel itself.

According to the school's public relations information, the Citadel is a state-assisted, comprehensive, liberal arts college in a military environment. To many southern families it is the finest education the country has to offer. Conroy calls it the last place in America where a boy from Brooklyn can learn to become a southerner, and where a southerner can learn to become a confederate. For the freshman "knobs" (nicknamed for their mandatory shaved heads) at the Citadel, however, to the question, "What is the Citadel?" there is only one right answer: "Sir! It is a fortress of duty, a sentinel of responsibility, a bastion of antiquity, a towering bulwark of rigid discipline, instilling within us high ideals, honor, uprightness, loyalty, patriotism, obedience, initiative, leadership, professional knowledge and pride in achievement."

That discipline, perhaps, is one factor which contributes to the depth of feeling that the Citadel seems to arouse in both alumni and outsiders. Alumni tend to talk about the Citadel in hushed, reverent tones and often consider the "wearing of the ring" their finest achievement. Citadel graduates—a group that includes senators, governors, and CEOs—are bound to each other in brotherhood. (That this charge is taken seriously is borne out by the commonly held belief that a Citadel ring is a guarantee of a good job, somewhere within the umbrella of the Citadel's old-boy network of alumni.) Loyalty to the Citadel as an alma mater can be measured by the fact that a recent four-year fund-raising campaign netted $27 million, from a school that graduates only 500 cadets a year. To the world beyond the Mason-Dixon line, however, the Citadel is at best an anachronism. When the popular press attempts to explain the school, terms such as "idiosyncratic," "eccentric leftover," and "dinosaur" find their way into print. Writer Ellen Willis was even more vitriolic, calling it "a vicious institution, devoid of redeeming social value, that exists for the sole purpose of transmitting authoritarian brutality from one generation of suckers to the next."

The passions aroused by the Citadel focus, for the most part, on two important characteristics. The Citadel is a military school unaffiliated with any of the U.S. Armed Forces; in other words, its educational objectives are pursued under a general military model. The style of education employed at the Citadel is known as adversative, which means that the students, or cadets, live in a very regimented atmosphere and experience rigorous "holistic"—meaning physical, emotional, and intellectual—training. This philosophy holds that the experience matures cadets and builds confidence in those who survive the process; in fact, a popular description of upperclassmen at the Citadel is "nine foot tall and bulletproof." The Citadel intends that when a man is graduated, he will know with certainty from that moment on that he will be able to handle whatever else life may offer.

This transformation is accomplished in a calculated fashion. The freshman, or "plebe" year, is designed to be nine months of sheer misery. "Freshman" is actually a rarely used term—the common terms include "knob," "wad," "waste," "screw," "dumbhead," and "abortion."

Freshmen must ask permission to eat, sleep, cough, scratch, or leave a room. They must obey any order from an upperclassman, assume a peculiar "brace" position when spoken to, and are permitted only three replies: "Sir, yes sir," "Sir, no sir," and "Sir, no excuse sir."

They are often prevented from sleeping or eating, having no freedom or privacy (there are no locks on doors and no curtains on windows), and are harassed, ridiculed, and subjected to extreme physical stress as a matter of routine. It is considered the sophomores' duty to run out any individual who does not measure up to the "Citadel Man"; in fact, it is a point of pride every year among the 17 companies at the Citadel as to which can drive out the most. Although hazing has officially been outlawed, there are still reports of upperclassmen putting cigarettes out on knobs' arms or dunking a knob's head repeatedly in a toilet. The Citadel's response to these charges is that they were made by those who sought excuses for dropping out of the school and that the administration has not been able to substantiate any of the charges. For those who endure until the end of the first year, supposedly, this baptism of fire lends a self-confidence and a feeling of shared experience that defines the rest of his life. One alumnus observed that "at the end of the nine months a miracle as strange as birth takes place. The cadet looks in the mirror, and in a moment of supreme madness, decides he loves the place." The Citadel's numbers seem to bear this out. The graduation rate is 37 percent higher than the national average; among African-American cadets it is 135 percent higher. The Citadel is rated in the top four schools in the United States in the graduation rate of football recruits (among colleges that grant football scholarships). The *Chronicle of Higher Education* reports that 83.3 percent of the Citadel's freshman athletes graduate, compared to 56.1 percent nationally. Among African-American athletes, the figure jumps to 90 percent, twice the national average.

A second controversial aspect of the Citadel is its reverence for the past. Conroy said that "the Citadel was very comfortable with the nineteenth century, but has had some trouble adjusting to the twentieth"—an opinion echoed in many descriptions of the school. The fact that Citadel cadets fired the first volleys in the Civil War is recalled repeatedly on campus as a defining moment of the corps' existence. Black cadets were not admitted to the corps until 1966; the school was embroiled in the 1990s in a well-publicized, prolonged legal battle to keep women from enrolling. To its supporters, adherence to tradition is a vital part of the environment cherished by the Citadel and coeducation was not part of that definition. In the 1960s, while drugs and riots ruled many of the nation's campuses, Citadel cadets were polishing their shoes and learning to clean an M-14; today the Citadel has a reputation in the South as a good place to send one's son to rid his mind of modern influences such as MTV.

Citadel supporters are determined to hold tight the ways of their collegiate forefathers. In 1979 the Citadel Board of Visitors elected Admiral James B. Stockdale—not a Citadel graduate, or even a southerner—to the presidency of the college. Stockdale attempted to put an end to hazing plebes, to erase the school's "macho" image, and to reorganize the structure of command. He lasted less than a year, stating when he left that the Citadel was "locked in pre-Civil War concrete." Perhaps even more telling: in the mid-1990s, the school—one of only two publicly supported all-male military colleges in the country—was in a legal battle over the admission of its first female cadet, Shannon Faulkner. When the news of a temporary stay issued by an appeals court was announced over the school's intercom system, the reaction, according to one alumnus on campus at the time, "was just like winning the World Series. People were yelling and screaming and slapping high-fives."

The Citadel found itself in the middle of a controversial issue—the right of a state-supported organization to define itself versus the right of an individual to be included. Although, since 1966, approximately 3,000 women students have earned graduate and undergraduate degrees, the Citadel continued to fight the application of Faulkner to be admitted as a full-fledged cadet.

After a two-and-a-half year battle in federal courts, in 1995 two Supreme Court justices rejected a last-ditch appeal by the school to prevent Faulkner from becoming a cadet. Along with over 20 males, Faulkner dropped out of the Citadel in the first week. However, women have been accepted for admission as cadets since Faulkner. Finally, after the United States Supreme Court ruled in 1996 that the other state-funded all-male military college's ban against women was unconstitutional, the Citadel announced that it would "enthusiastically" welcome women to the corps of cadets.

Further Reading: *The Lords of Discipline* by Citadel alumnus Pat Conroy (New York: Bantam, 1980) is considered the foremost account of what life as a Citadel cadet is really like, even though the plot is technically fictional. *The Boo*, also by Conroy (New York: Doherty, 1970), is a compilation of anecdotes collected from Citadel alumni. Both books give the reader a deeper understanding of the unique environment of the military college. Walter Fraser's *Charleston! Charleston!* (Columbia: University of South Carolina Press, 1989) places the history of the Citadel in context within the city of Charleston. *Fort Sumter 1861* by Albert Castel (Gettysburg, Pennsylvania: Historical Times, 1976) offers a detailed account of the events which led up to the Citadel's involvement in the beginning of the Civil War.

—Wendy Sowder Wippel

CITY UNIVERSITY OF NEW YORK
(New York, New York, U.S.A.)

The City University of New York (CUNY) is a state- and city-supported university system comprised of ten senior colleges, six community colleges, and one technical college. With schools throughout the five boroughs of New York City, the total enrollment for these urban colleges is over 210,000 students with 25,000 faculty. Today the CUNY college system is the third largest public university system in the country. The four original CUNY colleges were City College, Hunter College, Brooklyn College, and Queens College.

City College of New York
(New York, New York)

Location: Upper Manhattan in the Harlem area.

Description: The oldest of the CUNY colleges, City College is an ethnically and racially mixed college offering liberal arts and sciences curricula in its graduate and undergraduate programs.

Information: Enrollment Management
City College of the City University of New York
Convent Avenue and 138th Street
New York, NY 10031
U.S.A.
(212) 650-6419

Visiting: Admission to campus is by valid student I.D. Contact phone number above for tours.

Formal higher education was beyond the reach of the average American in the nineteenth century. Townsend Harris was affected by this fact and worked to change it. Born in 1804 in Washington County, New York, Harris came to New York City at the age of 13 to work in a dry-goods store. When he, his father, and his brother formed an import partnership, Harris developed a successful business in china and earthenware. Never marrying, he lived with his mother, who encouraged him to continue educating himself. After becoming fluent in French, Spanish, and Italian, and studying literature, history, and science, Harris became active in politics. In 1846 he was elected president of the New York City Board of Education where his first concern was the development of a free college.

The idea of a free academy began at the end of the eighteenth century in New England with the Jeffersonian idea that education was the path to cultivated citizenry. With the age of Andrew Jackson in the 1820s, the notion of a common school grew as immigrants began to trickle into the country, and social classes were less defined. The demographics of New York City were changing rapidly as immigrants from Ireland and Germany were arriving; yet the city had no public schools and only two universities—Columbia University and the University of the City of New York (now New York University). Harris proposed the development of a liberal arts school for the sons of tradesmen rather than the sons of landowners. Although he had the support of his fellow Democrats, there was considerable opposition to this controversial idea. Newspaper editorials warned that educating the masses would only lead to class tensions and jealousies between the working class and the elite. Despite its opponents, the proposal for the free academy passed the state legislature and was accepted by the majority of the voters in New York City in 1847.

James Traub, in *City on a Hill*, which covers the history of City College, describes Harris's goals:

> Harris's ends were actually . . . conservative . . . ; he had no intention of upending the social order. The notion that higher education might be a means of social mobility, a premise that City College came to vindicate as perhaps no other college did, seems not to have occurred to Harris. Quite the contrary; should the new academy succeed, he wrote, it "would soon raise up a class of mechanics and artists, well skilled in their several pursuits, and eminently qualified to infuse into their fellow-workmen a spirit that would add dignity to labor."

Harris favored building the new school on a site on 23rd Street near Lexington Avenue, a location then considered uptown and away from the bustle of activity. As excavation of the lot began, Harris resigned his position as president of the board of education. Following the death of his mother, his grief was so great that he no longer had the stamina to look after his affairs. His place was taken by Robert Kelly, a Columbia University graduate, who made daily visits to the building site and pushed the project to its completion, within the $50,000 budget set by the Free Academy Act. The building, designed by James Renwick, the architect who later designed St. Patrick's Cathedral, was completed by January 1, 1849. It was red brick, stood four stories high, and housed 34 classrooms, a library, a chapel, and a large assembly hall.

The Free Academy started its first year with 143 boys of 12 years or older and was headed by a West Point graduate, Dr. Horace Webster. He admitted the school's course of study was rigorous; it included mathematics, history, *belles lettres* [literature], and languages. Natural sciences could be chosen as electives, but bookkeeping was a required course, due to its practical application. Each student was tested once a day in each of his subject areas and any signs of lack of interest could lead to expulsion.

The next ten years saw a steady growth. The board of education provided financial assistance, but help also came in the form of private donations. By the end of its first decade, the Free Academy's library had 9,000 volumes, and the school was empowered to confer a bachelor of arts degree. The Free Academy had graduates going out into the world and entering such fields as medicine, architecture, teaching, engineering, and law.

With the dawn of the Civil War there was some pressure to introduce military science. The faculty deemed it impractical for the school but agreed that students who went into the Union army should be permitted to pass, while two alumni who opted to join the Confederate army were expelled from the Alumni Association "as traitors to their country."

Following the war, the Free Academy saw two major changes. The first was a change in the name of the school, since the term "academy" was deemed misleading for students who were receiving education at the college level. In 1866 it was agreed that the institution would become the College of the City of New York. The second major change was the resignation of Dr. Webster as president of the college. After 20 years as head of the school, the 75-year-old Webster retired and 33-year-old West Point graduate General Alexander Stuart Webb succeeded him. With an illustrious military career behind him, Webb took charge of the college in 1869 as its second president and embarked on yet another battle, when, in that same year, opponents to the idea of a free college began to stir again.

When the school began to offer courses leading to a degree and changed its name, it attracted new opposition. Charles Dana had become owner and managing editor of *The New York Sun* in 1868. The newspaper had previously been one with Democratic leanings, but Dana, a disillusioned liberal, turned it into the voice of conservatism and big business. As early as 1869, *The Sun* began its attack on the College of the City of New York. Dana called for the abolition of the college as a means of cutting taxes. In 1876 a bill was introduced in the New York state legislature calling for closing the school. The bill supported the use of taxpayers' money to fund elementary education but not higher education. The bill did not pass. In 1878, New York voters were asked to choose between a reduction in their taxes and the maintenance of free public higher education. They voted overwhelmingly to continue free public higher education. In that same year, a bill was proposed in the state legislature to change the college's admission policy. Up to that time, young men had to have attended one of the city's public schools

for one year before they could be considered for admission. In 1878, the college's board of trustees voted to ask the legislature to pass an act that would admit all boys—including those who had attended private and parochial schools—who could pass the entrance examination. A bill embodying this change was finally signed into law in May 1882.

Toward the end of the nineteenth century the college underwent more changes. The czarist pogroms in Russia and Poland resulted in a massive Jewish emigration to the United States. Previously the college's students were a mixture of Scottish, Irish, and German Americans. In 1890 one-fourth of the College of the City of New York graduates were Jewish; by 1910 that figure had reached 70 percent. As the college population increased in size, pressures were mounting for more space and, in particular, more buildings. When the trustees introduced a bill into the legislature requesting $1 million to buy land and erect new classroom buildings, the opposition cried out again. Along with them came *The New York Sun* joking that next, "the city could buy each of them [students] a handsome house." Nonetheless, the bill was overwhelmingly approved by the legislature. In 1895 the college received $1,175,000 to build their new institution on a site in New York City.

As the planning for the new college commenced and the search for a new site began, General Webb retired in 1903. Gone were the West Point men who had dominated the college since its founding and in their place came John Huston Finley, a Princeton professor. Under Finley's leadership the present site of the college at 138th and Convent Avenue in Manhattan was chosen and construction of new buildings began. All five structures stand today and are listed in the State and National Register of Historic Places. Finley also redesigned the curriculum. Geometry, physics, chemistry, and history were required courses but now six areas of study were offered in either the arts or sciences and options for electives were broadened. With the new buildings and a new curriculum, Finley brought the college into the twentieth century. Before the 75th anniversary of the institution in 1922, the college was visited by two distinguished men. In October 1920, Franklin Delano Roosevelt, then Democratic candidate for vice president, spoke to the students on national politics; in 1921 physicist Albert Einstein lectured on his theory of relativity.

Ten years after taking charge of the growing college, Finley resigned, and Sidney Allan Mezes became the new president. His administration saw further attacks on the school when the Real Estate Board of New York argued that free higher education was more costly to the taxpayers than sending the young men to neighboring Columbia University. Mezes defended his institution, demonstrating that the operating costs were among the lowest of those at any of the tax-supported schools in the country. When Mayor Hylan of New York launched an attack on the college in 1923, the Supreme Court upheld the right of the state to provide free education to its youth. The school won yet another victory when its budget was increased.

The College of the City of New York continued to grow and by the 1940s had over 8,000 students. In 1938 a study showed that the majority of freshmen entering the college were first-generation immigrants, with 40 percent having fathers who were laborers, unemployed, or not present. The college was, more than ever, providing education to the economically disadvantaged.

Women were beginning to trickle into City College. In 1930 the School of Business began to admit women. In 1938 the School of Engineering, followed by the School of Education in 1943, became co-ed. After World War II the College of Liberal Arts and Sciences approved a proposal to admit women. In autumn of 1951, 150 women registered for classes, making City College entirely coeducational.

In the 1960s the Jewish population began to decline in the college while the African-American and Puerto Rican student population began to increase, once again reflecting the migration and immigration patterns in New York City. But some thought that change had not come quickly enough. Only two percent of City's day students were black, and fewer still were Puerto Rican. When campus tensions mounted with white radicals protesting Vietnam, the Onyx Society (a black power group) and PRISA (a Puerto Rican organization) demanded an increase in minority enrollment. Splinter groups were formed and became militant. Over 100 incidents of campus bombings and arson took place between 1968 and 1969. Demonstrations escalated, racial violence erupted, and in spring 1969 President Buell Gallagher called in 200 police officers to patrol the campus. The police presence only increased the activism. The violence culminated in a fire which destroyed the Finley Student Center. President Gallagher resigned the following day. On May 19 the new president, Joseph Copeland, agreed to withdraw the police, institute a quota system, and to consider creation of a School of Black Studies.

When City University of New York (CUNY) began its first semester in 1970, it was operating under an open admissions policy, and planned to increase the enrollment of poor and minority students. Under this new policy, any city high school graduate who applied was assured a place in one of the system's 16 senior and city colleges, regardless of grades.

During this period of turmoil, one of the most controversial members of the faculty, Leonard Jeffries, joined the faculty of the School of Black Studies. As chairman, he began to lecture on the faults of the curriculum and its reflection of racial hatred. Espousing an Afrocentric view of history, he joined the lecture circuit in 1989. By 1991 Jeffries was gaining national attention and criticism for his speeches. James Traub wrote, "[Jeffries] railed against the Jews who controlled Hollywood, and the Jews who financed the slave trade, and the Jews who ran the affairs of City College." When CUNY fired him, Jeffries sued. He had been reappointed to his chairmanship every three years without opposition. He argued that his dismissal was based entirely on his lectures and thus clearly violated his right to freedom of speech. He was awarded $400,000 and reinstated in the department. However, in April 1995, a federal appeals court in New York City ruled that City College could legally demote Jeffries (thereby overturning its own previous ruling).

In its relatively short history, City College has produced many famous graduates, including author Upton Sinclair, philosopher Morris Cohen, actor Edward G. Robinson, and songwriter Ira Gershwin. Jonas Salk, developer of the polio vaccine that bears his name, is another renowned alumnus, as is former general and chairman of the Joint Chiefs of Staff Colin Powell. Julius Rosenberg, later executed for espionage, received his degree in engineering from City College. To date the college counts eight Nobel Prize winners as alumni: Leon Lederman, Arno Penzias, and Robert Hofstadter, who won the prize in physics; Julius Axelrod and Arthur Kornberg in physiology or medicine; Herbert Hauptman and Jerome Karle in chemistry; and Kenneth Arrow in economics.

Today City College is one of the most ethnically and racially diverse of any American college. Its mission remains the one identified by Dr. Horace Webster in an 1849 address:

> The experiment is to be tried, whether the children of the people, the children of the whole people, can be educated; and whether an institution of the highest grade, can be successfully controlled by the popular will, not by the privileged few.

Hunter College (New York, New York)

Location: Midtown Manhattan, New York City, at 68th Street and Lexington Avenue.

Description: A self-contained urban college of 20,000 students. Graduate and undergraduate studies are offered in liberal arts and sciences; there are also graduate programs in nursing and social work.

Information: Office of Admissions
Hunter College
695 Park Avenue
New York, NY 10021-5085
U.S.A.
(212) 772-4490

Visiting: Admission to campus is by valid student I.D. Contact phone number above for tours.

When Townsend Harris established the Free Academy for boys in 1847, a similar school for the education of girls was discussed. The matter was explored as early as 1849, but it would be another 20 years before the Female Normal School, a teachers school for girls, would open its doors in New York City. Establishing such a school would require a scholar with insight and drive; such a man was Thomas Hunter.

Hunter, the founder and first president of the girls school, was born near Belfast, Ireland in 1831. Employed as a teacher in Ireland, he was dismissed after publishing several revolutionary pamphlets in support of the independence of Ireland from Great Britain. After immigrating to New York in 1850 at the age of 19, he secured several teaching jobs. Hunter became principal of Public School 35 in New York City; he established a night school for adults there in 1866. Recognizing the need for more teachers, Hunter proposed a school for girls. He soon discovered that the New York Board of Education had approved the idea of a girls' school in 1851, and he was put in charge of establishing the city's first teaching school, or normal school as it was then called.

Space for eight classrooms was leased in a building located on Broadway and Fourth Street in lower Manhattan in 1870. As with the boys at the Free Academy, the girls started at age 14 or older. The school attracted over 1,000 students. Within a year the staff had to be enlarged from two professors and three tutors to three professors and 21 tutors. The course work included mathematics, physics, French, English literature, history, drawing, bookkeeping, and writing.

A year after the opening, Hunter decided to look for another location to give his school a permanent home. The present site was chosen for a new building. Today, the location is in the heart of Manhattan; in the 1870s it was barren farmland with goats grazing nearby. One student commented that the only sidewalks in the area were the ones that surrounded the school. Only partially finished, the school opened at its new location in September 1873. Over $1 million was spent to construct the Gothic structure which contained classrooms and a chapel with plans to finish the gymnasium and the upper floors later. The money to construct the building was provided by the taxpayers, and again Charles Dana spoke out in his newspaper *The New York Sun. The Sun* argued that the city had been through several difficult fiscal years and what the people of New York needed was not tax dollars going to another free school.

Regardless of its critics, the school performed amazingly well and in 1881 J. Edward Simmons of the board of education proposed to raise the status of the school to a degree-granting institution. The New York state legislature passed the bill and the Normal College, like its brother school City College, now granted a degree instead of a license after the successful completion of five years of study.

As the institution approached the twentieth century,

Hunter decided to upgrade the curriculum. To meet with state requirements, a three-year high school program was offered as well as a four-year liberal arts program that led to the A.B. degree. Therefore, after seven years of continuous study from the age of 14, a young woman could graduate with a bachelor's degree. This made the school the first free women's college in the nation to grant a college degree. At the age of 75, Hunter retired in 1906.

The Normal College began a summer session in 1910, primarily for the remedial students in the high school division, and that autumn night classes were offered for working girls who desired to further their education. Once again there was talk of a new building, and several years later Dr. Hunter's dark, Gothic structure was replaced by a series of Tudor-style units. A lighter and more fashionable limestone rock was chosen over the dark brownstone or brick facades of the nineteenth century; the cornerstone was laid in 1912. The buildings included a chapel, gymnasium, and offices, with cloisters connecting the library with the chemistry laboratories.

With a new building, a new curriculum, and state recognition, a name change seemed due. At the instigation of the alumnae, the name of the institution was changed from Normal College to Hunter College after its founder. The new name became official on April 4, 1914. In October 1915, five days before his 84th birthday, Dr. Hunter died.

As enrollment continued to rise, overcrowded classrooms became a problem. The new structure fell into disrepair by 1925, and pressures mounted for another new building. A site in the Bronx, a borough almost twice the size of Manhattan, was considered. An estimated 28 percent of the students at Hunter College came from the Bronx, a rapidly expanding borough. West of Fordham University, a plot of land called the Jerome Park Reservoir sat close to the new 200th Street subway station. The new school in the Bronx opened in 1932 but failed to alleviate the overcrowding in the Park Avenue building. Debates about the construction of a new building continued, but Hunter College's president, Eugene Colligan, delayed. Fate intervened on the night of February 14, 1936. A fire broke out and destroyed the limestone building. The students were moved to temporary quarters in leased space throughout the city. Plans for a new building began, but this time, rather than Gothic or Tudor academic style, the building would be functional and modern. The result was a 16-story skyscraper. The previous building had cost $1 million. This new structure would cost nearly $6 million. Famed critic of urban architecture Lewis Mumford commented that, although he found the old Hunter College building "possibly the ugliest on Park Avenue; the new one is certainly the handsomest modern structure the avenue can show." The skyscraper school merged nicely with the fashionable apartment houses along the avenue; its facades Mumford

Hunter College, City University of New York

described as "kind to the eye." The ground floors he considered the best interiors in the city with "polished lavender-grey marble walls and handsome white-metal lighting bowls." The lunchroom could serve 1,000 students. Mumford maintained that the large auditorium was "better in many respects than Radio City Music Hall." He concluded that Hunter College was in better shape to meet the demands of the future "than any other college in the country." In autumn of 1940, the new building was visited by President Franklin D. Roosevelt, New York State Governor Herbert Lehman, and New York City Mayor Fiorello La Guardia.

As the prospect of a two-ocean war loomed in 1941, military planners saw the advisability of recruiting women for the armed forces. In 1943 the U.S. Naval Center (Women's Reserves) moved into the women's college in the Bronx, which began to be called the "USS Hunter." Under the leadership of Captain William F. Amsden, Hunter College in the Bronx became a naval establishment training over 2,000 women every two weeks. The boot camp prepared over 80,000 WAVES, and 5,000 SPARS and women Marines for military service by 1945.

Following the war, the severe shortage of nurses prompted Hunter College to offer a nursing program that led to a B.S. in nursing. The Bronx campus initiated a two-year college level course for returning GIs, marking the beginning of coeducation at the school. Although graduate studies had been introduced in 1921 for both men and women, it was not until 1964 that the college became officially coeducational. In 1968 the Hunter branch in the Bronx became a separate four-year institution named Lehman College.

The theater that Mumford compared to Radio City Music Hall fell into disrepair during the 1970s. In 1993, the Hunter College Playhouse was renovated and renamed the Sylvia and Danny Kaye Playhouse in gratitude for the couple's contribution of $1 million for the renovation. Opening week featured opera singer and Hunter graduate Martina Arroya.

Among the other graduates who have gone on to success are: opera star Regina Resnick, financial self-help author Sylvia Porter, congresswoman Bella Abzug, film critic Judith Crist, and actress Ruby Dee. Hunter has also produced two Nobel Prize winners: Rosalyn Yalow, who received the prize for physiology or medicine in 1977, and Gertrude Belle Elion, who was awarded the prize in 1988 for physiology or medicine.

Brooklyn College (CUNY)
(Brooklyn, New York)

Location: The Flatbush section of south central Brooklyn between Ocean Parkway and Flatbush Avenue.

Description: An undergraduate and graduate college with enrollment of approximately 13,832.

Information: Director of Admission
Brooklyn College of the City University of New York
1602 James Hall
Brooklyn, NY 11210-2889
U.S.A.
(718) 951-5921

Visiting: Admission to campus is by valid student I.D. Contact phone number above for tours.

In 1898 the population of the city of New York increased considerably after the merger of its five boroughs. The Bronx, Brooklyn, Queens, Staten Island, and Manhattan were now called the greater City of New York. As City College and Hunter College began to accept students from these outer boroughs, the two institutions found it increasingly difficult to manage all the students. Brooklyn was the largest borough and had over one-third of the population of the greater City of New York. It was in Brooklyn that President John H. Finley of City College advocated establishing the first free college outside of Manhattan.

In 1917 the president of City College, Finley's successor Sidney Mezes, authorized offering evening courses to male students in Brooklyn; by 1917 an evening school was introduced, starting with 200 students. Classes were held at a high school and students completed their first two years in Brooklyn; then men finished their remaining two years at City College and women at Hunter College. By 1925 enrollment exceeded 2,000 students, and the need to open a new college in the borough had become apparent. In 1930 the New York Board of Education approved the establishment of Brooklyn College. It was to consist of a combination of the faculty of Hunter College and City College. Though it was nominally the first public coeducational college in New York City, classes were segregated by sex. The college did not yet have its own buildings, so classes were held in rented space located in five different buildings in the downtown business district in Brooklyn. The struggle for a permanent home was met with the same opposition that City College and Hunter College had previously faced—the unpopularity in some quarters of free higher education for everyone. When the idea of purchasing land for building Brooklyn College was proposed, Stewart Browne, the president of the United Real Estate Owners Association, remarked "These ideas about educating the masses are so much nonsense . . . education for morons can only lead to the collapse of our system and revolutions."

The decision to build the new college had coincided with the Great Depression. Banks were afraid to provide loans during the financially unsound economy. A 40-acre site had been selected in Flatbush, Brooklyn, with an initial asking price of $4,750,000. Because of the country's financial straits and the delay in the board's decision, the owners brought the price down to $1,600,000. The board of higher education could not pass up the deal and supported the purchase of the land. In the meantime, President Franklin D. Roosevelt had initiated his New Deal policy to provide relief to the ailing economy. New York Mayor Fiorello La Guardia took a trip to Washington, D.C. with "incomplete plans which no one looked at anyway" and met with the president. The two men talked and Roosevelt was willing to grant a loan of $5,500,000 from the Federal Emergency Administration of Public Works. Later that year, on October 2, 1935, Mayor La Guardia broke ground for the new campus with a silver-plated shovel. The construction was completed two years after the groundbreaking, and the buildings were opened for classes in 1937.

Brooklyn College was the child of City College and Hunter College; its administration and curriculum mirrored its parent institutions. While President William Boylan was responsible for establishing the campus facilities, President Harry D. Gideonse was responsible for creating an identity for Brooklyn College. When Gideonse came to Brooklyn College in 1939 he already had an impressive list of credentials. As a professor of economics, he taught at Columbia University, Rutgers University, and the University of Chicago. He had published numerous books and articles on economics and international affairs.

The reorganization of the departments of the college was an early priority as was renovation of campus facilities. However, World War II interrupted his construction plans. To break down the barriers between faculty and administration and also to enhance the curriculum, he expected administrators to teach a class; he himself taught a popular course called "Freedom and Order."

The issue of freedom was to arise early in Gideonse's tenure and to continue for a number of years. In response to the 1930s scare about Communist activity in education, the New York state legislature established a committee in 1940 to investigate subversive activities in New York City's school. Known as the Rapp-Coudert Committee, the body concluded that 30 members of the staff at Brooklyn College were members of the Communist Party. Three of the 30 resigned, 15 were named in public, and the others were never identified. Gideonse asserted that no teacher would be dismissed for membership in a political party. In 1952 the senate's Internal Security Subcommittee returned to the subject of Communist infiltration of higher education. Of the staff from Brooklyn College summoned to appear before the committee, three retired to avoid appearing, and the six who used the protection of the Fifth Amendment were fired by the board of higher education. Gideonse reaffirmed his position of 1940 that membership in a political party should not be grounds for dismissal. He was one of the few who early voiced objections to the tactics of Senator Joseph McCarthy in his pursuit of Communists in government and education. Not until 1980 was there a determination that injustice had been done to the fired faculty members. The board of trustees, successor to the board of higher education, provided pensions to those faculty members still alive and death benefits to the survivors of those who had died.

In 1940, Gideonse began a review of the college's curriculum, which had been fashioned after its parent institutions, Hunter College and City College. The curriculum was heavy on required courses. Gideonse recommended a major require 30 credits, with the remainder of the course work constituting electives related to the major chosen by the student. Although this curriculum has become standard in many colleges today, it was a new concept in higher education when Gideonse introduced it in the 1940s. The president also concentrated on Brooklyn College's two-year vocational program and fought to have the state award students an associate in arts degree with the option to continue their studies toward a B.A. Brooklyn College thus became a pioneer in the idea of the community college.

When the Middle States Association of Colleges and Secondary Schools visited the campus in 1955 to review its accreditation, the committee called Brooklyn College an institution with "great vitality, sound traditions, scholarly competence and farsighted vision," adding that it was a college "willing to experiment." However, Middle States found the facilities inadequate, which caused *The New York Times* to respond, "If the college could reach such heights with 'inadequate facilities' what could it attain in the years ahead if it had adequate facilities?" Following the Middle States' report, Gideonse oversaw the construction of an auditorium, a theater, a library, and a student center, all of which were completed by 1962. By the time he retired in 1966, Gideonse had doubled enrollment, increased the campus facilities, and turned Brooklyn College from a borough branch campus to a national university.

When the CIA came to the campus to recruit graduates in 1966, they were met with protests from student groups comprised of SDS (Students for a Democratic Society), the Dubois Club, and Youth Against War & Fascism. The following January, U.S. Navy recruiters met with a similar demonstration. In October 1967 an anti-war protest in Boylan Hall resulted in police intervention, media coverage, and the arrest of 60 students.

Increasing minority unrest led to 200 black and Puerto Rican students storming the office of the president in April 1969. They presented him with a list of 18 demands, including an increase of minority faculty and students. Their demands were greeted with indifference. On April 30, 1970, members of the Puerto Rican Alliance took control of the president's office again, with similar demands. This time the new president, John W. Kneller, listened. In 1968 only ten percent of the students were members of a minority group. Ten years later this had increased to 30 percent of the students.

Humorist Sam Levenson, who was graduated from Brooklyn College in 1934, summarized the importance of the college in the lives of the children of immigrants:

We were the children of peddlers, tailors, first-chance Americans, and everybody pointed to the city colleges and said, "This is your opportunity; take it.". . . Brooklyn College to me and to many other children of immigrants represented the Statue of Liberty.

Queens College (Queens, New York)

Location: Near the Long Island Expressway in Flushing, Queens.

Description: Enrolls over 18,000 students in its graduate and undergraduate divisions.

Information: Director of Admissions
Queens College of the City University of New York
65-30 Kissena Boulevard
Flushing, NY 11367-1597
U.S.A.
(718) 997-5600

Visiting: Admission to campus is by valid student I.D. Contact phone number above for tours.

While Brooklyn College was growing at a steady rate, the borough of Queens looked to its municipal leaders for a free institution of higher learning. Queens was the largest borough in square miles, but it lagged behind Brooklyn in population. Yet the migration from Manhattan had begun in the 1930s, and Queens needed to meet the demand for educational institutions.

In 1936 the New York Board of Education took the first steps to remedy the problem. A year earlier, the New York Parental School, an institution consisting of nine buildings for truants and delinquents, had been closed permanently. Under the board of education's control the school had remained vacant. A resolution was adopted by the board of education in 1936 to appropriate $500,000 to establish a college on the premises. The property, located in Flushing, Queens, was not far from Flushing Meadows, the selected site of the 1939 World's Fair.

The first president of Queens College was Paul Klapper. Born in Romania, Klapper arrived in New York with his parents at the age of seven. Like many children of immigrants in New York, he attended City College from which he was graduated in 1904. Klapper was a prolific writer on the subjects of teaching and education and had had a solid career in education, which included the post of Dean of Education at City College. Unlike its sister institution Brooklyn College, Queens College's faculty was not a combination of faculty from Hunter and City

Colleges. Klapper could start afresh by selecting faculty and designing the curriculum (which he patterned after the University of Chicago). In fall of 1937 the first 400 students entered Queens College. Three years later, in 1940, the college was earning a reputation nationwide, and the board of education unanimously approved a raise in Klapper's salary. He declined. The country was coming out of the Great Depression and New York City had suffered fiscally; Klapper recommended that any additional funds be put toward staff salaries and to provide more teachers. Earning $15,000 a year, Klapper was the lowest paid president in the four municipal colleges.

In 1945 Klapper designed a massive expansion program that would allow the college to more than double its student capacity. His building program called for the construction of a new library, a science building, and a recreation center at a total cost of $5 million. By the tenth anniversary of the college, in 1947, enrollment hit record numbers with 4,000 students; 23 new faculty members were added that year. To meet the demand for additional space, five barracks-style buildings were erected with a state loan of $125,000. Klapper retired in 1948 and returned to teaching, at the University of Chicago.

In 1958, following the 20th anniversary of the college, enrollment had increased to over 10,000. In the 1970s the curriculum was liberalized and all required courses were removed except English. However, in 1980, under President Saul Cohen, another curriculum change reinstated basic liberal arts requirements.

Jazz trumpeter Louis Armstrong spent the last 28 years of his life in a house one mile from the campus. In 1983, following the death of his widow Lucille, Queens College became the owner of his personal papers, recordings, and photographs. The Armstrong House, a historical landmark, is administered by the college. The Louis Armstrong archives are housed in the Benjamin Rosenthal Library at the college.

The college recently completed the construction of Aaron Copland School of Music, a $38 million structure that houses classrooms, studios, faculty offices, and a 491-seat concert hall.

The late writer Michael Harrington taught at the college, as have geologist Barry Commoner, mathematician Dennis Sullivan, and composer Thea Musgrave.

City University of New York

In 1961 the City University of New York was formed to govern the four main colleges: City College, Hunter College, Brooklyn College, and Queens College. Today the CUNY municipal system comprises six other senior colleges: John Jay College, Herbert Lehman College, Bernard Baruch College, York College, Medgar Evers College, and the College of Staten Island. Community colleges are Manhattan Community College, Bronx Community College, Hostos Community College, Kingsboro Community College, La Guardia Community College, Queensboro Community College, and the New York City Technical College.

Also established under the CUNY system was the Graduate School and University Center. The graduate school draws on the faculty of the CUNY colleges in addition to researchers from the New York Botanical Gardens, the Metropolitan Museum of Art, and the American Museum of Natural History. Offering doctoral studies, the center also offers select master's degrees and certificate programs.

The Graduate School and University Center is located in midtown Manhattan across from the New York Public Library. In August 1995 it was announced that the graduate school would move into the former B. Altman Department Store building, located a few blocks south of its present location.

In an effort to increase minority enrollment the policy of "open admissions" was instituted by CUNY in 1970. A controversial move, it guaranteed that all New York City high school graduates would gain admission to one of its colleges. Opponents argued that open admissions would result in a decline of standards in the municipal college system. Supporters argued that it followed in the tradition of free colleges, providing higher education to all. More important, in the spirit of the civil rights movement of the 1960s, it was viewed as a method of desegregating the New York universities.

In 1976, CUNY, citing severe financial constraints, started charging tuition. In his book, *City on a Hill,* James Traub described the trauma:

In 1976, with New York City having come within a whisker of bankruptcy, CUNY's budget was slashed by a third. The system actually shut down for the first two weeks in June. City [College] fired fifty-nine nontenured faculty members . . . To reduce the flow of students to the senior colleges, and to raise their level, admissions standards were changed to admit the top third, rather than the top half, of graduating

classes. And in a decision that was no less shocking for being inevitable, CUNY ended its tradition of free tuition. That tradition, at City College, was over 125 years old. Tuition would be only $900 a year, and state grants were generally available to cover much of the cost; but a higher education was no longer available to all who qualified.

Today the CUNY system continues to suffer from budget cuts, tuition increases, and faculty layoffs. Critics charge that CUNY had lowered its standards through open admissions. City College President Yolanda Moses credits the CUNY system with a rigorous emphasis on standards and a continuing concern for minority students. "City College," she says, "was founded in 1847 to educate the children of the whole people. Today we still accept the challenge."

Further Reading: S. Willis Rudy's *The College of the City of New York: A History 1847–1947* (New York: City College Press, 1949) provides a comprehensive account of the first 100 years of the college. James Traub discusses the fate of open admissions at City College in *City on a Hill: Testing the American Dream at City College* (Reading, Massachusetts: Addison-Wesley, 1994). Samuel White Patterson's *Hunter College* (New York: Lantern Press, 1955) covers the 85-year history of the college from 1870–1955. Hunter College President George N. Shuster writes of his experiences in *The Ground I Walked On* (New York: Farrar Straus, 1961). Murray Horowitz's *Brooklyn College: The First Half- Century* (New York: Brooklyn College Press, 1981) provides an exhaustive account from the college's founding to the present day. A thorough bibliography of writing by and about President Harry Gideonse was compiled by the Brooklyn College librarians under the editorship of Alex Preminger in *Urban Educator* (New York: Twayne, 1970).

—Patrice Kane

CLAREMONT COLLEGES
(Claremont, California, U.S.A.)

Location: In Claremont, 35 miles east of Los Angeles.

Description: A consortium of five undergraduate colleges and one graduate school, enrolling approximately 4,400 undergraduate and 1,800 graduate students.

Information: Admissions Office
Pomona College
550 North College Avenue
Claremont, CA 91711
U.S.A.
(909) 621-8134

Admissions Office
Scripps College
1030 Columbia Avenue
Claremont, CA 91711
U.S.A.
(909) 621-8149

Admissions Office
Claremont McKenna College
890 Columbia Avenue
Claremont, CA 91711
U.S.A.
(909) 621-8088

Admissions Office
Harvey Mudd College
Claremont, CA 91711
U.S.A.
(909) 621-8011

Admissions Office
Pitzer College
1050 North Mills Avenue
Claremont, CA 91711
U.S.A.
(909) 621-8129

Admissions Office
Claremont Graduate School
Claremont, CA 91711
U.S.A.
(909) 621-8069

The Claremont Colleges are a community of six private colleges, inspired by the colleges of New England and by Oxford University. On adjacent campuses in southern California, the traditions of New England and English education continue to flourish.

A community of scholars founded the first college, which generated a series of residential colleges linked by place and by a vision of quality education. This consortium shares the diverse assets of larger community, while each college preserves the personality of an individual school.

Forty years after the Gold Rush, the frontiers of southern California attracted settlers from the eastern United States, many lured by the Santa Fe railroad's promotion of available fertile land. Emigrants traveled west on excursion trains to view and purchase sites of former Spanish ranchos. In 1887, the railroad advertised townsites and sold lots along its route through the San Gabriel Valley. As part of the land boom, the General Association of Congregational Churches of Southern California founded a college and preparatory school in Piedmont, also known as North Pomona. Named Pomona College, it was incorporated on October 6, 1887. The new school was coeducational and nonsectarian, although established on Christian principles.

The Congregationalists promoted Pomona as a residential college of the New England type—on the Pacific Coast. This venture attracted scholars such as the first dean, who saw a notice in a Congregational paper about the New England college in California.

Students—27 in the preparatory department and three in the collegiate department—began attending classes in a rented house in 1888. Unfortunately, the land boom collapsed that same year. In nearby Claremont, a new hotel stood empty. One of its investors, a Pomona trustee, offered to donate the Hotel Claremont and 260 lots of surrounding land to Pomona College. The move was to be temporary, but the college remained permanently on the site. Despite the relocation, Pomona College retained its original name.

Pomona's first class was graduated in 1894. The school survived financial difficulties in the 1890s and grew to 507 students by 1908, with 60 percent now in the collegiate classes. By that time, Pomona had established a reputation for outstanding academic courses and had established the first chapter of Phi Beta Kappa in southern California in 1914.

The community of Claremont grew along with the college. The town agreed to close streets so the campus could be unified. The main thoroughfare, College Avenue, was widened, and eucalyptus trees were planted on both sides of the street. By 1915 the college had six buildings that are still in use today, including a library donated by Andrew Carnegie in 1908.

Pomona College, Claremont Colleges

As a focus of the community, Pomona College maintained a religious foundation. Most members of the board of trustees were Congregationalists, and most teachers were Congregational ministers. The college's motto was "Our Tribute to Christian Civilization." The YMCA was active on campus, students had to take work in the religion department, and an annual Day of Prayer for Colleges was observed.

Pomona College began the transition from a single college to a group of colleges, thanks to its resourceful president, James A. Blaisdell. A professor from Beloit College in Wisconsin, Blaisdell became the college's fourth president in 1910. This Congregational minister brought together Christian principles and a love for edu-

cation. The gates of Pomona are inscribed with his invitation: "Let only the eager, thoughtful, and reverent enter here." Dean E.C. Norton voiced the opinion of many, praising Blaisdell as a seer who could translate dreams into reality.

Blaisdell expanded Pomona College to 685 undergraduates by 1919, and he raised sufficient funds to secure the college's future. In the 1920s, he resisted the demands to admit more students and to expand Pomona College. He envisioned Claremont as a community of centers of learning, with education funded by individuals, not governed by the state. He communicated his concept to another transplanted midwesterner, Ellen Browning Scripps. Scripps, born in Illinois in 1836, was a publisher and supporter of women's suffrage in the late nineteenth century. She helped her brothers found the newspapers which became the Scripps-Howard newspaper chain.

In 1923, Blaisdell wrote a letter to philanthropist Scripps, describing his sincere hope

> that instead of one great, undifferentiated university, we might have a group of institutions divided into small colleges—somewhat on the Oxford type— around a library and other utilities which they would use in common. In this way I should hope to preserve the inestimable personal values of the small college while securing the facilities of the great university.

What became the distinctive Claremont Group Plan was modeled on Oxford University, with colleges as individual corporations grouped around an academic center. The colleges would thrive as unique and separate schools, yet they would unite to share common facilities. The dream of a succession of private colleges required money for land and buildings. Scripps provided the initial funding. Before the colleges had incorporated, she spent $250,000 for 250 acres of land to implement the Group Plan. The land was initially held in the name of Pomona College and then conveyed to Claremont Colleges. Scripps was in her nineties when she purchased the Claremont acreage, sight unseen. She also made available $500,000 to establish Scripps College. Her largesse inspired others to acquire property for the Group Plan for future college development.

Blaisdell's idea was a product of the 1920s. Wealthy Californians, including many Pomona alumni, were intrigued by the colleges. Pomona had just completed a capital campaign for $3 million, and investors willingly came forward to support a consortium. Over the next 40 years, private and corporate contributions led to the founding of five private colleges.

The Claremont Colleges began when a board of trustees filed articles of incorporation as Claremont Colleges, October 14, 1925. All but two of these men were members of the Pomona College Board of Trustees. Blaisdell was chosen president in 1925; he retained his position as president of Pomona College until 1928. This central coordinating corporation received a $1 million bequest from its first board of fellow's chairman, Colonel Seeley W. Mudd, in 1926.

Blaisdell compared the concept of Claremont Colleges to the United States. The central institution would act like the federal government, and the separate states would agree to join forces. He felt that the colleges could cooperate voluntarily, so for years Claremont Colleges operated without a formal constitution. New undergraduate colleges would be organized as Pomona was, emphasizing individual educational goals. They would remain smaller than Pomona's limit of 800, set in 1927.

Scripps College, which was incorporated June 12, 1926, opened in 1927 with 50 students. The board of fellows conveyed land to the new college from the Pomona holdings. The college adopted a motto from Dante, *Incipit Vita Nova* (Here begins a new life). The buildings of the Scripps campus reflected California's influence. Instead of copying the monumental Classical Revival style dominant at Pomona, Scripps achieved an aura of Spanish charm associated with the Mediterranean climate.

Claremont Colleges was an inclusive organization, with one of its roles the issuing of graduate degrees. Pomona had awarded over 80 master's degrees by 1925. The new graduate school administered this program and enrolled its first four students in 1925. Initially, except for courses in education, graduate courses were taught by faculty from the undergraduate colleges.

Claremont Colleges' graduate school began granting master's degrees in 1928. It appointed its first permanent, full-time professors outside the field of education prior to Blaisdell's retirement in 1936. Unusual in American higher education, the school is not part of a university. The undergraduate colleges provide faculty to teach some graduate courses, and graduate faculty may reciprocate at the colleges. Upperclassmen may attend graduate classes. The graduate school is financially independent from the other schools and appoints its own faculty and staff.

Throughout its first decade, the consortium survived conflicts over the Claremont Colleges as separate but not competing institutions. The members agreed to fund shared capital facilities, of which the infirmary was the first, in 1929. The Mabel Shaw Bridges Auditorium was built in 1931, located on Pomona land, and Harper Hall followed in 1932. Yet member colleges sought autonomy, following Pomona's example. Pomona was a complete college, mature before the Group Plan, and it continued to maintain a separate identity in academics and student activities. The need for a third undergraduate college was voiced in 1927 and planned as a men's college. The plans were promoted in 1929 and again in 1940, but halted first by the Depression and then by World War II.

A 1942 operating agreement, based on voluntary associations, created an intercollegiate council that replaced the board of fellows. One continuing issue was the name of the central institution, which went through five changes over its first four decades. Finally, the official name became the Claremont University Center (CUC) in 1967. The consortium agreed on enrollment limits in 1942, choosing to grow by adding colleges rather than by expanding the existing colleges. The colleges began and remained small, compared to the large schools on the West Coast, such as Stanford University and the University of Southern California. The existing colleges helped the three new schools started after the war, offering space in their facilities and even waiving service charges for joint services to Pitzer College in its first year. Scripps graciously exchanged its athletic facilities with the newly established Harvey Mudd College for adjacent, vacant land. Honnold Library, constructed in 1952, was another joint facility. Colleges shared use but retained ownership of their own books.

The Claremont Undergraduate School for Men was founded June 4, 1946. A class of 86 arrived that September, mostly veterans who temporarily lived in the basement of Bridges Auditorium. The college was incorporated as Claremont Men's College (CMC) in 1947 and grew to 325 students by 1948. It finally became Claremont McKenna College in 1981.

The Cold War and population boom influenced the founding of the two post-war colleges. The colleges agreed that the new schools added strength by expanding constituencies. Harvey Mudd College (HMC) aimed to offer an education for socially responsible engineers. Pitzer College, planned since 1959 as a women's college, would emphasize social sciences.

Officials anticipated the impact of baby boomers in the 1960s. They founded the next college December 14, 1955, naming it after chairman of the board of fellows Harvey S. Mudd, son of Seeley Mudd. The Mudds had helped to organize other colleges, and his family and friends pledged generous financial support.

Harvey Mudd College was planned as a technical school, to provide the nation with new engineers and to add science and engineering to the Group Plan. Harvey Mudd College was the first private college of science and engineering founded since 1900. Although its campus is only 15 miles from one of the nation's premier science institutions, the California Institute of Technology, Caltech welcomed the new school. Many graduates of Caltech have served on the HMC faculty.

The second post-war college, Pitzer, was incorporated February 21, 1963. Russell K. Pitzer funded the first two buildings. A 1900 graduate of Pomona College, he had helped establish CMC and HMC. Pitzer was the first independent college for women founded since Bennington. The first class of 153 entered in 1964.

The increased number of potential students sustained the colleges, with a total enrollment of 2,973 by 1965. Every college had sought expansion to attract top students and faculty. In 1948 Pomona was over its limit of 800 students with 1,100. Scripps asked to increase its limit from 225 to 325 and then to 400 in 1962. CMC requested an increase to 600. In 1958, HMC planned for 270, a number reached in 1965.

The concept of the affiliated colleges attracted other California institutions. La Verne College, six miles from Claremont, sought affiliation. In 1964, Immaculate Heart College began inquiries about purchasing land in Claremont. After acquiring 20 acres, Immaculate Heart planned in 1971 to move as a neighbor, not a member of the consortium, but the move did not occur. The School of Theology left the University of Southern California, and Rancho Santa Ana Botanic Garden also relocated to Claremont.

The social revolutions of the late 1960s had an impact on the Claremont Colleges. The colleges hosted "Claremont-Ins" (love-ins) and rock concerts, along with peace marches and antiwar demonstrations. Political activists Tom Hayden and Angela Davis were both visiting lecturers. Although student rebellion was limited compared to actions at larger schools, two buildings were bombed in 1969.

Students and administrators discussed changes in policy. In 1964 over 96 percent of first-year students were Caucasian. The Black Students Union and United Mexican-American Students (now Chicano Studies), both established in 1969, sought increased minority recruitment and curriculum changes. Students and even some faculty conducted sit-ins to protest injustice. All the Claremont schools have increased diversity in their student populations, with a current average of 40 percent minority students. In 1964, single-gender residence halls were the norm. Now most residence halls are coeducational.

Women have shared Claremont history from the outset. Both Pomona and HMC were planned as coeducational colleges. Scripps was founded by an enterprising woman and began with women comprising half of its board of trustees. Scripps has since had two women presidents. Two of the gender-specific colleges became coeducational: Pitzer in 1970 and CMC in 1976.

The colleges remained similar yet diverse. A major fundraising effort initiated more cooperative efforts. In 1965, the Ford Foundation announced a single grant of $5 million, if the colleges raised $15 million in matching funds within three years. A joint Challenge Committee agreed that each college would pursue an individual campaign, expanding the total goal to $81 million over seven years. A constitution in 1967 also symbolized the strength of a combined educational center; it also set maximum enrollments at 1,300 for Pomona and 800 for the other four undergraduate colleges.

Previously, the Ford Foundation had declined a 1962 application for a grant, citing a lack of group cooperation. The colleges still pursued separate academic programs. For example, the Tri-College Science Program (Scripps, Pitzer, and CMC) was the first completely integrated undergraduate department. Pomona had voted not to participate in a common science center in 1954. Built in 1955, the new joint center was followed by a second science building in 1968 and a new Joint Science Center in 1992.

Claremont has succeeded in founding five private colleges in 40 years, funded by private and corporate contributions. Blaisdell sought a place of strength and loveliness, a community which would inspire its citizens to seek order in their lives. Scripps had predicted, "I am thinking of a college campus whose simplicity and beauty will unobtrusively seep into the student's consciousness and quietly develop a standard of taste and judgement." The campuses reflect planning and vision.

Lines of trees lead the eye to the northern mountains, and the buildings blend with the landscape. Covering one square mile, the six affiliated schools exist as what appears a seamless community. The Scripps campus is on the National Register of Historic Places.

The experiment has thrived for 70 years. The Group Plan has allowed the individual colleges to embark on innovative educational programs. Claremont Men's College sponsors eight research institutes on campus. At Pomona and HMC, students share research with faculty. Harvey Mudd College's Engineering Clinic Program, begun in 1963, teams students with faculty to solve problems of government, business, and industry.

Each college emphasizes critical thinking. Scripps said:

I am not in sympathy with the so-called education imparted by an austere professor behind a desk to rows of docile students facing him, with a textbook as their only means of communication. Rather I like to think of a circle of teachers and students exchanging ideas and creating a mental capital . . . which no textbook can supply.

Further Reading: William Clary, a Pomona graduate and college official, wrote a detailed history of the university center, *The Claremont Colleges: A History of the Development of the Claremont Group Plan* (Claremont, California: Claremont University Center, 1970). Joseph Platt's *Harvey Mudd College: The First Twenty Years* (Santa Barbara, California: Fithian, 1994) is a lively narrative covering recent history. For an earlier perspective of Claremont's largest college, see *Granite and Sagebrush: Reminiscences of the First Fifty Years of Pomona College* by Frank P. Brackett (Los Angeles: Ward Ritchie, 1944).

—Charlene Strickland

COLLEGE OF MEXICO
(Mexico City, Mexico)

Location: Mexico City, in the southern part of the city.

Description: Publicly funded autonomous research center with 359 students and 306 faculty.

Information: Secretario Academico
Camino Al Ajusco #20
Mexico, D.F.
(5) 645-4721
Fax (5) 645-0464

El Colegio de México (COLMEX, the College of Mexico) was created on October 3, 1940, out of the Casa de Espana. Established a couple of years earlier, the Casa was composed largely of artists and professionals. It yielded to an institution, COLMEX, that would become important in research and graduate education in the humanities and, especially, the social sciences.

For progressive President Lázaro Cárdenas, the pressing motivation behind these institutional creations was to rescue and attract Spanish intellectuals at peril from their country's Civil War. Founders such as Alfonso Reyes and Daniel Cosío Villegas sought to create a research center capable of excellence and objectivity, which they viewed as beyond the reach of Mexico's own public university (UNAM), which was mired by ties to politics and the professions. The university actually aided COLMEX's formation, with the understanding that the new institution would not compete on the university's main teaching turf.

Major expansion came in stages. In the early 1960s Cosío Villegas led the way. In 1966 economist Víctor Urquidi took the reigns and presided a decade later over the institution's move to much more ample facilities in the south of Mexico City. Urquidi continued effectively as president, for a decade beyond that. The ascension of Mario Ojeda, and then Andrés Lira, continued the string of estimable academic figures.

When COLMEX's centers added teaching, it was mostly at the graduate level. As of 1996, COLMEX had only 63 undergraduates. Graduate enrollments were 6 time greater (106 masters, 120 doctoral candidates, and 70 specialized degree students); enrollment is equally divided between the sexes. There are almost as many professors. Of the 306 professors, 296 are full-time, but only 151 are permanent employees of the institution, so that the student/professor ratio is closer to 2:1 than 1:1. In any event, such figures reflect COLMEX's status as one of a breed of institutions that has in recent decades proliferated throughout Latin America: freestanding social-science centers devoted mostly to research. In fact, COLMEX assumes mammoth importance as the oldest and probably the broadest and best of the breed; particularly unusual is the strong inclusion of humanities alongside social science.

Although most nonaffiliated research centers are private, and some are public, COLMEX's status is subject to different interpretations. The College of Mexico's own lawyers insist it is public and point to factors such as the public agencies that created it, the constitution of the board, the principal source and restrictions on the funding, and appointment of the college president by the president of Mexico. On the other hand, until 1993 Mexico's most prominent listings of institutions put COLMEX in the private camp, citing especially its status as a Civil Association.

Not including its more specialized programs, COLMEX has seven centers: African and Asian affairs, demography and urban development, economics, history, international relations, literature and linguistics, and sociology. History was first, in 1941, soon followed by sociology and then literature and linguistics. Doctorates are given in Spanish linguistics and literature, Latin American history, sociology, and population studies. Masters are given in economics; demography and urban studies; and studies on Asia, Africa, and the Pacific Rim; and an undergraduate degree is given in international relations.

Over 70 percent of student applicants are rejected. Those admitted face a more structured graduate program than counterparts at other Latin American institutions. The vast majority of full-time faculty members boast advanced degrees, usually Ph.Ds. Almost half the full-time faculty are incorporated into the competitive National System of Researchers, a proportion far higher than at any other social research institution. The College of Mexico is credited with saving the nation from a more serious "brain drain" from academia.

Beyond Mexico, the impact of COLMEX's foreign graduates has been enormous in select institutions and fields of study (such as demography and economics). Moreover, COLMEX played a major role in the creation of Latin America's two main social science networks: the Faculty of Latin American Social Science (FLACSO), with a presence in more than ten countries (including Mexico); and the Latin American Council of Social Sciences (CLACSO), which functions throughout the regions. Within Mexico, COLMEX has been a model for a loose network of colleges in various states. Some, such as the college of Northern Frontier and the Colegio in

Michoacán, are quite successful. Within Mexico City itself, CIDE (Center of Research and Teaching in Economics) has followed the COLMEX model in most respects—including quality—and rivals the senior institution in size. The College of Mexico faculty routinely offer courses in the city's universities. And as the Mexican university system entered a period of major reform, COLMEX provided vital precedents: evaluations of performance; differential rewards; pressure to publish; applied research for the public, for-profit, and nonprofit sectors; mixed public and private funding; international contacts and norms; empirical research; and such.

Yet even COLMEX cannot escape many of the factors that limit the otherwise spectacular success of Latin America's freestanding research centers. Small size constrains efforts and results; COLMEX is a giant among these centers but that still leaves it tiny compared to leading universities. With a 1996 budget of only $17.5 million, it covered only some activities and fields of study. Its library (660,000 volumes) is at once impressively large for Latin America and yet small compared to even average U.S. universities. The teaching program is small in part because it is extraordinarily generous with the teaching load placed on faculty. Many teach just one course per year or one every two years; some can escape teaching altogether. And even with an uncommonly low student/teacher ratio, the degree completion rate is low in some centers. While the number of published professional papers and popular policy articles are impressive, and although the publication output overwhelms what Latin America's universities manage per capita, the profile is modest by international academic standards. Much of what is written is subject only to in-house review and is published in-house. International academic standards dictate a scrupulous peer-review, and juried publications.

Also problematic, research epitomizes COLMEX's role as a think tank for the Mexican government, its relative autonomy notwithstanding. The close relationship with the government is clear in other ways as well, including the government's role in selecting the institution's leadership and in financing. In return, the government gets research that is on topics of its choosing that can be used to support the government's own agenda. Beyond that, it is common for COLMEX's administrative leaders, faculty, and students to get recruited directly into government positions. Impacts in fields such as economics, international relations, and demography are notable, but they are even notable in the humanities (such as in the drawing up of school texts). Additionally, the institution offers seminars for government officials.

Naturally, the overall success and direction of COLMEX has depended greatly on adequate financing. The bulk of income is from the government. That means contracts and also unusual funding for Latin America, annual subsidies, which provide some level of guaranteed salary. The government funds have never been sufficient, though. Without tuition (COLMEX students get scholarships) or significant domestic corporate donations, the main financing has been through international philanthropy.

The College of Mexico's leaders have taken a very positive view of the impact of this non-Mexican philanthropy. They regard it as having been crucial to COLMEX's early existence, later to its international academic credibility, and now to its continued excellence. By the end of the 1960s, foreign sources had fallen to just one-fifth of COLMEX's total income, three-quarters of that from just two giant foundations, Rockefeller and Ford, but the funding has remained pivotal for quality and innovation. While foreign foundations have been crucial to the creation and sustenance of many Latin American private research centers, their primary recipient has been COLMEX. Today Rockefeller and Ford Foundations are joined by some U.S. foundations, including Hewlett and MacArthur, and Sasakawa (Japan), Konrad Adenauer and Friedrich Ebert (Germany), and the International Development Research Center (Canada).

Several trends are appearing to move other Latin American research centers somewhat closer to the structure of COLMEX. With redemocratization in many Latin nations, centers have moved to partnerships with governments. They rely increasingly on government money, though contracts and cosultancies remain important. With government support, some institutions have moved into formal graduate education. And, in general, centers that aspire to achieve greater size, influence, and quality of scholarship have COLMEX as an enduring example of what can be possible.

Further Reading: For perspectives on the institution within the context of the range of Latin America's freestanding research centers, see Daniel C. Levy, *Building the Third Sector: Latin America's Private Research Centers and Nonprofit Development* (Pittsburgh, Pennsylvania: University of Pittsburgh Press, 1996).

—Daniel C. Levy

COLLEGE OF WILLIAM AND MARY
(Williamsburg, Virginia, U.S.A.)

Location: Adjacent to Colonial Williamsburg, 150 miles south of Washington, D.C., and 50 miles from Richmond and Norfolk.

Description: A state-supported, four-year, coeducational, residential university.

Information: Office of Undergraduate Admission
P.O. Box 8795
Williamsburg, VA 23187-8795
U.S.A.
(804) 221-4223

Visiting: Group information sessions, followed by guided tours, are available; no appointment is necessary.

The College of William and Mary is the second oldest educational institution in the United States, preceded only by Harvard University. Founded in 1693 by a royal charter, it answered a long-standing need for a school of higher education in Virginia and the surrounding colonies. Originally, in 1617, colonists planned to establish a college that would educate and Christianize Indian children. Ten thousand acres in Henrico, Virginia, were endowed by the Virginia Company of London for the college grounds, at a location 12 miles south of what is now Richmond. But in 1622 an Indian uprising killed George Thorpe, the man named to construct the school, as well as 347 other colonists. The town of Henrico was destroyed, the charter revoked, and Virginia became a royal colony.

The plans for a college were therefore abandoned, although the need for such a school persisted. Aware that colonists were often reluctant to send their sons back to England to be educated, Anglican clergy in Virginia proposed in 1690 that a college should be formed consisting of three schools: grammar, philosophy, and divinity. The Reverend James Blair, a Scottish clergyman who was head of the Anglican Church in Virginia and commissary of the bishop of London, was one of the chief proponents of the establishment of the school, and it was he who traveled to England in 1691 with instructions from the General Assembly of Virginia to secure a charter for the college. Blair subsequently met with the king and queen and garnered the support of the archbishop of Canterbury. He also arranged to have part of the income from an estate of the Honorable Robert Boyle, the renowned philosopher and chemist, put aside to help fund the college,

specifically to help educate Indian children. The churchman's skill at fundraising would also lead him to a less conventional source of income: He negotiated a £300 donation to the college when he assisted in the acquittal of three Virginians on trial for piracy in London.

On February 8, 1693, with a grant of £2,000 and an endowment of 20,000 acres, the charter was granted. The document set forth three primary purposes for the college: the education of the white youth of Virginia, the training of ministers for the church, and the conversion of Indians. The charter also provided for the revenue of a penny per pound tax on tobacco sent from Virginia and Maryland to countries other than England. In return for his efforts, Reverend Blair was named president of the college, a position he held until his death in 1743.

The development of the College of William and Mary proceeded: a site for the college was established in what was called the "Middle Plantation," between the York and James Rivers. On November 16, 1693, the General Assembly of Virginia voted to charge an export duty on furs and skins to support the college. Construction of what was simply called the "College Building" began at a bricklaying ceremony in August 1695. Two years later, two of the building's wings were completed and lessons for young, grammar school boys began. They were taught by Reverend Blair, a grammar master, a master of arts, and a writing master; the subjects of instruction were reading, writing, Latin, and Greek. College-level instruction would not be fully established until 1729.

The College of William and Mary was immediately popular. For its first commencement in 1700, it is said that people came not just from Virginia, but from the colonies of Pennsylvania, New York, and Maryland. The growth of the school was noted in England: in 1706, a London publication, *Post Boy,* included a notice that said the college "is so crowded with Students, that they begin to think of enlarging the College, for it seems divers from Pennsylvania, Maryland, and Carolina send their Sons thither to be educated."

In 1699 the colonial capital of Virginia was moved from Jamestown to the Middle Plantation, which was then renamed Williamsburg. Legislators were pleased to observe the benefits that this arrangement would confer upon the college; the Act of 1699, which outlined the development of Williamsburg, noted: "It will prove highly advantageous and beneficiall to his Majesty's Royall Colledge of William & Mary to have the conveniences of a towne near the same." Indeed, the presence of the capital gave students access to a center of culture and government. Moreover, from this time forward, the

College of William and Mary

fortunes of the school and the town were closely linked; they would thrive and suffer together.

The original campus consisted of three buildings, all of which are standing today. The main building (the College Building) is now known as the Sir Christopher Wren Building in honor of the renowned British architect. It is believed that he drew the plans for this building, although he had no involvement in their implementation. Hugh Jones recorded in 1724 that the building was

> first modelled by Sir Christopher Wren, adapted to the Nature of the Country by the Gentlemen there; and since it was burnt down [in 1705], it has been rebuilt, and nicely contrived, altered and adorned by the ingenious Direction of General Spotswood; and is not altogether unlike Chelsea Hospital.

The Wren Building would be restored after two other fires in 1859 and 1862. One of the greatest losses in these fires was the destruction of most of the original records of the college. In addition to the distinction of being designed by Wren, the structure is notable for being the country's oldest building to serve in continuous academic use.

In 1723 the building known as the Brafferton was constructed to house the Indian school. It is named after the English estate of the school's benefactor Robert Boyle. While the Indian school gives William and Mary the claim of having created the first integrated educational institution in the colonies, it was not ultimately successful. Although in 1712 the school had 20 Indian pupils, including the sons of tribal royalty, it did not thrive. As Mary Newton Stanard noted in 1912, the boys "returned to idolatry and barbarism"; a more recent interpretation by the college president Thomas Graves in 1976, explained that "when these William and Mary students went back to their tribes, they did not want to hunt and fish any more as normal braves, but preferred just to sit around."

The third building in the original campus is the President's House, constructed in 1732. Together with the Wren Building and the Brafferton, it completes the third point of a triangle. The fully restored trio is considered an outstanding architectural achievement and is a tourist attraction in its own right.

The College of William and Mary was the only college operating in the South in 1775 when the American Revolution began. Because of its strategic location, it was occupied by military units several times. This was the norm rather than the exception, as seven of the nine existing colonial colleges were occupied by troops; in fact, William and Mary was the last college to be occupied. The college was commandeered at different times by British and American troops. In May 1781, Virginia was invaded by Lord Cornwallis, and college classes were suspended until 1782. In late June, British troops marched into Williamsburg and stayed there until July 4, using the President's House as their headquarters. Next, American troops entered the city, bringing the French with them; from September 1781 to June 1782, the college buildings were used to house wounded French soldiers. On November 3, 1781, the President's House was gutted by fire during this occupation. Fortunately, the French government gave £12,000 to pay for the damages, and the house was rebuilt in 1786. The college also suffered financially because of the war: in England, Boyle's Brafferton estate had been seized by the British; the income from the estate, which supported both William and Mary and Harvard, was sorely missed.

Meanwhile, the school's most notable alumnus, Thomas Jefferson, was working to promote its welfare in the state assembly. In 1779, three years after the Declaration of Independence and 17 years after he was graduated from the college, Jefferson proposed a bill that would have given the state the power to select the college's trustees and chancellor. The idea of a public university was not a popular one, however, and Jefferson's bill did not pass. Jefferson found other ways to use his influence and was instrumental in reducing the dominance of the Anglican Church at the college. While he was a member of the college's board of visitors, they voted to do away with two professorships in theology and one in classical languages that "involved the study of Scripture." The board replaced these faculty chairs with positions in the sciences and modern languages. With the abolition of these chairs, there were no British-born or British-educated professors on the faculty of the College of William and Mary.

As a member of the board (and now serving as Virginia's governor) Jefferson also participated in the creation of a school of law in 1779, the first of its kind in the United States. He supported the appointment of George Wythe as the first law professor. Wythe, a signer of the Declaration of Independence and Jefferson's former teacher, held the chair until 1790. The future president also helped to introduce the elective system of study and the honor system, two other William and Mary "firsts."

Thomas Jefferson is one of three U.S. presidents to have attended the College of William and Mary; he is joined by James Monroe, who was graduated in 1776 and John Tyler, a graduate in 1807. The college also lists an impressive number of graduates who were prominent figures in the American Revolution. Four of the signatures on the Declaration of Independence belong to William and Mary graduates, and 16 members of the Continental Congress were alumni. John Marshall, the first chief justice, was also a William and Mary graduate, and George Washington was the college's chancellor from 1788 until his death in 1799. Thus the university is able to refer to itself as the "Alma Mater of a Nation." The impact of William and Mary collegians in the revolution is made all the more striking by the fact that only one colonist in 1,000 was college educated. The school's academic distinctions were further enhanced by the founding in 1776 of the honorary academic society Phi Beta Kappa. The first organization of its kind, PBK now includes 228 chapters and 360,000 members.

The college's leadership role and its general fortunes would be diminished with the removal of the state capital to Richmond in 1780. This change brought the school to relative obscurity during the next 100 years. In 1849 the enrollment was shockingly low, with only 21 students attending William and Mary. Soon, the Civil War would threaten the school's very existence. During the war, with the entire faculty and nearly 90 percent of the student body enlisted in the Confederate army, the school was closed from 1861 to 1865. In May 1862, Federal troops marched on Williamsburg; four months later drunken Union soldiers set fire to the Wren Building. In the spring of 1865, the college was fortified, and cannons were placed inside the main buildings to ward off a possible Confederate raid. Even after the war ended, the faculty found conditions too difficult to continue; in 1868 they were forced to suspend classes until the damaged campus buildings were rebuilt and repaired. Classes resumed in October 1869, but the law school remained closed until 1920.

The determination of the college's president, Colonel Benjamin Ewell (elected 1854), kept the school alive during a desperate quarter century, from 1860 to 1888. Financial failure closed the college in 1881, but Ewell persisted in maintaining the school's charter. Finally, in 1888, his petitions to the general assembly resulted in an annual appropriation of $10,000 for the training of teachers. At the same time, a new president was inaugurated; Lyon G. Tyler, son of U.S. president John Tyler, took over the reins of an institution that soon grew in academic reputation, if not in financial security.

Continued financial problems resulted in the transfer of all college property to the commonwealth of Virginia in 1906, the college thus becoming a state-supported institution. The next year, with the help of the Carnegie Corporation, new funds were raised and a library was built (a section of the Wren Building had served as the library). Over the next several decades, many other buildings were added, including dormitories, a gymnasium, a dining hall, a physics and chemistry building, a classroom building, and an infirmary. With these improvements, the college began to take on the shape of a modern campus. Another modernization at William and Mary occurred in 1918, when it became the first Virginia college to become coeducational.

In 1920 the law school was reopened, giving further evidence of the improvement of William and Mary's status. An even greater event would more fully reestablish the college: the commencement of the restoration of colonial Williamsburg in 1926. This project was the combined effort of the college, the Colonial Williamsburg Foundation, and philanthropist John D. Rockefeller Jr. It resulted in the faithful restoration of the buildings of the original campus and the renaming of the College Building as the Sir Christopher Wren Building. A sunken garden was also created at the back of the Wren Building as a tribute to Thomas Jefferson. It is said he had expressed the wish that an undisturbed view of the countryside should be seen from this spot; the college has honored this wish with a large open area known as "Jefferson's Prospect."

The college expanded in 1930, by including a campus in Norfolk, a branch which would eventually become independent and be known as Old Dominion University. The William and Mary satellite called Christopher Newport College began as a junior college and became a full four-year school in 1968. On the main campus, the 1960s brought several important developments: in 1964, William and Mary was authorized to grant doctoral degrees, and in 1967, it was declared a university, although it retained its original name.

Today the university considers itself a "public ivy," and maintains the policy that all classes must be taught by professors (rather than teaching assistants). The school has six academic divisions: Arts and Sciences, Business Administration, Education, Law, and Marine Science. Not surprisingly, the history department is considered to be one of the school's finest, and is a sponsor of the Institute for Early American History and Culture. Two-thirds of its 5,300 undergraduate students come from Virginia, the remaining third from all over the world. The 1,200-acre campus, which is divided into "ancient," "modern," and "new" areas, now includes 40 major buildings, as well as Lake Matoaka and the College Woods.

Further Reading: *The Colonial Colleges in the War for American Independence* by John F. Roche (Millwood, New York: Associated Faculty, 1986) provides an account of the nine colleges that existed during the American Revolution and the role that they played in its events. *Colonial Virginia: Its People and Customs* by Mary Newton Stanard (Philadelphia: Lippincott, 1917; reprint, Detroit: Singing Tree, 1970) gives a brief account of the founding of William and Mary. Volume one of *American Higher Education,* edited by Richard Hofstadter and Wilson Smith (Chicago: University of Chicago Press, 1961) includes a condensed version of the college's 1693 charter. *Colonial Williamsburg: Its Buildings and Gardens* by A. Lawrence Kocher and Howard Dearstyne (Williamsburg, Virginia: Colonial Williamsburg, 1949) and *Williamsburg Today & Yesterday* by Grace Norton Rose (New York: Putnam, 1940) are slim volumes that give the history of the main buildings on campus. *Vital Facts: A Chronology of the College of William & Mary* (Williamsburg, Virginia: College of William and Mary, 1921; revised edition, 1993) is a detailed chronological listing of events in the history of the college.

—Karen Price

COLUMBIA UNIVERSITY
(New York, New York, U.S.A.)

Location: Columbia's main campus is in the vicinity of 120th Street, in northern Manhattan, New York City.

Description: A private university incorporating 15 professional and academic schools, and enrolling approximately 20,000 students.

Information: Office of Public Information and Communications
Columbia University
Low Memorial Library, Room 304
535 West 116th Street
New York, NY 10027-7017
U.S.A.
(212) 854-5573

In 1746, the General Assembly of New York sanctioned the first in a series of public lotteries to fund a college within the American colonies, and five years later, when the total sum of £3,443 had been raised, a board of trustees was selected to organize an institution. Trinity Church then offered to deed to the trustees a portion of King's Farm, a plot of land in what is now southern Manhattan, that it had acquired in 1702 or 1703 for the express purpose of establishing a college. The offer was accepted, and on October 31, 1754, King George II chartered an educational institution in New York City to be named "King's College."

Even before the charter was enacted, the trustees offered the presidency of the college to Dr. Samuel Johnson, a Congregational minister widely respected in both Britain and the colonies for his scholarly achievements. Dr. Johnson accepted, and oversaw the examination of candidates for entrance to the college in the summer of 1754. He began instructing eight students that year in the schoolhouse of Trinity Church. Not until 1760 was the first college building raised on the new campus.

The War of American Independence wrapped King's College in a cocoon from which Columbia University emerged approximately eight years later. On a May evening in 1775, the college's second president, Myles Cooper, was chased from his home, while still in his bedclothes, by a mob of citizens enraged by his loyalist speeches and writings. Cooper was afforded time to escape when a young alumnus of the class of 1774 scolded the crowd for acting indecently in the name of liberty. That brave man was Alexander Hamilton, the first

U.S. Secretary of the Treasury. Probably not more than two years later, the college building was seized by revolutionaries and used first as a barracks, and later as a hospital. The college itself effectively ceased operation until 1784, when the New York state legislature enacted a new charter granting the school the status of a university with the name of "Columbia College."

For almost three years, Columbia was controlled by the Regents of the University of the State of New York, during which time a small faculty was organized, and two classes were graduated. However, the regents soon realized that they could not effectively manage the several schools under their jurisdiction, and so they recommended that each college in the state be designated a corporation to be governed by an independent board of trustees. Alexander Hamilton is the probable author of a legislative act to that effect which was passed on April 13, 1787. Columbia was a private institution once again.

The college's newly appointed trustees elected William Samuel Johnson, son of the first president of King's College, the first president of Columbia. The younger Johnson was an influential lawyer and politician before his appointment; he served simultaneously as the U.S. senator from Connecticut during his 16-year tenure as head of the college. Johnson's primary accomplishment at Columbia was the founding of the medical school in 1792, the direction of which he assigned to Dean Samuel Bard, who had been with the school since its reformulation under the regents. Seven medical professors were hired, and the foundations for two new buildings laid; however, a shortage of funds long retarded development of the new program.

For the first half of the nineteenth century, Columbia stagnated under inept leadership. The most memorable event of that period was a subdued riot on commencement day, 1811. Provost John Mason, the acknowledged head of the school, persuaded President William Harris to refuse a diploma to a student named Stevenson who had read a controversial political essay—at odds with Mason's views—at the graduation ceremony. When Stevenson demanded his diploma, Mason instructed a nearby city marshal to arrest him, but Stevenson's peers and the attendant audience jumped to his defense, and the marshal was forced to retreat. Several of the students involved were found guilty of rioting. (Stevenson did not receive his diploma until 1816, when he was graduated from the College of Physicians and Surgeons.) Hardly had the deleterious effects of the riot on morale at the college abated when nine prominent New Yorkers, including three alumni, organized the University of the City of New

Columbia University

York (later New York University), having declared Columbia out of step with the liberal ideals of a democratic nation. By the late 1840s, Columbia still enrolled fewer than 100 students and was deeply in debt.

Despite Columbia's financial difficulties, the trustees determined to move the school to a new campus in 1856. Thirty-two years earlier, the state legislature had donated to the college a botanic garden, situated where Rockefeller Center is now located in midtown Manhattan, with the intention of providing an endowment. However, the trustees had retained the property and now planned to relocate their college there. The property at King's Farm was sold, and Columbia moved into the vacated quarters of the Deaf and Dumb Asylum, at Fourth Avenue and 49th Street, with the intention of remaining there only until a new plant was constructed on the planned site. The

Civil War prevented the trustees from realizing their plan (although the college did not rally behind the war effort to the extent that many other institutions in the North did), and Columbia remained on the grounds of the old asylum until its move to Morningside Heights in the mid-1890s.

Columbia was rejuvenated by Frederick A.P. Barnard, a graduate of Yale, who resigned from his presidency at the University of Mississippi when the Civil War began and accepted an offer to head Columbia in 1865. Barnard instituted sweeping changes at the college. He favored a practical curriculum over the traditional liberal arts education, at a time when the liberal arts college was still regarded as the center of the American academy. In 1883, he organized a women's program at Columbia; from that, Barnard College for women opened in 1889. Frederick Barnard also determined that Columbia should be modeled on the German research universities of the late nineteenth century, thus leading a trend in American education. Barnard's innovative ideas and enthusiasm soon attracted massive donations, as well as bright faculty and students. Between 1857 and 1889, Columbia's endowment rose tenfold, the number of teachers rose from 14 to 203, and enrollment rose from less than 150 to 1,712.

However, not everyone's impression of Columbia in the 1880s was a positive one. Professor John W. Burgess, who was persuaded to leave Amherst for Columbia and who was instrumental in founding Columbia's School of Political Science, recorded his early dismay. He found the faculty very odd: "I could not imagine upon what principle they had been brought together. . . . The students were rich loafers with no appreciation of anything scientific or intellectual." Another professor told Burgess, "I do as little as I can for these dunderheads and save my time for research."

Seth Low, a wealthy socialite and an alumnus of the class of 1870, was elected president of the college in 1889, following Barnard's death. Low was a skilled fundraiser who made considerable progress toward realizing Barnard's vision of Columbia. Most importantly, Low orchestrated the college's move to a new campus that was capable of sustaining a large and complex university. The trustees had contemplated a move uptown at least since 1872, when the corporation purchased ten acres at 160th Street and the Hudson River. That property was sold in 1889, however, while several costly buildings were erected on the 49th Street campus. Around the same time, however, it became apparent that Columbia would soon outgrow its confines there, as the expansion begun under Barnard continued unabated. Therefore, in 1894, the trustees approved the purchase of the old Bloomingdale Insane Asylum and surrounding property near 120th Street, where the present Morningside Heights campus is located. The asylum's buildings were promptly renovated for academic use, and the various branches of the college gradually moved into their new home.

Departments and schools proliferated before and during Low's presidency. King's College claimed the first professorship in law, established in 1773, but neither Columbia nor any other school in America had any systematic law course until at least 1858, when Theodore Dwight joined the faculty at Columbia. The school acquired its own facilities only in 1873, and Dwight remained the sole member of the faculty until 1875. The University of Physicians and Surgeons, organized at King's in 1767, separated from Columbia in 1807 but reunited with it in 1891. During the 1880s, the School of Mines, organized in 1864, added courses in civil, mechanical, and electrical engineering, and a department of architecture. In 1896, in recognition of these other developments, the trustees retitled the institution, "Columbia University in the City of New York,"

although the title was not legally attached to the corporation until 1912.

Nicholas Murray Butler was elected president of the university in 1902, having already established a successful career at Columbia. Having earned both his undergraduate and graduate degrees there in the 1880s, he returned from a trip to Europe to take a position as professor of philosophy. He was named dean of the philosophy department in 1890, and acting president upon Low's retirement in 1901. Butler's accomplishments as an administrator at Columbia, as an educational innovator of national stature, and as a statesman were so astounding that Theodore Roosevelt referred to him as "Nicholas Miraculous." Butler was a man of fame and prestige who claimed to have known 13 U.S. presidents personally, and who himself was the Republican vice-presidential candidate during William Taft's unsuccessful run for re-election in 1912.

Immediately upon his election as president of Columbia, Butler declared that the university was in pressing need of money, and so he devoted himself to fundraising. He solicited $16 million in donations during his first ten years in office, and by the time of his departure, he had raised more than $120 million. One of his most notable successes was the acquisition of $1 million from Joseph Pulitzer in 1904, with which the Columbia School of Journalism was founded. Pulitzer had offered the money to Harvard, but only on the condition that he could appoint an advisory board to help develop a curriculum. President Eliot of Harvard hesitated, whereupon Butler stole the opportunity.

In the early years of his administration, Butler heavily favored practical and professional curricula and specialized courses of academic study. His ambitions were twofold: to provide students with educations of definite application and to transform Columbia into a research university of the German variety. In 1905, he recommended that students move directly into professional programs after just two years of undergraduate study; at the same time, courses were added in such workaday subjects as "practical poultry raising." Thus, Butler was a proponent of transforming America's teaching colleges into modern universities. At Columbia and elsewhere, there was a backlash against those changes. In an effort to revive the liberal arts college at Columbia, Professor John Erskine inaugurated the Great Books course in 1916, and three years later, he organized a course in contemporary civilization.

Butler's emphasis on practical courses had positive and lasting effects at the university. For example, in 1886, even before assuming the presidency, Butler became involved with the Kitchen Garden Club, an organization associated with the church of St. Marks-in-the-Bouwerie, which trained schoolgirls in the practical skills of gardening and home economics. At the same time, Butler advocated the introduction of manual training programs into the New Jersey public school curriculum, and he approached members of the club with an offer to coordinate his efforts with theirs. The organization changed its name to the "Industrial Education Association" and elected Butler president in 1887. Shortly thereafter, Butler organized a practical course on teaching for public school instructors, held Saturday mornings on Columbia's campus. The trustees initially objected to women entering Columbia's classrooms, but the course proved enormously popular, and opposition faded quickly. In 1889, the Education Association was renamed "The New York College for the Training of Teachers," otherwise known as the Teachers College.

The evolution of the university's capacity as a research institution is demonstrated in the contribution that Columbia's faculty made in the development of the atomic bomb. Discussions between Enrico Fermi, I.I. Rabi, and others at Columbia led to the first experimental investigation of nuclear fission in the United States, on January 25, 1939. Several of the professors involved in the project at Columbia and Princeton Universities contacted President Roosevelt that fall, and the following year the National Defense Council issued one of its first research grants to Columbia. A financial link between government and university research programs was thus established; such links have since heavily influenced the American academy. The famous Manhattan Project was born, and, by 1944, there were approximately 1,450 people at Columbia working secretly to develop the atomic bomb. (Ironically, Nicholas Murray Butler had shared the Nobel Peace Prize in 1931 for his efforts in behalf of disarmament and international peace.)

In 1955, all federal funding for defense-related research conducted at American universities was put under control of the Institute for Defense Analysis (IDA), which made Columbia one of its chief beneficiaries. Moral objection to the university's involvement in military research peaked during the Vietnam War and partially provoked the famous Columbia riots of 1968. Between April 23 and 30, the Students for a Democratic Society (SDS), and a number of Columbia's African-American students occupied five buildings on the Morningside Heights campus. They promised to leave only if the administration severed ties with the IDA, and ceased building the Morningside gymnasium, which displaced African-American families in the Harlem community adjacent to Columbia. Administrators gave up hope of finding a peaceful solution when the occupation was entering its second week, and they ordered the police to take the buildings by force early on the morning of Tuesday, April 30. Dozens of students who resisted arrest were clubbed, and 524 Columbia students were arrested.

After the return of peace to the campus, Columbia continued on the course fixed by President Butler late in his administration. In 1996, approximately 87 percent of Columbia's students were enrolled in graduate or professional schools. Columbia's continued commitment to research is indicated by the fact that between 1955 and 1996, 15 professors earned Nobel Prizes while working at the university, the largest percentage in physics. During the same period, investment and donations raised the university's endowment to $2.2 billion. Today, Columbia is one of the wealthiest and most prestigious universities in the country.

Further Reading: *A History of Columbia University, 1754–1904,* edited by Brander Matthews, John B. Pine, Harry Thurston Peck, Munroe Smith, and Frederick P. Keppel (London: Macmillan, and New York: Columbia University Press, 1904) is probably the best of several books that cover the history of Columbia from its beginnings through 1901. *Columbia: Colossus on the Hudson* by Horace Coon (New York: Dutton, 1947) covers the same period as well as the first half of the twentieth century. There is scant material on later developments at Columbia, but *Crisis at Columbia: Report of the Fact-Finding Commission Appointed to Investigate the Disturbances at Columbia University in April and May 1968* (New York: Vintage, 1968) covers the riots of 1968 in thorough detail.

—Christopher Hoyt

COMPLUTENSE UNIVERSITY OF MADRID
(Madrid, Spain)

Location: Just north of the old, central section of Madrid.

Description: As state institution under the jurisdiction of the Ministry of Education and Science, enrolling approximately 127,000 students in undergraduate, graduate, doctoral and professional programs.

Information: Universidad Complutense de Madrid
Universitaria, 28040 Madrid
Spain
(1) 49-02-56
Telex: 41857

Sixteen years after Christopher Columbus discovered the New World in 1492, the Universidad Complutense de Madrid was founded. But the world's third largest university can trace its roots back more than seven centuries when King Sancho IV of Castille founded a study center in Alcalá de Henares.

Universities, or centers of higher education, were extensions of monastic schools and medieval colleges and have their origin in the eleventh and twelfth centuries in western Europe. Universities were first formed in France, England, and Italy. In the thirteenth century, universities began to appear on the Iberian Peninsula. The first was a school of general studies at Palencia, which later moved to Valladolid, followed by one in Salamanca. On May 20, 1239, a royal warrant established a school of general studies in the town of Alacá. (It would be 206 years before the school acquired the status of university and 543 years before the school was permanently transferred to Madrid because of financial difficulties.)

According to the royal warrant, the University of Alacá was to have "all those franchises that the 'Etudium,' [school of general studies] of Valladolid possessed," so that "the tutors and scholars to be will come here to study."

While this is the first documentation for the foundation of the University of Madrid, there is not enough additional information from the period to give an indication of the university's operations. However, information is available about one of the other Spanish universities—the University of Bologna—where only students of law and theology were admitted.

In 1348, Spanish rulers regulated and organized all the study centers in Castille as part of a reorganization of all the country's laws. The centers of higher learning were confirmed as a "council of tutors and scholars formed with the intention and purpose of acquiring knowledge." Under this reorganization, students were taught grammar, rhetoric, dialect with Aristotelian logic, mathematics, geometry, music, and logic. The method of teaching was repetition and discussion; the language of instruction was Latin, which allowed the exchange of students throughout Europe. A professor was assigned to each subject. Known as a tutor, the professor received a salary, was exempt from paying taxes, and did not have to serve in the Spanish army. A rector was employed to oversee the school itself, but he had no authority in academic matters or the granting of degrees; those functions fell within the province of the university's chancellor.

Students were chosen to fill vacancies at the school by examination by representatives of the region's cathedrals. All students had to be at least 19 years of age and were given 7-year grants to cover food, clothing, and lodging.

While the university had been established by a king, the religious figures of the area played a key role in its creation and development. The school was built at the request of don Gonzalo Garcí Gudiel, the archbishop of Toledo. Two future archbishops of Toledo also played important roles in the development of the Complutense: don Alfonso Carrillo and Francisco Jiménez de Cisneros.

Before being named archbishop, Bishop Carrillo intervened in the marriage of Isabelle and Ferdinand, which made possible the unification of Spain. After being named archbishop in 1446, he held a special favor toward Alcalá. Not long after his appointment as archbishop, Carrillo argued for the construction of a house of studies in the city. He entrusted the house of studies to the Franciscans and ordered three positions be made available for teachers for the study of grammar and the arts. He obtained the money to fund the teachers from Pope Calixtus III; in 1459 the funds were increased by Pope Pius II.

Cardinal Jiménez de Cisneros, who was born in a village near Madrid, first had contact with the study center as a youth when he studied there. He went on to complete his education in Salamanca, obtaining a bachelor's degree in law. He rose through the ranks as an archpriest and vicar general, later deciding to become a Franciscan friar in 1484. In 1492 he emerged from the Franciscans to be Queen Isabelle's confessor, and three years later became the archbishop of Toledo. In 1498, the development of Complutense University began at Alcalá as land and buildings in the area were bought. A year later, the first stone was laid for the university.

While construction had begun on the university, Cisneros also promoted the development of a printing press in the university's city. The press was used to print philosophical and religious books for the school. Years after the college was established, Cisneros tackled another project that would bring him and the Complutense fame. From 1514 to 1517, the printers worked on the "Complutense Polygot Bible," a Bible that contained Hebrew, Greek, Latin, and Chaldean characters in one book. The project began in 1502 when Cisneros began work on the first polygot Bible. For the undertaking, he hired most of the great experts on the four languages to teach at the university. He chose to produce the Bible in the original languages, saying, "No version can faithfully translate all the force and propriety of the original." Most of the Bibles were destroyed when a ship carrying them to Rome was wrecked.

Although many popes gave money to Cisneros to construct the university, he still was faced with difficulties in seeing it completed. Often he had discussions with the authorities at Salamanca who wanted to halt construction and have all the funds diverted to their school to challenge the superiority of the University of France. The construction of the university took a decade, and in the summer of 1508 the College of San Ildefonso was complete. The school officially opened July 26, 1508, with 500 students. For students to graduate, they had to pass a corresponding exam before a group of graduates from the university.

The College of San Ildefonso became the major college of Complutense. It was located in the main university building; beside it were the rectory and the university's library, one of the most important in Europe. In the following year, smaller colleges for theologians, Franciscans, philosophers and others were opened in the university. Following Cisnero's death in 1516, another college opened for the study of Greek, Latin and Hebrew.

Royalty and religious figures often visited the school, a tribute to its standing among centers for higher education. In 1514, Cisneros and King Ferdinand both attended the school's graduation. Another king, Charles V, declined to sit in his usual seat of honor, sitting instead in the choir to be with the nation's men of learning. Similarly, King Francis I of France during a visit to the city paid Cisneros tribute, saying that the University of Paris was the work of many kings while Complutense was the work of one friar (Cisneros) over a short period of time. Pope John Paul II visited Complutense on November 3, 1982, and reminded members of Spain's science and cultural societies of the school's importance. He encouraged students to "build the utopia of a new world." A few years later, the Pope was given a facsimile copy of the Complutense Polygot Bible from the Rector Francisco Bustelo.

After Cisneros's death, the university faced more turmoil, a foreshadowing of its future. During his tenure, the university had become well known and had begun to attract students from all over Europe, even competing with such schools as the University of Paris. Now, there were disputes between students and town residents, which eventually led to the school's departure to Madrid. According to some, moving the university to Madrid, which was not Spain's capital at the time, first was suggested by the bishop of Palencia. But that suggestion was rebuffed by Madrid Governor Francisco de Prado, who thought the students would be out of place in a city about to become the nation's capital. "You can't mix the striped cloaks of the philosophers with the august purple of the princes," he said. Prado got his wish, as the university was not moved until October 15, 1822. The restoration of absolutism returned the university to Alcalá, but the school's opening only delayed the inevitable.

During the sixteenth and seventeenth centuries the school had been renowned. King Philip II sent his son Charles, half-brother John, and nephew to study at the university. He also made 40 scholarships available to the sons of royal servants to study there as well. By the mid-1600s, the university was composed of the College of San Ildefonso and 35 other minor colleges that were set up in their own buildings or in the surrounding convents. Along with its educational growth, artistic and architectural changes came as well. The College of San Ildefonso was rebuilt and a chapel and great patio for the university also were constructed. During that time, Alcalá became the model for urban development and architectural style. But it was its scholarly acclaim that Complutense became know for. The school even served as the model for the first university established in the New World, the University of Santo Domingo.

While Philip II was impressed with the university, he nonetheless established a royal study center in Madrid in the mid-1500s. The center, called the Imperial College of Madrid, was run by Jesuits. The school taught grammar, theology, and rhetoric and educated many royalties. In 1624, the royal study center was promoted to the level of university despite the objections at Complutense and the University of Salamanca. The Jesuits taught at the royal university until they were exiled from Spain in 1767 for their beliefs and teaching methods.

About 1770, the idea of establishing a larger university in Madrid began to develop. The first step toward the move of Complutense to Madrid came with the faculty of medicine being sent to the Calle Atocha Hospital in Madrid. While Complutense flourished during the 1600s and 1700s, its decline had begun in part because of the Inquisition and censorship of new ideas in academia, violence, limitations within the colleges for faculty salaries and areas of study, and the lack of newer fields such as science. In 1786 no more than 450 students remained at the school, about one-quarter its earlier attendance. The admission process remained selective and college life rigorous. It was during this time that the university graduated its first woman as a doctor. Maria Isidra de Guzman y la Cerda was examined in philosophy and letters in 1785 and received her doctoral robes.

Fiscal problems and the Napoléonic wars led to the university closing its doors for a year in 1810. Town officials fought to keep the university but its fate was sealed in 1821 when it was recommended that the central university be established in Madrid to teach theology, law, natural history, botany, mathematics and other studies. Plans for the university's move to Madrid lasted from 1836 to 1845. The university's library was formed by combining the libraries of Alcalá, the royal study centers, and the colleges of medicine and pharmacy. On October 29, 1836, a royal decree made the University of Madrid a reality, stating that "the University of Alcalá will be transferred to Madrid where the corresponding lands will be given, so that it will be an establishment worthy of the capital and the Monarchy." The transfer was carried out in November, with several colleges moving immediately. The university sold its buildings in Alcalá, but the town residents did not honor the sale, reclaiming the buildings and confiscating all the articles in them to be sold or burned, including a cross of gold and glass, which was sold in 1839, that had been given to Cardinal Cisneros by Leo X. In 1842, the students were transferred from Las Salesas to the Norviciado, and the two buildings became the central places of study in the center of the growing city. By 1860, the university was well established with 40 percent of Spain's 2,465 students studying at Complutense de Madrid.

During the next half century, the university moved toward a more secular role in the community and in 1869, Rector Fernando de Castro incorporated many of the proposals set forward by a group known as the Institute of Free Education, among them coeducation and incorporating sports into the educational system. Castro, in effect, opened the university doors to every Spaniard for the first time.

During this time of change toward educational freedom and independence, Alfonso XII decided to consolidate the university, ending its array of scattered buildings in Madrid. By royal decree, on October 20, 1911, Alfonso XII ordered a University Campus to replace the decrepit building on Atocha Street. The king bought several plots of land on the La Montcloa estate and in 1928 construction plans were drawn.

Building committee members visited the United States to see several universities to use as models for construction. Architect López Otero began work on the buildings, which were a combination of traditional art and modernist experiments of plants and buildings. The project won acclaim at the International Exhibition of Barcelona in 1929. Unfortunately, the campus was on the front-line during the Spanish Civil War and many of the buildings, documents, and scientific archives were damaged. Otero worked to reconstruct many of the buildings after the war.

The latter half of the 20th century has seen several members of the university community honored internationally. Juan Ramon Jiménez won the Nobel prize for literature in 1956 and three years later former physiology student Severo Ochoa won the Nobel Prize for medicine.

Today, students wanting to attend the University of Madrid must obtain a secondary school certificate or its foreign equivalent, go through examination orientation, and pass an entrance exam. The school has grown from a small study center to a large research institution with nearly 130,000 students being taught by 5,500 teachers and professors. The university is so large that it is contained within a section of Madrid known as University City. In 1992, the university granted bachelor degrees in 31 majors and had 232 department courses. It is the largest university in Spain.

Further Reading: Rogélio Perez Bustamante's work, *A Brief History of the Complutense University of Madrid*, gives a quick review of the first 700 years of Spain's largest university.

—J. Cameron Tew

COOPER UNION FOR THE ADVANCEMENT OF SCIENCE AND ART
(New York, New York, U.S.A.)

Location: On Third Avenue in Manhattan's East Village.

Description: A private, independent, nonprofit institution enrolling 1,000 students in architecture, art, and engineering schools.

Information: Office of Admissions and Records
The Cooper Union for the Advancement
of Science and Art
30 Cooper Square
New York, NY 10003
U.S.A.
(212) 353-4120

The Cooper Union for the Advancement of Science and Art, established in 1859, was conceived and founded by New York businessman and philanthropist Peter Cooper. Cooper, who had risen from a modest background to become a giant of industry by the mid-nineteenth century, believed that traditional forms of apprenticeship had broken down in the industrial era and this conviction led him to establish Cooper Union as an institution that would fill in the gap by providing, tuition-free, practical education to the working classes of New York City.

The origins of Cooper Union can be traced to the late 1830s, when Cooper first spoke to friends and colleagues about his ideas for an educational institution designed specifically to respond to the needs of working-class citizens. At about this same time Cooper acquired, by way of an outstanding debt that was owed him, a lot measuring 16' by 22' on the northeast corner of Third Avenue and Seventh Street. Over the course of the next 13 years (from 1839 to 1852) Cooper purchased 16 more oddly shaped parcels of property surrounding the original lot with the intent to build what he called the Union at that location.

During these years plans for the design and scope of the Union began to take shape, although several significant alterations to these plans would occur before the school opened its doors in the fall of 1859. In general terms, Cooper imagined the school not simply as a college or university or even a secondary school but as a "Union" where city workers, as well as their children (ages 14 and up), could gather for discussions and attend classes, lectures, and debates, and where trade unions and other similar organizations could hold their meetings. In his early plans for the Union, Cooper, who had served as trustee for the Public School Society of New York but had received little formal education himself, placed great importance on popular lectures, dialogue, visual aids, and demonstrations as methods of teaching and less importance on semester-long courses, drills, and examinations. Over the course of the planning process, however, advisors convinced Cooper that traditional methods of instruction would be necessary for the Union to become a viable institution of learning. Cooper's hand in the formation of the Union, though, was still apparent. It was Cooper who insisted the Union be structured as a resource institution that would respond to the particular needs of working-class students and not an institution that would doggedly stand by traditional academic principles in the face of a rapidly changing social climate.

By 1853 Cooper had accrued enough property to begin construction on the Union's main building, now called the Foundation Building. A small ceremony accompanying the laying of the cornerstone took place on September 17; the gathering was attended by the mayor and covered by *The New York Times*. Fittingly, Cooper, who had spent many of his early years as a laborer, outperformed the mayor when it came time to lay the bricks, as was noted by the *Times* reporter:

> His Honor used the trowel as delicately as he would lift a pea on his silver fork. Mr. Cooper, on the other hand, handled the implement and laid on the mortar with as bold and workmanlike a hand as though he had been brought up to the business; indeed, as a bystander observed, he took to the mortar like a brick.

Six years after the laying of the cornerstone, construction was completed.

Structurally, the Foundation Building was ahead of its time. Facing Third Avenue and the Bowery, it was one of the first buildings to be supported by iron girders (the iron being produced by Cooper's iron production company). One notable feature to the building was a ventilation system run by a large steam-powered fan. Another feature was a large, empty shaft running from the basement of the building to the top floor. Cooper, who was somewhat of an inventor himself, realized that elevators would be available in the not too distant future, and thus he left space for them. Building costs totaled $630,000

Cooper Union

and were paid for in full by Cooper himself, even though this sum was more than double the $300,000 he had allocated for those purposes.

True to his entrepreneurial nature, Cooper wanted to make all-inclusive the scope of the Union's educational facilities and this led to some overly ambitious plans for the Foundation Building. Among other things, the building was conceived originally to include a museum, a cosmorama (or observatory), meeting and debate rooms, a roof-garden which would be used for summer concerts, and an entire floor with alcoves for statues. In fact, Cooper was so certain the museum would be an integral part of the Union that he purchased a gigantic stuffed whale to be the centerpiece of the museum collection. Upon considering the advice of his closest advisors, however, Cooper donated the whale to the Museum of Natural History, and the space allotted for the museum eventually became a public reading room. Cooper's advisors also convinced him to install a laboratory in place of the proposed cosmorama and additional classrooms in place of meeting rooms.

A similar narrowing process took place in the conception of the Union's academic offerings. Specifically, it was decided that the main emphases of the Union's "curriculum" would consist of courses, lectures, and workshops in applied science and political science, for which all classes would be taught at night; in art and design for women, for which all classes would be taught during the day; and in technology and science. Cooper envisioned the latter as a separate entity within the Union, but this was not achieved during his lifetime.

Plans for the night school and day school, however, would be immediately realized, save for the fact that courses in political science were put on hold, as difficulties were encountered in the hiring of suitable instructors. The art school for women became a reality in 1858 when Cooper permitted the New York School of Design, an already existing but financially troubled institution, to use the Union's facilities while the Union itself was still awaiting its charter. This arrangement was forecast in the Union's original deed of trust. Cooper had added a clause in the deed that, should any reputable art school for women wish to utilize the Union's facilities, such a school would be welcome. The school was later fully incorporated into Cooper Union, with its founders and administrators staying on in the capacity of an advisory board.

On April 13, 1859, having already passed the charter application, the New York State Legislature passed an amended charter. On April 29 Cooper and his wife executed the deed of trust for the property. Classes began in November of the same year.

Classes offered that fall filled up during the first day of enrollment, and this apparently caught administrators and instructors by surprise. In the spring of the following year more than 1,100 students had enrolled in courses; that number reached nearly 1,500 by 1864. By 1888 the Union had solidified its presence in the community and enrollment reached 3,000. In fact, by the latter decades of the nineteenth century, the Union was receiving twice as many applications for enrollment in the women's art school and four times as many for enrollment in the night school as they were able to accept. The first post-secondary degrees were awarded in 1864; those receiving degrees were two clerks, a coachmaker, an engraver, and a machinist, respectively.

News of Cooper Union and its practice of admitting women to classes that were traditionally intended for men caused quite a stir in the city. Cooper and Abram Hewitt, Cooper's son-in-law and the Union's chief administrator, were adamant that female students should be afforded equal footing with male students in every regard. Toward this end, they stipulated that any female students wishing to attend night courses in science could do so provided they supply a letter of recommendation from a minister or employer. This arrangement—that respectable women would be walking about in the city at night, and not just in the city but in or along the Bowery, a district renowned for its questionable activities—caused much consternation among the moral overseers of the city. Hewitt, though, was able to make a positive report on their "experiment" in 1865:

> we believe that both sexes are the gainers by learning together. Of course there will be found evil-minded people everywhere, even in churches, but in six years we have not had a single case of scandal at Cooper Union, and we should as soon think of excluding the young men as the young women.

The Union's unblemished track record in regard to providing a safe environment for young women considerably calmed the fears of doubters.

Although Cooper was by no means a feminist, his views on the education of women were progressive for his time. He was keenly aware of the dilemma for working-class women in New York City's highly industrialized setting: that female laborers accounted for a growing percentage of the work force in the city and that, if these women were to be employed in the better jobs available to laborers, they would need the same access to education afforded to men, access that was usually denied them. Initially, Cooper's efforts to provide practical education for women were focused primarily on offering instruction in art and science; however, as new employment opportunities opened up for women in the fields of telegraphy, stenography, and photographic art, Cooper was always the first to suggest that courses be taught in those areas. As Peter Buckley, a historian at Cooper Union, has observed, Cooper's practical philanthropy in effect blinded him to the chauvinism of the day.

While Peter Cooper was the person responsible for the establishment and financing of Cooper Union, it was

Hewitt who was primarily responsible for the day-to-day operations of the institution, and it was under his direction that the Union evolved from the somewhat vaguely defined—albeit progressive—enterprise it was in 1859 into the more narrowly defined educational institution it is today. As secretary of the board of trustees, Hewitt oversaw finances, the hiring of instructors, and was also influential in the design of the school's educational format. Hewitt supported the idea that the Union be structured in such a way as to offer more formal instruction. The board of trustees was apparently in agreement with Hewitt, for it reiterated his concerns in its annual report of 1866.

At about this time a tradition was born at Cooper Union. When the Foundation Building was conceived, Cooper had insisted that basement space be allocated for a large lecture hall, his logic being that a room below street level would best shield its inhabitants from the commotion of the city. Lectures were scheduled irregularly in 1863; the tradition of Saturday evening lectures was in place by 1868. Although the Union had only minimal funds with which to attract potential speakers, Hewitt worked diligently to bring in professors, inventors, and newspapermen to address the "Great Hall." Topics for these lectures ranged from government and politics (by 1866 the board of trustees had decided that instruction in political science would best be accomplished through lectures in the Great Hall), travel, cuisine, and psychology, among others. Notable speakers included Abraham Lincoln, who spoke on the topic of slavery in a campaign speech in February 1860; and John Tyndall of England, who gave an awe-inspiring lecture on, and demonstration of, electric light in 1872. Attendance at these Saturday night gatherings averaged 1,500.

In 1864 it became a distinct possibility that Cooper Union would merge with Columbia University. Upon the recommendation of Hewitt, a clause had been added to the Union's original deed of trust stating that, until funds could be secured for the establishment of a polytechnic school at Cooper Union, classrooms in the Foundation Building would be available to any reputable institution for the purposes of offering such instruction. There is evidence that suggests Hewitt had had in mind all along the merging of Cooper Union with a larger institution (and, in fact, neither he nor Cooper were averse to the notion of placing the Union's facilities and resources in more capable hands). With Cooper's blessing, Hewitt, who was an alumnus of Columbia, proposed these measures to trustees at Columbia. Hewitt believed that such a merger would empower both institutions: Cooper Union would gain from a close affiliation with a respected and established institution of classical learning such as Columbia; Columbia would gain from the widening of its educational focus to include the pragmatic curriculum of Cooper Union. Hewitt was also motivated by a vision of

uniting the working classes of New York City with "men of science and learning" in one educational enterprise, thus cultivating a better social and cultural environment in the growing metropolis. To Hewitt's dismay, little interest was shown on the part of Columbia and discussions ceased.

Four years later, however, the new president of Columbia requested that a dialogue between the two schools be re-opened. This time it would be Cooper who would put an end to the possible merger (a merger that would have resulted in the subordination of Cooper Union). When, during preliminary discussions, it became apparent that very significant alterations would have to be made to the Foundation Building for it to function as the school of science and technology that Columbia wished to obtain, Cooper became stubbornly averse to the idea. Hewitt regretfully declined any further discussion on the topic.

The histories of Cooper Union and Columbia University crossed paths again in the mid-1890s. At that time Columbia moved from its location in midtown Manhattan to Morningside Heights. Hewitt seized upon the idea of purchasing the vacant educational facilities left behind by Columbia for the purposes of expanding Cooper Union (while additions had been made to accommodate more female art students in the early 1890s, all other departments were severely constrained by space). Toward this end, Hewitt sought financial backing from wealthy members of New York City society, with the goal of raising $3 million. His argument for those who would listen was that the waiting list to gain admission to Cooper Union was long and presumably would be even longer if applicants thought they would be admitted sooner. His fundraising efforts failed, however.

Although Cooper himself was always willing to pay for any expenditures that exceeded the yearly budget, the financial resources necessary for growth simply were not available. In order to pay the Foundation Building's operating costs, rooms on the first and second floors of the building were rented out as storefronts, and this arrangement contributed even more to the school's severe shortage of space.

A successful venture at this time was the establishment of a Museum of Decorative Arts, now named the Cooper-Hewitt Museum. Founded by Hewitt's daughters, the museum enjoyed the generous support of patrons from its inception in 1895. The Cooper-Hewitt Museum fell under Cooper Union's administration until 1976, at which time it was transferred to the Smithsonian Institution.

Events that took place at the turn of the century brought financial security to Cooper Union. In addition to other gifts from patrons of the Union, Hewitt received an endowment gift of $100,000 from Andrew Carnegie in 1901. Hewitt met with Carnegie soon after to further explain the particular needs of the Union; Carnegie then donated an additional $200,000. After more discussions with Hewitt, Carnegie agreed to make yet another donation of $300,000, provided that the Cooper-Hewitt family match his donation. By restructuring family finances, they were able to do so. In the span of a year Cooper Union's endowment grew from $958,000 to well over $2 million. By the mid-1930s endowment had reached $12 million.

These gifts allowed trustees to cease the practice of renting out space in the Foundation Building. The increase in endowment also led to enhancement of the school's science facilities and to the broadening of its curriculum, for nearly coinciding with the school's much improved financial status was the restructuring of the school of science to include undergraduate day courses (this was a significant step in the process of becoming the college it is today). The school of science soon after developed into the present-day Albert Nerken School of Engineering.

School administrators narrowed the Union's educational focus to that of a fully post-secondary school. The final reorganization took place in 1975 when the Department of Architecture in the Art School became a separate degree-granting entity within Cooper Union.

Further Reading: Historical accounts of Cooper Union can be found in the biographies of the two men most responsible for establishing and shaping the institution: *Peter Cooper, Citizen of New York* by Edward C. Mack (New York: Duell, Sloan and Pearce, 1949), and *Abram S. Hewitt* by Allan Nevins (New York: Harper, 1935).

—Christopher Hudson

CORNELL COLLEGE
(Mount Vernon, Iowa, U.S.A.)

Location: Mount Vernon, in eastern central Iowa, on U.S. Highway 30, approximately 15 miles east of Cedar Rapids and approximately 200 miles west of Chicago.

Description: An independent liberal arts institution affiliated with the United Methodist Church.

Information: Cornell College
600 First Street West
Mount Vernon, IA 52314-1098
U.S.A.
(319) 895-4000

Visiting: With advance notice, a visit can be arranged at most times during the academic year. There are several options for visits including Student-Parent Preview Days, Individual Overnight Visits, and Individual One-Day Visits. To learn more about these options or to make reservations for a campus visit call (800) 747-1112 or (319) 895-4477.

Unlike many institutions of higher learning, Cornell College was founded without major support from church or state or magnanimous philanthropy. (In fact, the college was into its 40th year before a donation of more than $25,000 was received.) Cornell College grew from the dream of native North Carolinian George Bryant Bowman (1812–88), a circuit riding preacher who had come to Iowa from Missouri in 1841. While serving as pastor of a Methodist church in Iowa City, Bowman, believing that people required education as well as faith, determined that there was a need for a church school. He became one of the founders of Iowa City College, but the school closed shortly after its founding in 1843 because it lacked sufficient funds and patronage.

Undaunted, Elder Bowman still sought a suitable location for a Christian college. Legend had Bowman riding the circuit in Linn County and stopping upon the crest of the hill where Mt. Vernon now stands. Awed by the magnificent vistas of prairie and forest, he envisioned the multitudes that would come if he could build a Christian college on this spot. Bowman began to plan for his college, and, during a July 4th celebration in 1852, where "a plethora of edibles" was served, ground was broken for the new school. A month later a deed was obtained for land, and in September the Methodist Episcopalian

Church assumed guardianship of the new institution, the Iowa Conference Seminary.

In the fall of 1853, the school opened in the old Methodist Church in Mt. Vernon, and on November 14th of that year, a "large and commodious" seminary building was ready for the students who marched in procession through the town to take possession of their new quarters.

The first college catalogue listed faculty for the following posts: a professor of language; a professor of mental and moral science and belle lettres; a preceptress; a teacher of painting and embroidery; and a teacher of instrumental music. The Reverend R.W. Keeler of the Upper Iowa Conference was named president and served until he re-entered the ministry two years later. Samuel M. Fellows was then elected president.

Miss Catherine Fortner, the preceptress recommended by Governor Slade of Vermont, had been sent as a missionary teacher to Iowa, as "suitable instructors were not numerous at this time in the West."

Dr. David H. Wheeler, professor of languages and Greek, was subsequently appointed U.S. consul to Genoa. His distinguished career included writing several books, editing the New York Methodist, and serving as the president of Allegheny College.

The faculty taught the first class of 161 students, a remarkable number considering the inadequate transportation and communications systems and the scattered settlement patterns that existed in Iowa at the time. Getting to the school presented only one hardship. Not only were students expected to rise at 5 A.M., they had to furnish their own beds, lights, and mirrors. Tuition costs were $4.00 to $5.00 per quarter, and board $1.50 to $1.75 weekly.

In 1855, the board of trustees voted to reorganize the Iowa Conference Seminary into a four-year college. Mount Vernon College was considered as a new name. Instead, the college was named Cornell after William Wesley Cornell, a wealthy New York iron merchant known for donating generously to the Methodist church. However, Cornell contributed only a small sum of money to Bowman. Cornell was a distant cousin of Ezra Cornell who would endow Cornell University in Ithaca, New York, in 1865. William Cornell was not consulted about the naming of the college and was offended. Years later, Professor William S. Norton recalled that the Cornell's legacy consisted of "little but a good name and a few books."

The Iowa Conference Seminary was opened as Cornell College on August 27, 1857, with 294 students, 7 faculty, and the seminary building which housed the chapel, music recitation room, and dining and kitchen areas. Some women students boarded on the second floor;

Cornell College

teachers and a few male students boarded on the third. The college had constructed the seminary building, and later College Hall in 1857 with the help of local residents. The brick used in construction was made on campus and sand for the mortar transported from the Cedar River.

When College Hall was completed, the seminary was converted to the Ladies' Boarding Hall. Here, for almost 30 years, women endured austere conditions, even having to pay extra to have firewood cut and brought into the building. "Old Sem," as the building was known, burned in 1924, leaving only the masonry walls, It was rebuilt in its original style and today houses the administrative offices.

A wonder of its age, Bowman Hall opened in 1885 and offered young ladies hot and cold running water on each floor, indoor plumbing, gas lighting, heat, and a dining room that could seat 200 people. Bowman Hall, now Bowman-Carter, has served as a residence for women, except during World War II when it housed men of the Naval Flight Preparatory School.

Most male students boarded in town. The Cornell Boarding Association Hall (South Hall) was built as a men's dormitory in 1873, but men preferred to be out from under the watchful eyes of the faculty so the building was designated for academic purposes. Men did not live on campus until 1929 when Guild Hall, a former hotel, was purchases by the college. Today, 95 percent of Cornell students live in one of nine residence halls or college-owned apartments.

Cornell's library has occupied various locations around campus, beginning with the seminary building in 1854. Dr. Stephen N. Fellow, residing therein noted that his room, 10 by 16 feet was his "bedroom, sitting room and parlor and not being sufficiently utilized became the library room." Donations of "readable and instructive" books were requested from friends of the institution to form the nucleus of a library collection to which students would have access at "trifling expense." Request for books appeared in each of Cornell's catalogues for its first decade.

In 1904, a Carnegie library was constructed, the first time that the library enjoyed exclusive use of a building. This building is now the Norton Geology Center and Anderson Science Museum. Cole Library, named for the college's ninth president, was constructed in 1957, the library collection having outgrown the old Carnegie building. The library underwent a major renovation in 1994–95, which allowed for automation of major library functions. Since 1904, the college library has also served as the town library. The University of New Hampshire is the only other library to serve its community in this manner.

Perhaps the most important place on campus to many alumni is the King Chapel, named for William Fletcher King who served from 1863–1908 as acting president and president. In 1874, King was vacationing in Europe when the board of trustees resolved to build a chapel.

However, $15,000 in subscriptions was needed before work could begin. The cornerstone was laid in 1876, but money did not come in rapidly enough to pay labor and material costs, and the college treasury was drawn down. Contractors went bankrupt, and Cornell was obligated to assume the mechanic's liens. The trustees mortgaged the campus in order to secure a loan to pay off its debts. Additionally, the faculty donated one-quarter of their salaries to alleviate the debt.

Despite this precarious financial position, the chapel was completed over the next eight years. The upper story was finished when the first-floor chapel opened on April 1, 1878. By early summer 1882, the auditorium was open. Prior to the installation of electric lights in 1898, this room was illuminated by a chandelier of 350 sperm whale oil lamps which dripped; consequently, few people sat in the center section. Today the auditorium is used for assemblies, lectures, concerts, and an occasional religious service.

The chapel has many stained glass windows, but most panes are of clear glass upon which designs are painted and baked according to a process invented by Louis Tiffany.

During Cornell's first years, the college course was classical; a scientific course was added in 1860, and a civil engineering course in 1873. At one time, Cornell included a primary department (middle school) and a preparatory department which "prepared" student from two or three high schools to enter Cornell or get ready for careers in teaching or business. The primary department was discontinued in 1866 and the preparatory in 1921.

Cornell has offered courses in support of teacher education since 1872. Its department of sociology was established only six years after the University of Chicago established the first such department in the nation. Cornell was also one of the first colleges to offer a choice of degrees. In addition to its bachelors of arts and sciences degree, Cornell has awarded a Mistress of English Literature (last conferred in 1865), a Bachelor of Philosophy (first conferred in 1881), a Bachelor of School Music (conferred 1925–45), and a Bachelor of Special Studies (first conferred 1872). The last master's degree was awarded in 1936.

Cornell was a pioneer in women's rights; of the first class of 161 students, 57 were women. Cornell was the first college west of the Mississippi to admit women, and the women were accorded the same rights and privileges as male students.

In 1871, Harriette J. Cooke became the first woman in the United States to be awarded a full professorship with a salary equal to that of her male colleagues. Cooke arrived from Massachusetts, and "brought the best culture for women which New England then afforded, as well as an exceptionally forceful personality, and rare natural aptitudes for her profession." She was Dean of Women from 1860 until her resignation, and she held chairs in German and history.

Minority groups have had a presence on campus for some time. African-Americans attended high school or college, although the first African-American male was not graduated until 1909, the first woman in 1964.

Many early graduates traveled as missionaries in China, Japan, Korea, and the Philippines, and encouraged foreign students to attend Cornell. Four Japanese-Americans detained in internment camps attended Cornell during World War II. The increase in minority population on campus began in the late 1950s.

Over the years, dominant features of student social and cultural life have changed. From 1853 to the 1920s, literary societies engaged Cornell's students in weekly oration, debates, lectures, or dramatic readings followed by lively socials. The first and oldest literary society in Iowa and possibly west of the Mississippi was the Amphictyon Literary Society, founded November 18, 1853. Women on campus could belong to the Aesthesian Literacy Society, originating in 1870. This association aimed to "elevate the mind and develop the talents." At one time there were as many as 20 societies chartered at Cornell, the last of which disbanded in 1927.

Students have found enjoyment in athletic pursuits since the early days of the college. After the Civil War, Congress authorized the detailing of regular military officers on college campuses. Military drill gave male students the opportunity to develop their "health, discipline, bearing and manners at comparatively small expense." The Spanish-American War drew officers away from the campus, but after the confilct ended, Cornell was reluctant to continue the military drill. President Kind reasoned that athletics provided more variety and were better suited to developing college spirit than military drill and could be more easily adapted to women.

Cornell athletes took part in all Olympic games between 1924 and 1964; eight Cornellians were members of Olympic wrestling teams. Cornell College won the National Collegiate (NCAA) and the National AAU championships in 1947, the smallest college as well as the only private college to do so.

Over the years, Cornell has manifested a close relationship with the town of Mt. Vernon. President Lincoln's call for volunteer soldiers early in the Civil War elicited the formation of three full companies and a large percentage of a fourth from Mt. Vernon. Almost every able male student enlisted in the Union army. Only two Cornellians fought for the South.

Cornell has gained national attention for its distinctive academic calendar featuring One Course-At-A-Time (OCAAT), instituted in 1978. Under this plan of study, students study one subject for a three-and-a-half-week term, followed by a four-day break. There are nine terms in an academic year that extends approximately from the beginning of September through May. Students must complete eight terms in one year. The ninth term can be used for travel, the pursuit of recreational or cultural activities, special study, or an additional course at no charge.

Cornell College graduates have made outstanding contributions in many fields. Among distinguished alumni are Leslie M. Shaw, governor of Iowa 1898–1902 and U.S. Secretary of the Treasury 1902–07; Raymond Asa Kent, president of the University of Louisville, 1929–43; Lee DuBridge, former president of the California Institute of Technology; Marjorie Holmes, author of inspirational poetry and fiction; James Daly, actor; Donald E. Fehrenbacher, Pulitzer Prize-winning historian; Nancy Price, author of *Sleeping with the Enemy*; and David Hilmers, astronaut.

Cornell College announced in October 1993 that it had raised over $63 million for its Program for Cornell College, which is based on a $20 million challenge grant made by Cornell trustee and graduate Richard Small and his wife Norma of Boca Raton, Florida. This challenge grant is the largest ever made to an Iowa undergraduate institution.

Cornell's motto *Deus Et Humanitas* (God and Humanity) was said to be Elder Bowman's personal credo, *Humanitas* being a "liberal education, humane and gentle conduct toward others, philanthropy, kindness, and politeness"—ideals to which Cornell College has been committed over the years.

Further Reading: The *Cornell College Catalogue 1994–96* (Mt. Vernon, Cornell College) has a brief but informative history of the college and its major buildings. Cornell's Home Page (http://www.cornell.edu) provides statistics and facts about the college and a self-guided tour of Cornell's historic campus. Profiles of two individuals prominent in Cornell's history, George Bryant Bowman and William Fletcher King, can be found in Pauline Grahame's "Elder Bowman," in *Palimpsest* 17 (1937) and King's own lengthy and detailed *Reminiscences* (New York: Abingdon Press, 1915). Early histories of Linn County, Mt. Vernon, and Cornell College can be found in *The History of Linn County, Iowa* (Chicago: Western Historical Company, 1878) and *History of Linn County, Iowa: From Its Earliest Settlement to the Present Time*, edited by Luther Albertus Brewer (Chicago: Pioneer Publishing, 1911).

—Kathleen M. Conley

CORNELL UNIVERSITY
(Ithaca, New York, U.S.A.)

Location: Ithaca, New York, 200 miles northwest of New York City.

Description: A comprehensive Ivy League university with a total enrollment of approximately 20,000 students, of whom 6,000 are pursuing graduate or medical degrees.

Information: Cornell University
410 Thurston Avenue
Ithaca, NY 14850-2488
U.S.A.
(607) 255-5241

The tale of Cornell University is a tale of two men, with two visions, who jointly founded one visionary university. Conflict between those two ideals (reflected in the fact that Cornell today is the only university to be both a private Ivy League institution as well as the recipient of a New York state land grant) as well as animosity from the established system, almost destroyed the fledgling institution. In the end, however, the commitment of the university's supporters endured, building what has become one of the world's most respected seats of learning.

The years following the American Civil War were a period of great optimism and progress in the northern United States. Much of the nation was changing from pioneer towns to cities with business and industry, with an explosion of financial opportunities for those astute enough to recognize them. Along with the development of business and industry came an interest in and appreciation of higher education. Sixty-nine land grant universities were established following passage of the Morrill Act in 1862. Those men and women lucky enough to have made their fortunes during these boom years often saw, more clearly than others, the need for practical education. They generously endowed private universities, or better yet, started one of their own. New England, especially, had its share of these friends of higher education—idealists with a distinctive brand of liberal-democratic philosophy. These men and women believed that man by nature is good, that history evidences progress, that science is a God-given tool for understanding the universe, that man's most basic duty is to help his fellow man, and that enlightenment will conquer poverty, disease, and superstition. In short, through education and cooperation, man could build an earthly paradise.

Such an idealist was Ezra Cornell. The eldest of 11 children born to a potter, Cornell enjoyed little formal education. The Puritan roots of his parents showed in him: he was rigid in outlook, dour, earnest, taciturn, and possessed of a strong work ethic. He left home at 19, eventually settling in Ithaca, New York. His skills in business and the mechanical arts evidenced themselves quickly. By the age of 23 he was managing a flour mill; at 24 he designed and executed an engineering marvel of the time—a tunnel through several hundred feet of solid rock above some falls near Ithaca, thereby supplying water for numerous factories below. In 1843 he met Francis Smith, part owner of Samuel Morse's patent for the telegraph, and impressed Smith by designing a machine that could rapidly lay wires underground. Cornell's subsequent involvement in the booming telegraph industry led to his becoming chief stockholder in the Western Union Telegraph company, with an accompanying worth of about $4 million. He was then elected to the state senate, where he met Andrew White.

Andrew D. White was born into a privileged family and, proving an eager and able student, hoped to enter Harvard or Yale. His father, however, dismayed at his son's abandonment of the family's Episcopalian faith, enrolled Andrew in the church-affiliated Geneva College in New York State at the age of 16. White was immediately advanced to the sophomore class, but he found the other students unmotivated and the classes undisciplined. The next year he feigned departure for Geneva but hid at a friend's house and prepared for entrance examinations at Yale. He passed easily.

Educationally, however, Yale proved to be another disappointment. White chafed at the set curriculum of classic languages and literatures, the educational method of reciting by rote, and the lack of any meaningful interaction between instructors and students. Following his graduation in 1853 he traveled extensively throughout Europe, and came home three years later one of the best educated men in the country. He was elected, in 1863, to the New York state senate, where he met Ezra Cornell.

White and Cornell did not initially become friendly. They shared the idealistic, egalitarian views of the liberal democrats of their era and an enthusiasm for science and higher learning, but little else. Cornell was brusque and self-righteous, an unpolished, self-made man with little use for aesthetics or frivolities. He had, for some time, envisioned a university dedicated to applied science, an institution that would help mankind solve the problems of agriculture and engineering, and usher in the glorious new age of progress and prosperity. At his university, the

Cornell University

benefits of this higher education would not be limited to the sons of the well-to-do. He saw clearly the need for technological education for the masses. He had, however, no patience with idlers. Solving his problems through trial and error, he had worked his way to the top. His university would be available to all—men and women, rich and poor—but it would not be free. Their education would be paid for through manual labor on the part of the students themselves.

White, on the other hand, had endured his college years by dreaming of building an American university that would rival the beautiful architecture and bountiful libraries of the great European institutions. His institution would be free of any specific religious influence and would offer a superior education, promoting intellectual discourse between students and faculty and allowing students the freedom to explore their intellectual interests. He spurned the traditional concept of the university, which was to transmit, rather than increase, knowledge, and which was only intended to serve society's elite. He dreamt of a university that would teach "truth for truth's sake," where students could choose their own curriculum.

Fate threw Ezra Cornell and Andrew White together. Both men were elected to the state senate in the fall of 1863. Cornell was appointed chairman of the committee on agriculture; White became chairman of the committee which oversaw education. Cornell had recently presented the town of Ithaca with a public library; as chair of the committee on literature, White was involved in approving its incorporation. The generosity of the gift, and Cornell's arrangement for its administration, impressed White. In choosing a board of trustees, Cornell had included political enemies as well as allies and pastors of both Protestant and Catholic churches.

The Morrill Land Grant Act had just been enacted and several existing New York colleges lobbied earnestly for the promised funds. When, in 1864, Ezra Cornell initiated a bill calling for splitting the land grant money equally between the two of them, White buried the bill and bided his time, ostensibly committed to keeping the money together. Meanwhile, however, Cornell had made the decision to commit $300,000 to do whatever "shall do the greatest good to the greatest number of the industrial classes of my native state." He summoned White to a meeting of the trustees of one of the spurned colleges at which the demise of the institution, due to lack of the hoped-for funds, was expected to be announced. Cornell offered to donate a 300-acre farm and $300,000 to the college if it would relocate to Ithaca. White countered with an offer of his own. If Cornell and his supporters would apply for the whole grant, and add to it the farm and the $300,000, White would approve that request wholeheartedly.

Thus was the university conceived. A few months later White introduced the formal bill into the state senate proposing the establishment, at Ithaca, of Cornell University. The purpose of the university was to be "the cultivation of arts and sciences and literature, and the instruction in agriculture, the mechanic arts and military tactics, and in all knowledge," with the stipulation that the university be controlled by no religious sect, that the institution would receive the Morrill Act money and Ezra Cornell's endowment of $500,000 (he had since increased his pledge), and, each year, that one student from each state assembly should receive a full scholarship.

Immediately the plans were attacked from all sides. The already-established colleges in New York, having hoped for a portion of the Morrill Act monies, sent agents to Albany to lobby against the bill's passage. (They also encouraged media vilification of the "godless" university.) Some accused Ezra Cornell, already a rich man, of attempting to increase his fortune. Cornell refused to enter the battle, writing to his son that "I shall not go into fits to induce the State to accept $500,000 of my money," and telling White during one senate session, "If I could think of any other way in which half a million dollars would do as much good to the State, I would give the legislators no more trouble." In fact, at one point, he threatened to give the money to Harvard. Eventually, however, opposing forces were exhausted or appeased, and on April 27, 1865, the governor signed the bill that created Cornell University.

Cornell and White promptly set about turning their dreams into reality. They quickly reached an informal agreement on respective responsibilities: White handled the educational plans; Cornell managed the finances and facilities. Cornell went west to locate Morrill Act lands. (If no federal public lands existed within a state, the state was given land scrip in the amount they were entititled to, to buy lands in other states. Cornell's share amounted to half a million acres.)

White devoted himself to writing by-laws. Mindful of the requirements of the Morrill Act (and Cornell's aspirations) that the money be devoted to education in the agricultural and mechanical arts, still committed to establishing an oasis of intellectual stimulation and freedom, and in agreement with Cornell's stated desire (and now the university's motto) to "found an institution where any person can find instruction in any study," White established the early hallmarks of Cornell University—a broad curriculum, an elective course of study, a system of young and enthusiastic resident professors, supplemented by some of the world's most eminent thinkers and scholars as visiting lecturers, and a require-

ment for physical training and manual labor (but no other code of student discipline). Since these attributes were, for the most part, a radical departure from the universities of the day, considerable attention was paid to the embryonic college at Ithaca. (Over 2,000 letters were received in response to a single letter Cornell wrote to *The New York Tribune,* explaining that students could work their way through the university doing farm or factory labor.)

White was elected the first president of Cornell University. He scoured American universities for ideas and for brilliant young men to serve on the faculty; he then departed for Europe to outfit the institution he envisioned, purchasing chemicals, microscopes, laboratory equipment, pictures, statues, scientific collections, and trunks and trunks of books. He returned with a few more professors as well. Ezra Cornell, at home, supervised construction of the buildings and supplied the rooms with furniture and chalkboards. On October 7, 1868, the university celebrated its Inauguration Day, with 412 men passing entrance examinations. Women were to be admitted as soon as appropriate accommodations could be arranged.

The fledgling university continued to receive considerable attention, much of it negative because of its implication that it was superior to existing universities, its nonsectarian status, its lay president, and a host of disgruntled political opponents of Cornell and White. The attention of those early years, however, brought some students (and faculty) to Cornell from as far away as Japan, drawn by its egalitarian stance or its innovative ideals. For the students, the early years were rugged but rewarding. Classes were seriously overcrowded; classroom temperatures were sometimes as low as 40 degrees. Dissections were performed in the furnace room. On the other hand, faculty-to-student ratios were enviable, and students were free to pursue their own intellectual interests. Courses were offered in the traditional classics, as well as non-traditional subjects. Early bulletins offered courses in not only French, German, Spanish, and Japanese languages, but Mantchoo, Sanskrit, Turkish, and Tartar as well. Cornell awarded its first degrees in veterinary medicine and journalism and the first P.h.D.s in electrical and industrial engineering. It established the first four-year schools of hotel administration and industrial and labor relations. It endowed the first chairs in American literature and American history; it established the first departments of economic entomology and of architecture.

Reality, however, took its toll on the founders' dreams. White's lofty dreams of a campus full of architectural wonders fell to the reality of a limited budget. Student behavior forced the gradual addition of a student code. The chaotic accumulation by many students of unrelated courses prompted more structured, although still flexible, curricula. The work-study program proved unworkable for most students and gradually died out. Faculty members who had initially accepted abysmally low salaries for the thrill of being part of the new university began demanding increases. In truth, by the mid-1870s, the university's finances were desperate, exacerbated by the fact that the country was in the throes of an economic depression. The land scrip was being held in the hopes that land prices would recover, the original endowments had been spent on facilities, and at some points the treasury was so empty that faculty salaries could not be met.

The university's burdens were compounded by the fact that Andrew White, being more a dreamer than an administrator, had tired of the day-to-day struggles of actually running Cornell and had gone abroad. The trustees, and Vice President Russel, struggled to keep the university functioning, but faculty unrest grew and enrollment dropped from a high of 561 to 384. Russel was not liked by the faculty and was publicly perceived as hostile to religion. Pressure from the public, the faculty, and Russel's enemies among the trustees eventually resulted in his dismissal. The controversy, however, forced President White to come home.

Ironically, White's return coincided precisely with the onset of a scandal. Jennie McGraw (donor of the famous carillon that has rung out over Cornell's campus since its inauguration) was the unmarried daughter of an early, wealthy benefactor of Cornell, John McGraw. She inherited his sizable estate upon his death in 1877. Although McGraw was nearly 40 and suffered from tuberculosis, Willard Fiske, a professor at Cornell, courted her and wed her, amid rumors that White encouraged the match in order to bring her fortune to the university.

McGraw died two months after the marriage and indeed left the bulk of her money to the university. Mr. Fiske, however, having been advised that there were legal problems with the university's claim and, apparently feeling used, filed his own claim to the money. The Great Will Case, as it came to be called, drew Cornell again into the national limelight. Although Fiske won, only the lawyers involved really profited. And although the university lost the case, a minor ruling, stating that its endowment funds could be used for any purpose, effectively put the university back on solid ground. Other friends of the university stepped in to build the library McGraw had promised in her will. Moreover, White was back in the president's office, overseeing the fruition of his lifelong dream. Cornell again prospered.

One of the nation's largest universities on its day of inauguration, by 1909 Cornell's enrollment was second only to that of Columbia University, whose president wrote that Columbia's growth had ceased, "unless it shall . . . modify its plan of instruction in a more or less distant imitation of . . . Cornell University." Columbia was not the only college to notice Cornell's success. Slowly but steadily, private and public American universities adopted many of Cornell's once radical features. Cornell could no longer protest the archaic and elitist nature of the older universities—through Cornell's influence, it had disappeared. The Cornell Idea had become the Cornell Tradition.

Cornell continued to grow, doubling enrollment in the first decade of the new century, finally reaching in 1913 Ezra Cornell's dream of 5,000 students (which few believed would ever be realized). The events of the new century, however—two world wars with a long and difficult economic depression sandwiched in between—shook the philosophical foundation on which Cornell and White had built their dream. The inherent goodness of man was now eminently suspect, science alone had proven desperately inadequate for world prosperity, technology had been all too easily appropriated for warfare, and the earthly paradise that those idealists had imagined as just around the corner seemed now exceedingly removed.

Cornell University, however, survived. And although inevitably changed by world events, the university's commitment remained to Ezra Cornell and Andrew White's dream of a place where students could pursue their own interests, where learning was used to benefit mankind, and where "any person can find instruction in any study." Jacob Schurman, who led Cornell into the 20th century, wrote that "a People's University, if it is true to the spirit of our age, must hold all subjects equally reputable, and provide instruction in all alike . . . The analysis of soils is as important as the analysis of literature . . . In God's universe there is nothing common or unclean, and whatever is known about it must have a place in the curriculum." Under that philosophical umbrella, Cornell added schools of forestry, medicine, and veterinary medicine, as well as programs in city planning, aerial engineering, and most controversially, home economics (at which Eleanor Roosevelt was a regular speaker).

A natural outgrowth of Cornell's commitment to practical application of scholarly instruction was the establishment, in 1992, of the nation's first collegiate program in hospitality management, later to become the School of Hotel Administration. The Hotel School offered a curriculum designed to supplement a general education with management training with a service industry focus. Although the first class consisted of only 21 students, the school met a need and, fostered by the hotel industry, interested students soon strained the school's resources. Even during the height of the lean Depression years, the Hotel School still placed all of its graduates in jobs.

The Hotel School today is an embodiment of the Cornell philosophy. Within the Hotel School alone there are nine different majors and over 150 different courses. The school is a living lab, as the school's students run the prestigious Statler Hotel, including three restaurants and a full banquet service. Students learn every facet of the hospitality industry, from acting as intern housekeepers to launching a virtual restaurant chain. The Hotel School maintains a close relationship with the industry, facilitating field trips and co-op arrangments that immerse students in the real world of hospitality and service. In addition, the Hotel School boasts the most comprehensive library of hospitality resource materials in the world.

The site on which Ezra Cornell chose to build—a hill overlooking the Cayuga Lake valley, in an area surrounded by natural gorges and waterfalls—makes the Ithaca campus one of the great natural beauty. But students today, as students in Cornell's time, are not drawn simply for beauty. Interdisciplinary study is still a Cornell hallmark, as is an emphasis on undergraduate education. (Nobel laureates can be found teaching introductory courses.) Students come from every state and over 100 countries to choose from over 4,000 courses, including 50 languages, making Cornell's wish to found "an institution where any person can find instruction in any study" an attainable goal. Cornell remains true, as well, to the founding dreams of Andrew White, who envisioned a school where students would be motivated by their own intellectual fervor. Emily Dunning Barringer, a graduate of the class of 1897 and the first female American ambulance surgeon, wrote: "We were . . . a whole community of people making tradition. Here was an institution dedicated to mental freedom. That is Cornell's greatest gift to its sons and daughters."

Further Reading: Three publications cover Cornell's history: Morris Bishop's *Early Cornell, 1865–1900* (Ithaca, New York: Cornell University Press, 1962) and *A History of Cornell* (Ithaca, New York: Cornell University Press, 1962); and Waterman T. Hewett's *Cornell University, A History* (New York: The University Publishing Society, 1902).

—Wendy Sowder Wippel

DARTMOUTH COLLEGE
(Hanover, New Hampshire, U.S.A.)

Location: In Hanover, approximately 120 miles northwest of Boston, Massachusetts.

Description: A private liberal arts college enrolling approximately 4,000 undergraduate students. Dartmouth also has graduate programs in business, engineering, medicine, and 18 academic disciplines.

Information: Office of Public Affairs
Dartmouth College
Hanover, NH 03755
U.S.A.
(603) 646-1110

The roots of Dartmouth College can be traced to the unlikely source of Moor's Indian Charity School, founded in 1754 at Lebanon, Connecticut, by the Reverend Eleazor Wheelock, a Congregational minister educated at Yale. Frustrated by a lack of support for his project and a scarcity of Native American pupils, Wheelock determined to move the institution to the province of New Hampshire, where authorities had offered him land and support. Wheelock eventually drafted a charter for a new school, and New Hampshire governor John Wentworth then submitted it for the approval of the authorities in Great Britain. On December 13, 1769, King George III officially sanctioned an institution

> for the education and instruction of Youth of the Indian Tribes in this Land in reading, writing, and all other parts of Learning which shall appear necessary and expedient for civilizing and Christianizing Children of Pagans as well as in all liberal arts and sciences and also of English Youth and any others.

Wentworth significantly amended the charter drafted by Wheelock. He dismissed the proposal to name the school Wentworth and instead suggested that it be named Dartmouth in honor of William Legge, the Earl of Dartmouth, who was secretary of state for the colonies, and both benefactor and trustee of the school. More importantly, Wentworth incorporated the institution as a college, rather than a school or academy, as suggested by Wheelock, and he removed a proposal to have a coordinate board of trustees in Great Britain. Notably, the charter also specified that the college would be nondenominational at a time when most colleges and universities were sponsored by churches.

In 1770, Wheelock traveled up the Connecticut River, deep into territory stilll settled by Native Americans, in search of a site for the college. He chose 3,300 acres centered in Hanover, and there erected a single log hut to house the college. The trustees elected Wheelock president, and that year he ran the school with the assistance of just one other man, Bezaleel Wood, a fellow graduate of Yale. The college's location was remote; Governor Wentworth traveled to the commencement ceremony of 1771 via a single trail cut into the virgin forest specifically for the occasion, and President Wheelock chose for the school motto, *Vox Clamantis in Deserto*, "The Voice of One Crying in the Wilderness." Among the four students graduated in the first class was John Wheelock, son of Eleazor, who was elected the second president of Dartmouth when his father died in 1779.

The Continental Congress awarded Dartmouth funds during and after the American Revolutionary War as a reward for conciliating Canadian Indians, and so the college grew quickly in size and stature. Dartmouth Hall and College Chapel were completed by 1791, and 49 men were graduated that same year. In 1797, Dartmouth opened a medical school, the fourth in the country, under the direction of Dr. Nathan Smith, a physician and surgeon of excellent reputation. Daniel Webster was graduated with the class of 1801 and went on to become a powerful congressman who backed President Lincoln throughout the Civil War. Six years later, Sylvanus Thayer was graduated; he later organized the United States Military Academy and the Thayer School of Civil Engineering at Dartmouth.

Dartmouth was literally divided by a power struggle between the trustees and Wheelock, who was forced out of office in 1815, and immediately replaced by Reverend Francis Brown, of the class of 1805. The following year, Wheelock persuaded the New Hampshire legislature to declare the institution public, to change its name to Dartmouth University, and to select a new board of trustees. When the college's trustees refused to relinquish power, authorities of the university forcefully seized the chapel, libraries, and museum. The college survived on funds provided by John B. Wheeler, a wealthy New Hampshire merchant and farmer, and for a short while the two corporations existed side-by-side; in August 1818, the college graduated 30 students, and the university eight.

Meanwhile, the trustees of the college had filed suit in the Court of Common Pleas, Grafton County, New Hampshire, and eventually appealed their case to the United States Supreme Court. On October 10, 1818, Webster, assisted by Joseph Hopkinson, forcefully argued for the right of Dartmouth to retain its independence from the

Dartmouth College

state, and on February 2, 1819, Chief Justice John Marshall announced the court's decision in favor of the college. The university was dissolved immediately, and the college reunified. The spring term opened with 150 undergraduates. Webster received fulsome praise at the especially festive commencement ceremony held that summer.

Nearly a decade of ephemeral presidents passed between the death of Brown in 1820 and the election of Reverend Nathan Lord, the college's sixth president, in 1828. Lord's principal achievements were financial; he raised $30,000 by the late 1830s, thus bringing the college out of debt for the first time since the War of Independence. By the time of his departure during the Civil War, the college's assets exceeded $200,000. The town of Hanover and Dartmouth College evolved gradually during the same period, as marked by the establishment at the college of the first national chapter of a Greek letter soci-

ety in 1842, and the opening of a railroad station in Norwich, just across the river from Hanover, two years later.

The citizens of Hanover were staunchly Unionist, and 652 Dartmouth alumni and undergraduates joined the Union forces when the Civil War began, the highest percentage of men associated with any Northern school. However, President Lord published several pamphlets on the divine right of slavery, and public resentment of him and his opinions mounted as sons of Hanover and the college lost their lives battling the Confederacy. Lord resigned in 1863, and the trustees elected Reverend Asa Dodge Smith, of the class of 1830, to succeed him as the seventh president of Dartmouth.

Dartmouth evolved into a modern and complex institution between Smith's election and World War I. Elective courses were added in 1869, and their number increased in 1882; the Latin Scientific Course, leading to the degree of

Bachelor of Laws, was added in 1879; the formerly independent Chandler School of Science and Arts, founded in 1851, was incorporated into the college in 1892; and the Tuck School of Administration and Finance was organized in 1900. The college plant, which for several decades lagged behind the academic development of Dartmouth, was rapidly improved around the turn of the century. By 1909, there were 35 buildings on campus, with a combined value of more than $1.3 million, and the endowment had reached nearly $3 million. During the same period, student enrollment jumped from under 200 to 1,107, and the number of college officers rose to 107.

The Industrial Revolution and the rise of modern science at the end of the nineteenth century brought rapid changes in American society, which were reflected in changes within the academy. The increasing number of professions was paralleled by a proliferation of specialized courses and graduate programs, and the success of German research universities spurred educational institutions in America to devote ever greater proportions of their resources to seminal science. The undergraduate college and the classical curriculum of the nineteenth century were not only eclipsed by these developments, they were threatened with extinction. The presidents of Stanford and Columbia Universities both predicted that the college would disappear from the American academy in practice, if not in name. Dartmouth was put in a particularly difficult position by these changes, for it could neither afford to ignore them, nor did it have the size or resources to keep pace with such immense institutions as Harvard and Columbia.

Ernest Martin Hopkins, of the class of 1901, was inaugurated as the 11th president of the college in 1916, and during his tenure of 29 years, he fought doggedly to maintain the centrality of the humanities at Dartmouth and of the liberal arts college in general, despite the transformation of the American academy. Hopkins' traditional ideas about education were somewhat surprising given his background. He was the first head of the school who was neither a clergyman nor an academic. Hopkins was a business executive with AT&T whose ties to the college since graduation were limited to his founding of the alumni council and editing of the alumni magazine. Despite his background, Hopkins held firmly to the notion that a college education should be designed to produce men of good character and broad intelligence, not specialized intellectuals or prepared professionals.

While the administrators of most American universities began to employ faculty members based solely on their scholarly reputations and their ability to produce original research, Hopkins assembled a faculty of qualified men devoted to teaching. Contrary to the spirit of the times, Hopkins held that a Ph.D. "tends to unfit a man for teaching," and he hired many men who had not yet completed graduate school, "before [they have] become wholly permeated by its ideals and subject to influences antagonistic to the college purpose." For example, the name plate beneath a portrait of David Lambuth, which hangs in the college's Sanborn House, identifies him as a "Teacher of English at Dartmouth," not a professor. On the same note, a student memoir from the Hopkins era describes Lewis Dayton Stilwell, a history teacher who led provocative discussions both inside and outside of class, as having dismissed a suggestion that he publish his ideas with the remark, "[Maybe] after I have retired for a while. Right now I am working on a new lecture I think the guys will like."

The atmosphere and institutional character of Dartmouth were also deeply affected by Hopkins' devotion to the liberal exchange of ideas. At the height of the Red Scare of the 1920s, he allowed William Z. Foster, a prominent American Communist, to speak on campus, and he condemned raids against American leftists. A more famous incident, which drew the ire of alumni and the attention of the national press, involved Hopkins' defense of a politically controversial mural painted in the reading room of the Baker Library by the Mexican artist, Jose Clemente Orozco, whose leftists views were public knowledge. The mural, which covers 3,000 square feet, and which was completed in 1934, depicted the glory of pre-Columbian Aztec culture and the horrors of brutal colonization. When the National Commission to Advance American Art and the Daughters of the American Revolution criticized Hopkins and the mural, he responded, "I had not supposed that art was restricted by race or time, and I do not think that it is." Hopkins stood firm against his many opponents, even refusing Orozco's offer to alter the mural.

The Hopkins era was also a time of ostensible growth at Dartmouth, fueled by the financial prosperity of the nation that followed World War I. During the 1920s, Hopkins more than tripled the budget for instruction, and he orchestrated diverse building projects that greatly improved the plant. The Baker Memorial Library was completed in 1928, and was soon well stocked, thanks to the Sanborn Library Fund of $1 million, which was made available the following year. Among the many other buildings completed during the same period were six new dormitories, the Sanborn English House, the Carpenter Fine Arts Building, the new Tuck School unit, and Dick's House, Dartmouth's infirmary.

John Sloan Dickey succeeded Hopkins as president of Dartmouth in the fall of 1945, and within ten years he began the transformation of the college into a research university, the move which Hopkins had so long resisted. The faculty that Hopkins had assembled in the 1920s was aging, and nearly half of Dartmouth's instructors retired between 1954 and 1966. As positions were made available, President Dickey filled them with scholars with modern views. A prominent example of the new generation of instructors at the college was John Kemeny, later elected president of Dartmouth; he was hired in 1952 to head the mathematics department when he was just 27 years old.

While Kemeny proved to be a teacher and administrator of ability commensurate with the international reputation he achieved as a scholar, it is indicative of Dickey's administration that Kemeny was given a powerful position based exclusively on the outstanding reputation he had established as a graduate student at Princeton.

A portrait of Dartmouth students, based on a 1955 report by faculty members under the auspices of the American Association of University Professors, was not an attractive one. The report said:

> There prevails among many undergraduates on this campus an intellectual apathy, a negative attitude hardly to be dignified by the term anti-intellectualism. Deep-seated indifference, casual unpreparedness, and habitual absenteeism are among the symptoms. Few of our students ever do any academic work beyond the prescribed minimum.

In the 1950s and 1960s, the curriculum at Dartmouth came more nearly into line with the programs at most research universities, when its departments organized courses in such specialized subjects as international relations, Chinese language, city planning, and Latin American studies. In addition, the administration initiated an "independent reading program" in 1958, although it survived just ten years. Students were to choose from among great books, such as Plato's *Dialogues,* Chaucer's *Canterbury Tales,* etc. and were to read these works in their leisure time but with limited, if any, faculty guidance. Provost Donald Morrison voiced the suspicion that the focus of college education would be "shifted from teaching to learning, and [that] colleges [would] begin to think of their task as one of *enabling students to learn without being taught.*" The historian Charles Sykes suggests that the reading program—which was advertised as a means of reinvigorating undergraduate education at a time when the emphasis on research at American universities was drawing public concern—was actually a means of reducing the number of hours that instructors were required to be in the classroom. Thus, Sykes interprets the development as symbolic of the trend at Dartmouth and other schools to appease and retain reputable scholars at the sacrifice of student concerns.

Sykes sees a certain cynicism in the administration's willingness to leave the students on their own in the reading program:

> the notion of transferring responsibility to students was somewhat undermined by the administration's knowledge that student motivation was one of the chief problems at Dartmouth. Without a blush, administrators now had to extol the sagacity of the very students they had derided not only as anti-intellectual, but as apathetic, unprepared, and often absent.

Sykes also interprets the student unrest at Dartmouth of the late 1960s and early 1970s as a response to a feeling of neglect and disenfranchisement within the college, combined with the more commonly noted social and political concerns that sparked protests across the United States during the same period. However, the ostensible causes of the student movement at Dartmouth were indeed racial and political, not academic. The Students for a Democratic Society (SDS) organized protests against the Reserve Officers Training Corps (ROTC) at Dartmouth, as at other schools, because they opposed the implied complicity of the college in the Vietnam War. At the same time, Dartmouth's Afro-American Society demanded such racially specific actions as the hiring of black administrators, and the organization of a Black Studies program.

The most serious act of student rebellion at Dartmouth was the occupation of the administrative offices in Packhurst Hall by the SDS, beginning at approximately 3:15 P.M. on May 6, 1969. Later that day, Grafton County Sheriff Herbert Ash announced through a bullhorn that the students were legally bound, by an injunction hastily issued by a local judge, to vacate the building. Most of the students remained steadfast. Police from New Hampshire and Vermont were called in to remove the students by force if necessary, and at approximately 3 A.M., on May 7, they broke through the front doors and arrested 54 people, including 40 Dartmouth students, none of whom resisted. Forty-five of the protesters were sentenced to 30 days in jail, which was an unusually harsh punishment for nonviolent protesters at that time.

Professor of Mathematics John Kemeny was elected Dartmouth's 13th president in January 1970. He restored peace to the campus by siding with the protesters on most issues. Kemeny's stand was surprising, for, in 1969, he had urged stern punishment of SDS members who blocked army recruiters from their offices at Dartmouth, and in that same year he had opposed a denunciation of the war in Vietnam that was circulated by the faculty on the grounds that schools should remain apolitical. Yet when students organized a general strike at Dartmouth to protest the incursion of U.S. troops into Cambodia, Kemeny joined them. He canceled all classes scheduled for May 5 through the 10th, declaring in a radio broadcast, "There comes a time when there are priorities over and beyond that which we have traditionally considered the fundamental purpose of the institution."

Kemeny expressed his social consciousness in other ways during his tenure. For example, he successfully orchestrated the admission of women to Dartmouth, beginning with the class of 1976. In order to accommodate approximately 1,000 women without displacing any of the 3,000 men enrolled in the college, Kemeny instituted what became known as the "D-plan," a year-round academic calendar. Thus Dartmouth was able to substantially increase student enrollment without having to hire new faculty or raise new buildings. Kemeny also called for the reintroduction of a curriculum centered around the liberal arts, which, he declared, "still seems the best hope of returning our civilization to fundamental principles of morality"; however, he was unsuccessful in his attempts to stem the tide of specialization.

David McLaughlin, an outstanding graduate of the class of 1954, succeeded Kemeny as president of Dartmouth in 1982, having served on the school's board of trustees for 11 years. Despite his close ties to the college, McLaughlin was an unlikely candidate for the presidency, and his election rankled many members of the faculty. McLaughlin was an industrialist who brilliantly oversaw the 1970s expansion of Toro, a company that builds lawn-mowers, snow-blowers, and similar equipment. His background in business was not a sufficient preparation for his duties as president of the college, however. For example, he showed little understanding of the pressing issue of curriculum development felt acutely at Dartmouth; in his inaugural speech, he naively stated that Dartmouth had never wavered from Eleazor Wheelock's ideal of a liberal arts education. McLaughlin resigned in 1986, having been widely perceived as an ineffective leader, despite his considerable financial accomplishments and the introduction of a sorely needed new building program.

The trustees elected James O. Freedman, Dartmouth's 15th president in 1987, having been impressed by his previous success as the president of the University of Iowa. In October 1988, Freedman publicly declared that Dartmouth must recognize its identity as a university, despite its title, and devote its resources to research and expansion. In his first two years in office, Freedman modestly increased the size of the faculty, and helped to secure a 20 percent increase in research grants flowing into the school.

Freedman did not escape a controversy which had begun before his arrival. In 1980, the *Dartmouth Review,* a privately funded newspaper staffed by students, began publication. In 1983, the paper sent a reporter to the class of a black professor of music, William Cole, and subsequently published a negative evaluation of his classroom performance. Though Cole then suspended his classes, he said, until he received an apology from the reporter, he was reprimanded later only for banging on the reporter's dormitory room door late at night. Five years later, the *Dartmouth Review* once again questioned Cole's teaching abilities. The controversy resulted in Freedman's stating that the *Review*'s reporters were not covered by the First Amendment's protection of freedom of the press. *The Wall Street Journal* quoted a news release from Dartmouth's administration calling the *Review* "sexist, racist and homophobic," but it went on to editorialize that "We suspect the students' true crime was presuming to assess scholarship at their college."

Although Dartmouth is known for its undergraduate education, it has offered post-baccalaureate degrees for over a century. It conferred its first Ph.D. degree to a candidate in the classics department in 1885, but a doctoral program in the modern sense did not appear until 1960, when the college authorized the development of a Ph.D. program in the medical school, a move which led to an interdisciplinary doctoral program in molecular biology. Shortly thereafter, departmental programs in mathematics and physics were authorized, and since that time doctoral graduate study has been undertaken by all departments in the sciences and in psychology.

Further Reading: A well-written but tediously detailed history of Dartmouth from its beginnings through the 1920s can be found in the two-volume collection, *History of Dartmouth College* by Leon Burr Richardson (Hanover, New Hampshire: Dartmouth College, 1932). An abridgment of the same information is available in "A Description of Dartmouth College," in *The Dartmouth College Bulletin* (Hanover, volume 1, number 5, 1936). The development of Dartmouth into a university since 1920 is carefully analyzed in the provocative book *The Hollow Men: Politics and Corruption in Higher Education* by Charles J. Sykes (Washington, D.C.: Regnery Gateway, 1990).

—Christopher Hoyt

DOSHISHA UNIVERSITY
(Kyoto, Japan)

Location: On two campuses, at Imadegawa (in the city of Kyoto) and Tanabe (also in Kyoto Prefecture).

Description: A private Christian university that originated as an English school in 1875; the first university in Japan to admit women students; now, with around 22,000 students, one of the largest and most prestigious universities in the country, linked with a women's college and a number of schools for younger students.

Information: International Center
Doshisha University
Imadegawa-dori Karasma-Higashiiru
Kamigyo-ku, Kyoto 602
Japan
(75) 251 3260

Doshisha University (*Doshisha Daigaku*) is the largest and best-known of a group of educational institutions, privately owned by the Doshisha Board of Trustees, which offer courses based on Christian principles, from kindergarten to postgraduate research, at four sites in Kyoto Prefecture. All these bodies trace their origins to a small English-language school, the Doshisha Eigakko, founded in Kyoto in 1875 by Niijima Jo. Niijima's extraordinary career spanned the years when Japan was first transformed by modernisation along western lines, and his outlook still influences the university and its associated schools. Niijima was born (as Niijima Shimeta) in Edo (now Tokyo) in 1843. At that date, the city was the headquarters of the hereditary Tokugawa shogunate, which had ruled Japan since 1603 in the name of the powerless emperor, then still resident in Kyoto, and in alliance with provincial *daimyo* (lords), one of whom employed Niijima's father as a secretary. During Niijima's childhood this traditional hierarchy increasingly came under threat, first from the pressures of the United States and European powers, which succeeded in opening Japan to trade and communciation with the west, then by traditionalists who resented the shogunate's apparent weakness in the face of such pressures. Growing up into a newly turbulent and confused society, Niijima studied at the shogunate's naval academy, where the curriculum included "Dutch studies" (that is, studies of western thought through the medium of the European language then best known in Japan), and was deeply impressed by two western phenomena in particular, a

Dutch ship which he saw in 1860, and extracts from the Bible, which he read in a Chinese translation.

Even though overseas travel was still forbidden, in July 1864 Niijima boarded a U.S. ship, the *Berlin,* at Hakodate, one of the few ports open to foreign trade, and transferred at Shanghai to the *Wild Rover,* on which he served as a cabin boy. After arriving in Boston, Massachusetts, in July 1865, he was sponsored by Alpheus Hardy, the ship's owner, as a student at Phillips Academy, Andover, between October 1865 and June 1867. He converted to Christianity in December 1866. By adopting a religion which was then still illegal in Japan, he signaled his final break with national traditions and began his career as an advocate of internationalist and humanist principles.

Niijima went on to study philosophy and geology at Amherst College from October 1867 until he was graduated in 1870, the first Japanese person ever to earn a degree from a western university. After studying at Andover Theological College between October 1870 and June 1874, he became the first Japanese to be ordained as a Protestant minister, joining the Congregational Church (now the United Church of Christ). He was known at that time as Joseph Hardy Neesima and dressed in western clothing. Yet events were to show that he had by no means abandoned his commitment to his native country, where the shogunate had been overthrown in 1868 by a regime that sought to combine carefully controlled reforms, such as permitting Christian worship and introducing western industrial and administrative practices, with a revival of national culture.

During 1872 Niijima had been employed as an interpreter by Tanaka Fujimaro, who was investigating American and European educational systems as a member of the Japanese government's Iwakura Mission. However, rather than join hundreds of other Japanese of his age and background in working directly for the state, Niijima preferred to retain his independence and his international connections. He received $5,000 in donations through the Congregational Mission Board, meeting in Rutland, Vermont, in October 1874, and then returned to Japan, after an absence of ten years, in the following month. His intention was to establish a school offering instruction in English and in Christianity at Osaka, a plan supported by the government minister Kido Takayoshi, among other notables, but the hostility of that city's administration forced him to turn to Kyoto instead. In spite of Kyoto's historic status as the imperial capital (up to 1868) and as the center of Japanese Buddhism, he received valuable support from Yamamoto Kakuma, chair of the Kyoto prefectural assembly (whose sister he married in January 1876).

The Doshisha Eigakko opened in November 1875. "Doshisha," coined by Niijima from three Chinese characters, literally means "same-purpose-association"; "Eigakko" means "English School." This was perhaps an ambitious designation for what began as a class of eight students learning the language under two teachers, Niijima himself and an American missionary, Jerome D. Davis. In April 1876, they were joined by Dr. Dwight Whitney Learned, a Yale graduate, and in September they moved the school to the Imadegawa site that is still the center of Doshisha activities. This second Eigakko, which began with just two small buildings for teaching, next to a dining hall, included among its first intake most of the members of the so-called "Kumamoto Band" of 35 Christian converts. These were students from the city of that name in Kyushu, who had studied English and Christianity under Captain Leroy Lansing Janes and other Americans until the closure of their Yogakko, or School of Western Studies, earlier in 1876 under pressure from local traditionalists.

Whether or not Niijima intended it as a deliberate riposte to such opponents, he must have known that his opening of a sister institution, officially recognised as Doshisha Jogakko, or Women's School, in April 1877, would cause controversy in a country where women had traditionally been prevented from studying outside the home. The school's growing reputation was further enhanced during 1878, when Learned gave the first lectures in economic theory ever heard in Japan. During the remaining 12 years of his life, Niijima maintained a consistent policy of expanding his school and making innovations in its curriculum at the same time as seeking official recognition and social respectability for its activities. In February 1883 the two schools were incorporated within the Doshisha trust, with Niijima as its president; in September 1884 Doshisha's first brick building was completed—it is now used by one of the junior high schools associated with the university and is protected as an Important Cultural Property. The university chapel followed in June 1886 and its library in November 1886 (both are also now Important Cultural Properties). In November 1888 Niijima launched his campaign for university status, with financial assistance from alumni and from some local and national politicians, and in July 1890 the Harris Rikagakko, or school of science, was opened with funding of $10,000 from an American businessman, J.N. Harris (in yet another brick building which is now an Important Cultural Property).

Niijima died in January 1890, his hopes for university status for the school unfulfilled, but his own reputation as an educational pioneer secured. The importance of individual self-fulfillment, combined with commitment to social activism, which he and his American colleagues had tried to instill in their students, was to have its greatest impact on Japan in the generation following Niijima's, as Doshisha graduates, members of a very small elite of Japanese who had experienced higher education, rose to prominence in a variety of professions. Abe Isoo, for example, one of the Kumamoto Band, became a founding member of Japan's first Socialist party in 1901, and he was later a campaigner against war and militarism and a prominent adviser to the nascent labor movement. More conventionally, Ukita Kazutami, another member of the band, taught at Doshisha itself between 1894 and 1897 before becoming a teacher of political theory at what is now Waseda University in Tokyo; he was a major influence in the brief period of constitutional liberal politics known as "Taisho Democracy" between 1912 and 1926.

Of all the Kumamoto Band, the best known, outside the rather narrow circles of Japanese Christians (who still number less than 1 percent of the population), are probably the Tokutomi brokers, Iichiro, whose pen name was Tokutomi Soho, and Kenjiro, who wrote as Tokutomi Roka. During his long career as a publisher, magazine editor, and historian, Soho moved from a position favoring liberal democracy for Japan to support for militarism and nationalism, starting out as a popular radical journalist and ending up banned from public life during the U.S. occupation. Roka, by contrast, was among the first Japanese writers to seek personal expression through writing serious fiction; he became notorious both for publicly rejecting his older brother's traditional authority over him, and later for visiting the Russian writer Tolstoy and then trying to create a utopian community based on his anarchist principles. Both brothers abandoned the conventional Christianity they had taken up in Kumamoto, yet both retained in their divergent careers a commitment to public affairs and a self-confidence in asserting their views, which might well not have been encouraged or developed in any other Japanese educational institution of the time.

Yet another Kumamoto student, Kozaki Hiromichi, had gone to Tokyo after graduation from Doshisha to take part in Christian missions there but returned in 1890 to succeed Niijima as president and to help to continue his legacy of academic innovation and independence from Japanese nationalism. One year later, the Doshisha Seiho Gakko (school of politics and law) was established and quickly became a vehicle for introducing American and European concepts in the social sciences.

In 1893, a symbol was created for Doshisha, one that recalled Niijima's association with Amherst College in the United States. The symbol consists of three inverted equilateral triangles in white on a purple background, thus uniting the colors of Amherst College to an Assyrian symbol of the Earth. The design can also be interpreted as a representation of the Christian trinity or of the cultivation of mind, spirit, and body. A more tangible representation of Doshisha's religious orientation came in 1894, when the Clark Theology Building (now Clark Memorial Building) was opened to house what was still the school's largest and, in Japanese terms, most distinctive faculty.

As the twentieth century began, government regulations were to have a major impact on Doshisha. In 1904 the trust was required to limit its activities to its theological school and its liberal arts school under the terms of the government's Senmon Gakko Rei, an ordinance regulating the group of "specialist schools" to which Doshisha, still not a university, was compelled to belong. In 1912 the trust was permitted to reorganise its schools as a single "Daigaku Senmon Gakko," a specialist school with university characteristics but without university status. It was composed of three faculties (theology, politics and economics, and English literature), and had a preparatory department and a women's college.

From 1919, when Learned was appointed as the last non-Japanese president of the school (but not of the trust), Doshisha entered what can be described as the second phase of its history. Its pioneering role inevitably declined in relative importance as more and more institutions of higher education were created throughout the country, while its graduates' influence also tended to decline as Japan moved from the enthusiasm for westernisation typified by Niijima's outlook into a period of increasing nationalism. At first, expansion and innovation remained the school's hallmark. In 1920 university status was achieved at last under a law passed by the Diet two years before, making Doshisha the only university in Japan to have a Christian theology department, and a graduate school was established. Two years later the trust created a separate Keizai Senmon Gakko (school of economics) at Iwakura in Kyoto, the first Doshisha institution to be separate from the Imadegawa campus; it also formalised its long-standing relationship with Amherst College, which still operates staff and student exchanges with Doshisha. In 1923 it took a step which even Niijima had not contemplated, and which some universities in the west were then still resisting: it became the first Japanese university to admit women to four-year courses aimed at full degrees (although the Women's School continued to offer two-year diploma courses).

As an independent, Christian institution, with close ties to the United States, Doshisha University could not avoid coming into conflict with the authorities during the 1930s, when Taisho Democracy gave way to a series of weak and corrupt governments presiding over militarisation at home and colonial wars in China. In 1935 Yuasa Hachiro, a nephew of the Tokutomi brothers who had himself graduated from Doshisha in 1908, was appointed as the tenth president of the university, but he left only two years later because he found it impossible to accept the increasing power of the military training instructor seconded to the campus by the army. While he took refuge in the United States (where he had once been both a ranch hand and a university student), Doshisha was forced into line with other universities, as Japan launched its war on the United States and the European colonial powers.

Kyoto escaped bombing during World War II but was as affected by shortages of personnel and resources as other cities. By 1944 Doshisha was reduced to a single liberal arts faculty and a separate, temporary industrial school, teaching electrical and chemical engineering in support of the war effort. Yet it was also in 1944 that the university was able to establish what is now its Institute for the Study of Humanities and Social Sciences (Jinbun Kagaku Kenkyusho), one of the leading research bodies in these fields in Japan, evidence that private universities retained some freedom of action even in wartime.

In 1946 Yuasa Hachiro returned from exile to resume the leadership of the Doshisha group of schools. Working within the liberalised education system introduced by the U.S. occupation authorities, the Doshisha trust established two junior high schools—one for boys and one for girls—in 1947 and a high school, a girls' high school, and a commercial high school in 1948. It then reorganised the university once again. Faculties of theology, letters, law, economics, and education were created in 1948; engineering and commerce were added in 1949; and the graduate school was reopened in 1950. After the education faculty was closed in 1951, the university developed the undergraduate teaching structure it retains today. In 1950 Yuasa departed for Tokyo, where he became founding president of the International Christian University, now one of Doshisha's friendly rivals in the select group of privately owned, church-linked universities with international networks of alumni and supporters.

Doshisha University now began what might be called its third—and current—phase. On the one hand, it operates on a significantly larger scale than ever before, and with a broader range of courses, but as an integral part of a greatly expanded higher education system, for which it receives a subsidy from the national government amounting to around 9 percent of its budget. On the other hand, it maintains its distinctive traditions—including its theology department, its chapel, and its Amherst connection—but in a secularised Japan where its religious character probably matters less to most of its students (and perhaps staff) than its high placing in academic league tables, its prestigious and beautiful Kyoto location, and its cosmopolitan atmosphere.

Between 1951 and 1987 it hosted the Kyoto American Studies Seminar jointly with Kyoto University (a state institution); in 1958 it created its own Center for American Studies; and in 1973 it inaugurated the Associated Kyoto Program, which brings students from 15 liberal arts colleges in the United States to Doshisha for their junior years abroad. In another area of scholarship, its Science and Engineering Research Institute, founded in 1959, has become an important center for research on recycling and other aspects of the new discipline of environmental engineering. In addition, in 1986 several departments of the university were moved to a second campus at Tanabe, outside the city of Kyoto, which they share with the Doshisha International High School (opened six years earlier), Doshisha Women's College, and one of the four Doshisha junior high schools.

One hundred and twenty years after the original Doshisha Eigakko opened on what is now the Imadegawa campus, the trust which Niijima founded has become one of the most successful academic enterprises in Japan. Thousands of students have benefited from its activities over the years and gone on to make valuable contributions to Japanese society. It is undoubtedly a very different institution from the purely Christian academy Niijima envisaged. Whether the university can still entirely serve the same purpose from which its name originated remains to be seen. Even so, while Doshisha has changed as modern Japan has changed, its survival and flourishing in an environment that is at best largely indifferent and at worst is hostile to its founding principles has been a remarkable achievement.

Further Reading: Tokutomi Kenjiro's 1901 novel *Omoide no ki,* which includes a memorable account of student life at Doshisha in its early years, has been translated into English by Kenneth Strong as *Footprints in the Snow* (Rutland, Vermont, and Tokyo: Charles Tuttle, and London: Allen & Unwin, 1970). Irwin Scheiner's *Christian Converts and Social Protest in Meiji Japan* (Berkeley: University of California Press, 1970) covers the careers of a number of Doshisha professors and alumni among the wide range of both moderate and radical Japanese Christians.

—Patrick Heenan

DUKE UNIVERSITY
(Durham, North Carolina, U.S.A.)

Location: Durham, North Carolina, 275 miles from Washington, D.C.

Description: A private university, enrolling approximately 11,000 students in undergraduate, graduate, and professional schools.

Information: Director of Undergraduate Admissions
Duke University
2138 Campus Drive
Durham, NC 27706
U.S.A.
(919) 684-3214
Fax (919) 681-8941

Visiting: There are regularly scheduled orientations for prospective students and guides for informal visits. Visitors may sit in on classes and stay overnight at the school. To arrange a visit, contact the Hosting Office at (919) 684-3214.

At the beginning of the nineteenth century, North Carolina had no public education. To assist families that could not afford private schools, in 1826 the state treasury established funding for common schools. The schools proved academically unequal to private schools, and private schools continued to thrive. In 1840, there were 2,700 private academies in the South, twice the number of those in New England. At the beginning of the nineteenth century, citizens of North Carolina decrying a 75 percent literacy rate amongst whites, began a vigorous program of establishing academies. From the humble beginnings of one such private academy—Union Institute in Randolph County—Duke University was born.

Union Institute was created in the town of Trinity when local Quaker and Methodist communities in Randolph County set up a society to raise money and plan curriculum for a secondary school that would ensure that their children grew up literate, an uncommon goal in their agricultural section of the state. The first constitution of the society stated:

We the people of Randolph and adjacent counties . . . believe that ignorance and error are not only the bane of religious but also of civil society, that they oppose a formidable front to the march of internal improvement, as well as to all the arts and sciences and rear up an almost impregnable wall between man and the happiness he pants after.

In 1839, classes began with a mixture of Quaker and Methodist boys and girls. But by 1851, Union Institute was converted to a normal college for the education of teachers, which was increasingly the accepted method of training teachers. The school became officially affiliated with the Methodist Church when the Quaker students moved to the newly developing Quaker boarding schools in 1856. It then set about to graduate its quota of "teachers and preachers," a major goal of southern colleges of the day. In 1859, its course changed once again from a teacher-training college to a liberal arts college, whereupon its name was changed to Trinity College. Braxton Craven, Trinity's first president, resided over and substantially guided these changes until his death in 1882. He was followed by the brief tenure of Marcus Wood, 1883–84, and a period of three years where no president was appointed.

Trinity changed with the leadership of John Franklin Crowell, president from 1887 to 1894. Possessing a first-class education from Dartmouth and Yale and an abiding commitment to raising the standards of American post-secondary education, he took the helm of a school in rural North Carolina characterized by constant financial struggles, few resources, a faculty uninformed by new teachings, and a narrow view of the aim of education. Crowell began restructuring the curriculum of Trinity College by using European and the best American schools as models. This meant emphasizing a free exchange of ideas, rather than the traditional recitation of information. He bolstered the study of science, which was quickly becoming the new word in higher education. Crowell was the first to plant the seeds at Trinity of the university idea.

Crowell's subsequent changes to the curriculum were dramatic and beneficial, but the provincialism of the town of Trinity interfered with the kind of academic and intellectual contact needed for the optimal exchange of ideas. The college was academically behind the other developing institutions in the state, such as Wake-Forest College, Davidson College, and the University of North Carolina at Chapel Hill. In addition, it was in debt much of the time. Crowell saw the school's rural location as a problem. By locating the college in a larger city, it opened access to jobs, endowment opportunities, and a more educated population.

Crowell permanently changed the character and the future of the small, rural school; by relocating, Trinity College was thrust directly in league with the Duke fam-

Duke University

ily, millionaires many times over from the manufacture of tobacco.

The Duke family of Durham rose from extremely humble beginnings as tobacco farmers. Washington Duke, after the Civil War, recognized the potential of bright-leaf tobacco as a high-quality strain of smoking tobacco, and maximized its production and distribution, which made the family the holders of one of the few fortunes in the state. Washington Duke followed the tenets of Andrew Carnegie who believed that those fortunate enough to attain great wealth should give much of it to the public.

The other tobacco fortune in the city belonged to Julian Carr, who owned the powerful Durham Bull Tobacco Company, and who had declared that he wanted a Methodist University in Durham and was already a trustee of Trinity. The two families' confluence of a common religion and massive wealth proved fortuitous for the struggling Trinity College. In 1892 the two magnates, hearing of the efforts of the college to occupy a site in Raleigh, combined their resources; with Duke offering $85,000 for buildings and Carr providing 60 acres of his land, they spirited the college away from all other bidders and brought the college 90 miles to the thriving industrial city of Durham.

As the patriarch of the family and a staunch Methodist, Washington had actually been supporting Trinity since the mid-1880s. At first, the contributions were given as a matter of course along with the many other donations to worthy causes. But after the college moved to Durham and became more solid academically, Washington's sons, James and Benjamin, became more enthusiastic about the institution and took significant pride in its scholarly advances. Ben Duke had written friends that he believed Trinity had come to the point "to warrant the claim that it is the best institution of learning in the South." In 1903, both his son and daughter were attending the school.

Growth, sophistication, financial support, stringent academic guidelines, and a student body from all over the South, brought new challenges. In 1903 an esteemed and long-time Trinity faculty member, John Spencer Bassett, began a discussion in print on the state of race relations in the country, especially in the South. Bassett wrote an editorial in a student scholarship publication, the *South Atlantic Quarterly,* "The place of every man our American life is such a one as his virtues and capacities may enable him to take. Not even a black skin and a flat nose justify caste in this country." Bassett survived the ensuing firestorm of protest, especially from southern alumni, and the numerous calls for his resignation, due to the good graces and sensible attitudes of both the Dukes and the college administration.

The so-called Bassett Affair is legendary in the history of Trinity College; it was the first test of the institution's stand of academic freedom. The incident laid a foundation of liberalism. A few years later, President Theodore Roosevelt visited the campus and gave a speech to 15,000, citing the Basset Affair:

> You stand for all those things for which the scholar must stand if he is to render real and lasting service to the State. You stand for Academic Freedom, for the right of private judgment, for a duty more incumbent upon the scholar than upon any other man, to tell the truth as he sees it, to claim for himself and to give to others the largest liberty in seeking after the truth.

During the first quarter of the twentieth century, Trinity began a law school, made further improvements to its curriculum, added athletic programs, accommodated more graduate students, and increased its library holdings. In 1908 the North Carolina Methodist Conference included Trinity and Vanderbilt under the classification of university.

Although women had been at least ten percent of each class since the mid-1890s, there was a movement afoot in 1904 to build an entirely separate school for them. The president at the time, Dr. James Kilgo, insisted that unless there was a separation of sexes in the classes, men would not come to Trinity. The administration didn't implement the idea until the greater number of female applicants after World War I spurred sentiment that women's education should be separate but equal.

The college was growing and the university status was taking hold. Trinity had become a primary recipient of funds from the Duke family, and it was clear that by the mid-1920s, James B. Duke had ambitious goals for the college. Duke reflected on why he was so invested in the university:

> I was born in North Carolina and I am sixty-six years old . . . It is time I was beginning to think about a monument. I want to leave something to the state that five hundred years from now people can look upon and say Duke did that. Every man owes something to the state he was born in, and this is what I want to leave North Carolina.

In December 1924, James B. Duke endowed over $40 million to the institution. When its name was changed to Duke University, speculation was that J.B. Duke "bought himself a university." Administrators at Trinity College were thinking of a name change as early as 1890 because there were several other institutions with the same name. When speaking of the reasons for his gift, Duke said that he "recognize[d] that education, when conducted along sane and practical, as opposed to dogmatic and theoretical lines, is, next to religion, the greatest civilizing influence."

The new university set out to develop Trinity College for men, a coordinate college for women, a law school, a school of religious training, a school of education, a school of business administration, a school of engineering, a graduate school of arts and sciences, and a medical school.

From its simple unambitious beginnings as Union Institute, Duke University now had money, stature, and presence. The institution's aims, as outlined at the time, exhibited a broad scope academically and its curriculum was directed at fulfilling the needs of a range of students from different regions and economic classes. No longer a repository for training teachers and preachers from the South, Duke University shed its parochial beginnings and began to fulfill the aspirations of earlier Trinity College presidents, that it become a major, voluntarily supported research university, perhaps the first in the South. The new charter stated:

This university in all its departments will be concerned about excellence rather than size; it will aim at quality rather than numbers—quality of those who teach and quality of those who learn. It will be developed with a view to serving conditions as they actually exist. It will be for the use of all the people of the state and section without regard to creed, class, or party.

Additional acreage was acquired for expansion. In fact, the university came to own 8,000 acres of woodland, much more than was originally needed, but which proved quite useful for further expansion and for creating the over 7,000-acre Duke Forest. Buildings were planned for two separate campuses: the East Campus became the Women's College, with several new buildings constructed in American Georgian style, similar to the structures and design of Jefferson's University of Virginia; the West Campus housed several quadrangles containing castle-like buildings, built from grayish-green, North Carolina stone in a distinctive Tudor Gothic style. West campus, the home of the men's Trinity College and graduate and professional schools, was dominated by the 210-foot tower of Duke chapel, containing 77 stained-glass windows and a magnificent 5,000 pipe organ. The leading landscape design firm in the nation, Olmsted Brothers of Boston, was hired to lay out the grounds. The founder of the firm, Frederick Law Olmsted, designed Biltmore Gardens in Asheville, North Carolina; Central Park in New York; and many other well-known outdoor settings.

An interesting note is that one of the architects on this project in the heart of the South was Julian Abele, an African American. He was the designer of Harvard's Widener Library and the Philadelphia Museum of Art.

In addition to physical expansion, there was also academic expansion. A medical school was established in 1930, the School of Law was reorganized, and new graduate programs were added. But President William Few (Duke University, 1924–40; Trinity College, 1910–24) believed that the heart of a great research university lay in the undergraduate college of arts and sciences. So he began to scour academic departments throughout the country and abroad, to hire a superior teaching force; he also set about to upgrade the requirements for acceptance.

Besides emphasizing the importance of the arts and sciences, Few, in accordance with James B. Duke's dictum about the importance of religion, was also strongly committed to maintaining the religious dimension in campus life. By keeping a friendly, but not constraining relationship with the Methodist Church, he believed that religion could be a subject for study and an aspect of life.

Though he himself was deeply religious, Few would not allow religious zealots to compromise his equally important and dearly held convictions about academic freedom. Duke's location in the so-called "Bible Belt" often left the institution vulnerable to the assaults of fundamentalists. In the wake of the Scopes trial in Tennessee, there was an outcry from certain quarters in the South for laws against teaching Darwinian theories about evolution. Few, at a meeting of the Educational Association of the Methodist Episcopal Church in 1927, introduced a resolution that expressed opposition to all legislation that would interfere with the proper teaching of scientific subjects in American schools and colleges. Few believed that the School of Religion should guide the entire institution toward the "further duty of mediation between the religious conservatism of this region and the great intellectual ferment of the age" but not dominate its modes of inquiry.

Trinity College had long aspired to add a medical facility because, for one, North Carolina did not have a full-fledged, four-year medical school. When the aspiration came to fruition in 1930, hardly anyone suspected that it would become one of the strongest areas of the university. Duke University Medical Center now comprises clinical, training, and research programs, and the hospital is a major tertiary care facility. The center has a comprehensive cancer center, an eye center, a federally supported general clinical research unit, and other highly advanced treatment centers.

Separate but equal worked for the women's coordinate college at Duke from when the concept was established in 1924 and took root in the Georgian-style East Campus, until 1972 when the idea of separate education for women became a relic. Under the leadership of Alice Baldwin as first president, the women's college thrived as an intellectual beacon for southern women. Baldwin encouraged students to broaden their horizons of expectations and consider careers as well as marriage. Given the norms and expectations of the times, Baldwin never denigrated the role of homemaker and mother and made sure the women students conformed to the strict Methodist rules of the time, which included no smoking, no dancing, and maintaining utmost propriety. Of course, these rules were enforced far more stringently on the female students than the male students.

The Quakers, the Methodists, the visionary presidents of Trinity College and later Duke University, and the Duke family all contributed to the double goal of creating a major research university in the South and a place where religion could thrive. Duke is now a major center of learning, with many of its schools and departments consistently ranked among the nation's best. Its library holdings are the eighth largest among private universities in the United States, with 4.5 million volumes. The Duke University Museum of Art contains collections of medieval sculptures, Greek and Roman antiquities, African art, American and European paintings, the Nancy Hanks collection, and other fine acquisitions. Duke University Press, founded in 1921, publishes scholarly books, journals, and software in the humanities and social sciences, as well as policy studies, regional and trade books, and textbooks. *The South Atlantic Quarterly,* mentioned above as the outlet that Bassett used to speak out against discrimination in 1903, is the second oldest humanities journal in the nation.

The Duke Forest covers 7,700 acres and is used for research, protection of wildlife and rare plant species, and recreation. The Primate Center is the only university-based facility in the world devoted to the study of prosimian primates and is the world's largest colony of captive endangered primates. The mission of the Duke University Marine Laboratory at Beaufort, North Carolina, is educa-tion and research in basic ocean sciences, marine biomedicine, biotechnology, and coastal resource management.

All of these attributes and properties of the university exist comfortably alongside the Duke Divinity School, a major training facility for Methodist clergymen, which also anchors the university as a meaningful and contributing member of the community. Few's vision that the great purpose and aim of the university was to bring together education and religion in the "generous service of humanity" appears to have been borne out in succeeding generations.

Further Reading: John Franklin Crowell's *Personal Recollections of Trinity College, North Carolina, 1887–1894* (Durham, North Carolina: Duke University Press, 1939) covers Crowell's seven years as president of Trinity College and the developments he oversaw. Douglas M. Knight's *Street of Dreams* (Durham, North Carolina: Duke University Press, 1989) reviews the dramatic changes that the decade of the sixties brought to the campus. Also drawn from that decade is a collection of narrative and verse by William Blackburn, *A Duke Miscellany* (Durham, North Carolina: Duke University Press, 1970). *James B. Duke, Master Builder* by John W. Jenkins (New York: Doran, 1927) gives insight to the major benefactor of the university.

—Marcia Horowitz

EBERHARD KARLS UNIVERSITY OF TÜBINGEN
(Tübingen, Germany)

Location: Tübingen, Germany, 25 miles south of Stuttgart.

Description: A state university enrolling approximately 26,000 students at all levels.

Information: Zentrale Studienberatung
Universität Tübingen
Wilhelmstrasse 11
72074 Tübingen
Germany
(7071) 29255

Akademisches Auslandsamt
Universität Tübingen
Nauklerstrasse 14
72074 Tübingen
Germany
(7071) 295403

Guided Tours: There are no official university tours

When Count Eberhard of Württemberg founded the University of Tübingen in 1477, he accepted a great risk. His territorial possessions—and thus his income base—comprised only about half of the later kingdom of Württemberg, and the new university was located in an area that was already well provided with academic institutions, notably at Basel, Freiburg im Breisgau, Heidelberg, and Ingolstadt. The count, however, intended to have his own school, not only because of the attendant prestige, but also in order to control the formation of the officials who would administer his country.

In the beginning, financial arrangements followed the custom of the day. Part of the endowment of the collegiate church of Sindelfingen, located in the vicinity, was dedicated to the university. Pope Sixtus IV agreed to this transfer of funds in a bull dated May 11, 1476. As a result, Abbot Heinrich Fabri of Blaubeuren, acting as papal legate, on March 11, 1477, officially declared the university to have legal existence. On February 22, 1484, Emperor Frederick III granted the necessary imperial confirmation.

Lectures were held starting October 1, 1477. The original teaching body consisted of three professors of theology, three each of canon law and secular jurisprudence, two of medicine, and four masters of the humanities. Being an independent ecclesiastical corporate entity (*uni-versitas studii generalis* [university for general studies]), the university possessed authority to change its constitution and to adjudicate the law within its confines. It was autonomous in financial and administrative matters, could act as its own commercial agent, and enjoyed freedom from taxation. When in 1482 the financial ties with the Sindelfingen institution were fully severed, it could look forward to a prosperous and successful future. A refurbished constitution, adopted on December 20, 1491, established a pay scale for the professoriate. The founding period of the university had concluded.

The effort that had gone into creating the statutes of the University of Tübingen quickly received recognition elsewhere, as they served as a model for the constitution of the University of Wittenberg in Saxony. Founded in 1502, the University of Wittenberg for generations thereafter was considered an off-spring of the school of Tübingen. Both institutions were headed a by a *rector,* who was assisted by a chancellor. Until 1817 the chancellor was identical with the professor who occupied the first chair of theology; beginning with the Reformation, he also acted, in the name of the sovereign, as the official supervisor of the university. Financial matters were directed by a *syndicus;* at his side as a controlling body he had a *collegium deputatorum,* which consisted of four representatives of the faculties.

Soon Tübingen was able to hire as teachers a number of prominent scholars who earned the university substantial renown. Among them were the jurist Johann Vergenhans, author of a world chronicle; the theologian Gabriel Biel, propagator of the pietistic movement of *devotio moderna* in southern Germany; Johannes Heynlin, one of the most important preachers of his time; the philosophical traditionalist Konrad Summerhart; the poet Heinrich Bebel; the mathematician and astronomer Johannes Stoffler; and for a short time also the humanists Johannes Reuchlin and Philipp Melanchthon. All these men attracted students in great numbers. An imposing building, the *Bursa,* newly erected in 1478–79, provided lecture rooms and residential facilities. It was characteristic of the tolerant and scholarly atmosphere of the institution that representatives of the two controversial intellectual trends of the late Middle Ages and the early modern period, nominalists and realists, peacefully lived and taught in the same place. Not before the nineteenth century would the humanities radiate again from Tübingen as strongly and as far as they did during the time leading up to the Reformation.

In 1534 Duke Ulrich—Württemberg had become a duchy—introduced the Reformation. Since the university

Eberhard Karls University of Tübingen

opposed the move, several reformers had to be brought in from outside. Through Melanchthon, who stayed on for a month, the change received a Lutheran tilt. A substantial number of professors still resisted the Reformation and had to be dismissed. The refusal in particular of its chancellor, Ambrosius Widmann, to adopt the new faith created great problems for the university, as it could not confer degrees without his cooperation. It was only in 1556 that Widmann yielded his rights to the university senate.

One consequence of the Reformation was the founding of an institute for the education of a Protestant clergy. In 1536 Duke Ulrich created the *Evangelisches Stift,* which in 1547 moved from the *Bursa* to the former monastery of the Hermits of St. Augustine and in 1557 received its ultimate financial and administrative charter. The *Stift,* more than any other single part of the university, has over time established Tübingen's reputation. Its five-year curriculum (two years of philosophy, three years of theology) molded its students into a homogenous body that for several centuries shaped the intellectual and religious life of

Württemberg. It counted among its alumni not only famous theologians such as Jakob Andreae, Johann Albrecht Bengel, Ferdinand Christian Baur, Friedrich Theodor Vischer, and David Friedrich Strauss, but also eminent personalities working in other disciplines, such as astronomer Johannes Kepler, philosophers Georg Wilhelm Friedrich Hegel and Friedrich Wilhelm Joseph Schelling, novelist Wilhelm Hauff, and poets Johann Christian Friedrich Holderlin and Eduard Morike. After 1650 Philipp Jacob Spener's influence was instrumental in introducing the opinions and attitudes of German pietism into the *Stift.* Later on the thoughts of the Enlightenment and the French Revolution, the philosophy of Immanuel Kant, the ideas of the Left Hegelians and of nineteenth-century revivalism equally found a receptive climate there.

Until the Thirty Years' War, Tübingen had the reputation of being the most important university city in the Lutheran part of Germany. Andreae, chancellor of the university, played a significant part in the conception of the Formula of Concord, which in 1577 ultimately summarized the teachings of the Lutheran position. Although, or perhaps because, it had the reputation for being a fortress of orthodoxy, the university attracted the sons of the nobility of northern Germany as well as those of various regions of Hapsburg Austria. In 1594 a *Ritterakademie* [knight's academy] (*collegium illustre*) opened its doors to them. It subscribed to a new educational philosophy, offering a curriculum comprising instruction in the sciences, knightly exercises such as fencing and horsemanship, foreign languages, and later in geography and martial knowledge. The *Akademie* quickly rose to prominence and counted as many as 121 students in 1601. Due to the war that began in 1618, it had to be closed in 1628, but it enjoyed a late flowering between 1653 and 1688.

The university suffered severe damage during the Thirty Years' War. In previous decades lectures had been held on occasion at locations in the vicinity because of sporadic surges of the pestilence. Now the plague played absolute havoc with the university's activities. In 1635 fully half of the teaching faculty died from the disease, among them Wilhelm Schickard, inventor of a mechanical calculator. Material loss resulting from military action was heavy as well. The libraries were stolen, and the school's economic base was largely destroyed. For decades thereafter the university was attended by no more than 250 to 350 students at a time, and even fewer in the early eighteenth century. As a rule its professors were recruited from only a few families during this period, which proved detrimental to the university's intellectual climate.

A short period of renewal occurred in the mid-eighteenth century, when Duke Karl Eugen temporarily took a personal interest in the university. Its statutes were modernized, an observatory was installed in the castle above the city, a scientific laboratory was established, and the anatomic facilities were enlarged. In 1767 the duke made himself *rector* of the university, and two years later he renamed it *Eberhardino-Carolina,* in honor of its founder and himself. Starting in 1775, however, he unfortunately turned his interests to a newly created academy in the duchy's capital of Stuttgart. This competitor, though, survived only until 1794. Its demise saved the University of Tübingen.

During the nineteenth century, more important developments took place. Württemberg emerged from the Napoléonic turbulence with considerable territorial gains and was granted the status of kingdom. With the manifestation of a new bureaucratic spirit the university's rights and privileges were somewhat curtailed.

All changes were not unwelcome, however, as a certain liberalization and diversification occurred. The first university clinic to be established in Germany was created in 1805 and put up its 15 beds in the *Bursa*. In 1817 a doctor of medicine was made chancellor, a break from the tradition which hitherto had ordained that the office was to be held by a theologian; in the same year a Faculty of Catholic Theology was added in order to cater to the

needs of the population of the newly acquired territories, largely Catholic; and a Faculty of Political Economy was founded to improve the training of future administrative personnel.

Over time, nevertheless, the reactionary climate of Metternich's age made itself very much felt at Tübingen. Liberal student fraternities were prohibited, and in 1825 a state commissioner was appointed whose mandate was the supervision of the university's activities. In 1828 the teaching faculty were declared to be civil servants and were henceforth paid directly by the state. New university statutes were adopted in 1831; they remained in effect until 1912.

Few professors thereafter dared to be politically active or to propagate unconventional ideas. Of those who did, a goodly number were forced to resign, among them such famous personalities as statesman Robert von Mohl, theologian David Friedrich Strauss, and poets Ludwig Uhland and Friedrich Theodor Vischer. The revolution of 1848 as a consequence found enthusiastic support among students and liberal members of the faculty. From 1849 on, though, repressive measures again stifled all reform aspirations.

Ideological containment, on the other hand, was not identical with academic stagnation. For the first time the confines of the medieval town were left when a new anatomical institute was built in 1832–35. A decade later, an entirely new university campus was started in the valley of the Ammer Creek with the construction of a lecture hall, botanical and chemical institutes, and a medical clinic. United in 1863 for the first time in Germany in a faculty of their own, the sciences experienced ever greater specialization. The arts and humanities, formerly considered the handmaid of theology, now grew to be independent. In 1876 the student enrollment reached 1,000 for the first time.

The student body underwent remarkable transformation. By the turn of the twentieth century, the number of theology students, who for centuries had been in the majority, comprised only a quarter of all students registered at Tübingen. In 1859 yet another change occurred. The first woman, a zoologist, who had been admitted by special permission, obtained a doctoral degree. From 1904 on, female students were admitted into the university on the same basis as males. Tübingen was the sixth university in Germany to admit women. Remarkable growth appeared in the medical facilities as well. While at the beginning of the nineteenth century the university clinic had had to fight to keep its few beds, in 1913 a substantial number of teaching hospitals gave treatment to 53,000 patients.

Such diversification and expansion required statutory changes. A new university constitution, adopted in 1912, extended representation in the decision-making bodies to various classes of teaching faculty who were not chair-holding professors.

Germany's defeat in World War I meant that, from 1918, the university was confronted with severe social problems. To meet them, it ventured into social activities on a vastly larger scale than it had ever done before. A student service corporation was founded in 1920 (*Tubinger Studentenhilfe;* from 1930 *Tubinger Studentenwerk*). This corporation administered the student restaurant (*Mensa*) and the dormitories, as well as the typewriting and bookbinding facilities. The unstable political climate of the Weimar Republic was reflected in considerable political tension, which led to occasional flare-ups among the students. In 1925 at Lustnau, a suburb, there even occurred a bloody confrontation between left-wing and right-wing students. The teaching faculty, mainly conservative in outlook, succeeded in maintaining its homogeneity, however, and at the 450th anniversary of the university's founding (in 1927) the celebrations took place in a peaceful environment.

When the National Socialist regime established itself in Germany in 1933, the University of Tübingen did not offer any remarkable resistance. The academic decision-making bodies, in particular the two chambers of the senate, were abolished and replaced by an arrangement that reflected the so-called *Führerprinzip,* meaning that henceforth directives from above had to be followed. Some disciplines that were considered ideologically important, such as biology and history, received special support. On the other hand, in 1942, the university lost control not only of its material property, acquired from the time of its founding, but also of its legal independence.

Even the student complement shrank. The manpower demands of World War II resulted in the reduction of the number of students, which in 1940 reached the low of 889; for the first time the share of female students reached 50 percent. When in 1944 the Allies approached Strassburg, that university was evacuated, and a considerable number of its students and professors were transferred to Tübingen.

Fortunately the university did not suffer any physical damage during the war; it was one of the few German universities to escape destruction. It thus was able to resume its teaching activities as early as autumn 1945, only a few month after the armistice. Some dire consequences of the war resulted nevertheless. Twenty-nine of Tübingen's professors, a full third of the teaching body, were purged during the denazification phase of the Allied occupation for having had ties with the National Socialist regime. The efforts of the new German government of South Württemberg to replace the dismissed faculty members with new professors, and of the university to reinstate its former employees, dominated the first years after the war.

During this time the university also endeavored to develop new forms of learning. The introduction of a *dies academicus,* a day of lectures of a general nature, and the founding of the *Leibnizkolleg,* which offered specific courses in the humanities, testified (and still testify) to its intentions. But the quick growth of the student body soon reduced such efforts to little more than tokenism. Until 1949 a rigorous admissions policy kept the number of students below 3,500. By 1954, though, it had risen to over 5,000 and by 1962 to over 10,000.

In 1958 a general development plan was adopted according to which the natural sciences were to be concentrated in an entirely new complex of buildings some two miles from the traditional site of the university. Moreover a new medical center was to be erected. Both plans have largely been realized. The natural sciences moved to their new quarters north of the city (Morgenstelle) in 1975; vast new clinical buildings were occupied in 1989. Unfortunately the construction of dormitories has not kept pace with the demand, putting great strain upon the residential capacity of Tübingen with its 50,000 inhabitants. In 1973 the number of students reached 15,000 and in 1982, 20,000.

In 1978 a new University Act, passed by the Baden-Württemberg legislature, inaugurated a profound reform of the university's administrative structure. It provided for a president, who replaced the *rector,* and three vice-presidents. A Full Senate (63 members) and a Small Senate (39 members) represent the various segments of the university.

In 1995 a total of 26,000 students were registered in 17 faculties. The university employed about 9,000 people, of whom some 700 were professors and another 1,300 were full-time teaching members of different and varying status. As German students do not pay tuition, the university's operational funds were provided by public funds, i.e., the federal government and the *Land* of Baden-Württemberg. In 1995 its budget amounted to roughly DM900 million ($680 million), of which two-thirds went to the two faculties of medicine. Its libraries comprised about 6 million volumes. Today, as it has been over various periods of its existence, the University of Tübingen is considered one of the most important and most renowned institutions of higher learning in Germany.

—Udo Sautter

ÉCOLE NATIONALE D'ADMINISTRATION
(Paris, France)

Location: Central Paris.

Description: A state-run institution of higher learning, responsible for the education of France's senior civil servants and politicians. Students are admitted only after a series of rigorous competitive examinations called *les concours*.

Information: École Nationale d'Administration
13 rue de l'Université
75007 Paris
France
(49) 26 45 45
Fax (42) 60 26 95

École Nationale d'Administration (ENA) was created in 1945 by the government of Charles de Gaulle. It is responsible for the recruiting and training of the administrative class of civil servants in France. It was created as part of a series of reforms introduced by Michel Debré, the Minister of National Education aimed at modernizing the French civil service.

Since the French revolution, successive governments have always expressed an interest in the recruitment and training of civil servants. Law schools had traditionally been responsible for training France's administrative elite but with the establishment of the École Polytechnique and École Normale by the Revolutionary Convention (1793–95), new training schools known as *grandes écoles* provided specialized training for key sectors of the civil service. Napoléon established the modern French educational system. It was characterized by a strong centralized structure and rigid selection procedures based on entrance examinations known as *les concours*. As the last of the *grandes écoles* to be founded, the ENA is seen by some in France as the fulfillment of the Napoléonic dream for the creation of a uniform cadre of "grands commis."

The École Polytechnique was created to train the country's state engineers and the École Normale to train teachers. Both schools featured rigorous entrance examinations, strong school spirit, and a close association between the schools and their respective ministries since particular ministries of the French government had a larger say in determining the curriculum of these state schools than did the Ministry of Public Education. These schools would serve as the model for many institutions of higher learning in the nineteenth century and finally, the ENA.

The idea of establishing a *grande école* for France's civil servants had been seriously advocated as early as 1836 and was vigorously debated throughout the remaining century. Under Hippolyte Carnot, Minister of Public Instruction, the École Nationale d'Administration was established in 1848 as a preparatory school for all branches of the administration. It was modelled after the École Polytechnique, Carnot's former school but it survived only for 18 months, a victim of the political instabilities of the Second Republic, the opposition of the law faculties who feared losing their prestige and students to such a school, and the intransigence of the civil servants who likewise feared that their future promotions could be threatened by better-trained candidates.

Following the failure of the first ENA in 1849, all further attempts to create a *grande école* were suspended until France's defeat to Prussia in 1870. Once again, internal instability and political turmoil led to urgent calls for better training of France's administrative elite so as to prevent a similar humiliation from occurring. More importantly, the radical tendencies which the Paris Commune had brought to the forefront, led a group of private citizens to found their own institution, the *École Libre des Sciences Politiques* in 1871–72, which became known as the "Sciences Po."

Although it has often been seen as a *grande école,* the Sciences Po was a private-run institution, who feared the more radical elements in French political society and who wished to provide France with a corps of politicians and administrators who were sufficiently trained to deal with the demands of an industrializing society. Fearful of the state monopoly over the educational system, they believed that by training the country's administrative elite, they would not only break this monopoly, but would have greater influence over the running of the state. Soon after its founding, the Sciences Po became so entwined with the system of recruitment of *grand corps*, that the two became almost undistinguishable.

At the same time, similar changes were taking place in the French civil service. Fearful that a radical shift in the government could irrevocably alter the country's direction, each ministry and *corps* developed a greater autonomy. They also grew in importance in the early years of the Third Republic. Their members often served as the final authorities in administrative law, as the controllers of state finances, and as advisers on foreign policy. The *grands corps* slowly created a network of regulations, customs, and decrees which so intimidated politicians that they eventually established their own independent recruitment examinations (*concours*). Graduates from the

École Nationale d'Administration

École Libre des Sciences Politiques were the only ones who knew how to work amidst such a network, and became so indispensable as a link between the politicians and the bureaucracy that the school had a virtual "intellectual monopoly" over the senior civil service.

Each ministry and each corps not only administered its own examinations, it set the standards in the selection of candidates. Such a degree of training was required even to pass the *concours* that few candidates could ever hope to be sufficiently prepared to pass. Moreover, so much specialization was required to pass one particular exam that they were little prepared to serve in any other administrative sector. As a result of this utter dependency, many civil servants had a greater loyalty to their respective *corps* than to the state. These closely knit groups soon monopolized the French administration. The *concours* were often guilty of emphasizing obsolete or irrelevant knowledge and testing in such a way as to bias results in favor of the sons of the *grands corps* members. They became virtually impenetrable—open almost exclusively to sons of the well-to-do.

Such a system survived for well over half a century. It was not challenged until the 1930s when the Great Depression plunged France into a series of crises. Reformists within the civil service itself called for a complete overhaul of the system. They charged that the system of recruitment and promotion was inefficient, undemocratic, and biased. They demanded an alternative to the privately run Science Po in favor of a system similar to that of the École Polytechnique and military schools, which had only one uniform entrance exam regardless of where the candidate would eventually be posted.

In 1936, a bill calling for the re-establishment of a state-run École Nationale d'Administration was introduced by the Popular Front government. It called for the fusion of all *concours* into one examination which would determine the postings for each candidate as was the tradition in most of the *grandes écoles*. Once again, the corps, law faculties, and the civil servants opposed such provisions and were able to put sufficient pressure that the bill was significantly modified. By the time the Chamber of Deputies had adopted it, the bill called for little more than a nationalized version of the Sciences Po and left the separate *concours* of the *grands corps* and ministries untouched. Before the bill could take any effect, France was overtaken by the events of World War II.

As had been the case in 1849, the attempts at reform in 1936 demonstrated that such a reform entailed the reorganization of the entire civil service. No other civil service was so entrenched, so fragmented, and better able to oppose changes than the French. As it happened, the opportunity for such a massive restructuring occurred in the aftermath of the German invasion and Vichy regime. Many of the state institutions and entrenched interests of the *grands corps* had been discredited as a result of the Vichy regime. The postwar era was a propitious time for undertaking such reforms for as General De Gaulle later admitted, the creation of the École National d'Administration in 1945 "saw the light of day . . . in an atmosphere of scepticism on the part of the major bodies of public service and the parliamentary milieus."

One of De Gaulle's most important advisors and one of ENA's principle architects was Michel Debré. He appreciated the reality that such reforms implied more than the creation of a *grande école* for the corps. An entire reorganization of recruitment, training, and promotion system was required. Traditional structures had to be maintained so as not to engender the similar opposition which had defeated ENA's predecessors.

In 1945, he introduced major changes in the recruiting and curricula to modernize as well as democratize the civil service. The ENA was to follow the traditional structure of a *grande école* but with new features which were to destroy the previous geographic and social monopolies which had characterized previous generations of French civil servants.

The ENA was created by means of an ordinance on October 9, 1945. De Gaulle and Debré consciously avoided a vote in the assembly fearing that its members would not feel entirely at ease with the creation of such an institution. It was an important tactical measure and showed the importance of the school and the civil service reforms to the stability of the Fourth Republic. Its proponents sought to widen the training of future servants and open access to the corps to all who could demonstrate themselves capable, regardless of rank, background, or association.

Rather than close the École Libres des Sciences Politiques, Debré nationalized it under the new name l'Institut d'Etudes Politiques. Eleven similar institutes were to be opened in the French provinces. Tuition was free and the curriculum was to provide a broader training to enable students to pursue careers outside state service if they so chose. Moreover, it was no longer necessary for students from outside Paris to move to the capital in order to acquire the necessary education to gain admission to the ENA. All institutes were to offer equivalent preparation to all those wishing to write the entrance exams. The ENA became the sole means of recruiting for all levels and departments of the French civil service, including the prestigious *grands corps*. They maintained their position in the organizational structure of the administration, but they could no longer operate their own entrance examinations though they were guaranteed the right to select the top graduates of ENA.

The *concours* remained the central admission prerequisite with a few innovations. There were to be two categories of examinations, one for the young men and women who had received their education at Institut d'Etudes Politiques or the provincial institutions affiliated with provincial universities. It was hoped that these provisions would recruit students from every region and class of the French nation and end for all the traditional prerequisite of an elite Parisian education.

A second category was created with a special *concours* for more mature candidates who had at least five years of experience in the civil service but who did not have the academic qualifications. This was intended to prevent the "intellectual nepotism" of political science students and to facilitate a meritocracy so that lack of formal training in political science could no longer impede promotion, and could also draw more competent civil servants who had been previously barred by their lack of formal education. All of these measures were in response to former criticisms of the entrenched elitism of the *grandes écoles*, which critics had pointed out tended to place greater emphasis on formal education and disregard practical experience and ability.

Though there were two entrance examinations, all candidates for the civil service corps were to take the same competitive final examination after their 18 months of study. This one *concours de sortie* replaced the multiple competitions which each administrative body had used to fill postings. This new system, inspired by the polytechnical system, enabled successful candidates to choose between posts in the *grands corps de l'État* or the provincial departments of the prefectorial corps, according to how they were ranked following the final examinations. It was hoped that this system would minimize the co-optation which had prevailed in the *grand corps* while providing a more democratic, centralized, and less subjective means of determining the hierarchy of postings.

Intended to make the selection more democratic and efficient, Debré also argued that it was the best means by which to ensure a uniformly trained cadre of loyal servants to the state. One of ENA's chief missions was to teach future administrators the state's responsibilities to the people while fostering a renewed sense of service. At the time, Debré's reforms were praised as ingenious, a balanced compromise between tradition and change.

A growing chorus of protest erupted in the late 1960s about the ENA. Ironically, many of the attacks were made by former graduates. In April 1970, a group of students wrote a letter to *Le Monde* in which they denounced the ENA for its tendency to protect senior administrative postings for a co-opted minority, what they labelled an "esprit de caste." The following year, the students of the "Charles de Gaulle" class wrote to the Prime Minister Chaban-Delmas (himself a graduate of the ENA) to demand changes to the way postings were assigned. As a means of expressing their dissatisfaction, they refused to accept entry into the highly coveted *grands corps.*

The students were protesting the inequality in career opportunities. Those who graduated at the top of their class were assured a position in the *grand corps* and other important ministries of finance, interior, and foreign affairs while those with lower rankings were assigned to social affairs, education, and agriculture. They also objected to the "bonuses" paid to officials of the *grands corps,* which made for an inequality in salaries. They called for the creation of a single uniform corps, an end to the control over certain posts by the *grands corps,* and for equity in salaries. Six out of the 68 students in the "Charles de Gaulle" class could have chosen careers in the *grands corps* and though some did break with the class solidarity, the protest highlighted many of the problems and criticisms which not only the ENA but the entire French system of higher education faced.

The ENA's course program covers two years. Students are expected to serve under a senior administrator for a period of practical training in an administrative post. This was to cover a range of subjects which any similar civil servant would encounter throughout a normal career and enable the student to prepare a short thesis on a subject of local interest. The second year is a period of study divided in four major sections: general administration; finance and economics; social administration; and foreign affairs. After introductory courses, each section offers specialized courses and seminars that are taught by university teachers, high-ranking civil servants, and persons with special experience.

All critics generally agree that the problems lie more with the broader structure of the French educational system than with the ENA in particular. The Block-Lainé Commission of 1969 which had studied the question had also advocated the creation of a unified corps of administrators which would base promotion on work performance rather than academic performance.

Part of the problems lie with the 1945 reforms. By accepting the traditional belief that those who serve the state must be selected according to the most demanding academic criteria, ENA's architects had accepted the educational model of the *grande école.* By incorporating the hallmarks of this system—the *concours, the corps,* and postings based on rank—they indirectly legitimized the formation of elites and denied the promise of any promotion from the ranks since performance at ENA determined a student's entire career. The ENA has also only achieved mixed results in so far as the broadening of the social and geographic background of its candidates. The nationalized Sciences Po, the Institut d'Études Politiques de Paris, still had a preponderant role in providing students for the ENA.

In spite of such criticism, few dispute the role the ENA has played in the development of the Fifth Republic. Many of its graduates have been appointed to various ministries and advisory posts. Many others have gone on to have brilliant political careers, including three former prime ministers—Fabius, Chaban-Delmas, and Rocard—and Presidents Giscard d'Estaing and Jacques Chirac.

Further Reading: The following sources all provide information: W.D. Halls, *Education, Culture and Politics in Modern France* (Oxford and New York: Pergamon Press, 1976); F.P. Ridley and Jean Blondel, *Public Administration in France* (London: Routledge, 1964; New York: Barnes and Noble, 1965); Thomas R. Osborne, *A "Grand École" for the "Grand Corps": The Recruitment and Training of the French Administrative Elite in the Nineteenth Century* (New York: Columbia University Press, 1983); Ezra N. Suleiman, *Politics, Power and Bureaucracy in France: The Administrative Elite* (Princeton, New Jersey: Princeton University Press, 1974); Michalina Vaughan, "The Grandes Écoles" in *Governing Elites: Studies in Training and Selection,* edited by Rupert Wilkinson (New York: Oxford University Press, 1969).

—Manon Lamontagne

ÉCOLE NORMALE SUPÉRIEURE
(Paris, France)

Location: École Normale Supérieure de Ulm/Sèvres is located in central Paris, in the heart of the Latin Quarter, only a few blocks from the Sorbonne. École Normale Supérieure de Cachan is located on the southern outskirts of Paris, in Cachan, a ten-minute train ride from central Paris. École Normale Supérieure de Fontenay/Saint-Cloud is located a few miles southwest of Paris, in Fontenay-aux-Roses, a 15-minute train ride from central Paris. École Normale Supérieure de Lyon is located in central Lyons.

Description: Four advanced teacher training institutions administered by the Ministry of Education, enrolling approximately 3,000 students (800 students at the E.N.S. Ulm/Sèvres, 450 at the E.N.S. Fontenay/Saint-Cloud, 1,150 at the E.N.S. Cachan, and 674 at the E.N.S. Lyon) and offering graduate and postgraduate studies in the humanities and sciences. The Écoles are among France's *grandes écoles,* a set of specialized higher education schools accessible by competitive examination and which, in parallel with the university system, are designed to select and train elites for the higher ranks of public service.

Information: E.N.S. Ulm/Sèvres
45 rue d'Ulm
75230 Paris Cedex 05
France
(1) 44 32 30 00

E.N.S. Fontenay/Saint-Cloud
31 Avenue Lombart
92266 Fontenay-aux-Roses Cedex
France
(1) 41 13 24 00

E.N.S. Cachan
61 Avenue du President Wilson
94235 Cachan Cedex
France
(1) 47 40 20 00

E.N.S. Lyon
46 Allee d'Italie
69364 Lyon Cedex 07
France
(7) 72 72 80 00

Now comprising four distinct schools with separate entrance examinations and specified fields of study (sciences at Cachan and Lyon, humanities at Ulm and Fontenay), the École Normale Supérieure (ENS) arose as a unique institution from the French Revolutionary government, the National Convention, in 1795. Its creation is inscribed in the First Republic's attempts to set up a national public education, theoretically in the spirit of the Enlightenment and the Revolution, but mostly, at a more practical level, to fulfill the immediate needs of the young republic and its citizens. In the early days of the republic, one of those urgent needs consisted of providing the new public educational system with its teachers' teachers, in other words, with a higher corps of republican instructors capable of recruiting and training in turn the future teachers of the primary schools. Robert J. Smith described the goals of the institution: "Ultimately the *normalien* was to become the intellectual model for the transformation of illiterate and parochial provincials into well-informed citizens loyal to a democratic and republican nation." This first version of the École Normale of Paris—which did not earn the qualification of "Supérieure" until 1843—however failed to live up to its noble intentions. Lacking funds, credibility, and hope for a long future given the context of financial crisis and political chaos, it was closed in May 1795, only four months after its inauguration.

If the school's abortive beginnings can in large part be attributed to the economic and political uncertainties of the regime, they must also be tethered to the contradiction that lies at the heart of this product of republican enthusiasm and idealism, a contradiction which resonates to this day in the French educational system and which is a key to understanding its strengths and weaknesses. The École Normale Supérieure indeed epitomizes the unresolved tensions between a democratic approach to education and a fundamentally elitist structure which, in its attempt to abolish prior privileges, paradoxically fosters new hierarchies and new forms of exclusion. While its underlying principle is to make instruction "for French citizens uniformly accessible throughout the whole Republic," as Joseph Lakanal, the representative of the Committee of Public Instruction at the national convention and the father of the École Normale stated in his address to the convention in October 1794, the École Normale Supérieure, like the rest of France's *grandes écoles,* also reflects a two-track configuration geared to distinguishing power elites from the greater number and to producing an intellectual aristocracy.

This apparent incongruity, however, elucidates the reemergence of the École Normale under the Empire.

École Normale Supérieure

While the original version of the school participated in what Smith called "a national educational crusade at the primary level," the École Normale that reopened in 1810 as a part of Napoléon's educational reforms was now designed to train the professors of the secondary and university levels. As such, it targeted a much more limited part of the population and was openly dedicated to the education of the country's bourgeois youth and to the production of a loyal and competent ruling class.

Smith writes that

Napoléon's École Normale resembled a secular version of the Jesuit colleges of the Old Regime. The students' uniforms, their compulsory attendance at chapel, and the rigid daily schedule of a boarding school (an *internat*) reflected the military and authoritarian values of the regime. The Emperor intended that the *normalien* should be schooled rather than educated.

In spite of constraining links with Napoléon's autocratic regime, the *école* managed to preserve and develop the democratic and liberal tradition that had existed at its creation. An emphasis on intellectual freedom, independent reflection, and critical discussion led the École Normale to become what Smith describes as "a haven for intellectuals eager to exchange ideas as well as to earn academic degrees."

Such a progressive faction was regarded as increasingly suspicious by a more reactionary regime. The conservative wave that followed the Bourbon restoration of 1814, however, spared the École Normale and even improved its status with several favorable measures that increased the school's autonomy in relation to the university. But as the regime grew more reactionary in the 1820s, the École Normale became too much of a threat in the eyes of ultra-Catholic hegemony. As Smith wrote, "The *normaliens* seemed too proud of their learning, too little inclined to be submissive to traditional authorities, and too much attached to the philosophical ideas of the Enlightenment." The school was consequently closed in 1822 and remained so for the next eight years.

In 1830, one of the first decrees of the July Monarchy was to restore the École Normale, which had by then become a symbol of intellectual and spiritual liberty; its reopening in August 1830 was part of the new regime's rebuttal of years of ultra-Catholic coercion. From this point on the star of the École Normale was on the rise. It received the eminent title of "École Normale *Supérieure*" in 1843—a title which made official the school's strict dedication to the training of university and royal colleges' professors. It was relocated to the heart of the Latin Quarter, significantly close to its academic counterpart and rival, the Sorbonne, in 1847. The presence of distinguished personalities such as Victor Hugo and Adolphe Thiers at the ceremonial inauguration of the École Normale Supérieure's new quarters at the 45 *rue d'Ulm* connoted the growing prestige of the institution.

The dominant political position of the *normaliens* during the Revolution of 1848 reflected the school's well-established and privileged status in French society. Largely siding with the jeopardized bourgeois Republic and against the working-class insurgents, the *normaliens* confirmed their faith in liberalism, civil liberties, and moderate democracy and asserted their opposition to "socialism, authoritarianism, or plutocracy."

In the conservative context of the Second Empire, the École Normale's liberalism and intellectual independence naturally reappeared as a threat to be contained, and the school once again suffered from what Smith described as "the regime's insistence upon political and religious orthodoxy." "This was a period when serious study and independent work were discouraged . . . Instead of savants, who might become troublesome, the government preferred to turn out 'modest professors.'" As it had in the past, the school, however, succeeded in keeping its progressive tradition alive and in maintaining its identity and integrity against official pressures and constraints.

In the later years of the Second Empire and by the beginning of the Third Republic, the regime's wariness towards higher education and advanced studies abated and was gradually replaced by a genuine concern with the advancement of national education. Such a shift revived the importance of the École Normale Supérieure and placed the school's graduates at the pinnacle of a fast-growing educational system whose need for qualified teachers was urgent.

When, by the 1880s, education became the pivotal term of the Third Republic's promotion of new ideas and new standards of living, the *normaliens* came to occupy not only the higher ranks of the educational apparatus, but also the higher ranks of the political and administrative spheres. Smith explained that the École Normale Supérieure became an important source for national leaders, scholars, and schoolmasters, though that situation did not last much past World War II.

After World War II, the political role of the *normaliens* declined because of the competition of the scientific *grandes écoles* and mostly of the ENA (L'École Nationale d'Administration), founded in 1945 with the specific function of providing training for the higher ranks of civil service. The intellectual leadership of the school remained nonetheless prominent. Such crucial figures as Henri Bergson and Jean-Paul Sartre graduated from the École Normale Supérieure, and their enduring influence upon French culture and western philosophy underscores the importance of the institution in the production of an intellectual elite. The growing isolation and marginalization of the great intellectuals under the Fifth Republic, however, explains the *école*'s loss of the strategic political role it enjoyed during its golden age. Today's *normaliens* choose, for the most part, a career in academia, where they still constitute the elite of the profession.

Since its revised statute of 1810, the *école*'s curriculum has evolved from a two-year course of study to a four-year training program which, to this day, only consists in providing additional preparation for the basic degrees granted by the university—the license at the end of the first year, the *maîtrise* at the end of the second, and, most importantly, the *agrégation* at the end of the third year, the highest national competitive examination for the professorate. Once *agrégés,* fourth-year students usually embark upon doctoral research.

The fact that the École Normale confers nothing but the title of *normalien* to its graduates—a title nonetheless stamped with an aura of great cultural and social prestige—points to one of the enduring originalities of the school. To this day, and though they are undoubtedly privileged by the quality of the additional training they receive at the school (the most eminent professors teach at the ENS) and by the financial support they are granted throughout their entire course of study, the students of Écoles Normales Supérieures have always competed with the non-*normaliens* in the academic system. The four branches of the ENS indeed do not deliver a diploma; they merely provide additional training and funding to a selected group of students who, in return, sign a ten-year contract with the Ministry of Education, a contract which comprises four years of paid and top-quality training and six years of public service. The *agrégation* remains the ultimate goal of the *normalien*'s four-year course of study as a trainee-professor. The *normalien agrégé* is then almost guaranteed swift advancement at the university level.

An interesting issue is the status of women in an institution that remained reserved for male candidates until the creation, by Jules Ferry in 1880, of the École Normale Supérieure d'Institutrices de Fontenay-aux-Roses. This institution was specifically designed to form a higher corps of female professors whose function would be to train the future female teachers of the primary schools. It thus not only wished to compensate for the lack of attention granted to women in the academic world but also for the neglect of the primary level of education. The equivalent institution for boys, the École de Saint-Cloud, was created in 1882.

In 1881, the École Normale Supérieure de Sèvres was founded to provide a female equivalent to the École Normale Supérieure of the *rue d'Ulm*. Interestingly however, nothing officially prevented women from taking the entrance examination to the exclusive *rue d'Ulm*. A few bold women challenged the rule and the *rue d'Ulm* was forced to open its doors to female candidates. Today, Sèvres and Ulm, just as Fontenay and Saint-Cloud, have fused, constituting France's two highest academic institutions in the humanities, while Cachan and Lyons provide superior training in science. The differences between Ulm/Sèvres and Fontenay/Saint-Cloud have decreased over the years, though Ulm/Sèvres has kept the prestige granted by a longer history and a more strategic role in French politics and intellectual development.

Further Reading: Robert J. Smith's *The École Normale Supérieure and the Third Republic* (Albany, New York: State University of New York Press, 1982) provides a detailed and clear account of the school's history, with an emphasis on its golden age and its role in French politics during the Third Republic. W.D. Halls' *Education, Culture and Politics in Modern France* (Oxford and New York: Pergamon Press, 1976) has a chapter on France's "Grandes Écoles" with a rather informative section on the École Normale Supérieure.

—Dorothée M. Bonnigal

ÉCOLE POLYTECHNIQUE
(Paris, France)

Location: Located on rue Pailaiseau, in the suburbs, 20 miles south of Paris. Throughout much of its history it had been located in central Paris on Montagne Ste. Geneviève.

Description: A professional training school for many of France's engineers and civil servants. It is a *grande école,* one of the specialized French institutions of higher learning.

Information: École Polytechnique
91128 Palaiseau
CEDEX
France
(69) 33 47 37

The École Polytechnique, a state-run professional training institution for many of France's engineers, civil servants, and senior managers, was created during the French Revolution on March 11, 1794. Originally called the École Centrale des Travaux Publics, it was renamed École Polytechnique in 1795. Students refer to it colloquially as "Le X" and to themselves as *polytechniciens.* Since its founding, it has become one of the most prestigious institutions in France and is part of an alternative higher educational system to the universities which the French call *les grandes écoles.*

The school's revolutionary founders believed education would play an important role in the survival of the republic. They mistrusted the church-run universities, which they regarded as woefully inadequate in their teaching of mathematics and science. In 1793, they were abolished and reduced to mere faculties. In their place, the revolutionary convention established centralized state schools such as the École Polytechnique and the École Normale (to train the country's teachers). They would become the models for *les grandes écoles.* The École Polytechnique was established in order to meet the need for better trained scientists and engineers. Over 400 candidates were chosen from nationwide examinations. After a three-month introductory course (*cours révolutionnaires*) one third entered the state service immediately; another third were given a one-year course; and the final third were given the full two-year program.

Under Napoléon the modern system of French higher education was firmly established. Universities remained small and limited in their curricula. State schools gained increasing importance in the training and education of

French citizens. École Polytechnique was granted military status and subject to the directives of the Ministry of the Army, rather than the Ministry of Public Education. The school was moved to Montagne Ste. Geneviève, where it remained until 1976. Its internal operation was modeled on military discipline, after citizens complained about the students' rowdy behaviour. Students entering the École Polytechnique were selected according to the most exacting intellectual criteria and were guaranteed employment either in the military, the state engineering corps, or the civil service. The school also produced some of France's most eminent scientists of the early nineteenth century: mathematicians Denis Poisson and Louis Poinsot, physicists Jean-Baptiste Biot and Etienne Louis Malus. Thus was fostered an impression of service to the state by the most capable and best qualified candidates. Napoléon then gave the school a new motto: "*Pour la patrie, les sciences et la gloire*" (For country, science, and glory).

The École Polytechnique continued to reflect these republican values during the restoration of the monarchy in France (1830–48), when many students openly opposed the monarchy. The school was closed four times during this period and was stripped of its military status. Students took to the streets in 1830 to protest the imposition of school prayers and mass. The École Polytechnique was reinstituted as a military school following the disturbances, although student rioting led to more closures in 1832, 1834, and 1844. Continuing their opposition to the monarchy, the *polytechniciens* did not look favorably upon Napoléon III and the Second Empire (1852–70).

In the nineteenth century, École Polytechnique was one of only a handful of schools in France that provided a rigorous curriculum of mathematics and science and counted some of the country's best scientists as its instructors. While the school was open to all, the combination of tuition and rigorous entrance examinations (called *concours*) prevented many poorer students from applying. Only affluent families could send their children to the best schools which would prepare their sons for the *concours.*

Candidates prepared for the entrance examinations for at least two years after receiving their *baccalauréat,* taking special classes created for that purpose. Only a small percentage of applicants were admitted to the school (300 of 1,800 in the modern era). The examinations have been standardized over the decades, but almost half are still devoted to mathematics. Over the years, the *concours* came to represent more than just admission to a school. Acceptance implied admission to France's elite, if not in the civil service then in private enterprise. It was by far the most "bourgeois" institution in France. In the 1850s, over 70 percent of its students came from the upper middle classes, while 19 percent were children of liberal professionals. Only 1 percent came from the working class.

Although intended to supply the country with technical experts, the school's curriculum provided a broad training in science and mathematics, along with other non-scientific subjects. Students were taught a foreign language (English, German, or Russian), as well as introductory courses in economics, social sciences, history, literature, architecture, and artistic design to help them understand the modern world.

This academic curriculum was also complemented by rigorous athletic and military training, activities which played an important role in developing a legendary *esprit de corps*. Students were given officer cadet status and spent their two years of study in what some have termed "a living unit." They studied, slept, and lived together in groups of eight. Rituals, traditions, and a common language unique to *polytechniciens* fostered mutual respect and cooperation. This legendary spirit was (and still is) unusual in France where boarding schools were the exception rather than the rule.

A student's career options were also determined by his final standing (*classement de sortie*). The top students were offered places in one of the highly prized technical corps of the armed forces. The rest were offered places in the army or other sectors of the civil service. Those entering the technical corps of the civil service were subject to another two years of specialized training. École Polytechnique provided only a general scientific education and did not include a period of practical training. The two most highly coveted corps were the corps of mining engineers and the corps of civil engineers. Recruitment into these corps was usually reserved for the top students.

École Polytechnique has always been a model for the French system of higher education. Other *grandes écoles* with similar structures and characteristics were instituted by the state in order to provide specialized training in given fields. All featured the *concours* as a criteria for entrance. All sought to develop bonds of fellowship which would be maintained long after the training period was over. Furthermore all encouraged a broad introduction in a variety of artistic, scientific, and technical subjects.

The virtual monopoly of *polytechniciens* over state positions ensured that the school would always enjoy the patronage of the upper middle classes, but, in the mid-nineteenth century, the school faced competition from other technical schools which were being created to meet an increasing demand for industrial engineers. École Centrale des Arts et Manufactures, founded in 1829, was the first such school to train engineers for private indus-tries. Given École Polytechnique's strong association with service to the state, employment in industry was deemed socially degrading. This had created a problem in many industries where scientifically trained graduates were increasingly in demand. École Centrale, attempting to attract students, modeled itself on the École Polytechnique, making it attractive to many lower middle class families who also sought to increase their social prestige. Since its students were shut out from state service they were destined to become industrial engineers.

The industrialization of France after 1870, coupled with the emergence of new industries and fields of scientific research particularly in physics and chemistry, led to new calls for the creation of more technical training faculties to meet private industrial demand. Moreover, such calls were usually accompanied by severe criticisms of École Polytechnique's curriculum. Many felt that this had become as entrenched and aristocratic as the *ancien régime* universities that it had replaced.

Between 1882 and 1909, a host of new engineering schools and faculties were opened throughout France. These included the Parisian École Supérieure de Physique et de Chimie (1882) and the École Supérieure d'Électricité (1894). Also established were new engineering faculties at the provincial universities at Grenoble, Lille, Lyon, Nancy, and Toulouse. These institutions trained as many as 120 engineers annually up to 1914 and over 200 after 1919.

Emphasis in their curricula was placed on pragmatic applications of scientific knowledge directly to industrial problems. After a solid introduction to physics and chemistry in the first 18 months, students specialized in either chemistry or physics, with extensive exercises in the laboratory as well as an introduction to research techniques. The program also included a three-to-six-month period of apprenticeship, called a *stage*, giving the student practical knowledge of industrial operations. This curriculum was unprecedented in the French system of higher education, in its response to the immediate needs of French industry, which had previously relied almost exclusively on the expertise of one of the state engineering corps.

Between 1890 and 1914 industrial engineers gained increasing social importance. New organizations and the "professionalization" of industrial engineering provided a new challenge to not only the prestige of the École Polytechnique but also to its monopoly over the state corps of engineering. The school responded by criticizing the pedagogical foundation of the new technical schools (referred to collectively as the *grandes écoles des science appliquées*). They argued that the curricula of the *grandes écoles* were too narrowly based and short-sighted because they did not encourage deductive thinking necessary for problem solving. Advocates of the École Polytechnique felt the *grandes écoles* did not provide the cultural and educational instruction needed for leadership.

Industrial engineers responded with their own criticism of the École Polytechnique. They argued that lack of inductive learning was archaic and left the *école*'s graduates ill-prepared for the scientific and technological activities involved in industry. Moreover, *polytechniciens*' traditional disdain for industry inhibited France's economic development. They called for an end to the École Polytechnique's monopoly over the training of engineers for state corps, arguing that this change would lead to the replacement of *polytechniciens* with scientifically trained engineers.

This debate reflected several changes that were affecting the École Polytechnique. Between 1890 and 1914, the strong association between the army and the school, which had been strengthened after France's defeat in the war of 1870, waned. Several internal problems in the military led to new reforms, such as the military law of 1905, which required prospective candidates to spend one year in the ranks before entering the school. This regulation not only deterred many from pursuing military careers, including posts in the once much-coveted corps of engineers, but it led many to resign from their positions. Decline in advancement opportunities brought on by reforms, the relatively small material advantages, and particularly the decline in social prestige, made a career in the corps much less attractive than it had been throughout the nineteenth century.

At a time when industrial engineering gained in social prominence and considerable monetary rewards, many *polytechniciens* overcame their disdain for private industry only to find that industrialists were reluctant to employ them since they lacked the necessary scientific and technical skills. Ironically, this situation was to change dramatically during the interwar period. École Polytechnique's prestige was restored as a result of World War I.

Many of the French commanders had been graduates of the École Polytechnique, including Marshals Fayolle, Foch, Joffre, Manoury, and General Nivelle. A grateful nation restored a new measure of respectability to the *polytechniciens,* a respectability of which industrialists were quick to take advantage. They soon discovered that students of École Polytechnique were ideally qualified to suit the needs of industry, because their common bonds to fellow graduates in the civil service proved to be far more valuable than their training. Indeed, there developed a practice of what the *polytechniciens* called *pantouflage*, a practise of resigning from a civil service post to take up lucrative employment in industry or trade.

The state corps of engineers also gained prestige in the interwar period. The military demand for engineers and the effort that was required to rebuild the country after four years of destruction reaffirmed the importance of the state corps of engineers, but despite this resurgence, military service was becoming a less attractive career option for *polytechniciens*. By 1924 only one-quarter of graduates went into the army, as more lucrative careers were to be found in other sectors of the French bureaucracy as well as in business.

Several reforms have been instituted since the end of World War II to alleviate some of the problems in the system—the most notable problem was the development of entrenched elites while the school attempted to preserve and maintain the notion of meritocracy. Increasing social demands for democratization and administrative modernization have brought many changes to the École Polytechnique, including a move to the suburbs of Paris. A second separate entrance examination, introduced in 1969, allowed a small number of candidates from technical schools to gain access. Women have been admitted to the school since 1972 though their numbers are small.

Yet, despite these changes and the modernizing reforms of the French system of higher education in 1968 and 1984, the École Polytechnique has remained true to its traditions. The *concours* has remained as the only acceptable means by which to evaluate prospective candidates. Attempts have nevertheless been made to broaden the access of the school to middle-income and working classes. In 1850, an unlimited number of scholarships were made available to students, subject to a means test, who passed the entrance examinations. This enabled one-third of students to get scholarships. That number grew to one-half in 1881 as more and more French secondary schools provided their students with a better grounding in mathematics. By 1926 nearly two-thirds of the student body were given in scholarships and finally in 1930, the school was made entirely free.

The *école* is still semi-military in character and continues to be a major training center for the upper echelons of the armed forces and senior engineering personnel employed by the state. Students must still sign a ten-year engagement to serve the state in a civil or military capacity (though about half opt for the practice of *pantouflage*). The main outlets for graduates still remains the state engineering corps as the Génie Militaire (Army Engineering), Génie Maritime (Naval Engineering), Ponts et Chausées (Bridges and Roads), Artillery, and Mines, which were established throughout the eighteenth and nineteenth centuries. Though today many graduates do not choose to enter the military, the notion of service to the state predominates, and many find themselves employed in other technical sectors of the civil service known as the *grands corps technique de l'État*, such as the École National Supérieure des Télécommunications. This includes state monopolies and nationalized industries, economic and technical services, and research in state-owned laboratories of la Centre nationale de recherches scientifiques (the National Centre for Scientific Research). Since 1945, many graduates have abandoned the practice of *pantouflage* and have gone directly into private industry.

École Polytechnique has produced three presidents of the Republic—Sadi Carnot, Albert Lebrun, and Giscard d'Estaing. Among other notable *ex-polytechniciens* are Captain Alfred Dreyfus, the Nobel laureate and physicist Henri Becquerel, Georges Sorel, and the economist Jacques Rueff. More importantly, graduates are to be found in the upper echelons of France's ministries, public and private industries, in every walk of life including the church.

Further Reading: Although there is no history of the *École Polytechnique* in English, various aspects of the institution in the context of French education are covered in W.D. Halls' *Education, Culture, and Politics in Modern France* (Oxford and New York: Pergamon Press, 1976), Fritz Ringer's *Edu-cation and Society in Modern Europe* (Bloomington: Indiana University Press, 1979), Terry Shinn's "From 'Corps' to 'Profession': The Emergence and Definition of Industrial Engineering in Modern France" in *The Organization of Science and Technology in France, 1808–1914*, edited by Robert Fox and George Weisz (Cambridge and New York: Cambridge University Press, 1980), and Michalina Vaughan's "The Grandes Écoles" in *Governing Elites: Studies in Training and Selection*, edited by Rupert Wilkinson (New York: Oxford University Press, 1969).

—Manon Lamontagne

EMORY UNIVERSITY
(Atlanta, Georgia, U.S.A.)

Location: Suburban Atlanta, about five miles northeast of downtown.

Description: A private, coeducational institution affiliated with the United Methodist Church and enrolling 10,983 undergraduate and graduate students.

Information: Emory University
South Oxford Road N.E.
Atlanta, GA 30322
U.S.A.
(404) 727–6123

Emory University in Atlanta, Georgia, is one of America's wealthiest and most respected institutions of higher learning. It has an impressive endowment of about $750 million and physical assets of nearly twice that amount. The university's graduates have achieved distinction as statesmen, doctors, religious leaders, business executives, university presidents, and as members of many other professions. Two of the university's most distinguished graduates, Dumas Malone and Tom Rivers, both attended Emory in 1906. Malone went on to become the Pulitzer Prize-winning biographer of Thomas Jefferson and an editor of the important reference work, *Dictionary of American Biography*. Rivers went from Emory to Johns Hopkins Medical School and became one of America's pioneering virologists. Some 42 years later, in 1948, an Emory alumnus, Alben Barkley, was elected vice-president of the United States.

Emory has not confined itself to influence in the academic world. An institution affiliated with the university, the Carter Center (named for former U.S. president Jimmy Carter) has some 13 programs devoted to promoting world peace and human rights throughout the world. Emory and its benefactor Robert Woodruff donated to the federal government the land on which the Centers for Disease Control, the nation's foremost agency for tracking and preventing diseases, is built.

Emory's development into a major university did not come easily. The university had to overcome numerous obstacles, including war, inadequate financial support, and even outright hostility. Throughout its history, which has spanned more than 160 years, Emory University's development has reflected the major trends in higher education in the American South.

The university was founded as Emory College on December 10, 1836, but its beginnings are rooted in a meeting of the Georgia Methodist Conference, held in Washington, Georgia, in 1834. Dr. Stephen Olin, a representative from Randolph-Macon College in Virginia asked conferees for money to support his college. The conference was ready to support Olin's request when a preacher named Allen Turner stood up and said that Georgians didn't need to send money out of the state, but, rather, should use it instead to establish their own college. The conference decided to vote Randolph-Macon their support, but within a year it began acting upon Turner's exhortation, establishing a manual labor school at Covington, Georgia, with Alexander Means as superintendent and 30 students in attendance. In November 1836, the school's trustees, led by Ignatius Alphonso Few, petitioned the Georgia legislature to expand their original charter to include "college privileges." Two years later, Emory College began admitting its first class of students, all males. Located in Oxford, Georgia, 40 miles east of Atlanta, the college was named for Bishop John Emory of Maryland, who had presided at the 1834 Washington conference and who, in the following year, was killed in a carriage accident.

Few was elected to serve as both president of the board of trustees and first president of Emory College. Fifteen students arrived in Oxford for the college's first year. Their costs included $5.00 for lodging, $3.00 for fuel (firewood), $40.00 for tuition, and about $85.00 for meals for the entire year—lower fees than at any comparable institution in the state. These costs reflect Emory's humble beginnings, which were marked by a constant struggle for survival. During Few's presidency (1840–48), for example, faculty salaries had to be cut and the trustees had to stop giving perpetual scholarships. When George F. Pierce assumed the presidency in 1848, he found the college heavily in debt, with inadequate buildings and equipment and professors who received only about 77 percent of their salaries. Pierce, however, managed to raise money for a new building to house a library, classes, science demonstrations, and an auditorium. On February 25, 1852, the cornerstone was laid for the $15,000 structure.

By 1860 it seemed that Emory's fortunes would change for the better. Enrollment rose and the college was beginning to pay its own way. Then the Civil War erupted, forcing the college to cease operation. Its students were sent off to war and its buildings were used as a Confederate hospital and later as Union headquarters. The war destroyed the college and wiped out its endowment. To give a boost to Emory when it reopened in January 1866, the Georgia state legislature provided funds "to finance the

Emory University

educations of indigent and maimed soldiers"; those funds helped pay the tuition of Emory's 120 students. The following year, Luther M. Smith, an Emory-educated lawyer and professor of Greek, became the college's sixth president. Under his direction, Emory began implementing a more "practical" education, adding to its four-year curriculum a three-year program that did not require Latin or Greek. Under Smith's leadership, the college revived, but the president disagreed with trustees over policy and resigned in 1871. Under his successor Osborn I. Smith, the college's seventh president, Emory faced more difficult times. In 1873 the country's economic crisis caused a drop in Emory's enrollment, and a policy of generous but foolish tuition exemptions led to a serious reduction in the college's income; however, Emory did manage to find money for four buildings, including the prayer chapel.

The administration of Smith's successor, Atticus Greene Haywood, marked a turning point in Emory's history. In the words of historian Thomas English, the author of *Emory University, 1915–1965: A Semicentennial History,* Haywood "accomplished much by internal organization, and by an active campaign of publicity, he brought Emory's needs to the attention of the public. Most significantly, Haywood attracted the eye of George Seney, a New York City Methodist banker-philanthropist, who had read a pamphlet containing the president's 1880 Thanksgiving Day address, in which he talked of a restored South, the end of slavery, the hope for improved race relations, and a revived economy. Seney gave Emory $75,000 to establish an endowment, $5,000 towards repayment of its debts, and $50,000 for the construction of a new building.

Seney's generous gift helped, but Emory remained a poor college. By the turn of the century it was still in debt and its physical plant remained inadequate. A change of direction came in 1899, when Asa G. Candler, the brother of Warren Akin Candler, who had served as Emory's tenth president from 1888 to 1898, was elected to the college's board of trustees. Four years earlier, Asa had sent the very first keg of Coca Cola syrup to his son, who was a student at Emory University. Instead of attending college, Asa Candler had become a pharmacist. In 1888 he acquired the rights to Coca Cola, and two years later he began marketing the soft drink, a shrewd move that made him a millionaire. In 1914 the Methodist Episcopal Church, South, wanted to establish a university east of the Mississippi. Atlanta offered the church $500,000 and the use of Wesley Memorial Hospital and Wesley Memorial Church. Asa Candler wanted to have the new Methodist Church located in Atlanta with a transplanted Emory University as its academic center. Candler's wishes became the catalyst of what is considered the single most momentous event in Emory College's history. In a letter to the educational commission of the General Conference of the Methodist Episcopal Church, South, which was planning for the new university, Candler offered "the sum of a million dollars for the endowment of such an institution, the plans and methods of which are to be definitely directed to the advancement of sound learning and pure religion." Candler also gave the university the tract of land upon which to build the new university: seven acres northeast of Atlanta.

The commission voted to accept Candler's offer and it made him the chancellor of the yet-unnamed university. A committee was established to negotiate with the trustees of Emory College to make Emory the "academic department" of the new university. The Emory College trustees officially approved the amalgamation plan and suggested that Emory University be selected as its name "so as to preserve and conserve the assets of history and traditions of Emory College and enlarge its usefulness to the M.E. [Methodist] Church, South, and at the same time

promote the success of the new University." The university's charter was granted on January 25, 1915, and bylaws were adopted by the interim board of trustees on January 12, 1916.

The educational commission had set aside $500,000 of Candler's gift for the establishment of a School of Theology, and on September 23, 1914, that became the first organized division of the new university. The following February, the school was named in honor of benefactor Asa Candler, who also became the university's first president. In 1916 the Candler School of Theology moved into the first two academic buildings completed on the new campus. The same year, the university established the Lamar School of Law (named after alumnus L.Q.C. Lamar, who went on to serve in the U.S. House of Representatives, in the U.S. Senate, and as an associate justice of the U.S. Supreme Court).

During World War I, Emory College remained in Oxford, but with the war's end, the move to Atlanta began. The last faculty meeting of Emory College in Oxford took place on June 4, 1919, after which the faculty began preparing for the summer quarter which was to begin in late July, at the new Atlanta campus. The first four buildings—a classroom, a dormitory, and two temporary frame structures to be used as an assembly and dining hall—had been completed in 1917. By June 1919, 14 houses "suitable for use by members of the faculty as their homes" were ready for occupancy.

In the summer of 1919, Emory admitted the first women to candidacy for baccalaureate degrees in education and for graduate degrees. Two years earlier, Eleonore Raoul became the first woman admitted to the university when she enrolled in the School of Law. Chancellor Candler was adamantly opposed to coeducation and the admittance of Raoul, and she is said to have enrolled when he was out of town.

Candler resigned in 1920 and was succeeded by Harvey Warren Cox, a professor of philosophy and dean of the Teacher's College of the University of Florida. "With the coming of President Cox," wrote historian Henry Bullock, the author of *A History of Emory University,* "the University emerged from a period of changing leadership unparalleled in the institution's history and entered one marked by unified leadership and well-planned progress."

One of the major changes occurred in the university's curriculum. It became increasingly specialized, moving away from the strictly liberal arts education Emory offered in the past. As James Harvey Young, Charles Howard Candler Professor of American Social History, Emeritus, at Emory University, explained, "The history of the curriculum of Emory College in Atlanta reveals an ongoing contest between the demands of specialization, in an even larger number of disciplinary options, with the demands of general education." In 1919 the university established the School of Business Administration and the graduate school. Two years later, the university moved to improve the course of study in the College of Arts and Sciences, putting into effect a new curriculum that increased the number of free electives. Emory made important curricular changes in 1925, creating a Junior Division for the first two years, during which students acquired a general background, and a Senior Division for the last two years, during which students specialized.

After the move to Atlanta, the university began to address the problem of the inadequate library building. For the first seven years after the move, the library had been located in the basement of the theology building, much to the inconvenience of its faculty and students. In 1924 Candler donated money towards the construction of a new library building, and two years later, the Asa Candler Library was dedicated. The administrative offices, however, took over the ground and first floors, severely restricting the space for books and library services. The situation did not change until the construction of the new administrative building in 1955. To meet the need for constructing the new administrative buildings, Emory launched a campaign in 1925 with the slogan: "Ten million dollars in ten years." Three million of that amount was to be used for constructing buildings and the rest was to be added to the endowment, which stood at a comparatively meager $2 million. The campaign got off to an impressive start with $750,000 raised in less than three years after its launch. Several buildings were constructed between 1927 and 1936, the university's centennial year, including a temporary dining hall and chemistry building, both in 1927, and in 1937, Glenn Memorial, which was to serve as both a church and an auditorium. The university did raise money and some new buildings were constructed, but the Depression of 1929 dashed all hope of meeting the goal. The Depression, in fact, crippled the university. Its income declined steeply; salaries were slashed; enrollment plummeted; and the operating budget was cut drastically. Not until 1935 did the situation begin to improve. Historian English wrote, "Prudent management of its resources had enabled Emory to weather the storm, and the institution was to emerge from the ordeal, from a sense of hardship honorably shared and overcome, with a greater unified strength than it had possessed before."

When World War II broke out in 1939, Emory once again moved to action. In 1941 it revived the medical unit that served in World War I and organized a commit-tee of national defense. The following year, it began to offer a number of "war emergency courses," including military law and chemical warfare. In 1943 the U.S. Army sent medical trainees to Emory and the Navy instituted a college training program at Emory known as V-12. In recognition of the university's contribution to the war effort, a 10,700-ton cargo ship was christened the M.S. Emory Victory.

Major change came to Emory after the war. In 1946 Emory began offering doctoral courses in a wide range of subjects. The student body became more cosmopolitan, as the university began to recruit students from all over the country. The university opened its enrollment to women on an equal basis with men. In 1962 Emory moved to end racial restrictions.

After World War II, Emory's history was marked by two major episodes. The first was the 1946 donation by Emory University and Robert W. Woodruff of land on which the Centers for Disease Control was built. (The center actually opened in 1960.) Then in 1979 Woodruff, who had attended Emory College in Oxford and later headed the Coca Cola company in the 1920s, gave Emory University $105 million, the largest gift ever given to an American educational institution. Ironically, as a freshman in 1908, Woodruff, who left Emory before the first term ended, wrote to his father, complaining that his eyes "fairly ached" from studying. The university used the donation to establish Woodruff scholars and Woodruff professors, adding greatly to Emory's prestige. Moreover, the Woodruff gift has allowed Emory to move from the status of a regional university to one that has attained national and international stature.

Further Reading: Beth Dawkins Bassett's essay, "Once Upon a Time in Newton County" (*Emory Magazine,* March 1987, pp. 21–51), provides a succinct and interesting introduction to Emory's history. Henry Bullock Morton's *A History of Emory University* (Nashville, Tennessee: Parthenon Press, 1936) provides an exhaustive, detailed account of the university's history. Thomas H. English's *Emory University, 1915–1965: A Semicentennial History* (Atlanta, Georgia: Emory University, 1966) provides a detailed treatment of a specific period in Emory's history.

—Ron Chepesiuk and Mary Elizabeth Devine

FEDERAL INSTITUTE OF TECHNOLOGY
(Zurich, Switzerland)

Location: In the canton of Zurich in northern Switzerland, on the bank of the Limmat river on the northern tip of Lake Zurich.

Description: One of only two institutions of higher education directly funded by the federal government.

Information: Eidgenössische Technische Hochschule
Ramistrasse 101
Zentrum, 8092
Zurich
Switzerland
(1) 632 11 11

The *Eidgenössische Technische Hochshule* (ETH) is one of two universities of technology in the Swiss Federation. It was the first federal institution of higher learning to be created in 1854 under provisions of the 1848 Constitution. Its smaller sister institution is the École Polytechnique Fédérale à Lausanne (EPFL); the two remain the only institutions of higher learning that are funded by the federal government. All other universities are funded by their respective cantons, the member states which make up the Swiss Federation. Since its founding, the institute has been called upon to represent the ideals of a federal university in which cultural, linguistic, and religious diversities are reconciled and represented. It has played an important role in the training of engineers and scientists for not only the Swiss Federation but also for many industrial nations. Many of its graduates, such as Max Born and Albert Einstein, have had world-renowned scientific careers.

Switzerland is a confederation of 26 member states (cantons) of diverse languages, cultures, and religions. There are three official languages: German, spoken in 65 percent of the cantons; French, spoken in 18 percent; and Italian, spoken in 12 percent. The member states are almost equally divided between Catholics and Protestants. Given such diversity, education has always been the responsibility of the cantons.

The humanism of the fifteenth and sixteenth centuries inspired the founding of Switzerland's first university at Basel in 1460 in the German-speaking part of the federation. From 1550 to 1620, the university had its golden age. The Reformation had a profound impact on the university and on many other cantons. Calvin established his *Schola genevensis* as a theological school. Throughout the seventeenth and eighteen centuries,

most cantonal colleges and academies that had been created were for theological training. Their training tended to be classical and Latin-based.

With the invasion of French soldiers and the declaration of a Swiss Republic in 1848, many critics of the cantonal educational system called for the creation of a federal non-denominational institution. Chief among them was Phillippe-Albert Stapfer who was inspired by both the French centralized schools and the German universities. His dream of a federal university was a victim of the political struggles between federalists and centralists that dominated the Swiss Federation until the new constitution was adopted in 1848.

Switzerland, like the rest of Europe, was embroiled in an ideological debate about the role education was to play in its modernization. With the country's rapid industrialization in the 1830s, the need for technical schools was becoming apparent, especially in the northern German-speaking parts of the federation. The canton of Zurich had established its own *Kuntschule* to provide better training in mathematics and science to its artisans and entrepreneurs. Similar schools were also established in Bern in 1779, and in Lucerne in 1829. This rapid industrialization led to more liberalization and centralization. Several commissions studied the idea of intercantonal railways, and the harmonization of taxes, tariffs, currencies, and armies. Among the ideas was Stapfer's federal university which would serve all Swiss cantons.

In the meantime, several cantons undertook their own educational reforms. In the industrial north, new universities were created. In 1818, the University of Basel was reorganized along the lines proposed by the German philosopher Wilhelm von Humboldt. He advocated freedom of instruction, autonomous administration, and the free play of the scientific mind. Zurich also used the Humboldtian model when it created its university in 1833. Basel and Zurich were followed by Bern the following year when it enlarged its school of theology to create a university. Geneva also expanded its Calvinist seminary, which officially became a university in 1873.

Proponents of the federal university faced great hostility from these institutions and cantons. The religious and cultural differences in Switzerland made the idea of a single national university difficult to establish. Cantons considered the training of pastors, judges, and teachers to be too important to relinquish to a central authority. As for greater scientific and technical training, the Humboldtian model left little room for practical training. The proposal for a technical institute was soon added to the list of items to be studied by the constitutional commission.

Despite the hostility of some cantonal representatives, the Swiss Federal Constitution of 1848 did recognize the role of education in developing a national civic pride, in preserving liberty, and in maintaining order. Clause 27 of the constitution reserved the right of the confederation to establish and fund institutions of higher learning. A federal university and technical institute were officially recognized. It would take another seven years before Zurich's institute was created. In the intervening years, the proponents of a federal university would be defeated in the national council of 1851, but in a spirit of compromise, the proposal for a polytechnical institution was adopted.

With the hopes of a national university dashed, all efforts were turned to shaping the technical institute. Two of the most important driving forces were General Guillaume H. Dufour (who was to preside over the founding of the Red Cross in 1864), and Alfred Escher, a railway magnate from Zurich. Dufour was a great admirer of the French École Polytechnique. His original plans for the Federal Institute of Technology had been modeled on the French engineering school. Dufour called for a highly centralized administration. Obligatory courses in mechanical and civil engineering, chemistry, and applied sciences were to be spread over three years. The first year was to be devoted to theory, the second to practical application, and the third to specialized branches of engineering. The institute was to grant its own diploma and be administered by a committee which reported directly to the federal council.

Dufour's original plans were modified by the president of the federal council, Alfred Escher. Escher had been one of the chief proponents of a federal university based on the German model and was less disposed to following the Parisian model of the École Polytechnique. He proposed more autonomy for the university professors and administrators, though a federal committee would still oversee the institute. Escher was also successful in winning the institute for his canton of Zurich, which had lost its status as the nation's capital to Bern. In July 1854, the Swiss federal council sanctioned the creation of the Eidgenössische Technische Hochschule (Federal Institute of Technology). Its creation is ranked as one of Escher's greatest political achievements.

The Swiss Federal Institute of Technology opened in October 1855. It consisted of five teaching divisions called *Abteilung*: architecture, engineering, mechanics, chemistry, and forestry—each of which awarded its own diploma. A general branch, featuring chairs in natural sciences, literature, and political sciences, was also included in order to provide a broader education.

Within a decade after opening its doors, the Federal Institute was widely recognized in Europe and the United States as a center for the study of engineering and the sciences. It was to serve as a model for the Massachusetts Institute of Technology and other polytechnical schools around the world. Its reputation was largely built on the calibre and reputation of its teaching staff. The internal disruptions that followed the revolutions of 1848 enabled the Swiss institute to attract many renowned professors, such as the botanist Oswald Heer, the literary historian Theodor Vischer, the Italian libertarian Francesco de Sanctis, the renowned art historian Jacob Burckhardt, and the architect Gottried Semper.

Burckhardt joined the faculty in 1855. He previously had taught in his native Basel at the university. He remained in Zurich for only three years before returning to Basel. His study of the Italian Renaissance published in 1860 remains as of one the most influential works on Renaissance art and history. Semper was an eminently successful practitioner of the Neo-Renaissance style in Germany. Born in Hamburg, he had studied in Paris and Munich. After designing the Dresden Opera House, he was forced to flee Germany following the revolutions of 1848. On the recommendation of Richard Wagner, Semper was appointed professor of architecture in 1855. While in Zurich, he designed the main hall of the Federal Institute and the Winterthur city hall. He left Zurich in 1871 for Vienna, where he designed the theater buildings for the *Ringstrasse*.

The Federal Institute expanded quickly in the first decades. A mathematics section was added to the natural sciences division in 1866 and an agriculture division in 1871. A few years later, a superbly equipped laboratory was established by the physicist Heinrick Weber, with the help of the engineering tycoon Werner von Siemens. From 231 students in 1855, the institute grew to 741 in 1880, and over 2,000 in 1905.

The city of Zurich also underwent a considerable transformation. It grew from a small Swiss town into a cosmopolitan city. In 1856, oil lamps were replaced by public gas lights, which were replaced by electric lamps in 1880. In 1893, Zurich incorporated numerous wards in the surrounding vicinity and expanded quickly to 120,000 inhabitants. By the turn of the century, Zurich was not only Switzerland's most important commercial city, but was also one of Europe's most dynamic cultural centers. Many intellectuals from all academic and political spheres flocked to Zurich. Among them were Leon Trotsky, Rosa Luxembourg, and later, James Joyce.

It was not surprising then, that the institute should attract a young student who would give the school an international reputation for excellence. Albert Einstein enrolled in the mathematical and natural science school for teachers in 1896. He had taken the entrance examination a year earlier when he was just 16. The exam covered a wide range of subjects. Einstein failed to reach a high enough standard in languages, history, literature, and art, though he had done very well in mathematics and sciences. After a year at a school in Aarau, some 20 miles west of Zurich, he received his diploma, which allowed him to enter the Federal Institute. Einstein was joined in

1896 by three fellow students with whom he developed lifelong friendships: Marcel Grossman, a dedicated student and son of an industrialist; Michelangelo Besso who was to join Einstein at the Bern Patent Office; and Mileva Maric, whom Einstein married in 1902. In an era where few women were enrolled in sciences, Maric was indeed unusual, but women had been admitted to the University of Zurich since the middle of the nineteenth century and the Swiss were open to the education of women.

Einstein was, from all accounts, a typical student at Zurich. He was very particular about what lectures he attended, much to the consternation of some of his professors. Fascinated by direct experimentation, he worked most of his time in the physical laboratory until an accident in his third year diminished his enthusiasm for direct experience. By his own accounts, Einstein benefitted from excellent teachers particularly in the area of mathematics.

The Federal Institute had always attracted strong mathematicians such as Elwin Bruno Christoffel, who taught from 1862 to 1869. His work on differential geometry contributed greatly to the mathematical construction of the general theory of relativity. Herman Minkowski, who taught from 1896 to 1902, was the most influential teacher for the young Einstein. Minkowski had won the great Paris Prize for mathematics in 1882 when he was just 18. Einstein was to pay special tribute to him, acknowledging that his lectures provided the mathematical form for the theory of relativity.

As for his physics professors, Einstein had less admiration. The chair of the department was Heinrich Weber who taught at the institute from 1875 until his death in 1912. He was one of the pioneers of the science of electrical engineering, but he was somewhat old-fashioned in his approach to physics. A frosty relationship developed between Weber and Einstein. In his memoirs, Einstein described Weber's lectures as "outstanding and a magnificent introduction to theoretical physics," but he characterized his professor as old-fashioned. Feeling that such lectures taught little that was current in theoretical physics, Einstein elected not to attend them and instead read the works of Helmholtz, Maxwell, Botzmann, and Hertz.

Einstein was able to enjoy a relative freedom of choice until a few months before taking his final examinations for which, he recalled, "one had to stuff oneself with all the rubbish whether one wanted to or not." Admittedly, he had more freedom at the institute than in his native Germany, but he was also saved by the careful, copious notes of Marcel Grossman. Einstein passed his final examinations and was graduated in 1900. Out of total of six points, Einstein obtained a final average of 5.5 in theoretical physics; 5 in practical physics; 5 in the theory of functions; 5 in astronomy; and 4.5 for his diploma paper.

His friend Grossman was appointed a professor at the institute while Einstein was himself overlooked for any appointments. Once again, his good friend Grossman came to his aid and found Einstein a post at the Bern patent office. He returned to the institute 12 years later. In the intervening period, he married Maric, acquired Swiss citizenship, and, most important, developed his general theory of relativity.

Einstein was finally appointed to the chair of theoretical physics at the institute in 1912. Still relatively unknown outside the world of physics, Einstein was already garnering attention throughout Europe as a theoretical physicist. Madame Curie and Jules Poincaré, both eminent scientists, had high praise for Einstein, calling him one of the leading theoreticians of the future. They were quick to point out that despite the frosty relationship between Einstein and Weber, the institute would "reap great honour" in appointing the mathematical physicist. Einstein's teaching days were short-lived, for, as Curie and Poincaré had forewarned, Einstein's research work was becoming valued throughout the world. After one year of teaching, he left Zurich for a professorship at the University of Berlin, membership in the highly prestigious Prussian Academy of Sciences, and the directorship of a new physics institute.

The institute of technology also played a large role in helping Switzerland enter the world economy. Aided by a protectionist policy throughout most of the twentieth century, new enterprises in light mechanics, chemistry, and food production developed alongside the traditional textile and agricultural industries.

In the 1930s, a new chair and laboratory devoted to improving textile equipment and techniques were set up at the institute. Research there eventually led to the introduction of new automatic weaving techniques with synthetic fibers which have revolutionized the Swiss textile industry.

Similar research in the fields of organic and inorganic chemistry has had a comparable impact on the growth and development of the federation's pharmaceutical industry. In a country where arable land has always been in demand, the opening of an agricultural division in 1869 has vastly improved Switzerland's agroeconomy. Research undertaken by Ernest Laur in collaboration with local agricultural association led to more efficient production techniques, which in large part helped Switzerland overcome food shortages during two world wars. The agricultural school's research had also helped develop the sylviculture industry in Switzerland.

From eight divisions in 1854, the institute has grown to more than 20 divisions, most of which grant diplomas (equivalent to the American Master of Science degree) and Doctor of Science degrees. It presently has over 11,000 students working toward degrees in architecture, engineering, mathematics, and science with more than half in the engineering division.

Students who enter the institute tend to be older than their North American counterparts and are graduated after completing four and a half years of study (nine semesters), which includes diploma work and a practicum outside the institute. The institute is affiliated with many of Switzerland's top research institutes and continues to be internationally recognized as a center of scientific research and learning.

Further Reading: Although there is no history of the Federal Institute of Technology, references to it will be found in Frederick S. Allen's *Zurich, the 1820s to the 1870s: A Study in Modernization* (Lanham, Maryland: University Press of America, 1986) and Paul S. Bodemhan's *The Education System of Switzerland* (Washington, D.C.: U.S. Department of Health, Education, and Welfare, 1982). For information about the institute's most illustrious graduate, read Carl Seeling's *Albert Einstein: A Documentary Biography*, translated by Mervyn Savill (London: Staples Press, 1956) and Michael White and John Gribbin's *Einstein: A Life in Science* (London and New York: Simon and Schuster, 1993).

—Manon Lamontagne

FEDERAL UNIVERSITY OF RIO DE JANEIRO
(Rio De Janeiro, Brazil)

Location: In Rio, the state capital of Rio de Janeiro, on a three-mile-long island in Guanabara Bay just east of Rio's Northern Zone and four miles north of Centro, the city's business, government, and cultural center.

Description: The Federal University of Rio de Janeiro is Brazil's largest federal university and one of the nation's oldest public universities. It enrolls over 30,000 undergraduate and graduate students, who pay no tuition.

Information: Federal University of Rio de Janeiro
Avenida Brigadeiro Trompowski s/n
21941 Rio de Janeiro, RJ
Brazil
(21) 290 2112

Visiting: Contact the university at the above location.

Throughout the nineteenth century, Brazilian higher education was limited to the privileged classes who studied in private institutions. These schools emphasized professional training, generally in the fields of law and medicine. But Brazilian intellectuals sought the creation of a true, multidimensional university based on a Western European model. Their hopes were enlivened in the last part of the nineteenth century with the establishment of the Brazilian Federative Republic and the drafting of a constitution in 1891 that mandated federal support of secondary and higher education. But Brazil's government failed to fulfill this role. After the turn of the century, pressure increased for a public university. States, municipalities, and professional organizations responded to the demand by establishing nearly 30 pub-

lic and private colleges in the two decades surrounding 1900. Because most of these institutions were professional schools, pressure continued to mount for a true university.

Not until after 1910 did the federal government become increasingly involved in regulating higher education, and only in 1920 did the government make its first significant attempt to fulfill the promise of its 1891 constitution. That year, the government organized the University of Rio de Janeiro (the predecessor of the Federal University of Rio de Janeiro). The school was formed by uniting three of Brazil's traditional independent professional schools under one administration, combining the Polytechnic Institute of Rio de Janeiro (Brazil's oldest school in the field of engineering), with schools of law and medicine. United under a weak administration, these three disciplines remained semiautonomous. Also, professional training—the three schools' purpose prior to their unification—remained the express central purpose of the University of Rio de Janeiro; the pursuit of research and general knowledge were de-emphasized.

Although the Federal University of Rio de Janeiro has always considered its ancestor Brazil's oldest university, many Brazilian and American scholars maintain that the University of Rio de Janeiro was simply an administrative reorganization. Prominent Brazilian educator Fernando de Azevedo lamented that the establishment of the University of Rio de Janeiro "did not amount to any change in the structure and methods of higher education [in Brazil] . . . and was no more than a grouping of three institutions for training of professional men." Others similarly contended that the establishment of a true university in Brazil occurred only in the 1930s, after the government expanded its role and more actively directed the development of higher education. But despite this, the University of Rio de Janeiro's founding was symbolically significant as it represented the federal government's first solid attempt to address the educational mandates of its constitution. Further, through the creation of this university, the government constructed a model which it hoped would guide development of future Brazilian universities, both public and private. In fact, the prevailing characteristics of the University of Rio de Janeiro were reflected in the organization of Brazil's universities for the next 50 years. More immediately, the university served as an organizational model for the University of Minas Gerais. This school, founded in 1927, also combined existing schools of law, medicine, and engineering under a new central administration.

Just as the initial impetus for the establishment of the University of Rio de Janeiro came from the federal gov-

Federal University of Rio de Janeiro

ernment, significant academic and organizational changes at the university awaited the government's initiative, and a new government.

The 1930 revolution initiated a period of modernization and centralization in Brazil. Known as Estado Novo, the "New State" viewed education reform as central to its modernization program. The national government assumed an active role in all levels of public education, making efforts to standardize instruction and guide students from secondary school into the nascent public universities. The new, more activist government laid the legislative groundwork for Brazil's modern university system. In 1931 legislation detailed the organization and purpose of public universities by setting mandatory curriculum for all fields, directing the organization of academic departments, reemphasizing professional training and mandating a further unification of existing professional schools into the university system. In essence, the new regime's legislation created a model for all Brazil's public universities.

This legislation guided the University of Rio de Janeiro's development in the 1930s. In 1937, the departments of the Federal Technical University were added to the University of Rio de Janeiro, which then changed its name to the University of Brazil. Two years later, the departments of the University of the Federal District (in Rio) were transferred to the University of Brazil, and a department of philosophy, sciences and letters was formed to train secondary school teachers and to offer courses in science and the liberal arts. To fill this department, the government recruited many foreign professors for the university, which enabled the University of Brazil to emphasize scientific research in various fields. The government intended the University of Brazil, with its new organization and purpose, to be its model for all the nation's institutions of higher education.

In an effort to increase the number of trained technical personnel, the Brazilian government continued to develop a network of federal universities in the 1940s. In the next decade federal universities grew to enroll over one-third of Brazil's higher education students. Throughout the 1950s, federal expenditures on higher education increased, universities expanded their fields of study, and the government gradually eliminated all student fees and tuition at public universities.

In 1964 a military takeover of the government further expanded the federal role in education as the new regime tried to direct education for its modernization campaign. The new government aggressively expanded higher education, viewing it as the key to advancing Brazil; accordingly, universities received a greater proportion of the education budget. Economic growth, an expanding middle class, the demands of a technological society, and government efforts to increase access to higher education brought rapid growth to the nation's universities in the 1960s and 1970s. To handle this increase, the government federalized many state, municipal, and private institutions of higher learning in a campaign to make the public university central to Brazil's modernization. The federal universities remained the linchpin of this government scenario.

The government's activism brought significant change to the University of Brazil in the 1960s. In 1965, the university was reorganized as the Federal University of Rio de Janeiro. In 1968 the government launched an intensive university reform effort. These reforms again reorganized the Federal University of Rio de Janeiro using a North American model. Specialized academic departments and institutes were created; these held responsibility for all levels of education in their respective disciplines, from introductory courses to graduate level work, including research and professional certification if relevant. Also, additional independent professional schools were merged into the Federal University of Rio de Janeiro. The university also adopted the U.S.-style semester and credit systems and initiated a "basic cycle" of two years of broad-based coursework to precede specialized education in all fields.

Consolidating teaching and research tasks into discipline-specific departments facilitated research and expanded graduate education. More significantly, in the Federal University of Rio de Janeiro, the government attempted to establish its model research university. The university's role as a research institution was simultaneously encouraged by various federal agencies, which began funneling increasing resources to the university for science and technology research. These funds enlarged the number of science researchers, expanded the university's laboratories and libraries, increased the number of faculty and the proportion holding advanced degrees. By the late 1960s, over 60 percent of Brazil's higher education students were enrolled in public universities, and the Federal University of Rio de Janeiro—Brazil's largest

federal university—enrolled over 20,000 students. These statistics reveal the government's success at increasing access to free higher education, but developments in the next two decades jeopardized these achievements.

During the 1970s, public universities were overwhelmed by a doubling of enrollment. By the early 1980s economic stagnation and demographic factors had curtailed the increases in enrollment, but the government's inability to meet the explosive demand for higher education in the 1970s meant that Brazil's public universities now only enrolled approximately 30 percent of the nation's students, a figure that remains constant into the 1990s.

In the 1980s the Federal University of Rio de Janeiro faced financial problems, which led to hiring freezes, reductions of operating expenses and cutbacks in capital improvement plans. This led the university to initiate lucrative agreements with corporations, government agencies, foreign foundations, and foreign governments. These alliances, following 60 years of government encouragement, are the most recent step in the school's development into a true multidimensional research university.

In its early years the Federal University of Rio de Janeiro represented a mere reorganization of nineteenth-century Brazilian models of higher education. But since its inception, the school has evolved into a diverse, modern university. More than any other Brazilian school, the Federal University of Rio de Janeiro's history has illustrated the centrality of the Brazilian government's role in developing the nation's modern university system.

Further Reading: English language sources on the Federal University of Rio de Janeiro are scarce and many of the most thorough are also the most dated. Fernando de Azevedo's *Brazilian Culture* (New York: Macmillan, 1950) briefly portrays the school's founding from the perspective of an insider. Daniel C. Levy's *Higher Education and the State in Latin America* (Chicago: University of Chicago Press, 1986) describes the role of Brazil's government in the development of its modern university system.

—Michael Mundt

FREE UNIVERSITY OF BERLIN
(Berlin, Germany)

Location: In Dahlem, western Berlin, Germany.

Description: A state university enrolling about 55,000
                     students in undergraduate and graduate schools.

Information: Free University of Berlin
                     International Office
                     Brümmerstrasse 52
                     14195 Berlin
                     Germany
                     (30) 73900
                     Fax (30) 838 73901

The Free University of Berlin has been, since its founding in 1948, attached to Germany's break from the rule of National Socialism and World War II. A free university was not intended to mean an "open university" but one that participated in the new liberal western democratic society. "Truth, Justice, Freedom" has been the motto for nearly 50 years in the biggest university in the German capital.

Following a memorandum by Wilhelm von Humboldt, King Frederick Wilhelm III founded a university at Berlin's Unter den Linden in 1810 that strove for independence from the state while being supported by it. This model of independent research and education of youth has been the dominant university design from the nineteenth century until today.

Within its first 100 years, Berlin's Frederick Wilhelm University developed into one of the biggest and most important institutions of higher education in the German-speaking world. In the late years of the Empire before World War I, the university had a fruitful relationship with a number of other institutions like the Emperor Wilhelm Society, the Technical College of Charlottenburg, and the Prussian Academy of Sciences. There were plans to remove the university from the narrow space of the city center and relocate it in Dahlem, near the Emperor Wilhelm Institutes. But the idea to found a "German Oxford" was destroyed by World War I. The consequences of the war, the unfulfilled revolution, and economic inflation deeply affected the ability to conduct scientific research at the university. Nonetheless, world-class research was carried out for awhile following the war as the high number of Nobel prize winners from Berlin and Dahlem indicates.

After 1933, the National Socialists controlled policy at the universities and used their administrative and physical power to oust their opponents, especially Jewish professors and students. This forced exodus cut back dramatically on the scientific potential of the university.

Berlin suffered heavily from the effects of World War II. Large parts of the inner city were completely destroyed. The reopening of Berlin's university in 1946 was a monumental achievement. The university was located in the Soviet sector, but students from all sectors of Berlin and its surroundings began their studies there. In the following years, however, the confrontation between East and West increased in Berlin, and the university became deeply influenced by the Soviet Union and the East German authorities. Students were admitted largely on their social background, and preference was given to students from the working class and farming community. Student admission also depended on involvement in certain political activities and membership in mass organizations. Nonconformist political activities were repressed and those students were relegated, imprisoned, or abducted.

Students formed a growing opposition against this policy. In the summer of 1948 hundreds of students went to the western sector and demanded in a demonstration near the Potsdamer Platz the establishment of a free university in West Berlin. The idea to found a free university during the heightened political strain of the Berlin Blockade was a most remarkable one. Among others, Ernst Reuter, West Berlin's mayor, strongly supported the idea of founding a university.

Lectures started at the new school in the winter term of 1948–49. About 2,000 students joined the community of teachers and learners. Since the students had initiated the founding of the university, they were granted seats and votes in the Academic Senate, which was an enormous achievement. The Free University was supported by the financial and non-material help of American institutions like the Ford Foundation. Their donations helped to construct central buildings, the university library, the student village, Schlachtensee, and the Clinic Steglitz. Because of the destruction of the inner city, the university was looking for buildings and development area at the suburbs. Dahlem became an option since the American army had vacated buildings there to relocate to western Germany.

The number of students grew steadily through the 1950s. Faculty buildings were erected as well as the first student refectory. A number of formerly private villas in Dahlem were used by the university. The university grew steadily although the first years struggled with difficulties and an uncertain financial situation. Soon the Free University developed into a full university that offered most of the academic subjects, including medicine. However, engineering was only offered at West Berlin's Technical University.

The building of the Berlin Wall in 1961 affected the Free University strongly. Until then, one-third of the students had come from East Germany and East Berlin. After the wall, this was no longer possible. Moreover, the new student generation was not caught in the thought-patterns of the 1950s. In the middle of the 1960s, a student movement took shape in Berlin. The growing number of students, confronted with the insufficient options to influence university decisions; the entanglement of parents, politicians, and institutions during the time of time of National Socialism; the new scientific study of Marxist ideology; and the war in Vietnam all contributed to a strained situation that could not be solved in a conventional way. The shooting of a student during a demonstration against the Shah's visit in 1967, and the assassination in 1968 of Rudi Dutschke, one of the most influential speakers of the students, stirred both the university and the city and led to reconsiderations on all sides. West Berlin's senate agreed upon a fundamental university reform. The new constitution of the so-called "group university" allowed professors, assistants, students, and employees to participate in the decision-making process of the university. With this, the state hoped to bring the protesting students back to the university. At the same time, large amounts of money were invested in extending the university. The new distribution of power was met by the resistance from professors, and according to a decision of the Federal Constitutional Court some changes in the regulations had to be made after some years.

In the seventies both the influence of political groups and of the state administration increased. Structural reforms at the Free University, however, largely continued. The main problem of the 1970s was the continuing growth of the university. The educational policy, the high youth population, and the political and social climate attracted a student body that, in its open-minded independence and non-conformity, differed from that of many West German universities. With the integration of the Teacher Training College, the student number rose to over 30,000. About half of these students came from West Germany and 7 percent from abroad. At the same time the university opened a newly built complex for the humanities and ultra-modern institutes for the natural sciences.

The 40th anniversary of the Free University saw another form of student protest. The study situation had worsened in the 1980s as the number of students increased to about 60,000 while the university was less supported by the state than before. After a long student strike the situation improved.

With the falling of the Berlin Wall in 1989 the historical reasons for the separation of the Free University have abated as well. It is now up to the Senate of Berlin to take over the responsibility for the universities in East and West Berlin. This will also have consequences for the Free University, which is currently the third biggest university in Germany.

At the Free University, students can study subjects in the humanities, the social and natural sciences, and medicine. About two-thirds of the 55,000 students are enrolled in the social sciences. With its university clinics Steglitz and Rudolf Virchow in Wedding, and with subjects such as physics, chemistry, and geoscience, the university has taken a top position in the Federal Republic. This is also true for the faculties of economics, law, and politics. "Small subjects" like religious studies, ethnology, the study of Asian and Ancient cultures, aesthetics, and musicology are also represented at the Free University.

Today the Free University is the most important place of education for physicians in Germany. Both hospitals treat more than 90,000 in-patients annually. In the outpatients' departments, more than 100,000 people are being helped. Moreover, about 150,000 first-aid cases are treated each year. The technical equipment of the hospitals matches the latest developments. The university has two dental clinics in Wilmersdorf and Wedding that treat 7,000 to 10,000 patients each year.

The Free University offers state or academic degrees in more than 90 subjects. The education of 5,500 foreign students helps to spread Germany's and Berlin's reputation abroad. Annually about 1.500 guest professors come to the university that has partnership contracts with some 50 universities worldwide. The university is involved in European community programs that enable integrated study at different European universities.

Research at the university is financed partly by its own means, partly by third parties such as foundations, enterprises, and authorities. These means have increased from 40 million marks in 1981 to 103 million marks in 1991, and can be understood as a sign of the research potentials and future achievements of the Free University of Berlin.

—Wolfgang Holtkamp

GALLAUDET UNIVERSITY
(Washington, D.C., U.S.A.)

Location: In Washington, D.C., about seven miles northeast of the Capitol Building.

Description: A university for the deaf established as the Columbia Institution in 1857.

Information: Visitors' Center
Gallaudet University
800 Florida Avenue, NE
Washington, DC 20002-3695
U.S.A.
(202) 651-5050 (voice & tty)
Fax (202) 651-5704

The roots of Gallaudet University trace back to a modest school for the deaf and blind organized by Amos Kendall, a politician who served in two presidential administrations and a philanthropist who made a fortune through investments in Morse's telegraph. In 1856, a man whom Kendall refers to in his records only as "an adventurer" brought a number of deaf children with him from New York to Washington, where he solicited funds with which to found a school for the deaf. The project nearly collapsed when the man was legally accused of mishandling the money he had collected, and most of the children in his charge were returned to their parents. Five of the youth fell under Kendall's guardianship, however, for they were émigrés without families to take them back.

Kendall and the other trustees of the incipient school agreed to go forward with their plans even without their original leader, for they were still impressed by the need to educate the children in Kendall's care, as well as 20 or 30 deaf, blind, and retarded children residing in their district. Kendall donated a house and two acres of land from his expansive estate, known as "Kendall Green," and he singly paid to furnish supplies and a superintendent. Then Kendall persuaded the U.S. Congress to incorporate his little school under the name of "The Columbia Institution for the Instruction of the Deaf, Dumb, and Blind" on February 16, 1857.

The following May, Kendall retained Edward Miner Gallaudet to serve as the new superintendent of the Columbia Institution, while he assumed the presidency. Gallaudet was then just 20 years old, and had headed no institution, either educational or other. He was, however, the son of Thomas Hopkins Gallaudet, who in 1817 founded the first permanent school for the deaf in the United States, the American Asylum at Hartford (Connecticut) for the Instruction of the Deaf and Dumb. The elder Gallaudet married one of his deaf pupils, Sophia Fowler, who gave birth to Edward on February 15, 1837. Thus, while Edward Gallaudet was only a young teacher of the deaf at his father's school when Kendall approached him, he had almost literally been raised for the post he was granted.

When Gallaudet arrived, the Institution was essentially a small boarding school located in what was still a rural section of Washington. During his first year in office, Gallaudet and three assistants, aided by three servants, instructed 12 deaf and 3 blind children. Even eleven years later, when the last class of blind students were transferred to a school in Maryland, there were fewer than 60 students total.

Gallaudet spoke to Kendall and the trustees about founding a college for the deaf from the time of his arrival. His plan was well received, but progress toward its realization was slow. In 1864, Gallaudet drafted a proposal that the Columbia Institution be allowed to grant college degrees. Senator Grimes of Iowa presented Gallaudet's plan to Congress that spring, and it was enacted into law on April 8. The National Deaf-Mute College was inaugurated on June 28. Kendall ceded the presidency to Gallaudet at the inaugural ceremony, and died five years later, at the age of 80. The college also granted its first degree on inauguration day, an honorary M.A., awarded to John Carlin, an influential deaf painter and deaf advocate.

The college existed in name and intent only until later that year, for it was entirely without facilities, professors, and students. In 1865, a federal grant of $26,000 was set aside for the purchase of 14 acres adjacent to the original campus at Kendall Green, under the stipulation that the land be used for the instruction of male pupils studying horticulture, agriculture, and mechanics. The college began operating out of a small house on the acquired property that September, having enrolled 13 students. Two years later, Gallaudet hired landscape architect Frederick Olmsted to draw up site plans for the new campus. Still another year passed before Congress appropriated funds sufficient to begin construction, and the Main Building did not open until 1871.

The curriculum and manner of instruction at the college were revised in its first few years of operation. Seniors in the first class at the college received a traditional training; they studied anatomy, physiology, zoology, logic, mental philosophy, evidences of Christianity, English literature, and aesthetics. Gallaudet traveled to Europe in 1867 to study the methods by which the deaf were instructed

Gallaudet University

abroad, and upon his return, he issued that courses in speech and lip reading should be taught at the institution, despite the fact that speech was possible only for a minority of deaf students. That year, the directors voted to allow some hearing people to teach various courses, and in 1891, they created the Normal Department, a program devoted to the training of hearing teachers of deaf students.

The directors of the institution granted women the right to enter the college in 1887, on a provisional basis. They had been moved by a young woman's paper calling for the right of women to enter deaf schools which the author read at a convention of the American Instructors of the Deaf. The first six women to enroll were housed in Gallaudet's own home, for the college had no other appropriate facilities. Women enrolled in later classes were accommodated elsewhere, but a dormitory was not constructed for women until 1917.

In 1878, the faculty wrote to the board of directors asking that the name "National Deaf-Mute College" be changed, both because it was somewhat distasteful, and

because it was inappropriate; 23 of 52 students enrolled that year were in fact capable of speech. However it was not until 1894 that the name of Gallaudet College was officially adopted for the school, in honor of Thomas Gallaudet. The Kendall School and the college were then defined as the two divisions of the institution. The elder Gallaudet is a hero to the deaf in this country, for he traveled to Europe in 1815, 52 years before his son's venture, in order to study the methods by which deaf children were taught in England and France. He himself became expert in pantomime, and he was instrumental in the development of American Sign Language. His statue has adorned the Kendall Green since 1889.

While the college remained quite small for many years—the class of 1891 had only one graduate—its alumni did well professionally. A member of the class of 1869 became the principal of the Western Pennsylvania Institution for Deaf Mutes. An alumnus of the class of 1872 edited and published a newspaper in Massachusetts. Jamini Nath Banerji, who attended the Normal School in

1895, founded one of very few schools for the deaf in India, and of course, many graduates taught the deaf at institutions across the United States.

President Gallaudet retired in the spring of 1910, having served 53 years at the institution. He died seven years later, at the age of 80. The directors elected Dr. Percival Hall the next president of the college. After being graduated from Harvard with a bachelor's degree, Hall enrolled in the Normal Department at Gallaudet. He spent two years teaching at the New York School for the Deaf, and then returned to Gallaudet, where he served the institution in various capacities before assuming its leadership: he was Edward Gallaudet's secretary for several years, a mathematics teacher, head of the articulation program, and then head of the Normal Department.

The college was doing badly in many respects when Hall took over, despite Gallaudet's great achievements. The plant was overcrowded and generally in poor condition; teachers were underpaid and often left the college to take better salaries elsewhere; and only half of the students entering the college were graduating. Hall coped with these problems throughout his administration, but progress was slow. The college remained financially strapped, as the nation passed through the Great Depression and two World Wars during Hall's tenure. He is remembered today for having diversified the curriculum at the college, and for establishing a research department in 1937. Hall retired on May 7, 1945, having worked at Gallaudet for 50 consecutive years. He died eight years later, at the age of 81.

Dr. Leonard M. Elstad was elected the next president of Gallaudet, 22 years after being graduated from the Normal Department in 1923. After receiving his degree, Elstad held teaching and administrative positions at several schools for the deaf, including the superintendancy of the Minnesota School for the Deaf. Elstad succeeded in doing for the College what his predecessors had only dreamed of. In 1955, he successfully solicited the House Appropriations Committee of the U.S. Congress for funds sufficient to back a major renovation of Gallaudet's plant. Between 1955 and 1969, 18 new buildings were raised on campus, and six new areas of study were added to the curriculum. Thanks to these improvements, the Middle States Association of Colleges and Secondary Schools accredited Gallaudet in 1957. Five years later, Elstad oversaw the formation of a program for deaf students leading to a master's degree in education.

Gallaudet has prospered since Elstad's retirement in 1969. Dr. Edward C. Merrill Jr. was elected Gallaudet's fourth president that same year, and he oversaw the foundation of several new departments in the college: the School of Education and Human Services, the School of Communication, and the College of Arts and Sciences, each of which was granted its own dean. Dr. Merrill's two immediate successors served brief terms: Dr. W. Lloyd Johns resigned before his formal inauguration, having

been elected president in 1983. President Jerry C. Lee served between 1984 and 1987. It was during Lee's administration that U.S. President Ronald Reagan signed the Education of the Deaf Act, which accorded Gallaudet the rank of university, whereupon the Consortium of Universities of the Washington Metropolitan Area granted Gallaudet full membership.

The only episode of substantial student unrest at Gallaudet followed the trustees announcement of March 13, 1988, that they had selected Dr. Elisabeth A. Zinser to serve as Gallaudet's seventh president. Gallaudet students and deaf advocates from around the country were outraged that several qualified deaf candidates had been passed over in favor of Zinser, who can hear. A protest evolved into a "Deaf President Now" (DPN) movement, which shut down the university for a week, and attracted the attention of the international press. The protesters demanded the resignations of Zinser and Jane Bassett Spilman, chairperson of the board of trustees, and pushed for the election of Dr. I. King Jordan, the deaf dean of the College of Liberal Arts and Sciences.

At least eight groups publicly urged the university's search committee, formed in September 1987, to pursue and elect a deaf president. The DPN movement was eventually organized by one of those eight groups, known as the "Ducks." The Ducks were six deaf men associated with the National Association of the Deaf who originally met to discuss various issues including, but not limited to, the need for Gallaudet to elect a deaf president. When the search committee reduced a pool of 67 applicants to six qualified semi-finalists the following January, three of whom were deaf, the Ducks stepped up their advocatory activities from mere letter-writing. They contacted members of Congress and the press, and they organized a rally to take place March 1 on campus.

Deaf advocates from across the country gathered at Hotchkiss Field, the Gallaudet football stadium, where stickers and yellow buttons reading "Deaf President Now" were distributed. Numerous speeches were delivered, in sign language, first at the stadium, and later at the Kendall School, where the rally moved when the weather turned bad. Rebelliously signing "Deaf President Now," the crowd marched across campus, and then gathered again on the mall. There, Gary Olsen, head of the Ducks, told them to be proud of their deafness, thus resounding one faculty member's statement that a hearing president represented the "dark ages of paternalism" and the notion that deaf people are pitiably handicapped and must be cared for by hearing people.

When the board of trustees announced their selection of Zinser on Sunday, March 8, a group of protesters marched to the Mayflower Hotel, where Spilman was staying. Before Spilman could address the crowd, which was large and vocal enough that the police had been called in to contain the situation, Olsen led a march to the White House and the Capitol. The marchers returned to

Hughes gym around midnight, where protests continued and several members of the Ducks formulated a strategy for installing a deaf president, even as their cause appeared lost. They decided to block five entrances to the campus that Monday morning, and thus they succeeded in shutting down the university.

The protesters threw their support behind I. King Jordan, one of the three deaf semi-finalists selected by the search committee. Jordan initially announced that he would abide by the committee's decision, but he joined the protesters on Thursday, the fourth day that the university was shut down. Jordan's change of mind came when he realized that the DPN movement was a legitimate promotion of deaf people's civil rights. That same day, Zisner announced her resignation, and Spilman followed suit Friday morning.

The protesters marched to the Capitol a second time that Friday, to press their demand for a deaf president. The press openly expressed their support for the DPN movement, which was commonly compared to the black civil rights march in Selma, Alabama. The board of trustees met again that Sunday at the Embassy Row Hotel, and there decided to offer Jordan the presidency, which he happily accepted. Within a week, the backers of the DPN movement had accomplished their objective, and ushered in a new era at Gallaudet.

Further Reading: The only monographic history of Gallaudet is *Gallaudet College, Its First One Hundred Years* by Albert W. Atwood (Washington, D.C.; Gallaudet College, 1964). The DPN movement is recorded and analyzed in fine detail in *Deaf President Now! The 1988 Revolution at Gallaudet University* by John B. Christiansen and Sharon Barnart (Washington, D.C.: Gallaudet University, 1995).

—Christopher Hoyt

GEORGETOWN UNIVERSITY
(Washington, D.C., U.S.A.)

Location: On a 104-acre campus overlooking the Potomac River in the historic Georgetown district, a ten-minute drive from downtown Washington, D.C.

Description: A Roman-Catholic, coeducational institution, with an enrollment of nearly 12,000 undergraduate and graduate students from all 50 states and 110 foreign countries. The undergraduate ranks number about 5,600 students, divided almost evenly between men and women.

Information: Office of Undergraduate Admissions
Georgetown University
Washington, DC 20057-1002
U.S.A.
(202) 687-3600

Visiting: Contact the Admissions Office for a schedule of tours offered Monday through Saturday.

A Jesuit institution originally founded for men, Georgetown University is one of the most influential learning institutions in the United States, partly because of its location in the nation's capital and partly because of its graduate and professional schools. Georgetown's Walsh School of Foreign Service is the largest school of international relations in the world and the oldest in the United States. The Georgetown campus is steeped in history, having attracted political notables from George Washington to Bill Clinton.

Georgetown dates its founding to 1789, the year that saw the establishment of the United States of America. In actual fact, 1789 was the year land was acquired for the school; it did not open for another two years. The school's founding father was John Carroll, a Maryland native who had joined the Jesuit order (Society of Jesus) in 1753. Carroll had been teaching in Europe when Pope Clement XIV began suppressing the Society of Jesus, in response to pressure from European governments anxious to achieve more power over the church within their countries. The action drove Carroll back to the American colonies. There, he became an ardent supporter of the American Revolution, which seemed to promise the opportunities to restore the Jesuit order in America and free Catholics from the discriminatory treatment suffered by the religious minority.

After the American victory in the revolution, Carroll saw far-reaching possibilities for Catholic education in the new republic. In 1786, he wrote a prospectus for his proposed college, citing as its mission: "to unite the means of communicating Science with an effectual Provision for guarding and preserving the Morals of Youth." The prospectus also noted that "the Seminary will be open to Students of every Religious Profession." In 1789, the same year he was named the first bishop of the American Catholic Church, Carroll secured the title to 60 acres of land overlooking the village of Georgetown, a prosperous tobacco port in Maryland. He wrote: "We shall begin the building of our Academy this summer. In the beginning we shall confine our plan to a house of 63 or 64 feet, by 50, on one of the most lovely situations imagination can frame. . . . On this Academy is built all my hopes of permanency and success of our religion in the United States." As he prepared to receive students, Carroll was pleased to learn that the nation's capital would be established in the neighborhood, giving the school added prominence.

On November 22, 1791, the school welcomed its first student, William Gaston, who later would represent North Carolina in the U.S. Congress. The school included an institute to train candidates for the Jesuit order and a separate lay school of three divisions, comparable to modern-day elementary school, high school, and college. Elementary-level students studied reading, writing, grammar, arithmetic, geography, and beginning Latin. College-level students focused on Latin, Greek, and English literature, natural science, and philosophy. By 1793, the lay school had 60 students and the faculty had seven members. Tuition was about $44 a year; board was an additional $133. Four years later, Georgetown College received its first visitor of distinction when retired president George Washington arrived to visit two nephews who were enrolled as students.

Despite its ideal location, the school was plagued with poverty, insufficient faculty, and low enrollment for its first two decades. By the turn of the nineteenth century, the campus consisted of two unimpressive buildings, "Old South," a country schoolhouse, and "Old North," an austere, unfinished structure. Enrollment had reached only 76, less than a fourth of whom were sufficiently advanced for college-level instruction. By 1806, enrollment had fallen to 34, and Carroll, now an archbishop, recommended temporary suspension of the school. The situation did not improve until 1812 when the task of saving the school was assumed by three energetic Jesuits: Father John Anthony Grassi, who became the school's

Georgetown University

president that year, and his successors, Father Peter Kenney and Father Thomas Mulledy.

A native of Italy, Father Grassi resisted calls to move Georgetown College to the thriving metropolis of New York, predicting that the then-backward city of Washington would become an international center. He revitalized the faculty and repaired and enlarged classrooms and living quarters. He warned against complacency, advocating self-criticism as the means to continued improvement. During the War of 1812, the college inhabitants could see the flames as the British set fire to Washington. Fortunately, the college was spared invasion. The year 1814 brought welcome news: Archbishop Carroll announced that the Society of Jesus was formally restored worldwide, giving new impetus to Jesuit activities. A year later, Georgetown College was officially chartered by the U.S. government.

In 1817, the college welcomed more distinguished visitors. Eight Native American chiefs, in Washington to discuss land matters with President James Monroe, stopped at the college to thank the Jesuits for their missionary activities in Indian territories. Father Grassi had been succeeded by the Irish-born Father Peter Kenney, who strengthened the capabilities of the faculty by sending several teachers to study in Europe. Father Thomas Mulledy, president from 1829 to 1837, raised academic standards, reorganized the curriculum, further improved the quality of the faculty, and began an advertising campaign to promote enrollment. Georgetown College was now firmly entrenched.

In 1841, under Father James Curley, Georgetown began planning an astronomical observatory, only the third such installation in the United States. The three-story brick structure was completed in 1844 and astronomy was added to the curriculum. In 1842, English novelist Charles Dickens visited America and described Georgetown College as "delightfully situated, and, so far as I had an opportunity of seeing, well managed. . . . The heights in this neighborhood, above the Potomac River, are very picturesque; and are free, I should conceive, from some of the insalubrities of Washington. The air, at that elevation, was quite cool and refreshing, when in the city it was burning hot."

True to Archbishop Carroll's intent that the school be open to students of all faiths, Protestants had comprised nearly 20 percent of the student body in the first ten years the school was open. By the 1830s, Jewish students were attending Georgetown. The school's nearness to Washington gave a cosmopolitan flavor not only to the student body but to the faculty as well. Among the professors were Jesuit emigres from Italy, Germany, Poland, and Belgium. Until later in the nineteenth century, however, the student body continued to be comprised of boys from 10 to 16 years of age.

In the late 1840s, an anticlerical movement in Italy drove out several eminent Jesuit scientists who immigrated to America and became welcome additions to the Georgetown faculty. One was Father Benedict Sestini, former head of the Roman College Astronomical Observatory and a brilliant physicist and mathematician. Another was Father Angelo Secchi, who stayed at the school only a year and later became director of the Vatican Observatory in Rome. Others included Torquatus Armellini, John Baptist Pianciani, Joseph Ardia, Michael Tomei, Antonio Maraschi, and the brothers Francisco and Salvatore Tongiori, all highly respected in theological and philosophical circles.

In 1849, Georgetown established its first professional school when a group of doctors excluded from the Washington Infirmary by an insiders' clique asked the college to provide them with medical facilities. The college leased a building in downtown Washington for classrooms, a dispensary, and a six-bed infirmary. This was the beginning of the Georgetown School of Medicine. Three years later, Georgetown embarked on further advances when Father Bernard A. Maguire became head of the school. A youthful and dynamic administrator, Father Maquire improved the curriculum, developed new student organizations, and took other steps to keep both the students and the faculty performing at a high level.

The Civil War caused a devastating interruption in the school's progress, leaving the school, in Father Maguire's words, "nearly ruined." Despite its cosmopolitan surroundings, Georgetown was effectively a Southern school. Four-fifths of the Georgetown alumni who served in the war fought for the Confederacy. Enrollment fell from 313 in 1859 to a mere 17 in the autumn of 1861. For a time, Federal troops were billeted on campus; later, school buildings were converted into hospital facilities for wounded soldiers. In 1866, Father Maguire resumed his presidency and worked to rebuild the school. Buildings were repaired and enlarged, the campus was relandscaped and, by 1867, enrollment was up to 250. Symbolizing the nation's reunification, Georgetown adopted blue and gray as its official colors.

The recovery of the school itself was indicated in 1870, when Georgetown established its second professional school, the School of Law, funded by local attorneys. Then, in 1873, Georgetown came under the direction of one of its most renowned presidents, Reverend Patrick Healy, son of a New England ship captain and a former slavewoman. Nicknamed the "Spaniard" by his students for his dark good looks and his imperious demeanor, Healy not only maintained the school's academic improvements, he also implemented scientific studies well beyond those found in most other colleges. He ordered construction of a splendid Flemish Renaissance building to house a new library, classrooms, and laboratory facilities; the building is now known as Healy Hall. He also founded the Georgetown Alumni Association in 1880.

In 1889, Georgetown University celebrated its 100th anniversary. The centennial ceremonies were attended by U.S. President Benjamin Harrison and Secretary of State James G. Blaine, among others. Guests were greeted by the inscription: "Congratulations, Venerable Mother . . . You alone, among all the colleges, have lived as long as the republic." Speakers stressed the importance of future progress, appropriately symbolized by Thomas Edison's new multicolored electric lamps adorning the historic Old South Building.

The school began its second century under the leadership of Reverend Joseph Havens Richards, the son of an Episcopal priest. Richards introduced graduate courses in arts and sciences. He also enlarged law and medical school facilities. World-renowned astronomer Father John Hagen joined the faculty, bringing new vigor to the astronomy department and renovating the observatory. In 1892, groundbreaking ceremonies started construction of the new Chapel of the Sacred Heart, a modest English Gothic structure financed by alumnus John Dahlgren at the cost of $40,000.

At this time, more than 100 students were enrolled in Georgetown's medical school. In 1873, facilities were expanded to allow for studies in bacteriology, histology, and analytical and practical chemistry. Up to now, the medical school had refused to accept females, but when an ambitious young woman named Louise Taylor applied in 1898, the school allowed her to take an anatomy course, making her Georgetown's first coed. A university hospital was established that same year. Georgetown's School of Law also was prospering, graduating more than 100 students in 1891 alone. Georgetown's law students were distinguishing themselves in intercollegiate debating. The school's athletes, meanwhile, were also achieving renown, especially in baseball and football.

The beginning years of the twentieth century saw even more rapid progress at Georgetown. The Washington Dental College was absorbed in 1901, and a nursing school was established in 1904. By 1914, total enrollment neared 1,400, a far cry from the 17 students recorded little more than a half-century earlier. Of the new total, some 900 were law students. As dean of the Medical School from 1901 to 1927, Dr. George Kober led his school through an era of reform that was to revolutionize medicine. Georgetown achieved additional distinction as its observatory added seismological equipment and began recording earthquakes, up to then a field of study that had received little attention.

Professional school enrollment declined somewhat during World War I, and the student body was mobilized by law into the Students' Army Training Corps. In 1919, Georgetown's Preparatory School separated from the university and was relocated to suburban Maryland. That same year, Father Edmund A. Walsh established the Walsh School of Foreign Service to prepare students for diplomatic or international business careers. Enrollment in foreign service studies reached 500 within just five years. In the late 1920s, Georgetown's football team achieved its highest level of performance to date under Coach Lou Little. The construction of several new facilities on campus evidenced the university's continued growth.

Even the Great Depression failed to stop progress at Georgetown. The graduate school was formally established during those years under the presidency of Father Arthur O'Leary. During World War II, the main campus became a testing place for the Army Specialized Training Center. As is to be expected, enrollment in most of Georgetown's professional schools dropped during the war, although the medical school maintained its prewar enrollment level and began engaging in vital research. In 1944, the graduate school for the first time opened its doors to women.

In the post-war years, enrollment doubled as the G.I. Bill provided new opportunities to those who otherwise could not have afforded a college education. By 1949, Georgetown's School of Medicine was conducting important research into arthritis and cancer. It was at the Georgetown Medical Center in the 1950s that Dr. Charles A. Hufnagel made unprecedented advances in the treatment of arterial defects and the use of artificial valves. Georgetown also pioneered the use of the artificial kidney and curative operations on the human brain.

There have been periodic clashes at Georgetown between the principles of academic freedom and the university's Roman-Catholic tradition. In a 1950 commencement address entitled "The Sacred Fetish of Academic Freedom," Georgetown President Hunter Guthrie provoked considerable consternation when he said:

> Freedom must be limited by belief in God, by faith in the omnipotence of truth, and the beneficence of justice. Freedom springs from truth but still truth is rarely freedom's offspring. . . . [Academic freedom is] the soft underbelly of our American way of life and the sooner it is armor plated by some sensible

limitations, the sooner will the future of this nation be secured from fatal consequences.

In 1992 a strategic planning document reinforced the school's open-admissions policy to ensure class, cultural, and religious diversity in the student body as well as the faculty. A Jesuit dean noted that "a person's religion plays no part in hiring, tenure, promotion, the awarding of grants, or the securing of funds. In fact, most of us don't know each other's religious beliefs."

Today, in addition to professional schools of medicine, law, foreign service, and nursing, Georgetown has schools of business and of languages and linguistics. The campus contains some 60 buildings in addition to a recreation complex and athletic fields. Historic Old North, completed in 1795, still stands today. President George Washington once addressed the students from its south doorway. More recently, President Bill Clinton, a 1968 graduate of Georgetown's School of Foreign Service, spoke from the same location during the week of his inauguration.

The best-known building on campus is the Flemish Renaissance structure Healy Hall, which has come to symbolize the university. One of its parlors houses the university's art collection, which includes works by Gilbert Stuart, John Neagle, and John Wollaston, as well as such European masters as Sir Anthony Van Dyck and Luca Giordano. Georgetown's three libraries together hold more than 1.7 million volumes, including the Woodstock Theological Library, one of the best Roman-Catholic collections in the nation. The spiritual center of Georgetown University is the Dahlgren Chapel of the Sacred Heart, a dignified English Gothic structure dedicated in 1893.

Further Reading: *Georgetown University, First in the Nation's Capital* by Joseph T. Durkin (Garden City, New York: Doubleday, 1964) provides an interesting and informative account of the university's history, particularly its first century. The conflict between religion and secular education, with references to Georgetown, is discussed in the following two books: *Catholic Higher Education, Theology, and Academic Freedom* by Charles E. Curran (Nortre Dame, Indiana: University of Notre Dame Press, 1990); and *From the Heart of the American Church: Catholic Higher Education and American Culture* by David J. O'Brien (Maryknoll, New York: Orbis, 1994).

—Pam Hollister

GEORGIA AUGUSTUS UNIVERSITY OF GÖTTINGEN
(Göttingen, Germany)

Location: In Göttingen, Germany.

Description: A state university of 30,000 students with faculties of Protestant theology, law, medicine and dentistry, mathematics, history and philology, physics, economics, chemistry, earth sciences, biology, agriculture, social sciences, education, and forestry.

Information: Georgia Augustus University
Wilhelmsplatz 1
Göttingen 39-4341
Germany

Göttingen as a place derives its name from a village in what was to become the Prussian province of Hanover, known from mid-tenth-century documents. The late medieval town developed in the fourteenth century, but was unremarkable until its world-renowned university was built. The town has now come to exist primarily on account of its famous university, the Georgia Augustus, founded in 1734 and opened in 1737 by the Kurfürst George Augustus, elector of Hanover and King George II of England (the Kurfürstentum was united with the English throne from 1714). Although one of the youngest universities of old Germany, only older than Erlangen (1743), by 1777 it was Germany's largest and best-administered university, with over 3,000 students. Thirty Nobel Prize winners have taught or studied at it. The university and the famous names associated with it, some of whom are commemorated by statues distributed throughout the town, are what give Göttingen its continued renown.

Town officials attempted to found a university first in the 1540s. It was another 200 years before king George II agreed on the town as the site of a university to be built in his honor. The small village was chosen specifically because of its remoteness and available land—the low cost of living, for example, compared to Berlin, was an advantage to students. Another advantage of the new university was its riding hall and stables—not common in city universities. Court architects created a dazzling modern university, in the neoclassical style. Its charter specified complete freedom of inquiry, and students were given the uncommon privilege of library use (the standard was a library restricted to faculty). The famous library was housed from 1809 in buildings from a late thirteenth-century Dominican monastery.

The university was endowed by a deed dated December 7, 1736, and immediately established its reputation by appointing such outstanding figures to its professorial chairs as Albrecht von Haller and Christian Gottlob Heyne, who were among the foundation appointments, J.L. von Mosheim, the noted theologian and ecclesiastical historian, the jurist G.L. Böhmer, and the classical scholar J.M. Gesner. The actual work of founding the new institution was left by King George II to Gerlach Adolph von Münchhausen from Halle, later to become Hanoverian Resident in Great Britain and Hanoverian prime minister in 1765.

It is largely due to Haller and Münchhausen that Göttingen developed its liberal tradition, favoring intellectual academic freedom against the prevailing authoritarianism of the German university system. Münchhausen reformed the method of appointing professors along the lines already adopted by Douze in the Low Countries, relying on a lay appointing committee. Students were successfully attracted away from Halle, Helmstedt, Jena, and Leipzig, and the 1734 statutes enshrined the liberal principles which were originally the foundation for Göttingen's success, to which it has invariably remained faithful, and which still distinguish it today.

The ceremonial opening took place three years after the statutes had been promulgated and the first students admitted, on September 17, 1737. The celebrated philological seminar was founded, as well as the equally famous observatory, the botanical garden, and the library. Haller's appointment was itself a strident declaration. He was an early academic surgeon, whose craft was still commonly rated with that of the barber as inferior to that of the physician. (In Great Britain not even anatomy was systematically taught before 1705, and chairs of clinical medicine were not established there until 1741.)

The most important subjects at Göttingen in the eighteenth century remained those of the law faculty, but Göttingen was not founded merely for the training of administrators. In 1751 the university became the home of Hanover's royal society (*Königliche Sozietät der Wissenshaften*), a research institute that aspired not to teach but only to discover. By adopting the academy, founded by Haller and divided into three sections devoted respectively to the physical sciences, mathematics, and history linked to philology, the new university at Göttingen united teaching and research, now commonly associated with universities. This combination in the same institution was an important innovation.

The Göttingen library quickly grew; by 1900, it held half a million volumes, with over 5,000 manuscripts.

Georgia Augustus University of Göttingen

There was also a mathematics institute, another eighteenth-century research foundation joined to the university, among whose members were Karl Friederich Gauss and Bernhard Riemann.

So many teachers and scholars of world renown were associated with Göttingen's university even in the eighteenth century, that there is a danger of seeing the institution's history in terms of individual achievements. But in the history of Göttingen the sum in truly greater than the parts. The exacting scholarly research into classical antiquity and the obsessive urge to publish characterized Gesner's *Philologishes Seminar* and spread to classical scholarship throughout Germany. But this took place against the backdrop of research undertaken in the natural sciences. Although the work of scholars such as historian August Ludwig Schlözer, lawyer Johann Stephan Pütter, or economist Johann Beckmann, can be weighed for individual achievement, Göttingen's university is chiefly known for bringing individuals together for concerted action and for fostering academic values throughout all

research and teaching activities of the university. Napoléon himself respected these values, the interdependence of teaching and research, at the university of Göttingen, choosing it to be an institution of world rank when Helmstedt, Giessen, and Marburg were closed in Westphalia between 1806 and 1813.

With the new great hall built for the 1837 centenary barely completed, a new generation of Göttingen scholars backed a formal protest against the abrogation by King Ernest Augustus of the 1833 liberal constitution of Hanover. (Ernest Augustus, the fifth son of George III of England, had studied at Göttingen.) The seven professors to protest, known as the "Göttingen Seven," were removed from office on December 14, in spite of widespread sympathy throughout the German academic world, and they were by no means isolated in their indignation. Led by the Germanist W.A. Albrecht, the other six signatories of the protest were F.C. Dahlmann, classicist, historian, and liberal politician; the theologian Heinrich Georg August Ewald; the literary historian G.G. Gervinus; the famous brothers Jacob and Wilhelm Grimm, who also had been students at the university; and the physicist Wilhelm Weber. Ernest Augustus succeeded in imposing his new constitution in 1840, but Göttingen has always been proud of its seven protestors. It was in consideration of this precedent that another group of Göttingen professors made a protest in 1957. Led by C.F. von Weizsacker, 18 atomic physicists warned the German chancellor, Konrad Adenauer, that they would have nothing at all to do with the development of atomic weapons. Since Göttingen's Nobel Prize winners include names such as Max Born, James Franck, Werner Heisenberg, and Max von Laue, the views of the university's physicists have naturally come to carry weight.

The immediate result of the 1837 dismissals, however, was intellectually destructive and led to a further decrease in student enrollment, which had already been halved between 1823 and 1834. On the other hand, the 1848 liberal disturbances throughout continental Europe increased Göttingen's standing, and since Hanover's annexation by Prussia in 1866, the university, upgraded in status, again prospered. Shortly after the turn of the century there was a teaching staff of 121 and a student population of 1,529. At this time, the library holding contained the richest collection of modern literature in Germany— the library had been much rebuilt and extended between 1879 and 1882—and much new construction was undertaken in the early years of the twentieth century.

Meanwhile, Göttingen had gestated two other widely known cultural developments. The first was the formation of a group of student poets called the Göttinger Hainbund, also known as the Göttinger Hain or the Göttinger Dichterbund. This student league became deeply interested in the newer emotional forms of poetry emerging in the work of Friedrich Gottlieb Klopstock, especially his odes, which had been published in collected form in 1771. The league members reacted against what they regarded as the artificial elegance of the verse of Wilhelm Wieland (1733–1813), and rallied to the *Göttingen Musenalmanach*, the university publication. The story is that the group spontaneously gathered on a moonlit walk on September 12, 1772, and made a vow of everlasting friendship that was sealed by a dance around an oak tree, and then met regularly to read poetry. Many of its members went on to make important contributions to German poetry, drama, or fiction. The poet and translator Johann Heinrich Voss was one of its members and, from 1775, was editor of the *Göttinger Musenalmanach*. Others included H.C. Boie, L.P. Hahn, G.A. Burger, L.H.C. Holty, and J.M. Miller. Contemporary with the cultural phenomenon known as *Sturm und Drang* in Germany, the Göttinger Hainbund is culturally linked to the whole western European movement known as pre-romanticism.

The *Göttinger Musenalmanach* itself had been founded in 1770 and was edited by Boie until 1775, at first jointly with F.W. Gotter. Klopstock's work was featured from the second issue on, and from the third the poetry selection was closely associated with Göttingen Hainbund. Voss took over the editorship in 1775, but the almanac was losing its importance, although it continued publication until 1804, later under L.F.G. von Geockingk. Voss founded another almanac in 1775, and a competing *Göttingisches Magazin für Wissenschaft und Literatur* was published from 1780 to 1785, co-edited by G.C. Lichtenberg, professor at Göttingen from 1775, and G. Forster.

A further academic group of huge importance to emerge from Göttingen was that associated with Albert Eichhorn and devoted to setting New and Old Testament exegesis in its cultural context. From this arose the history of religions as an academic discipline in its own right. The foremost representative of this liberal historical school was probably Hermann Gunkel, who had taught at Göttingen from 1885 to 1888, when his academic differences with the more conservative A. Ritschl obliged him to move to Halle. The core of his method was to use old eastern cultures and literatures to contextualize the study of the Old and New Testaments, taking into account in his exegeses the late Jewish and Hellenistic environments in which the Christian scriptures were formed. This method led Gunkel to detract from the specific individuality of the canonical texts and their authors. Associated with Gunkel in Eichhorn's Göttingen group was Johann Franz Wilhelm Bousset, who came to Göttingen as a *privatdozent* in 1890, and was made a professor of New Testament exegeses in 1896. Beginning in 1897, he edited the influential *Theologische Rundschau*, and from 1903, with Gunkel, the *Forschungen zur Religion und Literatur des Alten und Neuen Testaments*. The school, which was massively important in religious studies, included many other figures, notably J. Weiss and E. Troeltsch, and inaugurated modern biblical exegesis, which situates the sacred texts in their environmental origins.

Innovations in departments continued as well. In 1939 came the incorporation of the forestry college, and in 1952 agriculture was separated from natural sciences. A social science faculty was inaugurated in 1962. New subject areas, already in existence, were formally established in 1980 after the incorporation of a teacher training college in 1978.

The university remained open during World War I, in spite of extremely low numbers of students. After the war, returning veterans swelled its numbers. Soon Göttingen and its university were among the first to support the new Nazi Party, beginning the university's decline as an intellectual center. Most of the mathematics faculty, for example, were Jews forced to leave in 1933, and the university never regained its status as a world leader of mathematics. The university celebrated its 200th anniversary in 1937 as a university stripped of its academic freedoms, a place of numerous Nazi ceremonies and speeches. Nonetheless, the 1945 defeat of Germany brought the opportunity for a new beginning, and Göttingen, its buildings undamaged by World War II, was among the earliest of the German universities to reopen. Political troubles surfaced again in 1955 with a defeated ministerial attempt in Lower Saxony to bring back some teaching staff discredited by their earlier national socialist activities.

In 1946 Göttingen became Lower Saxony's university, and the state acquired sufficient territory in the north of the town for the construction of the necessary new hospitals and institutes for agriculture, forestry, chemistry, and earth sciences. The humanities remained housed in the town center, where the state and university library was rebuilt and opened in 1992. In 1980, there were 14 different disciplines taught, of which 6 corresponded with the earlier faculties. The student population has risen from 5,000 in 1950 to over 30,000 in 1990. Göttingen survived the 1968 student disturbances throughout Europe with comparatively little change, although further impetus was given to the structural reorganization integrating the university's management and streamlining the agglomeration of institutes, faculties, and seminars.

In 1990, a commission of examination declared the University of Göttingen among the best in Germany, and certainly the best in Lower Saxony. Its declared aim is to continue its academic work in research and teaching unencumbered by any form of political interference.

—Claudia Levi

GUILFORD COLLEGE
(Greensboro, North Carolina, U.S.A.)

Location: Guilford College is located in Greensboro, North Carolina, west of the center of North Carolina. The college is two hours by automobile from the Blue Ridge Mountains and about three and a half hours from the Atlantic Ocean.

Description: An independent, four-year college with 1,650 students, affiliated with the Society of Friends, or Quakers.

Information: Guilford College
5800 West Friendly Avenue
Greensboro, NC 27410-4173
U.S.A.
(800) 992-7759

Visiting: Guided tours of the campus are available Monday through Friday by appointment. For more information, call the phone number above.

Established in 1837 by the Religious Society of Friends (Quakers), Guilford College is the third oldest coeducational college in the United States. It was then known as New Garden Boarding School and was a preparatory school rather than a college. Not until the 1880s did school officials change the institution from a prepartory boarding school to a college.

The first years were important for Guilford College, which became the first coeducational school in the South, enrolling women decades before schools such as the University of North Carolina at Chapel Hill. In the first year, 25 boys and 25 girls enrolled at the small school in Guilford County. The principle of coeducation extended to the faculty as well; Jonathan Slocum and Nathan Hill taught the boys and Catharine Cornell and Harriet Peck taught the girls.

The opening of New Garden took several years. In 1830 the North Carolina Quakers became concerned about the lack of educational facilities in the state. After deciding in their yearly meeting to finance a boarding school, the Quakers began to raise money to build a school that would accept young men and women to learn to be teachers, and who would be allowed into the school regardless of their ability to pay.

For six years, North Carolina Quakers worked hard to raise the money needed to open the school. During the first three years, they were granted a charter by the state legislature; they set up a working plan to run the school and a complete set of rules to govern its students before a single building was constructed or tract of land bought. The school's trustees decided that the school would include a boarding school house to accommodate nearly 50 students, who could attend for $50 a year to be paid in quarterly installments.

In 1834, the trustees bought a 100-acre farm near New Garden and the old school house of Jeremiah Hubbard, one of the boarding school's staunchest advocates. Elihu Coffin bought 70 acres beside the tract and donated it to the school. Another 58 acres were purchased in 1838. The trustees began building New Garden Boarding School in 1835. The building, which was school and home to students for many years, had three front doors. On the east side was the entrance for the boys, on the west the entrance for the girls, and the central entrance was for faculty and visitors. Inside the building were separate school rooms for boys and girls and above were separate lodging quarters. The building also served as the dining hall, superintendent's office, book room and parlor. The original building, later named Founders Hall, was used until its demolition in 1971.

The founders of New Garden School received full value for the $7,686 they paid for the building in 1837. A new Founders Hall was built for $1.3 million in replication of its predecessor. It houses a dining hall, a student center, and offices for administrators.

Founders Hall was not the first building to replace its namesake on the campus. King Hall, the school's meeting house, was built in 1871. In 1881 it was given to the school by the state's Quakers. The building was named King Hall after the Baltimore Quaker Francis King who supported the founding of the school. Four years after its donation, King Hall burned down. From its burned bricks King Hall II and Archdale Hall were constructed. King Hall II housed the library, president's office, and classroom until it too burned in 1908. It was replaced two years later by King Hall III, which served as the college's main classroom space for 60 years. In 1949, a front was added to the building and 20 years later its rear was demolished, to the joy of many former students, who recalled its high ceiling and antique appearance. The building was chilly in the winter and its back staircase reminiscent of the small stairs found in a lighthouse.

Archdale Hall, dubbed by students Phoenix Hall after the mythological bird, is now the oldest building on campus, built in 1885. Francis King persuaded administrators to name it after John Archdale, a Quaker who served as North Carolina's governor from 1694–96. Except during

181

Guilford College

World War II when Archdale housed women, it was a men's dorm. In 1965, it was turned into faculty offices. It is one of 30 principal buildings on campus, including 6 dorms.

In its early years, New Garden Boarding School accepted students from ages 8 to 23, and each student's studies were individually tailored. Most classes would be considered elementary school material now, but some students did college-preparatory level work. Only Quakers were allowed to attend the boarding school until 1841, when its founders chose to admit other students because of a lack of funds to operate the school.

From the beginning, all students had to adhere to strict rules of conduct. The sexes were kept separate. Students were expected to dress in a conservative manner and not to use profane language; music and dancing were forbidden. Dancing finally was allowed on campus in 1933, after years of petitions by students. The board of trustees decided that whatever evil others might see in dance, they did not. Students had demanded the right for years, say-

ing that students at UNC Chapel Hill were given an advantage by learning such social graces. Guilford's decision to permit dancing came several years before other schools in the South.

One rule that took longer to relax was the required chapel. Until 1915, students were required to attend chapel six days a week as well as Sunday meeting. In 1940, the requirement was dropped to four days a week plus Sunday meeting, with voluntary silent meeting on Tuesdays. Even with required chapel and threats of punishment, there were discipline problems. Students in the 1920s threw spitballs at speakers in chapel. Later generations read newspapers and played cards during convocation. In 1968, the faculty, not wanting to suspend students for skipping chapel, met with the student legislature to form a compromise. In 1969, mandatory attendance at chapel was eliminated.

Fifty-one years after the first students attended New Garden, the school officially closed its doors. In its place came Guilford College, using the same buildings and teachers, but with a different focus. With Lewis Lyndon Hobbs at the helm, Guilford had an administrator who spent a good portion of his life at the school. At the age of 15 he attended New Garden for eight years before leaving for college in 1872. He returned to New Garden in 1876 as an assistant teacher and moved up the ranks to principal of New Garden. In 1885, Hobbs began preparing students for college level course work. In 1888, Hobbs became president of the renamed Guilford College. On August 15, 1888, Guilford College opened its doors to 191 students, with 69 in college and the others taking preparatory classes. The preparatory school continued until 1924.

The first college faculty mirrored New Garden's first faculty with five women and four men. But the number of women students troubled Hobbs, since only 62 were enrolled. In his first report Hobbs noted, "The girls should have advantages equal in every respect to those offered to boys." To accomplish this he requested an art department to be located in the new science building and a women's gymnasium to be built. Today, 52 percent of the college's students are women.

Under Hobbs' guidance, the faculty offered students three four-year degree tracks: classical, scientific, and Latin-scientific. In the scientific degree program, the language requirement of Greek and Latin gave way to German, providing the first opportunity to a student to be educated without being drilled in classical languages. There also was a three-year teacher's course and students could spend a year at the college learning a vocation, such as accounting or telegraphy.

In 1910, the curriculum was changed to allow students to have majors, minors, and electives. This allowed students to pursue their interests and was a departure from the traditional classical study and rote memorization.

While the curriculum underwent changes under Hobbs, the grounds also were being transformed. During his 27-year tenure as president, seven buildings were built. The first was the YMCA, constructed in 1891 where Dana Auditorium now stands. Memorial Hall, King Hall III, the Library, and New Garden Hall were others.

Guilford College's most famous graduate, conservationist T. Gilbert Pearson, who became president of the National Audubon Society, traded his egg and stuffed bird collection for tuition to the school in 1892. That collection became part of the school's natural history collection. While in school, Pearson edited the Guilford Collegian and founded the Athletic Association. From 1899–1901 he taught biology at the school, but left when he couldn't negotiate a higher salary. In 1904, he was named secretary of the Audubon Society.

The construction of the Hege Library in 1909–10 was among the most important changes to the campus. An original Carnegie library, with money donated by Andrew Carnegie, it is one of the few Carnegie structures still in use as a library. Its most recent expansion in 1989 doubled the library's size to more than 70,000 square feet. The library contains more than 220,000 items from books, videos, CD-ROMs, and journals.

The Friends Historical Collection, which is housed in the Hege Library, is the center for the study of Quaker history in the southest United States. It is the second largest in the United States, below Philadelphia. Established in 1937, the collection includes the written records of Carolina Friends, printed and microfilmed copies of other Friends records, personal and family papers, printed materials by and about Friends worldwide, and sources for the study of Quaker family history. There are articles of clothing from Nathan Hunt, founder of New Garden Boarding School.

After Hobbs retired, Thomas Newlin assumed the reins of the school from 1915 to 1917. His tenure was clouded by troubles with the school's board of trustees and the students. He inherited a school in financial disarray and had eight faculty members leave. He tried to leave after a year and was fired the following year. His name was not mentioned often on campus and his portrait was not hung with the other presidents in the library until 1982.

In 1918, Raymond Binford took over Guilford College, as many people questioned whether the college should be closed in favor of the preparatory school. Binford had taught at the school from 1900–14, so he was familiar with the campus. However, he did not realize the debt the college had incurred. Among his major accomplishments was setting up an endowment drive that helped the school survive financially and put to rest talks of closing the school. Archdale was renovated and a laundry and heating plant were built in 1927.

Also, Binford implemented the Freshman Week, where freshmen came to school earlier than returning students to get acclimated to campus. But his most important contribution was the revision of the core curriculum. Under his plan, students took courses (math, English, science, and foreign languages) and cultural classes (art appreciation, philosophy, and religion). While some faculty resisted the change, Binford was complimented by administrators from other schools. Guilford became one of the first North Carolina colleges to implement an honor system in 1931.

A Quaker practice, the art of discussion is employed by all the large decision-making bodies on campus—administrative and faculty committees as well as the student senate. "What you see here that you don't see at other places . . . we don't vote," Guilford provost Dan Poteet explained. "Instead, all different views are listened to with equal respect and decisions are reached by 'sense of the meeting.' The process is one of stating issues and asking people to respond, keep responding, keep responding, until there is a sense that everyone addressing the issue agrees on how to approach [it]—or perhaps agrees that enough other people agree so that they might step aside."

By the time of Guilford's centennial celebration, Binford had been replaced as president because of failing health by Clyde Milner, the dean of the college. The school was reaching record enrollment, with many local students attending school while living at home. Known as a brilliant speaker, formal engagements became commonplace at Guilford, including a reception at the president's house to begin each school year. This was far different from the school's humble beginnings when dressing up was frowned upon.

On May 24, 1937, Guilford College celebrated its 100-year anniversary. Two thousand people were on hand to hear Arthur Morgan, chairman of the Tennessee Valley Authority, speak and 55 members of the centenary class received degrees.

Later in Milner's tenure, the school would once again show its strong belief in Quaker pacifism. The trustees did not allow the college facilities to be used by the military during World War II, and nine Japanese Americans were admitted as transfer students, most from the West Coast. Three of the students became mainstays on Guilford's basketball team, with Edward Hirabayashi being named all-conference.

During the war, enrollment dropped by half and the graduation numbers reached a low of 20 in 1944. When the war ended, Guilford faced a new problem—it was deluged by college applicants. Within two years, enrollment reached 600 as students took advantage of the G.I. Bill. This meant crowding in the aging facilities, which could not be repaired during the war. Those problems began to ease as the college-fund drive raised money that was used to build a dining hall and new dorms.

In 1953, the college assumed control of Greensboro's Evening College. Even before that, the Center for Continuing Education was established in 1947. It was the first adult education program in the southeast to offer fully accredited academic opportunities. Today, non-credit classes are offered, as well as six degree programs that can be completed entirely through evening classes, which 450 adult students use.

In 1965, 31 years after beginning as president, Milner stepped down to be succeeded by Lyndon Hobbs' grandson, Grimsley Hobbs. During his presidency, unrest was common with the Vietnam War protest and the college moving away from its role of "in loco parentis." As students began holding keg parties in dorms and Bryan Hall was turned into the first co-ed dorm, some alumni and parents questioned the school's Quaker affiliation. Hobbs was able to overcome such problems and implemented the fourth major change in the school's history, allowing non-Quakers to serve on the board of trustees.

Athletics, always popular at Guilford College, received accolades as well. The men's basketball team won the NAIA national championship in 1973, as did the women's tennis team in 1981. The golf team won the national championship in 1989, finishing second in the three previous years. Among the players on the 1973 championship team were NBA stars M.L. Carr and World B. Free.

Athletics were important, but the athletes were students as well, Carr said when he set up a scholarship in 1986. "When I look back at where I've been and where I am now, I realize how fortunate I was to have people around me at Guilford College who looked beyond M.L. Carr the basketball player and showed an interest in me as a person."

In 1981, William Rogers began his 15-year tenure as Guilford president. A tenuous relationship with Quakers over changes in Hobbs' administration were eased with the formation of the Friends Center in 1982. It was set up to have Quaker ministers steer Quaker youth to the school, if interested. Also, a new college logo was created in 1987 for the 150th anniversary. It was designed by Rogers and features a large black oak that stands adjacent to New Garden Hall. The tree is registered as the largest black oak in North Carolina and is more than 200 years old.

Donald W. McNemar, the former headmaster of Phillips Academy in Andover, MA, became the seventh president of Guilford College on June 1, 1996.

"Guilford is a remarkable institution. The college's strong academic program, inclusive environment, and commitment to service learning are very special educational assets," said McNemar. "It is a distinctive educational community based on the Quaker principles of respect for the individual and collaborative learning."

Further Reading: Alexander Stoesen's *Guilford College: On the Strength of 150 Years* (Greensboro, North Carolina: Board of Trustees, Guilford College, 1987) is a detailed pictorial history of Guilford College until the 1980s. Dorothy Lloyd Gilbert's *Guilford: A Quaker College* (Greensboro, North Carolina: Guilford College, 1937) is an extensive history of the school's first 100 years.

—J. Cameron Tew

HARVARD UNIVERSITY
(Cambridge, Massachusetts, U.S.A.)

Location: In the city of Cambridge, Massachusetts, across the Charles River from Boston.

Description: The oldest university in the United States, a private institution with nearly 21,000 students (including both undergraduate and graduate students).

Information: Harvard Information Center
Holyoke Center
1350 Massachusetts Avenue
Cambridge, MA 02138
U.S.A.
(617) 495-1573

Visiting: For information about guided tours, which leave from Holyoke Center, telephone the number above.

Harvard University, established more than 150 years before the United States Constitution was written, was founded on the model of traditional European universities, but it has pioneered several distinctive features of American higher education during its centuries of growth and change. It is now one of the wealthiest and most famous universities in the world, yet its main buildings are still where it all began, in Harvard Yard on Harvard Square.

The university originated as a public foundation owned and supervised by the Great and General Court, the government of the English colony of Massachusetts Bay, which decided in October 1636 to spend £400 on a college for the advanced training of young men, especially for the ministry of the colony's official Congregational Church. Newtowne, the colony's capital until the establishment of Boston in 1630, was selected as the location for the college, which was to be administered by a board of overseers, half of them church ministers and the other half lay magistrates. The overseers bought the house and one-acre cow yard which formed the nucleus of the modern Harvard Yard; they also appointed the first master, Nathaniel Eaton.

By 1638, when the college admitted its first students, Newtowne had been renamed Cambridge, for the English university of which Eaton was an alumnus, and in 1639 the college itself was named in honor of Eaton's friend John Harvard. A graduate of Cambridge, Harvard had come to Massachusetts as a Congregational minister but had died in September 1638, leaving half his fortune and a library of 400 books to the new college.

Eaton did not remain in Cambridge long. He was alleged to have beaten an assistant master with a cudgel, and there had been complaints that his wife, who was in charge of the kitchens, had not provided enough beef for the students. After the couple were dismissed in 1640, the college stood empty for one year but was revived by Henry Dunster, the first person to be appointed president; he organized the teaching of liberal arts, philosophy, and the "learned tongues" (Latin and ancient Greek). In 1650 his efforts were recognized with the General Court's granting of the charter, still the basis of Harvard's administrative arrangements. It created a corporation, composed of the president and the teaching staff, under the Court-appointed overseers.

By 1690 Harvard was admitting around 22 students a year. Its president at that time, the influential Boston theologian Increase Mather, sought to revise the charter so that the corporation would have a majority of church ministers to keep a close eye on what was taught, but both the Governor's Council in Boston and the King's Council in London rejected his proposal as an intrusion on their powers. Indeed, the King's Council went further, expressly forbidding Mather to require that the teaching members of the corporation should all be members of the Congregational Church. Mather, overruled and outvoted, left Harvard in 1701, while many of the more conservative overseers and teachers who had supported his plans departed to New Haven in Connecticut, where they founded Yale University to be a bastion of orthodoxy against the dangerous toleration practiced at Harvard.

In 1708 Harvard confirmed the worst fears of such conservatives by choosing as its president John Leverett, who was neither a minister nor even a strict Congregationalist. However, he was by no means a radical innovator. Examinations continued to consist of a series of oral tests and a Latin essay, on the traditional western European model, but he did appoint an instructor in Hebrew, and he gave permission for private lessons to be offered in French. He also presided over a notable expansion of the college beyond its original three buildings: Massachusetts Hall, the oldest structure now standing in Harvard Yard, was opened in 1720.

By that year Harvard had around 120 students, who had acquired a reputation for swearing, rioting, and gambling, and thus gained the college the nickname "godless Harvard." When the religious revival known as the Great Awakening erupted across New England, the college became an obvious target for reproof by such ministers as

Harvard University

George Whitefield, who came to Cambridge to demand reforms in 1740. However, the college authorities refused to impose religious oaths on their students (such as those already in effect at Yale), permitted some of their staff to publish pamphlets answering Whitefield's accusations of backsliding, and proclaimed their uprightness by building Holden Chapel, opened in 1744, inside the Yard. Conservative Congregationalists remained unconvinced at first, but eventually Whitefield himself was sufficiently reassured to contribute money and books to the college library, given its own new building after Old Harvard Hall, which had contained a previous library as well as lecture rooms, burned down in 1765. The rapid recreation of the library, along with the building of Hollis Hall in 1763, and of a new Harvard Hall in 1766, were signs of the college's steady expansion.

In 1771 63 students were graduated from Harvard, its largest class, just as Massachusetts was beginning to enter upon its leading role in the American Revolution. Between 1770 and 1773 the General Court met in the college buildings rather than in Boston, which was under the control of British soldiers, and in 1774 the revolutionary provincial congress met in the Meeting House on Watch Hill inside Harvard Yard to create a new government in place of King George III's officials. In the following year George Washington took command of the Continental Army somewhere in Cambridge, although opinions differ as to whether the event took place on the town's common or inside Wadsworth House, which was then the home of the president of Harvard. Because of these and related disruptions, the college's commencement ceremonies were suspended from 1774 to 1781, and for one academic year, 1775–76, its classes were held in Concord, Massachusetts.

In 1779 the Watch Hill Meeting House was the location for the convention that wrote the constitution of the commonwealth of Massachusetts (the oldest constitution still in force in the United States) on the basis of a draft text by a Harvard graduate, John Adams. This document, which went into effect in 1780, made Harvard into a university and established a new and much larger board of overseers, composed of the governor, lieutenant governor, council, and senate of Massachusetts, and the ministers of six Congregational churches in and near Cambridge. In 1781 the new board established the Harvard Medical Institution, the first alternative in New England to traditional medical apprenticeships and only the third medical school in the United States. It was moved in 1810 to Boston, where it has since become the famous Harvard Medical School. This new departure into vocational education can be seen as the first of the many changes which would transform Harvard into an institution independent of state and church alike, devoting its enormous intellectual and financial resources to teaching and research in a variety of subjects beyond the imagination of its founders, and continuously evolving to meet the challenges of industrialization and urbanization.

The elimination of the Congregational influence on the university proceeded in stages over almost 50 years. Between 1804 and 1806 both the presidency of Harvard and the professorship of divinity were given to Unitarians, the first non-Congregationalists to hold either post. The Congregational Church responded by creating its own seminary at Andover, while many puritan families began to send their sons to other colleges, leaving the Harvard Divinity School, founded in 1819, to be dominated by Unitarian teachers for generations. The rule that the ministers on the board of overseers had to be Congregationalists was at last abolished in 1843, and the ministers' seats were removed altogether in 1851. Even after that reform, however, attendance at morning prayers remained compulsory for all students.

Independence from the state of Massachusetts took a little longer to achieve as Harvard was cut off from public funds. Harvard's annual tuition fees had risen steadily during the early nineteenth century—for example, from $20 in 1807 to $55 in 1825—and it had become probably the most expensive college in the United States, at least for those who could not win any of the several scholarships. The numbers of undergraduates steadily increased—necessitating the building of three new halls: Stoughton in 1804, Holworthy in 1812, and University in 1815—but political resentment of the university's wealth and prestige also increased. In 1823 the Jeffersonian Republicans took control of the state from the Federalists and abolished the state grants to Harvard, which had risen to $10,000 each year. Thus the university was forced into a position of financial self-reliance, which has continued since, but Massachusetts officials dominated the board of overseers until 1851, when their numbers were cut down to five, the ministers (as has been mentioned) were removed, 30 seats were opened to election for six-year terms by the state's house and senate, and the university's president and treasurer also became ex-officio members of the board. In 1865 the five state officials were removed, and the right to choose the 30 elected overseers was transferred to Harvard alumni, meeting in Cambridge on commencement day. The university created by the colony of Massachusetts for the training of ministers became, and has remained, a private and secular institution.

These administrative changes were merely the background to the substantial reforms of Harvard's academic activities, which have long been associated, perhaps a little unfairly to others involved in the changes, with Charles William Eliot, president of the university from 1869 to 1909. New subjects had already been added to the curriculum before his appointment, with the creation, for example, of professorships in law in 1815, in French and Spanish in 1819, and in the sciences, gathered within the Lawrence Scientific School in 1847. Eliot himself had taught in this school for 15 years, helping to improve its status by taking part in its conversion from a three-year to a four-year program of studies and in the raising of its at first relatively low standards for admission. As president, however, he saw to an acceleration of the rate of change, to a large extent under the influence of the innovations already taking place in many universities in Germany, a country Eliot knew well and admired. Thus in 1871 Harvard appointed the first professor of political economy in the United States; in 1872 it established a pioneering Graduate School of Arts and Sciences; in 1879 it set up an Annex for women students, which was to become Radcliffe College in 1893; in 1886 it became the first American college to abolish compulsory chapel; and in 1890 it brought all the undergraduate courses in the Yard under a single Faculty of Arts and Sciences.

The purpose of this faculty was to facilitate the elective system, which is probably Eliot's, and Harvard's, greatest and most distinctive contribution to the pattern of higher education in the United States. Undergraduates had been permitted a steadily greater degree of choice among the subjects they would study until 1886, when the only limits left in place, apart from the practical matter of avoiding clashing schedules, were that courses had to be "liberal" (nonvocational) and that introductory courses were to be taken before advanced ones. By 1904 every large college in the country had introduced at least some elements of the elective system. One side effect of the system, bitterly resented by Eliot's critics, was that the studies in classical Latin and Greek, which had been central to the European university tradition ever since the Renaissance, and therefore to its offshoots in former colonies, began a decisive decline in status. Eliot's last great innovation was the creation of the Harvard Business School in 1908.

There is a certain irony in the fact that this overhaul of the university's work took place during the same period that saw a revival at Harvard and elsewhere of medieval architectural styles. The new buildings put up during Eliot's presidency included the enormous neo-Gothic Memorial Hall, opened in 1878, on a site to the north of the Yard, to honor Harvard graduates killed in the Civil War and two Romanesque halls (Austin and Sever) designed by Henry Hobson Richardson.

Eliot's successor, Abbot Lawrence Lowell, left his own mark on the university and on higher education across North America. In 1914 he revised the elective system by introducing the distinction between majors and minors, which has since become standard in universities both in the United States and in Canada, and which has also begun to feature in the curricula of European universities in recent years. But his stance on academic freedom was perhaps even more crucial for the future of higher education. Even when the United States was at war with Germany in 1917–18, Lowell refused a gift of $10 million to Harvard because its donor wanted the gift to be conditional on the dismissal of Hugo Munsterberg, a professor of philosophy who publicly supported Germany. This was a courageous stand, even for a university presi-

dent who was better placed to resist such pressures than his colleagues in poorer colleges.

Nevertheless donations kept coming. A Harvard graduate who drowned during the sinking of the *Titanic* in 1912 was commemorated the following year with the opening of the Harry Elkins Widener Library, which is a component of one of the largest university library system in the world; the Fogg Art Museum, founded in 1895, was able to move into a larger building on Quincy Street in 1927; Edward S. Harkness funded the construction of new undergraduate accommodations between the Yard and the Charles River starting in 1928; and the Memorial Church, which now honors Harvard alumni killed in the two World Wars, was opened in 1931. When he retired two years later, Lowell looked back on a presidency which had been less radical than Eliot's but which had significantly expanded Harvard's resources and consolidated its reputation for independence.

The next president, James Conant, was another innovator. During his first six years he and his colleagues abolished class attendance records and the traditional rank list and introduced national scholarships in order to broaden Harvard's population. After spending much of World War II supervising research on radar, chemical weapons, and the atomic bomb for the federal government, Conant returned to Cambridge. Back at Harvard, he established general education courses for undergraduates and committed the university to its long-standing policy of accepting federal government research contracts only if their content and results were nonclassified.

However, under Conant's successor Nathan Pusey, president from 1952 to 1970, such contracts became a major source of funding for Harvard, as for many other American universities, especially in the areas of science and engineering. This unprecedented involvement, however indirect, in government policies was to be one factor in the wave of protests which swept across American campuses during the years of the Vietnam War. In his January 1969 annual report, Pusey mentioned that Harvard had been free of the sort of major protests that had erupted at other schools. "Fortunately," he wrote, "difficulties of the unsettling kind now being experienced on many college campuses have remained relatively minor here." Such complacency was shattered in April of that year when 300 students seized University Hall, Harvard's main administration building and remained there for 17 hours. Nine university deans were ejected from their offices. In what proved an extremely controversial decision, Pusey summoned the police; 400 state and local policemen cleared the students from the building. Pusey retired as president in 1970.

One result of the protesters' demands was the hiring of Derrick A. Bell Jr., the first black professor at Harvard Law School, in 1969. In 1990 Bell requested an unpaid leave of absence until the school appointed a woman of color to its tenured faculty (the appointment was not made, and after his two-year leave of absence expired, Bell was no longer on the faculty). The law faculty again made history in 1973 when Professor Archibald Cox was appointed special prosecutor in the Watergate case. Cox was fired by President Nixon on October 20; even though the firing was ruled illegal, Cox did not seek to regain his position and returned to the Harvard faculty.

By 1971, when Derek Bok became president, Harvard was facing its first serious financial crisis, since spending on energy and other supplies was rising rapidly just as federal funds were dwindling, from 40 percent of university income in 1967 to 25 percent in 1974. Bok presided over financial retrenchment and also over another revision of the curriculum, the introduction in 1978 of compulsory "core" courses for all undergraduates. At Harvard, as at other universities, these courses have been the focus of debate, both about the choice of core subjects and about the view of civilization that the choice may (or may not) imply, ever since. Bok's successor, Neil Rudenstine, presided over the largest fundraising effort in the history of higher education. In 1994, the university announced its intention to raise $2 billion by mid-1999.

Harvard University marked the 350th anniversary of its foundation in 1986. A single house and cow yard in a small colonial town have given place to a sprawling range of buildings; a publicly owned seminary training ministers for a small area of the eastern coast of North America has given place to a self-governing university employing and teaching people from all over the world; and, through some, at least, of its alumni and its teachers it has already had a considerable indirect influence on both the public life and the culture of the United States in particular. In recent times, for example, Henry Kissinger, Secretary of State to President Richard M. Nixon, and John Kenneth Galbraith, the economist who served as ambassador to India under President Kennedy, have been perhaps the most noted among the many members of the Harvard faculty who have contributed to public policymaking. Six U.S. Presidents—John Adams, John Quincy Adams, Rutherford B. Hayes, Theodore Roosevelt, Franklin D. Roosevelt, and John F. Kennedy—studied at Harvard, as did many other leading figures in government, business, and science, while those of its alumni who have contributed to American literature include the Transcendentalists Ralph Waldo Emerson and Henry David Thoreau; the novelist Henry James and his brother William, a pioneer of experimental psychology who went on to teach at the university; the poets T.S. Eliot, e.e. cummings, Robert Frost, and Robert Lowell; and such modern novelists as John Dos Passos and Norman Mailer. Harvard has produced more than 30 Nobel laureates, from T.W. Richards (chemistry) in 1914 to Seamus Heaney (literature) in 1995. Probably the best known is James D. Watson, who won the prize for medicine or physiology in 1962 for describing the structure of DNA.

Harvard continues to try to balance tradition with innovation, the heritage of successive generations with the needs and interests of the contemporary United States and the changing world of which it is a part.

Further Reading: Samuel Eliot Morison's *Three Centuries of Harvard, 1636–1936* (Cambridge, Massachusetts: Harvard University Press, 1936) is still well worth seeking out, for it is a fascinating narrative which blends local detail with attention to broad social change. The following 50 years are well-surveyed in Richard Norton Smith's *The Harvard Century: The Making of a University to a Nation* (New York: Simon and Schuster, 1986).

—Patrick Heenan

HEBREW UNIVERSITY
(Jerusalem, Israel)

Location: Mount Scopus in Jerusalem.

Description: Private multi-disciplinary university enrolling approximately 22,00 students in undergraduate, graduate, and professional schools.

Information: Hebrew University
Office of Academic Affairs
Mount Scopus
Jerusalem, Israel

The idea of a Jewish university in Palestine had animated Jewish thinker and leaders for centuries. Near the end of the Middle Ages the Jewish communities in Sicily (1466) and Mantua, Italy (1564) asked the political authorities for permission to establish universities only for Jews. Apparently unsatisfied with the traditional religious education offered in the yeshiva (i.e., a school to train rabbis, organized around the study of the *Talmud*) and excluded from attending Christian universities, these communities hoped to offer Jewish students the same opportunities to study secular subjects such as medicine and science that were available to Christian students. Growing intolerance of Jews by the Roman Catholic Church doomed both efforts.

In the nineteenth century, European universities opened their doors to Jewish students; however the number admitted were kept in proportion to the number of Jews in a given country's total population. Demand far exceeded opportunity, and with the rise of Jewish Nationalism or Zionism in the late 1800s, the idea of establishing a university for Jews in Palestine was reborn. The call for a secular, multi-disciplinary institution of higher education was issued in 1882 by a German professor of mathematics, Herman Shapira. His plan called for a university with three faculties: theology, theoretical sciences (classical liberal arts and sciences), and practical sciences (engineering, agriculture, chemistry). He presented his ideas at Zionist conferences in 1884 and 1897 but both the Zionist movement and the Jewish public believed the idea of a Jewish university to be without practical value for that time.

Shapira inspired a generation of young scholars and Zionists who were led by Martin Buber, Chaim Weizmann, and Berthold Feiwel. In 1901 they urged participants at the Fifth Zionist Congress to open a Hebrew University in Palestine, and in 1902 they set forth their proposal in *Eine Judische Hoschschule* (A Jewish University). In this pamphlet, known as the founding docu-

ment of Hebrew University, the three idealists argued that such a university was integral to establishing a homeland in Palestine because it would, "promote the revival of the national language, become the focus of Jewish literary, artistic, and scientific work, . . . and become the cultural center" of Judaism. Moreover it would keep Palestinian Jews from going abroad for their education and attract European students who were denied admission to continental schools.

In 1913 Wiezmann and his allies won support for ideas at the Eleventh Zionist Congress and a committee, led by Weizmann, began to develop concrete plans for a Jewish university in Jerusalem. Key members of the committee included Baron Edmund de Rothschild, a major financial backer of the project, Nobel laureate Paul Erhlich, and Dr. Judah Magens. World War I interrupted the work of the planners. However, the work was resumed in 1917 when the British occupied Palestine and issued the Balfour Declaration which pledged official support of a Jewish homeland in the Middle East. In June 1918, even as the war continued, 12 foundation stones, representing the 12 tribes of Israel, were laid on the summit of Mount Scopus. It would take seven years to raise funds, hire faculty, design curriculum, and erect buildings so that the new school could operate. On April 1, 1925, it officially opened.

Hebrew University's character and its course of development were set during the struggle to establish the school and keep it functioning during the first half of the twentieth century. Bitter in-fighting over administrative and academic control of the university as well as the changes in Middle Eastern politics caused by World War II marked the early history of this first Jewish institution of higher education. The new university was at the center of conflict between Zionists and non-Zionists, intellectuals and colonists, and Arabs and Jews. According to Arthur A. Goren, a professor of Jewish history, the founding of the university was the product of competing intellectual and political ideologies:

What should be the character of the university—a great public institution, academic haven for victims of discrimination and instrument of nation-building? Or should it be an elitist institution, above Zionist politics, a lodestar for the far-flung Jewish world whose scientists would take their place among the honored members of the international community of scholars? Finally, what balance should be struck between the fervor for Jewish cultural renewal and the pursuit of science.

Hebrew University

The main conflict of the early years centered on two different conceptions of the university's mission and how it should be governed. From the earliest discussion in the 1910s, champions of the university disagreed about its role and its work. On the one side were European Zionists and intellectuals who hoped to create a top-rated research university with the sciences and Judaic studies as its cornerstones. On the other side were those who hoped the university would serve both as a refuge for scholars displaced or excluded by European anti-Semitism and as a comprehensive teaching university that would train new generations of Palestinian Jews.

The latter group, based in Palestine, was led by Judah Magnes, first chancellor of Hebrew University and fellow Zionist, Vladimir Jabotinsky. They argued that the school should be a home for students denied the opportunity for advanced education in anti-Semitic Europe. It should be a center of undergraduate and professional training in the humanities and sciences that would anchor a small but growing population of Jews in the Middle East, thus furthering the creation of a Jewish homeland in Eretz Israel. Magnes believed that the study of Judaism—its history, language, religious texts, archeology—should be at the academic heart of the proposed school. He was supported by historian David Yellin, Jerusalem-born educator Ahad Ha'am, and the nationalist poet, Chayim Nachman Bialik. Moreover, this faction hoped to improve Arabic–Jewish relations by establishing an academic center for the study of Arabic and Islamic social, economic, and cultural life. Not only would this build bridges of reconciliation between the two peoples but it would help Jewish students better understand their neighbors.

The competing faction in the creation of Hebrew University offered a different vision for the institution. This group represented European Zionism and intellectuals who adhered to the research ethic of continental higher education. It was led by Chaim Weizmann, president of the World Zionist Organization. He elicited the support of European scholars such as Albert Einstein and Paul Erhlich, and philanthropists such as Rothschild. Einstein and Weizmann believed that only a research university would attract the best young minds and faculty away from European and American schools to Palestine. In particular, Weizmann first wanted to establish research centers in the biological and chemical sciences that would anchor a strong medical school. Rothschild gave his financial support on the condition that the school be organized around a cluster of research centers, much like Pasteur Institute. If successful, Hebrew University would become internationally respected and the center of Jewish culture and thought. In this respect the two men opposed the Magnes goal of creating a comprehensive teaching university, because they feared that such a body would diminish the ability of its faculty to conduct high quality research, and result in a third-rate institution or in Einstein's words, a *Baueruniversitat* (a peasant's university).

The struggle over the definition and curricular direction of the university yielded compromises. Weizmann successfully raised funds and hired faculty to staff the chemistry and microbiology institutes in 1923 and Magnes did the same for the Institute of Jewish Studies in 1925. The university opened with these three research centers but no degree programs. Even so, voices were calling for undergraduate and advanced degree programs. The *Yishunov* (the Jewish community in Palestine) was especially loud in asking for undergraduate instruction (in order to keep local students from going abroad for university training), and student interest surpassed the founders' expectations. During the 1925–26 school year, a committee under the guidance of professor Selig Brodetsky was charged with charting a new path that would allow for more teaching without sacrificing research. The committee recommended that regular instruction be introduced at the master's and doctoral levels in 1927 for the humanities and in 1931 for the sciences.

During the late 1920s and 1930s the curriculum and creation of departments tacked between research and teaching interests. The Weizmann faction established the research-oriented departments of natural history and hygiene (including bacteriology) in 1926. The Magnes party created the department of archeology in 1926 and a humanities faculty (history, classical and modern languages, and philosophy) in 1928. Physics and biological science and cancer research followed in the early 1930s, as did education. By 1940 there were 1,000 undergraduates who were pursuing advanced degrees (however, no undergraduate degrees were awarded until after 1949), and more generally, Hebrew University was being transformed into a comprehensive university that trained undergraduates in liberal arts and professional programs.

One of the loudest critics of the "pure research" ideal was the Palestinian Zionist, Berl Katznelson. He rejected the apolitical position of the university; its failure to pro-

vide leadership in developing Jewish culture and meeting the needs of the community; and its dismissal of the Yishunov as a partner in determining the school's research and pedagogical priorities. Katznelson urged Weizmann and other university officials to make the school more responsive to the local population and situation. He lobbied for a school of education and a school of agriculture in the 1930s. He was a vocal advocate of establishing centers to study Arabic societies and urged the creation of a social science faculty to train prospective civil servants for the new state. After World War II, Katznelson pushed the university to rebuild its medical school and begin training a new generation of physicians and medical researchers to replace the thousands who had been lost in the Holocaust. Although his concrete plans were often put aside or reworked by university officials, his goal of transforming Hebrew University into an institution that would serve the interests and needs of the Israeli state and society was eventually realized during the post-war era.

Curriculum and mission were not the only subjects of dispute among the Weizmann and Magnes factions. The rival groups also disagreed about the school's administrative structure. Sponsors of the research university ideal wanted to control Hebrew University from Europe. Historian David Myers argues that Weizmann and his party looked upon local leadership with "paternalistic skepticism." According to their thinking, the Palestinian group, headed by Magnes, lacked the intellectual training and administrative know-how to effectively run the university. However, the Jewish settlement in Palestine and the Magnes party rejected this position as an attempt to subordinate the university to nationalist politics. In short, the new school was caught up in the larger battle about who should control Palestinian affairs, European-based Zionist executives or a self-governing Jewish community in Palestine. It was initially resolved in 1935 when Magnes was unceremoniously stripped of his powers and "booted upstairs" to occupy the figurehead role of president by a special committee, appointed by the Weizmann-controlled board of governors.

The final resolution of these internal disputes and the growth of the university occurred amid, and partially as a result of, heightened Arab-Jewish conflicts, World War II, and the founding of Israel in 1948. In 1929, when Arabs rioted in Palestine, Magnes broke with other Zionists in his efforts to create peace. He used his office of university chancellor to accomplish this goal. He also engaged in private diplomatic efforts to stop the violence and resolve the ethnic-religious tensions between the two populations. Many viewed him as a traitor to the Zionist cause and as a threat to the freedom and independence of the university, insofar as he had aligned the university with a specific political position. In short, Magnes' pacifism and break with Jewish nationalism subverted his leadership among university supporters and it was probably one of the factors that led to his removal from office.

The rise of National Socialism in Germany in 1933 and World War II created new challenges for Hebrew University. Hitler fired all non-Aryan professors (primarily Jewish) and closed higher education institutions to Jewish students. As Germany was the seat of learning for world Jewry, these actions were viewed with alarm. Magnes and leaders of the school in Jerusalem hoped to make the university a haven for German scholars and students. Moreover, the influx from abroad would bolster the university's faculty and allow administrators to build the curriculum. Unfortunately, the school could not raise the financial resources to hire the majority of the exiled scholars, nor could Weizmann and Magnes persuade more than 20 faculty and 100 students to make Hebrew University their home. England, Turkey, and the United States were the sites commonly chosen by those who made it out of Germany.

The war years actually increased the fortunes of Hebrew University. The Arab revolt that had disrupted Palestine since 1936 abated as both Jews and Arabs served in the British forces. The university became the hub of scientific activity for the Middle Eastern theater. Quartz crystals, necessary for radio transmission, were produced by university technicians. University chemists developed a chemical compound to extinguish fires on airplanes and helped devise techniques to repair radio transmission tubes. Specialists in tropical medicine trained American and Australian medical personnel to diagnose and treat malaria, and they prepared anti-typhus vaccines for the growing number of war refugees and soldiers stationed in the Middle East. Substantial financial gifts during the war allowed the university to expand. The Hassadah hospital and medical school were built north of the original buildings on Mount Scopus. The Institute of Jewish Studies was given funds for a new building and an Institute of Archeology with a museum was built. Finally, an agricultural school and experimental station were established at Rehobot (on the coastal plain of Israel, south of Tel Aviv).

The turmoil and violence that had characterized Arab-Jewish relations prior to the war were renewed in 1946, and the university was literally in the middle of the conflict. Arab attacks on Jewish residents engendered counter-attacks by the secret Jewish army known as the Haganah, for which many students fought. During 1946 and 1947 the British government, which controlled Palestine, and the United Nations studied the geo-political crisis in the Middle East. Britain had allowed the violence to go unchecked during this period, and, once the decision was made to divide Palestine into a Jewish and an Arab state, the rulers of the Mandate were powerless to stop its escalation.

The Mount Scopus campus was located on the outskirts of Jerusalem. On one side was the Judean desert and what would become the Arabic nation of Jordan. On the other was an Arab controlled neighborhood of Jerus-

alem. Not only did the university occupy strategic high ground, but the only road from Jerusalem to the north ran through the campus. Whichever side—Jewish or Arab—controlled Scopus possessed an advantage in the War of Independence. Hebrew University was the scene of protracted fighting from December 1947 (after the Partition Resolution passed on November 29) through June 1948. In January, classes on Mount Scopus were canceled and temporary classrooms were found in the city. Students and staff guarded the university and the hospital, which was still in use. Much of the fighting took place along the road, when convoys from Jerusalem brought supplies and changes of staff for the guards and hospital. Sniper fire, machine guns, and grenades greeted the heavily armored buses but usually inflicted limited damage. On the morning of April 13 the lead vehicles of the convoy were ambushed. Seventy-seven died and 20 were injured. The Mount Scopus campus closed that day. In early summer, Judah Magnes, who was terminally ill, negotiated a settlement whereby Mount Scopus would be neutral territory in the Arab-Israeli battle for Jerusalem. This was Mangnes' last act on behalf of the university he had helped to establish.

With the 1949 armistice between Jordan and Israel, the faculty and administrators of Hebrew University began to rebuild. Classes and offices were located in over 40 different buildings in Jerusalem. The exigencies of nation-building took priority in the plans of the university. Israel's leaders called upon the university to provide the professional training and scientific research needed by a modern state. A law school was started to provide the necessary education of lawyers, judges, and clerks for Israel's civil service. Social science programs were added and the education department expanded to meet the need for a new generation of school teachers. The agricultural campus at Rehobot was enlarged in order to help reclaim the semi-arid land within Israel's borders and increase its productivity.

In the early 1950s the board of governors and the faculty decided to build a new campus in the heart of Jerusalem. The makeshift facilities were inadequate for the growing student body and tasks of the university. The Mount Scopus campus was not available. It had been severely damaged during the fighting in 1947 and 1948, and after the partition of Jerusalem, it fell under Arab control. Building began in 1954, and the Givat Ram campus opened in 1956. Jerusalem was reunified following the 1967 war, and the Mount Scopus campus was gradually rebuilt. Givat Ram was the primary campus until 1981 when the Mount Scopus campus was completed.

Hebrew University has become one of the most important universities in Israel and the Middle East. It is a leader in agricultural research and is especially noted for its programs in Middle Eastern and Jewish studies. It has an internationally respected archeology department. A university archeologist, Eliezer Sulenik, was instrumental in acquiring the Dead Sea Scrolls and then studying them. Faculty members have surveyed the Temple Mount in Jerusalem and conducted important excavations at Hazor, Masada, Tel Miqne, and Jericho. Currently there are approximately 22,000 students studying at Hebrew University, a third in advanced degree programs. The school offers numerous courses of study and degrees ranging from classic liberal arts to medicine, business administration, law, and applied science.

Further Reading: Norman Bentwich's *The Hebrew University of Jerusalem, 1918–1960* (London: Weidenfeld and Nicolson, 1961) and Lotta Levonsohn's *Vision and Fulfillment: The First Twenty-Five Years of the Hebrew University, 1925–1950* (New York: Greystone Press, 1950) provide insider (and somewhat partisan) accounts of the early years of Hebrew University. A more current article by Yaacov Iram fills in details about the changes in curriculum and organization during the pre-independence period ("Curricular and Structural Development at the Hebrew University, 1928–1948," *History of Universities* [1992] XI: 205–41). David Biale's essay, "The Idea of a Jewish University" and Bernard Wasserstein's article, "The Arab-Jewish Dilemma" (both in William M. Brinner and Moses Rischin, editors, *Like All the Nations? The Life and Legacy of Judah L. Magnes* (Albany: State University of New York Press, 1987) offer insights into the role played by Judah Magnes in the founding of the university. The scholarly journal, *Judaism* devoted an issue to the origins of Hebrew University (vol. 45, spring 1996).

—Stephen Ellingson

HOWARD UNIVERSITY
(Washington, D.C., U.S.A.)

Location: In the Shaw neighborhood of northwestern
                     Washington, D.C.

Description: Howard is a public university that enrolls nearly
                     6,000 new students each year in its
                     undergraduate, graduate, and professional
                     schools.

Information: Office Admissions
                     Howard University
                     2400 Sixth St. N.W.
                     Washington, DC 20059
                     U.S.A.
                     (202) 806-2755

In November 1866, leaders of the First Congregational Society met in Washington, D.C. to discuss the foundation of a theological seminary intended to train "preachers (colored) with a view to service among freedmen." One of the 11 men present at the group's second meeting was General Oliver O. Howard, a white Civil War hero and Commissioner of the Bureau of Refugees, Freedmen, and Abandoned Lands, more commonly known as the Freedmen's Bureau. Howard's national stature and his enthusiasm for the education of African Americans led to the proposal to name the new institution the "Howard Theological Seminary." Plans quickly evolved for an institution of broader educational purpose, and so the newly elected trustees temporarily changed the name to the "Howard Normal and Theological Institute," and then finally settled on "Howard University" on January 8, 1867.

Howard's charter, a bill passed by Congress on March 2, 1866, makes no mention of the University's special service to African Americans. It calls for only the establishment of "a college for the instruction of youth in the liberal arts and sciences," and Howard's non-exclusive commitment to the education of African Americans has ever since been maintained by historical precedent. Howard's charter makes no mention of gender either, and indeed the university has been coeducational since its inception.

The trustees organized and opened Howard astoundingly quickly. Even before the university's charter was enacted as a congressional bill, General Howard purchased a small plot of land and a building to house the seminary and normal school, using funds allocated to the Freedmen's Bureau. In March 1867, Reverend Charles Boynton was elected president of the university, and together with the trustees, he decided to open Howard on May 1 of that year. The first students enrolled were four white girls, the daughters of two trustees. Meanwhile, Howard searched for a much larger site on which to build a permanent campus. He selected the 150-acre farm of John Smith in June 1867, and the trustees consummated the purchase within the month.

Approximately 91 acres were resold in order to recoup part of the $150,000 outlay, and the remainder of the land was reserved for the new campus.

Construction on the new site began promptly. The main building, a dormitory, medical building, and hospital were all in progress by the fall of 1867. The medical department opened in November 1868 with a faculty of two black and three white professors, all well qualified despite their relatively low salaries. The law department opened in January 1869 with a part-time faculty of four. The theological department opened in 1870; agricultural, military, commercial, and music departments soon followed.

President Boynton remained in office only 150 days before he resigned over conflicts with General Howard, who was then elected president himself. For one conflict, Boynton believed that blacks and whites should seek separate identities, and congregate in separate churches, whereas Howard favored amalgamation of the races. More importantly, Boynton was discouraged by Howard's legal problems involving the university. Between 1869 and 1872, Howard delivered nearly $530,000 to the university from the Freedmen's Bureau, which he headed. A congressional investigation was undertaken while he served as president of the school to determine whether his actions constituted a mismanagement of federal moneys. Although Howard was acquitted in 1871, the controversy was bad for the university. The Freedmen's Bureau closed in 1872, and the university was denied federal funds for seven years following. Howard resigned in 1873 when the War Department opened a second investigation into his activities as a federal employee.

Before leaving office, Howard recommended that the black lawyer John Langston, dean of the law department, serve as president pro tem until he could return, or until a permanent replacement could be found. Despite the university's implicit mission to educate African Americans, there was some controversy surrounding the appointment of an African American to the presidency. Langston was allowed to serve as acting president for a year and a half. However, when the post was offered for permanent appointment following the formal acceptance of Oliver Howard's resignation in 1875, the trustees elected the Reverend George Whipple rather than Langston. Their reasons are not fully known, but it is

Howard University

argued that they believed a white president could effectively solicit more funding than a black, which may have been true at the time.

Langston resigned from his position as dean of the law department after he lost the presidential election to Whipple, and the program staggered without him. The department was closed for the 1876–77 academic school year,

and then the executive committee fired all members of the department in 1880. The underqualified Dean Richard Greener, who held the post that Langston had vacated, was dismissed along with his faculty. A new faculty was hired the next fall, and the law department resumed operation that same year. Until 1926, law classes were held in a series of buildings downtown rather than on campus, and the convenience of the new location drew desperately needed students. Benjamin Leighton was appointed dean of the law department in 1881, and he eventually managed to restore strength and order to the program.

In the five years that followed Whipple's resignation in 1875, four more white men were elected president of Howard: Frederick Fairfield, Edward Smith, William Patton, and Jeremiah Rankin. Despite its lack of singular leadership, the university prospered in many respects during the time of fleeting presidents, and then through the 1910s. Many graduates of Howard's preparatory program were admitted into excellent undergraduate programs at Harvard, Williams, and other elite institutions, and many graduates of Howard's professional schools did exceptionally well in their careers. Robert Terrell and James Cobb, for example, who were graduated from the law program in 1889, together opened one of the first professional offices in downtown Washington that was black owned and operated. The university was growing, too, albeit more slowly than the trustees desired; dentistry, pharmacy, nursing, commercial, and other programs were added. Enrollment in the professional schools rose steadily as well.

Howard contributed substantially to the American effort when World War I erupted, despite the disappointment the university's community felt with Woodrow Wilson's maintenance of segregation in the military, and with his tolerance of segregationist ambitions amongst U.S. congressmen. University faculty and students helped develop and lead the Black Officers Training Camp at Fort Des Moines, Iowa, and approximately 200 of 1,250 candidates at the camp were from Howard. The university also established new programs to train radio operators and other civilian technicians useful to the military. An undetermined number of Howard graduates served and died in France, most of them in the Ninety-Second and Ninety-Third Divisions of the Army.

Following the war, President Stanley Durkee bolstered the university's explicit commitment to the service and education of black Americans. Durkee believed that Howard should devote itself to black causes by doing more than simply educating qualified black students denied their due opportunities at other universities infected with racism. Durkee considered it the responsibility of Howard's medical school to train black doctors to work in poorly served black communities, for example, and he described the law school as "the servant principally of a particular racial group."

Dr. Mordecai Johnson was president of Howard from 1926 until 1960, and he was the first African American to hold the appointment permanently. Johnson and the university benefited enormously from an amendment to Howard's charter, passed by Congress in 1928, on the eve of the Great Depression. The amended charter guaranteed substantial federal funding for the university, excepting its religious programs. Representative Daniel Reed of Dunkirk, New York, spoke persuasively to Congress of the need and benefit of an institution that would serve and elevate America's black population. Opponents charged either that it was improper to give special economic preferences to blacks which were not afforded whites, or that it was wrong to use federal moneys to fund an institution serving the population of Washington alone. The amendment passed by nearly three votes to one.

President Johnson wisely used the new federal funds to develop Howard's infrastructure, especially where changes were needed for the professional programs to receive accreditation. The law school hired new reputable scholars and opened day classes, and the schools of medicine, dentistry, and pharmacy each paid for several faculty members to study at America's finest institutions in order that they might later return with their acquired knowledge. As a result of these and other actions, all of Howard's professional schools were accredited by the end of Johnson's administration. In addition, the undergraduate colleges were greatly improved by the hiring of new professors, and by the consequent reduction in student-teacher ratio.

The Great Depression temporarily retarded Howard's maturation, for both federal funding and enrollment fell between 1930 and 1932. Several building projects were halted, and teachers' salaries were cut by a total of 15 percent. However, the effects of the Depression were not particularly severe at Howard, on the whole. The Public Works Administration, one of the federal agencies created under the heading of U.S. President Roosevelt's New Deal, allocated more than $2.25 million to Howard in 1933 for the construction of a chemistry building, utilities plant, library, and classroom building. The next year, teachers' salaries were raised 5 percent, and Johnson secured funds to hire 27 outstanding new scholars to invigorate several departments.

While the university enjoyed its newfound prosperity and stature, Johnson was under attack for his public expression of communistic ideas, and for the supposed mishandling of federal funds. U.S. Representative Alfred Bulwinkle of North Carolina publicly questioned whether the government ought to finance an institution whose president supposedly preferred communism to religion, and Representative Robert Hall of Mississippi called for a congressional investigation to determine whether Johnson was mismanaging federal funds by creating a tense, divided institution. In the fall of 1934, the General Alumni Association took the latter charges seriously enough to call for an independent investigation. Johnson defended himself vigorously against these criticisms, and in most cases he either defeated or made peace with his detractors.

In the years surrounding World War II, Johnson invested heavily in Howard's undergraduate programs, thus marking a change from the university's emphasis on its professional schools. In 1941, a new scholarship program was introduced to help qualified undergraduates in financial need, and a new standardized system of testing and evaluation was instituted to draw the best high school students from across the country. The following year, the trustees agreed to reduce course loads for liberal arts teachers, and to better their tenure and retirement programs. Then in 1946, the College of Liberal Arts was subdivided into five semi-autonomous programs, each responsible for establishing examinations, public lectures, and a curriculum more suited to its own discipline.

Several Howard administrators and professors held important positions during World War II. Two of the most important were Dean Hastie of the law school, who was a civilian aide to the Secretary of War, and Dr. Ralph Bunche, who worked for the Office of Strategic Services and the State Department, and then as an advisor to the U.S. delegation that negotiated the establishment of the United Nations. Dr. Bunche won the Nobel Peace Prize in 1950 for his role in bringing about an end to the Arab-Israeli war. In addition, about 300 soldiers trained on Howard's campus, and an indefinite number of Howard students and alumni served in the armed forces during the war.

Howard blossomed in the post-war years. In 1955, the university inaugurated its first doctoral program. Johnson approved stipends of $1,000 for each of three teaching fellows in the department of chemistry, and in 1958 Howard became the first predominantly black university in the country to award a Ph.D. Two years later, the department of physics introduced a doctoral program, and the dentistry program began planning a graduate program. Enrollment at Howard quickly doubled following the war, reaching more than 6,000 by 1960. The administration responded to the influx of students with an aggressive building program costing $17 million. Modern facilities were constructed to house the departments of architecture, engineering, fine arts, and biology, and the schools of law, pharmacy, medicine, and dentistry, as well as house the administration.

The medical program was substantially improved following the 1951 publication of an embarrassing article in the *Journal of the American Medical Association* reporting that many graduates of Howard's medical school were failing state boards. Johnson and his administrators implemented a variety of curative measures, including the hiring of new teachers and auxiliary personnel, the increasing of faculty salaries and research funds, the provision of new facilities and equipment, and the fuller integration of the medical school with Freedman's Hospital. When nearly 15 percent of the medical school's graduates taking state board examinations still failed in 1955, school administrators began requiring more and better written work.

In 1955, Johnson reached the age of 65, and thus according to a university policy that he had himself endorsed, he was forced to tender his resignation. However, the trustees appointed him to another five-year term to be served while they searched for a suitable replacement. His eventual departure was met with anxiety and sorrow, for Johnson had transformed Howard from a small, mediocre institution into a competitive and internationally respected university.

James N. Nabrit Jr. took up the responsibilities of the presidency in September 1960, and was inaugurated on April 26 of the following year. Nabrit was secretary of the university for 17 years prior to his appointment to Howard's top office, but it was his outstanding record as a civil rights leader that earned him national honor and respect. Nabrit was a lawyer who prepared or argued several of the most important civil rights cases in American history, including Brown v. The Board of Education. He brought his racial views to bear on his administration, in accordance with his declaration that "since Howard University is bound by its traditional service to the Negro people, it must continue to direct a large part of its efforts toward the training and development of young men and women who have been handicapped by segregation."

Ironically, several influential student groups at Howard doubted Nabrit's devotion to the black community. In 1967, Professor Nathan Hare and a small group of Howard students organized the Black Power Committee (BPC), which "pledged to revolutionize black universities and to defeat the colonialist administrators who rule on behalf of the white power structure, and to create black universities to serve black people." The BPC and other groups began to stage protest and walk-outs regularly on campus to promote their ambitions for the university. In the summer of 1967 and the fall of 1968, Vice President Wormely expelled or suspended more than 90 protesters. New demonstrations were staged to protest those punishments, and from there the situation escalated. In March 1968, approximately 1,500 students occupied the Administration Building for five days, during which they demanded that Wormely and Nabrit resign, that the university reverse Wormely's punishments, and that Howard be more thoroughly devoted to black issues. The administration flatly refused the first two demands, but the crisis ended when ground was given on the third.

Since Nabrit's departure in 1969, the university has delicately balanced its two purposes, to educate American youth and to serve the black community. Dr. James Cheek, who was elected president the year Nabrit resigned, devoted himself to Howard's building program. He oversaw the addition of three new campuses, several buildings, and the addition of several new departments. Enrollment, employment, and the university's budget all rose during Cheek's administration. Upon assuming office in 1989, Dr. Franklyn Jenifer pledged to make Howard a center for research into the issues facing black America. Howard's newest president, Patrick Swygert, spoke to both concerns in his convocation speech, delivered September 29, 1995. "[Howard] University must continue to be a place where African Americans and others can come to study, free of oppression of any type, stripe or kind. [And] this university must engender and nurture an environment that celebrates African-American culture."

Further Reading: The only monographic history of Howard is *Howard University: The First Hundred Years* by Rayford W. Logan (New York: New York University, 1969). The narrative is awkward at times, but quite thorough. Internet users can also find a brief, but useful history online at http://howard.edu.

—Christopher Hoyt

HUMBOLDT UNIVERSITY
(Berlin, Gemany)

Location: In Berlin's historical "Stadt Mitte" (city center), a borough of the former East Berlin sector. The university is located past the Brandenburg Gate on a main thoroughfare, *Unter den Linden*.

Description: A self-governing trust of the city-state since the 1992 academic reorganization, the university was founded in 1810 (as Friedrich-Wilhelm-Universität) and now enrolls about 24,500 full time students and offers 224 courses of study. Nine percent of the student body comes from abroad.

Information: Humboldt-Universität zu Berlin
Unter den Linden 6
10117 Berlin
Germany

The concept of a university for Berlin was first promoted at the end of the eighteenth century. Johann Gottlieb Fichte, progressive (pre-Romantic) scientist and Friedrich Schleiermacher, a humanistic theologian, influenced Wilhelm von Humboldt's plans for a "universitas litterarum," a school which would combine teaching and research and provide comprehensive education.

Four traditional faculties—law, medicine, philosophy, and theology—were offered in October 1810 when the university opened under the name of Friedrich-Wilhelm-Universität. Berlin's university was housed in a palace built by Friedrick the Great for his brother, Prince Heinrich, in 1748 in a restrained neoclassical style. The entrance gates facing Unter den Linden are now flanked by statues of educator Wilhelm von Humboldt and his brother Alexander, who explored South America. Wilhelm is in deep thought, holding a book in hand, while Alexander is sitting on a globe with the dedication, "Second Discoverer of Cuba," a gift from the University of Havana. From its foundation to 1948 the University at Berlin was named Friedrich-Wilhelm University and referred to as "Berlin University."

The Charité evolved from the hospital for the plague and contagious diseases that was built in 1710 outside the city walls. It became the university's medical school in 1829. The school of veterinary medicine which had opened in 1790, and the Museum of Natural History were also added to the medical school. Professors and researchers such as Hufeland and Johannes Müller were on the medical faculty.

Under Friedrich II (Friedrick the Great, 1740–86), Prussia became a major power in Europe. This philosopher/warrior king and others, such as Moses Mendelssohn, Gotthold Ephraim Lessing, and Friedrich Nicolai turned the Prussian capital of Berlin into a center of the Enlightenment in Germany. The grand structure which became the university, as well as the State Opera in the Forum Friederianum, the Old Library, and Saint Hedwig's Cathedral were all built along Unter den Linden during Friedrich II's reign. By 1806, Napoléon had defeated Prussia, and the French monarchy occupied Berlin.

Rector, Professor Dr. Kurt Schröder, speaking at Humboldt University's 150th anniversary in 1960 (which was a joint celebration for the 250th year anniversary of the Charité) stated, in a university Senate declaration, *Humboldt Universität: Gestern-Heute-Morgen*, that the university opened its doors during a time of ardent patriotism against foreign rule, during a "peoples' movement" which was destined to shake up the bonds of "feudal absolutism" and "bring about the will of the people against the remnant social structure of the middle ages by its striving for social change and scientific progress." Staunchly Communist, the celebrants at Humboldt in 1960 (just one year before the Berlin Wall was erected) expressed pride in the history of "their" university, which claims 27 Nobel Prize winners: among them, Albert Einstein and Max von Laue.

Rebuilt and renamed after the ravages of World War II by the German Democratic Republic (GDR) and the Soviet regime, and overcoming the intellectual decline of the Nazi years, Humboldt University would "once again," Schröder declared, become the great institution of learning set out by its founders, renowned for scientific achievements. Two prominent founders of "scientific Socialism," Karl Marx and Friedrich Engels, had been students at the Berlin University during its first century.

The declaration of the founders stated that the university was to be an "institution for the whole Fatherland, the work of a free and great national spirit . . . a new type of university, in which the unity of research and teaching would be the grounding principle." This university would not be like classical-imperial (*römish-kaiserlich*) universities of the past, endowed with "privileges," but rather, a university which would give the study of natural science its due allotment and would promote knowledge for the national betterment of the German people, while paying attention to the achievements of other cultures.

Since the storming of the Bastille in Paris, July 14, 1789, the German people had watched the development of personal freedoms, the undercutting of the feudal sys-

Humboldt University

tem, and the rise of free enterprise. They were ready to overthrow the double yoke of a foreign ruler (Napoléon) and the "backwardness" of their own feudal system. The professors and students were participants in a movement toward German unity and sympathized with Wartburg student demonstrations in 1817. Wilhelm von Humboldt wrote that one of the first proposals, a "mission," of the university should be the promotion of a single German language. Philosopher Johann Gottlieb Fichte and others argued that only through "the Volk," a collective, living, nationalistic force of German-born citizens with its own culture, traditions, and language could unity be achieved. Early professors included Jakob and Wilhelm Grimm, linguistics and literature; George Hegel, philosophy and dialectics; Friedric Karl von Savigny and Eduoard Gans, law; mathematicians Karl Jacobi and Peter Gustav Lejeune-Dirichlet; physicists Heinrich Magnus and Johann Poggendorf; chemist Martin Klaproth; and others in agriculture and forestry science.

In the revolution of 1848, Berlin's professors and students stood on the side of the people. Despite defeat at the hands of the Prussian monarch, and with the reactionary alliance of the rising bourgeoisie with the junkers (landed aristocracy), the university's humanistic "people's movement" was dealt a blow in their ideology about unification.

What the revolutionaries had long struggled for was partially achieved by the founding of the German Empire in 1871. However, "Unity, Justice, and Freedom" was granted by decree of a ruling monarch, the King of Prussia. Prussian King Wilhelm I became Emperor of Germany, not only of the Prussian people. Prussian Prime Minster Otto von Bismarck was his Imperial Chancellor, and Berlin became capital of the Empire.

Humboldt University, however, continued to play an important role in the development of scientific study, especially in the natural sciences. In the second half of the nineteenth century, prominent scientists had high regard for the Berlin university.

Humboldt University was an early leader in the field of chemical research. August Wilhelm Hoffmann, one of its well-known and respected professors, served as rector in 1880–81, aborted a potential crisis by denying the foundation of an anti-Semitic student society proposed by Treitsche and Stöcker. After Hoffmann's death in 1892, Emil Fischer, the Ordinarius of Würzburg was appointed rector. His research into the chemistry of carbohydrates and his discovery of phendylhydroxins led the way in the field of organic chemistry for Germany. Researchers' demands for better facilities led to the building of the largest and most modern institute for chemical research in Germany in 1910 on Hessischen Strasse, replacing the old Institute on Georgenstrasse. Inorganic chemistry also found a respectable nice at Berlin. Progress was made in the fields of radioactive chemistry, biochemistry, and physics. Researchers such as Alfred Stock, Otto Hahn, and Franz Fischer were pioneers in these fields.

Turn-of-the-century Berlin became a cultural mecca, attracting writers and artists, many of whom joined with Edvard Munch and August Strindberg in an artistic alliance in 1898 called the "Berlin Secession," after a scandal caused by a Munch exhibition. Artists such as Käthe Kollwitz depicted the social misery of the lower classes; Expressionists Wassily Kandinsky and Emil Nolde brought Berlin into the avant garde.

The university continued building throughout Germany's political changes. Christopher Isherwood, whose stories about turn-of-the-century Berlin was inspiration for the stage show "Cabaret," wrote that the architecture of the nineteenth century was "so pompous, so very correct." These buildings were restored from their post-war rubble.

During the Weimar Republic (1918–33), state authorities refused to grant professorships in some instances, especially to Jewish academics; there were still elements of Prussian anti-Semitism and social democracy at work. Many conformist professors who were rightists yet against the Weimar Republic, did nothing, although there were incidents of open hostility at some universities (e.g., Heidleberg, Marburg). With the rise of the National Socialist Party, several colleagues and students left Berlin, Lindemann and Franz Simon, who later found success in England, were two of the first to leave.

Jacobus van Hoff in 1901, Emil Fischer in 1902, and Walther Nernst in 1920 were honored with the Nobel Prize. Berlin University during the first two decades of the twentieth century reached its highest success in the field of chemistry. After Fischer's death in 1919, many of his students left the university for appointments at other universities.

The 1920s, characterized by economic crisis and the rising tide of Fascism, brought a decline to Berlin's university, as well as to other academic institutions throughout Germany. Intellectual emigration from Berlin preceded the physical devastation of Humboldt University during World War II.

The National Socialist Party came into power in January 1933. Political suppression followed the burning of the Reichstag building (government offices) in February; by March, hundreds of thousands of brown and black shirted SA and SS troops paraded through Berlin. By the end of the first two months of Hitler's arrival, hundreds of literary and artistic people had left Germany. The Civil Service law of April 7, 1933, forced more than 1,000 scholars from their academic positions as "politically unreliable" or "non-Aryan," although categories were not finally determined until the Nuremberg Laws of 1935. Max von Laue, Nobel-prize-winning physicist at the university, remained in Berlin signing petitions, pleading with Nazi officials, and sending news to "refugee colleagues." He wrote to Einstein in America expressing both joy at the ground-roots support for fleeing intellectuals in England and the USA, and shame and bitterness over the fact that remaining in Berlin meant resistance against academic and political oppression. Those who were left in the universities were mainly conformists and right-wing members of fraternities, or members of the Nazi party who were gaining influence. Hitler found support at all academic levels, making education serve his purpose: highly centralized, anti-intellectual, subservient to war preparations, and vocational. Only racially "acceptable," physically fit youth who were in service to the "Hitler Youth" were admitted to universities after 1933.

Boris Schwarz, a young Jewish violinist in Berlin, who had played chamber music with his father's friend, Albert Einstein, matriculated to Humboldt University in 1933, working toward his doctorate in musicology when, within a year, his German engagements were canceled, radio programs stopped inviting him to play, German students switched to other teachers, and his Jewish students vanished. In March 1936, although his dissertation had been accepted, he was refused admission to the oral examination and could not graduate. He joined Einstein in America.

On May 10, 1933, students burned books by authors who displayed an "un-German spirit." The works of Heine, Marx, Bernstein, Einstein, Freud, Kafka, Remarque, Hesse, and Brecht were among those reviled by student committees (Asta) controlled by the Nazis; books were thrown into bonfires at universities of the Third Reich. Humboldt University ultimately became a center for anti-Hitler propaganda; students and professors were imprisoned and executed for their activities. Lilo Herrman, Arvid Harnack, Mildred Harnish, Herbert Baum, Harro Schulze-Boysen, George Groscurth, and Robert Havemann were among the resistance leaders.

When the Soviet sector was established in Berlin in 1945, Berlin's university was in shambles—a university with few walls, fewer books, and educators with Nazi orientation who had to be dismissed. Socialist Realism allowed for the preservation of the national heritage;

Humboldt University was spared reconstruction in the "wedding cake" style of the Russian pseudo-classical, highly decorative style produced by architect Hermann Henselmann. The university was "reconstructed," however, with Soviet educational methods.

The Soviets set up a German Administration for Education in the summer of 1945, reorganized and renamed the university, and prepared the way for a communistic foundation of education under the 1946 "Law for the Democratization of the German School," which proposed to make the young "capable of thinking for themselves, acting responsibly, able and willing to serve the community." The education was to be free of militarist, imperialist or racial ideology, and at the early stages, communist ideology was not thrust forward, but made inroads along the whole system.

Humboldt University was reopened in January 1946, offering courses in seven departments. Conflicts over course structure and politics led to schisms in staff and student body and ultimately led to the dismissal or flight of academics and scholars to the western sectors, particularly after the opening of the Berlin Free University in 1948. The German Administration issued rules severely regulating the admission of students to the university in 1947, prioritizing the children of the urban and rural working class, if they had not been associated with or been members of the Nazi party, and those persecuted by the Nazis. Non-proletarians who had not been Nazis were next, and third on the list were those who had been members of Hitler Youth only. *Vordienstanstalten,* offering matriculation courses to mature students was a benefit for returning ex-political prisoners and servicemen.

"Arbeiter-und-Bauren Fakultäten" (Workers and Peasants Faculties-ABF) were instituted in 1949 for the working class who had not passed entrance exams (abolished by 1963); Marxist version of social science became compulsory in August 1950; and the university was brought under central control of the SED's Ministry of Higher Education in 1951. Economics and the needs of the party and state were priorities in course planning, and the German two-term academic year was changed to a Soviet ten-month academic year in a decree issued in February 1951.

The 1950s and 1960s were punctuated by a number of repressive and relaxed periods for intellectual freedom in the GDR. Communist playwright Bertolt Brecht returned from exile; Wolf Biermann (*The Glass Harp*), Christa Wolf (*The Divided Sky*), Hermann Kant (*Die Aula*) all had periods of favor with the government and periods of disfavor from 1956 after Khruschev's exposé of Stalin until the Hungarian revolution during the late 1950s.

In 1962—a year after the Berlin Wall was erected—until December 1965, another period of relaxation allowed students, teachers, writers, artists, and intellectuals a respite from the censorship fostered by Paul Fröhlich, influential Leipzig district secretary in the 1950s and 1960s.

Robert Havermann, chemistry professor at Humboldt University, an "experienced functionary" according to John Dornberg (*The Other Germany: Europe's Emerging Nation Behind the Berlin Wall*, Doubleday, 1968), and a member of the Communist Party since 1932, anti-Nazi resistance worker, concentration camp survivor, charter member of the SED, lost his faith in the party when Stalin's "sins" were exposed by Khruschev at the XXth Soviet Party Congress. He began "shocking" party members with his lectures at the university based on his doubts, and he became a symbol of the era. His lectures, every Friday, brought students from all over the GDR to Berlin to sit in his overcrowded lecture hall, in the aisles, to hear Havermann say that "Socialism cannot be realized without democracy." His lectures catalyzed the young East Germans. A mixture of philosophy, physical, bio- and photochemistry, his ideas were heresy to the "ideologues" and functionaries who kept a hard Stalinistic party line.

After riots at rock concerts and long-haired students playing Beatles music caused a stir in the sector, the December 1965 Plenary meeting of the Central Committee found Christa Wolf defending her colleagues who chose to loosen ideological interpretations, an indication of the Cold War thaw to come, although Walter Ulbricht's party-line leadership was still severe.

In 1965, Beirmann, a singer of raucous political songs (like Bob Dylan), was not allowed to perform any longer in the GDR, and self-exiled to Prague; Havermann was fired from his university post, expelled from the Party, and purged from the GDR's Academy of Science. A new law, "Lex Biermann" was put into effect to prohibit writers from publishing their works in the West before first offering them to East German publishing houses.

The "Third Higher Education Act" in 1968–69 changed the structure of Humboldt University. Traditional faculties were abolished and replaced by sections, having councils on which sat academic staff members, representatives of the Soviet SED, the German FDJ, and industrial or other groups tied to a section. Marxism/Leninism, History, Mathematics, Languages and Literature, Sciences, Chemistry, and Marine Engineering were typical sections. Research was commissioned by industry; sections providing for an economic need got better endowments. The university was still headed by a rector who did not have the power of former German university rectors. There was a "Ministry for Universities and Vocational Colleges" in Berlin which detailed and regulated every aspect of university life, from admittance to stipends, to where and how students spent their summers at work camps.

The unification of Germany in 1990 made Berlin a city with three universities. Humboldt developed a new framework with the help of the Central University Staff and Structural Commission and the Structural Development and Appeals Commission created by Berlin's legislative assembly. Courses have been redesigned and staff has been subjected to personal and professional evaluation. In July 1991, "Humboldt v. Berlin" was a test case to challenge the "fire and rehire" method used by the Berlin government to boot old Communist Party professors with links to the STASI (State Security apparatus) from their tenured positions. The case failed to overturn the practice.

Humboldt today has 11 faculties and two centrally administered institutions—the Museum of Natural History and the Great Britain Center. It maintains academic respect in scientific research, and covers all fundamental disciplines in mathematics, the natural sciences, agricultural science, the humanities, the social sciences, and medicine. A special research group, the "Quantification and Simulation of Economic Processes;" two special graduate colleges (Mathematics and Biochemistry); an innovative college of theoretical biology; and participa-tion in international fairs and symposia keep Humboldt University linked to its illustrious past.

Further Reading: No English-language histories of Humboldt University exist. John Dornberg's *The Other Germany: Europe's Emerging Nation Behind the Berlin Wall* (Garden City, New York: Doubleday, 1968) begins with a dramatic account of the days preceding the building of the Berlin Wall and reveals insights into the people and politics of the early Soviet city-state of East Berlin. *The GDR: Moscow's German Ally* (London: Allen and Unwin, 1983) by David Childs, gives a comprehensive account of the education system and daily life in the GDR.

—Carol Shilakowsky

ILLINOIS INSTITUTE OF TECHNOLOGY
(Chicago, Illinois, U.S.A.)

Location: Illinois Institute of Technology is composed of four campuses in and around Chicago, Illinois, a northern midwest state of the United States. IIT's main campus is a 120 acre campus located on Chicago's near South Side at 33rd and State streets. The downtown campus is located at 565 West Adams Street in Chicago's Loop district. The Daniel F. and Ada L. Rice Campus is a 19 acre campus in Wheaton, Illinois, a suburb 25 miles (40 km) west of downtown Chicago. The Moffett Campus is a 5 acre campus located in Bedford Park, Illinois, a suburb 10 miles (16 km) southwest of downtown Chicago.

Description: The Illinois Institute of Technology (IIT) is a private, coeducational university offering both undergraduate and graduate degrees. IIT is one of the leading scientific and technical schools in the United States and is particularly noted for its architecture program at both the undergraduate and graduate level. In 1996 the total student enrollment was 6,287.

Information: Office of Public Relations
Illinois Institute of Technology
3200 South Wabash Avenue
Chicago, IL 60616
U.S.A.
(312) 567-3104

Visiting: Office of Admission
Illinois Institute of Technology
3300 South Federal Street
Chicago, IL 60616
U.S.A.
(312) 567-3025 in the U.S.
outside of Chicago (800) 448-2329

Chicago, Illinois, a city of approximately 3 million people, is located on the southwest shore of Lake Michigan and is the midwest center for transportation, finance, industry, and culture. Chicago, nicknamed "The Windy City" for its bombastic politicians and boastful citizens who wanted to host the 1893 World's Fair, has a colorful reputation based on its history of gangsters, stockyards that were the setting for Upton Sinclair's novel *The Jungle* (so horrifying that it inspired U.S. government regulation of meat processing plants), and one particular cow infamous for starting a devastating fire. By the 1870s Chicago had a population of almost 300,000 people and

had become a center for, among other things, railroads, meatpacking industries, and farm machinery manufacturing. On October 8, 1871, however, the city was ravaged by a fire that began when, legend has it, Mrs. O'Leary's cow kicked over a lantern. Strong winds, dry weather, and wooden construction that dominated the city combined to produce a fire that destroyed roughly 4 square miles (10 sq km) of downtown Chicago, leaving approximately 100,000 people homeless and causing millions of dollars worth of damage. Rebuilding of Chicago began almost immediately, with stricter building codes in place, and, interestingly, out of this devastation came the opportunity for Chicago to be a center for architectural innovation and experimentation.

The Illinois Institute of Technology (IIT) traces its history back to the last decade of the nineteenth century. In 1890 the Armour Institute of Technology was founded in Chicago as a polytechnic school to educate local students and provide skilled workers and leaders for the community. In 1940 the Armour Institute of Technology merged with the Lewis Institute (founded in 1896) to become the Illinois Institute of Technology. The name Illinois Institute of Technology was also formally adopted in 1940. The Institute of Design (founded in 1937 as the New Bauhaus) joined the school in 1949. A fourth merger took place in 1969, when the Chicago-Kent College of Law (originally incorporated as a school in 1888) joined IIT. At the time of Armour Institute of Technology's establishment in 1890, Chicago had recovered from its "great fire" and become home to an architectural renaissance. The work of architects Daniel H. Burnham, John W. Root, Frank Lloyd Wright, Louis Henri Sullivan, and Dankmar Adler transformed the city-scape and became a style known as the first Chicago School of Architecture. The firm of Burnham and Root was noted for its development of skyscrapers, using steel skeletons to support buildings. Burnham emphasized the concept of a beautiful, integrated city in which wide streets, open spaces, and tall buildings worked together to form a balanced whole. Adler and Sullivan also became known for their work with skyscrapers and improvement of technical standards. Coming to the forefront of architectural theory of the time was the idea that the form or design of a building should express or aid its function. By the early twentieth century Chicago had established an international reputation as a city of architectural achievement and possibilities. It was to this city that the world famous German architect Ludwig Mies van der Rohe came in 1938 to teach, design, and create at the Armour Institute of Technology.

Illinois Institute of Technology

Mies van der Rohe was born in Aachen, Germany, in 1886. Although he was apprenticed to several architects, he never received any formal architectural education. In the early years of the twentieth century, Mies developed his belief that the actual supports of a building should be emphasized as a main architectural feature. He sought to take technology to its highest degree of development, ultimately transforming elements of industrialization into art. Mies associated with many leading architects of the time, such as Hendrik Petrus Berlage, Walter Gropius, and Le Corbusier. Following World War I, numerous painters, sculptors, and writers sought a universal expression of art; their international aim influenced the direction of architects who also began to create a unifying, international style. This international style was encouraged at the Bauhaus school, where Mies became director in 1930. Here he promoted the ideas of simple, functional design and an appreciation for the brick, steel, and glass building materials themselves. The totalitarian government of Hitler's Nazi Germany, however, soon stifled this period of creativity, and Mies immigrated to the United States in 1937. In 1938 he accepted the position as head of the School of Architecture of the Armour Institute of Technology with the assurance that he could design buildings for the campus as well as teach.

As an instructor, Mies encouraged disciplined learning, teaching students to begin by learning the basics of drawing, then to learn about the qualities and characteristics of building materials, and finally, to learn the principles of construction. The Armour Institute of Technology's original campus, with an area of 7 acres and 5 buildings, was marked for expansion with the merger of Lewis Institute and the formation of the Illinois Institute of Technology in 1940. Mies directed the creation of the new 120 acre campus on the near South Side of Chicago. State Street, a main thoroughfare running north/south through the city, was to divide the campus roughly in half. For Mies it was the opportunity to apply on a large scale his crisp, rectilinear forms, echoing the gridlike pattern of Chicago's streets; to use brick, concrete, and steel structures and walls of glass to blend technology into art; and to create a balance between open, natural spaces and man-made construction. Alumni Memorial Hall (constructed 1945–46) was Mies's first classroom building built on the campus. It lies to the west of State Street and now houses classrooms and labs used for civil and environmental engineering classes. This building established a pattern for other buildings on campus with its use of "module" space. These module spaces were large, open areas that could be used for classrooms, offices, or labs while retaining a flexibility to accommodate future changes in the school's use of the building. Perlstein Hall, also constructed 1945–46 and situated on the west of State Street, features a small, interior courtyard. The landscaping of the area around the building includes trees native to the midwest and was done by Alfred Caldwell, a student of Mies's, to Mies's designs. This building now houses administrative offices, including the president's office, as well as classrooms and labs. Wishnick Hall (constructed 1945–46) and Siegel Hall (planned in 1946 but not constructed until 1956–57) demonstrate Mies's use of line, rectangular forms, and steel, brick, and glass. Both buildings are now used for classrooms and labs. Wishnick Hall also contains the Center for Excellence in Polymer Science and Engineering.

Lying to the east of State Street is the Robert F. Carr Memorial Chapel of St. Savior. The chapel was constructed from 1949 to 1952 and is unique among Mies's works. It is believed to be the only building Mies created to house religious services. Also to the east of State Street is the Commons (constructed 1952–53). This building is a focal point of student life since it houses the university bookstore, a convenience store, a post office, and an eatery. It is a glass-walled structure in which Mies exposed the actual steel framework. Throughout the 1950s, apartment buildings by Mies were added to the campus. They are collectively called the IIT Apartments and lie to the east of State Street. Carmen Hall (constructed 1953), Bailey Hall (1955), and Cunningham Hall (1955) are all noted for their use of reinforced concrete and glass. In the 1940s and 1950s, Mies also worked on the IITRI Materials Technology Building, which lies to the west of State Street. This building is part of the Illinois Institute of Technology Research Institute and houses the Instrumented Factory of Gears; the Center for Synchrotron Radiation Research and Instrumentation; the Midwest Laser Center; and the Productivity Center. From 1950 to 1956, S.R. Crown Hall was constructed on the campus to the west of State Street. This building is considered one of Mies's masterpieces. The exterior is remarkable for its clean lines, four outside columns, girders, and expanses of glass, while the interior is known for its open, flexible, module space. S.R. Crown Hall now houses IIT's College of Architecture and the Graham Resource Center, the architecture library. In 1958 Mies retired from his position at the Illinois Institute of Technology, leaving it an internationally known showcase for the "Miesian" style.

Other notable buildings on campus include Main Building (constructed 1891–93) and Machinery Hall (constructed 1901), both buildings lie to the west of State Street and were originally part of the Armour Institute of Technology. Also to the west of State Street is IIT Research Institute Tower, which was constructed 1963–64. This 19 story building is the tallest on campus and houses offices for the school's research affiliate, Illinois Institute of Technology Research Institute as well as the

school's Institute of Design. The Paul V. Galvin Library and Hermann Union Building Hall, both to the west of State Street, were completed in 1962. These buildings are visually reminiscent of S.R. Crown Hall. In 1966 an athletic complex, called Keating Sports Center, was added to the east side of campus. This facility contains, among other things, a weight room, tennis courts, and a pool. It is the site for competition of the Illinois Institute of Technology's varsity-level Scarlet Hawks in such sports as women's basketball and men's swimming. Residence halls with cafeterias and computer facilities as well as fraternity houses are among the other buildings that lie to the east of State Street.

The Illinois Institute of Technology runs on a semester calendar, with the regular academic year extending from August to May. In 1996 the student body totaled 6,287, of which 1,959 were undergraduate students; 3,062 graduate students; and 1,266 law students. Approximately 70 percent of the student body is male, 30 percent female. The Illinois Institute of Technology prides itself not only on teaching about technology but also providing access to it. Among the technologies available to students are hardwire linking from all the residence halls to the campus computer network; 11 wind tunnels for use in basic research; and the William F. Finkl Interactive Instructional Network (IITV) that provides instruction at more than 20 TV receiving sites. This unique distance-learning technology has a live "talk-back" system to provide immediate interaction with the on-campus IIT classrooms. Leon Lederman, a winner of the 1988 Nobel Prize in physics, is accessible to students through his teaching of such classes as freshman physics. Although over half of the freshmen come from Illinois and other areas of the midwest, IIT is currently at work on an international initiative program to attract students from all over the world. A campus radio station, a newspaper, and a yearbook are media resources available for students to run as well as use.

The Illinois Institute of Technology is composed of six different colleges. These colleges are Armour College; College of Architecture; Institute of Design; Institute of Psychology; Chicago-Kent Law College; and Stuart School of Business. Among the bachelor's degrees offered by IIT are chemical engineering, architecture, English, history, mathematics, accounting, psychology, and marketing management. Master's degree programs include architecture, chemical engineering, civil engineering, biology, psychology, management science, and operations research. Doctoral degrees are offered in such areas as electrical engineering, mechanical and aerospace engineering, physics, psychology, and management science. The Chicago-Kent College of Law offers law degrees and a master's in labor law.

The Illinois Institute of Technology's downtown campus houses the Chicago-Kent College of Law and the Stuart School of Business. This 10-story building is equipped with up-to-date technology, classrooms, and a library. The Daniel F. and Ada L. Rice Campus in Wheaton, Illinois, offers upper-level undergraduate classes geared to complement the curriculum of the community colleges in the area. This campus also offers graduate classes and continuing education classes for professionals. The Moffett Campus in Bedford Park, Illinois, is the site of the National Center for Food Safety and Technology.

Further Reading: There are brochures, maps, and encyclopedia articles about the Illinois Institute of Technology and Mies van der Rohe. The Illinois Institute of Technology's website, www.iit.edu, provides much information, including a calendar of current events and directions to the school. Books with information about IIT and its famous architect include Rolf Achilles's *Mies van der Rohe: Architect as Educator* (Chicago: Illinois Institute of Technology, 1986); *The Mies van der Rohe Archive: Robert F. Carr Memorial Chapel of St. Savior, S.R. Crown Hall, and Other Buildings and Projects*, edited by Franz Schulze (New York and London: Garland, 1992); and *The Mies van der Rohe Archive: Metallurgical and Chemical Engineering Building (Perlstein Hall) and Other Buildings and Projects* edited by Franz Schulze (New York and London: Garland, 1992). A general history of the university is covered in Irene Macauley's *The Heritage of Illinois Institute of Technology* (Chicago: Illinois Institute of Technology, 1978).

—Anne C. Paterson

INDIAN AGRICULTURAL RESEARCH INSTITUTE
(New Delhi, India)

Location: In India's capital, New Delhi.

Description: A government-funded institution of research and post-graduate studies in agriculture with 24 departments and approximately 600 students.

Information: Indian Agricultural Research Institute (IARI)
New Delhi 110012
India
(11) 575 4595

In the second half of the twentieth century, India underwent a tremendous transformation. For much of its history, it was a largely rural society of poor peasants living barely above subsistence level, with small sectors of urban craftsmen, merchants, bureaucrats, and idle rulers and landlords. The country was also plagued by periodic famine. In barely forty years, between 1950 and 1990, India developed a large industrial base, created the third largest pool of scientific and managerial personnel in the world, became a leader in the computer industry, began to export technology, saw the rise of a middle class over a hundred million strong, and found the resources to produce enough food for its greatly-expanded population. The results have been uneven. Vast new social problems emerged; other, older problems were not solved; and there is till a long distance to go to bring every citizen a better life. Yet, certainly what has been termed "the Green Revolution" is one of the great events of the twentieth century, and, even more certainly, one of the least known. For an institution that could symbolize this great transformation, there may be none better than the Indian Agricultural Research Institute in New Delhi. This flagship of agricultural research enabled the country's great leap in production.

When peoples of Asia, Africa, and the Pacific began to achieve their independence from Western colonial domination in the years after World War II, none were more ready than the Indians. Despite ruinous, bloody riots and massacres that had torn the sub-continent apart in the years before 1947, India had a body of well-educated, capable political leaders who wanted the chance to bring their enormous, new (but ancient) nation into the twentieth century. The country was connected by one of the largest rail systems in the world; it had a number of good educational institutions, many hospitals, functioning courts with learned judges and lawyers, and a well-trained, disciplined military and police force. Such

institutions were certainly not existent for the large majority of new nations that emerged on the world scene between 1945 and 1975. Despite a strong colonial legacy than inherited by most African nations, India still lagged in many areas, and the new leadership was only too aware of it.

Though Mahatma Gandhi had preached agrarian simplicity and self-sufficiency for many years, rejecting the industrial civilization that he felt had created so many social ills, most of the new leaders of India, from Jawaharlal Nehru down, believed that the country's future lay in following the paths taken by Japan, Russia, and the USA in transforming their agrarian societies into industrial ones. Even after Gandhi's assassination in 1948, there were a number of voices raised for keeping to his preferred path. However, from his death on, much talk echoed his ideals, but few attempts were made to put them into practice.

Though the British rulers had made many contributions toward India's modernization, they had neglected a number of fields, for both financial and political reasons. India, with its vast pool of labor, was not allowed to compete with British industry. Similarly, the development of science and technology was ignored. The educational system, from primary school through university, through impressive on paper, was weak from lack of funds and skewed in two directions. Primary and secondary education were marked by extremely low standards for most Indians, with a few excellent, mostly private or religiously-run, urban schools that produced the bulk off the top university students. British efforts in education emphasized good universities without building a mass base from which to draw as many of the country's top talents as possible. (It must be noted that before World War II, British education in the United Kingdom itself was not much different.) Indian education was also skewed because the British envisaged education in India as a way to produce the bureaucrats and clerks needed to run the vast administration of hundreds of million of people, spread over more than a million square miles, encompassing a vast conglomeration of ethnic groups, religions, languages, castes, and tribes. As for scientists, industrial managers, and agricultural experts, these were always provided from the metropole.

Agriculture was another area of neglect. While the British must be credited with the development of a large canal and irrigation system and with the rise of the Punjab as the modern "food basket" of both India and Pakistan, their efforts in agriculture over all were limited. British funds were limited also and the Raj preferred to use them to protect its investments (via the military, legal system, and civil service) and not meddle in complicated questions of land tenure and class structure.

At independence, in order to industrialize, India had to face two enormous problems. First, how could the country get the expertise to build and manage all the factories necessary for industrial society? And second, if millions of workers were to be removed from agriculture, how would the food supply—always a risk of failure throughout India's history—be maintained? Better yet, how could it be increased? For a country like Japan, the answer had laid in rapid development of export industries so as to be able to import increasing amounts of food. The European method was to build an army and navy and try to conquer the territories needed for food production. America had had the expanding frontier. India had none of these options. Since 45 percent of its territory is arable land, much of which is among the world's most fertile, but whose production ratios in 1950 were abysmally low, India could only choose to boos internal agricultural development. There would have to be land reform as well, to distribute land to the farmers who would actually do the work, and to put idle land back into production. To produce, the country's farmers would have to learn new methods, utilize new kinds of seeds, and irrigation technology would have to be made available. A whole new range of practices and products, specific to the problems of Indian farms, would have to be developed. India needed a vast new program of agricultural research and extension.

In 1950, the Indian government set aside two million rupees a year for agricultural research and education in the whole country (which then included Pakistan and Bangladesh). This sum was equal to U.S. $644,000. The central facility was to be the Imperial Agricultural College and Central Research Institute in Bihar. The American philanthropist and steel magnate Henry Phipps retired in 1901 to use his money for humanitarian purposes. Phipps, who gave money to establish foundations to fight tuberculosis and mental disease in the United States, surprisingly, on a visit to India, donated $150,000 toward the establishment of this new institute. As a result, the site became known as "Pusa," an acronym for "Phipps + USA." The Imperial Agricultural Research Institute awarded an associateship after a two year course at post-graduate level. Most graduates went on to teach at one of the many other agricultural colleges that were built between 1905 and independence. None of these lower-level colleges engaged in research or extension work.

In 1934 a massive earthquake in Bihar destroyed every single building at the Pusa campus. As a result, the Imperial Agricultural Research Institute was moved to its present campus of 1600 acres in New Delhi, a site which then was on the outskirts of the city. It became the strongest agricultural research facility in India with "one of the best agricultural libraries in Asia, much good equipment, and the largest staff of any such institution in India," according to Campaign Against Hunger. But until the decision was taken to make an all-out effort to transform Indian agriculture, the institute, which changed from "Imperial" to "Indian" along with the rest of the country on August 15, 1947, remained a place of limited interest.

India's agriculture problems were on a giant scale, so it was no wonder that Indian leaders looked to other giant nations, namely the United States and the Soviet Union, to seek solutions. Collectivization in the Soviet Union may have had its good points, but it had involved the deaths of millions, and Soviet agriculture was, even so, not a model of efficiency. The American model was both less coercive and more successful: American society, however, was so different from India's that there was a real question as to whether American methods could work in Asia. Despite some misgivings, India turned to the United States for assistance in building an agricultural revolution.

American agriculture had been transformed by a combination of the land grant universities which had strong agricultural research departments and engaged in extension work, the U.S. Department of Agriculture, and the County Extension Offices with their agents for education and improvement of life for the rural population. This structure was now transferred to India. In 1948, a pilot project was begun at Etawah in the state of Uttar Pradesh. With an American expert acting as "midwife" the Indian Community Development program was born. Extension education was the chief element of that program. Within 4 years there were 55 intensive development "community projects" around the country. These in turn led to the nation-wide system of block development. This program ran under the auspices of an Indo-American Technical Cooperation Fund developed through USAID and aided by millions of dollars from both the Ford and the Rockefeller Foundations, plus funding from UN agencies, and the World Bank. The program covered the entire nation by the early 1960s. Blocks consisted of roughly one hundred villages. Each had a center with research and experimental stations, staffed with Indian specialists on everything from youth clubs to poultry raising, seed improvement to milk production. The fundamental research and experimentation was done at the Indian Agricultural Research Institute (IARI) in New Delhi—the flagship of the whole vast effort. However, differing local needs and conditions required local experimentation and feedback for the central researchers. New varieties of wheat, rice, millet, sorghum, or sugar cane, improved breeds of animals, insecticides, chemical fertilizers, tube-well installation manuals, designs for cold storage units—all these things came from the Institute and were propagated from the block offices by extension agents who bicycled out into the myriad villages.

To lead this vast effort, the IARI was remodeled. In 1958, the post-graduate school was inaugurated with Rockefeller Foundation money. The Indian government intended "to make this new graduate school into India's principal center for education research workers and teachers for all her agricultural colleges, leaders for the extension services, and competent men for other government posts requiring advanced training in agricultural sciences." The IARI was designated one of the national institutions "deemed to be Universities." An American professor of agronomy from North Carolina, Ralph W. Cummings, who had conducted extensive research in Latin America, was appointed the first dean. American agricultural scientists were sent to be visiting professors in fields that had not yet been developed in India. The Rockefeller Foundation donated a large amount of money to expand the library and sent an American specialist in agricultural libraries to New Delhi. The foundation also paid for Indian scholars' study trips to the United States, Mexico, and several Asian countries where crucial agricultural research and development was occurring. The IARI staff attends international conferences and workshops to gain and share knowledge as well as develop confidence in their own abilities. Admission for graduate students was highly competitive because there was only 150 places per year. Once admitted, the students followed a credit course system modeled on the U.S. pattern.

By 1965, the IARI had awarded 395 M.S. degrees and 132 PhDs. Six years later there was a total of over 1000 graduates. Mexican dwarf wheat varieties associated with the work of Dr. Norman Borlaug (Nobel prize, 1970) were brought to India and cross-bred with Indian strains at IARI. The knowledge needed to make these high-yield, disease-resistant types of wheat available to the mass of Indian farmers was accumulated at a feverish pace in the 1960s. The subsequent soaring of India's wheat production is a matter of history and one of the most positive stories of this era. Yields in many part of the country doubled. Certain areas of the country, particularly Punjab, Haryana, and western Uttar Pradesh, changed beyond all recognition. Good shoes, cigarettes, ball-point pens, television sets, bicycles, motorbikes, and fine brick houses became a common sights in villages. The consumer goods produced in Indian factories became available to millions of people with more dispensable income than ever before, thanks to this "Green Revolution." A vast array of Indian-made agricultural equipment—tractors, threshers, pumps, sprayers, fertilizers—was adopted by the village farmers. This equipment, while aiding in the leap in production, also points to the underside of the Green Revolution. It put large numbers of agricultural laborers out of work. If they could find work in new industries or services, the change was not bad for them, but many could not. By the 1970s, India had become self-sufficient in food, and its industrial program was able to expand beyond the wildest dreams of those who had greeted Independence in 1947. The IARI not only played a vital role in this great, rapid transformation, but it may also serve as a symbol of the whole effort. For this, it ranks among the foremost institutions of higher learning in the world.

The IARI produced a talented body of professionals over the years, graduates who staffed the agricultural universities (also on the American model) established in each state in India. It is a center of learning not only for Indians but for graduates from such countries as Egypt, Kenya, Nepal, the Philippines, Sri Lanka, Tanzania, and Thailand. Exchange students from Europe, America, and Australia are regularly found on itscampus. The IARI produces Dr. Swaminathan, the first-ever recipient of the World Food Award, the agricultural equivalent of the Nobel prize. Other famous graduates include Dr. B.P. Paul, the internationally-known rose breeder, Dr. A.B. Joshi, the wheat breeder, Dr. A.M. Michael, known for developing irrigation systems which minimize water loss, and Dr. G.S. Sirohi, a plant physiologist who also conducted research in the Arctic. IARI graduates work as experts in the U.S. Department of Agriculture, with the UN's Food and Agriculture organization and as leading scientists in many international research institutes. Many IARI graduates have emigrated to North America, Europe, and Australia, joining over one million professionals India has sent broad since the 1950s. In the heady days of the intense drive to raise agricultural production, the IARI was a showpiece toured by international leaders who visited New Delhi.

Today the IARI has 711 research professionals in 24 departments. There are 119 technicians and nearly 3000 other staff. The number of graduate students is around 600. The facilities include India's Central Seed testing Laboratory, a water technology center, the Wheat project Directorate, a nuclear research laboratory, and divisions of soil science, plant physiology, vegetable crops, floriculture and landscaping, entomology, microbiology, genetics, biochemistry, agricultural engineering and many more. The IARI maintains then regional research stations in the different agro-climate regions of India. The library has increased to over 600,000 volumes, and IARI publishes several bulletins and journals in related fields. From early days, the IARI began a genetic materials collection to preserve the numerous varieties of sorghums, pearl millets, and small millets fond in the subcontinent. Later collections include insects, fungi, nematodes, and the germplasm of agriculturally useful microbes. Besides the tremendous success in wheat production, IARI researchers also developed new varieties of rice, hybrid sorghum, corn, pulses (lentil-like, nitrogenous plants that are high in protein and a vital part of the average Indian's diet) tomatoes, mangoes, and roses.

Further Reading: Although there are no specific histories of the institute, its development is treated in *Campaign Against Hunger* by E.C. Starkman, Richard Bradfield, and Paul C. Mangelsdorf (Cambridge, Massachusetts: Belknap Press of Harvard University Press, 1967) and Sterling Wortman and Ralph Waldo Cummings Jr.'s *To Feed This World* (Baltimore: Johns Hopkins University Press, 1978)

—Robert Newman

INDIANA UNIVERSITY
(Bloomington, Indiana, U.S.A.)

Location: In the small university town of Bloomington, fifty miles south of Indianapolis.

Description: A state university with eight campuses, enrolling approximately 91,000 students in undergraduate, graduate, and professional schools.

Information: Office of Admissions
Indiana University
Bloomington, IN 47405
U.S.A.
(812) 855–0661

Visiting: Guided tours of the Indiana University, Bloomington campus are available year-round. For more information and tour scheduling, call (812) 855–3512.

From the foundation of Indiana as a state in 1816, Hoosier legislators envisioned a comprehensive system of public education that would be crowned by a state university. Article 9 of the Indiana Constitution stated that it

shall be the duty of the general assembly, as soon as circumstances will permit, to provide by law for a general system of education, ascending in a regular graduation from township school to a state university, wherein tuition shall be gratis, and equally open to all.

Four years later, in 1820, the state assembly chartered the Indiana Seminary, but classes at the new institution did not begin until 1825.

The lawmakers selected Bloomington, located in sparsely settled Monroe County, as the site of the new institution because they felt that its isolation from the boisterous and, presumably, immoral Ohio River communities would protect students from worldly evils and provide an idyllic atmosphere for a place of higher learning. This choice, however, proved to be problematic; isolation, primitive roads, and repeated failure to find an adequate and clean water supply would hinder the growth of the university throughout most of the nineteenth century. As the state's population boomed, improved transportation by stagecoach and, in 1854, by rail, brought an ever-increasing number of students to Bloomington. They found severe water and housing shortages, and as late as

the 1890s, battled the threat of malaria and typhoid from the school's wells.

The school also faced serious academic obstacles during its first sixty years. Although Indiana Seminary was nominally changed by the legislature to Indiana College in 1828, and to Indiana University in 1838, these new names did not reflect an actual expansion in the curriculum or in the mission of the school. During these early years, instruction was concentrated on the classical curriculum of ancient languages, personal morals, and religious commitments. By the 1830s classes in philosophy, mathematics, and history were added to the ancient languages. The first six presidents of the university were ministers who maintained tight administrative and curricular control of the institution, stressing the moral development of the youth in its care. Weekly sermons were given in the university chapel by the president on topics of religion and morals. When not attempting to persuade the state legislature to appropriate more money for the university, these presidents were often involved in doctrinal debates with other ministers in Bloomington and the surrounding countryside.

The narrow conception of the role of the university held by its early presidents was fueled by fears that the state legislators, who controlled funding of the institution, would prohibit growth and development during these nascent years. Legislators in the nineteenth century were wary of raising taxes to support higher education, and politics in the frontier states tended toward egalitarianism with little thought to promoting higher learning for the few. In effect, Indiana University in its early years was a state university without public support and, consequently, remained a static, classically oriented institution of little import to the intellectual and economic development of the state.

Another blow to the potential development of Indiana University came in the 1860s when the institution was denied a share of lands distributed by the Morrill Act. The state legislature used this land act to bolster the newly formed Purdue University in West Lafayette. Without funds to promote agricultural and scientific courses, Indiana University was forced to limit its academic focus to the liberal arts and the professions. This failure to meet the changing needs of students exacerbated the already difficult task of securing money from the state's elected officials.

A rare progressive note during these early, struggling years was the fact that Indiana University became the first state university to admit women. Sarah Parke Morrison, daughter of a university trustee, was the first female to

Indiana University

graduate in 1869. Morrison opened the door for other female students; in the year following her admission to the university 12 more women were enrolled.

Not until the 1880s did Indiana University begin its transformation into an institution that would live up to its university designation. A catastrophic fire on July 12, 1883, destroyed most of the existing campus on the south side of town, and led to the decision to relocate the university in Dunn's Woods on the east side of Bloomington. The fire proved to be a blessing because it forced the university to construct new and more modern buildings that would provide the physical plant for a larger and more forward-looking institution. In 1884 the cornerstones were laid for Wylie and Owen Halls, two buildings that form the nucleus of what is now called the "Old Crescent." In 1980, these nine buildings were placed on the national Register of Historic Buildings and continue to serve as the aesthetic heart of the university.

David Starr Jordan became president in 1885, breaking the succession of minister presidents. Before his departure (to become the first president of Leland Stanford University) in 1891, Jordan put into motion the transformation of Indiana University from a provincial enclave to one of the best-known universities of the American Midwest. Jordan, a world-renowned ichthyologist and an 1872 graduate of Cornell University, instituted a full-scale system of elective courses and brought in new and talented faculty trained in the renowned academic institutions of the East. He increased the number of faculty from 18 to 29 during his tenure and stumped through the state, county by county, seeking support for the university.

Jordan's work was continued by the next two presidents, John Merle Coulter and Joseph Swain. These three presidents brought Indiana University into the modern era of university education. They increased state responsibility for institutional funding by constant and persuasive lobbying. As more funds were made available, they continued to widen the university's range of academic subjects and directed increasing portions of the budget toward the development of the sciences. In 1895, Indiana University took a leading role among its neighboring midwestern institutions. In April of that year, the presidents of state universities in Illinois, Indiana, Ohio, Michigan, Wisconsin, Minnesota, Missouri, Iowa, Kansas, and Nebraska met in Evanston, Illinois, and formed the North Central Association of Colleges and Secondary Schools with the aim of developing communication between these state institutions and uniform accreditation standards. This organization publicized the work of Indiana University and give its faculty and trustees a clearer perspective on the development of higher education outside of their own state.

The first third of the twentieth century was a time of great expansion at Indiana University. Under the 35-year tenure of William Lowe Bryan, a talented experimental psychologist, the work begun by Jordan, Coulter, and Swain saw fulfillment. To publicize the work of the university, Bryan established a university press bureau in 1903. Although the school granted its first graduate degree in 1882, it wasn't until Carl H. Eigenmann was appointed dean of the newly formed graduate school in 1908 that graduate studies at Indiana University became formally organized. The early 1900s also witnessed the formation of a number of departments that added to the university's growth and prestige. During these years Bryan presided over the formation of the medical, music, architecture, engineering, and business schools as well as the expansion of the law school, which had been established in 1842, abolished in 1877, and then reestablished in 1899. In 1914, after much political wrangling and competition between Indiana University and Purdue University, a teaching hospital was opened in the capital city of Indianapolis as part of Indiana's medical school.

In particular, the music curriculum experienced a meteoric rise; after becoming a separate department in 1904, it was established as its own school in 1921 under the enthusiastic leadership of Dean Winfred Merrill. Merrill worked tirelessly to lay the groundwork for a strong music program at Indiana by encouraging orchestral and vocal music performances, strengthening the administration of the music school, and hiring qualified instructors. The completion of the Music Building (1937) and Auditorium (1941) further boosted the music program by providing facilities for more students and larger productions. After World War II, the music school, now led by Wilfred Bain, continued to build on its reputation. The late 1940s saw the hiring of more talented and diverse instructors, and the beginnings of an extensive opera program that, by the late 1950s, became the largest in the nation. In 1956, the music school enrolled nearly 600 students and the competition to get into the school became extremely heated. The excellent reputation of the music school was enhanced by international concert tours that promoted the university as a center of music study and instruction. By 1994, the school was tied with Julliard and Eastman for top national ranking by a *U.S. News and World Report* study. Currently the school of music sponsors nearly 1,000 recitals, concerts, and operas each year.

During Bryan's 35 years as president, academic development was paralleled by physical growth. The university added 40 new buildings to its physical plant, including a new library building and the Student Building; with its prominent clock tower, the Student Building is one of the most recognizable landmarks on the university's Bloomington campus. After World War I, during which new construction was put on hold, Bryan continued the physical expansion of the university. A new stadium, women's dormitory, and an expansive student union (which, with later additions, would become the largest student union building in the world) was added to the campus. Much of the building program was enhanced by funds made available from the federal government as part of its nationwide effort to spur the economy during the Depression of the 1930s.

When Bryan retired in 1937 he humorously commented on the difficulties of expanding the scope of the university during these watershed years, saying that "is it not reasonable for a man to still be alive after having made thirty-five budgets at Indiana University." During the Bryan presidency, state support increased by more than $2 million.

The next university president also proved to be an exceptional leader: Herman B Wells, an Indiana native, Indiana University graduate, former banker, and dean of the business school. For the next 25 years Wells led Indiana University through a period of growth that built on the Bryan years and pushed the institution further into the national and international spotlight. Because of a new retirement plan for faculty instituted by Bryan, Wells found himself replacing nearly half of the department heads. Attempting to avoid the tendency to recruit from within, Wells scoured the nation for talented young scholars to broaden the background and outlook of the faculty.

Furthermore, using an extensive self-survey of all constituencies in the institution, Wells developed policies that furthered the administrative efficiency and scholarly reputation of the school. A personnel office, administrative council, student health and counseling services, larger library and research facilities, and standard admission procedures were all created as a result of the survey.

Indiana University experienced a tremendous influx of students after World War II as a result of the GI Bill which, in an effort to ease the transition back into civilian life, offered ex-soldiers an opportunity for higher education. The need for student housing, which boomed as the enrollment doubled during the years immediately after the war, was initially met by temporary structures such as Quonset huts and mobile homes. This housing shortage spurred the construction of permanent facilities and added greatly to the number of students the university could absorb.

In the post-World War II era the character of Indiana University slowly transformed from one based in midwestern social mores to an increasingly cosmopolitan and international outlook. Wells carefully recruited foreign scholars who were refugees from war-shattered Europe; this spurred the intellectual life of both the academic and Bloomington community. Wells also staunchly backed the work of Alfred Kinsey, who pioneered research in human sexuality beginning in 1938. Kinsey's establishment of the Institute for Sex Research in a traditionally conservative community and state became a major test of academic freedom, research, and publication. The institute's survival and the national recognition it received cemented Indiana University's status as an institution of national and international repute. In retrospect, Wells wrote about the controversy over university backing of the Kinsey Institute:

> Time has proved that the defense was important, not only for understanding sexual activity, but also for the welfare of the university. It reinforced the faculty's sense of freedom to carry on their work without fear of interference, and it established in the public mind the fact that the university had an integrity that could not be bought, pressured, or subverted.

Wells retired in 1962, having set a course for the succeeding presidents; during the past 30 years the university has continued to expand and solidify its place as one of the largest and best-known research and teaching institutions in the country.

As Indiana University's academic reputation flourished so did the variety and quality of student life and campus traditions. Athletics at the university have grown from humble beginnings in the 1890s, when university teams played loosely organized schedules with other state and regional teams, to become highly organized and skilled competitors in the Big Ten conference. Basketball, in particular, has become a major focus of institutional pride. The Indiana Hoosiers men's basketball team has won five National Collegiate Athletic Association (NCAA) national championships, second only to the University of California, Los Angeles' ten national titles.

The Little 500, an annual 50-mile bicycle race established in 1951 to raise scholarship money, has become one of the most popular campus events. Held each spring, the Little 500 has garnered national attention. In 1979, the popular movie *Breaking Away* used the race as a backdrop for its story about growing up in small-town America.

From the beginning the goal of Indiana University, as outlined in the 1816 state constitution, has been to become the apex of the state system of education in Indiana. In the last 30 years, the transformation of extension campuses into full-fledged branches of the university has helped achieve this goal. The creation of branch campuses in Indianapolis, Ft. Wayne, Gary, Kokomo, New Albany, Richmond, and South Bend has been instrumental spreading the accessibility of higher education in the state of Indiana. Currently, 80 percent of Indiana's population lives within 50 miles of an Indiana University campus. Over 17,000 faculty and staff are employed throughout the state. Indiana University maintains some 22 major schools within the university structure and grants degrees in over 850 programs. Across its campuses, the student body now numbers over 91,000, making it one of the largest institutions of higher learning in the United States.

Further Reading: The most comprehensive history of Indiana University from its founding in 1820 to 1970, including an entire volume of primary documents concerning the most crucial events and issues in the university's history, is Thomas D. Clark's *Indiana University: Midwestern Pioneer* (4 vols., Bloomington: Indiana University Press, 1970–77). A much less detailed but highly informative account of the university up to 1990, supplemented with hundreds of photographs from the university archives, is Dorothy C. Collins and Cecil K. Byrd's *Indiana University: A Pictorial History* (Bloomington: Indiana University Press, 1992). An informative first-hand account of IU during its most impressive years of growth and development is Herman B Wells's *Being Lucky: Reminiscences and Reflections* (Bloomington: Indiana University Press, 1980).

—Alexander Urbiel

INDIAN INSTITUTES OF TECHNOLOGY
(Bombay, Delhi, Kanpur, Kharagpur, Madras, India)

Locations: In five cities in India: Bombay, Delhi (in an educational complex in south Delhi that includes Jawaharlal Nehru University), Kanpur, Kharagpur, and Madras.

Description: A chain of five state technological institutes enrolling approximately 13,600 students in undergraduate and graduate programs.

Information:
Indian Institute of Technology, Bombay
Powai, Bombay 400076
India
(22) 5782545

Indian Institute of Technology, Delhi
Hauz Khas, New Delhi 110016
India
(011) 666979

Indian Institute of Technology, Kanpur
IIT PO
Kanpur 208016
India
(512) 214151

Indian Institute of Technology, Kharagpur
PO Kharagpur Technology
Kharagpur 721302
India
(3222) 2221

Indian Institute of Technology, Madras
Madras 600036
India
2351365

In 1956, Prime Minister Jawaharlal Nehru traveled to Kharagpur to deliver the first convocation address at the Indian Institute of technology, which at the time was the only one of its kind. Nehru praised the institute as a "fine monument of India, representing India's urges, India's future in the making." Part of Nehru's plan for his country's future was to found a chain of Indian Institutes of Technology (IITs), a goal he ultimately achieved with the help of other countries: IIT Bombay opened in 1958 with the assistance of the Soviet Union, IIT Madras in 1959 with the aid of West Germany, IIT Kanpur in 1960 with the sponsorship of the United States, and ITT Delhi in 1963 with the help of Great Britain. Today the institutes are among the finest of India's universities.

The IITs were conceived even before India won independence from Britain. By 1945, the government had determined that the key to developing Indian industry was to educate top-notch scientists and engineers in the country's own universities. Deciding that existing engineering colleges could not produce such graduates, the government chose to establish new schools and to pattern them after the Massachusetts Institute of Technology. The Department of Education, Health, and Lands appointed a committee to determine how many institutions the country would need and what specific form their programs would take. N.R. Sarkar, a former member of the viceroy's council, headed the twenty-four-member committee, which included leaders in the field of engineering, science, industry, and finance. They convened on April 11, 1945.

The Sarkar Committee considered recommending the establishment of a single main institute and a number of satellite schools. They decided, however, that India's technological need would be better served by the founding of at least four separate institutions, to be built in the north, south, east, and west of the country.

A subcommittee tackled the question of how closely the proposed institutes should follow the model of MIT. In his study of the IITs, Kim Patrick Sebaly writes that the subcommittee drew up a list of goals which the Indian Institutes should adopt, and that the list was similar to the "statements of purpose" set forth in MIT's 1945 *Bulletin*. The six goals of the subcommittee's list were to strengthen student's characters, give them a solid foundation basic engineering, train them to conduct accurate experiments, and teach them to write and speak clearly on technical subjects.

Sebaly notes that the subcommittee also recommended the adoption of specific features of MIT's program. Like the Massachusetts Institute of Technology, the IITs were to require fundamental courses in science and the humanities as well as in engineering. Specialization would not be encouraged. As was the case at MIT, only in their last two years would students concentrate on a particular subject, and in their fourth year they would write a thesis.

However, Sebaly observes that the IITs were not slavishly to follow MIT's lead. The subcommittee also recommended, for instance, that IIT students spend 300 hours on their theses, while MIT students spent 120 hours on theirs. Furthermore, the subcommittee advised that IIT students should receive practical experience in industry as well as training in workshops, suggestions that deviated from the MIT model.

The Sakar Committee's plan for the Indian Institutes of Technology, submitted in March 1946, was a revolu-

217

tion in the country's engineering education. To that point, said the committee's report, engineering colleges failed to "integrate mathematics, science and humanities with the specialized professional subjects." The schools lacked such courses because, in the words of the Sakar Committee, "the purpose of engineering college programs was limited to supplying recruits to government departments responsible for the maintenance of civil works located in the provinces." The IITs were to educate creative engineers who were also well-rounded scientists, engineers who would be the leaders in India's technological development.

Later committees refined the Sakar's proposal. In 1950, for example, a committee composed of members of the All-India Council for Technical Education and the Inter-University Board decided that the IITs should grant degrees in four kinds of engineering: civil, mechanical, electrical, and telecommunications. In their first two years, all students would take the same courses, and in their third year they would concentrate on their chosen type of engineering, with students who and chosen the same type of electives in their field of specialization. In their fourth year, they would take electives in their field of specialization. The committee also recommended that the institutes offer a master's degree in each of the four kinds of engineering. The refining and improving of the program continued over the years because one of the qualities which were to set IITs apart from most Indian universities was the power to try out new ideas. Unlike other government-funded schools, the IITs were to make their own decisions in all, academic and administrative matters.

In 1951, the first Indian Institute of Technology opened at Kharagpur. Five years had passed between the publication of the Sakar Committee's report and the opening of the institute. Among the problems that caused the delay were lack of qualified Indian instructors and insufficient funds for equipment and books. These problems were solved with the help of other countries, though the first IIT had no single sponsor nation, as did later Indian Institutes of Technology. While visiting professor came to Kharagpur from the former West Germany and other nations, the University of Illinois supplied the most assistance, sending ten professors for two years and welcoming twenty three Indian students and teachers, who did research or received graduate education at Illinois. The university also gave about $200,000 worth of equipment to IIT Kharagpur.

Lack of equipment and instructors also postponed the opening of the second IIT. Prime Minister Nehru petitioned UNESCO for assistance, and one of its participant nations agreed to help. The Soviet Union gave technical equipment to the new school, sent experts to install the equipment, and published books to be used at the institute. Soviet professors designed and set up laboratories, helped develop departments, taught courses, and designed a graduate program which, like those in the

Soviet Union, stressed specialization. The USSR also granted fellowships to Indian professors. With this assistance, the second IIT opened in Bombay in 1958.

The success of collaboration with the USSR led Nehru to seek aid from West Germany in the founding of the third IIT, to be located in Madras. The German government gave equipment and texts to the institute and sent professors to help establish it. They shaped its program to emphasize the German system of practical experience in workshops, and they opened communication between the new school and the region's industries in hope that the institute could help solve their problems. Germany also gave scholarships to Indian professors, who studied for two years in Germany before returning to the new Indian Institute to teach. Thanks to this help, IIT Madras opened in 1959.

India looked to the United States for aid in establishing the fourth institute. The U.S. provided substantial assistance, including equipment and books, experts to design the new institute" laboratories and plan its library, visiting professors to teach some of its courses, and fellowships to Indian professors. A consortium of nine American universities also helped shape the new IIT's curriculum so that it would closely follow the American system of engineering education. With this program in place, IIT Kanpur opened in 1960.

These were the four Indian Institutes of Technology envisioned by the Sakar Committee; Kanpur in the North, Madras in the South, Kharagpur in the East, and Bombay in the West. The fifth was an unexpected development.

In 1961 Delhi University opened its College of Engineering with the help of British funds. Industries in Great Britain then contributed a surprisingly large sum, approximately £400,000, to help equip the new college. This increase in funding enabled the College of Engineering to become IIT Delhi in 1963. Great Britain continued to sponsor the institute in many ways, especially by extending fellowships to Indian instructors and sending professors to Delhi to help shape its program. They designed a curriculum that stressed practical experience, since industry in India, unlike that in Great Britain, was not developed enough to provide that experience to new graduates.

Collectively, the Soviet Union, West Germany, the United States, and Great Britain supplied over $17 million worth of equipment to the Indian Institutes of Technology. The four sponsor countries sent over 150 full-time visiting staff and 300 short-term consultants to India. More than 230 Indian professors received fellowships to study in sponsor nations.

Each of the four countries left its imprint on the IIT it helped establish. Because of the influence of Soviet experts, the graduate program at Bombay stresses specialization. Thanks to German professors at Madras and British professors at Delhi, the curricula of those IITs place particular emphasis on practical experience. Of all the sponsor nations, the United States had the most influence, shaping the program, the teaching methods, and the administration at Kanpur. But none of the four countries made the profound imprint on the institutes that the government had anticipated in 1961, when proponents of the IIT project had assured the Indian Parliament that the "assistance of different nations to four IITs would help to produce alternative patterns in order to develop different methods of training high level technical personnel." No country could introduce radically "alternative patterns" because the institutes had been dedicated to the MIT model from their inception.

Today the IITs, which the government has named Institutes of National Importance, are among India's most prestigious universities. For each incoming class, the institutes regularly receive up to a thousand times more applications than they have places available. The IITs grant nearly 60 percent of India's Master of technology degrees and 75 percent of its doctoral degrees. Graduates of the Indian Institutes of technology are respected around the world.

However, India has paid a price for that respect. Because industry has not developed as the government had hoped, many IIT graduates, unable to find attractive positions at home, go abroad to countries eager to employ them. In 1987 and 1990, S.P. Sukhatme conducted studies of this "brain drain" from IIT Bombay and concluded that 30.8 percent of the institute's graduates emigrate and do not return. The other IITs' rates of brain drain are no doubt similar to Bombay's. Speaking of India's loss of highly-trained professionals to other countries, Delhi educational consultant D. Biswas observed that "India has repaid through export of human capital more than the total aid it received from abroad." However, Professors P.V. Indiresan and N.C. Nigam of the institute at Delhi are confident that the IITs will yet be at the heart of the industrial growth that will slow the brain drain. If Indian industry had developed, Indiresan and Nigam write, "IIT graduates would have formed the core of creative scientist-engineers required for such an effort. They will do in the future, provided the goals of excellence are preserved and supported."

Despite the numbers who emigrate, most IIT graduates do find careers in their homeland. Many work in India's atomic energy, space, and defense programs, while others are employed in telecommunications. Most of the staff of the government's research and development laboratories graduated from an IIT, as did most of the employees in national science and technology departments. The majority India's science and engineering teachers, too, received their degree from an IIT.

The first Indian Institute of Technology, Kharagpur, stands on the site of the former British prison of Hijli. In the institute's first convocation address, prime Minister Nehru spoke of the location's symbolic value: "Here in the place of that Hijli detention camp stands this fine monument of India. . . . This picture seems to me symbolic of changes that are coming to India." Today at least one of those changes has been realized, for the Indian Institutes of technology are fulfilling Nehru's prediction that his country would one day educate its own "scientists and technologists of the highest caliber."

Further Reading: A detailed account of the establishment of the IITs will be found in Kim Patrick Sebaly's doctoral dissertation, *The Assistance of Four Nations in the Establishment of the Indian Institutes of Technology, 1945–1970* (Ann Arbor, Michigan: University of Michigan School of Education, 1972).

—Carol Whitney

JAGIELLONIAN UNIVERSITY
(Krakow, Poland)

Location: In the center of downtown Krakow.

Description: A state university of 16,650 students. The second-oldest central European university, after the University of Prague.

Information: Jagiellonian University
Golebia 24
31-007 Krakow
Poland
(12) 22 10 33

The foundation of the Jagiellonian University at Krakow is normally dated to 1364, when its charter was issued by the last of the Piast kings of Poland, Casimir the Great, although the charter was probably a confirmation of an earlier 1362 foundation. The 1364 charter was followed by a bull of Urban V in the same year, making the foundation both secular and ecclesiastical, and the Jagiellonian University made the celebration and the 600th centenary of its foundation a pretext for a reorganization in 1964. In 1364, the right to bestow degrees was reserved to the royal chancellor, and the crown was responsible for salaries. But the new university languished after Casimir's death in 1370; among many problems, there was great difficulty in finding good faculty from abroad. It was resuscitated only by King Wladyslaw Jagiello, who in 1397 procured a bull from Boniface IX instituting a faculty of theology. In 1400, fortified by the wealth inherited from his wife, he issued a new charter for the whole university, which flourished under the Jagiellonian dynasty.

Krakow, listed by UNESCO in 1978 as one of the world's 12 great historic cities, had been the capital of the Polish state since 1037. After Krakow developed as a market town in the tenth century, Boleslaw the Brave built the first Polish cathedral on Krakow's Wawel Hill, overlooking the Vistula River, in the early eleventh century. It is there that the royal insignia are kept, and that a series of kings lived and are buried. The earliest lectures were given in the immediate vicinity of the royal castle, probably in or near the cathedral school, although university buildings in the present old city were begun certainly before 1370.

The capital until 1611, Krakow today is still Poland's third largest town. The fifteenth-century Gothic *collegium maius* with an arcaded courtyard and ground-floor lecture rooms still stands in the center of the town. Originally endowed in 1400, it was used in that year for the opening ceremony of the university. It now houses the Institute of Art History and the university museum's famous collection of scientific instruments, particularly astrolabes, telescopes, and globes, including those which must have been used by Nicholas Copernicus during his period as a student at Krakow from 1491 to 1495.

The older university buildings, blending with the adjoining medieval marketplace, Europe's oldest, and including the fifteenth-century college of law and the 1449 *collegium minus,* make the small town center one of the most attractive in Europe. A college of medicine collapsed during the fifteenth century, but the new college in the Bracka, whose existing buildings date from 1883–87, was originally opened in 1464. The town walls were pulled down in the nineteenth century, and now the old city is encircled with avenues and park-lined fringes leading to the small 15-acre Wawel Hill and the castle, which dominates the town.

The university's original 1364 constitution was based on the University of Bologna, clearly envisioning a graduate student body, with rector and professors to be elected by the students, and no master eligible for the rectorship. The rector had full civil and some criminal jurisdiction. The principal subject was to be law, and the papal bull not only expressly excepted theology from the papal privileges bestowed on the university, but it also refused to endorse the royal chancellor's jurisdiction, insisting on Episcopal rights. In cases of serious misdemeanor, clerks were to be referred to the bishop's tribunal and others to the royal courts. Salaries were a charge on the tax on salt from the Bochnia mines.

When the restored university actually opened in 1400, the original constitution had been altered to reflect the changed conditions created by the Polish-Lithuanian union of 1385. The clause requiring the rector to be a student disappeared, and the rectors were in fact masters. The model had become Paris rather than Bologna, and the masters now clearly acted in common as a corporation. Colleges of jurists and of arts were founded on the German model for masters, not students, and in 1433 the faculty of medicine was reorganized. By the 15th century there were also student halls with small endowments, at least one of which was to accommodate 100 students. Under the 1397 arrangements, salaries, as in Prague, Leipzig, and the other German-speaking universities, were now provided through the bestowal of ecclesiastical benefices. The chancellor was the bishop of Krakow.

Krakow's original foundation is generally now seen as part of a movement of political unification of ethnic Poles and the consequent need for educated national-minded

Jagiellonian University

Polish administrators. The 1364 charter was the product of more than a decade's careful gestation. East of Paris, Krakow was preceded north of the Italian peninsula only by Prague (with the exceptions of Grenoble and Avignon). The overwhelming need for administrators explains the concentration on the law faculty, to which a privileged position was accorded, with five chairs in Roman law and three in canon law. In 1397 the balance shifted, and 11 chairs in theology were created, with 8 in canon law. In the fifteenth century the undergraduate faculty of arts, operating in the two old city colleges and preparing students for the higher faculties of canon law, civil law, theology, and medicine, had 22 poorly endowed chairs.

When the university opened, 205 students were matriculated in the first year. Students came from throughout Poland, but also from Hungary, Silesia, the southern German-speaking provinces, and the northern territories of

what is now Switzerland. Just under half of the fifteenth-century intake was foreign. Recruitment, fluctuating between 35 and 110 during the decade following 1400, increased to 150 in 1411. It thereafter seldom sunk to 100, probably on account of the difficulties being experienced by Prague. From 1408 the doctrines of Wycliffe had gained a strong hold among the Bohemian students, and the university there supported the king against the bishops in his attempt to withdraw from allegiance to Gregory XII. In 1409, in the wake of a movement to change the voting strengths led by Hus in favor of the Bohemians and to the disadvantage of the Germans, about 1,000 Germans left Prague, mostly for Leipzig or Vienna, but also for Krakow, where matriculation in the years 1408, 1409, and 1410 reached respectively 35, 57, and 88.

Matriculations suddenly bounded up to 388 in 1483. On the whole the university, much supported by Wladyslaw's queen, Jadwiga, whose fortune had enabled her widower to found it, tended to moderate conciliarism in the matter of papal powers. It supported Felix V at the Council of Basel, and was finally left alone in support of Nicholas V in defiance of king and episcopacy until unity was restored in 1449. In July 1448, the masters appealed for support to the universities of Paris, Vienna, Leipzig, Erfurt, and Cologne.

Through the sixteenth century, the university had a large student body from other countries. Its principal attraction for foreigners lay in its interest in mathematics and astronomy, in which it had two chairs. No other university north of the Alps had a chair in either subject before 1500.

The university was also deeply concerned with the promotion of Christianity in Lithuania, to which Queen Jadwiga, known as the "planter of the Catholic faith in Lithuania," was particularly committed. During the fifteenth century no less than six of the bishops of Wilno were *magistri* of Krakow. As might be expected of Europe's easternmost university, many of the Polish *magistri* had studied abroad, especially in Bologna and Padua; gifts from those who had studied in these places originally formed Poland's own early philosophical and theological manuscript collections. The Poles had formed their own "nation" at Bologna in 1265, providing a dozen rectors before 1500.

The university also was associated in the late fifteenth century with the early enclaves of enthusiasts for Latin and Greek literature, notably those centered on the Greek poet Callimachus and the German promoter of the classics, Conrad Pickel. In 1473, the first printing press in Poland was set up, intimately linked with the university. Krakow's publishers issued numerous textbooks alongside a stream of Latin and Greek classical texts, and they also published the first books in Hungarian. Lectures were instituted in Greek from 1499 and Hebrew from 1528. The teaching of rhetoric was reformed on Renaissance lines in 1518. By the first half of the sixteenth century there were some 200 matriculations a year, making the university an important community in a town with a population estimated at some 20,000.

The university had by now reached the peak of its international eminence, having for a century attracted almost half of its students from foreign countries. The consequences of the Lutheran schism took their toll as the university hardened its reaction to the new theological thinking which the schism brought in its wake. Between 1548 and 1554 sanctions were applied to maintain Aristotle's authority in philosophy. Although sharp controversy had arisen within the university, the reform of studies in 1603 confirmed the university's hostility not only to Lutheranism, but also to those forms of study, as of the pagan literary classics, thought conducive to heresy.

At the same time the university fended off the Jesuit attempt to achieve ascendancy within the Polish educational system, forcing the order to close its college in what is now the university's *collegium broscianum*. The mix of students within the university also changed, as the student population became less elevated in social rank, and dissenting schools as well as new universities were opened elsewhere in Lithuania and Poland. Astronomy and mathematics courses, which had been so well-respected at the turn of the century, lost something of their impetus. A 1516 plan to reform the Julian calendar had come to nothing, and the content of astronomy moved off in the direction of predictive astrology. Slow to adopt new ideas, the university suffered declining student enrollment. The most distinguished faculty in the early seventeenth century was medicine, in which there were six chairs, including one of anatomy and medical botany.

Between 1655 and 1657 Krakow was occupied by the Swedes and the general assembly of professors voted on July 11, 1656, to shut down the university. It remained closed until the city was restored to Polish dominion on August 24, 1657. The university was again paralyzed by the renewed Swedish occupation of Krakow from 1702 to 1709, although it recovered sufficient vigor to branch out into classes in French and German in 1713. Later eighteenth-century developments included attempts to found chairs in natural law and the law of nations, experimental physics, and mathematics. More recent philosophical thinking entered the curriculum with the reform of the faculty of philosophy in 1765.

The reform of the university itself did not occur until the creation in Poland of Europe's first Ministry of Education on October 14, 1773. The reform, the first since the Middle Ages, was entrusted to Hugo Kollataj, a Krakow graduate, politician, and philosopher. He scrapped the medieval four-faculty structure in favor of two colleges. The moral college contained literature, law, and theology, and the physical college was made up of the physical, mathematical, and medical schools. Except in theology, Latin was abandoned in favor of Polish as the medium of instruction.

The name was changed to the Crown's Central School, and in 1783 it took over the supervision and management of local primary and secondary education. In accordance with the spirit of the Enlightenment, Kollataj prescribed practical tasks for the reformed Central School, which was charged with serving the everyday welfare of the community in agriculture, industry, hygiene, health, and education. Among the results were a graduate college for teacher training set up in 1780; Poland's first medical clinic, founded in 1780; the botanical gardens of 1782; the chemical laboratory of 1783; and the observatory of 1787. French physiocrat economic theory flourished, and the reformed Central School began to specialize in applied technologies, like surveying and the exploitation of electricity.

The Crown's Central School came to an end in 1794, with the occupation of Krakow by the Prussian army on June 15, 1794, by the Austrians from January 5, 1796, and the subsequent partition of Poland. An attempt to close the university was thwarted, but lectures in Polish were discontinued, as was the financial autonomy of the institution. Germanized, the university was united with the Lyceum transferred from Lwow, with the majority of chairs held by German speakers. After Napoléon's defeat of Austria, Krakow became part of the Grand Duchy of Warsaw in 1809. From 1809 to 1815 the university became the Central School of Krakow, again under Hugo Kollataj, subordinated to state authority on the French Napoléonic model. In 1815 the Duchy of Warsaw was dissolved and Krakow, under the dominion of Austria, Russia, and Prussia, became nominally a republic. In 1818 the university was reorganized with theoretically extensive internal autonomy, and again became the Jagiellonian University. In fact supervision was progressively tightened with Foreign Minister Prince Metternich of Austria clearly fearful of student nationalist sympathies. Nonetheless, the Krakow "learned society" was opened in 1815 in association with the university. In 1873 it became the Polish Academy of Science. The "Republic of Krakow" as nationalist activists called it, was incorporated into the Austro-Hungarian Empire in November 1846, and in 1853 German became almost the unique language of instruction. The university was a provincial academy educating loyal subjects of the Austrian monarchy. After Austria's defeat and the regaining of Polish self-government, Polish was again allowed as the principal language of instruction in 1861. From 1870 to 1918 the university gradually became Poland's great seat of learning, vastly increasing in size, and growing from about 400 students in 1850 to 1870 to over 3,000 in 1914.

Between 1918 and 1939, the Jagiellonian University supplied Poland on a large scale with scholars, teachers, and professional practitioners of law and medicine. Its series of specialized institutes was created, including nursing, physical training, pedagogy, agriculture, pharmacy, and Slavonic studies. Although Warsaw was now a bigger city, Krakow's university was quite influential. After the German invasion on September 6, 1939, 183 professors and lecturers were arrested at Krakow on November 6. Many died at Dachau or Sachsenhausen, and the university was systematically despoiled. Students continued their studies through an underground network. (One such student, Karol Wojtyla, later became John Paul II, the first Polish pope.) Liberated by the Red Army on January 18, 1945, the university opened again and inaugurated its new academic year on March 19. Some 12,000 students entered for the academic year 1946–47.

Polish higher education was reorganized between 1949 and 1954. The university did away with the institutes of medicine and pharmacy, then physical training, agriculture, forestry, and finally theology, which was transferred to Warsaw. Five faculties remained: law; philosophy and history; philology; mathematics, physics, and chemistry; and biology and natural science. The 600th anniversary celebrations in 1964 inaugurated yet another reorganization of the university's structure to build, as its 1975 handbook put it, "a new model of Socialist higher education." Recruitment was partly to be determined by national economic needs and the social origin of candidates. Paid work in state-owned factories was compulsory in long "vacations," and about 70 percent of students received some form of public financial aid.

One of 12 universities now in the city, Jagiellonian today is responsible to the Ministry of Science, Higher Education, and Technology and regulated by basic statutes first issued in 1958. There are five faculties, each containing a number of institutes; the teaching functions of former departments are gradually being transferred to the faculties. There is a purely advisory senate, including non-academic representatives, with a rector appointed triennially. The library is the richest in Poland and functions as a national library. It contains some 2 million volumes, and 10,000 manuscripts. Social and economic pressures in Poland are certain to force another reorganization of the Jagiellonian University, and both its antiquity and its prestige insure that it will play an important part in Poland's future higher education system.

Further Reading: For the early period of the university, the most important work is Hastings Rashdall's *The Universities of Europe in the Middle Ages,* three-volume revision, edited by F.M. Powicke and A.B. Emden (Oxford: Oxford University Press, 1936). For the general history and the twentieth century, see especially the revised edition of Leszek Hajdukiewicz and Mieczyslaw Karas' *The Jagiellonian University* (Krakow: Wydawnictwo Uniwersytetu Jagiellonskiego, 1978). Another detailed, extensive treatment is *Crawco and its University* by Jozef Duzyk and Stanislaw Salmonowicz, translated by Marianna Abrahamowicz (2nd edition, Krakow: Wydawnictwo Artystyczno-Graficzne, 1966), which is nicely illustrated.

—A.H.T. Levi

JAWAHARLAL NEHRU UNIVERSITY
(New Delhi, India)

Location: Jawaharlal Nehru University is located in southern New Delhi, bordered on the west by the exclusive Vassant Vihar residential area and on the east by the Indian Institute of Technology. Its southern perimeter is dotted by the buildings of the rapidly expanding Vasant Kunj residential complex.

Description: The university awards mainly advanced degrees in the sciences, social sciences, and the humanities. The only undergraduate degrees offered on campus are in languages. It currently has seven schools, each with various centers, and offers undergraduate and graduate recognition to off-campus institutions such as the National Defense Academy, Pune. Jawaharlal Nehru University is one of the select 12 universities funded by the Indian federal government.

Information: Jawaharlal Nehru University
New Delhi 110067
India
(011) 6107676, (011) 6167557

Visiting: Write to the Office of the Registrar at the address mentioned above for further information.

Inaugurated in 1969, Jawaharlal Nehru University (JNU) was designed as a tribute to the memory of the visionary first prime minister of independent India, Jawaharlal Nehru. In its short history, Jawaharlal Nehru University has gone beyond its founding ideals of humanism and international understanding. Jawaharlal Nehru University is widely regarded in India as the leading center for higher learning in the country. Although it suffers from the malaise of fiscal shortages plaguing all Indian universities, JNU still evokes admiration for the high standards it maintains despite resources which are inadequate and thinly stretched. More than history and a collective sense of its past, JNU is famous for its vibrant and deeply political campus life and for the quality of graduate education it offers. Its small body of about 4,000 students looks to the future rather than to the past.

A thousand-odd acres of rocky, scrubby land make JNU an oasis of calm yet rugged beauty in a city which is slowly choking itself to death through unplanned growth and rampant pollution. As New Delhi fumes and belches toward unsuitable urban growth, JNU is a reminder—though a besieged one—of the virtues of simple living and high thinking. Its campus spreads out like a calm invitation to reflection and sociability and its students accept and cherish that aspect of JNU. An open-air amphitheater situated among the rocks and the serene heights of the Parthasarathy plateau (the highest point of the campus) are the unexpected delights that campus explorers may stumble upon.

The main gate opens unpretentiously onto a bougainvillea-lined road which winds through the campus and loops around it in an inner circle. Following this road, one can reach all the major subdivisions of the JNU campus. Jawaharlal Nehru University is famous for its campus life and imaginative architecture has contributed to the involvement of students in campus life. The national competition for the architectural design attracted 68 prominent architects. C.P. Kuckreja, the winner, designed the student and faculty residences in appealing red brick which went well with the rocky nature of the terrain. The academic complex is a pleasing quadrangle with creeper-covered walkways leading to each building and to the eight-story library. Maintenance funds being low, the insides of most buildings look shabby and in need of paint. In compensation for the shabbiness, the walls are richly decorated with a wallpaper of posters—changed frequently—urging students to "study and struggle" and to join in various causes of national and international appeal. The walls of the library canteen are especially popular with campus groups for publicity purposes.

Student and faculty residences are interspersed interestingly; both groups enjoy their privacy without isolation from each other. A total of 16 such residential sectors is envisioned, and construction is one of the permanent features of the campus. One of the problems with the elevated and rocky nature of the campus is that it faces a chronic water shortage, being located in the arid southwestern margins of New Delhi.

Jawaharlal Nehru University residential complexes are named for the geographical divisions of India. The student residences or hostels are named for the rivers of each sector. So, the hostels are named after the rivers Ganga, Sutlej, and Jhelum in the Uttarakhand or northern sector. One of the newest hostels is Narmada hostel in the sector called Dakshinapuram. Life in a JNU hostel is spartan at best. Meals are basic and there are few frills. To be a commuter student, though, would remove one from the other activities that compensate for the austerity. Student sociability centers around the tea stalls outside the hostels. One of the best-loved watering holes is Ganga

Jawaharlal Nehru University

Dhaba, the tea stall outside Ganga hostel. Here, summer evenings are especially busy when students gather in small groups. The socializing continues till late into the night and conversation ranges from idle reflections on the day gone by to serious strategizing for the next student's union election. Some critics point to the contradictions between the deadly serious political talk that suffuses the student body and the reality of the small children who serve tea to those sitting around discussing inequalities in Indian society. Yet, the intensity of political life on campus is not all abstraction. Many students leave campus not only with a degree but also with a permanently changed outlook on life. It is said that in order for problems to be solved, their existence must first be acknowledged. In this regard at least, the politicization of campus life has led to a fierce refusal in a section of the student body to let certain social and political issues be brushed under the carpet. Feminism, minority rights, social and economic justice are all debated fiercely among students in formal and informal gatherings.

It is this intense engagement with politics that has endeared JNU to many, and to others, including fearful parents, marked it as an unruly bastion of Marxist revolution. Student activists scoff at the criticism, pointing out (with some justification) that politics in JNU is issue-based and intellectual and does not result in the kind of rowdyism and bullying tactics that are a standard feature of student politics in other Indian universities. Like all major universities in India, student politics in JNU is serious business. Most major Indian political parties have their student wings, and campus leadership is often a stepping-stone to national-level politics. Jawaharlal Nehru University politics are vociferously left-of-center, although in recent years, right-wing student groups have also made advances in the polls. Political involvement is celebratory in spirit and generally anti-administration. The students' union election is preceded by days of debates and meetings. After-dinner hostel meetings keep students involved and informed. The Election Commission ensures that expenditure is kept to a minimum and that the election is based around issues and ideology. The counting of the votes is a major occasion of celebration. All parties and their supports camp outside the counting office and cheer when their candidates are announced to be leading. The festive atmosphere lasts all night long and morning usually finds both victors and vanquished exhausted.

Twice in the last 15 years, JNU student politics has come under scrutiny. In 1983, a student agitation based around campus issues such as admission policy and living conditions escalated into a full-fledged confrontation between students and administration. Students besieged the vice-chancellor's office and attacked administrative personnel and even some faculty. This outbreak of violence resulted in the police entering the campus to break up the agitation and to arrest the leaders. Many students were expelled, some were suspended. 1983 still lives on in JNU student mythology as a watershed year. To a large extent, it was. Since then, many changes were made in admissions policy and administrative measures. Radical students argue that the new admissions policy discriminates against those from a rural background and thus dilutes the stated national character of JNU. Administratively, a Grievance Redressal Mechanism began operations to prevent university issues from spilling into violence again. Student activists argue that these new measures restrict student activity on campus and have resulted in a greater bureaucratization of the university.

Jawaharlal Nehru University is also perhaps the only university in the world where a student's union election centered around democracy in another country. In 1989, the JNU students' union was led by a communist coalition. In June, when the incidents on Beijing's Tiananmen Square hit world headlines, the students' union, following the directive from party headquarters, refused to condemn the Chinese government's crackdown on the protesting students. A coalition of other students then led a demonstration to the Chinese embassy. Later that year, control of the students' union passed to a loose confederation of left-wing students called Solidarity. Solidarity denounced the previous union's record on Tiananmen and also pledged to refocus on campus issues. The coalition fell apart less than a year later, but it did initiate an agitation to undo some of the restrictive administrative measures passed after 1983. The agitation achieved few concrete goals, but it succeeded in restoring to the campus a participatory culture in student politics, which had dwindled in the years since 1983. Immunization camps for the children of the construction workers and a campaign against the construction of the Tehri dam in northern India, were not all-out successes either. However, they did somewhat reduce the criticism that JNU politics paid more attention to Che Guevara, Malcolm X, Ho Chi Minh, and Noam Chomsky than it did to local and national issues. The politics of affirmative action split the campus in 1989 and divided many students. Many students in the coalition objected to a new government policy reserving jobs for underprivileged groups in society. The divisions on campus reflected the divisions in India, and some conservative groups withdrew support to the union coalition. The polemical nature of JNU politics continued with a major controversy in 1996 when students objected to a right-wing national leader, L.K. Advani, being invited to the campus. The invitation was withdrawn, but it set off a debate over the right of dissent in a university and the freedom of expression. A national daily called for a crackdown on the students and suggested that one way to keep JNU students away from politics would be through reducing the number of social science and liberal arts courses and instituting more technical and managerial courses. Student activists are not likely to be swayed by these criticisms, but the incident drew attention to the divisions that exist in the student body.

Jawaharlal Nehru University culture shuns glamour and appearance as unnecessary distractions (though there are always students who enjoy "the bourgeois life" condemned by activists). Focusing on issues and beliefs, stressing intellectual rigor and substance over style and refusing to privilege the middle class over the rural and working world, JNU student politics prepare many for public life. It is here that future civil servants, academics, and politicians learn to place their ideas to clash or mingle with others and to test the strength of their own convictions against the beliefs of others.

Politics and activism are not just external grafts on to the campus culture; they have deep roots in the founding vision of the university. In 1969, when the Indian government founded JNU, it was to actualize Nehru's vision of an ideal university, an institution that in his own words, "stands for humanism, for tolerance, for reason, for the adventure of ideas and for the search of truth." If the process of realization has left many of the original founders, particularly the more conservative ones, dissatisfied on ideological grounds, the academic excellence of the institution has lived up to expectations. A talented contingent of researchers and professors have made their home in most JNU departments. Renowned historians Romila Thapar and Bipan Chandra taught here, and among its widely respected faculty are the political scientist Zoya Hasan and the economists Prabhat and Utsa Patnaik. Academic excellence has led to an international reputation for JNU and it attracts scholars and graduate students from a variety of countries. Some departments are better known than others: the departments of history, political science, sociology, and economics are leading centers in their fields. Departments combine rigor with flexibility and interdisciplinary methods are encouraged. Jawaharlal Nehru University is also home to the National Institute of Immunology and the UNIDO Centre of Genetic Engineering.

Standing on the outer periphery of New Delhi, JNU is at the center of intellectual life in India. Scholars find it a stimulating core of academic excellence. Its relatively small community of students lead a robust—if somewhat detached—collective existence, and its many non-academic visitors find craggy, strong beauty in the rolling campus as they come to meet friends and relatives or to lose the grime of New Delhi for a while in strolls along JNU's shaded paths.

Further Reading: There are few books centered around Jawaharlal Nehru University. This is because it is a relatively new university. The most useful publications are from JNU, especially its *JNU News,* published bi-monthly. Detailed, if somewhat official, information can be found in *JNU: Retrospect and Prospect* (New Delhi: Jawaharlal Nehru University, 1986). General studies on Indian higher education help put the development of JNU in a national context. *Higher Education in India: Conformity, Crisis, and Innovation* by G. Ram Reddy (New Delhi: Sterling Publishers, 1995) and *Higher Education in India: In Search of Quality* edited by K.B. Powar and S.K. Panda (New Delhi: Association of Indian Universities, 1995) talk about some of the problems with university education in modern India. The current chancellor of JNU, Prof. M.S. Gore has also analyzed India's higher education policy. See *Indian Education: Structure and Process* by M.S. Gore (Jaipur: Rawat, 1994). *Academics and Politics* by Subhash Chandra Ghose (New Delhi: Northern Book Centre, 1993) analyzes the political activities of Indian university students.

—Sharmishtha Roy Chowdhury

JOHNS HOPKINS UNIVERSITY
(Baltimore, Maryland, U.S.A.)

Location: In the Homewood neighborhood of Baltimore, Maryland; two additional campuses in Baltimore, one in Washington, D.C., additional facilities in the Baltimore-Washington area, China, and Italy.

Description: Johns Hopkins has approximately 16,000 students in undergraduate, graduate, and professional programs.

Information: Office of Admissions
Johns Hopkins University
3400 North Charles Street
Baltimore, MD 21218
U.S.A.
(410) 516-8171

Baltimore merchant Johns Hopkins's bequest of $7 million in 1873 for the establishment of a university and a hospital was the largest philanthropic gift of its time. The third son of Samuel and Hannah Hopkins, Johns was born at Whitehall, the family tobacco plantation in Maryland's Anne Arundel County. His unusual first name came from his great-grandmother, Margaret Johns, who married Gerard Hopkins in 1700. Johns's parents were active members of the West River Meeting of Friends (Quakers). The Quakers were abolitionists, and in 1807 Samuel Hopkins freed all the slaves on his plantation. As a consequence, Johns was forced to leave school at the age of 12 to work in the family tobacco fields. Five years later he was sent to Baltimore to work for his uncle Gerard Hopkins, a wholesale grocer and commissions merchant. The apprentice progressed smoothly until 1819 when Johns, who had fallen in love with his cousin Elizabeth, announced plans to marry her. His uncle (her father) forbade the union as did the Society of Friends. Although the couple agreed to accede to her father's wishes, they also pledged never to marry anyone else.

The strained relationship between Johns and Gerard grew more uncomfortable when Johns wanted to expand the grocery business to include the sale of liquor. Gerard was opposed, but Johns was convinced that there was money to be made in the whiskey trade. Many of the grocery's customers wanted to barter homemade liquor for food and other items; Johns saw no reason why he should not accept the liquor and sell it. He set out on his own with financial backing and help from his brothers, his mother, and her brother, selling Hopkins' Best Whiskey in Mary-

land, Virginia, and North Carolina. Johns had learned well from his Uncle Gerard and the fledgling business was soon bringing in large profits. Hopkins then expanded his interests into the banking industry and into the Baltimore and Ohio Railroad (B&O). His early support for the railroad stemmed from his personal experience of moving goods via Conestoga wagon on the rocky terrain of the Shenandoah Valley. Hopkins was soon the largest stockholder with an estimated 15,000 to 17,000 shares. In 1847 he was elected to the B&O board of directors; by 1855 he was chairman of the railroad finance committee. When the Civil War broke out, Hopkins, an avowed Unionist and abolitionist, used his considerable influence to override wishes of the numerous Southern sympathizers on the B&O board so that the railroad could be used by the Union army.

It is generally believed that Hopkins's disappointment at the early termination of his own education, coupled with his dismay at the city's inadequate medical resources in the face of cholera and yellow fever outbreaks, led him to draw up a foundation to fund a university and hospital. The bequest carried few restrictions other than the hospital was to admit everyone who needed its services, regardless of their ability to pay. A board of 12 trustees was appointed in 1867 but did not meet until 1874, a few months after Hopkins's death. In February of that year, the board began its search for a university president. In doing so, the board consulted three existing university presidents: Charles W. Eliot of Harvard, James B. Angell of Michigan, and Andrew Dickson White of Cornell. Each heartily recommended Daniel Coit Gilman of the University of California.

A native of Norwich, Connecticut, Gilman graduated from Yale and remained on its staff for many years. He played a significant role in the development of the research-oriented Yale Scientific School (later known as the Sheffield Scientific School), taught geography, reorganized the Yale library system, and served as superintendent of the New Haven school system. During that time, he declined several offers from other institutions, including invitations to serve as president of the University of Wisconsin in 1867 and the University of California in 1870. When the University of California made a second offer in 1872, Gilman accepted. However, when the opportunity came to head and develop a new university in Baltimore, Gilman was eager to escape California, where coordinating the loosely organized consortium of collegiate and trade schools had proved to be an administrative nightmare. On May 1, 1875, at the age of 44, Gilman was sworn in as the first president of the newly established Johns Hopkins University.

Johns Hopkins University

In the year before the new university opened, Gilman traveled and conferred widely in England and continental Europe. His first priority was the recruitment of a small but distinguished research faculty. He was able to promise unusually high salaries, complete freedom in academic matters, and an environment conducive to original research. Answering his call were mathematician J.J. Sylvester, physicist Henry A. Rowland, chemist Ira Remsen, biologist H. Newell Martin, and classicists Basil Lanneau Gildersleeve and Charles D. Morris.

Gilman was equally determined to recruit an outstanding group of students for Johns Hopkins and to offer them financial support. Each of the first 20 fellows was awarded an annual grant of $500. One observer remarked, "Probably no expenditure of $10,000 in American education has ever had so large and enduring a return from the investment." Among the first fellows were historian Herbert Baxter Adams (founder of the American Historical Association), economist Henry Carter Adams, and zoologist W.K. Brooks. (Later scholars included Christine Ladd-Franklin and M. Carey Thomas, both pioneers in higher education for women, philosopher and educator John Dewey, philologist Maurice Bloomfield, social scientist Thorstein Veblen, historian Frederick Jackson Turner, and Woodrow Wilson, who went on to become president of Princeton University and of the United States.)

After inaugural ceremonies in October 1876 at which noted English biologist Thomas Henry Huxley spoke, classes were held for the first time in a small cluster of buildings on Howard and Little Ross Streets in Baltimore. The curriculum was centered around teaching laboratories and student research. From its inception, Johns Hopkins University exacted stringent entrance requirements; of the 89 students in the first class only 12 had not completed undergraduate studies elsewhere. These 12 were enrolled in a 3-year undergraduate program; not until 1907 did the university formally adopt a 4-year program for undergraduates. However, the undergraduate school was always an integral part of the university as a whole. Among the most important of the early innovations at the undergraduate level was the institution of the "group system," a set of seven coherent curricula designed to meet different student needs and goals. The group system aimed at a compromise between the randomness of free elective courses and the conformity of the traditional prescribed curriculum. Concurrently, Hopkins was the first school in America to develop a system of faculty advisors to help the undergraduatse deal with the new freedom in an institution with very few rules and regulations. Such freedom of choice resulted in highly creative paths to doctoral degrees as well as the combination of programs such as A.B./M.A. and A.B./M.D. Although the hospital would not open for another decade, the nation's first coherent pre-medical program already was in operation at Johns Hopkins.

The school's emphasis on research meant that a variety of scholarly journals had their origin at Johns Hopkins. In 1877, Remsen launched *American Chemical Journal,* in 1878 Sylvester started *American Journal of Mathematics,* Martin and W.K. Brooks started *Notes from the Biological Laboratory* in 1879, and the *American Journal of Philology* was introduced under the editorship of Gildersleeve in 1880. From the school of historical studies, Henry Baxter Adams produced a series of monographs in 1882 entitled *Johns Hopkins University Studies in Historical and Political Science.* Over the next five years, the university also initiated the *American Journal of Archaeology* and the *American Journal of Psychology.* In conjunction with his founding of the Modern Language Association of America in 1883, A. Marshall Elliott began publishing *Modern Language Notes* three years later. All this activity called for a central publication unit, so in 1879, Gilman laid the plans for the founding of Johns Hopkins University Press. Dating to 1879, the press is the oldest North American university press in continuous operation. The first publication to carry its imprint was Sylvester's *American Journal of Mathematics.*

Through the efforts of two pioneers in medicine, John Shaw Billings and William Henry Welch, the Johns Hopkins Hospital opened on Broadway and Monument Streets in May 1889. Billings, who headed the Surgeon General's Library and would go on to serve as the first director of the New York Public Library, was a genius in design. He recognized that the function of the university and the hospital must be intertwined with the focus of the medical school; the hospital pavilion's design is a testament to his vision and expertise. Welch received his medical training at Yale and then studied in Germany. In 1883 he joined the faculty of Johns Hopkins University as professor of pathology. With his influence, William Osler came to the hospital as physician-in-chief and William S. Halsted came as surgeon-in-chief. Henry Mills Hurd, a psychiatrist and proponent of medical reform, served as the hospital's first superintendent.

While the university and hospital were growing, building plans for the medical school were stymied by lack of funds when the B&O Railroad suddenly ceased paying dividends on its common stocks. A group of young women who were spearheading Baltimore's educational reform movement came to the board with a proposition. They were M. Carey Thomas, Mary Garrett, Elizabeth King, and Mary Gwynn. Thomas's and Gwynn's fathers were Johns Hopkins University trustees; King's father was president of the hospital. However, it was Garrett who had the financial resources, having inherited a substantial fortune from the former president of the B&O Railroad. The four women met with several members of the board of trustees and pledged $200,000 for the building of the medical school. After forming the Women's Fund for the Higher Medical Education of Women, they conducted a nationwide fundraising campaign. Garrett made the first contribution of $10,000 and by October 1890, the Women's Fund had collected $100,000. This money was offered to the Johns Hopkins trustees with a monumental stipulation: women must be admitted to the medical school. The trustees reacted with dismay; Gilman was particularly adamant that the school not be coeducational. The board made a counter-offer that they believed would deflate the women's efforts: if the women could raise the entire $500,000 needed to open the medical school, the board would agree to admit women. Ultimately, Garrett contributed an additional $306,977 to bring the fund to the required amount.

Faced with growing pressure from the university, the hospital, and the community to open the medical school, the board had little choice but to accept Garrett's endowment as well as her additional conditions. Entering students were required to have a bachelor's degree or its equivalent, a knowledge of French and German, and a certain amount of previous medical study. The trustees had planned to institute these standards gradually, but Thomas, Garrett, King, and Gwynn insisted that the requirements be in place immediately. They also stressed strongly that not only were women to be admitted but that they were to be held to the same high standards of admission as men. Although all conditions were accepted on December 24, 1892, Garrett did not completely trust the board. Therefore she added a stipulation that the entire endowment sum would return to her estate if any portion of the conditions were violated in the future.

The Johns Hopkins Medical School entrance requirements were revolutionary, to say the least. At the time, a person desiring to enroll in a medical college did not even have to meet the requirements set by most liberal arts institutions. The school's goals were also lofty. At the university's commencement exercises that June, William Henry Welch, who would serve as the medical school's first dean said:

The aim of the school will be primarily to train practitioners of medicine and surgery. . . . It is not only or chiefly the quantity of knowledge which the student takes with him from the school which will help him in his future work; it is also the quality of mind, the methods of work, the disciplined habit of correct reasoning, the way of looking at medical problems. . . . The medical school should be a place where medicine is not only taught but also studied. It should do its part to advance medical science and art by encouraging original work, and by selecting as its teachers those who have the training and capacity for such work.

Fourteen men and women made up the medical school's first class when it opened in the fall of 1893. In keeping with the teaching philosophy of the university, the medical students attended laboratories rather than lectures, and original sources were consulted rather than textbooks. The medical school's emphasis on the scientific approach was often a subject of controversy, even among its faculty. William Osler was particularly opposed to its scientific focus and would eventually leave for a chair at Oxford in 1905. In spite of the board's fears, the high admission standards attracted students and instructors with excellent credentials. As a result, the school quickly outgrew its accommodations.

Welch retired as dean in 1898. Osler moved into the office for a year and then Howell took over the position. One of Osler's noteworthy accomplishments was the establishment of the nation's first medical residency program. Another was his seminal work, *Principles and Practice*. After the Reverend Frederick T. Gates, a principal advisor to John D. Rockefeller, read it, he was moved to recommend that the millionaire and philanthropist devote much of his fortune to medical research. The result was the Rockefeller Institute of Medical Research, which opened in New York City in 1904 with Welch as the first board president and a Hopkins graduate, Simon Flexner, as its first director. The Rockefeller-funded General Education Board also made it possible for the medical school to implement its revolutionary and controversial program of offering full-time clinical appointments. In a short period of time, the medical school was also publishing scholarly journals. *The Bulletin of The Johns Hopkins Hospital* made its debut in 1889. Welch founded the *Journal of Experimental Medicine* in 1896; J.J. Abel followed with the *Journal of Pharmacology* in 1909.

Gilman retired as the university's president in 1901 to become the first president of the Carnegie Institution, which was founded the following year by philanthropist Andrew Carnegie in part to support research in biology and chemistry. Years later Baltimore satirist H.L. Mencken (not renowned for offering kind words) wrote of Gilman:

He built no gaudy buildings and he set off no scintillant sky-rockets. But into such building as he had he drew quickly a faculty of the first water, and presently they were hard at work making a university out

of brains. . . . Gilman is seldom heard of today, but he was probably the most genuinely distinguished man, save perhaps Poe, who ever lived in Baltimore.

Gilman was succeeded by Ira Remsen. During Remsen's 11-year term, construction of new facilities for the undergraduate, graduate, and extensions schools was begun on what now constitutes the Homewood campus in north Baltimore. Remsen also enlisted state aid to establish a school of engineering.

The medical school continued to build on its reputation. Abraham Flexner, brother of Simon, published a report entitled *Medical Education in the U.S. and Canada* in 1910. Generally credited with engendering a massive upgrade of medical schools, Flexner recommended that schools use the Johns Hopkins Medical School as a model. During this period the departments of urology, pediatrics, and preventive medicine opened. The latter was initially headed by Perrin Long, who developed the use of sulfa drugs in the treatment of infection. In addition, the Phipps Psychiatric Clinic and the Wilmer Institute of Ophthalmology were founded.

Remsen was followed by Frank Goodnow, who occupied the presidency from 1913 to 1929. Goodnow's two prime interests resulted in failure. A graduate-level institute of law eventually closed in the 1930s for lack both of funding and of an interest in a program that was focused on the societal effects of law rather than the training of lawyers. Likewise, the so-called Goodnow Plan, which called for eliminating the first two years of the undergraduate program, met with opposition and was abandoned. However, in 1916, under Welch's direction, the School of Hygiene and Public Health was established. Here Elmer V. McCollum discovered vitamin D in 1922, and pioneering work in biomedical statistics, preventive medicine, public health administration, and epidemiology was carried out.

Goodnow's successor, Joseph S. Ames, guided the university through the Great Depression. Most of his energy was spent keeping the institution solvent. Ames was followed by Isaiah Bowman, trained as a geographer, who served as president from 1935 to 1948. Bowman was also a consummate fundraiser, bringing in over $1 million in endowments. During Bowman's term, the Applied Physics Laboratory in suburban Maryland was brought under the university's jurisdiction. Here, during World War II, scientists created a device called the proximity fuse, which allowed anti-aircraft shells to detonate near an enemy aircraft (previously shells would not detonate unless they hit the target); it was used extensively in the war in the Pacific. Researchers at Applied Physics were also involved in the development of the atomic bomb with the Manhattan Project.

Detlov Bronk, president from 1949 to 1953, attempted to revive Goodnow's idea of decreasing the role of the university's undergraduate program, but he also encountered strong opposition. On the positive side, the department of biophysics was established during his term, and the District of Columbia-based School of Advanced International Studies became part of the university in 1950.

After a short stint by Lowell Jacob Reed (1953 to 1956) during which the campus construction increased, the university installed its most dynamic and well-known president. Milton Stover Eisenhower, brother of President Dwight D. Eisenhower, is credited with tripling the institution's income and doubling its endowment during his 11-year presidency. Building construction flourished with the result that teaching and research space was also doubled. In addition to strengthening the undergraduate program, Eisenhower oversaw the founding of the departments of social relations, statistics, and the history of science. The engineering and philosophy faculties were merged with the arts and sciences division, the Evening College instituted a program in the history of ideas, and the medical school introduced an accelerated course of study.

Eisenhower's popularity contrasted sharply with the turbulent relationship between his successor, Lincoln Gordon, and the university population. Gordon, who served from 1967 to 1971, was faced with the campus unrest that so characterized the time. However, the upheaval was not without positive results. The university increased its involvement in the local community and a Center for Metropolitan Planning was formed. Women were admitted to the undergraduate program for the first time. Nevertheless, Gordon felt pressured to resign. Eisenhower returned for a ten-month period until a new president could be found.

Steven Muller was the university's provost and vice president when he was tapped to take over the president's office in February 1972. The first person to serve simultaneously as president of the university and of Johns Hopkins Hospital, Muller was particularly adept at fundraising. Under his leadership, a 1976 campaign surpassed its $100 million goal; another in 1985 reached its $450 million goal one year early. During his term, the university took over the administration of Baltimore's renowned music school, the Peabody Institute.

In 1990, Muller was succeeded by William Chase Richardson, who brought experience in public health to his presidency. During his five-year term, Richardson's greatest challenge was facing declining enrollment and a decrease in federal aid.

At the close of the twentieth century, the university boasts eight academic divisions: the School of Arts and Sciences, the G.W.C. Whiting School of Engineering, the School of Continuing Studies, the School of Medicine, the School of Hygiene and Public Health, the School of Nursing, the Peabody Institute, and the Paul H. Nitze School of Advanced International Studies. The university serves approximately 16,000 full-time and part-time students on three campuses in Baltimore, one in Washington, D.C., and facilities throughout Baltimore, and in China and Italy. On the main campus in the Homewood neighborhood of Baltimore, 3,400 full-time undergraduate students and 1,300 full-time graduate students attend classes. The university receives more federal research and development funds than any other university in the United States while the School of Medicine is first in the receipt of extramural awards from the National Institutes of Health. The School of Hygiene and Public Health is also first in research support from the federal government among all public health schools.

Further Reading: In-depth narratives of the early years of Johns Hopkins University can be found in *A History of the University Founded by Johns Hopkins* by John C. French (Baltimore: Johns Hopkins University Press, 1946) and *Pioneer: A History of the Johns Hopkins University 1874–1889* (Ithaca, New York: Cornell University Press, 1960) by Hugh Hawkins. For a treatment of recent years, see *Johns Hopkins: Portrait of a University* by John C. Schmidt (Baltimore: Johns Hopkins University, 1986). Also recommended are selected biographies of some of the men connected with the Johns Hopkins University, Hospital, and Medical School such as *The Life of Daniel Coit Gilman* by Fabian Franklin (New York: Dodd Mead, 1910), *Milton S. Eisenhower: Educational Statesman* by Stephen E. Ambrose and Richard H. Immerman (Baltimore: Johns Hopkins University Press, 1983), and *William Henry Welch and the Heroic Age of American Medicine* by Wimon Flexner and James Thomas Flexner (Baltimore: Johns Hopkins University Press, 1941, reprinted 1993).

—Mary McNulty

KEIO UNIVERSITY
(Tokyo, Japan)

Location: At two campuses in Tokyo (Mita and Shinanomachi) and three in neighboring Kanagawa Prefecture (Hiyoshi, Yagami, and Shonan Fujisawa); associated with three hospitals, in Tokyo, Mie, and Shizuoka Prefectures, and with schools for younger students in Tokyo, Kanagawa, Saitama, and New York State.

Description: The oldest private university in Japan, first established in an academy founded in 1858 by the prominent intellectual Fukuzawa Yukichi.

Information: International Center
Keio University
2-15-45 Mita
Minato-ku, Tokyo 108
Japan
(3) 3453 4511

Keio University (Keio Daigaku in Japanese) is the largest and best-known section of the Keio Gijuku corporation, an educational body which also operates nine schools for younger students, a two-year nursing college, and three hospitals. Since university and corporation alike originated in a private academy founded in 1858 (though each was formally established somewhat later), Keio plausibly claims to be the oldest private educational institution remaining in Japan. The development of the Keio group of schools over the following 14 decades or so has kept pace with the enormous changes in Japanese society over the same period; it also has largely kept faith with the principles laid down by their founder, Fukuzawa Yukichi, who hoped that his work would help students to realise their individual potential and to become leaders in improving their society.

Fukuzawa was born in 1835, the son of a samurai (warrior) who served as an official of the Nakatsu domain in what is now Oita Prefecture, on the southern island of Kyushu. At the time of his birth Japan had been controlled for more than 200 years by the Tokugawa dynasty of shoguns, who directly governed around one-fourth of the country and closely supervised the daimyo, the hereditary provincial lords whose domains covered the rest of Japan. Although their feudal order partly depended on the exclusion of almost all European people and books, which might subvert it, during the eighteenth century Japanese scholars had begun to be permitted to study techni-

cal and scientific works from overseas. By the 1830s there was a rich tradition of *rangaku,* or Dutch studies, so called because the texts which they used were mostly in Dutch, the language of the only European state which had commercial relations with Japan. It was to this tradition that Fukuzawa turned when he left home, in 1854, to study gunnery in Nagasaki for one year and then to study Dutch, anatomy, physics, and other sciences at a private academy in Osaka.

After three years in that city he moved once again in 1858, this time walking all the way to Edo (now Tokyo), where the lord of the Nakatsu domain had an estate, at Teppozu (now Akashi-cho). There Fukuzawa founded his *gijuku,* or academy, using domain funds to train his fellow-officials in Dutch, in a single room of the domain's *yashiki,* the large building which was both its lord's Edo residence and its government's office for relations with the shogunate. However, a visit to the foreign merchant community in Yokohama, established only four years earlier after the Tokugawa shogunate had been pressured into opening relations with other western powers, convinced him that English would be a more useful language, and three years of travel as a member of the first official Japanese delegations to the west confirmed that conviction.

On his return to Japan in 1863 Fukuzawa reorganised the academy at Teppozu as a school of English and also prepared the first of several editions of his influential book *Seiyo Jijo (Conditions in the West),* published in 1866. In a later book, *Gakumon no susume (Encouragement of Learning),* published in serial form between 1872 and 1876, he argued that *jitsugaku,* "practical learning" of the kind conducted in his academy, was superior to traditional Confucian learning, which made its students into "rice-consuming dictionaries," unable to satisfy the needs of everyday life. Through these and other writings, as well as through *Jiji Shinpo,* the newspaper he founded and edited, Fukuzawa popularised the phrase which he himself had coined—*bunmei kaika,* "civilisation and enlightenment"—to encapsulate the material and spiritual advantages that in his view the west already possessed and that the Japanese should try to acquire through such education.

Fukuzawa found a large and enthusiastic audience for his views, especially after the Meiji Restoration of 1868, when the Tokugawa shogunate was overthrown and replaced by a new regime largely composed of relatively young, low-ranking samurai who like Fukuzawa had visited the west, had witnessed the decline of China, Japan's historic exemplar, and had become determined to trans-

Keio University

form Japan. Instead of accepting their invitations to join them in public office, Fukuzawa preferred to continue teaching at his *gijuku*. In 1868 he used the proceeds from his writings to make himself and his school financially independent of the Nakatsu domain (which, like all the other domains, was to be abolished only three years later) and gave the school the name "Keio," commemorating the fact that in Japanese terms 1868 was the fourth year of the Keio era (though it became the first year of the Meiji era following the change of regime).

It was characteristic of Fukuzawa that he went on teaching throughout 1868, even when all other schools in the city had been closed and battle was raging at Ueno, in northern Tokyo, between the new imperial army and supporters of the Tokugawa family. May 15, the date on which the Battle of Ueno began, is still marked every year at Keio by a public lecture and other events honoring Fukuzawa's dedication to scholarship, which is also expressed in the Keio Gijuku's Latin motto, adopted about this time: *Calamus Gladio Fortior* ("the pen is mightier than the sword").

In 1871 Fukuzawa relocated the Keio Gijuku to a hill-top site in Mita, in southwestern Tokyo, which is still part of the university's main campus. With support both from the city council, whom Fukuzawa had advised on reorganising the police force, and from the leading government minister Iwakura Tomomi, Fukuzawa was able to persuade the lord of the Shimabara domain to sell the land to him, and the new campus remained his personal property until 1898. There, as at Teppozu, he continued to put the teaching of English first, but he supplemented it with introductory courses in both sciences (mathematics, physics, and chemistry) and humanities (geography and history), which prepared the approximately 100 students for more advanced study. Even so, the *gijuku*'s courses provided only the equivalent of a contemporary high-school education, and many of its alumni went on to further study at the government's Imperial University (now the University of Tokyo) before beginning their careers.

In these early years Keio Gijuku was run on a cooperative basis, with older students helping to teach first-year students and all students taking part in administrative and maintenance work. Fukuzawa carried on innovating, for example by adding a *yochisha,* an elementary school, to the *gijuku* in 1874, and, after coining the word *enzetsu* to translate the English word "elocution," having an Enzetsukan, an Elocution Hall, erected on the campus in 1875. This building, which is now an Important Cultural Property, is believed to have been the first purposefully built lecture hall in Japan.

Keio's students soon acquired a reputation for defying tradition. In 1885, for example, it was reported (in Fukuzawa's own newspaper) that more than half wore western clothing rather than Japanese, and students became notorious for regularly eating beef, which was forbidden by Buddhist principles, although even they preferred to keep

visits from the local butcher secret and to greet his arrival with the traditional knocking of flints, a ritual act believed to avert evil.

By the 1880s Keio stood alongside what are now Waseda, Meiji, and Chuo Universities as one of the leading private academies in the Japanese capital, with Fukuzawa and his colleagues providing training for men (but not yet women) entering careers in business and the professions, notably law. From 1887 those colleagues included three American scholars: the legal expert John Henry Wigmore, the literary critic William S. Liscome, and the economist Garrett Droppers. They had been recommended to Fukuzawa by Charles William Eliot, president of Harvard University, and were paid out of funds gathered by A.M. Knapp, a missionary of the American Unitarian Church. They all taught exclusively in English, providing college-level courses, initially lasting three years, in law, economics, and literature to around 60 students a year.

Their college-level section of the *gijuku* formed the basis of the Keio Gijuku Daigaku Senmon Gakko, an official designation, meaning "Keio Academy University-level Specialist School," which was conferred in 1890. This was not yet fully equivalent to the status of degree-giving university, which was then reserved for publicly owned institutions, but was nevertheless important, both as a sign that Fukuzawa's efforts were appreciated by the ruling oligarchy and as a justification for raising further funds for Keio Gijuku from the well-laced alumni who had already begun to support it. Many of them, after all, worked in institutions—the examination-based civil service, the westernised legal profession, large industrial enterprises—which had not existed when Fukuzawa started teaching in 1858 but which he had advocated through his teaching and writing. Largely due to their support, the college remained open in spite of a drastic but temporary fall in student numbers between 1890 and 1895, which led some of the staff to suggest abandoning the college.

In 1898 the Daigaku Senmon Gakko was made organisationally separate from the rest of the *gijuku*'s activities and converted into a five-year college when Fukuzawa created a single Keio Gijuku corporation. The new body, a mechanism for Fukuzawa to pass on his legacy to a new generation, took over the ownership of the Mita campus and supervised the elementary school, the high school, and the university as distinct entities, which shared a single campus, a common academic calendar, and Fukuzawa's basic principles. In the same year the corporation established the university's fourth faculty by separating political science from law. At Fukuzawa's death in 1901 he and his colleagues could look back with understandable satisfaction over 43 years of academic and literary achievements that had contributed to the transformation of their country, and especially of their city, almost beyond recognition.

Fukuzawa's colleagues maintained his program of westernising innovation after his death. Occasionally, this took forms that he might well not have recognised, such as the university's rugby football club, the oldest in Japan, which was founded in the year of his death by Edward Bramswell Clarke, a Briton who taught English at Keio, or the annual baseball games between Keio and Waseda, another private university in Tokyo. The baseball games first were played between 1903 and 1906 but have become a nationally popular event since their revival in the 1920s. But the general trend was to expand and improve the Senmon Gakko's academic provision, partly in order to prepare for recognition as a university, but also to secure its long-term future as an independent institution. To begin with, only 11 days after Fukuzawa's death the corporation assisted in founding an *Ijikai*, a supporters' society mainly composed of alumni, which has given Keio crucial financial assistance over the years (it now has nearly 25,000 members, many in prominent positions in public life and in business). The first projects the society helped to fund included the establishment of graduate schools within each faculty in 1906, among the first in any private university in Japan; and the building, between 1908 and 1912, of what is now the Old Library, a large red-brick structure, with an octagonal tower, which has since been designated an Important Cultural Property. Unusual for a university library anywhere, it has always been open to the general public as well as to staff and students.

In 1917 Keio expanded beyond Mita for the first time, with the foundation of a medical school at Shinanomachi, also in Tokyo. This school was to become closely associated with the main university hospital, founded three years later on the same Shinanomachi campus, and with a nursing college, all supervised by the first dean of the school, Kitasato Shibasaburo, a pioneering microbiologist who had been a close friend of Fukuzawa's and whose private research laboratory had been founded with funds provided by Fukuzawa himself. (In addition, in 1974 the school absorbed what became the Ise Keio Hospital in Mie Prefecture; it is also responsible for training at the Tsukigase Rehabilitation Center in the spa town of Izu-Yugashima, in Shizuoka Prefecture.)

In 1920 Keio was among the first of the private academies to be granted full university status, as Keio Gijuku Daigaku. It now had three faculties once again—law, literature, and economics, as in 1890—for the political science department was absorbed back into the first of these while retaining a separate curriculum. Physical expansion continued with the opening in 1934 of the university's Hiyoshi campus in Kanagawa Prefecture (the area, dominated by Yokohama, which lies to the west of Tokyo). This campus now is used for all general courses for first- and second-year undergraduates and to house the Graduate School of Business Administration. In 1944 an engineering faculty was created through the absorption of the

Fujiwara Institute of Technology, which had been founded in 1939 by Fujiwara Ginjiro, a Keio alumnus, using facilities at the Hiyoshi campus.

By the time that Fujiwara, a paper industry magnate, opened his institute, Japan had already been at war in China for eight years, and, through its alliance with Nazi Germany and Fascist Italy, was heading toward confrontation with the United States and its allies. The university's activities continued on all three of its campuses for the duration of the Pacific war (1941–45) until they were severely disrupted by the firebombing of Tokyo in 1945 and then, after Japan's defeat, by the transfer of most of the Hiyoshi campus to the Allied occupation authorities. However, under the terms of the liberalising education reforms sponsored by those same authorities, the Keio Gijuku corporation was revived and reorganised, so that from 1948 it was able to retrieve the Hiyoshi campus and to reopen its elementary school, its high school, and its university, now known as Keio Daigaku and open to both men and women. In the same year it introduced correspondence courses as a fully accredited alternative to regular teaching on campus.

Since 1948 Keio University has regained its position as one of the leading universities in Japan. Academic diversification has continued. For example, its library school, opened in 1950 with assistance and advice from the Allied occupation authorities, and endowed by the Rockefeller Foundation in 1951, has helped to modernise information systems in Japan; its faculty of business and commerce, established in 1957 to mark the centenary of the founding of Fukuzawa's *gijuku,* has since gained renown for consistently producing the largest number of successful candidates to become certified public accountants. Its business school, set up in 1962 on the model of its counterpart at Harvard and renamed the Graduate School of Business Administration in 1978, offers prestigious master's and doctor's degrees as well as non-degree courses; and the 1981 reorganisation of the engineering faculty as a faculty of science and technology has permitted an expansion of its teaching and research in these fields.

In addition Keio has acquired three more campuses. The Yagami campus, next to the Hiyoshi campus in Kanagawa Prefecture, was established in 1972 to house what has since become the science and technology faculty and its graduate school, and in 1990 two new faculties, of policy management and environmental information, were opened on a fifth campus at Shonan Fujisawa, also in Kanagawa Prefecture. The buildings at this site are equipped with computer networking facilities, allowing the integration of courses between the two faculties and the encouragement of language learning. Most recently, in 1990, the university has created the Keio Academy of New York in Harrison, New York, a high school for both Japanese and non-Japanese young men and women between the ages of 15 and 18, who can apply for automatic entry to the university after graduation from the academy. Meanwhile in Japan the Keio Gijuku corporation now controls a total of four senior high schools and three junior high schools in addition to its original elementary school, its nursing college, a foreign-language school, and the university. Among the university's students—roughly 26,500 undergraduates, 3,000 postgraduates, and 15,000 students studying through correspondence courses—there are many who have previously studied at one or more of the associated Keio institutions.

Shortly before his death Fukuzawa Yukichi summed up his outlook in a piece of calligraphy, preserved at the Mita campus: *Dokuritsu Jison Gei Shinseiki* (which may be translated as "Welcoming the new century with independence and self-respect"). Approaching another new century, the university he founded, owned, and closely supervised is still perceptibly influenced by his principles. For example, its pioneering use of interactive technology at the Shonan Fujisawa campus is in the spirit of the enthusiasm for "civilisation and enlightenment" which he, his university, and many of its alumni have done much to encourage, while its programs for academic exchange and cooperation with 38 universities in the United States, Britain, China, Germany, and other countries are an expression of a strong and widespread commitment to internationalism in a country all too often misrepresented as wholly inward-looking. Just as Fukuzawa's original *gijuku* was at the forefront of Japanese education in the 1850s and 1860s, so now Keio Daigaku is among the most prestigious and successful of Japanese universities.

Further Reading: Eiichi Kiyooka's English version of *The Autobiography of Fukuzawa Yukichi* (Tokyo: Hokuseido Press, 1934), a classic of modern Japanese literature, is available in a revised edition (New York and London: Columbia University Press, 1966). Carmen Blacker's *The Japanese Enlightenment: A Study of the Writings of Fukuzawa Yukichi* (Cambridge: Cambridge University Press, 1964) is an interesting survey of his main interests and activities.

—Patrick Heenan

KYUSHU UNIVERSITY
(Fukuoka, Japan)

Location: Fukuoka, Japan, one and a half hours southwest of Tokyo by air.

Description: A national university enrolling approximately 15,000 students in undergraduate, graduate and professional schools.

Information: Admission Division, Student Bureau
Kyushu University
6-10-1 Hakozaki
Higashi-ku
Fukuoka 812-81
Japan

The university is situated in the ancient port city of Fukuoka on Kyushu, southernmost of the four mainland islands in the Japanese archipelago. Kyushu has been for centuries a crossroads of cultures and was Japan's first point of contact with Chinese, Korean, and European civilizations. Today a city of over 1.2 million people, Fukuoka is the center of government, commerce, and education on Kyushu. Kyushu University is the largest of the city's 11 four-year colleges and universities.

Kyushu University was founded in 1911 as Kyushu Imperial University, the fourth government-sponsored university created under the educational reforms of the Meiji Era. Today it is one of 98 national universities operating under the jurisdiction of the Ministry of Education, Science and Culture.

During its first eight years, Kyushu University consisted of a faculty of engineering and a faculty of medicine, the latter created by incorporating the respected Fukuoka Medical College, founded in 1903 by Dr. T. Omori. The university's first graduation was held in the summer of 1912.

The faculty of medicine provided the nucleus of what would eventually become the largest center for medical education, research, and clinical care in western Japan. In similar fashion, the faculty of engineering, together with the faculty of agriculture (established 1919) and law and letters (established 1924) formed the broad base upon which future university programs would be built.

During these years, growth occurred in a number of directions. Buildings were constructed and the number of faculty in all departments increased. Among the new facilities were a marine biological station, orthopedic surgical workshop, roentgen and microscopic-photography laboratory, and a fishery research laboratory. A building was constructed for the faculty of agriculture, whose resources also included a university farm and the university forests. The forests, acquired beginning in 1912, offered an invaluable resource for teaching and research. Today four remain, including three on Kyushu and one on Hokkaldo, Japan's northernmost island, totaling 18,000 acres.

During its first decade Kyushu University attracted a number of faculty members from among the relatively small number of Japanese scholars who had studied overseas. Public demand for higher education at that time was intense, with graduates going on to fill responsible posts in the civil service and other fields.

In 1920 the first university library was created, staffed by a director and several library assistants, and in 1925 the position of university librarian was established. Also in 1925 construction was completed on buildings to house the faculty of law and letters, established two years earlier. The next year saw the retirement of president Bunji Mano and the appointment of Gintari Daikuhara to succeed him.

During these years, affiliated research institutes and laboratories were established at various sites on the island to support the main work of the university. These included the Institute of Balneotherapeutics, created as part of the medical school in 1931 in the town of Beppu, known throughout the world for its therapeutic hot springs; Amakusa Marine Biological Laboratory, established in 1928 (and later attached to the faculty of science) in Tomioka, a small seaside town about 120 km. south of Fukuoka on the largest of the Amakusa Islands.

In 1939 a number of departments, including physics, chemistry, and geology, were consolidated in a new faculty of science. A department of mathematics was added in 1942.

Major changes occurred following World War II. Post-war educational reforms included the National School Establishment Law, which called for one national university to be created in each prefecture, or national administrative division. The word "imperial" was deleted from the names of existing universities, and Kyushu, like its sister institutions, adopted a democratic system of governance.

Today, the president is elected to a four-year term by the university's professors and assistant professors from among their number and may be reelected to one additional term. Under the president, a university council, made up of the deans from each faculty, directors of the library system, hospitals, and other organizations attached to the university, considers and approves "all

Kyushu University

important affairs" of the university. In addition, each faculty chooses a dean from among its members,

Post-war reorganization created eight distinct faculties at Kyushu: letters, education, law, economics, science, medicine, engineering, and agriculture. The length of the undergraduate course of study was increased from three years to four, with the initial portion composed of general education.

The graduate school was reorganized in 1953 to include the following divisions: letters, education, law, economics (previously within the faculty of law and letters), science, pharmacy, engineering, and agriculture. Added later were the divisions of medical science (1953), dental sciences (1974), and mathematics (1994).

In addition, two interdisciplinary graduate programs—engineering sciences (1979), and social and cultural studies (1994)—emphasized cross-fertilization and the "sideway

relation" between established fields of study and their related boundary areas.

By 1956 the university had almost 5,500 graduate and undergraduate students enrolled in its eight faculties and seven research institutes and departments, covering most fields of natural and social sciences and humanities. Its physical size had grown to 384 acres.

The library has grown to more than 3 million volumes, including more than 1.6 million in Japanese and Chinese and almost 1.4 million in other languages. It includes the central library, medical library, Ropponmatsu Library, and the libraries of the faculties and research institutes. The university publishes 83 journals, as well as the quarterly Kyushu University Library Bulletin.

As in the past, Kyushu serves as a gateway for the international exchange of people and ideas. Since its founding, the university has accepted foreign students, mostly from

Asia and primarily in medicine, engineering, and agriculture. An International Student Center was established in 1985 to provide Japanese language and cultural training. In addition, the international student residence, a community building, and a living facility for foreigners engaged in research or teaching at the university help support the international exchange of ideas and culture.

Cooperative agreements with 26 universities in Asia, Europe, Canada, the U.S., and Brazil, and many more individual faculty initiatives, enable hundreds of faculty to teach, conduct research, or study abroad.

The university's campuses include the main Hakozaki campus and hospitals campus (including a 1,300-bed hospital), both in the older, eastern section of Fukuoka; Ropponmatsu campus in the southwestern part of the city (which consists of the Graduate School of Social and Cultural Studies and the Institute of Languages and Cultures); and Chikushi campus in the southern suburbs (graduate school of engineering sciences and various institutes and centers). There is, in addition, a 140-bed hospital campus at Beppu.

—Bette Noble

LAVAL UNIVERSITY
(Quebec, Canada)

Location: Most facilities are on the outskirts of Quebec City, with some schools inside the city and at Ste. Anne de la Pocatière.

Description: The oldest Francophone institution of higher education outside Europe; a secular, multi-faculty university with about 25,000 full-time and 11,600 part-time students.

Information: Université Laval
Cité Universitaire
Quebec, PQ
GIK 7P4
Canada
(418) 656-2131
Fax (418) 656-2809

Laval University (L' Université Laval in French), formerly the Grand Séminaire de Quebec, has been at the center of Francophone culture in North America for more than 330 years and has changed as the culture has changed. From 1663 to 1852, when it enjoyed a monopoly of higher education throughout what is now the province of Quebec, it was the principal guardian of the conservative French Catholic tradition, which long survived the conquest of New France by the British. From 1852 to 1970, endowed with charters both from the British monarchy and papacy, it developed into a more diverse and complex institution, adapting to the growth of science and industry and coping with competition from rival universities, while still transmitting a distinctive Catholic culture to its students, many of whom went on to leading positions in the church, and in business and politics. Since 1970 it has operated under a provincial charter, losing much of its exclusively Catholic identity while increasing its commitment to maintaining Francophone culture—just as the province itself has.

The university is named for Monsignor François-Xavier de Montmorency-Laval de Montigny, more commonly known as Bishop Laval, one of the most important figures in the history of Francophone Canada. He was a loyal subject of King Louis XVI but, as a Jesuit, he was also a devoted follower of the pope, from his ordination as a priest in 1647 onwards. While it would probably be anachronistic to infer that he was conscious of any great contradiction between these two loyalties, nevertheless, like Jesuits in other Catholic countries, he was clearly able and willing to defy secular authority for the sake of

the faith, as became apparent after he was sent in 1659 to New France.

Laval arrived in Quebec, the capital of the colony, armed with orders from the royal court to manage the religious affairs of the settlers and the natives, but he was also made an honorary bishop, as well as vicar apostolic of New France, by the pope. He soon proved his independence of the secular power by objecting to their turning a blind eye to the sale of alcohol to the natives and by securing the replacement of the corrupt governor. But his most lasting contribution to the developing life of the colony was the foundation in 1663 of the Séminaire de Québec, which absorbed a small Jesuit college established in 1635. The seminary intended to serve a dual function as both a home for elderly priests and the colony's only training center for their younger successors, and was to be financed by tithes from parishioners. It was located in a magnificent building, next to the bishop's palace and the cathedral of Notre-Dame and close to the royal fortress.

Laval directly contributed more than any other individual to the formation of a Francophone Catholic island in the North American sea of English and Spanish. The parish priests trained at the Séminaire played a crucial role until as recently as the 1960s as keepers and transmitters of French Catholic tradition. Laval went on to become the first bishop of Quebec, in 1674, holding office directly from the pope rather than from any French religious superior. This factor also would prove significant in the development of Quebec, providing the formal basis for the self-confident activism of a church increasingly staffed by priests born and raised in the province and not afraid to stand up to both French governors and their eventual British successors.

Laval himself retired to the Séminaire in 1688 and, after another eight years as bishop, died there in 1708. Over the half-century between his death and the British conquest of New France, the Séminaire remained the only institution of higher education in the colony. Perhaps inevitably, it expanded somewhat beyond Laval's strictly theological aims, to offer some limited teaching in the classics and humanities to the sons of those among the landowning elite who did not wish, or could not afford, to send the students to France. Most of the student prepared for entry to Laval by attending *collèges classiques*, privately endowed schools for the sons of the wealthy which were also staffed by priests.

In 1754 the French colonial governor moved from Quebec to Montreal; five years later the British arrived at the former capital, taking over the city after a battle on the Plains of Abraham at its edge, and in 1763 the French

Laval University

royal court, finally accepting the loss of the colony, called home all its officials and many other leading members of the settler society. Throughout this upheaval the Catholic church, based at Notre-Dame cathedral and the Séminaire, maintained the autonomy that Bishop Laval had won for it. Its priests continued to minister to the 50,000 or so Francophone settlers who remained and their posi-

tion in the life of the province was confirmed when the British parliament passed the Quebec Act in 1774, which guaranteed the religion and language of the Francophones but excluded them from official posts and the learned professions.

In a largely rural society, increasingly estranged from the commercial outlook and ethnic diversity which came to characterize Montreal, the largest city in the province, its rival Quebec City and the Séminaire within it, took on more importance than ever. The priests trained there carried to the countryside not only the strict, somewhat puritanical version of Catholicism which had been favored in pre-revolutionary royal France, but also the political quietism that accompanied it. They helped to ensure, for example, that there was little protest when New France was divided into Upper and Lower Canada in 1791 and that the rebellion of the *Patriotes* against British rule, in 1837, was almost entirely limited to Montreal, where it was swiftly defeated. Indeed, after the French Revolution of 1789, which led to the abolition of the monarchy and the disestablishment of the church there, the Séminaire and the *collèges classiques* alike welcomed a number of priests exiled from France, whose conservative outlook reinforced the tradition already established in the schools.

Since the Catholic Church in Lower Canada—roughly equivalent to modern Quebec—was conspicuously obedient to the British "powers that be," the Séminaire was not merely permitted but positively encouraged to expand its horizons, as the initial ban on Francophone admission to the professions was reduced and then abandoned. The people of Quebec City, the country districts, and the French-speaking areas of Montreal obviously needed lawyers and doctors who could speak their native tongue, and the church was understandably anxious to supervise their training if it could. At the same time the secular authorities appeared to favor a policy of Anglicization. The suppression of the Society of Jesus by the papacy had led to the transfer of the Jesuit estates in Lower Canada to the provincial legislature, which voted in 1801 to apply the revenues from the lands to providing instructions, in English only, through new schools and a university. Thus began decades of political and legal controversy, culminating in 1843 in the opening of what is now McGill University in Montreal, an Anglophone institution which, from the outset, has attracted many Francophones seeking access to the dominant culture of what was British North America.

The Francophone community took a long time to respond to what many of its intellectuals perceived as a serious threat to their culture. The mostly urban Anglophones, led by wealthy and powerful individuals, perhaps found it easier than most Francophones did both to accept that higher education would have to be expanded as industrialization progressed, and to gather funds to pay for it. In any event, the province's first Francophone university was established in 1852 by the simple (and cheap) expedient of renaming the Grand Séminaire, the section of the Séminaire de Québec devoted to training students, as L'Université Laval. (The Petit Séminaire, the residence for retired priests, continued as a separate institution.)

The British imperial authorities approved of the new university probably because it had become obvious that transforming the Francophone majority into Anglophones was neither practically feasible nor politically desirable. They arranged for Laval to receive a royal charter from Queen Victoria in December 1852, but, recognizing that the Catholic Church was unwilling to surrender control, they included in the charter provision for the bishop of Quebec to be the university's visitor (a post peculiar to universities created in the British tradition, in which a distinguished figure acts as a kind of court of final appeal in academic disputes).

Laval initially had a unique structure, designed to preserve the established system of Francophone education. Its arts faculties was composed of the *collèges classiques,* which was now affiliated to the university and provided undergraduate teaching as preparation for the bachelor's degree. Holders of that degree were then admitted to studies in one of the other three faculties: theology, civil law, or medicine. This system was not affected by the expansion of the arts faculty in 1860, when specialized schools of agriculture and pharmacy were added.

In 1867 the province of Quebec joined the new Dominion of Canada, on condition that the new federal authorities take over the British guarantee that its distinctive heritage of Catholic faith and French language would be protected, specifically by making education a provincial rather than a federal matter. It proved to be impossible to implement a secular education system open to all, so the province continued with its existing division between an Anglophone Protestant system and a Francophone Catholic system, each administered by private bodies but subsidized from the public purse. This was obviously a recipe for continued controversy, both between the two language communities and within them. Thus, for example, in 1873, after McGill University succeeded in obtaining government funds to open an engineering school, it was widely expected that Laval would accept funds for a Francophone equivalent. Instead, the university turned down what it said was an inadequate offer from a government which it did not want intervening in its affairs, and the money went to the Montreal Catholic School Commission instead.

The university went even further. Jealous of its historic monopoly, it campaigned against a proposal to establish another Francophone university, to be located in Montreal, even though the Catholic Church authorities supported it. In 1876 Pope Pius IX intervened in the dispute, which was becoming an embarrassment, by issuing a pontifical charter for Laval. This charter made changes in Laval's formal relations with the church, by conferring the power to grant full theological degrees and making the bishop of Quebec its apostolic chancellor, but it also required Laval to create its own branch in Montreal, a compromise which the university evidently found acceptable. With the arts faculty reorganized as a wholly internal body—although it still recruited most of its students from the *collèges classiques*—Laval could now begin to compete directly with the "godless" and Anglophone faculties of McGill in both major cities of the province.

By 1901 Laval, on its two sites, had a total of 1,175 students, compared to 1,208 (still including many Francophones) studying at McGill. Yet nearly 35 percent of Laval's student body were preparing for the priesthood and almost all the rest were in the law and medicine faculties, apart from just 39 individuals studying sciences, in contrast to McGill, which was already one of the leading centers for scientific research in North America and whose alumni dominated the commercial and political life in the province. Laval did make some adjustments to the industrial and commercial transformation of Quebec, by creating a school of surveying in 1907 and a school of forestry in 1910, both located in Montreal, but after more than 50 years as a university it was still unable—mainly because its conservative Catholic decision makers were unwilling—to offer the full range of academic disciplines.

By 1915 the long-standing mutual suspicion between the Anglophone education sector, led by McGill, and the Francophone schools, dominated by Laval, had worsened as it became clear that the latter's traditionalism was becoming an obstacle to further growth. McGill had an endowment of 6.7 million Canadian dollars while Laval had only $15,000 as its endowment, an indication that, as elsewhere in the western world, universities in Quebec would prosper if, and perhaps only if, they offered scientific and vocational courses which would attract government and business funding and increase the numbers of students. Once again the funding and content of education became a burning political question. The controversy contributed to the decision to separate the original Laval University in Quebec City from its Montreal branch. An independent corporate body, l'Université de Montréal, was established in 1920, absorbing a number of vocational schools in what was (as it is today) the largest city in Quebec.

The provincial government, well aware that McGill enjoyed a better academic reputation and stronger finances than its Francophone rivals, was nevertheless compelled to be evenhanded, and in 1920 gave $1 million each to McGill, Laval, and the new university in Montreal. Laval, now entirely based in Quebec City, was saddled with a reputation for being more conservative, or even reactionary, than its former affiliate and now rival. It decided to supplement the government's grant by launching its first public subscription drive in the same year, perhaps partly to raise its public profile but more concretely to finance a new science faculty, centered on a new school of chemistry, that could compete directly with the two universities in Montreal.

Meanwhile the government pressed ahead with reforms of both educational systems, so that by 1923 significantly larger numbers of students were staying on at school and then going on to higher education. Laval joined with the other institutions—universities, colleges, and technical schools alike—to respond to rising demand by expanding and diversifying. Within ten years it had established seven more specialized schools within the arts faculty—forestry in 1920 (replacing the school in Montreal); letters and science in 1921; music and nursing in 1922; philosophy in 1926; and social sciences in 1930. By 1929 the two Francophone universities between them had 3,857 students, among whom the proportion of theology students had fallen to about 17 percent, while more than half the total were enrolled in science or technology courses. Although almost all the former were at Laval and the majority of the latter were at Montreal, nevertheless these combined figures do suggest that the composition of the university had significantly shifted within just a generation.

Between 1936 and 1941 Laval University was reorganized once again. Apart from the music school, which remained within the art faculty, the specialized schools were transformed into independent faculties—thus incidentally creating Canada's first social sciences faculty—and in 1939–40 the graduate school was established for advanced study and research. Even after reforms and innovations had taken effect, however, the two Francophone universities still suffered from a relative lack of applicants, unlike McGill, which continued to expand and even began to attract French-speaking students. The main reason for this difference was that the publicly funded Catholic school system still did not provide sufficient education to prepare students for university, a function which was still almost exclusively performed by the expensive and exclusive collèges classiques.

Laval University, still balancing the requirements of tradition with the demand for scientific and professional training, was now among the leading universities in Canada, receiving wider recognition when Louis St. Laurent, who had both graduated from Laval and taught in its law faculty, became Canada's most prominent Francophone politician. As a member of Mackenzie King's Liberal government from 1942 ha gave vocal support to the imposition of conscription for service overseas during World War II. Then, as prime minister himself from 1948 to 1957, he took Canada into NATO, sent Canadian troops to permanent posts in western Europe, and introduced hospital insurance and equalization payments between the richer and poorer provinces—in the face of strong opposition from Quebec's provincial government.

St. Laurent also helped to launch Laval's second public subscription drive in 1948. In response to the sharp rise in the numbers of students and applicants, which threatened to place excessive strain on the resources available in the narrow streets and fragile buildings of the old Latin Quarter of Quebec City, the university authorities sought funding for a construction program, started in that year, aimed at unifying the university on a single 190-hectare campus, known as the Cité Universitaire, located in the suburb of St. Foy on the Plains of Abraham. (Although the Cité Universitaire is now its main site, the university has retained ownership of the Séminaire building in the Latin Quarter, within the walls of Old Quebec, the only fortified city remaining in North America. The building forms an integral part of the World Heritage Site, protected by federal and provincial conservation laws; the museum inside it, which is affiliated with the university, holds one of the leading collections of historic objects in Canada.

Relocation to the new campus gave the university the opportunity to expand and diversify still further as the unwieldy arts faculty was broken up. A separate faculty of letters came to include a school of languages and institutes of history and geography, a faculty of sciences was created to take in the schools of chemistry, mines, electricity, and pharmacy, and a faculty of commerce was also established. Still another faculty, that of agriculture, which includes a school of fisheries, was organized on its own separate campus, at Ste. Anne de la Pocatière.

Laval entered the 1960s larger, more diverse, and more widely respected than ever in its history, just in time to be swept by the winds of change generated by the reforms of the Catholic Church introduced by the Second Vatican Council; by the "Quiet Revolution" which modernized the institutions of Quebec and woke secular nationalism from its long slumber; and, to a lesser extent, by a brief eruption of student revolt across the developed world. Questions of identity became crucial. If Catholicism no longer defined Francophone culture, what did? And if that culture was to be "Québeçois," how would it deal with French-Canadians outside the province and non-Francophones—whether native peoples, Anglophones, or immigrants—inside it? Laval's staff and students played a leading part in offering answers to these questions, often through publications of the influential Presses Universitaires Laval, a publishing affiliate established in 1950. A few gave support to the terrorist Front pour la Liberation de Québec, but most contributed to political and social change through the Liberal Party, then dominant in the province, the newly founded separatist Parti Québeçois or the still vibrant Catholic press and social networks.

Individuals connected to the university thus responded to the new conditions in Quebec in various ways, by taking part in controversies which have by no means ended even now, but for the institution itself the key change came in 1970, when the royal charter of 1852 and the pontifical charter of 1876 were superseded by a new charter, provided by the provincial legislature. Nowadays, although the historic affiliation to the Catholic Church remains in place, it is more formal than substantive, apart from the faculty of theology. The special link with the *collèges classiques* has been broken, to permit entry from

any of the province's *collèges d'enseignement général et professionel* (colleges of general and professional education, or CEGEPs). Competence in French is now an absolute requirement for admission to "primary" courses, aimed at bachelor's degrees, but may be waived for students working toward master's degrees or doctorates.

Since 1970 the university has continued to grow, receiving both federal and provincial funding while competing with McGill, the Université de Montréal (now much larger than its parent), and several newer schools for research contracts and benefactions from the private sectors. Even now 93 percent of its students are from the province of Quebec itself, many of them no doubt choosing it in preference to its rivals because of its location, both literal and metaphorical, at the heart of "La Belle Province."

Yet precisely because it is now a fully modern, secular university, as open to free thought and debate as any other, Laval can no longer claim, as it once could, to transmit a unified, self-contained, and untroubled culture. Today Laval is perhaps best represented, at least beyond Quebec, by the Liberal Party politician Jean Chrétien, one of its most distinguished alumni. Between 1980 and 1982, when he was the federal justice minister under Pierre Trudeau, he joined the fierce campaign to prevent the Parti Québeçois, then in control of the province, from winning a provincial referendum on separation from Canada. He then led the government's successful efforts to remove control of the federal constitution from the British parliament. Prime minister from 1993, he again led the pro-Canadian forces to a victory (albeit a narrow one) in another referendum called by a Parti Québeçois government. Educating both federalists like Chrétien and separatists, and worldly enough to secure funding from both, Laval has clearly come a long way from its origins as Bishop Laval's bastion of the Roman faith and the French crown in the wilds of New France.

Further Reading: There are numerous books in English on the history of Quebec, including the development of the seminary and the university, such as *The Canadian Frontier, 1534–1760* by W.J. Eccles (New York: Holt, Rinehart and Winston, 1969), *Lower Canada 1791–1840* by Fernand Ouellet, translated and adapted by Patricia Claxton (Toronto: McClelland and Stewart, 1980) or *Quebec: A History 1867–1929* by Paul-André Linteau and others, translated by Robert Chodos (Toronto: James Lorimer, 1983).

—Patrick Heenan

LEIPZIG UNIVERSITY
(Leipzig, Germany)

Location: Leipzig, Germany, a city of more than 500,000 inhabitants (northeast of Weimar, east of Halle, and about 180 kilometers SSW of Berlin); a medieval trade route crossroads near the Elbe.

Description: From 1946 to 1990, within the former GDR, Leipzig University was the largest university in Eastern Germany. It was named Karl-Marx University from 1952 to 1990. Today, Leipzig is the largest institution of higher learning in the Sachsen free state (Saxony), with over 23,000 staff and students. Enrollment for 1995/1996 was 19,876 students in 14 faculties.

Information: Leipzig University
Augustusplatz
04109 Leipzig
Germany
(341) 97 108

The *Universitas Lipsiensis,* founded by dissident German professors and students who left Prague University during the early stages of the Hussite movement, officially opened on December 2, 1409, with a ceremony in the Refrectorio of the St. Thomas Church.

Prince Friedrich I ("The Quarrelsome") of Meissen and his brother Wilhelm, hoped to establish a university in Leipzig, on "true" German soil, an institution as prestigious as that in Prague, modeled after the universities in Paris and Bologna (*studia generale*). After royal approval was received, Johannes Boltenhagen, rector of the University of Prague, and the corporation of scholars from Prague arrived en masse in their homeland at Prince Friedrich's invitation and instituted the *hochschule* at Leipzig. In July, the corporation was given a house for professors, the abandoned Rathaus (Town Hall) of the city council, the earliest sign of the Prague corporation in Leipzig. In September, Pope Alexander V issued a papal bull, and the celebration at St. Thomas Church in December gave the church's seal of approval to the corporation-directed university, a first for a university supported by the Roman church. The pope named the bishop of Merseberg chancellor.

Several factors kept the masters, students, and institution together during the first decades: humanism rather than scholasticism taught in the *Artistenfacultat* (Arts Faculty or Humanities); the election of a deacon, who immediately organized studies even before the school

was officially recognized; statutes brought with them from Prague; the election of a new rector, Johannes von Munsterberg, a Silesian; and a lingering hope that they could someday return to Prague. Three hundred and sixty-nine students were matriculated during the first semester. As was the custom in European universities, students were organized into nations. The four nations of Leipzig University—Meissen, Saxony, Bavaria, and Poland—contained the German elite as well as serious scholars.

Two houses, *collegium major* and *collegium minus* established the university's place in Leipzig. A third college, the *Frauen Kollege* or *Jungfrau Kollege* (*Collegium Beatae Mariae Virginis*—College of the Blessed Virgin Mary), was established in 1422 by a master of the former Prague Polish nation who had his own funds. Three Silesian and one Prussian professor served as masters of this small house across from the Polish *Marienkapelle* (St. Mary's Chapel). In 1416, the first rector, von Munsterberg, died, and endowed this house for Silesian or Prussian students and professors. It later became a college building for the Cistercian abbey.

Most students lived in endowed houses, where they led disciplined lives with their master; they ate with him, they spoke Latin only, and in theory, they lived sheltered lives. A Swedish student at Leipzig in 1424 wrote home: "I live in the 'Kleinem Kollege.' At supper one is in charge of his own bowl and jug. Food is ample and good, also beer and wine. For savings and maintenance I need six groschen a week, because I must buy the drink myself. The Ordinarius reads from . . . [the Bible] each morning between 5 and 7 A.M. Whoever wants to be prepared must already be up by 4 A.M. Haec est vita laudabilis!"

In the early days of the University of Leipzig, the heart of its self-governance was the *Artistengakulat,* with professors who held bachelor's and master's degrees from all the various faculties of Prague University. The bishop of Merseburg, the university's chancellor, arbitrated in spiritual matters; the rector and university jurists were leaders in matters of secular law. The education and lifestyle of the new Leipzig students were different in 1409 from the usual *studia generale* founded by the church in other cities. The students and professors were already seeking progress from scholasticism in their adherence to humanistic teachings. Their constitution, although allowing for separate nations, pledged allegiance to the university above all. Autonomy from church and state put the scholars at Leipzig in a special position.

From the beginning, the university had books at its disposal. As a book handling trade center, the city was one of the first to see new books as they became available and to hear new ideas. In 1462, Peter Luder, a wandering lecturer of the period, who was at Heidelberg for a time, then at Erfurt, came to Leipzig. His lectures were the first to bring the newer humanistic ideas to the university. He lectured for three hours on Terence, the Roman comedic poet, gratis, and charged 25 groschen for his course on rhetoric. Luder left for some unknown reason in the summer of 1462 for Padua. At the same time, Samuel Karoch had matriculated at Leipzig. Karoch promoted the spreading of humanism from Ingolstadt to Basel and Tübingen, Erfurt, Heidelberg, Cologne, and Vienna. Like Luder, Karoch was an inspirational and persuasive speaker.

Italian wandering lecturer, Priamus Capotius, who published *Oratorio metrica . . . in alma Lipsensi universitate habita* and Jacobus Publicus brought the written word of humanistic ideas to the professors and students of Leipzig, but the most important of these wandering lecturers was Konrad Celtis who came to Leipzig in 1486 and published *Ars versificandi et carminum*. Celtis was the first poet of German humanism in print; he taught first-level Greek in 1487, and also interpreted and edited the tragedies of the Roman writer Seneca.

Leipzig became a place for changing opinions, discussion, reading, and thought. Marcus Brandis published *Liber der Philosophia Platonis* in 1488, opening the way to the study of Plato in Leipzig. An early graduate of Leipzig, known as Niavis, wrote a small conversational book for students covering everything from initiation ceremonies to the proper method of combing one's beard: *Latinum ydeoma pro novellis studentibus*. The oldest copy known was printed hastily in Heidelberg under the title, *Manuale scholarium* and was published in 1857 as *Heidelberger Gesprächsbüchlein* by Friedrich Zarncke, who did not know the book's Leipzig origin. The book has played an important part in the study of the differences between modern life and an older society. Niavis died in 1514 as a clerical worker for the city of Bautzen.

A fourth college appeared at the university in 1426, the *Bernhardiner Kollege* for the education of monks of the Cistercian monastery near the *Frauen Kollege*. But the theology faculty was becoming an unpopular place for students to matriculate. In the 10 or 15 years preceding 1485, not more than 50 theological lectures took place at the university. The study of religion at Leipzig became a joke: cliques formed in student houses where the students were pious between 4:00 A.M. and 5:00 A.M., just enough time to save their souls; the most famous group of irreverants, under the master Johannes Fabri de Werd, was the "Schwabische Bund."

The end of the humanistic period at Leipzig University coincides with the emergence of Richard Crocus and Petrus Mosellanus. Leipzig, for all its interest in Greek did not have a Greek professor. The Bible, translated from the Greek, brought fame to Erasmus of Rotterdam, and caused controversy as his version differed from the Latin. The Polyglot Bible had been translated at the Alcala de Henares in Spain, and was used in the study of Greek and Hebrew.

Richard Crocus (Croke), a British scholar and student of Aleander at Paris, took the position of Greek professor at Leipzig in 1515. His *R. Croci Britanni Acadamiae Lipsensis economium congratulatorium* was published in 1516. Students of Crocus included leading Leipzig theology professor, Hieronymous Dungersheim von Ochsenfurt. Crocus was followed in the position by "Petrus Mosellanus," who was born Peter Schade from the Mosel region, and was brought to Leipzig University by Caspar Borner.

The Reformation came to Leipzig as to other German towns after Martin Luther preached there; due to the abolition of Roman Catholic monasteries in Saxony, Herzog (Duke) Moritz von Sachsen gave St. Paul's monastery, including its extensive library, to Leipzig University in June 1543. Rector Caspar Borner had professors and masters study and note the volumes, and he accumulated the collection of four other Leipzig monasteries, as well as manuscripts, fragments, and letters from libraries throughout the Saxony-Thuringer area. Following Borner, Joachim Feller became librarian in 1675. He integrated more book collections, and created a handwritten catalog for the university. A later librarian, Christian Gottlieb Jochers, who served from 1742 to 1758, and who became famous for his respected lexicons, completed an alphabetical and inclusive university reference catalog.

In 1833, the library came under the jurisdiction of the Ministry of Culture. Ernst Gottfried Gersdorf, the director of the university library, reorganized the library on "scientific principles." By 1888, the library had expanded so much that a new building, the *Bibliotheca Albertina,* was planned according to designs by respected Leipzig architect, Arwed Rossbach. The *Albertina* was completed in 1891, on Beethovenstrasse, near the scientific institutes, but two-thirds of it was destroyed during World War II.

Its 453-year existence makes Leipzig's the second oldest German university library. Because of its special collections, the university library is now in demand by national and international scholars. Medieval handscripted works, papyrus, and coin collections from antiquity, legal briefs in Latin, fragments of handwritten Bibles from the famous Codex Sinaiticus of the fourth century have all been assembled and catalogued throughout the vast system which serves the university, greater Leipzig, and other towns in Saxony.

The decline of the university in the late seventeenth century was somewhat relieved by the music studies provided to the university by the cantor of the Thomas Church, Johann Sebastian Bach, who was also the head of church music for St. Paul's Church at the university. The elitist university music faculty looked down on Bach for his lack of university training, although students were eager to join the conservatory and choruses he led. Bach was not the city council's first choice for the position he held from 1723 to 1750, and the university consistently thwarted his ability to earn the extra fees he needed to support his family. Today the university houses a collection of ancient instruments at the Grassi Museum, which has been restored from World War II damages and contains about 4,000 old instruments. Concerts of Bach's music are performed and recorded by Leipzig musicians using this collection.

A student at Leipzig from 1765 to 1768, Johann Wolfgang Goethe was inspired to write *Faust* in Auerbach's Keller, a student haunt owned and run by the family of Heinrich Stromer-Auerbach, rector of the university in 1508. Other outstanding students of the university include: artist Martin Schongauer; philosopher and mathematician Gottfried Wilhelm Leibniz; dramatist and critic Gotthold Ephraim Lessing; historian Leopold Ranke; composers Richard Wagner and Robert Schumann; and philosopher Friedrich Nietzsche.

Teachers associated with the long history of the university include: German lecturer and linguist Christian Thomasius; theologian and philosopher Christian August Crusius; jurist and statesman Karl Fridrich Wilhelm von Gerber; philosopher Johann Gottlieb Fichte; novelist Jean Paul Richter; poet Christian Fürchtegott Gellert; and philosopher Friedrich Wilhelm von Schelling.

The medical faculty was established in 1415, doctors were in practice by 1438, and the "theater of anatomy" was operational by 1784. The "Trierschen Instituts," a teaching institute for birthing was opened in 1810 with a "healing institute" for diseases of the eye following in 1820. In the middle of the nineteenth century, numerous clinics were founded to research disease, anatomy, hygiene, stomatology, psychiatry, nervous disorders, and children's health, with still more added in the twentieth century. In 1906, The Institute for the History of Medicine became the first of its kind in Germany, named for its founder, Karl Sudhoff; today it houses many old medical instruments and archival papers.

Over 40 years of Soviet Communist suppression began with a student council vote in 1947 which scandalized Soviet military authorities when votes for the election numbered 500 less than the 1,100 SED (the Communist-sponsored Socialist Unity Party) student membership. German universities had a long tradition of liberalism, one that the Soviets endeavored to wipe out by replacing faculty and administrators and arresting and imprisoning liberal students. Leipzig was one of the important centers of the tumultuous events of 1989 that led to the reunification of Germany. September 1991 saw the reestablishment of the *Vereinigung von Foderern und Freunden der Universitat Leipzig* (Union of Sponsors and Friends of the University of Leipzig), who pledge, "now and forever," to be members and friends of "Alma Mater Lipsiensis," and to support its teachings and research.

—Carol Shilakowsky

LORÁND EÖTVÖS UNIVERSITY
(Budapest, Hungary)

Location: Budapest, Hungary, on the Pest side of the Danube in the inner city.

Description: A state-run university enrolling approximately 12,400 students in undergraduate, graduate, and professional schools.

Information: Rector
1364 Budapest, V
Egyetem-tér 1-3
POB 109
Budapest
Hungary
(1) 267-0820
Fax (1) 266-9786

Visiting: A guidebook to the university library is available at the library. For university tours, contact the above phone number.

Lóránd Eötvös University (*Eötvös Lóránd Tudományegyetem*) is the oldest continuously operating university in Hungary. It is also the nation's most prestigious university. Attempts were made in the Middle Ages to found universities at Pécs (1367) and Óbuda (1389), but political instability and successive wars made their existence impossible. In the sixteenth century, Hungary was torn into three parts by the northward invasions of the Turks and the eastern expansions of the Hapsburgs, and subjected to the tumultuous events of the Protestant Reformation. Overcoming these obstacles, the Jesuit Order managed to establish a college in Nagyszombat in 1561. During the subsequent Counter-Reformation, Nagyszombat (now Trnava, Slovakia) became the center of Hungarian Catholicism. At the forefront of the movement was Cardinal Péter Pázmány who had been named Primate-Archbishop in 1616. Cardinal Pázmány was responsible for the reconversion of many Hungarian magnates who had gone over to the Protestants; he was also a leader in the subsequent cultural and educational improvements. In 1635, Pázmány transformed the college at Nagyszombat into a university with faculties in theology and philosophy. A faculty of law was added in 1667.

The Turks, who lost control of Hungarian territory in 1686, left the country in ruins. The city of Pest had a population of under 4,000 when the Hapsburgs took over and brought with them Italian and Austrian Baroque art forms and ideas. As an enlightened despot

of the eighteenth century, the Empress Maria Theresa took the university under her wing and granted it complete university status in 1769 and also established a faculty of medicine. In 1777 she moved it and its library to Buda Castle. There the university was placed under state control. The management and material foundations of the new Buda University were also modernized and improved. In 1784, her son, the Emperor Joseph II, moved the university to its present location on the Pest side of the Danube in a former Pauline monastery designed by Matthias Drenker.

The Pest university library, today known as the Central Library, grew out of the Jesuit College Library founded in 1560. It contained many manuscripts given to the Jesuits by noble families fleeing the Turkish invasion and remains a repository for 11 medieval manuscripts from the world-renowned collection of King Matthias Corvinus. Of special interest to students of medical history is the Abucasis Codex. Among the 160 other medieval manuscripts and miniatures is an eighth-century Beda fragment (the oldest manuscript in the collection), a tenth-century Greek *Gospel* from Constantinople, a 1340 manuscript of Dante's *Divine Comedy*, six fourteenth-century antiphonals and over 1,000 incunabula which add to the collection's depth. Currently, the library holds 1,400,000 volumes and 40,000 manuscripts. It is a particularly rich source of early Hungarian printed works (to 1711), medieval and Christian history, philosophy, and psychology. The Central Library is also home to the Pray, Kaprinay, and Hevenesi Collections of Hungarian history. The first catalogue of the library was published in 1780–81 by Gregory Pray just before the move to Pest, at which time it became a state-owned institution and was housed in a former Franciscan monastery.

The Hungarian Jacobin movement of 1795 was squelched by the Hapsburgs and their political conservatism gained enough strength through the Holy Alliance of 1814–15 to stem educational progress for the first four decades of the nineteenth century. Professors sympathetic to the ideals of the French Revolution were removed from Pest University by the Hapsburg government.

In the 1830s and 1840s. those seeking Hungarian independence called for a general liberalization of the educational system and the use of Hungarian instead of Latin in the classroom. An 1844 law did introduce Hungarian as the general language of teaching, but because of the continued conservative curricula offered, many Hungarian students went abroad for their university education, mostly to schools in the German sections of the Hapsburg Empire.

Loránd Eötvös University

During the Revolution of 1848, students at Pest University again formally demanded educational reforms and the result this time was Act XIX "On the Hungarian University," which guaranteed freedom of teaching and learning. (The university was now under the control of the Ministry of Public Education.) When the revolution collapsed, however, the Hapsburgs reinstated repressive measures. Once again liberal professors and students were removed from the university and the limited self-government of Pest University was revoked. German became the language of instruction; yet, certain German educational notions, such as free choice of curricula within certain limits, were also introduced and the philosophy faculty became a true university faculty instead of a preparatory school.

About ten years later, the Hapsburg monarchy lost some of its influence and the effect at Pest University was autonomy and the reinstatement of Hungarian as the language of instruction. After the *Ausgleich,* or Compromise, of 1867, Hungary became a partner in the Hapsburg Empire and the new economic and political-social condition engendered reform of higher education. The university began to expand departmentally and physically.

In 1873, the city of Budapest was created by the union of Obuda, Pest, and Buda. The new city became the cultural, political, intellectual, and commercial heart of the new imperial Hungary. Now known as Budapest University, the school became Hungary's most prestigious seat of learning.

Egyetem-tér, or University Square, is only a few blocks from the Danube River near the Elizabeth Bridge in the Inner City district of Pest. Off of the square are the University Church, the Central Library, the Central University building with the law school, and the faculty of arts. The first three are noted for their significant architecture. The oldest of them, the University Church, is considered an outstanding example of Hungarian Baroque and a forerunner of Hungarian architectural style in general. Its architect, the Austrian Andreas Mayerhoffer, brought a full-blown Baroque style to his work in war-torn Pest. The church was finished in 1756 except for its towers which were added in 1768 and 1771. In 1786, the Emperor Joseph II removed it from the control of the Pauline Order and in 1849 it was the site of the Hungarian parliament. In the late nineteenth century it became part of Budapest University, then in the midst of its expansion. A new university library, called Central Library, was designed and built by Antal Skalnitzky (or Szklaniczy) and Henrik Koch between 1873 and 1875 in the neo-Renaissance style. The Central Building and the Law Faculty are neo-Baroque and were built in 1898–99, opening in May 1900. This domed building was designed and built by Fülöp Herzog and Sándor Baumgarten with neo-Baroque features reminiscent of the late eighteenth century and Mayerhoffer.

Other university buildings in the neighborhood housed the faculties of engineering and technology. The impor-

tance of these sites and the change in educational priorities in the twentieth century is implied by the almost continuous expansions which took place there in the 1880s and 1890s. Shortly after 1900, all the available space was exhausted and the faculties relocated to new buildings on the Buda side of the city in Müegyetem Rakpart designed by the university's own architects: Gyözö Czigler, Alajos Hauszmann, and Samu Pecz.

The arts faculty has remained in the inner city on a site once occupied by a thirteenth-century parish school. This was followed in 1717 by a secondary school established by the Piarist Order at the request of the City of Pest. This school, one of the first in the city, became well-respected for teaching and developing the Hungarian language as well as the sciences. In fact, physicist Loránd Eötvös studied there between 1857 and 1865. Early in the twentieth century, however, the building had to be removed to make way for the construction of the first Elizabeth Bridge. The present building, begun in December 1913, was completed in February 1917 by architect Dezsö Hütl. In 1948, the Piarist school was nationalized. The order was given another school in Budapest and the university's arts faculty took over the complex in 1950. The *Egyetemi Szinpad* (University Theater) is also located there.

With imperial status before World War I, the Hungarian government was able to commit more resources to its educational system and one result was a decrease in the number of Hungarians studying abroad. Yet conservative forces at the university restrained progress in most disciplines causing turmoil particularly in the law and philosophy faculties. After 1900, the situation was equally reactive in the sciences where politics, not ability, was the requirement for professorship. Reform movements appeared again in 1918 and 1919 when women and progressives were freely admitted to the university. In 1921, Budapest University became known as Péter Pázmány University in memory of its founder. Progress was once more stymied when Nicolaus von Horty was named regent of Hungary in 1920. He dictated extremely rightist policies through World War II and once again progressive students and professors were banned from the university. Although in honor of its 300th anniversary in 1935, the university was presented with the gift of two completely equipped observatories, law education remained the dominant disciplines into the thirties.

The Hungarian public education system, like other Hungarian social, political, and economic institutions, was reorganized after World War II when the nation fell under Soviet Russian influence. It was then headed by a Ministry of Education and an advisory body called the National Council for Public Education. The National Council instituted changes on all educational levels, particularly the secondary, which now included three types of schools: the Latin or grammar, the modern, and the secondary with a science major. Since then, the proportion of law students has decreased while those of the social and physical sciences, particularly medicine, have increased and relationships between the university and Hungarian industry have been established. In 1949, Péter Pázmány University became Loránd Eötvös University in honor of Hungary's greatest theoretical and experimental physicist. Between 1870 and 1890, Eötvös studied and published in the areas of capillary phenomena and the measurement of surface tension, developing the renowned Eötvös reflection method. His so-called Eötvös Law, which recognized the correlation between surface tension and molecular weights of liquids measured at different temperatures, was fundamental to Einstein's work on relativity. Eötvös also designed the Eötvös Torsion Balance (Pendulum) which measures minute changes of gravity and determines the distribution of masses in the Earth's crust. In 1872, he was appointed to the chair of theoretical physics at Budapest University. He was also responsible for the founding of the university's school of geophysics.

In 1951, the faculty of medicine was detached from Loránd Eötvös University and established at the Medical University of Budapest. During these middle years of the century, the Eötvös Normal School was the principal teachers' training school in Hungary. It was supervised by the University Council which also maintained the Middle School Teachers Examination Committee while a professor from the university served as president of the Middle School Teachers Training Institute. Its curriculum was expanded to include the preparation of technical specialists as well as teachers. The government also required that a certain proportion of students come from working-class backgrounds. The regular length of study was five years followed by two years of research and a thesis if the student desired. Programs for foreign students were also initiated in the 1950s and the university now maintains cooperative agreements with 30 universities.

Since the Loránd Eötvös University was founded by an individual, not the state, it has guarded its autonomy and is still considered an independent legal entity. Although today it is a state-run, nonprofit university, it still maintains controls of its land and resources in cooperation with the Ministry of Public Education. Internal administration is overseen by the university council, made up of the rector, prorector, deans, and prodeans. The present faculties include law and political science, science, arts, and teaching, with attached institutes and postgraduate centers for sociology and social policy, experimental biological research, law, and political science. In 1995, there were 1,817 on the teaching staff and 12,373 students.

Further Reading: K. Polinszky and É. Széchy's *Higher Education in Hungary* (Bucharest: UNESCO CEPES, 1985) provides a broad history of Hungarian education with a socialist flavor. Another brief account will be found in *Universities of the World Outside U.S.A.* edited by M.M. Chambers (Washington, D.C.: American Council on Education, 1950).

—Cynthia Ogorek

LUDWIG MAXIMILIANS UNIVERSITY OF MUNICH
(Munich, Germany)

Location: In Munich.

Description: A state-supported, coeducational university with 60,000 students and faculties, and over 200 affiliated institutes.

Information: Ludwig-Maximilians University
Geschwister Scholl-Platz 1
80539 München
Germany
89 21800

The Ludwig-Maximilians University of Munich is now Germany's second largest university, with a teaching staff in the early 1990s of 3,425 and a matriculated student population of 63,888, surpassed in size only by the Free University in Berlin. It was founded in 1472 by virtue of a bull solicited by Ludwig der Reiche, issued by Pius II from Siena on April 7, 1459, and by a charter from Ludwig himself, duke of Upper and Lower Bavaria and count palatine of the Rhine. First established at Ingolstadt, what is now known as the University of Munich was moved to Landshut, northeast of Munich on the Isar River, as the Ludwig-Maximilians-University in 1800 by the elector Maximilian Joseph IV, who ruled Bavaria from Munich. The university was transferred to Munich by Ludwig I in 1826.

The delay between the original bull and the university's original opening in Ingolstadt in 1472 was occasioned by the duke's war against Albert of Brandenburg and the emperor Frederick III, but, after the opening, 489 students matriculated within the year. In the following two years, the number of students increased until the end of the century, with a peak of 266 in 1514, just before the outbreak of schism split the German-speaking lands into two groups.

Ingolstadt, some 40 miles north of Munich, had been the seat of a royal villa from the early ninth century, and received its charter of civic incorporation in the mid-thirteenth century. Thereafter, it swiftly grew in importance, becoming the capital of a dukedom which was eventually merged with that of Bavaria-Munich. Its fortifications, erected in 1539, withstood the siege by Gustavus Adolphus of Sweden in 1632. The French surrendered the town to the Austrians in 1743, and the university's move to Landshut, caused essentially by a need for a reform so radical as to require relocation, was hurriedly undertaken when the town was again threatened by the French, who besieged it for three months in 1800. After the French victory, the fortifications were dismantled.

The university statutes were adapted from those of the University of Vienna, founded by the Hapsburgs in 1365. Vienna had been the institution hitherto most frequented by Bavarians in search of a university education. The inaugural brief of January 1472 referred to Ingolstadt's new institution as a papally approved *universitas et studium generale* and endowed it with all the privileges which used to be bestowed at Athens and still were at Bologna and Vienna. The bishop of Eichstatt became *ex officio* chancellor, and the ceremonial opening took place on June 26, 1472. A project to make the Ingolstadt church of St. Mary's collegiate fell through. Modeled on the Vienna scheme, it would have given university chairs to its canons, who would therefore be salaried by their benefices, but the endowment was presumably inadequate.

Ecclesiastical revenues were nonetheless used to support the academic foundation, being diverted from a fund that supported some of its beneficiaries to hear mass daily and say a stipulated number of prayers for the souls of the dukes, and also provided for eight psalm singers and an organist to sing over the ducal grave. Such an annexation of a pious bequest required the highest ecclesiastical sanction, duly granted by the bishop of Eichstatt in 1454 and by Paul II in 1465. The university professor of theology seems to have held a prebend at Eichstatt.

A draft charter projected the division of the student body into nations as at Vienna, of Bavarians, Rheinlanders, Franks, and Saxons, but the plan was modified in successive drafts and then abandoned; in 1472 there were neither nations nor consequential student participation in university government. There were two chairs of theology, three of jurisprudence, one of medicine, and six of arts. Professorial appointments were reserved to the duke. Voting was by faculty, with all regent masters having membership of their faculties and at first of the university's general council, for which four years standing as a master was later required.

Very early the faculty of arts split into two opposed camps, nominalists or followers of the *via moderna* of Ockham's followers (emphasizing the transcendance of the divinity), and realists, or followers of the *via antiqua* of Aquinas and Scotus (emphasizing the rationality of divine revelation and divine law). Each camp had its own dean, council, registered students, chest, and *bursae,* or student hostels. The two factions were not officially recognized, since they shared only a single faculty vote, and were forcibly reunited in 1478 at the insistence of the duke, who had ordered the installation of a single dean in October 1477. The *antigui* group attempted to split away again after Ludwig's death on June 9, 1479.

The son and successor of Ludwig der Reiche, Georg der Reiche, carried on his father's patronage of the university, and founded a college not for masters, as was normal in Germany, but for eleven poor students under a regent. The model was that of the Paris foundations, and the institution was known as the Collegium Georgianum. The students were to come from 11 different towns: Landshut, Ingolstadt, Launingen, Wassenburg, Burghausen, Schärding, Braunau, Oetting, Wemding, Hilpolstein, and Weissenhorn. The university was also remarkable in imposing an oath of fidelity to the pope on every student admitted, a condition known formerly only at Caen 22 years earlier, but later revoked there. Ingolstadt, ruled from Munich by Duke Wilhelm IV of Munich from 1508 to 1550, was at the center of resistance to the schism instigated by Luther's refusal to submit to the bull *Exsurge, Domine,* of June 15, 1520. Wilhelm IV, initially inclined to be sympathetic to Luther, turned hostile to the schism, whether from fear of a peasant revolt, or from a desire for an Austrian Habsburg alliance, or even from a possible ambition eventually to become emperor. Ingolstadt not only did not revoke the oath of loyalty to the Rome see, but its rulers were to invite the Jesuits to the university in 1556 with the pope's blessing.

Among the important figures connected with the university in its early years were the poet Conrand Pickel (Konrad Celtis), fiery in his repudiation of Italian claims to cultural superiority, who advanced at Ingolstadt the claims of the lyric poetry of Roman antiquity, and his opponent Jakob Locher, who had been taught by Pickel. Locher quarreled with the Ingolstadt theologians, and was to receive the poet's laurel from Maximilian I in 1497. In addition to the outright hostility of *moderni* and *antiqui* (which did not die down until about 1513), the first four decades of operation brought about the predictable tensions between town and university, mostly concerning clashes between civil and ecclesiastical jurisdictions and exemptions, and between artists and theologians, concerned in 1499 with ceremonial precedence. Noteworthy disturbances occurred in 1507, and a new tax regime was imposed in 1508.

Much more significant than interior tensions however, the university became a leader in the opposition to Martin Luther during the Reformation. Johann Maier of Eck, known from his birthplace as Johann Eck, was Luther's fiercest opponent. From 1517 he was vice-chancellor as well as a professor of theology at the university and a canon of Eichstatt. In 1518 he was obliged against his will to assume the rectorship. It was he who was charged with the publication of *Exsurge, Domine,* in Germany, who disputed against Luther at Leipzig in 1519, holding the primacy of the pope over a general council, and who led the literary pamphlet war against Luther, Carlstadt, and the theology associated with the schism. Consulted about the disputation, Paris decided that Eck had won,

and the Ingolstadt senate made him a financial award. During the plague of 1521 Eck left Ingolstadt and visited Rome, returning after the death of Leo X in December 1521. The university formulated the Bavarian religious edict of March 5, 1522, and was a body steadfastly anti-Lutheran from April 1522. There were ecclesiastical prosecutions for heterodoxy in the city and brief incarcerations of students for under a week for publicly breaking the Lenten fast in 1569.

Numbers at the university began to decrease. In the plague years the numbers were low, only 69 in 1521 and 114 in 1539. In 1521 the university virtually deserted the town, and in 1539 the jurists again fled. In 1549, another plague year, the jurists and unmarried arts students left the town, and the university did not resume full activity for a period. By 1548 the university had reached a state of financial crisis and an appeal was made to Paul III, who on October 24, imposed a tax on the clergy to last three years. However, it was never paid to the university. A new set of regulations in 1555 suggests that the university was felt to be in decline, and there is no account of any centenary celebration such as might have been expected in 1572. A 1555 commission appointed to look into the university's affairs found evidence of financial disorder.

It was at the request of Wilhelm IV that the Jesuits, whose formal foundation as a religious order dated only from 1540, were first invited to teach in the university, and for the next two centuries the history of the university largely centers on its relationship with the Society of Jesus, or Jesuits. They became responsible in 1571 for the arts course, opened a secondary school in the town, and taught in the theology faculty after Wilhelm IV asked Paul III to send Jesuit professors of theology. Wilhelm IV's successor, Albrecht V, was less favorable to the new order, but the emperor Ferdinand in 1555 hoped that they would found their own college in Ingolstadt. A *Capitulatio de erigendo novo collegio theologico in usum Societatis Jesu* was issued in December 1555, and in July 1556 six Jesuits with 12 pupils and servants arrived in Ingolstadt, blessed by the pope before departure from Rome. Tension between the Jesuits and the diocese first arose in 1558, but when the university was ordered to send two theologians to the Council of Trent in 1561, one of those chosen was a Jesuit.

Twenty demands by Jesuit provincial made in 1571 were mostly met, and Duke Albrecht strengthened their hold on the university in 1573. Later a clash with the university resulted in a partial Jesuit withdrawal for two years. The university senate invited the Jesuits to return, and in 1576 the Jesuit college was incorporated into the university. In the following year the duke wrote to the magistrates on behalf of the Jesuits, obtaining charitable status and consequent tax exemptions for their college and seminary. Albrecht V died on October 24, 1579 and under his son and successor, Wilhelm V, who was even more friendly to the Jesuits, there was peace between the order and the university. The Jesuits took over the teaching of Greek in 1582, and a year later the papal nuntius endowed their seminary, to which the duke forced other religious orders to send students.

Student numbers ran at an average of 201 new entrants a year. Notable was the increase in the number of foreigners, particular of noble extraction. Fifteen Polish nobles were admitted with the Silesian prince Alexander in 1580. The plague returned in 1562 and 1563, when most of the university left for Kelheim, and then, when the plague reached that town, for Pfaffenhofen. The student body normally elected nobles as rector, who, in spite of a petition to Sixtus V in 1586, were not allowed to be married until 1642.

Maximilian I, son of Wilhelm V, succeeded his father as duke in 1597, and became elector in 1623, ruling until 1651. Although himself a pupil of the Jesuits, he acted against their encroaching hegemony at Ingolstadt. A pact was concluded in 1613, giving both the university and the Jesuits the right to exclude students from classes. The era of the Thirty Years' War (1618–48) was nonetheless marked by a general lassitude in the university. The canonization of the Jesuit founder in 1622 was celebrated, but the bishops were now appointing substitute vice-chancellors, incidentally including five Jesuits among them. The general inertia continued after the war in spite of a disciplinary edict from the Kurfürst in 1654. An effort was made to prevent Bavarians from studying elsewhere than at Ingolstadt, which, it was noted in 1703, provided all the necessary facilities even for nobles to acquire skills at riding, dancing, and fencing. Salaries were in arrears, and it was found necessary to issue regulations about opening hours, prostitutes, the issue of house keys, and the need to increase the number of night watchmen.

In the early eighteenth century, the elector Maximilian Emanuel, ruler from 1679 to 1726, formed an alliance with Austria against England and France. The university buildings were used for billetting and as a hospital, while teaching continued in private houses of the professors. The rectors were now professors, and there was an annual recruitment of around 145 students. After the reign of the elector Charles Albrecht from 1726 to 1745, Maximilian Joseph III became elector from 1745 to 1777. During this period, only the legal and medical faculties at Ingolstadt appear to have withstood comparison with the mediocre standards obtaining elsewhere in German-speaking territories. The Jesuits were suppressed in 1773, but some ex-Jesuits were retained as teachers at the university. There were disputes over the order's property, but the Jesuit library and natural history collection passed to the university.

Talk of the need to move the university began as early as 1769, but fear of imminent invasion by Napoléon's troops caused the final decision to be made suddenly. Munich was a possible destination, but the small size of Landshut was the attraction that finally swayed the authorities, and the move was sanctioned on November 25, 1799. A fifth faculty of natural and social sciences was now added, and the Napoléonic reorganization of the university took place (as well as its physical relocation to Landshut in 1800). In 1805 Napoléon turned electoral Munich into a royal capital, declaring the Holy Roman Empire dissolved in 1806. Faculties disappeared, and the goals of the university became to service the needs of the state. Ultimate responsibility lay with the ministry of education. Teaching was arranged in a general section with four classes, philosophy, mathematics/physics, history, and art, and a special section with classes in religious teacher training, law/history, economics and administration, and medicine. The professoriate became civil servants, and received a pension on retirement. Degrees took four years, only after which was foreign study licensed. From 1807 degrees were bestowed not with imperial and pontifical authority, but with royal authority.

In 1815, when Munich had a population of about 45,000, Ludwig I, still crown prince, began to redesign the city. He acceded to the throne in 1825 and soon imposed a reactionary regime, lending his weight to the university circle surrounding Görres, Baader, and Schelling. Ludwig I had moved the university to the old Jesuit college in Munich. The 1814 statutes were provisionally kept, to be replaced by the new regulations of 1838 which stipulated five years of study for a degree. The university's fine building on the Ludwigstrasse by Gärtner was erected between 1835 and 1840 (its large assembly hall by Bestelmeyer replacing Gärtner's smaller original, finished in 1909). The university protested against the government's first appointment of a Protestant minister, and it was briefly closed early in 1848. That year it sent seven deputies to the university reform commission at Jena.

The university continued to expand its fields of study, adding a technical school in 1868, and increasing the Protestant faculty while maintaining a strong Catholic faculty. Now functioning as a state-supported institution, enrollment averages 60,000 students in undergraduate and graduate programs. Offering a traditional arts and sciences education, students can choose from 20 departments, including musicology, veterinary sciences, and Far Eastern studies. The university employs nearly 3,500 teachers.

—Claudia Levi

MARTIN LUTHER UNIVERSITY OF HALLE-WITTENBERG
(Wittenberg, Germany)

Location: At Halle in Saxony-Anhalt (Sachsen-Anhalt) on the Saale River, 20 miles (32 km) northwest of Leipzig in the former Eastern Zone of the unified Federal Republic of Germany.

Description: A state-controlled coeducational institution of higher learning formed in 1817 by the merger of the University of Wittenberg (founded in 1502 as an institution of the Catholic Church) and the University of Halle (founded in 1694 as a center of German Protestant Reformation). Its present name was adopted in 1933. The university was under the German Democratic Republic (GDR) administration until 1990. About 11,000 students enroll annually in faculties of: mathematics-science-technology, philosophy, law, theology, economics, agriculture, and medicine.

Information: Martin-Luther Universität Halle-Wittenberg
Rector: (Rektorat)
Universitätsplatz 10
06099 Halle (Saale)
Germany
(0345) 55-21001/02
Fax (0345) 55-27075

Martin Luther University of Halle-Wittenberg is the largest and oldest institution of higher learning in the province of Saxony-Anhalt. Its administrative history began in 1817 when two earlier universities, the University of Wittenberg (universitas vitenbergensis) and the University at Halle (universitas halensis), were merged under Prussian control following the Napoléonic occupation (1813–14). Prussia could not support both universities.

The University of Wittenberg is the older of the merged universities, and has an eventful history in the annals of educational theology. Wittenberg, located 42 miles northeast of Leipzig and 55 miles northwest of Berlin on the Elbe River, served as capital of the duchy Saxe-Wittenberg (1273–1422) until the House of Wettin gained control of the city in 1423.

Various forms of Humanism were embraced by the north German princes; their educational policies reflected "new ways" of thinking. The University of Wittenberg was founded by the elector Frederick II (Frederick the Wise) of Saxony in 1502 as an institution of humanistic learning. Wittenberg later became the site of Martin Luther's crusade to reform the Catholic Church. Through the teachings of Martin Luther, Johan Bugenhagen, and Philipp Melancthon, the University of Wittenberg became a catalyst and center for the Reformation in Germany.

Martin Luther was born in Eisleben, Germany, November 10, 1483. He received a bachelor of arts degree from the University of Erfurt (notable for its humanistic education) September 29, 1502, and received his masters degree January 7, 1505. On July 2, 1505, returning to the university and his law studies, Luther was hit with a sudden bolt of lightening during a thunderstorm. It knocked him to the ground as he prayed, "Ste. Anne help me. [and] I will become a monk." His medieval Christian belief in the renunciation of the world to gain God's favor was typical of his time. He entered the Augustinian monastery in Erfurt on July 17, just weeks later. His parents were upset with his leaving them.

His monastic life was characterized by deep bouts of anguish because of his sins; struggles with Satan; and the fear of God. Eventually, through the scriptures, he found peace. In Saint Paul's Epistle to the Romans text, "The just shall live by faith," Luther became convinced that he must have perfect faith and experience his own true fellowship with God. That was the cornerstone of his teachings.

"Faith," in the Middle Ages had been belief in the impersonal, supernatural powers of God. Luther's challenge to the structure of Catholicism led to an interpretation of Christianity that made God accessible directly to humans, without interference from priests or pope, through prayer. He studied theology at the University of Erfurt and was ordained, celebrating his first Mass May 2, 1507.

Luther brought his theories with him when his confessor and superior, Johan von Staupitz, sent him to teach at the new University of Wittenberg in 1508. He received a baccalaureate in Bible study from Erfurt in 1509, and was sent to Rome on a mission by his Augustinian order. In Rome, he became aware of the personal luxuries of the Pope, the injustices of the papal court, and the plight of poor parishioners and prelates; he was outraged. Luther returned to Wittenberg as professor of Bible literature, receiving his doctorate in theology from the University of Wittenberg, October 19, 1512 (where he was given a house which later became a barracks and is now a museum).

Luther lectured at Wittenberg on the Psalms and from St. Paul's Epistle to the Romans (1513–17), and became convinced that there was no way man could gain special favors from God (especially not through the purchase of indulgences), but he believed that man could find a "gracious God" by accepting what God has done for him in the life, death, and resurrection of Jesus Christ. He became parish priest in Wittenberg, preaching what he believed,

Martin Luther University of Halle-Wittenberg

having affinity with the early Augustinian piety influenced by St. Paul. His idea was not to break from the Catholic Church, but to "reform" it according to scripture.

Luther was a powerful preacher in his own German language. In 1517, John Tetzel (1495?–1519), a Dominican monk, born in Saxony and educated at the University of Leipzig, was sent by the Holy See (Pope Leo X) to sell indulgences (sin-pardoning tickets) in central Germany. The money collected was to be used to help build St. Peter's Basilica in Rome. Frederick the Wise forbid Tetzel to enter his domain. Luther railed against Tetzel by nailing an invitation on the castle church door in Wittenberg on October 31, 1517, for all to debate with him—as was scholarly custom—in speech or writing, regarding the question of indulgences. Luther also attached his famous 95 theses which argues that the Pope could not pardon sins, only God could, and that sinners who repented had no need to purchase indulgences. The unrepentent could not profit by such device, according to Luther, who proceeded to protest other Church doctrine in his theses. These documents were first written in Latin.

Luther meant them to serve as intellectual debate. The distribution of Luther's theses spread quickly over western Europe (due to Gutenberg's printing press and the capability of printing German translations), and a controversy raged among the German princes who were sympathetic, disliking papal interference, and the faithful who attacked Luther. The castle church door was burned during the Seven Years' War (1756–63) and named the "Black Board" ("Schwarzes Brett") by students of Wittenberg University; the monumental brass door which can be seen today with the original Latin text and figures of Luther and Melanchthon (designed and hammered in brass by August Klober of Berlin) was erected in 1858.

Luther was summoned to Rome. His "heretical" display had to be addressed. (Tetzel, himself, issued 100 counter theses.) But Wittenberg University and the Saxon elector intervened, insisting that the German prelate and scholar must be interviewed on German soil. Luther was questioned at the Diet of Augsburg by Cardinal Cajetan (Tommaso de Vio) in October, 1518. He refused to retract his views unless he was proved wrong from Holy Scripture, appealing from Cardinal to Pope and from Pope to the Council.

Legal matters for the Church had been handled by university jurist-prelates, as most universities were extensions of the Church, but at Wittenberg, a long history of civil jurists had prevailed, with titles of "Gutachten," consultants, advisers, experts of arbitration proceedings, providing legal council to princes and citizens of free states. The earliest of these jurists was Henning Göde (ca. 1450–1521) who gained the life title of "monarcha iuris" and wrote the legal statutes for his day ("Konsilien die praxis"). Göde and Hieronymus Schürpf, also professor at Wittenberg, were Luther's legal advisers during these trials. Melchior Kling, a Wittenberg law professor, 20 years after Göde's death, wrote 109 "Consilia" (statutes), and Wittenberg Ordinarius, Matthias Wesenbach, who began open practice as "Gutachter" in 1576, also made history in German "Konsilien" (statutory) literature.

During Luther's trial period, Carl von Militz, a German papal legate rebuked Tetzel's 100 counter theses for their "exceptional language" and "improper procedure," and Luther agreed to refrain from further discussion pending arbitration by German bishops. That silence was broken when Luther responded to a challenge of German Catholic theologian Johann Eck to debate the age of the papacy and its divine origin at Leipzig in July 1519.

In 1520 Luther wrote his three great treatises: "An Address to the Christian Nobility of the German Nation," "On the Babylonian Captivity of the Church," and "The Liberty of a Christian Man." In the same year, Pope Leo X issued a bull condemning Luther's doctrines and threatening him with excommunication. Luther had 60 days to recant, but instead, burned the bull and a volume of canon law on December 10, 1520, outside the walls of Wittenberg under an oak tree in the presence of students, professors, and citizens.

Charles the V (Holy Roman Emperor) convoked his first diet of princes and representatives of free cities in 1521 at Worms, where Luther was asked, once again, to recant. Luther issued his famous statement, "Here I stand, I cannot do otherwise," and was placed under the ban of the Empire.

By order of Frederick the Wise, Luther was hijacked and placed "for safe keeping" in Wartburg Castle near Eisenach under the pseudonym, "Junker Jorg." It was there Luther wrote the treatise, "On Monastic Vows," and translated the New Testament from the Greek text of Erasmus into German. He later translated the Old Testament, with the help of Johannes Bugenhagen, professor of theology at Wittenberg and lifelong friend.

In 1522, Luther returned to Wittenberg to mediate a dispute which had arisen between his followers (who were destroying Catholic churches) and political authorities (so-called Peasant Wars). His tract against the unruly "faithful" led to rejection of his views by some of his followers. In 1525, he married Katharina von Bora (1499–

1552), one of several nuns who came to Wittenberg under the influence of his teachings; she bore him six children.

Luther's later career was prodigious, writing Bible commentary, tracts, sermons and hymns, including "A Mighty Fortress Is Our Lord." Emperor Charles V was too busy fighting the French, Turks, and the Pope to deal with Luther, and he was left alone to expound his stated beliefs. With the help of his colleagues, Johann Bugenhagen and Philipp Melanchthon, Luther revised his Bible translations and furthered the cause of Protestantism.

The University of Wittenberg was critical during the first stages of the Reformation. It was where Luther lived, taught, studied, and preached. He attracted a number of like-minded theological reformers to Wittenberg, of whom Philipp Melanchthon was especially prominent.

Educated at the Latin school of Pforzheim (1507–8), the University of Heidelberg (1509–11), and at Tübingen (1512–14), where he began teaching, Melanchthon published "Rudiments of Greek Grammar" ("Institutiones gramaticae Graecae") the first of his many textbooks for elementary schools and universities in 1518.

On August 29, 1518, four days after meeting Luther on his arrival to Wittenberg, Melanchthon gave an inspired inaugural address, "De corrigendis adolescentiae studiis" (On Correcting the Studies of Youth), which attracted the interest of Luther, who was to become his friend and colleague. Melanchthon had already seriously questioned scholastic theology and ecclesiastical morality through his own readings in Wessel, William of Ockham, Aristotle, and the Bible. He turned to the study of theology and received his bachelor's degree in Wittenberg in 1519, the same year he assisted Luther with the debates at Leipzig. His was the voice of clear arguments against the primacy of the pope.

Melanchthon was never ordained, although he received his degree in theology and taught the subject. His "Loci communes rerum theologicarum" (Commonplaces of Theology"), first published in 1521, and his lectures on St. Paul's Epistles to the Romans, were the first systematic statement of Protestantism and provided logical, argumentative force to the Reformation.

While Luther was away at Wartburg Castle, Melanchthon served as leader of the Reformation. Luther had said to Melanchthon, when he was summoned to Worms: "my dear brother, if I do not come back, if my enemies put me to death, you will go on teaching and standing fast to the truth; if you live, my death will matter little."

In 1526, Melanchthon became professor of theology and was sent to unify the constitutions of the newly reformed churches with 27 other commissioners. At the Diet of Augsburg in 1530, with Luther still outlawed, Melanchthon delivered the "Confession," a conciliatory effort to delineate 21 articles of faith drawn up with Luther's help. His "Apology" followed a year later. For his work in training teachers, writing textbooks, and reorganizing schools and universities, Melanchthon was named "Preceptor of Germany." His "Unterricht der Visitatoren" ("Instructions for Visitors"), a basic school plan, was published in 1528. Enacted into law, it established a Protestant public school system in Saxony. Melanchthon also helped to establish universities at Marburg, Königsberg, and Jena, and instituted fundamental reforms in Greifswald, Wittenberg, Cologne, Tübingen, Leipzig, Heidelberg, Frankfurt-Oder, and Rostock.

Melanchthon developed beliefs contrary to true Lutheranism and was later accused of crypto-Calvinism, being more rationalistic and humanistic than evangelical in his tolerance of Catholic ceremony ("adiaphora," matters of no great consequence to the acceptance of evangelical doctrine). He broke with Reuchlin, who remained a Catholic Humanist, and was accused of heresy by antihumanist Lutheran theologian, Flacius Illyricus.

Luther died in 1546; Melanchthon in 1560. Both were buried in the "Schlosskirche" in Wittenberg where pilgrims can view their professorial houses, now museums, and other remnants of the Reformation and the history of Wittenberg University.

The University of Halle, founded by Frederick III, the elector of Brandenburg (later King of Prussia) in 1694 as a center for Protestant theology, has been called the first "modern" university. It renounced religious orthodoxy in favor of objectivity and rationalism, scientific attitudes, and free investigation. Canonical texts were replaced by systematic lectures and disputations by seminars. German instead of Latin was the language of instruction; an elective system replaced the formalized curriculum. Professors were given virtual control of their class rooms. This relative liberalism was adopted by the University of Göttingen a generation later, and by most American universities. Jurist Christian Thomasius and theologian August Hermann Francke were distinguished faculty members,

and the university was always innovative and progressive. At the Francke Institute in 1717, J. Juncker opened the first university clinic; in the middle of the 1800s Dorothea Christiane Erxleben was the first woman in any German university to receive a doctoral degree.

The French Emperor twice suppressed the university during Napoléonic Wars, and the victor, the Prussian king, could not afford to keep both universities running. The Universities of Wittenberg and Halle were merged in 1817. The university was renamed Martin Luther University of Halle-Wittenberg on November 10, 1933 under the National Socialist dictatorship of Adolf Hitler. The university was under the Soviet Ministry and German Democratic Republic Ministry of Education from 1946 to 1990 and went through the same problems as other universities in the eastern sector: faculty loss; ideological reorganization; upheavals and student unrest, yet managed to stay open and expand.

In April 1993, through the integration of the "Pädagogische Hochschule" (teacher's college) of Halle-Köthen, and the division of the Technical College of Merseberg, the mathematics-science potential of the university became augmented. For the first time in its history, the university was able to offer an engineering component. Because of its new faculty, the university will be able to formulate more interdisciplinary curricula and institutions.

Further Reading: There have been many books written about the German Reformation, Martin Luther, and Melanchthon. D.H. Lawrence provides vivid sketches of the Reformation and its people in *Movements in European History* (London: Oxford University Press, 1921).

—Carol Shilakowsky

MASSACHUSETTS INSTITUTE OF TECHNOLOGY
(Cambridge, Massachusetts, U.S.A.)

Location: On the banks of the Charles River in Cambridge, Massachusetts.

Description: A private university enrolling approximately 10,000 students at the undergraduate and graduate levels.

Information: Mr. Michael C. Behnke
Director of Admissions
MIT, Room 3-108
77 Massachusetts Avenue
Cambridge, MA 02139-4307
U.S.A.
(617) 253-4791

Visiting: Tours depart from the Information Center at 10 A.M. and 2 P.M., Monday through Friday, except holidays. For more information, telephone the Information Center at (617) 253-4795.

From its beginnings, the Massachusetts Institute of Technology—private, independent, and nonprofit—has been the antithesis of the isolated ivory tower. Its mission is pragmatic, linked to current events and the solving of real-world problems. The MIT emblem depicts the scholar and the craftsman side by side, and the school has as its motto *mens et manus*—mind and hand. The school's mascot is the beaver, to represent industriousness and renown for its engineering and mechanical talents.

The reason for MIT's success is simple: its scholars are, and have been since its inception, on the cutting edge of research. The school's roster of firsts is long and distinguished: MIT researchers created the first chemical synthesis of penicillin and Vitamin A; they developed new types of artificial limbs, high-speed photography, and magnetic core memory, which led to the creation of digital computers. In classrooms and laboratories, students and professors diagrammed bridges and highways, designed skyscrapers, developed sophisticated navigational and electronics equipment and, during the Cold War, created missile defense systems.

Boston Tech, the forerunner of the Massachusetts Institute of Technology, was founded in 1861, when wooden ships still plied the Atlantic and horse-drawn carriages rattled over cobblestone street near the school's original Boston campus. Today, the school can proudly boast of being "the only private U.S. university that is federally designated as a land grant, sea grant, and space grant institution."

The school was founded by William Barton Rogers, a scientist and educator. Rogers had graduated from the College of William and Mary in Virginia. His father taught natural history but William was not primarily interested in a career as a traditional classroom teacher. He was captivated instead by the era's enterprising industrial spirit. Rogers was also influenced by ideas advanced a century earlier by Benjamin Franklin, who had foreseen the need for schools devoted to science and technology. Rogers took the idea one step further, envisioning an industrial school that would approach science, steel making, and bridge building with the same sophistication and depth that Harvard College had already brought to the study of the humanities.

The school's beginnings were halting, but were sustained by its founder's tenacity and vision. In 1859, Rogers asked the Massachusetts legislature for permission to start a polytechnical school. The legislature rejected Rogers's first two proposals, but agreed, in 1861, to grant the school a charter after Rogers had persuaded benefactors to donate $100,000. Two years later, the school qualified for a portion of the federal land-grant money which the state had received through the Morrill Act, though plans for building were delayed by the Civil War. On February 20, 1865, just as the war was ending, Boston Tech's first students began classes in a rented section of the downtown Boston Mercantile Building. Rogers was named Boston Tech's first president.

The school originally had three sections: a society of arts—a short-lived program in which inventors and industrialists lectured students; a museum of technology, which acquired only a few trinkets and quickly faded away; and a school of industrial science, which prospered and gradually grew into the modern university. The industrial school focused on finding ways to use science for the betterment of industry, business, and society, making Boston Tech unique among its contemporary trade schools for linking theoretical science to applied uses. Other schools, meanwhile, concentrated simply on teaching students.

The school, called Boston Tech for its first 55 years, centered on Rogers's pioneering emphasis on scholarly laboratories, in which teachers used diagrams to clarify lecture topics and involved students in the performance of experiments. The laboratories' purpose was two-fold: to provide a setting for instruction, and to allow the class, led by the teacher, the chance to break new ground in research.

Massachusetts Institute of Technology

Success, setbacks, and new opportunities came quickly for the school. In 1869, two professors, Charles W. Eliot and Francis H. Storer, revolutionized the teaching of inorganic chemistry by publishing a popular textbook. Only a year later, Rogers suffered a stroke and stepped down as president, just as the school awarded its first 14 degrees. Rogers assumed the presidency again, from 1879 to 1881. He died in 1882.

John Daniel Runkle was acting president during Rogers's absence, and had to deal with an early threat to MIT's independence. Charles Eliot had become Harvard's president in 1869, ad the following year proposed a merger with Boston Tech. Runkle declined. Harvard didn't give up, though, and made another unsuccessful bid for Boston Tech in 1878.

In 1904, Eliot proposed yet another plan for merger of the two schools. This time, Boston Tech's governing body, the Corporation, ignoring alumni and faculty disapproval, accepted. But the Massachusetts Supreme Court blocked the merger, saying it violated school charters. At last, in 1959, Harvard and MIT forged a durable compromise, establishing a Joint Center for Urban Studies.

Women had, almost from the beginning, been allowed to take classes at Boston Tech's Lowell Institute evening classes, though their futures in the technical field were assumed to be limited. In 1871, Ellen Swallow was admitted as the school's first regular woman student. She would later become a faculty member and founder of the home economics movement.

Another graduate, Katherine Dexter McCormick, helped lead the women's suffrage movement and, after women won the right to vote in 1920, was elected vice-president of the League of Women Voters. It was not until the 1960s, however, that large numbers of women were enrolled at the school.

As the end of the nineteenth century approached, inventors discovered new ways to harness electricity. In the 1870s scientists had devised methods to derive power from electrical generators and motors. In 1879, Thomas A. Edison unveiled his incandescent lamp and an accompanying dynamo, which fed electricity to the lamp. Three years later, Edison opened the world's first central electric power plant in New York City.

Boston Tech soon absorbed the new techniques, causing major changes in the school's focus. The same year Edison's power plant opened, MIT's Charles Cross, an 1870 graduate, established the school's first electrical engineering course. By the end of the decade, Boston Tech was also offering its first course in chemical engineering, a discipline which focuses on finding uses for natural products such as coal, gas, and water. In 1887, Edison donated equipment to the school for use in the teaching of electrical engineering. The famous inventor later declared, "I have found the graduates of the Boston Tech have a better, more practical, more useful knowledge as a class than graduates of any other school in the country."

But even as its scholars were working on the cutting edge of technology, Boston Tech's campus was becoming outdated. In 1909, the school's sixth president, Richard Cockburn Maclaurin, a physicist and mathematician, decided to move the school to Cambridge. He chose a site along the banks of the Charles River with a view of the stately homes on Boston's Beacon Hill.

Welles Bosworth, a Boston Tech graduate, designed the buildings at the campus's center. Bosworth created a concrete dome for the library, in imitation of the dome Thomas Jefferson had designed for the University of Virginia. Bosworth added some of his own touches as well. He linked the buildings together via an "infinite corridor" in order to demonstrate that the school's diverse specialties are driven by a common purpose.

The "infinite corridor" connects five of the school's main buildings and is about three football fields long. Twice a year, its axis coincides with the elliptical plane, which is the sun's apparent path through the sky. When the alignment occurs—at 4:19 P.M. on November 12 and 4:49 P.M. on January 31—sunlight fills the corridor. Hundreds of students and professors line the hall for the event. Later additions to the Cambridge campus were designed by some of the century's most noted architects, including Alvar Aalto, Eduardo Catalano, Eero Saarinen, and MIT graduate I.M. Pei.

In 1916, the newly renamed Massachusetts Institute of Technology held a gala celebration to christen the new campus. A 21 gun salute greeted 500 New York alumni who arrived. The playfulness that characterizes many MIT activities was also evident. A group of MIT's first graduates from 1870 walked slowly with the aid of canes until, suddenly, they tossed them aside and nimbly jumped rope.

The alumni in question were drawing on an old, still living tradition of pranks, or, as they are known on campus, "hacks." A hack differs from an ordinary college gag. Hacks are clever, harmless jokes. Famous MIT hacks include the emergence of an expanding balloon from the football field during a Harvard-Yale football game, the placement of a mock police cruiser atop the library dome (complete with a box of jelly donuts on the front seat) and the measurement of the Massachusetts Avenue Bridge in "Smoots," the height of a fraternity brother named Smoot. Smoot's old fraternity still makes sure the measurements are fresh and readable.

With the onset of World War I, MIT was in a better position than ever to fulfill William Rogers's goal of practical usefulness. The United States severed diplomatic ties with Germany in 1917, and MIT President Maclaurin immediately wired the War Department and promised MIT's help. The school immersed itself in war-related research, creating training programs for pilots and flight and radio engineers.

The period between the world wars was a period of photographic innovation at MIT. In 1934, Harold Edgerton and Kenneth Germehausen devised a new form of electrical circuitry that paved the way for high-speed photography. Edgerton also perfected the modern stroboscope, which emits light beams as narrow as .1 millionth of an inch as often as 100 times per second. The device had many scientific applications, but it was also utilized for art. The stroboscope enabled photographers to take clear pictures of a speeding bullet or step-by-step photos of a single golf swing. Most school children have encountered such pictures in their science texts. A number of Edgerton's photos were considered both artistically and scientifically significant.

During World War II, former MIT Dean of Engineering Vannevar Bush was appointed to the commission responsible for war-related activities. Bush, who had invented a predecessor of the analog computer, played an important part in guiding the nation's wartime science policy and helped position MIT for its integral role in the war, which solidified the school's reputation as a topflight research institution.

The core of MIT's war effort was its radiation laboratory, known on campus as the Rad Lab. Primarily, it focused on the development of radar, a crucial instrument that gave the Allies a key advantage over the Axis powers. Though radar was not itself invented at MIT, many of the major advances were made there. The Rad Lab laboratory started small, taking up about 15,000 square feet, but quickly developed into a massive facility. At its peak, it took up 15 acres and had a staff of 4,000. Only the Manhattan Project atomic bomb research team was larger. Though research on the atomic bomb was conducted elsewhere, the school provided much of the expertise that made the Manhattan Project a success.

The Rad Lab made major contributions to the Allied war effort, It turned out a total of 150 military systems, including devices that could spot enemy submarines and airplanes, and enabled bombers to hit targets at night. Edgerton developed ultra-high speed stroboscopic photography for night reconnaissance. Charles S. Draper devised a more accurate gunsight and, after the war, started MIT's instrumentation laboratory, which developed rocket-steering systems later used in the Apollo space program. Immediately after the war, MIT formed the research laboratory of electronics, a peacetime version of the radiation laboratory. At the same time, the school created the laboratory for nuclear science and engineering.

During the war, MIT's Jay W. Forrester had begun work on what would become the Whirlwind I computer, the largest, fastest, and most powerful of the early electronic computers. It included a device that translated symbolic commands and performed tasks. In the 1950s, Forrester used Whirlwind as the basis for an early-warning air-defense system.

The war had solidified MIT's contractual relationship with the government, and, in its aftermath, administrators developed similar links with industry. In 1948, the school created the industrial liaison program, which called for corporate sponsors to pay MIT researchers for working on their companies' technical problems. Scholars at MIT had sometimes to extend themselves beyond the institution's customary areas of expertise, but administrators justified the work by saying the income kept the school independent.

Meanwhile, university researchers continued their trailblazing work. In 1948, Claude Elwood Shannon, an MIT Ph.D. recipient who was later an MIT professor, developed a mathematical theory of communication that would be known as information theory. His work focused on the myriad language options from which people select to communicate. This work, of major importance to the study of communication, also opened new paths of research in mathematics. Practical applications were soon found in the areas of telecommunications and automation.

The Cold War's Soviet threat brought many government contracts to MIT. In 1952, MIT's Lincoln Laboratory—a Lexington, Massachusetts-based, federally-sponsored center for research on electronics—developed plans for a computer system that would alert the United States in the event of a military attack. Six years later, the Lincoln Laboratory used radar astronomy to map Mars's surface and Venus' atmosphere.

In 1956, William Shockley became the first MIT alumnus to win the Nobel Prize, for his development of the transistor radio. Many others followed, including Charles H. Townes (1964, for the invention of the laser), Robert S. Mulliken (1966, for chemistry), and Paul Samuelson (1970, for economics), who also wrote a best-selling economics textbook. To date, 28 individuals associated with the school as faculty, staff, and alumni have won Nobel Prizes. Twelve of these individuals are currently on the faculty and one on staff.

Nor is the Nobel Prize the only measure of MIT's international reputation. The school boasts numerous faculty at the top of their respective fields, one of the best known being Avram Noam Chomsky, a linguist who was also an outspoken opponent of the Vietnam War. Chomsky revolutionized linguistics studies by focusing on explanatory principles instead of methods of classification, the typical subject of study. His writings include books on the Vietnam War (*American Power and the New Mandarins,* 1967), on Middle East (*Peace in the Middle East,* 1974), and on terrorism (*The Culture of Terrorism,* 1988).

Massachusetts Institute of Technology has stayed on the cutting edge. During the 1950s, Bob Mann, the head of the school's Design Center, began assigning students to design tools for use by the disabled. Such assignments gave students a chance to work with real-life needs in mind. This line of research led, naturally enough, to the design of artificial limbs. One of the most interesting projects was the design of an artificial knee, one that would be able to respond to the thought commands of its user. More than 20 years of research and advances in technology led finally, in 1990, to the development of a working model.

The university continues to break ground in other areas as well. In the late 1950s, Richard Feynman, Nobelist and MIT graduate, had predicted the design of incredibly small devices. Though the public may since have grown blasé about microchips, researchers at MIT are currently working on techniques that would enable them to engineer at the molecular level. Should this research prove successful, the practical consequences would be profound. Tiny, extremely sensitive devices could be designed that would do everything from detecting diseases and pollutants to making suggestions during food preparation.

While quantifying an institution's reputation is difficult, the school's statistics remain impressive. A Gallup Survey of international leaders ranked MIT as one of the leading universities in the world, in a class with Oxford, Cambridge, Princeton, and the Sorbonne. Massachusetts Institute of Technology registers more patents each year than any other American university. In 1995, MIT had the top-ranked graduate school in management and engineering, and was tied for first place with four other graduate programs in economics, according to *U.S. News and World Report.* In a survey of Ph.D. rankings, the MIT program in economics shared first place with Harvard, Princeton, Stanford, and the University of Chicago. The MIT Sloan School of Management ranked first in academic reputation and placement success. Among engineering schools, MIT ranked first in aerospace, chemical, civil, mechanical, and nuclear engineering.

With the benefit of hindsight, William Rogers's early predictions of the school's success seem prophetic. Years before his initial proposal to the Massachusetts legislature, Rogers had envisioned the future of the institution he was to found:

I doubt not that such a nucleus-school would, with the growth of this active and knowledge-seeking community, finally expand into a great institution comprehending the whole field of physical science and the arts with the auxiliary branches of mathematics and modern languages, and would soon outshine the universities of the land in the accuracy and the extent of its teaching in all branches of positive knowledge.

MIT's adaptability and innovation have allowed it to realize Rogers' vision, and make it one of the world's most important universities. The school has diversified to such a degree—in architecture, economics, business management, computers, and oceanography—that, at the end of the twentieth century, it is helping to lead the country out of the industrial age and into a new, high-tech global economy driven by computers and high finance. The school now offers degrees in the humanities and social sciences, but it is its focus on industry, technology, and science that has shaped its mission, and that accounts for its stellar reputation.

Further Reading: Samuel C. Prescott's *When M.I.T. Was "Boston Tech"* (Cambridge, Massachusetts: Technology Press, 1954) gives a detailed history of the university from its founding in 1861 to its move to Cambridge in 1916. *M.I.T. in Perspective,* by Francis E. Wylie (Boston: Little Brown, 1975), provides a more general overview up to the mid-1970s. Those wishing an overview of more recent achievements at MIT may consult *Up the Infinite Corridor: MIT and the Technical Imagination,* by Fred Hapgood (Reading, Massachusetts: Addison-Wesley, 1993).

—Bill Coyle

McGILL UNIVERSITY
(Montreal, Canada)

Locations: On the historic main campus at Sherbrooke Street West and elsewhere in and around the city of Montreal.

Description: Private Anglophone university chartered in 1821; now with about 30,000 students.

Information: McGill University
845 Sherbrooke Street West
Montreal, PQ
H3A 2T5
Canada
(514) 398 4455

McGill University, an Anglophone institution in a largely Francophone province, has long since weathered the political, legal, and religious controversies that surrounded its foundation in the early nineteenth century, to become one of the leading universities, not only in Quebec but in the developed world. Its survival and flourishing are the result of the generosity and goodwill of its many benefactors among the former Anglophone commercial and professional elite, and of the uniquely bilingual and multicultural character of Montreal.

The university's origins are complex and not a little bizarre. While most sources agree on assigning its foundation in the year 1821, when its first royal charter was issued, a law providing for its creation and financing had actually been passed 20 years earlier. The history of McGill can therefore be said to have started in 1801, when Montreal, the largest city in what was then called British North America, was the metropolis of Lower Canada (roughly equivalent to modern Quebec). That province, then as now, was largely populated by French-speaking Roman Catholics and was governed from Quebec City, but the numbers of English-speaking immigrants were already rising sharply, especially in Montreal itself, while the only institution of higher education in the province, the Séminaire de Québec, located in Quebec City, was controlled by the Catholic Church and was exclusively Francophone. The legislature of this divided society was unexpectedly given control of the large estates formerly owned by the Society of Jesus (the Jesuits), which the Catholic Church had just dissolved (temporarily, as it turned out), and passed a law to establish a Royal Institution for the Advancement of Learning. This Anglophone learned society would be based in Montreal and would operate a university college under a provincial charter, as well as three grammar schools to prepare students for entry to it.

The schools were duly established, but the college was not. The sponsors of the Royal Institution had a great deal of enthusiasm and some expertise to offer, but their ambition to use the new institutions to teach English to Francophones made them unpopular, and they lacked the funds to activate the charter, largely because of the £49,000 available from the Jesuit Estates Fund between 1801 and 1831, £37,000 disappeared into spending for "general purposes" (including bribery and corruption), leaving barely enough for the three schools for younger students. The French colonists who had endowed the Jesuits cannot have dreamt that the revenue from their lands would eventually either line the pockets of Protestant politicians or be spent on educating Protestant boys.

In 1813, while the Royal Institution was still being starved of funds, the Protestant elite in Montreal received news of the death of one of their number, the Honorable James McGill. He had been born in Scotland in 1744 but had settled in the city in the 1770s, becoming one of its prominent and wealthy fur traders. In his will he assigned to the Royal Institution a remarkable bequest of £10,000 and a 46-acre estate (Burnside Place), providing that the money was to be spent on a university, one college of which was to be named for himself, to be built on the estate. Its location on sloping ground between Mount Royal and the St. Lawrence River promised to put the college close to the center of the city's business and social life, and it seemed that at last the legislation of 1801 could be put into effect. Accordingly, the sponsors established themselves as trustees of the bequest, formally opened the Royal Institution in 1819, and in 1821 proceeded to establish the University of McGill College under a new charter, granted by King George IV of Britain.

However, these were empty gestures. In the meantime, relatives of McGill's wife's first husband had taken charge of Burnside Place and McGill's money and refused to surrender them. The charter had become legally necessary to ensure that the ten-year limit which McGill had placed on his bequest could be observed, but it took nine years of court cases (1820–29), proceeding all the way to the Privy Council in London (then the highest court for colonial disputes), for the trustees to obtain Burnside Place, and then another eight years (1829–37) for them to obtain all the £10,000 bequeathed 24 years earlier. This bizarre and expensive litigation rendered both the Royal Institution and the college little more than letterheads, although one faculty was established in the

McGill University

interim, in 1829, by the simple expedience of ceremonially taking possession of the estate and announcing that henceforth the Montreal Institute of Medicine, founded quite separately in 1821, would be known as the medical faculty of the college. The medical faculty, the only part of the college which had any staff or students at all, did not use a building on the estate until 1833 and departed to a more convenient site in 1841.

In 1839 the trustees, celebrating victory in the last of their legal battles, at last initiated the building of the rest of the college at Burnside Place, although there were still some more complications to sort out before they could proceed. They could only afford to do so by selling off part of the land, accepting a grant from the provincial government, and persuading Queen Victoria, the college's visitor (a kind of one-person court of final appeal, peculiar to universities in the British tradition), to dismiss the Reverend John Bethune, the profligate and barely educated principal whom they had appointed to help prepare for the new institution. In 1843 they formally established the faculty of arts, with just 20 students, in the building which the faculty still occupies today.

In 1852, under a new royal charter issued by Queen Victoria, the Royal Institution was merged into the college. As a result the members of the university's board of governors, which controls its finances, also serve formally as trustees of the Royal Institution even today. From the outset, they largely restricted themselves to financial administration, enhancing the endowment by attracting further gifts and bequests from William Molson, head of the brewing dynasty; Sir William Macdonald; Lord Strathcona; and other leading members of the Anglophone commercial community in Montreal.

As for academic affairs, the governors saw to the establishment of a law faculty in 1853, and then placed most matters in the capable hands of Sir William Dawson, a geologist from Nova Scotia who was principal of the college from 1855 to 1893. Dawson's own work as a practitioner and promoter of scientific thinking helped to make McGill better known. He was one of the founders of the Royal Society of Canada, and he was the only person ever to preside over both the British and the American Associations for the Advancement of Science, but he was perhaps better known in his lifetime for his work on fossil plants and his stubborn resistance to Charles Darwin's theory of evolution by natural selection.

As principal of McGill, Dawson was effectively at the pinnacle of the system of Anglophone Protestant schooling in Lower Canada, providing education for a small but relatively prosperous and influential minority separately from the Francophone Catholic population, who were served by their own school system and, also from 1852, by Laval University in Quebec City (successor to the Grand Séminaire de Québec). Dawson and his colleagues took their responsibilities seriously. Not content with just training high-achieving students for the professions, the

central function of universities since the twelfth century, they proved themselves true Victorians with a number of significant innovations, responding both to the wishes of benefactors and to the increasingly complex needs of the rapidly developing Anglophone community, most of whose members retained a deep-seated loyalty to Britain and to Protestantism. In 1861 they used a large gift from William Molson to fund the creation of the first of McGill's many libraries. In 1865, 1873, 1876, and 1880 respectively they welcomed the theological colleges of the Congregational, Presbyterian, Methodist, and Episcopalian churches as affiliates. In 1878 they opened a faculty of applied science, complete with laboratories and trained technicians, and supplemented it in 1882 with the Redpath Museum, the first purpose-built museum of natural history in Canada. Today, it is perhaps better known as the place to see skulls and other remains from the Iroquois settlement, Hochelaga, which stood on the campus site in the late sixteenth century, as well as an oyster shell, found by Dawson himself on Mount Royal, which proved that the region was once under the sea. They created the McGill Normal School, to train teachers for the Protestant education system, and started a network of colleges capable of preparing students for McGill examinations, on the pattern of the University of London. They admitted women students to the university, from 1884 onwards (as did the University of Toronto), just four years after London had become the first university in the British empire to do so.

The many distinguished men and women who graduated from McGill during Dawson's era made their own contributions to Canada's development, both before and after Lower Canada, renamed Quebec, joined in founding the new country in 1867. The principal's own son, George Mercer Dawson, was the leading surveyor of Canada's two borders with the United States (along the 49th parallel and with Alaska) and of the route of the Canadian Pacific Railway, the completion of which was the condition for British Columbia's also joining Canada (rather than continuing as a separate colony or even, as many had predicted, joining the United States). The bill to fund the railway was sponsored in the federal parliament by a fellow-alumnus, Sir James Alexander Grant, who was not only a politician but a wealthy and influential doctor whose patients included governors-general of Canada and Princess Louise of Britain. Another McGill-trained physician, William Osler, taught at the university before finding greater fame as the author of *The Principles and Practice of Medicine* (1892), a standard textbook throughout the English-speaking world until the 1920s.

While most McGill alumni, then as now, came from Anglophone backgrounds there was an important minority of students from the Francophone population even in Dawson's day, many of them defying the hostility of parents, friends, or priests to gain access through McGill to the rest of the world's second largest country. Perhaps the most prominent among them remains Sir Wilfrid Laurier, the first French-Canadian to serve as federal prime minister (from 1896 to 1911). Like his successors Louis St. Laurent; Pierre Trudeau; or Jean Chretien, in more recent times, he was vilified both by nationalists on the Francophone side and by anti-Quebec elements on the Anglophone side of Canadian society, but he succeeded in making a lasting impact. He was responsible for the financing of Canada's second transcontinental railway, the creation of the provinces of Alberta and Saskatchewan, and the compromises on schooling in the western provinces which did much (though critics said not enough) to protect the interests of Francophones there. His unsuccessful moves to introduce free trade with the United States and downplay Canada's dependence on Britain were derided at the time as, among other things, evidence of his having been corrupted by McGill's cosmopolitan atmosphere, but they can now be seen to have been simply too far ahead of their time.

Meanwhile back at the campus, James McGill's remains had been transferred in 1875 from the Old Protestant Cemetery to a new grave, marked by a gingko tree, in front of the arts building, and in 1885 the college had taken the name McGill University. Dawson's ambitious program of modernization, analogous to similar reforms at London, Oxford, Cambridge, or Harvard, was continued by the next principal, Sir William Peterson. When he took over in 1893 the university had more than 1,000 students, and was already renowned for having the most advanced laboratory equipment of any university in the world.

Peterson appointed Ernest Rutherford to a professorship in 1898. Rutherford's experiments at McGill, conducted in collaboration with Frederick Soddy (also an eventual Nobel laureate), and his preparation of the classic text *Radio-Activity,* published in 1904, give McGill some claim to being the place where nuclear physics was born, even though Rutherford returned to Britain in 1907. Peterson also helped to establish three more affiliates. Of these, McGill College in Vancouver has since become independent, as the University of British Columbia; Macdonald College, founded in 1907, continues to thrive on its own extensive Montreal site, where it specializes in agriculture and food science; and Royal Victoria College, opened in Montreal in 1899 with funds from Lord Strathcona, has lost its teaching function and is now a residence for women students.

Two great fires on the campus, both unexplained, occurred in 1907. The buildings housing the medical and engineering faculties were both completely destroyed, but were quickly replaced with gifts from the university's increasing number of benefactors. By 1915 the university's endowment, continually enhanced by the Molsons, Macdonald, Strathcona, and others, stood at 6.7 million Canadian dollars, which made it one of the richest educational bodies in Canada, let alone in Quebec, where the Francophone Laval University (then on two sites, in Montreal and Quebec City) had just 15,000 Canadian dollars. Expansion continued throughout World War I, when many McGill alumni went to fight in Europe. They are commemorated by the university's sports stadium, which is named for Captain Percival Molson, who died in battle in 1917.

In 1920 McGill's finances were further enhanced with its first major grant from the provincial government, a fund of 1 million Canadian dollars given partly because Laval University and the new Francophone University of Montreal had each received the same amount and the politicians feared accusations of discrimination. McGill continued to prosper between the two world wars, notably during the principalship of Sir Arthur Currie, who had been the commander of the Canadian soldiers in World War I and who therefore had unparalleled connections in the federal capital, Ottawa. The university's scientific schools in particular benefited from greater interest among benefactors and students alike. Otto Maass, himself a graduate of McGill, was at the forefront of the university's increasing interaction with government and commerce, serving not only as Macdonald Professor of Chemistry and supervisor of McGill's first graduate students in science, but also as a leading member of the Defense Research Board and president of the Pulp and Paper Research Institute. The interwar years also saw, for example, the creation of the McGill Social Science Project, set up by Leonard Marsh in 1930, which quickly made its name as the source of controversial reports on many aspects of Canadian life.

Student numbers more than doubled between 1939, the year that Canada followed Britain in declaring war on Nazi Germany and Fascist Italy, and 1948, rising from 3,400 to more than 8,000. Mature students returning from military service made up a large proportion of the increased enrollment. Cyril James, principal from 1940 to 1962, shrewdly used this rise in the numbers and composition of the student body to argue successfully for increased funding from the federal government and to persuade it, and other benefactors, not to neglect the humanities or social studies while building up the politically more fashionable and commercially more relevant science faculties.

During the 1960s and 1970s McGill was affected, although to a less extent than the Francophone universities, by the combined impact of worldwide student revolt and Quebec's "Quiet Revolution," which saw the secularization of education, the rise of the separatist Parti Québécois, and eventually, after it came to power in the province in 1976, the flight of around 100 major corporations from Montreal to Toronto. McGill, long since oriented far more toward the whole of Canada and to other English-speaking countries more than to Quebec itself, was insulated from events to some extent, although it had to fight proposals to link provincial funding with increased use of French. During these years many Canadians, both at McGill and beyond, came to appreciate that this Anglophone but cosmopolitan university has contributed just as much to the special character of Montreal—which differs in significant ways from Quebec City or the countryside—as the Université de Montreal, where the nationalist mood was more prevalent. It was also in this time of change that Leonard Cohen, another McGill alumnus, first found fame through the poems and songs which have formed his own distinctive contribution to the continuing Quebec renaissance.

Today, McGill is at peace with the city and the province. Perhaps its combination of federal, provincial, and private funding has so far avoided excessive interference by any one of these three sources. As in the days of Sir William Dawson, Ernest Rutherford, or Otto Maass, its staff and students can still work on research of importance far beyond the boundaries of Montreal or Quebec. The days when it could be dismissed as a bastion of British imperialism, or of Anglophone arrogance, are long gone, and all but the most extreme separatists have accepted that it plays a valuable dual role. McGill is the university of choice for the Anglophone minority, which may be less wealthy or powerful than in Victorian times but is still an integral part of the Montreal scene; and it serves Quebec as one of many vital links to the rest of Canada, and to the Untied States, with which Quebec must cooperate whether it remains part of Canada or not.

Further Reading: Stephen Leacock's *Montreal: Seaport and City* (Garden City, New York: Doubleday, 1943) still evokes the city's history and atmosphere at least as well as more recent publications and includes an entertaining chapter on McGill. More specific and detailed histories include Stanley B. Frost's two-volume work *McGill University for the Advancement of Learning* (Montreal: McGill-Queen's University Press, 1980–84).

—Monique Lamontagne

MICHIGAN STATE UNIVERSITY
(East Lansing, Michigan, U.S.A.)

Location: East Lansing, Michigan, 90 miles west of Detroit.

Description: A state university enrolling approximately 40,000 students in undergraduate, graduate, and professional schools.

Information: Office of Admissions and Scholarships
250 Administration Building
Michigan State University
East Lansing, MI 48824
U.S.A.
(517) 355-8332

Visiting: The MSU Student Alumni Foundation conducts campus tours year-round, except during term breaks, registration, holiday weekends, and final examination weeks. Call (517) 355-4458 for more information.

One of the initial public calls for the founding of a college to teach future farmers in Michigan was made at the state's first public exhibition and celebration of agriculture. At the first Michigan state fair in 1849, orator E.H. Lothrop noted that although 90 percent of the state pursued agriculture as a profession, there existed no school that taught the art and philosophy of this vocation.

The impetus behind Lothrop's speech had come from the Michigan Agricultural Society, founded in the same year. One of its main goals was to establish a college where students could learn scientific agriculture. Under the leadership of secretary John C. Holmes, the Michigan Agricultural Society petitioned the state legislature for an agricultural college.

The Michigan state legislature, in turn, petitioned the United States Congress for a land grant. Previously, land had only been granted to each state as it was admitted to the union for the establishment of one university to prepare men for the learned professions. Such a university was founded in Michigan during its admission as a state in 1837. The University of Michigan trained men in nearly every field except that in which four-fifths of the state's population was engaged—farming.

Before the gift of land from the national government, the state included in its second constitution a provision that "the Legislature . . . shall, as soon as practicable, provide for the establishment of an Agricultural School." Although both the University of Michigan and the Michi-

gan Normal College (now Eastern Michigan University) wanted the agricultural college, the state's agricultural society decided that a separate school should be established. On February 12, 1855, Michigan Governor Kingsley S. Bingham signed the law that founded the Agricultural College of Michigan.

The college formally opened on May 13, 1857, with dedication services held in the chapel of College Hall. Located where the landmark Beaumont Tower now stands, College Hall was the first building in the United States built specifically for instruction in scientific agriculture. The day after the services, 63 students started classes. This number, almost unprecedented for the opening day of a new college in the United States, grew to 81 in a few weeks.

The unique curriculum of the school was comprised of two-thirds science and one-third liberal arts classes. "Agriculture" was not one of the classes offered by the school. At that time, agriculture was a newly emerging field of study and had no precedent in the curriculum. Most of the students had already acquired basic farming skills at home. In the classroom they were to learn the theoretical scientific principles upon which agriculture was based, in classes such as animal and vegetable anatomy and physiology, mineralogy, botany, chemistry, and veterinary science. They learned to apply these principles in laboratories, experimental farms, and eventually during a lifetime of farming.

Manual labor was required of all students—and of professors—from the first day of classes until 1896. Students spent nearly as much time in the fields as they did in the classroom, about 15 hours a week. They earned up to eight cents a day for performing specialized tasks under the watchful eyes of their professors. At first, these tasks largely consisted of removing stumps, clearing the land, and even constructing and repairing the buildings of the college itself.

For the first decades of its existence, the college suffered an identity crisis: few people in the state knew it was a college. The campus at that time barely resembled a civilized settlement, much less an institution of higher learning. It covered 676 acres of forest about three miles west of the state capital, Lansing, itself no more than a small frontier village. In addition to its primitive location, the college faced serious financial problems in its first years. The state board of education, at the time the governing body of the college, believed that the experimental farms would make the school a self-sustaining institution. In order to control spending, in 1860 the board converted the college to a two-year vocational school that would

Michigan State University

teach only farming skills, ignoring the "extraneous" liberal education then offered.

The college received a new lease on life when, in the midst of the Civil War, President Abraham Lincoln signed the Morrill Act. This act provided land grants to support in each "loyal" state a college "where the leading object shall be, without excluding other scientific and classical studies and including military tactics, to teach such branches of learning as are related to agriculture and the mechanic arts . . . in order to promote the liberal and practical education of the industrial classes in the several pursuits and professions in life."

The prototype for the 72 land grant colleges and universities would be the Agricultural College of Michigan, the school that had initiated the petitions that led to the Morrill Act. The state received 250,000 acres of land. The land was sold and the profits deposited in an endowment fund that secured the financial future of the college. The state senate, led by Michigan State's first president, Joseph Williams, then restored the four-year curriculum.

Finally on solid financial footing, the college grew rapidly, at first focusing on scientific agriculture and then expanding to more accurately reflect the land grant mission. The college was one of the first to admit and grant degrees to women. In 1870, ten women enrolled, studied agriculture, and worked the fields; they did not disrupt campus life and proved studious and well behaved. The general sentiment seemed to be that they were a good influence on the rest of the students. In 1896 a separate curriculum for women was established. In classes such as nutrition, meal planning, and dress design, in addition to the liberal arts classes, women were taught skills that were considered relevant to their prospective careers. To further embrace the mission of the Morrill Act, a mechanical engineering department was added in 1885.

One of the integral philosophies of the college was that it existed to enrich and educate the farming community at large, especially within the state of Michigan. In the 1860s, leading scholars and professors such as Robert C. Kedzie and William J. Beal began sharing their agricultural research with Michigan farmers. They traveled to six communities throughout the state to teach, listen to, and work with the farmers. These "Farmers' Institutes," held each year during the college's winter break, were the forerunners of an extension service that has expanded to become one of Michigan State's primary missions.

The Hatch Act of 1887 gave federal funding to establish an agricultural research station at each land grant college. In 1894 the first "Short Course" (adult continuing education) for creamery managers helped Michigan agricultural workers realize that the college was beneficial to their businesses. By 1982, the university counted 14 field stations and 3,000 research projects.

The school year initially spanned the summer months so that students and professors could work the farms and fields on campus during the growing season. However, this schedule was found incompatible with those in the rest of the academic world and so the school year was altered to run from autumn to spring.

By the late 1890s, enrollment had dropped, and many of its outstanding professors left for other land grant institutions. The national economic depression, the ever-present malaria from the still-forested swamps, and the general rowdiness of the student body led to such a falling off of public confidence that a rumor surfaced suggesting that the governor planned to turn the college into a sugar-beet farming prison camp.

With the change in the century came the beginning of a two-decade upswing at the college, which was renamed the Michigan Agricultural College (MAC) in 1907. The manual labor requirement had been abolished, and departments of veterinary medicine (1909) and business (1925) were added. In those two decades, the number of faculty increased five-fold and the number of students quadrupled. This explosion was partly due to the school's president, Jonathan Snyder, a dogged promoter of MAC, who visited prospective students' homes whenever possible, at times traveling by bicycle if there was no livery stable in the student's town.

The college continued to expand its extension and cooperative functions during the first decades of the new century. The passage of the Smith-Lever Act of 1914 established the Cooperative Agricultural Extension Service, which provided for an agricultural agent from the school to be placed in each county. In the spring of that same year MAC held its first Farmer's Week. This annual event, which featured meetings, lectures, discussions, and demonstration sessions by livestock associations and other groups, drew great crowds to East Lansing. A farmer's day, held annually in late July, also educated, assisted, and entertained many Michigan citizens.

The college also grew physically. Private donations and gifts created Olds Hall, the union, a library (now Linton Hall), a stadium, and Beaumont Tower. Under the direction of President Robert Shaw and Secretary John Hannah in the 1930s, growth was stimulated by New Deal agencies. The National Youth Administration supplied funds for jobs for 12 percent of the student body. Funds from the Public Works Administration helped finance Abbot and Campbell Halls, the auditorium, the music building, Olin Health Center, and Jenison Fieldhouse. The Works Progress Administration backed the construction of sidewalks and roads, Farm Lane bridge, the track and field facilities, in addition to improving the union and the football stadium. Those entrusted with the building and maintenance of the campus still strove to preserve the tradition of informality in the grounds' appearance. Dedication to this ideal throughout the various expansions of the campus has resulted in what students and visitors often have judged the most beautiful campus they have ever seen.

The college's new name, changed to the Michigan State College of Agriculture and Applied Science in 1925, reflected the increasing emphasis on education beyond agriculture. From its founding and especially after the Morrill Act, the school was committed to providing a broad liberal education in addition to the one in agricultural and mechanic arts. In the first century of its existence, one of the overriding trends was toward a broader education encompassing all fields.

The man who became president of the college in 1941, John Hannah, was largely responsible for the development of Michigan State University from a relatively small agricultural college to a major American university. Hannah, who had overseen the building programs at Michigan State as its secretary during the thirties, assumed the presidency on the eve of World War II. To prepare for the war, the work of those students who were leaving for duty was accelerated, and women were trained to fill the positions the soldiers vacated. In addition, the college trained some 10,000 air cadets, engineers, language and culture specialists, and reservists as part of the massive war effort.

In the waning years of the war, Hannah began to make plans to reorganize the curriculum for the time students would return. In a 1946 interview with the *Detroit News* he said of his, and the school's, renewed philosophy of education that "our task is to make not merely better farmers or veterinarians or engineers but better citizens, capable of appreciating the finer things of life, able and willing to take their part in shaping the destiny of their country." This new philosophy was realized in the Basic College with its two-year curriculum of classes in natural science, humanities, social sciences, and English required for all students.

Michigan State continued its commitment to extension and continuing education. The Kellogg Center for Continuing Education, the nation's largest facility for hotel, restaurant, and institutional management studies, and the first major facility for adult residential education, was erected in 1951. In 1959, Alfred and Matilda Wilson gave the university their Meadow Brook estate, located in Oakland County north of Detroit. With this property and additional funding from the Wilsons, an extension college for training teachers, engineers, and businesspeople was established. Wishing to preserve its autonomy, the university named the new school not Michigan State University—Oakland, but simply Oakland University.

Enrollment exploded during Hannah's 28-year administration, from 6,300 in 1941 to 40,820 in 1969. The curriculum and the size of the campus grew as well. The College of Communication Arts and Sciences, the first of its kind in the nation, was established in 1955. The Honors College (1956) and the College of Human Medicine (1964) were added. Fifty-six new buildings, including the Kresge Art Center, a cyclotron, and a food science building were constructed. The college was renamed twice during Hannah's tenure: Michigan State University of Agriculture and Applied Science in the institution's centennial year of 1955, then simply Michigan State University in 1964.

As enrollment grew, MSU was competing with other organizations for state funding. When raising student fees was proposed, Hannah responded that the university should not reject talented people because they lacked funds. He said that such action would "create an upper class of the sort for which there is no place in a democracy." He also opposed student loans on the grounds that students would be saddled with onerous debt as they tried to begin their careers and start their families.

Late in his presidency Hannah was caught in a difficult situation associated with the then-escalating Vietnam conflict. In its April 1966 issue, *Ramparts* magazine reported that the university had hired at least five CIA (Central Intelligence Agency) agents as "police administration specialists" and had given them faculty rank. Hannah responded that the university's staff had "well-founded suspicions" that CIA agents were on its staff. However, he denied that the university had deliberately acted as a "spy operator" for the CIA.

Michigan State University continues to engage in important scientific and technical research. Since 1964, it has been a member of the Association of American Universities, an elite group of 58 of the nation's leading graduate research universities. Research in the early days of MSU helped lead to the development of hybrid corn, the homogenization process of milk, and a cure for brucellosis (better known as undulant fever, a debilitating disease for humans, acquired by direct contact with infected animals or animal products). More current research has focused on anticancer drugs, crops that produce biodegradable plastic, and turf for indoor athletic arenas.

The largest university in the state and the sixth largest university in the nation in 1993, Michigan State consistently boasts a student body numbering around 40,000. It is the only university in the country offering three medical schools (the College of Human Medicine, the College of Osteopathic Medicine, and the College of Veterinary Medicine). The main campus is an eclectic mix covering 2,100 acres that includes aspects of a botanical laboratory, city park, farmlands, and ivy-covered college buildings. An additional 3,100 acres includes experimental farms, research facilities, and natural areas.

At the close of the twentieth century, the pioneer land grant university remains dedicated to the ideals of the Morrill Act: to provide access to a practical and liberal education for the widest number of people. It was used as the prototype for the land grant colleges because of its precedent-setting agricultural curriculum. In the past century and a half, MSU has increasingly emphasized the need for a broad understanding of the philosophy and practice of the liberal arts and sciences.

Further Reading: Madison Kuhn's excellent *Michigan State: The First Hundred Years, 1855–1955* (East Lansing: Michigan State University Press, 1955) is an authoritative account of the founding and history of Michigan State University. Kuhn and Lyle Blair produced a condensed version, called *A Short History of Michigan State* (East Lansing: Michigan State University Press, 1955) for the school's centennial. Particularly informative for recent history are Paul Dressel's *College to University: The Hannah Years at Michigan State, 1935–1969* (East Lansing: Michigan State University Press, 1987), which also explores the curriculum and ideals of the land grant institutions in depth, and *A Memoir,* by John A. Hannah (East Lansing: Michigan State University Press, 1980).

—Cindy Mertz

MOUNT HOLYOKE COLLEGE
(South Hadley, Massachusetts, U.S.A.)

Location: An 800-acre campus located along the lakes in suburban South Hadley, 90 miles west of Boston.

Description: A women's college with approximately 2,000 students, offering graduate and undergraduate studies in liberal arts and sciences.

Information: Office of Admissions
College Street
South Hadley, MA 01075
U.S.A.
(413) 538-2023

The opening of Mount Holyoke Seminary in 1837 marked the establishment of the first women's college in the United States. Its founder, Mary Lyon, was a teacher on a mission to create affordable and accessible education for women. Lyon was born in 1797 in Buckland, Massachusetts, one of eight children from a deeply religious family. At the age of 17 she secured a job for 75 cents a week teaching summer session classes to school children in Buckland. In 1817 she attended Sanderson Academy in nearby Ashfield, paying her tuition from her savings and money earned by selling quilts. In 1821 she decided to enter a seminary school for young women in Byfield, north of Boston. Against her family's wishes she used her inheritance to finance her studies there.

After graduating from Byfield she secured a teaching position at Sanderson Academy, where she met Zilpah Polly Grant, who founded Ipswich Seminary in 1828; in 1830 Lyon joined her friend and became assistant principal. When Grant took a leave of absence due to poor health, Lyon was left in charge of the academy. It became apparent to her that the Ipswich Seminary was not adequately endowed and would not be a permanent school for women. In 1833 she decided to leave Ipswich to establish a permanent educational institution for women. Distributing a series of pamphlets and articles, she began to raise funds and recruit students. In "School for Adult Females," she described how costs would be kept to a minimum by having students perform all the domestic duties. "Address to the Christian Public" argued that idle young women would prove more valuable in society as qualified teachers. In September 1834, a formal organization was created to concentrate on the establishment of the seminary. A group of ministers and educators began to search for a location for the school. Meanwhile, Lyon

was knocking on the doors of her neighbors in Ipswich asking for donations.

Early in 1835 Reverend Joseph B. Felt and George W. Heard were surveying the towns near the Connecticut Valley, where the idea of a women's school was strongly supported in Sunderland, South Deerfield, and South Hadley. When the committee announced that at least $20,000 would be required to start the school, South Hadley responded overwhelmingly at a public meeting, and the money was raised immediately. Reverend Edward Hitchcock, a committee member and Amherst College professor, suggested a name for the school. Combining several Greek words meaning "all the powers of woman—physical, intellectual and moral," he suggested Pangynaskan Seminary. Lyon and the committee disliked the name, and opted for a simpler one, a name that described the location of the school. Outside of South Hadley stood a mountain called Mount Holyoke. In April 1835 the name Mount Holyoke Female Seminary was chosen.

Construction was being planned even as Lyon continued fund-raising. In 1836 she mailed hundreds of letters to women in New England pleading for money, hoping for donations of $50 or $60 to furnish a dormitory room; however, the response was bleak. The country was in the midst of an economic depression and times were hard. Lyon decided personal visits could prove more profitable; accordingly, she made personal pleas at schools and to individuals, and slowly money began to trickle in. Opening day was set for autumn 1837. There were over 200 requests for admission for a school that could accommodate 80. Lyon accepted 50 women; the others were put on a waiting list. Acceptance was contingent upon the student's providing money or furnishings for one dormitory room.

The building which housed the college stood five stories high. The dining room was located in the basement. The first floor housed the seminary hall in the south wing and the library, two parlors, and the principal's rooms in the north wing. The upper three floors were dormitory rooms, 16 to a floor. Suitable for two occupants, the rooms measured 18 feet by 10 feet, with a 5-foot lighted closet. Each room was furnished with a bed, chest of drawers, table, chairs, washstand, mirror, and an open Franklin stove for heat.

The school opened with eight women on November 8, 1836. Charging $60 a year, Mount Holyoke Seminary became the first school to offer college-level education to women (with the exception of Oberlin College in Ohio which was a coeducational school). The seminary had

Mount Holyoke College

one principal, Mary Lyon, two instructors, and three student assistants. The curriculum included literature and philosophy (in 1845 Latin would be added as a required course). Lyon also emphasized the study of the sciences for women. A deeply religious woman, she viewed the sciences as a study of the works and creations of God. A seven-course study in science and chemistry was required of all women. These courses involved lectures, recitation, and laboratory work. The laboratory method was very important to females, according to Lyon, since "they have a less number of years for the pursuit and as their time must be more occupied with other things." A guest lecturer, Reverend Edward Hitchcock of Amherst College, visited the seminary once a year to speak on the latest advances in chemistry, physiology, and geology.

As principal, Lyon also drilled the women on domestic responsibilities. An alternating group of 14 students rose at 5:00 A.M. each day to prepare breakfast. Another group performed the clean-up, and another scrubbed floors and stairwells. Having students perform these chores eliminated the need for servants and introduced an element of equality to the student body. Students were also expected to walk one mile a day. Monday was a recreation day which meant that no classes were held. However, Lyon disliked idleness. The students were expected to do their laundry and sewing on Monday. In addition to studies and housework, each student practiced religious exercises. Two half hours of silent prayer (one in the morning and another in the afternoon) were required during the day. On weekends study and recitation of the Bible was required. On Sunday the women were expected to attend two church services. Non-believers and "lost souls" were converted by Lyon at religious revivals at the school.

The poet Emily Dickinson arrived at Mount Holyoke Seminary to study as a 17-year-old. She described the average school day as beginning at six, breakfast at seven, study at eight, followed by devotions at nine. Classes and music practice took place until 12:30 when the main meal, dinner, was served. The meal was followed by more classes, then a daily inspirational lecture from Principal Lyon at 4:30. Supper was at six, followed by silent study until 8:45. Dickinson finished one year and then returned to her home in Amherst, Massachusetts. Like two-thirds of the women, she did not return after her first year. Only 10 percent of students were graduated. The reasons for dropping out were usually lack of money, marriage, homesickness, or illness.

When enrollment had increased to 120 students by 1840, the trustees approved the addition of a new wing to the main building. However, disaster struck. A terrible typhoid epidemic hit the school. Forty women became ill and nine died. Accusations were made against the seminary that the girls were being worked too hard or that the facilities were unsanitary. Enrollment dropped when the school reopened in October.

With only 80 students enrolled, the school had to recruit another 40 women from a waiting list.

Lyon's health had been affected by the typhoid epidemic of 1840, and by 1846 she was declining rapidly. Now 50 years old, she was plagued by colds and lung problems. In late February 1849 she fell gravely ill and died in bed at the seminary on March 5, 1849. Her successor was Mary W. Chapin, an 1843 graduate of the seminary. On the day of her appointment, November 18, 1852, the board approved both a four-story addition to the main building and the erection of an observatory.

Health problems at the school continued in the 1850s. Another typhoid epidemic struck the seminary during the 1852–53 term. A serious fever in 1854 put 140 women under doctor's care and resulted in one fatality. Teachers and administrators were especially conscious of the health problem, since women's education in general was coming under attack from such sources as the *New York Ledger,* which published an attack on education in an article titled "Murdering Girls at School." Mount Holyoke was taking great care of its facilities when, in 1857, three students died of scarlet fever, followed by two more cases of typhoid. Mount Holyoke decided to appoint a school physician, Dr. Mary A.B. Homer. Realizing that physical exercise was a method of combating illness, the board began to raise funds for the construction of a gymnasium. Construction began in 1863.

In 1861 the seminary fulfilled one of Lyon's wishes by moving from a three-year program to a four-year course of study. Following the Civil War, the school was in debt for $25,000. Building facilities, long out of date, were desperately in need of renovation. The trustees immediately began to campaign for funds and approached the state legislature. They were granted $400,000 because the seminary had demonstrated a high standard of scholarship and character. The outstanding debt was paid and improvements were made: steam heat replaced the open stoves; an elevator was installed; the old oil lamps were removed to make way for gas lighting and chandeliers.

With so much emphasis on the study of science, in 1870 the trustees addressed the lack of a science building. A local businessman, A. Lyman Williston, donated $10,000 for construction of one. Alumnae created the Mary Lyon Fund to supplement the donation. On June 1, 1875, the cornerstone was laid for the building, called Lyman Williston Hall, which would cost $50,000. Three floors were dedicated to lecture halls, classrooms, and science displays; the top floor was an art gallery. Williston patented an invention for this building that would be used on campuses everywhere. Called the "Mount Holyoke Adjustable Arm Rest," it was a convenient movable desktop allowing students to take notes.

Celebrating the 50th anniversary of the school, whose campus had expanded from 15 to 50 acres, alumnae pressed for the seminary to become recognized as a college. The curriculum was revised and new by-laws were established. On March 8, 1888, the school officially became a college under the name Mount Holyoke Seminary and College. Mary Brigham, an alumna, was chosen the first president of the college. Tragically, she was killed in a train accident outside New Haven that June. Elizabeth Storrs Mead of Oberlin College and Abbot Academy in Andover, Massachusetts, was appointed in her place.

Changes marked the last years of the nineteenth century at Mount Holyoke. The 1893 commencement ceremony saw the graduates wearing caps and gowns for the first time and the word "seminary" was dropped from the name of the school, making it Mount Holyoke College. In 1895 Mary Lyon's tradition of students performing the domestic duties of the school ended. Money was allotted to employ domestic workers.

A fire broke out in the gymnasium in September 1896 and by morning the main building lay in ruins. A serious year of rebuilding began. Countless gifts were received, due to the fire and in honor of the centenary of Lyon's birth to be celebrated on February 28, 1897. This money supplemented an endowment fund of $80,000. John D. Rockefeller donated $40,000 toward the building of a dormitory. Within a year four new dormitories were ready (Brigham, Safford, Porter, and Pearsons), and Rockefeller Hall was nearing completion. At the original site of the main building the new Mary Lyon Hall was also nearly finished.

As the new century approached, Mount Holyoke was involved with two presidents, one of the United States and one of the college. In 1900, the college was visited by President William McKinley, whose daughter Grace was a graduating senior. The president was presented with an honorary degree, and he participated in the commencement exercises by handing out the diplomas to graduates. With the new century came a new president for the college. Mary Emma Woolley, the daughter of a Congregationalist minister, was one of the first women to receive a degree from Brown University. A former professor at Wellesley College, Woolley was inaugurated as president of Mount Holyoke in May 1901. One of her first acts as college president was to appoint her companion from Wellesley, Jeannette Marks, as professor of English at Mount Holyoke. The favoritism that Woolley showed the demanding Marks (in housing and in course assignments) did not go unnoticed by colleagues.

By the end of her first decade at Mount Holyoke, Woolley doubled enrollment. The school's endowment grew to $300,000 and six new buildings were added to the campus. A member of the Massachusetts Women's Suffrage League, the president established the Equal Suffrage League at the college (which included 200 students and almost two-thirds of the faculty). In 1930 Woolley was rated one of 12 "Greatest Women Living in America" by *Good Housekeeping Magazine*. In her company were Jane Addams, Helen Keller, and Willa Cather.

The 1930s brought the Great Depression and difficult years for the country and for Mount Holyoke. Enrollment was dropping, and the college was operating in the red. To prevent layoffs, the faculty, with the exception of Marks, took a voluntary 10 percent pay cut. Woolley announced she would retire in 1937, the centennial year for the school. Rumor suggested the board of trustees wanted her to leave office earlier. Now in her seventies, Woolley's attention to the college was waning, and rumors circulated that both her physical and mental health were deteriorating. As early as 1932 "the Committee on the Succession to the Presidency" was established. In 1936 the committee announced that Roswell Gray Ham of Yale University was to be Woolley's successor. Married with two sons, and an ex-marine, Ham was the first male president of Mount Holyoke. Both Woolley and Marks were outraged at this action. They argued that the college had worked for a 100 years to prepare women for leadership roles and that this appointment defeated that purpose. Together they launched a campaign to overturn the appointment of Roswell Ham. Their appeals were met with indifference. The country was suffering through the Depression, and alumnae cared more about the college's financial problems than about women's issues. Mary Woolley never returned to Mount Holyoke after her retirement. The new president began rebuilding and restructuring the school. More male faculty were hired. Modern, functional buildings were added, the designs of which steered away from the academic Gothic look. Enrollment began to increase and, in 1948–49, a series of dormitories set along the lakes that would accommodate the growing student population was built. Originally called Lakeside, the dorm complex would later be named Louise Terry Hall.

Mary Lyon's emphasis on the study of science continues. One-fourth of the students major in a science. Today the college ranks number one for graduating the most women who go on for a Ph.D. in scientific fields. The biographical book *American Men and Women of Science* lists 99 women who are Mount Holyoke graduates. The oldest academic building on the campus is the John Payson Williston Observatory. Built over a century ago, it houses the latest in scientific equipment and includes a 24-inch reflecting telescope and an eight-inch Alvan Clark telescope. For the study of physics, Mount Holyoke offers the only particle accelerator at a college in the United States.

Gone are the evangelical revivals and in their place are the interdenominational services of Eliot House. The chaplins of Eliot House serve all religions and the Kosher/Hallal kitchen prepares meals according to the dietary traditions of the Jewish and Muslim faiths. Students of all denominations and beliefs can experience Wa-Shin-An in the Japanese meditation garden and teahouse.

Mount Holyoke has attracted faculty members who have distinguished themselves in literature and politics.

In 1967 John Irving joined the faculty as assistant professor of English. During his next 11 years at Mount Holyoke he would write four novels, the fourth becoming a bestseller. In 1985 Shirley Chisholm, first black woman to serve in the House of Representatives, spent a year at Mount Holyoke as guest lecturer.

Mount Holyoke remains the only school among the Seven Sisters Colleges that does not admit men. Honoring Mary Lyon's traditions and goals, the college continues to educate women to become leaders in society. Graduates of Mount Holyoke include Elaine Chao, director of the United Way; Nancy Gustafson, Metropolitan Opera soprano; economist Shelby White; and Olympic Gold Medalist Holly Metcalf. In 1989 the oldest living black graduate spoke at commencement. Frances Williams entered Mount Holyoke in 1915. Author Wendy Wasserstein was graduated from Mount Holyoke. Her play *Uncommon Women and Others* tells of six Mount Holyoke women during their college years, when they were full of ambitions and feminist aspirations; six years later they reunite to examine actual achievements in the real world.

Mount Holyoke's founder, Mary Lyon, was honored in 1987 when she appeared on the two-cent stamp. Feminist Lucy Stone (class of 1839) and writer Emily Dickinson have also appeared on postage stamps. Other alumnae featured on postage stamps include Frances Perkins (class of 1902), who served as Secretary of Labor under President Roosevelt, and Virginia Apgar (class of 1929), the first female professor at Columbia University Medical School.

Further Reading: A good biography of Mary Lyon is Elizabeth Alden Green's *Mary Lyon and Mount Holyoke: Opening the Gates* (Hanover, New Hampshire: University Press of New England, 1979). Arthur C. Cole's *A Hundred Years of Mount Holyoke College* (New Haven, Connecticut: Yale University Press, 1940) provides a thorough history of the college from 1837 to 1937. Anna Mary Wells covers the life and career of Emma Woolley in *Miss Marks and Miss Woolley* (Boston: Houghton Mifflin, 1978).

—Patrice Kane

M.V. LOMONOSOV MOSCOW STATE UNIVERSITY
(Moscow, Russia)

Location: Within the city of Moscow.

Description: A comprehensive university, better known as Moscow University, or "M.G.U.," enrolling more than 30,000 students in undergraduate and graduate programs.

Information: Head of the International Education
Department
Moscow State University
Moscow, 119899
Russia
(95) 939 4220
(95) 939 3510

Moscow State University was founded by an imperial decree in 1755 from Empress Elizaveta Petrovna, daughter of Peter the Great. The decree is said to be in response to the "Report to the Senate" of Count Ivan Shuvalov. The proximity of the young count to the empress may have been another factor. Count Shuvalov, Gentleman of the Bedchamber and lover to the middle-aged Elizaveta, occupied quarters adjoining hers. Shuvalov brought much in the way of cultural advancement to the city. Elizaveta agreed when Shuvalov told her that he and Mikhail Lomonosov, now remembered as the father of Russian science, wanted to form a university in Moscow.

Lomonosov, a member of the Academy of Sciences in St. Petersburg, was the son of a peasant fisherman who had first come into that city a poor youth, later to become an important figure in geology, meteorology (the study of iceberg formation), literature, philology, rhetoric, and history.

The university, open within a year, was located in a building on Red Square, with faculties in philosophy, law, and medicine, and a preparatory school for prospective students. The only university in Europe without a faculty of theology, it was, at Lomonosov's insistence, open to all races, all religious groups, and all social classes other than serfs.

The first university students came from the seminaries, which presented the only source of university-ready students in Russia at the time. Lectures were in Latin. Students wore green uniforms with red collars, lived in a dormitory, and were closely regulated and supervised by faculty. A majority of the faculty were products of the German Enlightenment. Lomonosov was known for quarreling with such men, but they influenced one of the first important graduates of the university, Denis Fonvizin, civil servant, translator, political satirist, and leading playwright of the 1770s and 1780s.

From the beginning, teaching at the new university fostered consideration of the era's concept of natural law, which asserted that there is a kind of law innate in human nature. Because this newly imported theory implied that power came from the people and not from God, this idea would bear upon relations between the autocracy and the universities it governed well into the next century, setting a precedent of contention between academy and state that would end only after the death of Lenin.

At the advent of the nineteenth century, Moscow University was still the only university in Russia, with no more than 100 students. Fifty years after the founding of Moscow University, few landowners were willing to send their sons to Moscow to be educated. Those members of the gentry who were educated were usually given tutors or sent to foreign schools.

During the reign of Catherine II, a Commission for the Establishment of Public Schools was set into motion, but did not really begin work until after her death. Her son, the emperor Paul, authorized in 1800 the reopening of the university at Dorpat (a German university conquered by Peter the Great), a year before he was strangled; the university at Dorpat reopened in 1802. There was also a Polish academy at Vilnius, which was made a university shortly after a national school system plan was announced in 1803, under the next emperor, Alexander I. Universities at Kazan, Kharkov, and St. Petersburg were added, and each of the six universities was given responsibility for an educational region.

The University Statute of 1804 granted autonomy (similar to that of other European universities) to Russian universities, allowing professors to take charge of their universities and educational regions and allowing for the creation of learned societies such as the Moscow University Society of Russian History and Antiquities, the Moscow University Society of Mathematics, the Imperial Mineralogical Society, and others. A new faculty of philology was added to Moscow University that same year.

In 1786, Moscow University had moved to a classical-style building at the corner of Bolshaya Nikiskaya Street and Mokhovaya Street (later renamed Herzen Street and Marx Prospekt by the Communists). The building was damaged in 1812 during Moscow's temporary fall to Napoléon and the great fire that came with it. Rebuilding began in 1817 with a new, Russian Empire-style facade. Another building was added on another corner of the same intersection in 1833. It would later become the House of Culture.

Moscow State University

With the victory of Russia over Napoléon and France, the Russian autocracy was at its zenith. Emperor Alexander I, who expanded the educational system and public access to it, took a new view of the intellectual life of his nation. When, in August 1816, the aging minister of Popular Enlightenment, Count Alexis Razumovsky, asked to be relieved, Alexander I replaced him with Prince Alexander Golitsyn, the over-procurator of the Holy Synod of the Russian Orthodox Church and leader of the Russian Bible Society. In October 1817, Golitsyn's post became "the Ministry of Spiritual Affairs and Education," which operated under the principle that a proper education must be based upon "Christian piety." The bearing of this religious notion on the intellectual character of the Russian university system took little time to show itself. In 1820, a publication at St. Petersburg University led to the firing of the author and four other professors, the replacement of many other non-compliant university professionals, and a temporary end of autonomy for all Russian universities.

Nicholas I came to power in December 1825 to face immediately the first of the eventually successful series of Russian rebellions, the Decembrist Uprising, which was quickly swept aside, but not without the notice of both emperor and populace. He wasted no time in ensuring that the universities were in check. Changes in the conduct of academic affairs were made subtly, beginning with improvements. Incompetent professors were sent into retirement, and the salaries of others were raised, some of them tripled. New institutions were opened. However, the new emperor's advancements were intended to establish a pedagogy that advanced the principles of "orthodoxy, autocracy, and nationality."

History was now dedicated to proving that the Russian Orthodox Church and the Romanov czars were the font of Russia's greatness. Michael Pogokin, professor at the University of Moscow, later seen as the first real professor of Russian history, would offer up the vision of Russia as "a gigantic machine . . . directed by the hand of a single man, the Russian Tsar, the earthly god."

These policies served more to drive young Moscow intellectuals out of the lecture hall and into circles, informal discussion groups at various places throughout the town, than it did to turn the tides of change. The young intellectuals who attended those circles were still moved by the same beliefs that had moved the Decembrists a few years earlier. They included Micheal Bakunin, the father of revolutionary anarchism; Ivan Turgenev, author of *Fathers and Sons,* a tale of young revolutionaries; Mikhail Lermontov, author of *A Hero of Our Time,* the seminal collection of stories of a disaffected Russian officer; and Ivan Goncharov, author of *Oblomov,* in which the character of a Russian noble is the quintessential "superfluous man." While most of the people who attended the circles were at one time or another enrolled at Moscow University, the official line imposed upon the professors there was not acceptable to these young intellectuals, who would be leaders of Russian intellectual and literary life for a generation.

Once again, German philosophers attracted the attention of young, activist Russians. This time it was such thinkers as Fichte, the liberal nationalist who postulated a universal will as the source of all things, and Hegel, most noted for his dialectic of thesis and antithesis and his influence on Marxism and existentialism, who tempted the minds of the young away from the autocratic, orthodox, nationalist line. Alexander Herzen, the founding father of populism and another of the disaffected students, would write in exile on socialism and revolutionary ideas in Russia. His books were first issued in French. When the Russian translation appeared in the early 1860s, it was dedicated to the students at Moscow University.

Professors who did not promote "orthodoxy, autocracy, and nationality" were not entirely absent from the scene. Timothy Granovsky, who began teaching in 1839, became one of the few popular professors at Moscow University, not by attacking the current Russian system, but by pointing out non-Russian issues such as the shortcomings of the medieval French and English legal systems in such a way that his students could readily understand that the Russian system was vulnerable to the same arguments. Granovsky became a regular celebrity, attracting crowds of admirers to his public lectures. At one point, he reported in a letter that he had been accosted by Metropolitan of Moscow Philaret, prelate of the Russian Orthodox Church, who told him, "I am informed that you are a harmful professor—that you darken the minds of the loyal sons of our sovereign."

In the second half of the nineteenth century, Moscow University advanced Russia's reputation in science. The physicist A.G. Stoletov, known for his work with ferromagnetism, founded the Russian Institute of Physics at Moscow University. Physiologist I.A. Babukhin, who discovered electrical organs in fish, brought Moscow University to the forefront of microscopic neuromuscular studies.

The first years of the reign of Alexander II, from 1855 to 1865, saw the emancipation of Russia's serfs in 1861, as well as a relaxation of the government's controls over Russian universities. The new emperor recognized the danger of student uprisings. Universities were opened to anyone who could pass the entrance examinations, scholarly materials were allowed to flow more freely into the country, and the curators and inspectors who had held academic life in check under Nicholas were replaced and no longer had duties outside of the university itself. Uniforms were done away with, and the professors and councils of universities were again granted autonomy. Long hair and beards, even then symbols of rebellion, appeared. University officials were no longer quite so sure of their dominion.

Alexander II would grow more conservative with time, but, though financial support for Jewish students was cut off in 1875, the reforms of his first decade as emperor would largely stay in place until his assassination in 1881. It would be Alexander III, his father only recently murdered by terrorists, who would put a stop to the academic freedom that Alexander II had brought.

The University Statute of 1884 stripped the Russian rectors and deans of their autonomy. The grip of educational district officials on students, university councils, and internal administrators was strengthened. The ministry of education was given the right to influence courses. Tuition was increased and the students were put back into uniform—the better to be identified by police and educational authorities—and denied the right to belong to certain kinds of student organizations.

University autonomy would advance and decline again under Nicholas II. The beginning of the overall disastrous Russo-Japanese war brought student strikes to Moscow, complete with talk of armed demonstrations, in early 1905. Russia experienced a failed revolution in 1905, but it was the workers of Moscow whom czarist forces shelled into submission in December of that year. The utter failure of the Russian war effort against the Japanese served to alert the Russian government to a need to improve education nationwide. At the university level, this meant lifting some of the restrictions imposed on faculties and administrations in 1884. Academic councils were again allowed to control the appointment of professors, rectors, and deans. Students also were allowed greater freedom.

Unfortunately, the Ministry of Education did not modify its approach. The ministers of education between 1908 and 1914, A.N. Schwartz and L.A. Kasso, were particularly heavy-handed. Restrictions on Jews were brought back, and meetings of university students were forbidden. Rectors and professors were fired at the pleasure of the ministry. These measures were not accepted by Russian scholars; nationwide student unrest was the result, though some professors seem to have had a hand in the demonstrations. Moscow University's uprising of 1911 was the most furious.

A few Russian intellectuals greeted Lenin's regime with open arms; the vast majority rejected it. Moscow

University again proved to be the least cooperative. Immediately after the revolutions of 1917, universities in Russia were granted autonomy, but in the summer of 1918, the Commissariat of Enlightenment, a giant organization formed to preside over all educational, scholarly, scientific, and artistic activity in Russia, took control of all institutions of higher learning except for the Academy of Sciences. In October of that year, universities stopped granting graduate degrees, and professors who had ten years' tenure at the same institution or who had been appointed for 15 years or longer were dismissed. At Moscow University, 90 professors lost their positions, but when elections were held to fill the vacant posts in the first part of 1919, the only one of the 90 not reinstated was the only Communist among them.

Although the Eighth Party Congress of 1919 declared the intent of the Communist Party to change the educational system from "a weapon of class domination" to "a weapon for the Communist rebirth of society," the universities maintained some autonomy for a number of years. A 1921 statute reestablished many of the restrictions of the czarist university statute of 1884 and gave power over faculty selections officially to the Commissariat of Enlightenment and effectively to the Communist Party. Official surveillance of the social science faculties was started between 1921 and 1922. In spring 1922, hundreds of professors from Moscow University went on strike to protest the new regulations. Seven were deported, and, as surveillance continued, more were dismissed and deported.

The new government strove to bring young people from working families to the universities, and to rid higher education of the humanities and pre-Communist social science faculties. The Institute of Red Professors, established in 1921, worked to produce Communist professors. The steps taken worked gradually, however, and it was the late 1920s before the Bolshevik measures really took effect.

In order to bring more working-class students to the university, the Bolsheviks declared open admissions for anyone over 16 years of age, a practice that did not work. The failure was partially due to professors' refusal to allow unqualified students into seminars and partially due to the general orientation of workers and peasants, who not only took little interest in academic matters, but had no means of feeding, clothing, and housing themselves if they left their jobs for the university. A more successful approach was the creation of Workers' Faculties to provide a step between the factory or the field and the university, but this effort still had mixed results. The percentage of peasants among university students went from 14.5 in 1914 to 22.5 percent in the 1923–24 academic year, but the number of workers and craftspeople dipped from 24.3 percent to 15.3 percent. During the Stalin years, more harsh measures were taken to try to turn the universities from preserves for the intelligentsia to

institutions for the masses, but Khrushchev, in 1958, would confess that a solid majority of students were from non-peasant, non-worker families.

By 1957, though then as now most commonly called simply "Moscow University," or "MGU," Russia's leading institution of higher education had officially become the M.V. Lomonosov State University, its main campus occupying a spot overlooking the Lenin Hills, which commands the most scenic view of Moscow. The main building, a towering 787 feet of "Russo-modern" architecture, was built between 1948 and 1953 at a cost of 3 billion rubles, which in the 1950s was more than three-quarters of a billion U.S. dollars. At that time, there were 1,900 laboratories and 15,000 rooms. The teaching staff numbered some 1,800 and the students 17,000, at least 13,000 of whom were in the sciences. The 4,000 liberal arts students were educated in an older building near the Kremlin. The curriculum was identical with that of universities all over the Soviet Union. Soviet citizens attended free of charge and received a government salary, although tuition was charged from 1941 to 1956. By the 1960s, though the population of the working class on matriculation was noticeably slipping, the Soviet Union rated second only to the United States in terms of the percentage of the total population studying at universities.

The end of the Soviet Union has brought gradual change to Russian universities, especially because the old guard of the faculties has been free to remain. The same instructors who taught Marxism and Leninism now teach the social sciences and anthropology. However, the abolition of the centralized schedules and curricula has left Russian universities in a confused state. Furthermore, the professors who were entrenched as part of the old guard still hold sway, partly because of their numbers and partly because it is they who have experience managing universities. When Moscow State University elected a rector in 1992, the old vice-rector won.

M.V. Lomonosov Moscow State University boasts a faculty of well over 8,000; 26,000 undergraduate students; and 5,000 doctoral students in 20 academic departments. It has more than 100 laboratories, a computer center, botanical gardens, and museums of anthropology, soil science, and rare books. One U.S. study ranks Moscow University as the second-best university in Europe.

Further Reading: It is difficult to find any literature that encompasses the history of Moscow University. What material there is tends to be very slanted either toward or against the Soviet regime. Especially useful for the czarist era are *Young Russia: The Genesis of Russian Radicalism in the 1860s* by Abbott Gleason (New York: Viking, 1980); *Years of the Golden Cockerel: The Last Romanov Tsars 1814–1917* by Sidney Harcave (New York: Macmillan, 1968; London: Hole, 1970); and *Russia Since 1801: The Making of a New Society* by Edward C. Thaden (New York: Wiley, 1971).

Thaden's work is also useful for its information on the communist era. *Inside Russia Today* by John Gunther (New York: Harper, 1958; revised edition, 1962) provides a close look at Moscow University during the Khrushchev regime. *Education and Society in the New Russia* edited by Anthony Jones (Armonk, New York: M.E. Sharpe, 1994) is an excellent collection of essays on conditions and movements in the immediately post-Soviet Russian educational system.

—Robert Schoenberg

NATIONAL AUTONOMOUS UNIVERSITY OF MEXICO
(Mexico City, Mexico)

Location: In the southern part of Mexico City.

Description: Public institution with 263,891 students.

Information: Secretaría Administrativa
Ciudad Universitaria
(Torre de Rectoría 5 piso)
México, D.F. 04510
(5) 616-0205
Fax (5) 616-1538

The Universidad Nacional Autónoma de México (UNAM, National Autonomous University of Mexico) is the most important higher education institution in Mexico and , arguably, in all Latin America.

The Royal University of Mexico was the first university to function in the Americas, though universities in Santo Domingo and Lima were chartered a bit earlier by the Spanish crown. Fray Juan de Zumarraga, the municipality of Mexico City, and the Viceroy Antonio de Mendoza were main forces behind the new institution's founding in 1553. The first students were four brothers of the de Castilla family, descendents of King Don Pedro. For matters ranging from academic structure to individual rights, the model was the University of Salamanca in Spain. The first subjects were theology, arts and grammar, and law. Because evangelizing the native population was a major concern, indigenous languages were taught; but of course the main language was Latin, the main texts European.

As the university grew, students held an honored place apart from the general population, the emblems of their particular school or faculty as badges of honor. Most of the professors were affiliated with religious orders, gaining their posts through rigorous examinations. The university gained pontifical status in 1595. But religion also brought early challenges to the institution, including struggles between church and crown, with the latter usually having the upper hand. Another challenge came from the Jesuits, who arrived in 1572 and founded their own colleges. Their success intensified protests from the university, fearful of competition. The university got royal protection through a decree that only it could grant academic degrees. Juan de Palafox y Mendoza, Bishop of Puebla, felt compelled to carry on the fight in the seventeenth century and help get further statutes for the university's privileged status. Jesuits remained the exception to the decline of higher education into conformist thinking

in that century. Expulsion of the Jesuits in the next century was a blow to Mexican education; the university played no major role in the country's cultural flowering.

As the colonial era closed, a trend toward secularization led to the creation of new professional schools and to curriculum reforms. But the struggle for independence hurt the university, which found itself occupied by Spanish troops for six years. With independence, the institution briefly became the Imperial and Pontifical University of Mexico but mostly it became a pawn in the titanic liberal-conservative struggle that contributed to the country's political instability and economic weakness. It was chronically closed and was definitively shut down in 1865.

Only separate professional faculties continued to operate until 1910 when followers of the positivist movement, who had such an impact from Europe to the New World, established the university anew—only to see it crumble in the cataclysmic revolution launched just months later that engulfed Mexico in violence for two decades and more. Into the 1930s demands of revolutionary solidarity or commitment to practical education for the masses were not compatible with university ideals of autonomy and advanced learning. When the university was granted first partial and then full autonomy, the price was elimination of government subsidies. Further, creation of a National Polytechnic Institute, which remains the other giant institution in Mexico City, broke the university's near monopoly on higher education.

By the mid-1940s, however, the regime settled into a postrevolutionary pursuit of political stability and economic growth and thus entered, with the university, into a modus vivendi that has, for the most part, held over the next 50 years; in fact, the first half of that period marks a golden age probably unmatched since the university's early years.

The modus vivendi was shored up by careful internal governance. Though UNAM's council has power to make academic rules, it includes the rector as president, and representatives of deans as well as faculty, students, and workers. In any case, the highest authority is a U.S.-style governing board; composed of 15 distinguished Mexicans, it appoints the rector and directors and deans. Moreover, since the early 1970s, rectors have come not from the (generally leftist) social sciences but mostly from the hard sciences; the re-election of some is testimony to a stability quite at odds with the situation in most of the institution's history since independence from Spain.

A first measure of the contemporary university's importance lies in its unrivaled size. Sprawling over 1,803 acres on the main campus alone (University City,

National Autonomous University of Mexico

built in the early 1950s and famed for its murals), UNAM commands an annual budget that reached (before the 1994 peso devaluation) 1 billion U.S. dollars—greater than a federal aid to 27 of 31 states and greater than the budget for some federal ministries. If all its students are counted, then UNAM is among the largest universities in the world. But over 40 percent of the students are in UNAM's network of high schools, some even at junior high school.

The UNAM slipped from near-monopoly to having roughly 10 percent of Mexico's higher education enrollment; some of the decline is a natural result of enrollment growth and national modernization. With the creation of public universities in every state, and the proliferating technical and agricultural institutions, UNAM could not have met the nationwide demand that would have made the university too large to manage. It also created National Professional Schools of its own on the outskirts of the city. Still, the creation of another public multi-university in Mexico City (The Autonomous Metropolitan University, 1974) was also a pointed effort to achieve academic reforms impossible at the UNAM and often failed at its own professional schools. And elite private universities have increasingly attracted students from the best high schools and provided them with a strong leg up on

the best jobs that require modern economic and technological skills. Private enrollments now approach 20 percent of the Mexican total.

Offsetting UNAM's slip in proportional size is the fact that it is still much greater in size than any other institution and has unrivaled breadth. A "mega-university," UNAM has 13 doctoral granting schools, varied other faculties and units, and a research network of 25 institutes, 14 centers, and 7 programs.

These research sites speak to UNAM's unmatched weight in the most advanced academic work. Begun in 1929, the sites often afford good facilities and protection from tensions afflicting the teaching faculties. They make a disproportionate contribution to UNAM's hold on one-third of all the places in the nation's competitive National System of Researchers. Similarly, and dating from about the same starting point, UNAM has one-fourth to one-third of the nation's graduate enrollments, and some of its science, medical, and engineering specialties have international reputations. At the undergraduate level, UNAM retains a superiority in many of the same fields, where elite private universities hardly challenge, and for the pre-university levels some facilities rank high.

Unfortunately, however, academic quality is compromised in several ways. Research, itself too variable across and within units, is strongest in the units separated from the teaching faculties and thus does not contribute enough to teaching. Part-time professors outnumber full-time at least three to one even though the latter is often more a formal title than a functional reality, and whereas most part-timers had been esteemed professionals now many are merely college graduates with no distinguished academic or practical knowledge to offer. (UNAM has roughly 23,000 professors, depending on definition of categories.) Moreover, much graduate education is but an ad hoc extension of undergraduate programs, and doctoral enrollments reach only 1,547 (roughly 70 percent of the nation's total.) At the undergraduate level, lax entry requirements are followed by lax rules on attendance, exams, and other matters, policies defended largely by a perceived threat of student disruption.

The UNAM continues to exert a huge influence beyond its own institutional borders. It has been the academic model for most public universities in the Mexican states and was influential for many private universities, in part because of its prestige and because almost all the private universities must be recognized by either the government or UNAM; in fact, the bulk of private high schools in Mexico City are accredited by UNAM, another source of UNAM's influence. Over the years, UNAM has also educated many of the academic leaders for other Latin American countries.

The university's Centro Cultural Universitario is a leader in its class. The UNAM houses dance and theater companies and a major orchestra. It owns and manages historical buildings and museums, the country's second largest concert hall, and largest libgrary system (164 libraries with over 4 million volumes), and the leading film collection in Latin America. Its sports facilities are Mexico's' largest and it boasts leading professional teams.

A major consequence of frustrated academic reform is academic laxity, at least in the social sciences and business-related fields where the contrast is sharp to elite private universities that have gained much of the prestige and an increasing percentage of good professors. Rigor remains greater in the exact sciences and medicine; elite private universities that compete in medicine do well but their numbers are rather limited. Entry to UNAM's secondary education still provides an automatic pass into its higher education, curriculum often remains weak and dated, students who do poorly (through lack of effort or ability) routinely just retake courses, and, despite all this, drop-out rates are high.

The prospects for reform, though, have improved in higher education in the 1990s. Resources and rewards are increasingly tied to performance, evaluation and competition are gaining ground, more consideration is given to links with a modernizing economy, and the North American Free Trade Agreement (NAFTA) gives new impetus to these processes as it also stimulates a notable increase in UNAM's contacts with U.S. and Canadian institutions. Opposition to the reforms appears now a defensive, delaying operation. But in Mexico's increasingly diverse and competitive higher education system, UNAM's stature and role will depend on how rapidly and well this institution effects its own reforms.

Further Reading: A useful introduction in Spanish and English is the UNAM's own *National Autonomous University of Mexico* (Mexico City: UNAM, 1981). A political analysis highlights Daniel C. Levy, *University and Government in Mexico: Autonomy in an Authoritarian System* (New York: Praeger, 1980). For more statistical information, see UNAM, *Agenda Estadística 1994* (Mexico City: UNAM, Dirección General de Estadístico, 1995).

—Daniel C. Levy and José María García Garduno

NATIONAL UNIVERSITY OF IRELAND
(Republic of Ireland)

Location: Three campuses in urban areas (Dublin, Cork, and Galway) and one in a semi-rural area (Maynooth).

Description: A four-campus, government-sponsored university system with total enrollment of approximately 31,000 students in undergraduate and professional programs (including programs at St. Patrick's College, Maynooth, for training clergy).

Information: University College, Dublin
Belfield, Dublin 4
Dublin
Ireland
(1) 706 7777

Information Office University College, Cork
U.C.C. Cork
Cork
Ireland
(21) 902371

University College, Galway
Admissions Office
U.C.G., Galway
Galway
Ireland
(91) 24411

St. Patrick's College, Maynooth
Registrar's Office
Maynooth
Co. Kildare
(45) 658 5222

Visiting: Guided tours of the campuses are available at all four colleges. For more information, call the phone numbers above.

As the new chancellor of the National University of Ireland (NUI) in November 1921, Eamon de Valera delivered a speech to students in which he said of the 12-year-old university: "A nation's university should not be a machine for casting standard types and stamping them off. Nor should it be merely a venerable seat of learning." To be worthy, he went on in his speech, NUI "should throb with the living fires of a nation's soul." When de Valera spoke of this dream, the fate of Ireland as a country had yet to be decided, and debate about political and cultural issues raged. As Ireland formed as a nation, so formed the National University of Ireland, which would train and educate the members of the new republic.

In 1921, the struggle for national independence was at a critical stage, and de Valera, whom Donal McCartney calls the "generally acknowledged leader of nationalist Ireland" accepted the candidacy for the chancellorship of the university. De Valera was then the president of the Irish Free State; in addition, he was also the president of Sinn Fein, the Irish nationalist movement which achieved independence for the Irish Free State in 1922.

The National University of Ireland was formed amidst heated debate over Irish education. In the years preceding the signing of the Irish Universities Act in 1908, which established the NUI, several options for higher education existed in Ireland, but many believed there was no place for the Catholic majority to gain the tools needed to advance in Irish society.

Indeed, at least 75 years before NUI, efforts had been strenuously made to achieve just such a goal. According to T. Corcoran, an early professor at the NUI, the seeds were planted for a national university system as far back as 1845: in that year Sir Robert Peel, prime minister of England, secured the passage of a law to erect and endow from public finds two colleges in Ireland. They were Queen's College of Cork and Queen's College of Galway. Together with Northern College at Belfast, the three colleges became Queen's University of Ireland in 1850. In terms of administrative duties, though, these colleges were not represented by local or regional bodies. Therefore, early nationalist figures vocally opposed the Queen's College system. Soon after, Ireland saw the formation of its own Catholic University; it was supported exclusively by donations from Irish parishes. But even with the Catholic University in place by the 1850s, the educational needs of the vast majority of the Irish population remained unserved.

An attempt at modification was made in the Royal University Act of 1879: this act expanded the university senate of Queen's College, and increased the "teaching power" in both the Queen's Colleges at Cork and Galway and the two Catholic University Colleges in Dublin. Then with the implementation of the Irish Universities Act of 1908, the Catholic University Colleges of Dublin and the two Queen's Colleges were made into three constituent colleges of a new national university—National University of Ireland. Within six months of that act, recognition status was accorded the National Ecclesiastical College of St. Partrick, Maynooth.

National University of Ireland

As de Valera well knew, the incorporation of the former Queen's Colleges and the Catholic University into one national university system represented an investment in Ireland's future as an independent nation. The National University of Ireland grew with the years. "De Valera's NUI, like the Chancellor himself," writes McCartney, "had indeed had a revolutionary youth, followed by academic maturity." Part of this academic maturity was reflected in the growth of the physical plants of all four colleges; part of it in increased course offerings; and part in the expanded process of self-government among the system's colleges. While the chancellor's office was appointed for life or until resignation, the office of vice-chancellor rotated between the presidents of the different colleges. This decision, made early in the history of the NUI, helped to alleviate friction between sister colleges.

However, in the twentieth century each college maintains its own strong regional flavor and represents the unique culture and history of the distinct areas of Dublin, Galway, Cork, and Maynooth. When de Valera was still a young man with a degree in mathematics, he wanted to teach, and so lobbied heavily for the position of chair in mathematical physics at the Queen's College at Cork, in the south of Ireland. "Energy, zeal, capacity," and "devotedness to learning" were among the qualities ascribed to the young de Valera in the race for the UCC teaching position. Despite all his efforts to obtain the teaching position, he failed. By 1917 he was still writing about mathematical equations not from a university post but, due to his activities on behalf of Irish freedom, from his cell at the Lewes Jail.

Later political opponents of de Valera joked that UCC,

and its president in particular, had much to answer for, in not accepting de Valera as professor of mathematical physics. They had thereby changed the course of modern Irish history. The famous Easter Rising of 1916 ended de Valera's teaching aspirations for good. However, although his patriotic commitment grew, his love for the university, scholarship, and learning never waned: it would be only a few short years before de Valera would return to the National University of Ireland.

Today the UCC, situated on the banks of the River Lee, enrolls over 10,000 students in eight different faculties. According to a UCC document, women are 54 percent of the student body. The Boole Library—so named for George Boole, fist professor of mathematics at Queen's College, Cork (now UCC)—was established in September 1983 and currently holds over 600,000 books. Among other renowned buildings are the Crawford Observatory, the Medical Building, and the Honan Chapel. The Honan Chapel, built in 1915, has a unique mosaic floor with signs of the zodiac, the river of life, and various animals. In addition, the campus features a science center, built in 1971 on the site of the former county jail buildings, and the Stone Corridor, which functions as a covered walkway in the main quadrangle. The Stone Corridor contains Ogham stones, an early coded form of the Irish language, that record genealogical statements of the period 300–600 A.D.

When the Irish University Bill was passed in 1908, the success of the new university would depend on how it was received in fractious Ireland of the turn of the century. Therefore, the role of the chancellor—the chief officer of the university—took on an added importance. With the cultural and political divisions in Ireland at the turn of the century, one of the issues the early chancellor faced was the issue of compulsory Irish as a subject that was essential for matriculation within the NUI The issue was resolved with an NUI Senate vote: "essential" Irish was affirmed. While not the rule by the late years of the twentieth century, Celtic studies still flourish at each site of the NUI

Another campus is that of the University College, Galway (UCG). Situated on the banks of the River Corrib in the western Ireland city of Galway—rich in Gaelic culture—the UCG honors the importance of Ireland's two official languages, English and Irish (Gaelic). Of the two, English is the more common. Yet at UCG, founded in 1845 as "Queen's College Galway," Gaelic culture can still be studied and examined in its element. There are seven faculties at UCG: arts, Celtic studies, commerce, engineering, law, medicine, and science. With a student population of 6,500 in 1993 the college strives to bring the older Gaelic culture of Ireland—in music, song, and language alive in this western city. This goal is reflected not only in the city and its environs, with its proximity to the Irish-speaking Gaeltacht, but in the programs of the UCG itself. Along with its programs in major disciplines

and professions, the UCG prides itself on its faculty of Celtic studies. In addition, the UCG's Hardiman Library, which is primarily a teaching library, holds Galway's oldest documents, as well as serving as a UNESCO-designated folklore archive.

Indeed, the diverse programs at the UCG may very well reflect de Valera's words to the students of 1921 when he requested a university that reflected the nation's history and soul. Perhaps no other campus among the constituent colleges of the National University of Ireland does so as intently and so well as University College, Dublin. With the successful passage of the Irish Universities Act, which became law on August 1, 1908, it was established as a constituent college of the National University of Ireland: its new name was University College, Dublin. Originally the Catholic University, which originated in 1851 in the face of the long-established Protestant University, the UCD represented Ireland's ancestral Catholic and Irish culture. This history is reflected in the current holdings of over 1 million books at the UCD library, which include a special collection of Celtic languages and literatures. The largest of the NUI constituent colleges, UCD had a total of 15,854 students enrolled in full or part-time study in the year 1993–94.

Currently the main campus in Belfield, Dublin, houses the faculties of arts, Celtic studies, commerce, law, agriculture, and other faculties. The Graduate School of Business is housed at Blackrock, Dublin, while the medicine, architecture, and veterinary schools are housed at Earlsfort Terrace, Richview, Clonskeagh, Lyons Estate, and Ballsbridge, respectively.

The three constituent colleges of the National University of Ireland—University College, Dublin, University College, Cork, and University College, Galway—have carried on the dream set forth by de Valera: the dream for a university system that would make available a quality education for the country's population. But in addition to the programs offered at the three constituent colleges, the NUI also has a recognized college, St. Patrick's College, Maynooth.

Located in the town of Maynooth in County Kildare, St. Patrick's, founded in 1795, was originally a training college for Catholic priests. Lay students were admitted in 1966–67, and are now by far the largest part of the college's 1994–95 total enrollment of 4,119 students.

Within the structure of St. Patrick's are three institutions: The College of the National University of Ireland, the Pontifical University, and the seminary. The College of the National University of Ireland awards degrees in arts and sciences—with bachelor of arts, bachelor of science, master of arts, master of science, and Ph.D. programs. The Celtic studies program offers courses in modern Irish, and middle and old Irish literature and language for a degree. A variation on the program is offered though a study of Welsh language and literature. A wide range of post-graduate degrees is available. Masters in science, education, and many other programs are available, and doctoral work is available as well. As of 1994, a new program was instituted: a B.A. in music.

The Pontifical University awards degrees in theology and philosophy. All seminarians attend the Pontifical University at some stage of their studies. Lay students also attend undergraduate and post-graduate courses through a joint program of B.A. in theology in conjunction with the National University. The seminary's own courses on the formation of priests are outside the academic coursework.

The buildings are divided into two sites: the north campus was developed in the 1970s, its facilities were designed for NUI courses. The south campus is the site of the original college founded in 1795: it is the base for the seminary. Offices and classes for the Pontifical University are located here, and administrative offices as well.

It would be fair to say that at the end of the twentieth century, the words of Eamon de Valera have rung true: "Standing here on the threshold of the future," he said in his original 1921 speech to the NUI students, "we may well salute it, and resolve together to make our dreams for our university and our nation come, every one of them, true."

Further Reading: T. Corcoran's *The National University of Ireland Handbook* (Dublin: National University of Ireland Press, 1932) provides a detailed account of the founding of the university through 1932. An excellent arrangement of graphs and charts demonstrates the growth of student population and teaching faculties up to 1932. *The National University of Ireland and Eamon de Valera* by Donal McCartney (Dublin and Dover, New Hampshire: University Press of Ireland, 1983) examines the history of the NUI through the chancellorship of Eamon de Valera. Another comprehensive account of the National University's history will be found in *Towards a National University: William Delany SJ, an Era of Initiative in Irish Education* by Thomas J. Morrissey (Dublin: Wolfhound Press, and Atlantic Highlands, New Jersey: Humanities Press, 1983). The role Mr. Delany played in the ultimate formation of the National University of Ireland is closely examined.

—Rosemarie C. Sultan

NATIONAL UNIVERSITY OF SAN MARCOS
(Lima, Peru)

Location: In Lima, Peru's capital and chief administrative, commercial, manufacturing, and cultural center. The university is five miles west of Lima's Plaza de las Armas, the city's center.

Description: Peru's oldest, largest, and most prestigious institute of higher education. The university enrolls over 35,000 students in a wide variety of undergraduate and graduate programs.

Information: National University of San Marcos
295 Avenida Republica de Chile
Lima
Peru
(14) 314 629

Visiting: Contact the university at the above location.

Shortly after Spain's arrival in the New World, it began organizing institutions of higher education modeled on Europe's universities. Spain viewed these schools as effective means of extending its political, religious, and cultural influence in its colonies. The important role the Spanish Crown intended for these universities plagued them with a tumultuous history.

Since the 1540s, Spaniards in Peru had desired an institution of higher education to advance their career ambitions and social status. The citizens of Lima argued most vocally for the establishment of a university in their city of grand churches, great government buildings, elaborate hospitals, and large monasteries. Founded in 1535, Lima was the capital of the Viceroyalty of Peru, which included all of Spanish South America. The young city was Spanish America's most important political, commercial, and religious center. The Spanish Crown shared the vision of Lima's citizens, realizing that educated men were needed to fill the New World's governmental and religious bureaucracies, but the government was slow to act.

Instead, the Dominican Order in Peru took the initiative. The Dominicans saw a university as a way to train missionaries to convert natives, but also as a means to gain colonial influence by educating men not only in religious but in secular topics. In 1548 the Dominicans opened a college in Lima. Friar Tomas de San Martin, director of Peru's Dominican Order, soon formally appealed to King Charles V to sanction this school as a university; the Dominicans, as they had achieved at the University of Santo Domingo, wanted royal legitimacy

for their education efforts. King Charles, content to avoid the drain on the royal treasury, issued a decree in May 1551 chartering the school as the *Pontifica y Real Universidad de San Marcos de Lima* (Pontifical and Royal University of San Marcos of Lima). This decree modeled the school on Spain's noted University of Salamanca. However, the Dominican Order only allotted 350 pesos for the project. The school floundered, only offering instruction in grammar. Despite their inability to fund the project, the Dominicans battled with Spain's kings for years to maintain control of the school, hampering the university's development. Indeed, although the university was the second sanctioned in the New World (after the University of Santo Domingo), it did not grow to its intended status until the Crown asserted its power.

Throughout Latin America, universities were the focal point of the struggle between the Spanish Crown and the religious orders. This battle is illustrated in the government's efforts to gain control of the nascent university in Lima. In 1569 Francisco de Toledo assumed the post of viceroy of Peru, instituting an efficient, repressive government. De Toledo wanted the university at Lima to serve its grand purpose of extending the Spanish Empire's influence in the New World, but on a local level he viewed the school as a means of fostering loyalty to the Crown by creating opportunities for Peru's growing number of Creoles.

In 1571, under the direction of King Phillip II, de Toledo ordered the school secularized and limited the involvement of the Dominicans. That same year, Rome attempted to reassert its authority by issuing a papal bull sanctioning the university. However, de Toledo, acting with the force and treasury of the Spanish Crown, acted decisively in 1574, when he formally founded the University of San Marcos, then provided the university with a substantial endowment and removed the school from the Dominican convent where it had been housed. Faculty and administrators were recruited from the University of Salamanca. Between 1576 and 1578 the school became a multidisciplinary university as de Toledo authorized the expansion of its programs to include philosophy, theology, law, canon, medicine, and Quechua, the language of Peru's indigenous people. In 1582, de Toledo further expanded viceregal control over the university by weakening the authority of the university's rector (the head administrator), whom the Dominicans still had influence in selecting. Nonetheless, the church's leverage in the university, as in all Latin American universities, remained for nearly three centuries. Dominican, Augustinian, Jesuit, and Franciscan Orders all maintained chairs which influenced the university's curriculum, and theology remained the most significant curricular offering. After Peru's viceroy and the religious orders arrived at a working compromise, the school became an organizational and curricular model for most Latin American universities founded in the 1600s.

By the early seventeenth century many scholars praised the University of San Marcos' distinguished faculty, but later critics have decried the stress the school placed on Scholastic education to the detriment of rational and applied science, math, medicine, and engineering. After the 1640s the university made some efforts to counter its Scholastic emphasis by augmenting its programs in medicine and math. The traditional curriculum was again challenged in the late eighteenth century, when the Enlightenment's ideals permeated intellectual Peru, weakening traditional ecclesiastic influence in education. Several professors at the University of San Marcos espoused these new doctrines. Peru's viceroy accordingly redeveloped the university's curriculum to emphasize natural science and medicine, established a library, reformed the professorial selection process, and tied the rector to the viceregal bureaucracy, although this last act was more consistent with politics than with the Enlightenment. While the Crown responded to the introduction of the Enlightenment's ideas into the university, these ideals would profoundly affect the Spanish Empire. The movement for independence from Spain grew in the early nineteenth century, and the University of San Marcos' rectors took a vocal part in the movement as the school agitated for political change.

After a series of revolts, Peru gained its independence in 1824. Thereafter, education received increased attention as the new nation searched for its path to progress. After 1850 Peru's government initiated expansive modernizing reforms in all areas of government. These efforts, which swept the newly independent republics of Latin America, emphasized educational reform. In Peru the government centralized control of all levels of education, established public schools, founded two additional universities, and sought to restructure higher education along a Napoleonic model. In 1855, the government reorganized the University of San Marcos in an attempt to make it a truly multidisciplinary, modern university. Five independent private colleges were added to the school, and the next year an independent medical school joined the campus, allowing the school to offer a comprehensive medical curriculum for the first time. But many faculty at the university fought the increasing government influence in their institution by claiming that the school's sanctioning prior to the establishment of the Republic of Peru conferred on it the privilege of self-determination. It took over a decade and a more potent minister of education for the government to effectively strengthen its control over the University of San Marcos and to quash this concept of "privilege." Thereafter, the struggle became irrelevant as the govern-

ment's instability weakened its control over the university. Despite some reforms, for the next half century the University of San Marcos, like universities across Latin America, remained a traditionalistic institution that primarily served the socio-economic elite. Several historians have noted the pressing need for academic reform in Latin American universities of the late 1800s. Their primary criticism was that these schools—unlike their counterparts in the United States and western Europe—served not the interests of students, but those of the state and church.

By the early twentieth century, activists inside the University of San Marcos initiated efforts to reform the institution. But their activism transcended the university and reflected the greater movement for social change in Peru. After 1900 the university became a center of political and social protest. This movement was initiated by a coterie of progressive professors and the university's increasingly activist student population. In addition to fundamental university reform, they called for increased access to education for the masses, agrarian reform, and legal protections for Indians and workers. These ideals began a long tradition of student activism which spread to most of Peru's universities and profoundly altered the political landscape of the nation.

In 1909 University of San Marcos students demonstrated for the release of political prisoners and protested Peru's dictatorship. In 1916 the radical student organization at San Marcos grew into the Peruvian Student Federation. Led by San Marcos' students, this body incorporated students from all Peru's universities, thereby creating a new political force and directing future student protests. In 1919 the student federation demanded extensive university reforms including a modernizing of the curriculum, the removal of incompetent tenured professors, the elimination of government interference in the university, scholarships for underprivileged students, and student involvement in administration. Early in the year the students merged their demands with the interests of Peru's workers and organized the nation's first general strike. This strike halted most commercial activity in Lima and led the government to establish an eight-hour day for the nation's workers. When the students called another general strike four months later to address their remaining demands, the president broke the strike by arresting 3,000 workers and closing the University of San Marcos for the rest of the year. These strikes hastened the electoral defeat of the president and ushered in a more democratic leader, President Augusto Leguia.

Realizing his debt to the students, Leguia drafted laws meeting most student demands, reorganized the entire education system, dismissed over 20 unpopular professors at the University of San Marcos, and gave the school greater autonomy. This alliance between Leguia and San Marcos' students was short-lived; one year later, when students protested Leguia's civil rights abuses, he closed the University of San Marcos for a year and removed its rector. Two years later a student/worker protest at the university descended into a riot and Leguia sent troops to close San Marcos, leading to the arrest of several students and the death of one. The university was again closed in 1924 and 1925. Leguia rescinded the school's autonomy in 1928, by which time most of the students' gains inside and outside the university had been reversed.

But the radical environment of the University of San Marcos did produce a more durable effect on Peru's political system. San Marcos student Victor Raul Haya de la Torre served as president of the Peruvian Federation of Students in the early 1920s. In 1924, with a group of Peruvian intellectuals, he founded the American Popular Revolutionary Alliance (APRA). APRA called for the same broad reforms in Peruvian society which San Marcos' students sought. Leguia quickly banned the party. The regime's hostility to APRA led to the repeated closings of the University of San Marcos in the 1920s, culminating in the 1932 closing of the university for three years in response to its continued association with APRA. When the school reopened it had less than 600 students. The University of San Marcos remained a center of protests and maintained a close relationship with APRA as it continued to advocate social change and became Peru's most influential political party.

After World War II the demand for higher education grew as Peru became more urbanized and its middle class expanded. By the 1950s the government began significantly increasing the number of universities to meet this demand. By the early 1960s the influx of middle-class students had renewed criticisms that Peru's universities were isolated from the needs of a modern society. In response, the government increased the universities' emphasis on science to address Peru's lack of trained technicians and increased funding for research at universities. In 1969 the government fundamentally altered all the nation's universities by uniting them into a university system and creating a National Council of Peruvian Universities to align the schools' goals with the state's goal of national development. Under this law, the University of San Marcos was reorganized and an academic department system was introduced.

In the 1990s university enrollment continues to grow while budget constraints limit the flexibility of universities. Since the 1960s, the level of spending per student has plummeted, a greater number of instructors are part time and professional training and instruction is emphasized over research. Amid these fundamental challenges facing Peru's university system, the University of San Marcos's self-proclaimed purpose is to contribute to Peru's modernization. The university remains the largest and most prominent of Peru's 26 national universities, enrolling over 35,000 students and offering masters degrees in 45 fields and doctoral degrees in 17. Its academic departments publish 19 journals and operate 3 prominent museums in Lima. The University of San Marcos' challenge for the near future remains the definition and fulfillment of its role within Peru's perennially turbulent political environment.

Further Reading: Jean Descola's *Daily Life in Colonial Peru* (London: Allen and Unwin, 1968) offers the most detailed history of the University of San Marcos' colonial years. John Tate Lanning's *Academic Culture in the Spanish Colonies* (London and New York: Oxford University Press, 1940) provides an overview of Latin American universities and briefly describes the early years of San Marcos. *Peru: A Short History* (Carbondale: Southern Illinois University Press, 1978), by David P. Werlich, covers the reform movement in early twentieth century Peru and offers a brief history of San Marcos.

—Michael Mundt

NEW SCHOOL FOR SOCIAL RESEARCH
(New York, New York, U.S.A.)

Location: In the Greenwich Village neighborhood of Manhattan in New York City.

Description: A private university with approximately 30,000 students in six undergraduate, graduate, and continuing education divisions.

Information: Office of University Communications
The New School for Social Research
838 Broadway
New York, NY 10003
U.S.A.
(212) 229-5667 or (212) 260-9932

The New School for Social Research arose indirectly from the actions of two Columbia University professors who openly defied university president Nicholas Butler's policy by actively opposing World War I in 1917. James McKeen Cattell, a highly regarded professor of psychology and a pacifist, and Henry W.L. Dana, assistant professor of comparative literature and a Socialist, played leading roles in antiwar protests and encouraged young men not to register for the draft. Both were dismissed by the board of trustees.

With their dismissal, professor of history Charles Beard, asserting the right of all people to dissent, resigned from the Columbia faculty. The economist James Robinson, who had a strong interest in cultural education, followed him soon thereafter, and the two set about founding a school designed to be "the antithesis of Nicholas Butler's Columbia." Having gained a pledge of $10,000 a year for ten years from Whitney fortune heiress Dorothy Straight, Beard and Robinson urged Herbert Croly, a founder of the magazine *The New Republic,* to bring the enterprise to the discussions he regularly held concerning projects that caught his attention. Among those to be found at such meetings were jurist Learned Hand; future justice of the Supreme Court of the United States, Felix Frankfurter; philosopher John Dewey, who felt that education was a moral necessity, a life-long process of "study and exploration" to be applied to every facet of a person's life; economist Thorstein Veblen, who supported the separation of research from undergraduate education; and associate editors of *The New Republic* Walter Lippmann and Alvin Johnson, who would become the first president of the New School in 1921.

The New School for Social Research opened in 1919 in a row of brownstones on West 23rd Street in New York City's Chelsea district. The first class boasted 200 adult students. The professed focus of the New School was, as its name implied, research, but a lecture series was offered. Early students, enrolled in the school's unaccredited courses, were presented with, among other notables, economist John Maynard Keynes, philosopher Bertrand Russell, and historian and political activist W.E.B. DuBois.

The intent of the founders was to create an environment organized in precisely the way other American universities were not. The installation of full-time administration was avoided until 1922. The oldest-known document pertaining to the school, a 1916 letter from Emily Putnam (the first dean of Barnard College) to James Robinson, is signed, "Yours in Anarchy." Charles Beard, who feared that a large endowment would lull the radical impetus of the school to a languid acceptance of the status quo, was averse to establishing any kind of set address at all. In the beginning years, he was successful in rejecting endowments but unsuccessful in avoiding the establishment of a home for the school.

The original scope of the school was intensely focused, and the goals were lofty. Of the 127 courses offered between 1919 and 1923, the overwhelming majority were in economics, political science, history, philosophy, and anthropology. By 1922, it had to be acknowledged that the lofty goals had not been met. The students had not thrown themselves into research for its own sake. Worse, the expectations of the intellectual left that World War I would prove a watershed of western history had not come true; the New School and its "respectably radical" community of thinkers had not proven as influential as had been hoped, and a financial collapse seemed to be forthcoming.

The New School was originally financed by nearly $300,000 worth of individual pledges to support the school for ten years. Disillusioned donors soon began withdrawing their funds, and the upstart academy found itself on hard times. A number of tactics and economies saved the day. Professors were attracted because teaching hours were limited to three to five hours per week, thus allowing some to devote more time to research and others to treat their classes at the New School as a second job. Fringe benefits were eliminated and salaries were raised. All of these stratagems allowed the school to attract professors from the most prestigious universities in the northeastern United States, while it acquired a somewhat unconventional student body. The New School for Social Research broke with other schools of the day and fully welcomed—indeed actively sought—Jews and women.

New School for Social Research

Nearly two-thirds of the early student body were women, and at least a quarter of the students had what appeared to be Jewish surnames.

The leadership of Alvin Johnson, teacher, economist, and editor, who had been made the first president of the New School in 1921, would see the fledgling institution through four decades of financial troubles and would broaden its interests to include the arts and humanities. Nearly every move the New School for Social Research made from 1923 until 1963 would bear Johnson's stamp.

The first issue Johnson faced concerned the very nature of the school. Was it to be a place for teaching or a place for research? The course that took the New School out of its troubled waters outraged its most important founders. With the closing of the research division in 1922, Beard, Robinson, and Croly departed. Veblen, however, stayed on. To his chagrin, since he was primarily interested in research and working with select students, his fame as a writer and social critic brought hordes of students to his classes. To drive away as many as possible, since he believed that students were interested in entertainment rather than education, Veblen mumbled through his rambling lectures. When Johnson finally dismissed him in 1925, the shift from founding ideals (unfettered research) to the principles of survival as an institution (paid teaching) was complete, if temporary, in Johnson's mind.

By 1926, only one-third of the courses offered were in the areas of public policy, the social sciences, and vocational training in social work and education. (From 1919 to 1922, nearly 75 percent of courses were in those categories.) Most courses now addressed cultural themes. The school's 1927–28 catalogue explained that the policy was to offer "whatever seriously interests persons of mature intelligence."

In 1930, the school moved from the rented row of brownstones on West 23rd Street to a new building of its own at 66 West 12th Street in Greenwich Village. The land for the building was sold by Daniel Cranford Smith, a retired businessman and a New School student, with the mortgage financed in such a way that the New School could arrange for a comfortable loan. Smith, in return, was given a penthouse in the new structure at a nominal rent and free courses for the rest of his life. Boasting murals by Jose Clemente Orozco and Thomas Hart Benton, the building, designed by Joseph Urban and considered an outstanding example of the International Style, has since been renamed the Alvin Johnson Building. The Orozco works are still on view on the seventh floor.

New York in the twenties was home to a large population of young people and families moving upward in social status. Though they lacked cultural education, many had the desire and the money to get it. For a reasonable price, one might hear poet Robert Frost, jurist Felix Frankfurter, writer Thomas Mann, or philosophers Bertrand Russell and John Dewey. Teachers included Martha

Graham and Doris Humphrey (modern dance), Aaron Copland (music), and Frank Lloyd Wright (architecture). James Baldwin (author of *The Fire Next Time* and *Blues for Mr. Charlie,* among other works), Mario Puzo (author of *The Godfather*), and William Styron (author of *Sophie's Choice* and many other novels) were all drawn to the writing program during the 1930s and 1940s.

This interest in culture did not mean that the New School had abandoned social sciences. Founded in the midst of the post–World War I Red Scare, setting its roots in the economic boom of the 1920s, funded entirely by student fees and the contributions of its own staff, the upstart school had to take advantage of every opportunity. In the twenties, the predominant opportunity was a revolution in the arts and humanities. In the thirties and early forties, however, it was provided by the Nazi takeover of Germany and then most of Europe.

With a grant from businessman and philanthropist Hiram Halle, Johnson, himself an anti-fascist activist, began to actively recruit a "University in Exile" from the German intellectual and activist community. This group took the name of the Graduate Faculty of Political and Social Science in 1934, the year after they began operating. Nominally part of the New School, the Graduate Faculty was separately funded and administered, thus allowing for funding from various refugee aid organizations, notably the Rockefeller Foundation and the Emergency Committee in Aid of Displaced German Scholars.

Still not full accredited by New York state, the Graduate Faculty started with 18 refugee scholars. By the summer of 1939, as Johnson managed to find more and more funding, there were 33 refugee faculty members. Then came the fall of France in 1940. The New School offered to take on over 100 of the resultant deluge of scholars. By the end of the war, Johnson and the New School had saved 167 scholars and their families.

The Graduate Faculty not only brought with it a mighty stack of credentials and major scholarly reputations, but it also allowed the granting of the New School's first degrees. Graduate degrees became available in economics, philosophy, political science, psychology, and sociology under a provisional charter from the New York State Board of Regents, which meant that the board of regents actually conferred the degrees for the New School. Emphasis was given to "interdisciplinary study and broad theoretical learning in the social sciences."

The émigrés had left Germany for predictable reasons. About half were Jewish, and the group had a decidedly leftist, social-democratic bent. The first dean of the Graduate School, Emil Lederer, had long concerned himself with the effects of technological development and the rising power of corporations. Gerhard Colm, another of their number, argued that the state should take direct action to ensure high levels of employment. Also among the German exiles was Weimar-era director Erwin Piscator, who founded the Dramatic Workshop. Its impact on

American culture was immense and is still felt. Writers Tennessee Williams and Arthur Miller worked on film scripts. Actors Marlon Brando, Harry Belafonte, Rod Steiger, and actress Shelley Winters emerged from the Dramatic Workshop. Piscator, however, was openly a Marxist, the type of political position that would draw attention to the New School after the war.

In February 1942, a free French academy, which actually taught its classes in French, opened as a temporary and independent part of the New School. Under Harvard art historian Henri Focillon, *L'École libre des hautes etudes* granted degrees by the authority of Charles DeGaulle, who also gave financial and political support, thus making the *École* an official organ of the French resistance. At one point, 65 French, Belgian, and Russian émigré instructors were teaching more than 200 courses to nearly 1,000 students. Not associated with the New School since briefly after the war, *L'École libre des hautes etudes* still exists on its own as a proponent of French culture in New York City.

In 1941, the New York State Board of Regents awarded the New School an absolute charter, in effect allowing the school to confer degrees on its own. In 1943, the Senior College was founded, offering the second half of an undergraduate degree to returning veterans and other adults who had completed two years elsewhere. That same year, the Adult Education division was split into the School of Politics, under Hans Simons, and the School of Philosophy and the Liberal Arts, under Clara Mayer. Mayer had been associated with the New School since its beginnings. The daughter of a wealthy New York real estate agent, she had recruited several family members to the school's cause and had helped enormously in the school's financial crisis in 1922.

Immediately after the war, the emergence of Greenwich Village as a creative center fed a new wave of creative students to the New School's adult division, particularly in writing and the visual arts. Arts programs continued to expand, although, for financial reasons, Piscator's Dramatic Workshop became a separate entity in 1949. Piscator himself fled the country in 1951 to avoid being called by the House Committee on Un-American Activities. During the McCarthy era, the New School kept some of its leftist posture, and in the 1950s, it came out against what Johnson and others described as a "new witch hunt." At least four avowed Marxists were allowed to go on teaching, since they denied being members of the Communist Party or any other secret organization. However, revelations in Johnson's private letters showed that he had been holding regular meetings with the FBI since the 1930s to report on faculty members.

In the midst of the McCarthy era, the New School found itself in the midst of an embarrassing incident of its own making. The Orozco murals, which were hung in a room sometimes used as a cafeteria, contained a section presenting heroic depictions of Lenin and the Russian Revolution. In 1951, the trustees told the administration to cover that section; later they ordered it removed. Objections were raised, and an argument followed in which it was pointed out that anyone who wanted to see the murals had a right to do so; however, the board concluded that their presence in a public place (the cafeteria) "violated the liberties of those who found them objectionable." Finally a compromise that pleased no one was reached. The "Soviet section" would remain covered whenever the cafeteria was in use. As Peter M. Rutkoff and William B. Scott commented in their history of the New School, "at the very time that McCarthy and his ilk had largely discredited themselves, the New School had managed to appear both cowardly and stupid."

The McCarthy era, however, did not stop progress at the school. Innovation continued. The Human Relations Center, which offered the first day classes "aimed exclusively at meeting the educational needs of mature women," was opened by the adult division in 1951. It was renamed the Vera List Center in 1987.

After many years of turbulence, John R. Everett took over as the fifth president of the New School for Social Research in 1962, and the first president, Alvin Johnson, fully retired in 1963. Though he had officially retired at the end of the World War II, the governance of the school had never been successful without his approval. Bryn Hovde, Johnson's immediate successor as president, had resigned largely because he had never been allowed to truly assume authority. The third president, Hans Simons, was one of the German exiles of the University in Exile, brought in and promoted to be head of the School of Politics by Johnson himself. The fourth president lasted but a single day in his office. His successor Henry David, appointed in 1960, relieved Johnson's head of the School of Philosophy and Liberal Arts, Clara Mayer, which proved a disastrous mistake. As Rutkoff and Scott pointed out, "In one stroke the New School lost its most loyal administrator, the generous financial support of her family, the backing of its German-Jewish constituency, and the loyalty of much of its most effective faculty."

Everett's appointment, though he was himself a Johnson protégé, represented a sea change. From this point forward, though it would maintain the principles of its founders, the New School for Social Research would go steadily, quickly, and aggressively forward to become a major modern university. In pursuit of that goal, the Institute for Retired Professionals opened in 1962 to serve older citizens. Two years late the J.M. Kaplan Center for New York City Affairs, the first academic center dedicated to a single city, opened. Parsons School of Design (established 1896) was acquired in 1970 and became the third major division of the New School, the others being the Graduate Faculty of Political and Social Science and the Adult Education Division. The fourth major division, the Graduate School of Management and

Urban Policy, opened in 1975. The Seminar College, now called the Eugene Lang College, was established in 1978 as the first complete undergraduate school.

At least partly because of its founders' belief that education should be applicable to the present, the New School for Social Research is still very much a work in progress.

Further Reading: Peter M. Rutkoff and William B. Scott's *New School: A History of the New School for Social Research* (New York: Free Press, and London: Collier Macmillan, 1986) provides a thoroughly researched and well written account of the school's history. Claus-Dieter Krohn's *Intellectuals in Exile* (Amherst: University of Massachusetts Press, 1987) provides a history of the professors who fled Nazi-dominated Europe and found an intellectual home at the New School for Social Research.

—Robert Schoenberg

NEW YORK UNIVERSITY
(New York, New York, U.S.A.)

Location: In the Greenwich Village neighborhood of Manhattan.

Description: The largest private university in the United States with a total enrollment of approximately 49,000 in undergraduate, graduate, professional, and non-credit programs.

Information: Office of Undergraduate Admissions
22 Washington Square North
New York, NY 10003
U.S.A.
(212) 998-4500

In the early 1800s, many Americans were concerned about the quality of education in the country, and nowhere was this truer than in the nation's largest metropolis, New York City. Fallout from the Industrial Revolution and the 1825 opening of the Erie Canal had swelled the size of the city of New York and its working class. There was little educational opportunity for this group, and Columbia University, like Harvard, was regarded as an aristocratic institution, offering a limited and strictly classical education to very few people (about 100 students in 1829). In addition, it was strictly sectarian, with close ties to the Episcopal Church.

When Andrew Jackson assumed the presidency of the United States in 1828, the balance of power in the country shifted from the landed gentry to the farmers of the west and the working class of the east. Fortunately there were those among the well-born class who were wise enough to recognize that it would be in the country's best interest to widen the scope of higher education to prepare a wider segment of the population for this new society.

At this time American colleges were almost exclusively administered and staffed by members of the clergy, and were largely aimed at training new clergy. But as the country grew, there grew a desire to loosen the sectarian control of the educational system. Many families wished their sons to receive a college education to prepare them for occupations other than those in the church. In addition, the growing mercantile class distrusted the clergy as administrators and teachers of science and rational thinking. The year 1828 brought news of the founding of a new London University aimed at practical instruction for the middle class. This news added impetus to those who favored a practical course of study for the class of people referred to then as "mechanics."

Despite the anti-sectarian sentiments of some New Yorkers, the first person reputed to have spoken of the idea of a university in New York was the Reverend Alexander Gunn, who allegedly mentioned his plan to the Reverend Jacob Brodhead. These two brought other men into the discussion and the first meeting, of which no formal record remains, took place on September 23, 1828. More than a year later, on December 2, 1829, an editorial in the *New York American* mentioned a movement to create a university in New York, and on December 16, 1829, the first formal meeting occurred to deal with the subject. Among the nine founders of the university at these first meetings were two clergymen, one banker, one lawyer, two merchants, two physicians, and one man of leisure. On December 30 the meetings became formalized, with Reverend James M. Mathews, a former pastor of the South Dutch Reformed Church, elected as chairman, and John Delafield, a member of a wealthy banking family, as secretary. A public meeting was planned for January 6, 1830, at which 38 local citizens were invited to meet with the founders.

The meeting was successful and exciting for founders of the new university because General Morgan Lewis, the son of a signer of the Declaration of Independence, attended. Though Lewis had not been formally invited, the group was so thrilled by his appearance that they elected him chairman of the meeting. One of the founders, Reverend J.M. Wainwright, read a long paper on the "Expediency and Means of Establishing a University in the City of New York," which was later distributed to the public; it is considered the first printed source of the university's history. The meeting attendees appointed committees to pursue various tasks, including applying to the state legislature for a charter. They also created a standing committee of nine people to oversee the general affairs of the university; John Delafield became head of the committee to solicit subscriptions.

In response to the need to show donors tangible plans for the proposed university, the subscription committee presented an organizational outline of the proposed university to the standing committee on January 14, 1830. This report was published in newspapers and included three important features: all university offices were to be open to all denominations; all areas of science and literature were to be taught; and professors were to depend mainly on fees collected from their students. This financial arrangement, modeled on the German system, was intended to be "an important stimulus . . . to constant improvement and attention to duty." The university was to be a joint-stock corporation with shares selling for $25

New York University

each. The shareholders were then to elect a board of 32, which would control the direction the institution would take. On July 29, 1830, approximately six months after the initial forming of the subscription committee, John Delafield reported that the target $100,000 had been promised to the university. (Subsequently, when less than half the pledged amount had been collected, speculation arose that Reverend Mathews had padded the list with false subscriptions to make certain that the drive would not appear to fail.) The shareholders were then invited to a meeting on July 31, to nominate members of the first council of the university.

On October 15, 1830, after much work by the nominating committee, 175 people were certified as subscribers and a list of nominees for office was approved, creating the first council of New York University. At the council's first meeting on October 18, it elected Albert Gallatin, former secretary of the treasury under Thomas Jefferson, as its first chair. He was a strong believer in the need for both nonsectarian university control and a practical course of study. He expressed this belief in a letter to a friend in 1833: "It appeared to me impossible to preserve

our democratic institutions and the right of universal suffrage unless we could raise the standard of general education and the mind of the laboring classes nearer to a level with those born under more favorable circumstances."

Among the many jobs facing the new council were organizing the university's plans for instruction. In September, the first council, the original standing committee, had decided to convene a group of eminent scientists and teachers from around the country to obtain their advice on the direction the new university should take. Approximately 50 distinguished men joined the council for this extended meeting which began on October 20, 1830, at City Hall. Among the attendees were Edward Livingston, soon to become Jackson's secretary of state; S.R. Betts, judge of the Federal District Court in New York City; and Henry E. Dwight, president of Yale.

According to historian T.F. Jones:

John Delafield suggested certain topics for discussion: the ways in which the examples of European universities should be followed in the United States; the importance of extensive libraries; the advantages and disadvantages of lectures or recitations in teaching; the importance of introducing instruction in English Literature and Government, etc.

Professor Vethake of Princeton suggested the abolition of a rigid curriculum, an idea which later evolved into the elective system. Vethake also proposed to replace the A.B. degree with the baccalaureate in literature for those graduates who had studied the classics, and the baccalaureate in science for those who had studied science. He also proposed the general examination for degree granting. Albert Gallatin also suggested a name for the practical course of study, which he called an "English College," one in which neither Greek nor Latin would be required.

By late November the council had named the new school the University of the City of New York. They made several other decisions as well, resolving that the council, chosen by the shareholders, would remain the ultimate authority with a president as chairman; and a chancellor, who would be elected every four years. On January 31, 1831, Albert Gallatin was named president, Morgan Lewis vice-president, John Delafield secretary, and the Reverend James M. Mathews chancellor. On this same day, the council completed a long application for incorporation to the legislature of New York state. Thus, four months later, on April 21, 1831, the University of the City of New York was incorporated.

The chancellor and a group of instructors were inaugurated on September 26, 1832, and instruction began on October 1 with 108 students in a rented building, Clinton Hall, at the corner of Nassau and Beekman Street in what is now referred to as Greenwich Village. In 1835, the university finally moved to Washington Square into a new building which was demolished in 1894 when a new structure, Main Building, was erected on the east side of Washington Square Park. Today the main Washington Square campus contains more than 30 buildings. The stone for some of the early buildings was cut by convicts in the prison at Sing Sing. The use of convict labor precipitated one of the city's first labor demonstrations—the Stone Cutters' Riot, during which the city's masons marched in protest.

One of the university's most famous instructors was also one of its first. In 1832, Samuel F.B. Morse was hired as a professor of sculpture and painting. In his studio in University Hall, he developed the first working telegraph. Samuel Colt of "revolver" fame was also a member of the faculty. Colt was a lodger in the Gothic tower of the university, as were poet Walt Whitman and artist Winslow Homer.

The university has expanded considerably since its beginning, adding schools and diversifying its student body. New areas of instruction were added early in the university's history. As early as 1835, the school of law, headed by Benjamin F. Butler, attorney general of the United States, opened. In 1854, an engineering school was added, and in 1890, the first school of pedagogy in the United States opened at the university. (There had been other teacher-training institutions, but this one was the first that was on a par with the professional schools in law, medicine, etc.) From the first, the school of pedagogy admitted women; in 1887 the school of arts and sciences admitted them. In 1890 the university revised its charter and severed itself from the close clerical and political ties that had resulted from the original joint-stock funding of the institution. Although independence from the clergy was one of the primary goals of many of the founders, it took almost 60 years for that to be realized.

In 1892 the university bought 18 acres on Fordham Heights (later called University Heights) in the Bronx, and in 1895 the undergraduate University College and the engineering school moved to this new campus, which had been designed by Stanford White. At the same time, the original building at Washington Square was razed and the Main Building, which still stands, was erected there. Soon after, on July 8, 1896, the university's name was changed to New York University.

During World War I, NYU trained field soldiers, officers, and ambulance drivers, which helped offset a reduction in the enrollment of young men. By the end of World War I, the university had added another campus in lower Manhattan's financial district, and it occupied other buildings in Brooklyn and Newark, New Jersey. During World War II, classes were filled with women, who replaced absent soldiers.

The university underwent a historic restructuring, as the result of a self-study undertaken in the 1950s. Heretofore the university had been run by a single official, the chancellor. Now the administrative responsibilities were to be assigned to a president, while the chancellor would direct academic affairs. The council became the board of trustees in 1955, and in 1956, NYU had its first president.

The 1970s brought a serious financial crisis to the university. In an effort to increase the university's endowment and decrease its deficit, President James M. Hester (president from 1962 to 1972), formed a commission to study the crisis. The result was the sale of the University Heights campus, as it was deemed too costly for the university to support two large campuses. Selling the campus enabled the university to devote its energies to one location. At the same time, Hester saw the need for a library and wanted one that would serve as a focus for the remaining Washington Square campus. This aim he accomplished with the building of the Elmer Holmes Bobst Library and Study Center, designed by Philip Johnson. This large, airy building, with its many-storied central space, was completed in 1973 and contains more than 2.5 million volumes.

In 1984, NYU's board of directors embarked on a major fundraising effort. Pledging to raise $1 billion in 15 years, the university instead reached its goal five years ahead of schedule, in 1994. Interestingly, after the goal was reached, the university received what may be the single largest gift any American university has ever received—the late Sir Harold Acton's estate, La Pietra, in Florence, Italy, estimated to be worth between $300 million and $500 million.

Rather than keeping the money in the university's endowment, the board chose to use the funds to make major improvements in many areas of the university, among which were additions to the faculty, including many scholars from such institutions as Princeton, Harvard, Stanford, and Chicago. The university spent $600 million on academic programs and more than that amount on construction and renovations, including the opening of a neural science center, a new performing arts center, an institute of mathematics, and an Italian studies center.

Though it has been in existence only since the mid-nineteenth century, NYU has produced an impressive list of alumni, including former New York mayor Ed Koch; the late New York senator Jacob Javits; authors Joseph Heller and Lillian Hellman; philanthropist Avery Fisher; economist Alan Greenspan; and Nobel laureates Gertrude Elion and George Wald. Wald shared the prize in medicine or physiology in 1967, and Elion shared the prize in medicine or physiology in 1989.

One school that has brought particular attention to NYU is the Tisch School of the Arts, especially its film and television program. In a recent *U.S. News and World Report* ranking (based on views of scholars and performing arts professionals), the film program was tied with the University of Southern California for first place; the drama program was second only to Yale. Among the alumni of the graduate division have been directors Martha Coolidge, Spike Lee, and Martin Scorsese.

One hundred and sixty-five years after the idea of creating a university for the city of New York first emerged, New York University has become the largest private university in the United States.

Further Reading: *New York University 1832–1932,* edited by Theodore Francis Jones (New York: New York University Press, 1933) provides an exhaustive view of the university's first 100 years. *The WPA Guide to New York City*, edited by Lou Gody and others (New York: Pantheon, 1939) offers information on the university in the context of New York City in the 1930s.

—Joan Wilder

NORTHEASTERN UNIVERSITY
(Boston, Massachusetts, U.S.A.)

Location: In the Back Bay section of Boston, between the Museum of Fine Arts and Symphony Hall.

Description: A private, independent, nonprofit institution enrolling approximately 15,000 students in undergraduate and graduate schools.

Information: Office of Undergraduate Admissions
Northeastern University
150 Richards Hall
Boston, MA 02115
U.S.A.
(617) 373-2211

Visiting: Campus tours led by undergraduate guides are available. Call the Admissions Office at Richards Hall at (617) 373-2211.

In the late 1800s, the philosophy that was to become the cornerstone of Northeastern University represented two firm beliefs: education should be affordable, and all educational institutions should be responsive to the needs of the community. This philosophy varied radically from that espoused by the traditional institutions in Boston at the time. The established classes provided by Harvard, Boston University, and the Massachusetts Institute of Technology (MIT) were available to serve the scholarly elite, students whose family wealth allowed them the luxury of an expensive four-year education. These institutions served their purpose but a significant number of students were excluded.

The seedling idea for Northeastern University began as a random selection of classes offered by the Boston Young Men's Christian Association (YMCA), called the Evening Institute For Young Men. Classes included English literature, vocal music, mechanical drawing, parliamentary law, penmanship, bookkeeping, arithmetic, and several languages. The classes were free, open to all, regardless of sex, occupation, race, creed, or color. They provided a growing service to the community of tradesmen, mechanics, and students in the Boston area. By 1895, class sizes were growing rapidly but women were now excluded. Seven hundred and thirty-three students enrolled in 24 classes. A new YMCA building was built on the corner of Berkeley and Boylston Streets to support the increase in enrollment.

It was clear to the directors of the Boston YMCA that a more organized and systematic approach to educational work was necessary. In May 1896, the board appointed a full-time educational director, Frank Palmer Speare, who brought to the task his experiences as a teacher in public and private schools as well as an enthusiasm for the promotion of education. Speare departmentalized courses under the headings of business, drawing, language, music, science, and physiology; he increased the complexity of the examination and admissions system, instituted a reporting system, and added a large amount of equipment. Within one year of his appointment, Speare prevailed upon the directors of the Evening Institute to establish an Evening School of Law that would better serve the needs of those studying for the bar examination. Traditionally, a prospective attorney prepared for the bar by reading law in a law office. However, legal knowledge was becoming extensive and specialized and a student aspiring to a law career was often restricted to the practice on which his mentor concentrated. Speare's program, initiated on October 3, 1898, had two objectives: preparation for the bar examination of the commonwealth of Massachusetts, and an accumulation of legal knowledge for professional use in business, court procedures, and other areas of work. The growth and development of the program of legal study was affirmed in 1904 when Massachusetts incorporated the Evening Law School of the Boston Young Men's Christian Association with the power to grant LL.B. (Bachelor of Law) degrees. This acceptance of the law school reinforced the YMCA board's belief that institutions with unique ideas could compete with more traditional schools.

At the same time, in Cincinnati, Ohio, a movement was underway that would have significant impact on the foundation that was to become Northeastern University. Dr. Herman Sneider, a former engineer from Lehigh, Pennsylvania, began working on a theory for the preparation of engineers. It was Sneider's belief that technical students should have some way of relating the outside world to their study of methods and practices. In 1906, at the University of Cincinnati, Sneider was given permission to offer an experimental program known as "cooperative engineering." Six pairs of mechanical, electrical, and chemical engineering students were teamed with 15 Cincinnati companies for a six-year work-study program. (Many skeptics felt this program was impractical, pointing out that a conventional engineering program could be achieved in four years.)

Reading about Sneider's work, Hercules Geromanos, dean of the Polytechnic School became convinced that the "co-op" philosophy was applicable to Boston students. In 1909, with the support of Frank Palmer Speare

Northeastern University

and the YMCA, Geromanos announced the first day school of "cooperative engineering." Eight students enrolled in the program and four Boston companies agreed to accept them: Boston and Maine Railroad, Boston and Albany Railroad, Boston Consolidated Gas, and Boston Elevated Railway. The students alternated between one week of study and one week of work at a pay rate of five to ten dollars a week. By 1912, the student body had increased to 70 and the cooperating companies to ten. The earn-as-you-learn idea had taken hold.

During the next few years, the YMCA Institute worked diligently to affirm its commitment to providing "co-operative education by day and adult education by night." In recognition of those efforts, the commonwealth of Massachusetts agreed to the creation of Northeastern College on March 30, 1916. Its purpose was to "furnish instruction and teaching in all branches of education in connection with the Boston YMCA and to do all things connected with or incidental to the purposes of its organization." Frank Palmer Speare was named the college's first president. Although two of the college's schools, the Evening

Law School and the School of Commerce and Finance, had previously been given degree-granting status they did so directly under their own names. It was not until March 20, 1920, that governor Calvin Coolidge gave Northeastern College authorization to grant bachelor's degrees in civil, mechanical, chemical, and electrical engineering.

Under Dr. Carl S. Ell, the new dean of the School of Cooperative Engineering, the Department of Cooperative Work and Student Affairs was established. Within the department, a strict policy of close contact between Northeastern and the cooperating companies developed. Ell was convinced that the period of classwork should equip the student with a unit of subject matter to apply on the job, but the time should not be of such length as to break the student's feeling of identity with the university. After much experimentation, it was decided that a ten-week plan provided the greatest benefit. The coordinators made visits once during every ten-week period to firms within a day's commuting distance of Northeastern. If the company was farther away, the coordinators traveled once or twice a year. In these meetings, the supervisors would review the student's progress and assist the employers in improving or adapting the program to best meet their needs and to keep abreast of the latest developments in their area of specialty.

Within a short time, world events affected the growth of Northeastern's cooperative programs. During World War I, the United States government took over the School of Cooperative Engineering and converted it into a Strategic Army Training Corps. Barracks and mess houses were constructed and new courses such as foreign trade, military French, and airplane mechanics were offered. During the Depression, cooperating firms were reluctant to employ students while family men were in need of work. Nevertheless, the Department of Cooperative Work continued to maintain relationships with the employers who found ways to use students for temporary jobs and special projects until they could resume their previous work-study relationships.

Northeastern's ability to maintain its cooperative service and commitment to the community during these difficult times expanded its educational influence. That influence was most notably reflected in 1936 when Northeastern changed its title from "College" to "University" and separated from its long-time affiliation with the Boston YMCA. This distinction allowed Northeastern University to begin to formulate a financial plan for its expansion into new buildings and property, and to propose a system of endowments to foundations and individuals. Many results of those efforts were realized under the new administration. As Northeastern's second president, Ell was responsible for the completion of the science hall (1941), student center and alumni auditorium (1947), Dodge Library (1952), Cabot Physical Education Center (1954), Haydon Hall (1956), and the graduate center (1959), in addition to increasing the school's assets from $2 million to $30 million.

By 1960, Northeastern's third president, Dr. Asa S. Knowles had begun to envision the university's role in cooperative education beyond the walls of the campus and the streets of Boston. The first step Knowles took was to change the Office of Cooperative Work to the Department of Cooperative Education, and the title of director to dean. According to Knowles, "Co-op is not just part-time work or a summer job. It involves a specific training program correlated with studies being pursued."

During his tenure, Knowles pioneered the addition of numerous cooperative relationships including mergers with the New England College of Pharmacy and Bouve/Boston's College of Physical Education and Physical Therapy. Knowles also extended cooperating graduate schools in law, accounting, business administration, and chemistry, at the doctoral level. But these changes still limited Northeastern's sphere of influence. Knowles wanted the virtues of "co-op" extended to the larger world.

In 1962, serving as its vice chairman, Knowles along with others organized the incorporation of the National Commission on Cooperative Education. The commission's purpose was to serve as the voice of cooperative education, particularly in Washington in hopes of attaining favorable financial support from the federal government. When President Lyndon Johnson's War on Poverty targeted higher education as a means of social mobility, the commission set to work. By 1965, the Higher Education Act included specific language for the introduction, support, and implementation of cooperative education.

When several institutions expressed interest in establishing cooperative education programs, the Ford Foundation's Fund for the Advancement of Education agreed to finance six colleges for a three-year period if Northeastern agreed to provide the guidance. Northeastern accepted the assignment and was given $143,000 in grant monies, with which the university opened its Center for Cooperative Education to provide direction and strategies for specific implementation to other institutions.

While the work of the commission stimulated interest in the Cooperative Plan of Education among legislators and administrators, some faculty members remained unconvinced. Both Knowles and the vice president of cooperative education, Roy L. Woodridge, understood the concerns, which were the result of an absence of scholarly material on the method. To ease the problem, Northeastern contacted the Ford Foundation with a proposal to establish a chair in cooperative education research at the university. A year later in 1968, Dr. James W. Wilson became the first research professor of cooperative education.

In the 1970s, recession and inflation triggered new interest in the cooperative method. In April 1972, a National Conference on Cooperative Education convened to explore issues concerning educators and employers: doubling of degrees granted since the 1960s but an increase in professional and managerial jobs by only a third; approximately 400,000 students who had taken out federally insured loans and then declared bankruptcy or refused to repay; the leveling off of federal government grants to education. An article published by Knowles in 1975 supported the view that cooperative education was well suited to meet these concerns. According to the plan, cooperative education, by its very nature, kept in close touch with staffing needs, served 75 to 80 percent more students without necessitating an increase in the institution's resources; it also lessened a student's dependency on government grants and loans because of its pay-as-you-go design.

From the discussions at the conference, a Cooperative Education Consortium of New England was established with Northeastern designated as the group leader and fiscal agent. Under this plan, the consortium guided participating schools in student placement procedures and provided counseling and financial assistance. During this time, the National Commission for Cooperative Education continued its work in Washington until, under a new Higher Education Amendment passed in 1976, cooperative education became an individual line item.

Knowles's belief in the worldwide influence of Northeastern's "co-op" program became a reality when he was invited to speak at the second Anglo-American Conference in England in 1973. By the close of his administration two years later, Northeastern was the largest private university in the nation in terms of enrollment, a leader in adult and cooperative education, and the owner of 330 acres of land with a total of 20 new buildings and $70 million in property value assets.

On May 13, 1975, Northeastern University elected its fourth president, Kenneth G. Ryder. During his tenure, the attitude toward cooperative education shifted from the traditional emphasis on the program's financial advantages toward its educational ones. With the rise in family income and the relative prosperity of the mid-1980s, financial considerations were less crucial than they had been. Ryder's philosophy focused on the transference of skills and the reinforcement of classroom experience. The first year of Ryder's administration coincided with America's Bicentennial and many visitors from around the world came to Boston, and also to Northeastern University. Ryder viewed this as a golden opportunity to increase the influence of Northeastern's cooperative education experience. The international exchange was expanded when, in the spring of 1980, 25 Northeastern delegates traveled to the People's Republic of China at the invitation of a delegation of Chinese scholars who had previously visited the university's Institute of Chemical Analysis, Applications, and Forensic Science.

In 1981, Northeastern hosted the Second World Conference on Cooperative Education. Educators, business, labor, and government representatives from 27 countries met to discuss how cooperative education could provide training and job experience to meet worldwide professional staffing shortages. At the following year's conference, Ryder was named founding chair of the new World Council on Cooperative Education. The council was charged with developing a worldwide awareness of cooperative education as an educational tool and strategy.

During these discussions with representatives of foreign countries, Ryder began laying the foundation for the international placement of Northeastern students. Because the world conferences made it possible for an understanding of the realistic employment needs of other countries, there was less confusion about where to place Northeastern students and more willingness on the part of companies to enter exchange arrangements, so that universities with exchange agreements could simply "swap" students.

While most international cooperative placements in the 1980s were exchanges, some direct placements were made. Many direct placements were made with Israel through the efforts of Stephen Kane, associate professor of cooperative education, who had developed numerous contacts during the mid-1970s. In most international placements, the pay was less and students had to be fluent in the language of the country. The students were required to complete two years of coursework at Northeastern, with grades well above average. For those students who met the requirements but could not afford the travel costs, President Ryder initiated a $100,000 fund to cover airfares and salary differences.

Currently, the Department of Cooperative Education and the International Cooperative Education Program are housed at the Stearns Center on Huntington Avenue. Every freshman is assigned a co-op advising team to aid in finding them appropriate work experience. All the colleges of the university offer cooperative opportunities. International students are often assigned to employers in their home countries.

From its beginnings in the YMCA building with an enrollment of eight to a 55-acre main campus with approximately 6,000 undergraduates and 2,300 employer locations in 27 states and 25 foreign countries, the Northeastern Cooperative Education experience has flourished. While the success of the program has been achieved in part by the dedication of leaders such as Frank Palmer Speare, Carl S. Ell, Asa S. Knowles, and Kenneth G. Ryder, it cannot be forgotten that these men would certainly not have achieved these results without the "cooperative" experiences of other men, women, and students associated with the Evening Institute, Northeastern College, and Northeastern University.

Further Reading: Northeastern University has published several comprehensive histories of its development. Chief among these are *The Origin and Development of Northeastern University 1898–1960* by Everett C. Marston (Boston: Northeastern University, 1961); and two volumes by Antoinette Frederick, *Northeastern University: An Emerging Giant 1959–1975* (Boston: Northeastern University, 1982), and *Northeastern University Coming of Age: The Ryder Years 1975–1989* (Boston: Northeastern University, 1995).

—Phyllis Brandano

NORTHWESTERN UNIVERSITY
(Evanston, Illinois, U.S.A.)

Location: Northwestern's main campus is located in Evanston, Illinois, approximately two miles north of Chicago. A second campus on Chicago's Near North Side primarily houses the university's professional schools.

Description: A private research university occupying two campuses, and enrolling more than 17,000 students in 12 academic divisions.

Information: Department of University Relations
Northwestern University
555 Clark Street
Evanston, IL 60208-1230
U.S.A.
(847) 491-4884

The Methodist Church founded Northwestern University in 1851 with the intention of educating youth from across the original Northwest Territory, and they named the institution according to that purpose. However, the church leaders were especially concerned to meet the educational needs of Chicago and its surrounding communities. There were already scores of colleges and universities in the midwest, including 12 in the young state of Illinois; yet Chicago had none. Nine members of the church met in a law office downtown in the summer of 1850 and drafted the university charter, which was approved by the governor the following January. That summer, the newly elected trustees decided to purchase a 379-acre site north of the city in Evanston, Illinois, where the present north campus lies.

The date of 1851 has been somewhat arbitrarily chosen as the year of the university's foundation, for like any complex institution, Northwestern came into being gradually. Clark Hinman was elected the university's first president in 1853, before there even existed a school over which to preside. His job was to raise an endowment of $200,000, half to be earned through the sale of $100 scholarships. Hinman died in 1864 at the age of 35, a little more than a year before the first building on the new campus opened for classes. That year, a faculty of two instructed ten students, principally in mathematics, literature, and religion. (The emphasis on religious and moral studies at Northwestern faded gradually in the early twentieth century.) To ensure future classes of qualified students, the university opened a preparatory program in 1856 which enrolled nearly twice as many students as the college through 1869.

Following more than a decade of financial difficulty, Northwestern embarked on an astounding period of growth. In 1869, the stately University Hall was completed. In 1869, the trustees voted to admit women on equal terms with men, and four years later integrated the Evanston College for Ladies, forming the Woman's College of Northwestern University. In 1870, the Chicago Medical College was integrated with Northwestern, which only then became a university in more than name. In 1873, Northwestern opened the Union College of Law in conjunction with the University of Chicago. The combined academic and financial strength of the two institutions permitted the law school to maintain standards and a curriculum comparable to those at Yale and Harvard in its first year of operation, and by 1876, it enrolled 134 students. Still more programs and buildings followed.

Northwestern's rapid expansion was perhaps too rapid, for the university fell on hard times in the mid 1870s. The Panic of 1873 and the depression that followed devalued Northwestern's land holdings and curtailed the influx of donations. The university was in debt for almost ten years and was unable to pay its professors in full for most of the same period. In addition, enrollment declined as competing educational institutions opened throughout the midwest. Thus, Acting President Oliver Marcy found it necessary to recommend to the trustees that the College of Technology be closed until a time when Northwestern could afford its proper equipage and staffing. Marcy determined that the university would be sustained by ensuring its high academic standing, for thus it would draw both students and benefactors. He pleaded with the trustees to do the following: concentrate spending on faculty and equipment; cease coeducation, for he believed that women were not capable of serious scholarship; and appoint a permanent president who would instill the university with vision and character. The trustees accommodated only the last request.

Joseph Cummings, former head of Wesleyan University, was elected president of Northwestern in 1881. His chief task was to raise funds to eliminate the university's debt of more than $200,000—Governor Evans promised $50,000 provided that the university contributed the remainder. Cummings accomplished his goal within two years, but he believed that only with more money would the university be able to maintain the high standards it claimed to have. To achieve that end, Cummings eliminated the requirement that students hold certificates from accredited secondary schools to take Northwestern's entrance exams. As a result, enrollment in the College of Liberal Arts rose 60 percent by the end of the decade.

Northwestern University

The closing years of Cummings's nine-year term marked the beginning of Northwestern's second period of expansion and improvement. By the end of his tenure, Cummings appointed six new professors, the Union College of Law became Northwestern's in full when the first University of Chicago closed in 1886, and a College of Dental and Oral Surgery was opened in 1887. The university also constructed several new buildings, most importantly the especially well-equipped Fayerweather Hall of Science and the Dearborn Astronomical Observatory. Cummings suffered a fatal heart attack on May 7, 1890, while finishing an annual report for the trustees which began, "Men die but institutions live on."

In 1890, the trustees elected Henry Rogers the next president of Northwestern, based on his great success as dean of the law school at the University of Michigan during the previous 11 years. Rogers particularly wished to modernize Northwestern in ways that would allow it to keep pace with the rapid technological and educational changes of the late nineteenth century. His initial steps were preliminary. First, he persuaded the trustees to step up their fundraising efforts in order that Northwestern's endowment might approach the daunting size of those of its academic competitors. Second, he more fully unified Northwestern's administration under his office, including the dental and law schools, which were previously almost fully independent. Other changes included the acquisition of the Woman's Medical School of Chicago in 1892, the introduction of doctoral programs, and the hiring of several prominent scholars to join the Liberal Arts College. Rogers also oversaw the construction of the Lunt Library, Swift Hall, the Music Building, and the capacious Fisk Hall on the Evanston campus. Rogers unexpectedly retired in 1900, probably because his ambition that Northwestern emulate such outstanding universities as Harvard and Yale had created tensions on campus. Northwestern's older professors apparently resented their younger, perhaps superior, colleagues.

Campus life at Northwestern in the nineteenth century principally revolved around literary, debate, and oratory clubs, and ever increasingly around fraternities and sororities. During the university's first decade of operation, the majority of students belonged to one of the academically oriented clubs. By 1895, more than 30 percent of Northwestern's students were members of one of the Greek letter societies. Athletics grew increasingly popular and well organized between 1855 and 1900 as well. Rogers was one of seven university presidents from the midwest who met to plan the regulation of intercollegiate athletics in 1895. They produced the Presidents' Rules, and a league which became the Big Ten in 1912.

The university continued to improve its capacity and record for seminal research in the period between Rogers' departure and World War I, and thus to come ever nearer to the stature of its east coast rivals. However, progress was slow for the first several years of the twen-

tieth century, for the university endured a period of ephemeral presidents. Acting President Daniel Bonbright served nearly two years before the trustees found a suitable replacement in Edmund James, but James left two years later, when he was offered the presidency of the University of Illinois, apparently frustrated by Northwestern's slow progress toward first-rate status. Two more years passed under Acting President Thomas Holgate, until finally Abram Harris began a ten-year period of service in 1906, thus restoring the leadership that the university badly needed.

During Harris's administration, Northwestern expanded and modernized in several ways. Numerous buildings were erected on campus, including the Swift Hall of Engineering, the Patten Gymnasium, Harris Hall, and the men's quadrangles. The addition of the Engineering Hall allowed the engineering program, canceled by Rogers, to resume. More significant still, was the opening in 1908 of the School of Commerce, the forerunner of Northwestern's prestigious Kellogg Graduate School of Management. The school was originally organized to train clerical workers for the increasingly complex businesses burgeoning in America between the Civil War and World War I. The original curriculum was accordingly practical: students learned commercial arithmetic, bookkeeping, ornamental penmanship, stenography, typewriting, and secretarial training.

Northwestern was temporarily but dramatically affected by America's entrance into World War I. All of Northwestern's fraternity houses were transformed into military barracks housing some 1,600 students serving in the Student Army Training Corps. More than 100 Northwestern faculty members took leaves of absence to serve as soldiers or civilian employees of the military. Professor John Hayford, of engineering, remained with the Advisory Board on Aeronautics in Washington, D.C. throughout the war. John Wigmore, dean of the law school, helped draft the selective service legislation. Professor Walter Scott of the psychology department helped formulate a method for placing military personnel according to their abilities, and for promoting officers according to their efficiency rather than merely by seniority. The medical school organized a unit of 241 individuals who treated some 60,000 soldiers in France. By the war's end, more than 2,800 Northwestern students, faculty, and alumni participated in the Allied effort, 65 of whom were killed.

A number of notable events unrelated to military matters also occurred at Northwestern during the war years. First, the preparatory academy was closed in 1917, for it was made redundant by the proliferation of good public schools. Second, the school of pharmacy was rendered to the University of Illinois, both because it was operating at a deficit and because it, too, was made redundant by the existence of a capable state institution. Lynn Hough was elected Northwestern's new president in 1917, after first

Harris, and then acting president Holgate resigned, each repeating the complaint of previous presidents that Northwestern's endowment was insufficient for the university to achieve its potential. In 1920, Hough oversaw the purchase of a lot on the corner of Chicago and Michigan Avenues downtown, where the medical and dental schools would be unified when the Montgomery Ward Memorial Building was completed in 1926. Hough resigned two weeks after the land transaction was completed, citing poor health.

In the period between the two world wars, Northwestern had an astounding run of large donations sufficient to fund the sort of improvements called for by many of its departed presidents, and sufficient to carry it through the Great Depression with little compromise. The university's good fortune may have been the result of deliberate actions; the trustees formed a financial campaign committee in 1919, and the following year the newly elected President Walter Scott created a publicity department to entice benefactors. By 1924, the committee had raised an impressive $8.5 million, $4 million of which was given in a single grant from Mrs. Elizabeth Ward specifically for the construction of the downtown campus building, subsequently named for her husband. While pleased with the results of the first campaign, Scott was disappointed that just $1 million was raised for improvements on the Evanston campus. He determined that another $5.7 million was needed for the undergraduate colleges to remain competitive. His hopes were more than realized, for between 1924 and 1930, Northwestern raised over $11 million for the Evanston campus, and over $5 million more for the professional schools. Then in 1928, Milton H. Wilson bequeathed to the university $8 million in his will, the largest single donation that the university had ever received.

President Scott spent a large portion of Northwestern's riches on new facilities. Four professional schools relocated to new buildings on the Chicago campus in 1926: the medical and dental schools moved into the 14-story Ward building; the School of Commerce into the Wieboldt building; and the law school into Mayer Hall and the Gary library. In 1929, plans were made to extend the Chicago campus by five more acres, purchased in 1927 for over $2 million, in order to build five hospitals to be associated with the medical school. Passavant Hospital was opened in 1929, but the others were delayed more than 30 years by the Great Depression, and then by war. The Evanston campus received a library, a chapel, women's dormitories, Dyche stadium, schools of music, speech, and education, and science laboratories.

World War II had a more profound effect on the university than did World War I. President Franklin Snyder was elected on September 1, 1939, the same day that the Nazis invaded Poland, and he soon integrated the university into the American war effort. In the summer of 1940, even before the United States entered the war, Snyder appointed a committee to determine how Northwestern's facilities might be utilized by the military. The psychology department worked with the army to determine methods for personnel selection. The university provided facilities and sometimes instructors for numerous training programs associated with the military, and reserve officer training programs swelled. Most medical and dental students were in the reserves, and the law school enrollment plummeted from 261 in 1939–40 to 57 in 1943–44.

The character of Snyder's ten-year term was chiefly defined by the war, but he is also responsible for nearly doubling the university's net assets and for hiring a higher rank of professors than the university previously retained. The campus was tense under Snyder, for he is reputed to have imposed his will on deans and professors. Snyder accused Professor Paul Schilpp of the philosophy department of behaving unprofessionally when he expressed personal views in class, for example, and he saw that Schilpp was neither promoted nor given salary increases commensurate with his excellent reputation as both teacher and scholar. No serious conflict between the two ever arose, but Snyder's heavy-handed treatment of Schilpp was an embarrassment to the university, and a source of anger among students and faculty sympathetic with the professor. The situation came to a happy conclusion when Schilpp was promoted to full professor in 1950, the year after Rosco Miller was elected Northwestern's 12th president.

Miller was a medical student, professor, and then dean of the medical school at Northwestern before accepting the university's highest office in 1949. During his 25 year administration, he exercised an executive style contrary to that of his predecessor. Miller created a tightly woven administrative hierarchy and delegated considerable powers to those holding lesser offices. He relied upon an administrative council, council of deans, and his immediate staff to keep him informed of the university's affairs, and to coordinate policies. Miller and the trustees generally concerned themselves only with issues related to the university as a whole, while the deans and various committees handled narrower matters independently. Moreover, Miller rendered many of the administrative duties associated with his office to Payson Wild, the vice president and dean of faculties, and devoted himself to managing the university's finances. On the other hand, Miller expected the deans to operate within the framework of a singular university, even when that entailed spending more money on a department than it brought in.

President Miller's goals were familiar: he pledged to raise more money with which he would improve faculty salaries and campus facilities. Miller did remarkably well, for the university raised more than $270 million in donations during his administration. An impressive $40 million of the university's acquired funds were set aside for faculty salaries. In 1961, the Evanston campus was extended by approximately 74 acres when the university filled in the shallow waters of Lake Michigan bordering the east side of the campus, and during the whole of Miller's administration, the university either built, purchased, or remodeled 51 buildings.

In the turbulent year of 1968, Miller faced the only serious case of student unrest ever seen at Northwestern. That May, a group of black students, both graduate and undergraduate, protested the university's "racist structure," and its exceptionally poor record for admitting African Americans; only 160 of 8,000 students were black. On April 12, they had made several strong demands for a degree of authority in decisions regarding admissions, hiring, and curriculum planning. The administration responded with outward sympathy, but made plain that they would relinquish no genuine administrative power. In response to the university's inaction, approximately 100 black students occupied the university business office on May 3. The trustees considered removing them by force, but they were dissuaded by the poor result of such harsh measures at other universities. They decided to negotiate, and the matter was resolved peacefully by the following evening. The administration conceded that it would give black students a voice in decisions that concerned them, while the students accepted the idea that the trustees and administration could not and would not relinquish their authority.

The years of Miller's presidency marked the decline of the university's athletic glories. The football team won the Rose Bowl in 1949, but they were not to return to it until 1995, when they lost to the University of Southern California. In the years between, there has been serious debate about whether Northwestern should withdraw from the Big Ten Conference, in which it is pitted against much larger schools that spend more on their sports programs, but Miller and others at the university have insisted on staying in. Frustrated with their losing teams, the Alumni Advisory Council recommended that Northwestern relax its academic requirements for student athletes, but the administration has refused all such suggestions.

One of Northwestern's most successful presidents was its 14th, Arnold Weber. He came to a fiscally foundering institution in 1985, and in his ten-year administration managed to both balance the university's budget every year and to hold down tuition increases to the lowest percentage of increases in major American universities. While Weber had reason to be proud of the university's achievements in research (research funds

increased from $64 million in 1985 to $155 million in 1993), he believed that undergraduate teaching was the main mission of the university. In a 1991 speech, he said, "From the founding of the earliest universities, teaching has been . . . the highest calling of the faculty. It remains so at Northwestern today."

Weber's tenure was not, however, entirely serene. Only three months after he took office, a group of students demanded that Northwestern divest itself of stock in companies which did business with South Africa. These anti-apartheid demonstrations produced arrests of over 120 student protesters. The following year, 32 students were arrested in similar demonstrations.

Another issue that prompted dissension on the campus was the denial of tenure to Barbara Foley, an assistant professor English whose Marxist beliefs caused her to lead a demonstration which prevented Nicaraguan contra leader Adolfo Calero from speaking at the university in 1985. Weber said, "They threw synthetic blood on him and ran a miniriot that prevented him from speaking." Foley was censured by the faculty. When she came up for tenure a few months later, the faculty recommended that she be granted that status, but the provost denied her tenure, and Weber upheld that decision.

By 1993, Northwestern had risen to 13th in the *U.S. News & World Report*'s ranking of national universities. In 1991, Weber had said, "as I reviewed the credentials of the incoming class and reflected on my own checkered academic career, I concluded that the only way I could get into Northwestern is as president—the mark of an outstanding university."

Further Reading: The only available history of Northwestern that covers events much beyond the turn of the century is *Northwestern University: A History, 1850–1975* by Harold F. Williamson and Payson S. Wild (Evanston, Illinois: Northwestern University, 1976). *The Evolution of Management Education: A History of the J.L. Kellogg Graduate School of Management, 1908–1983* by Michael W. Sedlack and Harold F. Williamson (Urbana: University of Illinois Press, 1983) is very thorough, but does not contain much information about university affairs beyond the Kellogg School. *Northwestern University School of Law: A Short History* by James A. Rahl and Kurt Schwerin (Chicago: Northwestern University, 1960) is similarly limited.

—Christopher Hoyt

OBERLIN COLLEGE
(Oberlin, Ohio, U.S.A.)

Location: Oberlin, Ohio, a community of 8,000, 35 miles southwest of Cleveland.

Description: A private, coeducational institution comprised of two divisions, with some 2,400 students enrolled in the College of Arts and Sciences and about 500 enrolled in the Conservatory of Music. The school offers bachelor's degrees in arts or music and selected master's degree programs.

Information: Admissions Office
Oberlin College
Oberlin, OH 44074
U.S.A.
(216) 777-8121

Visiting: Guided tours of the campus are available on weekdays throughout most of the year. Contact the Admissions Office for more information.

Founded in 1833, Oberlin College was the first college in the nation to admit women and one of the first to admit African Americans. Known for its abolitionist fervor, Oberlin was a stopping point on the Underground Railroad, transporting runaway slaves from the South to freedom in Canada. Today, the school is noted for its academic program and its outstanding conservatory of music, the conservatory being the first in the nation and today one of the most prestigious. The school retains a tradition of involvement in social issues which, at times, has earned it a reputation for radicalism among its critics. When the college celebrated its 150th anniversary in 1983, *The New York Times* wrote: "In its century and a half, while Harvard worried about the classics and Yale about God, Oberlin worried about the state of America and the world beyond."

Both the town of Oberlin and the college were founded in 1833 by two idealistic missionaries, the Reverend John Jay Shipherd and Philo Penfield Stewart. Shipherd was a revivalist preacher; Stewart was a one-time missionary among the Choctaw Indians. The two literally carved the town and the school out of the wilderness, and then began the challenging struggle for financing so common to the new colleges springing up on the nation's frontiers. The goals of the two men were to establish a model community of Christian devoutness and a college "to train teachers and other Christian leaders for the boundless, most desolate fields in the West." Both the school and the town were named for Johann Friedrich Oberlin (1740–1826), a French-born Lutheran pastor famed for devoting his life to helping the poor in the Vosges region of France.

The new school began providing instruction for students on December 3, 1833, receiving its charter on February 28, 1834. Four young men made up the first freshman class, among them James Harris Fairchild, who one day would become the school's president. Originally, the school was called "Oberlin Collegiate Institute," because Shipherd considered the name "Oberlin College" too pretentious for the modest level of instruction offered at the time. But in 1840 the school assumed the latter designation following its own detailed study showing its course of instruction to be comparable to that of Yale University.

Both the school and the town were governed by the "Oberlin Covenant," which reflected the strict moral standards of the founding fathers. The covenant forbade drinking, smoking, swearing, gambling, any liberties with the opposite sex, and any recreation or other pleasurable activities on Sunday. When one enterprising student attempted to rendezvous with a young woman, a group of his fellow students took him off for penitential prayer and a flogging.

On March 8, 1834, Shipherd published the school's first circular, stating, among its objectives: "The elevation of female character by bringing within the reach of the misjudged and neglected sex all the instructive privileges which hitherto have unreasonably distinguished the leading sex from theirs." Known as Oberlin's Magna Carta for womankind, this statement foretold not only instruction for women but equal opportunity with men in the pursuit of degrees.

Initially, women studied in Oberlin's "Ladies Department," paying their way by housekeeping, gardening, spinning wool, and making clothes. In 1835 the women of Oberlin College organized a Young Ladies' Association, the first women's club in any college. Two years later, four young women from the Oberlin Preparatory School petitioned and were given permission to join the men's freshman class. Three of them completed the full college course in 1841 and became the first women in the nation on record as earning bachelor of arts degrees.

The addition of women to the student body may have contributed to Oberlin's innovative establishment of a school of music. The school had choral singing almost from its earliest days. Then, in the mid-1860s, Professor George Allen, who had studied under famed American musician Lowell Mason in Boston, officially organized a

Oberlin College

music school at Oberlin. This marked the beginning of the Conservatory of Music, a full department of the college, and the first in the nation.

Oberlin's decision to admit women on an equal footing with men was revolutionary for the times. Even more revolutionary was its decision to admit African Americans. In 1835, just two years after its founding, the school was teetering on the edge of bankruptcy. Shipherd sought aid from two wealthy New York businessmen, Arthur and Lewis Tappan. The Tappans were staunch abolitionists who insisted, in return for their financial support, that Oberlin admit students regardless of color. The school's trustees agreed. As a consequence, African Americans became part of the Oberlin College student body at a time when the state of Ohio was still debating whether to admit black children to elementary and secondary schools and when several southern states held it a crime simply to teach African Americans to read or write. By the turn of the century, 128 African Americans had been graduated from Oberlin College, nearly half the total black graduates in the entire country. Mary Jane Patterson, who was graduated from Oberlin in 1862, one year before the Emancipation Proclamation, was the first black woman in the United States to earn a bachelor's degree.

In the years preceding the Civil War, both the school and the town of Oberlin became hotbeds of abolitionism. The town was a major depot on the Underground Railroad, the network of volunteers and safe houses helping escaped slaves to reach freedom in Canada. After the Civil War, more than 500 one-time Oberlin students went south to teach newly freed slaves struggling through the difficult days of Reconstruction. Historian-author Nathan Brandt memorialized Oberlin in *The Town that Started the Civil War.* A bestseller in its time, the book recounts a true episode, known as the Oberlin-Wellington rescue, which occurred in 1858. A fugitive slave named John Price was tracked down and captured by slave-catchers outside the town of Oberlin. A posse of 37 townspeople, including four students and one faculty member from the college, intercepted the slave-catchers at the nearby town of Wellington and freed the fugitive. He escaped to Canada, but the rescuers were indicted under the Fugitive Slave Act of 1850. They spent 83 days in a Cleveland jail, but their act of valor incited nationwide antislavery passions.

With slavery at an end, Oberlin College's humanitarian interests soon extended thousands of miles across the sea. In 1881, a number of the school's theology students traveled to the Shansi Province of China, not only seeking Christian converts but also hoping to found a school of higher education for the Chinese in that region. These pioneers were killed along with many other American missionaries during the turbulent days of China's Boxer Rebellion in 1900. However, the link they forged to Asia grew stronger over the years. The Oberlin Shansi Memorial Association today sends graduates and faculty members to teach in Asian countries and brings Asians to study at Oberlin. In 1989, Oberlin strengthened its historic bond with China by implementing a study-abroad program with Yunnan University in Kunming.

In its earliest years, the course of instruction at Oberlin College reflected a decidedly evangelical mission. Under the leadership of Charles Grandison Finney, a forceful revivalist who served as president of the school from 1851 to 1866, Oberlin earned a reputation for theological zealousness. Finney's successor, James Harris Fairchild, who served from 1866 to 1889, remained committed to the evangelical tradition, but favored a more moderate approach combined with greater social involvement. In his inaugural address he said:

College life, with us, is not peculiar, occupied with its own exclusive interests, pursuing its own separate schemes, and governed by its own code of duty and honor. Each student belongs still to the world. . . . The student still shares in the responsibilities of common life and is here for the purpose of a better outfit for the work before him.

Fairchild also believed that learning should be the means to an end, not an end in itself, and that teachers needed to establish a bond of mutual trust with their students rather than remaining distanced in their own scholastic world. "Oberlin's danger is that in a day of specialists, narrow men will be chosen [as teachers] and so character, manhood, womanhood and inspiring personal power will go," he said. "That would be a disastrous lapse from the Oberlin of former days."

Though Oberlin had been admitting women since 1837, it was not until 1879 that the first woman was appointed to the faculty. Amelia A. Field Johnston became principal of the women's department in 1879, a position in which she remained until 1894, when she became dean. She also taught medieval history from 1878 until 1907.

Another influential voice, later in the century, was Harry Huntington Powers, a French instructor from 1888 to 1892. Educated at the University of Wisconsin and at the Sorbonne in Paris, Powers achieved great popularity with his students but alarmed his teaching colleagues with his unorthodox views. His humanistic concept of Jesus went against traditional teaching and provoked lively debate. He urged the school to stretch beyond its evangelical roots and develop into a full-fledged university. In 1893, he wrote a futuristic article for the school magazine, the *Oberlin Review,* called "A Pedagogue in Wonderland," in which an Oberlin professor awakens after a 100-year sleep to discover a world in which all institutions and social conventions are judged by their benefit to the public good and in which private property and capitalistic enterprises are held under rigid public control. While Powers' unorthodox views were never widely accepted at Oberlin, his membership on the faculty is indicative of the school's tolerance for a variety of opinions.

The students of Oberlin, themselves, were not above urging change. By the late 1800s, many were complaining about the superficial level of instruction. They demanded higher admission standards, noting that many students left the school before graduation to complete their education elsewhere because Oberlin was admitting students who required secondary-level instruction. They pressed for a broader variety of elective courses and for more qualified teachers, including some who had studied at foreign universities such as those who could be found on the faculties of the nation's better-ranked colleges. A student editorial in the *Oberlin Review* criticized dogmatic teaching methods and advocated new instructors with fresh ideas:

> It seems inevitable that one who has taught for many years in the same channel should become intolerant of contradiction, while natural indolence on the part of many pupils leads them to accept without question the dictum of whomsoever their teacher may be. . . . How often do answers seem to be framed to fit the well-known view of the professor?

With the dawn of the twentieth century, America was in transition from an agrarian culture to a more urban, industrialized, and bureaucratic society. Oberlin's onetime religious zeal was rechanneled into the advancement of knowledge, a new intellectual sophistication, and a broadened involvement in social issues. At the turn of the century, Oberlin began to acquire a substantial body of art. The Allen Museum, named for the college's first benefactor in the arts, Dr. Dudley Allen, opened in 1917. It was the first college museum west of the Allegheny Mountains. The museum's collection includes artifacts from ancient Greece, Rome, and Persia, as well as works by major French artists—Courbet (*Castle of Chillon, Evening*) and Monet (*Wisteria* and *Garden of the Princess, Louvre, 1867*).

In the 1960s and 1970s, the school pioneered new services to meet the needs of minority and international students. These programs were quickly followed by the establishment of interdisciplinary majors in African-American, Judaic, Near Eastern, women's, and environmental studies. In another news-making move, Oberlin College, in 1970, opened one of the nation's first coeducational dormitories, earning itself a cover story in *Life* magazine.

Among the more noted Oberlin alumni today are television producer James Burrows ("Cheers" and "Taxi"), public interest lawyer Amy Gittler, author and screenwriter William Goldman ("All the President's Men"), civil rights activist Vernon Jones, pop artist Liz Phair,

award-winning columnist Carl Rowan, and conductor Robert Spano. The roster also includes John Langalibalele Dube, the first president of the African National Congress; Donald Henderson, head of the World Health Organization's successful program to wipe out smallpox worldwide; Nancy Hays Teeters, the first woman to serve on the Federal Reserve Board; John Vinocur, executive editor of *The International Herald Tribune*; and Sylvia Hill Williams, director of the Smithsonian Institution's Museum of African Art.

Additionally, there are three Nobel Prize winners among Oberlin graduates: Robert Millikan, who won the prize in physics in 1923 for his work on electrical charges and photoelectric effects; Roger Sperry, winner in medicine or physiology in 1981 for research on the brain; and Stanley Cohen, who shared the 1986 prize in medicine or physiology for the discovery and characterization of proteins that promote and help regulate cell growth.

Oberlin College today occupies 440 acres of land in the central business district of the town of Oberlin. The campus includes 20 academic buildings and 28 residence halls. The structures display a variety of styles, some reflecting the work of such noted architects as Cass Gilbert and Minoru Yamasaki. The oldest building on campus is Peters Hall, a fortress-like sandstone structure dating back to the 1880s and designed by two Akron, Ohio, architects who specialized in courthouses and prisons. The Gothic building was financed by Captain Alva Bradley, a Cleveland steamship owner, and Richard Peters, an Oberlin alumnus who went on to become a timber magnate in Michigan. The building's most impressive feature, a spacious, central court became a popular gathering place for bobby-sox dances in the 1950s and antiwar rallies in the 1960s. Periodic efforts by college planners to tear down the outdated and forbidding structure have been resisted by defenders of Peters Hall's historic and sentimental value.

Oberlin's Carnegie Library, which opened in 1908, came about largely through a case of fraud. Just when the school trustees were desperately seeking funds for a much-needed library, con-woman Chessie Chadwick duped a local bank out of $350,000 by claiming to be the illegitimate daughter of industrial giant Andrew Carnegie. Her fraud was exposed, and she was sentenced to ten years in prison. When Carnegie heard about the case, he generously stepped in to help the students who had lost their savings at the bank. Oberlin president Henry Churchill King went to New York to thank personally the industrialist to whom he mentioned the need for a library. King came home with the funds. Today, Oberlin's library of more than 1 million volumes has been moved to larger quarters and Carnegie Library now houses the admissions office.

Among Oberlin's newer buildings, Hall Auditorium opened in 1953 was labeled as "the most controversial building in Ohio," by *The Cleveland Plain Dealer*. Cass Gilbert had been the original designer, but the stock market crash of 1929 put a damper on his elaborate, costly plans. After a succession of architects and lengthy delays, the auditorium was finally completed, but it seated only 500 instead of the originally planned 4,000. Its curving limestone walls and white marble facade are beautiful in the eyes of some beholders but have been likened to a beached whale by others. Another controversial structure is that of Oberlin's Conservatory of Music, designed by Minoru Yamasaki and opened in the mid-1960s. The building's glistening quartz facades blend in with nothing else on campus.

At the heart of the campus is Tappan Square, a pleasant, tree-lined park, which carries the name of Oberlin's abolitionist benefactors. Most of the college buildings once lining the square have been razed according to the will of millionaire alumnus Charles Martin Hall, who favored open park space. Hall earned his fortune by discovering an economical method to extract aluminum from its ore, making the metallic element a common household item. The only structure left on the square is the Memorial Arch, built in 1903, to commemorate the Oberlin missionaries killed in China's Boxer Rebellion. Financed by the American Board of Foreign Missions, the neo-classical structure is designed as a triumphal arch of limestone embedded with polished red granite panels and discs. To many Oberlin students and graduates, Memorial Arch symbolizes the school's moral spirit, perhaps best summed up by Professor Walter Horton in 1961:

> If Oberlin should ever cease to produce graduates willing to go out on a limb . . . for new and risky causes on which the state of the world hangs balance, then it would no longer be Oberlin.

Further Reading: John Barnard's *From Evangelicalism to Progressivism at Oberlin College, 1866–1917* (Columbus: Ohio State University Press, 1969) provides a good review of the school's changing philosophies but is short on facts and contains little documentation. The same may be said for *Father Shipherd's Magna Charta: A Century of Coeducation in Oberlin College,* by Frances Juliette Hosford (Boston: Marshall Jones, 1937), regarding its review of women's progress at the school. *Oberlin Architecture, College and Town: A Guide to Its Social History* by Geoffrey Blodgett (Oberlin, Ohio: Oberlin College, 1985) offers brief, historic background on individual buildings, with photos.

—Pam Hollister

OHIO STATE UNIVERSITY
(Columbus, Ohio, U.S.A.)

Location: Columbus, the capital of Ohio and its largest city; regional campuses are located in Lima, Mansfield, Marion, and Newark.

Description: A comprehensive public university, enrolling approximately 50,000 students, that was established as a coeducational land grant school.

Information: Admissions Office
The Ohio State University
Third Floor Lincoln Tower
1800 Cannon Drive
Columbus, OH 43210-1200
U.S.A.
(614) 292-3980

Visiting: The Admissions Office offers two-hour tours on weekdays, as well as self-guided walks of the campus. The Office of Visitor Relations provides an alternate look at OSU with the tour "Tucked Away Treasures"; call (614) 292-0418 to make a reservation.

On April 18, 1870, the Ohio legislature passed the Cannon Act, authorizing the state's counties to raise money in order to secure potential sites for the Ohio Agricultural and Mechanical College. The creation of such an institution had been made possible by the 1862 Morrill Act of the United States Congress, which granted the state land scrip for 633,000 acres; the proceeds were to endow a system of higher education. Four counties actively sought to provide the site for the proposed college: Champaign, Clark, Franklin, and Montgomery. Franklin County was selected by the school's board of trustees, even though its support bid was lower than that of Montgomery County. The specific location chosen for the college was the 300-acre Neil farm north of Columbus, on what is today known as High Street. Legend has it that the decision to choose the Neil farm site was based on the presence of a good spring, water being regarded as a precious commodity.

Debate over the scope of the school's curriculum delayed its opening until September 17, 1873. The trustees were divided in opinion as to whether the school's focus should be vocational, as indicated by its name, or if it should offer a comprehensive course of study as was suggested by the Morrill Act. When the board was called on to vote on the matter, the comprehensive approach was confirmed by the narrow margin of eight to seven. Therefore, when the school began instruction it offered courses in agriculture and mechanic arts as well as in chemistry, geology, mining, metallurgy, mathematics, physics, English, literature, modern and ancient languages, and political economy. A class of 25 students, including two women, was enrolled that fall.

The first president of the fledgling institution was Edward Orton, who had come to Ohio to take part in a geological survey of the state. He also served as a professor at Antioch College and, for a short time, as its president. He left that post to take the helm of the Ohio Agricultural and Mechanical College, at a salary of $3,500. Orton was faced with a number of challenges, beginning with the fact that the college building was incomplete when classes commenced. However, his concern that the school would be unable to accommodate the number of incoming students was mitigated by the panic of 1873. As many as 80 student had been anticipated, but by year's end only 50 students were enrolled.

The first classes were held in a building lacking interior doors, part of its roof, and a floor in the chapel. Although a contract for the building had been signed two years earlier, requiring completion by November 1872, the college was unable to enforce these terms. A description by the architect indicates the type of facility the trustees had hoped to provide: "The Agricultural and Mechanical College of Ohio is designed, when complete, to be a three-story building, besides the basement and attic, and is to be of brick, with stone dressings above the basement story." The building would contain recitation rooms, professors' offices, two amphitheaters, and work rooms. In its unfinished state, the building was also to be pressed into service as a dormitory, housing half of the faculty and several students.

When the school began its second year, University Hall was finished and nine departments of instruction were in operation. Orton's attention was now focused on the heavy teaching load, the need to improve the library's collection and the geological museum, and the misleading effect of the school's name. This last item was addressed in 1878, when the school graduated its first class; the school was renamed the Ohio State University (OSU). The law providing for the name change also reorganized the board of trustees into a body of seven, and limited the president's salary to $3,000 and that of professors to $2,500.

At the same time, the curriculum was enlarged to include mine engineering and military tactics; military drill was also introduced as an elective, but it became compulsory in 1880. In 1879 the university offered its

Ohio State University

first free lectures in farming, thus launching the first extension service at OSU.

In its early years, OSU battled antagonism on several fronts. One faction consisted of other colleges in the area, which had hoped to share in land grant funds; they resented the increasing state aid the new college received. Some detractors argued that not enough attention was being paid to teaching farmers and mechanics, that too much emphasis was placed on other interests. Another criticism was that the school was a godless institution. The question of compulsory daily chapel attendance would contribute to the downfall of President Walter Q. Scott and cause problems for his successor, William H. Scott, each of whom served just two years: Walter Q. Scott from 1881 to 1883 and Walter H. Scott from 1883 to 1885. Walter Q. Scott was not renewed as president after he failed to enforce the university's chapel attendance policy; at the same time, he was labeled a communist for his criticism of land distribution in a capitalist society. In this hostile atmosphere, William H. Scott was pressed to assert the Christian, but non-denominational, status of the university. Required chapel attendance would be closely monitored during his tenure, although the policy was eliminated soon thereafter, in 1900.

A potentially controversial subject, the enrollment of women, generated little comment or activity on campus. The institution was coeducational from the outset, but men comprised most of the student body, and the school provided no special courses or facilities for women. Therefore, housing and meal arrangements for women were haphazard. In 1882 female students presented a petition asking for a "boarding hall." President Walter Q. Scott heartily supported their cause, but years passed and no action was taken. Likewise, the school was ten years old before female faculty members were hired. Women continued to enroll despite such inequities, and in 1886 Annie Ware Sabine became the first OSU student to be awarded an M.A. degree.

The university experienced great financial difficulties during its early years. While Ohio was one of the wealthiest and most populous states in the union, the general assembly failed to accept responsibility for the school's upkeep. One reason for such tightfistedness was active opposition to the school resulting from the Panic of 1873. Finally, in 1878, the legislature appropriated almost $16,000 for the school. This award was to fund the purchase of livestock and a solar compass, the development of a mechanical laboratory, and the construction of a dam on the Olentangy River. From this time forward, the legislature considered the school's needs on an item-by-item basis, giving as little as $1,350 in 1881, and as much as $15,500 in 1885.

In this improved yet precarious position, OSU saw marked growth. In 1891, student enrollment exceeded 500 for the first time. By then, football had been established as an organized sport, and the trustees had agreed to provide an athletic field and to start a school of law. A full electrical engineering course had also been added to the curriculum. These developments served to increase concerns regarding financial security and motivated the school to push for a one-twentieth mill levy for its support. Originally proposed in 1883 by William H. Scott, the levy came to represent the hope of continued growth.

The university was in desperate need of new buildings: the chapel was too small, the library was overcrowded, and several departments were lodged in cramped quarters. In March 1891, the legislature passed the Hysell Act providing for the levy the trustees had sought for so long. With this assurance, plans for two new buildings were commissioned, with building contracts awarded in October 1891 for a manual training (carpentry and woodworking) facility and a building to house the geological museum and library.

Progress of another kind was evidenced in 1896, when OSU ended a preparatory school program it had sustained since its inception. The program had served a large number of students who had attended country schools and were less prepared to enter the university than high school graduates. The trustees now felt that schools in the state had improved to the point that a preparatory school was no longer needed to provide students with an adequate background for college.

James Hulme Canfield assumed the presidency of the university in 1895 and soon saw its fortunes improve. The state legislature authorized the trustees to issue additional certificates of indebtedness for new buildings and improvements up to $300,000, to be repaid with funds provided by an increased levy. During Canfield's tenure, Townshend Hall was built to house the College of Agriculture and Domestic Science, the gymnasium and armory opened, and the number of female students rose markedly. With this in mind, Canfield urged the creation of a women's dormitory and the addition of restrooms for women in the older buildings. The dormitory did not become a reality until 1909.

Dr. Canfield's administration proved to be a short one, however, due to conflicts with some of the faculty and trustees; he resigned and was replaced by William Oxley Thompson, who served from 1899 to 1925; during his term as president, OSU saw great increases in enrollment, facilities, and revenues. In the academic year 1905-06 student enrollment reached a new high of more than 2,000. That same year the legislature passed the Lybarger Act, which distinguished the Ohio State University from other universities and gave it permanent priority as a technical and graduate school.

In 1907 the college of education was created; it was designed to admit students with two years of college work to prepare them as high school teachers and to provide training for school administrators. By the end of the twentieth century, education would become the most popular of the nearly 200 majors offered by OSU. The year 1907 was also marked by financial gains from state and federal sources: the Ohio legislature removed the cap on faculty salaries and granted $750,000 for special projects, while the federal government provided increased funding to $50,000 per year, by means of the second Morrill Act of 1890.

Thus the school saw continued growth, and by its 50th anniversary, in 1920, it could claim an enrollment of over 8,000 and an annual income of more than $1 million. The Ohio State University was now part of a college athletic association, with a director of athletics who served as head football coach. The university's newspaper, *The Lantern,* became a daily produced in the school's own print shop, under the aegis of the new college of commerce and journalism. A graduate school and the position of dean of women had been established. Perhaps most importantly, the Starling-Ohio Medical College had joined the Ohio State University as its college of medicine.

The school year 1921–22 included a number of significant changes at the university. It adopted a four quarter plan of operation rather than three semesters, and a point-hour ratio system was instituted to raise the requirements for graduation. The point system made it possible to weed out students who performed poorly, even though they officially were passing, and to award a degree "with distinction" to superior scholars. During the same period, a university news bureau was created to handle all publicity for the school. The need for such a department was confirmed by the public interest created the following fall by the dedication of the university's new athletic stadium, the first and largest horseshoe-shaped, double-deck stadium in the United States.

The Great Depression would curtail further improvements. The number of courses offered was decreased, faculty salaries were cut, and the size of the teaching staff was reduced. As hard times continued, further belt-tightening became necessary; the operating budget was again reduced and salaries were cut again and still again. In 1938 the Office of Student Aid was established to coordinate support for students. To help offset the reduction in state and federal appropriations, the University Development Fund was organized—a program designed to encourage gifts to the school by alumni and others. In spite of the Depression, a number of badly needed buildings were erected using Public Works Administration funds. They included dormitories for men and women, an addition to the journalism building, and a new faculty club.

The threat of war soon created new concerns on campus; six months before the bombing of Pearl Harbor, on December 7, 1941, some 3,000 students had registered for Selective Service. Special physical education classes were formed for those awaiting induction; in anticipation of a greater need for doctors, the freshman medical class was expanded. After the U.S. declarations of war, the university made further adjustments to wartime conditions. Courses were accelerated so that a year's work could be accomplished in nine months, and evening courses were instituted to train workers for vital industries. Research

facilities were made available for defense use, including secret work on the manufacture of liquid gases related to the atomic bomb project.

Near the end of the war, enrollment fell to its lowest point in 20 years. A trickle of returning servicemen, however, foreshadowed the flood of GIs that would engulf the OSU campus during postwar years. In 1945 a trailer camp was erected to provide housing for the thousands of veterans who would seek an education under the GI Bill. Classes were scheduled early and late to accommodate these new students. Of the 18,000 students and former students who had served in the armed forces during World War II, 691 had been killed.

When OSU marked its 75th anniversary in 1948, enrollment began to level off—after reaching more than 25,000. With the war over, the university was now able to respond to enrollment figures with a comprehensive plan for physical expansion. A medical center and music building would be the first of 15 new major buildings. Regional campuses were created to extend educational opportunities to other parts of the state: Marion and Newark in 1957; Mansfield in 1958; Lima in 1960; Lakewood in 1962; and Dayton (with Miami University) in 1964. Lakewood was subsequently incorporated into Cleveland State University and Dayton was reorganized as a separate school, Wright State.

In 1971, University Hall, the first building on OSU's campus, was razed to be replaced by a replica. It stands among four other historic buildings: Enarson Hall (1910), Hayes Hall (1893), Ohio Stadium (1922), and Orton Hall (1893). These four structures are on the National Register of Historic Places. The bustling, urban campus that now surrounds them is a vital part of modern Columbus. The university's 1,600 acres encompass art galleries, museums, gardens, and Mirror Lake, as well as the university medical center, the Arthur G. James Cancer Hospital and Research Institute, the university extension service, and an airport.

The Ohio State University has produced many graduates who have distinguished themselves in politics, the arts, and sports. Alumni include former U.S. senator Howard Metzenbaum; playwright Jerome Lawrence; author and cartoonist James Thurber; golfer Jack Nicklaus; Olympic champion Jesse Owens. Two Nobel laureates have been OSU graduates: Paul Flory, who won the Nobel Prize in chemistry in 1974 and William Fowler, who shared the Nobel Prize for physics in 1983.

Further Reading: A detailed record of the university's development is provided by James E. Pollard's *History of The Ohio State University: The Story of Its First Seventy-five Years, 1873–1948* (Columbus: Ohio State University Press, 1952). Additional information can also be found in volume 1 of *History of The Ohio State University* by Alexis Cope, edited by Thomas C. Mendenhall (Columbus: Ohio State University Press, 1920).

—Ruth Pittman

OREGON STATE UNIVERSITY
(Corvallis, Oregon, U.S.A.)

Location: Corvallis, Oregon, 85 miles south of Portland.

Description: A public, state-assisted university enrolling approximately 14,500 students in undergraduate, graduate, and professional schools.

Information: Office of Admission and Orientation
Administrative Services Building
Room B-104
Corvallis, OR 97331-2107
U.S.A.
(503) 737-4411

Visiting: Guided tours of the main campus begin at the Administration Building, Room A-150. Tours are available Monday through Friday from 8:00 A.M. to 4:00 P.M. year-round. For more information, call the phone number above.

Although it has been recognized officially as Oregon State University for less than 25 years, this public institution has persevered for well over a century. Founded on January 20, 1858, and chartered on October 27, 1868, as Corvallis College, the Oregon institution withstood 14 name changes and was sold twice before becoming the expansive 400-acre Oregon State University on March 6, 1961.

The Oregon institution had a difficult time getting started. In 1851 the Oregon territorial legislature passed an act ordering that a territorial university be "located and established at Marysville." During the same year Marysville changed its name to Corvallis, meaning "heart of the valley." Building materials were assembled on the selected site where Extension Hall now stands. In 1853 the territorial legislature named three commissioners to select the site in Marysville and erect the university. However, before construction of the new institution began, the legislature of 1855 changed the location of the university and ordered the building materials sold. Corvallis had lost its first bid at higher education.

A year after losing the promise of an institution, a community academy was established in Corvallis. Finally, on January 20, 1858, the school was commissioned as Corvallis College. Incorporated by six local citizens, it had no religious affiliation. For seven years primary and preparatory instruction were coeducational. Among its early teachers was John Wesley Johnson, who would later become the first president of the University of Oregon at Eugene.

Corvallis College's sole building and land was first sold in 1860 at a sheriff's auction to satisfy a mechanic's lien. It was sold again a year later to a Corvallis community board of trustees, on which each trustee was a member of the Methodist Episcopal Church, South. At the time, the college was only partly state-supported.

The church's Reverend William A. Finley, A.M., D.D. became the first president of Corvallis College in October 1865 and served until May 4, 1872. At the time, the college was merely a frame building on Fifth Street between Madison and Monroe. In fact, Finley worked in the college's only building. However, toward the end of Finley's term, in 1871, the Corvallis College Board of Trustees purchased a 35-acre farm on April 17. The land would be known 17 years later as the experimental farm, and now as Lower Campus.

In 1867 four students became the first class of collegiate standing to enroll at Corvallis College. In 1870, each Oregon state senator appointed one student older than 16 years of age to be enrolled for two years at the college. Each academic quarter the secretary of the state drew his warrant upon the state treasurer in favor of the college for $11.25 for each student attending.

The new agricultural curriculum began with 25 students whose tuition was paid by the state. Also in 1870, the first class—one woman and two men—graduated with bachelor of science (B.S.) degrees. They were the first degrees conferred in the far west by a state-assisted college or university. The following year the first bachelor of arts (A.B.) degree was obtained. In 1876 the first master of arts degree was conferred. The first professional degree, a master of engineering, was offered 31 years later. The first Ph.D. degrees—three in science and one in agriculture—were offered in 1935 during the school's 65th commencement. Graduate degrees would be offered in 1988 from the College of Liberal Arts along with the first masters degree in scientific and technical communication, and masters/doctoral degrees in economics. During Finley's term, course offerings included Greek, Latin, and moral philosophy. Freshmen learned by reading the works of Latin authors such as Sallust, Ovid, and Vergil, and Greeks such as Xenophon, Herodotus, and Homer. In addition to serving as the first president of Corvallis College, Finley taught Greek and Latin. After serving for seven years as president, Finley resigned in 1872 and moved to California, after much pleading from his wife, who found the rainy winters in the Willamette Valley hard to tolerate.

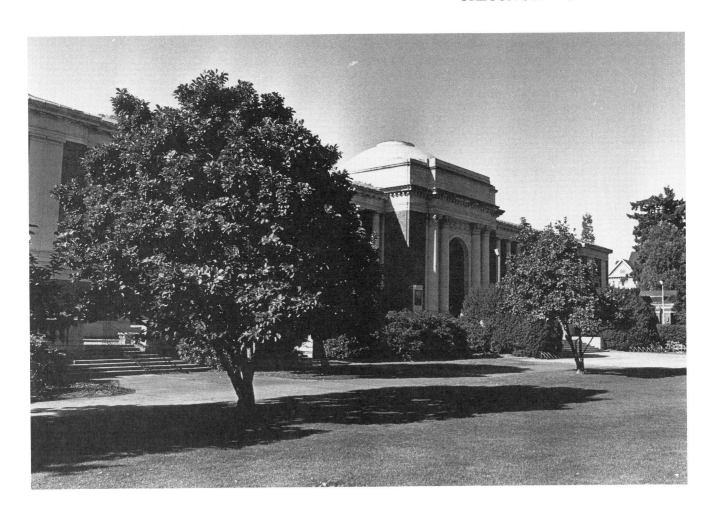

Oregon State University

Although full state support of the college began during Finley's term, on October 27, 1868, Corvallis College remained in the control of the Methodist Episcopal Church, South. The legislative assembly had temporarily designated Corvallis College the agricultural college of the state of Oregon and began making appropriations to maintain the institution. The institution became Oregon's first—and oldest—state-assisted institution of higher education. Its designation as an agricultural college was made permanent in 1870.

Finley's successor, Virginian Benjamin L. Arnold saw his cause as "the need for balance between education and training." Arnold sought to find the true meaning of an agricultural college for many years, and wanted to educate beyond the realm of farming. With limited financial and faculty support, and with Arnold and three teachers comprising the entire faculty, the president faced major obstacles. At one time Arnold headed the department of moral science; he also taught English and may well have taught physics and chemistry—all for an annual salary of $1,500.

When the state of Oregon assumed responsibility for Corvallis College on February 11, 1885, the Methodist Episcopal Church lost its control. In turn, the college's name was changed to Oregon Agricultural College (OAC). Three years after the name change, OAC was remodeled and fitted with a new tower. Money was tight, but, nonetheless, in 1888 the college prepared to move to a new campus. Near this time the new college seal was adopted by the State Agricultural College of Oregon Board of Regents on June 21, 1888. The seal is nearly identical to that of the state of Oregon, with the exception that it uses a wreath of Oregon holly rather than the 33 stars used in the state's seal. The role of agriculture is still recognized in the institution's official seal: a sheaf of wheat, a plow, and a pickax represent Oregon's mining and agricultural resources. The seal also features a British man-of-war heading west on the Pacific Ocean, signifying the departure of British influence in the region; an American merchant steamer symbolizes the rise of American power and commerce. The seal also shows a covered emigrant wagon being pulled westward by two oxen and the local topography with its mountains, forest, and seashore.

Now that OAC was fully state supported, the legislature accepted the provisions of the first Morrill Act, which President Lincoln had signed on July 2, 1862. This act provided grants of land to be used by the states for the sole purpose of establishing publicly controlled colleges. The bill gave each state 30,000 acres of federally owned land for each representative in the Congress of the United States to be used to finance educational programs; Oregon received 90,000 acres. The Congress defined the purpose of the land grant institutions in these words: "The leading object shall be, without excluding other scientific and classical studies, and including military tactics, to teach such branches of learning as are related to agriculture and the mechanic arts, in order to promote the liberal and practical education of the industrial classes in the several pursuits and professions in life."

Therefore, designated and adopted as an agriculture college, the OAC began instructing students in the arts and sciences. The Morrill Act's recommendations for agriculture college curriculum included mathematics, English, natural science, languages, military exercises, agriculture, and moral philosophy. But the OAC was so badly in debt that it would be nearly ten years before that curriculum was added. In fact, teachers were often unpaid, and many were forced to find other work to support themselves. In his first report to the governor of Oregon, Arnold describes the problems he faced:

When I took charge of this institution in the fall of 1872 I was met by three very serious embarrassments. First, the institution was in debt in every department. This, I may remark, has been removed. In the second place, there was no money and scarcely any resources. In the third place, there was no chemical apparatus; there was a tolerably good apparatus for physics. Of course all was paralyzed. Nothing could be done till an appropriation was made. An appropriation of $5,000 a year was made on the 15th of October, or rather the bill appropriating that amount was approved at the date.

Arnold divided the college into two departments, literary and scientific, and laid the foundation for OSU's curriculum. Each college had several schools. The literary department was composed of ancient and modern languages, history, and literature. The scientific department was composed of mathematics, engineering, practical mechanics and technology, physical science, and moral science. Arnold, however, would have to wait for state funding to provide more staff. Arnold realized the importance of scientific agriculture to the Oregon farmers, who at the time were prospering from abundant crops that couldn't last forever. One of Arnold's colleagues, English lawyer Wallis Nash (a neighbor and friend of Charles Darwin), had

come to Oregon in 1877 on behalf of a group of English investors. What Nash found in Oregon were farmers reaping the benefits of fertile land but doing nothing to ensure that prosperity. Farmers were paying only $5 an acre for good farmland and not having to worry about droughts, disease, or infestation. There were no threats of floods or storms and the winters promised to be mild. Farmers were building homes from fir lumber at $10 per 1,000 feet. Nash understood the magnitude of Oregon's prosperity when he learned that local travelers never packed a lunch. Instead, they would stop at a farmhouse where they would be offered a full meal consisting of hot meat, potatoes, cooked fruit, fresh bread, cucumber pickles, and jams and jellies. He wrote, "Where idleness and slovenliness were evident, even here the richness of the soil protected the settler from the want he seemed so thoroughly to deserve."

Nash was amazed at the difference between Oregon and English farmers. Hog parts that were eaten in Europe were fed to the dogs in Oregon. Deer was so abundant that only the hind quarters were consumed. Instead of raising cows for dairying, the farmers were feeding whole milk to the calves and importing butter and cheese. Farmers were planting crop after crop of wheat without rotating crops. When the soil was no longer fertile, the land was abandoned. If the Oregonians continued this way, Nash knew that the abundance could not last forever.

Arnold saw this future problem well, and in 1884 he proposed the establishment of an experiment station, similar to those in Europe at the time. He succeeded in his second attempt at the passage of a bill, which later became known as the Hatch Act of 1887. The Hatch Act established agricultural experiment stations in land grant institutions, such as OAC. Each experiment station received $15,000 annually in support from federal funds, boosting OAC's total operating budget by over 50 percent. The Hatch Act's goal was "to promote scientific investigation and experiment respecting the principles and applications of agricultural science." The OAC staff built its station on the 35 acres of farmland given by the citizens of Benton County in 1871. In 1901 the legislature funded OAC with an additional $10,000 for the establishment of a branch station located in Union, an eastern Oregon town where the land was high and dry, unlike that of the Willamette Valley. Since there were many other Oregon regions which vary in climate and topography, 15 branch stations have been erected to study them. The Hatch Act, therefore, ensured Oregon's abundant crops through educating farmers. Bulletins were published, with most of them focused on helping farmers solve problems from soil to weed control. Later, when mailed bulletins were not enough to solve problems of the farmer, county agents and cooperative extensions took over.

In addition to offering an agricultural curriculum, Arnold decided that one of the college's missions in the 1880s should be special studies for women who were to become homemakers. Margaret Comstock Snell was chosen as professor of household economy and hygiene for the fall term of 1889. Although she believed that skills such as sewing and cooking were important, she taught that they were only part of a well-rounded education. She wrote in a 1902 report:

> The senior class work in aesthetics is of the highest mental and moral value. Here the student is no longer left to "wander about in worlds not realized"; here she learns to know herself and something of her relation to the forms about her in the natural world, and in the world of art; here she learns to recognize all form in the universe as ideas of God—in the world of art, as man's ideas, seeking expression of himself to his fellow men.

Snell ran the first residence hall at OAC, Alpha Hall, and its kitchen. She reduced the per person cost of living in the girls' dormitory to under $1 per week. Snell died in 1923, but the shade trees she planted remain around Seventh Street (the former Episcopal Church), around the current Arts Center, and near her own home and apartments on Jackson and Monroe streets.

By 1883 the college's department of agriculture was well-established. It was the first in the Pacific Northwest. By 1908, professional schools of commerce, agriculture, household economy, and engineering had been added. The college later added to its curriculum schools of forestry (1913), mines (1913), pharmacy (1917), education (1918), basic arts and sciences (1922), and health and physical education (1931). In 1932 the school of science was established; however the school of mines was eliminated. At the same time, the school of health and physical education was reduced to a division. Also, major work in business administration was discontinued, but later resumed when the college of business was established in 1943. The college of liberal arts was founded in 1959 as the school of humanities and social sciences. In the 1970s the college of oceanography, the college of health and physical education, and the college of veterinary medicine were established. In the following decade, all schools within OSU were redesignated as colleges. In 1991, the college of education merged with the college of home economics to become the college of home economics and education.

The institution's course offerings have been just as varied as its changes in name and ownership. Referring to the university's mass and variety of its work, Spanish philosopher Ortega y Gasset wrote that it is "a tropical underbrush of subject matters." Oregon States University's school of business or commerce is one of the first 12 established in the United States, and the first in the Pacific Northwest. When Dean John Andrew Bexell founded the school of commerce in 1908 there were four members of the faculty, including himself. When he retired from active deanship in 1931, the school had grown to include 40 faculty members and the student population had jumped from 105 to 1,000.

Since its inception as an agricultural school, OSU has struggled with its label. The requirements of the Morrill Act were broad and ambiguous. Arnold reported to the governor and the legislature twice on the difficulty of setting a curriculum for an agricultural college. As writer James Groshong said of the institution, "Lacking models, then, the agricultural college of Oregon had to construct an identity for itself." During all its years, the institution was establishing its identity. The sixth president of OAC, William Jasper Kerr, continued the school's quest for liberal studies. However, in 1909, the state created the State Board of Higher Curricula to ensure that OAC and the University of Oregon in Eugene, only 40 miles away, were not duplicating curricula. The board assigned engineering and commerce studies to OAC and liberal arts to the University of Oregon in Eugene. By 1932 the changes were completed, and OAC had changed its name to Oregon State College.

During the years 1907 to 1932, while Kerr was president, the institution undertook major building construction. The list of buildings included the Memorial Union, the armory, the men's gymnasium, the women's building, a home economics building, Graf Engineering Laboratory, Dryden Poultry-Veterinary Hall, Covell Hall, and a building for the industrial arts. Finally, the William Jasper Kerr Library replaced the institution's first library, named after Ida Evangeline Kidder who had founded it. In fact, when Kerr came to OAC in 1907 he came to a 225-acre campus worth $229,000. When he left in 1932 the campus had expanded to 555 acres worth $7.5 million.

In 1961, when OSC became Oregon State University, developments occurred which led the institution back to its original liberal arts background. Under its new president, James H. Jensen, the first degree in English—a liberal arts field—was awarded at OSU. Later, other degree programs in liberal arts followed: history, art, economics, speech, political science, Russian studies, French, German, psychology, music, and sociology. Today, OSU's academic focus continues in liberal arts and sciences. It offers undergraduate and graduate programs in 12 colleges and two schools. In addition to its aforementioned land grant, OSU is also a sea grant and space grant university. (These grants are analogous to land grants and offer federal funds for student fellowships and research.) As OSU celebrated its 128th anniversary in 1996, the institution saw its mission as one to "teach, conduct scholarship and serve its constituents into the 21st Century." The institution vows to continue to lead Oregon and Oregonians as the state's only land grant Carnegie Research I University. (There are approximately 80 U.S. universities in this category. The Carnegie Foundation bases its ratings on the amount of federal research funds an institution receives and the number of Ph.D.s it graduates.) Although the university has no official motto, it has announced its intention is to provide "excellence in advancing knowledge and its application to practical problems, particularly those related to human resources, natural resources and the physical environment." Oregon State University had returned to the lessons of Benjamin Arnold who said, "If on the one hand the curriculum be less extensive than that of an ordinary college there is a loss of dignity and respectability, and with it a loss of the best young men and women, precisely those most needful for the present and future prosperity of the college."

Further Reading: James W. Groshong's *The Making of a University, 1868–1968* (Corvallis: Oregon State University, 1968) was published by the university to commemorate its centennial. A complete listing of OSU buildings and a chronological history timeline may be found in the *Oregon State University Fact Book* (Corvallis: Office of Budgets and Planning, 1994).

—Marla Bosworth

PHILIPPS UNIVERSITY OF MARBURG
(Marburg an der Lahn, Germany)

Location: Marburg an der Lahn, a city of 75,000 in central Germany, about 60 miles (90 kilometers) north of Frankfurt am Main.

Description: A state-run university of about 17,000 students, Philipps-Universität encompasses buildings ancient and modern stretching from the riverbank to the castle.

Information: Akademisches Auslandsamt der Philipps-Universität
(Foreign Students' Office)
Biegenstrasse 12
35032 Marburg
Germany
(0642) 28-1720
Fax (6421) 28-2500

Marburg an der Lahn (on the Lahn River) was once a great religious center of Europe. Its castle and the St. Elizabeth Church both date from the thirteenth century; the Elisa-bethkirche, oldest Gothic cathedral in Germany, contains relics of St. Elizabeth of Hungary and is the burial site for pre-Nazi leader Field-Marshal von Hindenburg.

With its hilly, twisted streets, Marburg features long flights of steps from the riverbank to the castle, portions of which are still used by Philipps University. Halfway up the hill, the old market square with its ancient courthouse and half-timbered houses is a glimpse into antiquity.

The climb is so steep that a public elevator whisks riders from the lower city to the upper section in a fraction of the time students of former generations spent puffing up the seemingly endless steps—quicker, but without the charming view over tiled roofs and the newer campus to the hills beyond.

The University of Marburg is not as well known to most foreigners as Heidelberg. The university was founded in 1527 by Landgrave Philipp the Magnanimous, at age 23 a nobleman in the German state of Hesse, and a political leader of the Protestant Reformation. The institution started with faculties of theology, law, medicine, and philosophy; there were 84 students taught by 11 professors.

Marburg was the first Protestant university in Europe and was soon drawn into conflict between reformers and Lutheran theologians. In the fall of 1529 Martin Luther, the Swiss reformer Ulrich Zwingli, and various followers met at the castle in what became known as the "Colloquy of Marburg," a high point in Hessian history although the talks were inconclusive, since their topic of disagreement was the transubstantiation at Eucharist, a subject that still arouses heated discussion half a millennium later.

For its first three centuries the university floundered, ranging from 30 students to 300. In one way its small size was probably a boon: plague epidemics in the sixteenth and seventeenth centuries several times forced the temporary removal of classes out of town and out of danger. Its small size did not exempt the institution from scandal; many times over the years, the local folks despaired over rampaging students, professorial shortcomings, and similar difficulties. As early as 1610, the populace was complaining about rowdy student behavior, necessitating an edict condemning shooting in the streets, window-breaking, and the like, and difficulties continued for hundreds of years after that. In the early nineteenth century social life ranged from wild drinking contests and duels to teas and dances with the local gentry. The town and the university's strengths ebbed and flowed for centuries, dependent on the political situation until the unification of Germany. After its first centennial, for example, the institution was joined with the university at the nearby city of Giessen for a time. Marburg achieved true stability only when the states of Hesse and Prussia were joined politically in the mid-nineteenth century.

The first major period of the University of Marburg's influence came when Friedrich Karl von Savigny arrived as a law student in 1797. He received his doctorate in 1800 and began to lecture, gaining great fame and respect as a jurist. The university's law school building is named after him. The famed Romantic writer Clemens Brentano came to town to visit Savigny, stayed until 1804, and the university became a "Paradise of Romanticism." One of Brentano's sisters, Kunigunde, married Savigny and another, poet/writer Bettina, visited often and wrote novels with reminiscences of Marburg. To that circle in 1802 came Jakob Grimm, the founder of German philology and author of dictionaries. His brother Wilhelm (collector of folk- and fairy-tales) followed in 1803. By 1808 they had all moved on to Paris and elsewhere, but their fame lives on in memorials as well as a Brothers Grimm museum.

The next period of renown for Philipps University came toward the end of the nineteenth century. Hermann Cohen arrived in Marburg in 1873 and Paul Natorp in 1880; together they founded the Marburg School of Philosophy, a branch of neo-Kantian theory and one of the brightest jewels in the university's crown. They carried Kantianism a step farther in an attempt to meld it with

Philipps University of Marburg

Marxism, and their fame drew students to the institution. Among the latter was Boris Pasternak.

Pasternak studied at the university for the summer of 1912; although his tenure was relatively short, it was a time of epiphany for the young man, who arrived at Marburg planning to be a philosopher and left certain he would instead pursue poetry. The cause of his change of direction came from an abortive affair of the heart; when a visiting friend from Moscow turned down his offer of marriage, Pasternak left Marburg in despair. His few weeks in the old city were memorialized in his auto-biography and poems. For example, an excerpt from "Marburg":

> Here lived Martin Luther. The Brothers Grimm,
> there. And all things remember and reach out to
> them: The sharp-taloned roofs. The gravestones.
> The trees. And each is alive. And each is an emblem.

T.S. Eliot planned to spend the summer of 1914 in Marburg on a fellowship from Harvard, but his arrival was ill-timed. He was only in residence for a couple of weeks before the outbreak of the war, and he left precipi-tously, landing instead at Oxford.

A third high point in the university's history came in the early twentieth century with theological scholars Rudolf Bultmann (student from 1907 to 1910 and later professor); Rudolf Otto from 1917, one of the best-known modern theologians; Old Testament scholar Karl Budde for the first quarter of the century; and Paul Tillich, the Protestant theologian who spent about a year in Marburg after World War I. Existentialist philosopher Martin Heidegger was professor of philosophy from 1923 to 1928; he in turn especially influenced Spanish philosopher and sociologist Jose Ortega y Gasset, who was a student in Marburg in 1910 and was given an honorary degree in 1952.

Over the years scattered arts and humanities faculty and students brought recognition to the university. Heinrich Schütz, in Marburg in the early seventeenth century, was the most important sacred music master in Germany until Johann Sebastian Bach. Heinrich Stilling in the late eighteenth century was a professor of political science and a friend of Goethe. Aldous Huxley lived in the city for two months in 1912 and used it as a setting for "Nuns at Luncheon." Erich Jaensch, also at Marburg for most of his career, was a famed psychologist who related personality to physiology.

From the very early days, many scientists have also owed a great deal to Marburg, whether as students or as researchers and professors. The first chair in chemistry in Europe was established at Marburg in 1609, with the post held by Professor Johann Hartmann.

The French physicist Denis Papin was at Marburg from 1688–95; there, in an attempt to stretch his meager coal supply, he invented the Papin pot, an early pressure cooker. He also theorized on steam-driven pistons, developed the centrifugal pump and attempted to navigate the wholly unsuitable Lahn River in a submarine in 1692.

In the next century Mikhail Vasilievich Lomonosov, the Russian chemist and writer, studied at Marburg. In Russia, he tried with a colleague to duplicate Benjamin Franklin's kite experiments—with disastrous results; he barely escaped with his life, and his friend did not survive. Lomonosov later founded Moscow University and it was his early interest in Marburg that helped lure Pasternak there two centuries later.

From 1839 to 1851, Robert Bunsen served as chemistry professor. He was a cofounder of spectroscopy and was responsible directly and indirectly for the discovery of several elements; still, he will be forever remembered by chemistry lab students as the developer of the Bunsen burner.

Theodore Zincke was professor of chemistry from 1875 to 1913 and in that time instructed not one but three Nobelists. Hans Fischer, researcher in natural pigments, was the 1930 chemistry winner. Otto Hahn, founder of the Atomic Age, won the Nobel Prize for chemistry in 1944. Karl Ziegler was awarded the chemistry prize in 1963 for his synthethis of polymers that formed a basis for plastics technology.

Emil von Behring was a turn-of-the-century professor of hygiene and world renowned for his investigations into blood serum therapy, especially against the dreaded killer diphtheria. In 1901 he received the first Nobel Prize for medicine ever awarded. Otto Schmiel in the early years of the twentieth century was well respected as an author of zoology and botany texts, and his contemporary Alfred Wegener was a famed geologist, Greenland explorer, and theorist of "continental drift."

Von Behring's Nobel Prize was the first associated with Philipps University, but it was far from the last. In addition to Zincke's students, Pasternak, and T.S. Eliot (the latter two admittedly of brief tenure at the university), biochemical pioneer and professor of hygiene Albrecht Kossel won in medicine for 1910. Ferdinand Braun, student and professor in math from 1868 to 1880, physicist and inventor of the oscilloscope, shared the 1909 physics prize with Guglielmo Marconi. Otto Loewi won the 1936 Nobel for medicine and Albert Butenandt, who had studied at Marburg, the 1939 Nobel for chemistry.

Philipps University of Marburg is so entwined with Marburg that separating them today is unthinkable. "It's not just a city but a medieval fairy tale. . . . It is hard to imagine a place that looks as much like a painting as Marburg," wrote Pasternak after his 1912 sojourn at the university. Parts of the citywide campus have changed little, at least in outward appearance, since the earliest days. The university still uses portions of the castle for functions, and the formerly secularized Kugelkirche (Dome Church), which served as a lecture hall for theology students in the very early years, has long been back in use as a Catholic church. The Old University, near the Lahn in the lower part of the city, looks positively ancient, but it was built in the late 1800s in Gothic style.

The university's most striking growth has come since World War II, especially in the last four decades of the twentieth century. Major construction projects in the early 1960s and after have expanded the campus with a new student union, a dormitory village (including the first residence for disabled students in the country), general lecture buildings, and a second campus of science and clinical buildings along the banks of the Lahn.

Several museums recall the history of Marburg and its university. The castle itself houses a collection of Celtic archeological finds ranging from tapestries to suits of armor. Separately housed collections cover mineralogy, art and cultural history, and the library has more than a million volumes.

Women were first admitted as undergraduates in 1909 and to the faculty in 1930. Today Philipps University of Marburg is highly ranked internationally for both graduate (law and medicine) and undergraduate studies (biology, engineering, humanities, physical sciences, and social sciences). Youth from around the world mingle in Marburg. Exchange programs bring students from France, Russia, Sweden, England, Italy, Japan, Spain, Poland, India, and the United States.

—Jeanne Munn Bracken

PRINCETON UNIVERSITY
(Princeton, New Jersey, U.S.A.)

Location: A 600-acre campus in Princeton, New Jersey, a city of about 30,000 residents, located within a 50-mile radius of both New York City and Philadelphia.

Description: An independent, highly selective Ivy League university of 6,300 total graduate and undergraduate students. The school emphasizes undergraduate education, a role reinforced by the absence of professional schools of law or medicine. The graduate school, established in 1901, offers doctoral programs in arts, sciences, and engineering.

Information: Admission Office
Princeton University
Princeton, NJ 08544
U.S.A.
(609) 258-5397

Visiting: Tours of the campus led by student guides are available daily during the academic year and at limited times during summer and holidays. Reservations are necessary for large groups. For more information, write to the Orange Key Guide Service, Maclean House, Princeton, New Jersey 08544, or call (609) 258-3603.

Chartered in 1746, Princeton University became the training ground for U.S. presidents James Madison and Woodrow Wilson, statesmen such as Adlai Stevenson and John Foster Dulles, noted authors F. Scott Fitzgerald and Edmund Wilson, and it provided a laboratory for world-renowned scientists including Albert Einstein and J. Robert Oppenheimer. The school survived British bombardment and occupation during the American Revolution, years of factionalism within the Presbyterian Church, and a long-time reputation as a country club for the privileged scions of the rich, and emerged as a respected center for scholastic achievement, scientific research, and international leadership. Princeton is often called the "school of statesmen."

Princeton was the fourth college established in the British colonies of North America. The school was first located in Elizabeth, New Jersey, then in Newark, finally moving to Princeton in 1756. Chartered as the College of New Jersey and known as Princeton College for most of its first 150 years, the school was the nation's first learning institution to emerge from the Great Awakening, an emotional religious fervor that spread through the colonies in the mid-1700s. For 50 years, the entire college was housed in a single structure, Nassau Hall, which still stands despite its bombardment during the American Revolution and two fires in later years.

Although its charter contained no reference to any religious denomination, Princeton's development was greatly influenced by its Presbyterian founders and by the Scottish evangelical John Witherspoon, who became president of the college in 1766. Witherspoon was an ardent supporter of American independence from Britain, and the school became a hotbed of revolutionary activity. At commencement ceremonies in 1770, students wore American homespun rather than British-made fabric, attracting considerable publicity. Following the Boston Tea Party, Princeton students gathered to burn tea over their own bonfire. Witherspoon, in fact, was one of the signers of the Declaration of Independence (the only minister on the list). Along with 30 other Princetonians, he also served in the Continental Congress. In 1777, George Washington led the forces that drove occupying British troops from Nassau Hall. Six years later, he returned to Princeton to be formally commended by the Continental Congress for his military leadership.

Among Princeton's early students were James Madison, Henry (Light Horse Harry) Lee, Charles Lee, and Luther Martin. Madison was later remembered as a quiet student who showed no hint of his presidential destiny, but his silence may have been attributable to ill health or his fear of public speaking. In any event, Witherspoon was so impressed that he tutored the young man in law and Hebrew. Additionally, Madison founded one of the first extracurricular clubs on campus, the Whig Society, which focused student attention on literature and debate.

A less illustrious graduate of Princeton was Aaron Burr Jr., son of the Reverend Aaron Burr Sr., the second president of Princeton and grandson of the dynamic theologian Jonathan Edwards, Princeton's third president. Young Burr arrived at the school at the age of 13 and came to be regarded as the most promising scholar of his era. He reportedly studied 18 hours a day and performed brilliantly at his commencement, giving an address titled "Building Castles in the Air." His political career reached a peak when he served as vice president to Thomas Jefferson, but it careened downhill when he killed Alexander Hamilton in a duel and later made an ill-fated attempt to carve out his own country in Louisiana and the southwest. The once-promising Princetonian was acquitted of charges of treason, but his reputation was in ruins.

Princeton University

Almost from its beginning, Princeton was a battleground between conflicting branches of Presbyterianism, a feud that led to the establishment of the Princeton Theological Seminary in 1812. This institution was to carry on the Calvinist tradition while Princeton College developed along more secular lines. Despite this action, religious conflicts continued to affect the school, centering chiefly on such issues as the interpretation of true Presbyterianism, revivals, and the school's position on slavery. By the mid-1800s, Princeton was under the presidency of John Maclean, an academic reactionary who believed that the school's prime mission was to defend religion. He prodded his faculty to prove that astrology and geology were compatible with literal interpretations of the Bible. With the end of the Civil War, however, Princeton's trustees sought ways to end the long-time religious conflicts and took a first step by seeking a new president.

The trustees chose a Scotsman in the Witherspoon tradition. The man they selected was James McCosh, who was to lead Princeton through one of its most formative eras. He arrived in 1866, at which time he found low teachers' salaries, campus buildings in disrepair, a curriculum woefully behind the times, and a school library that was open only one hour a week. He was dismayed to find the faculty exceptionally inbred, with more than 60 percent of its members holding degrees from either Princeton College or Princeton Seminary. He made first-rate teachers his top priority, stressing the importance of bringing vigor and excitement into the classroom. Upon hearing glowing reports of the academic credentials of individual teaching candidates, he would ask: "But, mon, is he *alive?*"

Among other renowned professors, McCosh brought in Columbia graduate William Milligan Sloane, the school's first genuine historian, who later held the presidency of both the National Institute of Arts and Letters and the American Historical Association. Another of McCosh's faculty additions was Rutgers graduate Alexander Johnson, who helped modernize the school curriculum by introducing public interest and social welfare issues. The appointment of the famed orator George Lansing Raymond to the faculty laid the groundwork for future achievements in that art by Princeton graduates.

McCosh brought in additional notables to strengthen instruction in the sciences. Cyrus Fogg Brackett, a Bowdoin graduate, had written impressively on the subject of evolution and generated considerable student interest in new theories on heat, energy, and electromagnetism. Dartmouth graduate Charles Augustus Young brought advanced astronomy to Princeton, establishing an observatory and designing an automatic spectroscope that would be used throughout the world. In 1873, McCosh created the John C. Green School of Science; following in the tradition of rival schools Yale and Harvard, this brought science studies into the forefront of the curriculum. McCosh held that no student should graduate from Princeton without studying natural history, physics, chemistry, astronomy, and geology or psychology.

McCosh taught psychology and philosophy, and was later credited by many students for their intellectual awakening. He also fought vigorously to eliminate the vicious student societies and class rivalries that had long created trouble at the school. They were largely replaced by a new institution, the "eating clubs" that remain a Princeton tradition to this day. These clubs actually took root in the 1840s when student protests against refectory food became frequent and disruptive. To solve the problem, the school sent students to eat in boarding houses around the town. Then, in 1879, a group of students calling themselves the Ivy Club received permission to incorporate and build their own quarters. This trend-setting move was quickly followed by the establishment of other clubs, bearing the names Cottage, Tiger Inn, Colonial, Elm, and Cap and Gown.

Financed by student food fees and alumni contributions, the new clubs were housed in elegant Tudor and Georgian mansions with stately dining rooms, wood-paneled libraries, and billiard halls. Such an aristocratic atmosphere advanced the image of the privileged, pipe-smoking college student with whom the college became forever associated and who was immortalized in the writings of 1917 Princeton graduate F. Scott Fitzgerald. Initially, the clubs were highly selective, advancing the idea that some students were better born than others. By the early 1900s, however, there were enough clubs to include the majority of students.

While McCosh made considerable strides, similar advances were occurring at other universities. Despite its transformation, Princeton faced serious troubles, particularly during most of the 1880s. Enrollment was declining.

Student disorder was on the rise, a backlash created by the destruction of the secret societies. The student newspaper, *Princetonian,* boldly published negative references to unpopular professors. McCosh was particularly dismayed by reports that a group of students attending a football game in New York City had fallen in with prostitutes and missed church the next morning. At the end of 1883, a discouraged McCosh threatened to quit, but he agreed to stay when the trustees offered to appoint new executive officers to take charge of discipline and ease the president's burdens.

In 1884, McCosh, then 73 years old, visited schools in Columbus and Dayton, Ohio; Chicago; Omaha, Nebraska; St. Louis, Missouri; and Louisville and Lexington, Kentucky. He returned home with a new recognition of the need for additional liberal reforms in Princeton's curriculum. He established a program providing entrance examinations in midwestern cities to bring in students from outside the region. His efforts met with success: enrollment increased and, when McCosh retired in 1888, some 600 students were attending Princeton. Eight years later, in 1896, Princeton College celebrated its sesquicentennial anniversary by changing its name to Princeton University; this action symbolized the school's belief that it finally belonged among the nation's top learning institutions, thus fulfilling one of McCosh's most cherished dreams.

Meanwhile, the long-standing conflict between Presbyterian liberals and conservatives was coming to a head, fueled by what became known as the Briggs case. Charles Augustus Briggs, a graduate of the University of Virginia and a professor at Union Theological Seminary, was a leading spokesman for the liberal faction, denouncing the critical doctrine of biblical infallibility in a collaborative religious publication, *Presbyterian Quarterly and Princeton Review.* Opposing such views was Francis Landy Patton, a brilliant graduate of Princeton Theological Seminary, who already had earned a reputation for fighting heresy when he was appointed president of Princeton in the late 1880s. When the American Presbyterian churches arraigned Briggs on heresy charges, Patton was appointed as chair of the tribunal that heard the case. He secured Briggs' conviction.

Presbyterian liberals, however, would not accept defeat. At Princeton the liberal faction opposing Patton rallied around a young faculty member and future U.S. president named Woodrow Wilson. As a student at Princeton, Wilson had not distinguished himself with high grades, but he was a prodigious reader and held offices in the Whig Society, on the *Daily Princetonian,* and in the football and baseball associations. Wilson was an ardent admirer of the reform-minded McCosh, of whom he once said: "He found Princeton a quiet country college and lifted it to a conspicuous place among the most notable institutions of the country." As a faculty member, Wilson led the drive to get Princeton moving again, winning valuable allies as aging trustees of the school were gradually replaced by other former students of McCosh. In 1897, Wilson headed the faculty committee that submitted a report to the trustees charging Patton with ineffective leadership and unprofessional administration. Two years later, another report to the trustees cited severe weaknesses in the curriculum and concluded: "The condition of scholarship among our students at the present time is one of demoralization." Money was collected from prominent alumni and trustees to purchase Patton's resignation and, in 1902, Woodrow Wilson was elected president of Princeton University setting the school permanently on a progressive course.

While Princeton may best be known for producing eminent statesmen, it would also become prominent in the realm of scientific research. The first step came in 1832 when noted physicist Joseph Henry joined the faculty. He was the first scientist to create an electromagnet, and, while at Princeton, he devised a magnetic relay from his office that signaled his wife to have his lunch ready. Later in that century, the ever-progressive McCosh established Princeton's School of Science and raised many eyebrows by defending Darwin's theory of evolution.

Early in the 1930s came the establishment, a few miles west of the campus, of the Institute for Advanced Study, the nation's greatest "think tank" at that time. While not officially connected with the university, the institute attracted some of the world's most eminent physicists to Princeton's campus. Albert Einstein had an office and workshop at the university and was known to roam empty classrooms scribbling equations on blackboards. A graduate student was assigned to follow him and copy the equations lest something of value be accidentally erased. Some of Einstein's mathematical formulas are actually preserved today in leaded windows in Jones Hall where, over a fireplace, Einstein's mysterious maxim is inscribed: "God is subtle, but He is not malicious." Later came such notables as John von Neumann, Eugene Wigner, Leo Szilard, Leopold Infeld, George Placzek, Leon Rosenfeld, and Niels Bohr.

Physicist (later Nobel laureate) Eugene Wigner did not stay long. He was later to describe Princeton as "an ivory tower [where] people did not have any normal thinking about the facts of life and so forth and they looked down upon me." The others fared better, becoming increasingly involved in the research concerning atomic fission. It was on a blackboard in Princeton's Fine Hall that Bohr drew for Rosenfeld his calculations about the critical role of Uranium 235 in the fission process. The research carried out at Princeton was to figure significantly in the making of the atomic bomb. Following World War II, the celebrated Robert Oppenheimer, "the father of the A-bomb," came to Princeton as director of the institute and remained there until 1966, one year before his death.

Affording Princeton further renown in the field of atomic research was astrophysicist Lyman Spitzer Jr.,

who inspired construction in the 1950s of Princeton's Plasma Physics Laboratory for the study of fusion-generated electricity. By 1982 Princeton had a $300-million Tokamak Fusion Test Reactor and a $135-million annual operating grant from the U.S. Department of Energy. "Tokamak" is the Russian acronym for toroidal magnetic chamber, which is a doughnut-shaped vacuum container designed to hold plasma within a twisting magnetic field. In December 1982, the Princeton reactor made history when it produced its first magnetically confined plasma.

As curricula and teaching philosophies underwent two-and-a-half centuries of change at Princeton, its campus grew from a single structure into one of the most stunning arrays of buildings and landscaping to be found at any university in the nation. The campus is known for its elegant Gothic and colonial architecture that is reminiscent of a medieval college. The oldest building, of course, is historic Nassau Hall, built in 1756, which houses administrative offices. Nassau also contains Charles Willson Peale's famous portrait of Washington at the Battle of Princeton and paintings of King George III, William III, the school's presidents, and U.S. presidents Madison and Wilson. On Cannon Green behind Nassau Hall are situated two cannons used in the American Revolution and the War of 1812.

Among other notable buildings is the beautiful medieval University Chapel, which opened in 1928, and replaced two earlier chapels, the second having been destroyed by fire. The current structure was modeled after King's College in Cambridge and has a chancel built of wood from England's Sherwood Forest. The chapel seats 2,000 on pews made from army surplus materials originally intended for gun carriages in the Civil War. There are more than 1,000 memorials in the chapel to the donors who funded its construction. Princeton's library system has some 5 million volumes housed in 22 special libraries, the main one being the Harvey S. Firestone Memorial Library, named for the noted industrialist who sent five sons to the university. The school also has its own art museum, whose primary purpose is to give students access to original works of art, thus enhancing learning and research. Princeton's art collection ranges from the ancient to contemporary and includes works from western Europe, China, and Latin America. The John B. Putnam Jr. Memorial Collection of twentieth-century sculpture includes pieces by such masters as Alexander Calder, Henry Moore, and Pablo Picasso.

Also of interest is Prospect House, once the residence of the school's president, which is now a dining hall and social facility for faculty and staff. The residence was built by Colonel George Morgan, explorer, gentleman farmer, and U.S. agent for Indian Affairs, and was acquired by the university in 1878. The gardens at the rear of the house were laid out by Mrs. Woodrow Wilson, who brought in Canadian evergreens to serve as a backdrop for her colorful flowers. Another special point of interest is the Woodrow Wilson School of Public and International Affairs. This memorial to Princeton's most illustrious graduate helps prepare students for leadership roles in public service and is an appropriate embellishment to a university known as the "school of statesmen."

Further Reading: *James McCosh and the Scottish Intellectual Tradition* by J. David Hoeveler (Princeton, New Jersey: Princeton University Press, 1981) offers substantial information about the school from its founding days through Mc-Cosh's 20-year tenure and beyond. *A Place Called Princeton* by Samuel A. Schreiner (New York: Arbor House, 1984) paints a more light-hearted, anecdotal portrait of the school, but still provides useful historic information. *Princeton Reflections* by the trustees of Princeton University (Princeton, New Jersey: Princeton University Press, 1982) offers very little historic information but contains stunning photographs of the campus and specific architectural features.

—Pam Hollister

PURDUE UNIVERSITY
(West Lafayette, Indiana, U.S.A.)

Location: Purdue University is located in West Lafayette, Indiana, a midwestern, state of the United States. The city of West Lafayette lies on the west bank of the Wabash River; the city of Lafayette lies on the east. Together the cities have an approximate population of 72,000. West Lafayette is roughly 60 miles northwest of Indianapolis, the state capital.

Description: Purdue University is a public school offering associate, bachelor's, and master's degrees, as well as doctorates and professional degrees. The total enrollment of the West Lafayette campus is approximately 35,000. The campus here is made up of 1,579 acres, including a university-owned airport. There are also four regional campuses offering degrees ranging from associate to doctorate: Purdue University Calumet in Hammond; Purdue University North Central near Westville; Indiana University-Purdue University Fort Wayne in Fort Wayne; and Indiana University-Purdue University Indianapolis, in Indianapolis. Purdue also runs a Statewide Technology Program.

Information: Visitor Information Center
Purdue University
504 Northwestern Avenue
West Lafayette, IN 47907
U.S.A.
(765) 494-4636

Visiting: See above.

The city of Lafayette, in the west central part of Indiana, was founded on the east bank of the Wabash River in 1825. It was named for the French General Marquis de Lafayette who was visiting America at that time. West Lafayette's history begins in 1845 when it was founded on the west bank of the Wabash as the town of Kingston. In 1866 the town's name was changed to Chauncey, and in 1888 it was renamed West Lafayette. The area quickly gained importance as a commercial and transportation center for the surrounding agricultural region. Today Lafayette has a population of approximately 45,000. West Lafayette has a population of approximately 27,000. Lafayette is the seat of Tippecanoe County, named after the 1811 Battle of Tippecanoe in which Indian forces under Tecumseh were defeated by U.S. forces led by

General William Henry Harrison (later the ninth U.S. President). The battlefield is a national landmark several miles north of the city.

The origins of Purdue University lie in the Land-Grant College Act of 1862. This act, commonly known as the Morrill Act after its sponsor Justin S. Morrill, was signed into law on July 2, 1862, by President Abraham Lincoln. The act granted lands to any state for the establishment or the support of a college that would teach agriculture and engineering, called "mechanic arts." Today each state has at least one school that was developed through the Morrill Act, and Purdue University is that school for Indiana. In 1869 Indiana's General Assembly agreed to situate Indiana's land grant university near Lafayette and accepted $150,000 from John Purdue, $50,000 from Tippecanoe County, and 100 acres of land from area residents for the school. The assembly also agreed to name the school Purdue University after its generous benefactor John Purdue. Classes began in September 1874, with 6 teachers and 39 male students. The next year, Purdue University began admitting women, and it has been coeducational ever since. Purdue belongs to a group of schools known as the Big Ten. This association was started in 1895 when James Smart, president of Purdue, invited presidents of seven midwestern universities to Chicago to discuss regulating their intercollegiate athletic activities. The number of universities involved grew (today it is actually more than ten), and the Big Ten became known for their high academic standards as well as their fierce athletic competitions.

Founded to specialize in the teaching of agriculture and engineering, Purdue has the distinction of being noted for its fine agricultural and engineering programs even at the end of the twentieth century. Famous alumni to have graduated with engineering degrees include Neil Armstrong, class of 1955, who was the first man to step on the moon in 1969, and Eugene Cernan, class of 1956, who was the last man to walk on the moon in 1972. Other engineering graduates have also been an integral part of the U.S. space program. Those involved in the space shuttle program include John Blaha (degree received in 1966), Charles Walker (1971), Janice Voss Ford (1975), Gregory Harbaugh (1978), and Mary Weber (1984). No matter what their area of study, though, Purdue graduates have gone on to be leaders in their fields. Other famous alumni include George Ade, author and humorist; Booth Tarkington, author; Orville Redenbacher, businessman; Earl Butz, Secretary of Agriculture; D. Kirkwood Fordice Jr., a political leader and governor of Mississippi; Marilyn Quayle, lawyer and wife of U.S. Vice President Dan

Purdue University

Quayle; and Anne Stock, social secretary to First Lady Hillary Clinton. Nobel Prize winners associated with the university are Edward Purcell, for physics in 1952, and Herbert Brown, for chemistry in 1979.

The oldest building on campus today is University Hall, built in 1877 and located between Memorial Mall and Founders Park. Memorial Mall is the site of John Purdue's grave. Founders Park, dedicated in 1994, is an area of a little over two acres containing trees, walks, and a fountain. It was dedicated during Purdue's 125th anniversary year to commemorate all those who helped Purdue to grow in its early years. On the northern end of campus is the Ross-Ade Stadium, where Purdue University hosts football games. The stadium has a seating capacity of 67,861. The first game played here was in 1924. Purdue, however, had a football team long before that time. In 1891 the team acquired the nickname "Boil-

ermakers" after soundly defeating the football team from Wabash College, a neighboring school in Crawfordsville, Indiana. A local Crawfordsville newspaper ran a story about the game and used a number of unflattering terms to describe the Purdue team members, including "rail-splitters," "cornfield sailors," and "boiler makers." When Purdue students learned of this they were amused instead of insulted. They especially liked the image of a big, burly boiler maker—a worker who built boilers for steam engines—and the nickname "Boilermaker" stuck, becoming a source of school pride.

Purdue Memorial Union, which opened in 1924, lies to the southeast of Ross-Ade Stadium. The original Union building has had several major additions since that time. The Union houses such facilities as the Union Market food court, sandwich and snack shops, offices, bowling lanes, and hotel rooms for the Union Club. Located in the central area of campus is the Frederick L. Hovde Hall of Administration, which was dedicated in 1937. This building contains offices for, among others, the president, the Purdue Research Foundation, and the registrar. Directly behind this building is the Edward C. Elliott Hall of Music, dedicated in 1940. This hall seats 6,027 and can be toured. The hall also houses studios for WBAA radio, Indiana's oldest radio station, which was established in 1922. In front of the Hovde Hall of Administration is the Purdue Mall. The Purdue Mall Fountain, located here, was given by the class of 1939 in 1989 and is 38 feet high.

Purdue University has a history of meeting the needs of its student body. One example of this history is the Recreational Gymnasium, the first university building in the nation built entirely for students to meet their sports needs. Co-Rec, as it is known, was completed in 1957 and was expanded in 1981. The gym is on the west side of campus, where there are also intramural playing fields and tennis courts. In 1958 the Stewart Center opened; it is connected by a subwalk to the Purdue Memorial Union. The center houses such facilities as offices for student organizations; meeting rooms; the Loeb Playhouse, with 1,046 seats; and the Experimental Theatre, with 176 seats. The Hicks Undergraduate Library is an underground facility joined to Stewart Center. The Slayter Center of Performing Arts, dedicated in 1965, is one of the most striking structures on campus. It is an outdoor concert facility with a 200-ton roof, suspended from stainless steel cables that radiate from the top point of an enormous steel tripod. Surrounding the concert stage are "steles," irregular-shaped columns each of which is at least 20 feet high. The Mackey Arena for sports activities is at the north end of campus near Ross-Ade Stadium. The arena was dedicated in 1967 and has a seating for 14,123. Other noted buildings and structures on the campus include Lilly Hall of Life Science (1951), A.A. Potter Engineering Center (1977), Krannert Center for Executive Education and Research (1983), Maurice G. Knoy Hall of Technology (1984), the Bell Tower (1995), and Academy Park (1996).

Purdue University offers associate, bachelor's, and master's degrees, as well as doctorates and professional degrees. The university is composed of the following schools: agriculture; consumer and family sciences; education; engineering; health sciences; liberal arts; management; nursing; pharmacy and pharmacal sciences; science; technology; veterinary medicine. There is also a graduate school division. Associate degrees for two years of study are specifically offered at the schools of agriculture, consumer and family sciences, science, technology, and veterinary medicine. Four-year bachelor of arts and bachelor of science degrees are offered, as well as bachelor of science in specific areas, such as aeronautical and astronautical engineering, agricultural engineering, and forestry. The graduate school offers master's degrees and doctorates. Professional degrees conferred are doctor of

pharmacy and doctor of veterinary medicine. Total enrollment at Purdue is approximately 35,000, with about 28,500 of those being undergraduates. Men make up 58 percent of the student body, while women make up 42 percent. Over half of the undergraduates come from Indiana. The rest of the students are from other states (mostly in the midwest) and foreign countries. Of the foreign students, most come from Asia, Europe, or Latin America. Admission to Purdue is based on a number of factors including scores from the standard college admission tests SAT or ACT, high school grade point average and class rank, and recommendations.

As well as being a center for learning, Purdue University is also a center for research. Funding for research comes from the federal and state governments, industry, and foundations. There are more than 400 research laboratories on the campus. Among the major research programs are the Agricultural Research Programs; AIDS Research Center; Cancer Research Center; Center for Applied Ethology and Human-Animal Interaction; Center for Tax Policy Studies; Engineering Experiment Station; Purdue Rare Isotope Measurement Laboratory; and Purdue Research Foundation. Today the West Lafayette campus has an area of 1,579 acres, which includes the Purdue Airport. The airport is on the southwestern side of campus and has the distinction of being the first university-owned airport in the country. It was established in 1930. Housing for students at the university is available in school-owned and operated resident halls. The school also has apartments for married students. There are 43 fraternities and 24 sororities, all of which have chapter houses. There are also 11 cooperative homes. Students may live off campus in privately owned apartments. *The Purdue Exponent* is the school paper and is published five times a week during the fall and spring semesters. Free copies of the paper are available on campus and help keep the student body informed and united.

Purdue University has four regional campuses: Purdue University Calumet in Hammond, Indiana; Purdue University North Central near Westville, Indiana; Indiana University-Purdue University Fort Wayne in Fort Wayne, Indiana; and Indiana University-Purdue University Indianapolis in Indianapolis, Indiana. Purdue University Calumet is a 180-acre campus located in Hammond, Indiana, a city of about 84,000 and 25 miles southeast of Chicago, Illinois. Over 9,000 students are enrolled here and degrees offered are at the associate, bachelor's, and master's levels. Purdue University North Central is a 275-acre campus for commuter students. There are over 3,000 students, and at this campus they can receive any of several associate or bachelor's degrees. One master's degree program, in elementary education, is also offered. Indiana University-Purdue University Fort Wayne is in Fort Wayne, Indiana, a city with a population of approximately 170,000. The campus covers an area of 565 acres near the St. Joseph River. Students have the option of earning associate, bachelor's, and master's degrees from Indiana University or Purdue University. There is no school sponsored housing. Student enrollment is over 10,000. Indiana University-Purdue University Indianapolis is administered by the Indiana University system. At this combined university in Indianapolis, the capital of Indiana, Purdue programs are taught, and there are specific Purdue schools, such as Purdue School of Engineering and Technology. There are also Indiana University programs and schools. Degrees from the associate level to the professional level are offered. Enrollment is approximately 27,000, over 3,000 of whom are Purdue students.

Throughout its history Purdue University has worked to contribute to the community at large. One way Purdue aims to provide skilled workers for local economies is through the Statewide Technology Program. This program, overseen by Purdue's school of technology, brings together leaders from Purdue, local businesses, and communities to identify a need in that area's job market. To meet a region's need for a certain type of skilled worker, Purdue institutes programs taught by their technology faculty at existing sites in the area. These specially directed and easily accessible programs allow students to earn a Purdue associate or bachelor's degree without needing to move away from home and family. Often the students involved in the Statewide Technology Program are nontraditional; they are older, perhaps married and working, and seeking to improve their careers. Currently the program has over 1,600 students in 10 cities (Anderson, Columbus, Elkhart, Indianapolis, Kokomo, Muncie, New Albany, Richmond, South Bend, and Versailles) throughout Indiana.

Total statewide enrollment of Purdue schools is near 64,000 and is expected to keep growing. As Purdue looks to the future and plans for the students of tomorrow, Purdue alumni continue to contribute to every aspect of our society today.

Further Reading: Maps and brochures about Purdue University are available from the Visitor Information Center (Purdue University, 504 Northwestern Avenue, West Lafayette, IN 47907) or the Office of Publications (Purdue University, 1131 South Campus Courts-D, West Lafayette, IN 47907). Purdue's website, www.purdue.edu, also contains much information, including applications and admissions information. Robert W. Topping's *A Century and Beyond: The History of Purdue University* (West Lafayette, Indiana: Purdue University Press, 1988) provides a look at the development of the school; while his *The Book of Trustees, Purdue University, 1865–1989* (West Lafayette, Indiana: Purdue University Press, 1989) looks at those who influenced the growth of the institution. Othr books on specific Purdue topics are also available, such as John Norberg's *A Force for Change: The Class of 1950* (Wesat Lafayette, Indiana: Purdue University, Office of Publications, 1995).

—Anne C. Paterson

RADCLIFFE COLLEGE
(Cambridge, Massachusetts, U.S.A.)

Location: In Cambridge, Massachusetts, adjacent to Harvard University.

Description: A private college enrolling approximately 2,904 undergraduate students in conjunction with Harvard College.

Information: Office of Admission
Byerly Hall
8 Garden Street
Cambridge, MA 02138
U.S.A.
(617) 495-1551

Visiting: Guided tours are available. For more information, call (617) 495-8601.

After she had completed her undergraduate work in history at Smith College in 1879, Kate E. Morris, a bright, intellectual young woman from Hartford, Vermont, was enthusiastic about undertaking postgraduate work in medieval history. As a girl, she had lain awake nights "hating men," because they could go on to college when women could not; but in the year 1879 she read a circular advertising the beginning of an experiment in education for women. A group of professors at Harvard College, the circular read, had consented to give private instruction "to properly qualified young women who desire to pursue advanced studies in Cambridge." Thus Morris was among the first female students to enroll in the "Harvard Annex," which would develop into Radcliffe College.

As early as 1872 a group of women in Cambridge, Massachusetts, initiated efforts to make a place for women at the all-male Harvard College. Named the Women's Education Association, this group of Harvard-connected women worked during the 1870s as advocates for the education of women. With the arrival of the first class at the Harvard Annex in 1879, the first step was taken toward the long process of education for Radcliffe College women. Upon arrival in Cambridge, Massachusetts, Morris found herself in a class of 27 women. As she wrote in her letters, the varied female students divided into four groups. Some of them were completing a full four years of college courses; others were postgraduates in mathematics, modern languages, and history; yet others were teachers from Boston and Cambridge; and there were also the "Cambridge ladies" who Morris described as "polishing up some single study."

The young women stayed in rented rooms in Cambridge, and Harvard professors offered classes in private; initially there were no classrooms, libraries, or laboratories. Female students crossed Harvard Yard to borrow books from the Harvard library. Morris laughingly described herself as "a beast of burden" who ran across Harvard Yard to her rented rooms on Sparks Street in Cambridge with her arms full of books. Nonetheless, the early classes of private instruction had opened the door to educational opportunity for women, and in 1882 the Annex was legally incorporated as the "Society for Collegiate Instruction for Women." Elizabeth Cary Agassiz, the president of the Committee of Managers of the Harvard Annex, was appointed as the society's first president.

Agassiz described the instruction of women in Cambridge as "an experiment." But the experiment was becoming a reality. With over 200 women studying in the early program, the society purchased land and a building. But postgraduate work was not available, and the society still awarded a certificate, rather than a college degree. Morris, determined to complete her Ph.D. in medieval history after her first year of study at what was still familiarly known as the Annex, petitioned Harvard College for permission to do so, but permission was denied. Energetic and determined, she completed her Ph.D. at a different institution for women.

The rapid growth of the early "experiment" in instruction for women made it obvious by the 1890s that a formalization of the relationship between Harvard and the women's program of instruction should take place. Alumnae from the original classes, along with many distinguished persons, petitioned Harvard: their demand was that Harvard grant degrees to women. Thus, in 1893 Harvard entered into negotiations for the establishment of an independent college for women.

The meeting room at the Massachusetts State House in which the petition to grant a general charter to Radcliffe College was discussed in 1894 was filled beyond capacity—mostly with individuals who opposed the plan. But the petition prevailed, with Agassiz giving a compelling speech on successful past work and plans for the future. In 1894 Radcliffe College was formally incorporated and established as a degree-granting institution. Named for Ann Radcliffe, Lady Mowlson, the college's name reflected the efforts of the woman who in 1643 donated £100 to the first Harvard scholarship fund.

As reflected in its charter of 1894, Radcliffe College was to provide instruction for women students by Harvard professors, and to grant college degrees signed by the pres-

Radcliffe College

idents of Radcliffe and Harvard colleges. Along with the charter came the first Radcliffe College administration. Agassiz was the first president of Radcliffe College. During her administration, the physical plant of Radcliffe College developed. A gymnasium was built, and land was purchased for the future construction of dormitories. By the approach of the twentieth century, Radcliffe College had begun to make the words of Morris a reality. "Women," Morris wrote in a letter to a friend, "should know everything, should have every chance in the world for self-support." The twentieth century presented a time of reorganization and growth. Agassiz announced her suc-

cessor as president of the college at the turn of the century. During the 20 years that her successor, Le Baron Russell Briggs, served as part-time president of Radcliffe College (while also holding the post of Dean of Arts and Sciences), administrative tasks were largely performed by a succession of six women deans. One such dean, Agnes Irwin, helped to secure $75,000 from Andrew Carnegie for the building of Radcliffe Library. Even while President Briggs believed that education should not teach women to compete with men, Radcliffe College continued to grow.

Radcliffe's first full-time president, Ada Louise Comstock, assumed office in 1923. She guided the college through the boom of the 1920s, the Great Depression, and the early days of World War II. In her farewell address to the Alumnae Association in 1943, she remembered the difficult days around 1930:

And then there was a hard period of four years . . . President Lowell [A. Lawrence Lowell, president of Harvard] saw the defects of the relationship between Harvard and Radcliffe, as they have been seen recently, but the cure that was proposed, that of splitting Radcliffe off completely from Harvard, would, I think, have been fatal to Radcliffe . . . Mr. Lowell was a resourceful and determined man; and the struggle, for those four years, was pretty nearly incessant and at times gave us great anxiety.

In Lowell's view, Radcliffe was a drain on the Harvard faculty and facilities. An accommodation was reached when Radcliffe agreed to limit the size of its student body and to abandon any requests for extended privileges in the university.

Another historic event for Radcliffe occurred in 1943, when the Women's Archives (later named the Schlesinger Library) were established. Alumna Maud Wood Park gave papers, books, and memorabilia documenting the 72-year suffrage movement (1848–1920), encompassing the years when women struggled for, and finally won, the right to vote. Other documents Park donated related to the women's political and reform work after 1920. The Schlesinger Library holds the papers of a host of distinguished women: Susan B. Anthony, pioneer women's rights advocate; Harriet Beecher Stowe, author of *Uncle Tom's Cabin;* Charlotte Perkins Gilman, lecturer and advocate for labor; Julia Child, television chef and co-author of *Mastering the Art of French Cooking:* Betty Friedan, author of the book often regarded as the "Bible of the feminist movement," *The Feminine Mystique.* The library's collection also includes a series of interviews with Latino, Cambodian, and Chinese-American women.

While the Schlesinger Library began to document the impact of women on the history of America, one of the major social issues Radcliffe faced continued: the full admission of women into Harvard programs. In 1943 Harvard and Radcliffe made an agreement that President Comstock called "the most significant event since our charter was granted by the legislature in 1894." In the past, Radcliffe had paid individual Harvard faculty members for teaching at Radcliffe. Now Radcliffe would turn over 85 percent of its tuition to Harvard in a lump sum. With these terms each Harvard instructor would be obliged to teach at Radcliffe if his department decided that he ought to. While the agreement was a step in the direction of coeducation, it did not strictly require the integration of males and females. Since World War II had drained Harvard of both students and faculty, coeducation for all but freshmen classes was adopted as a temporary expedient.

With the arrival of the 1970s change accelerated at Radcliffe College. By 1970 Radcliffe graduates joined their male counterparts at Harvard for the first joint commencement. Separate dormitories were abolished in 1971, and by 1975 equal access for women and men became university admission policy. In a 1977 milestone agreement (sometimes referred to as the merger/non-merger), Radcliffe women were granted the rights and privileges of a Harvard education. Historian Dorothy Elia Howells described the terms:

Radcliffe delegates to Harvard responsibility for classroom instruction of undergraduate women and management of the house system subject to consultation with the President of Radcliffe. Radcliffe's financial responsibility for the education of undergraduate women includes payment to Harvard of all tuition money and close to one million dollars in 1977–78 from endowment income and from unrestricted funds for financial aid to undergraduate women students. This latter amount will increase yearly.

At the same time, Radcliffe College was reaffirmed as a separate corporate institution. Charged with promoting the higher education of women, Radcliffe College continues to promote educational opportunities for women and to sponsor research that seeks to understand and promote the work of women scholars on social and academic issues. One such program is the Radcliffe Seminars Program. Established in 1950, it is a pioneering program in the continuing education of women. The Radcliffe Seminars Program provides courses in liberal arts, child advocacy, health care education, and landscape design. According to Howells, the courses are for "mature women" who desire what Radcliffe president Wilbur Jordan called "an opportunity to share ideas with other adults in an organized way." The seminars are open to the public and enjoy a growing enrollment. The Radcliffe Publishing Course, established as a four-month course, has become since its inception in 1946 what some call "the shortest graduate school in the world." The program is designed to teach the procedures of publishing; it often acts as an entry card to the world of publishing for its graduates.

Even as it has successfully struggled toward full access to quality education for female students through its joint relationship with Harvard College, Radcliffe College has had to confront the stereotype of being an elite institution for white women of established classes. In fact, in the early days of the Harvard Annex, many of the young women who chose Radcliffe were, according to Howells, "the middle-class daughters of Massachusetts clergymen, teachers, and physicians." Many of the early students were teachers in Boston schools who commuted to their classes in Cambridge by horse-drawn car from Boston.

The women were not, by and large, daughters of New England's wealthy elite. Dr. Sally Schwager, author of a history of Radcliffe College, states that early Radcliffe commuters were quite different from "the tradition of finishing school and a year on the continent." Further, Schwager points out, this class difference was a source of irritation to the Harvard men of the 1890s. One alumna described the difficulties she face:

> It was inordinately difficult to persuade friends and relatives that it was suitable for a girl to go to college at all. My brothers were the seventh generation of Fuller boys at Harvard but no Fuller girl had dreamed of Radcliffe till I came along . . .
>
> I had two cousins at Harvard at the time and they threatened me that is I ever disobeyed the rule [of not going to Harvard Square] they's contrive to find it out and "fix" me. It was bad enough, they contended, to have the disgrace of a cousin at Radcliffe without running the risk of meeting her on the street and being obliged to cut her . . .
>
> I took a course with Mr. Copeland and my grandmother once said to him, "I hope you realize that my granddaughter is a lady though she does go to Radcliffe.

Indeed, the initial days of the Harvard Annex—with its course work for qualified women students in the 1890s—opened a wellspring of desire for education among people of all classes. Schwager cites a nineteenth-century letter of inquiry to the founders of the Harvard Annex from a woman in Malvern, Ohio, who wanted schooling for her ten-year-old niece. "I am quite illiterate myself," wrote the aunt, "but if money will give her an education, she will have it." Schwager also notes the father of a 16-year-old daughter in Sonoma, California, who wrote "to request the new program in the form of correspondence or reading lists." His daughter, he wrote, read only a 'jumble of books' and he wanted more for her, but he could not send her to the new school in Cambridge. Clearly, Radcliffe College struck a nerve in American society when it opened the doors to higher education for women in the 1890s.

Early Radcliffe women also struggled against nineteenth-century beliefs that women who pursued higher education lacked mental capacity or moral fiber. Many Harvard professors provided excellent instruction for Radcliffe undergraduates; yet allegations were made that "Radcliffe students didn't offer the 'mental resistance' necessary to keep sharp the edge of the professor's minds," according to Howells.

An interesting refutation to this argument was an account reprinted in the *Boston Post* of March 24, 1888. According to historian Howell's account, the Bowdoin Prize was the highest prize awarded for English dissertations from Harvard College. The prize carried a monetary award of $100. A smaller prize, also for work in English, was to be awarded to the women students whose work would be reviewed by the same judges. In the competition for the year 1888, first prize was given to a writer by the name E.B. Pearson. Pearson's name, however, was not found in the Harvard College register. When the news came out that the author was "a young lady" and a student in the Annex, the *Boston Post* reported

> Miss Pearson dropped at once from the Bowdoin prize of $100 to the humbler Annex prize of $30, thus paying $70 outright for the privilege of being a woman. The crowing fact is that the venerable Professor Torrey [the contest judge] is one of the few professors who have disapproved of the Annex . . . having held that neither the brains nor the bodies of women were equal to severe study.

Indeed, until 1959 the basement of Memorial Church, just outside of Harvard Yard, maintained the "Radcliffe room": a place with beds and an attendant who "ministered to women," because it was thought that the long excursion from Radcliffe Yard to Harvard Yard was too tiring for ladies.

More than 100 years of Radcliffe College scholarship have changed that impression. Internationally known for its academic reputation, Radcliffe College graduates include the writer Gertrude Stein and the poet Adrienne Rich.

Today, Radcliffe College argues for its continued importance. While Harvard College has the responsibility for undergraduate life, "Radcliffe provides a variety of programs for undergraduate women such as research partnerships, leadership training courses, career colloquia, and lectures on women's issues."

However, some suggest that Radcliffe has all but ceased to survive. *Boston Globe* columnist Alex Beam wrote,

> Radcliffe, which merged with Harvard in 1977, has for all practical purposees ceased to exist. Consider: Radcliffe has a lovely campus, but it has no students. The 'Cliffe ceded "day to day management of undergraduate life" to Harvard in the 1977 nuptials. Radcliffe—once called the "Harvard Annex"—has an administration building, but no faculty. It does have one tenured professorship, but it is not currently filled . . . There are cynics who suggest that Radcliffe exists only to support its active Alumnae Association, which promotes the college's putative existence in glossy mailings to tens of thousands of pre-1977 alumnae. "It's sort of like the Alumni Association for the Austro-Hungarian Empire," says one sardonic Harvard grad. "Their buildings remind me of Vienna—they have all these elegant facades. But there's nothing behind them." Even Radcliffe officials have a hard time explaining where the col-

lege fits in. Women apply to Harvard and are officially accepted by Radcliffe. They are taught exclusively by Harvard professors and live in Harvard dorms, some of them Radcliffe territories ceded in the Treaty of '77. Diplomas in hand they leave Cambridge as graduates of Harvard College.

Others, including Linda Smith Wilson, president of Radcliffe since 1989 and an important advocate for the continuing education of women, believe that the college will be needed more than ever in the next century and beyond. She said, "The role Radcliffe plays for undergraduates is to promote leadership, risk taking, and expectation of success [for women]." The expanded educational opportunities for women provided by Radcliffe College at the close of the twentieth century may

well be what Kate Morris asked for in her entry to the Harvard Annex in 1879: a place where women could excel, and succeed.

Further Reading: Dorothy Howell's *A Century to Celebrate: Radcliffe College, 1879–1979* (Cambridge, Massachusetts: Radcliffe College, 1978) provides a lengthy account of the founding and current history of the college. *Smith Grants Radcliffe's First Ph.D.,* edited by Margaret Farrand Thorp (Northampton, Massachusetts: Smith College, 1965) provides letters by Kate Morris, which detail her experience as one of the first female students at the Harvard Annex.

—Rosemarie C. Sultan

REED COLLEGE
(Portland, Oregon, U.S.A.)

Location: Across the Willamette River from the center of the city of Portland.

Description: A private, independent college of liberal arts and sciences, with 1,200 students and 125 faculty.

Information:
Public Affairs Office
Reed College
Portland, OR 97202-8199
U.S.A.
(503)777-7511
(800) 547-4750

Reed College is an intense and highly intellectual 1,200-student undergraduate institution on a 100-acre wooded campus in Portland, Oregon, but for all of its size, it attracts national attention.

Reed College was founded in 1909 by the board of trustees named in Amanda Reed's 1895 will, establishing "an institution of learning, having for its objects the increase and diffusion of practical knowledge among the citizens of Portland." The institution was called the Reed Institute. Mrs. Reed's 1904 bequest was for just under $2 million; in today's dollars, the gift would be worth over $50 million.

Simeon Gannet Reed had left all his wealth to his wife when he died in 1895, suggesting that she contribute at least some of it "to the beauty of the city and to the intelligence, prosperity, and happiness of the inhabitants." Son of a prosperous Massachusetts family, the 25-year-old Simeon Reed had settled in Portland in 1855; by 1880, he was one of the richest men in the city, having done well in navigation, mining, and real estate. Reed was known for honesty in business dealings, for loyalty to his friends and to Oregon, and for generosity in philanthropy. In 1887, the Reeds' pastor, the Reverend Thomas Lamb Eliot, suggested that they found an institute of "lectures and arts and music and museum." The Reeds liked the idea, and Mrs. Reed's will named the Reverend Eliot as chairman of the institute's first board of trustees.

Neither Simeon nor Amanda Reed specified exactly how their gift to the city should be spent. Mrs. Reed's only stipulation was that the new school be free from sectarian influence. By 1909, when the bequest was freed from the protests of disappointed relatives, the trustees were inclined toward the establishment of a liberal arts college. However free they were to do as they thought best, the trustees were mindful of the Reeds' preference for the practical and commercial rather than the artistic and the intellectual; accordingly, they sought outside counsel, including that of a John D. Rockefeller-sponsored national foundation known as the General Education Board. The board's secretary, Wallace Buttrick, spent several weeks in Portland taking stock of the city's educational needs. He concluded that there was a strong need for a "college of strictly collegiate rank," as opposed to the trade and technical schools, of which there were already several in the region. Buttrick said that such a college "would furnish ideals for the state." Thus encouraged, the trustees founded Reed College in 1909 as a liberal arts college, determined that it be of the best possible quality.

The first order of business was to find a president suitable for the college. Again the trustees turned east to Buttrick for help, and also to one of the leading educators of the period, Charles W. Eliot, president emeritus of Harvard University. One of the first names suggested was a former student of Eliot's, a 31-year-old professor of English and Argumentation at Bowdoin College, William Trufant Foster, who was at the time on leave from his position, and lecturing in educational administration at Columbia University. Already the author of three books and numerous articles, Foster had earned a reputation as a reformer. Reed attracted him because of the freedom it offered from alumni and from traditions and commitments made by others. When the trustees accepted Foster's condition that he be allowed to commit the college to the highest standards, he accepted the presidency.

Reed's first president arrived in Portland already on record as being deeply unhappy about the state of American higher education. For Foster, the problem lay with the quality of student life. It had, he thought, "somehow gone wrong." Among the issues that Foster thought accounted for the problems were the growth of intercollegiate athletics and the inappropriate attention to social life, both of which he believed took students' attention from intellectual pursuits. To those who thought that colleges were places for "gentlemen," Foster replied with contempt that gentlemen were "youth free from the suspicion of thoroughness or definite purpose." Reed was to be a place where students could "stop the nonsense and get down to serious work." Accordingly, there would be no fraternities, no sororities, and no intercollegiate athletics. Foster was uncompromising in his vision of a college in which "intellectual enthusiasm" by the students would dominate; his commitment to that single goal was so intense that some said it bordered on the fanatic.

Reed College

Foster set about starting Reed on the right path. He sought superior faculty and an intelligent and serious student body. Classes began in 1911, with a handful of faculty offering courses to 23 young men and 23 young women. Foster instituted campus practices that would clear the way for academic seriousness, and with an acute awareness of the importance of marketing, Foster quickly cultivated national support for his college through a vigorous public relations campaign.

In his first six years as president, Foster built a young and energetic faculty from the nation's best academic institutions: Harvard University, the University of Chicago, Stanford University, the University of California, Radcliffe College, Columbia University, and Williams College. Of the first dozen hired, only one was over 40 years of age, while several were under 30. From the beginning, the faculty was at the very center of Reed's academic development, and it has remained there ever since.

To guarantee that Reed started off with bright students, Foster personally assessed all applications, to be sure that students measured up on paper; he evaluated their motivations by interviewing them personally. Foster was particularly appalled by the widespread practice in many major schools of filling out their freshmen rosters with students who did not meet the stated requirements but who were admitted "on condition" or as special students. After World War I, inundated by increasing enrollments, a number of colleges seeking the highest quality students became very selective in their admissions. Reed started that way and has not changed.

Although students' courses were electives, Foster had constructed a system to make certain that students would remain serious and work hard. Each student was required to write a thesis and then to defend it in an oral examination by a group of faculty members. In their third year, students were required to take a comprehensive examination, the Junior Qualifying Exam ("Junior Qual"), before they could be admitted to their senior year. Sociologist Burton Clark wrote that these stringent requirements are more commonly found in a program for the master's or doctor's degree, not in an undergraduate college. Clark went on to say that when some of these requirements appear in an undergraduate institution, they usually apply only to honors students and that Reed had, in effect, made itself an honors college.

As if to make the point that every student was an honors student, the Reed faculty early on decided to de-emphasize grade awareness and competitiveness by the simple expedient of not informing students about grades until graduation. Not much was made of this policy, initially—it merited no mention in catalogues of the day—but eventually faculty and students proudly claimed it as a symbol that Reed was about knowledge for knowledge's sake.

Also from the very beginning, the president and the staff de-emphasized extracurricular activities. There was a sports program, including faculty as well as students, but it was strictly intramural. With the exception of a brief period at the end of the 1910s and in the early 1920s, when Reed sought to right its sinking ship by venturing forth into intercollegiate athletics, the absence of intercollegiate athletics has consistently remained a defining characteristic of the college. However, Foster supported organized social activities among the students, especially if they were democratic and campus-wide.

Reed's first president evidently (but erroneously) thought to do well for his school by doing well in the community—specifically by improving the moral character of the school's home city and its citizens. Foster thought of Portland as the "city-wide campus," and he took his various messages of civic enlightenment to the people in the form of free lectures and heavy faculty involvement in community affairs. In 1913, for example, he and 11 other speakers presented a lecture series at a downtown hotel on "Sexual Hygiene and Morals." Attendance at these and other such events moved from 3,000 in 1911–12 to over 48,000 in 1916–17. Despite the numbers, the city was less than grateful; when Foster resigned in 1919, the *Portland Telegram* wrote that he "has no tact."

While Reed College was receiving favorable reviews nationally (in large part because of Foster's writings about the school in various popular and academic publications) and high marks from other academic institutions, its reputation in its home community was anything but warm. Foster's "do-goodism," the irritating arrogance of his system of Simplified Spelling (more phonetic than elegant—with spellings such as "involvs" and "alfabetical"), and the lack of a home team to root for made it hard for the college to get local support. These problems did not soon abate.

The immediate consequence of Portland's animosity toward Reed was that the college's financial base crumbled. President Foster's virtues of uncompromising vision and stubbornness were perceived by many, some faculty included, as vices. Most of the original faculty had left by 1919; shrinking salaries made it hard for the rest to appreciate Foster's leadership. When he resigned in 1919, he was not asked to reconsider. The school barely survived the next two years, administered by small committees of faculty. When Richard F. Scholz took over two years later as Reed's second president, the college's staff consisted of eight faculty members and a librarian.

Scholz managed to accomplish much in his three years (he died in 1924, at age 43). He doubled tuition, better managed the endowment investments, dramatically increased outside funding, and improved relations with the city. He was able to recruit six full professors and a dozen new faculty in the lower ranks; of the six senior men, five remained permanently. As it happened (not accidentally), Scholz's hiring preferences served to concentrate academic strength and faculty power in the humanities. Scholz fully accepted Foster's founding premise about promoting academic excellence, but he thought the curriculum he inherited was overly elective.

Accordingly, Scholz and the faculty, after considerable deliberation, designed new courses in the humanities. The courses in history and world literature would be run along parallel time lines. In addition, students would take courses in the natural and social sciences. New freshmen thus found themselves fully involved with the humanities, to the exclusion of almost everything else, and only slightly less so as sophomores. In 1943 the two parallel courses were combined into one; and while there has been some occasional experimental tinkering since and a few new courses added (including a year-long sophomore sequence in Chinese Humanities in 1995), Scholz's strong emphasis on the humanities became—and remains—one of the hallmarks of a Reed education.

President Scholz's other major contribution to Reed was structural. Interested in "an honest effort to disregard old historic rivalries and hostilities between the sciences and the arts, between professional and cultural subjects," he sought integration of the faculty across related disciplines. To this end, he combined academic departments into four divisions of related subjects: literature and language; history and social science; mathematics and natural sciences; philosophy, psychology, and education. Some departments are housed differently now, but the basic four-part structure remains. Each division is responsible for upper-class instruction and for shepherding students through their majors.

Richard Scholz was Reed's second strong president as well as its second president. Since his death in 1924, Reed College has had 15 presidents. Four of these were "acting," and four others are considered to have been "interim." Paul Bragdon was president for 16 years in the 1970s and 1980s, and Richard Sullivan for 11 years in the 1950s and 1960s; the rest, including the "actings" and "interims," averaged three years each. The ones who lasted longest tinkered least with the basic Reed formula, and the ones who tinkered most, or tried to, were soon gone. Since Scholz, the faculty (almost always the senior members by far) has run Reed.

One of Foster's legacies (not necessarily the best) is that he refused to establish the rank of associate professor. There were full professors, assistant professors, and instructors. Turnover was high in the lower ranks and low in the higher rank, and the higher rank consisted of mostly men who had come to believe deeply in the Reed ethic. The rank of associate professor finally came to Reed to 1946, but by then the pattern of senior faculty dominance in matters of curriculum and student affairs was well established.

President Dexter Keezar, in the late 1930s and early 1940s, encountered enormous resistance to his schemes to develop more extracurricular activities for students and more courses with a practical orientation. Duncan Ballantine's attempts in the early 1950s to point the

institution in dramatically different directions (develop the student's whole personality, offer vocational preparation and avocational skills, and tighten up the permissive atmosphere) ran head-on into a wall of faculty opposition and student hostility.

Student life at Reed has run the gamut from highly social and somewhat organized in the beginning to highly individualized and, at times in its recent history, completely anarchic. Before World War II most of the student body came from the Northwest, from Oregon, and especially from Portland. After the war, the school's reputation drew applicants increasingly from other parts of the country and from abroad. But while accents may have become more varied, the Reed culture of seriousness, intelligence, and independence has remained self-reinforcing, more or less guaranteeing that student life would remain true to form: distinctive, nonconformist, and highly individualistic.

Reed worked for a long time to become a fully residential college. In the mid-1930s almost nine out of ten students lived off campus; by 1960, almost all were in residence. Now, all freshmen and half the entire student body live on campus, while most of the rest are within a mile. But no matter where students lived, over the years Reed students progressively isolated themselves from life outside the college, and in important ways, from each other as well. Students in the 1930s were involved in numerous clubs and activities, including formal dances and formal dinners. These involvements diminished over the next three decades, so that by the early 1960s the values of spontaneity and extreme individualism all but destroyed all formal student organizations.

Student conduct was for a long time somewhat substantively governed by "the honor principle," which in the beginning consisted of certain ideals that grew out of a sense shared among students of what behavior was appropriate for young adults engaged in serious pursuits. Over time, the idea of "shared" became less attractive for many, and "honor" came to have more to do with freedom than with accountability.

The experimentation, excitement, and turbulence which characterized American universities and colleges in the late 1960s and early 1970s came much earlier to Reed College and lasted much longer than anywhere else. The issues were mostly related to matters of governance, change, and student life. Richard Sullivan's presidency (1956–67) managed to eliminate most of Portland's animosity toward the college, and Portland in its way became more like the college in its embrace of the flavor of the times. There were numerous campus discussions about new curricular ideas, new programs, and even about opening a graduate school. This last proved to be extremely divisive in the Reed community. In the end, the faculty defeated the proposal by a narrow margin. However, hard feelings remained, and several faculty members resigned.

For students during the 1960s, the logic of the times and the logic of leave-us-alone individualism worked to take issues concerning student life further and further away from faculty scrutiny; this move was reinforced by the shift among humanities and social sciences toward more scholarly research and publication, toward, in other words, the position already occupied by faculty members in the sciences. This too meant reduced faculty involvement in student life.

Minority rule by senior faculty continued. For 30 years, off and on, from the 1960s to the 1990s, elections to the two key faculty committees were controlled by younger faculty who took the trouble to organize themselves and run slates of people committed to taking a long look at issues such as Reed's character and identity and curriculum. These elections generated much controversy but little change during this period; a black studies program came and went; there was talk of interdisciplinary programs and talk of some nonwestern curriculum ideas. None of these proposals were more than talk.

In the late 1960s, after Richard Sullivan's departure, there followed three interim presidents; the institution became unstable, and in 1971, Reed came very close to closing for financial reasons. The college wrote a new financial plan, which was followed by a radical reduction in the size of the faculty and a reduction in programs. Student life was in a state of anarchy and the honor principle virtually collapsed. Students managed to gain the autonomy they wanted, but in the process gave up their involvement in curriculum development. With the faculty withdrawn from issues involving student life and with the students withdrawn from issues involving curriculum development, Reed College entered a long and stressful period.

Under President Paul Bragdon (1971–88), finances improved dramatically and the college stabilized, albeit on the side of no major curricular revisions. Bragdon created Reed's first dean of students and a student life program; both took several years to gain enough faculty acceptance to make them viable. Power among the faculty eventually swung again toward a relatively new, younger faculty.

By the mid-1990s, while certain issues remained problems, Reed College appeared to have healed. A college publication listed a sampling of some 50 student organizations, and then commented: "The College recognizes that students have control of their own lives and can decide for themselves what organizations they want to create." The honor principle began to have shared meaning again—the preamble to the 1989–90 Community Constitution specifies that "dishonesty, intimidation, harassment, exploitation and the use or threat of force are incompatible" with the freedom necessary for inquiry and scholarship. The faculty no longer looked on the student affairs program as "neo-nannyism," and the curriculum took on a more contemporary look with the addition of Spanish, Chinese Humanities, and Chinese.

Graduates of Reed College perform very well in the nation's top graduate and medical schools, and Reed turns out such students in percentages and numbers that vastly exceed its size. It is, for example, second in the nation among all four-year private institutions in the number of graduates who have gone on to earn Ph.D.s in computer science, and Reed does not have a computer science department.

Reed's first Rhodes scholar was named in 1918. In 1921, three Reed graduates were at Oxford concurrently on Rhodes scholarships; in 1936, four were in residence at the same time. This tiny college in the northwestern United States has produced 30 Rhodes Scholars since 1918, a number met by only one other liberal arts college in the country. While Reed has been known since the 1920s for its strong humanities program, almost half its Rhodes scholars were graduated as science majors.

Reed College closes its ninth decade with its historic reputation intact. The atmosphere is intense, the intellectual demands are strong, and measuring by graduate school placements and accomplishments, Reed students are very well prepared in methods of inquiry and in the world of ideas.

Further Reading: Burton R. Clark's *The Distinctive College: Antioch, Reed & Swarthmore* (Chicago: Aldine, 1970) offers a sociologist's historical analysis of the origins and development of Reed College from the beginning to the early 1960s. Richard E. Ritz's *A History of the Reed College Campus and Its Buildings* (Portland, Oregon: Reed College, 1990) deals with the history of the campus's architecture.

—Richard Allen Chapman

RICE UNIVERSITY
(Houston, Texas, U.S.A.)

Location: Three miles from the downtown area of Houston, Texas.

Description: A private, coeducational university enrolling approximately 4,100 students in the undergraduate, graduate, and professional degree programs.

Information: Office of Admissions
P.O. Box 1892
Houston, TX 77251-1892
U.S.A.
(713) 527-4036
(800) 527-6957

Visiting: Tours are scheduled on weekdays at 11:00 A.M. and 3:00 P.M. and Saturdays, 10:30 A.M. No appointment is necessary. Please contact the Office of Admissions for additional information.

As a successful businessman and philanthropist with a lifelong interest in education, William Marshall Rice's dream was to establish upon his death an endowed educational institution. Initially, his ideas took form as a school for orphans, then as a high school, and finally achieved realization as a public library and Institution for the Advancement of Literature, Science, Art, Philosophy, and Letters. The Rice Institute of Houston (now known as Rice University) opened its doors to the first class of students on September 23, 1912.

The establishment of the institute through an endowment from the philanthropist's will was not without a share of intrigue, twice placing his plans in jeopardy. The first incident occurred in 1896, upon the death of Rice's second wife, Elizabeth.

For unknown reasons, Elizabeth declared herself and her husband to be residents of Texas, a community property state, which meant that she could bequeath half of their shared assets as she wished. Subsequently, she drew up a new will on her deathbed without William's knowledge and empowered her executor, attorney Orren Holt, to distribute those shared assets as per her direction. William Rice contested the will on the premise that neither he nor his wife were residents of Texas, realizing that her new will would significantly reduce the endowment available for the establishment of the institute.

During the probate and subsequent challenge to Eliza-

beth's will, William Rice died suddenly under mysterious circumstances. Charlie Jones, Rice's valet, and Albert Patrick, an attorney hired by Orren Holt to assist with the residency questions surrounding the probate of Elizabeth's will, were arrested, tried, and, after a lengthy, much-publicized trial, convicted of murder and forgery.

Patrick had forged a new will supposedly signed by William Rice, naming himself as the primary recipient of the inheritance; in coercion with Patrick, Jones had administered mercury pills to Rice in an attempt to kill him slowly. Then, when faced with the deficit of a large sum of money due to an unexpected business loss incurred by Rice, Jones murdered his employer with chloroform on September 23, 1900.

Eventually, an out-of-court settlement was reached in regard to Elizabeth's will; after all legal fees, commissions, taxes, and actual bequests were dispensed from both wills, the Institute was left with an initial endowment of $4,631,259.08. The original board of trustees invested funds carefully and by 1910, the endowment had increased to more than $7 million.

In January 1907, the search for the institute's first president commenced. Recommendations were received from institutions and individuals all over the United States; after one year, Dr. Edgar Odell Lovett, a professor of mathematics from Princeton, was named as president. Dr. Lovett's vision for Rice Institute, best found in his own words, remains an integral part of the University's mission today: "in striving with their help to combine in its personality those elements—largeness of mind, strength of character, determined purpose, fire of genius, devoted loyalty . . . from its walls shall go forth a continuous column of men trained in the highest degree, equipped in the largest way, for positions of trust in the public service, for commanding careers in the affairs of the world."

In order to study the design and operation of other renowned institutions of higher education, the board of trustees approved a request to send Lovett on a tour of schools throughout Europe and Asia. The importance of this trip was indisputable; not only did Lovett serve as an ambassador from the United States and as the first representative of Rice Institute at international conferences, but he also made important contacts around the world from which the institute would profit in the areas of faculty recruitment and academic support.

In 1911, construction of the institute began with the administration building. Lovett Hall, as it is now known, included classrooms, professorial and administrative offices, studies, lounges, and libraries. The president's office, located high above the building over a 30-foot sal-

Rice University

lyport, inspired the following limerick by Hubert Bray, a mathematics professor at Rice:

A great man is Edgar O. Lovett.
His office has nothing above it.
It is four stories high,
As close to the sky,
As William Ward Watkin could shove it.

The initial faculty complement, selected by the president himself, as culled from outstanding professors at universities and educational institutions throughout the United States and the entire world. Professors were recruited from Cambridge, Heidelberg, Harvard, British Columbia, and Yale. The mathematician recruited by Lovett, Griffith C. Evans, was recommended to the Institute by the Italian mathematician Volterra.

The salaries paid in 1912 were comparable to Harvard. Professors earned $4,000 to $6,000 annually; assistant professors earned $1,200 to $3,660; instructors were paid $900 to $1,500. The president's salary was $10,000, plus lodging.

Academic excellence was high among Edgar Lovett's priorities for the institute, and those standards of excellence remain in place today. According to 1993–94 statistics, over two-thirds of Rice students graduate in the fifth percentile of their high school classes.

In pursuit of these academic ideals, Lovett set into place fairly difficult admission requirements as well as a rigorous course of required study for all incoming students. He was determined to gear the institute's curriculum in the direction of generally recognized and accepted university standards.

Incoming freshmen requirements consisted of a high-school certificate of graduation or successful completion of entrance examinations, character references, and 14 high school units. All students were required to take chemistry, English, German, mathematics, and physics. The infamous "Math 100" was initiated as a requirement, consisting of advanced algebra, analytical geometry, and trigonometry, with calculus being added to the course description during the 1920s. As a result of the rigorous requirements and inadequate preparation in high school, approximately 20 percent of the first freshman class had failed so many of their subjects that they were asked to withdraw.

Although women were welcome at the institute—the charter directed that both sexes should attend—Lovett and a few of the faculty members felt some discomfort at having women in their classes, no doubt due to their own past experiences of all-male classes and separate educational facilities for women. During the first year of the institute's opening, classes were separated by gender. Women were to be off of the campus grounds by 5:00 P.M. Such was the concern about the sexes mingling that even the available benches weren't placed in any shady spots were a couple might be tempted to linger.

In the continued pursuit of academic excellence, an honor code was established at Rice almost immediately, as the president observed the codes successfully maintained at Princeton University and the University of Virginia. The honor code remains intact today with few modifications. The responsibility for upholding the code lies with the students; it is self-monitored and policed.

Initially, Rice offered only a bachelor of the arts and fifth-year degrees in engineering and architecture. Since that time, Rice has expanded it degree offerings to cover more than 15 different degrees and 42 areas of study.

Mirroring Lovett's concern with fostering academic excellence alongside social development, student clubs were established but not as offshoots of national organizations. Lovett forbade the establishment of social fraternities and sororities; instead, the students created their own organizations. Literary societies, the Rice band, the first student newspaper, and the first yearbook were in place by 1916.

As directed specifically in William Marshall Rice's endowment and the Rice Institute's charter, a public library was to be created. In 1915 President Lovett selected a library committee, comprised of faculty members and chairman Griffith Evans. The library budget was $10,000 in 1913. The facility itself was housed in varying areas including the administration building; Fondren Library, as it is known today, occupies its own building and boasts holdings of 1.5 million books in addition to 1.8 million microform titles; 13,100 periodicals; and 16,000 records, tapes, and CDs.

The advent of World War I in April 1917 brought a militaristic turn to life at the Rice Institute. The administration petitioned and received permission to establish a unit of the Reserve Officers' Training Corps. All men and women were required to participate in military exercises; all had to wear uniforms and engage in physical training. The once fairly lax schedule of the Rice student was severely restricted; his or her day began with a room inspection at 6:15 A.M. and concluded with taps and "lights out" at 11:00 P.M. with the entire timespan between carefully regulated and planned.

The 1917 Rice catalog states, "It thus appears that as far as may be consistent with the university programme of the Rice Institute, the conduct of the life of the place, including that of the campus and the residential halls, will be under military regulations, certainly as long as the war continues." Dissatisfaction with the military lifestyle mounted; in November, the student newspaper began printing letters of complaint and protest, their subjects ranging from the poor quality of the "mess hall" food to restrictions on free movement and access to problems within the operation and implementation of the ROTC program.

An underground publication, entitled *Tape*, appeared in early spring of 1917, leading to a rebellion and an eventual meeting of a representative group of students with President Lovett and the board of trustees. Changes to the original regulations were discussed and an agreement reached between the groups, although differences and a degree of dissatisfaction remained until the war ended in November 1918. One positive development from this "rebellion" was the organization of Rice's Student Association including a Student Council, the first governing body formed by and for the students.

The 1920s brought attention to other concerns of the institute, including finances and the overcrowded conditions on the campus. Proposals were introduced to charge tuition and limit enrollments, and public pleas were made for donations. Rice's economic plight remained much the same until the early 1930s, when cost-saving measures were introduced such as reducing faculty salaries, limiting enrollments, required on-campus residency for one year for each male student, and the initiation of student association membership fees.

In 1934, Eugene L. Bender bequeathed $200,000 to Rice Institute, helping to alleviate the financial difficulties. Other funds in the form of gifts and assets such as the Rancor Oil Field delayed the move to charge tuition until February 1966, at which time the Texas Court of Civil Appeals upheld the decision of the lower court, that being to enable Rice to charge tuition and also to admit students without regard to color.

The second president of Rice, William Vermillion Houston, was selected after a search from 1941 to 1945, with the board examining at least 20 candidates. Lovett stepped down from the presidency, citing health reasons, but retaining the title of president emeritus.

Dr. Houston's management style was unlike the previous president's, and the faculty were pleasantly surprised at the active role he took in visiting with them in their offices across the campus, discussing their problems and concerns, and gathering information. The new president also solicited the faculty's opinions as to the nomination of new professors to fill the rapidly expanding needs of the institute. A superior faculty complement was seen as key to producing well-prepared and educated Rice graduates, and Dr. Houston placed a high priority on this goal. Despite the fact that Houston was the president, he never left behind his first love, that of research in physics. A laboratory was created next to his office in Lovett Hall, where the professor-president could pursue his scientific interests whenever he wished.

The residential college system, established in 1957, was part of President Lovett's vision for Rice; however, the system wasn't established until well into the second president's tenure. The college system was to emulate Princeton by making the educational experience less formal, with colleges acting as small communities within the larger community of the university.

Initially, only four residential colleges existed; the total number has double to eight coeducational colleges, overseen by a faculty master and associates. The associates act as advisors and participate in the functions of their respective colleges, striving to encourage self-discipline, intellectual growth and development, and fellowship among the students.

Each college was equipped with a dining hall and public rooms as well as private living space for approximately 215 students. All first-year students were assigned a room in one of the eight colleges; this rule remains in force today.

Although the goals of the original colleges were never realized to their full potential, the colleges have proven to be successful in the overall mission of Rice University.

By the end of the 1950s, it appeared that Rice's university status would become a reality, as the activities and status of the institute were more fitting to a university than what was defined as an "institute." Despite some opposition from a small number of alumni and students, the Rice Institute became known as William Marsh Rice University, effective July 1, 1960.

In 1960, Dr. Houston resigned his presidency due to illness. The third president of Rice, Dr. Kenneth S. Pitzer, was appointed in 1961. His plans for Rice included increased attention to the graduate school, upgraded quality of faculty, a satisfactory method of evaluating the faculty's performance, improved facilities, and an increase in the undergraduate enrollment.

As seemed to be the sign of the times, an aura of dissatisfaction with the educational quality of Rice arose. Overemphasis was placed on good grades, the students complained, and an apathy existed as to learning in general. Some faculty members voiced their agreement with the students' criticisms, and the subcommittee on the program on undergraduate instruction of the academic planning committee reported that Rice's manner of grading seemed to demoralize the student population.

Faculty were encouraged to examine the performance of their students more carefully, as well as to review course workloads and content of their freshman and sophomore sections. Despite various attempts at changing methods of evaluation, the rigorous grading system remained in place and the high academic standards were upheld.

The question of charging tuition raised its head once again the decade of the 1960s. Dr. Pitzer proposed long-range plans such as the creation of new housing units and the establishment of law and business administration schools, none of which could be accomplished without increased revenue and all of which were necessary for Rice's advancement. William Marsh Rice's goal of an endowed, free institution of higher education came to an end in the face of necessary expansion and progress.

Further Reading: For additional in-depth detail as to the preparation and opening of the Rice Institute (prior to 1915), *The Book of the Opening of the Rice Institute* (Houston, Texas: Rice Institute, 1915) is a well-documented, three-volume reference. Sanford Wilson Higginbotham's *Man, Science, Learning and Education* (Houston, Texas: William Marsh Rice University, 1963) illustrates the events and reprints the lectures given by such notables as Margaret Mead and Brand Blanshard at the semicentennial festival.

—Mary Jane Isles

RUPRECHT KARLS UNIVERSITY
(Heidelberg, Germany)

Location: Heidelberg, State of Baden-Wurtemberg, Germany

Description: A state university enrolling about 25,000 students in undergraduate and graduate schools.

Information: Ruprecht-Karls-Universität Heidelberg
Grabengasse 1
Postfach 10 57 60
69117 Heidelberg
Germany
(06221) 54-1

Heidelberg's Ruprecht Karls University, the oldest university in Germany, was named after two princes: Elector Ruprecht I, who founded the university in the fourteenth century, and Grand Duke Karl Friedrich of Baden, who reconstituted it in the nineteenth century. Since then, it has enjoyed an international reputation. Students from more than 90 countries have enrolled at Heidelberg University.

The Golden Bull of 1356, issued by Holy Roman Emperor Charles IV, had granted Ruprecht and his descendants full rights in the imperial electoral college. Thus, he was the most powerful of the secular electors and became a vigorous defender of the interests of the Holy Roman Empire in the west. After the election of two rival popes in 1378, European Christendom was divided into two hostile camps. Italian cardinals had elected Urban VI as pope, whereas the French had chosen Clement VII, who ruled from Avignon. Germany's spiritual and secular leaders supported Urban VI, who presided in Rome. Thus, Europe's center of higher education in the fourteenth century, the Sorbonne, refused to examine German students. As a consequence, Paris became an inhospitable city for German students and teachers. Ruprecht I recognized this crucial situation as an opportunity. He offered asylum and protection to German scholars fleeing Paris. In 1386 the council of electors agreed to found a *Studium Generale* in Heidelberg, modeled on that of Paris, in accordance with the instructions and privileges already granted in a papal bull of foundation of 1385. The Dutchman Marsilius von Inghen, one of the leading scholars of his day, who had been the head of the University of Paris, became the founding rector of the new university. Within a year of its foundation the university registered 570 students.

Ruprecht I and his successors had a strictly practical interest in the university. In order to unite and consolidate the widely scattered Palatinate territories they needed an intellectual and cultural center. The university provided it by educating future ambassadors, counselors, judges, lawyers, and teachers. It also kept an unconditional allegiance to Rome, a tie which had brought the university theological and conciliar importance.

With the proclamation of the teachings of Martin Luther at court, in the city, and in the university by Elector Ottheinrich another major change occurred. The university was reformed from a stronghold of scholasticism into a Protestant state university. Its spirit was that of criticism and free research. Ottheinrich also supported the university library by collecting and donating books, leading to the renown of the *Biblioteca Palatina*.

Friedrich III, who succeeded Ottheinrich in the middle of the sixteenth century, favored Calvinism, and so the Palatinate reformed. Scholars from Switzerland, France, Denmark, and Holland found their religious belief professed only in Heidelberg, which came to be called "the Geneva of Germany." In his survey of the university's history, Diether Raff wrote:

Heidelberg became the first really international university on German territory and briefly played a similar role to that of Paris in the fourteenth century. The *Heidelberg Catechism* (1563) . . . carried the fame of the university out into the world wherever Calvin's teachings made an impact: to Holland, England, Scotland and finally to North America.

The Thirty Years' War halted this development. Heidelberg's city and university were on the verge of ruin. The library had given its treasures to the pope as spoils of war. The university, which was suspended between 1626 and 1629, became Catholic again and tried to win back some of its old reputation. But military actions of Louis XIV against the Palatinate in 1689 and 1693 devastated both the city and the university. The university was evacuated to Frankfurt and then in 1698 to Weinheim before it returned to Heidelberg in 1700. But it was not until 1728 that the university had a main building again. Called the Domus Wilhelmiana (after the elector of the period), it is now the Old University.

The material problems were accompanied by religious ones. A belated Counter-Reformation destroyed the hope of regaining the university's academic freedom. According to Raff, "Out of 28 chairs—occupied on the instructions of the [Jesuit] Order's superiors—a mere four were

Ruprecht Karls University

in Protestant hands by mid-century." Another blow was the electors' plan to develop their Mannheim Court into a center of intellectual and cultural life.

After the disappearance of the Holy Roman Empire under the influence of the French Revolution, the Palatinate with Heidelberg and Mannheim was assigned to Baden. Its ruler Karl Friedrich, who had been promoted from elector to grand duke by Napoléon in 1806, was an enlightened Lutheran who wanted to transform the former principalities into a unified nation. In 1803 he had proclaimed the famous Thirteenth Edict which stated that Heidelberg was the official university in his land. As Raff explained, "He invited poets, artists and scholars to his court and endowed his university—he had already declared himself rector *magnificentissimus*—with a modern, functional constitution." Since then, both the original

founding document of 1386 and the edict of 1803 are regarded together as charters of Heidelberg University, a view expressed in the double name Ruperto-Carola, Ruprecht Karls University.

From this time on "freedom of teaching" was the main principle at the university. Latin was replaced by German as the academic language in most disciplines. The first scholar to accept a chair was Friedrich Creuzer, a distinguished philologist from Marburg. Clemens Brentano also moved to Heidelberg which marked the beginning of the romantic movement there. With his friend Achim von Arnim, Brentano compiled Germany's best-known anthology of early German lyrical poetry, *Des Knaben Wunderhorn,* a collection whose influence can be seen in his own poetry and that of his friends. Joseph von Gorres, Friedrich Hölderlin, Joseph von Eichendorff, and Jean

Paul likewise discovered and praised the city with its incomparable natural surroundings.

Heidelberg also became a center for a particular form of southern German liberalism that attracted professors and students alike. A few hundred took part in the uprising at the Hambach Castle in 1832. Others joined in storming the Frankfurt Hauptwache in 1833. Students also enrolled in the student legion during the Baden Revolution where they fought to change the Reich's constitution. Four Heidelberg professors sat in the Frankfurt National Assembly and in the decades before 1871 the Liberals made the university the chief bulwark of the idea of unity in southwestern Germany.

The names of Robert Wilhelm Bunsen, Gustav Robert Kirchhoff, and Hermann Helmholtz are linked with the importance of natural sciences at Heidelberg University in the 1860s. Raff explains their contributions:

Bunsen and Kirchhoff discovered spectral analysis, opening up new avenues for scientific research, and Helmholtz fathered physiological optics and acoustics, the scientific theory of sound and colour perception and modern electricity theory.

When the university celebrated its 500th anniversary in 1886, its importance was beyond question.

World War I closed this period of intellectual and material wealth. The university recovered slowly from the intellectual isolation caused by the war. Only a minority was willing to continue the pursuit of intellectual freedom guaranteed in the constitution, continuing Heidelberg's liberal tradition as well as the spirit of sociologist Max Weber and poet Stefan George. This minority formed the "Association of University Professors loyal to the Constitution" (the Weimar Group), and laid the basis for the public's image of the university as a most progressive place with high intellectual standards.

In 1928 the university received a new set of lecture halls thanks to American benefactors whose involvement was initiated by Jacob Gould Schurman, U.S. ambassador to Germany from 1925 to 1930 and former student at Heidelberg. This "New University" with its motto "To the living spirit" substantially expanded the university's academic facilities.

However, the "lively mind" was soon extinguished with the coming to power of the National Socialists. Raff described the changes: "[The university was] now stripped of any autonomy and organized on the basis of allegiance to the Fuhrer . . . The inscription over the New University portal had been altered to read 'To the German spirit,' humanism having yielded to nationalism." Minorities were excluded. Thirty-six percent of the full professors and 21 percent of other lecturers had been victimized by the regime. Raff continued:

The number of Jewish students was drastically reduced. In the summer of 1933 there were 180 still enrolled, but in the winter semester of 1936/37 only 24, and they had to suffer considerable restrictions and harassment. Similarly, in 1933 the National Socialists also expelled the students who had allegedly been "hostile to the Volk and the State" in the final years of the Weimar Republic.

After the war the university was closed by General Eisenhower's Proclamation No. 1 in April 1945. The New University, lecture halls, the university library, the Marstall refectory, and a number of scientific institutes were requisitioned by the Allied troops. But only three-and-a-half months after the occupation of Heidelberg, the medical school was reopened; by the beginning of the 1945 winter semester theology and some of the natural sciences were being taught. By January 1946 all other faculties had been reopened and by the summer of the same year 600,000 volumes dispersed during the war had been returned to the university library.

During the following decades the number of students increased immensely. In the mid-sixties the university faced the problems of a mass university. Before World War II the student population was never more than 4,000; by 1962 it was 10,900 and remained constant until 1970, then increased to 17,500 in 1975 and to 23,000 in 1981; since the winter term 1982/83 the number has been around 26,000. With the increase in enrollment came reorganizing and replacing the traditional process of decision making. The traditional 5 faculties were split into 18, each of which is administered by a faculty board and a dean. New buildings were erected to meet the need for classroom and laboratory space in the university. Three large areas within the city can be singled out as university areas: the Old Town around University Square with adjoining areas to the east and west, the Bergheim district (where the teaching hospitals are located), and Neuenheim (where a new campus houses the natural sciences, the medical school and teaching hospitals, student halls of residence, and a large new refectory).

With these capacities the Ruprecht Karls University serves according to Raff both its "role as a place for free research and teaching, and as a state institution with a special responsibility to the public at large."

—Wolfgang Holtkamp

RUTGERS: THE STATE UNIVERSITY OF NEW JERSEY
(New Brunswick, New Jersey, U.S.A.)

Location:

New Brunswick Campus is made up of five smaller campuses located on both sides of the Raritan River in New Brunswick and Piscataway. The campuses are connected by a free university bus system. Students can travel along campuses to take classes. Camden Campus is located at the foot of the Benjamin Franklin Bridge just across the river from the center-city Philadelphia; the campus is easily accessible by public and private transportation. Newark Campus is 15 minutes outside New York City by public transportation.

Description:

A state university enrolling approximately 48,000 students in undergraduate, graduate, and professional schools. The 26 degree-granting divisions offer more than 10,000 courses in almost 100 major fields of study. The university has the honor of being one of the top public research universities in the country.

Information:

Rutgers–New Brunswick Campus
George Street
New Brunswick, NJ 08903
U.S.A.
(908) 932-1766

Rutgers–Newark Campus
Office of Communications
249 University Ave.
Newark, NJ 07102
U.S.A.
(201) 648-1766

Rutgers–Camden Campus
311 N. Fifth Street
Camden, NJ 08102
U.S.A.
(609) 225-1766

Visiting:

A self-guided walking tour of the original New Brunswick colonial campus is available. Tours of the Camden and Newark campuses are also available. For more information, call the phone numbers above.

From a humble beginning as a struggling colonial college, and subsequent decades of challenges and setbacks, Rutgers has grown into a major state university system with more than 48,000 students on three campuses. Rutgers has an unique history as a colonial college, a land grant institution, and a state university—signifying the triple traditions of American higher education. Only Rutgers University can claim this triple distinction in the United States. Founded in 1766, Rutgers predates many of the Ivy League schools.

The circumstances leading up to the development of the college were far from ordinary. In 1755 one rebellious party of the discordant Dutch Reformed Church declared its determination "to plant a university or seminary, in the Province of New Jersey, for young men destined for study in the learned languages and in the liberal arts, and who are to be instructed in the philosophical sciences."

Lacking any resources, and facing opposition from church authorities in the Netherlands, and from their local adversaries, these impassioned ministers relentlessly pursued their plan. They sought a charter for their college from successive governors of New Jersey but were rebuffed.

On November 10, 1766, William Franklin, the last colonial governor of New Jersey, granted their petition, and signed the charter, in the name of King George III of England, establishing Queen's College. The college was established to train young men for the ministry in the Dutch Reformed Church, and named in honor of Charlotte of Mecklenburg, consort of King George III. (Queen's college was the eighth institution of higher learning founded in the colonies.)

The battle was far from over. Even after the charter was granted in 1766, five years were to pass before the work of the college commenced. Although a board of trustees was established, they found problems with specific charter provisions and would not move on to establish the college. Another obstacle during this time was the occupation of New Brunswick by British troops.

One clergyman who took a leading role in the application for the charter and may be regarded as Queen's College founder was the Reverend Jacob Rutsen Hardenbergh—a colonel in the New York militia. He was one of the school's original trustees, serving in that capacity for 50 years. In 1785, he was elected the first president of Queen's College.

A revised charter was sought and granted by Governor Franklin on March 20, 1770. In May 1771, the board of trustees voted to select New Brunswick, over rival towns, as the site of Queen's College. Subsequently, modest funds were raised for the institution.

In November 1771, the first classes were held in a tavern in New Brunswick. The Sign of the Red Lion, on the corner of Albany and Neilson streets. The first, and for a

Rutgers: The State University of New Jersey

long time only tutor, at Queen's College was Frederick Frelinghuysen, stepson of the college's future president and nephew of Theodore, the clergyman-pioneer. Frederick was only 18 years old when he took on the teaching position. He had just received his bachelor of arts degree at Princeton, then known as the College of New Jersey.

In the beginning, the student body consisted of one sophomore, and a handful of freshmen. Frederick's task was to instruct students in the learned languages, liberal arts, and sciences. He was also expected to teach the English language grammatically. During these early years, the college developed as a classical liberal arts institution.

Queen's College held its first commencement on October 12, 1774. The Reverend Jacob Rutsen Hardenbergh chaired the graduation ceremony and gave a moving speech stating "that men of learning are of absolute necessity and extensive advantages to society." The entire graduating class consisted of one Matthew Leydt, age 19.

The War for Independence cast a dark shadow on the destiny of the emerging Queen's College. In 1776, the college's tutor John Taylor joined the Revolutionary Army as a captain, and was followed by a number of his students. The actual location of the college shifted as General Howe pursued Washington through New Jersey. Many times classes were held sporadically in private homes around the New Brunswick area.

From the beginning, hard times haunted Queen's College. In 1793, the board of trustees considered merging with Princeton. The measure failed by one vote. By 1795, in need of both funds and tutors, the trustees contemplated moving the college to New York. In the end, they closed the school. After the trustees raised $12,000 in 1807, they reopened the college.

One April 27, 1809, the cornerstone of the first building, Old Queen's, was laid by President Ira Condict. Original estimates called for the cost of $12,000 but when the building was completed, the total cost was nearer $30,000 and took 14 years to build. The building is considered one of the nation's finest examples of federal period architecture. (In 1976, Old Queen's was designated a national historic landmark.) When the elegant, three-story house was completed, it housed professors and their families, classrooms, a library, and chapel.

The War of 1812, and a depressed economy, dealt a crushing blow, forcing the college to close again. Colonel Henry Rutgers, an American military officer, philanthropist, and a public-spirited citizen, took an interest in Queen's College, wanting to turn the tide on its low academic and financial status. However, he felt the name "Queen's" was not appropriate to the patriot ideas he upheld.

In November 1825, amid a rebirth of the school, Queen's College petitioned the New Jersey legislature to change its name to Rutgers College in honor of the Colonel. This move occurred simultaneously with the election of Philip Milledoler as college president, the latter a pastor, and a personal friend of Rutgers. The legislature made the necessary amendments to the charter, and the octogenarian's name was given to the financially strapped college. At this point, Rutger's donations had amounted to very little.

The honor may have been bestowed with a double intent: to recognize a prominent member of the Dutch Reformed Church (since he was then president of its board of corporation) and to share in the benefactions of a person whose generosity had long been known, and possibly could become enduring by gift or bequest. This last hope was not completely realized. Rutger's known gifts, thereafter, included $200 for the purchase of a bell to be hung in the new cupola on the college building. He also deposited a bond for $5,000 with synod, with the stipulation that the interest be paid annually to the college in cash.

Since the Colonel was a landed magnate and contributor to numerous educational and religious projects, the synod and trustees expected that he might also use his considerable influence within the denomination. In fact, the adoption of the new name did have a significant impact since it symbolized the addition of a new group supporting the college. Originally, local men largely sustained Queen's College. Now, a powerful group from New York City, including Milledoler, Abraham Van Best, the Reverend John Knox, the Reverend Isaac Ferris, and others, gained prominent positions on the board of trustees. Their arrival brought additional resources to the school.

In 1841, the college catalogue announced the creation of a scientific or commercial course that allowed a student to select studies that had a direct bearing on his intended life purpose. Influenced earlier by Princeton and Union, Rutgers had made special provisions in 1810 for special students interested in the study of science, but records indicate students did not choose this option. During the next two decades, the course attracted only a small number of students but it set the stage for the future land grant college.

Rutgers College experienced a burst of energy never seen before or equaled afterward during the decade following 1862. During that period, college assets increased fivefold, relations with the Dutch Church were practically severed, and the Rutgers Scientific School was established and designated the land grant college for New Jersey.

In July 1862, Congress offered 30,000 acres of public lands, or land scrip to each member of Congress for their respective states. The proceeds were to be invested as an endowment for the support of a college. The movement to secure the grant for Rutgers originated in the faculty by Professor Cook and Professor Murray. Murray's report to the trustees revealed that the New Jersey legislature had accepted the land grant in 1863 and would now apply the proceeds—estimates were up to $160,000—to an existing college or a new institution.

Cook and Murray urged the trustees to seek the land grant designation since it would expand the offerings and facilities in the various areas of science. The response of the trustees was positive. They decided that the "Scientific Course of Study," approved back in 1810, should be established as a department in the college under the name of Rutgers Scientific School. Simultaneously, the trustees petitioned for the land grant designation.

Both Rutgers and Princeton University began an intensive campaign to win the grant. On February 23, President Campbell, Governor Vroom, and Professor Cook (the most active advocate) presented their case for Rutgers at a legislative hearing, along with the rival institutions of Princeton and the State Normal School at Trenton. The legislative committee responded in favor of Rutgers' request. Finally, the bill was signed by the governor on April 4, 1864, for the land grant college of New Jersey with departments of agriculture, engineering, and chemistry.

Most states offered financial assistance which supplemented the small income from land grant funds. Rutgers received no aid from the state. Although obtaining the grant was a worthy endeavor, since it offered a needed educational discipline, the grant curtailed the trustee's resources and may have impeded the college's growth for many decades.

In 1873, a faculty committee considered the formal development of graduate courses, but not until 1882 did the trustees approve an extensive list of faculty recommendations. To qualify for the master of arts or master of science degree, advanced students in residence were required to take approved courses, pass a comprehensive exam, and present an adequate thesis. A two-year course of study, including subjects in two similar disciplines, an examination, and thesis could lead to the doctor of science or doctor of philosophy degree. The first Ph.D. was awarded in 1884.

The installation of President Merrill Edwards Gates in 1882 brought an era of student discipline, a strictly prescribed curriculum, and the establishment of an honors system to encourage students' independent reading and studying. He also espoused the formation of strong Christian character in students. During his tenure, the quality of the faculty vastly improved, the student body expanded, and academic standards were strengthened.

After World War I, a transformation swept across both America and Rutgers as experimentation and uncertainty permeated the air. By 1925, the institution had changed dramatically. Three major campuses had sprung up, several colleges were endowed with various degrees of autonomy, two distinct student bodies had formed, and trustees granted extensive responsibilities to special agencies for certain colleges.

Up until now, Rutgers was solely dedicated to the education of men. In 1918, the creation of the New Jersey College for Women—now Douglass College—shattered that tradition. As early as 1881, the faculty had proposed to the trustees that young women be admitted, but the request was turned down. Continued appeals were also later rejected by the trustees.

Mrs. Mabel S. Douglass, a Barnard graduate, took up the challenge of establishing a women's college, and worked with great fervor, despite financial setbacks. When personal afflications caused her to withdraw from the movement, other organizations (State Grange, New Jersey Education Association, State Board of Education) lent their endorsements. At last, the Women's College became a department of the State University of New Jersey in 1918.

James Dickson Carr became the first African American to graduate from Rutgers in 1892. He later became an assistant district attorney for New York City. Paul Robeson, the third African American in Rutger's history, gave the valedictory address at the 1919 commencement. Robeson had been praised as possibly the greatest college football player of his time.

The swift development of the New Jersey College for Women, and the College of Agriculture (1921), brought an urgency to the bigger concern of developing an appropriate structure for the growing university. For almost five years, the president, the trustees, and the faculty bickered over these difficult issues. State relations, educational efficiency, and economy only made the issues more complex. Decisions also had to be reached on the role of the faculty in the conduct of the institution.

Sharp disagreements surfaced over basic principles leading to the growth of two factions. One faction, led by Leonor F. Loree, lobbied for a "businesslike" plan of organization, and greater seeking of public support. The opposing faction, led by President Demarest, argued for traditional practices in the academic community. He also preferred adherence to established state policies. After a series of committees, clashing viewpoints, behind-the-scenes activities, proposed and defeated plans, the board of trustees agreed to a faculty submission with some modifications.

Accepted was the faculty's proposal for colleges of arts and sciences, agriculture, women, engineering, and a school of education. The proposal for a school of physical and biological sciences, and graduate school were rejected. At the June 14, 1924, commencement, the title of Rutgers University, as authorized by the trustees, was first employed.

In 1945, the colleges and schools of Rutgers were collectively designated the State University of New Jersey by legislature. The same controversy and opposition that had characterized other changes in Rutgers history applied to this latter achievement. Although more turbulent times were still ahead, additional university achievements continued.

By 1946 Rutgers University and the University of Newark merged. Soon after, in 1950, Rutgers merged with the College of South Jersey and its school of law to create the Camden campus. In 1961, the University of Medicine and Dentistry of New Jersey—Robert Wood Johnson Medical School—was founded. Formerly, it was known as Rutgers Medical School.

President Edward J. Bloustein's goal to make Rutgers one of the nation's top universities was achieved in 1989, when Rutgers was invited to join the Association of American Universities (AAU), the most prestigious body of research universities in North America.

In 1990, Rutgers conferred its 250,000th degree, and in 1991, Rutgers marked its 225th anniversary.

From a humble colonial college, fighting off decades of financial woe, setbacks, and a heritage of internal discontent, the university has fared well. Today, Rutgers' forefathers would agree with pride that the accomplishments achieved in the past will continue well into the next century.

Further Reading: Richard P. McCormick's *Rutgers: A Bicentennial History* (New Brunswick, New Jersey: Rutgers University Press, 1966) provides an extensive account of the founding of the university. Another lengthy account will be found in *Bicentennial Year, The Story of a Rutgers Celebration* by George H. Holsten Jr. (New Brunswick, New Jersey: Rutgers University Press, 1968).

—Darlene Maciuba-Koppel

ST. JOHN'S COLLEGE
(Annapolis, Maryland, and Santa Fe, New Mexico, U.S.A.)

Location: The Maryland campus is located in the heart of Annapolis, the state capital, on the Chesapeake Bay. The Santa Fe campus sits at 7,300 feet above sea level in the Sangre de Cristo Mountains in north-central New Mexico.

Description: Founded in 1696 as King William's School, chartered in 1784 as St. John's College, it offers a unique all-required curriculum based on the reading and discussion of works of western civilization.

Information: St. John's College
Annapolis, MD 21401
U.S.A.
(410) 263-2371

St. John's College
Santa Fe, NM 87501
U.S.A.
(505) 982-3691

In 1632, King Charles I of England gave Cecil Calvert, the second Lord Baltimore, a small piece of land from the state of Virginia along the Potomac River. With this parcel, Calvert founded the state of Maryland. Thirty-nine years later Calvert attempted to charter a state college but was prevented from doing so by the Protestant-run lower house of the Maryland General Assembly who feared that Calvert, a Catholic, would turn the school into a Catholic institution. Finally, in the 1690s, Maryland's royal governor, Francis Nicholson, a member of the Church of England, convinced the legislature to open a "free" school. In fact, the legislature's intention was to open several such schools under the Petitionary Act for Free Schools. The word "free" refers not to the tuition policy, but to the school's goal to ensure its students freedom through education. Founded as King William's School, the institution called for basic instruction in Latin, Greek, and writing, with the expectation that its students would go on to study theology at the College of William and Mary in Virginia. Classes were held in a brick building near the State House in Annapolis.

The school struggled financially. Other than a 1732 endowment from Governor Benedict Leonard Calvert, the school did not receive any money, save from tuition. Many associated with the school found this situation maddening, knowing that the state was reaping profits from the growth and sale of tobacco. The assembly eventually approved the trustees' request to sell certain school properties that were not generating income; however, the trustees delayed the sale, pending another action circulating through the legislature.

Pressure was mounting to found two state colleges, one in Annapolis and another on Maryland's eastern shore. Other legislators wanted the state to open a series of free schools; they blocked each attempt to charter the two colleges. In the meantime, young men were leaving the state to attend colleges in Pennsylvania and Virginia. Finally, in 1784, after seven attempts, King William's School was chartered as St. John's College. However, the first students would not arrive for another five years as buildings were readied. (Two years earlier, in 1782, Washington College was opened in Chestertown on Maryland's eastern shore.)

The state donated an unfinished governor's mansion and four surrounding acres. Now known as McDowell Hall, the structure was originally built by Governor Thomas Bladen in 1742. Construction costs quickly ran over budget, and Bladen was forced to abandon the project when the legislature refused to allocate more funds. Locals called the building Bladen's Folly. It suffered from water damage and was neglected for several decades. The board of visitors and governors of the college hired architect Joseph Clark, who designed the State House, to refurbish the building. Renamed McDowell Hall after the first president of St. John's College, the building is the nation's third oldest academic building in continuous use.

Four signers of the Declaration of Independence were among the college's founders: William Paca, Charles Carroll of Carrollton, Thomas Stone, and Samuel Chase. Paca was also the governor of Maryland at the time, and his name can be found on the charter. In spite of the presence of Jesuits, Presbyterians, Anabaptists, Episcopalians, Methodists, and Quakers on the founding board, St. John's charter states that students are to be admitted "without requiring or enforcing any religious or civil test."

The source of the college's name is open to debate. One assumption is that it was borrowed from the St. John's College of Cambridge University. Another theory is that the name has its origins in Freemasonic fraternity. The college seal bears a Masonic symbol; both John the Baptist and John the Evangelist hold honored positions among the Masons, although the fraternity is not a sanctioned Christian organization. Today, the popular belief is that the school was named for John the Evangelist.

In their search for a college president, or principal, as the position was known at the time, the board of trustees

St. John's Collge

expressed a desire for "A Stranger" or a "Great Character from Europe." However, one particularly influential trustee, the Reverend William Smith, one of the founders of the Protestant Episcopal Church in the United States, suggested a school of such decidedly American origins and character should be led by an American. Thus the board chose John McDowell in 1790. McDowell had come to St. John's the previous year as a professor of mathematics. Born and raised on a farm in Cumberland County, Pennsylvania, McDowell attended the College of Philadelphia (which would become the University of Pennsylvania) and practiced law for five years.

Under McDowell's presidency, the college gradually grew in reputation. By the beginning of the nineteenth century, 105 students had graduated, including Francis Scott Key, the author of the "Star-Spangled Banner"; George Washington Park Custis, stepgrandson of George Washington; and Fairfax and Lawrence Washington, two of the president's nephews. Other graduates would go on to serve as governors, judges, and members of the Maryland state legislature. However, at the turn of century the Maryland house of delegates voted to withdraw its funding, citing the school's neglect of impoverished students. This effectively put an end to the plan to join St. John's and Washington Colleges as the state's first university.

Weary of the constant battle for money, McDowell was easily wooed away by the University of Pennsylvania in 1801. He returned briefly in 1815, much to his regret. St. John's closed its doors in 1817 and then reopened the following year with alumni financial support. Led by Key and Robert Goldsborough, the alumni society was established in the 1820s.

In 1831, the dynamic presidency of Hector Humphreys began, bringing with it a revamping of the curriculum and the construction of two more academic buildings: Humphreys Hall and Pinkney Hall; and two faculty houses: Chase-Stone and Paca-Carroll. During his 26-year tenure, Humphreys added the instruction of modern science, increased the enrollment to 100 students, and brought the library collection to over 4,000 volumes.

St. John's was forced to close again during the Civil War. Most of its students set their studies aside to become soldiers in armies of the Union or the Confederacy. The Union Army used school property to set up a hospital, a way station, and barracks. The war years left the college ravaged. Although the federal government granted the school $4,666 in aid, the trustees were forced to raise an additional $11,500 to make the necessary repairs. St. John's reopened in 1866 with Dr. Henry Barnard as president. Barnard left after only one year to become the nation's first commissioner of education. He was succeeded by Dr. James C. Welling who increased the student body from 90 to 250. Welling left in 1870 to join the faculty of Princeton University. In 1884, a compulsory military program was initiated. It was during this period that extracurricular activities appeared for the first time in the form of a campus newspaper, literary societies, and athletics. The curriculum was divided between a study of the classics and technical courses in engineering and mining. Although other schools were offering elective courses, St. John's did not. Perhaps it was this fact that did little to improve the college's academic and financial standings.

Dr. Thomas Fell moved into the presidency in 1886 and established a prep school for the Naval Academy at Annapolis. By 1903, the state of Maryland was again making contributions to St. John's, which allowed for the building of Woodward Hall in 1899, Randall Hall in 1903, and a gymnasium in 1910. In 1905, the quality of the cadet corps influenced the U.S. War Department to name St. John's to its list of six leading military colleges. However, by the close of World War I, the nature of American education was changing, even at St. John's where military training was abolished, and electives were offered for the first time.

The board's decision to invest heavily in real estate during the 1920s came to a disastrous conclusion with the stock market crash and ensuing economic depression. Several of the college's buildings had been mortgaged, and operating funds were virtually nonexistent. In desperation, the trustees brought two academic reformers, Stringfellow Barr and Scott Buchanan, to the campus in 1937 with the charge to revamp the curriculum in such a way that it would attract new students. Barr would then serve as the college's president from 1937 to 1946, while Buchanan held the office of dean. Barr and Buchanan introduced a discussion group style of study based on the Great Books of the Western World, a program derived from the philosophies of Robert M. Hutchins, president of University of Chicago. The unified, all-required, no-electives curriculum, which abolished departments and majors, attracted national attention. Among the new recruits was the college's first African-American student, Martin A. Dyer, who enrolled in 1948.

Richard Weigle took over as president in 1949, and, during his 30-year tenure, the school's reputation grew within educational circles. Women were admitted to St. John's College in 1951. New dormitories were built. Mellon Hall and Francis Scott Key Auditorium were opened in 1959. By the 1960s the college was faced with the need to expand its physical plant to accommodate the demand for admissions. Fortunately, a donation of land at the foot of the Sangre de Cristo Mountains in Santa Fe, New Mexico, by John and Faith Meem allowed the board to open a second campus in 1964. Weigle headed both campuses until his retirement in 1980. Each campus is now headed by its own president. The school as a whole is governed by a board of visitors and governors.

Today, the curriculum is overseen by the joint committee on instruction. It continues to be a non-elective, interdisciplinary program based upon the reading and discussion of 130 great books on topics such as literature, philosophy, theology, political theory, history, and economics. Students are encouraged to attend classes on both campuses. Transfers are allowed at the end of each semester.

St. John's approach to education remains unique. There are no lecture courses, no text books, no written finals, and no departments. There are no professors. Faculty members are referred to as tutors. In the classes, students discuss the Great Books, which are at the heart of the college's curriculum, in chronological order. The first year is devoted to Greek authors; the second year explores works from Roman, Medieval, and Renaissance periods; third year considers books of the seventeenth and eighteenth centuries; and the fourth year covers the nineteenth and twentieth centuries.

St. John's Maryland campus, situated in the historic town of Annapolis, boasts several spots of historical significance. Admissions, alumni, and administrative offices are housed in the Carroll Barrister, once the residence of Charles Carroll, the Barrister, a cousin of the signer of the Declaration of Independence and St. John's founding board member of the same name. Charles Carroll, the Barrister, was the principal writer for the Declaration of the Delegates of Maryland, adopted on July 6, 1776. This document would eventually become the first 45 articles of the Maryland Constitution, which Carroll also helped to write. The last of the Revolutionary period "liberty trees," so named because of the meetings frequently held under its branches by the American colonists, also stands on the St. John's campus. During the U.S. bicentennial celebration, the tree, a tulip poplar, was officially deemed to be over 200 years old. Forestry experts estimate its exact age to be somewhere in the realm of 400 years.

St. John's library has its origins in the first public library in the United States, founded in Annapolis by the Reverend Thomas, an Anglican clergyman who created some 111 libraries in England and the American colonies. According to historical accounts, when Sir Thomas Lawrence, the secretary of Maryland, visited the future Queen Anne to ask permission to name Maryland's new capital in her honor, Bray accompanied him in the hope of securing financial support for the building of a library there. The future queen gave Bray 40 guineas (the equivalent of 44 pounds) with which he was able to establish a library with 1,095 volumes in the new capital. In 1696, the state assembly moved the library to the new state house. When the building burned in 1704, the books were moved to King William's where they were held when the school became St. John's College. Two hundred and eleven of the books remain, seven in St. John's library, the balance in the Maryland Hall of Records in Annapolis.

In the June 17, 1996, issue of *National Review,* William F. Buckley Jr. reflected on his experience as a commencement speaker at St. John's College: "What follows is a lullaby to the forlorn on the theme of: Believe it or not, some American students learn . . . What St. John's does is go exactly in the opposite direction of what virtually everybody else is doing . . . Did you ever see a dream walking? Go to St. John's, Annapolis."

Further Reading: *St. John's "For Ever,"* a special issue of the *St. John's Review* (Annapolis, Maryland), volume 40, number 2, 1990–91, is a collection of essays by Charlotte Fletcher, librarian of St. John's College from 1944 to 1980. The essays cover the early colonial years of Maryland, the struggle to charter a college, and the tenure of John McDowell, St. John's first president. For comments on the current situation, see "St. John's Clings to Classics" in *The New York Times* (January 10, 1993, p. EL18).

—Mary McNulty

SEOUL NATIONAL UNIVERSITY
(Seoul, Republic of Korea)

Location: Seoul National University's main campus, the Kwanak Campus, is situated approximately ten miles from Seoul, in the southern outskirts of the capital city at the foot of majestic Kwanak Mountain. The university's medical campus, the Yongon Campus, is located in the center of downtown Seoul, while Suwon Campus, the agricultural campus, is located about 24 miles south of Seoul in Suwon City. All three campuses are easily reached by subway; the Kwanak Campus is accessed by SNU Station, Line 2; the Yongon Campus is accessed by Hehwa Station, Line 4; and the Suwon Campus is accessed by Suwon Station, Line 3.

Description: A state-sponsored major teaching and research center comprised of 16 colleges, 4 graduate schools, and 71 research institutes and supporting facilities, with a total enrollment of approximately 28,000 (20,000 at the undergraduate level; 8,000 at the graduate level). With 1,400 faculty members, the faculty to student ratio is 20:1. The ratio of men to women is almost 4:1.

Information: Office of International Affairs
Seoul National University
Kwan-Ak-Gu
Shillim-Dong San 56-1 (151-742)
Seoul
Korea
(0)2 880 8633

Although efforts to educate the general public did not begin until late in the nineteenth century in Korea, education was always highly valued. The influence of Confucianism is largely responsible for this reverence; according to Confucian tradition only high-level scholars who had studied and passed rigorous examinations in the Confucian classics could attain positions within the government. Since social and economic power were achieved almost exclusively through the acquisition of these government jobs, the importance of scholarship was tantamount to success, if not survival.

Historically, access to education was primarily limited to male children of the upper class who were taught at Buddhist temples. The Koryo Dynasty (936–1392) promoted classes to teach the children of the aristocracy the Confucian classics. State schools in the capital and prov-

inces, established during the Choson Dynasty (1392–1910), eventually began to compete with the growing number of private academies established by out-of-favor scholars and former government officials. However, a tradition-based bias persisted; women were still excluded from formal schooling and Chinese texts and characters were still emphasized.

Beginning in 1895, a western-style program of education was set in place—a regular system of primary and middle schools, teacher training colleges, foreign language institutes, technical and commercial colleges, medical school, and other professional training institutes was established and greater importance accorded the Korean language in schools. Christian Protestant missionaries greatly influenced the direction of education in Korea. These missionaries opened elementary and secondary schools and three colleges, but it was their invitation to school children of all genders and classes that signified real progress.

Although some pressure for educational reform came from the Japanese in the mid-1890s, no substantial advances occurred during the period in which Japan ruled the country, from 1910 to 1945; education was directed at the Japanese living there, which meant, of course, that all classes were taught in Japanese. Liberation from Japan in 1945 allowed Korea the opportunity to begin to address educational policies that would reflect its new independence, but this was no easy task. According to Jongchol Kim, author of *Some Essays and Thoughts on Korean Education,* "The status of higher education at the time of Korean Liberation from Japanese rule is shrouded with obscurity. According to the official statistics, there were 19 institutions of higher learning in the south with a total of 7,819 student enrollments and 1,490 faculty members." A groundswell of public support for the expansion of institutions of higher learning eased the process somewhat.

For a brief three-year period from 1945 to 1948, the U.S. military government in Korea and the United Nations supervised the creation of a democratic educational system based on western models. The prime directives of this system, however, actually came from Korean nationals working on the newly organized Korean Committee on Education (organized in September 1945) and the Council of Education (November 1945). The resulting system, generally known as the 6-3-3-4 plan of school organization (six years of elementary school, three years of middle school, three years of high school, four years of college), most closely resembled that of the United States at the time.

Seoul National University

Although colleges and institutions of higher education already existed, the new republic lacked a national, state-operated university. Supporters hoped to combine Kyong-song Imperial University and nine other public and private colleges to create South Korea's first national university, but the leftist branch of both the faculty and the student body vehemently opposed such a move. Despite protests and organized strikes, some of which had violent moments, the state-operated Seoul National University (SNU) and its 491 faculty members opened its doors to 4,500 students on October 15, 1946. Only a few months later the first graduation exercise took place on March 6, 1947, when 34 students graduated from SNU medical college.

Throughout its history, the university has reorganized several times with the goal of providing the best opportunities for learning to its students. The 1948 constitution guaranteed Koreans the right to education and the development of a national university symbolized the new government's democratic vision for its people. The

Education Act of 1949 and later the Charter of National Education listed the country's educational goals, including enrolling all children in elementary schools and emphasizing teacher training and scientific and technological education. State-operated and privately run educational institutions were to be closely monitored by the Ministry of Education, the central administrative organization of education in Korea, first organized in 1948. Literacy courses became compulsory. The Korean War (1950–53) arrested the government's efforts to stamp out illiteracy, but once the war was over, the development of both education in general and the national university continued.

Politics again interfered during the 1960s. The student revolt of 1960 powered the demonstrations against President Syngman Rhee that eventually lead to his downfall, and the ensuing military government (1961–63) enacted numerous radical reforms to the educational system, most of which were nullified once that regime passed. University organizers recognized the need to establish long-term goals and plans for SNU, including the reorganization of component colleges and schools within the university and raising its standards for faculty members. In addition, various organizations were created to address the diverse needs of students, faculty, and alumni, as well as the public. A newspaper was founded in 1952, and nine years later, a press was created to help university faculty members publish their work. Today, the university newspaper has a circulation of approximately 30,000, and the SNU Press has its own printing and typesetting facilities and has published more than 600 books.

Since 1963 the Ministry of Education has allocated research grants to individual scholars and university departments or projects. At the time, SNU was receiving almost a quarter of the grant allocated to public and private educational institutions. The SNU Development Foundation was established in 1991 to finance student scholarships, research and charitable projects, and cultural and athletic activities on campus. The foundation solicits contributions from alumni, corporations, and others.

Occupying approximately 2.5 square miles, the university's main campus, Kwanak Campus, offers its students the amenities typical to large schools—athletic facilities, recreation centers, dormitories, and dining halls—and houses most of the administrative offices of both the school and student/student-related organizations. In addition to all of these facilities, the Kwanak Campus is home to the university library, the largest library in East Asia, with a collection of 1.6 million volumes.

The university library consists of three collections, older texts, contemporary texts, and special texts. The bulk of the older texts deal with law and East Asian studies and primarily came from the Kyungsung Imperial University. The contemporary collection is composed of books and documents collected since 1945, including 8,000 periodicals. University library organizers hope to increase the collection each year until, by the year 2001, the collection will have 20,000 volumes. A database network connects the university library with other networks throughout the world, allowing library users to tap into on-line sources. One project that is currently in the works will connect the university library to all the other university libraries in the nation, making it the center for library research. Branch libraries operate at the other campuses, namely the colleges of law, medicine, and agriculture.

Once a part of the university library, but now independent, the Gyujanggak Archives has the largest collection of classical texts in the nation, with 3,833 works. Among these are 175,000 ancient books, 50,000 rare documents, and 17,800 wooden printing plates, many of which have been declared national treasures. As such a precious resource is incredibly valuable to those in Korean and Asian studies, the archives are open to the public as well as SNU students and visiting scholars. Founded during the Chosun Dynasty in 1776 as part royal archive, part court library, and part policy research center, the entire collection was transferred to SNU in 1946 when the university was created. Since then, the collection has been cataloged, and in 1993, it was made into an independent library.

Completed in 1992, Seoul National University Museum exhibits talismans of archeological history, contemporary art, and folklore, among other subjects. The museum's holdings include over 100,000 archeological items of Paleolithic, Neolithic, and Bronze Ages, and rare artworks from the Three Kingdoms to the Chosun Dynasty to present day.

The Yongon Campus, located in the heart of Seoul's downtown, is home to SNU's medical school, research library institutes, and other organizations related to medical science. The college of medicine, the college of dentistry, the college of nursing, the graduate school of public health, and the university hospital are all located there. Twenty-four miles south of the capital city, in Suwon City, lies the agricultural campus. Students enrolled there in either the college of agriculture and life sciences or the college of veterinary medicine take advantage of an experimental farm and the veterinary hospital, complete with a livestock experiment station and modern facilities. An arboretum sprawls for nearly 111 square miles of the campus.

Competition is keen to enter SNU and the four other privately operated universities which together comprise the top five schools in South Korea—Yonsei, Korea, Ewha Women's, and Sogang. To qualify for consideration, applicants must have completed 12 years of school or the equivalent and have passed the Scholastic Aptitude Test (SAT). Applicants are screened for admission into SNU on the basis of their test scores on the SAT and entrance examinations given by the university in January of each year, as well as the quality of their high school records and an interview with someone from the university. Students are admitted to a department or school (the university's 16 colleges are subdivided into these two categories). Students are expected to complete their studies within six years, although a one-year extension is granted to foreign students.

Tuition and fees in U.S. dollars range from $2,300 to $2,500 per year, plus another $800 for books and living expenses. Scholarships are available.

—Elizabeth Taggart

SMITH COLLEGE
(Northampton, Massachusetts, U.S.A.)

Location: Ninety-three miles from Boston and 54 miles from Hartford, Connecticut; 125-acre campus in western Massachusetts located at the foot of the Berkshires with Amherst College and University of Massachusetts nearby.

Description: The largest private women's college in the United States with 2,600 students enrolled in 35 major fields of study, a member of the "Seven Sisters" women's colleges. The coeducational graduate school offers master's degrees in seven areas of study.

Information: Office of Admissions
Northampton, MA 01063
U.S.A.
(413) 584-2500
Fax (413) 585-2527

Visiting: Campus tours conducted by Smith College students are available through the admissions office. Contact the university at the address above.

During its early years, Smith College was recognized as the educator of the elite's daughters, as was Harvard for schooling the elite's sons. Today, the 125-acre campus designed by Frederick Law Olmsted maintains a student body of 2,600 from every state in the United States and 65 countries. The predominantly Protestant enrollees gave way to other faiths including Catholic, Buddhist, Muslim, Jewish, Christian Science, Hindu, and Quaker. It is the largest independent women's college in the country, with an endowment to match. Founded by Sophia Smith more than 124 years ago for the purpose of educating women to take a dynamic role in society, Smith College has surpassed its original aspiration.

Sophia Smith was born on August 27, 1796, in Hatfield, Massachusetts, the oldest daughter of seven children of Joseph and Lois (White) Smith. She was educated at Hatfield School, where boys were taught in the morning and girls in the afternoon. In 1836, when she was 40 years old, Smith became deaf, a condition which denied her social interaction and profoundly deepened her sensitive and introspective personality. Her father died the same year, leaving $10,000 to each of his surviving children, all of whom remained unmarried and continued to live at the family home.

At age 65, Smith was the last of her family, and wanting to dispose wisely of her inheritance, she turned to her young Unitarian pastor, the Reverend John Morton Greene, for guidance. A graduate of Amherst College, Greene believed that education would be the salvation of mankind. Although anxious for spiritual advice and earthly direction, Smith's independent nature led her to refuse Greene's initial suggestion to bequeath her fortune to two local institutions of higher learning, Amherst and Mount Holyoke (Greene's wife's alma mater). Greene, aware that Vassar College had just been chartered, then suggested that Smith fund the first college for women in New England that would have the same high standards and stringent academic programs as colleges for men.

Greene then consulted with the presidents of Amherst, Harvard, Williams, and Yale. These educational leaders declared that offering women higher educational opportunities was a "dangerous experiment." Smith then decided to leave the bulk of her fortune to an institution for deaf-mutes. But seven years later, a bequest by John Clarke enabled the Clarke School for the Deaf to open in 1868 in nearby Northampton, and she felt obliged to bestow her legacy elsewhere. Greene then renewed his campaign for a women's college as the beneficiary for Smith's largess.

Smith determined that leaving her inheritance to establish a women's college was the best way for her to fulfill a moral obligation. She expressed in her will:

I hereby make the following provisions for the establishment and maintenance of an Institution for the higher education of young women, with the design to furnish for my own sex means and facilities for education equal to those which are afforded now in our colleges to young men. . . . It is my opinion that by the higher and more thoroughly Christian education of women, what are called their "wrongs" will be redressed, their wages will be adjusted, their weight of influence in reforming the evils of society will be greatly increased; as teachers, as writers, as mothers, as members of society, their power for good will be incalculably enlarged.

The type of college envisioned by Sophia Smith resembled many other old New England colleges in its religious orientation, with all education at the college "pervaded by the Spirit of Evangelical Christian Religion, [but] without giving preference to any sect or denomination."

With her consent, Reverend Greene presented the plans to Professors W.S. Tyler and Julius H. Seeyle for review. After their enthusiastic endorsement was

Smith College

obtained, Smith named the three to the board of trustees in her will. In a last revision of her will, shortly before her death from a stroke in 1870, she directed that the college be located in Northampton, a larger and more accessible town than Hatfield. Her bequest to the new women's college amounted to $393,105.

After her death, Greene, Tyler, and another trustee, Professor Edwards A. Park of Andover, undertook a campaign for additional funds so that the new college would start off on a sound financial basis. Smith College, then, started out with approximately $500,000 in principal, interest, and contributions.

Receiving its charter in 1871, Smith College then opened four years later. Sophia Smith's will also directed that no more than half of the bequest should go for building; the trustees agreed that they "had no desire to repeat the too common mistake of investing the greater part of their funds in brick and mortar." The trustees further stated that "the requirements of admissions will be substantially the same as at Harvard, Yale, Brown, Amherst, and other New-England Colleges." Although Smith College, and its suburban Philadelphia counterpart, Bryn Mawr College, had set stringent admission standards, without establishing preparatory departments to assist students who were insufficiently prepared (a common practice in other women's colleges of that era) they had difficulty in adhering to their lofty standards.

At a time when most people held narrow views of women's abilities and their suitable place in society, Sophia Smith showed not only concern for the particular needs of young women, but also faith in their still undeveloped powers. After outlining the subjects that continue to be the backbone of Smith's curriculum, Sophia Smith commented:

And in such other studies as coming times may develop or demand for the education of women and the progress of the race, I would have the education suited to the mental and physical wants of women. It is not my design to render my sex any less the feminine, but to develop as fully as may be the powers of womanhood and furnish women with the means of usefulness, happiness and honor now withheld from them.

Smith's first class, convened in 1875, was composed of 14 students and 6 faculty, under the direction of President Laurenus Clark Seeyle. College Hall, a Victorian Gothic building, served as the administrative and classroom building, and dominated the head of Northampton's Main Street. During the college's first two decades, it was not at all unusual for students in their 20s and 30s to be enrolled. Instead of a dormitory, students lived in a cottage where life was more familial than institutional. Thus began the "house" system that, with some modifications, the college still employs. For study and worship,

students used the town's extensive public library and various churches.

In his inaugural address, President Seeyle laid down the school's educational policy. He declared that the admission standards were as high as those of the best colleges for men and that a truly liberal education would be fostered by a broad curriculum stressing the humanities, the fine arts, and the natural and social sciences. Some 15 years later, he remarked:

The college is not intended to fit woman for any particular sphere or profession but to develop by the most carefully devised means all her intellectual capacities, so that she may be a more perfect woman in any position.

Its small campus was planned to make the college part of what Reverend Greene called "the real practical life of a New England town, rather than a sequestered academic preserve."

A major difference between Smith and other women's colleges was in the emphasis on the classics, particularly Greek and Latin. The primary rationale for this curriculum rests in the ancient languages' cultural value. In an era in which men's education was focused increasingly on vocational studies, women's education concentrated on instilling cultural pursuits. Accordingly, Smith College started with a well-equipped department of fine arts, and with a strong emphasis on English literature.

Seeyle served Smith College for 35 years. During his administration, the college prospered: its assets grew from the original bequest of $400,000 to more than $3 million; its faculty to 122; its student body to 1,635; and its buildings to 35. Alumnae Gymnasium was opened, and was the site of the first women's basketball game. The facility now houses the College Archives and is connected to the William Allan Neilson Library. Currently, the library consists of 1.3 million items consisting of a main collection, rare book rooms, nonprint resources center and women's history archive. The Smith College Museum hosts an abundant collection of 24,000 pieces from ancient times to the present, with concentration on nineteenth- and twentieth-century American and European art. Mendenhall Center for the Performing Arts comprises two theaters, a TV studio, dance studios, recital hall, practice rooms, and an electronic music studio. Sage Hall, home of Smith's music department, houses a concert hall that is considered one of New England's finest. A Japanese garden, greenhouse, and arboretum add architectural diversion. Paradise Pond, with its Japanese teahouse, waterfall, and island accessible by rowboat has been a favorite of Smith students for years. Overall, the campus architecture consists of neo-Gothic, neo-Romanesque and modern architecture, coexisting with a pleasing mix of clapboard houses and ivy-covered buildings.

Smith's second president, Marion LeRoy Burton, assumed office in 1910. A graduate of Yale Divinity School, President Burton used his considerable business acumen to help the college raise $1 million, which he employed to increase faculty salaries and improve the faculty-to-student ratio. He also contributed to a revision of the curriculum and initiated a college honors programs to recognize outstanding students. Burton was also instrumental in organizing a cooperative admissions system among Smith, Mount Holyoke, Wellesley, and Vassar, the finest women's colleges of the day and the core of what is now known as the Seven Sisters colleges. His accomplishments are commemorated today by Burton Hall, the science building that his fund drive helped to finance. By 1915, Smith students were spending from $350 to $1,850 a year on tuition, books, and room and board. The college also was well on its way to becoming one of the largest women's colleges in the world.

In 1917, William Allan Neilson, Smith's third president, began his 22-year tenure. Smith College historians credit him with firmly establishing Smith College as one of the leading educational institutions in the United States, and also developing it into an institution of international reputation with a concern for the world that went beyond campus limits. Between two world wars, he brought many important exiled or at-risk teachers, scholars, lecturers, and artists from troubled countries to the college. In 1924, the Junior Year Abroad program was conceived at Smith.

A year later, after Nielson's retirement in 1939, Herbert Davis took office, continuing what would be a century-old tradition of Smith appointing male presidents. During his administration, he reaffirmed the contributions a liberal college could contribute to a world in turmoil. Soon after the 1941 bombing of Pearl Harbor, the college opened the first officers' training unit of the Women's Reserves (WAVES) on its campus. The college also added a summer term from 1942 to 1945 so that some students could graduate more quickly and go on to government, hospital, or military service. President Davis's administration was marked by an intensified academic life, reflecting his belief that serious study was a way of confronting the global threat.

Benjamin Fletcher Wright came from Harvard to become Smith's fifth president in 1949. By then, the college had resumed its regular calendar and completed several necessary building projects including a new heating plant and student recreation center named for retiring President Davis. During President Wright's administration, Smith's financial position was strengthened greatly. By 1950, a $7 million fund drive was completed. Again, campus facilities improved, and faculty salaries were raised. The college's first on-campus house of worship, the Helen Hills Chapel, was completed. By this time, Smith's Alumnae Association had grown to be a most devoted and active group. Before President Wright's term

ended, the college received a large gift for constructing a new faculty office and classroom building which now bears his name.

Smith's fifth president also had roots in the Ivy League. Thomas Corwin Mendenhall was installed as president in 1959, when both the country and college were experiencing peace and prosperity. The cultural changes ushered in during the 1960s brought a revised curriculum to Smith to accommodate the needs of an increasingly independent and ambitious student body. College-wide requirements were set aside and independent study encouraged. The college made more varied educational experiences available to Smith undergraduates by extending cooperation with four neighboring colleges. Smith also joined other private colleges in the northeast to develop the Twelve College Exchange Program. The college added buildings equipped with modern amenities to facilitate the study of the natural sciences, performing arts, and fine arts.

The impact of the women's movement had a profound impact on American society in the 1960s and 1970s. The times also served to confirm the original purpose of Smith College. In 1971, a committee of trustees, faculty, administration, students, and alumnae met to consider the possibility of Smith becoming coeducational. Vassar had begun to accept men for undergraduate study, and Yale, Princeton, and Dartmouth had started to admit women as candidates for degrees. The committee concluded that converting to a coeducational institution of higher learning would deflect from the founding purpose of the college: to make available the best possible education for women.

The college began its entry into its second century by inaugurating its first woman president, Jill Kerr Conway, who came to Smith College from Australia by way of Harvard and the University of Toronto. Her ten-year administration was marked by three significant accomplishments: 1) a large-scale renovation and expansion of Neilson Library; 2) the rapid growth of the Ada Comstock Scholars Program, through which women beyond the traditional college age could earn a Smith degree; and 3) a thriving fundraising program. In addition, the career development office was enlarged to better counsel Smith students and alumnae about career opportunities and graduate training. Responding to the growing importance on fitness and athletics for women, Smith erected Ainsworth Gymnasium and broke ground for new indoor and outdoor track and tennis facilities. In 1972, Smith College became the first women's college to join the NCAA, with tennis, basketball, and field hockey represented.

Former Bryn Mawr dean and history professor Mary Maples Dunn was installed as Smith's president in 1985. During the first five years in office, Dunn led the college to a successful realization of the largest fundraising campaign undertaken by a private liberal arts college. Of the $163 million raised, $18 million went to the expansion of the science center. President Dunn also lead a campus-wide effort to fight racism and directed the installation of Smith Design for Institutional Diversity. The Design's goals currently are realized with increased numbers of faculty, staff, and students of color; an annual symposium on racism; and a special fund to incorporate material about non-Western or neglected American cultures in courses throughout the curriculum.

Smith's basic curriculum in the humanities (its long-standing strength) continues, with majors or interdepartmental programs in computer science, women's studies, third world development, neuroscience, film studies, Latin American and East Asian studies, history of the sciences, and other emerging fields. The October tradition called Mountain Day endures and the particular day is named by the incumbent president. Classes are suspended and students are urged to climb a mountain, picnic, or observe the beauty of autumn.

On July 1, 1995, Ruth Simmons was appointed as Smith's ninth president. She is the third consecutive woman and the first African American (at Smith or any of the other Seven Sisters) to assume the office. A Fulbright scholar with a Ph.D. from Harvard, she also served as vice-provost of Princeton University.

Distinguished Smith graduates include Julia Child (co-author of *Mastering the Art of French Cooking* and host-ess of the popular television program, "The French Chef"); Betty Friedan (author of *The Feminine Mystique*); Meg Greenfield (editor, *Washington Post* editorial page and columnist for *Newsweek* magazine); Bettina Gregory (ABC News correspondent); Anne Morrow Lindbergh (author and wife of aviator Charles Lindbergh); Margaret Mitchell (author of *Gone with the Wind*); Sylvia Plath (poet and author of *The Bell Jar*); Nancy Reagan (wife of former U.S. president Ronald Reagan); and Gloria Steinem (feminist activist and author).

Further Reading: *The Insider's Guide to Colleges,* compiled by the staff of the *Yale Daily News,* (New York: St. Martin's Press, 1991), *Lisa Birbach's New and Improved College Book,* by Lisa Birnbach (revised and updated ed., New York: Simon and Schuster, 1992), *Notable American Women 1607–1950,* edited by Edward T. James (Cambridge, Massachusetts: Belknap Press of Havard University, 1971), *In the Company of Educated Women,* by Barbara M. Solomon (New Haven and London: Yale University Press, 1986).

—Michele Picozzi

STANFORD UNIVERSITY
(Stanford, California, U.S.A.)

Location: In Stanford, approximately 30 miles south of San Francisco.

Description: A private university that enrolls approximately 14,000 students. Almost 1,000 Stanford students are doctoral candidates, while the remaining 13,000 are evenly divided between graduate and undergraduate studies.

Information:
Admissions Office
Old Union Room 232
Stanford University
Stanford, CA 94305
U.S.A.
(415) 723-2091

Visiting: Guided tours can be arranged all year by contacting the admissions office at the above number.

Leland Stanford was a cofounder of the powerful Central Pacific Railroad, the company that built the western link of the first transcontinental railway. Stanford drove the spike that joined the two halves of the project. A political figure as well as a business tycoon, Stanford served a pivotal term as governor of California during the Civil War and later represented the state as a U.S. senator, from 1885 until his death in 1893.

For all his weighty contributions to West Coast progress, Stanford's legacy is dominated by his school of higher learning—Leland Stanford Junior University, built as a memorial to his only child, who died of typhoid fever just short of his 16th birthday, in 1884. Reports in the national press indicated that on the night following Leland Jr.'s death, Stanford dreamed of his son, who told his father, "Don't say you have nothing to live for. Live for humanity." When he awoke, Stanford is said to have affirmed, "The children of California shall be my children."

A decade earlier, in 1876, Jane and Leland Stanford had purchased land adjacent to the town of Menlo Park, on the San Francisco peninsula about 30 miles south of the city. Here they had 650 acres, which they named Palo Alto Farm. Eventually, the property would encompass 8,800 acres, and the Stanfords came to consider the farm their primary home. Almost immediately upon Leland Jr.'s death, the couple decided to use the farmland as the grounds for a tuition-free university.

As was his wont, Leland Stanford petitioned the best minds of the discipline to help lay plans for his university. He called on Harvard's Charles W. Eliot and Cornell's Andrew White, both of whom had been instrumental in leading American colleges away from their classical curriculum toward a more practical, democratic education based on the German model of a research-oriented faculty. Public infatuation with Stanford's proposal boosted his bid for the senate in 1885; meanwhile, his arch rival on the Central Pacific board, Collis P. Huntington, denounced the concept of the university as "Stanford's circus."

Despite Huntington's objections, the Stanfords heeded Eliot's advice and pledged to endow the university with $5 million, a remarkable figure, comparable to Harvard's endowment at the time; ultimately, the couple would contribute a precedent-setting $20 million to the university. In November 1885, a solemn ceremony took place at the Stanfords' San Francisco mansion, where 24 trustees were appointed. Leland Stanford's next step was to hire a president. Massachusetts Institute of Technology president Francis A. Walker turned him down but made recommendations for the physical layout of Stanford, suggesting the services of landscape artist Frederick Law Olmsted (who had designed New York's Central Park) and the Boston-based architectural firm of Shepley, Rutan, and Coolidge.

Olmsted wanted to build on the striking vista atop the foothills to the west of Palo Alto Farm, while Stanford demanded a more formal setting in the low-lying grainfields. Next, Olmsted proposed two diagonal thoroughfares leading from the quadrangle he designed to the nearby towns of Menlo Park and Mayfield; Stanford rejected that idea in favor of a straight road (Palm Drive) leading to the proposed community to be called "University Park," later renamed Palo Alto.

For the design of the Stanford buildings, Olmsted and the architectural firm's Charles Allerton Coolidge studied the sprawling, arched stone arcades of the Mediterranean. This time, their ideas coincided with those of Stanford, who wished to employ the noble Franciscan Mission styles that graced early California. Stanford University's cornerstone was laid on May 14, 1887—the birthdate of Leland Jr.—but construction on the primary quadrangle was painstakingly slow, as Senator Stanford's requirements in Washington made correspondence difficult. Olmsted and Stanford parted ways in 1890.

Coolidge and his crews completed the inner quadrangle by March 1891, leaving a lot vacant to accommodate Jane Stanford's plans for a majestic memorial church that

Stanford University

would serve as the campus centerpiece. By this time, Stanford had hired his president. Cornell's White had recommended a former protégé, Indiana University's 40-year-old president David Starr Jordan. "I might have found a more famous educator," a satisfied Stanford was quoted as saying, "but I desired a comparatively young man who would grow up with the University."

In his autobiography, Jordan detailed his two largest concerns about the job: the "discordant elements" inherent in "individualistic" California, and Leland Stanford's inescapable personal dominance over the project. Still, Jordan once explained, "When the evidence seems to be in, I like to say yes or no at once and take my chances." He accepted the day the offer was made. Jordan shared with Stanford an upbringing in upstate New York and a firm belief in career-oriented education and its opportunities for upward mobility. An enthusiastic Stanford presented his new president with a $10,000 yearly salary for life.

Despite Stanford's commitment to excellence, staffing a faculty so far from the East Coast's center of intellectual activity proved difficult. A majority of Jordan's first appointments were professors cajoled away from Cornell

and Indiana, and the nation's press began calling Stanford "the Cornell of the West." On October 1, 1891, approximately 500 students—more than double the projected enrollment—gathered in the quadrangle to hear Stanford and Jordan speak. Of the 559 admitted that first year, nearly half were freshmen of the "Pioneer Class" of '95. So-called special students made up another 147; critics of Stanford's tuition-free status suggested that this group had failed the University of California's entrance examination.

Jordan instituted the "major professor" system he had used at Indiana; in it students chose a faculty member as an advisor in creating an individualized course of study. "Any pre-arranged course of study is an affront to the mind of the real student," Jordan said. The university required just one class of every student: English.

In the spring of 1892, Stanford held its first commencement ceremony, culminating in the first of a soon-to-be-ritualized seniors versus faculty baseball game. In the summer of that year, the Hopkins Seaside Laboratory was opened as an advanced facility for the study of marine wildlife, funded by trustee Timothy Hopkins, surrogate child of the San Francisco hotelier and Central

Pacific partner Mark Hopkins. The younger Hopkins also helped fulfill Leland Stanford's dream of building the town adjacent to the university that came to be known as Palo Alto. After Stanford had been rebuffed in his attempt to co-opt Mayfield (the town denied his request that it shutter its dozen liquor purveyors), he had charged Hopkins with the development of Palo Alto. By 1893, Hopkins had overseen the design of the town and the arrival of its first 750 residents.

The young university had lofty goals but a paucity of resources. The beginnings of its library consisted of 3,000 volumes from the Stanfords' personal shelves. The university did not yet have a bookstore, a student union, or a housing authority. The first two dormitories, the men's Encina Hall and the women's Roble (later Sequoia) Hall operated by the Stanfords as private properties, were not nearly large enough to accommodate the overflow of early students. During the first year of operation, dormitory residents were charged $23 a month for room and board.

The early housing shortage resulted in many male students living at "the Camp," a series of whitewashed shacks previously occupied by campus construction workers. It was here that ideologues first fostered a "reverse class system" of sorts, in which refined culture was set aside in favor of the lifestyle of the common man. The "Roughs" of Encina Hall took up with those of the Camp and began what was to be an ongoing war of words with the "Frats." The campus hosted 5 fraternity chapters within its first year, 17 by 1898. By mid-decade, the men of the fraternities were challenging the Encina dwellers for control of the Associated Students of Stanford University (ASSU). Stanford had its first sorority by 1892, but only two more had joined the campus by the end of the decade.

In a decade marked by a steady increase in the numbers of women attending secondary schools, Stanford's first student body had 130 women. Still, at Stanford as elsewhere, women were not yet competing for the same careers as men. Jordan stressed that social evolution was marked by a commitment to the civilized home, one which could best be achieved under the watchful eye of a "wise, cultivated, and high-minded woman . . . To furnish such a woman is one of the worthiest functions of higher education," he wrote.

While Senator Stanford encouraged the children of Asian immigrants and black and Irish servants to apply to his university, few did. Apparently, only one black student enrolled in the early years. Students of Japanese heritage were by far the most populous minority on campus; by 1900, 19 Japanese-Americans were attending Stanford, enough to ensure the foundation of a Japanese Student Association.

In the spring of 1893, Senator Stanford presided over the second commencement ceremony. Several days later, he was dead at the age of 69. Stanford University's funding, which relied on the profits of the Stanfords' three California ranches, was suddenly held up in probate as the U.S. government filed a claim against the estate for its share of a $15 million loan made to the Central Pacific Railroad Company. Assigned a $10,000-a-month personal allowance, an enterprising Jane Stanford contributed most of it to the university. The community expressed its gratitude: merchants extended credit and faculty agreed to temporary cuts in pay.

After winning her battle with the government over her husband's estate and selling the family's share of the railroad company for $11 million (earmarked for the university), Jane Stanford set about completing her vision of the campus layout. At odds with her was President Jordan, who wanted to direct the available funds toward the faculty and the student body. Bowing to Mrs. Stanford's wishes, Jordan began referring to the coming years as "Stanford's Stone Age." In 1899, Mrs. Stanford instituted a new policy: with women comprising nearly half of the students, she ruled that the number of Stanford females at any given time would be limited to 500, arguing that "the University must be a place for men"—in part because it was a monument to her son. In 1903, Mrs. Stanford oversaw the grand opening of the multi-denominational Memorial Church, the majestic anchor of the Inner Quad. She guided the completion of other new buildings, including a gymnasium and the Thomas Welton Stanford Library, and she watched the growth of the Leland Stanford Junior Museum to its status as the largest privately held museum in America at the time.

For the next few years, however, a series of misfortunes at Stanford would lead to a wistful nickname for the class of '06—"Calamity Class." First, an epidemic of typhoid fever broke out in April 1903. Two hundred cases were diagnosed over the course of a few weeks, but the hard work of the community, the Student Guild in particular, limited fatalities to eight. Two years later, Jane Lathrop Stanford died at age 75. Upon completion of the Memorial Church in 1903, she had relinquished to her fellow board members the daily duties of running the university. Shortly after her death, the board of trustees put the faculty at ease by declaring the period of active construction to be near a close; in the wake of the ten-year probate proceedings, the faculty, once handsomely compensated, had yet to return to the national average in salary.

On April 18, 1906, the university, like the rest of the Bay Area, was rocked by the San Francisco earthquake. On campus, two people were killed; many of the newly completed buildings were severely damaged, including the Memorial Church, which would not reopen until 1913. Although the church's imported stained-glass windows had somehow survived the disaster, the church's resurrection would ultimately require half the total cost of repairs.

On that same fateful day, President Jordan had received an offer to become secretary of the Smithsonian Institution. Although he had coveted the job, he now declined it, saying, "I am sure my place is here . . . I shall stay with the poppies, the perfect sunshine, and the shadow of the great tremblor." Seven years later, after having successfully sustained the community's faith in the institution, Jordan stepped down to pursue his growing concern for global peace.

In 1908 Stanford acquired the Cooper Medical College of San Francisco and developed it as the Stanford Medical School, the first major academic addition to the university. Financing the facility quickly became a point of contention for many trustees, and in 1912 Stanford began its first campaign to raise money for its endowment. The university had begun charging out-of-state students a $30 tuition fee; those from in-state families still attended free of charge, with the exception of a few dollars for "syllabus fees."

Jordan became increasingly involved in international peacekeeping. In 1909 and 1910, he took his only two sabbaticals from the university to deliver antiwar addresses abroad; in the latter year he was appointed head of the World Peace Foundation. When Pioneer Class alumnus Herbert Hoover was appointed to Stanford's board of trustees in 1912, he offered the outgoing president a nominal chancellorship at Stanford. Jordan's longtime vice president, the geologist John Casper Branner, reluctantly agreed to fill the presidential vacancy, but only for two years, until his scheduled retirement.

An interim leader, Branner nevertheless made his presence felt as he argued for better faculty wages and the salvation of many programs (such as the department of art), a campaign he waged successfully, with long-lasting implications. Branner's sole defeat involved his recommendation that the university divest itself of the medical school. Not only did Jordan and Hoover disagree with him, citing the program's practical applications, but they also proposed the relatively young Dean of Medicine, Ray Lyman Wilbur, '96, as their candidate to replace Branner upon his retirement.

In over 25 years as Stanford president, Wilbur would leave an indelible imprint on the university. One of his first incentives was to revive flagging scholastic habits. By 1916, two-thirds of the student community were involved with fraternities or sororities; Wilbur admonished them to improve their grades or risk losing their charters. The most pressing issue of Wilbur's early tenure, however, was World War I.

In 1917, amid much fanfare, Stanford sent its 18-member women's unit for relief work to France. David Starr Jordan's high profile as a proponent of peace, as well as Herbert and Lou Henry Hoover's campaign for Belgian famine relief, marked Stanford as a stronghold of pacifism. But Stanford's close ties to the German educational community aroused the suspicions of many war supporters—the Stanford motto, *Die Luft der Freiheit weht,"* was German, rather than Latin—and Wilbur and others on campus felt impelled to stress their support of U.S.

involvement as the conflict worsened. By 1916, in an increasingly patriotic atmosphere at the university, Jordan's chancellorship was left unrenewed.

One important aspect of wartime culture on campus was the presence of Stanford's female students, who by now outnumbered the men who had not yet been called to duty. Reporters and editors at the *Daily,* for instance, were mostly women. Physically, the campus continued to grow, with a new main library, and a new art gallery serving as the cornerstones of another quadrangle. And former Dean of Medicine Wilbur helped launch the Stanford Hospital in San Francisco. Wilbur also moved into the first home specifically designated for Stanford's president, a mansion at "The Knoll" designed by Golden Gate Park architect John McLaren. Meanwhile, Hoover and his wife reaffirmed their commitment to their alma mater by breaking ground on their new home on nearby San Juan Hill.

Under Wilbur, the "major professor" system was disbanded, and quarterly classes replaced the semester calendar, ensuring nearly year-round activity on campus. In 1923, "Problems of Citizenship" became the first course at Stanford required of all freshmen. Most significantly, in 1920 the university began charging tuition of all its undergraduates—$40 per quarter, raised to $75 by 1922. Stanford was inevitably moving toward a position of greater exclusivity.

Enrollment during the 1920s nearly doubled, to 4,600 students in 1929, and the university itself seemed to be entering adulthood. Systematically, departments of study at Stanford were united under the various roofs of disciplinary schools: education, biological sciences, law, letters, etc. Additionally, a graduate school of business—the nation's second, after Harvard's—was founded in 1924.

With Stanford's healthy endowment (which for a time was the country's largest), the trustees' fiscal conservatism was waning, as the university attempted profit-making experiments with various properties of the Stanford estate. In 1926, the Ryan High Voltage Laboratory was opened on Stanford Avenue with funding provided by several entities interested in electrical research (including the city of Los Angeles). One of Stanford's prized library holdings, the Hoover War Collection, was established by its namesake in 1919. The increasingly visible Hoover, formerly director of the U.S. Food Administration and Calvin Coolidge's secretary of commerce, won the Republican nomination for the U.S. presidency in 1928. Before a partisan university community, Hoover delivered his acceptance speech at Stanford Stadium, where it was broadcast to a huge radio audience. On election evening, his victory was announced from the lawn of his home at San Juan Hill, accompanied by 2,000 jubilant students' rendition of "Hail, Stanford, Hail."

Granted a leave of absence by the university, Wilbur joined Hoover in Washington as secretary of the interior. Hoover's presidency soon suffered the disaster of the Wall Street collapse. However, Stanford was thriving, both fiscally and in the public imagination (homegrown athletes had won four gold medals in the 1928 Olympics), and few anticipated the upcoming hardships.

One of the ironic results of the Depression era at Stanford was the university's makeover into the "country club" of California schools, as fewer and fewer middle- and lower-class children could afford to forego hourly wages in exchange for education. With the number of male applicants dwindling significantly, in 1933 the board of trustees voted to rescind Jane Stanford's long-standing limit on the number of female students. By the end of the 1930s, the annual admission of over 1,700 female students had created an urgent need for expanded dormitory facilities.

Despite campus unrest at schools across the nation, the strong-willed Wilbur would not permit any censorship of topical discourse. In 1934, the so-called No-Fault policy went into effect, a controversial measure by which failing students could remain in school on their own determination. Earlier, in 1931, *Time* magazine had solidified the university's growing reputation as an elitist enclave ("more than half [the men] own automobiles"), and the *Chaparral* had eulogized the erstwhile working-class champion, the "Rough." Stanford was now often called "the Harvard of the West."

Although Stanford began to falter financially—its endowment income dropped to 75th in the nation in 1933—the university was consistently able to attract highly qualified staff members. The physicist Felix Bloch, for example, joined the university in 1934 and went on to become Stanford's first Nobel laureate in 1952. Beginning in 1937, the brothers Russell and Sigurd Varian conducted research that would lead to their invention of the klystron tube, a microwave generator that would in turn facilitate the invention of radar and launch the West Coast's microelectronics industry. In 1938, a new auditorium and library were dedicated in the name of the man who made the buildings possible: retired Dean of Education Ellwood Cubberley, an $8,000-a-year professor who bequeathed a grand total of $770,000 in stocks and bonds to the university.

As World War II loomed, the trustees convinced President Wilbur to remain in his office through the university's 50th anniversary ceremonies. Wilbur, a fervent supporter of U.S. intervention in World War I, encouraged students not to hasten to enlist: "An engineering student who can . . . make an airplane go 20 miles faster per hour is worth 100,000 men in uniform," he said. Upon Wilbur's belated retirement in September 1943, Donald B. Tresidder, '19, a former president of Yosemite Park, became Stanford's fourth president.

Despite Stanford's long experience with Asian studies, in May 1942, the campus gave in to nationalist sentiment, sending its Japanese Americans (including a retirement-age history professor, Yamato Ichihashi) to internment camps. By 1943, the Stanford campus was hosting some

2,400 soldiers under the auspices of the Army Specialized Training Program, with the president's house on the Knoll serving as a Women's Army Corps (WACs) barracks for trainees. Once again, the depletion of the number of men on campus left vacancies for women to fill: Janet McClanahan ('44) could assume the student body presidency only after an amendment to the university's constitution; the office floor at the *Daily* was reported to be covered with "lipsticked cigarette butts." However, also in 1944, Dean of Women Mary Yost ruled that sororities would be expelled from campus. When Tresidder was faced with the sudden loss of 3,000 student-soldiers to the war effort, he declared, "Our real business is not training men for war but training young people for peace. We'll go on with our original business." Tresidder was unable to see his commitment fulfilled: in 1947, at age 53, he succumbed to a heart attack.

On April 1, 1949, J.E. Wallace Sterling began a 19-year tenure at the helm of the university. By the end of his administration, enrollment had climbed to 11,400, and Stanford had returned to financial prosperity. Thirty new buildings were added to the campus during Sterling's stay ("the second Stone Age"), including the Tresidder Memorial Union, the Bowman Alumni House, and a sprawling science complex.

During the 1950s, other events on campus reflected the country's progressive atmosphere. The Stanford Museum, closed since the war, reopened to display its impressive new holdings. In 1958, Stanford opened its first overseas campus, in Beutelsbach, Germany. By 1961, Stanford had opened other extensions in Italy, France, England, and Austria. Through 1961, five Stanford scientists were awarded the Nobel Prize. Provost Frederick Terman created avenues of discussion between the university's researchers and California's applied-science industries, earning him the nickname "Father of Silicon Valley."

To accommodate the growing student population and a promising future, Sterling introduced his unprecedented "Plan of Action for a Challenging Era," a proposal for raising $100 million in three years. Before Sterling's arrival, Stanford had raised a total of $31 million in support money; in his 19 years leading the university, the figure reached $329 million.

At Stanford as elsewhere, the 1960s ushered in an unprecedented commitment to social activism. In 1966, students staged a sit-in at Sterling's office to protest the university's compliance with U.S. draft policies. A year earlier, the Stanford Sexual Rights Forum had become the first student organization to demand an end to discrimination based on sexual preference. Meanwhile, two fraternities challenged their national organizations over regulations which forbade the admission of black and Jewish members. In 1968, upon the assassination of Reverend Martin Luther King Jr., 40 black Stanford students burned an American flag on White Plaza.

Amid the upheaval, the university continued to erect new academic structures and to attain other academic achievements. The J. Henry Meyer Undergraduate Library and the Graduate School of Business building were completed; Dr. Norman E. Shumway's heart-transplant research was carried out for the first time; Stanford professors announced their success in reproducing DNA; and Nobelist Linus Pauling joined the faculty. But the well-liked Sterling retired in 1968, leaving the difficult job of holding together a divisive campus to former Rice University president, Kenneth Pitzer. As Pitzer took office, Stanford's faculty was displaying its own antiwar sentiment: the academic council stripped ROTC classes of their course credits, and the board of trustees ended the school's 20-year relationship with the Stanford Research Institute, citing the institute's classified work for the Defense Department. On October 15, 1969, 8,000 community members conducted a protest of the Vietnam War on the Stanford campus. Later in that school year, after more student demonstrations and an academic strike, a demoralized Pitzer resigned. Provost Richard W. Lyman accepted the challenge of the presidency, declaring, "A comfortable university is virtually a contradiction in terms. We exist to disturb and activate the minds of men and women."

As campus radicalism waned, another fundraising drive was begun in 1972, with a lofty five-year goal of $300 million. With 54,000 donors and 5,000 volunteers, the long campaign closed $4 million above projection. Acting swiftly on the financial windfall, the administration raised the number of endowed faculty members from 49 to 125 and directed $35 million toward student scholarships, fellowships, and loans. In 1978, the Herbert Hoover Federal Memorial was dedicated at Stanford, directing renewed attention toward the Hoover Institution on War, Revolution and Peace, a remarkable collection of 1.5 million documents most famously visited in 1975 by Soviet dissident Alexander Solzhenitsyn in preparation for his landmark study of the Bolshevik Revolution.

In 1980, the proven fundraiser Lyman stepped down from the president's post to accept the presidency of the Rockefeller Foundation. Vice President and Provost Donald Kennedy, a renowned biologist and commissioner of the Food and Drug Administration, took Lyman's place

and promptly established the Stanford Humanities Center.

More honors awaited Stanford and its alumni: the Supreme Court welcomed the appointments of four Stanford alumni: Sandra Day O'Connor, William Rehnquist, Anthony M. Kennedy, and Stephen Breyer.

The 1989 Loma Prieta earthquake in the Bay Area hit Stanford with $160 million in damages—750,000 books needed reshelving, and repairs to the Stanford Museum of Art forced its closure until 1997. In the wake of a nebulous financial scandal, Kennedy stepped down in 1992, making way for Gerhard Casper. Still, the university flourishes: of Stanford's 19 Nobel laureates, 11 continue an affiliation with the university. Fundraising has boomed: in 1994, Stanford was able to muster $226 million in a single year. By then, its overall endowment had topped $3 billion. Visitors to campus tour such landmarks as the 285-foot Hoover Tower, with an observation deck scanning the South Peninsula; the Rodin Sculpture Garden, with 20 works by the artist; and the Stanford Linear Accelerator Center, where research is conducted for the U.S. Department of Energy.

Further Reading: An interesting biography of the "founding mother" of Stanford is *Jane Stanford: Her Life and Letters* by Gunther Nagel (Stanford, California: Stanford Alumni Association, 1975), revised as *Iron Will: The Life and Letters of Jane Stanford* by Gunther Nagel (Stanford, California: Stanford Alumni Association, 1985). *The Stanford Album: A Photographic History, 1885–1945* (Stanford, California: Stanford University Press, 1989) has a comprehensive text by Roxanne Nilan, and includes photographs. Equally helpful is *The Stanford Century* by Linda Winthrop Peterson (Stanford, California: Stanford Alumni Association, 1991). Peter C. Allen's *Stanford: From the Foothills to the Bay* (Stanford, California: Stanford Alumni Association and Stanford Historical Society, 1980) offers many vignettes with profiles of members of the Stanford community. To view Stanford in relation to its environment, read Ward Winslow's *Palo Alto: A Centennial History* (Palo Alto, California: Palo Alto Historical Association, 1993).

—James Sullivan

STATE UNIVERSITY OF NEW YORK
(New York, U.S.A.)

Location: The central office is located in Albany, New York, the state's capital.

Description: A unified statewide system of 64 campuses enrolling approximately 400,000 students. It is the nation's largest single, most diverse multi-campus university.

Information: University Relations
State University Plaza
Albany, New York 12246
U.S.A.
(518) 443-5378

Although the State University of New York (SUNY) has roots dating from the 1700s, not until 1948 was the university actually created. The university has made dramatic progress since its founding. In less than half a century more than 1.4 million men and women have been graduated from SUNY.

When New York's state legislature held its first session after the American Revolution, a proposal was offered that a state university be established and that it be modeled on the French system of higher education, which featured many institutions controlled by a central administration. A state board of regents was appointed to oversee New York's educational programs (from the elementary grade to graduate and professional schools) and to start new colleges. The goal of developing a state university came up for discussion many times. However, the idea was usually dismissed in the early stages because a state university represented a threat to the enrollments of the private colleges and universities in New York State.

Before SUNY was created, there existed an unofficial form of public education, consisting of 138 private institutions, and 32 public colleges that acted independently of one another, without coordination or statewide goals and policy. The public colleges consisted of 11 teachers colleges, 6 agricultural and technical institutes, 5 institutes of applied arts and sciences, a maritime academy, and 9 other institutions managed for the state, under contract, by private institutions. Absent were public liberal arts colleges or research institutions. Consequently, each year thousands of New York's youth left the state to enroll in public universities in other states.

Before World War II, the state regents' support for higher education in New York was confined to providing funds for scholarships and to coordinating educational

policy with private institutions. The aftermath of World War II provided the impetus for the founding of SUNY. As servicemen returned, they applied to colleges in large numbers, thanks to the funds provided by the G.I. Bill. New York, however, was unprepared to accommodate the servicemen and minorities who were seeking places in colleges. Responding to the pressures from these groups to establish a free state university system, the legislature of the last state in the nation without a free university system began serious deliberations directed to creating such a system.

Governor Thomas E. Dewey proposed "The Temporary Commission on the Need for a State University," which was later approved by the legislature. The commission was a 21-member blue-ribbon assembly led by Owen D. Young, former chairman of the General Electric Company. The commission's 18-month study came to the following conclusions:

- Less than half of New York's high school graduates in the top 25 percent of their classes went on to college; the rest of the quartile, plus many other students qualified to benefit from a college education, simply could not afford the high tuition and room and board fees of private colleges and universities.
- Some members of New York's large minority groups had difficulty gaining access to educational facilities on an equal basis with white students.
- The state's higher educational student population had expanded to 310,000, or 50 percent above the prewar figure, as a result of veteran and expanded nonveteran enrollment and would continue to. Further expansion of existing institutions could not meet either the present or prospective demands.

Despite the commission's unanimity, opponents quickly appeared to plead that establishing a state university would force many of New York's private colleges and universities to close. Further heated debate occurred over the administrative issue as to whether the university would report to the governor or the board of regents. However, the commission's recommendations prevailed. On March 12, 1948, the legislature passed a law establishing the State University of New York, effective July 1, 1948. Governor Dewey signed the bill on March 30, and on August 16, he selected a temporary 15-member board of trustees for the new SUNY.

The SUNY board had a challenging task. Besides organizing the 32 public colleges into a distinct, coordi-

State University of New York, Albany

nated body, the board was ordered to plan the growth of two health and medical centers, overhaul the teachers colleges' curricula, and establish "such four-year liberal arts colleges, professional and graduate schools, research centers, or other facilities, including an integrated university located on a single campus, as deemed necessary." The board was also directed to develop a master plan "as a long-range guide to the localities and the state in establishing and developing community colleges."

Since SUNY's founding, an issue of nomenclature has caused confusion. A university publication explains:

The State Board of Regents, together with the State Education Department, come under the umbrella of the "University of the State of New York," a venerable title more than 200 years old. The emergence of the "State University of New York" has resulted in public confusion that exists to this day.

During the late 1940s and all of the 1950s, the country's youngest state university system focused on developing the structure, policies, procedures, and programs that would create a strong foundation for the university's future. SUNY's first president, Alvin C. Eurich (1949–51), oversaw the formation of the university's administrative staff, and the draft of the first SUNY master plan. The arrival of the 1950s brought welcome news. SUNY received its official accreditation from the Middle States Association. About the same time, the university created the Research Foundation of the university, a distinct corporation authorized to accept funds from public and private sources and to disburse them for research or relevant purposes at the campuses.

For a short time, enrollment remained steady, and then it slowly began to increase. SUNY's student population leaped from 30,910 in 1955 to 63,721 in 1959, a growth rate about three times the national average. However, constructing buildings to accommodate the students moved slowly, and space shortages were becoming a great problem. Although funding was available through $250 million in construction bonds, state policies were complicating construction progress. By the decade's end, the trustees claimed thousands of applicants were being turned away due to lack of space.

One of Nelson A. Rockefeller's first acts as new governor of New York in 1959 was to appoint a Committee on Higher Education, which would report directly to the governor and would study all the higher education needs in New York, as well as all higher education facilities. The committee's findings advised that, unless action was taken immediately, New York's students would soon not be able to obtain a quality public education in the state. "The State University," the 1960 report said, "appears to have less administrative and management freedom of operation than almost any other publicly supported institution or group of institutions in the United States." The

committee's chairman, Henry T. Heald, recommended that SUNY be released from the bureaucratic mandates that limited its effectiveness. Several important changes resulted: Legislation gave the SUNY chancellor more authority for unclassified civil service positions, and it allowed SUNY budget requests to be forwarded directly to the governor, instead of going through the state's education department. An amendment was also made to the education law which separated SUNY from the administrative supervision and control of the regents.

The Heald Committee also recommended that SUNY be granted greater freedom in beginning construction work to build needed instructional facilities. (At that point, enrollment exceeded 150,000 and was rapidly expanding.) The real driving force behind this construction proposal was Rockefeller and his dedication to SUNY's success. Due to his efforts, a semi-independent agency called the State University Construction Fund was set up to issue construction bonds to meet the university's massive building needs. Tuition, fees, and other university receipts would be used to pay the debt service with little more than the state's moral pledge that the bonds would be paid. With cost estimates of $3 billion, the project was heralded as the largest single construction program in the history of American higher education.

More changes were to come. Because of the Heald Committee's recommendation, the trustees announced a major decision to "establish a modest uniform tuition fee of $400 per year—effective in 1963." The monies were to enable SUNY to amortize its complete building process. Thomas H. Hamilton, the university's third president (1959–62), in concert with the trustees, guided the evolution of 11 colleges of education into multi-purpose arts and sciences colleges. Concurrently, the private University of Buffalo was brought into the SUNY system.

By the end of the 1960s, the Heald Committee had fulfilled its final mandates. The goal to expand the community college system was realized. Because of the committee's activities, there was a college within a reasonable distance of many of the state's residents. Four regional graduate centers had also been established—in Buffalo, Albany, Binghamton, and Stony Brook. Although, in the 1960s, the Heald Committee played an important role in SUNY's progress, Governor Rockefeller left the greatest impact on the university. Many times he used the strong influence of the gorvernorship in efforts to distinguish the university, and he made financial sources available to achieve its goals. Consequently, his administration brought the period of SUNY's greatest growth.

Samuel B. Gould (president and later chancellor, 1964–70) served during the swiftest and greatest growth period, as SUNY surged from 57 to 68 institutions, and from 150,000 to 286,000 students. The faculty itself grew from 9,800 to 14,900.

At the start of the 1970s, SUNY was offering more than 3,700 academic programs to over 321,000 students.

Fortunately, the greatest part of this construction program has been completed, since this new decade brought a problem unique to the university's history: severe budget restraints. SUNY reacted by decreasing enrollment goals, dismissing hundreds of employees, leaving many vacated professional positions unfilled, and eliminating several research programs. Tuition was raised to fund construction-in-progress. SUNY's monumental growth rate was slowing for the first time since 1948. The Chancellor's Panel on University Purposes (1970) and the University Commission on Purposes and Priorities (1975) were formed to determine how new cooperative alliances among the campuses could be educationally as well as fiscally beneficial. During the frequent budget crises, the campuses worked together under the SUNY name to make their needs known to the governor and legislature. By the end of the 1970s, SUNY had changed its major focus from building campuses to creating a more effective, efficient system. This new attitude resulted in the development of the Multi-phase Rolling Plan (MRP) in 1980. Its goal was to coordinate "SUNY's educational services and priorities with both public needs and available state resources."

Today, SUNY encompasses a unique system of traditional four-year colleges, research university campuses, academic health science centers, community colleges, colleges of technology, and specialized and statutory colleges. Besides four medical schools, SUNY operates three health science centers, specialized colleges of optometry, environmental science and forestry, and a maritime college. Empire State College, SUNY's nontraditional school, offers degree programs through self-paced independent study, and distance learning is available via mentors all over the state.

D. Bruce Johnstone, seventh chief operating officer (1988–94) was chiefly responsible for the planning document "SUNY 2000: A Vision for the New Century." The plan puts "special emphasis on SUNY as a key player in meeting state needs in health care, public education, economic development, social services, and the environment."

Further Reading: For a comprehensive view of the history of SUNY, consult *Sixty-Four Campuses: The State University of New York to 1985* (Albany, New York: Office of University Affairs and Development, 1985). Nelson A. Rockefeller's important role in the development of the university system is discussed in *The Rockefellers: An American Dynasty* by Peter Collier and David Horowitz (New York: Holt, Rinehart and Winston, 1976).

—Darlene Maciuba-Koppel

STRASBOURG UNIVERSITY
(Strasbourg, France)

Location: Strasbourg, the capital city of the Bas-Rhin Department, 250 miles (400 km) east of Paris, in the Alsace region of France at the Franco-German border, 2 miles (3.2 km) west of the Rhine River.

Description: Three autonomous, nonprofit institutions of higher learning established in 1970 under France's 1968 Orientation Act. These state-financed universities are successors to the University of Strasbourg founded in 1538 and chartered in 1621.

Strasbourg University I, also known as the Université Louis Pasteur, specializes in medicine, science, and economics. Strasbourg II, Université des Sciences Humaines, teaches theology, fine arts, and liberal arts. Strasbourg III is the Université Robert Schuman, which emphasizes the professional schools of law, business, and journalism.

Information: Strasbourg University I
Institute Le Bel
4 rue Blaise Pascal
F 67070 Strasbourg Cedex
France
(88) 41 53 99
Fax (88) 60 75 50

Strasbourg University II
22 rue Descartes
67084 Strasbourg Cedex
France
(88) 41 73 00, (88) 60 03 25

Strasbourg University III
1 place d'Athènes
B.P. 66
67045 Strasbourg Cedex
France
(88) 41 42 40
Fax (88) 61 30 37

In 1537, the city of Strasbourg called on humanist educator Johannes Sturm to revive three existing municipal schools, which were languishing in medieval scholasticism. Sturm came from Paris in 1538 to establish a *gymnasium,* a Protestant Latin school, influenced by the ideas of German educational reformer Philip Melanchthon.

Sturm's academic background was impressive. He had studied with Erasmus of Rotterdam and Thomas à Kempis. He attended the University of Louvain, where he also taught. A respected, learned man, who could at times be pedantic, Sturm directed the restructured *gymnasium* for more than 40 years. Sturm brought in important figures such as John Calvin and Martin Bucer, later adviser to England's King Edward VI. This respected classical secondary school was the forerunner of Strasbourg University. The *gymnasium* also served as a prototype for education throughout Europe.

In 1262, a revolt of the town burghers—aided by Rudolf von Hapsburg—against the bishopric, won the municipality of Strasbourg its own charter from the emperor, making it an autonomous city-state. As an inland port, Strasbourg became an important trade center on a route from Paris to the Rhine River. At the same time it became an intellectual center and experienced its first golden age. In 1210 Gottfried von Strassburg wrote the German poem *Tristan;* the great philosopher Albertus Magnus, equally interested in divine and natural knowledge, studied and preached in the Dominican cloister; and Meister Eckhardt expounded on his belief that there is a divine spark in each soul. By the latter half of the 1400s, Johann Gutenberg had left Strasbourg for his native city of Mainz, but he apparently made his earliest efforts in printing in Strasbourg.

By the time that Sturm arrived in Strasbourg to reform the city's educational institutions, the Reformation had taken hold in the community. According to historian Franklin Ford,

> It was the Reformation which changed the whole face of urban life in Strasbourg and thrust the town into a position of European prominence. Lutheranism had won the city with remarkable speed and ease, and the official abolition of the Mass in 1529 merely formalized the existing situation in a now overwhelmingly Protestant community.

Because of its location on the borderland of Catholic power, Strasbourg became a haven for French religious reformers and a place where debates raged between Lutherans, Zwinglians, and Calvinists.

The curriculum at the *gymnasium* consisted of ten classes (grades), each lasting one year under the "eye and hand" of a special master. All ten years were dedicated to the perfection of Latin, and six years to Greek. The classroom language of instruction was Latin, and the native German of the students was only permitted for catechism. Sturm himself wrote many textbooks and books on peda-

Strasbourg University

gogy including: *Book on the Right Method of Founding Schools for Literary Education* (1537) and *Classical Letters* (1565). Latin proficiency at the *gymnasium* was essential; studies were devoted to rhetoric and style. The education was cerebral and intellectual, with little attention to the body or to manners. It was not humanistic in the sense of Erasmus' "freedom" in education. It was an education which stressed piety, knowledge, and eloquence. Music, mathematics, and logic rounded out the curriculum. The Jesuit Order embraced it as a model to inculcate the minds of the young with the classical and religious training to which it adhered.

An imperial decree in 1566 transformed the upper classes of the *gymnasium* into an academy with two faculties: theology and philosophy. "Strassburg Academy" was given degree-granting powers, but the institution had to wait to become a full university because of the changing political climate. By the mid-sixteenth century, Strasbourg's tenuous allegiance to the Germanic Holy Roman Empire was beginning to crumble. During the Thirty Years War (1618–48), Strasbourg tried to remain neutral, yet delicately played the French Bourbon monarchy against the German Hapsburgs. And after Calvin and others had turned the school into a leading center of theological debate, Lutheranism became the orthodox religion of the community by town ordinance in 1598. Strasbourg then became as inhospitable to Calvinists as it already was to Catholics and to Jews.

Strasbourg Academy's Calvinistic professors and friends, threatened by censorship, petitioned for the school's conversion into a university, since a university charter would bring certain rights and immunities for the faculty. In 1621, after some municipal deliberation, the University of Strasbourg received its charter. Few students from predominantly German-Catholic Alsace enrolled, since the University of Strasbourg was traditionally a German-Protestant stronghold. In fact, it was recognized as an international university, attracting students from throughout Protestant Europe. Nonetheless, the municipal officers resisted any claims on their allegiance. To maintain the image of neutrality, in 1639, during the Thirty Years War, they dismissed Professor Joachim Clutenius from the university and took away his citizenship on charges of supplying military information to the German forces at the Rhine.

Although Strasbourg managed to remain neutral during the conflict by abandoning its Protestant allegiances, the city was nevertheless ravaged by the war. Plague and lack of trade due to its isolation devastated the city, while poor attendance at the academy/university (as well as its movement to seven instead of ten grades) lowered the university's prestige, despite the presence of renowned professors Bernegger and Clutenius and satirist Johann Michael Moscherosch, the protégé of several professors. By the terms of the Peace of Westphalia in 1648, the university, along with Strasbourg and the surrounding region, was transferred from the control of the Hapsburgs to the French monarchy. Despite these terms, it took years for the French to organize the particulars of what had been ceded to them.

France's Louis XIV claimed Alsace in 1681 and with it the University of Strasbourg. The document of surrender stated that the university was to remain Protestant and humanistic in nature even after the takeover brought French rule to Strasbourg and reasserted Catholic influence in the region.

Although France's right to Strasbourg was not officially recognized until 1697 by the Peace of Ryswick, the French influence was felt in the city and spilled over to the university. In the eighteenth century, the University of Strasbourg was a "cavalier's university" by reputation, where dueling, riding, dancing, and studying French and French culture—foreign to the German-speaking Alsatians and professors—became the fashion. The intelli-

gentsia and nobility who had clung to their German-Lutheran culture were becoming "Frenchified." As the university, which had already acquired a reputation as an international institution, became known as a center for "enlightenment," enrollment swelled. Students from Protestant Germany, Switzerland, the Netherlands, Scandinavia, and Russia—as well as from the "French Interior"—as the Strasbourgeois called the rest of France—made their way there. Talleyrand, Goethe, and Metternich all enrolled with Strasbourg's Faculty of Law.

The glory of the "Frenchified" Strasbourg University was short-lived as reforms in education began taking place in German universities across the Rhine. Other universities offered instruction in German, rather than in Latin, a faculty of philosophy that was elevated to major status, and a curriculum that included natural law. These were modern trends to which Strasbourg University barely gave lip service. Scientific research was gaining importance, and Strasbourg University could not keep up with the well-funded German universities that were amassing great libraries, recruiting the best thinkers, and establishing liberal and universal education. Funding for teachers at Strasbourg was in the hands of a secularized religious foundation called the *Thomasstift,* which limited the number of professorships, paid the professors little, and insisted that they be French natives and Protestant. Local Alsatian teachers, having ties to Strasbourg and Lutheranism, relied on student fees for payment. Reforms promoted by jurist Christophe Guillaume Koch, a law professor at the university, fell on deaf ears. The student population dropped, and regard for the university as an educational force suffered.

The academic life of Strasbourg revived dramatically with the arrival of German scholars and writers such as Wolfgang von Goethe, Johann Gottfried von Herder, and Jakob Lenz. Their work, especially as it related to the *Sturm und Drang* literary movement competing with the French literary hegemony (Molière, Racine, la Bruyère, Fénelon, etc.), was embraced by the Alsatian people and captured the "soul" of their region. Literary circles in Paris sought out these new writers, putting Strasbourg, once again, on the map. Within the politically charged environment of Alsace before the French Revolution, these writers brought life to the dying university. Yet the Alsatian elite, "Frenchified" for more than a century, remained royalists. Rouget de Lisle, a royalist soldier, wrote "La Marseillaise" in 1792 while stationed in Strasbourg, a song taken up by the revolutionaries. It has since become the French national anthem.

After the revolution, Strasbourg University experienced the impact of the newly formed French Republic. By 1790, schools became centralized under the French Ministry of Education. Tallyrand proposed a "new education" based on science in 1792. Study of geometry, calculus, physics, and the applied sciences was entered into the elementary curriculum. All universities were regarded as politically unreliable and were therefore suppressed. The end came to Strasbourg University with France's National Convention of September 1793. When the university returned in 1808, after Napoléonic reforms, it was as a French institution of higher learning, with a rector presiding over the faculties of "The Academy of Strasbourg." The rector's responsibility was to the ministry in Paris. Strasbourg Academy was responsible for training young bureaucrats by preparing students to pass examinations for governmental positions. It was not a remarkable school, except for its having five faculties. The National Academy in Paris had four, and there were three in most other academies. By 1818 Strasbourg Academy had added a Protestant theological faculty, and it was the center of higher education for two departments, Bas Rhin and Haut Rhin.

In the 1850s a number of Strasbourg Academy students formed two fraternities (Argentina and Wilhelmitana) dedicated to becoming the "sanctuary" of the German language and customs in the midst of an environment "totally steeped in French culture." A young pastor lamented to a professor that teaching German in Strasbourg was a "lost cause," and professor of theology, Johann Wilhelm Baum, warned that "it is all in vain. Another two years of this regime and Alsace will be irretrievably lost to Germany." This did not happen. The University at Strasbourg was given another chance—this time as a German institution. The annexation of Alsace to Prussia, the name of Bismarck's united Germany (1871), was possibly the result of prodding from the intellectual community in Germany who felt that once the Alsatian people were properly reeducated and reintroduced to their latent Germanic nature, they would assimilate easily within the German nation. Whether or not Bismarck was swayed by what he called a "professor's idea," the annexation took place. Building a national front through education was the next step to "giving the Alsatians back their true selves," and a strong push to restore the University at Strasbourg to its former glory—as a center for German culture in the Northern Rhineland. By late 1870, native French professors emigrated back into the interior of France and did not return to the classroom. The academy was in shambles as a result of the Franco-Prussian War. Eduard Reuss, a Protestant theologian, wrote to a colleague: "Our university library, as well as our city library is destroyed, and it is irreplaceable. Our lecture halls are sick bays, our students are scattered."

The provisional government of Germany supported the idea of beginning to organize a new university at Strasbourg. Heinrich von Sybel, a Bonn historian, was asked for his advice, which began a debate in the new national assembly, the Reichstag. The Alsatians hoped to keep former (French-speaking) professors employed, to retain courses in French, and to have control of the university rather than instituting a German-run school on the ruins of the old academy. Others argued for an institution dedicated to the promotion of the German language and culture. The debate was settled in favor of a bill put forth by Wilhelm Wehrenpfenning to establish a German university at Strasbourg. Meanwhile, in May 1871, the French National Assembly introduced a bill to incorporate the faculties of the defunct Strasbourg Academy into the Academy of Nancy—located in the still-French territory of Lorraine. The University of Nancy was developed to rival the great universities of Germany, yet to foster love of French culture and nationalism in the youth of Alsace. This was the impetus needed to hasten the German organization of their own University of Strasbourg.

Baron Franz von Roggenbach, a Catholic who was commissioned to organize the university, studied all aspects of the effect a new university would have on the region. He was sure that the former academy had failed due to "dilettantism" and "scientific superficiality." He offered chairs to Alsatians who had taught at the academy or at the Protestant seminary, but he did not introduce a Catholic theological faculty. New subjects entered the curriculum: economics and political science. The faculty of philosophy was divided: one humanistic, and one for natural sciences and mathematics. Roggenbach wanted more Alsatians to attend classes—the priority of this project was to assimilate the region into the German culture—but few had previously attended classes except for those at the Protestant seminary.

Roggenbach asked for 1 million German marks for laboratories, observatories, clinics, seminars, and institutes, and he hoped to establish an endowment for the university. The endowment was turned down by Bismarck and the Reichstag, which stated that funding was not available. The university would not reach the grand scale that Roggenbach had hoped for. He left, but the guidelines for future development were set in place.

Karl Ledderhose, the first curator of the university, dealt with the budget, staffing, and building construction; he also drafted statutes for the university. These statutes abolished student prisons and faculty policing, instituted faculty pensions, and officially divided the philosophy faculty as Roggenbach and the scientists had wanted. The university was granted full responsibility for governing itself in 1875. Prussian architect Hermann Eggert designed a master plan for the construction of new buildings. In 1874 he planned two campuses to appease the medical faculty who wanted their classrooms near the municipal hospital, as they already were, rather than at the proposed new site at Fischer Gate on the northeastern side of Strasbourg. Millions were appropriated to unify the scattered arrangement of buildings which made up the old university.

In April 1877, on the university's fifth anniversary, Strasbourg University officially became Kaiser-Wilhelm-Universität Strassburg. The modern university included new laboratories within the six buildings erected at the medical facility, and six new buildings at Fischer Gate, built in high Italian Renaissance style. The school gained fame as an *Arbeitsuniversität,* one noted for the seriousness of students and faculty, and for research. The faculties of medicine and law were highly regarded; Emil Fischer, later to win the Nobel Prize, studied chemistry with Professor Adolf Baeyer. The *Strassburger Kreis* (Strasbourg circle), a scholarly gathering of students, met at coffeehouses for evening discussions, and students gathered for discussions at professors' homes.

By 1887 the university professors, through published papers and general attitude, showed their hostility to the Reichstag's policies concerning the Alsatian territory, especially as it affected the university. Ledderhose resigned as curator; three professors left; rumors of university radicalism and Alsatian "francophilism" were widespread. This proved a significant turning point for the university. If professors spoke out against the Reichstag, thus "embarrassing" the government, there would be retaliation. The mission to "re-Germanize the Reichsland" (Alsatian territory) was the university's failure in the eyes of the government, which reassessed the situation by 1887, finding that Kaiser-Wilhelm-Universität Strassburg had, indeed, led the way as a modern university that would serve to glorify German education and would remind the Alsatians of their scholarly Germanic past.

Autonomy for the Alsatian region was in continual question throughout the twentieth century. Writers and artists were promoting the idea of a double culture, strongly tied to both the Gallic (French) and Germanic traditions, yet having a character and strength of its own. After World War I, the region was again in French hands, and on January 15, 1919, Strasbourg University became a French university after dismissing the German professors and reorganizing once again. Notable students were Louis Pasteur and Albert Schweitzer.

At the outbreak of World War II in September 1939, the government of France ordered the nonmobilized residents of Strasbourg to move immediately to locales in interior France. In the case of the University of Strasbourg, the move was to Clermont-Ferrand. Keeping the university open was, according to historian John E. Craig, a "matter of symbolic importance" because "it was now the most conspicuous reminder of *l'Alsace française.*" The existence of the institution was an embarrassment both to the German government and to their collaborationist allies in Vichy. The Germans opened a rival university in Strasbourg in 1941 and sent family members of students who had defected to Clermont to beg them to come home. One student said, "We would rather be Frenchmen and defeated than Germans and victorious." The institution became a

center for the *maquis* (the French resistance) in occupied France. German surveillance was heavy and sometimes punitive. Craig describes a 1943 raid:

> In November 1943 the Gestapo assaulted the university . . . before they were through the Germans had killed one professor . . . seriously wounded another, arrested about 350 members of the university community, and deported more than 100, including 8 professors, to concentration camps.

In June 1945, Charles de Gaulle, who symbolized the resistance, attended the last professors' convocation at Clermont. After 1945, the university was reestablished in Strasbourg. The manifesto of the university was to serve as a citadel of Franco-German culture (*La Nouvelle ligue franco-allemande* was established to help Alsatians heal). This development fostered unity in Alsace-Lorraine, as the European Council, founded in Strasbourg in 1949, worked toward European unity. Robert Schuman of the French ministry, for whom Strasbourg University III was named, was influential in the discussions of the postwar future of the university.

In 1991, Strasbourg University I, II, and III joined the city of Strasbourg, the Bas-Rhin department, and the Alsace regional office, to form Le Pôle Universitaire Européen, a cooperative dedicated to campus urbanization and to the general education of local "Strasbourgeois" students needing state job certificate training and improved linguistic skills.

Further Reading: John E. Craig's study of Strasbourg University, *Scholarship and Nation Building: The Universities of Strasbourg and Alsatian Society, 1870–1939* (Chicago: University of Chicago Press, 1984) presents a unique and scholarly view of the interaction between higher education and society, of nationalism and alienation as it relates to Strasbourg University in particular, and to the history of Europe in general. Franklin Ford's *Strasbourg in Transition* (New York: Norton Library, W.W. Norton, 1966) gives many details of the university's founding and its subsequent fate within the educational reforms of France and Germany between 1648 and 1789. *The Education of Nations* by Robert Ulich (Cambridge, Massachusetts: Harvard University Press, 1961) is a "comparison in historical perspectives" which recognizes the importance of Strasbourg University's history within the academic histories of France and Germany.

—Carol Shilakowsky

TATA INSTITUTE OF FUNDAMENTAL RESEARCH
(Mumbai, Maharashtra, India)

Location: The Tata Institute of Fundamental Research lies on the southernmost tip of Mumbai's (Bombay's) Colaba area. It is an enclave in the Navy Nagar district, one of the city's most exclusive districts.

Description: The institute offers no degrees. It is a community of advanced researchers and scientists working in the two broad groupings of physics and mathematics. There is also a dental research unit which has an ongoing project on the study and prevention of oral cancer. The institute's scientists have pathbreaking studies to their credit in mathematics, physics, astronomy, and computer science.

Information: Tata Institute of Fundamental Research
Homi Bhabha Road
Mumbai 400 005
India

Visiting: Write to the above address for further information.

Few centers of scientific research are as picturesquely located as the Tata Institute of Fundamental Research in Mumbai (Bombay). The Arabian Sea, crashing gray waves, and boundless horizons frame two sides of the TIFR campus. It is a small piece of land, but standing on the edge of the ocean, there is a sense of grandeur, space, and peace about the institution. Just outside the gates is the teeming metropolis of Mumbai; within the TIFR buildings, the pace is equally intense, but directed toward long-term research. The Tata Institute of Fundamental Research still commands respect in Indian scientific circles, although there are other centers these days for quality research, such as the various Indian Institutes of Technology. Its strength is its sharp focus on fundamental research. Engineering colleges and institutes cater to the demand for short-term technological research.

The history of TIFR is closely connected with that of science and scientific institutions in independent India. Its past is linked further to its founder, Homi Bhabha (1906–66), a physicist of great repute and extraordinary energy. Bhabha was born into an upper class Parsi family in Mumbai and educated at established centers, Mumbai's Cathedral School and Elphinstone College. He then went to Gonville and Caius College at Cambridge University

where he studied mechanical sciences. Soon after his success in the tripos, Bhabha went on to study theoretical physics at the Cavendish Laboratory. It was here that his active scientific career began. He worked with well-known scientists of the time such as John Cockroft and those in Niels Bohr's group at the Institute of Copenhagen. From 1933 to 1939, Bhabha lived in Europe, working on cosmic ray physics. The outbreak of World War II stranded him in India, where he was vacationing. He worked for a while in Bangalore at the Indian Institute of Science where his colleagues were other distinguished scientists such as Nobel Laureate, C.V. Raman and Vikram Sarabhai (who would succeed Bhabha as the head of the Department of Atomic Energy). During this period, he began active efforts to set up an institute of physics in India. In 1945, his perseverance paid off when the Tata family (one of India's richest industrial houses) agreed to finance a fundamental physics research institute of Bhabha's choice and design. The Tata's industrial empire began with investment in steel; Bhabha's aunt had married into this house. J.R.D. Tata (who played an active role in India's bid to become industrially self-reliant) encouraged Bhabha to create a scientific institution and the Sir Dorab Tata Trust followed this up with funds for the project.

Connected by birth to one of India's most powerful industrial families, Homi Bhabha was at ease with prominent politicians and national leaders. He was also a gifted administrator and TIFR was the product of his single-minded sense of mission about Indian science. Science under the colonial education system had either stagnated in university departments or experienced isolated bursts of glory under individual scientists. Bhabha's was an effort to build a community of scientists who would work in a collegial atmosphere, supporting each other intellectually and professionally. In this respect, his endeavor paid off. His recruitment efforts across India gained TIFR a team of talented scientists who lived up to Bhabha's expectations. The youthfulness of the TIFR recruits was an image of Bhabha's own youthfulness and energy (he was only 36 when he founded TIFR).

Bhabha's scientific talent, background, and connections came together particularly well in the period after India's independence from British rule in 1947. The Tata Institute of Fundamental Research benefited from the pro-science approach of the first generation of leaders in independent India. After independence, the problems facing India were vast. Poverty and the unequal distribution of resources weighed down the agenda of most administrators. The first prime minister, Jawaharlal Nehru, was especially convinced of the transformatory powers of sci-

Tata Institute of Fundamental Research

ence and technology. According to him, "The future belongs to science and to those who make friends with science." Homi Bhabha's efforts to build up a community of physicists at TIFR thus met with a sympathetic attitude in the very highest of government circles. Government funds completed, then exceeded the private contributions to the institute. Bhabha's personality ensured however that TIFR's academic culture maintained its autonomy and that the institution did not become a dull, marginal player in the competitive academic world. The Tata Institute of Fundamental Research was not to go the way of university science departments, and for a long time it did not have any university affiliations. However, once Bhabha became a senator of the University of Mumbai, TIFR did move toward integration and coexistence with the traditional system of science research in India, through university curriculum. Even today, TIFR offers no degrees; it is an institute for advanced research. Still, there is the provision for advanced physics graduate students to do their research here.

In 1955, funding for TIFR became an established part of government policy under the terms of the agreement (drawn up at Bhabha's insistence) between the state and federal governments and the Sir Dorab Tata Trust. The institute retained the Tata name but to this was added another title: National Centre of the Government of India for Nuclear Science and Mathematics. Its academic output grew rapidly in the 1950s. The construction of a digital computer was completed in 1959 and cosmic ray experiments and research were especially fruitful from 1947 to 1957. Theoretical physics and mathematics picked up momentum in the late 1950s. While Bhabha was often too busy with his multiple responsibilities to follow day-to-day developments at TIFR, he retained a lasting interest in the welfare of the institution. He attended TIFR Wednesday colloquia regularly and, from his position of power at the Department of Atomic Energy, ensured that TIFR did not become bogged down in bureaucracy.

Originally located on Peddar Road in Mumbai, TIFR moved in 1949 to Apollo Bunder, into the grounds of the Royal Yacht Club. Finally, in 1962 it shifted into its current residence in South Mumbai in the Navy Nagar area. Prime Minister Nehru himself, in recognition of the importance of the institution, inaugurated the new TIFR buildings. Homi Bhabha applied himself to the design and planning of the new location, with an eye to the minutest detail. At the new site, Bhabha was actively involved in planning the interior of the building, planting trees, and seeing to the layout of the Institute's gardens. He was open to the new architectural ideas that TIFR architect, Helmut Barsch of Chicago, presented to him. Barsch was given a free hand to design TIFR. Housing was extremely tight, but opposite the TIFR grounds, a residential complex for scientists has now come up. A lover of art, and a painter himself, Bhabha ensured that TIFR would not become a gloomy, dark shrine to science. The building is full of paintings in unexpected places. Some of his own collection hangs on the walls and in the small museum of the institute. M.F. Husain, one of India's leading artists, painted a mural on the wall of the central hall. Aesthetically, TIFR is a pleasing place, although many criticized Bhabha's and TIFR's attention to appearance in a country where there are few resources for day-to-day living.

Through Bhabha, TIFR is also connected to India's drive to generate atomic energy. This has been controversial in recent times, with accusations in world forum that this research is for military purposes. In the early days after independence, though, India's political and scientific concerns dwelt on the production of energy. Freedom from dependency on imported oil was a key political issue and science seemed to offer a way to achieve this national goal. Bhabha provided the leadership to this enterprise when he became chairman of the Atomic Energy Commission in 1948. In 1954, the AEC became the Department of Atomic Energy, again with Bhabha at its head. Under his leadership, research into atomic energy became a priority. In 1964, Bhabha said at the conference that for the developing world, "No power is as expensive as no power." Indigenization of technology was an imperative, especially in the 1960s when public finances became tight and imports of western technology became very expensive. The absolute independence from foreign control that Bhabha desired was not to be, at least not in his lifetime, and there were collaborations with France, Canada, and the United States in India's nuclear project. Still, there were advances as when the Atomic Energy Establishment (later renamed the Bhabha Atomic Research Centre or BARC), set up by Bhabha in Trombay, built India's first nuclear reactor, APSARA. It went critical in 1956. Tata Institute of Fundamental Research scientists built the control system for APSARA and many of its scientists such as R. Ramanna went on to become part of the DAE's leading scientific elite. The Tata Institute, along with BARC, became an active part of the Department of Atomic Energy's attempts to advance the research into nuclear physics in India. A major part of TIFR funding still comes from the DAE. The culture of independence and autonomy that Bhabha championed at TIFR also took root in the DAE. As Bhabha stressed, government funding did not necessarily mean a bureaucratic culture or excessive centralization, although with his death in 1966, some of the dynamism that had symbolized TIFR and the DAE faded. Bhabha had hoped to create independent scientific communities whose professional solidarity and vibrancy would see them through periods of weak or non-existent leadership. To a large extent, though, the success of TIFR and the DAE was dependent on his powerful personality and his personal and social links with the political and social elites and policy makers of independent India. With his unexpected death at the age of 57, in a plane crash at Mont Blanc, India lost an energetic champion of long-term scientific research whose skill at organizing indigenous scientific talent was unique.

TIFR continues to play a leading role in India's fundamental science programs. It has 400 scientists and its projects include the construction of the world's largest meterwave radio telescope and a high-energy cosmic-ray laboratory. A large library caters to the needs of its researchers. However, lack of funding restricts the easy movement of scientists to international forum. Sabbatical leave abroad is infrequent. Unlike Bhabha, the TIFR scientists of today do not have a completely free hand with state resources. Still, if Bhabha had been alive today, he would not have been ashamed of the institution he created. Given the current crisis in Indian higher education and despite inadequate resources, TIFR still lives up to its founder's aims. In 1995, the ceremonies and symposia that marked the 50th anniversary of the Tata Institute of Fundamental Research celebrated India's Renaissance man of science and the farsightedness of his vision.

Further Reading: *Homi Bhabha: Father of Nuclear Science in India* by R.P. Kulkarni and V. Sharma (Bombay: Popular Prakashan, 1969) is a straightforward narrative of Homi Bhabha's work both at the Tata Institute and at the Department of Atomic Energy. There is a comparative history of TIFR and Calcutta's Saha Institute of Nuclear Physics in *Building Scientific Institutions in India: Saha and Bhabha* by Robert S. Anderson (Montreal: Centre for Developing-Area Studies, 1975). An overview of India's science projects is in *Science in India: Institution-Building and the Organizational System for Research and Development* by Ward Morehouse (Bombay: Popular Prakashan, 1971). Another general work on Indian science is *Science and Indian Culture* by J.B.S. Haldane (Calcutta: New Age, 1965).

—Sharmishtha Roy Chowdhury

TECHNION—ISRAEL INSTITUTE OF TECHNOLOGY
(Haifa, Israel)

Location: On the western slope of Mount Carmel in Haifa, Israel. Technion City comprises 280 buildings on 300 acres overlooking the Mediterranean Sea.

Description: Large research university with 11,000 students. With more than 45,000 graduates by the late 1990s, Technion was a major contributor to the technological development of Israel.

Information: Technion–Israel Institute of Technology
Division of Public Affairs and Resource Development
Technion City, Haifa 32000
Israel
(04) 822-1513
(04) 829-2578

Visiting: Contact the university at the above addresses and phone numbers or through any of the Technion Societies. Societies are in place in Argentina, Australia, Austria, Brazil, Canada, Denmark, France, Germany, Great Britain, Japan, Mexico, South Africa, Switzerland, the United States, and Venezuela. The Coler California Visitors Center at Technion is open Sunday through Thursday from 8:00 A.M. to 3:00 P.M. Visits include an introduction by a Technion student with orientation at a physical model of the campus and an audiovisual presentation.

Technion was founded in 1924 and is the oldest university in Israel. By the 1990s, almost three-quarters of the managers of technological companies in Israel were graduates of the university. Technion comprises more than 250 buildings built on 300 acres, and boasts a student body of 11,000, with 700 faculty members. The faculty/student ratio in the mid-1990s was 15.8 to 1. There are 19 departments and 40 research centers and institutes. Technion's stated goals are education, leadership in technology and academia, contribution to human knowledge, and service to the economy and the general public of Israel.

When the fifth Zionist Council met in 1901, one of the issues on the agenda was the establishment of a Jewish university. Eleven years later, the cornerstone was laid for Technion's first building, and in 1924, the first class consisted of 16 students studying architecture and civil engineering. During these intervening years building was interrupted by a number of factors. Construction that had begun in 1912 stopped during World War I, and in 1916 the German army took over some of the partially finished buildings. Some of the early founders of the university argued over whether this should be a technical school or an institution of higher learning. Zionists in Germany who worked toward Technion's establishment discussed the language of instruction, and Hebrew won out over German. In 1925 a financial crisis prompted some affiliated with Technion to suggest a merger with Hebrew University in Jerusalem, but it was rejected. Technion's first graduating class took its examinations in Hebrew in 1928, and then engineers and architects were awarded their degrees in 1929.

In 1939 a Technion physics professor was sent to the United States where he organized the American Society for Technion (ATS), which continues to earn money for the university. At the New York World's Fair in 1939, a model of the main Technion building was part of a Technion exhibit. One of the university's founders was Albert Einstein. At a founding ceremony of the American Society for Technion, which pledged to raise funds for the institute, Einstein said, "I have seen with great satisfaction how the Technion fulfills the important task of developing the intelligence and expert knowledge of young people in the field of technology." David Ben-Gurion, the first prime minister of the state of Israel, saw Technion as an important leader in the building of the new state. In 1948, during the war for Israel's independence, the academic schedule was reduced, and the number of full-time students fell to 670. Wars continued to affect students over the years at Technion. In 1973 there was a five-month delay of classes after the Yom Kippur War. The president of Technion at the time was Amos Horev, who was the school's first Israeli-born president.

In 1909 German architect Alexander Baerwald designed a building to anchor Technion. Its style was European classical with eastern accents like a dome, since Palestine's Ottoman Empire left its mark on the country. Facilities on the 300-acre campus include an amphitheater and theater, audiovisual libraries, laboratories, music center, computer centers, a sports center and swimming pool, and student dormitories. In the dormitories for single students there were close to 3,000 beds. Also on the campus were a bank, shops, a day-care center, a synagogue, and a theological study hall.

In the late 1950s and early 1960s Technion shifted from a European-style school of engineering to a scientific research university based more on an American model. In 1953 the institute had outgrown its midtown

Israel Institute of Technology

Haifa location, and a site on Mount Carmel was selected by Prime Minister Ben-Gurion.

In the 1950s and 1960s women made up less than ten percent of the undergraduates receiving degrees at Technion. By 1995 that ratio had changed, and more than 25 percent of Technion's undergraduate degrees were granted to women. By the end of the century the student body population was increasing, and the university aimed to have close to 15,000 students.

The first academic unit established at Technion was the faculty of architecture and town planning. Together with the faculty of civil engineering, these departments trained students who went on to build the fledgling state of Israel. In 1949 Dr. Sydney Goldstein, chairman of the Aeronautical Research Council of Great Britain, joined the Technion faculty and formed the department of aeronautical engineering.

Technion offered 41 undergraduate degree programs. Most of the four-year undergraduate programs led to a bachelor of science in the sciences and engineering. In 1978 Technion added a three-year program toward a bachelor of arts in science, recognizing that other universities in Israel offered similar programs that were drawing potential Technion students away. The degree program in architecture was five years and that in medicine was six years with an intermediate B.A. or B.S. awarded. The 20 faculties/departments were: aerospace engineering, agricultural engineering, architecture, biology, chemical engineering, chemistry, civil engineering, computer science, education in technology and science, electrical engineering, environmental engineering, environmental science, food engineering and biotechnology, general option, industrial engineering and management, materials engineering, mathematics, mechanical engineering, medicine, and physics. Among undergraduates, the most popular concentrations are civil engineering, computer science, electrical engineering, and industrial engineering and management.

There were 61 graduate degree programs. Degrees offered include masters of science, engineering, business administration, and doctor of science. Of 2,800 graduate students, about 400 come from outside Israel. The percentage of graduate students in the general student population was between 25 and 30 percent in the early 1990s. During the large influx of immigrants from the former Soviet Union and Eastern Europe, Technion played a central role in absorbing the newcomers. Many were highly skilled, including 55,000 engineers who arrived among 500,000 Russian immigrants between 1989 and 1993. Technion offered job-development programs as well as retraining and educational programs.

Technion was the largest applied research center in Israel, and it was one of the world's only technological institutions that had a faculty of medicine. Technion opened its medical school in 1969. In 1973, the existing medical school merged into Technion as a faculty. In 1979 the 17-floor Rappaport Building was inaugurated to house laboratories, lecture halls, and library. There were 500 medical students, 200 graduate students, and more than 230 professors and researchers.

The faculty of aerospace engineering was the only one in Israel, and it brought the country to a position of leadership in aviation and aerospace. Its students built a communications satellite, as well as fighter aircraft and commercial aircraft. The supersonic wind tunnel at the university enabled the department to develop the Lavi jet fighter and the Kfir C-22 fighter.

Agricultural departments were essential in a region where self-sufficiency seemed impossible at first. Irrigation methods, harvesting equipment, pest-control techniques, and crop-protection systems pioneered at Technion were exported to farmers in Morocco, China, Russia, Spain, and elsewhere. Drip irrigation saved millions of dollars in the desert regions of southern Israel, and it was developed at Technion.

The computer science department expanded rapidly in the 1980s and trained many of the computer experts who went on to found and lead Israeli software companies. The Technion Energy Center created a giant solar energy collector and pushed the boundaries of solar power. With the help of Technion research, the parliament building in Jerusalem, the Knesset, was converted to solar energy. A hotel in a southern resort area saw a drop in its annual use of fuel oil from 48 tons to 3 after it switched to solar power. Technion scientists also investigated alternative energy sources, including solar ponds and methane gas, a by-product of farm animal waste.

Technion's budget in the late 1990s was nearing $200 million, more than half of which came from the Israeli government. Tuition and Technion societies provided some of the rest. Supporters of the university saw the funds as an investment in Israel's future. High-technology exports from Israel were valued at almost $5 billion at the close of the century.

Technion offers an international program for high-school students known as Sci-Tech. The six-week program allows students from around the world to work with Technion faculty and facilities on a variety of projects. Some work with robots, others study computer languages, and all are made to feel comfortable in a research environment. Technion also houses a Youth Center whose aim is to stimulate interest in mathematics and science among high-school students. Faculty members coach an Isareli team that participates in the International Mathematics Olympics and organized inter-city mathematics competitions. Many are also involved in training high-school graduates and army veterans so that they can pass Technion's rigorous acceptance regimen.

A program for exceptionally gifted students allows the university to work with students of promise in fashioning degree programs that have flexibility. Some undergraduates can undertake graduate-level research before completing undergraduate degrees, and others work toward B.S. and M.S. degrees simultaneously. The Technion Research and Development Foundation (TRDF) has registered hundreds of patents. A satellite designed and built by students, Gurwin-1 Technsat, was launched in the late 1990s.

Centers of Excellence were established at Technion in 1991 in many fields to allow inter-departmental cooperation and technological research. Some of these were: opto-electronics, which combined research in physics, electronics, and optics to focus on communications; space research; high-temperature superconductivity; environmental science and water resources; and complex fluids, microstructures, and macromolecules.

In 1992 the Technion Institute of Management was formed, and five years later the faculty of industrial engineering and management dedicated the new business school. One of its new courses of study was a master's program in information management engineering.

Technion has become Israeli industry's research and development department. Research in many fields pro-vides tools for corporations across the world. The high technology industries in Israel acquired their reputation in large measure from the work done by Technion students and graduates.

Alumni of Technion include the architect of Israel's Supreme Court; the general managers of Intel in Israel, Microsoft in Israel, Teva Pharmaceutical Industries, and Osem Food Industries Ltd.; presidents of Israel companies including Elron, Elbit, Israel Aircraft Industries, and Elscint; and government officials from the finance ministry and the defense ministry, among others.

Further Reading: A broad-based history of the university is *Technion: The Story of Israel's Institute of Technology* by Carl Alpert (New York: American Technion Society, 1982) provides a concise look at the university through the eyes of one of its most successful fundraisers.

—Fran Shonfeld Sherman

TUFTS UNIVERSITY
(Medford, Massachusetts, U.S.A.)

Location: Tufts has three campuses. The main one is a residential campus in Medford, a suburb five miles west of Boston. This campus compromises the College of Liberal Arts, Jackson College, the College of Engineering, the Graduate School of Arts and Sciences, the School of Nutrition Science and Policy, and the Fletcher School of Law and Diplomacy. The schools of medicine and dental medicine are on a campus in downtown Boston, near the Massachusetts Turnpike along with the Sackler School of Graduate Biomedical Sciences. The school of veterinary medicine is located in North Grafton, Massachusetts.

Description: Tufts is an independent, private, coeducational university. It has more than 8,000 students on its three campuses. Of these, approximately 4,500 are undergraduates.

Information: Tufts University
Medford, MA 02155
U.S.A.
(617) 628-5000
Fax (617) 627-3860

Visiting: For visiting information, contact the Office of Admissions at the above address.

The Universalist Church issued a charter to the Trustees of Tufts College in 1852. It was the 163rd institution of higher learning chartered in the United States, and it was built on land donated by Charles Tufts. More than a century later, Tufts is renowned as a center for teaching, as well as for research. In 1854 Tufts College had seven students and four professors and was led by president Reverend Hosea Ballou II. The college opened an affiliated medical school in 1893 on Boylston Street in Boston. The medical school was coeducational, and offered a three-year program. Four years later it moved to the remodeled Baptist Church on Shawmut Avenue. In 1899 the Boston Dental College joined with Tufts to form Tufts College Dental School. Realizing that the two schools had similar goals, they built a new building on Huntington Avenue in Boston for both the medical and dental schools in 1900.

In 1902, the faculty of arts and sciences was created. By 1906 women made up 70 percent of the entering class of College of Letters. In 1910 a change in the school's charter created a separate Jackson College for Women,

and students had the choice of a degree from Jackson or Tufts. The Fletcher School of Law and Diplomacy was founded in 1931 and was to be administered jointly by Tufts college and Harvard University. By 1945 every state in the United States was represented at Tufts, even though only five years earlier 80 percent of the students came from within 50 miles of Medford.

In 1952 the 100th anniversary of the Tufts charter was celebrated during the commencement week and again at a three-day centennial celebration in October. Among the dignitaries who joined in the celebration were the president of the Carnegie Institution, a Tufts alumnus; the presidents of Harvard and the University of Glasgow; and the Swedish ambassador to the United States. Leonard Carmichael, who had been president of the university since 1938, resigned at the end of 1952 to become secretary of the Smithsonian Institution. His tenure was marked by the expansion of scientific research at Tufts, combined with a continued focus on the education of undergraduates. The number of undergraduate students at Tufts during Carmichael's presidency rose from 615 in 1937 to 1,175 in 1950. His successor was Nils Yngve Wessel, who served as Tuft's president until 1966. Wessel was only 39 years old when he became the president. His goal was to maintain Tufts as, in his words, "a small university of high quality."

In 1955 Tufts officially became a university. Students and faculty applauded the change from Tufts College to Tufts University, saying that the name had finally caught up with the reality of the school. Undergraduate divisions were renamed colleges and graduate divisions were renamed schools in the updated charter. There were major expansions in the graduate schools in the early 1960s. The number of master's programs went from 21 to 31 and the number of doctoral programs went from 8 to 20. The Tufts–New England Medical Center became an unincorporated alliance in 1961, and by 1968 it was a Massachusetts nonprofit corporation. New degree programs were added in the 1970s, including a B.S. in engineering and engineering science that allowed more liberal arts courses for engineers. The Nutrition Institute was inaugurated in 1976, and the next year was the beginning of cross-registration and a five-year music degree with the New England Conservatory of Music. The School of Veterinary Medicine was authorized in 1978, and the Sackler School of Graduate Biomedical Sciences opened in 1980. The School of Nutrition absorbed the Nutrition Institute and the graduate department in nutrition. The Cabot Intercultural Center was inaugurated at the Medford campus in 1981, and the Large Animal Hospital opened at the Grafton campus in 1982, followed by the Hospital for

Tufts University

Small Animals at Grafton, which opened in 1985.

In 1990 the Tufts endowment reached a new high: $155,600,000. In 1995 Tufts was included among the country's top 25 schools in *U.S. News and World Re-port*. As a private institution struggling with increased costs, Tufts was an expensive place to study. Tuition and fees in the late 1990s were above $20,000 annually, with room and board costing an additional $6,500. About 39 percent of Tufts students received some form of financial aid.

On-campus housing is guaranteed for freshmen at the Medford/Somerville campus. This campus holds the College of Liberal Arts and Jackson College, the Fletcher School of Law and Diplomacy, the College of Engineering, the School of Nutrition Science and Policy, and the Graduate School of Arts and Sciences. Some of the dormitories are coeducational. Fraternities and sororities also provide housing for some of their members, but fewer than 15 percent of students join fraternities, and fewer than 5 percent join sororities. About 80 percent of the students live in university housing. Commuters make up only 8 percent of the student body. There are some special-interest houses available on campus that feature foreign languages or specific cultures.

When the university is not in session, Tufts opens its doors to outsiders for conferences. The residence halls are available as are lecture halls seating from 10 to 600 participants. Meals are offered in the dining halls, and special theme meals are available for catering. From may through August, Tufts also has summer programs for high school students and English as a foreign language programs.

On the Boston campus are the New England Medical Center, the Jean Mayer USDA Human Nutrition Research Center on Aging, the Tufts University School of Dental Medicine and Tufts University School of Medicine, the Health Sciences Library and Arthur M. Sackler Center for Health Communications, and the Rehabilitation Institute. The campus in Grafton holds the school of Veterinary Medicine and two animal hospitals. Tufts also has a fourth campus, located in Talloires, France, that has the university's European Center.

In the late 1990s Tufts had a full-time and part-time faculty of 617 in the arts and sciences. Of these, close to 300 were full-time faculty members in the school of arts and sciences while others taught in the engineering field. There were close to 400 other members of the faculty teaching either full-time or part-time in the medical, dental, veterinary, nutrition, law and diplomacy, and graduate science schools. The student/faculty ratio was 13:1. About 99 percent of the faculty hold doctorate degrees or its equivalent.

Tufts granted more than 1,000 bachelor's degrees annually in the late 1990s. Some of these students took advantage of specialized academic programs. These programs include double majors, independent study, internships, semester at sea, study abroad, and combined programs with the New England Conservatory of Music, the School of the Museum of Fine Arts, and the European Center in Talloires, France. The university offers remedial services such as tutoring as well as ROTC training for the Air Force, Army, and Navy. Graduate degrees are offered in 89 major fields of study.

Undergraduate majors include American studies, anthropology, archaeology, architectural engineering, art history, Asian studies, astronomy, biology, biotechnology engineering, chemical engineering, chemistry, child development, classics, communications, computer science, dance, drama, economics, education, electrical engineering, English, environmental studies, French, geology, history, international relations, mathematics, mechanical engineering, music, philosophy, physics, political science, psychology, religion, sociology, Spanish, and women's studies.

The five university libraries have 863,000 books as well as microforms, periodicals, journals, university archives, a media center, and government documents. There is a music library, and each department has specialized collections of materials. There are more than 250 microcomputers located in the libraries, classrooms, and computer centers. The campus has a computer network as well as special facilities including a computer-aided design laboratory. The academic computer services department runs three computer labs: the Eaton Computer Lab and the Mark Learning Resource Center both have PCs and the Jackson lab has Macintosh computers.

Tufts is a member of the National Collegiate Athletic Association, Division III. Its intercollegiate sports include baseball, basketball, crew, cross-country, field hockey, football, golf, ice hockey, lacrosse, sailing, soccer, softball, squash, swimming and diving, tennis, track and field, and volleyball. Club sports include rugby, fencing, sailing, water polo, ultimate frisbee, martial arts, and equestrian. There are more than 130 organizations on campus, including the student newspaper and radio station. Other popular clubs and groups include student government, film, choral groups, jazz band, concert band, marching band, opera, symphony orchestra, pep band, dance, and drama. Religious and cultural organizations include International Club, Hispanic-American Society, Afro-American Society, and the Asian Students Club. The students represent all 50 states as well as 63 foreign countries.

Tufts is among only 38 private universities with a Research I rating from the Carnegie Commission. The university focuses on teaching as well as research, and states on its home page on the internet that the university is dedicated to solving the most critical problems facing the international community.

Further Reading: The most complete history of the university is *Light on the Hill: A History of Tufts University 1852–1952,* by university archivist Russell E. Miller (Boston: Beacon Press, 1996). Tufts has an accessible and attractive web site at http://www.tufts.edu.

—Fran Shonfeld Sherman

TULANE UNIVERSITY
(New Orleans, Louisiana, U.S.A.)

Location: Approximately four miles from the central business district and the French Quarter of New Orleans.

Description: An independent university enrolling approximately 11,400 students in undergraduate, graduate, and professional schools.

Information: Office of Undergraduate Admission
210 Gibson Hall
Tulane University
New Orleans, LA 70118-5680
U.S.A.
(504) 862-8715

Visiting: To avoid conflicts with the university schedule, please call the Admission Office at (800) 873-9283 to schedule a campus visit.

The idea of Tulane University may have originated in Louisville, Kentucky, some 60 years before the institution was founded. Between 1818 and 1821, young Paul Tulane and his cousin traveled throughout the southern United States. Hearing that the first steamboat to ascend the Mississippi was to stop in Louisville, Tulane rode to meet it and was impressed by the Creole planters on board who were bringing their sons to attend college in Lexington or Bardstown. Years later he remarked: "It seemed a strange thing to me, and I remembered it; and I had not lived long in Louisiana before I thought I would like to see a good college built where the boys might be educated at home."

Tulane University began in 1834 when seven young physicians desired to open a medical college to provide better training to combat New Orleans' frequent epidemics of cholera and yellow fever. An advertisement for the school criticized the city's physicians, accusing them of acting selfishly and neglecting to educate others for the medical profession. Initially, the medical college had no buildings, property, or equipment; classes were held in private offices, and instruction was conducted in nearby Charity Hospital. However, 11 students enrolled in 1835, the year of its charter, and all graduated in 1836.

The school proved successful and soon had its own building in the city's business district. Impressed by the school's achievements, local civic leaders pushed for the establishment of a state university in New Orleans and presented a plan to do so at a meeting of the state constitutional convention in 1844.

When the state constitution was adopted in 1845, it stipulated that a university be established in New Orleans with four faculties: law, medicine, natural sciences, and letters. The university was to be named the University of Louisiana, and the Medical College of Louisiana was to constitute the medical faculty. Furthermore, the legislature would provide for the university's organization and maintenance but would not be under obligation to provide appropriations for its support. The University of Louisiana, absorbing the medical college, was incorporated by a legislative act on February 16, 1847. Shortly thereafter, a law department was added, and the collegiate department was established in 1851.

The constitutional decision not to mandate funding for the new university was a political one arising from tensions between the rural and urban lawmakers. "Country" legislators deemed the Louisiana State Seminary of Learning and Military Academy (the parent institution of Louisiana State University) in Rapides Parish near Alexandria to be the official state university. Nevertheless, between 1847 and 1861, the University of Louisiana received $117,000 in appropriations, most of the funds going to the medical school. An appeal to the citizens of New Orleans for money in 1850 brought the university's cash assets to $1,602.

Talk of secession was rampant during the late 1850s. The University of Louisiana advertised and drew many southern-born men away from northern colleges. During the Civil War, the university closed: many faculty members and most of the students were serving in the Confederate Army. The law school reopened in 1865, and the medical school soon thereafter. Although student enrollment had reached 400 in 1860, after the war it took 16 years for the enrollment to reach 217 students. Although the state constitutions of 1864, 1868, and 1879 provided for state support of the University of Louisiana, the economic devastation brought by the war made it impossible to actually collect the funds until 1883.

In 1877, David F. Boyd, president of Louisiana State University, strongly supported a plan to move the University of Louisiana to Baton Rouge and consolidate the two universities. The University of Louisiana's board acquiesced, but a popular vote was required in order to amend the state constitution. The people of New Orleans, however, did not embrace the idea of their sons attending school in Baton Rouge and soundly defeated the proposal.

In the nineteenth century, growth in business enterprise paralleled the growth in higher education. Private

Tulane University

benefaction now filled higher education's need for financial support once provided by the church or state. Beset by financial uncertainties and political pressures, the University of Louisiana was assisted, perhaps rescued, by the financial generosity of Paul Tulane. Tulane was descended from a line of French magistrates and lawyers. His father, Louis, prospered in the lumber exporting business in Santo Domingo but fled during a slave uprising in 1791 and settled near Princeton, New Jersey, in Cherry Valley. Paul Tulane was born there on May 1, 1801, received an elementary and private school education, and, at 15, went to clerk for Thomas White, a Princeton merchant. New Orleans, however, was to provide him the opportunity to amass a vast fortune.

On the aforementioned trip with his cousin, Tulane had observed the transportation of goods on the Mississippi River and assessed the potential of New Orleans as a major center of trade. Paul's older brother, Louis, was a successful fur merchant in New Orleans and, in 1822, Paul moved there. With financial assistance and encouragement from his father, he established himself as a dry goods merchant and traded up and down the Mississippi Valley.

By 1828, Tulane was worth $150,000, but his fortune was securely made when he joined a New Orleans tailor, Isaac Baldwin, in the mass production and marketing of men's clothing. Concerned that the coming war would bring unstable financial conditions to the South, Tulane transferred most of his liquid assets to the North. Tulane retired to Princeton in 1873, and, some years later, made the decision to financially support the cause of higher education in New Orleans where he had first become successful. He summoned U.S. Representative Randall Lee Gibson of Louisiana to meet with him and to accept the endowment of his New Orleans property, the income from which was to be used to support higher education. Gibson devised a plan by which a self-perpetuating board of 17 administrators selected from the best and brightest male citizens of New Orleans would oversee the bequest.

Two questions faced the board immediately. Should a new institution be established or should the University of Louisiana be strengthened? Should the institution be devoted to vocation and technical education or concentrate on the liberal arts?

Tulane had written to the board that he meant "to foster such a course of intellectual development as shall be useful and of solid worth, and not [be] merely ornamental or superficial." After much discussion, the board agreed to fortify the University of Louisiana and establish a vocational-technical school within the university, subject to Tulane's approval. The vote was close; two votes had determined that the new university would not be a technical school.

Tulane, however, did not approve; he objected to fostering the academic department of the University of Louisiana and wanted a new technological institute to be built. Eventually, because affiliation with the University of Louisiana was the only way to avoid paying taxes on the gifts to the institution, Tulane acquiesced to the takeover of the University of Louisiana, academic department and all.

In 1884, the legislature passed Act 43, which conveyed all property and control of the University of Louisiana, whose administrators had been supportive of the consolidation, to the Tulane Education Fund administrators. The people of Louisiana later ratified the act in a constitutional amendment adopted in 1889. Richard Henry Jesse, dean of the academic department at Louisiana State and later a senior professor of Latin at Tulane, spearheaded the merger. The resulting institution was renamed Tulane University of Louisiana. Tulane had objected at first to the naming of the university after himself. He suggested that Deosto, LaSalle, or Bienville might be good names, but he was prevailed upon to change his mind by Congressman Gibson who noted that these men had nothing to do with education.

Paul Tulane died on February 10, 1886, unmarried and childless, and the administrators fully expected him to leave the bulk of his estate to the university. His original and subsequent bequests had totaled over $1 million, allowing the university to increase its faculty and student enrollment and improve its facilities. At this time the Common Street campus consisted of a Grecian-type central building housing the medical school, flanked by east and west wings. However, the search for a will proved fruitless, and Tulane's assets of nearly $10 million were divided among his nieces and nephews.

The first president of Tulane University was William Preston Johnston, kin of Gibson, son of General Albert Sidney Johnston, who was killed at Shiloh, and president of Louisiana State University. Johnston's vision was that the new university would

cover the whole wide area of human knowledge,
rising through regular gradations, higher and high-

er, to the utmost attainments of the human mind . . .
It will have the ability, and therefore will have the
right, and should feel the duty of assuming the leadership in public education in the State.

Because Paul Tulane's letter of donation indicated the desire to advance the "promotion and encouragement of education among the white young persons of New Orleans," the door was left slightly ajar for the admission of women. Women attended classes through Tulane's adult education program, which offered lectures, discussion groups, and an extremely popular free drawing class. About this time, Josephine Louise LeMonnier Newcomb, the widow of a wealthy New Orleans sugar merchant, was searching for a fitting memorial for her cherished daughter, Harriott Sophie, who had died at the age of 15 from diphtheria. As Newcomb pondered various projects, her friend Ida Richardson, whose husband was professor of surgery at Tulane, suggested that part of the university be devoted to the higher education of women. Both women were aware of the growing movement to admit women to men's universities. On the advice of President Johnston, Newcomb made an initial donation of $100,000 "to be used in establishing the H. Sophie Newcomb Memorial College in the Tulane University of Louisiana." Established in 1886, Newcomb College became the first degree-granting coordinate college for women in the United States and served as a model for Radcliffe, Barnard, and Case Western Reserve for Women.

Professor Brandt V.B. Dixon was chosen as the first president of the women's college. The courses of study included classics, science, and modern languages, leading to bachelor of arts or science degrees. Courses in art, music, and "aesthetical gymnastics" were also offered. In 1894, additional donations by Newcomb led to the construction of a chapel, an art building and dormitory, and the Josephine Louise House, near the site of the original building, once a private residence, at the corner of Camp and Howard Streets. The chapel was a pet project of the benefactress, who ordered three stained-glass windows from Tiffany to adorn it. Today, the university owns 13 Tiffany windows, one of the largest collections in existence. Again, the purchase by Newcomb of Burnside Place in the Garden District allowed the women's college to move in 1891.

In 1907, eight women had attempted to enter the medical school, but were refused admittance. However, by 1911, women had been appointed to the medical faculty and, finally, in 1914, the faculty, with only one dissenting vote, allowed women admission. Lindal Hill Coleman, from Houston, Texas, was the first woman to receive a medical degree from Tulane. Bettie Runnels was admitted to the law school in 1897 and received her degree in 1898.

Other major changes were taking place in the late nineteenth and early twentieth centuries. The number of faculty and students doubled, the old campus on Common Street was abandoned, and land for a new campus was purchased in 1893 on St. Charles Avenue, across from Audubon Park, the current site of Tulane's main campus.

On January 27, 1894, the cornerstone was laid for the Arts and Sciences building (now Gibson Hall). When the academic department moved to the new campus, it split into the College of Technology and the College of Arts and Sciences. The College of Technology was in fact the engineering school, which now had its own building, faculty, and programs. At the time, the graduate school was small, offering doctoral degrees only in the basic medical sciences. Library resources were not adequate to support advanced research. At the time of the relocation, the library possessed only 15,000 volumes, including government documents.

Several other colleges made their appearances in the early years of the twentieth century. The School of Architecture, first in the area, was founded in 1907. The College of Commerce, established through the efforts of New Orleans businessmen, was established in 1914, and Newcomb moved in 1918 to a site adjacent to the uptown campus. The School of Social Work was added in 1927, the first of its kind in the Deep South.

Although blessed with the kindness of donors, Tulane's plans to expand programs and facilities required a more aggressive approach to fundraising. Tulane held its first endowment drive in the 1920s, bringing in $1,750,000.

After World War II, Tulane made a serious effort to strengthen its graduate programs, responding to the growing need for college and university teachers as the number of college students increased. The collections of three libraries, Howard Memorial Library, F.W. Tilton Memorial Library, and Newcomb College Library were merged in 1941 to provide the necessary support for the graduate school. Tulane developed guidance and financial assistance plans for graduate students through the doctoral level, and searched for and cultivated talent at the undergraduate level.

The 1950s and 1960s posed a further challenge for Tulane. The Supreme Court decision, *Brown et al v. Board of Education of Topeka,* prompted the Tulane administrators to address the possible admission of black students. Because the endowments of Tulane and Newcomb limited admission to white students, the university's board sought legal advice as to its obligations. In April 1961, the board issued a policy statement: "The Administrators of the Tulane Education Fund met Wednesday and noted that Tulane University would admit qualified students regardless of race or color if it were legally permissible." After a court challenge, Tulane was voluntarily desegregated by the board, and during the spring semester of 1963, black students were admitted without incident. Today, African Americans comprise nearly ten percent of the student body. Campus cultural diversity programs are funded through a grant from the Ford Foundation's Race Relations and Cultural Diversity Initiative.

Today, Tulane offers undergraduate, graduate, and professional degrees through its 11 colleges and schools. It has averaged one new building a year for the last ten years. The university supports nine libraries with 2.1 million volumes. Howard-Tilton Memorial Library houses several special collections, including the Latin-American Library, one of the world's foremost collections of primary and secondary source materials dating from the sixteenth century; the Hogan Jazz Archive; the Maxwell Music Library; the Louisiana Collection; and the Southeastern Architectural Archive. The Amistad Research Center houses the country's largest collection of primary documents on African-American history.

Throughout its history, Tulane has made numerous contributions to medical advancement. Dr. Andrew V. Schally shared the Nobel Prize for medicine and physiology in 1977 for his research on brain hormones. Dr. Schally and Dr. Akira Arimura, Director of the U.S.–Japan Cooperative Biomedical Research Laboratories, were ranked among the 28 top medical researchers in the nation, based on article citations between 1965 and 1984. Tulane's School of Public Health and Tropical Research offers the only degree in tropical medicine in the United States.

Tulane has had a number of memorable faculty members. Alcee Fortier, a proponent of Creole culture and professor of French, intimidated his students who failed to master proper French pronunciation. Robert Sharp, professor of English and Greek, is remembered for his ability to recite an entire Shakespeare play and involve his class wholeheartedly in the experience. Brown Ayres, a 24-year-old engineer and physicist, delighted students with his improvised laboratory gadgets.

Some of the many outstanding graduates of Tulane include Michael DeBakey, the cardiac surgeon who performed America's first heart transplant; Timothy John Robbie, president of the Miami Dolphins football team; Linda Wilson, president of Radcliffe College and a science advisor to the U.S. Congress; Harold Rosen, inventor of the first synchronous satellite; Robert Harling, playwright and author of *Steel Magnolias;* and Howard K. Smith Jr., a Rhodes scholar and ABC news co-anchor. Speaker of the U.S. House of Representatives, Newt Gingrich, received a master's degree in 1968 and a Ph.D. in modern European history in 1971 from Tulane.

In his first meeting with the board, in 1883, William Preston expressed his dream of creating a great Southern university by teaching youth well, espousing a community-oriented program of adult education, and developing human knowledge through research. As historian John P. Dyer notes, his views were "strongly prophetic of the type of institution Tulane eventually came to be."

Further Reading: *Tulane, the Biography of a University,* by John P. Dyer (New York and London: Harper and Row, 1966) is an extremely detailed, eminently readable, and comprehensive study of Tulane through the mid-1960s. Herbert E. Longenecker, a former president of Tulane, presents a succinct history in *Great Vision, Amply Justified, the Story of Tulane University* (New York: Newcomen Society in America, 1968). Philosophical history and statistical detail characterize the early years of Tulane in Edwin Whitfield Fay's *The History of Education in Louisiana* (Washington, D.C.: Government Printing Office, 1898). John Kendall Smith represents a detailed biography of Paul Tulane in *Louisiana Historical Quarterly,* volume 20, 1937.

—Kathleen M. Conley

UNITED STATES MILITARY ACADEMY AT WEST POINT
(West Point, New York, U.S.A.)

Location: West Point, 50 miles north of New York City, on the Hudson River.

Description: A publicly supported, professional college for men and women, enrolling approximately 4,300 students, who, as cadets, are in the United States Army, and who must serve six years on active duty after graduation. The military academy is under the general direction and supervision of the Department of the Army. It is also a national historic landmark.

Information: Director of Admissions
The United States Military Academy
606 Thayer Road
West Point, NY 10996-9902
U.S.A.
(914) 938-3308

Visiting: Visitors Center open daily, all year. West Point Museum, open daily, all year. Walking tours begin at Visitors Center. Guided tours provided by commercial service.

The United States Military Academy at West Point, New York, opened its doors on July 4, 1802, to ten "gentlemen cadets" who had no texts, no regular courses, and no discipline; they attended classes when they pleased, took vacations when they wished, took their meals in nearby homes, and lived in a barracks left over from the Revolutionary War. There was no four-year program; cadets were graduated at the pleasure of the superintendent. Two of the ten cadets were graduated from West Point after being there three months.

Almost 200 years later, the United States Military Academy at West Point hosts approximately 4,300 highly disciplined cadets of somewhat diverse backgrounds. Women and various minorities now account for 29 percent of the student body. Each cadet takes 15 required courses in mathematics, science, and engineering and 16 in social sciences, humanities, and public affairs; 4 intensive, summertime short courses in military science; and 11 year-long courses in physical education.

The 16,000-acre campus is an imposing array of parade grounds and great, gray-granite, fortress-like structures dominated by the stern Military Gothic of the Cadet Chapel. There are monuments to men with famous names, most of them graduates, most of them members of the historic cadet corps known as the Long Gray Line;

there are memorials to fallen classmates; and in the Old Cadet Chapel, built in 1836, one finds black marble shields inscribed in gold letters with the name, rank, and dates of birth and death of the senior American generals in the Revolutionary War.

West Point is a highly regarded academic and professional school with particular strengths in mathematics and engineering. Since 1922 West Point has produced more Rhodes scholars than all other colleges and universities in the nation, except for three. West Point is also a military post—the oldest, continuously occupied military post in the United States. It is a national historic site; and for many, it is a national shrine.

The academy opened as the Corps of Engineers at West Point, a strategically significant promontory on the Hudson River, 50 miles north of New York City, on hilly terrain already ringed with historic, Revolutionary War fortifications. Despite the fortifications, the British almost captured West Point, due to the perfidy of Major General Benedict Arnold, who offered to hand it over (along with General Washington and his staff) for a fee. (The inscription on Arnold's shield in the Old Cadet Chapel is chiseled out, except for the words "Major General" and "1741."

One clear lesson of the Revolutionary War was that the United States needed professionally trained military officers who were Americans, rather than French or Polish or German. However, anti-Federalist Jeffersonians wanted nothing to do with an officer corps made up of upper-class sons of the well-to-do. So, despite numerous proposals over the years, a military academy had to wait until Federalists were out of office and Federalist officers discharged from the army. Jeffersonians then could make appointments of instructors and cadets from all classes of people. Within two-and-a-half months of his inauguration, Jefferson ordered the immediate creation of a permanent military academy; less than a year later, Congress formally authorized the United States Military Academy at West Point, "for the purpose of training engineers." In the same legislative act, Congress reduced the size of the army and purged it of its Federalist officers. The idea behind both parts of this legislation was to shape a safe, non-aristocratic, standing army.

West Point is saturated with American history, and cadets know it well. They march past buildings named after President George Washington; Civil War generals Robert E. Lee, William T. Sherman, and Ulysses S. Grant; World War I general John "Black Jack" Pershing; World War II generals Omar Bradley, Douglas MacArthur, and Dwight David Eisenhower. They march past monuments in memory of fallen Union regulars in the

United States Military Academy at West Point

Civil War, fallen air cadets in World War II, fallen class-mates and all U.S. Armed Forces members who died in Southeast Asia. Two graduates became president of the United States (Grant and Eisenhower) and one, Jefferson T. Davis, became president of the Confederate States of America; West Pointers commanded armies in all of the country's wars (except the War of 1812); and several graduates have explored space and walked on the moon, including Edwin "Buzz" Aldrin and Frank Borman. The cadet corps has marched en masse to meals since 1815, and the corps' gray full-dress uniforms commemorate an 1814 victory by General Winfield Scott over British forces at the Battle of Chippewa, near Niagara Falls, New York. Because the Americans' uniforms were gray, rather than blue (the tailor was out of blue), the British thought that they were facing poorly trained militia instead of well-trained regulars.

The military academy had almost no impact on national affairs during its first 15 years, for reasons both administrative and political. Classes ran from April through November because the physical plant was not adequate for West Point winters. The Secretary of War from 1808 to 1813 was completely hostile to the idea of a military academy. His failure to issue "report to duty" orders to cadets who had been appointed to the academy meant that on the day in 1812 when war was declared, the United States Military Academy was empty.

Administrative reforms later that year put the academy on more solid footing by making faculty members exempt from duty requirements elsewhere and by making West Point a military academy for *all* branches of the army instead of just for engineers. In 1815, President James Madison sent a pair of officers to study military schools in France and Germany and to collect books and scientific instruments for use at West Point. One of the two officers, Sylvanus Thayer, was particularly impressed with France's *Ecole Polytechnique*'s outstanding teachers and scientists, its emphasis on mathematics, its small classes, and its blackboard drills for students. As West Point's first long-term superintendent (1817–33), Thayer had plenty of time to put into place much of what he learned in Paris. His ideas and practices had a profound impact on the academy, and had indeed, on the subsequent development of the naval and coastguard academies in the nineteenth century, and on the air force academy in the twentieth.

Thayer was appointed superintendent in 1817. His first days at West Point were inauspicious. Only 42 of 213 cadets were present for duty, and a number of them were "drinking and gambling and lounging about." Five of the faculty were under arrest for having protested his predecessor's policies, and six weeks after Thayer assumed command, his predecessor, Captain Alden Partridge, told a cheering cadet corps that he was taking his command back. It took several days for Thayer's letter about this turn of affairs to reach the Secretary of War and for a messenger to bring the reply to Captain Partridge: "You will deliver your sword to the bearer . . . and consider yourself under arrest."

Thayer immediately turned West Point into a military academy. Two days after he returned, this time firmly in charge, he ordered cadets to begin classes. He allowed no books of fiction, no newspapers, no unnecessary conversations at meals, and no trips to town. He established an extremely rigorous schedule for each academic day—every moment from reveille at dawn to lights out at 10:00 P.M. was accounted for. Cadets became soldiers as well as students. According to Thayer, being prepared for study assignments was a military duty. The shadow of Thayer's hand is very long indeed—cadets still face 16 hours a day of scheduled time, and being prepared for class is still a military duty.

Thayer's curriculum was equally formidable, and extraordinary in its own right. First-year students studied only mathematics and French. In the second year there was drawing, along with mathematics and French. Mathematics included algebra, Euclidean geometry, trigonometry, and logarithms during the first year, and geometry (analytical and descriptive), calculus, and "fluxions" during the second. Third-year students tackled mechanics, hydraulics, pneumatics, optics, magnetism, and astronomy, all under the heading of "natural philosophy," and in addition to ethics, fourth-year students learned civil engineering, field fortifications, the science of attack and defense, and principles of grand tactics.

The academy became the nation's first and, rather quickly, its most prominent engineering school. In 1830, 9 American colleges had West Point graduates on their faculties; ten years later, the number was 29; by 1860, West Point graduates were teaching at 78 institutions in 21 states. In addition, many of the nation's academic institutions used textbooks written (or translated from the French) by West Point faculty, and many academy-trained officers became civil engineers deeply involved in exploration, surveying, road and bridge building, canal design and construction, dam building, and railroad engineering.

West Point was not (and is not) simply in the business of turning out technically well-trained professionals, people with disciplined minds. To Thayer, the point of education was to develop character, and the way to develop character was to develop the soul and the body as well as the mind. *Character* meant military character: obedience to rules and schedules, unquestioning acceptance of authority, knowing one's place within a chain of command, commitment to duty, and commitment to being prepared at all times for anything that might happen or be needed. As it evolved, Thayer's definition of character as *duty* grew to include *honor* and *country.*

For the development of the mind, Thayer's approach required thorough and systematic preparations for performance, and then the performance itself. Classes were small, about 12 students each. The "Thayer principle of instruction" (as it has come to be called) was that every student would recite every day in every subject; that is, stand in front of the class, explain the theory involved in the day's lesson, and demonstrate its principles and practical operations at the blackboard, and do so according to a rigidly adhered-to formula; a mathematics class recitation might begin: "Sir! I am required to deduce a rule for extracting the nth root polynomials." Students were graded every day on their performance; at the end of four years, the cumulative grades for daily performance (and on the twice-yearly exams) determined class standing. Class standing—the rank order of merit—in turn determined a cadet's choice of branch of service and of duty location.

For the development of the soul, there was chapel. Attendance was compulsory. Officially nondenominational, services were essentially Episcopalian on the grounds that, as the army's first chief engineer, General Joseph Swift (and one of West Point's first two graduates) said it, such services "were deemed to be the most appropriate to the discipline of a military academy." Next, there was formal training in ethics that went beyond the classroom to include the thought-patterns and attitudes best summarized by West Point's famous honor code: "A cadet will not lie, cheat, or steal, nor tolerate those who do."

For the development of the body, there were athletics. Although athletics weren't available as such in Thayer's day, their development as a compulsory, four-year-long part of cadet life is certainly consistent with Thayer's scheme of things. In the early 1920s Superintendent Douglas MacArthur supplemented West Point's already excellent physical fitness programs with competitive athletic activities in which all cadets were required to partic- ipate. The idea was to develop some of the essential qualities of a fighting soldier: an aggressive, competitive spirit, the strength and endurance to surmount severe physical hardships, and the ability to lead.

At West Point, new students did not just "show up" for registration; they were civilians who reported for duty on an early July morning between the hours of 8:00 and 10:00 A.M. to become military cadets, and from that moment, their characters were under constant assault by smartly dressed, sharp-tongued upperclassmen wearing clean white gloves. The next six weeks were known as "Beast Barracks." In September, if they had survived the emotional, mental, and physical demands of "Beast Bar- racks," new cadets would become *plebes,* a Greek word which connotes "vulgar, coarse, common people": the lowest of the low. Plebes were subjected to severe mental and emotional stress by upperclassmen. This well- established (and notorious) custom has been known as "hazing." Congressional legislation in 1901 put a legal end to the forms of hazing which had become physical (and violent, after the Civil War), but almost two decades later, the "barking, hissing, and snarling" of upperclass- men drove one cadet to suicide. As superintendent, General MacArthur tried to halt the practice, without suc- cess. West Point continues to struggle with cadets who engage in hazing.

The first major American conflict after its founding— the American Civil War (1861–65), which pitted class- mate against classmate, had almost no impact on the activities at West Point. The war opened with West Point graduates firing at each other—P.G.T. Beauregard, a Con- federate general, had been superintendent of the academy (albeit briefly) just ten weeks earlier; the commander at the fort being fired upon (Fort Sumter) had been Beaure- gard's artillery instructor at the academy; and one of the Confederate officers firing a cannon had been graduated less than a year earlier.

By May 1861, three-quarters of the Southerners at West Point had resigned and gone to their home states. To staff the Union Army's officer corps, first-class cadets (seniors) were commissioned a month early. Early on, the engineering detachment of men and officers took the few remaining horses and left as well. Soon, every able-bod- ied officer had gone to war; however, they were soon replaced by the ever-increasing number of wounded. Apart from these departures, the routine at the academy proceeded as usual. Cadets were more interested in the increasingly popular sport of baseball—said to have been invented by West Point graduate Abner Doubleday—than in the war.

Early in the war a number of the military academy's graduates were charged with incompetence, charges that had some basis in reality. The West Pointers directing the Union's armies—George McClellan, Don Carlos Buell, Henry W. Halleck, and later John Pope, Ambrose Burn-

side, and Joseph Hooker—did a poor job. On the other hand, the armies of the Confederacy, which succeeded early on, were also commanded by West Point gradu- ates—Robert E. Lee, Thomas "Stonewall" Jackson, George Pickett, and James Longstreet. That the bonds forged at West Point were stronger than their sectional enmities is illustrated by the story that Grant sent con- gratulations across Petersburg's trenches to George Pick- ett on the birth of his child.

By the end of the war, West Pointers dominated the commands in both armies. Of the 296 graduates who sup- ported the Confederate states, 151 became general offic- ers, while in the Union Army the number was 294. Of the 60 most important battles in the war, all but five of the armies on both sides were commanded by West Pointers; in each of the other five, one of the commanders was a West Point graduate. West Point was one of the first insti- tutions to reunite after the war. In 1869, alumni from both sides formed an alumni association and chose Sylvanus Thayer as president.

After the Civil War, the intellectual and institutional in- breeding of the faculty turned the academy into a progres- sively rigid and unchanging institution, ever-mindful of its glorious origins and military traditions and out-of-touch with the real army's leadership needs. West Point ended up at the turn of the century more or less isolated from other colleges by its refusal to open up its totally pre- scribed curriculum, or to shift its emphasis from character building to the intellectual development of the individual.

When American entered World War I, once again a class was graduated early. The class of 1917 was gradu- ated in April, two weeks after the declaration of war against Germany, rather than in the usual commencement month of June. During this war, the high command of American armies was dominated by West Pointers to an even greater extent than it was during the Civil War. Of 38 corps and division commanders in France, 34 were West Pointers. The three field armies were all headed by West Point men, and the commander-in-chief of the American Expeditionary Force was academy graduate John J. Pershing.

After becoming superintendent in 1919—after the war's end—Douglas MacArthur asked, "How long are we going on preparing for the War of 1812?" MacArthur attempted a number of changes in faculty preparedness, in curriculum, and in the cadet corps' customary ways of doing things, but most were rescinded shortly after his term of office ended (two years early), or were resisted from the beginning by the governing board, the faculty, and the cadets.

American forces in World War II were led in both the- aters of war by West Point graduates. Forces in Europe were under the command of Dwight Eisenhower (who went on to become America's 34th president); those in the Far East were under the command of Douglas Mac- Arthur. Other West Point graduates who distinguished themselves in the conflict were Omar N. Bradley, George S. Patton, and Henry "Hap" Arnold.

After World War II, training programs and academic programs changed somewhat to reflect new technologies—for example, a sub-course was added in nuclear physics, as well as a course in applied psychology. In 1947, the earlier replacement of horse cavalry with mechanized armor led to the termination of horsemanship, polo, and the annual horse show at West Point. And questions about changing West Point and Annapolis to accommodate the new service that emerged from World War II were resolved in 1949 by the decision to open a separate academy for Air Force cadets.

Change finally came about under the superintendency of General Garrison Davidson (1956–60), in part because it had to: enrollments were declining and attrition rates were around 25 percent. West Point was not attracting students. Of those who came, too many left. The academy's image had been tarnished by the 1951 cheating scandal, which resulted in the expulsion of the entire varsity football team, including reserves. The cheating scandal, Davidson felt, came from a loss of perspective about why people were at West Point in the first place. In the area of military discipline and training, Davidson initiated a review of hazing practices and introduced changes in the way cadets were grouped together in companies, from how tall they were (a Thayer creation) to a combination of scholastic abilities, physical abilities, leadership potential, and height—for its day and for West Point, this was a radical change. In academics, Davidson urged faculty members to publish in professional journals and to keep current in their academic fields through occasional sabbaticals, and he required permanently assigned faculty members to obtain doctorates.

Davidson's regime ended before two events that profoundly affected West Point: the Vietnam War and another cheating scandal. The conflict in Vietnam was one of the few outside events to penetrate the otherwise isolated academy. Some new cadets arrived with a distrust of authority, rare for academy entrants; some upperclassmen hid wigs, which they wore on leave when in the company of long-haired civilian friends; and some of the faculty, mostly in social sciences, were quietly against the war. The class of 1966, which lost more members in Vietnam than any other West Point class, resigned at a rate 50 percent higher than classes from the 1950s and early 1960s. The second major scandal occurred in 1976 when 50 students were found guilty of cheating on an engineering examination. The reverberations of the scandal eventually led to the intervention of the Secretary of the Army.

In the end West Point changed. (One 1950s cadet refrain cynically referred to the academy as "120 years of tradition unmarred by progress.") Many of the reforms rejected or "studied to death" during the Davidson years were implemented by subsequent superintendents. Shifting to "positive leadership techniques over verbal abuse" almost immediately cut attrition rates during "Beast Barracks" from 10 percent to 5. "Beast Barracks" became "Cadet Basic Training." Mandatory attendance at chapel was ended by the Supreme Court in 1972. The prescribed curriculum was ultimately replaced by a core program of 31 academic courses plus 4 intensive short courses in military science and 4 year-long sessions of physical education. "Every cadet, every class, every day" is no longer required but it is still the standard for classroom performance.

By act of Congress, women were admitted to West Point (and to all the service academies) for the first time in 1976, 106 years after the first black was admitted (1870), and 99 years after the first black was graduated (1877). The top graduate in the class of 1995 was a woman.

West Point remains a military academy, of course, but sounds slightly civilian when it calls itself "the country's premier leader-development institution" and says that its mission is to train individuals "who will lead America into the twenty-first century."

Further Reading: Three books deal with the U.S. Military Academy in the context of all the service academies; all three are well documented and footnoted: *Liberal Education in the Service Academies* by William E. Simons (New York: Bureau of Publications, Teachers College, Columbia University, 1965); *Neither Athens nor Sparta?: The American Service Academies in Transition* (Bloomington and London: Indiana University Press, 1979); and *Soldiers and Scholars: Military Education and National Policy* by John W. Masland and Laurence I. Radway (Princeton, New Jersey: Princeton University Press, 1957). Ernest Dupuy provides a biography of one of West Point's most important figures in *Sylvanus Thayer, Father of Technology in the United States* (West Point, New York: The Association of Graduates, 1958).

—Richard Allen Chapman

UNITED STATES NAVAL ACADEMY
(Annapolis, Maryland, U.S.A.)

Location: On the south bank of the Severn River in Annapolis, Maryland; 33 miles east of Washington, D.C., and 30 miles southeast of Baltimore.

Description: A four-year service academy founded in 1845, as the Naval School.

Information: Candidate Guidance Office
United States Naval Academy
117 Decatur Road
Annapolis, MD 21402-5018
(410) 293-4361
(800) 638-9156

The Naval School, the forerunner of the Naval Academy, was founded in 1845, following a protracted struggle to demonstrate the need for an institution of its kind. Congress, the public, and many navy men alike long doubted the usefulness of academic instruction for sailors. Through the early nineteenth century, recruits were admitted into the navy very young, some just nine years old, and their entire education was practical and received aboard ship. An emphasis on workaday rather than academic instruction apparently explained the success of the British Navy over its colonial rivals, and the U.S. Navy emulated the British champions. Many of the earliest proposals for a naval school were advertised merely as a means to an orderly navy, for the young recruits were mainly incorrigible boys sent by schools and families unable to manage them.

Between 1800 and 1840, a number of individuals drafted a total of 26 different plans for a naval academy, but none was approved by Congress. Senators and representatives not only remained skeptical that sailors benefited from shore schooling, but they also worried that an academy would produce elitist officers out of spirit with contemporary liberalism. Two compromise programs were agreed to before the Naval School was organized. In 1813, Congress approved the appointment of schoolmasters to the navy's largest vessels, the 74-gun ships, but the program was a failure. Initially, teachers were paid and accommodated badly, and so the navy was unable to attract qualified men. Even after remuneration and facilities were improved and better teachers retained, the difficulty of educating children burdened with the duties of midshipmen proved insurmountable. Between 1821 and 1836, four shore schools (three of them housed in docked

frigates) opened, each running courses of one year or less to prepare midshipmen for their promotional exam.

The momentum behind the drive to found a proper naval academy was strengthened by two events. First, the U.S. Navy placed its first orders for steamships in 1839, and thereafter had an indubitable need for skilled engineers. Second, the esteemed Professor William Chauvenet, the head of the shore school in Philadelphia, formulated a plan for a two-year naval academy which might be opened without congressional sanction. Chauvenet's scheme was rejected by Secretary of the Navy John Mason, but a derivative plan was successfully instituted by Mason's successor, George Bancroft.

Bancroft moved quickly to establish the academy in the summer of 1845. First, he arranged for the U.S. Army to render Fort Severn to the U.S. Navy, where the Annapolis campus was soon located. Next, he dismissed half the navy's schoolmasters and reallocated their salaries to the inchoate school. He then appointed Commander Franklin Buchanan the school's first superintendent, and delegated him responsibility for its organization. Buchanan handled the job exceedingly well, and oversaw the inaugural ceremonies of the United States Naval School on October 10, 1845.

The school was originally housed in just eight small buildings already standing within the confines of Fort Severn, which was bordered by the Severn River and Annapolis Harbor on the eastern and northern sides respectively, and by bulwarks on its two inland faces. In 1845, a faculty of 7 instructed 36 midshipmen ranging in ages from 13 to 27. Programs of study varied in length according to the number of years each student had already served in the navy. The pupils received no military training per se, but were given a sound, general education thought to be well-suited to the duties of a naval officer; the curriculum included chemistry, ordnance, gunnery, steam engineering, history, composition, mathematics, natural science, geography, and either French or Spanish.

In 1846 Congress allocated $28,800 for infrastructural and academic improvement of the Naval School, despite Bancroft snubbing congressional authority when he created it. One may speculate that congressmen were loathe to appear insufficiently devoted to the military, for the Mexican-American War had begun just four months earlier. In any case, Congress continued to support the academy at Annapolis in their future budgets, and the school rapidly evolved: it was renamed the Naval Academy in 1850, the same year in which a fourth term of academic study was added. In 1851, Buchanan determined that the four years of academic study should run consecutively,

United States Naval Academy

rather than in pairs divided by two years at sea. Landfill added in 1853 extended the academy's grounds substantially on each of its two littoral fronts, and 29 buildings were raised on the campus between 1846 and 1861. By 1860, there were 28 members of the faculty, half of whom were civilian, and 281 midshipmen enrolled.

The rapid development of the academy was retarded by the Civil War, both because the navy devoted its resources to battle and because many cadets returned to the southern states from which they hailed. Following the Confederate attack on Fort Sumter, April 12, 1861, Superintendent George Blake worried that the civilian population of Annapolis would side with the South, and attack the school. Realizing that many of his students were either southerners or "little boys," Blake prepared to blow up the munitions on campus and flee with his pupils on the *USS Constitution,* which docked at Annapolis. His dire plan was not realized, however, thanks to the arrival of Union reinforcements who turned the campus into a military camp.

Blake requested and was granted provisions to temporarily move the academy to Fort Adams, in Newport, Rhode Island. Most of the students set sail for the new campus aboard the *Constitution* on April 26, led by the popular commandant, Christopher Rogers. Ten academy midshipmen were promoted to officers and commissioned to serve the Union Navy before the move, and 102 more just after. Thus, just 76 students remained in the first student body to reside at Fort Adams. The quality of education at the school declined severely during the war. Only 1,000 books were even unpacked at Newport, and new recruits were admitted only if they were literate. The faculty was constantly in flux, as its members were called into battle. Morale was severely battered by the loss of reliable leadership, the division of the departure of old mates for the Confederate states, and the general anguish of war. Meanwhile, the Annapolis campus was transformed into a Union Army hospital which proved so valuable that the academy remained at Newport even after Maryland was securely under Union control.

Following the war, Secretary of the Navy Gideon Welles determined to restore the Academy to its former stature, and to the haggard facilities at Annapolis. In September 1865, he wisely rendered responsibility for the renovation to Vice Admiral David Porter, whom he named the Academy's sixth superintendent. Porter was a man of demanding standards who asked specifically to head the school. He believed that a war with America's European rivals was immanent, and he expected to head the navy when that war began. Thus, he saw himself as training officers to serve under his command in battles not long in the future.

Porter secured generous funding for the academy through the political connections he had made in Washington during the war, and he used much of the money he had gathered to improve the campus. Shortly after taking office, Porter purchased three lots of land, totaling 81 acres, near or adjacent tot Fort Severn, and he embarked on

an ambitious building program. By 1869, the academy added an armory, engineering hall, chapel, chemistry laboratory, science building, and new midshipmen's residences. In addition, the former governor's mansion was transformed into a new library and offices for Porter himself.

Porter also reoriented the academy to provide an education more specifically geared toward naval duties. Most notably, he dismissed four civilian instructors and lured 21 bright naval officers to the faculty. He mounted a 13-inch gun on a sea-wall behind a classroom building, and cadets reportedly practiced their gunnery on it even while classes were held nearby. Porter retained two new gun boats on which cadets trained, and working models of sailing ships were constructed in a hall of the Department of Seamanship.

The academy fell on hard times in the years following Porter's departure for, at the same time, the navy's budget was drastically cut as national interest in the military waned. The number of fully commissioned ships fell from several hundred during the war to just 52 in the 1870s. Available positions for naval officers diminished, and the new superintendent, Francis Ramsey, responded with severe measures. In 1881, he instituted the practice of dismissing cadets whose academic progress was unacceptable, whereas previously they had simply been forced to repeat a year of study. The following year, Congress passed a resolution that the navy should appoint only as many officers from each graduating class as there were positions vacated the previous year. Graduates form the bottom of each class were dismissed with only diplomas and one year's severance pay ($950). Hundreds of men were turned away from the naval careers for which they spent six years preparing.

Morale at the academy, which obviously suffered under the draconian legislation of 1882, was improved by the acceleration of athletic programs at the school. Football matches against Johns Hopkins University in 1882–84 led to expanded seasons in the years following, and the navy "N" athletic letter was introduced by Cadet Dennis Michie in 1890. A goat was unofficially introduced as the school mascot in the army-navy game of the year. It was brought to the contest on a whim, and various other mascots were tried in succeeding years. Commander Colby M. Chester, commandant of cadets, is responsible for establishing a permanent place for "Bill the Goat." Colby had kept a goat aboard his ship prior to his service at the academy, and he persuaded the cadets to retain the goat as their own mascot.

The Spanish-American War erupted suddenly, when the Battleship *Maine* was blown up in Havana Harbor on February 15, 1898, killing 266 of her crew. It is still not known whether or not the Spanish were responsible for the explosion, but the war that Porter had predicted began nonetheless. The navy was short of junior officers due to the Congressional Act of 1882, and therefore the entire first and second classes from Annapolis were graduated early, and dispatched to the Caribbean. The Americans won the battle handily, and possibly the greatest change at the academy during the war was that the campus was partially transformed into an exceptionally civil prisoner camp. The captured Spanish Admiral Don Pascual Cervera y Topete and his crew were lodged in various buildings at the academy, and were allowed to visit Annapolis freely, having promised not to attempt an escape. The Spaniards were repatriated the following September.

Following the war in Cuba, the navy was rewarded with prestige, generous funding, and new territories in the South Pacific rendered by the Spanish, and the academy grew with the navy. Between 1901 and 1913, an entirely new plant was constructed, and the landfills of 1853 were extended still further north and east. The need for new junior officers in the fleet allowed the class of 1907 to graduate early, and in 1912, Congress provided that all graduates of the academy would automatically receive the status of ensign, thus eliminating the two-year probationary period of years past. In addition, the academy acquired a coat of arms in 1898, and a team fight song, "Anchor's Aweigh," in 1907.

It was during these years of growth and development that the academy offered its first postgraduate classes, designed to educate officers in burgeoning technological fields such as aviation and electrical engineering. The program was originally housed in two attic rooms, and was run by two instructors. In 1912, the Postgraduate Department of the Naval Academy was officially inaugurated, although degree-earning courses of study were then only completed at other institutions. It was not until after World War II that the school was moved across the nation to Monterey, California. Today, the Naval Postgraduate School educates approximately 1,800 students in 40 technical subjects.

The Naval Academy struggled with several issues during the period between the two world wars. First, the practice of hazing grew decidedly brutal in the early 1920s; plebes were routinely paddled by upperclassmen literally swinging from the ceiling, for example. Superintendent Henry Wilson, who assumed the leadership of the school in 1921, was a stern disciplinarian who brought order to the campus at the expense of creating a rather severe environment. In one instance, Wilson dismissed a midshipman wearing civilian clothes in town as he strolled with his new bride. At the same time, the United States ceased its production of new battleships for ten years by an agreement with the British and Japanese governments, thus reducing the number of officers' positions in the navy at a time when enrollment was soaring; between 1916 and 1919, an influx of patriotic recruits brought the student body from below 800 to more than 2,250. Ship production had hardly resumed when the effects of the Great Depression descended on the academy. Budget cuts in 1932 forced the navy to fire several civilian professors at the academy, and to commission only 216 of 413 graduates of the class of 1933. Happily, the men passed over were commissioned

the following year by an act of Congress, but the humiliating experience had a deleterious effect on the morale.

The Academy resumed an accelerated graduation schedule after America's entrance into World War II. The class of 1941 was graduated four months early, and a three-year curriculum was temporarily instituted beginning with the class of 1943. In addition, the admission and graduation of recruits was stepped up to meet the navy's personnel needs. Between February 1941 and June 1945, the academy produced 7,500 officers, 4,304 regular midshipmen, and 3,319 reservists. Academy graduates of the classes 1931–41 comprised the core of the navy's dangerous submarine, destroyer, and air squadron command, and approximately 12 percent of them were killed in action. However, except for the fact that many instructors were called into active duty and replaced by civilians, life for those young men remaining at the academy was little affected by the war.

The Academy graduated its first black midshipman, Wesley Brown, in 1949. Five blacks had been admitted to the academy previously, three shortly after the Civil War and two more in the 1930s, but all either failed out or resigned. Brown wrote of his experience at the academy in the *Saturday Evening Post,* where he reported having been subjected to extraordinarily harsh scrutiny during his first year. However, he claimed that after he passed through that trying time, he was thereafter treated fairly. "I never received special attention, either positive or negative," Brown wrote, "It was a lesson in democracy which many institutions could not imitate." Women did not win the right to enter the Naval Academy until 1976, and then only through an act of Congress that ran counter to the express wishes of the navy's leaders.

The academy has remained on a rather steady course since World War II. The campus was modestly extended by land purchases and new landfills in 1955, and more recently, the academy added the Nimitz Library, Rickover Hall engineering complex, and the Hendrix Oceanography Laboratory. The academic and practical curricula at the academy have evolved to meet the needs of a technologically advanced navy, of course. Classes in nuclear physics, jet propulsion, and electronics were added as early as the 1950s. The academy continues to enroll approximately 4,000 midshipmen, as it did in the late 1940s.

Further Reading: *The U.S. Naval Academy: An Illustrated History* by Jack Sweetman (Annapolis, Maryland: Naval Institute Press, 1979) is a well-written and readily available book covering all periods of the academy's development through 1979. *The Spirited Years: A History of the Antebellum Naval Academy* by Charles Todorich (Annapolis, Maryland: Annapolis Naval Press, 1984) is a very interesting book devoted to the formative years at the academy.

—Christopher Hoyt

UNIVERSITY OF ABERDEEN
(Aberdeen, Scotland)

Location: In central Aberdeen, 130 miles north of Edinburgh.

Description: A public university enrolling approximately 10,500 students in undergraduate, postgraduate, and professional faculties.

Information: University of Aberdeen
Regent Walk
Aberdeen AB9 1FX
Scotland
(01224) 272014
Fax (01224) 272086

Visiting: For information about touring the university, contact the university at the above address.

Few universities can claim a more intimate connection with the history and development of their region and people than the University of Aberdeen. For centuries, Aberdeen molded the opinion, beliefs, and character of Scots north of the River Tay. Aberdeen graduates provided most of the educated men in the north of Scotland. It has been said of the north in the nineteenth century that chances were that Aberdeen graduates would "baptise you, teach you, hire you, treat you when you were sick, draw up your will, and pronounce you dead."

It may also be said that Aberdeen has had a greater effect on the outside world than most other universities. The university for generations produced far more educated men and women than its lightly populated region could absorb, and in consequence its graduates have brought the benefits of an Aberdeen education to the ends of the earth.

In 1995, Aberdeen University celebrated the 500th anniversary of its founding in 1495 by William Elphinstone, Bishop of Aberdeen, under a bull of Pope Alexander VI, dated February 10, 1495. This charter had been requested by King James IV, and the foundation was officially laid for Saint Mary's College on September 17, 1505, with the promulgation of Bishop Elphinstone's constitution. It was renamed King's College shortly thereafter. Aberdeen was Scotland's third university after Saint Andrews and Glasgow and the fifth university in Britain. Note that, in the Scottish context, the university is the educational corporation and the college is the body of scholars—teachers and students—within the university.

Today Aberdeen also incorporates a second ancient university and college, Marischal College, founded in 1583. Marischal was often a fierce rival of King's College before their union on September 15, 1860, as the University of Aberdeen.

Alexander VI's founding bull noted the remoteness and barbarity of Aberdeen and the Scottish North, isolated "by firths and very lofty mountains" and "populated by rude and ignorant people." The bull authorized a *Studium Generale,* that is, a university, modeled on Bologna and Paris. Bishop Elphinstone's foundation was a medieval university primarily intended to spread literacy and the Gospel in this wilderness at world's end. It had four faculties: arts, law, medicine, and theology. The faculty of medicine, founded in 1497, was the first in the British Isles.

Elphinstone located the college in the sleepy Old Town of Aberdeen, a site dominated by the cathedral and monastic establishments. All officials and faculty of the college, except the Mediciner, were required to be ordained. The university's charter stipulated that the office of chancellor was to be held *ex officio* by the bishop. The university was to be supported by the revenues of an Augustinian hospital and several parishes. Liturgical ritual was integral to daily life. The importance of music was emphasized. King's College was tied more firmly to the church than any other university in Britain before or since, although it taught laymen as well as clerics. King's College remained staunchly Catholic until Protestantism was victorious. When that happened, King's found it difficult to adjust to the new religious climate.

On April 2, 1593, George Keith, Fifth Lord Marischal, a prominent reformer, founded another college and university in Aberdeen. Marischal and been on an unsuccessful commission to reform King's College to Protestant principles in 1582. When he became King's Commissioner for Aberdeen, Banff, and Kincardine in 1592, King's College came under his jurisdiction. His college, located in the New Town of Aberdeen, a vigorous commercial center and leading seaport of the kingdom, was probably intended to show King's College the path to reform by example. It was enthusiastically supported by the New Town's merchants as providing the educated men necessary for opening new European markets. The new foundation, Marischal College, had a single faculty: arts. It was funded by a number of confiscated church properties granted to the Lord Marischal by the king. Its practice was essentially the plan that reformers had attempted to impose on King's College. Marischal College was aggressively Protestant and required an entrance oath, eventually abolished in 1887, designed to exclude Catholics.

University of Aberdeen

Of the two colleges, Marischal was smaller, poorer, and had inferior buildings, but in the beginning its scholarship flourished, while that of King's languished. Early in the seventeenth century, the tide began to turn when Episcopalianism, favored by the king, arose as a moderate and conservative Protestant alternative to the more radical Presbyterianism.

When Patrick Forbes, a learned, pious man with great political and administrative skill, became Bishop of Aberdeen in 1618, he petitioned the king to improve the ruinous state of King's College. In response, the king sent a commission to examine both King's and Marischal Colleges. The commissioners were forcibly denied entrance to Marischal College, as Marischal saw the commission as interference by the bishop in the affairs of a rival college. The visitation of the commission resulted in the repair of King's College by using funds from the royal treasury and the restoration of offices that had been abolished by the reformers. Marischal received no royal largesse.

Bishop Forbes was an enthusiastic man who gathered to King's College a brilliant body of theologians who made Aberdeen first the most brilliant, and then the most oppressed town in the kingdom. Bishop Forbes and his coterie of Divines were so influential that they were respected by all and even influenced the teachings of Marischal College.

The bishop put the college library on firm footing, inspired benefactions, and introduced a printing press to Aberdeen in 1622. Most importantly, Forbes, a firm Presbyterian when consecrated bishop, became a leading proponent of the Episcopalian cause supported by the affirmative and vigorous "Aberdeen Doctors." These six professors, four from King's and two from Marischal College, put Episcopalianism on a firm philosophical footing and brought most of Aberdeen into its fold.

In 1638, the Covenant, a contract between God and Scotland based on Presbyterian principles, was circulated throughout the kingdom, and a majority in every town accepted it—except for Aberdeen. A commission came to implore and convince Aberdeen to sign. They were repulsed by the doctors, who argued, "If it were so, which we do not admit, why force it upon us?" In 1639, an army under Montrose came to force the town to sign. The chancellor of King's was deposed. The faculty was forced to sign the covenant, then deposed, and the Earl Marischal, chancellor of the rival college, was named governor of the town.

War between the Presbyterian Covenanters and the Episcopalian Royalists was the consequence. Aberdeen was conquered and would have been razed except for the intervention of the Earl Marischal. The town fathers were forced to sign the covenant, and Episcopalianism was suppressed. While these hostilities lasted only a year, they were the first in a series of religious wars waged intermittently throughout Scotland until the end of the Glorious Revolution in 1690.

The purge of King's College ended a decade in which Aberdeen was one of the most brilliant centers of culture, classical learning, and divinity in its time. Human learning was now disdained. One parson complained that the universal cry had become: "Downe doctrine and upp Chryste."

In 1641, King Charles I united the two colleges as "King Charles" or "The Caroline University." The union, which was marked by continual inquisitions, lasted until the restoration of the monarchy in 1661. (The only period when the colleges ceased operations in Aberdeen occurred during this period of union. In 1647, the plague struck and King's College students fled to Fraserburgh, while Marischal students were transferred to Peterhead.) Upon separation the colleges became acrimonious and confrontational rivals. Theology monopolized seventeenth-century Scottish thought, and perhaps the best that can be said for the two colleges is that they survived. Their survival and their maintenance of a measure of independent thought was in fact a triumph, as it has been said of the Presbyterian establishment during this time: "when the Scotch Kirk was at the height of its power, we may search in vain for any institution which can compare with it except the Spanish Inquisition." The rivalry between the colleges also impelled them to expand their curricula and erect new buildings in an attempt to outdo each other, with Marischal usually taking the lead.

In 1690, the Scots Parliament passed control of universities to the crown. It has been accurately said that "in the seventeenth century the Church ruled the Universities, during the eighteenth the Universities returned the compliment." Subscriptions to an oath of allegiance to the king and a confession of faith were demanded from university officials and faculty. Professorial positions were made competitive.

Aberdeen's universities cannot be said to have taken their oaths of allegiance seriously. The chancellor of Marischal College, the last Earl Marischal, and his younger brother, the famous Marshal Keith, rushed to the Jacobite cause in 1715. The Earl Marischal attended the raising of the standard on the Braes of Mar, which resolved to raise arms for the Old Pretender. The two brothers proclaimed James king at Aberdeen's market cross before the assembled universities. In retribution a royal commission in 1717 swept the universities virtually clean. Only one professor was left in his position. This was the fifth and last purge of the colleges. Never again has the university been officially involved in political issues. However, a legacy survives from the Jacobite rebellions. Many of the memorable songs and poems about the Jacobites appear to have been written by Aberdeen students and graduates.

This purge enabled the universities to concentrate on providing service to the community. The eighteenth century was a period of tremendous commercial growth for the city due to the improvement of the economic situation in Scotland as a result of the union of the English and Scottish Parliaments in 1707. Scotland had never been as prosperous before, and the universities reevaluated their role of educating the common man and providing an education suited to the needs of the people. In this, Marischal College led the way by placing a major emphasis on medicine and advancing the pure and applied sciences, coupled with modern philosophy. Some of Marischal's professors attained distinction and gave life to the intellectual culture of Aberdeen. Thomas MacLaurin, the one mathematician of the first rank to be trained in Britain, held the mathematics chair for eight years and produced some of his best work during that time. Patrick Copeland made Marischal famous for popular physics, erected an astronomical observatory, set up Aberdeen's first museum and, for three years starting in 1785, gave evening courses in mechanics to the public. The attempts of King's to move in a similar direction faltered as protests from its graduates kept it rooted in classical learning and philosophy.

In the eighteenth century, university curricula were standardized. Specialized teaching was introduced at Marischal, replacing the previous practice of "regenting," where each professor taught the entire curriculum. This destroyed the rigidity of education and gave professors the scope to expand their interests and depth of learning. Unfortunately, among Scottish universities, Aberdeen's colleges were slowest to change and, in change, King's was well behind Marischal. Regenting was not replaced by the specialized teaching of the professorial system at King's until 1799. It was the last Scottish university to do so. It is a measure of King's conservatism that Edinburgh, the youngest of Scottish universities, had been first to eliminate regenting in 1700.

Various attempts to unite the two colleges failed in the eighteenth century, as did attempts by both colleges to establish their own medical schools rather than just continue with lecture-based faculties of medicine.

The Universities (Scotland) Act of 1858 united King's and Marischal Colleges on September 15, 1860, as the University of Aberdeen. Arts and divinity were taught at King's. Law and medicine were taught at Marischal. King's buildings were expanded to accommodate the influx of arts students from Marischal, and a new library was built at King's. Aberdeen got, together with Edinburgh, a seat on the General Medical Board. The act of 1858 established universities as little scholarly republics in the midst of the secular world by providing a democratic structure of university governance, government funding, government building maintenance, and consolidation of bursaries to provide professors with adequate compensation. The importance of this act cannot be overestimated. It made the Scottish universities financially secure, public institutions free from government interference. Through the Representation of the People (Scotland) Act of 1868, the University of Aberdeen shared a seat in parliament with Glasgow University.

Medicine finally achieved a firm footing in the nineteenth century, and by 1893 Aberdeen had 367 medical students. Women were admitted to graduation in 1892, and the university took the rough outline of the form it has today with the establishment of a science faculty in 1894. It is interesting to note that the great majority of female graduates from 1894 to 1942 were over 40 years of age at graduation.

Aberdeen graduates have made their mark. Alumni have been governors of Newfoundland and Canada, Jamaica, Barbados, Lagos, Nyasaland, the Gold Coast, Ceylon, Hong Kong, the Straits Settlements, Queensland, Tasmania, South Australia, and the Windward Islands.

Men of letters associated with the university include: Dr. John Arbuthnot, originator of John Bull; Thomas Urquhart, translator of Rabelais and biographer of the Admirable Crichton; Arthur Johnson, "The Scottish Ovid"; John Skinner, songwriter acclaimed by Robert Burns; James Beattie, the poet; James Macpherson of Ossian fame; George Macdonald, teller of commonplace and mystical tales; and the novelist Eric Linklater.

Other graduates were instrumental in founding the College of William and Mary, the University of Pennsylvania, McGill University, and the Universities of Toronto, Manitoba, Saskatchewan, Alberta, South Africa, Capetown, Madras, Calcutta, Singapore, Hong Kong, Queensland, Western Australia, Sydney, Tasmania, and Otago, and the College de Marine in St. Petersburg.

Aberdeen alumni have dominated the field of tropical medicine through founding institutions for the study and treatment of tropical diseases: James Cantlie founded the Royal Society of Tropical Medicine and Hygiene; Patrick Manson founded the Hong Kong College of Medicine and the London School of Tropical Medicine; and John Simpson founded the London Hospital for Tropical Diseases.

Aberdeen graduates identified the causes of malaria and blood poisoning, discovered insulin, introduced the medical scanner, and founded the British Army Medical Corps. In 1949, the Nobel Peace Prize was awarded to Lord John Boyd Orr of Brechin, director of the university's Rowett Research Institute and professor of agriculture, organizer and director general of the United Nations Food and Agricultural Organization, president of the National Peace Council and the World Union of Peace Organizations.

The university is still centered about its old colleges and their architectural splendors. Marischal College, with its perpendicular facade, has been called the finest granite building in the world. King's College still retains its beautiful sixteenth-century chapel with crown tower hard by the old Cathedral, its lovely quadrangle, and its old Senator's Room and fine library.

Growth in recent years has centered around the King's College site, where there has been ample room for expansion. The spacious Old Aberdeen campus of King's College, once limited to the arts and divinity faculties, is now home to most departments. Here are the modern chemistry and physics buildings, the Queen Mother Library, science library, language laboratories, agricultural building, natural history building, refectories, residences, and gymnasium. Marischal College in the city center is today primarily devoted to administration. Today King's College and Marischal College have little identity except as the names of groups of buildings. Other university units include the clinical medical facilities centered at Foresthill, the athletic facilities at Seaton Park, and the Culterty Field Station, an internationally known center for teaching and research in animal ecology adjacent to the Forvie National Nature Reserve.

The university has shown tremendous expansion in the past 50 years. Between 1860 and 1955, the university graduated a total of 5,739 students, of whom 1,336 were women. In 1964, the student population had grown to 2,520, of whom 897 were women. Today British universities have embraced the concept of mass education, and Aberdeen now numbers over 10,500 students in undergraduate and postgraduate studies in four faculties that encompass 28 departments. The faculties are: arts and divinity; medicine and medical sciences; science and engineering; and social sciences and law.

Many Aberdeen graduates will have to find employment outside Scotland and even outside Britain. This has always been assumed. Scots regard themselves as a migratory race. The view that highly trained individuals are likely to leave Scotland to seek employment elsewhere is almost part of Scottish folklore.

Today the university is a forward-looking institution whose quality of education is strong. Aberdeen enters its sixth century, reflecting on its history, but more intent on developing and modifying the university to meet the needs of a changing world with a technological future. The university's dedication to this vision is shown by a particular emphasis given research and education in medicine, the sciences, and technology.

Further Reading: The following books cover different periods of Aberdeen's long history: John D. Hargreaves, editor, *Aberdeen University, 1845–1981: Regional Roles and National Needs* (Aberdeen: University of Aberdeen, 1989); John Malcolm Bulloch, *A History of the University of Aberdeen, 1495–1895* (London: Hodder and Stoughton, 1895); and Roger L. Emerson, *Professors, Patronage and Politics: The Aberdeen Universities in the Eighteenth Century* (Aberdeen: University of Aberdeen, 1992).

—Edward S. Margerum

UNIVERSITY OF AIX-MARSEILLE
(Marseille and Aix-en-Provence, France)

Location: The university has several campuses in Marseille, from the old central part of Marseille to outlying suburban territory. The research facility for geoscience and environmental studies is at the Technopole de l'Arbois campus north of Marseille. Aix-en-Provence is just northeast of Marseille.

Description: Three state institutions operated under the jurisdiction of the Minister of Education and financed by the state, offering undergraduate, graduate, and professional degrees.

Information: Université de Provence (University of Aix-Marseille I)
3, Place Victor Hugo
13331 Marseille Cedex 03
France
(91) 95-90-71

Université de la Méditerranée (University of Aix-Marseille II)
Jardin du Pharo
58, Boulevard Charles Livon
13284 Marseille Cedex 07
France
(91) 39-65-00
Fax (91) 31-31-36

Université de Droit d'Economie et des Sciences d'Aix-Marseilles (University of Aix-Marseille III)
3, Avenue Robert Schuman
13268 Aix-en-Provence Cedex
France
(42) 20-19-05

The educational heritage of the cities of Aix and Marseille is very old and is reflective of the Mediterranean heritage of the area. For over 2,000 years, educational institutions have continuously existed in the two cities. These schools have been the epitome of the educational state of the art for each era. Today, three modern universities exist in Aix and Marseille; they developed as a result of the changing needs of society and continue to meet the needs of the future. Although the goal today is to prepare students for the complex and technical modern world, their roots may be found in Greek schools and a medieval university.

Five centuries before Christ, Greek colonists founded the city of Phocea at the present site of Marseille. The schools established in the city continued to grow and flourish after the Roman conquest of the area. Aix, founded four centuries after Marseille, and located just to the northeast, became the capital of the Roman province of *Gallia Narbonensis Secunda,* the earliest center of Roman culture in Gaul, and its last refuge after Rome's fall. The region itself became known as Provence, from latin for the word "province." As a population and governmental center, Aix was also an important center of Roman education.

The Roman schools in Aix continued long after the Romans themselves were gone. The cathedral school at Aix, usually intended solely for the training of clergy, grew out of the earlier institutions. As as result, the syndics of the city of Aix retained a voice in appointing the *scholastics* who actually presided over the school, giving the school more secular atmosphere than usual. Some writers have referred to the school in Aix as a "university" before 1400, but the school itself appears to have been limited in scope and authority. The only example found of a law degree granted at Aix before 1400 (in 1302) seems to have been an exceptional event and was apparently done for political reasons.

Political and secular needs led to the founding of a real university in Aix. By the late fourteenth century, rulers required for educated administrators and judicial officials to handle the increasingly complicated affairs of state. At the same time, secular rulers were increasingly anxious to assert their power over religious authorities in their dominions, by means of schools which were not intended mostly for educating clergy. For these reasons in 1409, Louis II, King of Jerusalem and Sicily and Count of Provence, established a *studium generale* in his capital of Aix. The new school drew upon and grew out of the earlier cathedral school and included the traditional university's faculties of theology, law, and medicine.

The new school had to be recognized by papal bull to formally attain the status of university. Alexander V, just named pope by the Council of Pisa and in the shadow of the Great Schism, was anxious to secure his own position with the aid of a powerful ally such as Louis. Upon petition by Louis, the Pope issued a bull recognizing the University of Provence with all the faculties and privileges granted to earlier universities at Paris and Toulouse, and allowing it to grant degrees. To insure the new university's success, Louis decreed that all university students from Provence had to study at Aix or their degrees would not be recognized.

The letters patent for the university were issued in 1413, and established the government of the university. The archbishop of Aix was made the first chancellor of the university for the remainder of his life. Upon his death, a new chancellor was elected by the rector, masters, and licentiates—an unusual arrangement not repeated at any other French university. The rector was to be a "simple student," who had unlimited civil and criminal jurisdiction in all cases where one party was a doctor or scholar of the university. Those dissatisfied with the rector's decisions could appeal to a *doctor legens*. Eleven *consiliarii* assisted the rector, being elected annually by their predecessors. These men represented all three faculties, but were elected from among the students. The constitution was of a student-university; and the instructors had no great authority except in conferring degrees.

The Duchy of Provence was acquired by France in 1487. The continued existence of the University of Provence was confirmed by Louis XII, and Aix continued to be an important provincial center. It was, for example, the seat of a provincial parlement from 1501 to 1789, no doubt aided by the presence of the law faculty.

In 1603, Henry IV, created the *College Royal de Bourbon* in Aix for the study of belles lettres and philosophy, complementing the traditional faculties of the university, but not officially a part of it. This *college de plain exercise* became an important seat of learning, under the control of the Jesuit order. During the sixteenth and seventeenth centuries, the college served most often as a preparatory, but unaffiliated, school for the university. Only the university could grant degrees in theology, law, and medicine; but candidates for degrees had first to pass an examination in philosophy, which was only offered by the college. Universities often accepted only candidates who had studied in colleges legally affiliated with them, which in practice, required both college and university to be located in the same city. In 1762, the Jesuits were expelled from France, and in 1764, the *College Royal de Bourbon* was formally affiliated with the University of Provence as a faculty of arts.

The addition of the *College Royal de Bourbon* broadened the scope of courses offered at the University of Provence. Formal instruction in the French language was first offered at the college, with texts and a structured course of study. Physics later became a part of the curriculum at the college as a part of the philosophy course in the 1700s. Equipment for conducting experiments was purchased and the first course in experimental physics was offered at Aix in 1741. Newtonian physics, however, was only taught after 1755, when the physicist Paulian offered his first class and Newton's *Principia* and commentaries were purchased for the library.

The French Revolution, with its emphasis on the individual and an end to inherited privilege, saw the suppression of the universities. To the revolutionaries, universities represented bastions of corporatism and established interests. In addition, lands possessed by the universities and used for their support, represented a source of wealth to be tapped by the revolutionary government, just as property owned by the Church had been confiscated. In 1792, the University of Provence, along with 21 other universities, was dissolved. Specialized *ecoles,* with rigorous entrance examinations and open to anyone with talent, were eventually established to provide professional training in specialized areas. Even so, the government found it necessary to allow the faculties of law and medicine to continue in Aix and Marseille in the early 1800s.

Throughout the nineteenth century, additional faculties were established in Aix and Marseille to serve the changing needs of French society For example, Hippolyte Fortoul, later Napoléon III's Minister of Education, was the first dean and professor of a new faculty in French literature created in Aix-en-Provence in the 1840s. In 1896, the departmental council of the Bouches du Rhone founded a chair in the faculty of letters at Aix in the language and literature of Mediterranean Europe; their purpose was to assist the commercial exploitation of the region by French business. A new science faculty was established in Marseille to assist in the growing industrialization of the region. At about the same time, a special training program was established in the faculty of medicine to train doctors in colonial medicine for France's expanding colonial empire.

The most important development for the university in the nineteenth century, however, was the reestablishment of French universities in 1896. Facing competition from prestigious German universities following the Franco-Prussian War, French legislators were anxious to have their own universities. In 1896, a law was passed, establishing 17 autonomous regional universities financed largely by the state. The various faculties in Aix and Marseille were grouped into the new University of Aix-Marseille.

Through two world wars and a depression, the University of Aix-Marseille continued to grow. Increasing numbers of women and foreign students joined the student body, and a majority of students majored in the science, medicine, and law faculties. By the late 1960s, however, many students were gripped with a growing sense of the universities as cold, sterile places, which turned out graduates unlikely to get jobs. Individual faculties were nearly autonomous from university administration and the Ministry of Education often intervened directly among the faculties. Following riots among university students in Paris in 1968, a reform of French education took place. The *Loi d'Orientation de l'Enseignement Superieur* of 1968 divided the old faculties into smaller subject departments, reduced the power of the Ministry of Education, and established smaller universities, with strengthened administrations. In line with this, the University of Aix-

Marseille was divided into two institutions. Each university has differing areas of concentration of study and the faculties are divided as follows:

Aix-Marseille I: history; letters; psychology; sociology and ethnology; philosophy; mathematics; physics; chemistry; natural sciences; Anglo-American, Oriental, Slavonic, Romance, and Germanic languages; literature; and civilization.

Aix-Marseille II: economic science, geography, technology, medicine, pharmacy, dental surgery, tropical medicine, physical education, and oceanic sciences.

Aix-Marseille III: law, political science, applied economics, math and computer science, earth science, ecology, and technological studies.

Like all French universities, the three modern universities are administered by three elected boards, composed of elected representatives of the university community and appointed members from outside academia. The first is the board of administration (*Conseil d'Administration*), which determines general policy for the university, votes the budget, and approves programs and degrees. The second board is the scientific board (*Conseil Scientifiques*), which oversees research and teaching practices in the university. The final board is the board of studies and university life (*Conseil des Études et de la Vie Universitaire*), which advises the board of administration on issues and is concerned primarily with student life in all aspects, such as the library, medical care, and sports. All three boards jointly elect a president every five years from among the faculty of the university. The president represents the university in all official acts, administers university property, and hires all university personnel. He or she is also chair of all three boards and is responsible for law and order within the university.

In response to the increasingly technical nature of the world, the universities established the "Technopole de L'Arbois," an industrial and scientific park devoted to advances in the sciences. The site consists of 10,000 acres of land situated between Aix and Marseille. Access is easy from the International Airport of Marseille-Provence and a high speed train station is planned for the site. Backers hope the center will develop into a real partnership between university and industry to create the technology of the future.

The University of Aix-Marseille, in all its past manifestations and in all its present forms, has been a source of education and learning for the society which produced it. The emphasis has differed at various times, but the institutions, which have existed continuously for over 2,000 years, have strived to meet the needs which have arisen. Today, the three modern universities, with their different concentrations of study, provide education for the increasingly complex and technical Mediterranean world around it.

Further Reading: Hasting Rashdall's *The Universities of Europe in the Middle Ages* (Oxford: Clarendon Press, 1936) is the best starting point for information specific to the founding and early years of the University of Provence. A more modern complement, both in coverage and in publication date is *A History of the University in Europe* (Cambridge: Cambridge University Press, 1992). Other useful works that describe the French university system, with helpful information about the University of Aix-Marseille include L.W.B. Brockliss, *French Higher Education in the Seventeenth and Eighteenth Centuries: A Cultural History* (Oxford: Clarendon Press, 1987); George Weits, *The Emergence of Modern Universities in France, 1863–1914* (Princeton, New Jersey: Princeton University Press, 1983); and R.D. Anderson, *Education in France 1848–1870* (Oxford: Clarendon Press, 1975). The best source of information about the modern universities in Aix and Marseille, however, is through the Internet, using the universities' home pages: http://newsup.univ-mrs.fr/ (Universite de Provence); http://www.univ-aix.fr/ (Universite de la Mediterranee); and http://www.u-3mrs.fr/uIII/ (Universite de Droit d'Economie et des Sciences d'Aix-Marseille).

—Tim J. Watts

UNIVERSITY OF ALCALÁ DE HENARES
(Alcalá De Henares, Spain)

Location: Central Alcalá de Henares, Spain, 20 miles east of Madrid.

Description: An important university from the sixteenth to the eighteenth centuries, once attended by as many as 12,000 students and rivaling the University of Salamanca in importance. The university was transferred to Madrid in 1836 and restored to Alcalá de Henares in 1977.

Information: Universidad de Alcalá de Henares
Plaza de San Diego, s/n
28801 Alcalá de Henares
Spain
885 40 00

Visiting: Visits to the university and its historic sites can be arranged through the municipal tourism office in Alcalá de Henares.
Oficina Municipal de Turismo
Callejón de Santa María, 1
28801 Alcalá de Henares
Spain
889 26 94

The University of Alcalá de Henares has a long and impressive history, although the current institution bears little resemblance to the one that flourished for several centuries beginning in the early sixteenth century. The history of the city itself is closely tied to that of the university, and the one cannot be examined without the other. While the city's history is tied primarily to the university, Alcalá is also known as the birthplace of Catherine of Aragon, Queen of England, and Miguel de Cervantes, author of *Don Quixote de la Mancha*. Cervantes is the city's favorite son, and the central square is named in his honor. In addition, tradition holds that Christopher Colombus visited Alcalá to propose his expedition to Queen Isabel, and many argue that he returned to the halls of the university to report on his findings.

The history of the site itself goes back at least to Roman times when an important city developed in the Henares Valley at the confluence of two rivers, thus the early name *Complutum*. The alluvial soils in the area are very fertile and the land has long supported considerable agricultural production. Archeological remains from the area include a number of well-preserved mosaic floors, as well as ceramics, from this early period. The area later came under the control of the Moors, and from them the town gets the name *Alcalá*, or "the castle." Many other towns in Spain share this name, thus the addition of the name of the river valley, Henares.

It was in Alcalá on May 20, 1293, that Sancho IV, King of Castille, signed the documents that founded an *estudio general,* the earliest known educational institution to have existed in Alcalá de Henares, and a precursor to the modern university. Why Sancho would select this site, one with no tradition of educational activity, is an interesting question which some have attempted to answer based on some fabulous stories concerning the area. One history recounts how, in 711, the fabled table of Solomon, an immense green table with 365 legs, was found there. Like the fabled Ark of the Covenant, the table was thought to have been lost somewhere in the east. How it could have arrived in the Henares Valley is a mystery. The purported rediscovery of Solomon's table is said to have led to the construction of both a palace and a church at Alcalá by Don Rodrigo. This fantastic history and the rather spurious attachment to Solomon, a man of great wisdom, may have led Sancho to found the *estudio general* in Alcalá. A more probable explanation may be that the growing prestige of the university at Salamanca led Sancho to seek to establish an institution to rival it. Whatever the inspiration for Sancho, the creation of the school was ratified by the Archbishop of Toledo, Gonzalo García Gudiel. The institution benefited further from grants of land from the popes of the Catholic church, and it continued to grow and prosper into the fifteenth century. Unfortunately, the history of this early educational institution is essentially lost; not until the late 1400s does the history of the modern university begin to appear.

The dates associated with the foundation of the university vary greatly in historical accounts, as do the names of the principals involved. However, some dates are certain, and key individuals are well known. It was around 1495 that Cardinal Cisneros proposed transforming the *estudio general* into a university, and on April 13, 1499, Pope Alexander IV issued a papal bull conceding the transformation. The first students began studying at the university in 1508. In 1512 King Ferdinand recognized the university and granted his patronage.

Cardinal Cisneros had a vision for a university that would take as its principal mission the study of religion and the training of clergymen. He envisioned a reorganization of theological studies at the university. It did not take long for the university to establish its reputation in the area of religious studies, as well as in the study of languages and letters. Among the high points in the university's history is the publication, circa 1517, of the famous Polyglot Bible or *Biblia Complutensis,* which contained parallel texts in Hebrew, Latin, Greek, and Chaldean. The undertaking was very expensive, and only 600 copies were ever printed. Of those 600, only 3 were printed on velum. One of those copies can still be seen in Alcalá today. Modern biblical critics do not regard the text very highly and, in a sad turn of events, the original manuscripts no longer exist. Tradition holds that these manuscripts, along with other important documents, were sold by a university librarian to a fireworks maker to be used in the construction of rocket cases. It seems that the space they took up in the archives was needed for other purposes.

The university of Alcalá de Henares is also known for the contribution its scholars made at the Council of Trent. Among its well-known alumni are counted Saint Ignatius of Loyola and Saint Thomas of Villenueve.

In 1687 King Carlos II granted Alcalá the title of town, a distinction won in large measure because of the importance of the university. At its height the city boasted 38 churches, 21 convents, and 27 religious centers. During this period the university is believed to have grown to an enrollment of as many as 12,000 students. By the time Alcalá was granted the title of town, the university campus was well established, based on the carefully laid-out plans of Cisneros and his assistants.

Throughout the eighteenth century the university suffered a decline which corresponded to the loss of Spanish power and prestige throughout the world. Enrollments declined, and the stature of the faculty also suffered. The growth in importance and prestige of neighboring Madrid also led to a diminished position for Alcalá de Henares. These factors led to the transfer of the university to Madrid in 1836. The city of Alcalá de Henares suffered a serious decline thereafter. The decline of the town appears to have been so complete that, by as early as 1845, one handbook for travelers to Spain refers to Alcalá as "a poor and ignorant place; for the removal of the university to Madrid has completed its ruin, and, like Salamanca, it is a shadow of the past." The worst, however, was yet to come. The depth of Alcalá's decline came some years later, during the Spanish Civil War, when many of its architectural treasures were destroyed. Then nearly all of its religious structures were destroyed during the period from 1931–39, but many of the structures associated with the university survived. During the 1940s and 1950s the town was little more than a stopping point between Madrid and Guadalajara, but during the 1960s Alcalá began to benefit from the growth of the industrial sector and the spread of Madrid—Alcalá has now become essentially a suburb of the city.

In 1977 a royal decree restored the university and it now houses colleges of medicine and pharmacy as well as a polytechnical school and the Juan Carlos I botanical gardens. The re-established university also has a center in Guadalajara, including its summer language course in Spanish for foreigners.

While the university is no longer the prestigious institution it once was, many people visit Alcalá for its historical significance. The most important remaining sites in the city are associated with the university as it was planned by Cardinal Cisneros. The university was laid out in a careful pattern with two long perpendicular roads radiating from the central square. One road was planned to house the colleges and the other the book-dealers. Under the direction of architect Pedro Gumiel the major buildings of the university were constructed very quickly during the first half of the sixteenth century. Perhaps the most important building on campus is the Colegio Mayor de San Idelfonso (Saint Idelfonso's Residence Hall). Begun in 1537 and completed in 1553, the building has a distinct *mudéjar* style, drawing from the Moorish tradition. Especially noteworthy is the building's facade which is a fine example of Spanish plateresque. Rodrgrigo Gil de Hontañon, the architect of the Colegio Mayor de San Idelfonso, is also renowned for his work on the cathedrals in Salamanca and Segovia. Another important structural element at the site is the intricate and detailed ironwork of the building's grills.

Other structures of note include two residence cloisters, an assembly hall, and a chapel. Of these, the chapel is the most interesting. It contains striking elements of gothic, *mudéjar,* and Renaissance elements, including a coffered ceiling and interlacing arches. It has been termed one of the finest examples of the early Spanish Renaissance style. Many original elements from the building, including the altarpiece and the choir stalls, which disappeared after the university was moved to Madrid, have now been replaced. Cisnero's Tomb, the final resting place of the cardinal, is one of the focal points of the chapel. Its iconography is a unique mix of religious and secular, including the church fathers and allegories of the liberal arts. It is a fitting tribute to this Christian humanist and founder of the university.

Numerous other buildings erected during the sixteenth and seventeenth centuries were originally convents and colleges which were eventually annexed to the university. Among these are Saint Catherine's College, Saint Peter and Saint Paul's College, and King's College. Considerable restoration work has been done on these structures and most are open to the public, although many now house government and private offices.

Among the most important of the local buildings outside the university is the Palace of the Archbishops of Toledo. The structure was completed around 1534 and houses the archives of the kingdom. Among its most interesting exhibits are the Polyglot Bible and the constitution of the university. In addition to its archives, the building also houses a small archeological museum.

The glory of both the university and the city of Alcalá de Henares are long past, and only a flavor of those times remains today. However, the influence of this once-great institution can be seen in everything from Catholic church doctrine to the first universities in the Americas.

Further Reading: Most of the histories that deal extensively with this university and its history are available only in Spanish although it is discussed at least briefly in most major English-language travel guides. Even in the works in Spanish, this site and the university generally merit only a few paragraphs. Peter Lineham's *History and the Historians of Medi-eval Spain* (Oxford: Clarendon Press, 1993) contains a nice treatment of the founding of the university and the historical figures involved. A number of informational guides published by the Ayuntamiento de Alcalá de Henares are useful, especially one on patrimony and history and another on culture. The text in these publications is in Spanish, French, and English. The university itself has also published a number of pamphlets, maps, and guides discussing both the history of the university and its current status and configuration.

—Michael D. Phillips

UNIVERSITY OF ARIZONA
(Tucson, Arizona, U.S.A.)

Location: Tucson, Arizona, surrounded by the Santa Catalina Mountains and the Sonora desert.

Description: A state university enrolling over 32,000 students in undergraduate, graduate, and professional schools.

Information: Registrar and Director of Admissions
University of Arizona
Tucson, AZ 85721
U.S.A.
(602) 621-3237 (undergraduate)
(602) 621-3132 (graduate)

Visiting: Student Services provides information and campus tours from the Visitor Center. Information desks are located on the main floor of the Student Union Building.

When the Territory of Arizona was created in 1863, its legislature immediately began discussing a public educational institution. John N. Goodwin addressed the body on this topic, proclaiming that "self-government and education are inseparable. . . . The common school, high school, and the University should all be established and are worthy of our fostering care." In 1864, the creation of a territorial university was formally proposed and its constitution was written, a board of regents was established, and income from the sale of public lands was provided. Soon, however, the uncertainties of life in Arizona brought progress to a halt; Regent Gilbert W. Hopkins was killed by Apaches, an event which illustrated the more pressing concerns of the territory's settlers.

Plans for the university were put on hold until 1885. At this time, with the Apache wars drawing to an end, the legislature was ready to put in place its territorial institutions: the capital, an insane asylum, the state prison, a university, and a teachers' college. Tucson, which had been the capital from 1867 to 1879, was now competing with other communities for this status; the asylum and prison, with their appropriations, were also considered plums. The university, however, was looked on skeptically and many Tucson residents shared the sentiments of a bartender who sneered "What do we want with a university? What good will it do us? Who ever heard of a University Professor buying a drink?" Other practical concerns also made the idea of a university seem slightly ridiculous. Who would attend a university when there was not one high school in the territory?

Nevertheless, the legislative assembly passed a bill appropriating $25,000 for the school, stipulating that 40 acres of land must be secured for its location by the end of the year. It appeared that the funds would indeed lapse, when no offer of land was forthcoming. Only Jacob S. Mansfield, a Prussian-born merchant and a member of the board of regents, showed an interest in promoting the university's cause. Mansfield believed that the university would be beneficial to Tucson's development and proceeded to search for a potential location. In May 1886, he selected a site east of town, a piece of land owned by E.C. Gifford, Ben C. Parker, and William S. Read (who would become identified as gamblers and a saloon-keeper in university legend). It took Mansfield months to convince the men to donate the land to the board of regents, but they finally did so on November 27, 1886.

One year later ground was broken for the first university building. Soon the course of events hit another snag, as the regents ran out of money before the building was completed. It took four more years to acquire more funds from the legislature, at which time the building finally received its roof and windows. In 1890 the university was officially ready for business, having created a college of agriculture, a college of mines and engineering, and an agricultural experiment station. The inclusion of agricultural studies had been inspired by the Hatch Act of 1887, which provided an annual $15,000 grant for any land grant institution that had an experiment station.

When classes began in autumn of 1891, there were 6 professors and 32 students at the University of Arizona. Only nine of the students were of college rank; for the next 35 years the school would have to provide preparatory courses in addition to a college curriculum. Mining and agricultural courses were supplemented by enough liberal arts courses to satisfy degree requirements. Practically all activities were held at the new university building, which became known as Old Main. It provided space for classrooms, laboratories, the library, an assembly hall, as well as living quarters for students and faculty. A Chinese cook was hired to feed the residents.

These modest beginnings set the tone for some years. In 1895 the school's first graduating class numbered just three, two women and one man. For 20 years, the graduating classes did not exceed ten students; degrees were not granted until 1917. In part, the slow growth of the university was following the fortunes of the city of Tucson. By 1920, enrollment had grown to 1,000, while the city's pop-

University of Arizona

ulation reached 20,292. The construction of a new stadium and the creation of a school of music reflected a new optimism about the school's future. Such optimism proved to be short-lived, as the university soon faced the setbacks of the Great Depression, which resulted in staff and salary reductions. University President Homer L. Shantz struggled to fulfill his hopes for a building program and applied for a Public Works Administration grant of $800,000. Approval of the grant was a boon to the school, which gained a science building, a greenhouse, a women's gymnasium, an auditorium, a classroom building, and a museum; moreover, the city's unemployed were enlisted to complete this work and thereby benefited as well.

By 1939 enrollment had jumped to 3,000 and the University of Arizona had become a respected institution in the southwest. Not only had the university acquired the physical proportions of a legitimate university, it had established an excellent academic reputation in the sciences. In particular, tremendous advances in tree-ring research (dendrochronology) were achieved by faculty member Andrew E. Douglass, an astronomer. His interest in sunspot cycles led him to study tree rings and to develop the basic principles by which they are used to date historical and environmental events. This work led to the creation of the university's Laboratory of Tree-Ring Research in 1937.

Many of the fields of study that have reached the greatest prominence at the University of Arizona benefit from the school's location. The area's clean, clear skies make it a perfect place to study astronomy. A $60,000 gift from Lavinia Steward in 1916 financed the university's first observatory; ultimately, the growth of the city and its lights led to the relocation of the Steward telescope to the Kitt Peak National Observatory in 1963. Astronomical research facilities also include Flandrau Planetarium, the Lunar and Planetary Laboratory, and a multiple mirror telescope on Mount Hopkins. Construction of the Mount Graham International Observatory commenced in the 1990s with plans to build three new telescopes, including what is expected to be the world's most powerful binocular telescope.

The presence of the well-preserved pueblos of several prehistoric cultures (the Anasazi, Hohokam, Mogollon, and Sinagua) are vital resources in the university's anthropological and archaeological studies. Such work has also been complemented by UA's tree-ring studies, which provided a method for dating the construction materials found in the pueblos and other ancient sites.

Related exhibits are part of the university's natural history museum, the Arizona State Museum, including clay, stone, and bone artifacts from these indigenous cultures and tree-ring specimens that date as far back as A.D. 212.

The Sonoran desert and the Santa Catalina mountain range have facilitated environmental research of arid lands, as well as research in hydrology and mining. Other areas where the university excels are management information systems, optical sciences, and health professions. The College of Medicine is well known for its research relating to heart surgery, cancer, and arthritis.

A gift from alumnus C. Leonard Pfeiffer created the basis for the university's fine art collection. His donation of American works from the 1930s (by Edward Hopper, Stuart David, and Reginald Marsh) have been supplemented by the Kress Collection of paintings from the Renaissance through the seventeenth century, the Gallagher Memorial Collection of paintings by twentieth-century masters (Picasso, Rodin, Arp, Maillol, and Degas), and a large number of bronze and plaster sculptures by Jacques Lipchitz.

The UA campus now encompasses some 300 acres, supplemented by five separate agricultural centers. With more than 138 buildings, mostly made of red brick, it mixes traditional southwestern architecture with modern structures. Old Main, the first university building, has survived the repeated threat of demolition and now provides offices for the dean of students and other support services. The building's safety was assured in 1972, when it was named to the National Register of Historic Places. Seventeen other campus buildings are also on the register.

Further Reading: An early history of the University of Arizona is provided by *Tucson: The Life and Times of an American City* by C.L. Sonnichsen (Norman, Oklahoma: University of Oklahoma Press, 1982) and *A Photographic History of the University of Arizona* by Phyllis Ball (Tucson: University of Arizona Press, 1986). *Arizona: A State Guide,* complied by Workers of the Writers' Program of the Work Projects Administration in the State of Arizona (New York: Hastings, 1940) and *This Is Tucson: Guidebook to the Old Pueblo* by Peggy Hamilton Lockard (Tucson, Arizona: Pepper, 1988) give details regarding the school's subsequent development and its outstanding programs and facilities.

—Junelle Dupee

UNIVERSITY OF BARCELONA
(Barcelona, Spain)

Location: Barcelona, in the Catalan region of northeastern Spain.

Description: State-supported university enrolling approximately 70,000 students.

Information: University of Barcelona
(Universitat de Barcelona)
Gran Via de les Corts Catalanes 585
08007 Barcelona
Spain

The structure and history of the University of Barcelona have been influenced greatly by the persistent republican spirit of the Catalan region. Catalonia, situated on the northeast corner of the Iberian peninsula, has attempted to establish itself as an autonomous republic, free from the rule of the Spanish state, frequently throughout its history. The university has been affected by the contrasting movements toward Spanish centralization and regional autonomy since its founding in 1450. Freedom and self-government were the same issues that spurred the Spanish student protests that began in Barcelona 500 years later.

Higher education in Barcelona can be traced back to the thirteenth century. Informal academies of learning existed where scholars would convene to discuss topics of interest and importance. The University of Barcelona's immediate predecessor was the autonomous academy of medicine arts (*Estudio de Medicina y Artes*). This school was established in 1401 by Martin I, son of Martin the Humanist. Martin I (1374–1409) was the king of Sicily and prince of Aragon.

The University of Barcelona was founded in 1450 when the school was authorized by King Alfonso V of Aragon (Alfonso the Magnanimous), and confirmed by papal bull. Alfonso (1396–1458) liked to be known as the true renaissance king who promoted scholarship and enlightened activities. He opened literary soirees to the young people of Messina and developed a school in the library of Naples. This institution, opened in 1443, was intended to be "akin to the schools of Florence where youth could imbibe the new literary arts and the spirit of humanism."

The same spirit inspired Alfonso's financial backing of other institutions of higher education in his kingdom. He authorized the schools of Catania (1444), Gerona (1446), and Barcelona (1450). Much of this support was limited to giving his personal sanction and exercising his influ-

ence to secure papal approval so that these local schools could be raised to official university status.

For all his cursory backing of the creation of universities, Alfonso did not encourage his subjects to acquire academic training. The practical experience that men acquired abroad in law, theology, and medicine seemed to be sufficient for the king. Because Alfonso gave no financial or moral support beyond his own sanction and influence with the church, the University of Catania was the only school that actually came into being during his reign.

The University of Barcelona waited another 50 years after its official founding date until it truly began to function. In 1507 the general study, or university (*estudio general* or *universidad*) was created. It was yet another half century until the university was firmly established. The definitive organization of the University of Barcelona took place from 1559 to 1565.

As the Bourbon movement of centralization swept through Spain in the early eighteenth century, the Catalans saw their personal freedoms sharply curtailed, including their access to education. In 1714, Barcelona's three main military and government institutions, which had been in power since the thirteenth century, capitulated to the rule of Felipe V. Although all but one of the members of the replacement government were Catalan, they were merely puppets of the Bourbons.

By September 1714, this new government passed several laws that severely restricted the Catalan's personal and financial freedoms. The very next year, the government disbanded the University of Barcelona and moved it to a small, remote country town, Cervera. The only part of the old university that remained in the city was the grammar school. This was a minor part of the university, a kind of prepatory school. The scholars and professors—perhaps seen as a threat to the new regime—"could do little harm in that remoteness [of Cervera] except teach and study scholasticism."

The university remained in Cervera for more than 150 years, during the various revolutions and republican battles of the eighteenth and nineteenth centuries. The first national educational reforms, which signaled the beginning of a modern, unified educational system in Spain, took place in the middle of the nineteenth century. The first general education act was passed in 1857. The *Ley Moyano,* named for the minister responsible for it, provided the foundation for a national education system. The centralized, hierarchical, standardized Spanish educational system was based on this law until the late 1960s and early 1970s. Under the law, university education was to be completely under state control, with the

University of Barcelona

Catholic church completely excluded. Although the church had no official control over the educational system after the *Ley Moyano,* it still tried to influence curriculum, particularly in universities. This rift between the church and university professors still persisted in the late twentieth century.

Under the law, the country was divided into ten university districts, with a hierarchy of officials, including a king-appointed rector to oversee all education in each district. The universities' main function was not research but granting a qualification (*titulo*) to professional people. The curriculum was standardized across all universities; technical subjects were excluded.

Although the *Ley Moyano* was passed in 1857, its effects did not reach many universities, including the University of Barcelona, for years. In 1873 the University of Barcelona was officially re-established as part of the centralized, state-controlled educational system. In the same year, the university was moved from Cervera back to the city of Barcelona. Most of the buildings on campus on the Plaza Universidad date from this period.

The structure of the university and its role in the centralized system remained relatively unchanged until the 1930s. In 1931, Frances Marcia declared an autonomous Catalan republic and a new government, the *Generalitat.* Although the *Generalitat* had widespread powers, education remained for the most part under the control of the Spanish government.

The exception was the University of Barcelona, which was made into an autonomous institution in June 1933. The university was governed by a joint council of repre-

sentatives from the *Generalitat* and the Spanish state. Classes would be conducted in either of the two official languages of the republic, Castilian and Catalan. Eighty percent of the students and staff chose Catalan for their classes, indicative of the strong republican spirit of the Catalans.

In the 1950s and 1960s, students all over Spain got caught up in political movements. The University of Barcelona was one of the earliest institutions to experience student unrest. Influenced by the radical theories of doctrines such as Castroism and Neo-Marxism, students began to protest the autocratic rule of the university government. The Spanish University Union (SEU) had been officially in control since 1939, but students felt that they should have more say in the governance of universities. They demanded representative and independent associations that would be democratically administered.

The student turmoil begun in the mid-1950s, with one of the first large uprisings at the University of Barcelona. In 1956, several of the schools of the university were closed for two weeks because of strikes. Throughout the next ten years, there were more strikes, demonstrations, violence, meetings, and police action. The student movement had spread all over Spain by 1965, and it escalated to an extreme level at the University of Barcelona. In April 1966, after two days of student demonstrations and agitation the entire university was temporarily shut down.

Besides the issue of student representation, the sheer number of students was another reason for the uprisings. The sudden and tremendous increase in university enrollment across Spain was not accompanied by a simi-

428 INTERNATIONAL DICTIONARY OF UNIVERSITY HISTORIES

lar increase in resources. Students may have been protesting the effects of both overcrowding and thinly stretched budgets and staff.

Enrollment in the Barcelona university district jumped from 6,945 to 14,988, an increase of more than 115 percent from 1955 to 1967. To provide for the enormous influx of students, autonomous universities were created in existing districts. In 1968, the Autonomous University of Barcelona was created, along with autonomous institutions in Madrid and Bilbao. These universities competed with existing national universities.

The University of Barcelona has continued to grow at a tremendous rate, particularly in the last 30 years. In the late 1960s, about 4,000 students attended the university. By 1991–92, student enrollment totaled over 69,000.

The university was reorganized again in 1985 under the jurisdiction of the Generalitat of Catalonia. It remains a self-contained institution, financially supported by the Spanish state and the Generalitat. Although there still exists a hierarchy of administrators who govern the university, included among the ruling bodies are representatives of the staff and students. The students' fight for representation apparently has resulted in some changes in the structure of the University of Barcelona. The republican spirit of the Catalans is also reflected in the university today. The Catalan government shares control of the university with the Spanish state, and classes are still conducted in either Catalan or Castilian.

The University of Barcelona cooperates with many other universities all over the world. It participates in exchanges with schools in the United States, Europe, South American, Asia, and Australia. The university's outreach programs include the Andorran Studies Institute, the High Mountains Research Institute, the Inter-University Institute of Ancient Middle Eastern Studies, the Public Health Institute, and the Hispanic Studies Institute.

Further Reading: Although there is no authoritative, comprehensive account of the history of the University of Barcelona, bits and pieces can be found in various sources. John M. McNair's *Education for a Changing Spain* (Manchester: Manchester University Press, 1984) provides an overview of the Spanish educational system and covers the history of Spanish universities in general. Information about student protests of the 1950s and 1960s can be found in Victor Alba's *Catalonia: A Profile* (London: C. Hurst, 1975), which also gives a good description of the region and its republican impulses. Early history of the university is covered briefly in *Eighteenth Century Spain, 1700–1788* by W.N. Hargreaves-Mawdsley (London: Macmillan, 1979), *Alfonso the Magnanimous* by Alan Ryder (Oxford and New York: Oxford University Press, 1990), and the *Enciclopedia de la Cultura Espanola* (1962–68).

—Cindy Mertz

UNIVERSITY OF BORDEAUX
(Bordeaux, France)

Location:

In Bordeaux, southwest of Paris, on the west bank of the Garonne River.

Description:

Three autonomous, state-financed universities founded in 1970 under France's Orientation Act of 1968, which provided for reform of higher education. They replaced the former University of Bordeaux.

Université de Bordeaux I:
Enrolls approximately 26,000 students in science, physics, chemistry, mathematics and computer science, biology, earth sciences, law and economics, juridical studies, private law and history of institutions, public law and political science, economics and management studies, and general economic and social training.

Université de Bordeaux II:
Enrolls approximately 15,000 students in medical sciences, pharmacy, odontology, tropical medicine, public health, biochemistry and cellular biology, social and psychological sciences, applied human sciences, physical education, and oenology.

Université de Bordeaux III (Université Michel de Montaigne):
Enrolls approximately 17,000 students in letters and arts, philosophy, history, geography, language, literature and civilization of anglophone countries, foreign languages, Germanic studies, Iberian and Latin American studies, information and communication sciences, science, communications, and technology development and natural resources.

Information:

University of Bordeaux I
351 cours de la Liberation
33405 Talence Cedex
France
(56) 80-84-50

University of Bordeaux II
146 rue Leo Saignat
33076 Bordeaux Cedex
France
(56) 57-10-10

University of Bordeaux III
Esplanade Michel de Montaigne
Domaine Universitaire
33405 Talence Cedex
France

The University of Bordeaux was established during the fifteenth century when the English dominated France. Situated in the department of Gironde, in southwest France at the mouth of the Garonne River, the university was modeled after the *studium* existing in Toulouse. (*ad instar Studii Tolosani*). The University of Bordeaux was founded by a papal bull in 1441 but did not receive a direct royal confirmation until the reign of Louis XI in 1443.

Over the next four centuries, the university managed to survive tumultuous uprisings in the region, including those in the town of Bordeaux. To appreciate an institution's beginning struggles, subsequent improvements, and future goals, one needs to survey the area's unique development.

"Take Versailles, add Antwerp, and you have Bordeaux," is the way Victor Hugo described the city. He was impressed by the beauty of its tidal river as well as its eighteenth-century magnificence. In reality, Bordeaux played a major role in France long before anyone heard of Versailles.

Bordeaux's position on the Garonne was definitely a factor in its popularity as an important port. From the center of the estuary, Gironde, several streams ran north to the River Dordogne or south to the River Garonne. Dating back to some 300 years B.C., it was a small Celtic port, trading with the Phoenicians who brought tin from mines in Cornwall. Later, under Roman occupation, Bordeaux (known as *Burdigala* by the Romans) produced its first wine. This led to the beginning of a thriving wine region and was instrumental in Bordeaux becoming a popular commercial city.

Ausonius, a writer and native of fourth-century Bordeaux, describes it as "four-square and surrounded with walls and lofty towers, and celebrates its importance as one of the greatest educational centres of Gaul."

In 1137, Bordeaux's St. Andrew's Cathedral was the stage for a royal wedding. Eleanor, the oldest daughter of William X, Duke of Aquitaine, was to wed the French king's son, the future Louis VII. Eleanor's dowry, as heiress of Aquitaine, was opulent, encompassing nearly all southwestern France. Throughout their troubled 15-year marriage, the distinguished statesman Abbot Suger of St. Denis, attempted to restore harmony between them by suggesting policies to extend the domain. All good will was in vain, and in 1152, the marriage was annulled by the Council of Beaugency.

Eleanor regained her dowry and within two months married Henry Plantagenet (ten years her junior) Duke of Normandy, Count of Anjou. Henry inherited the English crown two years later, becoming Henry II of England. He and Eleanor reigned over southwest and central France, as well as England.

Bordeaux's prosperity was enhanced by this union, due to increased commerce with London; yet discord between England and France ensued and lasted for three centuries. The opposition which began with their marriage ended in 1453, at the Battle of Castillon, marking the last battle of the Hundred Years' War and the end of English domination.

In 1441, prior to the end of the Hundred Years' War, the University of Bordeaux was founded by a papal bull of Eugenius IV upon the petition of Archbishop Pey-Berland (1375–1458) an important spiritual and political leader, together with the seneschal and Aquitanian councillors of the English King Henry VI, and of the mayor and jurats of the city. Two years later it received royal confirmation. The foundation of the university was mostly the work of the municipality and was governed primarily by the masters. The only recognized student rights were in the enactment, which required that "two of the rector's four councillors should be bachelors." The archbishop of Bordeaux was named chancellor; upon his death, the chancellorship would pass to the archdeacon of Médoc. Apostolical conservators were the bishop of Bazas, the abbot of La Sauve, and archdeacon of Cernes. The preservation of royal privileges was delegated to the seneschal of Guienne (Aquitaine).

Under the University of Bordeaux's first statutes, dated 1443, there were four schools: theology, canon law, civil law, grammar and arts. The faculty of arts incorporated the existing college of arts and the town-school. Medical training was entrusted by the city to the Collège des Médecins (college of physicians). This medical college began in 1411. The new university was not able to change established customs until 1472, when letters from Louis XI imposed statutes, similar to those of Toulouse, stipulating medical education be dispensed by a university faculty and not practicing physicians. When a regent in medicine was established in 1491, the University of Bordeaux was complete.

None of the chairs was endowed, though the right of teaching was limited to their occupants; the professors were left to be supported by a fee of half a golden noble from each scholar. The prelates, nobles, and sons of doctors and masters were commonly excused from examination. During the sixteenth and seventeenth centuries the university was reduced to little more than an establishment for the sale of degrees.

The city, which continued to grow, saw a decline in its commercial life when English domination ceased. Streets were crowded and dirty and surrounding marshes became unsanitary. In 1585, there was an outbreak of plague. The mayor of Bordeaux, Montaigne, a well-known essayist who succeeded in pacifying rival religious factions in the area, fared poorly during this phase and preferred to seclude himself in his castle in

the country. No improvements were made to the city until the eighteenth century.

Claude Boucher, governor of Bordeaux from 1720 to 1743, had the vision and vigor to demolish the city's worst parts and begin rebuilding. Fortunately for Bordeaux, Boucher's fear of expanding vineyards did not ever succeed in passing a law obliging owners to uproot their vines. One famous French jurist and political philosopher, Charles Louis de Secondat, Baron de la Brède, known as Montesquieu, was not only a vineyard owner but president of the parliament of Bordeaux. Montesquieu's influence was instrumental in saving the prosperity of Bordeaux, which was built on wine.

Montesquieu (1689–1755), born in La Brède, near Bordeaux, returned to study law at Bordeaux University after studying in schools near Paris. He received his law degree at age 19 and went on to become a magistrate as well as president of the Bordeaux Parliament. He held his presidency for 12 years, taking part in the proceedings of the Bordeaux Academy, where he contributed papers on philosophy, politics, and natural science.

The work started by Claude Boucher was continued by Louis Urbain Aubert, Marquis de Tourny, governor from 1743 to 1757. He brought light and air into the city by creating spacious squares and wide avenues. During this rebuilding period Bordeaux was given a magnificent facade along the river as well as public gardens. During the second half of the eighteenth century Bordeaux became the most important port in France, with a lucrative trade in sugar and slaves with the West Indies, in addition to its wine exports. Such affluence brought more improvements to the city until 1789, when the Revolution brought the golden age to an end. Blockades, during the Napoléonic Wars, hurt the city's economy and it was not until the mid-eighteen hundreds that recovery began.

During the nineteenth century, work on one of the poorest departments in France, the Landes (south of Bordeaux in Aquitaine), was continued. Pine forests were planted on barren land and sand dunes secured. To eliminate unhealthy swamps, drainage methods were installed and forests extended. Landes became one of the richest departments from the export of wood and resin. Bordeaux, being the nearest city, increased its economic importance and continued to grow.

Prior to World War II, Bordeaux became so depressed that many wine estates were sold. Nearly every year in the 1930s was bad for Bordeaux wine, which was still its most important commercial element. It was not until the war ended and a new mayor, Jacques Chaban Delmas, took leadership that new industries arose. In addition to wine, the city attracted space and aviation industries, electronic and automobile plants as well as clothing, food, construction, medical goods, and paper-making factories.

After World War II, French educational institutions were out of step with the needs of a technological society. Provencial universities, including Bordeaux, were biased toward classics, emphasizing mathematics, Greek, Latin, and French philology, literature, and history. Science and technology were treated as less important. University systems remained much the same as when Napoléon conceived them.

In the early 1950s, France became aware of higher education's shortcomings. During Charles de Gaulle's regime, efforts to reform the education system began. He had two initiatives: the first was to change the curriculum, putting emphasis on postwar needs, focusing on science and technology; the second was encouraging students to attend provincial universities, thus de-emphasizing Paris. If successful he believed that these initiatives would position France as a modern nation in the new world order. During the period between 1956–57 and 1972, enrollment in higher education grew from 150,000 to nearly 700,000. While provincial universities, such as Bordeaux, managed to increase enrollment, Paris also continued to grow.

Student uprisings in 1968 forced changes to the university system, including replacing the *facultés* with *unités d'enseignement et de recherche,* or units of teaching and research (UER). Eventually, UERs were distributed among new institutions, including 43 universities in the provinces. Small city universities represented a unification of traditional *facultés.* Larger cities such as Bordeaux had the university divided into three parts.

President Georges Pompidou followed Charles de Gaulle and continued rebuilding the university system. Pompidou appointed Edgar Faure to continue France's rebuilding process. Faure, a minister of education under de Gaulle, passed a set of reforms authorizing political activity on campuses, streamlining both faculties and examination systems and providing student-faculty committees. The "Faure law" allowed considerable voice to students and faculty in the administration of individual universities.

In the early 1980s, Alice Saunier-Selte, minister of universities, enforced a decision to cut back graduate degree programs at the nation's 76 universities. Quite abruptly, 30 percent of all master's and doctoral degree programs, mostly in humanities and social sciences, were eliminated. Saunier-Selte felt this initiative was an

efficient way to end curriculum duplication and to restrict graduate education to major university centers such as Paris, Bordeaux, Grenoble, Lille, Lyon, Nancy, and Strasbourg. She hoped these would become "poles of excellence."

Throughout the turmoil, the universities at Bordeaux have grown and prospered. The three uiversities founded under France's Orientation Act of 1968 now have nearly 60,000 students.

Université de Bordeaux III (Université Michel de Montaigne) has an enrollment of nearly 17,000 students. Bordeaux III most closely resembles the traditonal French university. The curriculum is primarily classic in orientation, including letters and arts, philosophy, history, languages, and communications.

Université de Bordeaux II was established to give the region a medical university. Bordeaux II has an enrollment of approximately 15,000 students. Studies include medical sciences, pharmacy, public health, chemistry, biology, social sciences, and a regional institute of physical education. This university fills a historic void for the region.

Université de Bordeaux I, largest of the schools, enrolls nearly 26,000 students. This school focuses on the curriculum identified in the 1950s as critical to maintain France's competitiveness in the post–World War II environment. The university specializes in the sciences (physics, chemistry, biology, and earth science) as well as computer science, political science, and economics.

In an effort to meet the needs of the twenty-first century, France adopted, in May 1991, a plan called *Université 2000.* Its objectives are to admit more students and improve standards, to contribute to regional development, and to prepare for increasing competition and for entry into the European Community. As the twentieth century draws to a close, Bordeaux continues to extend its scope and activities, building and developing into a university that meets the needs of the region and France.

—Sandy Gladfelter

UNIVERSITY OF BUENOS AIRES
(Buenos Aires, Argentina)

Location: On a widespread campus in the capital of Argentina.

Description: A public university; enrollment in 1994 was 174,345.

Information: Secretaría de Extensión Universitaria y Bienestar Estudiantil
(Licenciado Martín Marcos)
Avenida Corrientes 2038
Buenos Aires
Argentina
(1) 953-0390

The University of Buenos Aires (UBA) was created in 1821 during the Argentinian independence period, when Argentina aspired to leave behind its colonial history and become a "civilized nation." Though Spain provided the model for Latin America's colonial universities, France was the main inspiration for the newly independent nations and their establishment of secular universities freed from Church influence. Thus, UBA was an heir of the French Revolution more than Argentina's own theologically oriented colonial University of Córdoba. And so the UBA emerged as a major antagonist in the liberal-conservative conflicts that marked much of Argentine politics in the nineteenth century.

The university's philosophical studies reflected the influence of French thinkers, such as Destutt de Tracy. Juan Aguero, the first professor for logic, metaphysics, and oratory, cast doubt on the authenticity of the gospels and taught about Jesus Christ as the philosopher of Nazareth, a figure like Plato or Socrates. Rather than a faculty of theology, UBA boasted a faculty of philosophy and humanities, as well as faculties of medical sciences, law and social sciences, mathematics and physics, and natural sciences. The university also controlled the national secondary schools.

The 1880s was a landmark decade for UBA's institutional identity. Named after an ex-rector and ex-president, the Avellanada law of 1885 established two hallmark principles for all Argentine public universities: autonomy and the absence of tuition. University governance would be entrusted fundamentally to professors. They could select new professors, create syllabuses, and organize the basic academic character and structure of the university. Meanwhile, to this day, students pursue their studies totally free of charge.

In the ensuing decades, changes in the character of the nation brought changes to the university. Argentina's land-owning oligarchy was yielding to forces of immigration, urbanization, and industrialization, all supported by the vigorous construction of railroads. Argentina enjoyed an unprecedented cultural and scientific opening. Again Europe provided inspiration. The philosophy of positivism gave priority to science and culture as ways to civilize society and achieve progress. The University of Buenos Aires eagerly created research institutes from ethnography to physiology and undertook a series of new practical tasks.

A growing and prosperous country also meant a growing and better endowed university. An expanding student body (from just 602 students in 1886, including those at the secondary level, to 9,352 by 1920) was treated to recreational student centers in various faculties. The first minister for public instruction saw in recreational centers a replica of the English and German student associations that prided themselves on developing morality and national leadership through physical discipline and guided activity. Meanwhile, libraries grew enormously, though laboratories did not develop at an equal pace.

For all the development, however, UBA remained predominantly professional in its orientation and activities. The great majority of the students enrolled between 1885 and 1930 chose the liberal professions, especially law, engineering, and medicine, as their ticket to social and economic (and often political) success. The university basically fostered change within the establishment.

The 1918 reform movement jolted that state of tranquility. This movement would have a major impact not only in Argentina but in much of Latin America. The ire and the triumphs of the young reformists focused on university governance. Co-gobierno would come to mean representation of three key groups—professors, students and graduates—on decision-making bodies (university assembly, high university council, and the faculty or school councils). It would also mean university autonomy, appointment of teaching staff by examination with renewed competition every seven years, easier access to courses, and updated teaching methods.

Reformist notions of expanded participation in university governance again reflected broader tendencies in Argentine politics. The nation had turned away from oligarchic and elitist political ideas, behind President Hipólito Yrigoyen, leader of the Radical Civic Union, as it adopted universal suffrage. This responded to the interests of the rising middle class, and the middle class was taking over the university. The principle of no tuition took on new meaning and sanctification. Moreover, students assumed a role as voice of the middle class, the nation, and progressive reform. Notions of national identity and anti-imperialism had a prominent place, even as the economy remained heavily involved in the export of agricultural products and supply of raw materials within the international market.

Despite the ferment, it was not until the 1950s that UBA finally abandoned its nearly exclusive professional profile. Academic reform now largely involved incorporation of research into the university's mainstream agenda. This, then, was an effort to move closer to the Humboltian model, and certainly the U.S. universities' mixing of teaching and research was another influence. The new emphasis was not meant to push aside other cherished principles, such as co-gobierno, autonomy, or academic freedom.

Compared to reforms launched in countries like neighboring Brazil, however, Argentine efforts were limited. A key difference was the far greater level of development of Argentine universities, led by UBA. Boasting a proud university tradition, and easily leading Latin America in terms of both total enrollments and percentage of the age cohort enrolled, Argentina was less ready to embrace foreign models. The logic certainly applied to UBA, the region's largest and possibly most prestigious university at the time. Besides, whatever joint efforts would otherwise have flowered were decimated by the political instability and violence that wracked the nation and its universities from the mid-1960s. So when international philanthropy offered up its large-scale projects for university reform Argentina mostly remained on the sidelines. This contrasted with its participation in many smaller but important earlier activities built around individuals and small units; for example, figures like Gino Germani played a role in importing empirical sociology.

The marginalization of large philanthropic projects meant there would by fewer efforts, with less success, on a variety of reforms: blending research with teaching at the faculties, integrating more natural and social science, shifting from professional faculties to academic departments, centralizing the internal academic and administrative apparatus of universities, pushing general studies as an alternative to immediate entry into a professional faculty, introduction of credit systems to allow students some mobility among academic units, and so forth. Actually, this reform package inspired a young scientist (Alberto Taquini) who had observed the U.S. system up close. He gained the ear of military rulers; these efforts would center not on UBA but on building a network of public provincial universities that would try to break with the UBA mold.

Increasingly, however, university reform and even basic functioning fell hostage to turbulent national politics. Dictatorial periods had repeatedly taken a toll (1930, 1946, 1955). In the 1940s and 1950s Juan Perón's style of populism brandished an anti-intellectual orientation. But it was the military governments of 1966 and especially 1976 that inaugurated the campaigns of terror and austerity that brought the worst nightmares in UBA's history. In between, the last incarnation of Perón's rule clashed with a growing revolutionary movement to produce a violent climate for universities.

The last period of military rule (1976–83) was so brutal and sustained that it dismantled much of the university's—and therefore the nation's—intellectual infrastructure. Argentina gained notoriety for the disappearance of intellectuals and students. Others were simply fired or forced out by the penury that sapped units throughout the institution. Many went into exile, often contributing notably to the academic life of other countries. Autonomy and academic freedom were demolished and stunningly stupid proscriptions were put into effect regarding subject matter and teaching methods integral to universities in the modern civilized world. Nearly the entire national budget for science and technology was funnelled through a national council that was dependent on the dictatorial executive and crippled the universities' research capacity.

The ousting of the military brought immediate normalization to UBA in terms of its autonomy and academic freedom. Repression and violence terminated.

Yet this would hardly mean a new period of tranquility. First, UBA plunged headlong into some of its debilitating prior practices. Unlike Chile, Argentina allowed redemocratization to be interpreted as license for a grand opening of university access; enrollments jumped from just over 100,000 to nearly 150,000 within a couple of years, convincing some leading professors that UBA would just not be a serious academic institution. Political parties and other factions once again came to be too influential in election of administrative leadership and in academic decision making.

Second, a furious debate emerged over the wide-ranging modernization agenda that seeks to obliterate some enshrined principles (e.g., free tuition) and reconceptualize others (e.g., autonomy). Public universities were threatened with becoming less public in the sense of entitlement to automatic, generous public subsidies entrusted to an autonomous entity. Instead, they would move into the market place more, seeking ample private funds and proving themselves accountable for their performance. To succeed in a more competitive environment, UBA and others would need to manage themselves much more efficiently on bottom-line, cost effective academic-economic measures than of on the political calculations that predominate too often in practice.

The prime promoter of the modernization agenda is the government, its neoliberal political-economic policies in step with powerful international banks and other agencies. The prime opponent is UBA, in step with most public universities and their constituencies. The University of

Buenos Aires' centrality results from its size, location in the capital, and simply its venerable status as leader of the university system; its central role probably also results from the perception that its practices are so much the target of the modernization agenda.

This is not to imply that the university stands as total and immovable opposition. On the contrary, important internal divisions and elements of the modernization agenda attract a sympathy or at least a decent hearing where earlier they would have been summarily dismissed. One example is evaluation, where Argentina makes more progress than most other Latin American nations. Another example of modified policy is the university's engagement in applied research for businesses as a way of increasing relevance and service. For example, UBATEC S.A. is a tripartite firm in which UBA, the government, and industry each holds about one third of the stock.

Any understanding of UBA's responsiveness to the modernization agenda, and of the great dangers that it faces if it does not respond much more, requires consideration of competition from other universities. Although most of the public provincial universities have basically followed UBA in structure and practice, some have been innovative, and have received rewards accordingly. But it is private universities that pose the most pointed challenge for UBA.

The University of Buenos Aires led a bitter but ultimately losing resistance to the legalization of private universities in 1959. (The battle actually pitted brother against brother, rector of the UBA versus president of the republic.) The university did succeed, however, in erecting barriers such as probation periods and proscription of public subsidization. With a few exceptions, including institutions that operated as safety nets for professors forced out of the more repressed UBA, private universities remained rather marginal to academic life. Even then, however, they were vivid examples of life with tuition instead of subsidy and they often showed the way into business-related fields of study that earned job-market success for graduates. Today, a growing number of new and old but expanding private universities aim to challenge UBA in a growing range of academic arenas, especially those related to the economy and the modernization agenda.

Nor is the challenge to the UBA limited to universities. In the 1960s and 1970s university problems led to the creation of dozens of private and public research centers. Many were headed and staffed by UBA refugees. Centers often grabbed the lead in research and elements of the modernization agenda such as the attraction of diverse income and differential rewards based on evaluated performance. As these centers face their own set of problems and limitations, a challenge for UBA is to attract some of their talent, develop joint relationships, and emulate their appropriate practices.

However great its difficulties are, UBA remains easily Argentina's leading academic institution. Three reasons are (1) its leadership in research; (2) its leadership in professional training; and (3) its size and breadth.

The University of Buenos Aires' leadership in research is remarkable given the university's turmoil and the rise of alternative institutions. But most centers are rather small and some have recently faded; only recently have a few private universities undertaken a serious research effort. The nearly 3,000 researchers at UBA represent about 15 percent of the nation's total. Yet UBA is not merely ahead in a nearly empty field. Argentina manages to stay around the top among Latin American nations. If that owes much to the high level of human resources produced even in distressed institutional and political environments, surely UBA deserves some praise for its role in the development of those resources. It also has managed to build some protection for research in its institutes and in its faculty of science. It has produced the country's only three Nobel Prize winners in science: Bernardo Houssay (1947), Federico Leloir (1970), and César Milstein (1984).

More ample success has been achieved in professional training. This fact gets obscured because of normative notions that universities are most appropriately about academic elite activities headed by research and graduate education. The university itself contributes to the fiction by its exaggerated academic claims. Its own statutes maintain that research is undertaken in all its faculties and departments. What UBA mostly does, however, today as historically, is produce professionals in a variety of fields. To be sure, its record there too is mixed as many faculties suffer from lax admissions and standards, poor staff, outmoded curriculum, and a terrible waste of resources. Additionally, the university continues to provide professional training in a given field even though so many graduates will not find work in that field; they would be better served by a somewhat broader education. Still, some faculties (e.g., philosophy and letters) do provide a fine education to broaden horizons and improve critical abilities. Moreover, Argentina is a nation with many proficient professionals, and no institution plays as large a role as UBA in training them. In several fields, UBA remains the preferred place to go.

Finally, UBA's importance relates to its enormous size and scope of activity. The University of Buenos Aires joins Mexico's national university as the two largest university-level institutions in Latin America. It is easily Argentina's most multifunctional, versatile, diversified, and complex university.

The University of Buenos Aires still holds 28 percent of the nation's university enrollments (compared to roughly two-thirds the 1920 total). Its budget is approximately $250 million. The university is made up of 13 faculties or schools. At the graduate level it offers 105 courses, 11 doctorates, 11 masters, and 114 specialized careers. It also has a basic cycle program for new students and a center for advanced studies, as well as two secondary schools. In terms of services to its students and the broader community, UBA has 18 libraries, a cultural center (*Centro Cultural Ricardo Rojas*), 8 museums, 5 assistance units, a clinical hospital, a health center, and a sports facility. To all this it adds distance education. Its best-known distance program is UBA XXI (twenty-first century), which includes optional counselling; a novel distance agreement was signed with the Federal Penitentiary Service.

Like the country it serves, the University of Buenos Aires has lived a tumultuous century. Like the country, it suffers from a profound sense of unfulfilled promises born in the prior century and repeatedly reconstructed since. Yet, also like Argentina itself, it has much to take pride in and seems to have entered a fresh period of reform.

—Marcela Mollis and Daniel C. Levy

UNIVERSITY OF CALIFORNIA
(California, U.S.A.)

Location: Nine campuses located throughout the state of California in Berkeley, San Francisco, Davis, Riverside, San Diego, Los Angeles, Santa Barbara, Irvine, and Santa Cruz. The original campus is located in Berkeley, east of San Francisco Bay and north of Oakland.

Description: A state university system currently operating on nine campuses. Eight of the campuses offer general education services; the ninth, at San Francisco, specializes in health sciences. The university system is tuition-free to qualified residents of California.

Information: Admissions and Relations with Schools
110 Sproul Hall #5800
University of California, Berkeley
Berkeley, CA 94720-5800
U.S.A.
(415) 642-3175

Visiting: Guided tours can be arranged year-round, by contacting the Admissions Office at the above number or at the appropriate campus. Information for UC campuses can be obtained at the following numbers: Los Angeles: (310) 825-4321; San Francisco: (415) 476-9000; Davis: (916) 752-1011; Santa Barbara: (805) 893-8000; Riverside: (909) 787-1012; San Diego: (619) 534-2230; Santa Cruz: (408) 459-2495; and Irvine: (714) 856-6345.

California legislators had already made constitutional provisions for a state university by the time the state was admitted to the union in 1850. Clearly, the architects of American's westernmost frontier envisioned a community that would require the progressive education of its future leaders.

In 1853, the state of California received 46,000 acres of land from the federal government for the purpose of raising money to form a "seminary of learning." In 1862, the federal government's Morrill Act made land grants available to states committed to establishing schools of higher learning in agriculture and the mechanical arts. California was awarded 150,000 acres, and in 1866 the state legislature drew up a mandate for an agricultural, mining, and mechanical arts college.

Independent of the state's plans, in 1853 two transplanted easterners, Reverends Henry Durant and Samuel H. Willey, helped establish the Contra Costa Academy in Oakland at a cost of $30,000. Their first site, at Broadway and Fifth Street, was a former fandango house. Two years later, the struggling school was incorporated by state charter as the College of California.

Upon announcement of the plans for the state university, Governor Frederick Low and the advisors of the College of California agreed on a merger: the state would take over the college's land in exchange for the promise that the state would establish a "complete" university, adding courses in the humanities to the practical sciences stipulated by the Morrill Act. On March 23, 1868, Low's successor, H.H. Haight, signed a new act forming the University of California—an event now celebrated in the UC system as Charter Day.

The transfer of property included the College of California's undeveloped land four miles to the north of its Oakland home. Many residents of that area supported the college's relocation and offered land for its use free of charge. To appease less enthusiastic neighbors, founding administrator Willey arranged a homesteading plan, reserving 160 acres for the campus and selling another 160 at $500 an acre. On April 16, 1860, nine trustees dedicated the site at a landmark christened "Founder's Rock."

After great debate, the town that sprung up around the anticipated campus was named "Berkeley," honoring George Berkeley, the Bishop of Cloyne, an early eighteenth-century teacher who had come to America to educate the New World's "aboriginal Americans" and who had been instrumental in outlining plans for Columbia University in New York. Streets of the new town running east-west were named for famed literary men (Brancroft, Dwight, Hawthorne), while streets running north-south were named for distinguished men of the sciences (Audubon, Bowditch, Choate). Frederick Law Olmsted, the renowned landscape architect who was in the midst of designing New York's Central Park and who would later draw plans for Stanford University, was enlisted to design the Berkeley campus. His blueprint, however, yielded only a few characteristics that remain today: the central axis that came to be known as Campanile Way and campus entrances at the south and east ends.

The newly established Board of Regents of the University of California presided over the university's opening in 1869. Graduates of the College of California had officially become alumni of the university one year earlier. Ten faculty members and 40 students were on hand for UC's inaugural year. Of those students, 12 graduated in 1873; the members of this charter class came to be known

University of California, Berkeley

as "The Twelve Apostles." The prestigious group included a future congressman and a future governor, lawyers, professors, financiers, and a minister.

In 1870, women were permitted to apply to the university; 17 were admitted. Henry Durant, president of the College of California, was chosen as president of the new university, replacing interim president John LeConte after the regents' first two choices (including Yale professor Daniel Coit Gilman) declined the invitation.

In establishing the university, the legislature had stipulated that state residents would be exempt from tuition as soon as the regents deemed their operating budget to be sufficiently funded. After three months at the Berkeley site, the university became tuition-free for Californians, a policy that remains in effect today. Over the years, supplemental services such as health care have been covered by an "incidental fee" (a little over $2,100 for California residents for the 1996–97 academic year). In addition, the Vrooman Act of 1889 provided the university system with 1 cent of revenue for every $100 of taxable property in the state. The figure was later raised to 2 cents per $100.

In 1872, Durant stepped down from the presidency, suggesting that the board of regents find a younger man to replace him. They did, in the person of Yale's Gilman. Gilman remained in his post a scant three years, however, during which time a campus construction supervisor was accused of financial mismanagement. Although Gilman himself was exonerated of any wrongdoing, he departed amid controversy in 1875, assuming the presidency of Johns Hopkins University. Although his stay was short, Gilman left a legacy at Berkeley. Gilman's expansive vision for the university was fitfully implemented over the next few decades as several presidents came and went. Between 1874 and 1894, five men held the top post—John LeConte, William T. Reid, Edward S. Holden, Horace Davis, and Martin Kellogg. None served longer than seven years.

By 1873, the Berkeley campus's North and South Halls, designed by David Farquharson, had been completed, and classes were moved to the new site from Oakland. The student body that first year in Berkeley included 199 students, of whom 26 were women. In

1881, another long-time campus fixture, Bacon Hall, was completed. Originally used as a library and art gallery, the magnificent Victorian Gothic building and its holdings were the gift of Oakland businessman H.D. Bacon.

From the beginning, gifts to the university were instrumental in its growth: eccentric San Franciscan James Lick, for example, funded the world-renowned Lick Observatory, established at Mount Hamilton, with $700,000 left in his will. In 1873, Dr. Hugh Toland presented the university with the medical college that bore his name, located across the bay in San Francisco. His generous gift included $100,000 worth of property. Also in San Francisco, Judge Serranus Clinton Hastings made the establishment of the Hastings College of the Law possible with a $100,000 contribution to the state treasury. In 1891, five scholarships for women were endowed by Mrs. Phoebe Apperson Hearst, an active participant in the growth of the university and a regent as of 1897. Hearst funded two buildings on the Berkeley campus (including the Hearst Memorial Mining Building, dedicated in memory of her husband, Senator George Hearst). At the turn of the century, she led an international search for an architect to design the campus layout. Another widow, Mrs. Jane K. Sather, memorialized herself and her late husband, Peder, with the donation of two of Berkeley's most recognizable landmarks—Sather Gate and the 307-foot-high Sather Tower (also known as the Campanile).

There was much international fanfare over Hearst's architectural contest, the application of which stated that the university sought a design with "no more necessity of remodeling its broad outlines a thousand years hence than there would be of remodeling the Parthenon, had it come down to us complete and uninjured." First place was awarded to Emile Henry Benard of Paris, whose $80 million plan was designed to create just such an imposing campus in the classical tradition. Critics, however, decried the exorbitant cost of his plan and its imposing design. A discouraged Benard left Berkeley not long after he arrived, and the campus layout has since evolved in piecemeal fashion.

After Benard's departure, the university's Bernard Maybeck, a guiding light in efforts to unify the campus layout, enlisted fourth-place contestant John Galen Howard to design Hearst's Memorial Mining Building. Howard was appointed supervising architect of the Berkeley campus in 1902, where he presided over the completion of 11 major buildings in 12 years. In 1914, work was begun on halls named for university presidents Gilman and Wheeler and geologist Eugene W. Hilgard, buildings which joined the Charles Franklin Doe Library, Agriculture Hall, and the Hearst Mining Building as the nucleus of the campus. Howard remained on campus until 1927, insuring a certain consistency of design, with most buildings erected in Greek or Roman styles in imported white stone.

In 1906, the newly completed Greek Theatre, the campus's outdoor venue, hosted a visit from the noted actress Sarah Bernhardt, who made a goodwill appearance in the wake of the San Francisco earthquake. Through the years, Berkeley's Greek Theatre has been the site of annual events such as Charter Day festivities and the "Big Game" bonfires that precede Cal–Stanford football matches. The reception building of the theater includes Flemish Gothic tapestry and fourteenth-century Italian marble bas-reliefs, donated by Hearst's son William Randolph Hearst, who had provided funding for the theater in 1903 and would pay for its full-scale renovation in 1957.

By its 25th year, the university ranked in the top ten in the nation in such categories as financial support and numbers of students, graduate students, and faculty members. Although UC was 3,000 miles from the United States' best-known education centers, the ambitious institution began to attract an impressive roster of faculty members. Many of its earliest recruiting successes involved the practical sciences for which the university was originally established. The College of Agriculture, for instance, had an auspicious beginning with the arrival of noted soil chemist Eugene W. Hilgard in 1875. In 1885, Samuel B. Christy was appointed dean of the pioneering College of Mining, which would soon be attended by students from all over the globe. Elwood Mead, recognized as a premier authority on civil engineering, led his college to prominence; it would soon be called upon by the U.S. government when the Hoover Dam was being planned.

In 1899, the university welcomed its first true long-term leader, as Benjamin Ide Wheeler began his 20-year presidency. He arrived to lead a campus of 2,000 students; by his retirement in 1919, the student body had tripled. As a condition of his acceptance of the presidency, the former Cornell University professor of Greek was granted complete autonomy regarding the staffing of faculty and administration. During his tenure, Wheeler began the university's lateral expansion, establishing many classrooms in the field rather than on campus. He presided over the foundation of the University Farm School at Davis (1905); Riverside's Citrus Experiment Station (1907); La Jolla's Scripps Institution for Biological Research (1912); and San Francisco's Hooper Foundation for Medical Research.

In 1898, the former Toland Medical College had combined with the university's Colleges of Dentistry and Pharmacy, taking advantage of the $250,000 grant appropriated by the state legislature to organize the "affiliated colleges." San Francisco mayor Adolph Sutro donated 13 acres of land at what was the westernmost part of the city, at Parnassus Heights, for a new campus. The Hastings College of the Law, though part of the new arrangement, remained in its downtown location; in 1939, San Francisco's College of Nursing would be added to the group.

At the turn of the century, California's Agricultural Society secretary Peter J. Shields led the call for the foundation of a university farm. Dubbed the "father of the Davis campus," Shields pursued the state legislature until he earned passage of a bill in 1905 calling for the establishment of the farming facility. One year later, after studying various climatic regions statewide, the legislature approved the purchase of 773 acres from Jerome C. Davis's farm in Yolo County, near Sacramento. Construction was underway by 1909; two years later, classes had begun. University agriculture students could take supplemental semesters on the new campus, while state residents who had completed grammar school could apply to a three-year school at Davis to learn the farming process. By 1922, the Davis campus became the first university extension to move toward independent course loads, offering its own four-year degree programs.

Somewhat grudgingly, Wheeler's administration began to explore the possibility of opening a second campus to accommodate residents in the southern half of California. Established in 1881, the Los Angeles Normal School was chosen as the site of an experimental arrangement in which the university would expand to include a southern branch. In 1919, Wheeler's last year, the normal school began offering two years of college instruction; five years later a full four-year education was available. In 1927, the regents renamed the normal school the University of California at Los Angeles, informally known as UCLA (the "at" was eventually dropped). In 1929, new campus ground was broken on 383 undeveloped acres in the Santa Monica hills. The previous landowners, Edwin and Harold Janss and Alphonzo Bell, agreed to sell the plot for $1 million; its market value was such that the three men made a gift of well over $3 million to UC. Their asking price was provided by revenues from a local bond issue. In 1927, ground was broken on the four Italian Renaissance buildings of the new campus quadrangle—Royce Hall, the college library, the chemistry building, and the physics-biology building. In 1933 the southern branch established its graduate division.

President Wheeler's great successes in broadening the university system were somewhat offset by increasing concern among the faculty over his omnipotence within the UC system. In 1919, the year of the president's retirement, the faculty staged its so-called revolution, wresting control of nominations for its new members from the administration. The reorganization was implemented the next year, following Wheeler's departure.

The university expanded rapidly, in direct correlation to the growth of its home state. As early as 1923, with the university scarcely a half-century old, its enrollment of 14,061 was the world's largest. By the close of the 1920s, the University of California could claim 40,000 graduates. Women played an important role in shaping the campus: nearly half of Berkeley's students at the turn of the century were women, or "pelicans," so nicknamed because of their starched white shirtfronts.

Wheeler's successor in the president's office, political science professor David Prescott Barrows, recognized the need to ensure a strong academic community for the university's booming student body, and he convinced the regents to operate under their first deficit budget. Their initial reaction to his half-million dollar proposal was that it still was not enough to assure the university's place among the best institutions in the country, and a pleasantly surprised Barrows found himself with $670,000 to allot.

William Wallace Campbell, professor of astronomy and long-time director of the Lick Observatory, succeeded Barrows in the presidency in 1923. By 1930, Robert Gordon Sproul had taken his place—in time to receive the results of a survey conducted by the American Council of Education which for the first time scored Berkeley among the finest institutions in the country.

Sproul was the first native Californian and the first Cal alumnus to accept the presidency. A student of engineering, vice president and comptroller of the university at age 34, and a secretary of the regents, he had been groomed for the job. Sproul's three decades in office were characterized by his pragmatic approach to the system's overwhelming expansion—it was the first major U.S. institution to move to a multi-campus plan. The energetic president would come to spend half of each year at Berkeley, one-third on the growing Los Angeles campus, and the rest at the other university outposts. By the 1950s, he had delegated sizable responsibilities to the holders of newly created chancellorships at Berkeley and Los Angeles and to the provosts of the other campuses. To assure dialogue among the campuses and their residents, Sproul instituted two yearly conferences, those of the California club and the all-university faculty.

Sproul's dedication to the university system was evident in his pursuit of the finest researchers and educators. Physics professor Ernest O. Lawrence had invented the cyclotron (the so-called atom-smasher) at Berkeley in 1929, paving the way for California's invaluable role in nuclear development. The Lawrence Berkeley Laboratory, located on "the hill" of the Berkeley campus, was established to conduct nuclear testing (toward peaceful ends such as nuclear propulsion and mining, as well as weaponry), with a second facility at Livermore, 40 miles to the southeast. Researchers at the LBL have been credited with the discovery of 15 chemical elements, including Berkelium and Californium, as well as the discovery of antimatter. Upon the outbreak of World War II, the university played an integral part in atomic research, opening the Los Alamos nuclear test facility on the desert floor of New Mexico. The university faculty, already the leader in Guggenheim Fellowships, would surpass Harvard by the end of the 1950s in memberships to the National Academy of Sciences as well.

Between 1944 and Sproul's departure in 1958, his administration set in motion an era of phenomenal

University of California, Los Angeles

growth, acquiring its new campus at Santa Barbara and expanding the curricula of Davis and Riverside to include the liberal arts. In 1931, Sproul had commissioned a comprehensive Carnegie Institute study of the university's options for expansion. He retired in 1958, two years before various subsequent studies were combined and implemented as "The Master Plan for Higher Education in California, 1960–75." In 1960, the California state legislature convened a special session to enact the provisions of the Donahoe Higher Education Act, a proposal which incorporated most of the master plan.

The State College at Santa Monica, originally specializing in the manual arts and home economics and later evolving into a normal school for teacher training, was established in 1891. Fifty years later it was annexed to the UC system. In 1954, the new campus, designed as a high-quality liberal arts facility, was relocated ten miles west of Santa Barbara, to 414 acres of beachfront in Goleta, California. By 1958, the administration had seen fit to quadruple UC Santa Barbara's (UCSB) original 2,500 enrollment ceiling. Today, UCSB enrolls more than 17,000 students. Its environmental studies program, launched in the wake of a major 1972 oil spill, is often considered one of the nation's best. It also offers programs unique to the UC system such as an advanced course in theological study and a doctorate in musical arts.

Home to the university's Citrus Experiment Station since 1907, Riverside established its own liberal arts college in 1954. Sproul enlisted former UCLA Dean of the College of Letters Gordon S. Watkins to direct a liberal arts venture at Riverside, where the basic academic design was simplified to accommodate four divisions: humanities, social sciences, life sciences, and physical sciences. Upon opening, Riverside's two-to-one ratio of students to faculty was unrivaled; the campus's commitment to excellence was recognized almost immediately, as the *Chicago Tribune* listed Riverside as one of the ten best undergraduate facilities in the country in a 1956 study. By the early 1960s, Riverside was converted into a general campus. Its unique aspects include the California Museum of Photography, the J. Lloyd Eaton Collection of Science Fiction, and the Rupert Costo Library of the American Indian.

In 1958, Sproul was succeeded in office by Clark Kerr, Berkeley's former chancellor, a deeply principled moderator who would weather the turbulent changes on the UC campuses of the 1960s. Upon Sproul's retirement there were 44,000 students enrolled in the University of California system; projections for 1975 showed 120,000 students, a figure which demanded direct action by the regents and the administration. To accommodate the rising costs of campus construction, Californians supported bond-issue ballot measures in 1956, 1958, 1962, and 1964. Among changes in the state education system were new admission standards that afforded the top 12.5 per-

cent of California students an opportunity to attend the university; an agreement allowing California's state colleges access to the university's extensive library system; and the establishment of a joint graduate board presiding over a cooperative doctoral program between the university and the state colleges.

Kerr continued Sproul's decentralization of the UC system, increasing the responsibilities of campus leaders to ensure more adaptable solutions to the problems facing the by-now enormous system. In addition to new programs at existing campuses, such as Davis's new law school and the engineering studies established at Davis and Santa Barbara, the university opened three new campuses—San Diego, Irvine, and Santa Cruz—with an eye on still more rapid expansion in the near future. Davis was made a general campus of the university in 1959, and its schools of law and medicine were launched in 1964 and 1965, respectively.

At Los Angeles, the 1950s and 1960s saw a campus building frenzy, as some 60 buildings were erected. By the early 1940s, the university's southern branch had already become the fastest-growing major university in the country. Some of the most important additions to the campus included the Marion Davies Children's Clinic (1962), the Jules Stein Eye Institute (1966), and the Pauley Pavilion (1965), an athletic facility where Lew Alcindor (Kareem Abdul Jabbar) and coach John Wooden would raise UCLA to new heights in intercollegiate basketball. An earlier UCLA basketball star, Jackie Robinson, had gone on to break the color barrier in major league baseball.

During these years, UCLA firmly established its preeminence in the sciences. Dr. Ernest O. Lawrence's cyclotron had been transferred to the Los Angeles campus in 1946, and UCLA became a pioneer in computer programming techniques with its $4 million investment into one of the first large computers at its Western Data Processing Center. Today, UCLA remains the only campus among the nation's top ten in research to be founded in the twentieth century. In 1950 and 1951, two professors, Drs. Ralph Bunche and Glenn T. Seaborg, won Nobel Prizes, for peace and chemistry respectively. In another discipline, librarians Lawrence Clark Powell and Robert Vosper raised the standard of the university's holdings to a level commensurate with the finest in the nation and played integral roles in the development of library services nationwide.

In 1959, La Jolla's Scripps Institution of Oceanography provided the base for another UC general campus. In 1956 and 1958, San Diego residents had voted overwhelmingly to offer the university 500 acres of prime land on the Torrey Pines Mesa at no cost, and the U.S. government had assured the donation of an additional 418 acres on adjacent Camp Matthews. The location's first college was named for former Scripps director Roger Revelle and its second for naturalist John Muir.

While the new campus became UCSD in 1960, the original Scripps Institution retained its name. Today, of all the nation's public universities, San Diego claims to have the highest percentage of undergraduates who go on to graduate school.

The general campus at Irvine, a few miles inland from southern California's Newport Beach, was opened in the fall of 1965. Its first 1,000 acres had been the gift of the Irvine Company in 1961. Soil scientist Daniel G. Aldrich Jr. was chosen as the campus's first chancellor. President Lyndon B. Johnson helped dedicate the campus on June 20, 1964, and the following year, Irvine welcomed its first affiliate, the California College of Medicine. Located amid one of the most densely populated regions of the country, Irvine specializes in urban planing studies. The campus also offers a graduate writing program and programs in neuroscience and atmospheric research.

Along with Irvine, Santa Cruz became the most recent campus to join the UC system, as the 2,000-acre Cowell Ranch overlooking Monterey Bay was selected for that purpose in 1961. Education at Santa Cruz began in 1965; in its earliest years, the facility added roughly one college per year, including its original liberal arts college, Cowell, and the Adlai E. Stevenson College (1966) for the social sciences. In addition, Santa Cruz now has charge of the Lick Observatory, as well as other unique departments such as the Institute of Tectonics, dedicated to the study of earthquakes. Like San Diego, Santa Cruz is based on the "cluster college" model, designed to help personalize the educational experience within a larger university system. By the early 1960s, the university system claimed 76,000 students, 40,000 employees, and a $.5 billion yearly operating expenditure. President Kerr had taken to calling the UC system the "Multiversity."

Although the UC system was undoubtedly a source of great wealth to the state, its expansion would prove to be the underlying theme of student rebellion. Student unrest in the 1960s became synonymous with the Berkeley campus. The so-called Free Speech Movement and other protests of its kind brought the university's name a measure of notoriety it retains to this day. Increasingly, the student body at Berkeley and elsewhere expressed anxieties over the faculty's emphasis on research, the administration's link with defense, and the difficulty of learning in large classes, often taught by teaching assistants. These issues were among those that erupted in 1964, as students employed the methods of civil disobedience on the Berkeley campus, where they crusaded for freedom of speech.

On several occasions Kerr had made a point of reiterating the campus policy that the university would remain disengaged from "all political and sectarian influence"— allowing freedom of campus speech was not to be confused with the administration's endorsement of its con-

tent. These speeches came to be known as the "Kerr Directives." Also during his tenure, the university lifted a 12-year ban on communist speakers on campus in 1963. Although he was sympathetic to the concerns of the individual, his authority made him a target nonetheless.

At the east end of the Berkeley campus, a strip of land at the intersection of Bancroft Way and Telegraph Avenue would provide the arena for the dispute. Students regularly set up various political and religious recruitment tables at that location, to the east of Sather Gate. In 1959, Kerr had asked that the Bancroft strip be transferred to the city, but the order had not been carried out. In the summer of 1964, when the administration discovered that the Bancroft strip was still within the bounds of the campus, they banned active solicitation along the strip in accord with the ban already in existence on the general campus.

On September 28, Berkeley students confronted the university, setting up unpermitted recruitment tables at Sather Gate. The regents announced they were prepared to allow some degree of on-campus recruitment, but by this time the students had resolved to seek unmitigated freedoms. Two days later, five students manning tables for the Student Non-Violent Coordinating Committee (SNCC) and the campus's Congress of Racial Equality (CORE) were ordered to appear for disciplinary hearings. As they were being cited, CORE member and former Berkeley student Jack Weinberg began rebuking the administration. Weinberg's speech galvanized the students, addressing their concerns not just about political freedoms but about the quality of campus life in general. Later that day, philosophy student Mario Savio led hundreds of students in accompanying the five recruiters to their disciplinary hearing. When Berkeley's chancellor announced their suspensions, Savio and other student leaders drew up a series of demands and christened their new-born organization the Free Speech Movement (FSM).

On October 1, Weinberg was arrested at one of the recruitment tables for refusing to identify himself. A police car was summoned; by the time it arrived, hundreds of students had gathered to block its departure. Overnight and into the following day, the police car holding Weinberg remained on the plaza amid the students' sit-in. California Governor Edmund G. Brown refused to send in the National Guard, fearing the incident would be identified with the recent civil rights demonstrations in the deep south. Later on the second day of protest, President Kerr agreed to moderate a meeting between his administration and student leaders. As 500 police officers stood ready to arrest the demonstrators, the two sides agreed upon a six-point settlement. Outside on the plaza, Savio mounted the besieged police car and called off the protest.

The crisis was not over, however. During the Thanksgiving holiday, the administration moved to discipline the main participants in the demonstration. Angry activists scheduled a massive protest for December 2, 1964. At that rally, Savio spoke: "When the operation of the machine becomes so odious that you can't take part," he said, "you've got to put your bodies upon the gears . . . and you've got to make it stop." One thousand demonstrators occupied Sproul Hall and stayed there through the night. At 3 A.M. on December 3, Berkeley's Chancellor Strong went through Sproul Hall asking the students to leave; those who did not were rounded up by over 600 law officers. Later that day, hundreds of faculty members passed a resolution calling for charges against all student agitators to be dropped and for the immediate implementation of freer campus speech codes. For several days, the campus was embroiled in picketing and its normal operations were disabled.

At a tense gathering at the Greek Theatre on December 7, Kerr publicly accepted a proposal drawn up by academic leaders. Shortly thereafter, Chancellor Strong, suffering from health problems, was granted a leave of absence. Berkeley had finally found an uneasy peace. By the spring of 1965, the FSM had disbanded in favor of more specialized movements. Protests, however, continued to have an impact on campus life: rallies for various advocacy groups were staged daily, and in March 1965, a campus visitor was arrested for displaying an obscenity on a placard, igniting the so-called filthy speech rallies. The 793 students who had been arrested in Sproul Hall went on trial in April. Most were fined for trespassing or sentenced to short jail terms for resisting arrest. Savio, Weinberg, and Arthur Goldberg were given 120 days in jail; their appeals reached the Supreme Court in 1967, where they were denied a hearing.

Berkeley's unrest did not significantly hamper the UC system's ability to attract faculty and students, but it did anger alumni and potential benefactors, who felt the university's prestige had been undermined. In 1966, gubernatorial candidate Ronald Reagan promised to control Berkeley's dissenters, claiming that Kerr had been too lenient with them. In 1967, the newly elected governor threatened to trim $35 million from the university's operating budget; he also called for tuition charges at UC, drawing crowds of thousands in protest in Sacramento. The UC budget for 1967–68 was eventually trimmed by more than $20 million. Reagan's motion to institute tuition fees was defeated, but he did secure an $81 per student rise in yearly incidental fees.

By 1968, Kerr had been coerced into resigning, but incidents of civil disobedience did not end with his departure. On the UCLA campus, students had staged a 1967 sit-in protesting on-campus interviews conducted by the Dow Chemical Company. In 1969, incoming UC president Charles Hitch was faced with the so-called People's Park incident, when thousands of students and residents occupied a parcel of Berkeley land, demanding that it be turned into a community park. In another Berkeley scene watched closely throughout the nation,

Reagan called in the National Guard to put down the protesters.

By the end of the 1970s, however, political idealism had dwindled on the Berkeley campus. Surveys at the time showed that 43 percent of the students considered themselves politically moderate, while 17 percent argued that the administration retained the right to ban certain speakers from appearing on campus. Still, some political issues continued to gather attention: on the Santa Cruz campus, 400 students were arrested in 1977 while protesting the university's financial holdings in South Africa. Other groups have sought an end to the university's affiliation with the Livermore and Los Alamos nuclear testing labs.

In recent years, the university has been the forum for protracted debate over affirmative action. In 1977, white student Allan Bakke sued the university, claiming that he was denied entrance to the Davis Medical School in favor of less-qualified minorities. The case reached the U.S. Supreme Court, which heard for the first time a "reverse discrimination" argument. The Supreme Court overturned California's ruling against the university's special admissions program, but at the same time the high court ordered Bakke's acceptance at Davis, indecisively concluding the issue. In 1995 the UC Board of Regents struck down its commitment to affirmative action, sparking renewed national debate over the decades-old policy.

With a total enrollment topping 30,000, Los Angeles now has the largest student population in the UC system, surpassing Berkeley. The UC system continues to grow at a remarkable pace: even its smallest general campuses, at Riverside and Santa Cruz, have approached or topped enrollments of 10,000 students in recent years. California's role in the Pan-Pacific community increasingly affects the makeup of its student body: Berkeley today has a higher percentage of Asian-Americans than Caucasians.

The faculties of the University of California continue to excel, to date having garnered 29 Nobel Prizes, with 18 of those laureates currently in residence. In addition, a record 241 members of the National Academy of Sciences grace the UC faculties. Ten percent of all federal funding for secondary-education research goes to the UC system, and ten percent of all Ph.D.s earned in the United States are earned at UC.

Wielding the considerable strengths of its numbers and its traditions, the UC system has risen to prestige in all aspects of university life. From an initial graduating class of 12, the university and its affiliates have spread to dozens of locations throughout California, the nation's largest state, where it provides services for over 150,000 students per year. Despite the inevitability of such an immense institution encountering periods of darkness in its collective mission, the University of California stands by its original motto—*Fiat Lux* (Let There Be Light).

Further Reading: Verne A. Stadtman, longtime editor of the California Alumni Association's monthly magazine, has written two essential, exhaustive histories of his alma mater: *The Centennial Record of the University of California* (Berkeley: University of California, 1967) and *The University of California 1868–1968* (New York: McGraw-Hill, 1970). A more casual source, *Cal: A Guide to the World's Largest University and the Bay Area* by Steven Warshaw (Berkeley: Endymion, 1983), includes a concise section on the Free Speech Movement, among other topics. Two pictorial histories of the university include short but efficient texts: *Photographic Guide to the University of California, Berkeley* by Benjamin B. Ehrich (Palo Alto, California: Pacific Books, 1969), and *The University of California: A Pictorial History* by Albert G. Pickerell and May Dornin (Berkeley: The Regents of the University of California, 1968). The Writers' Program of the Work Projects Administration in Northern California produced a helpful history, *Berkeley: The First 75 Years* (Berkeley, California: Gillick, 1941). Finally, *UCLA On the Move during Fifty Golden Years 1919–1969* by Andrew Hamilton and John B. Jackson (Los Angeles: Ward Ritchie, 1969) provides much information about UC's largest campus not found in the general texts.

—James Sullivan

UNIVERSITY OF CAMBRIDGE
(Cambridge, England)

Location: Sixty miles north of London, 80 miles northeast of Oxford.

Description: The second-oldest university in England, enrolling approximately 15,000 students in 31 autonomous colleges.

Information: The Registry
The Old Schools
Trinity Lane
Cambridge CB2 1TN
England
(01223) 332 200

The University of Cambridge was one of only two universities in England until 1825 (although there were four in Scotland, a separate kingdom until 1707), and even now it is one of the most socially prestigious and academically successful universities in the United Kingdom. It has unavoidably developed largely in tandem with the enormous social and economic changes which have transformed a small, marginal western European kingdom, first into the center of the world's largest colonial empire and a pioneer of scientific and industrial modernization, and then into a post-imperial country exposed to global competition and uncertain of its future. Along with the University of Oxford, the other "ancient university" of England, which is still customarily seen as its main rival, it has sometimes become disconnected from these changes, notably in the eighteenth and early nineteenth centuries, but it has retained throughout its intimate connections with leading individuals and groups in British politics and culture.

The origins of the university remain obscure. The first scholars to settle in what was then a market town on the Cam River appear to have arrived from Oxford, where some kind of advanced schooling already existed, around 1209. Their first meeting place was probably in or near the parish church, Great Saint Mary's, which had been built some time before 1205. By the time it was rebuilt in 1478, it was already being referred to as the university church. Graduation ceremonies were held in it until the opening of the university's Senate House in 1730; its bells were used to ring curfew for undergraduates at nine o'clock every evening until as recently as 1939; and it still receives financial support from the university today.

Such a close connection with Christianity is characteristic of universities founded in western Europe during the Middle Ages. Both Oxford and Cambridge were to remain formally linked to the Church—first in the Catholic tradition and then, after the Reformation, to the Episcopal Church of England—until the middle of the nineteenth century. From a very early stage they were also to be subject to interventions by officials of the secular state. The first reference to a chancellor of the University of Cambridge dates from 1226. The first known case of royal intervention took place just five years later, when, in the name of King Henry III, its scholars were placed under the authority of the town's sheriff and of the Bishop of Ely and were required also to obey their own masters. The first recognition of the university by a pope came in 1233 in the form of a bull issued by Gregory IX, which confirmed the scholars' autonomy.

Three religious orders, the Dominicans, the Carmelites, and the Franciscans, also began teaching inside their own houses in Cambridge during the later years of the thirteenth century. Relations among the various Cambridge bodies involved in education were not clarified until 1276, when the Bishop of Ely declared a fundamental division between priests, or "clerks," attached to parish churches, who were to be answerable to his archdeacon, and those engaged in study, who were to come under the jurisdiction of the chancellor while remaining within their own houses or halls. Thus formal recognition was given to the model of organization which the university, like Oxford, had borrowed from the Sorbonne (the University of Paris). Both have remained federations of self-governing colleges ever since.

Peterhouse is the oldest remaining college in Cambridge, although it does not use the word "college" in its title. It was given its present name in 1284 but had been founded in 1280 as an annex of Saint John's Hospital under the jurisdiction of Hugh de Baldsham, the Bishop of Ely, who is regarded as its founder. Next came Michaelhouse, founded in 1324 by Hervey de Stanton, and later absorbed into Trinity College; University Hall, founded in 1326, refounded 12 years later by Lady Elizabeth de Clare, and known as Clare Hall until 1856, when it became Clare College; King's Hall, founded by Edward III in 1337, and also now incorporated into Trinity College; Pembroke College, founded in 1347 as Pembroke Hall by Marie de Valence, dowager countess of Pembroke; Gonville and Caius College, begun in 1348 as Gonville Hall, named for its founder Edmund Gonville and intended for the training of priests to serve in his native county of Norfolk; and Trinity Hall, founded in 1350 by William Bateman, Bishop of Norwich, and dedicated from the outset to the study of law. The last of this

University of Cambridge

early group was Corpus Christi College, known locally as Corpus, which was founded in 1352 by two guilds of Cambridge citizens. Its Old Court, which dates from soon after its foundation, is the oldest remaining example of the courts, sets of rooms around a paved or, more commonly, grassed yard, which have come to characterize Cambridge college buildings and which resemble the quadrangles (or quads) of Oxford colleges.

Each college had its own accommodation for its scholars, its own library, and its own dining hall, the three basic features which still define the college in principle. Their presiding officers, known as regent masters, shared in the administration of the university, alongside non-regent masters, who were in charge of the smaller hostels connected to one or another religious order. At this period the university was chiefly concerned with discipline and finance and consisted of the chancellor and other officials elected by the masters. From around 1278 they began to acquire houses near Great Saint Mary's as bases for administration and teaching, but they did not have a dedicated headquarters

built until around 1350. This complex, extended and rebuilt several times since and now known as the Old Schools, has remained at the heart of the university's activities, as distinct from those of the colleges. Lectures were being delivered there as early as 1400, and the university library was located there from 1438 until 1842. Today the Old Schools house the university's registry and the meeting room of its council, among other official bodies.

By the time the Olds Schools were opened, the university's status had been confirmed by two important documents. In 1317 it was granted a royal charter; in 1318 its officers were freed by a bull issued by Pope John XXII from their former subordination to the Bishops of Ely. Such official recognition did not protect the university or the colleges from occasional outbreaks of popular resentment, notably in 1381, when the Peasants' Revolt spread across southern England. Corpus Christi College, then the wealthiest, was attacked and damaged by a crowd of its tenants, the university records kept inside Great Saint Mary's were burned, and the homes of several university officials were also pillaged. These disorganized protests culminated in a formal seizure of power over the university by the town authorities, the mayor and burgesses, who compelled the scholars to surrender the privileges granted by various kings. Prompt military action by the forces of the Bishop of Norwich, followed by judicial intervention to ensure the execution of the rebels' leaders and the restoration of the university's autonomy, restored the status quo. The uprising offers a salutary reminder that much of the enormous wealth of the colleges, at Cambridge as at Oxford, has been extracted, not only from distinguished patrons or charitable foundations, but also from their agricultural tenants, among whom were some of the poorest and most exploited people in England.

When not engaged in disputes with the town authorities or with their tenants, the scholars of Cambridge devoted themselves to the study of theology, law, and philosophy (known at Cambridge as moral sciences), the traditional subjects taught in all western European universities of the period. As the number of undergraduates steadily increased, four more colleges were founded. King's College was established by King Henry VI in 1441, one year after he had set up a school, Eton College, with which the college was to be long associated near the royal castle at Windsor. The construction of the famous chapel at King's began in 1446, but was not completed until 1526, by which time Henry's Lancastrian dynasty had given way to the Yorkists and then in 1485 to the Tudors. It is their version of the royal coat of arms, along with their symbol, the united red (Lancastrian) and white (Yorkist) rose, which appears above the chapel's west door. The chapel has since been enhanced with Flemish-style stained-glass windows, fan-vaulting, a sixteenth-century oak screen, a seventeenth-century organ, and a painting by Peter Paul Rubens, *The Adoration of the Magi* (1633–34), which was installed as recently as 1968.

The next foundation was Queens' College, established in 1448 by Andrew Dockett with the support of Margaret of Anjou, wife of King Henry VI, and later of Elizabeth Woodville, wife of Edward IV, who supplanted Henry in 1460. Its red brick Old Court, built soon after its foundation, still retains the appearance and atmosphere of the later Middle Ages. It was followed by Saint Catharine's College, called Catharine Hall until 1860 and still nicknamed Catz, which was founded in 1473 by Robert Woodlark, the provost of King's College (a post equivalent to master at other colleges); and Jesus College, founded in 1496 by John Alcock, Bishop of Ely, originally in honor of the Virgin Mary, Saint John the Evangelist, and the relatively obscure Saint Radegund, the patron saint of the nuns' priory which had previously occupied its site and the buildings of which, some still standing today, were incorporated into the college.

In the sixteenth century the University of Cambridge, like other universities in northwestern Europe, became a center of the humanist scholarship and reforming ideas which fed the growth of Protestant forms of Christianity. One of the earliest representatives of these tendencies, although he himself remained within the Catholic Church, was John Fisher, who was to become chancellor for life and who was also chaplain to Lady Margaret Beaufort, the mother of King Henry VII. She was persuaded to endow what is still called the Lady Margaret Chair of Divinity (in theology), the university's first dedicated professorship, which Fisher was the first to occupy. She also, uniquely, founded two new colleges. Christ's College was founded in 1505 with the intention of reviving God's House, built in 1446, while Saint John's College, known as John's, was founded in 1511 with a bequest from Lady Margaret, who had died two years before. John's incorporates what is now one of the oldest buildings in Cambridge, the twelfth-century School of Pythagoras.

It was probably also Fisher who brought the great Dutch scholar Desiderius Erasmus to Cambridge, where he introduced the study of classical Greek, an essential tool in the program of biblical criticism, of which he and his associates were pioneers. Erasmus resided between 1510 and 1514 in what was then a new part of Queens' College, the Cloister Court, and is said to have worked on his groundbreaking edition of the Greek New Testament there. Although the writings of the leading Protestant, Martin Luther, were to be publicly burned in Cambridge in 1520, and Erasmus, like Fisher, remained loyal to the pope, the investigations which he inspired were to lead many Cambridge teachers and students to conclusions similar to Luther's. Among these, Thomas Cranmer, one of the first graduates of Jesus College, was to be the most prominent, as archbishop of Canterbury (the leading church official in England) during and after King Henry VIII's creation of the Protestant Church of England.

The triumph of Henry's Reformation was symbolized at Cambridge in 1534 by a formal denunciation of the pope, the execution of John Fisher, and the appointment of King Henry's leading adviser, Thomas Cromwell, as vice-chancellor of the university. The same year also saw the granting of a royal charter to the Cambridge University Press, now the oldest printing and publishing company in the world. Two more colleges were founded during the early years of the Reformation. Magdalene was established in 1542 by Lord Audley in the buildings of Buckingham College, a Benedictine establishment dissolved by Henry VIII. Trinity College—not to be confused with Trinity Hall—was founded in 1546 by Henry himself, a statue of whom adorns its Great Gate. The Great Court into which the gateway leads is said to be the largest enclosed courtyard in Europe. Trinity remains unique in being headed by a master who is not elected by the college's fellows (academic staff) but is appointed by the Crown.

During the reign of Henry's daughter Queen Mary I (1554–58), England briefly returned to the Catholic fold. Many university and college officials were dismissed, and the Protestant victims of the Marian persecutions included three Cambridge-trained bishops, Thomas Cranmer, Hugh Latimer, and Nicholas Ridley, who were all burned in Oxford.

Yet another college was created under Mary, when Gonville Hall was refounded in 1557 by a physician named John Keys, who used the Latin form of his name, "Caius," in his scholarly writings. One of several university traditions is that the college is usually nicknamed Caius, pronounced "Keys." It is famous for the three gates which its founder had constructed for it, the Gate of Humility through which new undergraduates and visitors enter, the Gate of Virtue through which its fellows and students pass on everyday business, and the Gate of Honour, a triumphal arch through which undergraduates leave to receive their degrees.

The upheavals associated with the Reformation continued under Mary's sister and successor Elizabeth, who refounded the Church of England and also gave the university the Statutes of 1559 and the Charter of 1561, which regulated its activities up to the middle of the nineteenth century. But the religious reforms had already changed much more than the details of administration or the content of courses in divinity. In 1540 Henry had established five Regius professorships, posts which are still filled by the British prime minister in the name of the monarch, in divinity, Greek, and civil law, all of which were already being taught at Cambridge, but also in Hebrew and physic (medicine). In addition the dissolution of the monasteries and other religious houses and the dispersal of their lands and wealth among the nobility and gentry helped to alter the composition of the student body in both English universities, as more and more sons of landowners entered their colleges, displacing the poorer candidates. The medieval emphasis on theology and moral sciences began to give way to the humanists' emphasis on a broad, liberal education, including languages and history, and emphasizing individual study.

Nevertheless, Cambridge was still a mainly religious institution. Its teachers were all clergymen of the Church of England with many, sometimes most, of its undergraduates preparing to join the church too, and the spirit of the Reformation continuing to dominate Cambridge life and thought, perhaps especially in the last two foundations of the sixteenth century. Emmanuel College, founded in 1584 by Sir Walter Mildmay on the site of a Dominican friary dissolved by Henry VIII, was closely associated with the Puritan movement within the Church of England, whose adherents would break away in the following century to form separate, nonconformist churches both in England and in its North American colonies. Of the first 100 English university graduates to settle in New England more than 30 were from Emmanuel, including John Harvard, for whom Harvard University was to be named. Puritanism was also influential within Sidney Sussex College, founded in 1596 on the site of a dissolved Franciscan friary with money bequeathed by Frances Sidney, Countess of Sussex. This college's most famous graduate was Oliver Cromwell, who went on to become a parliamentary general in the English Civil Wars, one of the signatories of King Charles I's death warrant in 1649 and, as Lord Protector from 1653 to 1658, the king's replacement. Since 1961 Cromwell's head, cut from his corpse after the restoration of the monarchy in 1660, has been buried inside the college.

In spite of political and social unrest the seventeenth century saw the university flourish, both intellectually and architecturally. Henry More and other philosophers, forming the group since dubbed the Cambridge Platonists, developed the idea of religious toleration and integrated the proto-scientific thinking of Francis Bacon and René Descartes into the curriculum; Isaac Newton was a fellow of Trinity College, residing there from 1679 to 1696 while working on his *Principia Mathematica*. Saint Catharine's Church was rebuilt between 1674 and 1687, the Old Court of Clare College was constructed between 1638 and 1715, and Christopher Wren, who taught astronomy at Cambridge and whose uncle, the Bishop of Ely, was his first architectural patron, designed the chapel at Pembroke, opened in 1665, the chapel at Emmanuel, built between 1666 and 1679, and the library of Trinity College, completed in 1695.

The eighteenth century, in contrast, saw something of a decline, as the number of undergraduates fell, reaching its nadir in 1760; but change continued, if more slowly. Moral sciences came to include elements of mathematics, astronomy, and physics. Addenbrooke's Hospital, founded in 1740 with a bequest from Dr. John Addenbrooke, a fellow of Saint Catharine's, has housed the university's School of Clinical Medicine ever since, although it was moved into a new set of buildings in 1984. The university's Senate House was built between 1722 and 1730, to designs by James Gibbs and James Burrough, to be used for graduation ceremonies, some public lectures, and meetings of the Regent House, the governing body of the university. (It would be impossible for it to contain the entire membership of the senate, which is defined as all those who hold a master's degree or a doctorate from the university.) Meanwhile, those who were members of the nobility received their degrees without taking any examinations, and in general Cambridge, like Oxford, gained a reputation for leisurely living rather than for academic prowess.

The transformation of Cambridge into what has been jokingly called "the city of perspiring dreams"—in contrast with Oxford, "the city of dreaming spires"—occurred during the nineteenth century, as a rapidly modernizing and expanding British empire burst in upon the university's courts. New colleges were founded and new buildings were erected, some of them accommodating strange new subjects and new kinds of students, while many of the assumptions and habits which had typified university life for centuries were challenged and faded away at Cambridge as at Oxford, at Harvard and at many other leading universities. Throughout the century, too, the number of undergraduates increased, as the range of academic subjects widened.

The first sign of new life was a series of new buildings. Downing College, the first new foundation in more than 200 years, was established in 1800 with a bequest from Sir George Downing, who had died 51 years earlier. Its Greek classical buildings were constructed between 1807 and 1820 to designs by William Wilkins and then extended in 1953 and again in the 1980s and 1990s in a similar style. In addition, the front buildings of King's College were constructed in the 1820s to designs by William Wilkins which echo the frontage of the chapel, and John's became the first of the riverside colleges to expand across the Cam onto its western bank, with the building of its New Court and its covered Bridge of Sighs, both completed in 1831 in a neo-Gothic style.

While the colleges, apart from Downing, favored neo-Gothic styles, presumably because they fit better with their existing buildings, the university preferred to revive Classical styles for such buildings as the Fitzwilliam Museum, opened in 1848 to house prints by Rembrandt, pictures by William Blake, and paintings by Titian, Veronese, Rubens, van Dyck, Hogarth, Reynolds, Gainsborough, Turner, and Constable. By then Cambridge also had a railway station, built in 1845 by the Great Eastern Railway Company, which was compelled by the university authorities to locate its station at a distance from the colleges, because the noise and dirt of its trains.

But the modern world could not be kept entirely at bay. Queen Victoria's husband Prince Albert, chancellor of the university from 1847 until his death in 1861, encouraged the appointment of a royal commission to investigate both Oxford and Cambridge. Its report, published in 1852, directly influenced the shaping of new statutes, issued under an act of Parliament in 1856, which at last removed the traditional religious test from Cambridge life, except for divinity students, college officers, and members of the senate. From 1871, only divinity students and heads of houses were still required to be members of the Church of England. Further interventions by the national government ensured that, from 1877, the colleges would have to surrender some of their enormous incomes to the university and could no longer appoint fellows who did not teach, and that, from 1882, no college could dismiss a fellow merely for having married or left the Church of England. Almost 100 years after the French Revolution secularism had arrived in Cambridge.

However, this is not to say that the Divinity School, the oldest academic division of the university, immediately lost its importance. Indeed, it was moved in 1879 into a bigger building, now named for William Selwyn, its leading professor at that date, and two new foundations were devoted to religious studies. Selwyn College, founded in 1882 as a memorial to George Augustus Selwyn, the first bishop of New Zealand, required all its fellows to be members of the

Church of England; it did not become a full college of the university until 1958. Saint Edmund's College was established in 1896 as Saint Edmund's House, a college for Catholic students. It became a postgraduate institution in 1965 and changed its name in 1986, but it still has the only Catholic chapel in the university.

While divinity and the other traditional subjects of study survived intact, nineteenth-century Cambridge also underwent a gradual transformation into a center of scientific research and achievement, going far beyond established mathematical studies and even the work of Newton. This trend may be dated from 1833, when Professor William Whewell invented the word "scientist," or from 1851, when Whewell and others secured recognition for natural sciences as a faculty. Between 1863 and 1914 the area known as the New Museums Site became the home of many scientific laboratories and teaching rooms. Among these is the complex now called the Old Cavendish Laboratory, founded in 1874 by William Cavendish, Duke of Devonshire, then the chancellor. This was to be the university's center for experimental physics until 1973. It was inside the Cavendish that J.J. Thomson discovered the electron in 1897; between the two world wars, Ernest Rutherford pursued his research on the nucleus; James Chadwick discovered the neutron in 1935; and Francis Crick and James Watson worked out the double helix structure of DNA in 1953.

The nineteenth century also saw the university's first tentative steps toward widening access to its facilities. A Non-Collegiate Students Board was set up in 1869 to help and encourage those unable or unwilling to live in colleges. After becoming known as Fitzwilliam Hall in 1887 and as Fitzwilliam House in 1924 this organization was converted into Fitzwilliam College in 1966 and moved into a modernist building designed by Denys Lasdun. Three institutions for women have gone through a similar development, achieving their first success in 1881, when women were permitted to take university examinations for the first time, although they were still unable to take degrees. The first women's college, Girton, had been established by Emily Davies in the town of Hitchin in Hertfordshire in 1869 but four years later had moved to its present buildings designed by Alfred Waterhouse, more than two miles from the city center. It now admits both women and men. Newnham College was established in 1871 and moved into its present Dutch-style red and white buildings, which are unusual in not including a chapel, in 1875. Next, what is now Hughes Hall was founded in 1885 as a training college for women schoolteachers. It took its present name in 1949 to honor its first principal and was converted into a coeducational postgraduate college in 1973. Finally, in 1894 Homerton Academy, another teacher-training institution for women, founded in London in 1768, moved to Cambridge, taking over buildings abandoned by Cavendish College when it closed in 1892 (only 16 years after its opening) and becoming Homerton College. It remains exclusively devoted to teacher training but has admitted men since 1978.

The last of the great modernizing reforms of the university during the century was the development of the faculty of economics and politics, one of the leading centers of economic research and thought in the English-speaking world. There had been a professorship of political economy, the discipline which was to spawn both modern economics and political science since 1828, but the subject remained subordinate to moral sciences and to historical studies until after 1885, when the professorship passed to Alfred Marshall. His then-rare interest in linking academic research with the needs of industrialists and even labor unions inspired generations of British economists, while his campaign for an independent faculty at Cambridge met with success in 1903. Since then its members have included such influential economists as A.C. Pigou, John Maynard Keynes, and Joan Robinson.

By 1903, the University of Cambridge had moved decisively away from its medieval and early modern role as a loose federation of religious foundations providing the finishing touches to the molding of young gentlemen to become an assemblage of intellectual and material resources for the training of young men, and increasing numbers of young women, both in the traditional liberal arts and in the professional specializations of science, engineering, medicine, and law. During the twentieth century the university has further developed its strengths, occasionally creating new faculties, such as English in the 1920s, and social and political studies in the 1980s. These faculties have made notable contributions to their respective disciplines through the work of such critics as I.A. Richards, F.R. Leavis, William Empson, and Raymond Williams, as well as of such social scientists as Anthony Giddens, Quentin Skinner, and John Dunn. For most of the century Cambridge has also remained socially exclusive, partly because of the sheer expense of a Cambridge education, which has only slowly been made more widely available by government grants and scholarships.

The university's physical expansion has also continued. For example, in 1920 the university established the Scott Polar Research Institute to commemorate Captain Robert Falcon Scott, the leader of the second expedition to reach the South Pole, near which he and his companions died in 1912. Clare College commissioned two new courts across the river from its older building, the grey brick Memorial and Thirkell Courts, built between 1923 and 1955 to plans by Sir Giles Gilbert Scott. Scott also designed the new brown brick university library, opened in 1934, with its 160-foot high tower rearing up over the two Clare courts. Now the largest open-access library in Europe, it is also notable for its space-saving system of shelving books, within each subject, according to a system of four sizes. Meanwhile, the university's scientific faculties had already expanded across Downing Street onto the Downing Site, purchased from Downing College between 1896 and 1902 and developed between 1903 and 1939 to accommodate teaching and research in the life sciences, as well as the university's Museum of Archeology and Anthropology and Sedgwick Museum of Geology.

During World War II many leading Cambridge academics played crucial roles in enhancing the British war effort and incidentally influencing the postwar world as well. For example, Professor Sir John Cockroft of the Cavendish Laboratory was closely involved in the development of radar as well as in the British contributions to the development of atomic weapons and of civil atomic power, while Alan Turing and other young mathematicians used "Ultra" machines, direct ancestors of the digital computer, to break supposedly unbreakable German codes. In Cambridge itself, where little damage was sustained from bombing, accommodation was provided for the London School of Economics and three other colleges evacuated from the capital.

In 1948 women were at last allowed to take degrees and to become members of university bodies, 28 years after the University of Oxford had introduced similar reforms and fully 70 years after the University of London had been the first in Britain to do so. Six years later New Hall was founded to provide more places for women students. This turned out to be only the first of seven new colleges. Churchill College was opened in 1960 in honor of Sir Winston Churchill who, ironically, never went to any university. Churchill was followed by three colleges for postgraduate students only: Darwin College, founded in 1964 and given collegiate status the following year, which is housed in Newnham Grange, once the home of Charles Darwin; Wolfson College, established by the university itself as University College in 1965, but renamed eight years later to mark a large donation from the Wolfson Foundation (now admitting undergraduates as well, so long as they are over 21 years old); and Clare Hall, created by Clare College in 1966 but made independent in 1983. Two other colleges have brought the total number to 31. Lucy Cavendish College, founded in 1965, 40 years after the death of the campaigner for women's education whom it commemorates, remains unique in having exclusively female staff and restricting admission to women over 21; Robinson College, founded in 1977 with funds donated by the wealthy businessman Sir David Robinson, was opened in 1981.

While new colleges were opening, and the older colleges were expanding their accommodations for steadily rising numbers of students, the university too was growing and taking up still more space in the city. During the 1960s the arts faculties of the university were brought together in buildings spread across the Sedgwick Site. The most famous, or notorious, of the new buildings has been the History Faculty Library, designed by James Stirling and completed in 1968, which has been praised for its striking combination of large areas of glass with a structure of traditional red bricks but which has proved difficult and expensive to maintain. In addition, the university's scientific work moved to a new stage 1981, when Trinity College opened its Science Park on the outskirts of the city. This project, in which the university and other colleges also take part, is intended to close a perceived gap between academic researchers and the computing, pharmaceutical, and other companies which exploit their discoveries and which have relocated to the site.

This larger and more varied university now has a larger and more varied population of students. One reason has been the trend toward opening traditionally single-sex colleges to both men and women. In 1972 Church, Clare, and King's were the first to become mixed, and by 1995 only three single-sex colleges remained: Newnham, New Hall, and Lucy Cavendish, all for women. Another reason has been the enormous growth, in line with other British universities, in the numbers of postgraduate students in all of its colleges; they now account for one-third of its total of 15,000 students. A third, but so far less important, reason has been the abolition in 1985 of the university's entrance examination. It was widely believed that the examination had unfairly favored applicants from the public schools (British English for private schools), who could be specially coached and who might also have been able to take advantage of historic ties between their schools and the university. However, the system which has replaced it, depending on a combination of national examination results and interviews, has hardly altered the situation, for just under half of undergraduates still come from this small minority of schools, and the historic under-representation of northern England, in comparison with London, the southeastern counties around it, and East Anglia, the region in which Cambridge stands, continues today.

One more change in the nature of the university is that since World War II it has come to depend on public funds from national and local governments for most of its income. Partly in order to offset this reliance on public funds, the university launched its first general fundraising campaign in 1993, aiming to gather 250 million pounds by 2003. The campaign reached 60 percent of its target in its first two years, at least some of the money coming from its alumni; they, like Oxford's graduates, are still disproportionately represented in the ranks of the civil service, among judges and politicians, in the management of the media, and in other leading positions in British society.

The University of Cambridge has already undergone several major transformations during its history. An offshoot of the medieval church, training priests and lawyers, has become, in succession, a finishing school for the sons of the wealthy, a center of scientific excellence, and a modern university with an international reputation; an institution originally open only to a very small number of well-connected men faithful to the dominant religion has become accessible to a much wider range of people, teaching and studying an enormously wider range of subjects. The achievements of at least some Cambridge teachers and graduates, in politics, science, economics, and the arts, have affected British and even world history, for better or for worse. If the university can go on adapting to changing conditions as it has in the past, there may well be more to come.

Further Reading: Cambridge University Press has published an interesting anthology of writings about the university, *Cambridge Commemorated,* edited by Laurence and Helen Fowler (1984); *A History of the University of Cambridge* in four volumes, edited by Christopher Brooke (Cambridge and New York: Cambridge University Press, 1989–92); and the latest of several semi-official illustrated guides, Kevin Taylor's *Central Cambridge: A Guide to the Universities and Colleges* (Cambridge: Cambridge University Press, 1994). *My Cambridge,* edited by Ronald Hayman (London: Robson, 1977; revised edition, 1986), is a collection of memoirs evoking Cambridge from the 1930s to the 1960s.

—Patrick Heenan

UNIVERSITY OF CANTERBURY
(Christchurch, New Zealand)

Location: In Ilam, seven kilometers from Christchurch, South Island, New Zealand.

Description: An autonomous coeducational university offering undergraduate (first) and postgraduate (higher) degrees, with 11,000 undergraduate and postgraduate students.

Information: University of Canterbury
Private Bag 4800
Christchurch
New Zealand
(3) 3667001

The early settlers and planners of Christchurch were determined to bring the Anglican tradition and excellence in the educational system to this planned settlement. In 1848 in England a highly educated group formed the Canterbury Association and two years later published the "Scheme for the Establishment of Christ-Church College." After their arrival in New Zealand, great efforts were made to establish a university as quickly as possible. They did, indeed, want to remain part of the world, even though they felt on the edge of it.

In 1872 the inaugural address of the board of governors for the newly formed body, the Canterbury Collegiate Union, stated the policies of the existing University of New Zealand: to provide accessible higher education; to offer assistance to existing institutions serving the major communities; and to encourage talents without barriers of distance, wealth, or class.

Only a year later, 23 years after the founding of the settlement of Christchurch, Canterbury College was established as a constituent college of the federal University of New Zealand. It was the second university on the South Island and the fourth in New Zealand and Australia, following the universities of Otago, Auckland, and Melbourne. Christchurch, inhabited by 13,000 people, was located in the province of Canterbury on an alluvial plain sloping for 60 kilometers from the Pacific Ocean to the foothills of the Southern Alps.

The founders' specific intentions can only be surmised, but significant clues exist. First, the early promoters stressed the concept of a college as the "provincial edifice of education and culture." Second, the initial three chairs (departments) and academic subjects suggest educational priorities: chemistry; the classics, history, and English literature; and mathematics and natural philoso-phy. The Provincial Council Ordinance of 1873, dated June 16, 1873, is identified as the beginning of the college's legal existence. It stated that the college was "to provide a regular and liberal course of education."

For the following two decades, the board of governors was the provincial authority in most fields of education above the primary level. Their function was to manage an estate, maintain the number of institutions, and control the staffs. The 1873 reality was that the board of governors was the colony's largest landlord. Rental income totaling £3,000 came from the lands of poorer quality in the high country. In addition to Canterbury College, the board was responsible for the Canterbury Museum (1873–74), Canterbury Public Library (1873–74), Christchurch Girls High School (1876), Christchurch Boys High School (1877), Canterbury School of Agriculture (1873–80), and the School of Art (1879–80).

During the first two terms (June–November 1874), five part-time lecturers taught biology, modern languages, mental science (philosophy), jurisprudence, and political economy (economics). Three of these lecturers, an additional lecturer, and three young professors appointed as chairs (heads of departments) comprised the staff for the first full teaching session in 1875. Alexander William Bickerton (age 32) came from the Royal School of Mines (London) as the first professor of chemistry; John Macmillan Brown (age 28) from the University of Glasgow (Scotland) and Bailliol College (Oxford) became the first professor of classics and English; and Charles Henry Herbert Cook (age 29) as the first professor of mathematics and natural philosophy. This triumvirate became known as the college's foundation professoriate. They were paid £600 a year and could be dismissed at any time by the board of governors. It is said that these academic founding fathers were given "opportunities and functions which could never be repeated—the glories (and the perils) of a pioneer." The three offered complementary gifts: Bickerton gave promise of something approaching scientific adventure; Macmillan Brown, of lifting study to the level of an intellectual crusade; Cook, of an ability to hold the college to fundamentals, and to a sense of balance.

Students came, but with different skills and expectations than the founders had imagined. The initial 83 students arrived from provincial schools for part-time, late afternoon, and evening classes. Instruction was elementary; only a small percentage of the students were capable of matriculation or entered with the academic preparation suited for university study. Initially it was necessary to accept a majority of fee-paying students who were incapable of matriculation. Soon afterward, high schools

University of Canterbury

which could prepare students for a scholarly education were identified as feeder schools Christchurch Boys High School and Christchurch Girls High School were the primary feeders, while students from Christ College matriculated while still in high school. It was not until 1888–89 that matriculated students (165) outnumbered non-matriculated students (153).

Women attended on equal terms with men. In 1876 Helen Connon was the first matriculated female student to begin a degree course. In 1880 Connon and Anne J. Bolton received their bachelor of arts degrees; Connon is considered the first woman to win honors in the British Empire. Connon, who later served as headmistress (principal) of Christchurch Girls High School (1883–94), married Macmillan Brown in 1886.

Development of the government, staffs, classes, sites, and buildings of these institutions was piecemeal over the initial five years. Local architects, including Benjamin Woolfield Mountfort, who had designed the Canterbury Museum, submitted designs for the college buildings. However, extensive controversy prevailed, and physical development was slow.

Francis William Chapman Haslam arrived in 1880 to replace Macmillan Brown as chair of the department of classics. In vivid contrast to Macmillan Brown and his academic fervor, Haslam was a strong advocate of residential halls, an early promoter of student sports, and the founder of the Canterbury College Football (soccer) Club. He considered the "gentlemanly pursuit of style and elegance" to be an important element of university study.

By 1886 the growing number of students required the board of governors to provide better facilities. The college buildings in the center of Christchurch had opened in 1877, replacing temporary structures of wood and corrugated iron on Worchester Street. A Men's Cottage, nicknamed the Football Den, was provided in 1888; the first women's residence hall, the Helen Connon Hall, opened in 1918. In 1992, the residents of Helen Connon Hall were given the right of complete self-governance rather than having a resident warden. This system remained in effect until 1954.

Students were involved in clubs and societies. Macmillan Brown began the Dialectic Society in 1878 as a debating club and initiated social evenings of concerts and plays. The 1880s were considered the "golden age of drama," a tradition which continued with later professor of education James Shelley (1920–36) and honorary lecturer Miss (later Dame) Ngaio Marsh (1942–64).

By 1893, 375 students attended Canterbury College (176 women; 199 men) with four professional chairs; the department of engineering had been added in 1887. Eighty-six percent of the funding still came from rents from outlying properties, a financial resource unique to Canterbury. Canterbury had become the primary finishing school for teachers in response to the 1877 national policy of free compulsory education at the primary level and funding for public high schools, which created a great demand for teachers.

In the 1890s one of Canterbury's most distinguished graduates studied at Christchurch. During a year of postgraduate research prior to studying in Cambridge (England) on scholarship, Ernest Rutherford discovered his own scientific ability. Another significant graduate, Apirana Ngata of Ngati Porou, received his bachelor of arts degree on August 17, 1894. The first Maori graduate, he was honored at a centennial celebration in 1984.

After Macmillan Brown's departure in 1880, Canterbury's stature diminished. A new focus had to be established, and that was to be engineering. In 1894 three new chairs were introduced: engineering, biology, and modern languages. In response to the potential offerings in engineering, the Seddon government made a grant of £2,333 toward the building and equipping of an electrical engineering laboratory at the college. This grant signified a decision to locate the "special" school of engineering at Canterbury. The distribution of special schools throughout the university campuses was competitive: Canterbury and Auckland later vied for the forestry school; the medical school went to Auckland; new campuses for the agricultural schools went to Palmerston North and Lincoln; and architecture to Auckland.

In 1905, the training school for teachers was officially established at the college, continuing the trend for more general education rather than for scholarly degrees imagined by its founders. Enrollment dropped, reflecting the increasingly dense population in the north island. Enrollment did not rise significantly again until after World War II. Physical development was slow and funding for development scarce. The faculty initiated a fundraising drive in 1913 "to give the College what is most needed, a separate and adequate library." The drive brought in £1,760. The new library opened in 1916 and provided a greatly needed structure in the academic quadrangle.

Even though a professional board had been established in 1875, it was not until 1922 that the professorial board had direct representation on the board of directors of the college. The dominant presence of absentee upper-middle class volunteer academic men on the board of governors had slowed the pace of development, advancement, and academic excellence. The voices of the academic staff were not being heard.

The 1930s witnessed a decrease in the number of students from nearly 1,000 in 1925 to 780, with an accompanying decline in university spirit. In 1933 the college was renamed Canterbury University College. This name change was perhaps a forewarning of the ending of the provincial First Era of the college. Its primary financing no longer came from its landholdings, and it became more dependent on other sources of funds. The last construction of a permanent building had been in 1923; high priority given to the expansion of the library in 1936 was not fulfilled for 40 more years.

The academic reform sparked in 1939 resulted in the formation of the joint council of the professional board committee in 1944. They were to examine the postwar needs of the college. The end of this First Era—the first 75 years of existence—is cited as 1948 when the engineers supported the idea of a larger campus. The possibility of splitting the college into two locations was considered; conflicting views were heard about the advantages and disadvantages of expansion of the existing center city campus versus a major move of at least part of the college to a more rural site. A search was begun for a site to accommodate the 2,534 students as well as the projected higher enrollments.

On June 18, 1949, almost 76 years after the opening of Canterbury College, the official announcement of the intention to move was made. The chosen location was in Ilam, a spacious suburban site seven kilometers away. The move would take place in stages from 1960 to 1974 with priority given to the building needs of the School of Engineering.

However, the November 1949 defeat of the Labour government significantly affected academic development and planning throughout New Zealand. The educational priority was to house primary school children. Cutbacks were to the detriment of education; salaries were reduced and development curtailed.

Critics maintain that the academic value of the move to Ilam was scarcely mentioned. No comprehensive planning had been done and neither the professional board nor students had been consulted. In 1952, the staff expressed their dissatisfaction with the plan to move, for they feared a loss of academic excellence with the projected enrollment of 8,000 students on the 76-hectare site at Ilam. A well-attended, lengthy Association of University Teachers meeting was held on June 18, 1953. The academic staff voiced intense exasperation, but no formal recommendation resulted.

Progress continued slowly. In 1955 a reaffirmation of the plan to move was made, and plans were approved for the School of Engineering. The grounds would be developed in three main blocks: engineering, science, and arts/library. In 1957 the Canterbury University College was renamed the University of Canterbury. The modern buildings on the Ilam campus encompass approximately 155,000 square meters in a park-like setting.

In 1960, John Angus Erskine, a Canterbury College graduate in the 1890s, made a bequest to the university which established the Erskine Fund. This funding has enabled Canterbury staff in the fields of science, engineering, and commerce to study overseas and allowed academic visitors from overseas to come to Canterbury.

In 1961 the federal system of universities was dissolved, and the University of Canterbury became fully autonomous. During this time, Margaret Mahy graduated (1958) and became one of New Zealand's foremost writers for children and teenagers. She has received awards and acclaim for her more than 100 books. In 1993 she received an honorary Doctor of Letters (Litt.D) at the graduation ceremonies.

In celebration of the 1973 centennial and to express its gratitude to the city of Christchurch, the university presented the former downtown site and buildings to the Arts Centre of Christchurch Trust. These gifts to the community are now being used as a community arts center, theaters, galleries, craft rooms, and offices for community organizations.

In 1974 the Ilam campus was completed, although further construction continued for the next two decades. The reduction in national funding drastically increased the need for research and grants. As a centennial project for the School of Engineering, the Centre for Advanced Engineering was established in 1987 to undertake projects that would enhance engineering knowledge in the areas of national concern.

As another example of research, the Macmillan Brown Centre for Pacific Studies and the Macmillan Brown Library were established in 1983 as a bequest from Professor John Macmillan Brown, the foundation professor of classics and English. His four endowments offer research and visiting scholar programs to international scholars of Pacific societies and culture.

To celebrate the centennial of the Students' Association established in 1894, the Students' Association is now housed in a new Students' Union at Ilam. This union is a long-sought gathering place for students with a cafeteria, ballroom, and conference center. It also contains a 420-seat theater named for Dame Ngaio Marsh, an honorary lecturer in drama at the college in the 1940s. Marsh produced Shakespearean plays for sold-out audiences in Christchurch and other New Zealand and Australian theaters and instituted production courses at the college. A well-known author of detective novels, she received the Order of the British Empire (OBE) in 1948.

The Students' Union was initially funded by a student-initiated levy to help provide student services and is completely controlled by the Students' Association. Membership in the association is compulsory for enrolled students. The Association built the first specially designed day-care center in a New Zealand University and owns one-half share in the University Book Shop.

The current charter of the University of Canterbury requires the university "to advance knowledge by research and to maintain and disseminate it by teaching." This research function provides opportunities for scholarly studies, scientific investment, and solutions to practical problems.

In 1993, during the 99th year since Apirana Ngata was the fist Maori graduate at Canterbury College, Keith Ikin was named the first Maori liaison officer at Canterbury. He was assigned to work with Maori secondary school pupils, arrange orientation programs, and assist in specific departments in Maori concerns. In addition, a bicultural council named Kaunihera Tikanga Rua first met in late 1993 with the intention of advising the vice chancellor on bicultural development and cultural awareness in the university.

The Ilam campus was developed to accommodate 8,000 people. However, by 1993 it was as serving 11,000 students and 1,200 staff. In 1993 the law building opened, housing two floors of the new law library.

In addition to continuing physical development, the university remains committed to extending the educational opportunities to the community. Among its offerings are the non-degree community education courses, certificate courses, Elderhostel programs, and cultural events. In addition, lay people are involved in the governing bodies, professional associations, and review bodies.

Thus, the three guiding principals for the initial Canterbury College are still primary concerns for the contemporary University of Canterbury. Is higher education accessible? Is the university assisting institutions which serve the community? Are talents encouraged without barriers of distance, wealth, or class? In the words of Ian Leggat, the current chancellor of the university, "In the hard work and academic endeavours of staff and students 'liberty, light, and learning' [Disraeli's words] continue to flourish."

Further Reading: In honor of the university's centennial, N.C. Phillips edited a collection of historical essays: *A History of the University of Canterbury, 1873–1973* (Christchurch: University of Canterbury, 1973). Of special note are three contributions: W.J. Garner's "The Formative Years, 1873–1918," E.T. Beardsley's "Augustan Repose, 1918–1948," and T.E. Carter's "College into University, 1949–1973." Professor R.N. Tarling's introductory essay on New Zealand in *The Commonwealth Universities Yearbook, 1994* (London: Association of Commonwealth Universities, 1994) discusses the New Zealand university system in general and each university in specific detail. Two publications, *University of Canterbury—Guide to the Campus* (Christ-church: Printery, University of Canterbury, 1994) and *University of Canterbury—1993 Annual Report* (Christchurch: Printery, University of Canterbury, 1993) cover current issues and developments.

—Christine Farrow

UNIVERSITY OF CAPE TOWN
(Cape Town, South Africa)

Location: In Cape Town.

Description: An open university enrolling approximately 14,497 students in undergraduate, graduate, and professional schools.

Information: Office of Admission
Bremner Building
Lover's Walk
Rondebosch 7700
Cape Town
South Africa
(21) 650-2128

Visiting: Guided tours are available. For more information, contact the Office of Public Relations at (21) 650-3743.

The University of Cape Town, founded in 1829, was an educational venture by the Dutch and British citizens of South Africa, who had two ambitions for this institution. The first was that it be South African in its "fullest sense," a goal which it would take well over 150 years to begin to achieve. The other ambition was "to become a university as good as the best anywhere." This ambition has been more fully met—as evidenced by the academic reputation of the university over the past century. The university is currently embarked on a course to fulfill the first aim: to represent all of South Africa in its student body, its programs, its faculty, and its staff.

The University of Cape Town (UCT) is one of the oldest educational institutions in sub-Saharan Africa. It began as the South African College, a private venture of Dutch and British citizens. The small, private school consisted of three educational levels: a primary school for the early years of education, a secondary school for work at the pre-college level, and a small university section. By 1874, the lower classes of the college were severed from the university section. They were formed into the South African College schools. The university component of the South African College obtained its charter as the University of Cape Town in April 1918.

The newly chartered UCT entered the twentieth century with a school of medicine, engineering courses, a library, and a women's residence in addition to offering its previous college-level courses. The campus was settled on Groote Schuur, the estate of Cecil Rhodes, a British statesman and business magnate. Six hundred

students made up the UCT's enrollment in its initial year of 1918. In 1995, enrollment was over 14,300 students. From a single library the UCT built and maintained the Jagger Library which, together with its extensions, holds over 824,000 volumes and 7,400 journals. University faculties expanded to include impressive programs in ten faculties: arts, commerce, education, engineering, fine art and architecture, law, medicine, music, science, and social science and humanities.

But the twentieth century also saw the growth of South Africa's apartheid rules, designed to legally segregate white South Africans from blacks and those then designated as coloureds. Apartheid split the country apart—allowing banishments and detentions without trial, creating separate homelands for blacks, and making education virtually impossible to obtain for the majority of the population. Apartheid laws had serious and long-lasting implications for the UCT. Before South Africa made its difficult transition to democracy in the 1990s, UCT admitted black African and coloured students in small numbers up until the 1950s; however, the University Extension Act changed that.

In March 1957, the Afrikaaner-led National Party, which set up an efficient state apparatus to implement laws of apartheid, introduced the Separate Universities Education Bill. The object of the bill was the "closing of the open universities to non-white persons" according to the Academic Freedom Committee (AFC) of the UCT. The bill was dropped, and a later bill, the Extension of University Education Bill, was introduced before the South African Parliament on February 26, 1958. Despite opposition from the United Party and the Native Representatives, it passed into law. According to the AFC, "The Extension of University Education Act 45 of 1959," as it was named, effectively segregated the already primarily white universities by prohibiting any blacks who were not already enrolled to participate in the white universities as students.

The University of Cape Town firmly protested the Extension of University Education Act and its segregation policies. Not only did UCT students stage a large protest march through the center of Cape Town in 1959, but students protested outside of Parliament while the bill was being debated. Just as members from constituent bodies at the UCT pledged themselves at mass meetings "to continue to defend the ideal of the open university," so did the UCT chancellor and other high-ranking administration members sign a protest against the act at a meeting held on July 29, 1959. The protest read, in part:

University of Cape Town

We dedicate ourselves to the tasks that lie ahead: to maintain our established rights to determine who shall teach, what shall be taught, and how it shall be taught in this University, and to strive to regain the right to determine who shall be taught, without regard to any criterion except academic merit.

The government's attacks on the university broadened from exclusion of black students to more comprehensive restrictions on freedom of expression; accordingly, the volume of protest increased. In 1960, Professor C.W. Kiewiet spoke out in his T.B. Davie Memorial Lecture at UCT: he urged university members to "go beyond freedom to pursue knowledge for its own sake, and claim for scholarship today a greater and freer role in relieving mankind of inequality, injustice, deprivation, fear, ignorance, or anger." The task of the university, many believed, was to reach out to reform South Africa itself.

In 1961, the UCT initiated a triennial public lecture called "The Chancellor's Lecture." In contradiction to the Extension of University Education Bill, the lecture series pledged itself to uphold the principals of an open university: the education of women and men of all races. Distinguished lecturers in this series included Lord Butler, Master of Trinity College, Cambridge (1969), and the historian Dr. Leon Marquard (1973).

Yet lectures, protests, and remarks carried out by the UCT to protest restrictions on academic freedom may be overestimated when viewed in contrast to its real admissions practices for blacks, coloureds, and Asians well before the University Extension Act of 1959. In 1959—when the University Extension Act was made law—there were 39 black African students enrolled at the UCT, as opposed to a white enrollment of 4,471 students. However, many within the UCT as well as without did not hesitate to speak out about what they saw as the "true role" of the UCT. Humphrey Harrison served as the vice-president of the Students' Representative Council (SRC), the senior representative student body, from 1976 to 1977. According to Harrison, the UCT retained its position as a training ground for the white elite. The University of Cape Town, he wrote, "is often the natural progression for white matriculants of parents in the upper-middle income bracket, and few have ever had to work for a living or shoulder any responsibility. . . . From the protected environment of home and a fashionable school we move straight to the isolated and even cosseted sanctuary of a white university."

Yet that situation could not last; as South Africa moved toward a multiracial society, so did the UCT. After decades of civil unrest, an organized protest movement, and international sanctions, the apartheid laws that officially segregated the country were lifted. South Africa, which saw the imposition of a state of emergency in 1986, moved into a period in the 1990s during which F.W. de Klerk, elected president in 1989, ended the state of emergency, removed the ban on anti-apartheid political parties including the African National Congress (ANC), and released ANC leaders including Nelson Mandela, who would become the first black president of South Africa. Apartheid laws were repealed in 1991. In 1992 then-president of South Africa de Klerk and black leaders undertook negotiations leading to a transition to democracy in 1994.

Just as 1994 was the year of South Africa's transition to democracy, so teaching, research, and community service remained at the center of the UCT; but if one considers the actions of unity that took place at the UCT that year, it is clear the university was also moving into a new phase of its existence. "On May 13," reads the Vice Chancellor's Report for 1994, "we raised the new flag above the Jameson Hall . . . On July 20 we re-lit the Torch of Academic Freedom—34 years after it was extinguished in protest against the Extension of University Education Act." Because the emergence of a new South African site meant the development of a vastly different country, the UCT dramatically altered its policies on student admissions and support and in some cases, began to adapt curriculum to reflect the new nation.

Rather than resist the new climate in South Africa by maintaining a largely white student body, the UCT aggressively stepped up its outreach to black Africans, coloureds, Indians, and Asians: for the first time in its history, 1994 saw black students comprising a majority (52 percent) of the university's new enrollments. The figures, as documented in the Vice-Chancellor's Report for 1994, are as follows: 28.3 percent African, 16.8 percent coloured, and 6.8 percent Indian. The vice-chancellor attributes the shift in student enrollment to "desegregation strategies" initiated by the UCT during the 1980s and the 1990s. In his report he notes:

> Of the first year African students in 1994, about half were admitted via our special admissions programme. This access route takes the form of a test designed by our Alternative Admission Research Project (AARP), to measure an applicant's potential to succeed rather than his/her past educational experience. The tests are in the areas of language and mathematics, and offer students an opportunity to demonstrate their capacity to come to grips with information and use it.

The alternative admissions program is offered at 15 centers across South Africa. The vice-chancellor notes the results of the program up to 1994: "At the end of 1994, 1,609 students wrote the AARP tests, and 503 were recommended to faculties or admission in 1995." There is, he notes, a high correlation between the test results and a student's success at the UCT.

To assist students who have been admitted to the UCT from educationally disadvantaged backgrounds, the university developed the Academic Support Program (ASP), which is an inter-faculty teaching and research unit whose aims include "providing access to the University for talented but unprepared black students who do not meet standard admission criteria." A UCT document states: "In selecting students, we recognize that South Africa's racially segregated primary and secondary education systems are unequal in many respects. The school systems that cater for the majority of those classified 'African,' 'Coloured' and 'Indian' do not match the predominantly white school system." Once the students are in the university, the ASP works through a variety of programs to help those from "disadvantaged backgrounds to realise their academic potential."

The Academic Support Program has developed an array of "foundation or bridging programs," from introductory and augmented courses offered by the UCT departments as options to traditional first-year courses, to intensive tutorial programs in the arts, social science, and humanities faculties, through student preparation for the UCT's science, engineering, commerce, and medicine faculties, and even language development programs. The ASP was reconstituted as the Academic Development Programme (ADP) in 1994; in that year, it had more than 40 full-time staff and numerous part-time tutors.

While the Alternative Admissions Research Project and the Academic Development Programme have been implemented to change the composition of the UCT's student body to reflect the diversity of South Africa, the integration of the UCT's staff has been slow. In fact, while more women and people previously classified as coloured occupy administrative positions, according to a UCT document, they along with Indians and Africans are "underrepresented in differing degrees of different sectors" of the staff. As of 1993, fully 94 percent of the professors and associate professors were white, while 3 percent were African. Women made up 22 percent of the professorship. Apartheid as a social and legal phenomenon may be in South Africa's past, but "its legacy," a UCT document states, "lingers on."

Just as the dismantling of apartheid put new demands on the UCT's enrollment policies, so it put new demands on the UCT's academic programs and research aims. The university's academic programs have expanded to include subjects that reflect South African concerns. As of 1994, the UCT saw the institution of its Law, Race and Gender Research Institute. In addition, the UCT saw the faculty of science produce a document which demonstrated "the relevance of scientific research to improvements in the quality of daily life—ranging from access to a safe water supply to employment, health, and educational opportunities." Further, a Traditional Medicines Programme (TRAMED) was established as a new academic program. Part of the department of pharmacology, Tramed was established in 1994. Its goals include a "traditional medicines database for the Southern African region" and "access to traditional medicines information by researchers and traditional healers."

The implementation of these new academic programs and research initiatives reflect the hopes raised by Conor Cruise O'Brien while he was vice-chancellor of the University of Ghana. O'Brien called for the "liberation" of the African university "whose main and virtually sole function was to pursue European studies and disseminate European knowledge in Africa. . . . In transcending that narrow concept and in becoming more fully part of its environment, an African university becomes not merely more fully African but also more fully a university." New research initiatives reflect that hope.

Such changes in research, administration, programs, and student enrollment show the UCT to be a complex institution that echoes the words of its British and Dutch founders in a different, wider context. As the UCT enters the twenty-first century, there is a different, broader tone to its originally stated goal: "to be South African in its fullest sense" means that the university works to make itself ever more relevant in South Africa's changing world.

Further Reading: *The Open Universities in South Africa and Academic Freedom* compiled by the Academic Freedom Committees of the University of Cape Town and the University of Witwatersrand, Johannesburg (Cape Town: Juta, 1974) is a book-length study detailing the impact of the Extension of University Education Act and the response of the open universities. Sections on the concept of academic freedom, freedom of expression, and the international community give a comprehensive picture of the UCT. *UCT at 150* edited by Alan Lennox-Short and David Welsh (Cape Town: David Philip, 1979) offers a wide range of recollections, commentary, and critiques on all aspects of the UCT. Its faculties, student life, policies, and people are dissected and discussed in essays by a member of the UCT council, a senior lecturer in history, and a planning officer in the UCT administration, among others.

—Rosemarie C. Sultan

UNIVERSITY OF CHICAGO
(Chicago, Illinois, U.S.A.)

Location: The University of Chicago is located in the Hyde Park neighborhood of Chicago, seven miles south of the central business district, called the Loop. The 190-acre campus is situated on either side of the Midway Plaisance that connects Jackson and Washington Parks, and is just blocks away from Lake Michigan. The university is accessible both by car and public transportation.

Description: The University of Chicago is a private, coeducational, nonsectarian institution that opened in 1892. The university consists of an undergraduate college, graduate programs in the arts and sciences, and graduate schools in law, business, medicine, education, and the ministry. The university enrolls close to 10,000 students annually, including approximately 3,500 in the undergraduate college. More than 1,200 full-time faculty members teach and conduct research at the university. The university combines an emphasis on broad liberal arts education in its college with graduate schools known worldwide for high-quality research.

Information: The University of Chicago
5801 S. Ellis Avenue
Chicago, IL 60637
U.S.A.
(773) 702-1234

Visiting: The University Visitor Center is located on the first floor of Ida Noyes Hall, 1212 E. 59th Street. The center offers guided tours, maps, and schedules of university events. The office is open from 8:30 A.M. to midnight, Monday through Friday; 10:00 A.M. to midnight on Saturday; and 1:00 P.M. to 10:00 P.M. on Sunday. The center offers tours to the general public on Saturdays at 10:00 A.M., except on major holidays. The tours leave from Ida Noyes Hall. Metered parking is available in the guest lot just north of Ida Noyes Hall; enter the lot from Woodlawn Avenue between 58th and 59th Streets. For further information, call the Visitor Center at (773) 702-9192.

The University of Chicago was founded under Baptist auspices in 1891 as a private, coeducational, nonsectarian institution of higher learning. The impetus for founding the university came when the Baptist Education Society, a group of American Baptist ministers, convinced Standard Oil magnate John D. Rockefeller, himself a Baptist, of the need for a Baptist institution in the midwest. There had been a Baptist university previously in Chicago, also called the University of Chicago. It was founded by Illinois senator Stephen Douglas in 1857 as a Baptist mission school. After several financial setbacks, however, the school was forced to close its doors in the spring of 1886. Leaders in the Baptist community then began their efforts to found a new institution that would take the place of the old University of Chicago but also would be larger in scope and scale.

Thomas Wakefield Goodspeed, a faculty member at the previous University of Chicago and a prominent Baptist minister in Chicago, was a central figure in the founding of the university. He helped secure William Rainey Harper, a prominent Semitics professor at Yale, as the first president of the university. Harper impressed upon Rockefeller his desire to establish a prominent research university, not just an undergraduate college, in Chicago. Harper and others argued that the midwest needed a Baptist institution to foster higher learning in the region. Many Baptists, however, feared that the creation of a large-scale university devoted to scientific research would undermine the missionary spirit of the Baptist Education Society. Yet the founders of the university, and especially Harper, saw scientific inquiry as a means through which to unlock the mysteries of the universe and come closer to God. Science would therefore be used in the service of religion in the quest for truth, they argued.

Harper modeled his educational plan for the new university on the German university ideal. He wanted to establish professional and graduate programs devoted to research and scientific inquiry, thereby creating a center for advanced scholarship that would be respected worldwide. Harper and other founders were careful to note, however, that the University of Chicago would not be an ivory tower. Rather it would use scientific inquiry as a means to study problems of society and solve them based on these findings. The city of Chicago would serve as a laboratory in which scholars and students would make their investigations and formulate their conclusions.

Indeed, the university's charter stipulated that the school must be located in the city, so the Baptist Education Society selected Hyde Park, one of the neighborhoods on the south side of Chicago annexed in 1889, to situate the new school. Retail merchant Marshall Field donated ten acres for the original campus and later sold the university additional land as it expanded. Architect Henry Ives Cobb

University of Chicago

designed the Gothic Revival campus in the image of Oxford and Cambridge, with the enclosed quadrangles creating a feeling of insularity and detachment from the surrounding city, which the board of trustees hoped would foster a tight-knit community of scholars.

The university opened its doors on October 1, 1892, with an initial enrollment of 594 students and 103 faculty. The university opened at the same time that the World's

Columbian Exposition fairgrounds were being constructed in Jackson Park, just south of the campus. When visitors attended the exposition in the summer of 1893, they could ride the Ferris Wheel located on the Midway Plaisance and get a glimpse of the burgeoning campus to the north. The neo-classicism of the White City, as the exposition designed by Chicago architect Daniel Burnham was called, contrasted sharply with the grayness of the Gothic campus, leading many observers to comment on the sense of tradition and seriousness inspired by the use of Gothic architecture.

President Harper hired some of the most well-respected scholars from colleges and universities across the nation and the world to fill his new faculty. John Dewey, George Herbert Mead, and James H. Tufts helped establish the distinguished philosophy department. Dewey, also a leading theorist of pedagogy, worked with Harper to establish the university Laboratory Schools in 1896. The Laboratory Schools brought together several elementary and secondary schools in the city and incorporated them within the university. The Lab Schools, especially the University Elementary School founded by Dewey, employed Dewey's progressive theories of education, which stressed the need to relate teaching methods directly to children's experiences and make the teaching process a symbiotic one between teacher and student. The consolidation of education that Harper sponsored gave the university a complete educational system from kindergarten through graduate school and became an important influence on educational reform throughout the nation.

The university also established the first department of sociology in the United States. Scholars such as Albion Small, and later Ernest Burgess and Robert Park, made the sociology department one of the most influential in the nation, as the "Chicago School" pioneered research in immigration, race and ethnic studies, and urban community studies. Chicago sociologists compiled vast amounts of data on various regions in the city and used the evidence from their field investigations to produce richly textured studies of urban life. These studies often formed the basis of social policy and were crucial in aiding institutions such as the Chicago Juvenile Court in understanding the backgrounds of their clients. Scholars in social science departments worked closely with Chicago reformers such as Jane Addams, Florence Kelley, Graham Taylor, and Mary McDowell, who became head resident of the university-sponsored settlement in the neighborhood known as Back of the Yards, because of its proximity and ties to the stockyards. The university played a central role in linking the emerging disciplines of the social sciences with urban reform activities and municipal government in Chicago.

From the start, President Harper sought to expand the role of the university in the city. He launched the University Extension Program, the first in the United States. This program allowed nonenrolled students, particularly adults in other parts of the city, to take courses part-time and off-site. University faculty taught these courses, often in the evening, at libraries, churches, and union halls. Harper also sought university affiliation with other institutions in the city, including Rush Medical College, the Chicago Theological Seminary, the Chicago Institute Teachers' College, the Chicago Manual Training School,

and the YMCA. This program of extension and affiliation gave the university a prominent role in shaping intellectual life in all parts of the city.

When Robert Maynard Hutchins became university president in the 1930s, he continued this practice of linking the university to civic life throughout the city and even the nation. Hutchins launched the "Great Books" program, which brought together university faculty with city elites to read and discuss classic texts of western civilization. Soon librarians and public school teachers were trained to lead discussions, making the program more accessible and widely available throughout the city and later the nation. Hutchins also emphasized educational reform, and introduced his "New Plan" for the college curriculum in 1931. This plan established a core curriculum for general undergraduate education based on survey courses in the arts and sciences. This plan has been a model for other institutions across the nation as they adopted core curriculum requirements for undergraduate education.

The university also took advantage of changing technology to take a leading role in shaping the exchange of ideas. The first "round-table" discussion of public issues on radio took place on February 4, 1931, with three University of Chicago professors discussing prohibition. The success of the format led NBC to air the program nationwide on Sunday afternoons. By 1951, the "Round Table" was carried by over 100 radio stations and had the largest national audience of any discussion program. The university soon employed the radio, and later television formats, to broadcast noncredit courses in the humanities, bringing the work of its faculty to broader audiences.

The university's physical science departments earned reputations of distinction from the time of their founding. Scientific investigation had been one of the central features of the early university, and through the first decades of its existence, university faculty engaged in field research both in and away from the main campus. Biologists traveled to Woods Hole, Massachusetts, to conduct research at the Marine Biological Laboratory, botanists collected samples on the shores of Lake Michigan, and archaeologists journeyed to the Near East to participate in digs. These research trips led prominent university archaeologist James Henry Breasted to establish the Oriental Institute as a center for the collection and interpretation of the cultures of the Near East. The Institute, founded in 1919, acquired most of its museum collections as a result of archaeological excavations sponsored by the university, illustrating the intimate connection between research and museum exhibition at the Institute.

The physics department could boast the university's first Nobel laureate, Albert A. Michelson, who won in 1907 for his measurements of the speed of light. Two more physicists won the Nobel Prize in the 1920s—Robert A. Millikan (1923) and Arthur H. Compton (1927). The department gained new prominence after atomic bombs fell over Hiroshima and Nagasaki in 1945. Led by physicist Enrico Fermi, a team of scientists at the university initiated the first self-sustaining nuclear reaction under the football stands at Stagg Field, near the center of the university. The "Manhattan Project" launched a new partnership between the federal government and the university that shaped the future of scientific research. The university soon launched efforts to improve scientific investigation that would be useful to government and industry, and built several laboratories in conjunction with government and corporate sponsors, including the Argonne National Laboratory and the Enrico Fermi Institute. The university worked with NASA to build the Laboratory for Astrophysics and Space Research, linking university research with government-sponsored space flights.

At the same time that the Manhattan Project was bringing national attention to the university, student enrollment was declining, largely as a result of changing neighborhood conditions in Hyde Park. Economic and demographic changes, particularly the expansion of the "Black Belt" into Hyde Park, led many wealthier white residents to leave Hyde Park. Many property owners subdivided homes and became absentee landlords, often neglecting building upkeep and maintenance. By the early 1950s the university faced a 60 percent drop in student applications, and had trouble recruiting new faculty. In order to revitalize the neighborhood and ensure the continued prominence of the university, trustees and administrators worked with local residents to create the Hyde Park-Kenwood Community Conference. Members promoted urban renewal policies to address issues of crime, poverty, racial integration, and planning. The plan for redevelopment, approved by federal, state, and city governments, called for demolition of older, substandard buildings and the construction of new apartments, townhouses, and shopping areas. The cost for the entire redevelopment project, started in 1955, was over $300 million, with $46 million coming from the federal government, $29 million from the university, and $250 million from private investors. Several thousand residents were displaced in the process, but the partnership between the university and local residents became a model for promoting interracial and economically stable urban communities. The relative success of the urban renewal project enabled the university to maintain its reputation as one of the leading research and teaching institutions in the nation. Additional federal and private investment in the 1980s allowed the university to expand the scope of its research, especially in the physical sciences. Similarly, the university hospitals took on greater prominence in the 1970s and 1980s as other areas hospitals were forced to close their doors. The university maintains a strong presence in city affairs and public policy, and provides expertise in areas as diverse as legal aid, tax policy, housing, education, job training, and medicine. The university continues to combine its goals of rigorous research and teaching with its role in applying that research to the practical needs of the community and the nation.

Further Reading: There are several books that provide good histories of the founding of the University of Chicago. The best overviews are *A History of the University of Chicago: The First Quarter-Century,* by Thomas Wakefield Goodspeed (Chicago: University of Chicago Press, 1916; 1972), *Harper's University: The Beginnings,* by Richard J. Storrs (Chicago: University of Chicago Press, 1966), and *Hutchins' University: A Memoir of the University of Chicago, 1929–1950,* by William H. McNeill (Chicago: University of Chicago Press, 1991). The university published a series, "A Centennial View of the University of Chicago," in honor of its 100th anniversary in 1992. For a discussion of student life and athletics at the university, see *Stagg's University: The Rise, Decline, and Fall of Big-Time Football at Chicago,* by Robin Lester (Urbana: University of Illinois Press, 1995). Books dealing specifically with the social sciences and their role in city affairs include *The Chicago School of Sociology,* by Martin Bulmer (Chicago: University of Chicago Press, 1984), *A City and Its Universities: Public Policy in Chicago, 1892–1919,* by Steven Diner (Chapel Hill: University of North Carolina Press, 1980), and *The Chicago Pragmatists and American Progressivism,* by Andrew Feffer (Ithaca, New York: Cornell University Press, 1993). Books discussing the relationship between the university and the neighborhood of Hyde Park include *A Neighborhood Finds Itself,* by Julie Abrahamson (New York: Harper and Row, 1959), and *Making the Second Ghetto: Race and Housing in Chicago, 1940–1960,* by Arnold Hirsch (Cambridge: Cambridge University Press, 1983).

—Robin F. Bachin

UNIVERSITY OF CHILE
(Santiago, Chile)

Location: Santiago de Chile, with campuses in various parts of the city.

Description: Public university with approximately 18,000 students, undergraduate and graduate, and 5,000 faculty.

Information: Universidad de Chile
Avda Bernardo O'Higgins 1058
Casilla 10–D
Santiago
Chile
(2) 6781003

The University of Chile (UCH) stands as one of the crowning institutional achievements of nineteenth-century Chile: it organized and supported education at all levels, was the center of the country's intellectual life, introduced scientific knowledge, helped establish the professions, and formed one of the region's more enlightened and successful ruling classes. The foundation of Chile's other universities, starting in 1888, did not significantly lessen the UCH's importance over the next 100 years. The university continued to hold a near monopoly over intellectual life until the late 1920s and, even today, the UCH sits at the system's pinnacle. It produces half of all Chile's research, leads all universities in graduate education and the arts, and is still regarded as the national university within a system widely heralded as the model for Latin America. Indeed, the UCH is routinely included in any informed listing of the handful of the region's best universities.

The University of Chile was founded in 1842, during the administration of President Manuel Bulnes. It was not Chile's first university, however, The Royal University of San Felipe started functioning in 1757, and religious institutions of higher education existed before that. The Royal University (closed in 1839, shortly after the end of the colonial era) was one of the institutional bases upon which the UCH formed, but the new university would not be a mere extension of it. Under the leadership of Diego Portales, the newly independent government gained a stability and authority envied elsewhere in Latin American. This climate was propitious for the influx of many of the region's educational innovators, who were often inspired by European liberalism, the Enlightenment, and European university structures and practices. They supported public education against clericalism, and later in the cen-

tury joined with Chilean intellectuals who heralded the positivist ideology that helped reinforce state over church influence in education. Venezuela's Andrés Bello was a key figure in creating the UCH (*La Casa de Bello,* Bello's House), which of which he became the first rector. He is still widely cited throughout the region for his advocacy of the enlightening purposes of higher education and its service to the nation.

The University of Chile was founded to aid the developing nation-state in its efforts to modernize a traditional society, reinforce a sense of national cohesion, and serve capitalist modernization. Centralized and uniform public education was seen as the instrument that would foster such change, and the UCH was designated to lead the effort. This is why the UCH was designed to be the superintendent of education and a scientific academy, not a teaching institution. This design was similar in neighboring Argentina and Uruguay; the *Estado Docente* (Teaching State) would rely on the national university as its education arm. The teaching of the professions would continue to take place in Chile's National Institute, created after independence to assume the teaching mission of the colonial university and the seminaries. In its superintendent role over education, the UCH had the authority to grant the higher degrees of bachelor and *licenciatura* (first higher education degree, valid usually for professional practice), give exams for and certify the completion of secondary education, direct public education, and inspect both public and private educational institutions.

As the UCH was less a teaching institution than a scientific academy, its model was the Institute of France more than any university. The five original faculties or academies were philosophy and humanities, law and political sciences, theology, mathematics and physics, and medicine. They had 30 academics each and their tasks included the development of their fields, assistance to other institution's teaching, and advice to the government.

Over time, however, the UCH did in fact become predominantly a teaching institution. For one thing, scientific academies generally proved difficult to build securely in developing countries (though Chile's performance was far from the low end). For another, the UCH lost its supervisory role over secondary education. Catholic conservatives, raising the flag of freedom of teaching, led the charge against the UCH's authority. Although liberals prevailed in much of that bitter battle, a new law in 1879 reorganized the university according to its new teaching mission, and a trend was discernible regarding its supervisory role; by 1930, control had slipped away almost completely to the Ministry of Education.

But these losses did not usher in a period of decline, since the UCH developed such prominence in its invigorated teaching role. This teaching was oriented to preparation for professional practice, under the assumption that general education was provided at the secondary level—at least for the small minority that would enter higher education. The vast majority of the still fewer than 1,000 UCH students enrolled in the late 1870s studied the big three professions of law, engineering, and medicine. Another aspect of professionalism reinforced the teaching role: professional teachers gained power within an institution that achieved increased autonomy from the government.

The rise of teaching did not mean a one-dimensional enterprise. Ties to the professions were strong enough for the UCH to be dubbed, at least until the mid-twentieth century, a "professionalist" university. Moreover, the intention was more to join research with teaching than to exclude research. In the 1870s, rector Ignacio Domeyko (a Polish exile) promoted the Humboldtean idea of blending the two functions. Although the professionalist function became much more successfully institutionalized, the UCH achieved some research gains, mostly because of specific units or heroic individuals; in any case, the UCH certainly led in terms of what the nation was able to manage. Again foreigners and immigrants played a key role, above all in the exact and natural sciences. They also facilitated contact with leading institutions in Europe and the United States, and helped the modest development of laboratories and libraries. The *Annals of the University of Chile* earned praise for its scientific and educational articles over the years. Starting in 1954, a law earmarked 0.5 percent of national tax revenues to a fund created primarily for the construction of research facilities, and the UCH was given over half of the total.

A focus on research and (particularly since the 1950s) on the dream of blending it with teaching—a model now imported mostly from the United States—marked the crucial philanthropy that came from the Rockefeller and then Ford Foundations. It is revealing that Chile would become one of the very most favored countries for donors. This happened because Chile met so many of the criteria for giving. Most important was a desire for change combined with a reasonable chance of achieving it. While many elite private institutions elsewhere met the criteria, few national universities did. The rectorships of Juan Gómez Millas and Edgardo Boeninger epitomized the partnerships struck between the UCH and both foreign and domestic reformers. A joint project between the UCH and the University of California was the largest operation ever financed by the Ford Foundation in Latin America.

Another hallmark of reform, however, was expansion. This generally made it harder to build elite academic functions. For example, after years of building graduate programs and sending students abroad for advanced work, less than 10 percent of university professors would have doctorates as rapid growth necessitated hiring many with lesser qualifications. Growth was a response to accelerated expansion of secondary school, a rising middle class, and beliefs that a modern democratic society needed to overcome its elite restrictiveness. Indeed, Chile trailed in access behind Latin American nations at similar levels of economic development. As late as 1960 only four percent of the cohort group was enrolled (one-third of the Argentine figure). By 1974 Chile had reached 16 percent. The University of Chile thus played a major role in the social mobility of middle-class groups, especially as it did not charge tuition, but mobility did not reach the popular sectors.

To respond to increased demand without watering down its academic standards, the UCH created (in the 1960s) regional two-year colleges, emulating the institutional diversification California was undertaking. Another UCH motivation was defensive: to preserve its institutional weight within higher education. The University of Chile was now one of eight universities. Its monopoly had ended with the creation of the Catholic University of Chile in 1888. Five more private universities followed and a public technical university opened in 1947. The regionalization of UHC was an alternative to the creation of more universities.

The University of Chile lost ground more slowly and limitedly than did the national university counterparts in sister nations. Not until the 1960s did Chile's other universities gain full rights to grant professional degrees without UCH authorization. And compared to other nations Chile avoided massive institutional proliferation—until the 1970s.

The massive and multiple changes that the UCH and the whole system have undergone in the last few decades must be understood in the context of the nation's wretched political-economic transformations.

The 1960s saw the rise of inclusionary democratic reform in national politics. In higher education, a potent reform movement also developed. It had its radical wings, but noteworthy were non-extreme features that set it apart from student rebellions elsewhere in the region; furthermore, the UCH was home to neither the birth nor the most extreme strongholds of the Chilean movement. The movement found ample support from the Christian Democratic government as well as from a majority of university administrators and professors. The general goal was to attune universities more to social change. That meant increased access, but also such intrauniversity reforms as replacement of hierarchical chairs and professionalist faculties with more participatory departments (which, in turn, would be suitable homes for mixing in more research with teaching). The measures paralleled those championed contemporaneously in Europe. And many were implemented at the UCH and other Chilean universities.

The reform was anathema to the military rulers who grabbed control of the country in 1973. By then, the reform had indeed fractured into disparate wings including very radical ones. Enrollments soared from 55,000 to 145,000 from 1967 to 1973. The 1970 presidential elections brought Salvador Allende's socialist coalition to office, with a minority of the vote and a shaky mix of democratic leftists and revolutionaries. While the president himself exhorted students to study, many in his coalition favored those students who believed that the only progressive course was revolution. The university reached a highly politicized state.

But the military was bent on reversing not only the extreme manifestations of the pre-coup period but the entire thrust of reform. Ideas like connecting the study of law to sociology and help to the poor were regarded as dangerous. So the government obliterated the autonomy enjoyed historically by the UCH and its counterparts. The University of Chile had in fact gained almost complete autonomy from the government despite receiving roughly 90 percent of its funds from it; professors (eventually joined by students) had elected all university authorities, and the authority of the president of Chile to appoint the rector had remained symbolic. Now, for the first time in Latin American history, military officers (usually retired) were appointed rectors. Units perceived as leftist were closed and purges expelled perhaps 20,000 students, 25 percent of the teaching staff, and between 10 to 15 percent of the administrative personnel. Participation in governance by professors was sharply reduced and student participation was proudly terminated. The ideological control made for what esteemed Chilean philosopher Jorge Millas called the "watched" university.

Repression was widespread but not uniform. Reflecting its importance and leftist movement, the UCH was hit hard from the outset, much more than the Catholic universities. Still, it was not whipped as much as either the public technical university or the private University of Concepción. Some protection came from UCH rectors who were rightist and vehemently anti-communist but not violently anti-democratic. They defended institutional interests with help from powerful alumni holding similar persuasions. Moderate deans could be yet more resistant to repressive measures. But, annoyed at its inability to effect more counter-reformation, the regime launched a second wave of terror in 1976. Now the attack extended beyond leftists to centrists.

Until 1981 the junta's thrust remained essentially toward destruction. This fit with its repressive orientation. It did not, however, fulfill the "neoliberal," free-market orientations championed by the economists who had the president's ear. They set out to construct a new system based on competition among institutions, private funding, and ties to the job market. They decried the non-competitive position that the universities enjoyed for so long, ensured by their legal monopoly over credentials and

their automatic incremental funding from the government. They denounced universities' inequitably disproportionate consumption of the education budget: 40 percent of the financing for 4 percent of the total students (regressively benefiting from subsidies drawn from the taxes of poor Chileans in need of better basic education). The University of Chile was the number one target of financial attack since it was the largest university, with the highest per capita costs, though defenders legitimately pointed out that high costs had something to do with the institution's unmatched activities in research and cultural extension.

Elements of the neoliberal agenda clashed with what some military hard-liners wanted. Suggestions of autonomy, or even an institutional self-financing that could indirectly promote autonomy, unsettled many. In other respects, though, the neoliberal and repressive approaches complemented one another. Reducing subsidies limited the role of the state and provided neat pretexts for getting rid of people and programs the government opposed. Similarly, cutting the UCH into separate institutions and opening the market for the remarkable proliferation of new institutions diminished the UCH's political power and the threat that represented—for the government remained preoccupied with the danger of a future return to autonomy and leftist politics.

The 1981 law authorized creation of private higher education institutions at three different levels: universities, professional institutes, and technical training centers. It slashed public funding for the existing universities. The regional branches of the UCH were ripped away into new universities or professional institutes. The Santiago campuses lost more than half their 24 faculties, now clustered in two new metropolitan universities. By the time citizens pushed out the military government (1990), a system of 8 universities had become one of roughly 70 universities, 80 professional institutes, and 150 technical training centers. The university's enrollments had plummeted from their 1974 peak of 63,000 to just 18,000, and the government provided only 30 percent of the UCH budget. Once the government's main education arm, the UCH had fallen far from its monopoly over even higher education.

Nor were the UCH's losses all to the institutions created by the government plan. Many professors and graduate students either left academia or became refugees. A brain drain that hurt the UCH badly brought Chilean talent to universities throughout Latin America, Europe, the United States, and other continents as well. But Chile pulled a miracle out of the hat as many refugees remained in their country. They formed a network of private research centers surpassing any in Latin America, the region in which such centers grew and assumed an importance unparalleled anywhere. In this too, the UCH led, joined by the Catholic University of Chile and others especially as regime repression struck past the left to the center. The private research centers achieved a breakthrough in the quantity and quality of social research. Remarkably, with the help of the Church and international philanthropy, they also became major sites of opposition to military rule and major actors in the development of democratic alternatives.

Remarkable too has been the continuity of higher education policy as Chile has once again undergone political transformation. The democratic regime that so strongly denounces its predecessor's repression, and has restored university autonomy, has tacitly or explicitly endorsed many of its neoliberal reforms. Examples include competition among the extensive array of institutions (and within them) and ample private funding (with tuition). Continuity is also evident as private research centers remain. Those who expected a massive return to the UCH and other leading universities have been disappointed. For one thing, the centers have established reputations and networks, and many researchers are happy to avoid the bureaucracy or teaching responsibilities they associate with places like the UCH. For another, the democratic government was not about to increase subsidies to universities. Rather than a massive restoration of the UCH, then, one sees a variegated and uncertain process of adjustments and accommodations allowing links between research centers and the UCH, including sharing of personnel and facilities,

All in all, the UCH has done very well in adapting to the changes it has faced. In its early history it established missions unknown by its colonial predecessor. It then transformed itself into a fine professionalist university and proceeded to add a research component that surpassed the Latin American norm. Its reform was more academically serious and successful that most elsewhere. The repression it then suffered was more extreme and took a major toll. Nonetheless, the UCH showed a capacity for preservation even then. While critics see this as proof of how much waste had been present, a friendlier interpretation is that the institution handled its task with skill. As the new democratic government does not hand the UCH back its prior privileges, the university seeks to reconstruct itself and build new relationships with an array of other institutions. As it must compete for funds, it continues to come out at the top in attracting top students and research funds. With its restored autonomy, it has restored decency, academic freedom, and a degree of participation. Rector Jaime Lavados was a courageous voice for freedom and higher education in the long period so hostile to those causes, and the present head of the student federation, which is opposing government higher education initiatives, is a communist. But the UCH has not fallen back into disabling internal policies and it has managed to handle the challenges thrust on it by new economic realities. Indeed, the UCH leads the public universities' demands that the government ease the regulations that still handicap them in terms of financial flexibility. For international agencies and most independent experts on higher education policy, the UCH is the model national university for reforms vigorously promoted but still only sporadically achieved throughout Latin America and, for that matter, much of the rest of the world.

No Latin American university matches the UCH for prolonged stature. The national universities of Argentina and Mexico have enjoyed periods at the top, but have since been too wracked by compromising factors. They lay claim now to only mixed reputation within their societies. But the UCH, through its nation's good times and bad has maintained—deservedly—a high degree of respect.

Further Reading: The best English-language source for the history of the University of Chile, though not completely about the university, is offered in Iván Jaksíc, *Academic Rebels in Chile: The Role of Philosophy in Higher Education and Politics* (Albany, New York: SUNY Press, 1989). On the period of military rule, see Daniel Levy, "Chilean Universities under Junta," *Latin American Research Review* 21, no. 3 (1986).

—Daniel C. Levy and Andrés Bernasconi

UNIVERSITY OF COIMBRA
(Coimbra, Portugal)

Location: In a former royal palace in the oldest section of Coimbra, 120 miles north-northeast of Lisbon.

Description: A state university encompassing seven faculties and enrolling approximately 13,100 students.

Information: Director of International Relations Office
Paço das Escolas
3000 Coimbra
Portugal
35410, 35418, or 35420

Founded in Lisbon in 1290, the University of Coimbra is one of the oldest universities in Europe. By virtue of its near monopoly on higher education in Portugal, which it held for more than 600 years, the university played an integral role in the cultural life of Portugal. Scholars from Coimbra occassionally became prominent throughout Europe: for centuries, the destiny of the Portuguese nation was in the hands of those who had studied or taught at Coimbra. Among the many distinguished persons who passed through Coimbra's halls were Luís de Camões, Portugal's foremost poet, Antonio Egas Moniz, Nobel laureate in medicine, and António Salazar, premier of Portugal from 1932 to 1968. Throughout most of its history, the university had a reputation as a bastion of conservatism, both politically and scholastically. Reforms aimed at modernizing the curriculum were rare and often met with great resistance. The major exception occurred in the eighteenth century when long overdue reforms were undertaken. Today the University of Coimbra, though no longer the nation's sole institution of higher learning, maintains a preeminent place in Portugal because of its illustrious history and time-honored traditions.

The first universities on the European continent were established during the mid-twelfth century. The creation of a university in Portugal was paramount in helping to establish a national identity for the nation, which had thrown off vassalage to the Spanish monarch in 1139–40. Scholars brought from France by King Alfonso III at the close of the thirteenth century helped to germinate the idea of establishing a Portuguese university. In 1288 a petition to authorize the creation of a *studium generale* in Lisbon was sent to Pope Nicholas IV by several religious leaders including the abbot of Alcobaça, prior of the monastery of Sant Cruz in Coimbra. A papal bull establishing a university was issued in 1290. That same year a

royal charter was issued by King Denis, the founder of the university. Faculties were established in arts, law, canon law, and medicine.

Unlike other universities outside the Iberian Peninsula, the university at Lisbon came under close royal control, and its development was nurtured by the king. Teachers were appointed by the monarch. Students, however, held considerable power, for rectors (initially there were two) were elected from among the students and by the students. The election of rectors by the students remained in place for more than 200 years.

The university did not thrive in Lisbon. As was the case in many medieval universities, conflicts arose between the students and the residents of Lisbon. In 1308 the university was moved to Coimbra; a royal charter was issued in 1309. The sleepy town along the Mondego River was already a center of learning by virtue of its renowned monastery school of Santa Cruz. The university was established on the site of what is now the main library. For unknown reasons, perhaps because the town of Coimbra was still quite provincial, the university was moved back to Lisbon in 1338, only to be again transferred back to Coimbra 16 years later. The peripatetic university was once again moved back to Lisbon in 1377, where it remained until the mid-sixteenth century.

In Lisbon the university underwent few major alterations. In 1411 a faculty of theology was established with a chair endowed by Prince Henry the Navigator. Like most institutions of its kind, the curriculum of the university emphasized the study of canon and civil law and theology. In the 1430s Coimbra acquired ownership of its buildings, which had previously been leased by teachers. By the 1450s the university had about 1,000 students and was generally considered a medium-sized school, compared to others on the continent.

Student life was highly regulated by a code known as the *honeste se gerrere* which dictated proper behavior under four criteria. The all-male student body was not to have any contact with women. It was feared that such contact would tend to inflame relationships between the students and the townsmen. Bearing arms was prohibited, mainly to prevent fatalities when conflicts did arise. Simple apparel was proscribed, hence the statute issued in 1321 requiring students to wear gowns, a tradition that endured well into the twentieth century. Finally, students were to refrain from hurling insults at teachers and fellow students. In a highly chivalrous era, this rule was meant to assuage challenges to one's honor. Students were responsible for paying their teachers' lecture fees, according to a graduated pay scale set forth by King John I.

University of Coimbra

By the sixteenth century, preparations were being made to move the university back to Coimbra. The impetus for this move came from the growing awareness of the backwardness of education in Portugal. It was believed that in order to implement significant structural changes, the university should start anew; a chief proponent of this move was the Spanish humanist, Luis Vives (author of the 1531 work, *De Causis Corruptarum Artium,* one of the major early writings on education). By the 1530s some secondary and graduate courses were being taught at the monastery of Santa Cruz in Coimbra. The days of the university at Lisbon were numbered. The return to Coimbra came in 1537 under King John III. The university was housed in the royal palace of Alcáçova, which in the 1540s was refitted to house lecture halls. The university at Lisbon was effectively extinguished, not to be revived until the twentieth century.

The move to Coimbra did in fact lead to some changes. Teachers at Lisbon were not guaranteed jobs at Coimbra, and many did not move with the university. Most of the new faculty at Coimbra came from the University of Salamanca. The main curriculum was kept, but courses in each division increased dramatically, some doubling. New bylaws and ordinances reaffirmed and expanded royal control. Rectors, long elected by students, were now to be appointed by the king. The influence of the university in Portugal was enhanced in 1541 when a law was enacted prohibiting Portuguese students from acquiring degrees abroad.

A new college of arts was established in 1548. At first it functioned independently but later came under university control. The college was an important center for humanism; however the reforming spirit at the university was shortlived. The orthodox nature of the Counter-Reformation and the Inquisition caused many teachers to come under charges of being "Lutheran." Liberal humanistic education and free inquiry were eliminated. A further blow came during the 1550s when the college of arts was entrusted to the Jesuits and became an instrument of the Counter-Reformation. In 1559 a new Jesuit university was founded at Évora. Although it was much smaller than the one at Coimbra, it represented a challenge to Coimbra's monopoly.

Despite the ravages wrought on liberal education by the Counter-Reformation, a group of Jesuit scholars at Coimbra known as the "conimbricenses" became famous throughout Europe for their commentaries on Aristotle. These commentaries functioned as the main Aristotelian textbooks for Europe during the early seventeenth century, and their works were reprinted between 15 and 25 times. During this period the university remained conservative in its outlook. Further reforms were needed but were not implemented until the eighteenth century.

The great reforms of the eighteenth century came under the direction of the Marquis de Pombal, chief minister of King José I. The basis of Pombal's reform was the production of a new cadre of enlightened officials for the bureaucracies of the church and state. By the mid-eighteenth century the inadequacy of education in Portugal had become apparent, especially in the sciences. No longer contending with the University of Évora, which had been closed down in 1759, the University of Coimbra became the chief object of reform. In 1770 a panel of inquiry, known as the *junta da providência literária,* was set up to establish new statutes for the university. By 1772 the new statutes received royal assent. A university press was founded and new faculties were established in mathematics and philosophy. In addition, the existing faculties of theology, canon law, and medicine were modernized. In the sciences, experimental research was encouraged and the study of natural sciences, long neglected, was included in the new faculty of philosophy.

Another key element of the Pombal reforms was the addition of several new buildings and laboratories. A certain amount of significant new construction had occurred earlier in the century, during the reign of King John V (1707–50). Treasures brought from Portuguese Brazil financed most of these projects. The baroque bell tower, which came to be a symbol of the university and the town of Coimbra, was constructed between 1728 and 1733. At about the same time the magnificent baroque library of King John was built. New construction during the Pombal era went much further. In keeping with the reforms, an observatory and laboratories for physics and chemistry were built, along with a botanical garden and a museum of natural history. Many of the new buildings, including the chemistry laboratory and the natural history museum, were designed by the English architect William Elsden.

Upon the death of King José I in 1777, his daughter Maria succeeded. Maria I dismissed Pombal and endeavored to reverse many of his reforms. On the whole she was unsuccessful; however, she did manage to virtually crush the overall spirit of the reforms, and the university came under harsh criticism by dissatisfied students. Nevertheless, during Maria's reign and that of her successor, John VI, education in Portugal was advanced somewhat with the establishment of schools in Lisbon and Oporto. These schools were not universities but rather "technical schools" designed to offer courses outside the scope of those found at Coimbra. Also, in 1794 the University of Coimbra gained the power of inspection over all schools in Portugal, an authority that lasted until 1859.

Throughout the nineteenth century the university remained relatively stagnant. The only major change was the merging of the faculties of civil and canon law into one school in 1837. The new school of law gained some renown throughout Portugal as the school of choice for the sons of the wealthy. Thus Pombal's desire to provide a "training school" for the political bureaucracy was ful-

filled. Most of the new politicians entering service after the Portuguese revolution of 1820 were graduates of Coimbra.

Portugal underwent many political and cultural changes during the nineteenth century in its struggle to become a modern nation-state. As the only university in Portugal, Coimbra provided an intellectual venue for discussions concerning Portugal's future; both students and teachers were active in these debates. One of the most famous debates occurred during the 1860s. The "Coimbra question," as the debate came to be known, involved two schools of thought. One group, led by the poet Antero de Quental, attacked the prevailing norms of society in Portugal. Opposed to this group were the defenders of the status quo, led by the blind poet Castilho. By elucidating the controversies surrounding political and intellectual life in Portugal, the students and teachers at Coimbra played an integral role in fostering the cultural and political climate that ultimately led to the fall of the monarchy and the creation of the Portuguese republic in 1910.

With the advent of the republic came changes at the university and in university education in Portugal. Perhaps the most influential change affecting the University of Coimbra was the founding of two new universities in 1911 at Lisbon and Oporto. Coimbra's centuries-old position as Portugal's sole center of university education ended. Secularization was a hallmark of the new regime, and the school of theology at Coimbra was abolished. Moreover, rectors, appointed by the monarch since the final move to Coimbra, were made elective once again (this system lasted only until 1918–19 when they became government appointees). During this era the young António Salazar began his studies at Coimbra, matriculating in 1914. Salazar went on to earn a doctorate in finance and economics in 1918 and became a lecturer at the university.

The Portuguese republic proved to be a complete failure. In the course of 16 years Portugal had 45 different governments and only one president who completed a full term. Once again, students and teachers at Coimbra played an important part in the overthrow of the republic and the creation of the dictatorship in 1926. It was at Coimbra that the ideological tenets outlining opposition to the republic were nurtured. When Salazar became premier in 1932, he filled his cabinet with professors from the Coimbra law school.

Salazar never forgot his alma mater, and in 1948 he instituted a public works project to construct a new campus at Coimbra. This action was one of his more questionable endeavors, for many of the university's and the town's historically and artistically valuable structures were torn down. Buildings constructed as part of this project include the main library, and the faculties of arts, medicine, and science.

During the 1970s eight new universities were founded in Portugal, further diminishing Coimbra's preeminent position in higher education. Nonetheless, the university continued to expand. In 1975 the largest of the university's buildings, that for faculty of science and technology, was completed. In 1987 a new university hospital was inaugurated. The university's student body also increased during this period; between 1972 and 1995 emrollment at the university increased by more than 60 percent. Today the University of Coimbra retains significant prestige as a living testament to the Portuguese history by virtue of its position as the oldest institution of higher learning in the country.

Further Reading: The second volume of Hastings Rashdall's *The Universities of Europe in the Middle Ages* (Oxford: Clarendon Press, 1936) provides a well-documented study of the university's early years. Another valuable source for the university's beginnings is *A History of the University in Europe* (Cambridge: Cambridge University Press, 1992), edited by Hilde de Ridder-Symoens. The development of the university in the medieval and early-modern periods is best described in A.H. de Oliveira Marques's two volume *History of Portugal* (New York: Columbia University Press, 1972). *Pombal, Paradox of the Enlightenment* by Kenneth Maxwell (Cambridge: Cambridge University Press, 1995) provides an exhaustive account of the great reformer's work at Coimbra. The definitive work outlining the history of the university is *The University of Coimbra* (Coimbra: Office of the Rector of the University of Coimbra, 1988). The section on the history of the university was written by Professor Luis Reis Torgal and contains a thorough and unbiased account of the university's history. The text is complemented with many fine color photographs of the university's buildings.

—Jeffrey M. Tegge

UNIVERSITY OF COLOGNE
(Cologne, Germany)

Location: West of the town center and the Rhine River in Cologne, Germany.

Description: A large state university of 54,000 students with faculties of social and economic sciences, medicine, law, philosophy, mathematics and physical sciences, and education.

Information: University of Cologne
Albertus-Magnus-Platz
50923 Cologne
Germany
221 4701

The present University of Cologne is a twentieth-century institution arising out of the trade schools that flourished in Cologne (Koln) in the first decades of the century. Even the ancient University of Cologne is a much later foundation than is often supposed, having been founded long after Cologne had already become a center for learning, well over a century after the Dominicans and then the Franciscans had established their theological *studia* there. The medieval university, founded by a brief of Pope Urban VI dated May 21, 1388, was dissolved by the French on April 28, 1798, in the wake of their conquest.

When Cologne was incorporated into France by the 1801 Treaty of Luneville, it was only sufficiently important to become the chief town of an *arrondissement*. The medieval university was succeeded by a short-lived French Université de Cologne; there was no university in the town between the assignment of the city to Prussia by the Congress of Vienna in 1815 and the establishment of the modern institution by an agreement between the city of Cologne and the Kingdom of Prussia of May 29, 1919. Prussia did attempt to reestablish Cologne's university, but the project was thwarted by Berlin, and in 1818 the University of the Rhine was instead established at Bonn.

Today's large and distinguished university, which in 1995 had 54,000 students and a teaching staff of 1,870, has only a brief history. Its foundation dates from a first memorandum on vocational tertiary education of June 1879. The first independent institution was founded May 1, 1901, followed by the academy of practical medicine, opened on October 25, 1905, and the polytechnic for social administration on February 5, 1912. The new university, founded by the 1919 agreement, passed in 1953 under the jurisdiction of the Ministry of Education, and on April 1, 1954, to the control of the province of North-

Rhine Westphalia. In 1980 the Cologne departments of teacher training were incorporated into the university. A fine statue of the early thirteenth-century Dominican, Albert the Great, by Gerhard Marcks stands outside the building—although Albert died before the modern university was founded. Nonetheless, in 1988 the university celebrated its 600th anniversary.

The medieval university arose out of the desire neither of prince nor of prelate as in the rest of northern Europe, but, as was more usual south of the Alps, of the municipality itself to have within its walls an institution capable of bestowing degrees. There was already both the Dominican and Franciscan *studia*, established in the thirteenth century by friars drawn to Cologne by the excellence of Cologne's grammar schools, notably the cathedral school. The cathedral itself, with its relics of the three magi, was one of the most important places of pilgrimage in the west.

Albertus Magnus instituted the Cologne *studium* of the Dominicans in 1248, arriving from Paris with his distinguished disciple, Thomas Aquinas. The Dominicans, who favored a theory of knowledge in which the mind's activity was dependent on sense perception (in spite of the difficulties such doctrines created for an explanation of the immortality of the soul), differed in theological style from the Franciscans, who tended toward explanations of human knowledge in terms of direct divine illumination. Cologne, reflecting such theological discussions in Paris, soon became the leading forum for thirteenth-century intellectual debate on the central philosophical and theological issues of medieval Christianity.

By 1388 universities had been founded at Prague, Vienna, Heidelberg, and Erfurt. The merchants of Cologne naturally wished to underline and consolidate their city's importance and to service its administrative requirements with a tertiary institution of professional training. The patrician hold on civic authority was being challenged by the guilds, sometimes in alliance with, and sometimes opposed by, the archbishops. Although the patrician oligarchy had been challenged by the weavers in an uprising of 1370, which was suppressed, the city was to be ruled from 1396 by what amounted to an alliance between patricians and guilds in a new municipal constitution, the *Verbundbrief*. In the meanwhile, the merchants had solicited from the pope the brief founding the university.

The bull was proclaimed in December 1388, and the *studium* opened in January 1389 with 21 masters, 3 in theology, 2 in medicine, 1 in law, and the others in arts. Further privileges were soon granted by the Duke of Guelders in 1396 and by the Emperor Frederick III in 1442, but it was the city council that exercised the closest

472

University of Cologne

supervision and the greatest authority over the young institution. Most of the masters and students came from Paris and the German universities that had already been founded. As was usual, the teaching posts were funded from the annexation with papal permission of ecclesiastical prebends; the chairs of law and medicine and some posts in theology were funded from an endowment from the municipality. The pope created a prebend for each of the 11 monasteries, although masters in the arts faculty were expected to live from their fee income. In its first year the university received 738 students, the number having been swelled by the pestilence and quarrels that nearly emptied Heidelberg in 1387.

Professional appointments were entrusted to the elected rector and four municipal *provisores,* and the constitution was adapted from that of Paris—but without splitting into "nations," as had residually occurred in the older German universities, Prague and Vienna. Masters from all faculties were eligible for the rectorship, to pass between each faculty in turn. Civil jurisdiction belonged in minor matters to the rector, in more serious ones to the rector and deans, and in the most serious matters to the university itself. Spiritual jurisdiction was conferred on the abbot of St. Martin in Cologne, together with the deans of St. Paul in Liège and St. Salvator in Maestricht. A number of endowed student houses were founded, beginning with the *Bursa coronarum* established in 1430 for 12 poor students governed by a rector.

Matriculations fell off at Cologne from 1391, no doubt partly on account of Heidelberg's recovery, but admissions rose in the fifteenth century, reaching an annual figure of 1,348 in the five years following 1460. The religious orders kept coming, however, and kept the intellectual reputation of Cologne high, apparently coming near to achieving the sort of intellectual pre-eminence in the Rhineland which Paris was exercising in northern France. The fifteenth century was doubtless the period of the university's greatest ascendancy. In 1448 the university had sided with Nicholas V, who as pope was victorious over the conciliarist movement. By 1520 the common university opinion was hostile to the religious reformer Martin Luther. Its views were to be predictably ultramontane well into the sixteenth century. By 1525 political events in the wake of the Great Schism had virtually consummated the university's collapse, and its was to regain vitality again only during the period of the Catholic Counter-Reformation.

The most famous incident in the university's history, which also explains its abrupt decline, is the episode concerning Johann Reuchlin in the very early sixteenth century. Reuchlin was a Hebraist who thought that studying the sacred text in Greek and Hebrew mediated the religious experience of direct contact with God. Among his early works were a Hebrew grammar and dictionary and two cabalistic treatises in dialogue form. He came into prominence when a converted Jewish butcher called Johann Pfefferkorn became convinced that the conversion of the Jews could be effected by the destruction of their religious books. Pfefferkorn enlisted support for his view from the Cologne Dominicans and from Ortwinus Gratius, a teacher in the university arts faculty. Reuchlin had already published a consideration on the state of the Jews, and, alone of seven authorities consulted at the emperor's request on the likely effects of exercising coercion on the Jews, opposed Pfefferkorn in a report of October 1510. Confiscated Hebrew manuscripts were returned.

The dispute became bitter, and early in 1513 Reuchlin issued a virulent attack on the stupidity and senility of the Cologne theologians. In March 1514 Reuchlin published a selection of letters written in his support, *The Letters of Famous Men.* Then in October 1515 appeared the famous satirical attack on Reuchlin's opponents, *The Letters of Obscure Men,* mostly by Ulrich von Hutten but published anonymously, mockingly purporting to support the Cologne theologians by sarcastically congratulating them on their reactionary attitudes, and ironically flattering their self-importance. The letters were addressed chiefly to Ortwinus Gratius. Hutten attacked the Cologne Dominican inquisitor, Jacob von Hoogstraten, by name, and came to see Luther's schism in terms of a political movement by which Germany was throwing off the tyranny of Rome. The letters reflect the discredit into which the reactionary scholastics of the university had fallen by the early sixteenth century in the face of new learning. A second edition of the letters appeared with 7 more letters in 1516, and in 1517 there was another edition, with a further 62 letters. The European reaction to their publication, about which Reuchlin himself seems to have been embarrassed, makes clear why the university teaching

and scholastic positions they caricature had fallen in such low public esteem even before the schism broke out.

During the sixteenth century, the university adhered doctrinally to the *via antigua,* the positions inaugurated by Aquinas and Scotus, which relied heavily on human reason's capacities to reach truth, and was opposed to the fashionable Ockhamism of the late fifteenth century, which relied more emphatically on reason's feebleness and on the need for revelation. Cologne's position was not reactionary but advanced, since the Thomism of the *via antigua* seriously advanced confidence in rational human powers, and the way in which it replaced the *via moderna* mirrored the growing confidence in human nature also evident in the new cult of classical antiquity.

Cologne's Thomism was carried into the eighteenth century, during which efforts to reform the university had no great effect. As the Cologne institution declined, the new university at Bonn was growing. Although the formal foundation dates only from 1818, the academy founded at Bonn in 1777 became a university in 1786. Like Cologne, it was closed by the French. Cologne's university did not reopen as a German university until 1824.

Reorganization of the German university system in the wake of the Napoléonic wars had been radical. After the closure of Mainz and Cologne in 1798, universities in Bamberg, Dillingen, Duisberg, Rinteln, Helmstedt, Salzburg, among others, also were dissolved. Most of these universities, with the exception of Mainz, were scarcely missed. In their place arose three new great institutions, the reorganized University of Munich, the Royal Friedrich Wilhelm University in Berlin, and the Rhenish Friedrich Wilhelm University in Bonn.

In Bonn, there developed an evangelical theology faculty, intended to replace Cologne, and the best available talent was sought not for Cologne, but for Bonn. By the end of the century, both in Bonn and Cologne and throughout Germany, theology as a discipline, whether Lutheran or Catholic, was in serious decline. Law was in the ascendant. The numbers studying philosophy climbed slowly, while those studying medicine declined. These and other changes in the German university world are partly attributable to the introduction of compulsory military service introduced in 1867.

The university that was recreated in 1919 was supported by the state and remained successful until Hitler came to power. It was closed from 1933 to 1953. The new University of Cologne is today again a large and flourishing world-class institution offering a full range of disciplines and facilities, clearly anxious to claim continuity with its briefly illustrious late medieval predecessor. It has an international character, and again counts among the major institutions of higher education in western Europe.

—Claudia Levi

UNIVERSITY OF COPENHAGEN
(Copenhagen, Denmark)

Location: In the capital city of Denmark, in the heart of the city center, just northwest of the museums.

Description: A publicly supported university, enrolling approximately 25,000 students.

Information: The University of Copenhagen
Narregarde 10
Box 2177
DK-1017
Copenhagen K
Denmark
35 32 26 26

Erik of Pomerania, king of the Scandinavian Union (Denmark, Norway, and Sweden), during whose reign Copenhagen became the capital of Denmark, gained authorization from Pope Martin V in 1419 to found a university. The pope allowed the new institution faculties in the "inferior" fields of arts, medicine, and law, but not in the "superior" area of theology. An additional papal condition was that the university be established within two years. Preoccupied with wars, Erik was unable to meet the papal deadline. Finally, in 1438, frustrated by the politicking of the nobles and high clergymen of the *Rigsraad* (the Council of State), King Erik quit the throne for a life of piracy.

Half a century later, in 1448, King Christian I came to the throne of an unstable Scandinavian Union, forced to share his power with the *Rigsraad*. By 1470, he had lost control of Sweden. In 1474, he made a pilgrimage to Rome, where Pope Sixtus IV entertained him lavishly. With the help of Queen Dorothea (his wife and also the widow of his predecessor), he won papal authorization for the university, which was to have all four faculties, offering degrees in Roman law, canon law, philosophy, medicine, and, this time, theology. The new university was founded with the Bishop of Roskilde, Oluf Mortensen, as its first chancellor. In accordance with the authorizing papal bull, it was given its own jurisdiction, which gave it a large measure of autonomy. This status lasted until 1771.

The University of Copenhagen opened in 1479, with accommodations in the Town Hall. (The Swedes, having learned of the university coming to Copenhagen, had stolen a march on the Danes by founding the University of Uppsala in 1477.) The crown lacked funds, partially due to the war with Sweden and partially due to the extrava-

gant lifestyle of Christian I. Funding was largely provided by the Church, and many salaries were paid by providing housing and food from farms subject to the Church.

Christian II, who reigned from 1513 to 1523, was a progressive king, whose most successful reforms were in education, reforms which represented an effort to develop the peasants and artisans of Denmark into a middle class. Appalled by the ignorance of the clergy, Christian II issued an edict forbidding anyone to be ordained a priest who had not studied at the University of Copenhagen; he also began to separate the Danish church from allegiance to the papacy. The university, which had never managed to achieve popularity, ceased operations under Frederick I, Christian II's successor.

Not until 1537, when a civil war left Denmark in Lutheran hands, was the university reconstituted with Johan Bugenhagen, a scholar of Wittenburg, the university most associated with Martin Luther, a key figure in the new orientation of the university as an evangelical Lutheran institution.

Copenhagen had never been a school for the wealthy. The income of a beginning clergyman, which is what a recent graduate was most likely to become, was low; such positions would not attract members of the nobility. Some students were so poor that they could not afford tuition and housing costs, a condition alleviated for some 100 students when Frederick II established a scholarship fund in 1569. Admission criteria were not rigorous. If a student received a testimonial from the headmaster of his grammar school, he could be admitted and "deposed," a ceremony which took place when students entered the university. In his history of the university, Svend Erik Stybe describes this unusual ceremony:

> The students had first to be "deposed." This was to symbolize that they had put aside their old character in order to enter into a higher and more spiritual sphere. Their faces were blackened, a dunce's cap bearing two horns was placed on their heads, and they were given a long nose and a hunched back. They then had to behave as rowdily as possible, among other things by uttering the most abusive language they could think of. This would induce the "deposer" to flog them and tear off their disguise. Afterwards they would be washed clean, would put on ordinary clothes and seat themselves in the auditorium, where one of them would address the dean in Latin. A student thus "deposed" was called a *depositurus,* and from the final syllable of this word comes the name for Danish freshman—a *rus.*

University of Copenhagen

A student's program of studies was expected to last two or three years. Perhaps he would live in a professor's home; in addition to collecting rent the professor might supplement his income by providing tutoring services. A student's career might conclude successfully when his major professor issued a statement attesting to his competence. Three degrees were also offered by examinations. The baccalaureate and master's degrees were available in philosophy, and doctorates could be earned in medicine, law, and theology. Art was the province of the philosophy faculty and comprised what is now commonly called arts and sciences. Geography was a part of physics, and astronomy was a part of mathematics. The only law taught was Roman law, which had no direct bearing on life in Denmark, and so few studied it. Medicine was based on Galen's theory that illness could be cured by restoring the balance of the humors: blood, phlegm, black bile, and yellow bile.

The first of a long line of distinguished students and faculty members, astronomer Tycho Brahe, lectured at Copenhagen in 1574, a year after the publication of his *De Nova Stella,* in which he described his discovery of a new star in the constellation of Cassiopeia.

The University of Copenhagen expanded as it passed through the seventeenth century. Buildings were enhanced, most notably the *Konsistorum* (University Senate) building, which dated from the fifteenth century and which had been part of the bishop's palace before the Reformation; after the Reformation, the building was used as the residence for the university's treasurer. A student residence hall was added, and a students' church, Trinitatis Church, sporting a distinctive, round tower (the *rundetaarn*) was built with a library above it and an observatory above that. Another existing structure, which housed the library until the 1650s, was given a state-of-the-art anatomical theater, where lectures could be developed in conjunction with dissections. A botanical garden was added, as was a new building with an *auditorium superius* for theology lectures above and an *auditorium inferius* for philosophy lectures below.

The debate over religion did not end when the university was reconstituted as an evangelical Lutheran institution in 1537. The Society of Jesus (Jesuits) had emerged as the strongest force in the Counter-Reformation. Their reputation for excellence in higher education prompted some wealthy Danes to send their sons to Jesuit schools in other countries. The university's registers note several returned "Jesuit" students. No steps were taken against them; however, when one applied to be registered as a private tutor, he was required to submit to an examination on his theological views. In 1606, a Norwegian-born Jesuit, Laurits Nielsen (called Kloster-Lasse) attempted to start a Catholic Counter-Reformation in Denmark. King Christian IV forced him to appear before the Lutheran professors of the university, where Kloster-Lasse received a message from the king that he was to be expelled from the country.

During the seventeenth century, the University of Copenhagen began to break away from its reputation as an educational backwater, an achievement largely owed to a group of scholars related by blood and by marriage and loosely identified as the Bartholin family. The founder of the "dynasty," Thomas Fincke, mathematician and physician, professor from 1591 until his death at 95 in 1656, was a dominant figure at the university, but his descendants' reputations would overtake his. One of his daughters wed Ole Worm, another medical faculty member, who was the first to salvage the ancient artifacts that still lay scattered about Scandinavia. Worm's 1643 work on the interpretations of runes, though largely wrong, was seminal, and his accumulation of ancient artifacts made up the collection of Denmark's first museum. He was also the professor in charge of the botanical garden. From it, he produced a number of medicinal plants which he used in his medical lectures.

Fincke's other daughter married Caspar Bartholin, professor of medicine, author of an anatomy text, and father of Erasmus Bartholin, professor of geometry and medicine, and Thomas Bartholin, also professor of medicine. Erasmus Bartholin is best noted for his work with the refraction of light. To illustrate his lectures Thomas Bartholin dissected animal and human bodies; the human bodies were the corpses of hanged criminals, who were, by royal decree, turned over to the anatomical institute instead of being drawn and quartered. Thomas Bartholin is credited with discovering that the liver is not the governing organ of the body or the source of blood and with the discovery of the lymphatic system.

The Bartholin line's strong presence was not always to the benefit of the university. For instance, Niels Steensen, also called Nicolaus Steno, who had demonstrated that the heart was a muscle and that muscles consist of more than fibers, was denied the chair from which Thomas Bartholin had just retired. The chair went instead to Matthias Jacobaeus, who was connected to the Bartholins. Steensen would later demonstrate in Paris that his understanding of the brain was far ahead of that of his contemporaries. What the Bartholin era brought to the University of Copenhagen was empiricism. Until the seventeenth century, scholasticism, which saw faith and reason as the chief sources of knowledge, had held sway. Now, under the empiricists, observation and experience became that source.

Copenhagen was attacked by Sweden in 1659; the entire city defended itself, with the students fighting in the area surrounding the royal palace. Ole Borch, one of the school's future leading empiricists, who was a philologist, chemist, and botanist, became a war hero and was rewarded by the country with a lifetime income. He went on to do important work in the classification of plants. With no family to which to leave his considerable fortune, he left funds for the construction of a residence hall, *Borschs Kollegium,* which still stands.

The excitement of the defense of Copenhagen left the student body having a difficult time adjusting to the relative placidity of the scholarly life. They soon found another outlet for their aggressions. Frederick III had come to the throne in 1648. Beginning in 1660, with a meeting of representatives of the nobility, clergy, and bourgeois classes, he began displacing the nobility from their position of power. The university's students, not generally members of the nobility, began to turn on the servants of the nobles who had come to the meeting. Students—even those who were in no battles—had taken to wearing swords as part of their normal dress. Professors attempted to intervene in the disputes between students and the servants and to forbid the students to bear arms, but the king did not support the ban. After the king took absolute and hereditary power in 1661, the professors again forbade the bearing of arms by students, with the result that the students would simply take their swords off when they went to meet with professors. The custom of Danish students carrying swords lasted into the middle eighteenth century.

The man who is credited with founding Danish literature, Ludvig Holberg, came from Norway to attend the University of Copenhagen in 1702 and received a degree in 1704. The publication in 1711 of his history of Europe resulted in a government grant. In 1717, he was appointed professor of metaphysics at the university; in 1720, he was promoted to the chair of public eloquence, a lucrative position, which ended years of poverty. After writing about history, law, and philology, Holberg turned his talents to the theatre, for which he produced a number of satiric comedies, in the vein of Molière. Literary critic Edmund Gosse and B.W. Downs, author of *Norwegian Literature 1860–1912,* wrote in the *Encyclopaedia Britannica:*

> Holberg found Denmark provided with no books, and he wrote a library for it. When he arrived in the country, the Danish language was never heard in a gentleman's house. Polite Danes were wont to say that a man wrote Latin to his friends, talked French

to the ladies, called his dogs in German and only used Danish to swear at his servants. The single genius of Holberg revolutionized this system.

In his history of Denmark, Paulle Lauring observes that the reign of Frederick IV (1699–1730) marked the beginning of the intellectual life in Denmark. Credit for this activity and for the arrival of the Enlightenment in Denmark in the latter half of the eighteenth century must be shared by the egalitarian Pietists (they represented a movement within the Lutheran community that reached out to educate heretofore neglected classes of Danes) and by their old-guard, elitist opposition. It was, however, the traditions of Ludvig Holberg and the Bartholins that paved the way for the Enlightenment at the University of Copenhagen.

Unfortunately, the intellectual advancement of the university was interrupted by the fire of Copenhagen in 1728, which destroyed most of the university. The old *Konsistorum* building, and with it the archives, was saved by the students. The university was rebuilt relatively quickly. A new *Kommunitets* building, a new auditorium building, and a new anatomical theater, complete with specimens, had all been put into operation by 1740. The most irreparable damage was to the *rundetaarn* or round tower, of Trinitatis Church.

The Bartholins had firmly planted empiricism in the scientific studies at the university. Once empiricism became established, science flourished. The most noteworthy figure in medical and scientific study in the mid-to-late eighteenth century was Georg Kratzenstein, a young German scholar, who was wooed away from the University of St. Petersburg (Russia) with a position in experimental physics and the additional post of professor designate of medicine. An early experimenter with electricity, Kratzenstein had trouble finding a place to live. Landlords had heard that among his possessions was a machine to attract lightning. Kratzenstein lectured on physics, chemistry, and natural history. He was also instrumental in making the standards for medical education stricter. Elected rector of the university four times, he worked to improve the conditions of the tenant farmers who worked the estates that supported the university. He was also an advocate for Jewish students, the first of whom was admitted to the medical school in 1758.

Other reforms of the latter part of the eighteenth century included an increase in the number of professors, greater assurances that a professor hired for any position would be the best available candidate (and not simply a favorite of the king or some other important person), degree-examination requirements for grammar-school teachers and physicians, and abolition of the university's separate jurisdictional status. The most noteworthy change was a revision in the university's mission. In the past, the chief concern had been to train scholars in the fields of theology, law, and medicine; it was now in the business of training young men ready to begin to work as clergymen, physicians, judges, and senior civil servants.

The Napoléonic wars brought disaster to Copenhagen and to the University of Copenhagen. In 1807, the city came under heavy bombardment by the British, and most of the campus was damaged or destroyed. The old *Konsistorum* survived intact, as it had in the fire of 1728, but the university was left to make use of the partial buildings that were left standing and of whatever other accommodations could be found. As a result of the catastrophe brought on by the wars and by the collapse of the Danish merchant trade, the university endured in such conditions for the next quarter century, when rebuilding was finally begun.

It was precisely under such conditions that the university showed its best fruits of the Enlightenment. One of a wave of romantics, Hans Christian Ørsted, whose pantheistic leanings would not be disclosed until 1850, the year before his death, revealed in 1820 a demonstrable relationship between magnetism and electricity that would eventually lead, along with Faraday's discovery of induction, to electromagnetic theory, a new branch of physics, and to the development of every electrical and electronic device more complicated than a flashlight.

Librarian and literary history professor Rasmus Nyerup noticed the abilities of student Rasmus Christian Rask and enlisted his assistance in translating *The Younger Edda,* an Old Icelandic classic text, which was published in 1808, the year after the English bombardment. Three years later, Rask published a guide to the Icelandic language (a remarkably slow-to-change language). He would go on to light the way to understanding of the Indo-European language group. He was also an early experimenter with phonetic notation. Rask is generally regarded as the founder of the science of comparative linguistics.

Another distinguished student was Søren Kierkegaard, who studied theology at the University of Copenhagen from 1830 to 1840. Now recognized as the father of modern existentialism and a revolutionary in Protestant Christian thought, he would receive little notice outside of Denmark during his own life.

In 1874, Nielsine Nielsen, a schoolmistress, applied to become the first female student at the University of Copenhagen. She was admitted in 1875 over the protestations of Professor Matthias Saxtorph and others; Saxtorph denounced the "spirit of the time," which he called "Socialism, Emancipation, or Communism." Nielsen completed her program in medicine in 1884. In 1875 a royal decree had granted women admission to all examinations and degrees, except for those in the faculty of theology, to which they were admitted in 1905. In 1893 Anna Hude received the first doctorate awarded to a woman, but it was not until 1946 that a woman, Astrid Friis, assumed a faculty chair.

One of the most distinguished physicists of the twentieth century, Niels Bohr was associated with the University of Copenhagen as both student and faculty member. He received his Ph.D. in 1911. The first person to apply the quantum theory successfully to the problem of atomic structure, he was awarded the Nobel Prize in physics in 1922. Bohr became a professor of physics at the university in 1916; in 1920, he was named director of the newly created institute of theoretical physics, a post he held until his death in 1962. Active in the Danish resistance against the Nazis in World War II, Bohr fled to the United States, where he participated in the Manhattan Project, which led to the creation of the atomic bomb. Bohr's reservations about the power of such weapons led to his receiving the Atoms for Peace Award in 1957.

The University of Copenhagen continued to function throughout the Nazi occupation, though teaching was suspended for a week in 1943 to protest the deportation of Danish Jews. Many university professors were active in the resistance; a number of the professors were arrested, and, at one point, placed in a camp for about a month. Students protested the Danish government's accommodation with Germany, singing Danish national songs, as well as the "Internationale" and "It's a Long Way to Tipperary"; the several students who were arrested received suspended sentences. University people also helped with the underground press and the escape of the Danish Jews.

Students protested again in 1968, this time to claim a share of the power to determine university policies. In 1970, the 400-year-old system, in which professors ruled the university, was replaced with a system in which student representatives shared power. Historian Svend Stybe wrote that the ensuing negotiations led to "one of the most radical and pro-student university laws in the world."

Further Reading: *Copenhagen University: Five Hundred Years of Science and Scholarship* by Svend Erik Stybe (Copenhagen: Danish Ministry of Foreign Affairs, 1979) is a thorough history; however, sections require a working knowledge of Danish history. *A History of the Kingdom of Denmark* by Palle Lauring, translated by David Hohnen (Copenhagen: Host, 1960) is straightforward and covers its subject well, though it lacks an index.

—Robert Schoenberg

UNIVERSITY OF DUBLIN TRINITY COLLEGE
(Dublin, Ireland)

Location: Forty-acre campus in the center of Dublin, capital of the Republic of Ireland.

Description: Privately incorporated university, which receives substantial state funding. Approximately 11,000 full- and part-time students enroll for undergraduate and graduate degrees. Undergraduate admissions is through centralized state points system.

Information: Secretary to the College
Trinity College Dublin
Dublin 2
Ireland
(01) 677-2941

Visiting: Guided tours of the major buildings and grounds, including the Old Library and Book of Kells, start from Front Gate, College Green, at frequent intervals daily from April to October. At other seasons, tours are available by arrangement; inquiries to the phone number above or at the Porter's Lodge, Front Gate.

Attempts during the fourteenth and fifteenth centuries to establish a university in the English colony in Ireland had been frustrated largely by the insecurity of the colony under continual pressure from the hostile Gaelic and Anglo-Irish aristocracies. The successful foundation by the English crown of a university in Dublin in the last decade of the sixteenth century reflected the recent extension and securing of English rule in Ireland by the Tudor conquests, which had placed some three-quarters of the island under effective English military control. The establishment of a university was regarded as a necessary complement to the victory in arms, an instrument in the next phase of the conquest: the consolidation of English authority by means of a concerted campaign in the religious, intellectual, and cultural spheres, directed against the two primary obstacles to the security of English rule, native Gaelic culture, and the Roman Catholic religion.

Accordingly, a letter from the Dublin Corporation (the municipal authority) to the Privy Council in London in November 1591, petitioning for a university in the city, described the projected institution as "a means to plant religion, civility, and true obedience in the heart of this people." In her favorable reply to the petition the following month, Queen Elizabeth I deplored the fact that, owing to the lack of a university in Ireland, many Irish

were wont to attend universities on the Continent, "whereby they have been infected with popery."

On March 3, 1592, Elizabeth issued a charter for "the College of the Holy and Undivided Trinity near Dublin." The college was to be located on a site one-half mile to the east of the city walls, on the lands of the former Augustinian monastery of All Hallows, dissolved under Henry VIII and its lands turned over to the Dublin Corporation in 1538. Construction of college buildings commenced promptly and the first group of students matriculated in 1594.

The queen made no provision for the endowment of the college; funds for its establishment were raised by public subscription. The college was granted liberty to acquire and to hold property in perpetuity, to derive income from the collection of rents on those properties, and to be exempt from all taxes and exactions. In 1597, the first land grants to the college were made by the crown; they consisted of some 3,000 acres in counties Kerry and Limerick recently confiscated from rebel Irish landowners. By the late nineteenth century, Trinity College would be a major Irish landlord, owning property in virtually every county, which fact contributed to the contemporary criticism of the college by nationalist opinion.

Under the terms of the charter, the college was incorporated as *mater universitatis* (mother university), which raises a complicated question of the relationship between Trinity College and Dublin University. Dublin University is unique among universities organized on the British model in that, throughout the four centuries of its existence, it has always contained but one constituent college: namely, Trinity. Furthermore, there is no organizational distinction between college and university; the institution has always been a single corporation, with one provost, one governing board, and one administration. For all practical purposes, then, Trinity College and Dublin University are different names for one entity. Whatever aspiration may have been contained within the rhetoric of the charter—that Trinity College might in time spawn sister colleges within the one university—from the start the institution founded by Elizabeth's charter has been empowered to fulfill both the collegiate function of instruction and the university function of examination and conferment of degrees. The college historians, R.B. McDowell and D.A. Webb, suggest that Trinity might be regarded as being both the last of the British medieval universities and the first of the British overseas colonial colleges to be emulated by such New World foundations as Harvard and Yale. Recognizing that capital would be scarce in a precarious frontier colony and that only one

University of Dublin Trinity College

college would likely be viable, the founders of Trinity made certain that their college was granted the status and function of a university.

Akin to Harvard and Yale in its location on a frontier of Anglo-Saxon culture and Protestant religion, Trinity was imbued in its early years with a combative Puritan ethos, derived in part through its close association with Trinity College in Cambridge, the intellectual furnace of English Puritanism. The chief mission of the Dublin college was the training of a learned Protestant clergy, equipped to minister to parishes throughout the colony and to proselytize among the native Catholics. In accordance with the official state policy of assimilation of the Irish, Catholics were encouraged to attend Trinity, in the hope of their thorough anglicization and conversion to Protestantism. From an early date, provision was made for extracurricular instruction in the Irish language, both

as a welcome to Catholics and as a better preparation of the ordinands for their missionary work. Such instruction was abandoned in the wake of the political strife and polarizations of the mid-seventeenth century. Apart from a brief period in the 1680s, Irish language instruction would not return to Trinity until the mid-nineteenth century; not until 1908 would the study of Irish count toward a degree.

The first provost, Adam Loftus, Archbishop of Dublin, presided in 1594 over a collegiate community of three fellows and three scholars. By the 1620s the college had grown to include 16 fellows, 7 senior and 9 junior, the senior fellows with the provost forming, as they do to this day, the governing body of the college, the board. In the 1630s the number of scholars was fixed at 70, although students other than scholars (who as members of the foundation possessed certain rights and privileges) were admitted in ever-growing numbers. A four-year course of instruction led to the bachelor of arts degree. The great majority of students, being bound for the ministry, remained an additional several years to study for the master of arts degree and to contend for election to a fellowship while awaiting ordination and appointment to a clerical living. The college also awarded advanced bachelor's and doctor's degrees in divinity.

Although Greek was studied and Latin was the medium of instruction, the course contained next to nothing of the classical authors; as befitted a seminary, the ancient languages were regarded as the basis for the study of theology, moral philosophy, and scripture. The Reformation, not the Renaissance, was the chief influence on the curriculum. An early Trinity innovation was the importance accorded to lectures and tutorials as arenas of instruction, on an equal level with the hoary scholastic disputation.

In 1633, William Laud, Archbishop of Canterbury, was appointed chancellor of Trinity by King Charles I; he then initiated an effort to curb the college's independence by asserting tighter royal and Episcopal authority, as he had already done over the English universities. The result was the Laudean Statutes of 1637, a major revision and addendum to Trinity's original Elizabethan charter. The statutes assured stricter conformity to Anglican orthodoxy, and along with changes in curriculum brought to an end the Puritan temper of the college.

Laud's ally was his vice-chancellor, James Ussher, Archbishop of Armagh, former Trinity student, fellow, and Professor of Theological Controversies. The foremost scholar of Trinity's first century, Ussher, throughout his lengthy association with the institution, was devoted to the development of the college library. Ruined financially by the despoliations of the wars of the 1640s and 1650s, Ussher, upon his death in 1656, left to his daughter the legacy of his extensive personal library of some 10,000 books and manuscripts. Henry Cromwell, brother of the Lord Protector and Lord Deputy in Ireland, purchased the library in its entirety from Ussher's daughter for the state, in part out of contributions from the Cromwellian army in Ireland. Cromwell's intent was to use the purchase as the basis for a public library in Dublin that would also service a projected second college of Dublin University, to be named Cromwell College. With the restoration of the Stuart monarchy, the plans for both public library and second college were abandoned, but in 1661 the Irish Parliament persuaded King Charles II to donate the Ussher collection to Trinity College, a great enhancement of the college library, both in its breadth and in its numbers.

At about the same time, two incomparable medieval illuminated manuscripts, the Book of Durrow and the Book of Kells, were presented to Trinity College by Henry Jones, Bishop of Meath. The Book of Kells, regarded as the supreme work in the history of Irish art, is a handwritten manuscript text in Latin of the four gospels with supplementary material, rendered upon vellum (calfskin) pages in a beautiful insular-style majuscule script. The text is embellished by various types of illustrations, including scenes from the life of Christ, portrait pages of the evangelists, zoomorphic ornament and drolleries, and intricately decorated initial letters. Crafted about A.D. 800, most likely in the scriptorium of the Irish monastery of Iona, off the west coast of Scotland, the manuscript—referred to in 1007 as "the chief relic of the western world"—was preserved for at least six centuries prior to its presentation to Trinity at the monastery of Kells in County Meath, 40 miles northwest of Dublin. It remains to this day the greatest treasure of the Trinity College Library.

During the Jacobite War of 1690, the college was occupied by the royalist army of James II for use as a military barracks and prison for Williamite sympathizers; nearly all the fellows and scholars had previously fled to England for refuge. Some random vandalism occurred, but through the efforts of two Catholic priests, the library's holdings were spared molestation. The Jacobites evacuated Trinity and the city of Dublin following their defeat at the Boyne (July 1, 1690), and the college community soon thereafter returned.

The eighteenth century, the most splendid epoch of the Anglo-Irish Ascendancy, was a period of intellectual stagnation at Trinity. Of the 25 fellows elected from 1716 to 1734, not one published a single work in his lifetime. This scholarly stasis earned for Trinity the derisive agnomen "the Silent Sister," a sobriquet which, unfortunately, adhered to the college long after it ceased to be merited. The century was marked by a steady increase in the proportion of students intent on careers other than in the church, and the consequent development, especially in the latter part of the century, of such disciplines as classics, mathematics, medicine, and music.

The opulence of the Georgian Ascendancy left its enduring mark upon the physical face of the college through a program of extensive rebuilding which shaped the nucleus of the campus as it exists today. As a consequence, of the original Elizabethan and early Stuart structures, nothing remains, the oldest extant building being a red-brick residence hall, Rubrics, erected about 1700.

As a result of this vigorous spate of Georgian building, Trinity today can boast what art historian E.J. McParland has called "the finest *ensemble* of classical architecture in Ireland." While no single one of Trinity's Georgian buildings can lay claim to unrivaled eminence in its own right, the west end of the college campus is remarkable as a masterful stroke of architectural planning, for the harmony with which the buildings relate to one another and to the open spaces. It is therefore a surprise that the ensemble of Front Square—one of the most pleasing prospects of synthetic scenery in Ireland—did not derive from a master plan, but evolved piecemeal throughout the eighteenth and nineteenth centuries, each architect building upon the opportunities inherited from his predecessors. The centerpiece of the prospect, the Campanile, was not erected until 1855, on the site of an earlier range of buildings that had partitioned today's airy and expansive Front Square into two separate and comparatively cramped quadrangles.

The oldest and most important of the college's neoclassical structures is the Old Library, built from 1712 to 1732 to the design of Thomas Burgh. Commentators have remarked upon the weighty regularity and puritanical severity of this building, seen as redolent of the hardheaded, mercantile temper of the early Georgian age, in contrast to the more lightsome and graceful spirit of the later Georgian. The books, stored on the two upper stories, were insulated from the damp of the surrounding marshy ground (the River Liffey prior to later eighteenth-century reclamations came up to the college walls). In 1858, the flat plaster ceiling of the first-floor Long Room was removed and the two upper stories thereby thrown into one lofty space, surmounted by a new semicircular wooden barrel vault. The result was to augment the majesty of the Long Room; at 210 feet in length, it is one of the most striking interiors in Ireland, and described by McDowell and Webb as one of the two "most splendid university library interior[s] in Europe." (The other is the library of the University of Coimbra).

While the Trinity campus is renowned for its classical Georgian architecture, the finest single building at the college is of the nineteenth-century Italianate revival. The Museum Building (1853–57), the work of the same architects who raised the roof of the Long Room, was described by McParland as "one of the landmarks of Victorian architecture in Britain and Ireland."

The 1801 British Copyright Act extended to Trinity the status of a legal deposit, or copyright, library, entitled to claim one free copy of every printed item (books, pamphlets, maps, periodicals) published in the United Kingdom. The status was reaffirmed following the Anglo-Irish Treaty of 1921 and by subsequent copyright legislation in both Great Britain and Ireland. Despite early irregularities in the actual implementation of these rights, the privilege has resulted in the enormous growth and enrichment of the library's holdings. The resultant accumulation of books—the library currently adds 50,000 new volumes every year—required one-half mile of additional shelving. With a significant increase in student numbers (from 1,543 in 1939 to 3,500 in the 1960s), Trinity needed a new library building. The Berkeley Library (named for the eminent eighteenth-century philosopher and educator, who was collegiate librarian when work commenced on Burgh's Old Library in 1712) was completed in 1967 to the design of Paul Koralek. The first manifestation of twentieth-century modernism on campus, the Berkeley is notable for its cellular floor plan, affording secluded areas conducive to quiet study. Thirty years on, opinion concerning the Berkeley remains divided. The building indeed fulfills the original intention of erecting on campus a building as representative of the twentieth century

as the Old Library is of the eighteenth. As the two libraries stand at apices of a triangle with the museum around a connecting plaza, the viewer, in one glance, enjoys a visual lecture upon three centuries of Irish architecture.

The nineteenth century found Trinity in the forefront of innovations in new spheres of higher education. Early in the century, Trinity—which had provided instruction in medicine since 1711—introduced the practice of the clinical teaching of medicine. In partnership with the teaching hospital opened in Dublin in 1815, Trinity medical students were the first in the world to receive training in a hospital setting and in direct contact with patients. In 1841, Trinity opened one of the first schools of civil engineering in the world and established a professorship in the discipline. While at first a professional diploma course, in 1872 a degree of bachelor of engineering was introduced, the first degree course in Great Britain or Ireland outside the traditional faculties. An unusually large proportion of Trinity engineering graduates embarked on careers in the British overseas colonies, the advance guard of a large body of Trinity alumni of the nineteenth century who provided the sprawling reaches of the British Empire with administrators, jurists, doctors, and missionaries.

Modern research at Trinity in the physical sciences was pioneered by Sir William Rowan Hamilton (1805–81), appointed professor of astronomy in 1826 at the age of 21, a year before taking his B.A. A brilliant mathematician best known for his discovery of quaternions, Hamilton also accomplished important work in dynamics, geomagnetism, and optics. Later notable Trinity scientists include G.F. Fitzgerald (1851–1901), whose research into the contraction of moving bodies in the direction of their motion was employed by Einstein in developing the theory of relativity; and Ernest Walton (1903–95), Trinity graduate and professor, who at Cambridge in 1932 conducted crucial experiments in producing nuclear reactions by proton acceleration and thus launched the modern era of accelerator physics, for which work in 1951 he became the first Trinity alumnus to be awarded the Nobel Prize. Important work has been done in optoelectronics and laser physics, continuing a long Trinity tradition of research into the nature of light and vision. Trinity's second Nobel laureate was the startlingly innovative novelist and dramatist Samuel Beckett (Nobel Prize for literature, 1969), representative of the long history of literary attainment by Trinity alumni, extending back to such eighteenth-century figures as William Congreve and Jonathan Swift.

The 1800 Act of Union between Great Britain and Ireland designated Dublin University as a parliamentary constituency, entitled to return a member to the House of Commons at Westminster, a number later increased to two. Trinity returned an unbroken succession of Conservative and Unionist M.P.s, an apt reflection of the prevailing political ideologies within the corporation and among alumni and students. Most notable of these Dublin University M.P.s was Sir Edward Carson, who represented Trinity at Westminster from 1892 to 1918. A barrister who catapulted to fame with his cross-examination of another former Trinity student, Oscar Wilde, during Wilde's libel action against the Marquess of Queensberry in 1895, Carson rose to the leadership of the Unionist Party in 1910, and emerged as the most implacable foe of Irish Home Rule and the most important figure behind the retention of Northern Ireland within the United Kingdom.

Beneath this mainstream of Unionist opinion, there lurked throughout the nineteenth century at Trinity a minority undercurrent of nationalist sympathy, nurtured in the college debating societies and represented by such figures as Theobald Wolfe Tone, founder of the United Irishmen and progenitor of Irish republicanism; Robert Emmet, expelled from college in 1798 for his United Irishmen activities; the Young Ireland leader and journalist Thomas Davis; the Fenian leader John O'Leary; Douglas Hyde, Irish language scholar and founder in 1893 of the Gaelic League; and such literary figures as Wilde and John Millington Synge.

At the time of the Easter Rising of 1916, the college grounds possessed a small arsenal of rifles and ammunition in the custody of the college's Officer Training Corps. For fear that the store might be seized by the republican insurgents, and because of the strategic location of the campus in the heart of Dublin, the college buildings were held by a small number of the OTC cadets in the face of hostile sniper fire for two days until they were reinforced by regular British troops, who established in college a headquarters and emergency hospital for the duration of the week-long insurrection.

Under the terms of the 1922 constitution of the Irish Free State and under the later Irish constitution of 1937, Trinity was accorded representation in the Seanad, the upper (but less significant) house of the Irish parliament, the Oireachtas. Since 1937, Trinity has elected three Seanad members by vote of all registered graduates. In recent years, certain Trinity senators have been notable for articulating unconventional positions which might otherwise have gone unrepresented at the mainstream of Irish politics. Foremost among these has been Mary Robinson, Trinity professor and expert in constitutional law, who represented Trinity in the Seanad for some 20 years prior to her election as president of Ireland in 1990.

Women were first admitted to Trinity in 1904, despite concerns that their presence might imperil both the morals and the prudent marital choices of themselves and their male undergraduates. By 1914, women accounted for 16 percent of the student population. Progress in the realm of instruction and governance was slower: the first woman professor was appointed in 1934, the first woman fellow elected in 1965. In 1995, women comprised over 50 percent of the student body, but recent criticism has cited their marked under-representation among the fellows and on the board.

Throughout its history a thornier issue for Trinity than gender coeducation has been religious coeducation. The initial proselytizing welcome extended to Catholics evaporated in the anti-Catholic backlash following the Rebellion of 1641, as the earlier English policy of assimilation was supplanted by one of suppression. In the era of the Penal Laws, political and religious conformity was enforced at Trinity by the imposition of oaths of loyalty to the Hanoverian succession, abjuration of Jacobitism and repudiation of the Catholic doctrine of transubstantiation. These tests were required of all fellows (who were also required to take Anglican holy orders) and of all students prior to conferment of their degrees. Thus, while Catholics were effectively barred from college positions and from graduation, there was no formal ban to their enrollment in undergraduate courses (although college regulations required attendance at Anglican services), and during the eighteenth century a smattering of Catholics attended Trinity under these terms.

In 1794, as part of general relief legislation that sought to curry the loyalty of Irish Catholics to the English crown against the threat of a French invasion and to appeal to the perceived common interest of Catholic and Protestant against the revolutionary danger of French and Irish republicanism, the Irish Parliament abolished all religious tests for students at Trinity, thus opening the college's doors to adherents of all denominations and of none. The college remained an Anglican institution through retention of the Fellows' Oath, which included a repudiation of "pontifical religion." Over the next half-century Trinity became accepted as a suitable school for lay Irish Catholics, largely supplanting the old tradition of education in the Catholic colleges of the Continent. No less eminent a Catholic and nationalist figure than Daniel O'Connell, himself educated in the old manner at St. Omer in France, had his sons educated at Trinity.

In mid-century, however, attitudes hardened on both sides of the sectarian divide: Protestants concerned over a perceived Catholic encroachment in higher education represented by the Oxford Movement; Catholics alarmed by the assertive proselytizing activity in Ireland of evangelical Protestants. Within both camps there was also the growing tendency to equate Catholicism and Irish nationalism. At a synod in 1850, the Irish Catholic hierarchy warned its flock of the dangers of secular education and commenced an energetic policy of promoting a separate, but state-supported Catholic school system at all levels. Four years later a Catholic university, chartered by the Vatican, opened in Dublin. It was to this institution that those Irish Catholics who could afford the costs of a third-level education were strenuously encouraged to attend by their bishops to attend.

In 1873, in response to growing pressure from English Liberals and nonconformists against the concept of denominational education at the third level, an act of the Westminster Parliament abolished all religious tests and declarations of faith for any position at Trinity, save for admission to the divinity school (still essentially an Anglican seminary), thereby reconstituting the college as a nondenominational institution. Two years later, in 1875, the Catholic bishops intensified their objections to Trinity, condemning the introduction there of what they termed "purely secular education." This marked the beginning of the so-called ban by the Irish hierarchy on Catholic attendance at Trinity.

During the twentieth century, the ban was reiterated in increasingly severe terms. In 1961, the Archbishop of Dublin expressly forbade Catholic attendance at Trinity "under pain of mortal sin." From the 1940s, an official of the Dublin archdiocese was empowered to render decisions upon individual exceptions to the ban, which were granted only after grueling investigation into the circumstances of the request. Grounds for exception were limited to pursuit of a course of study unavailable in Ireland except at Trinity, or inability to meet the Irish language proficiency requirement of the National University, a circumstance ordinarily applicable only to students whose prior education had been received abroad.

In the late 1960s, the Irish government studied proposals to merge Trinity with University College Dublin into a new, two-college University of Dublin. In preparation for such an event, the two colleges prepared a plan for the allocation of certain faculties and disciplines between them to avoid redundance. Under such a plan, the continuing of an absolute ban against Trinity attendance would have proven impossible. Hence, in June 1970, the Catholic bishops formally announced the removal of the ban. The merger plans eventually were dropped, but the removal of the ban was irreversible. In the ensuing years, the proportion of Catholic students at Trinity has steadily and rapidly increased. In the 1990s, some 75 to 80 percent of students are from Catholic backgrounds, a figure roughly equivalent to the proportion of Catholics in Ireland.

As Ireland's oldest institution of higher education, Trinity College continues to occupy a special place in the life of the nation. The evolution over the last century of Trinity's complicated relationship to Catholic and to nationalist Ireland is typified in the careers of three of the college's alumni already cited: Edward Carson, whose Protestantism and uncompromising Unionism were dominant in pre-1921 Trinity; Douglas Hyde, son of a Protestant rector, champion of the Irish language and of a cultural nationalism which contributed immensely to the establishment of the independent Irish state, and who in 1938 was elected as Ireland's first president; and Mary Robinson, a Catholic, whose election as Ireland's seventh president in 1990 was widely seen as reflecting a liberalizing trend in contemporary Irish life and a more pluralist conception of Irish national and social identity. It is these latter values which Trinity College seems prepared to represent within a rapidly changing Ireland.

Further Reading: The standard history is *Trinity College Dublin 1592–1952: An Academic History* (Cambridge: Cambridge University Press, 1982) by R.B. McDowell and D.A. Webb; while the emphasis throughout is upon the college's development as an institution of higher education and scholarship, there is enough material regarding Trinity's broader place in Irish political and social history for the work to be authoritative in all areas. The college's quarter centenary was the occasion for the publication of two important volumes: *Trinity College Dublin: The first 400 Years* by J.V. Luce (Dublin: Trinity College Dublin Press, 1992), a briefer survey than McDowell's and Webb's that continues the account to the present day; *Trinity College Dublin and the Idea of a University,* edited by C.H. Holland (Dublin: Trinity College Dublin Press, 1991), an anthology by various contributors ranging widely over aspects of the college's history and traditions. Maurice Craig's classic *Dublin 1660–1860* (Dublin: Allen Figgis, 1952), an eminently readable architectural-cum-social history, contains valuable and well-indexed material on the college buildings and vignettes of college life in the eighteenth and nineteenth centuries.

—Lawrence W. White

UNIVERSITY OF DURHAM
(Durham, England)

Location: In a restored medieval castle and at other sites in the cathedral city of Durham in northeastern England.

Description: Established in 1832; formerly noted for training schoolteachers and priests of the Church of England, now a multi-faculty institution enrolling approximately 7,000 students in undergraduate and graduate programs.

Information: The Registrar and Secretary
The University
Old Shire Hall
Durham DH1 3HP
England
(0191) 374 2000

The University of Durham, established in 1832, occupies a special position in the development of higher education in the British Isles. It was the last British university to be created by a Christian church rather than the government or other secular private benefactors, and it maintained close links with the church even as Britain in general and other universities in particular became less and less religious. In addition, for many years it was the only university in northeastern England, maintaining a long association with the college which was to become the University of Newcastle. Thus, while its foundation set it apart from all later universities, its location also set it apart from the universities of Oxford, Cambridge, and London, in the prosperous metropolitan southeast of England, as well as from the separate education systems of Scotland and Ireland.

It is possible that there might have been a university in Durham long before 1832 if Thomas Hatfield, one of the wealthy and powerful prince-bishops who for centuries directly governed an autonomous "palatinate" from Durham, had not endowed a college at Oxford in around 1326 and provided scholarships for students from the city to go and study there. On at least two later occasions proposals were made for a university in Durham itself, in each case during a period when the bishop's palatinate powers were being challenged. In 1536 King Henry VIII's separation of the Church of England from the Catholic Church was met with an unsuccessful rebellion, known as the Pilgrimage of Grace, which the priests of Durham were suspected of encouraging. In retaliation, between 1541 and 1544 the bishops' powers were

reduced, the cathedral's treasures were confiscated, Hatfield's foundation of Trinity College, Oxford, was abolished, and plans were made for a university to take over the buildings of the dissolved monasteries in the city.

The proposal failed, but a similar scheme came much closer to fruition in 1657, eight years after the English Civil Wars had ended with the execution of King Charles I, the abolition of all bishoprics, and the creation of the short-lived British republic. A group of prominent Durham citizens petitioned the Lord Protector, Oliver Cromwell, for permission to use the cathedral and its attached buildings, then standing empty, for a new college; they got as far as selecting a provost and fellows (presiding officer and teachers) and planning a curriculum. The universities of Oxford and Cambridge, which then guarded their monopoly of the power to grant degrees, objected to the scheme, and Oliver Cromwell's son and successor Richard shelved the college.

In 1660 both the monarchy and the bishops were restored and no more was heard of a university until 1831, when the idea was revived by the dean and chapter, the governing body of Durham Cathedral. In 1832, with the support of William Van Mildert, the prince-bishop (then, like his successor now, an ex-officio member of the House of Lords), as well as Earl Grey, the prime minister, they secured the passage of an act of parliament and the granting of a charter by King William IV, allowing them to donate part of the cathedral's property to a university of which they would be governors and the bishop the Visitor, a largely ceremonial office. These arrangements were based on those at Christ Church, Oxford, where the college chapel doubles as Oxford Cathedral.

Durham is often referred to as England's third university, after Oxford and Cambridge. Yet it is also often referred to as England's fourth, on the assumption that London preceded it, for University College London had been opened in 1828. The difficulty can only be resolved according to one's definition of what a university is. Those who define a university as an institution which teaches advanced courses favor London over Durham. Those who emphasize the power to award degrees do the same, since the University of London, which absorbed the College in 1836, was granted that power the same year, while Durham received it a year later. But those who prefer the British legal definition of a university give Durham priority, since it received a royal charter four years before London did and, in any event, a college is not the same as a university.

The first classes at Durham, admitted from 1833 onward, were taught in a house owned by the cathedral (the

University of Durham

Archdeacon's Inn on Palace Green, near the castle). Professors of divinity, Greek, and mathematics, and readers in history and law were the first staff to be chosen by the dean and chapter, who also appointed a warden and a senate as executive officers. The extent to which these clerical governors involved themselves in the affairs of their new foundation, at least in its early years, is suggested by the fact that in 1835 they found it necessary to review and approve the purchase of a soup ladle, sugar tongs, and wine glasses for its refectory. As at Oxford and Cambridge in those days, officers, teaching staff and students alike were required to be members of the Church of England.

In 1836 Bishop Van Mildert died and the palatinate was abolished once and for all, a reform which was resisted by the dean and chapter even though it did not alter their positions in the cathedral or the university. In the following year, the university was given the right to award degrees in arts, theology, science, and—particularly fitting for an institution located near the coalfields and shipyards of northeastern England—civil engineering and mining. It was thus the first university in the British Isles to offer teaching in either of these last two subjects.

The general perception of the status of these degrees may be gauged by the fact that for many years the university offered both courses leading to its own degrees and courses leading to certificates which permitted students to take examinations at the University of London. The Bishop of Durham arranged with Lord John Russell, prime minister, to have this apparently embarrassing connection kept secret, even though it was standard practice for most of the university colleges founded in England during the nineteenth century.

Meanwhile the number of students at the university, whether on Durham degree courses or London certificate courses, continued rising at an unexpectedly rapid rate, making it necessary to provide more and more accommodation for them. The castle of the former prince-bishops, started in 1072, largely rebuilt in the fourteenth century but long left in ruins, was given to the university in 1837, restored to a usable state, and then opened for both teaching and residence in 1840. Bishop Hatfield's Hall (now Hatfield College), named in memory of the fourteenth-century prince-bishop, was opened in 1846, in a former inn, as a residence for poorer students; and another residential building, Cosin's Hall, was added in 1851, only to be closed down for lack of funds in 1864. In addition,

Saint Bede's College, a teacher training institution loosely affiliated with the university, was established in 1839, and Saint Hild's College, a sister institution to Saint Bede's which trained women to become schoolteachers, was opened in 1858.

The university's provision for the study of science, through lectures on engineering and mining and, from 1841, through the work of the university's astronomical observatory, was relatively meager, for Durham's academic strengths were in the arts and, overwhelmingly in terms of student numbers, in theology. Scientific provision tended to become the special preserve of the university's sections located at Newcastle upon Tyne, 16 miles north of Durham, which had developed after 1852 when a small medical college in that city was affiliated with the university, culminating in the opening of a College of Physical Science in 1871 and formal incorporation in 1874. The intention appears to have been to attract those young men from northeastern England who were considering a business or engineering career into academic training in the region rather than having them train in Germany or other continental European countries, as had been customary. The college was supported by such prominent local patrons as the banker Thomas Hodgkin and the steelmaster Lord Armstrong, and it appointed a professor of mining, one of the first in Britain, in 1880; however, its alumni, armed with University of Durham degrees, tended to be greeted with suspicion by many of the shipbuilding and engineering firms of the region, then one of the most advanced industrial centers in the world.

In 1871 Durham abolished the residential requirement which it had copied from Oxford and Cambridge, although in practice most students continued to live in accommodations either provided or licensed by the university authorities. More important, in the same year it joined with Oxford and Cambridge (again) in abolishing all religious tests for admission to its courses or membership in its senate, even though at Durham that body continued to be appointed by governors who were priests of the Church of England. (In contrast, London and all the universities founded later never had such tests.)

In 1895 Durham received formal permission from Queen Victoria to award degrees to women and did so for the first time the following year, 16 years after the University of London had become the first British university to do so, but 24 years before Oxford and fully 52 years before Cambridge. The first women alumnae were in fact trainee schoolteachers from Saint Hild's College, which perhaps suggests that the notion of women entering any profession other than teaching had still not reached the more conservative northeast of England, some 20 years after the country's first women doctors had started practicing in London.

The opening of a women's hostel, known as Abbey House, in 1899 was perhaps a sign of slightly more radical intentions, but women continued to be a small minority in the university for many more years to come. The numerical dominance of male theology students was reinforced by the opening of two more residential halls which were then reserved for their exclusive use, Saint Chad's Hall in 1904 and Saint John's Hall in 1909. In 1919 the three halls and the women's hostel were all renamed colleges—Abbey House became Saint Mary's, and the residential section of the castle was renamed University College. It should be noted that this was a purely nominal change, since, unlike the colleges of Oxford, Cambridge, or London, those at Durham have no teaching facilities of their own. At this stage the university was still housed entirely within buildings in the historic center of Durham, on a peninsula all but surrounded by the river Wear and in the shadow of the cathedral, although all the buildings which it acquired or had constructed after 1919 are located elsewhere in the city.

Meanwhile the longstanding relationships with the dean and chapter of Durham Cathedral and with the colleges at Newcastle upon Tyne had been placed on a new footing. In 1904 the College of Physical Science was renamed Armstrong College in memory of one of its chief benefactors, and in 1908 the institutions in both cities were reorganized into a federal University of Durham, composed of the Durham and Newcastle Divisions, as they were known, and with a new charter, resembling those of other British universities, providing for supervision by the city councils and local worthies as well as the cathedral authorities.

Unfortunately, although hardly surprisingly, these rearrangements of the academic furniture did little to endear the Newcastle colleges to the local magnates who might have patronized them but who still generally retained an inveterate hostility to what they saw as overeducated upstarts. Their attitude to Armstrong College in particular stands in sharp contrast not only with the generosity of those businessmen who endowed universities elsewhere in England and (even more so) in continental Europe, North America, and Japan, but also with that of the coal miners' associations, the leading labor unions of the region, which, in spite of the huge financial losses they had sustained during the General Strike of 1926, managed to raise enough money the following year to endow a research laboratory at Armstrong College.

Curiously, this new facility in Newcastle was built three years after the opening of the Dawson Building, the first of several in Durham which house scientific departments, an indication that, in spite of attempts to plan the federal university as a single unit, they were already competing to attract students in the same fields as early as 1924. Thus after 1937, when the Newcastle College of Medicine and Armstrong College were merged to form King's College, Newcastle, the new institution remained formally within the Durham federation but developed its own courses in the arts and social studies as well as in the natural sciences.

During World War II the industrial districts of Newcastle were bombed, but the university, in both cities, was undamaged. Both divisions were considerably reduced in size as most of their teachers and students (male and female) were conscripted for the war effort; but they resumed the pattern of expansion after 1945, encouraged by governments which, for the first time in British history, actively planned and helped to finance the provision of higher education formerly left almost entirely to the churches, local governments, businessmen, and other private benefactors. In Durham in 1959 a footbridge was built over the river Wear (using university funds although it is open for general use) in order to relieve pressure on the medieval Prebends Bridge. This event, which occurred just as the university authorities were beginning to plan a formal separation of the Durham and Newcastle colleges, may be taken to mark the beginning of a new phase in the university's history, as the Durham colleges and departments expanded, occupying more and more sites on both sides of the river and offering a wider range of subjects than ever before.

King's College, Newcastle was formally separated from the Durham colleges and became the University of Newcastle upon Tyne in 1963. In the meantime the remainder of the university, which retained the original title, had already opened Grey College for men in 1959, the Gulbenkian Museum of Oriental Art and Archeology in 1961, and its own Physics Building in 1962. In addition, Saint Aidan's Society for women (which, like Saint Cuthbert's Society for men, had been created in 1947 to cater to those students, around one-third of the whole body, who were not resident in any of the colleges) became a college in 1961. It is now noted for its dining hall and other buildings designed by Sir Basil Spence, the prominent modernist architect best known for designing Coventry Cathedral.

In 1963 the university was able to bring its administrative offices together on one site after purchasing the Old Shire Hall and other buildings vacated by Durham County Council. New colleges were added to the university—Van Mildert College for men in 1966, Trevelyan College for women in 1967, and a pre-existing Catholic theological college, Ushaw College, which was affiliated in 1968—and such new departments as applied physics and electronics, engineering science, economics, politics, and anthropology were also added during the 1960s, while the business school was set up in 1967. The latest addition to the university's residential provision, Collingwood College, opened in 1973, and Saint Hild's and Saint Bede's Colleges, both still owned by the Church of England rather than by the university, were merged as the College of Saint Hild and Saint Bede in 1976 but were then incorporated into the university in 1979. Most recently, in 1992, the university entered into a joint venture with Teesside University to manage a new institution, University College, at Stockton on Tees, a small coastal city south of Durham.

As it prepares to enter the twenty-first century the University of Durham has largely abandoned many of its traditions. Its connection with Durham Cathedral has dwindled to a ceremonial and sentimental level; it is no longer dominated by theology students but instead competes with other leading British universities across the whole range of academic disciplines, and among its 13 colleges only Ushaw College for men and Saint Mary's College for women retain gender discrimination in admissions. Nevertheless certain distinctive features remain. For example, like Oxford and Cambridge, but unlike most universities founded later, it admits students on the basis of interviews (by the colleges, not the university) as well as school examination results, it assesses their work almost exclusively by written examinations rather than by continuous assessment, and it assigns them to membership of its constituent colleges, albeit at Durham these are not teaching institutions. Accordingly it has acquired an informal reputation as a university mainly interested in competing with Oxford and Cambridge and eager to admit students rejected by those ancient foundations, although this is probably an unfair aspersion on all but a few of its approximately 7,500 students (including around 1,000 postgraduates).

Throughout its history the University of Durham, unlike the universities of Oxford, Cambridge, or London, has produced few alumni famous in politics, business, or the arts. Instead, like the universities in other parts of England outside the southeast, it has been more concerned with training priests, schoolteachers, doctors, engineers, and other professionals of the type who are much less celebrated but are at least as essential to the maintenance and improvement of society and culture (perhaps even more so). From the 1960s onward, like all other British universities, it has steadily increased its student numbers and the range of its courses in order to compete in national and international academic leagues. If, as a result, it has moved further away from its founders' intentions than any other British university established in modern times has had to, that is an indication both of how homogeneous British higher education is becoming and of how unusual Durham originally was.

Further Reading: J.T. Fowler's *Durham University: Earlier Foundations and Present Colleges* (London: Robinson, 1904) provides illuminating information about the university's earliest days, while C.E. Whiting's *The University of Durham 1832–1932* (Durham: n.p., 1937), published in honor of the university's centenary, brings the story of the university a bit further along. Both have been out of print for some years but may be obtainable at larger libraries.

—Patrick Heenan

UNIVERSITY OF EDINBURGH
(Edinburgh, Scotland)

Location: In Old Town, Edinburgh, Scotland.

Description: A public university enrolling approximately 17,000 students in undergraduate, graduate, and professional faculties.

Information: The University of Edinburgh
Old College, South Bridge
Edinburgh EH8 9YL
Scotland
(0131) 650 1000

Visiting: For information on campus tours, contact the Information Office at the above address.

The University of Edinburgh is Scotland's fourth oldest university, the first university founded in Britain after the Reformation, and Britain's first municipal university. Higher education began in Edinburgh in the mid-sixteenth century, when Mary of Guise, regent of Scotland, appointed two eminent scholars, who were paid out of the royal treasury to give public lectures in Edinburgh on canon and civil law, Greek, and the sciences. The town provided the Magdalen Chapel in the Cowgate for a series of lectures which lasted two or three years. This transitory foundation demonstrated the desirability of a university in Scotland's capital.

In 1582, the town council obtained a royal charter from James VI to establish a college of law, known as the Tounis (Town's) College. James also gave the college the income from an ecclesiastical benefice. The town council was also aided in establishing university finances by getting control of part of a legacy which had been left in 1558 by Robert Reid, bishop of Orkney. The charter of King James authorized the college to establish all faculties, although this document did not mention degree-conferring powers. While arts degrees were issued from the beginning, their legality was not made certain until an act of 1621. In 1617 James VI declared that it should be known as King James's College for all time. Over the main entrance to the university's Old Quadrangle the inscription "James the Sixth's Academy" may still be seen.

Instruction began at the college in 1583 under Robert Rollock, a Saint Andrew's graduate. Because many of the would-be students could not understand Rollock's lectures, which were given in Latin, a second appointment was made, that of Duncan Nairne, graduate of

Glasgow, as Latin tutor. Nairne's students could enter the degree program after a year of Latin tutelage and passage of an examination.

Instruction was done under the medieval regenting system, whereby each instructor taught the entire body of knowledge rather than a single specialized field. It is surprising that the university continued this practice because the Protestant reformers had advocated its abolition. The Edinburgh town council under the leadership of the local ministers had founded the college with the intention that it should produce good Christians who would be intelligent and responsible citizens using the academic views of Calvin. Under regenting, students should have a single instructor for their entire four-year academic course. In practice, faculty turnover was high and few teachers lasted as long as their students, largely because professors could find better jobs elsewhere.

The college soon had more students than any Scottish university had ever had. While intended as a residential college, from the very beginning, most of the students lived at home. This was in conformity with the beliefs of the Scottish religious reformers that virtue is best inculcated in the home. It was also necessary because the college had inadequate provision for boarders.

Even in its early years, the college had an international reputation and attracted a considerable number of foreign students, primarily Huguenots and English Puritans with the occasional Irish student. Most domestic students came from Edinburgh and southeast Scotland.

Until 1617, the university was located in "the Duke's House," built by James Hamilton, the second Earl of Arran (who was also known by his French title, Duke of Châtelherault), and buildings connected with the adjacent ruined Kirk O'Field, where Lord Darnley had been murdered. After 1616 the university constructed its first purpose-built building, a two-story structure serving as common hall and library. In 1642, a new library was begun. It included student reading rooms, available for an annual fee. Building continued throughout the century in a piecemeal fashion, producing a jumble of undistinguished buildings.

For its first 300 years, the university was indeed the town college. It was administered by the town council, which gradually delegated administration to college officials while retaining the right of final approval. The town funded the university from three major sources: (1) pre-Reformation church benefices, (2) a monopoly on funeral pall rentals, and (3) benefactions. The income was not great and was largely devoted to salaries and building maintenance. The principal and professors were supported

University of Edinburgh

by student class fees, and found it necessary to supplement these inadequate incomes with outside positions. The town council's oversight did not extend deeply into academic affairs, and the principal and professors had much freedom to improvise and innovate as they saw fit, though the town council kept an eye on the college, through appointment of rectors and, later, chancellors of their choice.

Despite the civil turmoil of the seventeenth century, the college continued to grow. In 1662, new students exceeded 100 for the first time and the total student body may have exceeded 500 during the Restoration. The standards for graduation were rigorous and attrition among the students was high. Usually no more than 50 percent of students were able to complete their degrees in the normal time. In the later seventeenth century, examination techniques were modified by group interrogation and a group thesis, to enable, in the words of D.B. Horn, "the doltish sons of influential parents" to obtain degrees. Some students augmented their studies by learning shorthand, French, German, Dutch, and Polish, all of which were taught in town.

The college in the seventeenth century was alternately dominated by Presbyterianism and Episcopalianism. Each change of theology was marked by the flight of students and the punishment of dissenting professors. Among the most notable events in this period was a protest in 1680 in the wake of the Popish Plot. The students, led by a self-titled "Secretary of State to all our Theatrical and Extra-literal Divertisements," publicly burnt an effigy of the pope in spite of the opposition of the college authorities, the town guard, and the regular army. The students involved were charged with treason by the Privy Council, as the Duke of York, the heir to the throne and a notable papist, was in residence at Holyrood Palace at the time.

As a result of this incident, the college was closed and only reopened when the students and their parents produced signed bonds of good behavior under pain of expulsion. Similar bonds were required of all incoming students for some years.

The college entered the eighteenth century as a pillar of Whiggery and the Presbyterian cause. The parliament of William III made a grant to the college to establish a chair of ecclesiastical history and provide divinity bursaries. In 1703, Queen Anne provided a further grant. These were the first substantial grants by the government to the college since the benefice grant of James VI.

The main interruption of university life during the century came when the Jacobite forces of Bonny Prince Charlie occupied Edinburgh in 1745. The university closed from June 1745 to December 1746 as many students and faculty left to join the Hanoverian cause.

Edinburgh, formerly a respectable arts college and divinity school, became one of the great universities in Europe through the leadership of principals William Carstares and William Robertson. In 1708, the archaic practice of regenting, wherein a professor would teach all knowledge, was replaced by specialized teaching. The quality and range of subjects taught, the ability of the professors, and the flexibility of the curriculum attracted students from Europe and the American colonies. Most of the foreign students were upwardly mobile members of the middle class, with a smattering of the nobility. Many were dissenters attracted by Edinburgh's policy of not requiring religious or political tests of students from outside Scotland. In 1789 Thomas Jefferson declared that for science, "no place in the World can pretend to a competition with Edinburgh." Benjamin Franklin had been even more sanguine in 1776: "At this time there happen to be collected a set of as truly great men, professors of the several branches of knowledge, as have ever appeared in any age or country."

Among the chairs established in the eighteenth century were: mathematics, public law, civil law, Scots law, universal civil history, rhetoric, belles lettres, medicine, anatomy, chemistry, midwifery, and natural philosophy. At the same time, old subjects were given new direction; Greek moved toward linguistics; natural philosophy embraced Newton before he was accepted at Cambridge.

A dozen medical doctorates were given in 1750, over 100 by 1800, and as many as 140 in the early nineteenth century. And yet this does not accurately depict the number of medical students. In the 1780s, 400 to 500 students were studying medicine annually.

The intellectual ferment spearheaded by the University of Edinburgh spread throughout Scotland in the form of the Scottish Enlightenment, and the university played a major role in providing the basis for Voltaire's comment: "We look to Scotland for all our ideas of civilization."

The meager finances of the university became its strength. Unlike the English universities which paid their professors living salaries from the universities' ample endowments, Edinburgh's professors received token salaries. Their livelihood depended on class fees collected from students, and they supplemented their income by writing. Excellent teaching was imperative to attract as many students as possible, and publication was often a necessity for a comfortable life. At the same time the university had a flexibility which permitted professors to offer courses in fields outside the scope of the older universities, such as literary criticism, psychology, political economy, sociology, and aesthetics.

Among the brightest stars in Edinburgh's galaxy of professors and alumni are included: Alexander Monro secundus, discoverer of the function of the lymphatic system and structure of the nervous system; the founders of the philosophy of common sense; Joseph Black, discoverer of latent heat and discreditor of phlogiston; Adam Ferguson, a founder of sociology; Francis Home, first to apply chemistry to agriculture and discoverer of the respiration of plants; William Rutherford, the discoverer of nitrogen; and the philosopher David Hume (whose conservatism is said to have impelled more than a few students to migrate to Glasgow's more liberal university).

Other Edinburgh luminaries include: biologist Charles Darwin, and his grandfather Erasmus Darwin; physicists Sir Edward Appleton and James Clerk Maxwell; Lord Joseph Lister, who introduced antiseptic surgery; authors Oliver Goldsmith, Sir Walter Scott—"The Wizard of the North," Robert Louis Stevenson, and Sir Arthur Conan Doyle (who is rumored to have modeled Sherlock Holmes on one of his medical lecturers); John Witherspoon, the only clergyman to sign the American Declaration of Independence and the introducer of literary studies into American higher education as president of Princeton University; architect Robert Adam; James Hutton, father of modern geology; Peter Mark Roget, compiler of *Roget's Thesaurus;* Ella Pringle, the first female member of the Royal College of Physicians; surgeon Elsie Inglis; and prime ministers Palmerston and Russell.

Edinburgh was a dazzling fixture of the Scottish Enlightenment. As an alumnus, Sir R.J. Mackintosh wrote in 1835: "it is not easy to conceive a university where industry was more general, where reading was more fashionable, where indolence and ignorance were more disreputable. Every mind was in a state of fermentation."

Edinburgh reached its apogee during William Robertson's principalship. Robertson was the most eminent historian of his time and a founder of the Royal Society of Edinburgh. Robertson revivified the senate, established committees to deal with urgent problems, and implemented their recommendations with infrequent dissent. Among his greatest contributions may have been initiating the rebuilding of the university.

The university's fabric had been crumbling for a century when the American visitor, Henry Merchant, declared its buildings "a most miserable musty pile scarce fit for stables." By 1760, a burgeoning student population made the situation critical. Piecemeal construction began. A new anatomy theater was erected in 1764 and the library of 1642 was raised a story. The senate in 1768 approved a committee report on new buildings needed. The university needed 14 classrooms, rooms for professors, a faculty meeting room, a chemical laboratory, a common hall, a new library, and a museum. The old library expanded a quarter century before was filled to overflowing. The town council enthusiastically tried to raise funds by subscription and failed. Only a chemistry classroom and laboratory were constructed.

In 1789, the town council raised £15,000 by subscription and began laying the foundation of the new college, based on the designs of Robert Adam, an alumnus and the leading architect of his day. In February 1790, a new anatomy theater was begun, incorporating "subterranean passages" for the surreptitious conveyance of dissection subjects. However, with the coming of the French wars, most of the subscriptions were never paid and Adam's planned buildings, modified and reduced through economic necessity, were not completed until 1832, using government funding.

From 1793 to 1858, the university consolidated and retrenched as the university senate wrestled with the town council over control of the university, a struggle which only ended with the Universities (Scotland) Act of 1858 which made Scottish universities the responsibility of the state. The wars increased the demand for people useful to the military. Emphasis was put on medicine. The government forced the college to establish chairs of forensic medicine, military surgery, and clinical surgery. Arts became static. Chairs in Celtic literature and antiquities (1807) and in intellectual power (1823) were rejected.

The student population began to decline after 1820. A senate committee in 1840 noted:

> Every profession is overstocked. There is not the same demand for the services of educated men as in former times. Schools, academies, colleges, have started up in every corner of the land. . . . Old establishments cannot afford to run the same race of popularity, and when they have attempted it, it has been at the expense of their dignity and usefulness.

Following a troubled half century for the university, the Universities (Scotland) Act of 1858 transferred university funding to the government, placed the institution on a firm financial foundation, and moved it toward modern needs. The curriculum was revised and, in 1889, parliament authorized the university to admit women, 20 years after the idea had first been proposed.

Today, the university, one of the largest in the United Kingdom, is still centered on its original site and maintains a close relationship with the town. Most visitors to Edinburgh's picturesque Old Town are unaware that students comprise about a quarter of its population. The 17,000 students are enrolled in eight faculties: arts, divinity, law, medicine and dentistry, music, science and engineering (including agriculture), social sciences, and veterinary medicine—staffed by 2,500 academics.

Edinburgh, while distinctly Scottish in character, continues to be the most cosmopolitan university in Scotland with high educational standards and a strong reputation in research. While the bulk of the students come from England and Scotland, about 10 percent come from Europe and the larger world. Approximately half the students are women.

The university has recently stated its mission as providing learning and inquiry toward the development of the individual, the health of society, and the national economy. Its international reputation is high. Its research and development projects provide almost a quarter of university income, about £46 million. The university is an active participant in cooperative projects with industry, business, and professional societies. Areas of particular strength include languages, medicine, microelectronics, biotechnology, and computer technology.

The university has invested heavily in high-technology such as artificial intelligence and speech technology, and has established a commercial subsidiary, UnivEd Technologies Ltd., to provide a liaison between the academic and commercial sectors. With a pool of 2,500 academic specialists from which to draw, UnivEd provides consultancy, state-of-the-art technology—including a Cray T3D, the most powerful supercomputer in Europe—and practical training for professionals, the government, industry, and business. UnivEd was awarded the Queen's Award for Expert Achievement in 1994.

Edinburgh is currently undertaking cooperative projects to improve the other sectors of Scottish education, expanding the university's services to non-traditional students and increasing its emphasis on postgraduate education. Postgraduates currently make up 27 percent of its population.

The university also has strong links with the local and national community. Edinburgh's continuing education program enrolls over 10,000 annually in courses, conferences, study tours, and summer programs. University Settlement runs community projects providing services to the disadvantaged, young, infirm, and elderly.

Edinburgh's stated aim is to promote diversity while maintaining excellence, an ongoing process of which it seems fully capable. In 1995, higher education funding council assessors placed Edinburgh in the highest level of British university education, with 75 percent of departments rated in the two highest ranks for research quality.

Further Reading: For a general historical overview, consult D.B. Horn, *A Short History of the University of Edinburgh 1556–1889* (Edinburgh: The University Press, 1967).

—Edward S. Margerum

UNIVERSITY OF FLORENCE
(Florence, Italy)

Location: Florence, Tuscany, a region in central Italy.

Description: A state university with an enrollment of approximately 55,000 students.

Information: Università di Firenze
Piazza San Marco
5 Firenze
Italy

Universities are considered one of the most innovative cultural advances of the thirteenth century. *Regnum, sacerdotium,* and *studium* are listed as the powers governing the world, according to Alessandro di Roes, at the end of 1200. However, in Florence—home to Dante, father of the Italian language—there is no trace of such an institution. Although we have proofs of the existence of schools with public teaching, Florence lacked a *studio* (or university) which was the main cultural institution of the Middle Ages.

It is only in the fourteenth century, a period in which the university tradition becomes less significant, that Florence sought to obtain a *studio*. On May 14 and 15, 1321 (rather late compared to other Italian cities), the city of Florence decided to create a *studium generale* with colleges of law, medicine, and fine arts. The *studio* had the same characteristics and regulations as the *studio* of Bologna. Among the most important regulations were: (a) the founding of a specific committee: the future *Ufficiali dello Studio;* (b) the establishment of a special academic fund; (c) a request to the pope and the college of cardinals to give permission to representatives of the clergy to attend the *studio* as students without losing their ecclesiastic benefits during their studies.

In Florentine academic history, the period from 1321, the year in which Dante died, to the end of the century was marked by a continual succession of deaths and resurrections. As with the University of Naples, the *studio* in Florence was created by political parties who alternated stages of strong support with periods of complete neglect.

In 1324 the *comune,* or city-state, of Florence rented various houses to accommodate a *studio* which was soon closed. It was reopened in 1349, after the plague, on a street still called *Via dello Studio.*

On May 31, 1349, Florence obtained from Pope Clement VI an official document founding the *studium generale.* In this document the pope authorized opening for the first time in an Italian university a faculty of theology.

Only in 1360 did the prestigious *studio* of Bologna open such a faculty, when Francesco di Biancozzo de' Nerli had already received a great deal of notoriety as the first graduate in theology from the *studio* in Florence. Francesco Petrarca was one of the many celebrated intellectuals whom the Florentine *studio* tried to obtain. Petrarca, however, declined the invitation.

In 1364 the Emperor Charles IV conferred on the *studio* in Florence the same recognition and privileges that the other *studi* in Italy already had obtained. The year 1366 was a prosperous one for the Florentine *studio* due to a general growth of interest in the improvement of the institution. Among its many eminent lecturers, Boccaccio stood out with his teaching of Dante.

At the end of the fourteenth century, the *studio* drew up new statutes, and its organization became more complex and efficient. Greek was introduced in the academic curriculum, and the field of medicine received more attention from the comune of Florence. Unfortunately, this condition was ephemeral and a series of ups and downs characterized the life of the *studio* until 1472, when Lorenzo de' Medici decided to move it to Pisa.

Although in the fifteenth century Florence upheld a cultural supremacy, Pisa was the center of academic education. Yet, there were prolific interactions between the *studio* and the group of intellectuals (*eruditi*) and artists living in Florence, as well as exchanges among the *studia humanitatis* such as linguistics, rhetoric, philosophy, and science with the city's artistic community.

The *accademie,* competing with the *studio* as centers for discussion, started as spontaneous meetings among the intellectuals and became unconventional study centers and research institutes that departed from the traditional medieval academic structures. Therefore, the *accademie* represented a constant point of reference which stimulated and enriched the cultural environment and the scholars, bringing together arts, letters, and science.

In the 1500s, even though the *studio* kept functioning regularly, the *accademie* became the more relevant and vital intellectual centers. The establishment of the absolute power of the Medici with Cosimo I meant the official recognition of the *accademie.* The *studio* itself accommodated three *accademie:* the Florentine *accademia,* the Crusca (founded in 1582), and the *accademia* of the Apatisti.

Few documents remain to testify to the cultural events of the 1600s. Evangelista Torricelli, the inventor of the barometer, ruled the faculty of mathematics, as a follower of Galileo. Many other famous scientists taught at the *studio.* In 1657 the first scientific *accademia* in western civilization was founded, based on Galileo's experimental method.

In the 1700s, although numerous and well-known historians could be found in Florence, the teaching of history was absent, except for a class in "sacred and profane" history. The fact that two history professors, Anton Francesco Gori and Giovanni Latini, gave lessons at home, highlights the lack of organization of the *studio* in this field.

The many historians present in Florence at this time preferred to share their knowledge in the *accademie,* such as La Colombaria, than in scholastic institutions. In middle schools and high schools, the only history taught was that taken from the classics. Information about medieval and contemporary history was taken from historians better known as literary scholars, such as Machiavelli and Guicciardini.

During the French-Bourbon domination, at the beginning of the nineteenth century, history was still not present as a discipline in university institutions, although it was taught in the *Accademia delle Belle Arti* of Florence by Gian Battista Niccolini.

Only in December 1859 were innovative reforms introduced by Cosimo Ridolfi, the minister of public education of the Tuscan Temporary Government. The *Istituto di Studi Superiori pratici e di perfezionamento* created a tenure position for history among the 11 positions already existing in the department of philosophy and philology.

This *Istituto di Studi Superiori* was intended as a post-university school and consisted of four sections: legal studies, philology and philosophy, medicine, and natural science. The intention was to create a school focused on specialization and research. It did, indeed, succeed in attracting professors and students from all over Italy. European scholars came to Florence not only to consult the *Istituto*'s libraries and archives, but also to meet the many Italian scholars attending the *Istituto*.

According to Eugenio Garin, "The doctors who created it [the *Istituto*] went back to the 'sperimentalismo' of Galileo's tradition, and the new course of Florentine culture moves itself dialectically between natural and historical sciences, in order to reach a synthesis by studying nature with an historical approach and history from a scientific one."

The *Istituto* became, with its energy and dynamism, the center of discussion between the old and the new and it was to leave a deep trace in the future of Italian culture. Of the above mentioned four sections in which the *Istituto* was divided, the best structured were those of philosophy and philology and medicine. Only in 1874 was the teaching of Italian literature activated by Adolfo Bartoli, the real initiator of the Italianist tradition in the *Istituto*. From his schools, many of the best scholars and philologists of the next generation were to come. Bartoli's main merit was the development of the "historical method" which was applied successfully to documents and texts on the origins of Italian literature.

After Bartoli's death in 1894, Guido Mazzoni succeeded him as teacher of Italian literature in the *Istituto di Studi Superiori*. Mazzoni was professor for 40 years, first in the *Istituto* and then in the *Facoltà di Lettere* (Liberal Arts College) after the transformation of the *Istituto* in *Regia Università* at the beginning of the 1924–25 academic year. A figure of outstanding culture and artistic sensitivity, Mazzoni succeeded in blending together the continuation of the Florentine "historical school's" tradition and the new cultural environment in Florence. As the secretary of the *Accademia della Crusca,* he defended the necessity of keeping this *accademia* alive.

Between 1924 and 1930, the intervention of fascism in the new university structure was widespread throughout the country and quite significant. Until 1940, the presidents (*Rettori*) of the fascist university, first Bindo De Vecchi and then Arrigo Serpieri, insisted on the development of the technological and organizational aspects of the university. Serpieri in particular was the personification of the regime in the world of academics. In the academic year 1938–39 Serpieri applied the racial laws by dismissing six Jewish professors. Among them were the philosopher Limentani, who died during his voluntary exile, and the historian Salvemini, who was forced into a long exile in the United States. Under the presidency of Serpieri, the "Cesare Alfieri" school became the *facoltà* of political sciences with the founding of the *cattedra del fascismo* (chair of fascism) and the strengthening of the socio-political element in every discipline. With both De Vecchi and Serpieri, a militarization of the university took place in concurrence with the wars in Africa and Spain.

In spite of strong pressure from the fascists, the University of Florence was able to maintain continuity in research and study throughout the regime's 20 years, according to the tradition of the old *Istituto di Studi Superiori*. Fascist propaganda touched only the surface of the academic structure, affecting only marginally the technical and scientific aspects of the University of Florence. The university succeeded in maintaining its dignity and coherence.

In 1934, Mazzoni retired and Attilio Momigliano, from the region of Piemonte, took his place as professor of Italian literature in the college of liberal arts in the University of Florence. He had a strong influence on the university, reconciling his background in the school of history in Turin with the new perspectives opened by the idealism of literary critic Benedetto Croce. Under his supervision, a new Italian generation of literary criticism was formed. After only four years, Momigliano, of Jewish origin, had to leave his position due to the application again of the racial laws. He never stopped his literary activities, and after World War II he resumed his teaching with a large following of students. In 1938, Giuseppe De Robertis substituted Momigliano. De Robertis came to Florence to collaborate at the *Voce,* the literary review created by the two Italian writers and critics Prezzolini and Papini. With De Robertis, the innovative wave of the new critical methods—applied both to the classic and to contemporary literature—entered the university.

Both Momigliano and De Robertis gave a specific and defined configuration to the literary aspect of the university. Among the scholars who followed and kept the great literary tradition of the college of liberal arts at the University of Florence, Walter Binni, student of Momigliano, carried out an intense didactic activity that joined his remarkable technical preparation with his personal critical methodology. This was based essentially on analysis of the "poetica" of important authors—Leopardi, Ariosto, Alfieri, and Carducci—and on the significant periods of literary history in Italy: that dating from "preromanticismo" to "decadentismo."

In 1967, a chair of Dantesque philology was created next to the one of Italian literature in occasion of the Dante celebrations that took place in 1965. Francesco Mazzoni was called to teach in this department.

The school of architecture was reopened during the difficult autumn of 1944. The German troops were moving behind the Gothic Line and half of Italy was still in the hands of the fascists. In the academic year of 1943–44, attendance was extremely reduced. The next year, the number of students in the school of architecture went up 300 percent, a tremendous figure for that tragic period. During the terrible winter of 1944–45, the students of architecture would cut the fingertips from the gloves they wore so that they could use a pen to draw the furniture for the Giardino di Boboli in Florence. It was common for students to work six hours per day. Among these students, Franco Zeffirelli emerged. He conveyed his taste for the baroque in his scene designs for Luchino Visconti's movies before becoming himself a celebrated film director.

The configuration of the university in 1924 brought a positive change in the field of mathematics. Before 1924, the college of science granted degrees only in chemistry and natural science. The presence of Giovanni Sansone in the *Istituto Matematico* contributed immensely to the development of the *Istituto*. He strongly believed that a library was a necessary tool to teaching, learning, and researching. Only one book was in the library of the *Istituto Matematico* when Sansone started teaching there in 1927. He worked so hard in collecting books that by 1962, the library owned 6,301 complete works and 275 mathematical periodicals.

—Antonella D. Olson

UNIVERSITY OF GLASGOW
(Glasgow, Scotland)

Location: The University of Glasgow is located in Glasgow's west end, where it has been since 1871. The university overlooks Kelvingrove park and museum, and is easily accessible by local bus routes and the underground train. Also in the Gilmorehill residential area are shops, restaurants, and cafes.

Description: The University of Glasgow is an independent, state-funded university with 13,500 full-time students, including 1,500 foreign students. There are also 2,600 part-time students at the coeducational university that was founded in 1451 for men only. There are 200 professors and 1,250 other faculty members.

Information: The University of Glasgow
University Avenue
Glasgow G12 8QQ
Scotland
(41) 339-8855
Fax (41) 330-4808

Visiting: The Visitor Centre is open from 9:30 A.M. to 5:00 P.M. from Monday through Saturday. From May to September it is also open on Sundays from 2:00 P.M. until 5:00 P.M. In the summer months there are also campus tours focusing on historical and architectural campus landmarks at 11:00 A.M. and 2:00 P.M. on Wednesdays, Fridays, and Saturdays. There are historical exhibits as well as interactive video displays at the Visitor Centre. For more information and tour prices, contact the Visitor Centre at (41) 330-5511.

The second oldest university in Scotland is the University of Glasgow. It is one of the largest and oldest universities in the United Kingdom. Glasgow is located in the Midland valley, a center in the fifteenth century of the political, cultural, and economic life of Scotland. The city became an archbishopric in 1492. King James II of Scotland petitioned Pope Nicholas V to found the university in 1451. The king worked with Bishop Turnbull to secure a papal bull from Nicholas. When Bishop Turnbull died in 1454 the university lost its major patron, but Turnbull's cathedral helped the university for many years. William Elphinstone, who became the rector of the University of Glasgow in 1474, kept the university in the public eye after Turnbull was gone.

Robert Henryson, a poet who was credited with bringing hundreds of words into the English language, taught law at the university in 1462. Some supporters hoped the university would specialize in legal studies, but they were outnumbered by those who believed Glasgow would be better served by a university that taught a wide range of subjects.

The church played a significant role in Scottish education until the mid-nineteenth century. Andrew Melville, a Presbyterian leader, created a charter for the university in 1575 that became the university's credo for 300 years. Since many colleges at that time trained boys who would be future ministers, Melville's work was pastoral as well as educational. Melville was at the university from 1574 until 1580, and in those years he transformed the curriculum and introduced teachers who specialized in particular subjects. The regenting system had been in place since the university's inception, meaning that students stayed with one regent or teacher for four years. That regent taught his students every subject. Melville had studied in France and Switzerland, and he was eager to bring up the level of Scotland's universities.

During the Reformation, ministers studied the "Book of Discipline," which established new rules for the education of Scotland's youth. Students were said to need a background in the arts, and then were to approach law, medicine, or divinity as a specialty. In the seventeenth century Scotland's universities were different from those in Cambridge and Oxford because they were open to students regardless of their rank in society. Parish and burgh schools in Glasgow provided students for the university, and they studied alongside their more privileged colleagues in Latin, which was the language of study until 1727.

In the early seventeenth century Oliver Cromwell installed Patrick Gillespie as principal of the University of Glasgow. These were exciting years at the university. Francis Hutcheson lectured in English literature and held the chair of moral philosophy from 1729 to 1746. Hutcheson showed the influence of Thomas Hobbes in his lectures.

Economist Adam Smith was educated at the university and later taught there. He arrived at the university in 1737 at the age of 14, and was appointed professor of logic in 1751. He also taught moral philosophy until 1763 and served as rector in 1787.

The medical school at the University of Glasgow has an international reputation. It opened a teaching hospital at the university in 1794. Two chemistry professors went from Glasgow to teach at the University of Edinburgh: William

University of Glasgow

Cullen and Joseph Black. Black studied at the University of Glasgow, and Cullen was one of his chemistry instructors. Black discovered "fixed air," or carbon dioxide. Joseph Lister did groundbreaking research in antisepsis at the university in the nineteenth century. Lister was the chair of surgery in 1860. Lord Kelvin was a professor of natural philosophy from 1846 to 1899 and he held the chair of the department. Other famous faculty members included James Watt, whose improvements on the original steam engine led to the engine's major impact on society.

The university was located on High Street in the center of the city until 1870 when it was moved to the west end of Glasgow. Finally in 1893 women were admitted to the university. In the 1990s, slightly more than half of the full-time students are women. Almost one-quarter of the students are 21 years old or older, and more than seven percent of the full-time students come from overseas.

The University of Glasgow's main building was designed by Sir George Gilbert Scott. A fine example of gothic architecture, the building has become one of Glasgow's landmarks. The university has one of the largest university libraries in the United Kingdom, with almost 1.5 million volumes on 30 miles of shelves. It carries more than 8,000 periodical subscriptions and keeps close to 300,000 volumes of periodicals. The library also boasts close to 20,000 maps, more than 30,000 manuscripts, and almost 10,000 theses.

There are eight faculties at the university: arts, divinity, engineering, law and financial studies, medicine, science, social sciences, and veterinary medicine. The rector is elected by the students every three years on the basis of academic achievements as well as personal appeal. All of the faculties are based on the main campus, except for the veterinary school, which is located four miles away, in Garscube. The university offers more than 100 academic departments in these 8 faculties. The university also has six affiliated teaching hospitals.

Degree programs at the university include those leading in three or four years to a bachelor's degree. An additional one or two years in the same subject may lead to a master's degree. To receive a doctorate, students must devote approximately three more years. For acceptance to the university, students must provide a general certificate of education (GCE) or its equivalent with five passes in different subjects. The subjects must include at least two at the advanced, or A, level, or four passes with at least three at the A level. Alternatively, international baccalaureate, European baccalaureate, and U.S. or Canadian high school diplomas are also accepted.

The university offers degree programs with several associated colleges. Students can study agricultural science, food production, and leisure in a program offered with the Scottish Agricultural College. In conjunction with the Glasgow School of Art, students may study architecture and fine art, or product design engineering. Teaching degrees are awarded to students completing study together with a program at St. Andrews College.

The university's career service department is open from 9 A.M. until 5 P.M. daily when the university is in session. It provides information on jobs and careers in Scotland and abroad. The department also tracks various business-related web sites that students can visit to gain information about any of hundreds of fields. Career areas are divided into categories of interest and into categories of study areas. They offer help for students putting together resumes and curricula vitae, and coaching for those about to begin interviewing. Students with disabilities are also welcomed at the university. Dyslexic students, for example, are given more time in which to complete exams.

The university's academic services unit consists of the library, media services, university archives, and computer services. The computing services maintains file servers as well as clusters of personal computers for student use. Color laser printing is available and video conferencing was introduced in the late 1990s. The staff offers software and hardware support as well as training courses and facilities.

The Hunterian Museum is on the campus of the university. Founded in 1807, it is the oldest public museum in Scotland. It was originally located on the university's campus on High Street, and moved with the rest of the university to Gilmorehill in western Glasgow in 1870. The Hunterian has permanent collections explaining the evolution of the earth, ancient Egypt, the Romans in Scotland, and Captain Cook's collections from the south seas. One of its most prized exhibits features an ancient clutch of dinosaur eggs. Another is a scientific experiment of Lord Kelvin's that began in 1887 and continues to this day. The museum displays the history of the university and tracks research done by faculty and students. It also offers many temporary exhibitions and a gift shop.

The Hunterian art gallery opened in 1980. It has an outdoor sculpture courtyard, a bookshop, and frequent exhibitions from its own private collection of prints. Paintings by Pisarro, Rembrandt, and Reynolds grace its halls. The gallery displays works from the estate of renowned architect Charles Rennie Mackintosh and from the estate of painter James McNeill Whistler. There is also a reconstruction of Mackintosh's own house.

Some of the special programs at the University of Glasgow are the Beatson Institute for Cancer Research, the Confederation of Scottish Business Schools, the Engineering Research Design Centre, the Hetherington Language Centre, the Institute of Soviet and East European Studies, the John Logie Baird Centre for Research in Television and Film, the Scottish Science and Technology Forum, university audio-visual services, university marine biological station, Wellcome History of Medicine Unit, and West of Scotland Science Park.

Four organizations for students of the university are very active. There are two student unions: the Queen Margaret Union and the Glasgow University Union. The Students' Representative Council is the official liaison between officials of the university and the student body. The Glasgow University Athletic Club, or GUAC, comprises 45 different sports and their organizations.

There are also myriad other clubs and societies at the university. Some of these are the aikido club; alchemist society; archaeology and astronomy societies; a musical and operatic club called the Cecilian Society; canoeing, curling, and cycling clubs; gaming society; orienteering and parachute clubs; and other sports, music, and ethnic clubs. The Scottish Country Dance Club was established in 1955, and is affiliated with the Royal Scottish Country Dance Society.

There are about 4,000 available places of residence for students on campus. These are reserved for full-time students working toward degrees. Those students who live far from the university are also given priority in room assignments. Residence halls vary from the student village on Murano Street that was completed in 1994 to such large traditional halls as Queen Margaret Hall and Dalrymple Hall near Great Western Avenue. Some of the dormitories offer full catering, while others have kitchenette facilities for student use. The dormitories are also a center of university social life, and each has its own annual events and parties. There are also facilities for married students and those with families. The university maintains a list of properties on campus, near campus, or near an underground station, that are available for rent.

As a major employer in Glasgow, the university plays a large role in the city's economy. It employs 5,000 people and has an annual budget of more than £170 million. Glasgow is the largest city in Scotland, with a population of about 740,000, and the faculty and students of the university have an intimate relationship with the city. The university's credo promises a learning and working environment that is free of discrimination. Industrial and commercial clients rely on expertise from the university. Research projects are often coordinated by leading businesses in conjunction with particular faculties. This intertwined existence has helped Glasgow immensely, and the university also continues to benefit.

Further Reading: Most histories of Scotland discuss the University of Glasgow at length. Some of these include the multi-volume *The Edinburgh History of Scotland* edited by Gordon Donaldson (Vol. 2, Edinburgh: Oliver and Boyd, and New York: Harper and Row, 1974), (Vol. 3, New York: Praeger, 1965). Other histories describing the university include *Scotland's Story: A New Perspective* by Tom Steel (London: Collins, 1984); *A History of Scotland* by Rosalind Mitchison (London: Methuen, 1970); *Scotland from the Earliest Times to 1603,* 3rd ed. by W. Croft Dickinson (Oxford: Clarendon,

1977); and *The Story of Scotland* by Janet R. Glover (New York: Roy, 1958). The university has an interesting and informative web site at http://www.gla.ac.uk. A short illustrated history available at the visitor center called *The University of Glasgow: An Introduction,* provides visitors with a short illustrated history of the University of Glasgow.

—Fran Shonfeld Sherman

UNIVERSITY OF GRANADA
(Granada, Spain)

Location: In the city of Granada, in southeastern Spain, near the Sierra Nevadas.

Description: Government-funded university with 53,000 undergraduate and graduate students.

Information: University de Granada
Cuesta del Hospicio s/n
(Hospital Real)
18701 Granada
Spain
(58) 243 063

The University of Granada's history has been inextricably linked with that of its city and of its region, Andalusia. The university was founded in 1526 to help integrate the culturally distinct former kingdom of Granada into the Castillian empire, an integration which proved difficult. In the late nineteenth century and early twentieth century, perhaps the most interesting part of the university's history, a new appreciation emerged of the culture of Andalusia. During that period, the arts flourished in Granada. The recentralization of power and repression of political dissent under General Francisco Franco, who ruled Spain from 1939 until his death in 1975, hindered the development of the university for much of the century. Since the early 1980s, the university has had increased autonomy in deciding its affairs and has grown significantly.

The University of Granada had its origins in Holy Roman Emperor Charles V's effort to integrate Granada, the last redoubt of Islam in Spain, into the kingdom of Castile. Because the kingdom of Granada remained the last Moorish stronghold in Spain for over 20 years, until it fell to Isabella and Ferdinand in January 1492, the city of Granada attracted many talented refugees in arts, letters, architecture, and engineering. The conquest of the kingdom of Granada signified the final defeat of the Moors in Spain and of Islam in western Europe.

Because of its illustrious past, Granada presented a challenge for the new Spanish rulers: how to incorporate a very advanced mercantile society with a religiously and culturally diverse population into the rest of their kingdom. Granada had been a center of learning in Moorish times, but building on this tradition proved difficult. While the current University of Granada is to some extent the continuation of the Arabic university of Yusuf I, founded in the fourteenth century, education in Granada before Spain's victory had been based on knowledge obtained from the great Arab centers of learning and from Jewish scholarship. The fall of Granada to Spain cut Granada off from these scholarly sources. In 1492, Ferdinand and Isabella expelled from their kingdom all Jews who would not convert to Christianity. In 1502, many Moors were forcibly converted to Christianity and remained in Spain. Those who did not convert were expelled.

Because Granada, as the last stronghold of Islam, had great symbolic importance for its Spanish conquerors, they lavished considerable attention on improving the city, but the social atmosphere proved to be a deterrent to scholarly endeavors. The Arab residents of the city distrusted the non-Arab Christian rulers, doubting that eight centuries of animosity could end easily. The Christian residents of Granada, on the other hand, found it difficult to understand why the Spanish rulers were so magnanimous toward the conquered people of Granada.

The ruler responsible for founding the University of Granada, Holy Roman Emperor Charles V (who reigned as Charles I of Spain from 1519 to 1556), was particularly torn by, on the one hand, his admiration for the tremendous achievements of the Islamic rulers of Granada and, on the other, his duty to convert the population to Christianity. He particularly admired the Alhambra, the fourteenth-century Moorish citadel overlooking the city, choosing to spend his honeymoon there. Charles had further ambitions for Granada in his early days as king of Spain. He started construction of a palace in Granada and, at one point, he planned to make the city the permanent site of his court.

While Charles sought to win favor with the population of Granada, as a fervent Catholic he was obliged to convert the people to Catholicism. Easing the minds of the city's conquered population, which included various cultures, while promoting Catholicism, proved difficult. In 1526, the same year that he started the process for creating the university, Charles V decreed that all Muslim ceremonies, usages, and customs were to be banned in Granada. Although Charles resisted the pleas of the Moorish nobles to rescind the edict, bribes to the chief imperial advisor and tributes to the emperor kept the edict from being enforced for the next 40 years.

The founding of the University of Granada grew out of Emperor Charles' 1526 visit to the city. He founded the new university as a way of maintaining the former kingdom's cultural richness. In November 1526, the emperor called a meeting of bishops and men of letters to make known his intention of creating a college of logic, philosophy, theology, and canon law. On June 14, 1531, in a papal bull, Pope Clement VII authorized the

University of Granada

founding of a "general school"; the bull described which degrees were to be conferred and granted. The bull also explained the procedures for conferring and granting degrees at Bologna, Paris, Salamanca, and other leading universities. The pope authorized a house of general studies, with a college of logic, philosophy, and canon law; a school for 100 boys; the Colegio Catalino; and the Colegio San Miguel. Although the university was to be open to students of all towns, religious backgrounds, and cultures, in the beginning the university was concerned solely with moral education and, in particular, religion. Not until 1549 did the rector propose adding chairs in a non-religious field, medicine, an area which later became a strength of the university.

Charles V did not continue to play a strong role in the development of Granada or the university. His ambition to create a universal empire involved him in continuous wars and prevented him from finishing his imperial palace in Granada. As Spain expanded in the New World, Spain's rulers shifted their attention to Seville, a major port for embarkation to America. Granada fell into neglect.

Despite Spanish efforts at integrating Granada and its surrounding region, Andalusia, the area maintained a separate culture and has been a site of unrest since the fifteenth century. Between the late nineteenth century and the end of the Spanish Civil War in 1938, there was almost constant turmoil. A regional identity developed by the mid-nineteenth century which worked against the success of federalism in Spain in the 1870s. The idea of federalism in Spain had been based on the equality of different areas; however, the different regions in Spain had not developed equally. Castile had long dominated other provinces, including Andalusia. Although the first attempt at federalism in Spain failed with the end of the First Republic in Spain in 1874, the idea of a Spain in which the regions had some autonomy remained important, particularly in Andalusia, for decades afterward. Although the University of Granada was noted for its programs in letters and medicine around the turn of the twentieth century, two of the most influential graduates of the university, Blas Infante and Federico García Lorca, studied law there during this period.

The importance of Granada before 1492 had a strong effect on these two students. Although both came from Andalusia, like most of their fellow students in Granada, they first became conscious of the richness of Andalusia's heritage at the university. Inspired largely by his education at the university, Infante became a leading Andalusian writer and nationalist after receiving his law degree in 1906. His contact as a student with outstanding Andalusian specialists formed in him a desire to recover the culture, history, and identity of the region. Like other Andalusians at the time, Infante believed that Andalusian history and culture had been suppressed by the impact of assimilation into Castile, an area for which Andalusian history was merely an appendage.

Another famous writer who studied at the University of Granada was Federico García Lorca, the most popular poet of the group called the "Generation of '27." He studied law at the University of Granada before transferring his studies in 1919 to the University of Madrid, in the city at the center of the Spanish arts world. Lorca studied law because his father wanted him to have a professional career, and the other faculties—medicine, science, and pharmacy—were unthinkable, given his interests. Even though he went to Madrid ostensibly to continue his studies, there is no evidence that he ever set foot in the university there. Under pressure from his family, Lorca did eventually complete his studies at Granada, in large part due to the leniency of the examining faculty, who even allowed him to take an examination after the deadline had passed.

Lorca's studies in Granada were to have a powerful effect on his life. He was strongly influenced by Don Martin Dominguez Berrueta, professor of the theory of literature and arts. Don Martin believed that Spanish universities needed to be reformed to meet the needs of contemporary Spanish society. He was particularly noted for developing close ties with his students and taking them on educational field trips, both actions almost unheard of in Spain at that time. During field trips conducted by Don Martin, Lorca first came into contact with the art of cities beyond Granada. Lorca's first book, *Impressions and Landscapes*, developed out of these trips with his art history class. Another professor, Don Ramon Guixe y Mexia, served as the model for the pedantic professor in Lorca's play *Dona Rosita*.

Lorca, like Blas Infante, was greatly influenced by the blossoming cultural atmosphere of Granada. The growing awareness of the distinctness of Andalusian culture and the presence of Moorish architectural treasures drew artists to Andalusia in the early twentieth century, Angel Gavinet, a poet associated with the "Generation of '98," was a native of Granada whose first book was *Granada the Beautiful*. Many other local writers from the "Generation of '98" were still living in Granada in the 1920s; many served as inspirations to younger writers and artists. Resident artists such as the composer Manuel de Falla attracted other poets, musicians, and intellectuals to Granada, giving it a cultural richness it had not had since Moorish times. The cultural life was so rich in the 1920s that Lorca founded a literary magazine which he described as "of Granadans and only Granadans." The first issue contained a drawing by Salvador Dali.

The history of Granada also played a key role in Lorca's intellectual development during his time at the university. Lorca, who was more interested in arts and literature than law, often spent time in the Alhambra and the Generalife or with the gypsies of the Sacromonte and Albaicin rather than in class. In fact, Lorca was so impressed by the Arab past of Granada that he at one time even suggested building a library for Granadan Arabic artifacts.

A few of the professors who most greatly influenced Lorca later played a major role in the liberal Second Republic, which lasted from 1931 until 1939. One of the professors closest to him was Fernando de los Rios Urruti, a professor of political and comparative law. Fernando de los Rios Urruti served as minister of justice and then minister of education during the Second Republic. Before that he had founded the Granada branch of the Socialist party, been a member of parliament for Granada, and served as president of the center of arts and literature. Professor Don Augustin Vinuales, who had urged other faculty members to examine Lorca leniently—he could only practice his true calling of poetry after he had pleased his family by obtaining his degree—served as minister of finance under the Second Republic.

The left-wing political opinions of some people connected to the university made their lives difficult during the Spanish Civil War, which began in 1936. When the right-wing nationalists took control of Andalusia in 1936, they executed many of their opponents. The best estimates available place the number of executions in Granada and its immediate vicinity at approximately 4,000, with August 1936 the bloodiest month. The most famous of those executed was Lorca, who had returned to Granada for a visit. Before he was shot, Lorca was kept for two or three days in the university's current law department building, then the governor's office and residence. Others connected with the university who were executed include the rector of the university, Salvador Villa; a professor of pediatrics, Rafael Garcia Duarte; a professor of political law, Joaquin Garcia Labella; a professor of pharmacy, Jesus Yoldi; and a professor of history, Jose Pananco Romero. Many of those artists and scholars who remained physically unharmed were deeply affected by the assassination of friends and acquaintances.

The political developments of the twentieth century had a strong influence a strong influence not only on the faculty of the University of Granada, but also on what students in Andalusia chose to study. In the first years of the century, equal numbers of students studied humanities and science. During the dictatorship of Primo de Rivera, from 1925 to 1930, the number of students studying science increased to 68 percent. During the Second Republic, 45 percent of students in Andalusia studied the humanities. After the Spanish Civil War, the percentage of students studying humanities declined gradually to 30 percent from 1951 until the 1970s.

The growth of higher education in Andalusia was fairly slow during this century, until at least the 1980s. Traditionally, university education in Andalusia has been reserved for the few. In 1910, 0.02 percent of the population in Andalusia had a university degree. By 1973 the percentage of Andalusians with such an education had climbed to a meager 0.34 percent.

Since 1983, the University of Granada has experienced the most rapid growth in its history, a growth strongly influenced by the law on university reform of 1983. Before the law passed, the Ministry of Education in Madrid controlled the entire national university system. The law on university reform granted autonomy to each state university, as long as it followed the guidelines and met the qualifications common to all state universities.

The University of Granada has continued to play a major role in the intellectual and cultural life not only of southern Spain, but also of nearby Africa, where it has branches in the Spanish cities of Ceuta and Melilla in Morocco. Currently, the University of Granada is the only European university with centers in Africa. It has traditionally maintained a strong relationship with the countries of the Maghreb, especially with Morocco.

The University of Granada consists of faculties, technical schools, and university schools. The length of time required for each program varies. The programs offered through the university schools require three years. In addition, there are three-year degree programs to receive the degree of diplomatura in fields including optics, optometry, chemical engineering, statistics, management, and labor relations. Five-year degree programs are offered for the degree of licenciado in law, science, philosophy, and letters, as well as a five-year program in engineering. The university offers a six-year medical program. Doctorates in law, science, medicine, pharmacy, and letters require a further two years of study and a thesis.

Further Reading: Although information about the university is in Spanish, two English-language books about its most famous graduate shed some light on the university: Ian Gibson's *Frederico García Lorca: A Life* (New York: Marion Boyars, 1989) and Francisco García Lorca's *In the Green Morning: Memories of Frederico* (New York: New Directions, 1986).

—Christine Margerum

UNIVERSITY OF ILLINOIS
(Urbana-Champaign, Illinois, U.S.A.)

Location: In the adjoining cities of Urbana and Champaign (combined population 100,000), approximately 120 miles south of Chicago, in east-central Illinois.

Description: The University of Illinois at Urbana-Champaign (UIUC) is a comprehensive, major public university enrolling approximately 26,000 undergraduate students. As a land grant institution, it offers undergraduate and graduate education, conducts research, and provides public service.

Information: Office of Admissions
10 Henry Administration Building
506 South Wright Street
Urbana, IL 61801
U.S.A.
(217) 333-3200

Visiting: Student-conducted tours of the campus are available when classes are in session and weather permits. Reservations are recommended and may be made by calling the Campus Visitors Center, (217) 333-0824.

The University of Illinois is one of the original 37 public land grant institutions created by the Morrill Act in 1862. This grant allowed for the provision of 30,000 acres of land for each congressman to be used for educational purposes. Illinois received 480,000 acres of land in Nebraska and Minnesota as its share, the sale of which was to provide an endowment for an industrial educational institution of higher learning. Illinois had lagged behind other states of the Northwest Territory in establishing a state university even though the Northwest Ordinance of 1787 had encouraged the founding of schools and the promotion of education. Early settlers in Illinois opposed the founding of a university and diverted available funds to other state operations.

Eventually the proselytizing efforts of Jonathan Baldwin Turner, an educator from Yale, who migrated west to teach Greek at Jacksonville College in 1833, helped rally support for higher education for the working classes in Illinois. Turner fought against prevalent and persistent assumptions that institutions of higher education offering courses other than in the professions of law or medicine were "Utopian schools" peopled by effete professors. He enlisted support from both Abraham Lincoln and Stephen

A. Douglas, political rivals, for a land grant to provide the endowment for a university for farmers and mechanics. Passage of the legislation necessitated site selection for the state university. Leading contenders included the downstate towns of Jacksonville, Bloomington, Lincoln, and Champaign-Urbana. Each institution touted its attractive features and the material gifts that it could provide to the new university.

Champaign was well-positioned when the legislature met in 1867. Due in part to the efforts of Clark R. Griggs and John Bricker, who represented Champaign County, a large percentage of legislators became convinced that Champaign was a fitting and proper site for the new state university. Champaign County, the lowest bidder yet the site "winner," was accused of employing a slush fund to "buy up correspondents of the press, editors and legislators" and overvaluing its bid. Presumably, the "buying up" included the liquid refreshments and sumptuous quail and oyster dinners proffered by Griggs and his cronies to the legislators of both parties.

Whatever factors persuaded the legislature, the new institution, chartered by the state of Illinois as the Illinois Industrial University, welcomed its first class of students on March 2, 1868. The board of trustees, established by state law, included the governor, state superintendent of public instruction, president of the state board of agriculture, and 28 other citizens. This number precluded doing business efficiently and was reduced in 1873 to 11 and later to 9 (1973). John Milton Gregory, a Baptist minister and former state superintendent of public instruction in Michigan, was chosen the first regent by the board. Gregory faced the challenges of establishing a curriculum, employing faculty, and developing a broad-based university while not antagonizing those individuals who desired to see the university consigned to imparting strictly practical knowledge.

When the university opened its doors to 50 students in March 1868, it had a faculty of two and the regent to teach 17 courses in the fields of agriculture, polytechnics, military science, chemistry, natural science, trade and commerce, general science, and literature. To encourage enrollment, only a grammar school education was required for entrance. Later, one year of preparatory education was a requisite for admission. All university classes were held in a single five-story building, a former female seminary surrounded by muddy fields. Students slept and studied in this same building, sometimes coming downstairs to recite in their bathrobes and slippers.

In the early years, the school fared poorly. Buildings and equipment were in need of repair; rainy weather and

University of Illinois

foraging cattle destroyed any emerging crops. In addition, no great demand for graduates of an agricultural college existed; the fields of business or engineering provided more remunerative employment.

Gregory labored to bring academic culture to rural central Illinois, confronting a few trustees and agriculturists who objected to the offering of academic courses in addition to the strictly practical. The student population continued to grow and included 24 women allowed admission by the board of trustees in 1870. At this time, the legislature approved the construction of a new building, University Hall, which stood on the present site of the Illini Union.

The late 1870s were a time of self-examination for the university. It granted no degrees until 1877. Earlier, only diplomas or certificates listing courses taken were awarded. The Illinois Industrial University lacked a song, official colors, and its motto, "Learning and Labor," was in English not Latin. Delta Tau Delta, the first fraternity at the university, was organized in 1871–72 but not officially recognized. Gregory pronounced fraternities silly, anachronistic, disruptive, and dissipating. Clashes with trustees and students led to Gregory's resignation in 1880.

Financial hardships beleaguered the university in the 1880s when Selim H. Peabody, professor of mechanical engineering and physics, was appointed the university's second regent. Some relief came from federal appropriations in the form of the Hatch Act of 1887, which provided $15,000 annually for the establishment of agricultural experiment stations, and the Morrill Supplementary Act, which provided incremental financing to land grant institutions.

Largely through the efforts of the faculty and alumni, the university slowly gained in stature. Peabody estimated that in 1889, the indefatigable faculty had attended over 100 educational, agricultural, or other gatherings and delivered over 200 addresses. At this time, the alumni, especially the Chicago chapter, effected two important changes. The name Illinois Industrial University was incongruous with the broad-based mission of the university. Since the mid-1870s, "Industrial" had connoted reform schools or manual labor schools for indigent or unruly students. Both alumni and students petitioned for a name change, and on June 19, 1885, the legislature officially approved the name University of Illinois. Second, alumni were instrumental in securing the popular election of trustees, approved in 1887. It was believed that this method would ensure that the board would have more alumni members who would have the best interests of the university at heart.

Criticized for strict policies including his continued opposition to fraternities and his struggle to maintain academic standards, Peabody was forced out by the board of trustees in 1891. The board then sought a strong administrator who would control student rowdiness and move the university forward. Previously, students had caused disturbances in chapel by loosing vials of tear gas and by staging a military rebellion over the dismissal of a cadet captain for poor grades.

Trustees offered the regency to the Reverend Washington Gladden, a prominent Congregationalist minister to Woodrow Wilson. During the search for a new leader, Thomas J. Burrill, dean of the College of Agriculture, who served as acting regent, greatly advanced the reputation of the university by acquiring unprecedented funding from the state legislature, opening the graduate school, starting the summer session, and developing extension teaching.

The next administrator, Andrew S. Draper, insisted that the title of his office be changed from regent to president. He continued building programs begun in 1892 and added the schools of law, library science, and medicine during his ten-year administration.

Draper enjoyed the support of Governor Peter Altgeld (1893–97), who increased legislative funding for the university during his tenure. Altgeld took a personal interest in the university, regularly attending board meetings and pronouncing his opposition to endowed universities as aristocratic, believing that the University of Illinois was a worthy representation of the citizens of Illinois.

At this time, the diversions of students reflected new interests. Intercollegiate activities grew to eclipse formerly popular literary societies by 1886. Fraternities were officially approved by the trustees in 1891. Sigma Chi was the first to receive sanction. The first sorority, Alpha Chi Omega, grew from the Alethanai Literary Society. Fraternities and sororities filled the social void in Champaign-Urbana and provided greatly needed room and board.

The colleges of agriculture and engineering both flourished. Under the capable direction of Dean Eugene Davenport, the agriculture college was reorganized. Appropriations increased, and the support of farmers was enlisted. A new agriculture building contributed to an increase in enrollment and the number of courses offered. After the turn of the century, the agriculture experiment station, established in 1876, had become the agricultural center of the state. Engineering, too, was well established when Draper arrived. Over 300 students were enrolled in 1894. A large appropriation provided the beginnings for an engineering experiment station. Both agriculture and engineering experiment stations focused national attention on university research.

The University of Illinois continued to prosper under President Edmund J. James, a native Illinoisan who served from 1904 to 1920 and who used public relations and legislative skills to secure significant state appropriations. James strengthened educational standards, emphasizing research and stressing the importance of a liberal education. He hired outstanding faculty often in competition with other institutions. President Charles Eliot of

Harvard University visited the campus in Champaign in 1908 to discover for himself why he was losing so many professors to Illinois. Sometime later, after James spoke to a gathering at Harvard, Eliot said to the group, "Men of Harvard, there is your competition of the future." Under James, course offerings were expanded, in 1905, the state geological survey was brought to campus, and in the following year, the College of Education was founded. Sixteen major buildings were completed before 1918, including the auditorium, the armory, and the first women's residence hall. Enrollment quadrupled, with many international students coming to the university.

Unlike the Spanish-American War, World War I involved the university extensively. The military department was reorganized and moved to the armory in 1914. In response to the establishment of the Reserve Officers Training Corps (ROTC) by Congress, a unit was established on campus in 1916. The University of Illinois was one of six schools chosen for military pilot training. Provision for student enlistment was made when the United States entered the war, and by the end of the term, 1,262 students had withdrawn from the campus.

James, suffering from poor health, resigned, and David Kinley, a long-time university administrator, was selected president in 1920. Facing the effects of wartime disorganization, financial difficulties, and increasing enrollment, Kinley nonetheless persevered in a building program. Smith Memorial Hall, the first university building constructed from funds that were not state-appropriated, was finished in 1921; Mumford Hall was built in 1924 and the new library was completed in 1926.

President Harry W. Chase, a progressive who followed Kinley, served for only three years. However, during his tenure he liberalized university statutes and student regulations.

The Depression touched the campus in 1932. Delinquent taxes in Chicago resulted in inadequate funds in the state treasury. Chase resigned and was succeeded by Arthur H. Daniels, acting president for one year. Although Daniels endeavored to improve the financial situation, the university considered borrowing federal funds for needed improvements.

Construction of new buildings slowed during President Arthur C. Willard's term (1934–46). However, University Hall was demolished, and the Illini Union was built. The Depression touched the campus in other ways. More students sought part-time work. Even the chimes in Altgeld Hall were silenced; the university could not afford to pay the chimes player.

In the post–World War II era, the University of Illinois, with other regional universities, benefited from state support of higher education. At this time, George D. Stoddard was named president, assuming leadership in the summer of 1946. He carried his reputation as an outspoken and liberal state commissioner of education in New York when he came to Illinois. His appointment

of young deans who occasionally clashed with veteran faculty and conservative elements in the community hastened his dismissal by the board of trustees, an event which occurred in 1953.

Unprecedented growth characterized the university's tenth decade when David D. Henry was selected as president. During his tenure, the graduate school grew rapidly, and federal support for scientific and technological research increased. The university was reorganized into the Champaign-Urbana campus, and the Chicago Circle and Medical Center campuses. The Chicago campuses merged in 1982 to form the University of Illinois at Chicago.

University Archivist Maynard Brichford notes that the recent rapid growth in telecommunications, campus networks, and supercomputer applications has been stimulated by federal grants, the generosity of manufacturers, and the rapid development of electronic technology.

Throughout its 128-year history, the University of Illinois has attracted outstanding faculty who have made significant contributions in teaching and research. More than 70 faculty members are members of the American Academy of Arts and Sciences, the National Academy of Sciences, and the National Academy of Engineering. The National Medal of Science was awarded to eight scientists while they were on the faculty. Congress established the Presidential Young Investigators Award to support research by faculty members embarking on academic careers. Twenty-six University of Illinois faculty have received this award.

The university boasts seven Nobel Prize winners, including two who were honored for work undertaken at Illinois. John Bardeen, who served on the faculty from 1951–91, was twice awarded the Nobel Prize in physics—in 1952 and 1972—the only individual to achieve this honor.

Throughout the decades, research has comprised a major thrust of the campus mission. From the Nuclear Physics Laboratory which began operations in 1940 to the National Soybean Research Laboratory established in 1992, more than 30 centers, institutes, and programs contribute to the development and dissemination of knowledge.

The first student in the United States to graduate in architecture, Nathan Ricker, did so from Illinois. Ricker, a renowned educator, designed several university buildings. Altgeld Hall, the only Romanesque building on campus, was designed by Ricker and James M. White and completed in 1897 with subsequent additions. Originally, it housed the university library; today it houses the mathematics department and its library.

"Alma Mater," standing in front of Altgeld Hall, is the university's most familiar symbol. Designed by sculptor and alumnus Loredo Taft and unveiled on June 12, 1929, it stood until 1962 behind Foellinger Auditorium. Romantically inclined students kept its throne "shiny and well-used." "Alma Mater" is flanked by "Labor and Learning," representations of the university's motto.

Clarence Blackall designed Foellinger Auditorium, the site of classes, lectures, concerts, and other special events. Built in 1907, its copper roof and cornice is reminiscent of Thomas Jefferson's rotunda on the University of Virginia campus. In 1984 the auditorium was completely renovated with funds provided by alumna Helene Foellinger.

Another domed building on campus, revolutionary in conception, is the Assembly Hall (1963) designed by Max Abramovitz, who served on the design team for Lincoln Center in New York City. The Assembly Hall is one of the two largest edge-supported domes in existence, spanning 400 feet in diameter and rising 128 feet above the floor. Musicals, concerts, commencement, and "Fighting Illini" basketball games are held in the Assembly Hall.

The largest academic building on campus, the Beckman Institute for Advanced Science and Technology, is a major research center wherein diverse research communities work together to explore relationships between areas of traditionally discrete scientific research. The Beckman Institute was constructed in 1989 on the site of the university's first building. A $40 million gift from alumnus Arnold O. Beckman and his wife Mabel M. Beckman supplemented by $10 million from the state of Illinois funded Beckman Institute, the recipient of the 1990 Laboratory of the Year Award by *R & D Magazine*.

From an initial collection of 644 books and government pamphlets purchased with $1,000 of state appropriations, the university library's collections include more than 8 million volumes, ranking it as the third largest academic collection in the nation after Harvard and Yale. The main library was designed by Charles Platt and completed in 1926 with several subsequent additions. The 27 tinted glass windows designed by J. Scott Williams of New York depicting Renaissance printers' marks decorate the main reference room. Quality and diversity characterize library collections. The Rare Books and Special Collections Library owns a complete first edition of Audubon's *The Birds of America* and comprehensive collections of works by and about Shakespeare, Milton, Abraham Lincoln, and Mark Twain. The Grainger Engineering Library Information Center, opened in 1994, is the largest engineering library in the country, housing more than 225,000 vol-

umes and 3,400 serials. Additionally, the library system includes the undergraduate library and more than 38 departmental libraries. The undergraduate library was built underground so as not to obstruct sunlight falling on the Morrow Plots.

The Morrow Plots and the Astronomical Observatory are designated National Historic Landmarks. The Plots, designated in 1968, are the country's oldest agricultural experiment fields in current use. The Astronomical Observatory received its status in 1990 primarily for research in astronomy conducted within the building.

Graduates of the University of Illinois have made significant contributions in business, education, research, and public service. Some notable alumni include Mary L. Page, 1878, perhaps the first woman graduate in architecture in the nation; Wallace Carothers, inventor of nylon and named by *Life Magazine* as one of the 100 most important Americans of the twentieth century; Charles Bowsher, head of the General Accounting Office and Comptroller General of the United States; James Brady, press secretary to President Ronald Reagan; Avery Brundage, president of the International Olympic Committee for several years; and Jack Kilby, inventor of the integrated circuit. Six college of communication graduates have won the Pulitzer Prize, including film critic Roger Ebert.

The University of Illinois, although a world-class institution, drawing international students and students from every state, still fulfills its original mission to educate the citizens of I llinois. Fully 93 percent of its undergraduates call Illinois their home state and contribute to the University of Illinois's status as the public flagship institution in the state.

Further Reading: Winton U. Solberg's *The University of Illinois, 1867–1894: An Intellectual and Cultural History* (Urbana: University of Illinois Press, 1968) offers a thorough and approachable history of the university's early years. Another treatment of the founding years is the detailed and scholarly *Illinois* by Allan Nevins (New York: Oxford University Press, 1917). An intimate and detailed view of campus life as seen through the pages of the *Daily Illini* is provided by Roger Ebert in *An Illini Century: One Hundred Years of Campus Life*. (Urbana: University of Illinois Press, 1967).

—Kathleen M. Conley

UNIVERSITY OF IOWA
(Iowa City, Iowa, U.S.A)

Location: In Iowa City, a town of 60,000 located 220 miles southwest of Chicago, Illinois, and 250 miles northwest of St. Louis, Missouri.

Description: A state university enrolling approximately 27,000 students in undergraduate, graduate, and professional schools.

Information: Campus Information Center
Iowa Memorial Union
Iowa City, IA 53342
U.S.A
(319) 335-3847; (800) 553-4692
(319) 335-3055

Visiting: The Old Capitol, the school's first building, is open every day except legal holidays and December 31. For group tours, call (319) 335-0548.

In the mid-1800s, pioneers settled the fertile fields west of the Mississippi River. They were Irish, German, and Yankees, who respectively, sought refuge from cataclysmic crop failures, intolerant government, and economic troubles. They practiced separate religions and knew unique histories, but they shared a belief in education. The German immigrants had left behind the best state-run schools in western Europe, and many of the Yankees had come from Massachusetts, home of the oldest public school system in the nation.

They had moved into the Iowa Territory near the end of a 25-year period that saw the idea of tax-supported education take hold in the United States. The founding fathers, particularly Thomas Jefferson, believed that education was crucial to a successful democracy. However, an organized, three-tiered educational system had been slow in coming. Ill-trained teachers held disorganized classes in cramped schools. Most colleges were small liberal arts schools run by religious groups, with the focus more on decorum than philosophy. Several such schools were scattered throughout Iowa.

Progress came steadily. Starting in 1804 with Ohio, the federal government offered new states free land for state universities. The Northwest Ordinance, which established guidelines for westward expansion, lured people from the 13 original colonies by stating that "means of education shall forever be encouraged." In 1847, only 59 days after Iowa became a state (and 52 years after North Carolina

opened the country's first state-run university), the Iowa legislature decided to build a state university in Iowa City, the state capital.

Iowa politicians soon discovered that deciding to build a school was easier than agreeing how to run it. Iowa's religious colleges offered curricula centered on Greek and Latin. In contrast, the legislature wanted the new school to provide Iowa with badly needed schoolteachers and professionals to help the economy. The governor, James Grimes, declared that it would be a mistake to create a liberal arts institution that would compete with the private colleges. What he believed was needed, according to the Stow Persons in *The University of Iowa in the Twentieth Century,* "was a practical scientific and polytechnical school to educate farmers, mechanics, engineers, chemists, architects, metallurgists, and geologists."

Even before the university opened, the legislature wrangled over proposals to establish five branches throughout the state. The governor resisted these attempts, and the 1857 constitution stipulated that the university was to remain at Iowa City, and "without branches."

The university opened in September 1855 with four faculty members and 124 students, including 41 women, enrolled in one of three departments. In addition to the collegiate department, which was the university proper, the school offered a normal department for prospective teachers, and the preparatory department for students found inadequately prepared for college work. Only the collegiate department had the power to confer degrees. Grimes had lost his battle for a practical curriculum, and, what Persons describes as "eastern clerical and educational interests" controlled the university curriculum, imposing a traditional liberal arts curriculum on the university.

Due to low enrollment, the collegiate and preparatory departments were closed from 1857 to 1860. New trustees also voted to exclude women from the collegiate department. However, this restriction provoked such opposition that it was not enforced, and it was repealed the following year. Since, in practice, women were never excluded, Iowa claims that it was the first public university in the United States to admit men and women "on an equal basis." From the first, the university was also open to minorities. (Alexander Clarke, an activist on behalf of civil rights for blacks, began his legal studies at the University of Iowa just after the Civil War at the age of 57.) However, because of Iowa's overwhelmingly white population, there were few nonwhite students (student housing was segregated until the 1930s).

Because of the elitist tradition of existing colleges, many legislators feared that university graduates would

University of Iowa

be contemptuous of manual labor. In 1858, they founded a State Agricultural College and Model Farm at Ames (today known as Iowa State University). In 1876, Iowa State Teachers College (now the University of Northern Iowa) opened in Cedar Falls. As the state legislators had feared, the university at Iowa City initially copied the more prestigious institutions in the east from which it drew its faculty. Until the 1890s, it functioned primarily as a liberal arts college offering a classical curriculum in a Christian environment. The first five presidents were Protestant clergymen, and students had to attend daily chapel and Sunday church services. The rules forbade drinking, card playing, gambling, profanity, entering a saloon, and attending the theater. Tobacco was not allowed in the classrooms or study halls.

Within the collegiate department, students followed a set program in Greek, Latin, mathematics, and science. Acting under pressure from the state legislature, the university added five professional departments: law (1865), medicine (1870), dentistry (1882), pharmacy (1886), and homeopathic medicine (1887). However, these departments offered only undergraduate courses, and admis-

sions and graduation standards were much less rigorous than those of the collegiate department.

Under the leadership of George MacLean, president from 1899 to 1911, Iowa turned to the Germanic model of a university. The pioneering American institution in this area was Johns Hopkins University, founded in 1876 as the first American university on the German model—with lectures to large groups, seminars for intensive research, and laboratories for experimentation. Inspired by Hopkins, established American schools also created graduate faculties and granted the M.A. and Ph.D. as earned (rather than honorary) degrees. MacLean was personally experienced in and an enthusiastic supporter of the German model, having earned a Ph.D. at the University of Leipzig in 1883.

Despite student indifference and faculty hostility, brought about by fears that MacLean's changes would adversely affect their professional lives, MacLean moved vigorously to turn Iowa into a research university. The six existing undergraduate departments became colleges. More rigorous standards were introduced into the five professional colleges, and their change into graduate programs began. The former collegiate department became the College of Liberal Arts, and postgraduate courses were assigned to a separate graduate college with its own dean. New subject-matter departments were created within these colleges; departments with related interests became schools.

The new departments were staffed by professors qualified to conduct research. When MacLean took office, only 26 percent of the professorial staff had doctoral degrees. When he left in 1911, more than half had an earned Ph.D. By 1911, 231 students were enrolled in the graduate college. Only 12 American universities had a higher percentage of students in graduate programs. Wisconsin was Iowa's only equal among public universities.

Neither the public nor the legislature was ready to accept MacLean's concept of a scholarly institution of graduate and professional schools. He was forced to resign in 1911, following changes in the makeup of the university's governing board. From 1870 to 1909, each of the three state schools was governed by its own board of regents, which hired and fired faculty, managed financial operations, and monitored students' lives. Under this system, the schools directly competed for funds and facilities. Impatient with the schools' rivalries and legislative lobbying, the legislature in 1909 placed the three schools under one board of education (called the board of regents since 1955). The members of the new board wanted to make their own hiring choices and forced MacLean and the other two presidents to resign.

The post-MacLean era was shaped by an effective working partnership between President George Jessup (1916–34) and Carl Seashore, dean of the graduate college from 1908 to 1936. Jessup was determined to make Iowa one of the top universities in the country. He was a superb politician and manager but not an intellectual. His manner was brisk and incisive, fostering the impression that he was in firm control. Arthur M. Schlesinger Sr., history department chair from 1919, once described Jessup as "a stock, square-jawed man who looked and acted more like a business executive or banker than a university president." Jessup remembered every political and civic leader who might be useful to the university and maintained close ties with them. He spoke to any group that would hear him, and he was careful to say nothing that would challenge or disturb his audiences.

Thanks largely to Jessup's personality, the relationship between the school's president and board finally stabilized. The board devoted itself to policy and left administrative matters to Jessup. Instead of delegating, Jessup kept much of the power to himself. Like the university's founders, he scorned elitism. He believed that a university should serve public needs and that extension programs, educational radio, correspondence courses, hospitals, and health clinics should bring the university's resources to communities throughout the state. At the same time, in his determination to improve the faculty, he offered high salaries to recruit the best professors.

Among the school's leaders during the Jessup years was Carl Seashore, the graduate school's dean. A native Iowan, Seashore earned a Ph.D. in psychology from Yale University. Firmly committed to the newer methods of experimental psychology, he visited pioneering laboratories in Berlin, Leipzig, and Göttingen before joining the Iowa faculty in 1897. As dean from 1908 to 1936, Seashore controlled admissions and approved proposed thesis and dissertation subjects. Central to Seashore's educational philosophy was his belief in the importance of recognizing and cultivating individual differences. In 1909, he said, "Keep each individual busy at his highest normal level of successful achievement that he may be happy, useful, and good." To move toward this goal, he provided institutional support for programs that integrated teaching, research, and practical service. Convinced that the methods of applied psychology could be useful in many fields, he encouraged isolated departments to work together.

Some of the most lasting innovations at the University of Iowa occurred in educational testing, child welfare, and speech pathology. During World War I, Seashore helped develop the Army's Alpha intelligence tests. In 1923, at his suggestion, President Jessup ordered that incoming freshmen take the Alpha test. Out of Seashore's proposal that high schools institute similar tests emerged the Iowa Testing Program. Everet Linquist, who directed the testing program from 1930 to 1969, developed the Iowa Test of Basic Skills, taken by millions of school children throughout the country. In the 1950s, Linquist invented an electronic machine to score and store objective test results. Because he feared that the consequent ease of objective testing would lead schools to emphasize isolated facts, Linquist developed test questions requiring comparison, inference, and judgment. In 1959, he became cofounder of the influential American College Testing Program.

The Iowa Child Welfare Research Station was also important. Established in 1917, the research station was the first American center to study the development of a normal child. As a result in his interest in physiology and psychology of normal speech, Seashore was directly responsible for the founding in 1925 of a pioneering clinic for the study of speech defects (now the Department of Speech Pathology and Audiology). Seashore personally supervised the education of Lee Travis, the clinic's first director. Later, James F. Curtis and Wendell Johns attracted scores of patients to Iowa City for work on cleft palates and stuttering. As part of their therapy, stutterers walked around the city startling passersby by asking questions such as "Does my stuttering bother you?"

Another innovation was the School of Religion, established in 1925. The first such school at a state university, it grew out of an effort to bridge the separation between church and state. Protestant, Roman Catholic, and Jewish leaders each chose and funded a professor, whose courses carried full academic credit toward graduation. Administrative costs, initially supported by the Rockefeller Foundation, were taken over by the university in 1938. Since 1970, the university has chosen the faculty, but churches and synagogues continue to provide financial support.

The university also broke new ground in the arts. Iowa was the first American college or university to accept artistic work in lieu of research theses. Though it has been widely imitated since, this procedure was revolutionary in the 1920s. Many schools offered courses in music, drawing, and painting, but they did not lead to advanced—or even undergraduate—degrees. The physical and biological sciences started the practice of requiring a research thesis for advanced degrees; the practice later spread to the social sciences and humanities. In any field, a dissertation was expected to follow a rigid scientific methodology: identify facts; classify data; and analyze expression or behavior.

The change began with George Stewart, a physicist, who acted as a graduate dean in Seashore's absences. Stewart believed that research was a creative act. Experiments started with a hunch, and conclusions were guided by insight and inspiration. As a result, Stewart thought the arts deserved the same academic respect as the sciences. The agreement of Seashore and other physical scientists lent credibility to this innovative philosophy.

In 1922, the graduate council revised the thesis requirement "to include artistic production, e.g., in literature, art, or music; the performance of a project, e.g., in education or sociology." The first master of fine arts degrees were awarded in 1925 and 1926 for two symphonic compositions and a painting. In 1929, the School of Fine Arts was founded with the goal of coordinating and integrating work into music, theater, and the graphic and plastic arts. The English department at first lagged behind the fine arts in accepting creative work. Norman Foerster, appointed director of the new School of Letters in 1930, finally persuaded the department to accept creative dissertations. The first master's degree was granted in 1931 for a collection of poems, and a doctoral degree was awarded in 1935 for a group of essays. Foerster was also influential in founding the Iowa Writers' Workshop, the most widely copied of the Iowa programs in the creative arts. Although the name was not officially used until 1939, the Iowa Writers' Workshop traces its beginnings to the first graduate courses in writing in 1936.

The two-year program is divided into poetry and fiction workshops that meet weekly—poets on Monday, fiction writers on Tuesday. The writers discuss and criticize one another's work. Students submit book-length manuscripts as theses. The workshop instructors tend to have unique teaching styles. Some give detailed instructions for improvement, while others leave the discussion to the writers, whose commentaries are sometimes devastating. The workshop developed a reputation as the finest writing program in the country under the leadership of Paul Engle, a published poet and native Iowan, who directed the workshop from 1942 to 1965. Saul Maloff, a former member of the Writers' Workshop, wrote in *Publishers Weekly,* "If any institution can be said to owe its life to the volcanic will and drive of one man, the poet Paul Engle, a native son, must be held accountable, for it was he who presided over its coming of age with a ferocious single-mindedness verging on monomania." Engle said that he recruited talented writers the way a coach recruits athletes, and he was remarkably successful in raising money to lure them to Iowa. After resigning as director in 1965, Engle established the International Writing Program, which brings prominent foreign writers to Iowa City.

In addition to a small core of tenured professors, courses are taught by visiting instructors who stay for a year or two. The faculty has included some of literature's brightest lights: poet Robert Lowell, novelist and poet Robert Penn Warren (twice winner of the Pulitzer Prize for poetry [1958 and 1979] and winner of the 1947 Pulitzer Prize in fiction for *All the King's Men*), novelist Vance Bourjaily, novelist Stanley Elkin, novelist and short story writer John Cheever (winner of the 1979 Pulitzer Prize in fiction for *The Short Stories of John Cheever*), novelist Kurt Vonnegut, novelist Philip Roth, novelist and short story writer Frank Conroy, and poet Galway Kinnel (winner of the Pulitzer Prize for poetry in 1983). Students, many of whom have come back to teach, have included novelist Flannery O'Connor, poet Donald Justice (winner of the Pulitzer Prize for poetry in 1980), and novelists Gail Godwin, John Irving, and Raymond Carver. More than 300 writers gathered in Iowa City in May 1986 to celebrate the workshop's 50th anniversary.

Since the 1960s, hundreds of other schools have created graduate and undergraduate writing programs, many initially directed by former Iowa Workshop participants. The master of fine arts degree has become almost a requirement for entry into a literary career. At Iowa, at least, students consider themselves free to write whatever they please, no matter how unfashionable. However, over the years, critics have charged that Iowa and other university writing programs encourage conformist writing designed to earn approval in the classroom. They believe that workshop graduates end up teaching writing at universities while publishing mediocre work in small magazines. During the 50th anniversary celebrations in 1986, Howard Moss, poetry editor of the *New Yorker,* noted that Iowa, the first of the writing programs, "has become a whipping boy for all that's wrong with any of them. It can't make you a writer. You're talented or not."

Since World War II, the university has continued to build on the foundations laid in the 1920s and 1930s. Enrollment continuously increased, from some 5,000 students in 1945 to a peak of about 30,000 in 1984. Enrollment in 1994 was 26,932. The practical applications of scientific research continued to be emphasized, most notably in the investigations into outer space of James

Van Allen of Iowa's Astrophysics Department. Van Allen and the department have contributed to NASA missions by building equipment and analyzing data. Van Allen himself is probably best known for his discovery of two doughnut-shaped zones of charged particles that encircle the earth, now called the Van Allen radiation belts.

Iowa's thriving Writer's Workshop and its continuing contribution to scientific research would seem to bear out Dean Seashore's view that the arts and the sciences make equal contributions to the academic world.

Further Reading: More than 325 photographs enrich the historical overview in John Gerber's *A Pictorial History of the University of Iowa* (Iowa City: University of Iowa Press, 1988). In *The University of Iowa in the Twentieth Century: An Institutional History* (Iowa City: University of Iowa Press, 1990), Stow Parsons presents a detailed narrative history. Larry Perl, a journalism school graduate, offers a jazzier style and more attention to student life *in Calm and Secure on Thy Hill: A Retrospective of the University of Iowa* (Iowa City: University of Iowa Alumni Association, 1978), based on a series of articles in the Iowa City *Daily Iowan.* Steven Wilbers' *The Iowan Writers Workshop* (Iowa City: University of Iowa Press, 1980) traces the history of this innovative and influential program. For a complete listing of books and magazine articles about the university, see Earl M. Rogers, *A Biliography of the History of the University of Iowa, 1848–1978* (Iowa City: University of Iowa Libraries, 1979).

—Jan Rogoziński

UNIVERSITY OF LEIDEN
(Leiden, Netherlands)

Location: Inside a former convent of White Nuns and in other buildings in the city of Leiden (also spelled "Leyden" in English or "Lijden" in Dutch), 30 miles southwest of Amsterdam.

Description: "Rijksuniversiteit te Leiden" in Dutch; the oldest university in the Netherlands, founded by William the Silent in 1575; historically famous as a center of Calvinist theology, Oriental studies, and botany; now a multi-faculty university, with around 17,000 students.

Information: Secretaris, Rijksuniversiteit
Stationsweg 46
P.O. Box 9500
2300 RA Leiden
Netherlands
(71) 27 2727

The University of Leiden, the oldest in the Netherlands, has been closely involved in many of the major events and movements that have shaped the Dutch nation ever since it was founded in 1575, during the struggle for independence from Spain. Today it is one of several institutions of higher education and has lost its unique role as the leading center of Dutch learning, but it retains a distinctive character nonetheless.

Until 1425 there was no university in any of the small states and principalities known as the Low Countries (modern Belgium, Luxembourg, the Netherlands, and northeastern France). The foundation of the University of Louvain (or Leuven) in that year provided some opportunities for higher education, but its adherence to the doctrines of the Catholic Church—a feature shared, of course, with all universities in western Europe at that date—presented problems for the already growing minority who questioned those doctrines and the enormous power and wealth of the Church. Over the years that minority became more organized into Lutheran and Calvinist groups that rejected Catholic authority altogether, and attempts to suppress them became more determined and brutal under both Charles V, Holy Roman Emperor and overlord of the Low Countries, and his son and successor Philip II, king of Spain.

Militant opposition to Philip's policies, led by William the Silent, prince of Orange, and others among his own Dutch officials, broke out in 1566–67 and again from 1572. Leiden, a center of Calvinist and other anti-Spanish

movements, was besieged by Philip's troops (for a second time) from May 1574 onward, but it was relieved with supplies brought on barges after the breaking of the dikes to flood the plain around the city. The end of the siege is still celebrated every year on October 3 with the eating of carrots and onions, the vegetables left behind by the retreating Spanish, and of herring and white bread, the first foods brought into the city by the rebels. This date may also be taken to symbolize the foundation of the university, which was first proposed by William the Silent in a letter dated December 28, 1574, addressed to the states assemblies of Holland and Zeeland. It was formally established by the two provinces the following year, in commemoration of the city's deliverance.

Johan van der Does, already famous as a leading defender of the city during the siege, and later renowned as a poet under the Latin pen name Janus Dousa, chaired a committee appointed by the states assembly of Holland which composed the charter for the new university (*Academia Lugduno Batava*) issued on January 6, 1575, in the name, somewhat bizarrely, of King Philip, since the rebels did not create their own government of the United Provinces until 1581. Its provisions appear to have been based on the examples of the Academy of Geneva, created by John Calvin himself, and the University of Louvain. The opening ceremony took place on February 8, 1575. Until 1577 the university was housed in the former convent of Saint Barbara, on the Rapenburg Canal; then it moved into the convent of the Faille-Mantled Beguines nearby; and in 1581 it also took over the convent of the White Nuns, on the canal's other bank. It is this historic building which, as the New Academy, is still the university's headquarters.

With just 2 students in 1575 and 14 in 1576, the new university's professors, influenced by four of their number who had moved to the city from Geneva, devoted their energies less to teaching than to quarreling with the city fathers over the university's rules and its relationship with the city's schools and churches. On June 2, 1575, William himself intervened to impose a new administration led by a rector, who, significantly, had to be a Dutch-speaker, and two or three curators appointed by the city. Three years later, when the States of Holland forced the university to give up administering the oath of loyalty to Calvinist doctrine which William had reluctantly imposed on staff and students alike, the superiority of the secular authorities over the dogmatists among the faculty was further reinforced. The university was probably unique in Europe at that date, and for two centuries to come, in not imposing a religious oath on its members.

University of Leiden

Perhaps partly because of this factor, by 1581 there were more than 40 students in Leiden, divided into two groups: those who studied theology, most of whom were "bursars," receiving scholarships provided by the provinces and living together in a seminary known as the States College; and those studying other subjects, who lived in private lodges.

In 1586, the city authorities successfully resisted the plans of the English Earl of Leicester, the temporary, unpopular, and ineffectual governor of the rebel provinces, to move the university to Utrecht and thus deprive them of "their only and most precious pearl." Instead they set about enhancing its value. The library, founded in 1587, gradually expanded to fill the convent of the Faille-Mantled Beguines—also known as the Old Academy (it now contains more than 2 million books), and the university embarked upon its own "golden age" just as the United Provinces expelled the Spanish and started theirs.

During the seventeenth century Leiden was probably the single most important and influential university for European Protestants, attracting students and scholars from England, Germany, and other countries as well as from the United Provinces, all of whom shared in teaching and research conducted mainly in Latin. Indeed, the average proportion of foreigners among the students at Leiden has been estimated to have been around 41 percent in the years up to 1601, around 43 percent between 1601 and 1625, and as much as 52 percent between 1626 and 1650, which would be extraordinary at any university even today. In addition, Leiden retained its primacy in the higher education of the Dutch nation, although other provinces founded a total of five more universities between 1585 and 1656, mainly because Holland remained the wealthiest, most populous, and culturally most influential province and Leiden the most cosmopolitan and most substantially endowed university.

Leiden's prestige was closely bound up with that of the Calvinist church. Although the church accounted for a relatively small minority of the population—probably no more than around 10 percent—it had been closely identified with the struggle for independence, and now, through its Leiden-trained ministers and its monopoly of legally approved religious services, claimed the right to admonish those secular powerholders whom it considered too tolerant or too lax, just as John Calvin himself had in Geneva. This was the context in which a theological debate among scholars developed into a nationwide political crisis. In 1603 the university appointed Jakob Hermanns—known in Latin as Jacobus Arminius—to one of its professorships of theology. In the following year he and his colleague Franz (Franciscus) Gomarus took opposing sides in a public debate on the question of salvation, Arminius arguing that human beings could affect their chances of salvation by their free acceptance of God's grace, Gomarus following Calvinist orthodoxy in asserting that each person's fate is predestined by God

regardless of individual acts. Arminius' rebellion against Calvin's doctrines might have remained a merely academic scandal if his death in 1609 had not been followed in 1610 by his supporters' decision to present a Remonstrance, a demand for toleration of their views, to the states assemblies of Holland and Friesland, the two provinces in which there were then universities and in which the training of ministers was therefore a political issue. The Arminians, or Remonstrants, won the support of the majority in both assemblies, only to find that the so-called Counter-Remonstrants, led by Gomarus and other powerful ministers, were supported by the other provinces, and crucially by Maurice of Nassau, William's son and his successor as military commander of the country. (He himself had given up his studies at Leiden in 1584 after the assassination of his father.) The subsequent crisis attracted international attention, with Britain supporting the Gomarists and France the Arminians, and was resolved in 1619 by the banishing of 13 Arminian ministers, the purging of the universities, and the execution of Jan van Oldenbarneveldt, the most important statesman in Holland and Maurice's former mentor. In the same year the synod of Dort (or Dordrecht) reasserted orthodox doctrine, which was imposed with renewed vigor on the universities and schools and, through them, on the country as a whole. Yet enough of the spirit of toleration remained to permit the leading Arminians to return from exile and create their own separate church in 1626: in the Netherlands, as in other countries in this period, the academic community was forced to be notably less tolerant than society at large. (The Arminians' own academy, the Athenaeum founded in 1632, became the University of Amsterdam.)

One of the scholars purged during the upheaval was Huig van Groot, better known as Hugo Grotius, who had graduated from Leiden in 1598, at the age of 15, and rapidly become known as one of the most brilliant scholars in the Netherlands. His support for Oldenbarneveldt led to his imprisonment and, following his escape to France in 1621, the loss of his talents to his nation, for he remained in exile until his death in 1645. It is one of the countless ironies of history that this particular Leiden graduate, widely regarded as the first scholar to formulate the principles of international law, is now probably better known, and exercises a greater influence, in the Netherlands as in other countries, than any other graduate of the university. Another side-effect of the upheaval was that the cultural supremacy of Holland over the other provinces was reinforced—to the extent that, like England within Britain, its name came to misrepresent the entire country—by way of the Staten Bible, the official translation into the form of Dutch prevailing in the province, which was commissioned by the synod of Dort and completed by scholars at Leiden. Like Luther's translation in German-speaking regions, or the authorized version in English-speaking ones, this version of the Christian scriptures had a formative influence on most people, but especially on writers and scholars, until well into the nineteenth century. Still another result of the triumph of orthodoxy may well have been the determination of the "Pilgrim Fathers," the founders of Massachusetts, to impose a similar orthodoxy in their new home, for they resided in Leiden between their departure from England in 1609 and their voyage to North America in 1620 and witnessed the rise and fall of the Arminian heresy and its disruptive effects.

As a direct offshoot of its theological concerns, Leiden soon became a center of European knowledge and research in languages and literatures. Joseph Justus Scaliger, a French Protestant scholar of Italian descent who was at Leiden between 1592 and 1609, when he died, was especially prominent in the study of Latin and Greek, not only in the service of theology but as a means for studying history, politics, and science as well, so that (for example) the study of the Roman historian Tacitus became the basis for study of politics and diplomacy in general, for Grotius and for many others. More distinctively, during the seventeenth century Leiden came to rival the ancient universities of Europe as a center for the study of the Semitic languages. Scaliger, although a classicist himself, encouraged the new discipline, while his colleague Raphelengius, professor of Hebrew, also served as university printer, ensuring that the press maintained fonts for printing texts in Hebrew, Arabic, Ethiopian, and other "exotic" scripts. These continued to be used on behalf of the university until 1712 by the Elseviers, the famous printing dynasty which had started in Leiden around 1581. The Sorbonne was the first European university to appoint a professor of Arabic; Leiden was the second, and it was at Leiden that Thomas Erpenius became one of the first Europeans to make a serious study of the grammar of Arabic and that Jacob Golius, one of many linguists trained by Scaliger, compiled one of the first dictionaries of that language to be published in Europe. Later, Albert Schultens continued in the tradition by pioneering the study of Hebrew, Arabic, and other Semitic languages as a single family.

The work of these scholars and their successors was appreciated not only within the academic community at Leiden but by the wider community of educated Dutch citizens involved directly or indirectly in the extensive trade between the Netherlands and its Muslim, Arabic-speaking colonies in what are now India and Indonesia. Golius was even appointed by the states general assembly of the United Provinces to conduct official correspondence in Arabic with the rulers of the Muslim territories of North Africa, with which the Dutch state was among the first in Europe to maintain diplomatic relations.

However, the university was not exclusively concerned with theology or the languages associated with it. It also gained a Europe-wide reputation in science and medicine. Its botanical gardens, founded in 1587 as a garden of medicinal herbs, in a field behind the New Academy, were laid out on rational principles devised by the French botanist Charles l'Ecluse—known at Leiden at Carolus Clusius—who not only led the way in the Europe-wide program of classifying and investigating the properties of plants, but was also credited with, perhaps as early as 1573, introducing the tulip, which now seems so typically Dutch, from its original location in Turkey to his garden in Leiden and from there across the country. Leiden was also the home of Willibrord Snellius, the mathematician who devised Snell's Law, the formula that describes optical refraction. Snell was the most influential among a number of Leiden mathematicians whose work was eagerly taken up and applied in the practical field of navigation, then so crucial to the wealth and power of the United Provinces.

From 1593 onward the university also had a Theatrum Anatomicum, a dissecting room, at first located in the Old Academy, which was one of the few in any European university. During the eighteenth century the number of foreign students in the university's faculty of medicine averaged around 400, making it among the largest and most cosmopolitan of the time and bringing great renown to its most important professor, Hermann Boerhaave, who taught there from 1701 until his death in 1738. An expert on human anatomy as well as on entomology, he carried out important research on perspiration and on the epidemiology of smallpox; his textbooks of medical principles were translated into numerous European languages. In the summer months, when work with corpses was impossible, the room was use to display the university's steadily growing collection of curiosities, such as Egyptian mummies, stuffed crocodiles, and other objects from distant lands.

Just as the university's golden age coincided with that of the Dutch nation itself, so its gradual contraction and decline during the eighteenth century occurred as the United Provinces fell further and further behind in economic and colonial competition with Britain. The city of Leiden itself suffered from the rise of rival centers of weaving and other industries, its population falling from a peak of around 100,00 in 1640 to around 30,000 in 1800. Economic problems in turn contributed to a mounting political crisis which, as in earlier times of trouble, came to focus on the struggle between the monarchical tendencies of the House of Orange and the republican tradition of the states assemblies. In these years the University of Leiden gained a reputation for conservatism which was enhanced by the writings of Adriaan Kluit, a professor of history who was a vociferous supporter of the claims of William V, the prince of Orange, who became absolute ruler in 1787.

However, following the French Revolution of 1789, the anti-absolutist Patriot movement was revived and, in 1795, with help from French troops, it overthrew William V and established the Batavian Republic. Like the other Dutch universities, Leiden was now opened to other teachers and students apart from the orthodox Calvinists who had dominated its first two centuries. But in 1806 the republic gave way to a new "Kingdom of Holland" ruled by Louis Bonaparte, brother of the French emperor Napoléon, and only Leiden and Groningen survived Napoléon's drastic reforms of the Dutch universities in 1810, which placed them under the strict supervision of a board of control, charged with assimilating their work with the principles of the French empire.

After the restoration of the *ancien regime* in 1813, when the Kingdom of the Netherlands was created under the Orange family, Leiden and Groningen were joined by a revived university at Utrecht to form the extant group of three state-controlled universities (alongside the municipal university of Amsterdam and two universities controlled by Christian churches). All three continued to be regulated by the Napoléonic system, which had two notable effects. First, the centralization of power at the national level, a trend advocated by Willem Bilderdijk, who followed Kluit in promoting an absolutist interpretation of history at Leiden, meant that the supervisory powers formerly exercised by the city of Leiden and the province of Holland were never revived. Second, the formal separation of the natural sciences from the arts allowed the three state universities to take part in the great academic sea-change which was to transform higher education all over Europe and North America during the nineteenth century.

Leiden also benefited from the prestige of being the oldest and most famous of the Dutch universities, a prestige which was enhanced by the creation of a group of national museums in the city, which were and are closely associated with the university. The first of these, the Museum of Natural History, was founded in 1820 on the basis of the royal collections donated to the university by King William I five years before. It was followed in 1821 by the Museum of Archeology and in 1837 by the Museum of Ethnology, this last being notable for its important and fascinating collection of Japanalia, a byproduct of the period (1639–1854) when the Dutch were the only Europeans permitted to trade with Japan.

Latin remained the language of instruction at Leiden, Groningen, and Utrecht long after it had been replaced by native languages at most other European universities, and the need to provide elementary instruction in Latin for most of the students entering from ordinary schools continued to take up time and resources that might have been devoted to developing instruction and research in the natural sciences, social studies, and other newer forms of learning. Even so, the university did not lack developments in these directions. It first acquired a chemical laboratory in 1859, a physiological laboratory in 1866, and a modernized astronomical observatory in 1868; a pharmaceutical laboratory was added in 1889 and separate laboratories for organic and inorganic chemistry followed in 1901 and 1918 respectively. The high standards of research achieved

with these new facilities may be inferred from the awarding of three Nobel Prizes to scholars of the university. Hendrik Antoon Lorentz, who had graduated from Leiden at the age of 16 and been appointed a professor at 24, was awarded the physics prize, jointly with his student Pieter Zeeman, in 1902, for their work on electromagnetism; Heike Kamerlingh Onnes received the same prize 11 years later, having liquefied helium and opening up the whole field of superconductivity; and Willem Einthoven, a pioneer of electrocardiography, was awarded the physiology or medicine prize in 1924.

However, for better or worse scientists are generally less well known to the public than their colleagues in other faculties, and between the two world wars the single most famous professor at Leiden was probably the historian Johan Huizinga, whose book *The Waning of the Middle Ages,* first published in 1919, is widely regarded as a classic. As rector of the university he not only presided over the continuing expansion in student numbers—which rose from 798 (including around 100 women) in 1900 to 2,410 (including around 800 women) in 1940—but became almost equally well known, at least within his own country, as an implacable opponent of the Nazi regime in neighboring Germany. He caused controversy as early as 1933, the first year both of his term of office and of Hitler's dictatorship, when he forbade the participation of a Nazi-dominated group of German students in an international conference on university property. This act alone marked him for punishment seven years later, when the Netherlands was invaded and incorporated into the Nazi empire.

Huizinga was by no means alone in his protests against the occupying power which, unlike in France and other countries, found very few collaborators anywhere in the Netherlands. At Leiden R.P. Cleveringa, dean of the law faculty, and his colleague B.M. Telders led courageous protests against the anti-Semitic decrees issued in October 1940, including the circulation of a petition signed by more than 70 percent of the student body. The university was closed in November that year and, once it was clear that its staff and students would not cooperate in converting it into a Nazi institution, it was formally "abolished" in November 1942.

The university reopened in September 1945, four months after the end of the war in Europe. Earlier that year Huizinga, who had been taken hostage in 1940 but later released, had died of natural causes, and Telders had been murdered at the Bergen-Belsen concentration camp, but Cleveringa and others, released from imprisonment, were able to restore the university to its former academic standing.

The past 50 years have been typified, at Leiden as at other universities across the developed world, by unprecedented expansion and transformation, as the university authorities have responded to changes in society. The single most striking change has been the rise in student numbers, from 2,924 in 1945 to 7,878 in

1965, and then to 17,190 in 1993. This process has necessarily altered the everyday experience of studying in Leiden as well as the social status of its graduates. As elsewhere the expansion was accompanied in the late 1960s by a brief and ultimately ineffectual outburst of student protest, which at Leiden culminated in the events of May 1969, when part of the headquarters building was occupied for 12 days and converted into a "discussion center" by student radicals. But the lasting effect of this historic change has been to make Leiden, like its counterparts in other countries, an institution concerned less with the training of a homogeneous national elite (although that process still continues to some extent) and much more with the education of a diverse range of professional specialists and the provision of research services to the government and private corporations.

Although Leiden has thus, inevitably, lost some of its unique character it remains the leading university in the Netherlands and a center of excellence in both the humanities and the natural sciences. Less tangibly but perhaps even more importantly, its teachers and students alike can lay claim to, and variously try to live up to, the Dutch tradition of independence and free thought which was inaugurated by William the Silent, the father of the nation and of the university, then betrayed during the Arminian crisis, only to be reaffirmed by individual scholars over the years and by the university as a whole during World War II.

Further Reading: M.W. Juriaanse's *The Founding of Leyden University* (Leiden: E.J. Brill, 1965) is a fascinating account of its early years, but the history of its golden age and the period since is scattered through general histories of the Netherlands, ranging both in age and quality; one of the best is Bernard H.M. Vlekke's exemplary study *Evolution of the Dutch Nation* (New York: Roy, 1945).

—Patrick Heenan

UNIVERSITY OF LONDON
(London, England)

Location: Senate House and several member institutions in Bloomsbury; other member institutions in South Kensington and other districts of Greater London; also in Wye, Kent, England; and in Paris.

Description: A federal university, with the second largest number of students among British universities, comprising 6 multi-faculty colleges, 9 medical schools, and 22 other specialist schools and institutes.

Information: The Registrar
The Senate House
University of London
Malet Street
London WC1E 7HU
England
(0171) 636 8000

The University of London is a federation of general colleges, medical schools, and other institutions of higher education which has grown up almost haphazardly since its formal creation in 1836, partly by absorbing several older institutions. It is the product of two interconnected processes: the development over several hundred years of formal courses in medicine, linked to the numerous hospitals in the British capital, and, from 1828 onward, the piecemeal creation of alternatives to Oxford and Cambridge, which until that year were the only universities in England (Scottish and Irish education being separate). Alternatives were needed for those groups whom the ancient universities, as they are known, have traditionally excluded, up to various points in the nineteenth and twentieth centuries: Catholics, Nonconformist Protestants, Jews, and the non-religious; women; men from working-class backgrounds; and people wishing to study near their homes, whether in London itself or in cities elsewhere in Great Britain and the British Empire, where "daughter" institutions were created. In addition the university has played a leading role in the long-term trend away from general education in the liberal arts and toward specialized professional training, at first (and still predominantly) in medicine, but later also in the natural sciences, social studies, and modern languages, all of which were long neglected or underrated at Oxford and Cambridge.

Among the 37 institutions which are now members of the University of London, the oldest by far are the medical schools attached to two medieval hospitals, Saint Bartholomew's and Saint Thomas's, affectionately known to generations of Londoners as Bart's and Tommy's. Bart's was established in 1123, Tommy's perhaps even earlier, although its present name and location appear to date from 1215. Although it is impossible to establish when either hospital first began training doctors, for lack of documentary evidence, both were almost certainly doing so by the time that they were taken over by the Corporation of the City of London, Bart's in 1546 and Tommy's in 1551. The formal organization of medical schools, complete with regulations, examinations, and certificates, was completed in the early eighteenth century, by which time there were five more hospitals in London: the Westminster founded in 1716; Guy's from 1726; Saint George's from 1733; the London from 1740; and the Middlesex from 1745. Guy's and Tommy's, which stood next door to each other, seem to have been the first to organize programs of lectures, beginning in 1768, while the London is believed to have created the first medical school organizationally separate from the hospital itself, in 1785. The medical schools of all these hospitals, as well as the school attached to the Charing Cross Hospital, founded in 1818, were to join the university soon after its foundation.

The training of barristers (lawyers who represent clients in court) has also been concentrated in London since the fifteenth century, or perhaps earlier, at the four colleges known as the Inns of Court and at the now-defunct Inns of Chancery. However, these have always been independent, rejecting an invitation to join the University of London in 1899. Instead they elected four members to its senate from 1900 to 1929, and after World War II they developed a cooperative relationship with the university's Institute of Advanced Legal Studies.

While medical and legal training was evolving in London, higher education in the liberal arts in England had long since become the exclusive business of Oxford and Cambridge. Their monopoly was broken from 1596, when Gresham College was established in Bishopsgate in London in the former home of the merchant Sir Thomas Gresham (1519–76), perhaps best known for the "law" of economics named for him ("Bad money drives out good"). Between 1660 and 1710 this college also served as the headquarters of the Royal Society, the influential learned society created by King Charles II. However, by 1768 the college had lost prestige and students alike. Gresham's home was demolished and the college named for him continued on a reduced scale and in a series of locations, until it was absorbed into the separate City University established in 1966.

University of London

It was against this background of success in professional education and relative failure in the teaching of the liberal arts that a true University of London was first proposed. On February 9, 1825, *The Times,* then the leading British newspaper, published an open letter setting out the proposal, written by the poet Thomas Campbell to his fellow-Scot, the politician Henry Brougham. He responded by inviting representatives from religious groups whose members were excluded from Oxford and Cambridge, including Baptists, Jews, and Catholics, to join in planning the new institution, which, like the older universities and the medical schools, would still exclude women. The London University which they devised, better known from the outset as University College, London, was opened in Bloomsbury in October 1828.

University College (usually abbreviated UCL) is still based in its original range of neoclassical buildings designed by William Wilkins, although several additional buildings have since been squeezed onto its site. It would eventually become, as it remains, the largest single member institution of the federal University of London, with which many Londoners still confuse it. Its departments now include the Slade School of Fine Art founded in 1871, which has trained such prominent British painters as Sir Stanley Spencer, and the Petrie Museum of Egyptian Archaeology, which commemorates the work of

UCL's first professor of Egyptology, Sir Flinders Petrie. Its most famous mummy, however, is not in the museum but inside a glass-fronted wooden cabinet near the college's main entrance. This is the "Auto-Icon" of the philosopher Jeremy Bentham (1748–1832), whose utilitarian and liberal principles greatly influenced the founders of UCL. His seated, embalmed body, fully clothed and with a hat on its wax head, has been on display since 1850, while his real head, which was displayed on a wooden platter between his feet until 1948, is now kept in a safe.

The founders of UCL appear to have envisaged that the college and the university would be one and the same thing (as Trinity College and the University of Dublin had been since 1598), but its right to be known as "London University" was challenged within one year of its opening. Almost as soon as Brougham and his colleagues began raising funds, a campaign for a rival college, which would follow Oxford, Cambridge, and Dublin in being open only to members of the established Church of England (and its offshoot, the Church of Ireland), had been started by a group of bishops and noblemen headed by the Duke of Wellington. Unlike the "godless" Bloomsbury foundation in 1829, this orthodox competitor was given a royal charter which included permission to call itself King's College when it opened two years later on the Strand, then the main street between the cities of London and Westminster. Part of its original building, designed by Sir Robert Smirke to fit with the facade of Somerset House, the government offices next door to it, was torn down in 1966, in spite of protests, to be replaced six years later by a Modernist block.

Neither the two new colleges nor the medical schools had any right to award degrees. In 1836 this crucial function was given to a separate board of examiners, appointed by the British government, which, under its own royal charter of November 1836, was to call itself the Senate of the University of London. Thus the federal university was created as the fourth university in England, just four years after the University of Durham had been founded as the third. Its dependence on the government—in contrast to its predecessors and its own member institutions—was confirmed by its being given office space inside Somerset House.

During its first two decades the new university became the national examining body, not only for UCL and King's but also for 30 colleges in other cities in Great Britain and Ireland as well as for 69 medical schools, including the 8 in London which have already been mentioned, the medical faculties of UCL and King's, which had created their own hospitals in 1837 and 1840 respectively, and the new medical school at Saint Mary's Hospital in Paddington, founded in 1854. In 1853 the university left Somerset House for another government block, Marlborough House, but moved on again only three years later to Burlington House. There in 1858 the senate began promoting the teaching of the

natural sciences on the basis of practical as well as written work by introducing examinations for the bachelor of science and doctor of science, building on the success of such institutions as UCL's Birkbeck Laboratory, founded in 1846 as the first university chemistry laboratory in the United Kingdom.

In the same year the university received its second royal charter, which opened its examinations, except in medicine, to all who wished to take them, regardless of the school or college at which they had studied. This was the origin of the distinction, formalized in 1900, between "internal" students, taught at the university's colleges and medical schools, and "external" students. Under this unprecedented arrangement the numbers taking examinations rose from 358 in 1855 to 1,459 in 1870. After 1865, many students who were living in Mauritius, Gibraltar, and Canada were allowed to take the examination in their home countries. In just 30 years the university had passed from being a local compromise between UCL and King's to being already one of the leading educational bodies in the British Empire, and not only through its own examinations. Its model of an examining university separated from teaching colleges was first borrowed for the Queen's University of Ireland (now the National University) in 1850. This was to be followed by the University of Toronto in Canada in 1853, the three university colleges of India set up at Calcutta, Bombay, and Madras in 1857, the University of New Zealand in 1874 and, in England itself, the Victoria University, established in 1880 to provide examinations for colleges in Manchester, Leeds, and Liverpool, all of which had used the London examinations until that year. (The Victoria University was abolished in 1903 and its three colleges became separate universities.)

As the University of London grew, two events signaled that it had at last gained official acceptance on equal terms with the three other English universities, the six in Scotland, and Trinity College, Dublin. In 1867 its graduates, who form the university's convocation, were given the right to elect a member of parliament to represent the university, a right which they exercised until the abolition of the university seats in 1950.

In 1870 the university moved into its first purpose-built headquarters, after three years during which the building was being constructed and the university officials worked in a house in Savile Row. The university building in Burlington Gardens now houses the Museum of Mankind, a branch of the British Museum, but the university insignia and the statues which were installed in 1870 can still be seen there.

In 1869 the university further extended its unique openness to types of students excluded from other British universities by introducing examinations for women, who until then had had access to higher education only at two small colleges which were located in London but did not belong to the university—Queen's College, founded in 1848, and Bedford College, founded in 1849.

At first the women's examinations led only to certificates of study, but in 1880 the university became the first in the British Empire to award degrees on equal terms to men and women, two years after UCL had become the first British college to admit women as full members. King's College, in contrast, kept women literally at a distance, offering lectures for them in Kensington, four miles from its main buildings, from 1878 and creating a formal ladies' department there in 1885. This became the women's department in 1902, King's College for Women in 1908, King's College of Household and Social Sciences in 1928, and Queen Elizabeth College, for both women and men, in 1953. At last, 100 years after its foundation, it became once again an integral part of King's College. Meanwhile, the availability of degrees brought a group of women's colleges into membership in the university. These were Bedford College (but not Queen's, which became a girls' school); the London School of Medicine for Women, which had been set up in 1874 and was later made into the Royal Free Hospital School of Medicine; Westfield College, founded in 1882; and Royal Holloway College, opened in 1886 in an enormous French Renaissance building, with its own picture gallery provided by its founder, the businessman Thomas Holloway, on Egham Hill (then in the county of Surrey, now in Greater London).

Between 1870 and 1895 the numbers of men and women taking the university's various examinations rose from 1,459 to 6,219. Even as this increase continued the university became divided by controversy over its structure, as UCL, King's, and 10 London medical schools, the 12 largest members of the university, sought degree-giving powers of their own. The whole system was investigated inconclusively by a royal commission in 1888, and in 1891 plans were made for a separate Albert University, which would provide both teaching and examinations on the traditional model for the 12 colleges, leaving the University of London as an examining board for a variety of smaller institutions. These were abandoned in the face of opposition within UCL and among politicians in favor of a second royal commission, which eventually led to the London University Act, passed by parliament in 1898.

The result was a new set of statutes for the university, which came into effect in 1900, the same year that its headquarters moved yet again, this time to the Imperial Institute, a grandiose neo-Gothic building in South Kensington. The senate was overhauled to represent alumni, teachers, the Inns of Court (as mentioned above), and local government bodies as well as the national government. The university was to have two categories of members: in London a variety of smaller colleges known as "institutions having recognized teachers," which had their courses validated by the university but remained separate; and those institutions which were full members of the federation. This second group included not only all the member institutions mentioned so far, but also six small colleges run by various Christian denominations (none now in the university); the South Eastern Agricultural College in the county of Kent, which had been founded in 1894 and which is now called Wye College; the Royal College of Science (incorporating the Royal School of Mines) and the Central Technical College, both in South Kensington; and one of the most famous and influential members of the federation, the London School of Economics and Political Science (the LSE).

The first institution of its kind in Britain, the LSE was established in 1895 by Sidney and Beatrice Webb, leading lights in the Fabian Society, an influential group of socialist intellectuals, using money left by their friend Henry Hutchinson to be used for the purposes of the society and its version of socialism. However, the Webbs rebuffed the efforts of their friend and colleague, the playwright George Bernard Shaw, to make the school an avowedly socialist institution, preferring to dedicate it to the impartial investigation of economic and social questions, thus attracting vital support from such conservative bodies as the London Chamber of Commerce. One has to wonder, not only what Hutchinson would have thought of the way that the Webbs interpreted his will, but why they believed that impartiality could be achieved in such inevitably controversial subjects. In any event, the LSE has been a lively forum of debate as well as a leading international center of teaching and research across the range of social studies, its staff having included such decidedly anti-socialist thinkers as Friedrich Hayek and Karl Popper alongside, for example, William Beveridge, a member of the Liberal Party whose famous report, *Social Insurance* (1942), laid the foundations for the British welfare state, and the political scientist Harold Laski, a prominent member of the Labour Party.

Now that the university, already the largest in the British Empire, was active in promoting teaching and research, as well as in examining their results, it expanded further, mainly by taking in several more institutions which had existed separately. In 1905 the Goldsmiths' Company gave their Technical and Recreative Institute, founded in 1891 at New Cross in south London, to the university, which renamed it Goldsmiths' College. In 1907 and 1910 respectively, UCL and King's gave up their independent governing bodies, becoming departments of the university itself. Also in 1907 the South Kensington scientific schools were merged, becoming the Imperial College of Science and Technology, and the East London College, originating in 1887 as part of the "People's Palace" group of schools created for the poor of the East End of London, joined the federation, being renamed Queen Mary College in 1934. In 1916 a School of Oriental Studies was created, taking over teachers, books, and other resources from parts of UCL and King's; it became the School of Oriental and African Studies (SOAS) in 1938. Birkbeck College, which had been founded as the London Mechanics' Institute in 1823 by George Birkbeck (later a member of the first council of UCL), was brought into the university in 1920. It continues to specialize in offering part-time and evening courses for people who wish to study for a university degree while working. The London School of Hygiene and Tropical Medicine was created in 1924 as an expansion of the School of Tropical Medicine created in 1899, and in 1929 it moved into its own building (which had become well-known for the larger-than-life-size reliefs of fleas and other disease carriers on its frontage). In 1925 the School of Pharmacy, founded in 1842, also joined the university.

The university's existing member institutions by no means stood still while these new members were being admitted. For example, while Imperial College led the way in promoting training and research in such new industries as aeronautics, chemical engineering, and petroleum geology, UCL and King's were among the first colleges in Britain to develop courses in electrical engineering; Sir Ambrose Fleming, a professor at UCL, collaborated with Edison and Marconi in work on lighting, power supply, and radio. In addition, the university as a whole made decisive moves into providing for postgraduate studies, awarding its first Ph.D.s in 1921, the same year that the senate created the first of the university's institutes for advanced study, the Institute of Historical Research (the IHR). However, the most outstanding result of the university's research efforts between the world wars was the discovery of penicillin by Sir Alexander Fleming (no relation to Sir Ambrose) at Saint Mary's Hospital Medical School in 1928.

The year 1929 proved to be a turning point in the university's history. As yet another new set of statutes came into effect, the non-university members of the senate were replaced by the heads of the larger colleges; a new body, the court, was appointed by the senate, the London County Council, and the government to administer the university's finances; and serious work began on the removal of the university's headquarters and some of its member institutions to a 10.5-acre site in Bloomsbury, near UCL, LSE, and the British Museum. In 1931, the Modernist architect Charles Holden, well-known for designing 40 stations on the Tube (the London Underground rail network), was invited to design the new university quarters, and produced a plan for a single huge structure of Portland stone, culminating in a tower, which would be the tallest building in the city. The tower and two wings at its base were completed in 1937. This building, known as the Senate House, now contains the university's main offices, its library, the IHR, and the School of East European and Slavonic Studies (SEESS). However, partly for financial reasons, a new "balanced" plan was agreed for a group of separate buildings, which together would represent only around one-third of Holden's original "spinal" complex.

Even as Holden's plans were being considered and reshaped the university continued its piecemeal growth.

In 1932 alone it took over the Slavonic studies department which King's College had founded in 1915, creating what is now SEESS, converted the London County Council's Day Training College for teachers into its own Institute of Education, and used an enormous endowment from the textile magnate Samuel Courtauld to open the Courtauld Institute of Art. While the institute itself introduced the discipline of art history to Britain, its galleries, which were at first housed separately, quickly became famous as one of the most important art collections in the country. The two parts of what is affectionately called simply "the Courtauld" were brought together at last in 1989 inside Somerset House, where the university had begun, and where such masterpieces as van Gogh's "Portrait of the Artist with Bandaged Ear" and Manet's "A Bar at the Folies-Bergère" now attract large numbers of visitors. Still another institute, the Institute of Archaeology, was founded in 1937, at the suggestion of Sir Mortimer Wheeler. All the while the numbers of "external" students were steadily rising, both in Britain and overseas. From 1920 onward it became possible to take the university's examinations in places outside the British Empire, and by 1937 there were nearly 5,000 students enrolled at 79 different "overseas centers" of the university, in an academic network which was then and still remains unique.

The outbreak of World War II in 1939 put a stop to all new building plans, as most of the university's schools and institutes were evacuated from London, and the Senate House was taken over by the wartime Ministry of Information. (It is believed to have provided part of the inspiration for the Ministry of Truth in George Orwell's novel *1984,* and indeed its tower appears as such in the feature film based on the novel.) During the war UCL suffered particularly badly from German bombing raids: its library and many other buildings were destroyed and its dome, the symbol of the college, was badly burned. As for the war effort, the university's greatest contribution to it was the work done by Lord Blackett of Imperial College, J.D. Bernal of Birkbeck, and other members of a group known as "Blackett's Circus," whose operational research techniques, developed for military purposes, were later to be adapted to industrial management.

The university began planning further expansion even before the war ended in 1945. The Warburg Institute, a re-creation of the Kulturwissenschaftliche Bibliothek Warburg, which had been brought from Hamburg after the Nazis seized power in Germany in 1933, was made part of the university in 1944 and has since pioneered work in the relatively new field of cultural studies. A new British Postgraduate Medical Federation, uniting several specialist institutes, was established in 1947, and the Royal Veterinary College, founded in 1791, joined the university in 1949. Four more institutes for advanced study were created as well—Advanced Legal Studies in 1947, Commonwealth Studies in 1949, Germanic Studies in 1950, and Classical Studies in 1953.

Along with the Warburg Institute and (for some years) the Courtauld Institute Galleries, all were eventually given space on the Bloomsbury site around the Senate House, where brick buildings designed by Holden took the place of his Portland stone masterpiece, never to be built. They were joined there by the Institute of Education (at first inside the Senate House), SEESS and the IHR (which are still inside it), SOAS and Birkbeck College, the Percival David Foundation of Chinese Art, a research institute and gallery created in 1950, and the University of London Union (ULU), which, along with the library inside the Senate House, is one of the very few university-wide bodies with which most of its students ever have direct contact.

As mentioned above, the university lost its examining powers for three colleges in Manchester, Leeds, and Liverpool in 1880, and between then and 1945 its links with colleges in Birmingham, Sheffield, Bristol, Nottingham, and Reading were also severed as, one by one, they too became independent "civic" universities. Between 1946 and 1971 the University of London entered the last phase of its special role as a "mother of universities." As the British Empire was transformed by the colonial independence movement, first into the British Commonwealth and then into just the Commonwealth, a total of eight colleges in the colonies that became Sudan, Ghana, Uganda, Zambia, Kenya, Tanzania, and Malawi were given special "internal" status, which helped them prepare to become national universities after independence. Similar provisions were made for the British colleges which have since become the Universities of Southampton, Hull, Exeter, and Leicester, as well as for a number of teacher-training colleges which have since joined other universities.

By the 1960s the internal structures of the university were coming under increasing criticism for what was seen as excessive centralization. A number of reforms throughout the decade gave greater powers over course content and postgraduate work to the larger colleges and made the university's boards of studies more representative of all the teaching staff, not just the more senior among them. Give that, for example, UCL, King's, LSE, and Imperial were now each as large and as complex as most of the ordinary British universities, it is perhaps not surprising that these changes were not considered sufficient, and in 1978 parliament introduced further changes through a new University of London Act. King's and UCL became autonomous institutions once again, in 1980 and 1977 respectively; the vice-chancellorship became a full-time salaried post; and the senate was reformed yet again, to give the member institutions greater representation and to provide seats for student representatives for the first time.

The two decades of internal upheaval were also a period of accelerated expansion in the University of London as in British higher education in general. The university's total number of students rose from nearly 54,000 in 1960 to around 64,000 in 1980, although within these figures there was a significant decline in the numbers of external students, mainly because most of the centers at which they had traditionally taken examinations had themselves become degree-granting bodies. New members joined the federation, too. An Institute of Computer Science, existing from 1964 to 1972, led the way in converting many of the colleges to new technologies; Institutes of Latin American Studies and of United States Studies, founded in 1965, completed the university's intellectual coverage of the world; and in 1969 the university took charge of the British Institute in Paris, which had been founded in 1894 as the Guilde Franco-Anglais and which still continues to provide courses in French studies for British students and in British studies for French students. Lastly, in 1970 Heythrop College, which specializes in Catholic theology, became the newest member of the federation and at the same time one of its oldest, since it traces its origins to an English Jesuit college established in Leuven (Louvain), now in Belgium, in 1614.

However, the same general process of expansion also brought new institutions into the field of higher education in the London region, breaking the degree-granting monopoly which the university had enjoyed since 1836. From 1964 onwards a number of polytechnics all over England were allowed to give degrees which were validated by a new government body until the 1990s, when all of them became independent universities, further reducing the numbers of external students taking University of London examinations. In 1966 three former colleges of advanced technology were reconstituted as the City University, Brunel University, and the University of Surrey, while a fourth joined the federation as Chelsea College. Finally, in 1969, the Open University was set up to provide "distance learning" through radio, television, and correspondence courses and to supplant the University of London both as the largest university in Britain (in terms of student numbers) and as the leading source of degrees for those combining employment with study.

The late 1960s were also notable, of course, for the eruption of student protests in major cities around the world, fueled by a combination of local grievances, rejection of the traditional professor/student hierarchy, and indignation about events in Vietnam, Czechoslovakia, South Africa, Rhodesia (now Zimbabwe), and other areas of conflict. In Britain the movement began at LSE in January 1967, when Sir Walter Adams, long associated with higher education in Rhodesia, was appointed its director; conflict spread to other colleges and universities throughout 1967 and 1968. Offices were occupied, classes were disrupted, and numerous demonstrations took place, but their only long-term effects were to increase student representation on university bodies and to give LSE and a few other institutions a misleading reputation for political radicalism. By 1970 the movement, always disorganized and chaotic, had petered out.

While still coping with the effects of frequent and complex internal reforms and greatly increased external competition, the University of London next had to face the problems created for all British universities from 1981, when Margaret Thatcher's government decided to cut public spending on higher education for the first time since the university itself had been created by such spending. One response was to encourage a series of mergers among member institutions. In line with changes in the pattern of National Health Service provision in London, the number of hospital-based medical schools has been reduced from the original 12 (all founded up to 1874) to 8, of which two have been reabsorbed into the colleges that originally created them, UCL and King's. The non-medical colleges were also reorganized. Royal Holloway and Bedford Colleges were amalgamated in 1985, and the "New College" thus created, known at first as RH&BNC but now simply as Royal Holloway, was located at Egham Hill, while the old Bedford College in Regents Park was sold off. In the same year Queen Elizabeth and Chelsea Colleges were absorbed into King's (which was briefly known as KQC as a result). In 1987 the IHR took over the Institute of United States Studies, and UCL absorbed the Institute of Archaeology; in 1989, Queen Mary and Westfield Colleges were merged.

An alternative response to the decline in public spending was to seek more funding from private sources, with the result that UCL, Imperial, and LSE, in particular, became larger and wealthier; there was speculation that they might eventually break away from the federation. For the moment, the university remains intact, but since September 1994 it has been governed under yet another set of revised statutes, which have given still more financial and academic autonomy to the larger member institutions. The court, which had grown to have 24 members, and the senate, which had an unwieldy total of 120, have been replaced by a single council, which it is hoped will be more efficient, although the headquarters is still known as the Senate House.

The university which the new council is to govern is still, after so many changes, one of the largest and most diverse in the world, comprising (as of 1995) nine medical schools, six multi-faculty colleges, nine specialist schools, and nine institutes; and, in a looser relationship, the London Business School, Jews College, the Royal Academy of Music, and the Trinity College of Music, the last of the "institutions having recognized teachers." Over the past one and a half centuries the numerous British colleges which the university fostered have become independent, the empire which it served has disappeared, and it is no longer even the only university in London. These developments may make it harder to appreciate just how radical, even shocking, it once was—perhaps especially in imperial yet insular Britain—to construct a university largely with public rather than privileged private funds, to operate it without regard for religion, gender, wealth, or other social divisions, and to make its resources available to anyone who was willing and able to benefit from them (not just in London but across the planet).

Further Reading: This essay could not have been written without recourse to Negley Harte's impressive book *The University of London 1836–1986* (London and Atlantic Highlands, New Jersey: Athlone Press, 1986), which, in spite of its title, gives comprehensive coverage of all the member institutions of the university from 1123 to its year of publication, enlivening the narrative with numerous anecdotes and vignettes as well as over 350 pictures. There are several histories of the leading member institutions, including *The World of University College London, 1828–1978* by Negley Harte and John North (London: University College, 1978); *King's College, London, 1828–1978* by Gordon Huelin (London: University of London, King's College, 1978); and *My LSE,* edited by Ronald Hayman (London: Robson Books, 1977), which is a collection of memoirs by former students.

—Patrick Heenan

UNIVERSITY OF LOUVAIN
(Louvain, Belgium)

Location: The three campuses form a triangle connecting the town of Leuven (Louvain), the new community at Louvain-la-Neuve near Ottignies, and Louvain-en-Woluwe, a suburb of Brussels. Each campus is approximately 18 miles from each of the other two.

Description: Divided by a dispute over language in the late 1960s, the Katholieke Universiteit te Leuven (KUL) and the Université de Louvain (UCL) each enroll over 20,000 undergraduate and graduate students. Five thousand of those enrolled at UCL study at the facility at Woluwe, which includes the faculty of medicine and several graduate research institutes in science and business.

Information: KU Leuven
22 Naamsestraat
B-3000, Leuven
Belgium
(16) 28 40 24

UCL Service des relations extérieures
Place de l'université, 1
B-1348 Louvain-la-Neuve
Belgium
(10) 47 81 01

UCL-in-Woluwe: (02) 764 41 28

Visiting: For information on guided tours, call the telephone numbers listed above.

In a country whose population is divided along linguistic lines (Flemish in the north, French in the south, and bilingualism in the capital city of Brussels), it is not at all surprising that Belgium's oldest and largest university found it necessary to divide itself in the same way. The language dispute can be traced to the fifth century, when some Frankish tribes held onto their Germanic origins, while others were influenced by the Roman traditions and the Latin language. Religion, too, played an important role in the history of Catholic Belgium, whose citizens never felt comfortable with either the Protestantism of the Dutch or the anticlericalism of the French Revolution. The University of Louvain is a testament to the influence of religion and language on intellectual thought.

The university was established on December 9, 1425, when Duke John IV of Brabant, with the support of the local magistrate, secured a papal bull from Pope Martin V to open a *studium generale* to train doctors, men of law, and eventually, theologians. A joint effort of the Church, the ducal authority, and the local officials, the university was intended to help unify the Belgian provinces. Scholars from the Low Countries would no longer have to study at Paris or Cologne. The university first opened with four faculties: arts (humanities), canon law, civil law, and medicine. The faculty of theology was added in 1432.

The growth of the university was slowed during the fifteenth century by plagues, economic hard times, and the instability caused by the warfare between the Hapsburgs and the Burgundians. However, the first half of the sixteenth century was a period of prosperity and glory for Louvain, with its theological quarrels with the ideas of Martin Luther. Desiderius Erasmus of Rotterdam (best known as the author of *Praise of Folly*) was on the faculty from 1517 to 1521 and dominated the side of the humanists, seeming to thrive on the controversy of his time. He once wrote to a friend about Louvain: "Its climate is not only agreeable, but also healthy; a man can study in peace and quiet, and no other university can rival its intellectual life, or the numbers and quality of its academic staff."

That Erasmus could have found peace and quiet at Louvain is a mystery in that he was frequently attacked by his conservative colleagues. When opposition from the faculty threatened the funding of his College of the Three Languages, Erasmus decided to establish a separate institute independent of the university. He set about recruiting teachers who would instruct theologians in Latin, Greek, and Hebrew as part of a liberal Catholic education, which would allow for more open interpretation of the scriptures. His critics regarded this idea as a threat to orthodox teaching and as an open invitation to heresy. Arguing that only the Vulgate, the Latin translation of the Bible, could be a source of dogma, they attacked his proposal for an original language edition of the New Testament as sacrilegious. Erasmus sought to make theology more critical by referring to original texts. He criticized the emphasis on ecclesiastical practices and advocated a return to a morality based on the gospels. While he reproached Luther for the sharpness of his style, he was open to at least some of Luther's ideas. When he refused to succumb to pressure to denounce Luther publicly, he was accused of collaborating with him. The university condemned Luther in 1519, and as his position as an independent reformer became more and more untenable, Erasmus felt obliged to leave Louvain for Basel, Switzerland, in 1521.

Erasmus was not the only thinker to meet with resistance at Louvain. Some of the university's most illustrious faculty suffered a similar fate. Gerardus Mercator, the renowned cartographer, a student and later a professor of geography, was driven out of the country in 1544. He and Andreas Vesalius, who modernized the study of human anatomy, taught side by side with classicists. Most of the teaching at Louvain during the sixteenth century was devoted to the study of antiquity and opposed to the idea of making knowledge accessible to the lower classes. Convinced that educating the masses would undermine the authority of the princes and the clergy, the university continued to perpetuate an intellectual elite. One of Louvain's most famous history professors, Justus Lipsius, dedicated himself to studying Seneca and Tacitus and to publishing editions of those writers and other classical figures.

During the Reformation, the great questions of the age had to do with free will versus predestination, the meaning of original sin, and the infallibility of the pope. The theologians at Louvain clung steadfastly to the ideas of Aristotle and Thomas Aquinas. Their contributions to this period included the creation of an index of censured books that became a model for the Catholic Church's Index of Forbidden Books, and the publication of a new Latin translation of the Bible, the "Louvain Bible" of 1547.

By the end of the sixteenth century, Belgium's population decreased as Calvinists emigrated rather than face the policies and practices of Philip II of Spain, who ruled the region and sought to wipe out opposition to Catholicism. As commerce slowed, Louvain's population went from 20,000 to 9,000; with the university no longer enjoying its former prestige, intellectual decay set in. Part of the problem stemmed from the reorganization of the bishoprics, whereby Louvain became part of the diocese of Mechelen (Malines) instead of Liège. In addition, it now had to compete against universities at Douai (under the Spanish Netherlands) and Leiden (a Calvinist university established to oppose Spanish Catholicism). When economic and political troubles occurred at the end of the century, the university at Louvain encountered difficulties in meeting professors' stipends. Following an attack on the town in 1572 by the Calvinist William the Silent, leading a revolt against the Spanish rulers, a garrison was sent to keep order. However, when the soldiers were not paid, they turned to vandalism. Furthermore, the plague of 1578 claimed the lives of many faculty members. Fewer and fewer students came to Louvain during these years.

A period of relative tranquillity followed the appointment of the Hapsburg archduke Albert of Austria as governor of the Low Countries. Shortly after his death, however, Louvain became embroiled in a dispute between the Spanish Netherlands and Louis XIII of France and Frederick Henry of Orange. In 1635 the townspeople and the students joined forces to take up arms against the Spanish governor.

The seventeenth and eighteenth centuries produced only mediocre scholarship. The leaders of the university officially rejected the Cartesian philosophy which had caught on in France in favor of the more traditional Aristotelian philosophy in 1652.

During the eighteenth century Austrian authorities sought to make reforms at Louvain in order to raise its standards. They withdrew the right of the university to appoint its own rector. After the French Revolution, control of Louvain alternated between France and Austria until 1797, when the university was closed after almost 400 years of existence. Many priests who had been teaching there refused to take the oath to the new French republic, and so were exiled. Students continued their studies in Brussels or in France.

In 1814 some of the former professors suggested reopening the university in its original form. The local authorities preferred a university based on the French model, and others opposed the idea of reopening the school altogether, citing Louvain's opposition to the Enlightenment. However, two years later, William I, king of the new union of Belgium and the Netherlands, established three state universities in the southern Low Countries: at Ghent, Liège, and Louvain. The university was officially reopened in 1817.

The liberals and the Catholics in the community did not like William's authoritarian government; many students joined the rebellion of 1830, part of a larger revolution ending the Belgium-Netherlands union and giving rise to the independent kingdom of Belgium. Disorder marked the next few years at Louvain. Some wanted a single state university for all of Belgium; others wished to retain only Ghent and Liège. In 1835, it was decided that only Ghent and Liège would be supported by the state. The bishops, who had established a Catholic university at Mechelen in 1834, took advantage of this opportunity to move their university to Louvain.

The new university was to continue the traditions of the old one, except that there were no ties to the state, as provided by Belgium's new constitution. Funds came from tuition and charitable contributions. Discipline was rigorous, and professional training was more important than scholarship. While French replaced Latin as the language of instruction, there were classes in Flemish language and literature that were not offered at other Belgian universities.

Some students, believing that Louvain had become too conservative, transferred to Brussels. Some conservatives on the staff felt that the administration was too liberal, and they sought positions at other universities. Internal struggles continued through the next few decades, with the conservatives gaining many concessions, such as the power to appoint faculty and to oversee lectures.

A new law in 1876 allowing the university to create its own examination encouraged experimentation in science courses. New schools opened in engineering and agronomy with the intent of improving Belgium's agricultural economy and preserving Catholicism among the peasants and industrial workers. As the student body began to come from the middle classes, student life became more relaxed. The university's need to expand to meet the needs of its growing population often resulted in financial strain.

Toward the end of the century, there was less emphasis on teaching and more on scholarly research. Study groups formed in theology and humanities classes, and student organizations began to develop. One group which called for promoting the Flemish language encountered resistance from the Walloon (French-speaking) students. Nevertheless, more courses were offered in Flemish and more documents were published in both languages as a result.

By 1900 more capital was found to resolve some of the university's financial difficulties and to build new facilities. New institutes were set up in bacteriology, pathology, and geology. Petitions for duplication of courses in both languages, however, were denied on financial grounds. This increased the tension between the two groups. Finally in 1911 more classes were added in Flemish, along with new courses in art history, dentistry, and banking.

When the Germans invaded Louvain in 1914, about one-third of the existing buildings were burned down. The university was forced to close for the duration of the war, since many of its professors had left to teach abroad, and the administration did not want to give in to German censorship. Professors who remained in Louvain busied themselves with research or with looking for books to replace those lost when the library was burned. When the university opened once again in 1919, Belgian bishops sent out an international appeal to rebuild the library. The Treaty of Versailles stipulated that the Germans had to compensate Louvain for any lost treasures.

As funds were secured from the bishops' appeals and from Belgian and American citizens, the university began to rebuild. More students matriculated than ever before, and women were accepted as students for the first time in 1920. Under pressure from Flemish groups, the duplication of classes in two languages was increased. Until 1923, Louvain was the only Belgian university which had classes taught in both Flemish and French. Nevertheless, tensions between the two groups over the language question continued to mount. When the administration tried to suppress the militant groups, the Flemings rebelled by boycotting the 500th anniversary celebration in 1927. By 1932, almost all classes were taught in Flemish as well as in French.

The town of Louvain had to be evacuated in May 1940 when Belgium was invaded by the Germans a second time. Once again fire destroyed many of the buildings, including the rebuilt library. The rector reopened classes at the university in July, but the community suffered many problems during the occupation. There was a large increase in enrollment because the University of Brussels closed in 1941 and because many young people preferred to register for classes rather than submit to forced labor under the Germans. The increase in the number of students from 4,600 at the start of the war to 7,700 by 1943 put a strain on the university's resources.

Students had to work under uncomfortably crowded conditions and endure shortages of materials, food, and heat. When the rector refused to release the first-year students to work in the German factories, he was arrested and sent to prison, although the sentence was soon commuted to house arrest. The vice-rector set up clandestine lectures and examinations for students who were not allowed to register officially. When the town was repeatedly hit by Allied bombs in 1944, many of the university's buildings were destroyed and some of the students and faculty killed. More damage was done as the Germans retreated, making it necessary for the town and the university to go about the task of rebuilding once again.

After the war, the university responded to the increased social needs of the students by assigning advisors and counselors to give them guidance. Academically, new institutes were set up in archaeology, art history, African studies, and other disciplines. In 1954 funds were allocated to establish a sister center of learning, Lovanium University, in the Belgian Congo in order to meet the needs of African students.

The language issue came to a head again in the 1960s. Despite the duplication of courses and the hiring of Flemish faculty, the administration continued to hold its meetings in French, and French culture prevailed. When, in 1960, the number of Flemings outnumbered the Walloons, the Flemish students and professors began to press for more autonomy. While some were willing to accept bilingual status for Louvain on the model of Brussels, the majority felt that this solution was unacceptable, since Louvain was in Flemish territory. The Francophone professors, on the other hand, wanted their children to learn French in school.

When the issue could not be resolved by dividing the university into two separate sections under separate deans, pressure mounted to transfer the French section to Wallonia, the French-speaking part of Belgium. The medical school had already moved its facility to Woluwe-Saint-Lambert, a suburb of Brussels, in 1965. Proponents of the move argued that Louvain was much too small a town to accommodate the increasingly large student body. Opponents feared that Louvain would lose its status as a world-class university. The debate divided students, faculty, bishops, and eventually the Christian Social party. In 1968 a plan was approved to separate the Katholieke Universiteit te Leuven (KU Leuven), which was to remain in Louvain, from the Université Catholique de

Louvain (UCL), which was to be relocated in French-speaking territory 15 miles southwest of Louvain in Louvain-la-Neuve, a community to be built between Wavre and Ottignies. A law passed in May 1970 recognized the existence of two separate universities, and the first stone was laid at Louvain-la-Neuve in 1971.

The division had some advantages. The new university, while a Catholic institution, was led primarily by lay people who abandoned the former authoritarian policies in favor of a new open-mindedness. State subsidies were increased, allowing for the expansion of the facilities at KU Leuven and the building of a well-planned university community at UCL. Each section was able to serve over 16,000 students by 1975. On the negative side, the decision to divide the existing library in half by allocating books with even-numbered call letters to one facility and books with odd-numbered call letters to the other has devastated the historic collection.

During the 1970s, nine faculties moved to the new campus at Louvain-la-Neuve, including theology, law, philosophy, economics, and science. Built on a 2,300-acre parcel of land, the new city boasts residential, business, and university sections. Twenty percent of its students come from over 100 foreign countries, many of them on scholarships aimed at benefiting third world countries. Université Catholique de Louvain also has a commitment to continuing education, offering outreach programs for teachers, professional people, and senior citizens. A large science park allows for cooperation between university research and industrial applications, such as pharmaceutical and agricultural products and informational technology. The first two years of undergraduate education serve as an introduction to the basic academic subjects from which the student chooses an area of specialization. Students who fail are provided assistance in choosing an alternative program of study. Clearly, the university's mission has moved forward from the perpetuation of an elite toward the education of a diverse student body.

The rural location of Louvain-la-Neuve has afforded the campus the space to create a large sports complex, an experimental theater, a museum, and the Bois de Lauzelle, a forested park ideally suited for nature walks. It is not surprising that this well-planned and well-maintained community has become one of Belgium's most popular tourist attractions.

Louvain-en-Woluwe, located on the outskirts of Brussels, has benefited as much from its proximity to the city as Louvain-la-Neuve has from its location in the country. Its hospitals and clinics serve a vast community, providing relief to the sick and education to those pursuing careers in medicine, dentistry, pharmacy, and public health. Its many institutes provide research in cancer, bioethics, cellular pathology, and organ transplants. Administratively part of the UCL, it has its own science park and its own partnerships with companies involved in medical research. Visitors to UCL in Woluwe can visit the Garden of Medicinal Plants, with its systematic classification of plants, or try their mountaineering skills on the climbing wall next to the sports center.

Katholieke Universiteit te Leuven has not been idle since 1970. It, too, has expanded its facilities and services. The human sciences section surrounds the heart of the city of Louvain, while the biomedical sciences occupy the west side of the city near St. Peter's and St. Raphael's hospitals. Katholieke Universiteit te Leuven has the added advantage of being surrounded by nearly six centuries of European history. Its many student cafés and its dynamic cultural life add to the charm of this old university town.

All three campuses of the University of Louvain can boast of the unique geographical position of Louvain within Europe. Brussels, the center of NATO and of the European Economic Community, has become Europe's unofficial capital. Its international spirit and cosmopolitan character have influenced the new University of Louvain: humanistic, practical, and accessible to all who wish to learn.

Further Reading: *The University of Louvain 1425–1975* by R. Aubert, A. d'Haenens et al. (Louvain: Leuven University Press, 1975) is a complete, balanced, and beautifully illustrated history of the university from its beginnings through the years of separation written on the occasion of its 550th anniversary. It gives a detailed account of its most famous students and faculty and of the movements that shaped its history. *Belgium: The Making of a Nation* by H. Vander Linden, translated by Sybil Jane (Oxford: Clarendon Press, 1920) is a valuable, if generalized, history of Belgium. Linden examines the social, economic, religious, and political movements that helped to shape modern Belgium. *Erasmus: His Life, Works, and Influence,* by Cornelis Augustin, translated by J.C. Grayson (Toronto: Toronto University Press, 1991), is an in-depth study of the life and writings of Erasmus and of the criticism of his contemporaries. Flora Lewis's *Europe, a Tapestry of Nations* (New York: Simon and Schuster, 1987) gives an excellent overview of the Belgian language dispute in the chapter entitled "Belgium: Divided by Language."

—Sherry Crane LaRue

UNIVERSITY OF MANCHESTER
(Manchester, England)

Location: About one mile from the city center, on Oxford Road. Manchester is about 180 miles north of London and 210 miles south of Edinburgh, Scotland.

Description: The oldest and largest of England's civic universities, with nearly 16,000 full-time undergraduate students and 4,000 postgraduate students.

Information: Registrar's Department
The University of Manchester
Oxford Road
Manchester M13 9PL
England
(161) 275 2113
Fax (161) 275 2209

Visiting: Call the Communications Office at the telephone number above.

The city of Manchester, England, was settled by the Romans in A.D. 79. They called it *Mamucium* (city of tents) and remained there for over 300 years. In 1359, Manchester became a market town, to which people flocked on market days to buy and sell. In the sixteenth century, Manchester saw the beginnings of a prosperous textile industry, and by the late eighteenth century, Manchester was the largest textile producer in the world, with the mills powered by the vast quantity of coal, which was both nearby and abundant. Located in the heart of Britain, on the River Irwill, lying almost exactly between London and Edinburgh, and accessible to the port of Liverpool, Manchester grew to be the central city in Britain's Industrial Revolution and a powerful international center as well.

One of Manchester's many prosperous merchants, John Owens, who died in 1845, left £96,000 for the founding of a college. Owens's will stated that the purpose of this endowment was "providing or aiding the means of instructing and improving young persons of the male sex (and being of age not less than 14 years) in such branches of learning and science as are now, and may be hereafter, usually taught in the English universities." Owens also wanted to found a school that was free from denominational tests and subscriptions. The only other institution based on similar foundations was University College in London. At its foundation in 1851, the institution was named Owens College.

The original college was located in the former residence of Manchester reformer and economist Richard Cobden on Quay Street. It had 62 students and 5 professors, with A.J. Scott as the principal. Owens College established its first scholarships, the Victoria Scholarship and the Wellington Scholarship, in 1852.

A library was established in the same year as the college, 1851. Just over 120 years later, in 1972, the university library joined with the John Rylands Library. The Rylands Library, established by the third wife of another wealthy Manchester merchant, John Rylands, brought with it an impressive collection of incunabula, Oriental manuscripts, papers of the famous critic John Ruskin, and material related to the pre-Raphaelites. The library presently contains almost 4 million volumes as well as important collections related to railways, private presses, and the Quakers.

One of the early courses offered at the college was geology. In 1851, the paleobotanist W.C. Williamson was appointed to teach it. In its first 100 years, the department of geology focused on the study of stratigraphy and paleontology. In the 1950s, England's first laboratories for the study of experimental petrology were opened at the university. Another first was the establishment of the first chair in organic chemistry in 1874; it was occupied by Professor W. Boyd Dawkins.

While the school did not fare well financially at first, it began to prosper in the 1860s. In 1870 the entrance age for students was raised to 16. In 1872, the much older Manchester School of Medicine (founded in 1824) merged with Owens College. By 1873, the college had outgrown its Quay Street facility and moved to new buildings on its present main site, on Oxford Road. The principal building, designed by Victorian architect Alfred Waterhouse, is still in use today.

In 1874, women were first allowed to attend special lectures specifically designed for them, but they were not permitted to attend classes with men. A vote to allow women was brought before the governors in 1877, but it was denied. The College of Women, which opened nearby that same year, was taken over by the university in 1883.

In 1880, the Victoria University was created under a federal constitution. Owens College was incorporated into this university, but it was still called Owens College, as one of the entities of the university. The other two colleges were the University College of Liverpool and the Yorkshire College at Leeds; both schools later became independent.

In 1903, when the university received a new charter, it was renamed Victoria University of Manchester. It became the first civic university in England, followed by

University of Manchester

schools in Birmingham, Leeds, and Liverpool. After the 1903 charter was granted, businesspeople and local authorities in Manchester became very interested in the school and began to make grants and private donations. The philosophy of the university in the early 1900s was to meet the needs of the community. With this eye toward practicality, in 1904 Manchester became the first British university to offer degrees in pharmacy. It also became one of the first institutions to grant a degree in commercial services. Much later, in 1965, the Manchester Business School was founded.

In 1905, the Faculty of Technology was incorporated into the Victoria University of Manchester. Originally developed in 1824 under the protection of the city of Manchester, this institution, now called the University of Manchester Institute of Science and Technology (UMIST), is financially and constitutionally independent from the Victoria University of Manchester, but it is academically fully integrated with the university. Though UMIST operates under a separate charter, first granted in 1956, with a supplemental charter in 1987, students who graduate from UMIST receive degrees from the University of Manchester. Some of the courses offered at UMIST include astrophysics, chemical engineering, total technology, and civil and structural engineering.

Several renowned scientific achievements have taken place at the University of Manchester. Probably the most notable of these achievements is that of Sir Ernest Rutherford, whose area of concentration was the nature of matter, and specifically, while he was at the University of Manchester, the atom and its radiations. He came to England from his native New Zealand and studied at Cambridge University's Cavendish Laboratory, where he investigated electricity and radioactivity. He took over the chair of physics at the University of Manchester in 1907 on the invitation of his predecessor, Arthur Schuster, himself a well-known researcher in the area of optics, the author of *The Theory of Optics,* and one of the first men to take x-ray photographs in England.

Rutherford won the Nobel Prize for chemistry in 1908 for his studies of radioactivity. In 1909, his studies of alpha particles and radiation led to his theory of atomic structure. He later said of the experiment, "It was almost as incredible as if you fired a 15-inch shell at a piece of tissue paper and it came back and hit you." In 1919, while at the university, he created the first artificially induced nuclear reaction. (In his honor, the rutherford, a unit of radioactivity, was named for him.) Rutherford had several accomplished assistants in his laboratory, including Georg von Hevesy, who won the Nobel Prize for chemistry in 1943 and Hans Geiger, who later developed the Geiger counter.

The university is also home to some of the world's most important astronomical research facilities. The research of Sir Alfred Charles Bernard Lovell, who was on the staff of the university, led to the construction of the Nuffield Radio Astronomy Laboratories, which are part of the university's department of physics and astronomy. The Jodrell Bank Experimental Station, as Nuffield is also called, was founded in 1945 and is located in Cheshire. It housed a steerable radio telescope which was the world's largest steerable parabolic dish until 1971. In 1951, Lovell became the professor of radio astronomy and director of Jodrell Bank. The laboratories now focus on the study of radio sources and the detection of neutral hydrogen in Earth's galaxy and external galaxies.

Also remarkable was the invention of the Manchester Mark 1 or MADM computer. This, the world's first stored program computer, was developed in the late 1940s by F.C. Williams, who took a chair in electrotechnics at the university in 1947; a colleague also involved in the project was Maxwell Newman, who was professor of pure mathematics. By 1949 the MADM was solving mathematical problems. In 1951, the team of computer pioneers at Manchester built an improved version and called it the Mark II, or MEG.

A direct result of the work of these men was the formation in 1964 of the university's department of computer science, the first computer department in a United Kingdom university. Its first class had 11 faculty and 20 students. By 1995, the department had 168 staff and 637 full-time students. It is the largest computer department in the United Kingdom.

By 1995, the University of Manchester was one of the largest unitary, noncollegiate universities in England, with more than 16,000 full-time undergraduate students and 4,000 postgraduates and a faculty of about 1,200. The school has nine faculties: arts, education, law, medicine, theology, science, economic and social studies, business administration, and technology. Within these faculties there are over 70 departments.

The campus covers 280 acres in Manchester, and has branches in other locations as well. Manchester University is home to the Manchester Museum, the University Theater, where the Contact Theatre Company performs, and to the Whitworth Art Gallery. The gallery holds renowned permanent collections of English watercolors, textiles, and wallpapers.

Further Reading: There is an informative article on the early days of the University of Manchester in *A Cyclopedia of Education,* edited by Paul Monroe (New York: Macmillan, 1913; republished by Gale Research Company [Detroit, Michigan], 1968). Edward Neville da Costa Andrade's *Rutherford and the Nature of the Atom* (Garden City, New York: Doubleday, 1964) explores the life and career of Sir Ernest Rutherford and includes information on colleagues and other important scientists of the period.

—Karen Price

UNIVERSITY OF MELBOURNE
(Parkville, Australia)

Location: The campus covers territory in two Melbourne suburbs, Parkville and Carlton.

Description: A public university enrolling approximately 28,000 students in undergraduate, graduate, and professional schools.

Information: Course and Careers Unit
P.O. Box 4048
University of Melbourne
Melbourne, Victoria 3052
Australia
(3) 9344 6543

When the foundation stone of the University of Melbourne was laid on July 3, 1854, it was so well concealed that it was never seen again. Although the stone holds no inscription, records indicate a copper plate underneath it reads in Latin, "This is the first stone of the University of Melbourne, instituted in honour of God for establishing young men in philosophy, literature and piety, cultivating the talent of youth, fostering the arts, extending the bounds of science." The lost inscription also names 23 men who were considered influential in the university's founding.

Some citizens of Melbourne had become determined to establish a university after Australia's first university opened in Sydney in 1852. One of the founding fathers was Sir Redmond Barry, a Supreme Court judge and graduate of Trinity College, Dublin, who was appointed the university's first chancellor. On April 13, 1855, during the University of Melbourne's opening ceremony, Barry told the crowd that he hoped that the university would become "the nursing mother and generous instructress of a race of distinguished scholars."

The university's true founder was Hugh Culling Eardley Childers, who arrived in Melbourne in 1850 at the age of 23 and served as vice chancellor during the university's early days. He had studied at Oxford and was a Cambridge graduate. Although Parliament rejected his idea for a unified system of education, his experience as the inspector of denominational schools in Australia earned him an appointment as auditor-general and as an official nominee on the Legislative Council.

In November 1852, Charles La Trobe, the lieutenant governor of Victoria, voted £10,000 for the establishment of a university for Melbourne. On January 22, 1853, the bill for establishment of the university was given royal assent. By February 1853 a bill had passed through Legislative Council which granted £20,000 annually for university buildings and another £9,000 annually for university expenses. The legislation specified that the university be "open to all classes and denominations of Her Majesty's subjects" and that "no religious test shall be administered to any person" before he became a student or office holder.

Childers authored the original draft of the bill for the university's establishment. The draft has since become one of the institution's most prized possessions. Childers later became Chancellor of the Exchequer in England.

Although the University of Melbourne is now considered a distinguished school by many scholars, it had very humble beginnings, which, ironically coincided with a period of prosperity for the country. On the minds of many individuals in the mid-1800s was the greed for gold. Furthermore, most of these people wanted to find gold and return to Europe with their fortunes. Gold fields were found within 100 miles of Melbourne, which helped to boost the city's population to 25,000 during the 1850s. Author W.H. Newnham would reflect years later that, "it is strange that though the university was built on the optimism and prosperity that came with the discovery of gold, those who made fortunes out of gold contributed practically nothing at all to its development."

The university's chosen site was in Carlton, a suburb of Melbourne. Professors had to travel toward town to the Carlton Hotel to pick up mail at the nearest carrier drop. Not until the late 1850s did Carlton become more populated. The site was bordered by Grattan and Swanston streets, Royal Parade and College Crescent. This area in 1852 was a rubbish dump split by a gully running north and south. Edward La Trobe Bateman was given the job of landscaping the area. There was much work ahead for a team of ex-convicts who lived on porridge, tea, and bread, and worked 12-hour days to improve the rubbish-filled swampland. Bateman's laborers brought in good soil, planted grass and greenery, and dammed the gully to form a lake.

Redmond Barry organized a competition for the design of the university's first buildings. Francis White, an architect from London won the contest with a design for a stone quadrangle with cloisters and a Tudor ornamental front. One of White's buildings was for the law school, which was raised in the middle of a paddock in 1855.

On the university's opening day, lectures began in the original Exhibition Building on William Street, since the university was still under construction. Only 16 students enrolled. The low attendance was attributed to the dearth of young men in Melbourne interested in noncommercial activities. In fact, the local newspaper, *The Age,* called the university a costly toy, "the very insanity of extravagance." *The Age* editorialized that it was ridiculous to spend a large sum of money to teach classics in a country that needed scientists, engineers, and geologists to develop harbors and unearth the minerals in the country's heartland. *The Age* also suggested that the prospective students would be better to attend Oxford and Cambridge—universities which cost only half as much to attend. *The Age* editorial writer commented, "For one-half the money the boy could be sent to Oxford or Cambridge, and maintained there in a sumptuous style."

Six months into the university's opening year, 5 of the 16 students had dropped out. The low student numbers may be attributed to the unsatisfactory state of secondary education in Melbourne. Many undergraduates found they did not possess the needed skills. In its 1859–60 reports, the University Council criticized the "inaccuracy of the training of all the young men who have hitherto come up." First-year students, said the report, "have so much to learn at the University, which should have been done at school."

In its first two decades, the University of Melbourne was one of the most secular universities among those in the British Empire. By being so, Melbourne's university removed itself from religious controversies. Of the 100 acres granted for university grounds in Carlton, a suburb of Melbourne, 40 acres were reserved for boarding colleges to be built by Protestant and Catholic denominations. These institutions, it was felt, ensured that young men would not lose track of the religious foundations of society. The state of Victoria considered all Christian denominations as equal and therefore decided to withhold the influence of any and all religious denominations. The university was allowed only four clergymen on its 20-member council staff. In addition, the council agreed that professors must not be clergymen. At least three of the first six professors were sons of clergymen. Even as late as 1910 the university defended itself as a secular university when the council rejected a motion for the university to confer degrees in divinity.

The University Council decided that the following subjects would be taught at Melbourne: mathematics, classical languages, natural sciences, and moral sciences. The selection of professors was done by a London committee which had also selected professors for Sydney's institution. Four professors from the United Kingdom were selected. Professor of mathematics, W.P. Wilson, professor of the natural sciences, Frederick McCoy; and W.E. Hearn, professor of modern history and literature and political economy, all came from Queen's University of Ireland. Henry E. Rowe came from Trinity College, Cambridge, to chair the classics and ancient history department. Unfortunately Rowe never had the opportunity to teach at Melbourne. After making the long sea voyage from Plymouth, England, he was so seasick that he died five weeks after reaching Australia.

The attraction for the professors in part was the salary—at least four times more than they were paid in the United Kingdom. Although the annual tuition was only £12, it was too high for the poor colonists who could not afford to send their sons to preparatory or secondary schools, while at the same time meeting their other expenses. To meet the needs of the poorer students, the council offered two £50 scholarships to the best students at the matriculation and the first and second year examinations. The best students at the final exams were also awarded two-year £100 scholarships. These scholarships were intended to enable students to study for a master of arts degree. However, since there were no free secondary schools, it would be 1865 before a workingman's son enrolled—the son of a quartz miner. Most of the students were sons of wealthy Melbourne businessmen: doctors, judges, government officials, or tradesmen. These students were taught from a broad curriculum—Greek and Latin for two years and geometry and "the Elements of Natural Philosophy and Astronomy" for one year. Other subjects included mathematics, history, political economy, science, and logic.

The university began offering a law course in 1857, mostly to defend itself from harsh criticism that the education provided was not useful. The two-year law course was composed of evening lectures given three times a week. Students who passed were entitled to practice as barristers and solicitors in the colony. During the first year of the law course offering, 39 students enrolled. The total number of students increased to 45 in 1858, and reached 110 by 1861. That year, architecture, civil engineering, and surveying courses were added to the curriculum. In 1863 Professor George Halford inaugurated a five-year medical course which later made Melbourne world-famous.

In 1881, after much discussion and argument, Melbourne became the first Australian university to admit women. By the early 1900s the number of students was fewer than 1,000. From 1900 to 1940 enrollment increased to 5,000. Then after a decline during World War II, it rose to nearly 10,000 in 1948. In 1995 enrollment grew to its highest numbers ever, at over 30,000 students, with a teaching and research staff of approximately 5,000. The university has grown to 11 faculties and the School of Graduate Studies and the Melbourne Business School. Nine university residential colleges and three halls of residence are situated close to the campus.

The University of Melbourne has come a long way from its swampy start. The potpourri of architectural styles reflects 14 decades of the university's history: from the classical tranquility of the sandstone law cloisters and the older colleges to the modern lines of the Melbourne Business School. One of the original buildings is named after W. Baldwin Spencer, who established the school of biology. He was later known for his studies of the Aborigines. Built in 1887, the W. Baldwin

Spencer Building is spired and turreted. Today, it has a contrasting architectural backdrop—that of the tallest building on campus, the Redmond Barry Building. The university is dominated by tall and spacious buildings of the late twentieth century; there still exists, however, architecture dating from the institution's birth. Few drastic changes were made in the appearance of the university until after World War I. During the 20 years between the world wars, buildings were added, but with little logical planning. A master plan for the university's buildings and grounds was finally instituted in 1970. One of the interesting modern feats was the construction of the South Lawn over a car park. The car park earned a place in the *Australian Register of Historic Buildings*—the only car park to be listed.

At one end of the Law Quad lies Cussonia Court, named after the rare Cussonia tree which stands at its center. This tree replaced an old, diseased one. Another interesting tree on campus is called the Ginko biloba or maidenhair tree; examples are found outside the Faculty of Science Building on Masson Road. The trees on either side of the doors of the building are from one of the oldest known species of plant. The fossil remains of these trees have been discovered in Australia, dating back 250 million years. The species is unusual because one of the trees is male, the other female.

Perhaps John Bechervaise described the campus best when he wrote:

. . . though useful maps and aerial photographs are available, they cannot reveal cloisters and arcades, facades and sculptured plaques, enamels, and ceramic murals; all those inspired grace-notes which abound, in which one finds delight and subtle concepts of meanings and purposes.

During the institution's early years many scoffed at its motto, "I shall grow in the esteem of future generations." The foundation stone for the University of Melbourne may remain unfound, but the institution's influential educators and leaders will not be forgotten.

Further Reading: Geoffrey Blainey's *A Centenary History of the University of Melbourne* (Melbourne: Melbourne University Press, 1956) is a history of the early development of the university. The book also includes a number of rare old photographs. John Bechervaise's *The University of Melbourne: An Illustrated Perspective* (Melbourne: Melbourne University Press, 1985) includes photos of the newer buildings on campus. W.H. Newnham's *Melbourne's Biography of a City* (Melbourne: Cheshire, 1956; revised edition, Hill of Content, 1985) contains quirky tidbits about the university and its buildings. Also interesting is Michael Cannon's *Melbourne after the Gold Rush* (Main Ridge, Victoria: Loch Haven, 1993).

—Marla Bosworth

UNIVERSITY OF MICHIGAN
(Ann Arbor, Michigan, U.S.A.)

Location: The main campus is in Ann Arbor, Michigan, about 35 miles due west of Detroit. Other campuses are in Dearborn and Flint, Michigan.

Description: A public university that enrolls approximately 40,000 people in its undergraduate, graduate, and professional schools.

Information: Office of Undergraduate Admissions
1220 Student Activities Building
University of Michigan
515 E. Jefferson
Ann Arbor, MI 48109-1316
U.S.A.
(313) 764-7433

When the University of Michigan was established in 1817, Michigan was still part of the Northwest Territory on the western frontier of the United States. There were no more than 7,000 settlers in the region, most of whom were French fur traders. It was in this unlikely environment that Michigan Supreme Court Justice Augustus Woodward drafted a resolution to provide a public school system throughout Michigan. His plan was adopted on August 26, 1817, and that September Woodward attended the laying of the cornerstone of the first university building on Bates Street in Detroit.

Woodward's educational scheme was derived from progressive French examples; despite that, he pedantically titled the university, "Catholepistemiad, or University of Michigania." Woodward provided that the university was not to be governed or funded by a church, as was the norm at the time. Instead, the professors themselves were to manage the school, and the state was to finance it through taxation. Secondly, the university was to be the hub of a unified public education system. Woodward accorded the university president and professors the authority "to establish colleges, academies, schools, libraries, museums, athenaeums, botanic gardens, [and] laboratories" throughout Michigan. Thus, the university was cast from the start as a state institution intended to serve the public good. Finally, Woodward's curriculum emphasized science over classical studies, contrary to the programs at Harvard, Yale, and the other established schools in the East.

The university actually functioned only as a primary school and academy until 1837, the year that Michigan became the 26th state of the Union. John Pierce, who held the newly created post of the state superintendent of

schools, pressured the state legislators to fulfill their constitutional obligation to establish a proper university. The regents complied, and quickly decided to locate the university's main campus at Ann Arbor, on 40 acres of land donated by the city's residents. Eight more campuses were called for or established over the next nine years, but none long survived the transfer of all state funding to the central campus in 1846. The facilities at Ann Arbor emerged slowly; four professors' houses were built in 1840, and the next year the Main Building (later renamed Mason Hall) was erected.

In September 1851, the university enrolled its first students, all male: 6 freshmen, 1 sophomore, and 23 at the preparatory level. The atmosphere appears to have been more like a contemporary boarding school than a modern university. The students all lived in the capacious Main Building, and all followed a severe schedule that began with chapel service early each morning, and continued through the day with a rather more classical curriculum than Woodward envisioned. Their only free time was between dinner and 9 P.M., after which they were confined to the campus. The students at Ann Arbor in the 1840s played many boyish pranks as well. They built bonfires in the city streets, for example, piled hay in the chapel, and locked the dorm monitor in his quarters. Thus began an enduring tradition of mischief making at the university.

Much to the displeasure of the faculty, several fraternities established chapters at Michigan very early: Beta Theta Pi and Chi Psi in 1845, and Alpha Delta Phi in 1846. Their purpose was strictly social, in contrast with the literary societies they displaced, and the fraternities fostered the vices of drinking, smoking, and card playing, along with more wholesome activities. When the faculty tried to ban the fraternities in 1849, the townspeople of Ann Arbor defended the students, for they associated the Greek letter houses with their own secret societies, the Masons and Odd Fellows. The faculty eventually conceded to allow the fraternities on several conditions, most notably that each publish a list of its members.

Michigan evolved rapidly into a serious academic institution after 1852, when Henry Tappan began his tenure as the first of many extraordinarily competent presidents to reside over the university at Ann Arbor. A faculty quarrel forced Tappan out of a professorship in philosophy at New York University in 1837, and between then and his arrival at the University of Michigan, he published four books on philosophy and education. While the university had suspended its preparatory program, erected two new buildings, and founded a medical department before his arrival, Tappan had the vision to add a graduate program, and to

University of Michigan

change the university from a mere place of instruction into a serious research center. He eventually raised funds with which he founded the law school, increased the library's holdings, hired new faculty, built and stocked a chemical laboratory, and raised an astronomical observatory. Despite his successes, Tappan was forced out of office in June 1863, by a board of regents intent on taking back control of the university.

The Civil War erupted before Tappan's departure, with the Confederate attack on Fort Sumter on April 13, 1861. Tappan organized a rally at which he professed his unionist view to a public of divided opinion (an act that may have contributed to the regents' disapproval of him). A faction of inspired students immediately formed three companies and began drilling on the campus, and Tappan himself enlisted in a home guard unit for men over the age of 45. By the war's end, approximately 1,800 students and alumni of Michigan served in the Union Army; 290 died or were wounded.

Erastus Haven assumed the university's presidency mid-war, in 1863, and it fell upon him to guide the institution through the first several years of postwar expansion. In 1865–66, 1,205 students enrolled at Michigan, making it the country's largest university. Haven's term was a brief six years, but he oversaw the inauguration of the first teaching hospital in the country, the first instruction by seminar at an American university, and the guarantee of a state tax to fund the university continually. It was also during Haven's tenure that the first black men were admitted to Michigan, in 1868, with neither argument nor fanfare. Haven left in 1869 to take over as president of Northwestern University.

Henry Frieze, professor of Latin, served as president pro tem while the search continued for someone to fill the position permanently. Frieze's brief term was uneventful, except for two matters. First, the cornerstone was laid on the massive, classically styled, University Hall. The building housed offices, classrooms, a chapel, and an auditorium seating 3,000 people. Second, Frieze argued for and won the right for women to enroll at the university. Although several midwestern universities were already coeducational, former President Tappan had decided not to admit women, for he felt that serious scholarship was the business of men exclusively. A group of 13 women twice applied to the university in the 1850s, and the daughter of one of the professors attended classes without enrolling in the 1860s. However, it was not until January 1870 that the regents approved Frieze's proposal to admit women on an equal status with men. That fall, 33 women were admitted to study medicine, law, or literature.

James B. Angell accepted the presidency of the university in 1871, when he was just 42 years old. He remained 38 years, longer than any other president at Michigan. The university prospered during Angell's administration, largely as a result of his success in soliciting funds. In his first 20 years, the university's faculty increased from 38 to

more than 100 members, and the number of courses offered rose from 57 to 378. The school budget rose fourfold, and the enrollment topped 2,500, making Michigan once again the largest university in the United States. A new hospital, library, engineering building, and law building were all built during Angell's term, and he oversaw the introduction of many new programs of study, including dentistry, pharmacy, music, and nursing. Finally, Angell twice raised faculty salaries in order to more nearly approximate the standards of Harvard and Yale, and thus to retain fine professors often lured east by higher salaries.

A variety of extracurricular activities blossomed during Angell's term, including the first intercollegiate athletics, new fraternities and sororities, drama and music clubs, and several student publications. Coach Fielding Yost famously led the Michigan football team through several undefeated seasons in the early 1900s. There were a few incidents of disrespectful student behavior also, as was rather common at the Ann Arbor campus since its inception. In one instance, students rushed the evening performance of a traveling circus, only to find themselves in a rumble with its employees. Someone burned a sideshow tent, and the fight was only broken up when firemen turned hoses on the rowdies.

Following Angell's retirement in 1909, the university elected Harry Hutchins, dean of the law school, acting president. Plans to replace Hutchins with a permanent appointee were stalled by the onset of World War I. While the nation debated whether to enter the war, the students at Ann Arbor rushed into military training. The regents accepted a War Department proposal to form Reserve Officer Training Corps (ROTC) units on campus, and the first naval militia at an American university was comprised of about 55 Michigan men. All told, approximately 12,750 students, faculty, and alumni from the university served in the Army and Navy. Notably, Lieutenant Joseph Hayden, on leave from his professorship at Michigan, fired the last big cannon used in the war, at 11:00 A.M. November 11, 1918.

The two presidents to succeed Hutchins served only nine years combined. Marion Burton died in 1925, when he was just 50 years old, and having served only five years in office. In 1935, he was memorialized by the Burton Tower, for he is credited with having reinvigorated Michigan's research programs. Burton arranged financial partnerships with wealthy industrialists eager to tap the university's research capabilities, and he backed research sabbaticals and expeditions to such distant locations as Africa, Egypt, and the South Pacific. President Clarence Little lasted just four short years in the age of flappers and hip-flasks. He offended too many people with his outspoken, liberal views on birth control and euthanasia, and by favoring a compulsory course of classical study for freshmen and sophomores, contrary to the wishes of both students and faculty. Rather than battle the population he was elected to serve, Little resigned in 1929.

The university entered the Great Depression under the adept guidance of Alexander G. Ruthven. Because it was a state university, Michigan suffered the effects of the Depression more severely than its private rivals. The state legislature cut the university's funding by 15 percent in 1931, and faculty and staff salaries were consequently reduced. In 1933, further budget cuts forced the closing of 66 teaching and 26 nonteaching positions, and the remaining employees at Michigan suffered a second salary reduction. Then in 1935, the state legislature eliminated the mill tax by which the university had theretofore been funded. Ruthven effectively implored the state legislators to write the principle of the mill tax into their new plan, and thus he prevented the university's probable fall to mediocrity.

The university had not yet fully recovered from the drain of the Depression when the outbreak of World War II thrust Michigan into a new phase of development. With Ruthven still in charge, the university assumed an aggressive role in the United States' war effort. Michigan acquired 31 research contracts with the federal government, and yielded several important products. Three of the university's professors were involved in the development of the V-T fuse, a devise that causes a bomb or missile to explode shortly before reaching its target, thus making it more destructive. Professor William Dow and colleagues in the engineering department invented the "Tuba," a radar jamming device, and Professor Werner Bachman of the chemistry department found a method for mass-producing what was then the most powerful explosive known, RDX. In addition, the university's ROTC programs were expanded, and most of the fraternities were converted to soldiers' accommodations. Approximately 32,000 people schooled at the university served in the armed forces, 520 of whom were killed in action.

The university went through several changes after the war. Enrollment jumped 25 percent, largely due to an influx of veterans. In response, the board of regents initiated an $8 million building program that produced several dormitories, the Business Administration building, the Women's Hospital, the chemistry building, and more. A more abstract change concerned the students' growing expectation that they had a right to influence administrative decisions at Michigan. The rapid inflation that followed the nation's return to a peacetime economy had forced the university to raise tuition and fees substantially, and to double the percentage of the school's operating budget that tuition fees covered. Thus, the students came to see it as their right to influence the decisions that affected them on campus, as reflected in their new practice of evaluating the faculty of the Literary College, for example.

The 1950s and early 1960s were a time of relative prosperity for Michigan, ably guided by President Harlan Hatcher from 1951 until 1968. In 1956, the Kresge Foundation donated $3 million for a new medical research facility, and the Ford Motor Company donated $6.5 mil-

lion, along with the former estate of Henry Ford, where the university's Dearborn campus is now located. Hatcher solicited federal research grants worth millions of dollars each year at a time when many academicians argued against accepting task-specific grants, and when students were just beginning to protest the use of university facilities for military research. The scientific benefits of Hatcher's controversial policies are undeniable: Dr. Jonas Salk's polio vaccine was tested at the university's Survey Research Center, Dr. Robert Pidd of the physics department worked on the Phoenix Project to convert nuclear energy into electricity for the first time, and Professor Donald Glaser won the Nobel Prize for his invention of the bubble chamber, which produces a visible path of ionized matter in the trail of fast-moving subatomic particles.

Not humbled by such achievements, the students (and some faculty) at Michigan grew increasingly irreverent and rebellious. The students' impious ways and acts were by turns silly and serious. In 1952, Michigan's men staged the first "panty raid," later imitated at universities across the country. The casual beatnik aesthetic gripped the campus in the 1950s, and the Young Progressives flouted numerous university policies in their varied protests against the Korean War. In the 1960s, tension and impiety grew more severe, as protests erupted over various issues such as the war in Vietnam, military research conducted on campus, and the university's poor record in admitting and graduating minorities. The administration deflated most potential conflicts of the era through compromise and tolerance. They took no action against 37 students and professors arrested for occupying the draft board office of Ann Arbor, for example, and they withdraw the university from the controversial Institute for Defense Analysis. When the Black Action Movement (BAM) called a strike that successfully shut down large sectors of the university, the administration conceded to the principal demands of the group: minority aid, services, and numbers of staff devoted to their allocation were all increased.

Financial difficulties in the 1970s had an adverse effect on Michigan. President Robben Flemming, who took office in the fall of 1968 and left ten years later, was unable to protect the university's funding from harsh statewide budget cuts. Michigan suffered through several years of a hiring freeze and salary cuts while the nation experienced rapid inflation. The losses impacted severely on the university's quality of research and education. In 1966, Michigan had been ranked fourth in the nation. In 1975, it fell to 19th, and by 1980 it was 35th. Between 1971 and 1980, tuition nearly tripled for Michigan residents, and more than doubled for out-of-state students. Michigan's historic role as a state-funded university devoted to the public good was seriously compromised, probably forever.

Michigan's two most recent presidents have attempted to restore the university to its previous glory, but the full effects of their actions have not yet been realized. Harold

Shapiro rose through a series of administrative positions at Michigan to the presidency, which he assumed in 1980. He immediately embarked on a plan to streamline the university and recoup its standing by maintaining a smaller but better-paid faculty working in upgraded facilities. To guarantee Michigan's capacity for seminal research, Shapiro allocated more than $80 million for building projects and renovations, including a new hospital opened in 1986, a revitalized medical campus, new chemistry laboratories, and a $2.3 million renovation to Tappan Hall. Like Shapiro, James J. Duderstadt was a Michigan administrator and professor before he assumed the presidency in 1988. He espoused high ambitions for Michigan, which enrolled more than 36,000 students per year. His early goals included: the hiring of more women, increasing Michigan's endowment to $2 billion, upgrading the school's facilities, and restoring pride in the University of Michigan.

Further Reading: *The Making of The University of Michigan, 1817–1992,* by Howard H. Peckham, edited and updated by Margaret Steneck and Nicholas Steneck (Ann Arbor: University of Michigan, 1994) is an extremely thorough book that will bring the reader up to date on the university's history.

—Warren D. Rees

UNIVERSITY OF MINNESOTA
(Minneapolis and St. Paul, Minnesota, U.S.A.)

Location: Main campus in Minneapolis and St. Paul, Minnesota. Other campuses in Duluth, Morris, and Crookston, Minnesota.

Description: A state university enrolling a total of approximately 52,000; 38,000 on its Minneapolis/St. Paul campus.

Information: Office of Admissions
University of Minnesota, Twin Cities
240 Williamson Hall
231 Pillsbury Drive S.E.
Minneapolis, MN 55405-0213
U.S.A.
(612) 625-5000

Visiting: Phone VISITLINE at (612) 625-0000

In 1851, only two years after Minnesota formally became part of the Northwest Territory of the United States, its earliest European-American settlers decided to create a great university that they prophesied "would put Harvard in the shade." Badgered by Alexander Ramsey, governor of the territory and Henry Hastings Sibley, its representative in Washington, Congress passed an act reserving 46,080 acres of land "for the use and support of a university"; the two houses of Minnesota's legislature moved swiftly to choose a board of regents, which soon decided that all necessary steps must be taken to establish a preparatory department.

The *St. Anthony Express* (St. Anthony was the original name of Minneapolis) enthusiastically supported the project in an editorial: "We should start with the determination that not a single youth of either sex should be permitted to leave the territory to acquire an education for want of an institution at home fully endowed to meet the needs of this class." The university opened it doors on November 26, 1851, to an enrollment of 20 pupils. Fees ranged from $4 a quarter for such basic subjects as grammar and spelling to $6 a quarter for Greek, Latin, French, bookkeeping, and higher mathematics.

The university's first decade was a series of calamities, from the withdrawal of a gift of land by one of the regents to the effects on Minnesota of the financial disaster that befell the United States in 1857. The regents pressed on with their plans to erect the building known as "Old Main"; however, the school was forced to shut down in 1859, one year after Minnesota achieved statehood.

Though "Old Main" was indeed built, it stood neglected—as did all other considerations about the shuttered university—during the years of the Civil War (1861–65) and the concurrent Indian uprisings, both of which took young men away from the area.

Salvation came in two forms: the Morrill Act signed by President Abraham Lincoln in 1862 and the involvement with the university of entrepreneur John Sargent Pillsbury (who went on to found the milling company that still bears his name). The Morrill Act allotted to any state which was willing to set up an institution of higher education to teach agriculture and the mechanic arts 30,000 acres for each of its representatives in Congress. Minnesota's two senators and two representatives entitled it to 120,000 acres. John Sargent Pillsbury's involvement with the university began about the time the Morrill Act was signed. When Pillsbury came to Minnesota, he opened a hardware business. According to James Gray in his centennial history of the university, Pillsbury was on the brink of suing the regents for debts owed to him (including $5.50 for locks, nails, and iron used in the construction of Old Main). However, he was turned from potential foe to champion of the university, when Minnesota's first governor, Henry A. Swift, chose him as a regent. Pillsbury's initial reaction was that he was "not fit" for the assignment. He had no college education himself, but he educated himself by extensive reading. Gray describes Pillsbury's first visit, made with a committee of the legislature, to the decrepit "Old Main":

> The news was very bad indeed. Old Main was in the quite illegal possession of a group of casual folk who became surly at having their privacy invaded. As the committee members entered one room turkey flew at them in bewildered excitement; in another the squatters had improvised a barn loft; in the central hall the floor had been ruined by wood-splitting operations.

In addition to its physical decrepitude, the university was burdened with debt. To solve the problem of the deep debt, Pillsbury sold lands and negotiated compromises with creditors so that by 1867 every creditor had been satisfied. In that year the university had two faculty members and an admissions policy allowing both males and females to enroll. Within the first years of his tenure as regent (a position he held from 1863 until his death in 1901), Pillsbury had taken a dying idea and brought it to life.

William Watts Folwell, a graduate of Hobart College in New York became, in 1869 at age 36, the university's

University of Minnesota

first president. Folwell, who sometimes said he must sound like a "wild educational mutineer," had ambitious plans for the university. His "Minnesota Plan," adopted unanimously by the regents in 1870, called for three clearly marked educational phases: the Latin school (the elementary grades of today); the collegiate department, which would teach the disciplines needed for higher education; and the professional colleges. He advocated "throwing the usual work of freshmen and sophomores out of the proper University course and merging it into the old preparatory department." Believing that there was

a natural boundary between the first two and the final two years of instruction, he wanted the university to abandon the studies of the first two years, which he said were often "drudgery." Folwell encountered opposition on several fronts, ranging from the regents' refusal to move the university away from the center of a growing city to Lake Minnetonka and their unwillingness to approve construction of more buildings, including a library. The legislature refused most of his visionary ideas of expanding the campus and departments, but many of them eventually came to pass under future leadership.

Through much of the 1870s and 1880s, the university's enrollment numbered about 300. Though agricultural instruction was added to the curriculum, it was at first met with almost total indifference. As historian Gray wrote, "Though entrance requirements were modest (virtually anyone over 16 could apply) no one appeared. Farming, to the pioneer, was a matter of bending one's back over a hoe, not over a book." Despite efforts to impress members of existing agricultural societies, such as the State Grange, with the value of agricultural education, in 1880 no one enrolled in the agricultural college.

The university's second president came to be known as "Cyrus the conciliator." After coming to the university from Yale in August 1884, he served more than 25 years. Cyrus Northrop began his tenure with a $6,000 a year salary, double that provided by any other midwestern school, and a penchant for strong ideas. During his first decade as president, the student body grew to 2,000, and several specialized colleges were created: one for law, one for medicine, and another for agriculture. A School of Agriculture was created (so named to prevent confusion with the College of Agriculture which had attracted almost no students). It offered a two-year course open "to such boys as aspire to become successful and intelligent farmers." Women were admitted for summer courses in agriculture and home economics in 1894, and three years later they were admitted on equal terms with men.

Northrop proved so visible and powerful a figure on the university landscape that, according to Gray, "he was asked to be father, confessor, unofficial chaperone, unpaid employment agent, public sustainer of the spirit, and one man committee on student loans (from his own pocket)." He moved among the legislative and academic worlds with skill, building the university and hiring faculty who, for example, started the Minneapolis Symphony Orchestra and created schools for mines, dentistry, education, nursing, etc.

Northrop's successor, George Edgar Vincent, began his tenure in 1911 with an inaugural address that proved him a visionary:

We are coming to realize that good farming is not a robbing but a compensating of the soil; that it costs as much to plant bad seed as good . . . that public health is national capital; that juvenile delinquency comes less from depravity than from deprivation; . . . that industrial accidents are not lawyers' perquisites but costs of production; . . . that all idleness is not due to indolence; . . . that the United States must trust less to "manifest destiny" and more to constructive purpose.

With a gracious charm, wit, and natural gregariousness, Vincent grew to be among the best loved presidents in the university's history. One of his first moves was to create an "extension service" to bring the university to the people through night classes, correspondence courses, lectures, and other events in villages and towns throughout the state. Vincent tried other outreach techniques that he had learned from his father, a Methodist minister who had started the Chautauqua movement as a summer school training ground for Sunday school teachers. One such technique was University Week, which offered a week-long program of lectures and classes led by university professors in towns and villages. Another was the "University of the Air," broadcast throughout the Twin Cities (Minneapolis and St. Paul) on the campus radio station. Although Vincent would not allow his own voice ever to be broadcast on radio, he approved of spreading the word about the university through the then-new medium.

The outbreak of World War I brought uncertainty to the campus as many young male students went off to fight in the war or to work in munitions factories or on family farms. Several administrators went to Washington, D.C., to work in the government. Other faculty members were assigned various war-related tasks. Enrollment plummeted badly in 1917–18. Into this difficult environment came Vincent's replacement, Marion LeRoy Burton, who almost immediately suffered setbacks from war-related problems and tensions. Greatest among these was the state's Commission of Public Safety, charged with ferreting out German sympathizers. One of their targets was Professor William Schaper, head of the department of political science. He was fired by the regents for "his attitude," which made him "unfit to discharge the duties of his position." Even U.S. President Woodrow Wilson attempted to intervene on Schaper's behalf, but the firing stood, and the charges were not finally rescinded until 20 years later.

Once the war ended, so did issues relating to it. Burton launched a "comprehensive building program," which he asked the regents to present to the legislature. He wanted an auditorium, to be named after Northrop, and several buildings alongside it on a mall that had been designed decades before by Cass Gilbert, architect of the U.S. Capitol. With an enrollment of 8,000, the university was in dire need of new buildings and of repairs to existing ones. However, before he could see the plan through Burton accepted the presidency of the University of Michigan and left Minnesota in 1920.

Lotus Delta Coffman, remembered as originator of the university's College of Education, began his tenure as president in 1920, just as a fiscal crisis erupted. Despite record enrollments, the legislature offered the university a pitifully small budget, an action which caused faculty and students to protest vigorously and to point out what one student leader called "poor facilities, congested conditions, and inadequate teaching staff." The state legislators finally ended their opposition and passed a larger budget. The university was at last able to construct Northrop Auditorium with a group of buildings lining a mall in front of it, though considerations of cost forced modifications in Cass Gilbert's design. A welcome change occurred when the university persuaded the Northern Pacific Railroad to reroute its tracks away from several university buildings, thus reducing the terrible noise and vibrations that had plagued classrooms and laboratories.

In 1924 Coffman created a committee whose work led to the establishment of University College, aimed at gifted undergraduates; later he established the General College for those at the other end of the academic scale. The General College offered courses that connected the academy with real life situations. A developmental psychology course dealt with family life, a mathematics course looked at loans, etc. Though the college came to be known by such nicknames as "All Fools College," Coffman was proud of his contribution to helping students who learned at a slower pace. Another addition to the university was the Center for Continuation Study, where graduates could come for concentrated short courses. In 1936 the center offered its first courses; suggestions for courses from the public were often implemented. While physicians have used the center more than any other group, courses have been offered in such disparate disciplines as social welfare administration and mining engineering.

By 1933, the economy of the midwest was in a sad state. Coffman was worried about a student body that would dwindle because students could not afford to pay for their education. Accordingly, a plan was devised whereby students attended classes and in between worked at such jobs as examination-readers, cafeteria assistants, typists, etc. For their labors they received small stipends from both the federal and state governments. The plan, which came to be called the National Youth Administration, expanded to include graduates who were unable to find jobs and who came back to the university to assist with research projects. Dr. Maurice Visshcer attested to the invaluable assistance of these students when he remarked that many of Minnesota's cancer studies "could not have been carried on without this assistance."

Walter Catella Coffey served as president during the years of World War II, when enrollment peaked and then dramatically plunged as young men left to fight in the war. On the home front, an important discovery was made in the University of Minnesota's department of physics. As the chairman of the department wrote in a ledger book, "In March and April, 1940, [Albert O.] Nier established U 235 as responsible for the slow fission in Uranium." This proved a significant discovery in the creation of the atomic bomb. Meanwhile, Coffey's background as dean of the College of Agriculture (1921–41) helped the university win funding for a School of Veterinary Medicine within the College of Agriculture (veterinary medicine became a college in 1957). When Coffey relinquished his post in 1945, he reminded an audience of graduating seniors that there "is scarcely a

family [in Minnesota] with whom [the university] has not had instructional contact; the results of its research have made life better and more secure in rural and metropolitan areas alike."

By the time James Lewis Morrill came from Ohio State University to assume the presidency of the University of Minnesota in 1945, "University City" was the fourth largest city in the state. After the federal government passed Public Law 346, the so-called GI Bill, more than 16,000 former soldiers enrolled at the university. Total enrollment jumped from 15,000 before the war to 28,000 after it. The legislature was generous in giving the school the largest budget in its history. In order to help students cope with its ever-growing size, the university instituted a counseling service, which offered students at all levels assistance with academic and personal problems. In the 1940s, two doctors at the university, Dr. J. Charney McKinley and Dr. Starke Hathaway, created the Minnesota Multiphasic Personality Inventory, still the most widely administered personality test. Psychologists applaud its high level of validity in helping them diagnose levels of depression, anxiety, and low self-esteem.

The medical school, in particular, grew enormously during the postwar period and attracted four to ten times as much funding as other medical schools in the Big Ten. The Heart Hospital opened in 1951 to treat patients with heart problems. The first open heart surgery in the world was performed at the university in 1954. In other medical break-throughs, the university's medical division developed the first heart-lung machine in 1955. The first pancreas transplant occurred there in 1966, the first successful bone marrow transplant in 1968, and the first CAT total body scan in 1978. The university had cemented its important medical relationship with the world-famous Mayo Clinic when, after years of delay, the Mayo Memorial Hospital was dedicated in October 1954.

With the addition of three campuses outside the Minneapolis-St. Paul area—one in Duluth, one in Morris, and one in Crookston—the University of Minnesota became the largest university in the United States, according to the *Chronicle of Higher Education*'s 1993 figures, which showed a total enrollment of 51,880. In 1993, the university's endowment was $122 million, second among public institutions in the United States.

The University of Minnesota has had many distinguished faculty and graduates. Faculty member and agricultural expert Norman Borlaug won the Nobel Peace Prize in 1970, and Professor Dominick Argento won the Pulitzer Prize for Music in 1976. Graduates have moved to respected careers in communications and politics: both Eric Severeid and Harry Reasoner went on to distinguished careers in television news. Two former Minnesota senators and later vice-presidents of the United States, Hubert H. Humphrey and Walter Mondale, both attended the university.

Writer, radio personality, and University of Minnesota

alumnus Garrison Keillor lauded his alma mater at a 1992 alumni dinner: "To speak up for the University of Minnesota is like writing an ode in praise of the sun—you assume it's been done by smarter people. But let's say it anyway: the University is one of the glories of this state."

Further Reading: James Gray's *The University of Minnesota: 1851–1951* (Minneapolis: University of Minnesota Press; London: Oxford University Press, 1951) is a compre-hensive and detailed history of the university's first 100 years. Gray's *Open Wide the Door: The Story of the University of Minnesota* (New York: Putnam, 1958) updates and condenses his previous history. No general history of the university has appeared since.

—Frank M. Jossi and Mary Elizabeth Devine

UNIVERSITY OF MISSOURI
(Columbia, Missouri, U.S.A.)

Location: Columbia, Missouri, 125 miles west of St. Louis, Missouri, and 125 east of Kansas City, Missouri.

Description: Oldest campus in the state university system (Columbia, Rolla, St. Louis, and Kansas City). The University of Missouri enrolls about 23,000 students in undergraduate, graduate, and professional schools.

Information: University of Missouri-Columbia
Office of Admissions
130 Jesse Hall
Columbia, MO 65211
U.S.A.
(800) 225-6075 in Missouri
(314) 882-2121

Visiting: Guided tours of the campus are available year-round, Monday through Friday.

The University of Missouri is the oldest public university in Thomas Jefferson's Louisiana Purchase territory. A clause in the Act of 1820 admitting Missouri to the Union gave Missouri a land grant of two townships, the sale of which was to provide funding for a public university. By 1839, enough cash was available to endow a university.

The big question was where the University would be located. The Missouri General Assembly determined the award would go to the one of six counties offering the largest support in land and money, a competition the counties took seriously.

Logistics determined the Assembly's decision to limit the location to six central counties on the Missouri River. First, lack of roads made travel difficult. A central location came as a sort of equalizer since students from all parts of Missouri would have a relatively equal distance to travel by horseback. In addition, in the early years, most of Missouri's population was concentrated in and around St. Louis, and along the Mississippi and Missouri rivers because rivers formed a major transportation venue.

Boone County, one possible site, became the logical choice. While in 1840 the St. Louis census showed a population of 16,000, Boone County ranked next with 13,561. Wealth (defined by slaves, livestock, and cereal grain production), too, placed Boone among the top contenders.

Although Boone County calls to mind the log-cabin dwelling Daniel Boone, the Booneslick area population wasn't only composed of cabin dwellers. Under the Missouri Compromise, Missouri came into the Union as a slave state, leading a number of "bluebloods" from Kentucky to import their opulent Southern lifestyle to the area: tobacco crops, slaves, cash, and Whig politics. The county seat, Columbia, had a population of about 700 in 1840, a third of whom were slaves.

While many of Columbia's leading citizens belonged to the Whig political party, the state was predominately Democratic. These contrary political viewpoints would haunt the university financially for some years to come since the Missouri legislature controlled the purse strings.

Public transportation to Columbia was better than service to many other frontier towns. Jonas Viles described its location: "The town was on the stage route from St. Louis to Fayette and the West. In 1841 there was one regular semi-weekly river packet from St. Louis to Glasgow and in 1842 three, all stopping at Providence, Columbia's river port some fourteen miles away, with a regular stage to Columbia in 1843."

How did the university finally come to be awarded to Boone County? Chicanery. More than one county purchased land and inflated the value of the acreage as part of their "bidding package." Boone County just did it better. According to Jonas Viles, "Her subscription was $82,381 in cash and $35,540 in land, a total of $117,921." Although the value was overstated, the citizens' enthusiasm and dedication was not. At a time still touched by the Panic of 1837's seven-year depression, almost 900 people contributed money or land. Columbia gladly welcomed the new school—then named the University of the State of Missouri.

A board of state-appointed curators oversaw the university's organization. The board selected John Hiram Lathrop, a graduate of Yale, as the first university president.

Despite the lack of an official campus building, classes began April 14, 1841, under what is now the College of Arts and Sciences, the oldest academic division in the university. The first university catalog listed 77 students. Today's campus has 13 undergraduate and 5 graduate schools, 300 buildings, and about 23,000 students.

The first campus building was Academic Hall (1843), designed by Stephen Hills, Missouri state capital's architect. Today the only reminder of Academic Hall is a row of graceful columns, survivors of a fire in 1892.

In contrast to the campus beginnings (when the first building cost under $75,000), the most recent building cost $5.4 million. Named for Lee Hills, an alumnus who won the Pulitzer Prize, the building houses the School of Journalism's daily newspaper and other operations.

University of Missouri

In 1849 the library held only official documents, a set of Livy, some reviews, and Blackwood's magazine. Today the library system is made up of Ellis Library (main library) and seven branch libraries. The collection consists of 2.58 million volumes, 5 million microforms, 22,973 journal subscriptions, and special collections.

The Civil War caused problems for the developing university. Even before the war the largest number enrolled was 181. With the Civil War, things got so bad that the Board of Curators suspended operations in March 1862. The Academic Hall housed federal troops, officers resided at the president's house, and the Normal School served as a hospital. Horses were stabled in the campus enclosure. Despite this adversity, the university reopened in November 1862.

Incidently, one Civil War souvenir remains. Missouri's football team name "Tigers" comes from the Columbia Civil War militia organized to protect the town; they called themselves the Missouri Tigers.

Between the ravages of war and the always uncertain finances because of the dependence on legislative appropriations and political climates, the university struggled to stay open. Since the Missouri legislature presumed Columbia's "disloyalty" during the Civil War, the university faced a hostile legislature when asking for budget approval.

Finally, relief came when the Missouri Assembly located the College of Agriculture and Mechanic Arts at Columbia in 1870. With the college came a land grant for 330,000 acres. The university's survival was no longer in question.

With America's entrance into World War I, classes thinned as students and faculty left for service or to work in a war-related industry. Military training, which already existed on the campus, expanded with fraternity houses and dormitories becoming barracks.

World War I was followed by a period of calm with enrollment increases but with no appropriation increases to help the university move forward. Then the Depression hit. With a budget that had no extras to begin with, cutbacks struck hard and hit essential programs. But the federal Public Works Administration, developed because of the Depression, brought about one of the most extensive building programs in the history of the university.

World War II saw a healthy enrollment drop from over 5,000 in 1938 to 1,500 in 1943. In response to the war, the university developed educational programs for military services, the first such being a diesel motor school.

The surge of students on the GI bill came in the fall of 1946, catching the university with a shortage of instructors, classrooms, and housing. Barracks from Fort Leonard Wood were brought in to help relieve some of the crush.

As changes came to the physical side of the university with the addition of buildings and courses, so change came to the student body. From a predominately well-to-do male student body in the early days of the university, today men and women of all races and economic strata enjoy the opportunity to study at this public institution. However, the change took time.

The first Women's Rights Convention met in 1848 in Seneca, New York. Despite this national voicing of the demand for women's rights, female students took almost 30 years to show at the University of Missouri. Even then, a woman's right to be a student there came quietly with no grand acknowledgment, and with restrictions.

Female students first appeared in the 1868–69 catalog as the last item under the Normal College. Twenty-two names are listed under the heading of "Ladies." In 1869–70, the Normal College had 42 female students. By the 1870–71 catalog, the names of the female students were no longer listed separately from male students. Women were allowed to attend regular classes by 1871–72.

Easing female students into campus life came gradually but successfully. In the 1873 catalog, President Daniel Read said: "Finding . . . that the young women at 'the Normal' did no manner of harm, we very cautiously admitted them to some of the recitations and lectures in the University building itself, providing always that they were to be marched in good order, with at least two teachers, one in front and the other in the rear of the column, as guards . . . By degrees, and carefully feeling our way, as though explosive material was all around us, we have come to admit them to all the classes in all the departments, just as young men are admitted."

Mary Louise Gillette became the first graduate from the Normal School in 1870, and in 1874 a woman was valedictorian.

A setback came in 1876 with a new president, Samuel Laws, who seemed to prefer no female students at the university or at the very most a "separate but equal" situation. Laws's rules for female students included their wearing a uniform. A woman was appointed a principal of the ladies department, her main job being to ensure ladylike behavior.

Under Laws's administration, a new course of study designed specifically for women led to the degree of A.D.B., Artium Domesticarum Baccaluarea, adopted in 1880. The degree stressed courses in art, literature, and domestic chemistry and economy—all adapted to the "culture of woman." The A.D.B. degree proved so unpopular that only seven women ever took it.

Things have changed since then. The university opened co-ed dorms in 1977 and today women comprise about 50 percent of the student body. Another change in 1977 was the addition of a minor in black studies in the College of Arts and Sciences in response to the needs of black students.

With Missouri admitted to the Union as a slave state and a number of leading citizens of Columbia, Missouri being pro-slavery, admitting blacks to the university was a touchy subject for many years. Indeed, legally under the Missouri constitutions adopted after the Civil War, the official state policy indicated "separate but equal" schools. To account for unequal educational opportunities, blacks were shunted to other states with "out-of-state tuition" scholarships.

In the 1930s four black graduate students applied for admission to the university and instead of being admitted, found themselves referred to Lincoln University, an all black university. Lloyd L Gaines, who had applied for the School of Law, filed a writ of mandamus in the Boone County Circuit Court to force admission. The case went all the way to the United States Supreme Court where out-of-state tuition scholarships were declared unconstitutional. By the time the decision was handed down, Gaines had disappeared from the scene.

Finally, in 1950 three black students won admission in professional or graduate programs. Seeing that changes would be coming, the Board of Curators appointed a committee which created a set of rules for admitting black students. Basically the rules said that only if a course wasn't available at Lincoln University, would a black Missouri resident be admitted to the University of Missouri. All such restrictions were removed with the decision of the United States Supreme Court in the case of Brown vs. the Topeka Board of Education, declaring public school segregation unconstitutional.

At the same time the university struggled with social inequalities, funding, and growth, it was building a national and international reputation and becoming a school of choice. Now students come from every state and more than 100 foreign countries.

A major claim to international fame held by the University of Missouri is its school of journalism which was established in 1908. Its importance rests not only with the quality of the curriculum (rated by the Associated Press Managing Editor as one of the best in the nation in 1991), but with the fact that the school is the world's first school of journalism.

Although other educational institutions had given courses and had chairs of journalism prior to 1908, the University of Missouri holds the distinction of creating a school dedicated to teaching journalism. The board stressed the fact that the new school of journalism would be "coordinate in rank with the schools of law and medicine."

The establishment of the school of journalism came about despite controversy regarding the practicality of instruction in journalism sparked by Joseph Pulitzer's proposal to endow a school of journalism at Columbia University. Viles noted, "Disapproving editors expressed the opinion that journalism was a subject that could not be taught, that success in it required talent for it and a long apprenticeship under conditions that could not be duplicated in academic halls."

The controversy helped the university decide on three principles for the journalism school: first, a laboratory newspaper was needed for practical experience; second, teachers would be experienced newspapermen; and third, a broad liberal education would be emphasized.

These principles were followed from the beginning. The school's first dean, Walter Williams, was the editor of the *Columbia Herald*. Other newspapermen joined the staff: Silas Bent, *St. Louis Post-Dispatch;* Charles G. Ross, *St. Louis Republic;* and Frank L. Martin, *Kansas City Star.*

Classes began September 14, 1908, with 72 of the university's 2,944 students enrolled as journalism students. That same day an issue of the laboratory newspaper, *The University Missourian,* was prepared by the class.

Today the approximately 800 journalism students experience hours of practical laboratory work in a variety of media settings: print at *Columbia Missourian* (six-day-a-week general newspaper for Columbia and Boone County), *Missourian Weekly* (Wednesday, Sunday editions), and *Weekend* (magazine and entertainment supplement); radio and TV at KBIA (MU's public FM radio station which covers central Missouri) and KOMU-TV (NBC affiliate, broadcasting news and public affairs programs).

A broad liberal education was and is emphasized as the foundation for the journalism degree. When the school first opened, of the 120 hours needed for graduation, only 24 hours had to be in journalism. Today the bachelor of journalism degree requires 33 hours of journalism and 90 hours of non-journalism credits; at least 65 hours of the 90 non-journalism credits required of degree seekers must come from the College of Arts and Sciences.

The school of journalism retains strong links to the world of professional journalism. For instance, the Frank E. Gannett Foundation presented a gift on behalf of the country's largest newspaper chain; the result was Gannett Hall.

News directors come to the campus to select the national winners of Radio-Television News Directors Association's Edward R. Murrow Awards. The school is the headquarters for the Society of American Business Editors and Writers, the Missouri Interscholastic Press Association, and the national headquarters for Investigative Reporters and Editors Inc. The Pictures-of-the-Year competition selects the best photojournalism from news-

paper, magazine, and picture editing categories and a book, *The Best of Photojournalism,* is published annually.

A special annual event, Journalism Week, began in May 1910 as a conference of editors. During Journalism Week, classes are canceled so students and journalists can attend lectures and workshops given by faculty and visiting speakers. Also, the Missouri Medal of Honor, one of journalism's most prestigious prizes, is awarded.

The school of journalism boasts the Freedom of Information Center which indexes newspaper and magazine articles on information access and press freedom and responds to more than 1,000 requests from professionals for information. The importance of the center was recognized when it was established in 1958 with worldwide news coverage and a special commemorative U.S. postage stamp.

Distinguished graduates of the school of journalism include: Howard Lamade (1913 graduate) and his brother George (1916 graduate), publishers of *Grit;* Walter D. Scott, president and chief executive officer of NBC; Elmer Lower, head of NBC News; William Manchester, journalist and author of *The Death of a President;* Helen Delich-Bentley, maritime editor of the *Baltimore Sun;* James Lehrer, coanchor of the MacNeil-Lehrer Report; Marshall R. Loeb, editor of *Fortune;* and Seymour Topping, managing editor of *The New York Times.*

The school of journalism's first dean took the profession of journalism and its responsibility to the public seriously. Walter Williams wrote the journalist's creed which contains beliefs including: "*I believe* that the journalism which succeeds best . . . fears God and honors man; is stoutly independent, unmoved by pride of opinion or greed of power, constructive, tolerant but never careless, self-controlled, patient . . .; is a journalism of humanity, of and for today's world."

Somehow this philosophy (engraved on a plaque in Jay H. Neff Hall) makes it fitting that the original tombstone of Thomas Jefferson, author of the Declaration of Independence, and supporter of individual rights and freedom of speech, rests on the campus of the University of Missouri in Columbia.

Further Reading: James Olson's *The University of Missouri: An Illustrated History* (Columbia: University of Missouri Press, 1988) provides an interesting and well-illustrated account of the history of the university from the beginning until the 1980s. Another detailed account is Jonas Viles's *The Univeristy of Missouri: A Centennial History* (Columbia: University of Missouri, 1939) which deals extensively with the early history of the university. *A History of the University of Missouri* by Frank F. Stephens (Columbia: University of Missouri Press, 1962) is another inclusive history of the university.

—Vera-Jane Goodin

UNIVERSITY OF MONTPELLIER
(Montpellier, France)

Location: Montpellier, located in the Hérault department of southern France, approximately 750 kilometers south of Paris, 164 kilometers east of Marseille and 10 kilometers from the Mediteranean Sea.

Description: Three autonomous, state-financed universities founded in 1970 under France's Orientation Act of 1968, which provided for reform of higher education. They replaced the former University of Montpellier. University of Montpellier I consists of teaching and research units in law, medicine, pharmacy, economics, and social sciences; University of Montpellier II teaches science, engineering, technology, and business management; and University of Montpellier III focuses on arts and letters.

Information: Université de Montpellier I
BP 1017
34006 Montpellier Cedex
France
(67) 41-20-90

Université de Montpellier II
Place Eugène Bataillon
34095 Montpellier Cedex 5
France
(67) 14-30-30

Université de Montpellier III
Place de la Voie Domitienne
BP 5043
34032 Montpellier Cedex 5
France
(67) 14-20-00

"**B**ecause wisdom enlightens the human heart and leads it to virtue." In this way begins the papal bull issued by Nicholas IV on October 26, 1289, that acknowledged the existence of a *studium generale* comprised of masters and students of the town of Montpellier. The papal bull recognized and joined together the already existing faculties of medicine, civil and canon law, and the arts, and it served as the founding charter of the University of Montpellier. Sources which give 1220 as the date the university was founded refer to statutes confirming a university of medicine (described below).

The settlement of Montpellier developed between the eighth and tenth centuries and, as an inland port, played an important role in trade with the Orient. The merchants who dealt in spices and medicinal plants knew the therapeutic value of the products they sold; those who were better educated read the translations of Hippocrates. Thus students, drawn by the merchants' knowledge of medical science, were the basis of the first schools of medicine to form at Montpellier in the twelfth century. The town of Montpellier acquired a charter in 1141.

A medical school existed at Montpellier as early as 1137. After completing a course in the arts at Paris in that year, one Adalbert, later archbishop of Mainz, is said to have studied at Montpellier. According to the writings of Saint Bernard, the Archbishop of Lyons went to Montpellier to be cured.

Several possibilities have been suggested concerning the origins of a university of medicine: it was perhaps "an offshoot" of the famed University of Salerno; it may have resulted from the medical science that "survived the downfall of the Saracenic Empire" when Muslim fugitives, after a defeat by Charles Martel in 737, fled to the area that later became Montpellier; contact with the Jewish and Arabic schools of twelfth-century Spain or with the Jewish medical schools at nearby Arles and Narbonne could have led to its formation. In any event, a university of medicine was the first of the schools founded at Montpellier that were united by the charter of 1289.

The Arabic influence is exemplified in the Muslim philosopher and physician Abu Ali al-Husein ibn Sina (980–1037). Avicenna, as he was known in the west, was considered one of the greatest writers on medicine of the Middle Ages. His *Qanum-fi-l-Tibb* (*Canon of Medicine*), translated into Latin in the twelfth century, served as one of the chief texts in European medical schools from the twelfth into the seventeenth centuries; it was required reading at the University of Montpellier until the mid-seventeenth century.

The works of a Jewish physician, Moses ben Maimon (1135–1204), called Maimonides in the Christian world, were also renowned; a Latin translation of his *Guide* was taught at the University of Montpellier. An important Jewish colony was established in Montpellier, and it produced several able teachers.

Licenses to teach and to practice medicine may not have been instituted in Montpellier until the thirteenth century. An edict issued in 1181 by William VIII, lord of Montpellier, granted to all who so willed the right to teach medicine. A university of medicine is mentioned in statutes that were confirmed in 1220 by Cardinal Conrad and by a second cardinal in 1239; the statutes were confirmed by papal bull in 1242. These statutes were appar-

University of Montpellier

ently the first to provide for the appointment of a chancellor, nominated by the bishop and three masters, to preside over the university. In 1240, the masters appointed "arbitrators to interpret or modify these statutes." By 1272, King James I of Aragon, then overlord of Montpellier, forbade the practice of medicine at Montpellier by anyone who had not been examined and licensed.

In 1309, Pope Clement V declared certain books which he, upon the advice of his Montpellier physicians, considered necessary reading for students of medicine. The list consisted of works by the second-century Greek physician Claudius Galen, perhaps the most renowned of ancient medical writers and one whose influence continued into the eighteenth century; Avicenna; Constantinus Africanus, who brought his translations of Greek and Arabic works of medicine to Salerno; Isaac Judaeus; Rhazes, a Persian healer of the ninth and tenth centuries whose works were among those translated by Constantinus; Johannicius; and Hippocrates.

Several changes occurred in 1340. Students were required to attend lectures for two years in order to attain a bachelorship in medicine; bachelors and senior students spent the summer in practice. Before earning their bachelor degrees in medicine, students accompanied their doctors on visits to the sick and, under the doctors' supervision, experimented upon the patients. The length of time to obtain a doctor's degree was five years for masters of arts and six years for other candidates. In addition, a biennial anatomy class was authorized at Montpellier. For a period of several days, a doctor of medicine would lecture students as a surgeon dissected a cadaver.

The Montpellier surgeon Gui de Chauliac developed a method of surgery and published, in 1367, a treatise on anatomy. Most of his methods, however, were taken from the writings of the ancient physicians.

Will Durant in *The Age of Faith* describes the medieval student as a man "of any age. He might be a curate, a prior, an abbot, a merchant, a married man; he might be a lad of thirteen, troubled with the dignity of his years. . . . He encountered no entrance examinations; the only requirements were a knowledge of Latin, and ability to pay a modest fee to each master whose course he took."

The inception of a university of law at Montpellier dates from the 1160s when the noted jurist Placentinus, who had taught at Bologna and Mantua, fled to Montpellier, where he sought asylum from "the jealousy of less distinguished colleagues." Around 1230, licenses were being granted and increased the number of doctors and students of law at Montpellier. The bishop, supported by a royal brief, claimed control over the bestowal of licenses in canon and civil law (a right he also exercised with the medical school). By 1268, a college of doctors in law, backed by statutes issued by the bishop and the doctors, existed. When Pope Nicholas IV issued the bull recognizing the *studium generale* in 1289, the law school had only recently attained a degree of importance in its field.

The students of law soon began to resist the control exercised over them by both the bishop and the masters. In 1320, the bishop issued a proclamation against "secret conventicles and congregations," "confederations and colligations," and "scholars of one province against the scholars of another." Around 1339, with the aid of the cardinal legate Bertrand di Diaux, a compromise was reached: statutes, modeled after those of Bologna, allowed a "student-university of a very modified type."

One of the law university's most famous students was the Italian poet Francesco Petrarch (1304–74). Although Petrarch, who spent seven years at the universities of Montpellier and Bologna ("seven wasted years," he called them), detested law, it was during his days at Montpellier that he wrote the first of his poems that remain in existence today.

A university of the arts was confirmed in statutes of 1242. In his *Summa,* Placentinus hints that masters of arts existed at Montpellier as early as the end of the twelfth century. "The ancient faculty of Arts of Montpellier received its first statutes from a bishop of Maguelone: Jean de Montlaur, second of that name. They were dated from the sixth day before the Calends of April (March 27 on the ancient Roman calendar) in the year 1242. These statutes apply to the schools of grammar and logic." The statutes of 1242 recognized the authority of the bishop; they were not drafted by the masters. This was not a student-university.

A university of theology did not officially exist at Montpellier until 1421, when Pope Martin V issued a bull creating a *studium generale* in theology, with the bishop as chancellor. As early as 1263, however, a college had been founded for the Carthusian monks at nearby Valmagne by James I and may have served as the nucleus for the later university.

The University of Montpellier retained its position as one of the great *studia* of Europe until the end of the fourteenth century. The last half of the fourteenth and most of the fifteenth centuries, however, saw a general decline in many of the universities of Europe. "The fifteenth century was a period of decadence in the universities generally, though not equally so everwhere."

In 1362, the number of students attending the law university had declined from 1,000 to 100; the medical school also experienced a decrease in the number of students. Anna M. Campbell, in *The Black Death and Men of Learning,* states that the University of Montpellier was "destitute of lecturers and auditors because in the said *studium* where formerly a thousand students used to dwell, scarcely 200 are to be found today." Around 1390, the students were complaining against the masters, and enrollment of students at the university continued to decline.

The run-down condition of the university is exemplified by a student at the *Collège des Douze Médecins* (College of a dozen doctors), who, in 1422, described himself as its sole medical student. In 1494, the rebuilding of the *Collège des Douze Médecins* was a sign that the university's decline was near an end.

During the Renaissance, the university once again came to life. Charles VIII and Louis XII, influenced by their Montpellier physicians, offered support and granted favors to the university. In 1498, King Louis "made an annual grant of 500 *livres* to the *studium,* 400 of which were to be devoted to providing salaries of 100 *livres* per annum for four doctors."

In the sixteenth century, Montpellier was one of the most ardent centers of the Renaissance; the university included the five faculties of law and economics, medicine, sciences, letters and human sciences, and pharmacy.

In the 1530s, the writer François Rabelais, after a brief period of study at the medical university, was granted a bachelor of medicine. Soon afterward, he lectured on Galen and Hippocrates in the original Greek. The teachings of the Greek authors now took precedence; in 1567, after a petition by the students, Arabic authors were struck from the required readings. The Greek texts remained the principal source of teaching in the medical schools until the eighteenth century. In 1673, a doctor was "required on pain of suspension to cease teaching a doctrine contrary to that of Hippocrates, Aristotle, and Galen."

In 1552, a 15-year-old student from Basel, Switzerland, arrived in Montpellier to study medicine. For five years the young man, Felix Platter, kept a detailed account of his experiences in a journal that was translated into English in 1961. After his examination and matriculation on November 4, 1552, Felix was admitted to the baccalaureate program; he chose as his sponsor a Dr. Saporta, who would serve as his consultant throughout his years of study. Felix described his initial course as two or three lectures in the morning and the same number in the afternoon; the first dissection he attended was that of a boy who had died of a stomach abscess. A doctor presided, and a barber performed the operation. Many people, other than students, were present (" . . . even young girls, notwithstanding that the subject was a male"). Felix later described nighttime excursions to cemeteries to find bodies for dissection.

In his journal, Felix discusses more than his studies; he gives an account of the social history of the period immediately preceding the Wars of Religion (1562–98). His comments range from descriptions of public executions and the persecution of Protestants to such topics as Mardi Gras celebrations, travel throughout the region, and his surreptitious method of cooking eggs, which were forbidden during Lent.

After four years of study, Felix sat for his baccalaureate and was promoted to bachelor of medicine. He returned to Basel in 1557, married his childhood sweetheart, and became a distinguished physician.

Felix Platter, as a Swiss Calvinist, had been allowed religious freedom in Montpellier, a region sympathetic toward Protestants. Conditions changed, however, in the years between Felix's return to Switzerland and the arrival of the Huguenot theologian and classical scholar Isaac Casaubon (1559–1614). Casaubon's parents were ardent Huguenots (French followers of John Calvin) and, following the St. Bartholomew's Day massacre of August 24, 1572, Casaubon received his first Greek lesson in a mountain cave in the Dauphiné region of France while in hiding from fanatical Catholic armies. Nine years later, he became a professor of Greek at the Academy of Geneva, where he taught for 15 years. In 1595, he was appointed to a professorship at Montpellier and served for three years.

In the seventeenth century, the University of Montpellier continued to attract students from France and distant countries. Medical science had advanced to the point where a degree from a recognized institution was required for the legal practice of medicine in western Europe.

The French universities provided a model for teaching and research for Europe until 1793, when the National Convention suppressed all universities in France. Higher education was reinstated by Napoléon I in 1806. The University of France, a centralized system of education under the jurisdiction of a ministry located in Paris, encompassed schools of medicine, law, and pharmacy, and faculties of science and letters; primary and secondary schools were also under its control. Changes occurred in the late nineteenth century, including the separation of church and state in education (March 1882). In 1896, the system was reorganized into 23 districts or *académies,* each with its own university consisting of faculties of medicine, law, pharmacy, science, and letters. Concurrently, the *grandes écoles,* elite institutions leading to engineering, teaching, and civil service degrees, were created.

Other than the establishment of two-year *instituts universitaires de technologie* or IUT (university institutes of technology) in 1966, few changes occurred between 1896 and May 1968, when student unrest led to the *Loi d'orientation de l'enseignement supérieur* (Orientation of Higher Education Act). As a result of this act, the University of Montpellier, in 1970, was divided into three autonomous units: the Universities of Montpellier I, II, and III.

The University of Montpellier I enrolls approximately 18,500 students in law and social sciences; economics; economic and social administration; medicine; pharmaceutical and biological science; industrial pharmacy; odontology; alimentary, oenological, and environmental studies; and physical education and sport.

The University of Montpellier II (*Université des Sciences et Techniques du Languedoc*) enrolls approximately 11,000 students in basic and applied sciences; engineering sciences; business management; chemical engineering; and technology (in both Montpellier and Nîmes).

The University of Montpellier III (*Université Paul Valéry,* named after the nineteenth- and twentieth-century writer who studied at Montpellier) enrolls approximately 18,000 students in letters, arts, philosophy, and linguistics; Anglo-American, Germanic, Slav, and Oriental studies; human and environmental sciences; economic, mathematical, and social sciences; science of society; and Mediterranean Romance Languages.

Further Reading: For general information about the early history of the university and its times, consult *The Universities of Europe in the Middle Ages,* Volume II, by Hastings Rashdall (Oxford: Clarendon Press, 1942); *The Age of Faith,* Will Durant (New York: Simon and Schuster, 1959); *The Age of Reason Begins,* Will and Ariel Durant (New York: Simon and Schuster, 1961); *The Age of Louis XIV,* Will and Ariel Durant (New York: Simon and Schuster, 1963). For a detailed account of medieval medical study experiences at the university, see the autobiographical work *Beloved Son Felix: The Journal of Felix Platter, a Medical Student in Montpellier in the Sixteenth Century,* translated by Sean Jennett (London: Frederick Muller Limited, 1961).

—Susan R. Stone

UNIVERSITY OF MUMBAI (BOMBAY)
(Mumbai, Maharashtra, India)

Location: An urban campus located in the financial section of Mumbai (Bombay), on the southeastern shore of the city, formerly the old Fort Bombay.

Description: A government-funded coeducational university of over 220,000 students and over 130 affiliated colleges. Offers B.A., M.A., and Ph.D. degrees in liberal arts, technology, law, commerce, and medicine.

Information: University of Mumbai
University Road
Fort Bombay
Maharashtra State 400032
India
(22) 273623

In 1665, when British king Charles II took possession of the port and island of Bombay from the Portuguese (as part of the dowry of Princess Catherine Braganza of Portugal), the city was a small fishing village. Soon after, in 1668, Bombay became the official seat of the East India Company, a judicial system was established, and a hospital built—acts which marked the beginnings of modern Bombay. The city's population grew from 10,000 in 1668 to 110,000 in 1780, to 500,000 in 1850.

One significant development in Bombay as the population grew was the appearance of schools and colleges in the city. The Elphinstone Institution had its origins in a Christian school founded by Reverend Richard Cobbe in 1718. Opening its doors to Indians, it became known as the Charity School in 1820. In 1840 the school, which concentrated on the arts and sciences, changed its name to the Elphinstone Native Education Institution after Montstuart Elphinstone, the governor of Bombay from 1819 to 1827 and a pioneer in education. The Poona Sanskrit College was founded in 1821. Originally aimed at the education of the Brahmin class, the Poona College began to teach both Sanskrit and English in 1837, opening its doors to all classes. The Grant Medical College was founded in 1845, named for Sir Robert Grant, former governor of Bombay. It conferred a degree in medicine until the establishment of the University of Bombay.

In August 1852, the Bombay Association was formed. Comprised of educated members of the city's Hindu, Parsi, Muslim, and Jewish communities who sought to define the "wants of the people of this country, and the measures calculated to advance their welfare, and of representing the same to the Authorities in India and England," they petitioned parliament to adequately fund university education in India. A second petition was sent in 1853, pleading for the establishment of vocational schools and for a law school to train Indians for the profession. These two petitions resulted in *Wood's Education Dispatch,* which became fondly known as the "Magna Carta of the Indian Education."

Wood's Educational Dispatch was composed in July 1854, by Sir Charles Wood, later Lord Halifax. In this dispatch Wood outlined plans for a university system in India. Because of his efforts, the Department of Public Instruction was established in 1855. Two years later, the country's first university system was incorporated. In January the University of Calcutta was established, followed by the University of Bombay in June and finally the University of Madras in September, three schools modeled after the London University. To be patterned after the London University meant that the University of Bombay did not offer teaching but would perform as an examining institution, testing students presented from local schools and colleges. The colleges first affiliated with the University of Bombay were the Elphinstone Institution (including the college and high school), the Poona College, and the Grant Medical College.

When the universities of Calcutta, Bombay, and Madras were incorporated in 1857, they were not corporations of scholars but of administrators. With a chancellor and a vice chancellor, the syndicate appointed examiners, granted degrees, and maintained the budgets of each university. The syndicate also created the by-laws with the approval of the senate. Every member of the senate was a faculty member of the affiliated school's faculty of arts, faculty of law, faculty of medicine, or faculty of civil engineering.

To matriculate at the University of Bombay one needed to be at least 16 years old. Students were expected to pass written and oral examinations in English and Indian languages, and mathematics. For the bachelor of arts degree, the young men pursued a course of study for 22 months. Then they appeared for the first examination in arts, followed by another examination for the bachelor of arts.

A bachelor of law degree was granted to graduates with the B.A. who went on to study an additional three years in the law school. A licentiate in medicine would be granted after successful examination at the end of the second and fourth years of study. A master's degree in medicine involved two additional years of study beyond the

University of Mumbai (Bombay)

licentiate. A master of civil engineering required four years of study beyond the bachelor of arts, with two of those years being spent as a journeyman for an engineer.

The first matriculation examination was held at the University of Bombay in 1859. There were 132 candidates who appeared to be tested in languages and mathematics. Only 22 passed the examinations. The majority of those who failed lacked knowledge of the native languages. The British-inspired university system emphasized Indian as well as English languages. The reason for this emphasis was the belief that teaching and learning were best done in the native tongue. Sir Bartle Edward Frere, chancellor of the University of Bombay, believed that the object of education was "to enrich your own vernacular literature through the learning which you acquire in this University . . . the learning which can here be imparted to a few hundreds . . . of scholars, must by you be made available through your own vernacular tongues to the many millions of Hindustan."

In 1861 the matriculated students appeared for the first examination. Only seven passed. In 1862 six candidates appeared for the final examination for the bachelor of arts degree; only four passed. In addition, Grant Medical College presented candidates to the university, of whom only four passed. The first four to receive the bachelor of arts degree from the University of Bombay included Mahadev Govind Ranade and Ramkrishna Gopal Bhandarkar. An embarrassing error occurred when the names were posted. Initially only three of the names were listed as passing the exam. When Sir Alexander Grant of Elphinstone College noticed his student Bhandarkar's name was missing, he asked to have the test results examined. The results from another student's exam had mistakenly been interchanged with Bhandarkar's. The correction was made and Bhandarkar was awarded the bachelor of arts.

Ranade went on to become the first Indian judge on the Bombay High Court. A social reformer, he published two well-known books: *The Rise of Maratha Power* and *Essays on Indian Economy.* Bhandarkar became a teacher and researcher. He was knighted in 1911 and an institute in his name was established in 1919 called the Bhandarkar Oriental Institute.

The university was without a building of its own. For this reason the first convocation was held in the town hall. There the senate and the syndicate held their meetings, and university degrees were conferred there. In 1863 philanthropist Cowasjee Jehanghier offered to donate money toward the construction of a university hall, with his donation supplemented by funds from the government. The famed architect, Sir Gilbert Scott (architect of the Houses of Parliament in London), was called upon to design the buildings. Unfortunately, Scott, who had never visited India, performed all his work in England. Building plans were discussed via correspondence, a factor which caused so many delays that at one point Cowasjee Jehanghier grew impatient and threatened to withdraw his donation.

The government had settled on a site on the Esplanade opposite the Churchgate Street entrance, an area under development and with new roads. Thanks to Governor Sir Bartle Frere the century-old moat and fort ruins had been dismantled and the area was at the beginning of a building renaissance. Finally, on December 29, 1868, the cornerstone was laid by Chancellor Sir Seymour Fitzgerald. Afterward, due to government bureaucracy, the site was taken from the university and reassigned to the Bombay High Court. In November 1874, the Senate Hall was finally completed at a cost of Rs. 379,092. On March 4, 1875, the senate passed a resolution to rename the hall Sir Cowasjee Jehanghier Hall, in honor of his generous donation of Rs. 100,000 to construct it. The thirteenth-century French architectural structure stands 63 feet high. At the north end of the hall is a circular stained-glass window with the 12 signs of the zodiac. A gallery supported by ornamental brackets runs along the three sides of the hall. More stunning is the University Library and Rajabai Clock Tower (sometimes referred to as the Rajabai Tower Library), completed in November 1878 at a cost of Rs. 547,703. Built with funds from successful businessman Premchand Raychand, the tower was named in memory of his mother, Rajabai. Rising some 280 feet, the tower became the tallest building in Bombay. The ground floor has two wide rooms, a central hall, and a staircase. The tower forms a carriage porch 26 square feet in front of the building. The main building is 152 feet long with round open staircases leading to an upper floor used as a reading room with stained-glass windows. Above the carriage porch is a gallery extending 68 feet from the ground, followed by two more stages of galleries that combined rise 280 feet to the finial. Large figures carved from Porebunder stone depicting the different races and costumes of western India were set in the pillars above the first gallery. Above were similar statues showing different costumes and dress of the multicultural populace of Bombay.

On February 27, 1880, the ceremony opening the university building was held. The area around the Rampart Road had changed considerably during the past ten years. Besides the new university buildings, the High Court Building, the General Post Office, and the Public Works Building now graced the campus environs. The university ceremony prominently featured scientific exhibits because the University of Bombay had recently decided to offer a bachelor of sciences degree (first conferred in 1882). Exhibits included coral reef specimens, microscopes with blood samples, specimens of plants, and an electric light. Drawings illustrated new nineteenth-century inventions such as the microphone, the phonograph, and the telephone.

In 1883 the University of Bombay decided to admit women. The issue had first been raised in 1875 when Post Master Kharsedji inquired whether his daughter, Phiroze Sorabji, could appear for the matriculation examination. The syndicate replied that no provision had been made to admit women when the university had been incorporated. However, the issue was not forgotten. In 1878, London University became the first British university to admit women. The syndicate reconsidered, and in 1883 Chancellor Sir James Ferguson stated, "Their intellects are as acute, their power of assimilating knowledge as great and means of usefulness open to them by the acquisition of knowledge not inferior to those of men." Cornelia Sorabjee was admitted to Deccan College of Poona and became the first female graduate of the University of Bombay in 1888.

Tragedy struck the university campus when the bodies of two young women were found at the base of the Rajabai Tower on April 25, 1891. According to the coroner, 16-year-old Pherozebi Sorabji Kamden and 20-year-old Bachubai Ardeshir Godrej had died by being thrown from the top of the tower. A suspect was arrested, then acquitted by the Bombay High Court due to lack of evidence. Rewards were offered for information, and rumors circulated that there was a second suspect who was from a socially prominent family. The case was eventually closed and the murders never solved.

Changes were gradually made in the curriculum. The creation of the faculty of science in 1879 made the University of Bombay the first Indian university to offer a science degree. In 1887 French was recognized as a second language, and in 1892 the course leading to the B.A. degree was extended from three to four years. Kashinath Trimbak Telang, who became the first Indian vice chancellor of the university in 1893, was instrumental in these changes. His death at the age of 43 in 1894 led to a debate about Hindus and education. In a convocation address in 1894 Dr. Ramkrishna Bhandarkar discussed the high mortality rate among Hindi graduates. Also shaken by Telang's death was Mahadev G. Ranade. Speaking to the Bombay Graduates Association that same year, he argued that Hindi poverty and the competitiveness of the university system contributed to this death rate.

By the turn of the century the University of Bombay was still functioning under the 1857 constitution. Reform was imperative. The university now had 11 colleges affiliated with its program and over 4,000 candidates for matriculation. The Universities Act of 1904 affected all the universities in India. Its attempt to reform higher education in India received both criticism and praise. The act, the result of a two-year commission study, put all the universities under government control. It was disliked because it placed limits on the number of people in the senate and syndicate and controlled the approval of colleges affiliated with the universities. Supporters argued it made the universities teaching institutions as well as examining boards and provided assistance for teaching positions and equipment. The annual grant the university received from the government was Rs. 15,000, hardly enough to make it a teaching institution. In 1912 the government of Bombay's generous offer of an annual grant of Rs. 45,000 opened a new era for the university.

With this money lecturers from affiliated colleges were brought to the university to lecture M.A. students. Professors from Europe and the United States were invited to be guest lecturers and the role of the university library was expanded. Newly established research grants promoted publishing.

With facilities at the University of Bombay inadequate by 1914, consulting architect to the Bombay government, George Wittet, worked with the senate to design new buildings. Two buildings were to be constructed to the north and south of the university gardens. Although they were to be completed by 1920, financial difficulties caused numerous delays. The south wing was completed in 1922 at a cost of Rs. 450,000 and the schools of economics and sociology moved there in 1923. The north wing's eastern half was ready in 1923, but its western half was finished in 1937 for the Office of Registrar. With help from the government of India in 1952, the east wing was constructed for the new school of civics and politics.

Growing political unrest reached its peak in the 1940s, when students rallied to join Mohandas Gandhi's Quit India Movement in 1942. Students who participated in the freedom struggle were excused from class attendance provided they had recommendations from the principals of their schools. The university convocation, which was to be held on August 18, 1942, had to be postponed until February 10, 1943, due to political disturbances.

In 1947 India won its independence from British rule. Interestingly, this led to an increase in the number of women entering college. In 1930, 1,245 women were attending college. In 1951 and 1952 this number had increased to 9,167. That same year the country was divided into Pakistan and India, resulting in the displacement of persons from both countries. The University of Bombay sought to accommodate Indians migrating from Sind and Punjab in Pakistan based on their Pakistani educational records.

Another effect of the division of India and Pakistan was the loss of jurisdiction of the university's affiliated colleges. In 1947 there were 79 schools affiliated with the University of Bombay. In 1955 this number shrank to 31. In 1962, following the liberation of Goa, the jurisdiction

of the university was increased to Union territory, and the number of affiliated colleges began to rise. By 1980, over 131 colleges were connected with the university with enrollments of over 100,000. In 1949 the matriculation examination had been abolished, due to the government-imposed Secondary School Certificate Examination Act, which was enacted in 1948. Also in 1949 the university set up its own printing press in the former Indian Air Training Corps hangar building, which had been used during World War II. The increasing need for its own press was due to the growing publications of the university, including the *Journal of the University of Bombay* and the University Bulletin.

The University of Bombay celebrated its centennial in 1957. On February 3, an enormous torchlight procession of over 10,000 students, alumni, and faculty headed down what had been the old ramparts and forts less than a century before and entered the university gardens past the flood lit Rajabai Tower. A new coat of arms was designed for the university in honor of the centennial: it includes the Rajabai Tower above an open book that represents learning, and the university motto written in Sanskrit ("The fruit of learning is character and righteous conduct").

However, all was not peaceful at the university. In July 1977, the employees union, representing the non-teaching employees at the university, went on strike for 17 days over demands to change the pay scale. The government agreed in principle with the strikers and they returned to work. A second strike, which began on December 14, 1977, lasted 53 days. Ultimately, the workers won their demand for an adjustment in their "Dearness Allowance" (an income supplement).

An ambitious expansion program initiated in the 1960s continues. In 1962 the rector of the University of Bombay, Professor G.D. Parikh, envisioned a utopian campus with room to grow. It would contain a new university library, buildings for individual departments, a botanical garden, a herbarium, and a zoo. In 1966 the university acquired 231 acres in the village of Kole-Kaylan. When the government red tape finally cleared in 1969, construction costs had risen. On March 9, the cornerstone for the new science building was laid, and the building was ready for occupation in 1971. Progress was slow but continued and the Humanities Building was ready the following year, then the library in 1976. Work continued on the Kalina campus through the 1980s with many buildings yet to be added.

The two main libraries, the Rajabai Clock Tower Library and the Nehru Library on the Kalina Campus, hold over 600,000 books and journals. The Tower Library holds many old documents, including over 1,200 manuscripts on Islamic theology and Zoroastrianism, illuminated manuscripts in the Marathi language, and the diaries and personal records of old Bombay families. The Nehru Library, in contrast, has the most recent books in the sciences and social sciences.

The university has a long list of outstanding graduates who have made major contributions to Indian life and culture. They include: Mithan Tata, who became the first Indian female lawyer in the 1920s; Dhondo Keshan Karve, a woman's rights activist who founded the Widow's Home in 1898 and established the Society for the Promotion of Widow Marriages; Pandurang Vaman Kane, whose works include the five-volume history of ancient Hindu scripture, *History of Dharmasastra.*

Further Reading: The centennial year produced two good biographies of the university. T.V. Chidambaran, the chair of the Souvenir Volume Committee, published *University of Bombay (1857–1957) Centenary Souvenir* (Bombay: Bombay University Press, 1957), which contains photographs, reminiscences, and statistical information. S.R. Dongerkery, who was the Registrar of the University of Bombay, provides an exhaustive account of the university's history in *A History of the University of Bombay 1857–1957* (Bombay: Bombay University Press, 1957). University librarian Aroon Tikekar's *The Cloister's Pale: A Biography of the University of Bombay* (Bombay: Somaiya, 1984), which relies on Dongerkery's book, updates the history to the 1980s and provides many photographs, maps, and drawings.

—Patrice Kane

UNIVERSITY OF NORTH CAROLINA
(Chapel Hill, North Carolina, U.S.A.)

Location: Chapel Hill, North Carolina, about 24 miles east of Raleigh, North Carolina.

Description: A state university enrolling approximately 24,500 students in undergraduate, graduate, doctoral, and professional programs.

Information: Office of Undergraduate Admission
University of North Carolina at Chapel Hill
CB# 2200, Jackson Hall
Chapel Hill, NC 27599-2200
U.S.A.
(919) 966-3621

Visiting: Guided tours of the campus are available year round. For more information, call the phone number above.

According to legend, William R. Davie and a group of trustees set out one day in 1792 to find a suitable spot on which to build North Carolina's first state university. After an exhausting search, Davie and his companions sat down—possibly to rest from the summer heat—beneath a giant poplar near a hill known as New Hope Chapel. After they partook of "exhilarating beverages," and a picnic lunch, followed by a nap, the group was convinced by Davie that there could not be a more beautiful spot for a university. A tree near the center of the university was christened "Davie Poplar" in the late nineteenth century by Cornelia Spencer, the daughter of a prominent university professor, in honor of the father of the university.

While the legend is appealing, the creation of the University of North Carolina at Chapel Hill, the nation's first public university, dates back to 1776 when the state's constitution was drafted. The constitution stated "one or more universities" were to be started with state support and instruction provided at "low prices."

Before a university could be built, the Revolutionary War broke out and it was not until 1789 that the General Assembly chartered the University of North Carolina. Despite the charter, trustees were left to find money and land themselves. Davie, a state legislator who had pushed for the charter, took up the task of locating the university. He and 39 other trustees identified possible sites. In August 1792, 25 of the 40 trustees met to discuss several options. In the end, the group agreed to build the university within 15 miles of Cyprett's bridge in Chatham County. In December of the same year, the group's land

search committee chose New Hope Chapel Hill as the site. A central location and roads accessible to the eastern and western parts of the state played a role in the choice, but the site's selection was made in large measures because of the donation of more than 1,300 acres of land by 12 landowners. The land was to be used for the university and for firewood. As a token of gratitude, the trustees granted the donors the "respective priviliges [*sic*] of having one student educated at the said university free from any expense of tuition."

Four years after the charter was signed, Davie and the university's founding fathers watched on October 12, 1793, as the cornerstone of Old East, the nation's first public university building, was laid. The two-story brick building, which still stands and is listed as a National Historic Landmark, was first used as a dormitory, library, and classroom. Archibald Henderson, a UNC alumnus and mathematics professor, described Old East's architectural design in his 1940 book, *The Campus of the First State University*. John Conroy drew up the building's original design which

indicates a preoccupation with Oriental ideas in consonance with Moslem *mores*. In the East it was customary to bury the dead with head directed toward the east, to face toward the east in crying the *muezzin* (call to prayer) and to build temples and mausoleums fronting toward the rising sun.

Henderson speculated that the building's Orientalization had its beginnings with the Masonic Order, and that Conroy's design may have been influenced by Davie who became North Carolina's Grand Master of Masons in 1792. In 1822, a third story was added to the building, and it was lengthened to its present-day size sometime between 1845 and 1848. While it was first used for multiple purposes, as the university grew its sole purpose became that of a dormitory. It was closed in 1991 for a two-year renovation to celebrate the university's bicentennial.

Today, Old East remains a men's dormitory across the street from South Building—which houses the chancellor's office. Old East is one of 30 dorms and 151 major buildings on the 792-acre campus.

When Old East, then known as East Building, was finished in 1795 it was the only structure on campus for two years. Person Hall, long used as the chapel, was the next structure to be built, and the cornerstone for Main, now known as South Building, was laid in 1798; the building was not completed until 1814.

University of North Carolina

When the university opened its doors on January 15, 1795, it had no president or students. The Reverend David Ker, a Presbyterian preacher had been chosen as the first presiding professor the year before, but it would be ten more years before Joseph Caldwell was named its first president. The lack of students was resolved a month later when Hinton James arrived from Wilmington, North Carolina, on February 12. Today, a ten-story dormitory is named in his honor. By March, there were 40 more students. The university remained the only institution of higher learning in the state until 1837 when Davidson College was founded.

Before the Revolutionary War began, there had been nine colleges in the 13 colonies. All but one, the College of Philadelphia, were sectarian. Davie, who was brought up a Calvinist and was urged by his uncle to join the ministry, seemed opposed to having a religious leader at the helm. But when at least six of the seven nominees for presiding professor were ministers, he had no choice but to accept Ker's appointment. While Davie failed in securing a secular leader, he did convince leaders to offer science courses along with the classics. Science, English, and history made up the core courses of study, with the classics being offered as electives. In addition to philosophy, the

languages, mathematics, and history, students were offered courses in chemistry, astronomy, geography, philosophy of medicine, and agriculture and mechanics. For the first several years, students could receive a bachelor of arts degree. In 1875 a bachelor of sciences was added, and a year later graduate-level courses were offered for the first time. Three years later the university began providing courses in pharmacy and medical studies.

Along with strict academic requirements, the first university students also had to attend sunrise and evening prayers and Sunday religious services and adhere to stringent rules for student behavior. Monitors were appointed to make sure no students used profane language, gambled, or spoke ill of religion. Those who disobeyed the rules faced punishment, usually a suspension that ranged from two weeks to six months. Despite the strict rules, it was known widely that many students gambled, remained unruly, and threatened professors. These problems climaxed in 1799, when students rioted against campus regulations and against presiding professor James Gillaspie, who had become obnoxious to them. The students beat Gillaspie and stoned and threatened other faculty members. When the riot was over, about 35 of the university's 115 students withdrew, many promising never to return.

Students finally took control of monitoring their behavior 76 years after the riot. In 1875 the university adopted a student honor system. Students elected others from among themselves to try cases involving cheating and other infractions the faculty and trustees had overseen before. Each student was required to sign a pledge stating he had neither given nor received aid during an examination. The system has survived for nearly 120 years, even when, in 1936, a widespread cheating ring involving many prominent student leaders was discovered to have been in existence for two years. Franklin Graham, university president at the time, told the student council, "The honor code belongs to the students. It is your responsibility. Blow the lid off it if you have to, but get to the bottom of it." When the investigation was completed, more than 100 students were expelled, including most of one fraternity.

With the 1799 riot, Gillaspie resigned and Joseph Caldwell assumed the university's reins again, at the request of the students. Caldwell had replaced Ker in 1796, but he had given up the position of presiding professor six months after assuming the job, remaining on the faculty as a professor of mathematics. His second tenure as head of the university lasted much longer, culminating in 1804 with his appointment as the first president of the university.

With Davie retiring to his South Carolina plantation, Caldwell assumed an even greater role in guiding the university. He moved to restore the classic curriculum making Latin and Greek required subjects. In 1812 he withdrew as president and resumed his professorship in mathematics, only to return to the presidency four years later, the same year the university conferred an honorary degree on him.

During the early nineteenth century, the university's appearance began to take shape. Main Building was completed in 1814 and housed two literary societies, boarding rooms, and classrooms. Old West, designed as the sister building of Old East, was completed in 1823. In addition, stone walls were constructed along many paths by piling field stones together. Similar stone walls remain a centerpiece of the campus.

Shortly after Caldwell's death in 1835, a monument was created in his honor on the north side of campus. It was replaced in 1858 by a new marble obelisk, on the site where Caldwell, his wife, and her son from a previous marriage, Professor William Hooper, are buried. Caldwell Monument is part of a unique designing quirk that has several buildings and monuments located in a straight line through the longitudinal center of campus. Also part of this unique symmetry are Davie Poplar; Silent Sam, a bronze statue erected in 1913 to honor Confederate soldiers; Old Well, a university symbol that had been a primary source of water; South Building; Wilson Library, which was completed in 1929; and the Bell Tower, which was finished in 1931 and stands 167 feet tall and contains a dozen bells ranging in size from 300 pounds to 3,500 pounds.

In the late spring of 1847, a current of excitement ran through Chapel Hill as a U.S. president visited the campus for the first time. It was not President James K. Polk's first trip to the university, since he was born in Mecklenburg County, North Carolina, and had graduated from Carolina in 1818, where he earned first honors both in mathematics and in the classics and finished first in his class. The campus was given a facelift for his visit, with a coat of tan wash applied to the buildings. At the chapel, Gerrard Hall, which had been enlarged for his visit, he was welcomed by the president of the university, David Lowry Swain. Over the next two days, Polk renewed acquaintance with the campus. Accompanied by college friends he strolled past the buildings of his youth, and with his wife returned to his old dorm room on the third floor of South Building.

As momentous as Polk's visit was to the campus, less than 15 years later scores of Carolina graduates and students would take part in a war against the nation Polk had led. During the Civil War, the university was one of only two Southern universities to remain open, but students and faculty were few. The university's fortune became graver when Swain, a former governor of North Carolina, was thrust forward to meet General William Tecumseh Sherman to discuss terms of surrender for Raleigh, the state's capital. During that meeting with Sherman, an old correspondent and former college president, Swain was assured the university and its property would be safeguarded.

On April 17, 1865, Sherman's forces entered the village with a handsome 30-year-old general, Smith B. Atkins, at their head. Two days later, Atkins called upon Swain, and there encountered the president's 21-year-old daughter, Ellie Swain. It was love at first sight for both, which meant hard times for Swain, who, some said, was consorting with Union soldiers. The Union brigadier made Ellie Swain a present of a spirited riding horse, and every evening he dispatched the regimental band to Swain's house to serenade her. In three weeks, Ellie was engaged to the enemy commander who was occupying the town; in four months, they were married. So incensed were Confederate loyalists that Cornelia Spencer (a nineteenth-century professor's daughter) noted in her diary, "[wedding] invitations were spat upon in one or two houses."

This episode set the stage for the next visit by an American president, since Swain, despite his loss of popularity, still held office when Andrew Johnson came to Chapel Hill in 1867. Johnson, once viewed in the South as a renegade, had redeemed himself with his native section by the time he arrived in Chapel Hill in 1867 by vetoing the Reconstruction Acts, though his veto had been overridden by Congress and military rule imposed. A few years earlier, the University of North Carolina had the largest enrollment of any college or university in the United States except Yale. But when President Johnson and his party attended the 1867 commencement, the number of "distinguished guests" seated on the stage of Gerrard Hall outnumbered the graduating class, a total of only 11. After Johnson's visit, the reconstruction governor removed Swain as president of the university in 1868. Not many days later, the horse General Sherman had given Swain as a present bolted, hurling him to the ground, and he died shortly thereafter.

While the Civil War shut many universities, that fate did not befall the University of North Carolina until 1870, when a shortage of students forced its closure. It remained closed until 1875 when Mrs. Spencer and others pressed for its reopening. She wrote a series of scathing articles in North Carolina publications blasting those who had forced its closure. Her writings and work are credited with the reopening of the university. When she received word in March 1875 that the university would open again she gathered a group of friends and went to the attic of South Building, then in shambles, and rang the bell to sound the news.

By the time of its centennial celebration, the university had been renovated and refurbished. It was still a small school, not yet considered among the elite institutions of higher learning in the nation. As the twentieth century neared, major changes began to occur. In 1897, Mary McRae was the first of five women to enroll in the university; a year later Sallie Walker Stockard became the first woman to earn a degree from it. The university was awarded North Carolina's first chapter of Phi Beta Kappa (the national scholarship fraternity) and James Horner Winston became its first Rhodes Scholar. A milestone occurred in 1915 when the university's enrollment topped 1,000 for the first time. By 1930, enrollment had risen to 2,600 students.

Other social changes came later. Like many universities across the country, the school was forced to desegregate in the 1950s. In 1952, Harvey Beech, who earned a law degree, became the first black man to graduate from the university. However, in 1955 when a federal court ordered that admission requests be processed without regard to race and color, the university appealed the decision. The appeal failed, and in 1959 three black men from Durham—brothers Leroy and Ralph Frasier and John Brandon—became the first blacks to earn undergraduate degrees. Blyden Jackson because the first black full professor at the University of North Carolina-Chapel Hill. While the university is more diverse than ever, with women making up 58 percent of the students and blacks about 10 percent, struggles continue.

By 1993, the university's bicentennial, its reputation had grown internationally, as *U.S. News and World Report*'s survey of American colleges has consistently ranked it among the best colleges in the nation and among the best research universities. One man who single-handedly brought fame to the university was basketball star Michael Jordan, who enrolled as a freshman in 1982. On October 12, 1993, when President Bill Clinton delivered the University Day speech, he became the fifth U.S. president to speak at the campus. Even on a campus that regularly features protests and performers, this was a banner day—including flags from 80 of North Carolina's 100 counties and 100 seedlings from Davie Poplar Jr. given to 100 students from North Carolina's 100 counties.

On the 32nd anniversary of President John F. Kennedy's University Day speech, President Bill Clinton spoke of the university's founders: "Tonight, we honor this university's heroic builders and believers. We meet as their heirs a dozen generations after our nation and this university were founded—and we meet at another moment of change."

Further Reading: William Snider's *Light on the Hill* (Chapel Hill: University of North Carolina Press, 1992) offers a lengthy account of the university from its founding until the late 1980s. Kemp Battle's two-volume account of the *History of the University of North Carolina* (Spartanburg, South Carolina: The Reprint Company, 1974) gives an extensive view of the university from 1789 until 1912. Albert Coates provides a more personal view of the university in *A Magic Gulf Stream in the Life of North Carolina* (Chapel Hill: University of North Carolina Press, 1978). A pictorial and written history can be found in William Powell's *The First State University* (3rd edition, Chapel Hill: University of North Carolina Press, 1992).

—J. Cameron Tew

UNIVERSITY OF NOTRE DAME
(Notre Dame, Indiana, U.S.A.)

Location: The University of Notre Dame is located in the midwest region of the United States at Notre Dame, Indiana, adjacent to the city of South Bend, Indiana, and approximately 90 miles southeast of Chicago, Illinois.

Description: The University of Notre Dame was founded in 1842 by Father Edward Sorin, a priest of the Congregation of the Holy Cross. Chartered by the state of Indiana in 1844, the university was governed by the Holy Cross order of the Catholic Church until 1967, when governance was transferred to a predominantly lay board of trustees. At present, the university is an independent, national Catholic university with a student body of 10,500. The university programs include extensive undergraduate and graduate studies, as well as a law school and a business school. Notre Dame has earned world renown for its achievements in intercollegiate football.

Information: University of Notre Dame
Public Relations and Information
317 Main Building
Notre Dame, IN
U.S.A.
(219) 631-7367
Fax (219) 631-8212

Father Edward Sorin, a Catholic priest and missionary, arrived at the present site of Notre Dame University on a cold, winter day in November 1842. With him were four of his fellow brethren of the order of the Congregation of the Holy Cross (CSC). Sorin, the religious superior and advisor of these men, had been granted the church-owned land (totaling 524 acres) with the stipulation that he build a religious novitiate and a college within two years. Under frontier conditions Sorin and his small group fulfilled the agreement; by December 1844 the Notre Dame community encompassed five buildings, including the Main Building, the novitiate, and a chapel. Sorin began accepting pupils in 1843, and in 1844 John D. Defrees, a South Bend attorney and state senator, secured a comprehensive charter of incorporation for the school as a degree-granting university from the Indiana legislature.

In the early decades, the Main Building comprised the entire University of Notre Dame. Its rooms served both as classroom and dormitory space. All boys and young men who applied for admission were accepted. Tuition for education and for room and board (all students boarded) was rarely fulfilled with cash, but more frequently through trade of goods (such as pigs or cows) or through physical labor (one boy's father, a carpenter, agreed to build the church steeple). The school included three levels of instruction: the Minim Department, the Junior Department, and the Senior Department. The Minim Department taught the youngest boys elementary arithmetic, reading, grammar, and history. The Junior Department, a college preparatory division, taught Latin, Greek, English, history, and composition. The curricula of the Senior Department, the collegiate division, consisted of four years of humanities, poetry, rhetoric, philosophy, modern languages (French, German, Spanish, or Italian), music, and drawing. In the early decades, the Senior Department never attracted more than a dozen students yearly. The needs of local families during this period largely precluded schooling in anything except the essentials. Sorin's main desire was for the school to instruct young men to be good, Catholic citizens. Although his vision included the development of the collegiate division, the development of the preparatory divisions fulfilled both his desires and the needs of the larger community during this era.

When Sorin founded Notre Dame, he founded a frontier colony. With little capital and meager resources, Sorin developed Notre Dame into a self-sufficient community. He and the members of his community erected the first buildings and farmed the land. Within two years of their arrival, 120 acres of wheat, potatoes, and corn were under cultivation. The Notre Dame farm buildings grew to include an ice house, a pigsty, a slaughterhouse, a cow barn, a hay barn, a sugar house, a horse shed, a wagon shed, and a tool house. Notre Dame produced their own lime and brick beginning in 1843, using the rich marl deposits in the soil. The yellow brick, used in all early buildings and known commonly as "Notre Dame brick," made Notre Dame's campus distinctive and brought in revenue on the market. Sorin invited Sisters of the Holy Cross to the community in 1843 who assumed many of the domestic tasks of the institution. A manual labor school taught orphans and other poor children trades such as carpentry and leather working. Sorin channeled his energies, not solely to the development of the University of Notre Dame, but to the development of an entire community.

Under Sorin's direction the school grew both in numbers and in quality. In 1844, Notre Dame consisted of five buildings, eight faculty and 25 students. Nearly 50 years

University of Notre Dame

later, in 1893, Notre Dame had grown to include 24 buildings, a faculty of 52, and a student body of 542. The University of Notre Dame had six presidents between 1842 and 1893: Father Edward Sorin (1842–65), Father Patrick Dillon (1865–66), Father William Corby (1866–72), Father August Lemonnier (1872–74), Father Patrick J. Colovin (1874–77), Father William Corby in a second term (1877–81), and Father Thomas Walsh (1881–93). However, the real authority during this time was Sorin; upon relinquishing his post as president, he retained authority over the community as Provincial of the Congregation of the Holy Cross in Indiana and later as Superior-General of the CSC in Europe and in the Americas. Sorin's vision made possible the magnificent Sacred Heart Church, with its 42 large, stained-glass windows and elaborate frescoes painted by the Italian artist Luigi Gregori, constructed between 1871 and 1888. When the school's Main Building burned to the ground in 1879, a tragedy which destroyed the entire school, Sorin's determination to rebuild bigger and better than before led the school in its rapid recovery. Sorin dedicated a large portion of his time and energy to found Notre Dame and continued to guide its development until his death in 1893.

The quality and popularity of college instruction advanced slowly. Under Father Walsh (1881–93), civil and mechanical engineering became regular four-year courses. Walsh procured the services of notable lay faculty, including Maurice Francis Egan (a poet and novelist reputable in U.S. Catholic circles) in literature, Albert Zahm (an influential pioneer of flight aerodynamics) in the sciences, and William Hoynes (a lawyer, an inspirational professor, and an excellent administrator) in law. Father Andrew Morrissey (1893–1905) revised and elaborated the college curriculum, raised the entrance requirements, and expanded the physical plant of the campus to accommodate more students. An average of 30 bachelors degrees were conferred per year during Morrissey's presidency, along with several masters. Father John W. Cavanaugh (1905–19) recognized the need for additional faculty, laboratories, professorships, and scholarships, and for an adequate library. He commissioned a building plan from architect Francis Kervik and witnessed the completion of the Lemonnier Library in 1917.

The 1920s were a definitive period for the university. James A. Burns (1919–22), the first university president with a doctorate, improved academic standards, restructured the administration, and strengthened financial support. He recruited faculty with doctorates and standardized college entrance and graduation requirements. He divided the university into five colleges—arts and letters, science, engineering, law, and commerce—assigning a dean and several department heads to each. When Burns came to the presidency, the preparatory divisions had accounted for nearly half of the total student body. With increasing enrollment (due in part to the post–World War I college boom), the presence of preps meant the rejection of college applicants due to a lack of dormitory space. Burns summarily did away with the first two years of the preparatory school, illustrating the new dedication of Notre Dame to the development of their collegiate division. Burns also contributed greatly to the financial status of the institution, bolstering the school's endowment with support from the General Education Board of the Rockefeller Foundation ($250,000) and the Carnegie Foundation ($75,000). Before 1921, the school's endowment never surpassed $100,000. With Rockefeller and Carnegie Foundation support, Burns instigated a $2 million endowment drive which he continued to direct after the completion of his presidential term.

Also during the 1920s, Notre Dame acquired national fame for its football program. Notre Dame's intercollegiate football career began inauspiciously in 1887, when they lost 0 to 8 to the University of Michigan. For the next 25 years, Notre Dame lost money on their football program. Football began producing revenue only in 1913, when Notre Dame upset Army 35 to 13. Knute Kenneth Rockne, captain of this winning football team, returned to Notre Dame football as full-time coach in 1918 and proceeded to place Notre Dame in the national news. He coached the team until his death in 1931, winning 105 games, losing 12, and tying 5. Rockne's flamboyant side-line manner and performance, his knowledge of football strategy, and his ability to motivate young men to extraordinary performance made him a fascinating persona for the growing numbers of sports fans. During this time period, football (and baseball)

acquired an unprecedented following, as individuals of all ages across the nation attended games and followed the successes and failures of their favorite team. It was Notre Dame's good fortune to acquire a number of superstars, in addition to Rockne, during the 1920s. For three years, a handsome George Gipp led Rockne's team in rushing, passing, and scoring; his untimely death in December 1920 led to the inspirational saying, "Win one for the Gipper." Rockne's 1924 team, which had a brilliant backfield known as the Four Horsemen in reference to the four biblical plagues of the apocalypse, took Notre Dame to the Rose Bowl. Throughout the decade, the team brought additional revenue to the school and placed Notre Dame in the public eye, attracting greater numbers of students and thereby furthering the growth of the college.

Football revenue, along with the funds acquired by President Burns, enabled his successors, Father Matthew J. Walsh (1922–28), Father Charles O'Donnell (1928–34), and Father John F. O'Hara (1934–40), to expend over $5 million on campus construction. Increased admissions had led to a campus housing shortage; the 1,000 students living in South Bend in 1922 represented a financial loss to Notre Dame and compromised the traditional residential atmosphere of the campus. Father Matthew Walsh alleviated the housing shortage with the construction of two temporary residences (Freshman Hall, 1922; and Sophomore Hall, 1923) and three permanent residences (Howard Hall, 1924; Lyons Hall, 1925; and Morrissey Hall, 1925). In addition to providing rooms for over 900 students, Walsh also placed a limit of 2,500 on enrollment. Father Charles O'Donnell provided more needed space when he ended the Minim program in 1929, and St. Edward's Hall became a dorm for 200 college men. The following year, a new football stadium (seating 59,074) graced the campus, a testament to both the glory of and the money in Notre Dame football. O'Donnell and his successor, Father John O'Hara, oversaw the further extension of the school's campus with the construction of a new power plant, water tower, infirmary, and three additional residence buildings (Cavanaugh Hall, Zahm Hall, and Breen-Phillips Hall).

The increasing revenue of the 1920s not only allowed for building projects but also created growth opportunities for the university's academic program. Although the Great Depression did affect the university's enrollment, Notre Dame neither cut salaries nor laid off faculty. In fact, the school managed to strengthen its academic programs. By the early 1930s Notre Dame had abandoned its grade, preparatory, and vocational schools and was concentrating on upgrading its undergraduate and recently founded graduate programs. Although Notre Dame had awarded masters of arts degrees throughout its history, its formal graduate school was not established until 1932. Respectability for a professor in American higher education largely demanded separation of religious and academic thought, as well as the possession of advanced degrees. For this reason, Notre Dame had recruited increasing numbers of degreed laymen to the faculty. In 1932 laymen outnumbered clerics nearly three to one; 20 lay professors possessed doctorates; 40 possessed masters. These numbers represent a profound divergence from tradition for an institution initially comprised solely of brothers, sisters, and priests of the Catholic religion; they also represent the school's aspirations to become a first-rate university.

The 1940s marked the return of high student enrollment, football success, and active presidential efforts to strengthen university status. After World War II, with 1.5 million veterans enrolling in American colleges on the G.I. bill, Notre Dame's student body increased dramatically. Veterans entered Notre Dame academics and athletics both as students and staff, including Frank W. Leahy as football coach. Leahy coached six unbeaten teams between 1941 and 1953, recruiting hardened veterans as players and earning a winning streak of 39 games. The graduate school also flourished after the war, with the acquisition of refugee scholars of war-torn Europe. Their emigration to the United States strengthened academic inquiry at Notre Dame and in numerous institutions of American higher education. Father John Cavanaugh (1946–52) built upon the postwar increase in students and faculty, increasing fund-raising efforts and strengthening the academic program. Cavanaugh created the Notre Dame Foundation in 1947, the first permanent university endowment, and carried the needs of the school to the American Council on Education and the Ford Foundation. He upgraded the quality of academics, emphasizing advanced studies and research and authorizing the construction of LOBUND (Labs of Bacteria at the University of Notre Dame). These labs have played a significant role in bone-marrow treatment for leukemia and Hodgkins disease.

Father Theodore Hesburgh accepted the presidency in 1952, determined to bring Notre Dame status as a great institution of higher learning. In a dynamic, 35-year presidency, Father Hesburgh secured a prominent place for Notre Dame in society and in academia. Hesburgh himself gained international renown through his academic, ecclesiastical, and civic duties (participating in numerous national academic and government agencies and serving on the boards of elite financial institutions). Hesburgh's goals for the university included building a first-rate undergraduate school, upgrading the graduate school, and reorganizing the institution as a modern university. He reformed the curricula and enforced tougher admissions requirements. He recruited visiting lecturers and permanent faculty of national academic standing. In 1960, the Ford Foundation selected Notre Dame as one of six rapidly improving universities to receive a grant of $6 million, if an additional $12 million could be raised from other sources within three years. This effort pro-

vided funds for the 14-story Memorial Library built between 1961 and 1963, a building that towers over the rest of the campus. Its 132-foot mosaic of Christ the Teacher symbolizes both Notre Dame's religious affiliation and its quest for academic greatness. Another campaign between 1967 and 1972 secured an additional $62 million, which endowed distinguished professorships, expanded graduate education, and provided minority scholarships and student loans. During Hesburgh's presidency, Notre Dame's enrollment, faculty, and the number of degrees awarded all doubled, the number of library volumes increased 5-fold, the endowment rose from under $10 million to over $400 million, its physical facilities grew from 48 to 88 buildings, its faculty compensation increased 10-fold and its research funding, more than 20-fold.

Hesburgh oversaw an era of astronomical growth for the University of Notre Dame. He also oversaw two notable changes in the structure of the university: the transference of university ownership to a predominantly lay board of trustees, and the admission of women. In 1967, the CSC community relinquished ownership of the university. Ties between the university and its founding order of the Catholic Church had grown weak during the past few decades. Of over 700 faculty members, only 55 were CSC priests or brothers. In addition, most of the university's $30 million operating budget came from secular sources. It had become increasingly clear to Hesburgh that the pursuit and realization of long-term fund-raising goals depended upon the assumption of a lay-oriented power structure. The CSC community relinquished ownership with the stipulation that Notre Dame's president continue to be a CSC priest and that Notre Dame's character as a Catholic institution of higher learning would not be abandoned without the approval of a joint committee composed equally of CSC priests and laymen. Regardless, the transference of ownership exemplified a serious break with tradition. With the acceptance of women five years later, the university accepted the characteristics of most modern American universities.

The university has continued to grow under the leadership of Father Edward A. Malloy (1987–present). The university is organized into four undergraduate colleges (arts and letters, science, engineering, and business administration), two schools (the law school and graduate school), and numerous research institutes. Admission is highly competitive, with five applicants for each freshman class position. The quality of undergraduate programs is evidenced in the success of its graduates in post-baccalaureate studies; Notre Dame ranks 18 among private universities in the number of doctorates earned by its undergraduate alumni. The graduate school, which encompasses 38 master's and 24 doctoral degree programs in 27 university departments and institutes, ranks among the nation's top 50 universities in number of doctorates awarded annually. Notre Dame's faculty continue to gain academic recognition; Notre Dame ranks in the top ten nationally among private universities in the number of National Endowment for the Humanities fellowships won by its faculty since 1985. The faculty, students, and academic capabilities of Notre Dame today, coupled with a history of religious and national football glory, make the school a notable university.

Further Reading: For general histories of the University of Notre Dame, see Arthur J. Hope's *Notre Dame: One Hundred Years* (Notre Dame, Indiana: University of Notre Dame Press, 1943), and Thomas J. Schlereth's *The University of Notre Dame: A Portrait of Its History and Campus* (Notre Dame, Indiana: University of Notre Dame Press, 1976).

—Beth Rillema

UNIVERSITY OF ORLÉANS
(Orléans, France)

Location: Orléans, in the central region of France on the banks of the Loire river, north of Paris.

Description: A state-run university established in 1970 as part of reforms of the French system of higher education in 1968. It serves the central region of France in four areas: letters and social sciences; law, economy, and management; applied sciences; and technology, energy, and materials.

Information: Château de la Source
BP 6749
45067 Orléans Cedex 2
France
(38) 41 71 71

Modern French universities such as the University of Orléans were created in the aftermath of the social and political upheavals of May 1968. The French university system differs greatly from the North American system. In France, every student who graduates with a *baccalauréat* (school-learning certificate) has a guaranteed right to register at an institution of higher learning. Some institutions called the *grandes écoles* limit their admission by competitive entrance examinations (*concours*). The vast majority of French 18- and 19-year-olds who exercise this right enter a *université* rather than undertake the special two-year preparatory courses which would be required to enter the *grandes écoles*. Since it was founded in 1971, the University of Orléans has been restructured and reorganized along the lines proposed by the Ministry of National Education while still maintaining its own autonomy and multidisciplinary approach.

The present University of Orléans was named after a medieval university that had existed from the ninth to eighteenth centuries but the current university has no direct connection with its medieval namesake. The medieval institution was renowned for its faculty of law, where Pope Clement V (1305–14) studied, but it was abolished during the French Revolution. Orléans and the central region of France would not have another university or institution of higher learning until the 1960s for higher education was to be consolidated and concentrated in Paris.

As he was for many aspects of modern French society, Napoléon was largely responsible for the French educational system. The traditional humanist ideal of universities dealing with the whole of human knowledge was replaced with his own concept of an imperial university. The university implied the entire educational system—primary schools, *lycées* (secondary schools), and faculties. Even the term *faculté* does not correspond to the North American understanding of the word. The 100 or so faculties which existed in nineteenth-century France were not associated with an independent institution but were grouped into academies, regional administrative structures that were under the control of the central educational authority. Poorly funded and staffed, they provided training for the *baccalauréat* (school-leaving certificate) or the *licence* (teacher's diploma). Professional and more advanced instruction was provided in one of the more prestigious *grandes écoles*.

Universities did not regain any status until 15 were created in 1896. They still lingered under the disadvantages of the nineteenth century. They were little more than a loose association of faculties grouped together as administrative bodies. There was little, if any, communication between disciplines and institutions despite the fact that most of them were concentrated in Paris, with decision making in the hands of the Ministry of National Education. However, individual professors could affect substantially a student's career, because they had the power to determine their own teaching and evaluating methods. These problems continued to plague the French educational system well into the twentieth century. In spite of repeated calls for a restructuring and updating of the entire system, such reforms were not forthcoming until student protests, caused in large part by serious overcrowding and high drop-out rates, forced the government to redesign radically the French university system.

The Fifth Republic was declared in October 1958 amid an atmosphere of educational reform. A succession of ministers of education introduced a number of measures aimed at dealing with the increasing problem of overcrowding in the Parisian universities. New academies were created in the outlying regions of the capital, including Orléans, in 1962 by Charles de Gaulle's Minister of National Education, Christian Fouchet. These institutions resembled their Parisian counterparts and suffered from the same organizational problems. Fouchet, however, did introduce some modest changes to the awarding of degrees. A two-year course was to constitute the first phase of higher education. Upon completion, a student would be awarded a diploma in science or in arts; any further education would have to follow the discipline chosen in the first phase. An additional year led to the *licence* (equivalent to a bachelor's degree) and a four-year course

University of Orléans

to a master's degree which was a mandatory qualification for all secondary teachers.

In response to criticism from businessmen that graduates (more often than not from faculties of law or letters) were insufficiently trained to meet industry's needs, Fouchet announced the creation of new institutes of technology (Institut Universitaire de Technologie–IUT) in October 1966. They were to provide a two-year practical course in preparation for industrial and commercial careers. Unlike the universities, they were given the right to select and limit admission based on academic records. Students who completed the course were given diplomas (Diplôme Université Technologie). Fouchet hoped that by reducing the first degree to two years, many students would complete their studies and enter the work force, but changes in the French economy in the 1960s made further education a prerequisite for finding work. The number of students quickly doubled from 1964 to 1968. The entire university system was overrun by a new generation of French students exercising their right to a free education.

The first student disturbances were at Nanterre, a bleak university campus on the outskirts of Paris. Desolate, ill-equipped, and severely overcrowded as it was, students often could not get into the halls to attend lec-

tures. Many chose simply to abandon their studies rather than study in such conditions, often at the expense of getting a good job. On March 22, 1968, 100 students occupied the university campus buildings at Nanterre to protest conditions.

Students throughout France were ripe for revolt. They were concerned about job prospects. There was a huge imbalance of students in the faculties of letters and law. With most graduates only trained for teaching, few could find careers in industry and commerce. Nearly half of the students in law and over a third in letters failed their first-year examinations. Only one third of students in France's universities were in the sciences and well over half failed their examinations. The drop-out rate among the sciences was almost 50 percent higher than that rate in letters.

Students blamed these failures on study conditions, teaching methods, and the curricula. They demanded more teachers and better teaching methods. Student/teacher ratios were significantly higher than in any other industrial country. Professors were seen as too authoritarian. Students accused them of paying more attention to research than to teaching. In France, the way to promotion lay through publication rather than by attending to students. Nonetheless, professors exercised an almost absolute control over their courses. Nor were the students pleased with the Fouchet reforms. They saw the new institutes and changes in degrees as little more than measures devised to meet industry's need for workers. They accused the new institutes of technology of producing second-rate degrees that led to mediocre dead-end jobs, while the promising careers were reserved for the graduates of the *grandes écoles.*

The unrest that started at Nanterre quickly spread. In May, police action against a meeting of sympathetic students at the Sorbonne touched off rioting. A strike by the Union nationale des étudiants de France (UNEF) was supported by the teachers' union and the all-powerful car workers at Renault. Both Prime Minister Georges Pompidou and President Charles de Gaulle were forced to cut short foreign visits to rush back and deal with the growing crisis. The protests quickly lost momentum as first the auto workers and later teachers were appeased with new collective agreements. As for the students, the de Gaulle government promised a commission which would study the question of reforms to the French educational system with particular emphasis on the student demands for more autonomy, participation, and interdisciplinarity.

In the aftermath of the student unrest, a commission studied the fundamental issues of curriculum, the organization of *facultés,* and the role universities were to play in French society. From this review new parliamentary legislation emerged that would mark a new and dramatic phase in the history of the French university. In November 1968, de Gaulle's Minister of National Education, Edgar Faure, introduced *La Loi d'orientation de l'enseignement supérieur.* The 100 or so faculties in existence were to be reorganized into 71 new universities and smaller university centers. The old faculty system was abolished, although the administrative structure of 23 academies was maintained. Each discipline was to be subdivided into *unités d'enseignement et de recherche* (UERs) which would correspond to a traditional faculty. The UER was to link teaching with research in order to develop the student's full potential.

The law also sought to meet the students' demand for more autonomy. Each university was given the authority to determine its own internal structure and to administer itself. The universities were to be run by committees or councils made up of elected representatives. The students, administrators, teachers, and support staff all had the right to vote. The highest elected body, the *conseil d'université,* was to include a number of prominent members of the region who were not associated with the university. Presidents were to be elected for a five-year term but could not seek a second mandate.

Each UER council was given the full authority to design its own programs of study, research, teaching methods, and systems of evaluation. They had to correspond to a national standard which would be set by the Ministry of National Education. They were also given greater autonomy over their own budgets and financial matters according to national limits and guidelines. The law also encouraged the active participation of students, teachers, and other staff in determining the direction of the university. Elections held among the teaching and research staff as well as for the university council were to be by secret ballot. Though this had been one of the chief demands on the part of students, their participation rates have been rather low.

The law also took great measures to reduce the formidable power which had rested in the hands of the professors. The new universities were to offer a multidisciplinary approach between arts and letters, science, and technology. It was hoped that this measure would also break down the traditional barriers between individual disciplines and introduce students to broader aspects of French society and culture.

The law of orientation has served as the basic structural model for the University of Orléans, which was created as a result of the legislation in 1971. Its three UERs offered courses in law, data processing, and technology. It chose to organize its courses in units of cycles rather than years, as was the case in many older universities. There were three phases of study: the first cycle of general study leading to an intermediate degree (*diplôme*), an additional year of specialization leading to the first degree (*licence*), and a fourth year leading to a master's degree which would then enable a student to pursue the doctorate.

Since the 1970s, the University of Orléans has been in a perpetual state of change and evolution. Although the 1968 law of orientation still remains the basic organizational structure, the university has been quick to respond to changes proposed by the Ministry of National Education. In 1973, changes were introduced to the intermediate degree. A new degree, the diplôme d'études universitaires générales (DEUG) was introduced for students who did not wish to pursue further studies after a two-year course. It was also intended to harmonize with the diplôme universitaire de technologie granted by the institutes of technology. A further aim was to streamline and reduce the number of students attending university as well as to deal with the high drop-out rate which still plagued the educational system.

Following the recession of the early 1980s, a new law, the Savoury law was passed in 1984. The *unités d'enseignement et de recherche* (UERs) were replaced with *unités de formation et de recherche* (UFRs). More than just a change in nomenclature, the law wanted to stress the importance of training (*formation*). Its chief proponent, Savoury wanted to encourage institutions of higher learning to address the critics in industry and commerce who argued that graduates were insufficiently trained to meet the challenges of a global economy and new technologies. The law provided for a greater role on the part of local industry and regional governments on the university councils.

The law also allowed universities to establish separate streams which involved more orientation and specialization during the first two years and led to the DEUG *rénové*. Further impetus to professional training was accentuated with the awarding of professionalized master's degrees.

The Minister of National Education left the decision to institute these changes up to each individual university. The University of Orléans was one of those which swiftly adopted the changes and completely reorganized in May of 1985. It established three UFRs in law, economy, and management; letters, languages, and human sciences; and in applied and natural sciences. It also includes a school of engineering and two institutes of technology.

The university awards national diplomas that are centrally sanctioned by the Ministry of Education. The period of study is organized in three stages (cycles). The first generally lasts two years and offers an initiation to the study and methodology of various disciplines. It leads to the first national diploma, the DEUG. The diploma is multidisciplinary and will enable students to qualify for further study in a wide range of areas: law, economics, communication, arts and literature, and social sciences.

The second stage consists of the *licence* (equivalent to a bachelor's degree) and is awarded after one additional year of study. The master's (*maîtrise*) is awarded to those who complete two more years after getting their DEUG and is usually taken by those who intend to continue into the third phase or wish to have a qualified teaching certificate. The third phase can involve as much as ten years of additional study and includes the *diplôme d'études approfondies* (DEA), which is itself a preparation and qualification for the doctoral thesis.

The institutes of technology (IUTs) are in fact separate institutions within the university framework. Their objective is to train high-level technical staff for France's industrial and private sectors. Admission is selective and competitive as is not the case in the rest of the university. Candidates, chosen based on their academic records and an interview, are offered a two-year intensive program in specialized areas such as chemistry, mechanical engineering, business administration, and computers. The program also includes obligatory work placements. Since many of the graduates find jobs, there is a high demand for admission.

The *École supérieure de l'énergie et de matériaux* is a school of engineering and is also a separate institution that offers more senior instruction for engineering students in the third stage. It awards the DEA, an engineering degree as well as a doctorate. The University of Orléans followed the recommendations to increase professionally oriented certificates upon completion of the first diploma.

The need for more practical training has also greatly influenced the course and subject matter at the UFRs. Though they still grant the traditional diplomas and degrees, many modern subjects have been added to the curriculum. Students in applied modern languages, for example, are encouraged to follow courses which provide them with career opportunities outside the field of education. In addition to two modern European languages, they must study economics, marketing, accounting, management, and business. Such courses have proven popular with students as they increase their job prospects not only in France but throughout the European community.

The university also offers French language and civilization courses for foreign students. Universities in France have always played an important role in providing courses for non-francophones. Its *Centre d'études pour étrangers* provides courses which lead to a certificate.

The French educational system has undergone fundamental changes since 1958. As France continues to draw closer to its European neighbors, new economic and technological changes have put a strain on the French institution of higher learning. At present, the enrollment of over 16,000 students at the University of Orléans and the practical need for longer periods of study and more professional needs may challenge the principles of free admission, greater autonomy and participation, and multidisciplinarity.

Further Reading: While no history of the University of Orléans exists in English, several books mention the university in the context of the rather turbulent history of French higher education in the twentieth century: Jean Capelle's *Tomorrow's Education, The French Experience* translated by W.D. Halls (Oxford: Pergamon Press, 1967), W.D. Halls's *Education, Culture and Politics in Modern France* (London: Pergamon Press, 1976), and *Reforms and Restraints in Modern French Education* (London: Routledge and Kegan Paul, 1971).

—Manon Lamontagne

UNIVERSITY OF OXFORD
(Oxfordshire, England)

Location:
The University of Oxford is located in the city of Oxford, Oxfordshire, England. The city is 56 miles northwest of London and has a population of approximately 150,000. Oxford is situated on the banks of the Thames and Cherwell rivers.

Description:
The University of Oxford is England's oldest university and is world renowned as a bastion of scholarship, eccentricity, and civility. The school is a unique composition of 36 colleges and 6 permanent private halls. Men and women undergraduate and graduate students are admitted in accordance with the individual college's requirements. Total student enrollment is approximately 15,000. The university buildings and grounds are spread throughout the city itself, which is a thriving metropolitan area.

Information:
University of Oxford
University Offices
Wellington Square
Oxford OXI 25D
England
(865) 270000

Visiting:
University of Oxford
External Relations Office
Wellington Square
Oxford OX1 2JD
England
(865) 270010l

Although the exact founding date for the city of Oxford is unknown, the city's development can be traced to several factors. The name, commonly believed to be derived from "oxen ford," hints that one reason for the city's development was as a convenient location for animals and their owners to cross the rivers in the area. Located in the developing economic and political center of England, Oxford's geographic importance was reflected in the ancient name for the city center: Carfax. This name, used even today, is thought to be derived from the Latin "quadrifurcus" or the French "quatre voies" and describes the four-cornered intersection of two main streets that have been here since Saxon times. The establishment of religious institutions and the area's political importance as a strategic location were other factors con-

tributing to the growth of the region. The Anglo-Saxon Chronicle of 912 contains the first written mention of Oxford, although by this time the settlement was probably over 200 years old. St. Frideswide's Priory, founded by the saint herself after divine intervention rescued her from an unwanted marriage, was established here in the eighth century. Today Christ Church Cathedral of Oxford University stands on the site of the ancient priory. Power struggles between the Danes and the Saxons enveloped the area during the tenth and eleventh centuries until political stability was achieved when the Normans conquered the area. Robert d'Oilly, the first Norman governor, oversaw the building of a castle, a wall surrounding the city, and the area's first three bridges, Folly, Magdalen, and Hythe, in the early twelfth century. In 1129 another priory, later called the Osney Abbey, was established in Oxford. Oxford University thus had as its birthplace a burgeoning center of transportation, religious, and political activity.

The exact founding date of the university, like that of the city, is not precisely known. Oxford is generally thought to have become a center for learning after 1167, when English students were no longer allowed to attend the University of Paris. Masters and students gathered in Oxford for the discussion of topics as varied as theology, the arts, and the works of Aristotle. As both the school and the city grew, tensions between the two groups arose, causing what became known as "town and gown" friction. In 1209 one dispute became so large that many scholars felt the situation unbearable and moved to the town of Cambridge. There they founded the University of Cambridge, a rival school still in existence today. The first recorded acknowledgment of Oxford University comes from a papal grant of 1214. This grant provided privileges, such as reduced rents, for the growing community of scholars and students who lived throughout the city. It was also at this time that Robert Grosseteste, a mathematician and churchman, became the first chancellor of the university. Grosseteste remained chancellor of the school until 1235 when he became bishop of Lincoln. Subsequently, for over 100 years, the bishop of Lincoln had influence over Oxford University thus adding to the school's religious character—noted even today in many of the college's names.

In these early days of the university, students lived in rented lodgings at hostels or halls, and classes were held in rented rooms or at churches. St. Edmund Hall (which did not receive official status as a college of Oxford University until 1957) was one such place of residence for students and has been in existence since the early thir-

University of Oxford

teenth century. The first colleges of Oxford University were created with endowments as housing for poor students unable to afford the rental expenses. The first three colleges of Oxford University were University College, Balliol College, and Merton College. Although all vie for distinction as the oldest, it appears that in 1249 University College was the first to be endowed. The quadrangle of this college contains a memorial to poet Percy Bysshe Shelley. He was, however, expelled from the school in 1811 for the publication of his pamphlet *The Necessity of Atheism,* which apparently expressed views offensive to the administration. Balliol College, generally thought to have been founded in 1263, was endowed by John de Balliol as an act of penitence. Many of the buildings seen here today are from the eighteenth and nineteenth centuries. Scorch marks on the quadrangle archway are from the burning of Archbishop Cranmer and Bishops Latimer and Ridley, who were killed for their Protestant beliefs. Members of Balliol College include Adam Smith, Aldous Huxley, and Graham Greene. Merton College, founded 1264 by Walther de Merton, the Bishop of Rochester, has many of the oldest surviving buildings of the university, some with work by Sir Christopher Wren. The gateway

tower was built in 1418; the college Hall dates from 1277; and the library, constructed 1371–78, is noted for being the first to store books upright on shelves. Merton's Mob Quadrangle is the oldest at Oxford (built 1304–78) and became the model for the university's other quadrangles (four-sided lawns surrounded by buildings). Famous Mertonians include Lord Randolph Churchill, Sir Max Beerbohm, and Japanese Crown Prince Naruhito.

Oxford University has continued to expand, and colleges have been added to the university every century since the 1200s. A chancellor is the honorary head of the university. The university, however, is actually run by the vice-chancellor, who is selected from the college heads on a rotating basis and serves for a four-year term. Two proctors, the Hebdomadal Council, and the Congregation make up the rest of the administration. Each college has its own statutes, although together the colleges are overseen by the university, which approves course content, sets examinations, and awards the degrees. In 1571 the university was officially incorporated by an act of Parliament. It is technically known as "The Masters and scholars of the University of Oxford" and properly called the University of Oxford, although the school is world renown as Oxford University. Students apply to and are admitted by individual colleges, each of which offers a variety of subjects to study. Tuition is paid to the individual college, although an annual fee is also paid to the university. The colleges have residence halls, dining facilities, libraries, and heads (known variously as dean, rector, warden, master, principal, and provost). It is one of the unique features of Oxford that the colleges have distinct personalities. Students are instructed in "tutorials," an intense and unique educational experience. In the tutorial, students (either individually or with one or two others) meet with a professor to discuss work done in the past week. The work may be an essay or the answer to a problem posed by the professor, and the sessions last an hour. During this time the student is expected to define, defend, and debate ideas with the professor. The aim of this teaching method is to create logical and independent thinkers. Undergraduate degrees normally take three years to complete, although some such as those in Arabic, biochemistry, engineering, and Japanese take four years. Two examinations are given. The first is called Prelims (preliminary) or Mods (moderations) and is typically taken in the first year of study. The second exam, Finals, is taken in the last year. Numerous graduate degrees are awarded by the university. The academic year lasts from mid-October to mid-June and is divided into the terms of Michaelmas, Hilary, and Trinity.

The long history of the school and its individualistic colleges combine to form a place noted for traditions and eccentricities. One university regulation prohibited students (even in the twentieth century) from carrying bows and arrows. The regulation probably stems from a 1355 town and gown dispute that led to rioting and fatalities on both sides. In the 1990s dressing for dinner was still required, although depending on the college, students may need to dress one way for the first seating of dinner and another for the second. In the Mertonian Time Ceremony, students of Merton College parade in full academic dress backwards through the quadrangle when the clocks are changed back to Greenwich mean time in the fall. The campus security officers, nicknamed bulldogs, are noted for their black suits, derby hats, and regal air. The university has also played a role in the history of the nation, when during the civil war of the seventeenth century it was refuge to Charles I and Parliament. During the 1800s the constitution of the university was revised, the academic quality improved, and religious testing abolished. The university only admitted men until the late nineteenth century, when five schools were established for women. Women, however, were not formally allowed to receive degrees from the university until 1920. The five women's colleges were Lady Margaret Hall (1878), St. Anne's (1879), Somerville (1879), St. Hugh's (1886), and St. Hilda's (1893). Oxford remained gender segregated until the 1970s when most of the colleges became coeducational. Today St. Hilda's is the only college that admits women exclusively.

Of the colleges, the most famous of those founded in the fourteenth century include Exeter (1314, one famous member of this college was J.R.R. Tolkien), Oriel (1326, noted for its library designed by James Wyatt in 1788), Queen's (1340, famous member: Joseph Addison), and New (1379, known as an excellent example of perpendicular architecture). Famous colleges established in the fifteenth century include Lincoln (1427, originally intended for the instruction of clergy to refute the Lollard beliefs of John Wycliffe's followers), All Soul's (1438, today admitting only fellows), and Magdalen (1458, where the chapel choir is known for its choral services). Brasenose (1509, perhaps named after an old door knocker), Corpus Christi (1517, featuring one of Oxford's most picturesque libraries), Christ Church (1546, containing both the Cathedral, the smallest in England, and Tom Tower, with a seven-ton bell cast in 1680 and originally belonging to Osney Abbey), St. John's (1555, famous member: Sir Tryone Guthrie), Trinity (1555, famous member: Sir Richard Burton), and Jesus (1571, famous member: T.E. Lawrence) are among the most well-known colleges from the sixteenth century. Pembroke (1624, famous member: Samuel Johnson), Hertford (1740, famous member: Evelyn Waugh), and Keble (1868, featuring the longest Hall in Oxford) were later noted additions to the university. The twentieth century has seen the establishment of such important colleges as St. Anthony's (1950, emphasizing graduate studies in the humanities and international relations), Wolfson (1966, emphasizing graduate studies in the natural sciences), and Green (1979, emphasizing graduate studies in all sciences). Most colleges have a student body of only 300 or 400. There are also six permanent private halls associated with the university. These schools were originally established to provide religious education. They are, with their original founding dates and religious association: Manchester College (1786, Unitarian), Regent's Park College (1810, Baptist), Mansfield College (1886, Congregational), Campion Hall (1896, the Society of Jesus), St. Benet's Hall (1897, Benedictine), and Greyfriars (1910, Franciscan).

Other famous features of Oxford University include the Bodleian Library, Ashmolean Museum, the University of Oxford Botanic Garden, and the Oxford University Press. The Bodleian is the principle library of the university and is entitled to a copy of every book printed in England. The library is one of the oldest functioning libraries in the world and dates back to the fifteenth century. The Ashmolean Museum, opened in 1683 as the first public museum in England, is noted for its art and archeological collections. The University of Oxford Botanic Garden, founded in the seventeenth century, today contains approximately 8,000 species of plants. The Oxford University Press, which came under control of the university in 1629, is a world-renown publisher of scholarly, religious, and reference works. One of its most famous publications is the *Oxford English Dictionary*.

Today Oxford University has a student population of approximately 15,000, made up of both men and women, public and private school graduates, and students from England as well as other countries. The school sponsors Rhodes Scholars, who are chosen from countries around the world for their intellectual ability, character, leadership qualities, and physical achievements. Oxford has contributed leaders to society in the fields of the arts, sciences, and politics. Prime ministers who attended Oxford include Clement Attlee, Harold Macmillan, and Margaret Thatcher. In existence for over 800 years, Oxford University is today internationally famous for its remarkable scholarship and traditions. An alphabetical listing of the colleges of Oxford follows: All Souls, Balliol, Brasenose, Christ Church, Corpus Christi, Exeter, Green, Hertford, Jesus, Keble, Lady Margaret Hall, Linacre, Lincoln, Magdalen, Merton, New, Nuffield, Oriel, Pembroke, Queen's, Rewley House, St. Anne's, St. Anthony's, St. Catherine's, St. Cross, St. Edmund Hall, St. Hilda's, St. Hugh's, St. John's, St. Peter, Somerville, Trinity, University, Wadham, Wolfson, and Worcester.

Further Reading: There are numerous guides, maps, encyclopedia articles, and books about Oxford University, school life, and the buildings and colleges. The Oxford University website, http://www.ox.ac.uk, is an excellent starting point for information. Information about the Bodleian Library is available in Ian Philip's *The Bodleian Library in the 17th and 18th Centuries* (Oxford: Oxford University Press, 1983) and *Bodleian Library, Oxford* (a booklet on sale at the library, Oxford OX1 3BG, tel: [865] 277000). Works about the university include V.H.H. Green's *A History of Oxford University* (London: Batsford, 1974) and *The History of the University of Oxford,* 8 volumes (Oxford: Clarendon, and New York: Oxford UniversityPress, 1984–94).

—Anne C. Paterson

UNIVERSITY OF PARIS
(Paris, France)

Location: Scattered sites in and around Paris, France.

Description: Thirteen autonomous, state-financed universities founded in 1970 under France's Orientation Act of 1968, which provided for reform of higher education. They replaced the former University of Paris, founded in the twelfth century.

Information:

Université de Paris I (Panthéon-Sorbonne)
12, place du Panthéon
75231 Paris Cedex 05
France
46-34-97-00

Université de Droit, d'Economie et de Sciences Sociales (Paris II)
12, place du Panthéon
75231 Paris Cedex 05 (Panthéon)
France
43-29-21-40

Université de la Sorbonne Nouvelle (Paris III)
17, rue de la Sorbonne
75230 Paris Cedex 05
France
40-46-22-11

Université Paris-Sorbonne (Paris IV)
1, rue Victor Cousin
75230 Paris Cedex 05
France
40-46-22-11

Université René Descartes (Paris V)
12, rue de l'Ecole de Médecine
75270 Paris Cedex 06
France
40-46-16-16

Université Pierre et Marie Curie (Paris VI)
4, place Jussieu
75252 Paris Cedex 05
France
44-27-44-27

Université Paris VII
2, place Jussieu
75251 Paris Cedex 05
France
44-27-44-27

Université de Vincennes à Saint-Denis (Paris VIII)
2, rue de la Liberté
93526 Saint-Denix Cedex 02
France
49-40-67-89

Université de Paris-Dauphine (Paris IX)
Place du Maréchal de Lattre-de-Tassigny
75775 Paris Cedex 16
France
45-05-14-10

Université de Paris X (Nanterre)
200, avenue de la République
92001 Nanterre Cedex
France
40-97-72-00

Université de Paris-Sud (Paris XI)
Centre scientifique
15, rue Georges Clémenceau
91405 Orsay Cedex
France
69-41-67-50

Université de Paris Val-de-Marne (Paris XII)
Avenue du Général de Gaulle
94010 Créteil Cedex
France
48-98-91-44

Université Paris-Nord (Paris XIII)
Avenue Jean-Baptiste Clément
93430 Villetaneuse
France
49-40-30-00

The University of Paris is one of the oldest universities in western Europe. According to historian Hastings Rashdall, "The university was not made but grew; a date for its formation would be misleading." The twelfth century, however, is generally acknowledged as the period of the university's inception.

The system of education that sprang to life in France in the twelfth century had its beginnings during the Carolingian dynasty (eighth–tenth centuries). Each abbey and cathedral maintained a school for the training of young monks and clerks, and the school was headed by a *magister scholarum,* or master. By the end of the ninth century,

University of Paris

the School of Remigius of Auxerre, a monastery school perhaps connected with the church of Saint-Germain-des-Prés, existed; it has been called the first school at Paris.

The eleventh and early twelfth centuries saw the emergence of cathedral schools in Paris. The teachers were not monks but members of the secular clergy. These schools, attached to the Cathedral of Notre Dame, were presided over by the chancellor of the cathedral. A man desiring to become a teacher would, after a sufficient period of study and upon the approval of his master, receive from the chancellor, free of charge, a *licentia docendi,* or license to teach.

The first known master of the Cathedral School of Notre Dame was William of Champeaux (1070?–1121). William, who lectured in the cloisters of Notre Dame, was one of the early leaders of the intellectual movement that contributed to the birth of the University of Paris. It was from the study of dialectic, or logic, that the University of Paris grew. The cloister school of Notre Dame seems to have evolved into a *studium generale* by 1127, when a statute was issued that limited the lodging within the cloister to "members of the cathedral body."

One of William's pupils was Peter Abelard, whose teachings during the early years of the twelfth century attracted students to Paris from throughout Europe. Abelard, who was criticized for teaching without having first served an apprenticeship with a master, taught between 1100 and 1140. Although Abelard has been called the "father of universities" upon whose life and work the University of Paris originated, there is no trace of a university or society of masters during the first half of the twelfth century.

The theologian Peter Lombard (1100?–60) studied at Paris and taught theology at the school of Notre Dame from 1136–50. His *Four Books of Sentences,* a collection of church teachings and opinions, were the standard textbook on theology in the universities until the sixteenth century.

As the number of students at the cathedral schools increased, so did the number of masters, who soon became too numerous to be housed within the cloister of Notre Dame. They spread to other areas of Paris, including the bridges of the Seine. There also existed famous external schools at two other churches—the Collegiate Church of Sainte-Geneviève and the Church of the Canons Regular of St. Victor's.

By the second half of the twelfth century, the number of schools had again multiplied. The population of masters and students in Paris became so numerous that they comprised a group apart.

Between 1150 and 1170 there arose, not a union of faculties, but a *Universitas magistrorum et studiorum,* a guild of teachers and students. Out of this guild, formed by the increasing number of students and masters at the cathedral schools of Notre Dame, originated the university. The cathedral schools can be considered the "cradle" of the University of Paris.

The custom of "inception" (or commencement) into the guild involved a formal ceremony admitting the newly licensed master into the society, in addition to recognition by both his old master and the other members of the group. Evidence that a guild existed in the twelfth century is found in a chronicle from the year 1214. In it, the English historian Matthew Paris wrote that the abbot of St. Alban's, while a student at Paris (probably no later than 1170–75), was admitted to a "fellowship of the elect masters."

In 1200, a tavern brawl resulted in the killing of five students by an armed band led by the Provost of Paris. The student population was so incensed that it threatened to withdraw from the city, and the masters appealed to King Philip II Augustus. The king, fearful that the masters might follow through with their threats, issued a charter that extended royal protection and goodwill to the students of Paris.

In 1208–9, the first written statutes of the University of Paris are mentioned in letters of Pope Innocent III, referring to an association of Paris masters and of the statutes they were sworn to obey. The oldest preserved statutes, however, date from 1215, the year they were presented by the papal legate Robert de Courçon.

The special treatment granted by the king to the Parisian students soon met with resistance from the bishop and the chancellor of Paris, who were accustomed to exercising control over the schools. A series of conflicts occurred between 1212 and 1231. At issue were the granting of licenses, jurisdiction over the schools, and the university's right to endow itself with statutes.

The conflict came to a head between 1229 and 1231. A tavern brawl, again involving students, erupted during the carnival of 1228–29. The regent, Blanche of Castille, after being informed of the disturbance by the bishop of Paris, sent royal sergeants to the scene. Several students were killed. On April 16, 1229, the masters resorted to an extreme tactic: they determined that, unless justice were obtained through the bishop of Paris and the regents within one month's time, they would dissolve the university and disperse. Their threat was ignored, and, as a result, scores of masters and students began to leave Paris. They traveled to Oxford and Cambridge, Rheims, Orléans, Angers, and Toulouse. (The University of Angers perhaps traces its beginnings to this migration.) The decline in the city's prestige and prosperity began to cause alarm.

The university and its colleges at this time had no permanent buildings or locations. They borrowed a church or convent for their meetings, and even these varied. Dispersal, therefore, was not difficult; the only property was the fees paid by the students.

The tactic proved effective; the masters and students soon gained the support of the pope. After the civil and ecclesiastical leaders of Paris submitted to the terms of reparations and guarantees for the future, the masters and students returned to the city. On April 13, 1231, Pope

Gregory IX issued a bull, the *Parens scientiarum,* which became the Grand Charter of the University. Until the Great Schism of 1378, the University of Paris received special treatment from the popes, who continued to discourage the foundation of schools of theology by other universities.

By the middle of the thirteenth century, the masters of the university had divided into four faculties: theology, canon law, medicine, and arts. The seven arts (the *trivium* and the *quadrivium),* part of the curriculum of the arts faculty, were the first step in a student's training; the *artistae,* or arts students, were the equivalent of modern-day undergraduates. The process of advancing from arts student into one of the "superior" faculties of medicine, canon law, or theology took seven or eight years.

The time required to progress through the superior faculties varied. The study requirements as stated by the faculty of medicine (around 1270–74) consisted of 32 months for the bachelorship and 5 to 6 years for the license. The required length of study for the faculty of canon law in the mid-fourteenth century was 48 months over a 6-year period for the bachelorship and 40 months for the license. In 1215, the length of study required by the faculty of theology, which was considered the most important of the superior faculties, was five years of initial study and eight years for the doctorate, and the doctor had to be at least 35. By 1366, the length of study had increased to 16 years; by 1452, it had dropped to 15.

Presiding over each of the four faculties was a dean. The arts faculty was divided into four "nations": French, Picard, Norman, and English, and over each nation was a proctor. The term rector came to be reserved for the head of the faculty of arts, and by the mid-fourteenth century, the rector was recognized as the head of the entire university.

The mid- to late-thirteenth century brought an influx of scholars from throughout Europe: Albertus Magnus from Germany, Bonaventure and Thomas Aquinas from Italy, Roger Bacon from England, and Duns Scotus from Scotland. The masters of the University of Paris, part of the secular clergy, opposed the right of the mendicants, members of the Dominican and Franciscan orders, to teach at the university because the mendicants had not taken an oath to obey the statutes of the university. Albertus, Bonaventure, and Aquinas were sent by Pope Alexander IV to defend the mendicant orders; they were successful in their mission.

About 1257, Robert de Sorbon, theologian and chaplain of King Louis IX, founded the Maison de Sorbonne as a dormitory to house 16 students who had attained the degree of master of arts and wanted to continue on to the doctorate of theology. The number soon increased to 36. Sorbon became the chancellor of the university in 1258. In 1259, the Sorbonne was sanctioned by the pope; it soon developed into a major center of learning and the "core" of the University of Paris. Toward the end of the thirteenth century, the Sorbonne was the administrative seat of the

university, and the city contained approximately 15,000 undergraduates. The word Sorbonne, although in reality the name of the building and not a college or university, was long used as a synonym for the University of Paris.

At the beginning of the fourteenth century, the faculty numbered more than 500, and the students, who came from many countries, were too numerous to count. Its prestige lay in the teaching of philosophy and theology. By the mid-fourteenth century, the city of Paris had 40 colleges and students from every country in Europe. The university had attained a reputation of excellence unsurpassed "in all Christendom" and was known as "the great school where theology was studied in its most scientific spirit."

During the thirteenth and early fourteenth centuries, the university did not actively concern itself with French politics. This soon changed: toward the end of the fourteenth century, its political influence and privileges, and later its pretensions, began their climb.

After the death of King Charles V in 1380, the university, by then accustomed to the favor of the Crown and an unprecedented degree of prestige, became increasingly involved in political affairs. In 1382, the university was asked to intercede on behalf of a group of rebels convicted in an uprising against "the tyranny of Anjou." The faculty of theology became the unnamed theological police of the Church, and by the fifteenth century, the power of the university was such that its approval was considered necessary in the resolution of a political crisis. In the early fifteenth century, the university sided with Burgundy in a dispute against Armagnac.

During the Hundred Years' War between France and England (1337–1453), the university aligned itself with England and acknowledged Henry V as king of France. The majority of the masters had, however, left Paris during the occupation by the English. (Many of them had fled to Poitiers, where a new university arose.) In 1430, the masters who remained in Paris were said to have initiated the idea to try Joan of Arc and to have provided one of their best prosecutors. The Parisian doctors who assisted at the trial had, however, been generously compensated by the king of England.

The University of Paris was involved in efforts to end the Great Schism of the Roman Catholic Church (1378–1417). Jean Gerson (1363–1429), appointed chancellor of the university in 1395, was one of the principals in the attempt to put an end to the conflict. One suggestion offered by the university and voted on by the four faculties was that a general council be formed to solve the dispute. Both sides of the papal schismatics, however, refused to admit to the council's authority. (The theory of conciliarism contended that a general council of the church had authority over the pope.) Jean Rousse, a master of theology at the university, presented the council's appeal. The regent ordered Rousse imprisoned and, although he was soon released, Rousse's arrest caused consternation among the clergy and the university. Once again students, masters, and doctors left Paris for other locations. This disbursement, however, marked the beginning of a decline in the university as a center of learning.

Superstitution was prevalent during the fourteenth century. When asked by King Philip VI for a report on the plague, the doctors of the University of Paris said it was caused by "a triple conjunction of Saturn, Jupiter, and Mars in the 40th degree of Aquarius said to have occurred on March 28, 1345." This pronouncement was accepted as the official cause. At the end of the fourteenth century, the faculty of theology succeeded in calling attention to the black arts (witchcraft), by then almost forgotten, and it failed to dispute the existence of demons.

During the fourteenth and fifteenth centuries, the special privileges long enjoyed by the university began to erode, and the government interfered more frequently in the university's business. As the need for revenue increased, government officials began to look askance at the tax exemptions that had been granted to academic ecclesiastics. In 1446, an edict from King Charles VII "proclaimed the jurisdiction of the Parliament in the suits of the university."

The reign of Louis XI (1461–83) brought a further decline in the influence of the university. Under Louis's policies, the character of the university began to change from ecumenical to nationalistic. In 1467, the king ordered the university to cease any interference in political matters, "even in letters to their relations"; in 1470, he ordered all scholars who were subjects of the duke of Burgundy to take an oath of allegiance to the Crown; and in 1474, he declared the rector of the university subject to the king. The international nature of the university, which had heretofore been protected by rulers who offered protection to its foreign students, waned.

During the reign of Louis XII (1498–1515), the university suffered a major setback. When it opposed an edict "limiting its privileges and guarding against their abuse" (which included tax exemptions), the Crown banned the right of cessation. Thus the university could never again exercise the "great instrument of academic aggression" that it had utilized so frequently in the past.

The studies in theology and philosophy, which had been so important to the university's reputation in its early years, began to deteriorate under Scholasticism. Consequently, the university contributed little to the humanistic spirit of the Renaissance.

While a student at the University of Paris in 1495, the great humanist Erasmus expressed his disappointment in the theological teachings: "Those studies can make a man opinionated and contentious; can they make him wise? . . . By their stammering and by the stains of their impure style they disfigure theology, which had been enriched and adorned by the eloquence of the ancients. They involve everything while trying to solve everything." The Sorbonne was later (in 1527) to condemn Erasmus's *Colloquies*.

The Sorbonne was disrupted by the religious conflicts that occurred during the Reformation and Counter-Reformation. After Martin Luther's break with the Church in 1520, the school reacted swiftly. The following year, it condemned Luther's *Babylonish Captivity*, and in 1523, it brought about the arrest of Louis de Berquin, a friend of Erasmus, for translating Luther's works. Six years later, de Berquin was burned at the stake for heresy.

The Sorbonne increasingly met with criticism and opposition. King Francis I objected to its narrow theological teachings and, in 1529, in an effort to provide studies in the humanities, he established the Collège Royale (later renamed the Collège de France). Tuition was free, and four "royal professors" were appointed to teach Greek and Hebrew; Latin, medicine, mathematics, and philosophy were soon added.

Francis's sister, Marguerite of Navarre, was summoned in 1533 to appear before the Sorbonne on a charge of heresy. She refused, and the king defended her actions. Marguerite was a protector of the religious reformers and a devotee of the arts and letters.

The sixteenth-century writer and physician, François Rabelais, personified the humanistic spirit of the Renaissance. His *Gargantua* (1534), which he dedicated to Marguerite of Navarre, drew condemnation from the Sorbonne for its satirical depiction of the clergy.

Censorship of publications was prevalent during the Inquisition, and the Sorbonne contributed to the stifling of ideas by issuing, in 1544, the first general list of condemned books. The Etiennes, a renowned publishing family whose first press was established in Paris around 1500, were often criticized by the Sorbonne. In 1552, one member of the family took his press and transferred it to Geneva; in 1566, another brought on the wrath of the Sorbonne by publishing a work comparing Christian miracles with Greek marvels.

Since the system of education in western Europe was under the influence of the Church, the disruptions that occurred during the Reformation directly affected the schools. Universities lost their international character because religious differences among countries prevented students from traveling far afield for their education. The number of students at the University of Paris remained high (6,000), but few came from foreign lands, and new and enlightening ideas were discouraged. Montaigne and Rabelais criticized the curriculum as being far removed from real life. At a meeting in Orléans in 1560, the chancellor for the Queen Mother, Catherine de Médicis, called for mutual tolerance between Catholics and Huguenots. A doctor of the Sorbonne responded by urging that the death penalty be imposed upon all heretics.

By the end of the sixteenth century, the University of Paris was in serious need of reform. It was still governed by the 1452 statutes, which remained untouched by the spirit of the Renaissance. In 1595, Henry IV set up a commission of six members to prepare new statutes to define the role of teachers, to reinforce discipline, and to start new programs. These statutes, which remained in effect through the end of the eighteenth century, were implemented in 1598. Under Cardinal Richelieu (1585–1642), new colleges, including the present site of the Sorbonne (completed in 1627), were constructed. He laid the first stone of the Sorbonne's chapel, where he is buried.

Religious conflicts continued throughout the seventeenth century. The University of Paris was troubled by theological strife stemming from the Jesuits and the Jansenists. In 1663, the Sorbonne affirmed the Gallican tradition, which granted French kings the right to appoint bishops and abbots. This position, upheld by Louis XIV but opposed by Pope Innocent XI, almost led to a split between the French Church and Rome.

After Louis XIV's death in 1715, Philippe d'Orléans, regent for the five-year-old Louis XV, ordered that the University of Paris be opened to all qualified students, with their tuition paid by the state. The Sorbonne, however, remained intransigent. It continued to condemn books, even some which had been printed with the royal imprimatur. In 1751, it objected to portions of the naturalist Buffon's *Histoire Naturelle* as contradictory to "the teachings of religion."

Following the expulsion of the Jesuits in 1762, the 500 colleges of France became part of the University of Paris. In 1767, the Sorbonne ordered the destruction of "every teaching threatening to shake the foundations of the Catholic faith."

With the French Revolution came the dissolution of all institutions of the *ancien régime,* including the Roman Catholic Church. On September 15, 1793, the National Convention abolished all universities in France and, for 13 years, schools specializing in different fields of learning supplanted them. In 1795, the Directory, a form of government consisting of five men with executive power, began a four-year rule that ended when Napoléon staged a coup on November 9, 1799. Under the Directory, teachers were instructed to "exclude from your teaching all that relates to the dogmas or rites of any religion or sect whatever," an attempt "to build a social order upon a system of morality independent of religious belief."

Between 1806 and 1808, Napoléon I established the Imperial or Napoléonic university (after 1815, known as the University of France). The university was divided into academies, each headed by a government-nominated rector. It was a centralized system of education that encompassed all teaching units in France, including the primary and secondary schools. In 1821, the Academy of Paris acquired the buildings of the Sorbonne; the reconstituted University of Paris became part of the Academy of Paris.

This system remained in effect until the final years of the nineteenth century. Teaching was secular, and professional chairs at the University of Paris numbered over 600; by 1885, there were nearly 12,000 students. Once again, the University of Paris was an important intellectual and scientific center. In 1886, the faculty of theology, which had been so important in the university's history, disappeared.

Changes occurred during the late nineteenth century. The minister of education, Jules Ferry, introduced the idea of the separation of church and state; this became law on March 28, 1882. Individuals and associations were allowed to found private institutions of learning, but they had to follow the rules set down by the National Ministry of Education. Under Ferry, in 1896, a system of 23 *académies* or educational districts was established throughout France. Each district had its own university, and all districts were centralized under one minister of education. The system of 23 universities, each with the same five faculties (law, medicine, pharmacy, letters, and science), remained virtually unchanged until the 1960s.

In addition to the universities, a system of elite institutions, known as *grandes écoles,* was created to train professionals in engineering and administration. Students could not transfer from university to *grande école,* or vice versa. The system still remains in effect. The *grandes écoles,* however, unlike the universities, escaped the reorganization that occurred after the 1968 student revolt.

In 1900, students in French universities numbered 29,300 (12,270 of them in Paris). Enrollment grew from about 134,000 in 1950 to approximately 500,000 by 1967. Because of the open admissions policy, the number of students continued to increase, but so did the number of dropouts. By 1967, overcrowded buildings, understaffed faculties, and obsolete teaching methods had brought about a high level of student dissatisfaction and unrest.

Unrest led to protests. A political correspondent for *Le Monde* wrote that "France is bored," words that had been used by the poet-politician Alphonse de Lamartine on the eve of the 1848 Revolution. Students were "bored"—not only with the antiquated school system but also with the "status quo of bourgeois life and its government."

Student unions in France had long wished for more student involvement in the establishment of university rules and policies. In February 1968, the *Union nationale des étudiants de France* (UNEF), an influential union that traces its beginnings to 1877, urged students to begin a series of minor protests. In March, a group of about 150 students on the Nanterre campus of the University of Paris marched through the administration building and protested the lack of student control over the university's faculties. The left-wing group attracted nearly 2,000 students to their cause before the campus was closed by the rector.

The students moved their efforts to the Sorbonne, and the events that would reshape the entire university system of France were set in motion. On May 3, 1968, the police, who had been summoned by the rector of the Sorbonne in conjunction with the minister of education, entered the central courtyard of the Sorbonne and began arresting students, members of a left-wing group, who had gathered there. The action of the police had perhaps been ordered because of the rumors that a right-wing group was planning to interrupt the meeting.

Word of the disruption spread throughout the city, and the Latin Quarter was soon filled with protesting students. During the next 24 hours, police clashed with students. Student leaders were imprisoned, and, in an unusual move, the Sorbonne was closed.

A week of student-police conflict followed. The Sorbonne, closed to all student activity, became an armed police fortress. The students tried repeatedly to free the Sorbonne from the authorities, but each march was unsuccessful. The student movement gained support among citizens and workers, and the revolt expanded to the provinces.

The European edition of *The New York Herald Tribune* reported, on May 7, "Paris Students Battle Police 14 Hours in Latin Quarter." The article called the Latin Quarter a "battleground" and parts of Paris "a city under siege." Clashes and student strikes continued to spread. Students used sticks and stones "and anything movable" to attack the police; the police employed nightsticks and tear gas. Injuries and property damage, including burned cars, overturned buses, and broken store windows, were reported.

Leaders of the student unions went to the powerful communist and socialist labor unions and asked for their support in staging a march. On May 13, nearly half a million people marched down the Champs Elysées in Paris. The government was forced to reopen the Sorbonne.

Strikes multiplied throughout France; by May 24, a general strike had the country in a state of near-paralysis. Negotiations between the de Gaulle government and the labor unions were unsuccessful. Then President de Gaulle made a move that helped to defuse the situation: he announced new elections within a month. Although students continued to protest throughout the summer, the movement lost momentum.

The students did, however, gain a victory. The government officials whom the students opposed were removed or shifted to less influential positions. The Gaullist minister of education was replaced by Edgar Faure, who vowed to reform the system of education. Faure's reforms resulted in the "Faure law," the *Loi d'orientation de l'enseignement supérieur* (Orientation of Higher Education Act), which led to a radical restructuring of the university system.

In 1970, the reforms set forth by the *Loi d'orientation de l'enseignement supérieur* of 1968 brought about the decentralization of the university system. The universities were reorganized into self-governing bodies, and students and teachers were granted a voice in the decision-making process. In addition, political activity was no longer forbidden on campus. The need for more graduates in the sciences and fewer in the liberal arts was addressed in the law that stated that the universities

would "associate wherever possible arts and letters with sciences and technics."

The faculties were replaced by more than 700 *unités d'enseignement et de recherche* or UER (units of teaching and research). The UER ranges from a single discipline (such as engineering or English) to interdisciplinary studies (for example, environmental sciences). Groupings of UERs became the foundation for the reorganized universities: 43 in the provinces (61 by 1975) and 13 in Paris.

The University of Paris, divided into 13 independent units, replaced the four faculties of letters, law, sciences, and medicine. Each university, with its own administration, faculty, and student body, has a primary focus. Paris I is a school of law, sociology, and economics. Paris III (the historic Sorbonne) emphasizes language and literature, and Paris IV, classical literature. Paris VI and VII, on the site of the old Paris wine market, comprise the new science complex. Paris XI, located in the former NATO headquarters, offers related studies in applied mathematics, economics, computer science, and management.

University policy is established by an elected council, consisting of teachers, students, and representatives from outside the university. The council elects the president, who replaced the rector of the old university system. The once powerful position of dean no longer exists.

An uprising of students, teachers, and administrators in April 1976 called for new leadership in France and protested Valéry Giscard d'Estaing's plans for university reform. The reforms to which students and faculty objected placed the blame for the country's high level of unemployment on an excessive number of liberal arts students; emphasis was to be shifted to technological and business studies. Both students and teachers rebelled against being told what they had to study or to teach, and most university rectors objected to the removal of the small amount of autonomy that remained with the institutions.

After the implementation of the 1976 reforms, only three percent of eligible students entered the new job-related programs (such as applied business Spanish and technical English translation). By 1981, the number increased to 15 percent. Additional reforms were introduced in 1981 favoring graduate degrees in the sciences at the expense of those in the humanities and social sciences. A five-year plan called for technological research and development as France's main priority.

In 1984, the public higher education service was formed to oversee university training after the awarding of the baccalaureate. In May 1991, Université 2000 was created to prepare for increased university enrollments and rising costs, to improve standards, to develop vocational training, to assist in regional development, and to prepare for increased world-wide competition.

In the fall of 1995, students of the Universities of Paris and throughout France demonstrated against overcrowded conditions. They demanded higher pay for the faculties and an increase in the number of professors. In spite of overcrowding, underfunding, and a loss of prestige to the *grandes écoles,* the 13 Universities of Paris continue to attract students from throughout the world.

The 13 universities, their student enrollment figures and principal courses of study are the following:

The University of Paris I (Panthéon-Sorbonne) enrolls approximately 40,000 students in economics, human sciences, and political and juridical sciences. The University of Paris II (Université de Droit, d'Economie et de Sciences) enrolls approximately 18,000 students in law, economics, and social sciences. The University of Paris III (Université de la Sorbonne Nouvelle) enrolls approximately 19,000 students in contemporary languages, literatures, and civilizations. The University of Paris IV (Université Paris-Sorbonne) enrolls approximately 24,000 students in civilizations, languages, literature, and arts. The University of Paris V (Université René Descartes) enrolls approximately 30,000 students in health sciences (medicine, dentistry, pharmacy, biology, etc.), human sciences, and law. The University of Paris VI (Université Pierre et Marie Curie) enrolls approximately 37,000 in exact and applied sciences and biological and medical sciences. The University of Paris VII enrolls approximately 30,000 students in exact, biological, medical, and human sciences. The University of Paris VIII (Université de Vincennes à Saint-Denis) enrolls approximately 27,000 students in human sciences, and science and technology. The University of Paris IX (Université de Paris-Dauphine) enrolls approximately 7,000 students in management sciences. The University of Paris X (Nanterre) enrolls approximately 35,000 students in juridical, economic, and human sciences, languages and civilizations, and technology. The University of Paris XI (Université de Paris-Sud) enrolls approximately 28,000 students in exact, biomedical, pharmaceutical, and juridical sciences and technology. The University of Paris XII (Université de Paris Val-de-Marne) enrolls approximately 22,000 students in juridical, biomedical, and human sciences. Finally, the University of Paris XIII (Université Paris-Nord) enrolls approximately 16,000 students in exact, juridical, medical, and human sciences, and technology.

Further Reading: No general history of the University of Paris exists in English, but general information about selected periods of the university's history can be found in A. Belden Fields, *Student Politics in France* (New York: Basic Books, 1970), *A Distant Mirror* (New York: Knopf, 1978), and several of the historical series by Will and Ariel Durant (Simon and Schuster), including *The Age of Faith, The Age of Napoleon,* and *The Reformation.*

—Sandy Gladfelter and Susan R. Stone

UNIVERSITY OF PENNSYLVANIA
(Philadelphia, Pennsylvania, U.S.A.)

Description: A private university enrolling more than 22,000 students, with 4 undergraduate and 11 graduate schools.

Location: The west side of Philadelphia, Pennsylvania, near the neighborhood of Schuyhill.

Information: University of Pennsylvania
34th and Spruce Streets
Philadelphia, PA 19104-6380
U.S.A.
(215) 898-5000
(215) 898-7111

Philadelphia was one of the largest and most prosperous of American colonial cities in the 1740s, with a population of approximately 12,000, and a thriving commercial trade centered around its ports on the Delaware River. Only a small minority of the city's youth were formally educated, however, and the quality and manner of instruction even for privileged children was quite varied. The William Penn Charter School enrolled 20 to 30 boys in a classical program, and as many again who studied a cruder English curriculum. The majority of boys and girls lucky enough to receive some schooling hired individual tutors working in their own homes. To the chagrin of Philadelphia's religious and social leaders, nearly all of Philadelphia's poor children received no academic training whatsoever.

The first attempt to found a school available to a wider population of Philadelphia's youth was headed by George Whitefield, an Anglican preacher who came to the city in 1739. Whitefield was a controversial figure among Philadelphia's clergymen, for his manner of sermon approached the ecstatic, but he was extremely popular with the masses; there are reports that as many as 18,000 people attended some of his talks. Whitefield had helped to develop several charity schools in Britain, and he began planning for one in his adopted city soon after his arrival. He organized a board of trustees, most of them religious men of no special standing, to oversee the construction of a single building where Whitefield and others could preach, and in which to operate a charity school. The trustees soon obtained a lease on a plot of land at the corner of Fourth and Arch streets, and by June 1740, they had begun constructing the largest building in the city, known simply as the "New Building" following its completion.

Despite the intentions and promises of Whitefield and the trustees, no school operated out of the New Building for nine years. Then in 1749, a second group of trustees purchased control of the New Building with the intention of realizing a school. The new trustees were, unlike the first board, 24 of Philadelphia's wealthiest and most influential citizens, and thus they possessed the means to actualize their ambition. They acted quickly; at a meeting held November 13, 1749, they signed the *Constitutions for a Public Academy in the City of Philadelphia,* a document drafted by their president and Philadelphia's leading citizen, Benjamin Franklin. Thus, Franklin is often titled "the founder" of the University of Pennsylvania, which evolved from the academy chartered that day.

Franklin's plan for the academy was unique in all of western education, for it rested responsibility for the school on a "voluntary society of founders" whose purpose was secular and civic. Other schools in Europe and the New World alike were under the patronage of a church, a government, or individual. The academy, on the other hand, was to be maintained indefinitely by a board of trustees answering to no higher authority, and dependent on no single source of funding. Franklin's innovative academy opened in January 1751 with an enrollment of 145 boys, and the Free School followed that September.

The trustees soon added a college, the antecessor of the modern University of Pennsylvania. In the spring of 1754, Dr. William Smith, a well-educated Scotsman just 26 years old, began teaching collegiate level courses in logic, rhetoric, ethics, and natural philosophy (science). The following summer, the provincial governor signed a new charter incorporating "The Trustees of the College, Academy and Charitable School of Philadelphia in the Province of Pennsylvania." A new school administration was soon organized, and Smith was named the college's first provost. Teachers were accorded the title of "professor," and the college ambitiously assumed the authority to grant any degree of higher education awarded in Great Britain.

The college evolved quickly after its foundation, although it remained rather small. A dormitory opened in 1765, and homes for two professors and the provost were purchased near the College Building, as the New Building came to be know. The directors of the college organized an innovative and rather modern curriculum, the first in the nation that was neither modeled on medieval tradition of the *studium generale* nor centered around religious instruction. Students enrolled in a regularized three-year program, and were ranked as fresh-

University of Pennsylvania

men, juniors, and seniors. They studied mathematics, physics, history, politics, economics, law, classics, and oration. A few medical classes were taught as early as 1765, and a faculty of four doctors, all awarded their medical degrees at Edinburgh, was assembled four years later. The college assumed the right to grant doctoral degrees in medicine in 1772, and thus emerged the nation's first medical school.

The old colonial college organized around Franklin's liberal plan was radically altered by the War of American Independence. Following the revolution, the Pennsylvania state government fell under the control of the zealously patriotic Constitutional Party, which scorned the Anglican and aristocratic connections of the college, and the hint of loyalist spirit in Provost Smith and several faculty members. In 1779, less than a year after the British departure from Philadelphia, the state assumed control of the institution, and renamed it the University of the State of Pennsylvania. A new board of 24 trustees was then appointed according state legislation: six state offices

were permanently adjoined seats on the board of trustees, as were the leaderships of each of six church denominations. The 12 remaining trusteeships were designated to specific individuals, including Franklin, and these 12 were to be filled by citizens of the board's choosing as they were vacated in the future, although the state retained the power to override the board's decisions.

Smith vigorously resisted his ouster. He refused to leave his house, which belonged to the university, until he was legally evicted almost a year after being stripped of office, and he made a series of legal appeals to regain his post. In 1789, a state legislative committee assigned to examine the case determined that the state indeed had no right to hold the College Building itself, for it was legally the property of the original trustees. Smith and those of the original trustees still alive were restored their school, and for a short while it existed again as before the revolution. The university continued to exist as a legally distinct corporation, but it was forced to move into a building belonging to the Philosophical Society.

The bureaucratic difficulties involved in having these two corporations, which shared some professors, students, and influence over the academy, proved unmanageable, and they united, or reunited, in September 1791. The two boards of trustees agreed to title the new institution the "University of Pennsylvania," and then each elected 12 members to remain on the unified board. When the new trustees met during the early months of 1792, they were faced with the difficult task of forming a single faculty, and thus with dismissing many professors. Ironically, Smith was terminated by a vote of 13 to 11, for he was less popular than the rival candidate for the professorship in Greek and Latin, Dr. Davidson.

The college fared badly in several respect for approximately three decades following the university's reunion. First, it was sorely underfunded because it attracted too few students; in 1804, there were only eight seniors and six juniors. Students preferred institutions with dormitories, of which the university had none since the Revolution, and many of their parents favored schools with religious affiliations. Second, the caliber of instructions was deleteriously lowered to match the capabilities of boys rushed through the academy and enrolled at the college when they were just 13 or 14 years old. Finally, the trustees exercised a domineering control over the college—even choosing textbooks and curricula—that left the professors disgruntled, and the atmosphere on campus tense.

While the college stumbled and degenerated, the medical school prospered. The faculties of the old college and university both were retained in the new medical school, and several of the doctors established excellent reputations that attracted prestige and students to the program. Nearly 2,000 medical doctors were graduated from the school in the first quarter of the century, and approximately 3,000 more attended a year of study and went on to practice without state licensees, especially in the south. It is interesting to note that the professors were, at that time, paid directly by their students; the members of the medical faculty were wealthy with salaries estimated to have been between $5,000 and $10,000, earned during the four-month school year.

The university moved into a splendorous new home beginning in 1802, even while the college declined. Eleven years earlier, the capital of the United States was moved from New York to Philadelphia, and the state government constructed a grand building to house future presidents. The work was a majestic example of new classicism; it was three stories of brick, stone, and marble, capped by a glass dome and cupola, and its facade was adorned with eight Corinthian pillars and two Palladian windows. The President's House was completed in 1797, at a cost of more than $110,000, and offered for rental to President John Adams, who declined the somewhat ungracious proposal. The U.S. capital was subsequently moved to Washington, and the state legislature put the building and several adjacent properties up for auction.

The university acquired the lots and building for the bargain price of $41,650, and remodeled the President's House for scholastic use. Then in 1829, twin Georgian brick buildings were completed on the new campus, into which the collegiate department and faculty of medicine relocated.

The university prospered in its new environs. A new provost and college faculty were selected in 1828, and enrollment rose to 125 within two years, thus bringing in sorely needed capital. In 1852, a School of Mines, Arts, and Manufactures was added, through which a broader range of scientific courses were taught. Two years later, the university organized a law school, having belatedly acted upon a petition to do so sent by the Philadelphia Law Association in 1832. By the end of the 1860s, the student body numbered more than 700.

The university was variously, although not extensively, affected by the Civil War. The majority of students enrolled in the medical school were southerners, and many left the university for the duration of the war, some to join the Confederate forces. Students enrolled in the college formed a Student Officers Training Corps, but most were between 14 and 19 years old, and so were mere cadets. The university was under serious threat when the Confederate Army seized most of Pennsylvania, and the Battle of Gettysburg was literally underway when the commencement ceremonies of 1863 were held, but Philadelphia and the university plant survived the war unharmed. Approximately 780 men associated with the university are known to have served in the war, 130 of them for the Confederacy, and the remainder for the Union.

The university moved to its third and present location after the war. The old quarters in and around the President's House had grown worn and crowded, and the medical facilities were not up to contemporary standards. Moreover, the neighborhood surrounding the university was depressed and worsening. Ten acres of swampy farmland west of Schuylkill were purchased in 1870, and four new buildings were constructed within as many years. They housed not only the university, but also a hospital associated with the medical school. All were built of a green serpentine stone collected in Pennsylvania's own Chester County, according to the plans of Thomas W. Richards, who later was appointed the university's first professor of architecture.

The university expanded modestly following the move. The awkwardly titled School of Agriculture, Mines, Manufactures, and the Mechanic Arts was reorganized, and given the graceful name of Towne Scientific School in honor of John Henry Towne, one of the trustees. A professorship in music was created in 1875, and a course leading to the degree of bachelor of music was organized the next year. The medical faculty considered establishing a dental program as early as 1874, and in 1877 proposed to absorb the Pennsylvania College of Dental Surgery. That schools' administration refused, but its faculty agreed to join the university if a dental department was established. One was in 1878, and the university began offering the degree of D.D.S. that same year. Just two years later, the dental school was moved into a new building, shared with the medical school.

Women won the right to enter the university piecemeal, beginning in the 1870s. The first two women admitted to the university were enrolled in the Towne Scientific School in 1876. They appealed directly to Frederick Genth, professor of chemistry, to allow them into his classes. He and the board of trustees agreed to do so. Ms. Carrie Kilgore was denied admission to the law school in 1871, and unsuccessfully appealed her case to the state supreme court. Then in 1881, she persuaded the state legislature to grant women the right to serve as lawyers. The law school admitted her that same year, and has ever since been open to women. The Graduate School for Women was organized in 1890, and the College of Liberal Arts for Women in 1933. The university was not fully coeducational until the 1970s.

William Pepper, elected in 1881, was the first provost of the university to be granted the authority ordinarily afforded a university president. By an amendment to the school charter, the trustees gave the provost executive authority over the board, and the presidency of each school faculty. Pepper, who remained in office for 13 years, famously used his power to guide the university through an unmatched era of expansion. Thirteen departments opened during his administration, including the prestigious Wharton School of Business Administration, the graduate school, and the Veterinary School. At the same time, the faculty rose from 55 to 300 professors and instructors, and the student body doubled, to nearly 2,000.

Like most American universities, Pennsylvania experienced a rush of applications in the first two decades of the twentieth century. Despite stepping up admissions requirements in order to curtail the influx, the university's student body jumped from approximately 2,000 in 1894 to more than 11,000 by the close of World War I. Provost Charles Harrison, Pepper's successor, oversaw an astounding building program organized to accommodate the swollen institution. Thirteen stately brick buildings were raised during Harrison's tenure, several of them massive, including the law and dental schools. The esteemed architectural firm of Cope and Stewardson designed the huge Residence Hall, which is actually an interlocking system of 31 houses encompassing five interior courtyards. The hall is a blend of Gothic and classical styles, and is constructed of Flemish bond brick complemented by white limestone.

The history of the university in the twentieth century has been one of almost continuous growth and achievement, but historians have yet to analyze modern events. A few diverse highlights of the neglected period must serve to indicate the broad course of the university's development into one of the nation's leading academic institutions. The School of Nursing was established in 1935, and stands among the nation's best three today. The world's first computer, the ENIAC (Electronic Numerical Integrator and Computer), was built at the University's Moore School of Electrical Engineering during World War II, and three scientists associated with the university won Nobel Prizes in 1972. The Wharton School is widely considered the best business school in the United States, and ten programs in the College of Arts and Sciences are ranked among the country's most elite.

Further Reading: *History of the University of Pennsylvania, 1740–1940,* by Edward Potts Cheyney (Philadelphia: University of Pennsylvania Press, 1940; reprint, New York: Arno Press, 1977) is an excellent book, and widely available. Of course, it contains little information about the university since the Great Depression. An interesting history focused on 17 individuals associated with the university can be found in *Gladly Learn and Gladly Teach; Franklin and His Heirs at the University of Pennsylvania, 1740–1976,* by Martin Meyerson and Dilys Pegler Winegrad (Philadelphia: University of Pennsylvania Press, 1978).

—Bob Adams

UNIVERSITY OF PISA
(Pisa, Italy)

Location: In the old section of Pisa, along the Arno River.

Description: A state university of 34,000 students with faculties of law, economics, letters, political science, foreign languages and literature, medicine, mathematics and sciences, pharmacy, engineering, agriculture, and veterinary studies.

Information: Università degli Studi di Pisa
Lungarno Pacinotti 45
56100 Pisa
Italy
(50) 590 000

Pisa, with Genoa and Venice, once had been one of the most important cities on the Italian peninsula, victorious against the Saracens, and in the second crusade, active in banking and trade throughout the Middle East. It had developed its own legal code, and rudimentary republican but aristocratic form of government, known as Ghibelline, on account of its imperialist sympathies before 1100. The war waged sporadically with Genoa throughout the twelfth century was decisively lost by Pisa in 1284. By this date Pisa's cathedral (begun in 1068 and consecrated in 1118), the baptistry (begun in 1153 and completed in 1278), and the Leaning Tower (begun in 1173) were all testifying to a grandeur that had passed.

Something approaching a university can be assumed by a reference to a "nuntius," or representative of the Pisan scholars, in 1194. In the thirteenth century another stray reference shows that Pisa was attracting scholars from as far away as Marseilles. The lawyer Bartolo di Sassoferrato, at Pisa from 1339 to 1343, writes of lecturing in Pisa's *studium generale* in 1340. The privileges of the *studium generale* were conferred on Pisa in a 1343 bull of Clement VI, which conferred on Pisa all the privileges of "Bologna, Paris, and other famous *studia generalia.*" (The university lists this as its official opening.) Another bull allowed beneficed clergymen to study at Pisa, and the foundation was confirmed by Urban V in 1364. Siena and Arezzo were erected into *studia generalia* at the same time. The conferment of the status of *studia generalia* on the Italian peninsula (never granted to Genoa or Mantua) did not imply the ascendancy achieved in northern Europe by Paris or Oxford over neighboring chapter or cathedral schools.

By 1438 Pisa was awarding degrees in virtue of both papal and imperial authority, although references to the

1343 opening ceremony make it unlikely that any imperial charter could have preceded the papal bull. It is clear that in the Italian universities generally, episcopal supervision, while never absent, gradually yielded to civic financial support and to municipal academic direction. The Florentines regarded the erection of their *studium generale* as an external recognition of civic sovereignty.

An understanding of the importance of the University of Pisa depends on some knowledge of the relationship between Pisa and Florence during the Renaissance. Although Renaissance Florence had its own developed forms of higher education, and although the neoplatonist discussions of the group known as the Florentine Academy, established by Cosimo de'Medici and entrusted to Marsilio Ficino, was at the center of the most exciting developments in European culture in the late fifteenth century, attempts in Florence to found a university met during the fourteenth and fifteenth centuries with only mediocre success.

Universities were institutions for the training chiefly of administrators, doctors, and, in Italy, of a markedly smaller group of theologians. In Florence itself altogether more radical attitudes to social and political life than those envisaged by the universities were being explored, and the Medici in Florence were rich enough to import officials from elsewhere. Florence was not, in the fourteenth and fifteenth centuries, a place in which a medieval university might be expected to function well, and certainly not to rival the established universities of Bologna and Padua. A resolution dissolved the University of Florence in favor of amalgamation with the University of Pisa; it explicitly mentioned the expense of accommodation in Florence, the distracting delights of the life of the city, the departure of Pisa's wealthier citizens, and Pisa's declining prosperity.

In the end, under Lorenzo de' Medici, a merger of Florence's classes of higher education with the University of Pisa took place on November 1, 1472. Pisa gained Florence's university. The city was in need of resuscitation; it had lost its eleventh-century commercial importance and military power. As a university it offered cheaper accommodation, first-class facilities, and magnificent architecture. Pisa also offered the advantage of deflecting from Florence what might have proved any unwelcome attention to the contents of the curriculum or the orthodoxy of the teaching. Hence, the history of the University of Pisa can scarcely be unraveled from that of Renaissance Florence.

Florence had been defeated by Pisa in 1315 at Montecatini. Seriously weakened by further military defeat in

University of Pisa

1325, by plague in 1348, by war with Milan, by war in 1375 against the papacy, by the revolt in 1378 of the day-workers in the wool trade, and by the threat of Visconti conquest in 1402, Florence became oligarchic, effectively controlled by a score of important families. They reversed its decline, and expanded its dominion in Tuscany, attaching much importance to the conquest of Pisa in 1406. Florence allied with Venice in 1425, and made peace with Milan in 1428. It was the failure of Florence's expansionist ambition to bring Lucca into its control which set in train the events which led to the assumption of power in Florence by Cosimo de' Medici in 1434.

Lorenzo de' Medici revived the Pisan *studio* only by moving much of the teaching away from Florence's own *studio* and by imposing a ban on Florentine citizens which prohibited them from studying other than at Pisa. The bull dissolving Florence's own university dates from 1471, as Pisa became host to the university of its conquerors from November of the following year. The University of Pisa was to become second only to Padua in reputation among the centers of learning on the peninsula.

The University of Pisa was placed under a Florentine board of governors and had a Florentine *provisor.* Lorenzo kept at Florence only a few teachers. A decree stipulated that there should be "three or four" teachers of grammar, and mentioned the need to provide for the teaching of the Latin poets and orators, but the bulk of

ordinary curriculum was henceforward to be taught at Pisa. The Florentine Grand Council had in 1471 nominated five representatives "to organize a worthy *studio* in the city of Florence, and not elsewhere," but the decree restored the *studio* at Pisa.

The immediate cause scarcely can have been the sudden realization that accommodation in Pisa was less expensive. It has been more reasonably supposed that Lorenzo, realizing the place that Florence occupied at the forefront of the peninsula's cultural life, was not prepared to see its future administrators go off to Bologna and Padua for their training. The use that Florence proposed to make of Pisa was similar to that which Venice had already successfully made of Padua. The arrangement had the advantage of going some way to appease the hostility still felt at Pisa by its treatment at Florentine hands since its recapture in 1406, and was made easier by the fact that the bishop of Pisa was a Medici on friendly terms with the pope. After 1509 the Florentine grand dukes were again to restore the University of Pisa, and it was to be there that Galileo, a native of the city, was to establish his European reputation between 1592 and 1610.

The statutes of both Pisa and Florence show that during the fourteenth and fifteenth centuries Pisa came increasingly under the control of its Florentine city-state board, as professorial salaries became less of a charge on the student purse and more on civic finances. That development also released the professors from their humiliating subjection to the student rector as had been first established at Bologna. Now both teachers and students became subject to civic authority. At Pisa, where the bedels were charged with noting the attendance and punctuality of professors, they reported not to the rector, but to the governing board of civic officials, which also retained the right of appointment. Benedict XII, pope from 1334 to 1342, refused to allow diversion of ecclesiastical revenues from the diocese of Pisa to support the *studium,* but much later Pope Sixtus V (1585–90) did allow a tax of 5,000 ducats to be raised from the clergy to support the *studium.*

For a brief period after 1338, the Pisa school was kept full by the migration from Bologna. Very swiftly, its student body split into at least two "universities," or regionally grouped student bodies, apparently with different leaders or *rectores* by 1340. It may be that the *rectores* ruled not different national groups, but students of different disciplines, jurists on the one hand, with medical students and artists on the other. The *rectores* enjoyed wide jurisdiction, extending to all civil cases and to all criminal proceedings except those for theft or homicide.

The plague of 1348 severely damaged the Pisan institution, which took a century to recover. At times, teaching seems to have been altogether suspended, and in any case no trace was left before Pisa recovered from the 1406 conquest by Florence. In the fifteenth century the University of Pisa was four times forced temporarily to move, in 1478 to Pistoia on account of the plague, in 1482 and 1486 to Prato for the same reason, and in 1495 again to Prato on account of the revolt in Florence. Teaching had originally taken place in hired rooms, increasingly paid for by the governing board, but Lorenzo de' Medici turned the corn exchange into a grand university building in 1492. The same building also housed a college founded by Lorenzo for poor students. When Lorenzo moved the teaching of the standard curriculum, he spared no pains to see that the revived university at Pisa was a success. Lorenzo himself moved for several months from 1473 to 1474 to Pisa, and the salaries were adequate to attract the finest professors.

By the end of the fifteenth century the student *universitates* had amalgamated at Pisa, and there was only one *rector.* The Italian pattern was moving in the direction of that of the northern universities as separate colleges of doctors and *universitates* of students adopted a structure nearer to that of a single university divided into faculties.

About student life at Pisa we know relatively little. The licentiate, awarded after private examination, led normally to the doctorate, which meant incurring additional expense and was sometimes therefore taken at a university where the charges were less. Paduan charges were lower than those at Bologna, until the sixteenth century when its degrees carried greater prestige. In the Italian universities investiture with the doctorate corresponded to the inception ceremony in northern institutions, and originated in a first ceremonial exercise of the powers attached to the new dignity in a way analogous to the reception ceremonies of the guilds of merchants and craftsmen. Presents, in time commuted to payments, had to be given by the candidate to the participating officials. At Pisa, in addition to fees, candidates were required to send each participating doctor a box of comfits of stipulated weight, as well as to pay for a banquet.

Lorenzo's second son, Giovanni, as Pope Leo X from 1513, was an active patron of the University of Pisa, but the institution declined again after his death, and by 1551 the city's whole population is estimated to have been under 10,000. Nonetheless, in 1581 Galileo entered the University of Pisa to study medicine and mathematics. He left in 1585 to study mathematics at Florence, holding a chair in that subject at Pisa from 1589 to 1592, when he left for Padua. It is unlikely that he ever dropped objects from the Leaning Tower. (While at Pisa, Galileo still believed that only bodies made of the same material accelerated at the same rate under the force of gravity, irrespective of differences in weight; he reportedly conducted experiments from the tower.)

The next major expansion of the University of Pisa took place in the nineteenth century, when the university embraced Italy's rising interest in science. In 1839 Italy hosted its first congress of scientists. Pisa, in response, assembled faculties in jurisprudence, philosophy, philology, medicine and surgery, natural sciences, and veterinary sciences.

In the nineteenth and early twentieth centuries, a number of political events affected the university. In 1848 several faculty and a large portion of the student body participated in the Austro-Hungarian War, which precipitated the university moving the faculties of theology and jurisprudence to Siena. In 1923, the fascists restructured the University of Pisa as a "Gentile" university, and it was not until the end of World War II that Pisa was able to return to its more open and avant-garde educational style.

In 1967, the university was divided into three distinct branches: the *Studi,* for professional study, the *Scuola Normale Superiore* for letters and sciences, and the *Istituti Pisani del Consiglio Nazionale delle Ricerche* (CNR). (Pisan Institutes of the National Council for Research). The CNR focuses on five sciences: biology and medicine, chemistry, physics, information and computer sciences, and environmental and earth sciences. There are 14 separate institutes within CNR, employing over 600 people. In order to modernize, the CNR began a large-scale program to build facilities to accommodate all the institutes. One of the largest research centers in Italy, the CNR invested millions of lire in the new center.

The university currently employs 300 professors (excluding the CNR), and 28,000 students attend annually. There are 20 degree-granting fields in 11 faculty divisions.

Further Reading: Basic information on the history of the University of Pisa is contained in Hastings Rashdall's *The Universities of Europe in the Middle Ages,* the 1936 edition in three volumes edited by F.M. Powicke and A.B. Emden (Oxford: Oxford University Press, 1895; revised edition, 1936). For the history of Pisa, see D. Herlihy's *Pisa in the Early Renaissance* (Port Washington: Kennikat Press, 1973).

—A.H.T. Levi

UNIVERSITY OF POITIERS
(Poitiers, France)

Location: In a mid-size provincial city of 83,000 inhabitants, 219 miles southwest of Paris.

Description: A state institution operated under the jurisdiction of the minister of education and financed by the state, offering undergraduate, graduate, and professional degrees to approximately 22,000 students.

Information: University of Poitiers
15, Rue de Blossac
86034 Poitiers Cedex
France
(49) 45 30 00

As a small provincial university, the University of Poitiers has endured and prospered for five centuries, due mostly to support from the city. Trough periods of revolution, reaction, and rebirth, the university has continued its educational mission. Among the notable persons associated with the university are writers Honoré de Balzac, François Rabelais, Joachim du Bellay, and philosopher René Descartes. Today, after a period of turmoil and reorganization in French education, the University of Poitiers combines the best of the old and the new. The old is embodied in the "Centre d'Etudes Supérieures de Civilisation Médiévale," a noted institution for the study of the Middle Ages; the new is represented by the "Parc du Futuroscope," a center for exploring and creating the future through technology.

The city has a long history. It was founded by the Gallic Pictones (hence the name), although the Romans referred to it as Limonum. The city was an early center of Christianity, with its first bishop St. Hilarius (360–367). Arian Visigoths made the city their capital, but it was conquered by the Franks in 507 and became the capital for all Frenchmen from Poitiers in 1577, in a document later know as the Edict of Poitiers.

The University of Poitiers's origins can be traced to the political needs of the medieval French monarchy. The university owes its existence to the Hundred Years' War (1337–1453) between England and France. During a period of defeats for the French, Paris fell to the English, along with control of the University of Paris, center of learning in France. King Charles VII was forced to establish his court in Poitiers in 1428, bringing with him those Paris faculty members loyal to his cause. Charles was anxious to counter the influence of the English and to attract French students to learn under French teachers. Using the exiled faculty as a nucleus, he established a new university at Poitiers. Charles was unable to obtain formal approval for his university from the pope, however, until March 31, 1431. In that year, Eugene IV issued a papal bull conferring upon the university at Poitiers all the privileges granted to the University of Toulouse and ordering the new university to be based upon the model of that university. In 1432, the University of Poitiers was formally and solemnly opened with a charter granted by Charles VII. The French king had obtained his French university.

Like the University of Paris, the University of Poitiers was composed of four faculties—arts, theology, law, and medicine. The actual constitutional arrangements for the governing of the university, however, were a compromise between those of the universities at Paris and Bologna, and differed from those outlined in the papal bull. There was one rector for the university and two law faculties—canon law and civil law. The law students, at least, were divided into four nations—France, Aquitaine, Touraine, and Barry—to represent the geographic origins of the students. Each nation selected a rector to represent its interests in the university. Selection was based upon a public disputation in which the candidates had to debate with all comers.

The actual governing of the university was done by the rector, assisted by a general congregation, composed of doctors, masters, and graduates of all faculties, except arts. The choice of rector apparently rotated between the nations and the faculties. In contrast with similar universities, however, the University of Poitiers had no formal connection with the local bishop and cathedral; instead, the treasurer of the Collegiate Church of St. Hilary was named to serve as chancellor.

The University of Poitiers continued to function after the Hundred Years' War ended and the University of Paris once again became the premier French university. One reason for its survival was the unusual amount of support it received from the city of Poitiers. By the standards of the time, the University of Poitiers was a large institution—300 to 400 students of varied background—which increased in size as time passed. To support the growing university, local residents made many generous donations. While most universities of the time had no buildings of their own, the city began building the university's "Great School" in 1448; 11 years later, the city also built a library. Teachers at other universities were dependent upon fees paid by students for their income; at Poitiers, salaries were paid to the faculty by the municipal authorities in an effort to attract the best teachers and to retain them. In return, the city was able to exert an unusual degree of control over the university, apparently with royal support. Because municipal authorities paid the teachers' salaries, they were also able to control who was hired and what they taught and also to correct what they viewed as abuses, such as graduation without sufficient residence or qualification. An associated college was founded in 1478 by Francoise Gillier, Lady of Puygareau and widow of an advocate-fiscal in the Parlément of Paris. The College of Puygareau provided for a prior and eight scholars in theology and arts.

Student life was given some structure, at least in the beginning, by the nations, which functioned as corporate social groups, theoretically representing the geographic origins of students. Germans were well represented at the University of Poitiers, and by the end of the fifteenth century, a large number were studying Roman law there. Things changed as more universities were founded, and rulers attempted to keep their subjects in their own countries. More and more students attended the institutions closets to their homes, leading to a regionalization of education. Poitiers ceased to attract foreign students such as Germans and drew more on French students from Poitou. During the sixteenth century, the student nations collapsed as meaningful groups. The authorities, who had come to view these groups as merely sources of trouble, finally outlawed them in 1629.

University education in France prior to the French Revolution was limited primarily to the wealthy and the socially ambitious. Since education, especially in law, was required for more and more positions and provided a boost to one's social standing, some faculties expanded rapidly during the seventeenth and eighteenth centuries. At Poitiers, for example, the law faculty doubled in size during the seventeenth century. Leading families were able to consolidate their status through law degrees and positions as lawyers. In smaller cities and towns such as Poitiers, lawyers became the new aristocracy and the leaders of urban society.

Although law was growing in importance, other faculties at the University of Poitiers did not fare so well during this period. It was not uncommon for some faculties to suspend teaching for extended periods of time. Most notably, the medical faculty at Poitiers did almost no teaching during the entire eighteenth century. Part of the problem may have been the small size of the medical faculty. At one point, only four undistinguished doctors comprised the teaching staff; at the same time, more prestigious institutions had over 100 doctors on their medical faculty, including several famous medical authors. Since the relative prestige of one's university played a role in one's success, there was little incentive to attend the medical faculty at Poitiers. By 1789, the only teaching faculties active at Poitiers were those of law and theology.

The French Revolution, with its emphasis on the individual and on an end to inherited privilege, saw the suppression of the universities. To the revolutionaries, universities represented bastions of corporatism and established interests. In addition, lands possessed by the universities and used for their support, represented a source of wealth to be tapped by the revolutionary government, just as property owned by the church had been confiscated. In 1792, the University of Poitiers, along with 21 other universities, was dissolved. Specialized *écoles,* open to anyone with talent, and with rigorous entrance examinations, were eventually established to provide professional training in specialized areas. Even so, the revolutionary government found it necessary to allow some education faculties to continue at Poitiers.

Throughout the nineteenth century, additional faculties, especially in science, were established as required to serve the changing needs of French society. The most important development in French education in the nineteenth century, however, was the reestablishment of the universities. Facing competition from German universities, especially following the French defeat in the Franco-Prussian War (1870–71), many French legislators were eager to recreate their universities. Debate centered on what form they should take. Reformers who favored efficiency wanted only five or six institutions to serve the entire nation. Smaller provincial faculties, like those at Poitiers, could be eliminated to free resources for larger ones. If small universities were to be retained, some questioned whether they needed to have all the faculties, especially in the sciences. Members of smaller faculties were opposed to the whole debate, fearing they would be disbanded or would lose all funding. They also disliked the possible loss of autonomy, since the formerly independent faculties might be made answerable to the new university administrations.

Nonetheless, the French legislature passed an education law in 1896, establishing 17 autonomous regional universities, financed largely by the state. The various faculties in Poitiers were reestablished as the University of Poitiers. The new university was a small, but important, regional institution, offering education in many areas. On the eve of World War I, in 1914, the University of Poitiers had about 1,000 students The faculty of letters had about 200 students, the science faculties had between 90 and 140, and the combined faculties of medicine and pharmacy had 39 students.

Through two worlds wars and a depression , the University of Poitiers continued to grow. Increasing numbers of women and foreign students joined the student body. Cooperative educational programs have been established with many foreign universities, including the University of Oregon, the University of Valladolid in Spain, and the University of Coimbra in Portugal. By the late 1960s, however, many French students were gripped with a growing sense that the universities were cold, sterile places, which turned out graduates unlikely to get jobs. Individual faculties remained nearly autonomous from the university administration. The universities did not even have their own budget as a whole, since it was divided among the faculties.

Following riots by students in Paris in 1968, French education was reformed. The *Loi d'orientation de l'enseignement supérieur* of 1968 divided the old faculties into smaller departments, or *Unités d'enseignement et de recherche* (UERs), reduced the power of the Ministry of Education, and established smaller universities with strengthened administrations. The UERs were combined with existing *Instituts universitaires de technologie* (IUTs) (two-year courses of study with technological emphasis) as the basic building blocks for the universities.

While the University of Poitiers was not divided into smaller universities, it did receive a new administrative structure. Like all French universities, it is administered by three boards, composed of elected representatives of the university community and appointed members from outside academia. The first of the board of administration (*conseil d'administration*), which determines general policy for the university, votes the budget, and approves programs and degrees. The second board is the scientific board (*conseil scientifiques*), which overseas research and teaching practices in the university. The final board is the board of studies and student life (*conseil des études et de la vie universitaire*), which advises the board of administration on issues and is concerned primarily with student life in all aspects, such as the library, medical care, and sports. All three boards jointly elect a president every five years from among the faculty of the university. The president represents the university in all official acts, adminis-

ters university property, and hires all university personnel. He or she is also chair of all three boards and is responsible for law and order within the university.

In response to the increasingly technical nature of the world, the university is establishing the *"Parc du Futuroscope,"* a scientific park devoted to advances in the sciences. Supporters hope to make it a center for applying science to the future. The University of Poitiers is a unique institution which remembers and honors its roots but looks to the future. It has endured through difficult times, but is establishing itself as a forward-looking institution serving the needs of its region.

Further Reading: Hasting Rashdall's *The Universities of Europe in the Middle Ages* (Oxford: Clarendon Press, 1936) is the best starting point for information specific to the founding and early years of the University of Poitiers. A more modern complement, both in coverage and in publication date, is *A History of the University in Europe,* edited by Hilde de Ridder-Symoens (Cambridge: Cambridge University Press, 1992). Other useful works that describe the French university system, with helpful information about the University of Poitiers, include L.W.B. Brockliss's *French Higher Education in the Seventeenth and Eighteenth Centuries: A Cultural History* (Oxford: Clarendon Press, 1987), George Weisz's *The Emergence of Modern Universities in France, 1863–1914* (Princeton, New Jersey: Princeton University Press, 1983), and R.D. Anderson's *Education in France 1848–1870* (Oxford: Clarendon Press, 1975).

—Tim J. Watts

UNIVERSITY OF ROCHESTER
(Rochester, New York, U.S.A.)

Location: In Rochester, 80 miles east of Buffalo, New York.

Description: A private university with over 9,000 undergraduate, graduate, and part-time students.

Information: Office of Admissions
University of Rochester
Rochester, NY 14627
U.S.A.
(716) 275-3221

Shortly after a small faculty and student body moved into a renovated hotel in Rochester, New York, and called it a university in 1850, Ralph Waldo Emerson observed that the professors of this fledgling but intrepid institution were "confident of graduating a class of Ten by the time green peas were ripe."

While such a hope seems modest by today's standards, Rochester was a city undergoing tremendous transformation in the first half of the nineteenth century. On the banks of the Erie Canal and the Genesee River, the city swelled during the 1820s with burgeoning industry and trade. With the new industrialism, the city filled with a restless transient population of adventurers, displaced workers, and tradesmen, who raised the ire of the city's established classes with their rowdy behavior.

As in much of the United States, the anxiety accompanying these sweeping social changes fanned the new evangelism of the Great Revival. After the religious fervor subsided in the 1830s, Rochester's major cultural characteristic was its plethora of churches, including several Baptist congregations. As these fiercely sectarian groups competed to attract members to their congregations, religious colleges sprang up beside the churches to provide "a Christian education for the gentleman of the particular denomination."

A small Baptist college existed in Hamilton, New York, several miles outside of Rochester. The college began in 1820 "for the purpose of educating pious young men to the gospel ministry"; by 1846 it was chartered by the state as Madison University (later Colgate). The school, managed by the joint jurisdiction of the state Baptist Education Society and a board of trustees, was viewed by the Baptist denomination of New York as one of its proudest possessions.

Not everyone on the 146-student campus was content with the location of the school. The remote town of Hamilton lacked the facilities enjoyed by urban schools such as Brown and Yale, and dissatisfaction with Madison's location was rife on campus. Madison trustee John Wilder, one of the most vocal proponents of moving the school, said, "We are advocating its removal on the grounds of its location, its dilapidated buildings, the badness of the roads leading to it, the smallness of its own library, [and] its distance from other large libraries." Were Madison to relocate, Rochester would have been the logical destination. For three years "removalists" and "Hamiltonians" debated the location of the school; however, in 1849 the New York Supreme Court issued first a temporary and then a permanent injunction against removal.

The failure to move Madison to a more cosmopolitan location launched the campaign to create what would be the University of Rochester. Wilder and William Sage, the son of a Rochester boot manufacturer, began an intensive public campaign to win approval for the new school, and scoured the countryside near and far to bring in funding for the new institution, raising a grand total of $142,000 between them.

The 24 trustees who constituted the school's managing body met for the first time in September 1850. Assembling a faculty proved no problem, since many of the best professors from Madison University moved to Rochester. The difficulty in finding a campus for the new school was solved by the procurement of an old hotel on Buffalo Street, the United States Hotel, which had been built to serve people traveling on the Erie Canal. The professors who abandoned Madison encouraged their students to do so as well, and so toward the end of October 1850, 28 refugees from Madison converged on Rochester. Sixty students in all answered the attendance call on the first day of class, a number which grew to 82 by the end of the year. Tuition in that year was $10 per term, with a $2 surcharge for "incidentals."

As the university grew, the trustees sought a permanent site for the school other than the hotel then serving as a campus. A prominent Rochester resident, Azariah Boody, offered eight acres to the east of the city as a site for the university; the trustees accepted the land in 1853 as the location for what came to be called the "East Avenue colony," a library built some years later and Anderson Hall, named for the school's first president Martin Anderson.

During the Civil War, the school suffered a serious—almost fatal—decline in enrollment and income as stu-

University of Rochester

dents rallied to the union cause. After Lincoln became the Republican candidate, students formed clandestine "wide-awake clubs" which held political rallies and met in the basement of school buildings for drills. President Anderson aligned himself fiercely with the union cause, but nonetheless urged students not to be moved by their emotions. Despite his pleas, 1 out of 12 undergraduates enlisted, as well as 85 of 198 Rochester graduates.

After the war, the university remained in perpetual financial crisis, but managed to avoid "all pecuniary embarrassment," in the words of President Anderson. The university saw modest growth during these years, including the erection of Sibley Hall (named for the wealthy Rochester benefactor Hiram Sibley) as the school library.

By the turn of the century, the city of Rochester had evolved into a robust, cosmopolitan center with 130,000 residents. Like the rest of America, the city was moving into an era of modern industrialism; the university, however, remained identified as a primarily Baptist institution, lacking a widespread appeal among the heterogeneous population of Rochester and the nation at large. After President Anderson announced his resignation in 1886, the trustees unanimously elected David Jayne Hill as president of the university in 1888 in the hope that Hill would bring to bear his administrative skills in tackling the ongoing fiscal difficulties of the school. During his tenure as president, however, deficits continued to grow and fundraising efforts foundered. He stepped down in 1896 after a brief and disappointing presidency.

Like most institutions of higher learning, Rochester faced an increasing demand from women to be admitted to the school. The 1848 Seneca Falls Convention, held a mere 50 miles from Rochester, had earlier called for equal education for women in the historic "Declaration of Sentiments," and one of the most vocal and vociferous advocates of women's rights, Susan B. Anthony, lived in Rochester. Toward the turn of the century, the chorus grew even louder. While undergraduate sentiment appeared to be against accepting women into the school, many faculty and friends of the school supported coeducation. In 1891, when Susan B. Anthony held a reception for 200 guests in honor of Elizabeth Cady Stanton, the nationally known champion of women's rights, many of the guests spoke in favor of bringing women into the school. Between 1891 and 1893, several women audited classes at the school. In 1893 Helen E. Wilkinson entered the freshman class with the tentative approval of the president. Her expenses were paid by Susan B. Anthony and some of Anthony's friends. Wilkinson had agreed not to matriculate and thus would not be eligible to receive a degree. After two years, poor health caused Wilkinson to withdraw, and in 1897 she died. In 1898, the trustees voted to make the university coeducational if those in favor of college training for women could raise $100,000. When she heard this news, Anthony reportedly cried, "This is better news to me than victory over Spain. It is a peace-victory, achieved only by the death of prejudice and precedents." In September 1900, 33 women registered for classes.

In 1900, Rush Rhees was inaugurated as president of the university. During his tenure, Rhees oversaw some of the most sweeping changes yet in the university. World War I saw the university's enrollment—and subsequently its income—fall sharply. Rhees and the trustees reacted by aggressively pursuing donations from bene-

factors. Rhees made the acquaintance of George Eastman, who had begun retailing cameras in 1888 and by the turn of the century had become one of Rochester's wealthiest citizens. While his total contributions to the University of Rochester exceeded $51 million, Eastman is perhaps best known for the contributions that founded the Eastman School of Music and the School of Medicine and Dentistry.

With plans for the Eastman School of Music completed by 1919, the first classes were held in 1921. Though Eastman described himself as a "musical moron," he nonetheless felt that music deserved an integral role in the leisurely pursuits of an advanced industrial society. So strongly did he hold these sentiments that Eastman contributed nearly $10 million to the music school and expressed his dedication in the inscription atop the Eastman Theater, "For the enrichment of community life."

Rochester's School of Medicine and Dentistry came to be when Eastman dedicated $30,000 per year to the Rochester Dental Dispensary, whose primary purpose was the care of poor children's teeth. At the same time as Eastman was making lavish contributions to the dispensary, Dr. Abraham Flexner—the author of a scathing indictment of the U.S. medical establishment in 1910—approached Rhees with the proposal for a medical school at Rochester.

The three met in February 1920, and later in the year publicly unveiled the project, a school for both the study of general medicine as well as dentistry. Contributions from the Strong family of Rochester funded the Strong Memorial Hospital, allowing Rochester to claim the distinction of having the first medical school in the country with both a school and a hospital. In 1925, instruction began for the first students, and in January 1926, Strong Memorial Hospital treated its first patient, Harry Commons, who was afflicted with stomach pains. Frightened by the number of attentive nurses and doctors at hand, the patient promptly left the hospital, only to return the next day for (successful) treatment.

The suggestion had been made in 1920 that perhaps the university had outgrown its campus on Prince Street, and a new movement began urging the university to relocate. George Todd, a wealthy Rochester resident, proposed the idea of moving the university to the grounds of the Oak Hill Country Club by the Genesee River several miles from the city. Rhees, Todd, and over 50 powerful Rochesterians met for a "reconnaissance" talk at Todd's home to discuss the expansion. They decided that $10 million would be required to erect a new campus, toward which Eastman donated $2.5 million. A fundraising campaign with the slogan "Ten Millions in Ten Days" sought donations from alumni and local citizens. The "River Campus" groundbreaking was in 1927, and the new campus was declared completed on a foggy October day in 1930.

Eastman, who committed suicide in 1932 at the age of 79, bequeathed the majority of his $17.6 million estate to the university, where it passed into a University Endowment Fund. In 1933 President Rhees wrote, "Income from these designated gifts has saved us from dire financial trouble during this year of Universal distress." Despite the munificence of the university's donors, the burden of the president's office had grown heavy for Rhees, now in his seventies. He announced his resignation in 1930, and in 1934 the presidential post passed to Alan Valentine, a graduate of Swarthmore College and a Rhodes scholar. Eastman's bequest allowed the university under Valentine's guidance to envision a more prosperous future, including the growth of graduate studies, expansion of scholarships, and a more comprehensive plan of study for the arts and sciences.

During World War II, the battles overseas permeated every aspect of university life. As in the rest of America, the university practiced drills, rationed, and sold war bonds. By 1943, one-third of the class of 1946 had entered the armed forces. The drop in enrollment, however, was offset by the arrival of the V-12 corps on campus, students who combined academics with training for the navy. Approximately 800 V-12 members arrived at Rochester, ushering in "naval and marine standards of discipline" to the campus throughout the course of the war. At the conclusion of the war, the university saw a remarkable inrush of students. While 5,600 were attending the university prior to Pearl Harbor, enrollment reached 6,420 by 1946, and 9,444 by 1950. University spending was on the increase as well, largely because of the huge growth in research funded by the government, industrial firms, and educational foundations during and after the war.

President Valentine unexpectedly announced his resignation in 1949, and a trustee search committee began the process of finding a replacement. That replacement was found in Cornelis W. de Kiewiet. Though born in the Netherlands, de Kiewiet was raised in South Africa, studied in Paris and Berlin, and chaired the modern history department at Cornell before assuming the Rochester presidency in June 1951. Under de Kiewiet's tenure, the Men's and Women's Colleges—formerly separated between the River Campus and the Prince Street Campus—were integrated into a single College of Arts and Sciences. To accommodate the consolidation of the two bodies onto the River Campus, the college underwent a major expansion, including the building of new residence halls and a greatly expanded offering of classes, including instruction on non-western civilization.

Student interest in politics at this time was tepid. While, during the late 1950s, civil rights became an issue with the forced integration of previously all-white fraternities on campus, not until the early 1960s did students begin to respond to the new political currents running through the nation. The year 1960 saw the establishment of a SANE (Committee for a Sane Nuclear Policy) chapter. In 1961, students began to picket Woolworth's in solidarity with southern lunch-counter protesters, and they protested at movie houses in Rochester whose southern franchises remained segregated. For the first time, students became active in the administration of the university, protesting tuition increases in 1961 and the de-emphasis on undergraduate classes. The dissent among students led to the formation of a Faculty-Student Policy Review Group to consider the sentiments of the students and make recommendations to the administration.

When W. Allen Wallis became president in 1963, one of his first acts was to confer an honorary degree on former president of the United States Dwight D. Eisenhower, who became the first former United States president so honored by the university. It fell to Wallis to steer the university through one of the most turbulent periods in American history, the Vietnam War era. Though many radicals and some conservatives were unhappy with Wallis's declaration that the campus should be open for discussion of all views but should avoid a commitment to political goals, Rochester emerged relatively unscarred from that era.

Until 1975, Rochester had always selected its presidents from a pool of candidates from outside the university. This tradition ended when Robert L. Sproull, who had come to Rochester in 1968, was inaugurated as president in that year. Sproull's strength as a fundraiser was evident when a campaign to raise $102 million actually raised $108 million. His years also saw Rochester taking a lead in medicine and in research. During his tenure, the Strong Memorial Hospital opened, the Cancer Center was constructed, and the Laboratory for Laser Energetics became a leading center for laser research.

G. Dennis O'Brien, president from 1984 to 1994, presided over a university whose undergraduate applications nearly doubled and whose student body became more diverse. Among the innovations O'Brien introduced was the "Take Five" program, which permitted students to take a fifth, tuition-free year while working for the bachelor's degree. He was instrumental in the establishment of the Frederick Douglass Institute for African and African-American Studies and the Susan B. Anthony Center for Women's Studies, both of which actually opened shortly after he retired from office. Another high point for the university during O'Brien's administration came when, in 1990, *U.S. News & World Report* ranked Rochester among the nation's top 25 universities; three years later the magazine placed it among the top 25 "best values" among America's universities.

In the years intervening between the time that Ralph Waldo Emerson made his observation in 1850 and the end of the twentieth century, the university has graduated over 75,000 living alumni, among them Nobel laureates,

Pulitzer Prize-winning poets, and world-class musicians. Were Emerson able to return to Rochester in spring when the peas are ripe, he would hardly recognize the school that has risen from such humble beginnings.

Further Reading: For an excellent account of revivalism in Rochester, read *A Shopkeeper's Millenium* by Paul E. Johnson (New York: Hill and Wang, 1978). One of the most comprehensive histories of the Univesity of Rochester available is *A History of the University of Rochester: 1850–1962,* by Arthur J. May (Princeton, New Jersey: Princeton University Press, 1977).

—Theodore Emery

UNIVERSITY OF ST. ANDREWS
(St. Andrews, Scotland)

Location: St. Andrews, Scotland, 45 miles north of Edinburgh.

Description: A coeducational institution enrolling 5,400 students in undergraduate and graduate schools.

Information: Public Relations
College Gate
St. Andrews
Fife KY16 9AJ
Scotland
(01334) 462530

Established as the outcome of a rise in nationalism and more specifically due to the exclusion of Scottish students from the universities of Oxford, Paris, and Orléans, the University of St. Andrews had its beginnings when a cadre of educators and scholars driven from France decided to locate a center of higher education in the coastal city of Fife, near Edinburgh in eastern Scotland.

Subsequently founded in 1410, the University of St. Andrews stands as the first university in the country's long history. The need for Scotland's premiere university came out of the period between 1378–1429, referred to in Europe as the "Great Schism." During this era, Scotland and France gave loyalty to Benedict XIII, the antipope of Avignon, France, in clear contrast to England which conformed to the doctrine of Pope Martin V in Rome. Scottish students traveled to Paris for their university training, but in 1408, when France abandoned its devotion to Benedict XIII, the antipope moved to Spain. Scottish scholars found themselves in a difficult position.

Learning centers in Spain were few and mediocre, and Scotland's remaining loyalty to the antipope was the antithesis to France's new consecration of the Roman pope. The University of Paris therefore made it difficult for Scottish students to continue, thus serving as impetus for Scotland to create a university of its own.

More a small association of scholars than a center of higher learning at the time of its establishment, the University of St. Andrews was incorporated in 1411 by charter and conferred with full university status two years later by papal bulls issued by Benedict XIII. The bulls gave the University of St. Andrews title to teach a number of faculties, including canon and civil law, theology, medicine, and the arts. It should be noted that despite its prior and unswerving devotion to Benedict XIII, the Scottish Church in 1417 was persuaded by the masters of the Uni-versity of St. Andrews to break away from the antipope and pledge faith to Pope Martin V. This desertion of Benedict XIII was likely based on pure economics, seeing that Benedict had been deposed in 1417, and no longer offered much usefulness to his followers.

Over the course of the next century, three colleges were developed on university premises. St. Salvator's was established in 1450, followed by St. Leonard's in 1512 and St. Mary's in 1537. By 1553, the three colleges had received a papal grant but, along with all other European colleges, suffered the consequences of the Reformation.

The Reformation, a period of religious resurgence in the European nations out of which Protestantism was created, had authorities in some cities reappropriating revenues previously intended for university theologians. Moreover, this intense period of religious, political, and economic turmoil manifested in growing ecclesiastical differences, prompting rapid student decline in many universities. Therefore, following the Reformation, the University of St. Andrews, a learning center predicated on Catholicism, lost its dominance as an ecclesiastical giant. By 1579, the colleges of St. Salvator's and St. Leonard's took the generic monicker of the Colleges of Philosophy, and the College of St. Mary's was limited to the study of reformed theology.

For the next century, the University of St. Andrews made great gains in reestablishing itself as a college of preeminence. During this time, the university boasted teachers the likes of renowned Presbyterian leader and scholar Andrew Melville and historian George Buchanan. Many of the college rectors have been equally well known, including novelist James M. Barrie and former South African prime minister Jan Christian Smuts.

By 1747, St. Salvator's and St. Leonard's colleges had merged to form the United College, an amalgamation that continues today. The United College houses all arts and sciences and the College of St. Mary's remains as the Divinity College. These buildings and all other college property has, since 1858, come under the charge of a supreme governing body of some 25 members culled from within the university and local municipal associations. These university overseers saw an opportunity to enhance the college's reputation as a distinguished learning center when in 1897, Queen's College in Dundee, Scotland, joined the University of St. Andrews to establish a "Conjoint School of Medicine." That association came to an end in 1967 when a separate University of Dundee was established.

The university has been coeducational since 1892; the first century of female matriculation was celebrated in

University of St. Andrews

1992 when two Women's Centenary Research Fellowships were established in the School of Physics and Astronomy and the Scottish History Department.

Today, the University of St. Andrews retains acclaim for its achievements in history, the humanities, and theology, but also boasts its reputation as a center for research in laser and solar physics, biological chemistry, neuroscience, psychology, and computer science. While these subjects may be modern, many are taught in buildings dating back to the fifteenth century. Located in the town center of St. Andrews, the university's library, administrative buildings, arts schools, and lecture halls stand in St. Salvator's Quadrangle on North Street, while St. Mary's College, off South Street, has its own quadrangle. One-half mile from the town center is where more modern campus buildings are situated, in which the physical and mathematical sciences are taught.

The university is just one of several internationally know sites in a community with a relatively small population of 16,000. Once an important medieval town and fishing port, St. Andrews is perhaps best known as the home of the Royal and Ancient Club, a prestigious golf authority established in 1754. Among the city's other notable landmarks are ruins of Scotland's largest cathedral and St. Andrews Castle.

Tradition as old as some of the town's landmarks plays a significant part of student life at the University of St. Andrews. Many scholars in the faculties of arts and science wear a scarlet undergraduate gown during special events. The robe-like costume dates back to the seventeenth century and infers degrees of seniority, depending on how far it is worn off the shoulder. Its present-day quality and texture saw beginnings in 1838 when students, as testimony to the cold weather of Scotland, made an appeal to university authorities to change the overgarment from a thin robe to a thick cloak. Students wearing the colorful gowns can be seen on Sundays during the Pier Walk when they stroll along the town pier.

Two other long-standing customs are popular on campus. Raisin Monday is based on a tradition that couples third- and fourth-year students with first-year students. The older students act as "parents" to the younger charges and as such help them better settle into campus life. Traditionally, the first-year students present their older guardians with a bottle of wine on Raisin Monday, a gift that has seen transmutation since the original gratuity of a pound of raisins.

The "parents" issue a receipt for the wine to the first year students. The acknowledgment, scribed in Latin, can be written on anything. Moreover, "parents" have the authority to dress their "children" in clothing inappropriate to the climate and march them through town. In contrast, the Kate Kennedy procession serves as more of a historical celebration. Each April, students dress to depict the individuals and events that have shaped both the city and University of St. Andrews.

Further Reading: For general background on the country, region, and town, see William Craft Dickinson's "Scotland from the Earliest Times to 1603" (London and New York: Thomas Nelson, 1961).

—Sharon Nery

UNIVERSITY OF SALAMANCA
(Salamanca, Spain)

Location: In the old section of Salamanca, 120 miles west-northwest of Madrid.

Description: A state institution under the jurisdiction of the Ministry of Education and Science, the university enrolls approximately 25,290 traditional and 25,290 correspondence students.

Information: University of Salamanca
Patio de Escuelas 1
37008 Salamanca
Spain
(923) 214518

The exact founding date of the University of Salamanca is unknown, but it is estimated to be in the year 1200 or shortly thereafter. What is certain is that the university is the oldest in Spain and one of the oldest in Europe. One of the earliest records of the establishment of the University of Salamanca dates from 1243. In a charter issued in that year by Ferdinand the Saint of Castile, the university was taken under the protection of the crown and its privileges confirmed. Although the university had existed for nearly a half a century, this year is usually considered its founding date.

Fortunately for the university, Alfonso X ascended to the Spanish throne during the middle of the thirteenth century, the important formative period of the University of Salamanca. Alfonso, known as "the Wise" or "the Learned," was a tremendous supporter of scholarship and the arts. Alfonso's interest in creating an educated populace helped the University of Salamanca grow. In 1252, the king continued the privileges granted to the university nine years earlier; this charter, confirmed by Pope Alexander IV, granted a substantial income to support the university. In the charter, the pope also gave graduates of the University of Salamanca the right to teach in any European university, except those in Paris and Bologna.

Alfonso the Wise is famous for his own writings, in addition to those produced under his patronage. In his administrative code, called *Siete Partidas,* Alfonso devotes an entire chapter to education. This part of the code presents an ideal for university organization, although it cannot be determined how much the University of Salamanca actually conformed to the idea. Under Alfonso's code, the university community enjoyed certain privileges as well as exemptions from regular laws. Known as the *fuero academico,* this part of the code

stated that students and professors were outside the jurisdiction of the regular courts. The students formed a self-governing body and elected a rector as their leader.

Although the university gained the support of both the crown and the papacy in words, actual financial assistance was relatively infrequent. Often grants from the king were promised but never paid. Professors did not receive their salaries and so refused to work. As a result of these troubles and especially after Alfonso's abdication, the university came close to financial ruin and closure during the last half of the thirteenth century.

The university found new life in the beginning of the next century under the reign of Ferdinand IV. In 1300, the king granted to the university one-third of the tithes collected in the Salamancan diocese. Called *tercias reales,* these tithes were previously earmarked for church construction and maintenance. Although it took more than 100 years for the revenues to be collected by the school on a permanent basis, the *tercias reales* provided the main financial support for the university until the nineteenth century.

For the first century of its existence, the University of Salamanca felt the influence of the monarchy more than that of the church. The papacy would approve the changes proposed by the king, but the impetus for reforms came from the crown. In the fourteenth century, however, the situation reversed. Four succeeding popes reorganized the university's departments, constitutions, and finances in various ways.

Pope Clement V authorized the establishment of chairs of Hebrew, Arabic, and Chaldean. He also granted additional revenues to the university. Pope John XII reorganized the administration of the university in 1334. He appointed the *maestrescuela* of the cathedral school as chancellor of the university. The office of the *maestrescuela* had recently assumed judicial powers over the *fuero academico,* the special privileges given to the university. From this point on, the *maestrescuela* slowly became the direct arm of the pope in the administration of the University of Salamanca.

Pope Benedict XIII was responsible for starting major changes at the university in the late 1300s. Benedict, the Spanish antipope, added new chairs, increased salaries, and reformed the university's constitutions. The modern statutes reflected the acceptance of Roman law in Spain. The changes made by Benedict lasted only a short time; soon after the new statutes were approved Castile transferred its support from Benedict, the antipope, to Pope Martin V. Martin, who upheld many of Benedict's directions for the university, later issued a new set of statutes.

University of Salamanca

The new constitution, which was issued in 1422, was the last given to the University of Salamanca by a pope.

Under Martin's direction the university had three leaders: the *maestrescuela,* the rector, and the *primiciero.* The *primiciero,* who was elected by the doctors and masters to preside over their meetings, was the least important and held the least power of the three leaders. The rector was the spokesperson of the students. The office alternated annually between natives of Castile and Leon. The rector, elected directly by the students, was obligated to swear obedience to the pope. The *maestrescuela* was the most powerful of the three heads of the university. The powers first granted to this position by Pope John XII had increased over the past century, and by 1422 the *maestrescuela* had become the guiding hand of the university. The direct representative of the pope, the *maestrescuela* acted as the judge for the university, granted degrees, and enforced the constitution.

In addition to these three leaders, the university was directed by a council, also elected by the students. The council of 20 *definitores,* consisting of 10 chairholders and 10 students of noble birth, directed the day-to-day business of the university and selected the *maestrescuela,* who was then confirmed by the archbishop of Salamanca and the pope. For the next 50 years this basic organization of the University of Salamanca was directed by two major forces: the students, who were represented by the rector and the *definitores,* and the church through the *maestrescuela.* The Spanish monarchy, which had enjoyed some control over the university in its first century of existence, had slowly lost its power until the 1470s.

The ascension of Ferdinand and Isabella to the throne in 1474 signaled the end of the line of weak Spanish monarchs. For the University of Salamanca, this marked the beginning of the process of modernization. The royal power merged with the forces of the students and the pope, resulting in a more contemporary university. The resumption of royal jurisdiction over the university meant that the powers of the students and especially the papacy were reduced significantly. It also meant an end to some of the abuses that had infested the university. Ferdinand and Isabella issued their first set of *cedulas,* or royal decrees, in 1480. The *cedulas* reasserted the crown's power and addressed the abuses.

A second set of statutes issued by the Catholic monarchs in 1492 further asserted their powers and limited those of the pope. Under the *Concordance de Santa Fe,* the jurisdiction of the *maestrescuela* was severely curtailed. The power that the Spanish crown exerted over the university continued to increase after Ferdinand and Isabella. Royal jurisdiction reached a climax in 1528, when Charles V claimed the right of appointing the *maestrescuela,* a move severely restricting the church's control of the university. By the end of the 1520s, the crown had a hand in virtually every aspect of university activity, including requirements and fees for degrees, content

of courses, examinations, texts, filling of chairs, and officials' conduct.

The sixteenth century saw a further consolidation of power in the monarchy, not only at the university but across the entire country. The Spanish Inquisition was an iron fist holding all of Spain in its grip from the end of the fifteenth century until the beginning of the nineteenth century; the University of Salamanca was securely clenched there. During the Inquisition some of the most infamous events in the history of the university occurred. Christopher Columbus presented the results of his voyages to a group of professors at the University of Salamanca; they scoffed at Columbus's idea that the world was round. Legend says that "they denied the earth was round, for if this were so it would have no stability. Columbus confounded them by tapping the famous egg . . . until the shell flattened at the pole and thus made it stand upright." Despite the erroneous judgment made by the professors in Columbus's case, the University of Salamanca was renowned for attracting the most learned men in Europe to teach there. Famous faculty members included Ignatius de Loyola, founder of the Society of Jesus (Jesuits); Calderon de la Barca, poet and dramatist; Peter Martyr, Dominican friar, who is the patron saint of the Spanish Inquisition; Copernicus, the astronomer; Nebrija, the humanist and writer; and Vesalius, the Belgian anatomist.

The famous writer Luis de Leon also taught at the University of Salamanca. One of the most brilliant literary voices of the Spanish Renaissance, Leon felt the brunt of the Inquisition during his tenure at Salamanca. Leon was an Augustinian monk, and so was denounced by the rival Dominicans, who were the executives of the Inquisition. Leon was imprisoned for nearly five years, during which time he wrote his prose masterpiece, *The Names of Christ.* Leon was never tortured by his Dominican captors, and although he was unjustly imprisoned, he eventually obtained justice. After he was released, the University of Salamanca welcomed the poet back, although he was not reappointed to the same chair he had held prior to his imprisonment, since it had been filled by someone else. Instead, Leon received a chair in another faculty. The classroom in which he lectured still stands today; the Hebrew text inscribed above the door translates, "Happy are thy men, happy are these thy servants, which stand continually before thee and hear thy wisdom."

Imprisonment of brilliant professors was not the only indication of the decay of the University of Salamanca during the Spanish Inquisition. Studies suffered tremendously because of the suffocating and closed-minded atmosphere. The statutes of the university were revised several times throughout the sixteenth and into the beginning of the seventeenth century. These statutes continued to reflect the university's domination by the crown that had begun with Ferdinand and Isabella. The royal statutes that were issued in 1538, 1561, and 1625 outlined the basic administrative organization of the university. These constitutions, each of which built upon and complemented the preceding ones, directed the course of the university until 1770.

Although the Inquisition severely affected the university, this period was not entirely detrimental. Most of the buildings of the present school were constructed during this time. The main facade is one of the most beautiful and notable examples of Spanish Renaissance decoration. The Plaza Mayor, which has been called "one of the lordliest public squares anywhere," is home to glorious arcades and staircases.

The university chose to focus on teaching traditional law and theology, while the rest of Europe was teeming with scientific and artistic advances. Scholars at the University of Salamanca were so preoccupied with defending Catholicism that they ignored the important intellectual confrontations of the Enlightenment that were occurring throughout the rest of Europe. When, to scholarly failures was added abusive administrative practices, such as favoritism in professors' salaries and appointments, the university experienced a steep decline.

Troubles extended beyond the classrooms and into the city of Salamanca. Students and townsmen had habitually feuded since the early days of the *fuero academico*. By the 1600s, the university had gained virtual economic and judicial independence from the city. Scholars had always enjoyed special privileges, including being exempt from many taxes and tools. The university controlled its own meat and wheat supplies and also enjoyed rent exemptions. Townspeople were understandably irritated by these favors. Tensions climaxed in the Great Riot of 1644. One November night, a fight broke out in the streets of Salamanca between a group of students and townsmen. The students killed one of the citizens, and the townsmen captured and tortured one of the students. The students, vastly outnumbered, retreated; citizens called by the alarm ransacked the students' quarters and took captive those who remained. The Salamancans waged another attack on the cloistered students the following day. The students fled again, tried to regroup, and were finally pacified by university and town officials. After the student who was captured first had been hanged, and several townsmen sentenced to public whipping, the volatile atmosphere subsided, but the rivalry between the city and the university continued.

The decline of the university endured into the early eighteenth century. Scholarship had decayed to a pathetic state. Classes were plagued by absenteeism by both students and professors, and, by 1736, even the requirements for graduation were reduced. In the 1760s and 1770s reforms were initiated by the monarchy and by the university itself. This reform movement culminated in the Plan of Studies (*Libro de Claustros*) of 1771. Under this plan, almost the entire university became more liberal in its orientation, even including its textbooks.

Although the reforms were far-reaching, further changes were necessary to make Salamanca a more modern university. The department of medicine was the spark of the second series of reforms. The medical school had been threatened in the late 1790s by a proposal to centralize all of the Spanish universities' medical departments. Under the United Medical Faculty, the university would be little more than a glorified prep school. The University of Salamanca vehemently opposed the plan. Its department of medicine united to fight the United Medical Faculty. Although the United Medical Faculty was created, the university's fight worked—Salamanca was under merely nominal control by the group. The United Medical Faculty lasted only until 1801, but the consolidation helped to modernize, to liberalize, and to lead the way to broader university reforms.

One of those broader reforms was the new plan of medicine for the university that was adopted in 1804. This led to the university-wide revised Plan of Studies in 1807. The new plan did not reflect an enlightened shift like that proposed in the plan of 1771; the 1807 Plan of Studies was a more radical administrative reorganization. Under the new plan, more emphasis was to be placed on science, law, and Spanish. The new Plan of Studies did not have a chance to prove its effectiveness. Shortly after the plan was passed, Charles IV abdicated, and Ferdinand VII ascended the throne. After the French invasion of 1808, the combination of war and poverty devastated the university. During the war, the University of Salamanca completely closed. Any reforms that could have moved the university out of its decline were thwarted. When it opened again, the university was a completely different and modern nineteenth century institution.

War provided another dramatic moment for the University of Salamanca over a century later. In the opening days of the Spanish Civil War, the university witnessed a chilling standoff between the Falangist general Millan Astray and the aging nationalist Miguel de Unamuro, for 35 years rector of the university. In a speech at the university in October 1936, Astray compared Catalonia and the Basque provinces to cancers in the body of Spain. Upon hearing this, Unamuro stood up and denounced Astray. This emotional outburst was the last time the frail Unamuro spoke in public.

This scene was but one of many dramatic moments in the history of the University of Salamanca, an institution that has been intimately tied to the ruling powers of Spain for over 700 years. In its early years, the university was controlled alternately by the students, the church, and the monarchy. It was one of the only universities in Europe during its glory days in the Middle Ages. Today the university has been called "just another provincial school," but if only because of its long and rich history, the University of Salamanca ranks among the grandest in the world.

Further Reading: George Addy's *The Enlightenment in the University of Salamanca* (Durham, North Carolina: Duke University Press, 1966) focuses mainly on the years from 1740 to 1808. The introduction contains a brief but comprehensive account of the early years of the university. Alfonso Lowe's *The Spanish: The Intrepid Nation* (Madrid: Gordon Cremonisi, 1975) is primarily concerned with the arts and letters of the Spanish Renaissance, but it also provides some information about the university. More a guidebook than a historical text, Dorothy Loder's *The Land and People of Spain* (Philadelphia: Lippincott, 1972) nonetheless mentions the city and the University of Salamanca.

—Cindy Mertz

UNIVERSITY OF SEVILLE
(Seville, Spain)

Location: Seville, Spain, the capital of the province of Andalucia in southern Spain.

Description: A state institution under the jurisdiction of the Ministry of Education and Science, enrolling approximately 34,000 in undergraduate, graduate, and professional schools.

Information: Universidad de Sevilla
Calle San Fernando 4
Sevilla
Spain
(954) 218600

The creation of a school in Seville was first proposed by King Alfonso X (1252–84), the ruler of Castile and Leon. Called "the Learned" or "the Wise" because of his patronage of scholarly pursuits, Alfonso had a special fondness for the city of Seville. The city was the most frequent seat for the king's court, which at one time resided there for eight consecutive years. One of Alfonso's most important contributions to Spanish arts and letters was his support of Arabic translations. He commissioned scholars to translate important works from Arabic into Latin. A long tradition of such translation in Toledo had existed since the twelfth century. Translators commissioned by Alfonso also worked in Toledo, but they were independent from the so-called Toledan School. Alfonso had ideas of founding a similar school in Seville that would serve not only as a center for translation, but as a general school for Latin and Arabic. Latin was needed to understand church matters while Arabic was needed for scientific and political reasons—manuscripts about astronomy, medicine, agriculture, and geography were all written in Arabic.

Alfonso first proposed the idea of a school in 1256, and a papal bull was secured in 1260 for the establishment of one in Seville. Soon more serious events, such as his election to the throne of Germany, disagreements with his sons, and fights with other principalities, came along to occupy the monarch, distracting him from thoughts of promoting scholarship. Alfonso X died in Seville without ever realizing his dream of establishing a school there.

After Alfonso came four kings of diverse character, none of whom promoted a school. After that, the court moved away from Seville. No longer the largest residence of the kings, the city's grandeur declined as did local interest in letters. Part of this decline was assuaged by the founding of the Colegio de San Miguel, the oldest school

in Seville. It educated young choral assistants, first in Latin and humanities, then in philosophy or liberal arts, and then in religion. Later students learned about music and Gregorian chant. This was the only school in Seville until the reign of Henry IV.

Henry IV was succeeded on the throne by Ferdinand and Isabella, who lived for a time in Seville. Ferdinand and Isabella made Seville into the center of commercial activity generated by exploration of Africa and the Americas. Amid growing prosperity and splendor, interest was renewed in the establishment of public schools.

At that time, Sevillian youths who wanted to pursue scientific or other learned careers had to travel long distances to obtain the proper training and education. Those who stayed in Seville did not receive an education and were limited to lower-class, nonprofessional occupations. However, many families could not afford the expense of an extended journey. Such travel was dangerous, and many of those who left Seville to become doctors, lawyers, or clergymen never came back. The city was in danger of slowly losing its brightest and most promising youth to cities with universities. For these reasons, the city leaders recognized that a university was necessary to perpetuate the emerging glory of Seville.

Two members of the city council, Archbishop Diego Deza and Rodrigo Fernandez de Santaella, were very interested in founding a school in Seville. Moreover, neither wanted to concede to the other the fame and renown that would fall upon one who established a place of higher learning, and so a long and bitter fight ensued between the two sides. Santaella, after much perseverance and personal expense, finally acquired, in 1472, the first buildings for what was to become the Colegio Mayor. The papal bull for the founding of this university was asked for in 1502 and granted by Pope Julius II in 1505. It is this institution that came to be known as the University of Seville. Diego Deza obtained another bull for the founding of an ecclesiastic school in 1516. The two men and their respective schools remained bitter rivals, arguing over who had more authority to grant degrees and whose courses of study were superior.

The school founded by Santaella, the Colegio y Universidad de Santa Maria de Jesus, was to teach arts, logic, philosophy, theology, canon and civil law, and medicine. By means of the 1505 papal bull, Santaella was given the right to form the university's constitution, and church benefactors were appointed to support the students and teachers. A second papal bull, granted in 1508, said that a degree from the University of Seville carried with it the same prestige and legitimacy as a degree from any university in the kingdom. This raised the university to the same level as the esteemed University of Salamanca, which had been the country's premier institution of higher learning for more than 250 years.

Although there was much enthusiasm for establishing a university in name, the real work of building and opening the school was not undertaken with so much pleasure. The constitution was not finished until 1509, and it was another seven years before the university existed legally. In 1516 the university finally accepted its first students; 17 were admitted on scholarships: 10 to study theology, 6 for law, and 1 who was as yet undecided. Only two professional chairs were established at first, one for theology and one for canon law, but before long other chairs were filled, and the university could offer a true general education.

In its early years, the university had numerous problems: incomplete buildings, uncertainty about the legitimacy of its degrees, rights and privileges questionable in the eyes of the monarchy and the church, and competition from other, more established, schools. As a result, it did not attract many students, and certainly not the brightest among the eligible youth.

The university slowly began to increase its financial strength, and consequently its student body, studies, and prestige. Two faculty members, Alonso de Campos and Doctor Sarmiento, helped the university to raise adequate amounts of money. The school grew, and in 1551 it officially became a university.

Within about 30 years the University of Seville was in a state of disorder. A papal bull issued in 1545 gave the administration the right to revise or add to the university's statutes whenever it deemed necessary. Minor chaos ensued, resulting in a school that was overburdened with debts and had divided academic departments.

Eventually, a commission was established to reform the university's statutes. Comprised of doctors, teachers, and other learned men, the commission's revisions were accepted and recognized by papal bull in 1621. This reform resulted in many improvements to the university, although many shortcomings remained. Latin, rhetoric, and poetry were not taught at the university—a surprising omission in a city that prided itself on its achievements in the arts and humanities.

Another serious fault of the university was in its religious education. At the more famous divinity schools, the university was located in the heart of the religious community. In Seville, the divinity students and faculty went to the university for classes but lived in distant convents. This made the religion department less powerful and prestigious than the general education department, which led to great rivalry between the two sides.

The university's focus was on practical and scientific studies. Rapid advances were being made in physics and natural sciences in the seventeenth century. Furthermore, the founders of the university were primarily concerned with providing an education that was related to everyday life. Thus, the school taught formulas rather than theories, and physics instead of metaphysics. The university's focus on practical education was explained in the statutes of 1621, which even stipulated that certain authors were never to be taught at the school.

Fighting among the various schools in Spain was fierce throughout the seventeenth and early eighteenth centuries. Each was connected to a different faction of the Catholic Church, a factor which gave rise to disputes not only over church doctrine, but about the teaching of church doctrine. Schools quarreled over whose courses were more fulfilling, whose professors were more respected, and whose degrees were more prestigious. This factionalism infected not only the religious departments of each school, but the arts, sciences, law, and medicine divisions as well. Such animosity, coupled with the fighting among departments at the university, led to a volatile atmosphere. In such a situation, academics were bound to suffer. By the middle of the eighteenth century, scholasticism and the arts in Seville were in a shambles.

The job of revitalizing education in Seville fell into the hands of Pablo Olavide, an official who came to the city government with an interest in both learning and public administration. He wrote a scathing indictment of the condition of the city's schools, which was presented in 1768. In this mandate, he emphasized the divisiveness and pettiness that plagued Seville's learned community. Spain was split into factions of many kinds, Olavide noted. It was a country divided by geography, language, religion, and social class. This divisiveness was draining the country of its lifeblood. Professors and, consequently, students at the universities were more concerned with promoting the doctrines of their own group and disparaging the views of other factions than with teaching basic fundamentals of education.

Olavide declared that universities in Spain were concerning themselves with frivolous and useless questions, a serious mistake in a time when knowledge was flourishing throughout the rest of Europe. Spanish youth were poorly taught and carried the lack of education to their future careers. These businessmen, lawyers, government officials, artists, doctors, and clergymen had been educationally corrupted, and the professional life of the country suffered as a result.

In response, Olavide proposed that the University of Seville occupy the old building that the Jesuits had left vacant upon their desertion of the city. The religious and secular parts of the university were to be separated; the university would be located in the basement and the seminary on the higher floors. The seminary actually served as a kind of boarding school for students with severe discipline problems. Olavide also proposed a new structure for the government of the university. A rector and three counselors would be elected periodically, and treasurer and secretary would be permanent positions to provide some continuity. Olavide also restructured the pay scale for professors and administrators and redesigned the courses of study.

These mandates were well received. In the following year, 1769, the university was reestablished and confirmed by papal bull. The University of Seville entered a new period of prosperity. The departments of theology, law, and medicine attained a new prominence and attracted illustrious professors to the faculty. Because the textbooks that had been used previously were grossly outdated, the most learned men of Spain were recruited to write new texts that would complement the courses taught at the university.

During the reign of Carlos III (1759–88), university reforms swept through the entire country. Rights, privileges, rules, and tuitions were standardized at all universities in Spain. During the same period, the University of Seville continued to grow. The department of mathematics was established and a library was opened; arts and literature flourished. The college of law was reorganized, an event that led to the reformation of the Sevillian bar.

Another series of reforms came after much political turmoil—the abdication of Carlos IV, the war for independence, and the revolution—that upset the course of learning at the university. From 1820 to 1823, three sets of university reforms were passed. The University of Seville initially profited from these reforms and, as a result, enrollment increased substantially. Chemistry and history departments were added and new equipment was acquired for the physics and mathematics departments. The college of pharmacy became accredited.

The prosperity did not last long, however. Studies and morale declined so rapidly that 20 years later more reforms were needed. The university counselor, Nicolas Maestre, was primarily responsible for the moral rejuvenation of the university. He reformed discipline and made examinations and grades more rigorous. Maestre stimulated an appreciation of good scholarship and a feeling of cooperation among students and faculty members. Under the direction of Maestre, the physical and intellectual splendor of the University of Seville also increased. New buildings, lecture halls, laboratories, and auditoriums were constructed, and existing structures were improved. Modern furniture and laboratory equipment were bought. The botanical garden was improved and the library was opened to the public.

Today, some of the university's buildings number among the greatest architectural and artistic attractions in Seville. The old university church, designed by F. Bartolome Bustamante, features Ionic columns and a sculpture of the Madonna and Child by Bautista Vazquez. Its paintings, sculptures, and funeral monuments are also of special note. The marble tombs of Don Fadrique Enriquez and dona Catalina de Ribera are very impressive, among others. One of the university's divisions occupies a former tobacco factory with a peculiar past. The old factory, which encompasses the second largest historical building complex in Spain, is a baroque and rococo square that incorporates a maze of courtyards. Moreover, it is the cigarette factory where Carmen, the protagonist of Bizet's opera of the same name, was said to have worked. The factory dates to the eighteenth century, but the university relocated there only a few decades ago.

Since 1940, the population of Seville has grown dramatically. From 281,000 at the beginning of the decade, it had risen to over 700,000 by 1990. When Seville-born Felipe Gonzalez was elected president of Spain in 1982, the ruling socialist party began to favor projects for the improvement of the underdeveloped south of the country. One of the major projects was the Expo '92 World Fair, which was held in Seville; the city's economy benefited from the spending of the 43 million visitors to the fair.

Further Reading: The university is mentioned briefly in a guidebook about Seville by Robert S. Kane, *Spain at Its Best* (Lincolnwood, Illinois: Passport, 1986), and in Dorothy Loder's *The Land and People of Spain* (Philadelphia: Lippincott, 1972).

—Cindy Mertz

UNIVERSITY OF SIENA
(Siena, Italy)

Location: In central Tuscany, about 30 miles south of Florence.

Description: A state institution enrolling approximately 14,000 students in undergraduate, graduate, and professional schools.

Information: University of Siena
Via Banchi di Sotto, 55
53100 Siena
Italy
0577-298000

A school in Siena, supported by a tax levied on landlords who rented rooms to foreign students, was first mentioned in a town document from 1240, but there is subsequent testimony that a school of Roman law was established in Siena as early as the eleventh century. Schools of grammar and medicine also existed, all serving as forerunners to the university. In the first half of the thirteenth century, a Bolognese teacher wrote movingly of a city-financed school of grammar and rhetoric in Siena: "This distant land is crowned Siena. I have been there at the feet of its philosophy, I have heard its teaching, I have drunk its milk and not without labor and expenses have I found the flower of precious knowledge." Accounts such as this were critical to the Tuscan school, which owed its existence to students migrating from other northern Italian universities in search of alternative educational sites.

The university at Siena was recognized by Holy Roman Emperor Frederick II in 1248 and Pope Innocent IV in 1252. The pope's approval exempted students and faculty from taxes and recognized them as members of an institution governed by common law. In 1275, the emperor and the General Council of Siena urged the city to help finance the university; however, the school often found itself without sufficient resources and for some time lacked a permanent headquarters. Under these circumstances, classes were conducted in a rented church or in the teachers' own houses. Despite these difficulties, the university played an important role in maintaining the public health of the city. Therefore, after 1250, the city's municipal council made paying the salary of the school's medical teacher its top priority. In the early fourteenth century, city elders began paying the salaries of teachers according to fame; a legal act also set standards of behavior for teachers, requiring, among other things, that they stay in the city and teach "faithfully." If a teacher failed to

do so, his caricature would be drawn on the walls of the town, making him the object of public scorn.

During this period the university was associated with two notorious criminal incidents. The first involved Benincasa d'Arezzo, a well-known law professor at the university who later, as a judge in Rome, was murdered by Ghino di Tacco; the episode was apparently so graphic that Dante mentioned it in canto six of *Purgatory.* Then, in 1321, a student in Bologna was sentenced to death after being found guilty of kidnapping a girl, prompting students there to flock to Siena in protest; Sienese authorities responded by financing their reception and granting them standard student privileges. Though Bolognese officials were quick to try to lure the students back, the incident helped enhance the reputation of its Sienese rival.

In spite of competition from schools at Florence and Perugia, the university enrolled a large number of foreign students, particularly from Germany, Spain, Portugal, and Burgundy. The reputation of the school depended heavily on the renown of its teachers, and among those attracted to the school were canon jurist Federico Petrucci, civil jurist Giovanni Pagliaresi, and the poet and jurist Cino da Pistoia. A concerted effort was to be made to further improve the university's prestige. In 1348, the governors determined to spend whatever sum was necessary to persuade the pope to confer *studium generale* status on the university. Though they failed, the city's concistory, or ruling magistracy, also had been working to secure legal recognition for the university. In this they were successful. In 1357, Emperor Charles IV made the Sienese school an official university of the Holy Roman Empire, allowing it to confer academic degrees.

In 1392 the Bishop of Siena suggested the foundation of a *Casa della Sapienza,* or residential college, to maintain and preserve the school; due to the depressed economic state of the town, however, the project languished. In the early fifteenth century the idea again surfaced, and this time, with the considerable help of Pope Gregory XII, the plan was implemented. The pope approved the refurbishing of several rooms of an old charity hospital known as Mercy House, and decreed that the building would host 30 poor students from Siena. When the first students were admitted, however, none were from Siena and all had to pay 50 florins a year.

As time went on, the official functions of the *Sapienza* changed. Funding for the university was suspended in 1411 due to recurrences of the plague, which had first reached the city in 1348 and eventually wiped out half its population. Funding was also cut due to the influence of the rector of the local hospital, who considered the paying

University of Siena

of teachers' salaries an inappropriate use of public monies. Local officials now expected the *Sapienza* to provide the university with administrative and financial support, and also to supply the state with intellectuals capable of handling transactions with foreign powers.

The *Sapienza* quickly became the most important division of the Sienese school; its patrimony included shops and houses in town and an estate with more than a 100 farmhouses on it. Being admitted was a privilege, one that often depended on the recommendations of emperors, popes, or cardinals, as the school began to evaluate candidates on the political benefit to be gained. In 1472, the *Sapienza* helped to established a new bank in Siena with a deposit of 300 gold florins; in the following year, government officials ruled that the college should assume the responsibility of building two houses every year, further increasing its role in maintaining Siena's economic well-being. The influence of the *Sapienza* is commemorated today in the university's seal, which pictures an *M* (for the original Mercy House) in a cross held by Saint Catherine of Alexandria.

The first half of the fifteenth century was a golden age for the university. A center of the new humanism, Siena attracted some of the world's greatest teachers. Among them were Antonio Panormita and Francesco Filelfo, who was paid a salary of 350 gold florins a year, the highest figure the university had ever paid. Also teaching at Siena was Marrasio, the author of *Angelinetum;* Aeneas Silvius, the future Pope Pius II, who wrote *Cinthia;* and Antonio Beccadelli, who wrote a collection of epigrams titled *Hermaphrodytus.* From 1396, Buccio da Spoleto lectured on Dante and gave public talks on *The Divine Comedy* from San Vigilio on major feast days. The activities of the university led to the introduction of the printing press in Siena. Henry of Cologne, a German printer, began such activity in 1484 by publishing a law text by Paolo di Castro; the books later printed in the town were primarily meant for the school's roughly 600 students.

The Observant Franciscan San Bernardino was a great champion of the university during this period. Once a student at Siena, he left the university with 12 classmates to devote himself to the care of the sick during a plague outbreak. Later in his life he often returned to the city to lecture, and always urged the Sienese to support their university, warning them that without the education it could provide, no Christian community was possible.

Students at Siena were required to enroll in long courses of study: seven years for degrees in arts, medicine, or philosophy, and five years for degrees in civil or canon law. Meanwhile, the behavior and performance of teachers was still closely monitored. During the academic year, which ran between October and June, teachers were required to have at least five students for their classes; otherwise, they were fined and forced to lead discussions in the public square.

Interest in such rules diminished over the years, as the school was forced to deal with more serious matters, crises created by fierce competition with the University of Pisa, and by a period of political instability that brought the region under Spanish dominance.

Siena's status as an independent republic was now threatened by Emperor Charles V, who had been appealed to for protection against Pope Clement VII in 1526. Between 1530 and 1540 these political disruptions took a serious toll on the university. Many writers and scholars went into exile and the school was left to fend for itself with few teachers and a restless student body. The university became host to so many Spanish and Portuguese students that the other students staged a revolt in 1541. The emperor waged war on the city in 1552, with aid of the duke of Florence, Cosimo de' Medici. Siena surrendered in 1555, and two years later it was ceded to Cosimo, who was made grand duke of Tuscany in 1569. Meanwhile, the school continued its decline, becoming a small, civic institution.

The university began to expand again under governor Francesco de' Medici, who in 1569 created a committee to find new resources for the school. Francesco was made grand duke of Tuscany in 1574; at this time he approved articles of association for the many German students in Siena, despite their being implicated in charges of "Lutheranism" by the Inquisition. His successor, Ferdinand de' Medici, introduced faculty reforms at the university, dividing teachers into groups (doctors, jurists, artists, philosophers, and theologians) based on their disciplines. He also instituted the use of competitive examinations for teachers, to avoid political nominations.

In 1591 new legal powers were given to the rector, or student leader, of the university. Siena followed the model established in Bologna of a student-dominated institution. Its rector was an important figure in the life of the town; ideally a foreign student, the rector was chosen by student representatives and prominent citizens. The status of this position was reflected in the entertainments that marked an election: a month-long schedule of celebratory dances, masked balls, and plays. The status of the rector is well illustrated by the accomplishments of German rector Giorgio Fuccaro (1593), who enacted new laws about instruction methods and formally requested an end to protectionism that favored the rival University of Pisa.

Changes at the university during the seventeenth century diminished the influence of the rector. Competitive examinations were abolished and new governors were put in place. The university was now under the control of aristocrats who were faithful to the grand duke. Among the members of this oligarchy was the renowned teacher Pirro Maria Gabrielli, who founded the scientific *Accademia dei Fisiocritici* in 1691 to compete with Florence's *Accademia del Cimento.*

Siena's medical school, a cornerstone of academic life at the university, was notable in the eighteenth century for its faculty, among them Paolo Mascagni, who wrote the famous *Grande Anatomia del Corpo Umano* (Anatomy of the Human Body). This work contained life-size anatomy tables that students still considered valuable a century later. However, the university's prosperity was destroyed by the French invasion of Tuscany in 1808, when the school was abolished and its dean pressed into service as the commissary of a new French medical school. Ferdinand III would eventually revive the university and transfer its legal, medical, physical, and theological colleges from the *Casa della Sapienza* to an old abbey near the church of San Vigilio.

Political upheaval, however, continued to affect the school's operations. After 1832, when the first *Risorgimento* (or national unification) uprisings took place, many Sienese students joined in the Young Italy movement in opposition to the grand duke. In July 1847, Ludovico Petronici, a medical student and known liberal, was killed by the police. The incident brought the tension between the authorities and students to a new high; a year later, 55 students and 4 teachers from Siena joined the Savoia army in the revolutionary battles of Curtatone and Montanara.

In 1851, Leopold II split the university in two: his decree kept the faculties of law and theology in Siena, and moved the colleges of medicine, philology and philosophy, mathematics, and natural science to Pisa. The provisional government that replaced Leopold II reorganized these two universities eight years later, but the changes tended to favor Pisa, especially in the humanities. After the plebescite to unify Italy, the new education minister, Terenzio Mamaini, suspended three teachers on the Siena faculty of theology for being reactionary; the archbishop promptly responded by resigning as administrative head of the university, which led to the faculty being abolished.

In 1862, however, with the passing of the Matteucci Law, the university was nationalized and, in 1875, an organization of citizens formed to assist the university in its development. The creation of the schools of pharmacy (1865) and obstetrics (1870) increased the medical school's reputation, which was also benefiting from the

services of the Hospital Santa Maria della Scala—later to become a university hospital. Developments in the law college included a law club that was founded in 1879 and, five years later, the introduction of the periodical *Studi Senesi*, which provided a forum for the research of law teachers and students.

Despite such progress, a proposal to abolish to university was presented in 1892 by minister Ferdinando Martini. This act incited a general strike by shopkeepers, and a protest committee was quickly formed representing every institution and group in town, including the seminary and the masonic lodge. Within a year, Martini's proposal had failed and expansion of the university continued; a new biology department was funded and built by the Monte dei Paschi. Later the work of the University Committee, the local hospital, the *Accademia dei Fisiocritici*, and other groups would support the university following the Gentile Law of 1923, which required small universities such as Siena to develop their own funding. In the years between World War I and World War II, the university proceeded to establish a faculty of political science.

One of Italy's most intact medieval towns, Siena has maintained the ancient beauty of its university. Today many of its departments are housed in centuries-old buildings. The arts and humanities faculties, for instance, are situated in the historical center of Siena, with one of the buildings linked by ancient passageway to the fifteenth-century Palazzo San Galgano. The medieval Servi Convent houses the departments of history, archeology, and art history, as well as various workshops.

Further Reading: Judith Hook's *Siena: A City and Its History* (London: Hamish Hamilton, 1979) provides many details of the early life of the university. Willis Rudy's *The Universities of Europe, 1100–1914: A History* (Toronto: Associated University Presses, 1984) discusses Siena in the context of other institutions.

—Melanie Wilson

UNIVERSITY OF SOUTHERN CALIFORNIA
(Los Angeles, California, U.S.A.)

Location: Approximately three miles south of the Los Angeles Civic Center.

Description: A private university enrolling approximately 28,000 students in undergraduate, graduate, and professional schools.

Information: Alumni Relations
Alumni House
University of Southern California
Los Angeles, CA 90089-5371
U.S.A.
(213) 740-2300

Visiting: The Alumni Association offers guided tours.

The University of Southern California (USC) was established on September 4, 1880, by members of the Methodist Episcopal Conference of Southern California on land donated by three civic leaders: Ozro William Childs, John Gately Downey, and Isaias Wolf Hellman. Ironically, these three men were neither Methodists nor educators, but they were indicative of the diversity which was to characterize the university's future development. Childs was an Episcopalian and a nurseryman/horticulturist, Downey was a Catholic and a former state governor, and Hellman was a German-Jewish banker and philanthropist.

Another person instrumental in founding USC was Judge Robert Maclay Widney, who worked diligently for the university's development after he settled in Los Angeles in 1868 and opened a law practice there. Eleven years later—after he secured the land donation from Childs, Downey, and Hellman—he saw his dream of a university realized. Widney House, the university's first building, which was designated a California landmark in 1955, is named for him.

The land was originally transferred to the Methodists by the three men as an endowment fund. All income from each individual lot was to be used to support and maintain the university. The deed stipulated that the majority of the board of trustees be members of the Methodist Episcopalian Conference, although the institution was created as a nonsectarian university. Further, the institution was to be incorporated as the "University of Southern California."

The *Los Angeles Daily Commercial* reported that "the establishment of this institution marks an era in the progress of the people of the Pacific Coast. It has outrun the railway, and established itself before the connecting link has been made between the Mississippi and the Southern California coast." The university's founders were aware of its significance to future generations, not only in southern California but throughout California and the west. As a result, they marked the laying of the cornerstone of the first building in 1880 by placing a series of documents that pertained to the new university inside that cornerstone. When a more permanent brick structure—usually referred to as Old College—was completed in 1887, the cornerstone was placed in it; there the documents remained until 1948 when Old College was torn down. One of the items chosen to be preserved for posterity was the formal invitation to the cornerstone ceremony that took place on September 4, 1880. The date was especially important in the history of Los Angeles because exactly 99 years before, on September 4, 1781, at the site of the present Los Angeles Civic Center, another group of pioneers had founded the City of Los Angeles.

In fact, when the university was established, Los Angeles was still considered a frontier town. There were no paved streets, no telephones, and no electric lights in the area. However, Los Angeles underwent a dramatic transformation after the 1876 completion of the Southern Pacific Railroad link from San Francisco. This important link with the transcontinental railroad increased trade and transportation and contributed to the city's prosperity and growth.

The philosophical position of the university's founders was inscribed in a stone placed at the northern entrance to the campus. They expressed their desire to create a university that was dedicated to:

the glory of God and the preservation of the Republic; an institution of Higher Learning dedicated to the search for and dissemination of the Truth; to freedom of thought and discussion; to intelligent unbiased analysis of the forces that have shaped the past and will mold the future; to the development of Manhood and Womanhood for Christian service and loyal citizenship.

The true vision of the university lies in its founders' desire that it be a great university, not just a small college or a religious college, but a major research university offering a solid education in the liberal arts. The university was founded on the belief that "a great university could transform Southern California into a commercial and cultural mecca."

The University of Southern California's motto, "Palman qui meruit ferat" (Let whoever earns the palm bear

University of Southern California

it), exemplifies the university's emphasis on merit. Accordingly, the first class, which consisted of five men and two women, encountered a challenging array of courses such as Latin, English composition, physiology, integral calculus, and civil engineering. Two courses of study in the College Department, the classical and scientific, led to either a bachelor of arts or bachelor of science degree. As early as 1885, the university announced that merit would be the sole criterion for admission, asserting that "no student would be denied admission because of race, color, religion, or sex."

Three schools established within 20 years brought USC to the forefront in teaching and research related to medicine. Founded in 1885, the USC School of Medicine is now ranked among the top 20 medical schools in the United States in terms of federal research funding; it has developed into a major center for cancer research and care, gene therapy, neuroscience, and transplantation medicine. The School of Dentistry, founded in 1897, ranks among the top ten schools nationally in funding for dental research. The last of the three, the School of Pharmacy, founded in 1905, is the only school of pharmacy in southern California and one of only three in the entire state. It was the first school to offer a doctor of pharmacy as its sole degree. About half of the practicing pharmacists in southern California are graduates of the school.

During USC's early years the Bovard family of Alpha, Indiana, made major contributions to the progress and development of the university. Nine of the 12 Bovard children became Methodist ministers, and all were interested in education. The first president of USC was Marion P. Bovard, for whom the Bovard Administration Building is named. He was appointed to the office in 1880, after being in charge of the Fort Street Methodist Church for two years. His brother, George F. Bovard, served as the university's president from 1903 to 1921, and another brother, Freeman D. Bovard, became vice-president of the university.

During the presidencies at the turn of the century, the university struggled to keep up with the demands it faced from the rapidly expanding communities of southern California. Los Angeles's population had grown from 11,000 in 1880 to 319,000 in 1910. During George Bovard's 18-year administration, student enrollment increased from 329 students to 4,600 students. In addition, the young university found itself struggling without major contributors or endowment funds. Thus, it had to rely on its own faculty, deans, presidents, and trustees for its growth.

This situation began to change, however, during the 1920s. President Rufus von KleinSmid, who was president for a quarter of a century, is often hailed as the man who built USC into southern California's only major private university. Affectionately known as "Dr. Von," von KleinSmid, who served for the 25 years between 1921 and 1946, is credited with many significant pioneering ventures. After only his first decade in office he had

brought the university to full national accreditation, established a graduate school, and begun working toward making USC a large, nondenominational university. In 1928 he was responsible for making USC an independent, nonsectarian institution. Until that year the university had been governed by the Southern California Methodist Conference, which elected the university's trustees. Although the conference controlled USC, it did not support it financially. After several failed fundraising drives, von KleinSmid proposed a resolution to amend the articles of incorporation; as a result, control of USC passed to a self-perpetuating board of trustees, ending the university's formal ties to the Methodist Church.

One of the most memorable additions to the university during the von KleinSmid years was the Doheny Memorial Library, completed in 1930. At the time, the university had over 15,000 students and 20 colleges and schools but no separate library building. The library is named for Edward L. Doheny, who was then one of the most important financial figures in the United States. By investigating the crude tar or *brea* found near Westlake Park, he discovered oil; he then donated a portion of his oil fortune to USC for the construction of its library. (Doheny was subsequently indicted in the Teapot Dome Scandal, which involved the illegal leasing of oil fields, but he was acquitted.) The Doheny Library provided more than just a needed physical facility. It gave the university a focal point for its expansion when the surrounding Alumni Memorial Park was created; there students still gather and there commencement exercises are held.

The von KleinSmid era also saw the establishment of the Department of Cinematography. Founded in 1929 by famed motion picture producer and director Cecil B. DeMille, with the cooperation of the Academy of Motion Picture Arts and Sciences, the department's curriculum was organized to cover all aspects of the movie industry. DeMille continued his support of the department throughout his Hollywood career. The department was the first in the nation to offer a bachelor of arts degree in film. Its first course, "Introduction to Photoplay," featured such faculty members as producers D.W. Griffith and Darryl Zanuck, and actor Douglas Fairbanks Sr. Even today, this school is usually regarded as one of the leading film schools in the United States. The regular faculty has always been augmented by lecturers and instructors who are distinguished in both theatrical and nontheatrical film. Today the program is known as the School of Cinema-Television. The list of USC students and alumni who have achieved fame in the motion picture and television industries could make up a large portion of a "Hollywood Hall of Fame." Among its former students are Robert Zemeckis (director of the Academy Award winner *Forrest Gump*), George Lucas (director of the *Star Wars* films), Ron Howard (director of *Apollo 13*), and James Ivory (of the Merchant-Ivory partnership that has produced such films as *Howard's End*).

Another school for the performing arts, the School of Theater, has produced well-known stage and screen actors, directors, and technicians who have received a wide range of honors including Tony, Obie, and Emmy awards. A third school in the area of the arts predates the other two. The School of Music, founded in 1884, is probably the principal music school west of the Mississippi. Its alumni include jazz musician Lionel Hampton, conductor Michael Tilson Thomas, trumpet virtuoso Herb Alpert, and opera star Marilyn Horne.

In addition to its renown in film, USC is also considered one of the premiere private research universities in the world. Its long tradition of active and research-oriented professors was recognized when USC Professor George A. Olah received the 1994 Nobel Prize in chemistry. Two alumni made history in the NASA space program. The first man to walk on the moon (in July 1969), Neil Armstrong, spent five years in graduate study in USC's aerospace engineering program. The fourth man to walk on the moon, Navy Lieutenant Commander Alan L. Bean, completed intensive graduate courses at USC's Institute of Aerospace Safety and Management.

Cognizant of its location in Los Angeles, a city with a significant minority population, USC has provided a variety of programs designed to improve the urban environment and the university's relationship with the surrounding city. The Center for Urban Affairs opened in 1969, offering both undergraduate and graduate degrees in urban studies. A year later the university established an undergraduate program concentrating on the biological aspects of such urban problems as pollution, community health, drug abuse, and decreasing world food supplies. The program was the first of its kind in the nation offered to students who were not science majors. Another creative program found a group of Spanish-speaking fifth graders serving as "guest lecturers" in classes in conversational Spanish, while a group of USC students conducted a bilingual course in first aid at a Los Angeles school. On another level, in 1985 the USC library received the H.F. Boeckmann II Latin American Collection, valued at approximately $1.7 million. It contains important materials published in Latin America, primarily from Mexico, Brazil, Central America, and the West Indies.

In 1969, USC was elected to membership in the Association of American Universities (AAU), which was founded in 1900 as an organization of universities in the United States and Canada considered preeminent in the fields of graduate and professional study and research. Today it is made up of 58 leading public and private universities.

The University of Southern California is also internationally famous for its athletic program. Since 1904, a total of 272 USC athletes have participated in the Olympics, more than any other university in the world. Olympians from USC have won 87 gold, 53 silver, and 46 bronze medals. A USC athlete has won a gold medal in every summer Olympiad in which one has competed since 1912, making USC the only university in the world with this distinction. The "Trojans," USC's nickname, was coined by journalist Owen Bird in 1912 to honor the athletic teams' spirit.

Further Reading: Manuel P. Servin's *Southern California and Its University: A History of USC 1880–1964* (Los Angeles: Ward Ritchie Press, 1969) is a detailed history of the development of USC through 1964. A less detailed but updated account is the USC publication *University of Southern California: Glimpses of History 1880–1995* (USC History Project, April, 1995). *The Pocket Profile 1995,* published by the University Public Relations Administration, provides statistical and related information.

—Judi Gerber

UNIVERSITY OF SYDNEY
(Sydney, New South Wales, Australia)

Location: Four campuses near the main business area of Sydney. The Conservatorium Campus and the St. James (law school) campus are in downtown Sydney; Cumberland Campus is at Lidcombe; Rozelle Campus (Sydney College of the Arts) at Rozelle; Surrey Hills (dentistry) campus at Surrey Hills, Orange Agricultural College is 242 kilometers west of Sydney at Orange. The faculty of agriculture also has outlying teaching areas at Camden and Narrabri. Astrophysics has various telescopes at sites outside of Sydney.

Description: A state university (with eight residential colleges) enrolling 30,000 students with 2,514 academic staff, 5,415 total staff.

There are faculties of agriculture, architecture, arts, dentistry, economics, education, engineering, health services, law, medicine, nursing, science, veterinary science, board of studies in music, and social work, College of the Arts, Conservatorium in Music, Agricultural College at Orange and numerous research institutes and Centres of Excellence as well as continuing education.

Information: The Registrar
University of Sydney
New South Wales 2006
Australia
(02) 9351-2222

Visiting: Museums and galleries are open at set hours. Guided tours are mainly run by the Chancellor's Committee, telephone (61) 02-9351-3927.

William Charles Wentworth's proposal in 1849 for the establishment of a university in New South Wales was met with indifference or hostility by Australians. Although the transportation of convicts had ceased, New South Wales society was still profoundly affected by the mores of a convict-based system with, on the one hand, profound suspicion of the rulers and the wealthy and, on the other, an ingrained expectation that the government should provide. This view was reinforced by religious antagonism between the Catholic Church, which was powerful among those of Irish descent, the Church of England, and the more powerful Protestant sects. Conflict over control of a university, over access, purpose, direction, and funding, was inevitable. Autonomy was a concept reserved for rhetoric. The prospect of a private university was remote. Private resources were inadequate and philanthropic impulses poorly developed. Any university with minimally acceptable standards would necessarily be founded by public act and subsidized by public money.

Wenworth, the lawyer son of a convict woman and an Irish ship's surgeon twice acquitted of highway robbery, embodied the colonial myth of Australian identity. His life-long commitment to colonial self-government underlay his belief that a university was essential—a belief not widely shared. The colony was still small—under 200,000 people, about a quarter resident in Sydney—and the newly introduced national education system as yet had produced few candidates capable of university entrance. Those who could afford professional training for their children sent them to Britain. While a local institution might be promoted as offering openings for colonial talent, in practice those able to avail themselves of its services would be a small ruling group, subsidised by scarce government resources.

The yardstick against which the proposal was measured was profoundly utilitarian; training was more acceptable than education. This underlay the first proposal which was for a graduate professional university covering medicine, engineering, and commercial pursuits with liberal arts to be provided by separate, affiliated colleges. Those who contributed to the debate were numerous. No single figure either then or subsequently ever dominated the shaping of the institution. The final proposal was formed from conflicting views and compromises. These have been the elements which shaped the institution from its origins to the present day. Utility, the problems of state funding, and state control though appointments to the governing body and the power to alter the governing act, conformity to international expectations, and the university's accessibility were continuing themes.

All agreed the university should be like those in England but disagreed on the particular model: either London where the university's role was only to examine and the colleges to teach, or a university which both taught and examined. Even more contentious was the issue of whether the school should be secular and what part the churches should play. Wentworth wished to exclude the clergy from teaching. While religious colleges might affiliate, the university should be a source from which "all may drink be they Christian, Mohamadan, Jew or Heathen."

By government act on October 1, 1850 the university was established—secular and nonsectarian with no religious tests for entry, open to all academically qualified

University of Sydney

subjects of the Queen resident in NSW without any distinction whatsoever. It was given the power to confer after examination the degrees of B.A., M.A., B.Laws and D.Laws, B.Med and D.Med, and to examine for medical degrees in medicine, surgery, midwifery, and pharmacy. Denominational colleges might be founded but had to be privately funded. A royal charter would be sought, but the inauguration was not delayed until it could be obtained. Only one-quarter of the governing body, the senate, could be clergy. The principal officer, the provost, was to be elected annually.

The government of NSW provided an endowment of £5,000 for building, stipends, scholarships and prizes, a library, and other necessary expenses. Additional resources had to be raised by fees. This factor immediately limited the university's scope as few candidates presented themselves. Only three foundations professors—classics, mathematics, and science—could be appointed. They were expected to supplement their stipend from class fees and extramural teaching and had tenure during good behaviour.

The vision for this public university, which was one of the most isolated in the world (an average of three months behind news from Europe), was perfectly summarised in the university motto "Sidere Mens eadem mutato." The only concession to the southern hemisphere was in adopting the calendar year for academic purposes which better suited the southern seasons. Conservative, traditional adherence to concepts, standards, and objectives developed elsewhere became dominant characteristics of the university, at times its strength and at others its weakness.

The first university appointments were remarkably well judged. The foundation professors firmly asserted university autonomy and British orthodoxy against a variety of local pressures and critically reshaped the intended structure to this end. Woolley, the first principal, with the full support of the second provost, Sir Charles Nicholson, promoted liberal arts as the core, indeed, as "the University properly so called" to which the special schools devoted to the professions were complementary. Liberal arts were directed to "the learner as an end in and of himself, his perfection as a man simply being the object of his education." The purpose was fundamentally moral based on "fixed and eternal principles." The university was to train gentlemen, to discipline the mind, and develop the power of independent reasoning, and the best way of providing such mental training was through maths and classics. It was to prepare statesmen and leaders for their tasks. The professional schools, on the other hand, had an end beyond the learner, in service to the community. Woolley also insisted that the teaching provided by the university was a necessary requirement for sitting university examinations, preventing the colleges from simply presenting candidates for examinations. University students did not have to belong to a college, and the colleges which appeared, although internally autonomous, had little influence on the university curriculum.

University instruction began at the downtown site which now houses Sydney grammar school, but in 1852 Grose farm, which was then some way out of the town of Sydney, was confirmed as the permanent site despite its inaccessibility, which made part-time or evening attendance inconvenient. The senate was determined to build an imposing public structure. The colonial architect, Edmund Blackett, designed a Gothic Revival structure to be built in stone; it was not opened until July 18, 1859, when only the front facade was completed. The opulence of the vision ran the university into debt, but, despite some criticism, it was accepted as reasonable in the heady post–gold-rush days, when icons of aspiring nationality were seen as desirable.

The university was still struggling to establish the importance of its role in the local community. It was under attack for its traditional and irrelevant undergraduate teaching which was restricted to Greek, Latin, mathematics, natural philosophy, chemistry, and experimental physics. Postgraduate teaching was virtually nonexistent. The masters program was largely nominal, and, although law and medicine were formally established in 1855, they were little more than examining boards. Colonial society was not impressed with the virtues of Greek and Latin. Practical relevance, not the alleged development of thought, was sought, and most were disinclined to pay substantial fees.

Only children of the wealthy could afford university despite the availability of 12 scholarships which should at least have covered the fees. Few students therefore enrolled, and fewer graduated. Between 1852 and 1860 only 109 matriculated and 33 graduated with perhaps 33 attending in any one year. Ignoring public indignation, in the name of maintaining standards, the professors sometimes failed up to half the candidates and publicly rebuked the students for their poor performance. A corporate university life, which might have attracted students, was slow to develop. Students came only to lectures and then dispersed.

As part of their effort to strengthen and integrate the university into NSW society, the foundation professors, John Woolley, Moris Pell, and John Smith, went outside the university and made a significant contribution to the education of the whole community from primary school to adult instruction both directly by extramural and evening classes, and indirectly. The matriculation examinations provided a state-wide standard. Each in his own way also served the practical needs of the economy, Pell as an actuary and an expert on rivers and railways, and Smith as a practical chemist and photographer.

Despite this, public support remained problematic. A facility paid for by all should be, but evidently was not, available to all. The requirement of attendance at lectures not only excluded non-Sydney residents but those who might through private study achieve the appropriate knowledge. Considerable expenditure, narrowly viewed, seemed to have produced insignificant measurable results. Social radicals felt that the money could have been better spent on schooling for the poor. A parliamentary enquiry in 1860 criticised building costs and the relationship with the affiliated colleges, which was seen as violating the principles of secular education. Critics compared the university's requirements unfavourably to those of the University of Melbourne.

Public indifference, state parsimony, and a narrow academic vision of the university curriculum combined to ensure that numbers remained low throughout the 1860s and 1870s, and the problem of persuading students to attend the university remained acute. In 1865 there were 46 students; in 1881, 51 matriculants and 14 graduates. Many courses were dropped for lack of student interest. Sciences were grudgingly accepted as part of the arts curriculum largely in deference to public opinion. Badham, the classics professor thought them "ornaments of the memory which may be required at any time of life." A separate faculty of science, however, required an additional endowment that the state refused. Slowly, nevertheless, a sense of internal community was developing, symbolised by the foundation of the University Union in 1874 and the traditions of debating and the annual Commemoration Day.

Transforming the university from a finishing school for gentlemen to a multifunctional institution that trained in specific professional skills was slow, and even by 1914 it was incomplete. The 1880s were a period of growth for the university, reflecting the general population increase, economic prosperity, and the results of an improving school system. In 1881 after a decade of stonewalling, women were admitted at the instigation of the chancellor William Manning, and they immediately took advantage of the change to enter arts, science, and medicine. They were slower to enter law since they could not practice before 1918, but by 1918 there were 641 women undergraduates—one-third of the total undergraduate population.

New interest in university development was stimulated by professors such as Liversidge and Charles Badham, who traveled the country to promote bursaries and easier access to university study. Badham's theme was that "The university was wherever the Professor might be and University hours were whenever the mass of students could attend." The university curriculum was changing. Evening classes were introduced in 1884 and additional lecturers were appointed to conduct them. Numbers rose steeply—284 in arts in 1890 with a quarter of all students studying at night. Extension lectures were also formally introduced in 1880, helped by Liversidge's report on the movement in England. This assisted the working class and elementary school teachers who wanted to improve their qualifications, and attempts were made to extend them to towns outside the capital.

The Challis bequest in 1881 and Thomas Fisher's bequest for the library together with a further £5,000

from the government enabled long-shelved plans for professional development to be implemented. A medical school and an engineering school were finally established as well as chairs in subjects such as modern history. Unfortunately this burst of private philanthropy did not mark a turning point in endowments, which remained rare and unreliable. It precipitated, however, a major shift to the professional faculties. The young foundation professor of medicine, Anderson Stuart, believed that technical learning trained the mind just as well as arts or science, and despite Manning's support for the arts as "the very essence of University education and the chief source of culture," his demands were largely met, which upset the university's finances and squeezed the other faculties. The medical school soon became so large, attracting more students than the arts faculty, that its needs took precedence over developments elsewhere, causing bitter internal division.

In the depression of the 1890s, however, the government once again cut the university's public revenues, requiring it to rely more on its own resources while putting impediments in the way of the university's ability to increase charges. The press again urged that it was still not catering to poor students but expected support for the wealthy. Although its graduates came to the university's defense and attempted to influence government and public opinion, the support was more moral than financial. Only engineering benefited from a substantial gift from the manufacturing family of Peter Nicol Russell.

As the university gradually recovered, the shift toward utilitarian subjects increased. The typical student background was changing. Middle-class and a few skilled working-class parents demanded the useful and the vocational. Science and scientific research were justified as essential to the nation's industrial and commercial prosperity. Close links with the professions in law and medicine were promoted. Professors were appointed from practicing professionals; quality in teaching did not necessarily follow. Student expectations were growing and criticism of lecturers was commonplace.

Internal dissatisfaction with the university's management structure was also developing. The senate was dominated by government appointees. Professors and undergraduates alike were aggrieved at their exclusion from senate decision making and its habit of ignoring their submissions. Disagreements arose over issues of vital importance to academic autonomy, such as freedom of speech, when the modern history professor, George Arnold Wood adopted the unpopular position of opposing the Boer War.

Education under the federation remained a state responsibility, and further professional and practical disciplines were introduced: dentistry (1900), agriculture (1908), and veterinary science (1908). They were followed by economics, commerce, and education, although only economics attracted a large number of students.

A major management restructuring to suit the needs of a much expanded university was overdue but did not occur until 1924. The result was a permanent full-time vice-chancellor following the English pattern, changes to the senate, and the creation of six new faculties, bringing the number to ten. It was not increased for another 50 years.

The staff was not satisfied. The professorial board was responsible for academic advice, but the senate's view of their authority in such matters conflicted with the board's. The senate interfered in new appointments, notoriously refusing to appoint Gordon Childe and deciding to sack the poet Christopher Brennan for marital indiscretions and drink. The dispute in 1943 over the appointment of Julius Stone to a law chair was both bitter and public. Senate interference in the selection process and attempts to block the appointment met an uncompromising assertion of professional board rights and conflict over the "rights" of the legal profession to be consulted. Racist (Stone was Jewish) and "nationalistic" (an Australian was hoped for) issues came into play. Professors felt they had particular rights and responsibilities, but a growing issue was that of the nonprofessorial staff who were aggrieved by their continuing lack of voice. By 1940 nonprofessorial academics constituted 75 percent of the total staff and their career prospects were diminishing.

Sharp growth in student numbers after 1919 meant for the first time courses were overcrowded, and proposals to cap numbers emerged. The legal status of matriculation made the university's ability to refuse access to any faculty to a matriculated student problematic, however. High enrollments in the expensive faculties aggravated financial difficulties. By 1924 there were 809 students in arts and science and 1,696 in professional programmes. Increased funding deferred the issue of access for a time. A generous bequest from Sir Samuel McCaughey in 1919 provided an income of about £15,000, which was used for salaries; the government also increased its grant and made a special allowance for new building. Although many members of the state parliament were by now Sydney graduates, this did not always produce a government sympathetic to university difficulties.

Funds were tight and attempts to raise money externally had only a limited success. The 75th anniversary appeal produced promises of only £350,000, of which £250,000 was a single gift from George Henry Bosch directed to medical education. With the depression, the financial problems got worse. A public enquiry into possible mismanagement instead recognised that on the basis of the numbers of students on scholarships and bursaries, the endowment was inadequate and the chairs established at government request not properly funded, although by comparison with Melbourne, the university was overstaffed. The proposed solution was to reduce the bursaries, and a reduction in government funding saw salaries cut by a "voluntary" ten percent and, later, a further five percent cut.

The problem of maintaining a sense of community in an institution under pressure from reduced resources but increasing numbers stimulated new bodies. The Lecturer's Association was intended to make the ideal community a reality by providing a focus which would bring the subprofessorial staff together in communal activities that would serve both mind and body. To improve interaction between different faculties the association sought to get one or another faculty to give talks on what they were doing. Common social activities were promoted.

Students suffered from similar problems. Growing numbers did not improve student participation in activities outside the classroom. College residents, the most active, were a very small percentage of all students— under 500 in all. Only unpopular senate decisions, such as a crackdown on the Commencement Day procession or the proposal to raise money for services by a general levy on students, united undergraduates, who typically responded with an appeal to the state government to change the composition of the senate. As jobs became harder to find, graduates associations were formed, but most were a passing phenomenon.

Throughput the inter-war period, the university was struggling to maintain its standing as a reputable international institution in circumstances which were pushing the costs and direction of research beyond its resources. Its staff had always had problems keeping in touch with developments which were so far away, and these were exacerbated by the increasing speed of new discoveries and the need for teams of researchers. Study leave was increasingly essential and became universal. A variety of external sources, however, enabled some research to be maintained. Although the main university focus was undergraduate teaching, the staff laid stress on the symbiotic nature of teaching and research and fought for a division of time which would permit scholarship. In 1942 the Ph.D. was inaugurated, but postgraduates went overseas for training.

The quality of the teaching was high and frequently updated. Stephen Roberts, for example, introduced the first fourth-year honours course in Australia. Slow moves toward small group teaching, however, were put on indefinite hold by the war. Attempts to meet specific training needs were mainly frustrated. Radcliffe-Brown's diploma in anthropology to train cadets for service in Papua/New Guinea was perhaps the most successful. A diploma in journalism, introduced at the request of the Journalists Institute, dwindled and died. Too few students completed university courses in country centres to make them financially viable. In 1938, however, a college of the university was established at Armidale, the second campus in the state.

Community service remained an expected academic contribution. Broadcasting provided a new form of sharing expert knowledge, which improved the general image of the university with the public. The cultural cringe, however, continued. Candidates for jobs from Britain always had the edge over local candidates.

In 1939 the university had 13,000 graduates, a student enrollment of 3,839, and 173 staff. The war effort persuaded the governments that university research was useful at least in science and science-related subjects, which was important for postwar university growth, but attempts to restrict "normal" scientific communication in the interest of "national security" even after the war caused renewed conflict with the academic community. Freedom of expression for academics was also tested when the professor of philosophy, John Anderson, attacked compulsory religious teaching and was censured in the NWS legislative assembly.

The university was still accessible only to the few. Students from state schools without scholarships were usually unable to attend even if they had matriculated. The need for army education, however, had led to the commonwealth government for the first time taking a part to supply its manpower need by financing students. This affected the social profile of students and the percentage from state schools. Quotas were imposed in medicine, dentistry, engineering, veterinary science, and agriculture. The growth of an intellectual community was noticeable.

Even so, in 1950 the public image of the university was still ambiguous and the rush of returned military to get a degree, which swamped classrooms (nearly 9,000 students), was not matched by state grants, although the commonwealth government continued and eventually extended its assistance. At this time, a third of all Australian university students attended the University of Sydney, but Sydney in 1949 received the smallest grant per student of all universities in Australia. The university received about 4.4 percent of the annual cohort of students until 1960 when there was a marked and sudden rise. A new emphasis on postgraduate training after 1946, despite the initially slow growth in numbers, led to a shift in university priorities.

The appearance of new universities, especially NSW and technical colleges, affected Sydney's position. Growth was to be accommodated by increasing the number of institutions, not allowing one to grow to an unmanageable size. Roberts, the new VC who was a clever politician, helped develop a new image for Sydney as the premier institution with the greatest range of disciplines, postgraduates, and research. Sydney took the cream of the students and was the first institution to select for entry on merit. The 1950–52 centenary celebrations helped, although the centenary financial appeal was a failure. Faculties sought outside funding. Research foundations such as the nuclear research foundation established by Harry Messel were able to draw on public expectations of immediate returns from science.

After the 1957 Murray report, which confirmed commonwealth commitment to university education, there

was a rise in staff numbers, and new areas of study were developed. The percentage of Australian-born or trained staff was increasing, and Sydney was employing more and more of its own graduates. By 1966 student numbers had risen to 16,000 and many came from state schools and poorer backgrounds. There was also a sharp rise in postgraduate students assisted by commonwealth scholarships. In 1963 they comprised 3.7 percent of total enrollment, and the plan was for an increase to 9 percent by the end of the decade and 14 percent in the 1970s. Such a high percentage, however, required increased funding which was not forthcoming, and 1,000 postgraduates in 1981 still only comprised 5.8 percent of total enrollment. Coursework for graduates proved popular. Most were local students—government efforts to encourage students to move from their home fell on stony ground.

Changes in teaching practices followed worldwide changes. A tutorial system was one way of improving learning and attempting to reduce failure rates. Restructuring disciplines led to the rise of the department and decline of the God-professor. The result of demands for participation was a rise in internal disagreements. Disputes within departments spilt over in a number of cases into stoppages and fights and in the economics case a student strike. Student support and activism, especially after 1967, took the authorities by surprise. Adaptation to new social conditions and changing cultural norms followed slowly and often after government pressure to take in a wider range of students, especially aborigines and those of a non-English-speaking ethnic backgrounds.

Reliance on the government for funding research made restructuring difficult, but common facilities such as SILLIAC and the Electron Microscope Unit were achieved and the library reached 2 million books by 1975. Bequests by Edwin Cutberth Hall for archeology, John Power for fine arts, and community support for modern Greek and Hebrew helped but represented a tiny fraction of the total required. In 1973 the commonwealth government's assumption of all funding for tertiary study increased government control of the direction of new development and pressure to comply with new state and federal rules on equal employment, antidiscrimination, health, and safety. The university's technical autonomy was finally curbed by the need to negotiate for what a decade later became called a "profile" of activities.

The 1975 change of government saw curbs on university growth. The 1980s saw undergraduate numbers slowly rising as the university moved from elite training to the multiversity. New areas such as women's studies got underway through combined efforts of academic and general women staff. The end to elitism came with the 1988 amalgamations, when the old university, under pressure from Canberra, was joined by Cumberland College of Health Sciences, the Teachers College, the Conservatorium of Music, and the College of the Arts. The centralised 1924 structure, despite its many subsequent modifications, was inadequate to cope with the sudden increase in size and in numbers of campuses; the consequent restructuring is still incomplete.

Further Reading: The official history in two massive volumes is *Australia's First: A History of the University of Sydney,* 2 volumes (Sydney: University of Sydney and Hale and Iremonger, 1995). See also S.M. Jack, "The Cultural Transmission of Science and Technology to Australia 1788–1989," in *Under New Heavens,* edited by Neville Meaney (Port Melbourne: Heinneman, 1989).

—Sybil Jack

UNIVERSITY OF TEXAS SYSTEM
(Texas, U.S.A)

Location: On more than 350 acres just north of the state capital and additional land acquired by gift and purchase, the main branch of the University of Texas System (UT System), the University of Texas at Austin, is located in the heart of beautiful Central Texas Hill Country. Additional parts of the main university campus include the J.J. Pickle Research Campus, a 476-acre tract eight miles north of the main campus that houses research organizations in engineering, science, and the social sciences; the Brackenridge tract, 445 acres bordering the Town Lake, where research is conducted in life sciences; and the Montopolis Research Center, 94 acres located in southeast Austin.

Description: The academic flagship of the UT System's 15 component institutions, the University of Texas at Austin, is a major, comprehensive research university with a broad mission of undergraduate and graduate education, research, and public service. With approximately 48,000 students in attendance, a full-time teaching staff of about 2,700, and about 15,000 staff members, the university's programs and professional schools generally rank among the top 20 programs and schools in the United States.

Information: Director of Information Resources
The University of Texas System
702 Colorado Street
CLB, Suite 5.104
Austin, TX 78701-3020
U.S.A.
(512) 499-4547

University of Texas at Arlington
P.O. Box 19088
Arlington, TX 76019
U.S.A.
(817) 273-2119

University of Texas at Brownsville–Texas Southmost College
Office of News and Information
80 Fort Brown
Brownsville, TX 78520
U.S.A.
(956) 544-8231

University of Texas at Dallas
P.O. Box 830688
Richardson, TX 75083-0688
U.S.A.
(214) 690-2111

University of Texas at El Paso
500 W. University Avenue
El Paso, TX 79968-0512
U.S.A.
(915) 747-5896

Public Affairs
University of Texas–Houston
7000 Fannin Street
Houston, TX 77030
U.S.A.
(713) 500-3033

University of Texas–Pan American
1201 W. University Drive
Edinburgh, TX 78539-2999
U.S.A.
(512) 381-2011

University of Texas of the Permian Basin
4901 E. University Boulevard
Odessa, TX 79762-0001
U.S.A.
(915) 552-2020

University of Texas at San Antonio
6900 North Loop 1604 West
San Antonio, TX 78249
U.S.A.
(512) 891-4011

University of Texas at Tyler
Office of Admissions and Student Records
3900 University Boulevard
Tyler, TX 75799
U.S.A.
(903) 566-7202

Visiting: The Visitor Center at the University of Texas at Austin provides information and assistance to visitors. Located in Sid Richardson Hall, adjacent to the Lyndon B. Johnson Library and Museum, it is open weekdays from 8 A.M. to 4:30 P.M. For information, telephone the Visitor Center at (512) 471-6498.

The Office of Admissions provides student-guided walking tours of the campus. Reservations are not required; weather permitting, tours leave from the General Information Desk on the ground floor of the Main Building at 11 A.M. and 2 P.M. on weekdays, and at 1 P.M. on Saturdays. Tours are not conducted during the last half of December, the first half of May, or on official holidays, but a self-guided tour brochure is always available.

For more information, or to schedule special tours, telephone the Office of Admissions at (512) 471-1711.

For visitor information for the other locations of the University of Texas, please contact those individual institutions (listed above).

Following its liberation from Mexico in 1836 and prior to its annexation by the United States in 1845, the independent Republic of Texas began pursuing the goal of education for its citizens. In 1839, under Texas president Mirabeau B. Lamar, the Congress of the Republic of Texas ordered that land be reserved for a university.

The same year another act of legislation allocated 50 leagues (231,400 acres) and funds for the endowment of two colleges or universities. Whether the funds had to be reallocated for frontier defense or there was disagreement as to the location or there was disagreement as to the location or future funding of the university, no further action was taken by either the Congress or the Texas legislature until 1858, when the legislature appropriated for the university the 231,400 acres of land granted in 1839; $100,000 in U.S. bonds left over from the $10 million paid to Texas as part of the Compromise of 1850; and one section of land out of every ten reserved to the state in grants made in aid to private agencies.

The Act of 1858 also created a body of ten administrators to control the university—the governor, the chief justice of the Texas Supreme Court, and eight others nominated by the governor. However, fate and history again conspired to delay the opening of the university; secession and the Civil War prevented the act from being carried out, and instead, most of the appropriated university funds were used for other state needs and not repaid until 1883. Meanwhile, the Constitution of 1866 demanded that the legislature establish an institution of higher learning as soon as possible, and so the Texas Agriculture and Mechanical College was created. As a result, the first state-supported educational institution to actually matriculate students was the Agricultural and Mechanical College of Texas, now Texas A&M University, which opened at College Station in 1876.

The long wait was making university supporters anxious. The Constitution of 1876 stipulated that the legislature, without further delay, establish, organize, and maintain a university of the highest caliber, and that popular vote would determine the university's location. An article of the same constitution made agriculture and mining a branch of the university and ordered the legislature to establish and maintain a college or branch university for black students, although no tax was to be levied and no money appropriated out of the general revenue for such a school or for buildings of the University of Texas. This proscription effectively prevented the establishment of a separate branch of the university for blacks. The constitution went on to authorize the allocation of the original 231,400 acres granted the university in 1839, but it repealed the gift of alternate sections of land granted railroads, instead substituting a million acres in West Texas.

An act passed on March 30, 1881, created a governing board of eight regents (later changed to nine); established admission fees, coeducation, and nonsectarian teaching; and called for an election to name the location of the university. The governing board met for the first time on November 16, 1881, and elected Ashbel Smith president, Alexander P. Woodridge secretary. Then, on September 6, 1882, the citizens voted to make Austin the site of the main university and Galveston the site of the medical department. A small, 40-acre tract on College Hill was chosen for the main campus, and on November 17, 1882, in a ceremony officiated by Ashbel Smith, the cornerstone of the west wing of the first Main Building was laid. This first building, known to all as the Main Building, for many years, served all of the university's purposes, from housing administrative offices to classrooms. Although classes were still being held in the temporary capital as late as January 1884, the university finally opened its doors in the new building on September 15, 1883. Eight professors, four assistants, and one proctor served the needs of 221 male and female students during the university's first year. Forty-four years had passed since members of the new Republic of Texas had first set in motion plans for a university.

From its first year, Main University offered upper level degrees. Divisions in instruction were termed departments and subject divisions within departments were called schools. Main University opened with an academic department (with six schools) and a law department. More schools and departments were added until, by 1994, the university had eight colleges and seven schools offering a total of about 100 undergraduate degree programs and 170 graduate degree programs. The colleges and schools were the College of Liberal Arts (1883); the College of Natural Sciences (1883); the School of Law (1883); the College of Engineering (1894); the College of Education (1905); the Graduate School (1910); the College of Business Administration (1922); the College of Pharmacy (1893 at Galveston, moved to Austin in 1927); the College of Fine Arts (1938); the Graduate School of Library and Information Science (1950); the Graduate

School of Social Work (1950); the School of Architecture (1951); the College of Communication (1965); the Lyndon B. Johnson School of Public Affairs (1970); and the School of Nursing (1976). The Division of Continuing Education, originally the Division of Extension (1909), changed to its present name in 1977.

By 1967, the faculty had grown to 1,800 and included 9 of the state's 14 members of the National Academy of Sciences. During the 1960s, the university established nearly two dozen endowed and named academic positions, as well as temporary lectureships, to lure high-profile academics to their departments. Today, for example, the University of Texas at Austin has more than 1,000 privately funded endowed faculty positions.

Care was taken to ensure the future financial security of the university and its component institutions. In addition to gifts and grants to the university made by alumni, other patrons, and fundraising efforts, the end result of the numerous legislative acts concerning the university was the establishment of the Permanent University Fund, the Available University Fund, and biennial legislative appropriations. The Permanent Fund is an endowment consisting of the proceeds of the sale of the 231,400 acres deeded to the university in 1839, the million acres granted in the Constitution of 1876, and a second million acres granted the university by the legislature in 1883, together with proceeds of sales or leases of this land. The Permanent Fund cannot be spent, but instead, must be invested in particular types of bonds, the interest of which constitutes part of the Available Fund, along with student fees, and other university revenues. Use of these monies is fixed by the legislature in biennial appropriation bills.

At the outbreak of World War I enrollment at the university had risen to 2,254, and then to 4,001 the first year after the war ended. By 1938, enrollment had increased to 11,146; it dropped during World War II to 8,794, but rose to 15,118 in the year following the war. To meet the demands of the growing enrollment the university had to physically expand, both in terms of classrooms and housing structures, but it was increasingly clear that the 40-acre campus was no longer large enough to accommodate such expansion.

In 1921 the university's regents briefly considered moving the campus to a 500-acre site on the banks of the Colorado River donated by George W. Brackenridge 11 years earlier in 1910, but the board's vote to move the campus was met by bitter opposition. In response, the state legislature voted to purchase additional land adjacent to the original 40 acres for $1,350,000. Among the lands acquired by the university were the former Blind Institute (later the Texas School for the Blind) in 1925; the Cavanaugh homestead on Waller Creek in 1930; and the grounds of Texas Wesleyan College and property on Whitis Avenue in 1931.

Other lands and lots were acquired throughout the university's history, and the campus land now totals more than 350 acres. The J.J. Pickle Research Campus, a 476-acre site eight miles north of the main campus, houses research organizations in engineering, science, and the social sciences. The Montopolis Research Center is located on 94 acres in southeast Austin. The main university also has attached to it the University of Texas at Austin McDonald Observatory site in Jeff Davis County, the University of Texas at Austin Marine Science Institute at Port Aransas, Winedale Historical Center near Round Top, the Bee Cave Research Center west of Austin, Paisano Ranch, the Sam Rayburn Library in Bonham, and the Institute of Geophysics in Galveston.

Many of the early buildings owe their Spanish Renaissance-style architecture to Cass Gilbert of New York, who designed the first library building, and Sutton Hall. Paul P. Cret of Philadelphia supervised the development of structures built between 1932 and 1945, many of which were temporary frame buildings because of the prohibition against using general revenue to construct university buildings. The increased enrollment after World War II necessitated yet another era of temporary housing and classrooms. Eventually, between 1950 and 1965, 19 buildings were constructed or acquired, and in 1965 the university was granted the right of eminent domain to acquire through purchase the lands adjacent to the existing campus.

African Americans finally gained admission to the university for the first time in 1950, following the U.S. Supreme Court's decision in *Sweatt v. Painter.* During 1966–67, 27,345 students were enrolled in the main university, including 4,307 graduate students.

On March 6, 1967, the Texas legislature voted to officially change the name of the main university to University of Texas at Austin. Celebrated alumni include Lady Bird Johnson, Walter Cronkite, Lloyd Bentsen, Bill Moyers, Frederico Peria, and Edwin Dorn. Among the distinguished faculty members of the UT Austin faculty are several Nobel Prize winners, including 1995 recipients Jean-Marc Bouju of the Associated Press for feature photography and Lucian Perkins of the *Washington Post* for explanatory journalism.

The facilities are top notch, including the fifth-largest academic library in North America, with approximately 7 million volumes, 5 million pieces of microfilm, 30 million pages of manuscripts, and on-line access to hundreds of databases and other electronic resources. The library has its own, separately administered system comprised of the General Libraries, the Tarlton Law Library, and the Harry Ransom Humanities Research Center. Of these, the General Libraries are made up of The Perry Caraneda Library (the main library); the Undergraduate Library; the Nerrie Lee Benson Latin American Collection; and the Center for American History, which includes the University Archives, the Sam Rayburn Library and Museum in Bonham, and the Eugene C. Barker Texas History Center.

University of Texas at Austin

Cultural and entertainment facilities include the Performing Arts Center (a complex of several theaters, performance halls, and workshop and rehearsal spaces); the Franklin C. Erwin Special Events Center (with a seating capacity of 18,000); the Archer M. Huntington Art Gallery; and the Lyndon B. Johnson Library and Museum, among others.

The student body at the University of Texas at Austin is composed of students from all 50 states. The average SAT score of freshmen in 1995 was 1217, more than 300 points higher than the national SAT average of 902. Estimated tuition and fees plus living expenses and associated educational costs totaled $7,614 for a student living at home, $10,606 with campus housing, and $12,188 with off-campus housing.

Although originally conceived of as a system of schools, the University of Texas System wasn't officially referred to as such until 1967. The state's system of higher education was reorganized then, combining existing educational institutions with newly established ones to form an entity which currently ranks among the ten largest systems of higher education in the United States. Today, the University of Texas System is governed by a nine-member board of regents selected from different parts of the state, nominated by the governor, and appointed by the senate for six-year terms; the board has been administered by both the presidential and chancellorship forms. Logan Wilson and Harry Huntt Ransom are among those who have served as head of the system's administration.

As part of the overall drive to streamline administrative and economic efforts among the university components, the health science centers, cancer center, and nursing school were organized in 1972, a by-product of which was the coordination of university-wide programs in specific health areas. Under the administrative control of these three medical units were several individual institutions.

Over the last 100 years, the UT System has grown to its present combination of 15 universities (9 of which are academic), 6 medical schools, health science centers, a cancer center, and a nursing school. Total student enrollment is approximately 147,374. With 69,000 employees, an administrative staff of 426, and an administrative budget of $30.4 million (supporting schools with a combined budget of more than $4.5 billion), the UT System ranks as the fifth-largest employer in Texas.

The University of Texas at Austin was both the largest and the oldest component institution in the system, and it included the University of Texas at Austin, McDonald Observatory at Mount Locke, and the University of Texas at Austin Marine Science Institute in Port Aransas. The other general academic institutions which combined to form the system were the University of Texas at Arlington, the University of Texas at Brownsville and Texas Southmost College, the University of Texas at Dallas, the University of Texas at El Paso, the University of Texas Health Science Center at Houston, the University of Texas-Pan American in Edinburg, the University of Texas of the Permian Basin in Odessa, the University of Texas at Tyler, and the University of Texas at San Antonio, which also included the University of Texas Institute of Texan Cultures at San Antonio. A brief historical sketch of each branch follows.

The University of Texas at Arlington. Established as Arlington College in 1895, the college first changed its name to Carlisle Military Institute in 1901 and then again to Arlington Training School in 1913 before becoming a junior college branch of Texas Agriculture and Mechanical College. The school changed its name several more times and in 1959 became a four-year college, awarding its first baccalaureate degree in 1961. The school joined the University of Texas System in 1965, adopting its present name in 1967.

The University of Texas at Brownsville–Texas Southmost College. Originally established in 1973 as an upper-level extension center of Pan American University in Edinburg, Texas, the University of Texas at Brownsville in 1991 joined Texas Southmost College—a lower-level, community college with a presence in Brownsville since 1926. The goal of this partnership was to offer students in the Rio Grande Valley the opportunity to pursue programs and degrees typical of a four-year college without sacrificing their opportunity to explore vocational, technical, developmental education, and continuing education classes more typical of a community college. More than 1,700 students study everything from one-day seminars to full credit courses. Both schools are located on the grounds of the historic Fort Brown, established by General Zachary Taylor in 1846.

The University of Texas at Dallas. Originally the Southwest Center for Advanced Studies (1961), the University of Texas at Dallas was established in 1969 by an act of legislation which enabled the privately funded graduate research center to transfer to the state of Texas. The school's first class of upper division undergraduates was admitted in 1975.

The University of Texas at El Paso. Established in 1913 as Texas State School of Mines and Metallurgy, the school is the second oldest component of the UT System. The first campus, located on land that is now part of the Fort Bliss Army post, was destroyed by fire. The school moved in 1916 to the present campus in the western foothills of the Franklin Mountains. Its Bhutanese architecture is unique among most American schools; the campus looks more like exotic Oriental castles than the modernistic, stacked cubes of classrooms erected on other campuses. Known as UTEP, the school first offered instruction at the post-secondary level in 1914 and awarded its first baccalaureate degree two years later, in 1916. The school then became a branch of the University of Texas in 1919, changing its name a year later to the Texas College of Mines and Metallurgy. In 1949, the school changed its name to Texas Western College. The present name was adopted in 1967.

The University of Texas–Houston. Founded in 1972, the University of Texas–Houston is an institution of the health sciences: medicine, dentistry, public health, nursing, allied health, and biomedical science. The university serves a student body of approximately 3,100, conducts biomedical research valued at $95 million per year, and provides health care through nearly 1.5 million outpatient visits and inpatient admissions per year.

The University of Texas Pan American in Edinburg. Located in the Rio Grande Valley, 75 miles from the Gulf of Mexico and South Padre Island, Texas, UT Pan American began in 1927 as Edinburg College. After six name changes, the university joined the University of Texas System on September 1, 1989. Today, more than 13,000 students are enrolled at the main campus in Edinburg, Texas.

The University of Texas of the Permian Basin. Authorized by the Texas legislature in 1969 as an upper-level university offering junior, senior, and graduate-level programs, the University of Texas of the Permian Basin achieved four-year status and began offering freshman level courses in September 1991. Enrollment is approximately 2,300; 70 percent are undergraduates, 30 percent are graduates. Many of the students commute from the surrounding Permian Basin region. Although most are older employed full-time or part-time, there has been a corresponding increase in the number of traditional, college-age students since the university achieved four-year status. The 600-acre campus is in West Texas, midway between Dallas and El Paso.

The University of Texas at San Antonio. Created by a mandate from the 61st Texas legislature on June 5, 1969, the school was designed to be a university of the highest caliber, offering undergraduate and graduate degrees. The first class was admitted in June 1973. The UTSA is one of the fastest-growing universities in the state, with an enrollment of approximately 17,000.

The University of Texas at Tyler. Created in 1971 as an upper-level university—Tyler State College—the school then became Texas Eastern University in 1975, joining the University of Texas System in 1979. The university's mission was changed by the Texas legislature in 1997 to include lower division classes, as well. Effective in the summer semester 1998, the university began enrolling freshmen and sophomore students.

Further Reading: For a closer look at the University of Texas System and its component institutions, see *In the Beginning of the University of Texas,* by Carl J. Eckhardt (Austin: University of Texas, 1979), and *A Source Book Relating to the History of the University of Texas* (University of Texas Bulletin 1757, 1917). For a concise summary of the individual component institutions, read *The New Handbook of Texas* (Austin: Texas State Historical Association, 1996).

—Elizabeth Taggart

UNIVERSITY OF THE SOUTH
(Sewanee, Tennessee, U.S.A.)

Location: Atop the Cumberland Plateau in Sewanee, Tennessee, between Nashville and Chattanooga.

Description: An independent institution affiliated with the Episcopal Church enrolling approximately 1,200 students and awarding degrees of baccalaureate, master of divinity, and doctorate of ministry.

Information: Office of Admission
University of the South
735 University Avenue
Sewanee, TN 37383-1000
U.S.A.
(615) 598-1238

Visiting: Call (800) 522-2234 or (615) 598-1238 to schedule an interview and a tour of the campus.

The University of the South, perhaps more than any other American university, suffered the effects of the American Civil War and the harsh economic circumstances of Southern Reconstruction that were to follow. Founded in 1857 and chartered in 1858, the formation of the University of the South came to a temporary halt in the early 1860s when one of the school's principal founders was called into military duty by Jefferson Davis himself. The war also took its toll on the school's property, as newly constructed buildings were razed by army battles and occupations. By the end of the Civil War, even the university's cornerstone had been destroyed, broken into pieces to be kept as war mementos.

The idea for the University of the South may be traced to an Episcopalian church convention in Tennessee in 1832, some 25 years prior to its actual founding and 36 years before the first class was held. During this convention the Reverend James Hervey Otey, who soon after became the Bishop of Tennessee, proposed that the Tennessee diocese establish an Episcopalian school of theology and classical learning. Although no immediate action was taken toward this end, only three years later Otey and the Reverend Leonidas Polk (who would later become Bishop of the Southwest, comprising Arkansas and Louisiana) began raising monies for the purpose of establishing a university that would be owned and administered jointly by the dioceses of Tennessee, Mississippi, and Louisiana. The idea to expand the base of financial

resources to Mississippi and Louisiana was, in retrospect, a step in the right direction; however, the economic climate of 1837 persuaded the two men to shelve their aspirations temporarily.

While Otey and Polk are credited with being the chief visionaries in the formation of the University of the South, their dream of a large-scale, church-sponsored university was essentially pragmatic. By the late 1850s the Baptist, Methodist, and Presbyterian denominations were responsible for establishing more than half of the institutions of higher learning in the south, and these denominations had become reasonably well established in southern society. The Episcopal Church had a much smaller membership in the south; Otey and Polk, who were both founding bishops of their respective dioceses, saw that the surest way to solidify the role of the Episcopal Church in southern culture was to establish, first, a school of classical learning that would lend prestige to the Episcopalian cause and, second, a theological school that would train young men to be ministers, teachers, and leaders in their communities.

In the wake of the first failed attempts to form a university that could achieve these goals, Otey and Polk helped to found the Female Institute in Columbia, Tennessee. The Female Institute was a modest success, but other attempts by Otey to establish Episcopalian centers for learning failed. Mercer Hall in Columbia and Ravenscroft College outside of Columbia were both short-lived owing to lack of financial support.

In 1851 Otey traveled to Europe for a full year to recover from a series of illnesses that had befallen him. There he visited with the Archbishop of Canterbury as well as going to several institutions of higher learning in England, France, Prussia, Switzerland, and other neighboring countries. These visits confirmed in Otey the desire to establish a university in Tennessee that was similar in atmosphere and purpose to those he observed in Europe. His visits were productive in another sense as well: he initiated several key relationships with scholars and administrators at European universities, some of whom would come to the aid of the University of the South in its crucial early years.

As the south reached new heights of prosperity in the 1850s, Bishops Otey and Polk again revived the idea of an Episcopal institution of higher learning that would combine the cultural values of the American south with the academic traditions of Europe. In the summer of 1856, Bishop Polk drafted a letter to the bishops of the other nine southern dioceses outlining his proposal for a church-sponsored university. In this letter Polk set forth

University of the South

in great detail the necessity of such an enterprise and suggested that the church's leadership take up the discussion in earnest at the general church convention in October of that year. Polk's proposal did indeed gain the support of church leadership, and in October a declaration of intent to establish a university was signed by all ten bishops of the southern dioceses.

The declaration further elaborated on the resolutions outlined in Bishop Polk's letter, most notably that the university would be owned and administered by all participating dioceses; that an initial endowment of $500,000 would need to be raised for the purpose of establishing the university; and that, ideally, the school would be located near Chattanooga (this region was chosen for its connection via railroad lines to major cities of the north and south).

On July 4, 1857, representatives from seven southern dioceses of the Episcopal Church met at Lookout Mountain near Chattanooga to elect officers and to found the university. The date chosen for this meeting was purposeful, as Bishop Otey's address to the crowd of nearly 500 onlookers implies:

We affirm that our aim is eminently national and patriotic . . . not of political schism. . . . We contemplate no strife, save a generous rivalry with our brethren, as to who shall furnish to this great republic the truest men, the truest Christians, and the truest patriots.

Otey's nationalist rhetoric, however, would soon be modified when his institution expressed its loyalty to the Confederate cause.

The next step was to secure property in a favorable location. At some time between the founding of the university in July, 1857 and the meeting of the executive committee in November of that year, a prominent geologist and civil engineer was contracted to investigate several possible sites in the general vicinity of the Cumberland Plateau, particularly Chattanooga, Huntsville, McMinnville, Cleveland, Atlanta, and Sewanee. The communities of Chattanooga and Huntsville campaigned by offering land, natural resources, and monetary gifts to the fledgling institution. Criteria for site selection included degree of elevation above sea level, water supply, availability of building materials, proximity to railroad lines and roads, temperateness of climate, and pleasantness of landscape; in the end, however, it was the generous offer of 10,000 acres of land and free shipping of 20,000 tons of freight made by Samuel F. Tracy of the Sewanee Mining Company and other local citizens that swayed the executive committee to choose Sewanee as the home of the University of the South. To this day, the 10,000-acre domain atop the Cumberland Plateau remains a key component of the university's unique character.

The name of the university was also chosen at the November meeting, after some deliberation. Other names considered were "The University of Sewanee" and "The Church University," each reflecting a different vision of the university's role. That committee members chose a grander and more inclusive title for the school attests to their more ambitious aim: to establish a university that would represent culturally the entire region of the south. The naming of the university also suggests that committee members believed they could create—in nearly finished form—an institution that would compare favorably with the more established universities of the north in regard to atmosphere, personnel, and financial resources. Bishop Polk stated as much in a letter written to cofounder Stephen Elliott, Bishop of Georgia:

There is no reason why . . . we might not in five years have a Church University which would rival Harvard or Yale. . . . A movement of some kind is indispensable to rally and unite us, to develop our resources and demonstrate our power.

This fierce sense of optimism among executive committee members, although crucial at the time of the university's founding, would prove to be an obstacle in the economically troublesome years that followed the Civil War.

On the heels of the November meeting, the State of Tennessee granted the university its charter on January 6, 1858. This accomplished, Bishops Polk and Elliott gave their attention to the work of raising revenues. As outlined in Polk's letter of 1856 to the bishops of the ten southern dioceses, their initial goal was to raise $500,000, a sum upon which they would draw interest and, in turn, use only the interest to fund construction and operation of the university. It was Polk's idea to raise this sum in one diocese alone and so demonstrate the feasibility of their goals to the remaining dioceses. This was nearly accomplished in the spring of 1859 as Polk and Elliott traveled through the Louisiana diocese soliciting financial support from wealthy plantation owners and others. By tour's end, the two bishops had raised more than $478,000 in cash, bonds, and promissory notes.

The apparent ease with which Polk and Elliott had raised the initial endowment for the university inspired trustees to make preparations for the laying of the cornerstone. The actual ceremony and accompanying festivities took place on October 10, 1860. As plans for the layout of the campus had not yet been finalized, the six-ton marble cornerstone was placed on large sandstone supports at the site's highest point of elevation. The ceremony began in the late morning as some 5,000 onlookers followed a procession of church and university leadership through the wilderness to where the cornerstone was temporarily laid.

Following the ceremony, trustees met to agree upon the constitution and statutes of the university, part of which stipulated that the board of trustees was to be comprised of the bishop, a clergyman, and two laypersons from each of the ten participating dioceses. The clergyman and two laypersons would be elected at their own diocesan conventions. The constitution and statutes also stipulated that each member of the board of trustees would have an equal vote. Arthur Benjamin Chitty Jr., a chief historian of the University of the South, notes that this arrangement was designed to "counterbalance the idealistic and spiritual thinking of the bishops against the hard practicality of the realistic laymen and would prevent domination by either group."

All of these detailed plans, however, were made nearly obsolete by the course of events that began in December 1860, when South Carolina seceded from the Union. Bishop Elliott of Georgia, who now resided in Sewanee, supported the secession of all southern states and actively campaigned for southern dioceses of the Episcopal Church to become independent of their northern counterparts. This action was formally taken at a special convention in Montgomery, Alabama in July 1861. The dilemma that the war between the North and South represented for the school's founders, however, is perhaps best manifested in the actions of Bishop Polk, who more than once declined the commission of major-general given to him by Jefferson Davis, reasoning that others were more qualified than he to serve in such a capacity and for such a cause. Later events would serve to change his mind. While in New Orleans in April 1861, Polk learned that his home in Sewanee had been burned to the ground by unidentified persons and that his wife and family had barely escaped. This incident occurred the same night that shells were fired against Fort Sumter in Charleston, South Carolina. Polk, who was a graduate of the military school at West Point, finally accepted his command in June 1861.

The war destroyed all hopes of opening the University of the South on a grand scale as a large, fully operational institution. Much of the landscape of the south lay in ruins, property values plummeted, and plantation owners were forced to cease production owing to the severe labor shortages associated with the emancipation of the slave population. The most critical consequence of the war for the university, however, was that its original benefactors were no longer able to provide the financial backing they had promised. This meant that a new fund-raising effort would have to be undertaken at a time when most, if not all, southern dioceses were barely able to finance their own essential operations. Also damaging to the cause of the University of the South were the losses of Bishops Otey and Polk. Otey succumbed to illness in Memphis in April 1863, and Polk died in battle in June 1864. Bishop Elliott, although managing to reconvene a portion of the board of trustees in October 1866, also died before resumption of plans to open the university actually took place.

Leadership then fell to the Reverend Charles T. Quintard, newly elected bishop of Tennessee and protégé of Bishop Elliott. At the Tennessee diocesan convention in September 1865, it was resolved that the diocese of Tennessee alone should take measures to establish a seminary at Sewanee. This attempt to establish a modest center for learning—in contrast to the original intent to create a bustling, fully operational university out of the wilderness—was necessitated by political and economic circumstances. Moreover, executive committee members were very aware of a clause in the deed to the property which stated that ownership of the domain would revert to its original owners if a school were not functioning on the premises within ten years of its donation. Although committee members clearly conceived of the theological school as merely the first step toward a larger enterprise, it was the establishment of a small-scale seminary at the site designated for the University of the South that essentially secured the committee's rights to the domain and made possible all later developments.

In January 1866, Bishop Quintard and two colleagues addressed to the remaining members of the executive committee a letter outlining plans by the Tennessee diocese to open a theological school. The three men also proposed that a boys' preparatory school be established at the Sewanee domain and toward this end called for all diocesan treasurers to collect on pledges made to the University of the South before the war. Characteristically, those individuals most involved in the formation of the university were overly optimistic. Although Quintard's letter was met with some enthusiasm, the monies promised to the school's founders were simply unavailable in the postwar economy.

Still, in February 1866, construction began on the first university building, Otey Hall, under the direction of George R. Fairbanks, commissioner of lands and buildings. This wood structure was built to house the activities of the divinity school and was financed primarily by the fundraising efforts of Quintard as he traveled through his diocese. In March a Dr. Merrick became director of the divinity school, but he left within a year. The basic means to instruct students now existed, but it is unclear whether any students attended the school during Dr. Merrick's short tenure.

Plans to reestablish the University of the South were considered on October 11, 1866. Bishop Elliott, in his last official act as third chancellor of the university (Otey first held the title and Polk succeeded him), presided over a meeting of 9 of the original 40 members of the board of trustees who had convened expressly to discuss the future of the university. While the number of members present was not sufficient to take formal action according to the school's constitution and statutes, those in attendance agreed that earnest attempts to resurrect plans for the university should be made. Notably, Bishop Quintard agreed to remain chief fundraiser for this undertaking.

Upon the death of Bishop Elliott, William Mercer Green, bishop of Mississippi, was elected fourth chancellor of the University of the South. Under his administration, the divinity school finally opened, and fundraising efforts for the university continued. At the behest of the board of trustees, George R. Fairbanks planned to travel to Louisiana to see which, if any, prewar pledges could be collected. Bishop Green addressed a letter to all previously associated dioceses requesting they resume their financial participation in the enterprise. In the spring of 1867, Quintard and Fairbanks traveled to Louisville in search of financial backing. Quintard also traveled to Georgia and South Carolina, but to no greater avail. Each of these fundraising efforts proved only mildly successful.

As it became increasingly clear that the economic climate in the south would remain hostile to their cause, the board of trustees resolved in August 1867 that the reach of fundraising efforts be extended to the Church of England. Bishop Quintard, now vice-chancellor of the university, was thus sent to England, where he quickly secured the endorsement of the Archbishop of Canterbury. Aided by other Anglican church leaders sympathetic to his cause, Quintard raised a considerable sum. A skilled and charismatic orator, Quintard augmented this income by preaching in pulpits throughout England, for which he received offertories. In total, Quintard raised approximately £2,500 over the course of his eight-and-a-half month trip to England. He also accepted books donated by Oxford University and Cambridge University.

On the basis of Quintard's success abroad, the board of trustees moved ahead with plans to open the university. Consistent with the trustees' new-found sense of restraint, a junior department was created to teach younger students at the college preparatory level. The executive committee pursued a headmaster and teachers for this purpose, and, in September 1868, the University of the South opened its doors to nine students, all of whom had been personally invited to attend the school. These male students (women were not admitted until 1920 and were not awarded degrees until 1971) ranged in age from 12 to 19, and it was not until a year later that a formal division was made between the grammar school and the junior department. By the fall of the following year, a total of 86 new students had enrolled and attended classes, and in the spring term of 1870 another 95 students were admitted.

Perhaps because of this apparent progress, members of the executive committee and trustees continued to overestimate severely their base of financial resources. Commissioner Fairbanks conveyed to the trustees his belief that a large stone structure, estimated to cost $30,000, could be financed over the period of its construction, approximately three years. In reviewing the institution's financial assets, the finance committee made the crucial error of estimating values at prewar rates. Additionally, it was not until the summer of 1870 that Fairbanks fully realized the complete loss of the prewar Louisiana pledges. One fact, however, was becoming increasingly clear to all involved: the plan of Otey, Polk, and Elliott to fund and operate the institution drawing only on the interest and investments gains from a large principal endowment was no longer attainable. Whatever aid could be gotten from the southern dioceses or from benefactors in England would have to be spent as circumstances required.

Following these miscalculations, the executive committee—now comprised only of Quintard and Fairbanks—authorized construction of several new buildings on the campus intended to accommodate the hundreds of new students projected to enroll at the university. Once they realized that these costs were beyond the school's financial means, the board of trustees was forced to seek a loan in the sum of $10,000 in 1872. The process of obtaining the loan from the New York-based United States Mortgage Company was a sobering affair for trustees; they saw that northern investors were reluctant to invest resources in southern enterprises. Still, the loan was successfully negotiated.

All was not grim, however. In the name of elevating the school's operations to the university level, the board authorized the creation of seven university departments that had been prescribed in the original constitution and statutes: chemistry, civil engineering, mathematics, metaphysics, modern languages, ancient languages, and moral science. Initially, professors were hired to teach in six of these departments. Also, in the years 1870–72 a village community began to grow and flourish at Sewanee. The number of leases granted by the university tripled over the course of this period, and the number of homes in the village alone reached 100. This expansion was owed in part to Quintard's solicitation of skilled laborers and their families during his fundraising trips.

The remainder of the 1870s saw several maneuverings on the part of university trustees to maintain credit ratings, including the reduction of faculty salaries and consolidation of high-level administrative positions. In order to pay off existing debts, a second loan from the United States Mortgage Company in the sum of $25,000 was secured. The timing of this loan may have been fortuitous. In the years 1878–79 a yellow fever epidemic in the region caused enrollment to fall off considerably, and the loss of income from student tuition would have been disastrous had reparations not been made on previous debts.

The university's finances were now largely under the supervision of the Rev. Telfair Hodgson, first dean of the theological department and later third vice-chancellor of the university. Under Hodgson's direction the university's financial standing finally stabilized. As a consequence, the next 25 years were devoted to the construction of permanent buildings on the campus. The first stone structure, Hodgson Library, was begun in 1876, followed by St. Luke's Hall in 1877. Thompson Hall (1883), Walsh Memorial Hall (1891), Hoffman Memorial Hall (1898), and Quintard Memorial Hall (1901), all designed in the architectural style of Oxford and Cambridge, soon followed. These buildings were financed through the gifts of benefactors.

The University of the South emerged from the dark years of Southern Reconstruction to become a thriving center of academic tradition and learning, and had ample cause to celebrate its 125th anniversary in 1981. Today, the university is home to a wide array of departments in the liberal arts and sciences as well as to a school of theology. Although significant changes have taken place since its founding in 1857, the University of the South has managed to maintain the unique blend of southern culture and Oxfordian spirit and architecture envisioned by its founders.

Further Reading: Two volumes detailing the history of the University of the South are *Reconstruction at Sewanee: The Founding of the University of the South and Its First Administration, 1857–1872,* by Arthur Benjamin Chitty Jr. (Sewanee, Tennessee: The University Press, 1954), and *History of the University of the South at Sewanee, Tennessee,* by George R. Fairbanks (Jacksonville, Florida: H. and W.B. Drew Company, 1905). Moultrie Gerry's *Men Who Made Sewanee* (Sewanee, Tennessee: The University Press, 1981), which has been republished with additional chapters by Arthur Benjamin and Elizabeth N. Chitty, offers a closer look at the personal lives of the school's founders and chief architects.

—Christopher Hudson

UNIVERSITY OF THE WITWATERSRAND
(Johannesburg, South Africa)

Location: Situated in Johannesburg, the largest metropolitan area and industrial and commercial center of South Africa. Also known as "The Rand," a 150-mile ridge located in northeast South Africa which contains the world's largest gold field, producing two-thirds of the world's gold. Located 31 miles from Pretoria, South Africa's capital.

Description: The main campus is at Milner Park in Johannesburg, occupying 168 acres, and includes the recently developed West Campus, where the departments of law, education, commerce, and a portion of engineering are located. The Medical School is located in Parktown, approximately five miles from the main campus.

Information: Admissions Office
Senate House Concourse
University of the Witwatersrand
Private Bag 3
WITS 2050 South Africa
Admissions (001) 716 8003
Main (011) 716 1111

Shifts in the local economic landscape and world events throughout the early part of the twentieth century have shaped the growth and direction of the University of the Witwatersrand. The school's roots have their origins in the South African School of Mines in Kimberley, which opened in 1896 and moved to Johannesburg in 1904. There it was incorporated into Transvaal Technical Institute. By 1910, it had been renamed South African School of Mines and Technology. Ten years later, it was named a university college, with university status established by Private Act of Parliament, Act. No. 15 of 1921. On March 1, 1922, the University of Witwatersrand officially opened with 6 schools with 37 departments, 73 academic staff members, and a little more than 1,000 students studying the arts, sciences, medicine, engineering, law, and business.

The combined discovery of the diamond fields of Kimberley and Griqualand West during the 1870s, followed by the unearthing of the gold fields of Johannesburg and the Witwatersrand in the 1880s spawned South Africa's first industrial revolution. As a result, within a single generation the foundation of South Africa's economy metamorphosed from an agrarian to a capitalist system based on mining. In response to these rapid economic changes, the initial effort was made within South Africa itself to establish the facilities for training professional men to meet the needs of the rapidly expanding mining industry. And herein lie the roots and evolution of the Witwatersrand University.

In 1890, the Council of the South African College elected to open "a School of Mines in South Africa" in Cape Town. A conflict then arose concerning the physical location of the college. Should the School of Mines be located in Kimberley, the mining town, or in Johannesburg, the mother city with a lengthy tradition as a center of education? Compromise was reached in the form of a 1894 parliamentary motion that proposed that professional training be taught at the South African College in Cape Town. It was then decided by parliamentary motion that technical and practical training would be conducted at Kimberley, and that Johannesburg should not be excluded if the necessary facilities could be provided. Because of the high cost of living the students incurred in Johannesburg, both the third- and fourth-year courses in mining were consolidated in Kimberley. In 1895, the Witwatersrand Council of Education was formed by the leaders of the gold mining industry of the Witwatersrand for the purpose of teaching English-language education.

Also in 1895, the Council of the University of the Cape of Good Hope met to discuss a proposal made by the Council of the South African College. The college set forth the following objective: "to bring within the reach of young men, throughout South Africa, the opportunity of qualifying themselves in their own country, for a profession which has hitherto been filled chiefly by experts trained elsewhere." Ultimately, this led to the founding in 1896 of the South African School of Mines in Kimberley, and endorsed by the De Beers Consolidated Mines. In 1896, J.S. Lawn, a distinguished graduate of the Royal School of Mines in London, was appointed as the first professor of mining, stationed in Kimberley. Later, he became principal of the South African School of Mines in Kimberley. Enrollment, however, was small through the 1890s, with only 12 to 14 new students admitted yearly. The South African War in October 1899 put an end to the school's activities until July 1900.

By August 1903, the Transvaal Technical Institute was established, replacing the Kimberley School. The same mining curriculum offered at the Kimberley School was followed at the new school. The first class met on March 29, 1904, in temporary quarters, which had first been

University of the Witwatersrand

used as a cigar store. The only academic awards the institute could confer on students were diplomas and certificates, not university degrees. Thus, the institute functioned more as a trade school than an institution aspiring to claiming university status. In July 1906, the school's name was changed to Transvaal University College. Two years later, the functions of the college were divided. Engineering and technical training along with law classes proceeded in Johannesburg and the arts and sciences were relegated to Pretoria.

Also in 1906, the sum of £200,000 (the value of his Frankenwald estate) was bequeathed to the college by Alfred Beit "to be applied towards building and equipping the university" to be called the University of Johannesburg. The gift, however, came with a provision: if the money was not used to establish this university within ten years of his passing, the money would be returned to his estate. However, the sole beneficiary of Alfred Beit's estate was his younger brother Otto. Apparently, Alfred Beit (a partner with Wernher in Johannesburg's largest gold mine) had in mind the building of a University of Johannesburg on the Frankenwald estate. It would then serve the educational needs of both Johannesburg and Pretoria. The Transvaal

government, though, did not consider Frankenwald a suitable site for a university.

As the former colonial secretary in the Transvaal government, General Jan Smuts was responsible for higher education there. He was keenly aware of and supported the government's plans for a reorganized system of national education. With this idea in mind, Smuts met with Otto Beit (Alfred's brother) during a London business trip. His strategy was to steer Otto Beit to giving favorable consideration to establishing a national university at Groote Schuur. Beit told Smuts that he no longer felt bound to Frankenwald and instead preferred the Groote Schuur site to found a South African university. In a letter to Smuts, Beit wrote from London on August 19, 1910, "I have fully discussed the matter with Sir Julius Wernher . . . and . . . provided the government renounces the legacy by my late brother of £200,000 for the Johannesburg University on the Frankenwald estate, be it either by Act of Parliament, or by any other means to the satisfaction of my legal advisers, I will give an equal amount for the scheme of which you now write."

The letter was accompanied by another letter to Smuts penned by Sir Julius Wernher, who wrote: "The idea of a South African University appeals to us very much on sentimental and practical grounds and we are glad that you are putting it forward. Assuming that the bequest . . . can be diverted, I shall be very happy to contribute say £200,000, and if it is found that £500,000 is necessary, Mr. Otto Beit and myself would find the difference of £100,000." Smuts clinched the deal by an enthusiastic cable of acceptance on behalf of the government which were now committed to the Groot Schur scheme for a national university.

During this time, strong rivalries existed between Pretoria and Johannesburg for the site of the proposed university as well as among other colleges, and the various colony governments would not make a move until a proposed Inter-Colonial Conference on University Matters had met and until the governments of South Africa had arrived at a decision on the question of university policy.

With the granting of responsible government to the Transvaal in 1908, with Pretoria as the seat of government, there was a demand for proper facilities for higher education. The situation was resolved by dividing the functions of the Transvaal University College. A dual system was then introduced under which engineering and technological training continued at Johannesburg, together with classes for the law certificate examination. The arts and sciences departments became the responsibility of the Pretoria branch. In 1910, the Transvaal Parliament passed an act that finally allowed the two institutions to become independent. The one in Johannesburg was renamed the South African School of Mines and Technology, while the one in Pretoria retained the title of Transvaal University College.

Then in April 1913, a parliamentary bill was introduced for the establishment of a new University of South Africa. Subsequently, the bill was withdrawn because the University Commission had requested the establishment of two universities, one in the south and one in the north. The Johannesburg School of Mines and Technology then would be recognized as the school of technology for both universities. Of the total Wernher-Beit endowment, £400,000 would go to Cape Town and £50,000 each to Pretoria and Johannesburg. At a conference in Capetown on December 17, 1915, attended by representatives of all the colleges, the minister informed those present that while they were welcome to discuss the details, they "could not deal with the principles, the government having decided to found three universities."

The worst feature of the new bill that incorporated the School of Mines with the other colleges was a clause stipulating that no development of any kind could be undertaken at any of them without the express permission of the Minister of Education. After much protestation in Parliament, the minister finally agreed that a constituent college could promote legislation "providing for the incorporation of such colleges as a university." Although the way was cleared for establishing a univer-

sity, not at Johannesburg, but at Witwatersrand, funds, nevertheless, were badly needed.

The city of Johannesburg donated the Milner Park site of 80 acres. Another 12 acres was given by Transvaal Consolidated Lands, along with generous financial support from the cities of Johannesburg, Reef, and Vereeniging together with the Transvaal Chamber of Mines, the Witwatersrand Council of Education, and the support from the general public. Ultimately, the Witwatersrand University owes its existence to the overwhelming civic support of the entire Witwatersrand community together with the 72-member Witwatersrand University Committee and the Witwatersrand College of Education. Nine new departments were established in 1917 to provide premedical and predental training. A men's dormitory, the first building erected on the new campus, was ready for the 1921 academic session.

On 1919, Jan Hofmeyr, at age 24, was appointed principal of the South African School of Mines and Technology. Later that year on August 1 by act of Parliament, the University College of Johannesburg was established. Three years later, the government transferred the Frankenwald estate to the university.

The academic staff, led by Hofmeyr as president, was composed of nearly 60 professors, senior lecturers, and lecturers. Because of a strike, the official opening ceremony was postponed more than six months when conditions returned to normal. Hofmeyr, who went on to play a greater role in South Africa's history, was succeeded in 1925 by Sir William Thompson, who held the president's post for two years.

The period between 1917 and 1922 marked a steady build-up of faculties and departments that afforded the university a broad academic base, thanks in part to the men who had come from the United Kingdom and who were typical products of the older as well as the younger universities.

On June 23, 1925, England's Prince of Wales (who was to become Edward VIII) made an official visit to the university to open the Main Block and to receive an honorary degree of doctor of laws. In 1928, Humphrey Raikes assumed the president's post, which he held until 1953. By 1939, the number of students had increased to a total enrollment of 2,544. The number of academic departments grew from 37 to 44, while the full-time academic staff expanded from 60 to 105 members. The school of dentistry opened in 1929, and the school of architecture and fine arts in 1940.

The slow progress in erecting buildings on the Milner Park campus reflected only one aspect of the very severe financial restrictions the university faced between the two world wars. The years of depression that preceded South Africa's departure from the gold standard in 1932 only made the problem of trying to make ends meet more difficult. As a result, the school was mired in a near constant state of bankruptcy. The only substantial source of revenue was from student fees, already the highest of any of the country's universities. In spite of the hardships, the university did graduate an impressive number of students. From 1922 to 1939, 2,998 students were awarded diplomas.

Four new buildings were built from 1925 to 1945 including the Isabel Dalrymple House (1928), a women's residence; the main library (which had been totally destroyed by fire in 1931 and was replaced with a separate fire-proof building); the Bernard Price Institute for Geophysical Research (1936); and Hillman Block (1940), which houses the departments of civil engineering and surveying. In addition, those years saw the completion of the Central Block that contained the Great Hall where graduation ceremonies were held and the Douglas Smit House (1945) where African medical students were housed.

The great technological strides that were gaining momentum throughout the world required trained engineers and scientists for industry and research purposes. The tremendous advances of the early 1940s caused South Africa to realize the need to manufacture and export more sophisticated goods. This realization spurred the country's push for both fundamental and applied research.

Prior to World War II, South Africa's government viewed the financial support of its universities as a "liability," with funding kept to a minimum. After the war, when rebuilding efforts peaked, civic leaders realized the vital services colleges and universities could provide for a country on the move, which led to a significant change in the government's position. To further that end, the Holloway Commission was formed in 1951. Two years later, it issued a report that placed the financial relationship between the state and universities on an entirely new footing. Now, it was the state's responsibility to provide the major part of the revenue required to maintain satisfactory minimum standards of university education. The expenditure per student at the university rose from R 170 in 1922 to R 219 in 1939 to R 713 in 1970.

During the 1950s and 1960s, the campus landscape expanded to include the Oral and Dental Hospital (1952), built at a cost of R 1 million and the John Moffat Building, which houses the departments of architecture, fine arts, quantity surveying, and building science. It is named in honor of a prominent Johannesburg architect who contributed R 200,000 to the university. The Humphrey Rivas Raikes, which is the home of the department of chemistry (1960), was named after the president who served the university for 25 years.

By the 1960s, the university was rapidly outgrowing the campus at Milner Park. The Johannesburg City Council donated a valuable open space called "The Oval." Renamed the Parktown Campus, it contains Ernest Oppenheimer Hall, the first half of the new men's residence, and the graduate school of business adminis-

tration which is housed in a gracious older building called Outeniqua. Also bequeathed to the university was a handsome private home known as Savernake. A donation of Dr. Bernard Price, it serves as the home of the university's president.

In 1960, the building to house the Nuclear Physics Research Unit was completed, as well as many other small structures to house equipment for such special purposes as the making of nitrogen and liquid hydrogen. In addition, three of the university's original buildings—the Physics Block, old Medical School, and South West Engineering Building, all built in 1922—underwent extensive remodeling.

The university's first development office to house permanent fundraising activities also was opened at this juncture. Wits's first computer was purchased in 1961, making it the second scientific computer in use in South Africa. During the next ten years, the original computer was replaced twice by more powerful and faster hardware.

In the late 1960s, an eight-story medical school building to house the clinical departments was completed. In addition, a new seven-story building for chemical engineering and metallurgy was constructed. These structures represented the first high-rise buildings on the university's campus.

Two central libraries—the Wartenweiler Library and the William Cullen Library—and 13 divisional libraries are located on the main campus. The Wartenweiler Library opened in April 1972 and is primarily an undergraduate teaching library for students in the arts. It contains 17,190 items. The William Cullen Library opened in March 1934 and serves the school's reference and research requirements. The university also has maintained a medical library since 1926. The campus also features 26 museums and 2 arts galleries, a theater facility, and a planetarium operated by the university.

The geology and mining engineering building and the Jan Smuts House were opened in 1962. The first Student Union building was opened in 1964, and three years later, a new social sciences building was built. In 1972, the Old Mutual Indoor Sports Center opened, named in honor of its major contributor, South African Mutual Life Assurance Society.

While other South African institutions for higher learning have varied their practices in admitting "certain categories of students," the university of the Witwatersrand is one of several South African universities that did not discriminate on grounds of "color, creed or race." However, this liberal policy was altered in late 1956, when the South African government introduced legislation in 1957 "to enforce apartheid on all universities in South Africa." The universities of Witwatersrand and Cape Town were most affected. The Extension of University Education Act that debarred non-Europeans from attending white universities passed in 1959.

Currently, the University of the Witwatersrand is composed of 10 schools with 99 departments among them. With 19,000 students served by 4,000 employees, including 1,250 academic staff, Wits now confers about 4,500 degrees annually.

Further Reading: General background can be found in *A Brief History of the University of the Witwatersrand, Johannesburg and Its Predecessors 1896–1972* (university publication, 1972).

—Michele Picozzi

UNIVERSITY OF TOKYO
(Tokyo, Japan)

Location: On three main campuses in Tokyo, at Hongo, Yayoi, and Komaba, with other institutes and observatories at several sites around Japan.

Description: "Tokyo Daigaku" (or "Todai") in Japanese; formerly Tokyo Imperial University, enrolling over 25,000 students, is the oldest national university in Japan and the alma mater of most Japanese prime ministers and leading figures in many other fields.

Information: University of Tokyo
7-3-1 Hongo
Bunkyo-ku, Tokyo 113
Japan
(03) 3812 2111

When the University of Tokyo was created in 1877 it combined the elements of an entirely new institution, based on non-Japanese models; an amalgamation of three existing schools, one of them already more than two centuries old; and the role of being the latest in a series of institutions created by successive Japanese regimes for the purpose of training government officials. That latter fundamental purpose has remained constant, and for more than a century alumni of the university have occupied many of the leading positions in Japan's politics and in public administration, as well as playing important roles in business and, indeed, in literature and the arts.

This enormously prestigious institution is the expression of a very old tradition in Japan. The very term *Daigaku,* which literally means "great learning" and which was chosen to translate the English word "university," had been known in Japanese as early as the eighth century, both as the title of one of the classics of Confucian thought imported from China and as the name of the first such institution, then located in what is now Nara, the first permanent Japanese capital, and later in Kyoto, the capital city from 794 to 1868. These older schools had been superseded during the seventeenth century by another Confucian institution, created and managed by the Hayashi family of scholars under the supervision of the Tokugawa shoguns who were the effective rulers of Japan, from their castle at Edo (now Tokyo), from 1603 onward. The Hayashi school, long known as the Shoheiko or Shohei Gakko (Shohei School) from its location on a hill in Edo called Sho-

heizaka, was taken over by the shogunate in 1797 and officially renamed the Gakumonjo, although its informal name remained in use.

Meanwhile, two other institutions had grown up in Edo to provide training in subjects developed in western countries but excluded by the Confucian conservatives of the Shohei Gakko. The Kaiseijo, or Kaiseigakko—the Development Institute or School, had been established in 1863 but could trace its origins to 1811, when a permanent body of scholars specializing in translating and analyzing European and American publications was created within the shogunate's astronomical observatory. In 1855 this group had been given a separate status, as the Yogakusho, the Western Learning Institute, renamed in the following year as the Bansho Shirabesho, the Institute for Investigating Barbarian Writings. At this point the main language studied and used was Dutch, which had been the one European language known to the Japanese since all other European powers had been excluded from trade and contact with Japan in the early seventeenth century. Within the next few years, however, training in English, French, and German was also developed, while the scope of the institute's activities was widened to include not only navigation, geography, and related subjects of relevance to the military and naval authorities, but also the sciences which, it was now clear, were playing a crucial role in the industrialization of the western powers. With around 50 scholars employed at the institute and around 200 students being sent from all over Japan to study with them, the institute set the pattern for treating higher education and research as matters in which the state could and should take a direct interest.

The other leading center of "Dutch" or "Western" studies was the Igakujo or Igakko, the Medical Institute or School. This had been created by the shogunate in 1863, on the basis of a smallpox clinic, the Shutosho, which had been privately established in 1858 and brought under government control in 1860. Its purpose was to build on the achievements of generations of medical scholars and researchers in Japan by organizing training in European techniques.

In 1868 the Tokugawa shogunate was overthrown and replaced by a new government, acting in the name of the emperor and pledged to modernize Japan. Edo, renamed Tokyo, became the capital in place of Kyoto, and in 1869 a new Diagaku was created by merging the city's existing government institutions of higher education at a single site. The Shoheiko, which claimed seniority both because of its age and because its staff hoped that Confucianism would continue to be the official ideology, was renamed

647

simply the Daigaku, while the Kaisei Gakko became the Daigaku Nanko, its Southern School, and the Igakko became the Daigaku Toko, its Eastern School, in reference to their locations on the new campus. The new institution proclaimed its commitment to modernization by employing numerous lecturers and instructors from Britain, the United States, France, Germany, and other western countries, although their numbers and influence would steadily decline over the decades, as the Japanese whom they had trained became able to take their places.

This first merger of the three schools lasted for only two years, before many of the former Shokeiko's Confucian scholars and facilities were transferred to the new Monbusho, the Ministry of Education, and the other two schools regained a measure of autonomy. The law, science, and literature faculties of the Kaisei Gakko occupied various buildings in the Kanda district of the city (it was at one of its departments, incidentally, that baseball was introduced to Japan in 1873, yet another augury of extensive westernization). Meanwhile the Igakko moved to the Hongo district of northeastern Tokyo, along with what is now the university hospital, founded in Kanda in 1868, to occupy part of the Kaga Yashiki, the former estate of the Maeda family, who had been hereditary lords of Kaga Province and whose wealth and power had been second only to that of the Tokugawa shoguns.

At this Hongo site, around one mile from the Imperial Palace, the present University of Tokyo was formally established on April 12, 1877, once again as an amalgamation of the Igakko, the Kaisei Gakko, and parts of the Shoheiko. The hybrid nature of the new institution is still reflected in its very appearance. All the buildings were constructed in the 1870s and later, using a variety of styles imported from Europe and North America; however, some of the formal gardens of the Maeda have been preserved within the university precincts, and one of the main entrances to the campus through the brick wall surrounding it is the Akamon, the Chinese-style Red Gate built for the Maeda in 1827, which has become a symbol of the university.

The former Shoheiko was no longer formally dominant within the university, organized on western lines into four faculties (law, literature, medicine, and science), each containing several departments. Those Confucian scholars who were appointed to teaching posts were no longer concentrated into one school; they offered courses in Chinese and Japanese literature, formed the nucleus of the university's Chinese studies department, set up in 1882, and occupied leading positions in the history department. Even so, the new institution, like its predecessor of 1869–71, was at the center of controversies over how far modernization should or could go before it threatened the integrity of Japanese traditions, and when the enthusiastic westernization of the 1870s gave way to a revived nationalism in the late 1880s, the character of the university was to be altered once again.

In 1886 the university was renamed Teikoku Daigaku, the Imperial University, under an imperial ordinance, giving it the twin objectives of training its students in arts and sciences and investigating matters necessary to the state. In the same year it underwent significant expansion by establishing a graduate school and absorbing the previously separate Kobu Daigaku, a college of engineering. This school then included among its staff Josiah Conder, who introduced European styles of architecture to Japan and helped to make Japanese traditional painting better known in Britain, his home country; and his compatriot John Milne, who brought the science of seismology to a country where it was still widely believed that earthquakes were caused by dragons or giant turtles. The transfer of the government's astronomical observatory to the university in 1888 and the absorption of the Tokyo Norin Gakko, a college of agriculture and forestry, in 1890, appeared to confirm its role as the national center for training across the range of academic disciplines imported from the west.

Meanwhile, however, those Confucianists who had regrouped inside the Education Ministry, notably in its textbook section, gained the attention of the Emperor Mutsuhito (referred to since his death in 1912 as the Meiji emperor), through the regular programs of lecturers at his court given by Motoda Eifu and others. After the emperor had made his first official visit to the university in 1886 he commissioned Motoda to investigate its neglect of traditional subjects such as Japanese literature, Confucian philosophy, and ethics. Crucial changes followed, which formalized the university's role as the national center for training social elites. In 1887 competitive examinations were introduced for civil service posts, tailored to the university's graduates. In 1889 the socially exclusive Dai-ichi Koto Gakko (First Higher School), founded 15 years earlier at the Tokyo School of English, was reestablished on a site to the south of the university, as the main conduit for students seeking to enter it. Finally, in 1890 Motoda and others drafted the Imperial Rescript on Education, the influential document displayed inside the university and all other educational institutions in Japan until 1945, which required that they promote the values of loyalty and filial piety.

Thus what had been envisaged by some of its founders, and its foreign lecturers, as a center for westernization became an integral part of the Japanese state's program for creating loyal subjects rather than active citizens. More concretely, the domination of the civil service by a network of Imperial University graduates, beginning around 1905, further ensured that the nationalist ideas favored by the leading politicians and officials would permeate the state, the university, and indeed, its sister institution, the imperial university which was established in Kyoto in 1897 and which necessitated yet another change of name for the older foundation, which became Tokyo Teikoku Daigaku in that year.

Even so, the university was still not exclusively controlled by traditionalists. On the one hand, scientific and technical subjects, if they were to be at all useful to the state, had to be taught in ways which unavoidably challenged inherited ideas, even if their staff and alumni had less social prestige or influence than those of the humanities departments. On the other hand, those departments also could not be hermetically sealed off from the liberal and even socialist ideas emanating from the west. These ideas were usually ignored by the government so long as they remained academic theories rather than inspirations to political action. In 1910, for example, Minobe Tatsukichi, a professor of political science, was allowed to publish a new interpretation of the 1889 Constitution which treated the emperor as just one of several organs of the state; in 1911 12 leftists, lacking his high social status, were executed on the false charge of planning to assassinate the emperor.

The government at this period also gave relative freedom of action to the literature faculty, which established its own position of enduring influence on Japanese culture, partly by exposing its students not just to foreign books and ideas but to foreign teachers, whom it went on employing into the more repressive 1930s. The best known of these were Basil Hall Chamberlain, the first professor of Japanese, and Lafcadio Hearn, an early professor of English, both of whom wrote extensively about Japan, thus pioneering what has since been formalized as Japanese Studies (and setting examples of independent thinking and readable prose which regrettably few of their academic heirs seem able to follow). As for the early students of the literature faculty, they included Natsume Soseki, often called the father of modern Japanese literature. After being graduated in 1893 and returning to succeed Hearn as professor of English in 1902, he resigned five years later to begin writing novels which are still read today for their evocation of Japan in the late Meiji period, caught in transition between familiar customs and disturbing new ways of life. He is commemorated on the Hongo campus by Sanshiro's Pond (another remnant of the Maeda estate), so named for the eponymous hero of his novel *Sanshiro,* which was partly based on his student years there. Later alumni of the faculty include the novelists Kawabata Yasunari, Inoue Yasushi, Nagai Kafu, Tanizaki Junichiro, and Mishima Yukio, each of whom has made his own distinctive contribution to literature yet has also shown the influence of his training in awareness of both classical Japanese and contemporary foreign literary forms and topics.

Tokyo Imperial University continued its expansion during and after World War I, most notably in 1916, when it absorbed the Institute for Infectious Diseases, along with its attached hospital, both founded in 1894; in 1918, when its Aeronautical Research Institute was established; and in 1919, when a separate faculty of economics was created. However, many of the university's buildings were destroyed by the Great Kanto Earthquake of 1923,

which devastated much of Tokyo and Yokohama; they were replaced by a range of neo-Gothic structures which dominate a large part of the Hongo campus and include the General Library, partly financed by a donation from the Rockefeller Foundation. In addition, from 1925 the center of the Hongo campus was occupied by a new building, the Yasuda Auditorium, which was funded by a donation from the businessman Yasuda Zenjiro. The building has been used ever since for graduation ceremonies and other special events. In the same year the establishment of the Earthquake Research Institute indicated that at last John Milne's work was being taken seriously by the government.

During the early 1930s the uneasy official balance between enthusiasm for westernization and hostility toward it shifted decisively toward hostility, as the Japanese state came more and more under the influence of military leaders and conservative politicians committed to confrontation with the European colonial powers and their ally the United States, especially over the future of China. At home the reassertion of the state ideology, based on the concept of Japan's unique *kokutai* (literally, "national body"), involved increased interference in the education system, and the imperial universities in Tokyo, Kyoto, and elsewhere were all purged of the minority of liberals and Marxists who had been appointed as lecturers in the more tolerant era which had begun before World War I. The removal of Professor Minobe from Tokyo Imperial University, and his dismissal from the House of Nobles (the upper chamber of the Diet), was the best-known case. The fact that he was being punished for ideas expressed in a book published 25 years earlier indicates how thorough the purge was.

The triumph of ultra-nationalism was strikingly celebrated in October 1940, when the Yasuda Auditorium was used for a state celebration both of the 50th anniversary of the Imperial Rescript on Education and of the supposed 2,600th anniversary of the enthronement of the first emperor and the foundation of Japan. In 1941, as the armed forces prepared to launch the Pacific War, the university was required to create an Institute of Oriental Culture (which still exists), then intended to help in assimilating the conquered peoples of East and Southeast Asia to the "Co-Prosperity Sphere" established by Japan. In 1942, somewhat more practically, a temporary Second Faculty of Engineering was established to contribute to military research. Although the university was closed and its students were conscripted into the armed forces and the munitions industry in November 1943, two further institutes were created, with obvious relevance to the Pacific War but little actual effect: the Institute of Research in Natural Sciences of the Tropics, set up in 1944 (but closed in 1947), and the Radiation Chemistry Research Institute, founded in 1945, the year of the first two civilian-targeted atomic bombs and of Japan's unconditional surrender.

Under the Allied Occupation (1945–52) the university, renamed Tokyo Daigaku in 1947, was purged yet again, this time to remove the professors who had collaborated with the militarist regime, and the Aeronautical Research Institute was closed. The latest major reorganization of the university took place between 1947 and 1949, in response to the educational reforms introduced by the Occupation authorities. The former First Higher School and another "feeder" school, the Tokyo Koto Gakko (Tokyo Higher School), were absorbed into the university and reorganized to form its College of General Education, later called the College of Arts and Sciences, the body of which provides teaching for the first two years of the university's four-year degrees on the First Higher School's former campus at Komaba. Education and literature were separated into two faculties and the university created five more specialist institutes, those of social sciences, science and technology, physiography, industrial science, and journalism and communication studies. But perhaps the reform with the greatest long-term impact was that the university, like others controlled by the state, was opened to women students for the first time.

This new "democratic" institution retained its predecessors' prestigious role as the Japanese university most favored by the political and social elites. If anything, its importance increased, for with the abolition of the nobility, the disgrace of the armed forces, and extensive land reforms in the countryside, very few alternative routes to power and influence remained open in a society which gave increasing importance to educational records. Thus, for example, while most prime ministers of Japan before and during World War II were either self-made men of the Meiji period—rural magnates or soldiers—most since 1945 have been Tokyo graduates with experience as lawyers and/or government officials.

Somewhat paradoxically, however, this eminently respectable place was also a breeding ground for Marxists and other radicals (including many prominent members of the Communist Party, legalized after the defeat). Many of its students took part in the riots which erupted in May 1960 in response to the government's decision to disregard the opposition parties and force the renewed Security Treaty with the United States through the Diet. Eight years later the university became one of the leading centers for the large-scale agitation by student radicals which spread throughout the higher education system. In March 1968 proposals to reform the intern program for medical students sparked off a student strike in every faculty, and in April the graduation ceremony was abandoned, and the student radicals disrupted the formal welcome to new students. In June the police removed the protesters and restored order, but a second occupation of the Yasuda Auditorium began in July, driving administrative staff out of their offices in the building. Eventually squads of riot police were brought in to take control of the campus, on January 18 and 19, 1969, but the damage

to the Auditorium and the continuing demonstrations elsewhere on campus meant that in 1969 the entrance examinations were canceled altogether. The building could not be used until May 1971. In the meantime anti-American demonstrations arranged for Okinawa Day, on April 28, 1969, failed to attract the large numbers which the organizers expected, and in August a new university law was passed, giving the administration extra powers to suppress student protests and impose penalties if they failed to do so. The physical damage is estimated to have cost around 136 million yen (then around $380,000, U.S. dollars), but the damage to the university's reputation, though probably severe at the time, did not outlive the protests themselves.

With the distance of time, the student movement of the 1960s appears to have been a minor diversion from the university's fundamental character, which has changed remarkably little since its foundation. There are now approximately 24,000 students, of whom around one-eighth are women, within its 9 faculties, its graduate school, its 12 specialist institutes, and its medical research facilities. Like their radical predecessors, few of whom failed to conform in the end, most of these students can expect to enter one or other section of what is known in Japan as the *Todaibatsu* (the "Tokyo University faction"), the informal network of alumni in leading positions in government and business. In spite of the high academic and social standing of such rival universities as Kyoto, Keio, or Waseda, and the huge general expansion of higher education since 1947, such alumni still account for approximately one-third of all those entering the leading grades of the civil service and for approximately two out of every five executives in the large corporations which form the decisive sectors of Japan's dual economy. Within their ranks those who studied in the university's law faculty are even more prestigious than their fellows, for about one-sixth of its alumni regularly enter central government service, while approximately two-thirds take up posts in private enterprise. These men (and a very small number of women) have contributed, perhaps more than any other single group of Japanese people, to the exceptional stability of the political and economic structures of their country, as well as to the pervasiveness of the highly conformist attitudes acquired during their four years of studying in the faculty, which, in spite of its name, teaches political science and economics as well as legal theory.

It is probably a safe conclusion that if the University of Tokyo had not been created when it was, Japan might have been a very different country. In particular, the adoption of a variety of western ideas and institutions, and their adaptation to the Japanese context—disastrously between the two world wars, with considerable success since 1945—owe much to the work of the university's teachers, foreign and Japanese alike, and of its alumni, whether in public service, in business, or (not least) in the field of culture. The impact of the *Todaibatsu* on the development of modern Japan is up to the Japanese people themselves, who are, formally speaking, its owners and clients. If the past 120 years or so are any guide, the university can and will be changed as Japan changes. In this sense perhaps the chief lesson that its alumni have taken away from their years at "Todai" is the importance of adaptability.

Further Reading: W.G. Beasley's impressive history, *The Rise of Modern Japan* (New York: St. Martin's Press, 1990; second edition, London: Weidenfeld and Nicolson, 1995), and Edward Seidensticker's two volumes covering Tokyo since 1867, *Low City, High City* and *Tokyo Rising* (New York: Knopf, and London: Allen Lane, 1983 and 1990) usefully explain the national and local contexts of the university's development. More specific aspects of its history are dealt with in *Confucianism in Modern Japan: A Study of Conservatism in Japanese Intellectual History* by Warren W. Smith Jr. (Tokyo: Hokuseido Press, 1959), and *Governing Elites: Studies in Training and Selection,* a collection of essays edited by Rupert Wilkinson (Oxford: Oxford University Press, 1969).

—Patrick Heenan

UNIVERSITY OF TORONTO
(Toronto, Ontario, Canada)

Location: On the Saint George campus in the city of
Toronto, at Scarborough 21 miles to the east
and Erindale 21 miles to the west, with a
number of specialist institutes and medical
facilities at other sites.

Description: The largest university in Canada, a federation
of universities and colleges in and around
Toronto, with a total of around 39,000 full-time
and 18,000 part-time students.

Information: The Provost
University of Toronto
Toronto, Ontario MSS 1A1
Canada
(416) 978 2011

The University of Toronto is a unique mixture of universities and colleges that has developed over nearly 170 years, from its beginnings as a college controlled by the Church of England, through decades of conflict as a secular institution rivaling the universities created by the Christian churches of Ontario, to a period of expansion and diversification as a federation including its former rivals. Its teachers and alumni have contributed a great deal to Canada, especially to its politics and literature, during the twentieth century, as the university and the country alike have moved decisively away from their roots in Christian faith and colonial reverence for Britain.

The oldest section of what is now the University of Toronto was established in 1827 at the suggestion of the prominent Anglican priest John Strachan, later to become the first bishop of Toronto. At that time Toronto was already a provincial capital, under the name York, while Ontario was then called Upper Canada. Because the new institution was granted a charter by King William IV, it was named King's College, but because it was the only institution of higher education in the province it was also known as the Provincial University. Strachan was its first president. Its governors and its teachers were required to be members of the Church, although its students were not. The intention was to create a collegiate body, along the lines of the medieval colleges of Oxford and Cambridge, in that part of North America that had remained loyal to the British crown.

The establishment of such an institution at that date, as well as its controversial dependence on public funds, reflected the privileged position of the Church of England

under the colonial constitution imposed by the British in 1791, which had made it the officially established church of Upper Canada and given it one-seventh of all the lands in the province. But its creation was also due to the local influence of what is known as the "Family Compact," a small group of wealthy citizens who then dominated the city's affairs and who favored the established Church of England against other Protestant churches that were associated in their minds with subversive tendencies toward American notions of democracy and republicanism. As the city grew, becoming ethnically and religiously more mixed and being renamed Toronto (in 1834), the influence of this elite was increasingly resented, and in 1837 they were the main target of a brief rebellion led by the city's mayor, William Lyon Mackenzie. The rising failed, but it played some part in influencing the British imperial authorities to enforce a union between Upper and Lower Canada (now Ontario and Quebec) in 1841. In these circumstances it proved impossible to operate the college. Its first students were not admitted until 1843, and it did not award any degrees until the following year.

In the meantime the Wesleyan Methodist Church had established its own rival body, Upper Canada Academy, at Cobourg in 1836. In 1841 it was renamed Victoria College and given the power to grant degrees. In 1850 it was designated a university, in 1854 it took over the Toronto School of Medicine, and in 1860 it created a law faculty. Despite the addition of faculties, theology remained the university's principal discipline, having been taught from the outset in a seminary for the training of the church's ministers. This seminary was to be renamed Emmanuel College and separated from Victoria University in 1925, the same year that the Wesleyan Methodists joined the United Church of Canada.

Controversy over providing public money raised from taxpayers of all denominations to King's College, a sectarian body, had helped to delay the college's opening, and debate broke out again after the union of Upper and Lower Canada, for the parliament of the united colony, based in Montreal, had a majority of non-Anglicans, principally the French-speaking Catholics of Quebec. In 1849 the parliament voted to sever the college's connection with the Church, so that from 1850 the college became a secular institution, the University of Toronto, and its faculty of divinity was closed. (Because of this important change in character and name many reference books give the date of foundation as 1849 or 1850 rather than 1827.)

The newly secularized university was intended by Robert Baldwin, the premier who had originated the change, to become a federation of Ontario colleges. However, precisely because it lacked religious tests for either staff or students, a then-radical feature which, among all the universities of the British empire, it shared only with the University of London, the churches rejected any association with it. Instead, in 1851 Bishop Strachan, who had given up the presidency of King's in 1848, created a new establishment to be owned and operated by the Church of England, the University of Trinity College, which had an almost entirely British faculty and was enthusiastically supported by the Tory (conservative) elements in the city. In 1852 Bishop Charbonnel of Toronto, head of the Catholic Church in Upper Canada, established the University of Saint Michael's College, operated by the order of the Basilian Fathers.

In 1853 the University of Toronto was reorganized along the lines of the University of London, which had been established in 1836 as an examining body serving a group of colleges. The Provincial College, as the teaching faculties were renamed once the medical and law faculties had been closed, was to be the only college in this system for more than 30 years, because the religious institutions still declined the implied invitation to join.

At first both the university's officials and examiners and the Provincial College's teachers and students carried on sharing the use of the original site of King's College, some distance from the center of the city, a position which probably enhanced the mutual suspicion between the conservative middle classes of Toronto and the allegedly radical teachers at the university. But in 1859 both institutions moved into a new Romanesque building on the 160-acre Saint George's campus, near the provincial parliament building in central Toronto; the area has been at the heart of the university's activities ever since.

With the creation of the Canadian federation under the British North America Act of 1867 the former Upper Canada had been reestablished as the province of Ontario and from then onward the provincial parliament, once again based in Toronto, had refused to make any further grants of aid to the three church-owned colleges, which therefore faced increasing financial difficulties. In 1881 the Catholic University of Saint Michael's College accepted a form of affiliation with the University of Toronto. This action gave it access to public funds but preserved its academic independence; however, the other churches still resisted compromise with what they saw as a "godless" institution.

In spite of such persistent hostility the provincial university steadily extended its influence and made itself part of the life of Ontario. In 1878 a new affiliate, the School of Practical Science, was opened to provide advanced training in engineering, and in 1884 the provincial parliament forced the Provincial College, against the wishes of its President, Sir Daniel Wilson, to admit women students on equal terms with men, one year after Victoria University had become the first institution in Ontario to award a degree to a woman. In the same year the chancellor of the

University of Toronto was able to boast that 51 of the 94 principals of secondary schools had been graduates of the university, trained in the province, and 73 of the 98 assistant principals had been educated at the university. Serious discussions started, also in 1884, on some form of federation among the various colleges and universities; they culminated in 1887 in the passage of the Federation Act by the provincial parliament, providing for a federal University of Toronto which would have supervisory and examining powers over whichever colleges elected to join it.

As a result, the Provincial College was renamed University College, and its medical and law faculties were reestablished, but the process of federation envisaged by the politicians was not so rapid as they expected. The first new members of the university, besides University College itself, were the Royal College of Dental Surgeons, established in 1875, which joined in 1888, and two small theological colleges, the Church of England's Wycliffe College, founded in 1877, and the Presbyterian Church's Knox College, established in 1844, which joined in 1889 and 1890 respectively. It was also in 1890 that the Wesleyan Methodist Victoria University joined the federation, moving from Cobourg to the Saint George's campus two years later. By 1891 the university was examining around 1,500 candidates a year. The Royal Conservatory of Music, which had been established in 1886, affiliated in 1896, and, finally, the Anglican University of Trinity College completed the federation in 1904. (Two prominent Ontario universities have never joined the federation: Queen's University at Kingston, founded by the Presbyterian Church in 1842, and McMaster University, which was founded in 1887 in Toronto but moved to Hamilton in 1927.)

In 1905 a center for part-time students was established on the Saint George's campus as the first stage in what was to become a major aspect of the university's teaching. From 1920 this center was the headquarters of the extension department, providing a range of courses for part-time students, some of whom took the university degree. In 1974 the department was divided into a school of continuing studies for noncredit courses and a separate school for part-time degree students, Woodsworth College. Part-time students now account for around 30 percent of the total student body, a proportion which is among the highest in Canada and significantly higher than the numbers in most universities in North America and western Europe.

Under the University of Toronto Act of 1906, the federation was formally reconstituted to regulate its relations with the provincial authorities and to take account of the informal division of labor which had developed among its constituent parts. Its finances were to be managed by a board of governors appointed by the provincial government but its academic affairs were to be conducted by a senate representing all of the affiliates, a system of joint control intended to remove the university's business from party political controversy. From 1910 Victoria, Saint Michael's, and Trinity were restricted to providing courses leading to theology degrees, which were to be granted by the universities themselves (which is why they have retained the designation "university"), alongside courses in classics, modern languages, Near Eastern studies, and ancient history, leading to degrees awarded by the University of Toronto. Knox and Wycliffe Colleges remained exclusively theological colleges serving the churches that had founded them, while University College and the extension department offered courses across the whole academic range, leading to University of Toronto degrees and certificates.

The secular affiliates had always been much larger than the religious ones in terms of student numbers, and under the leadership of Sir Robert Falconer, president from 1907 to 1932, they seized the opportunity to expand further. Faculties of home economics, education, forestry, social work, nursing, and hygiene were established on Saint George's campus between 1906 and 1926, and graduate studies were given a new emphasis, with increased provincial funding and a separate school opened in 1922. In addition the university acquired and helped to develop three notable non-teaching affiliates. The first of these, the University of Toronto Press, was established in 1901, expanded in 1911, and refounded as a commercial publishing company in 1945. It publishes learned journals, including the *University of Toronto Quarterly* (since 1931), academic books, and, perhaps most famously, the monumental *Dictionary of Canadian Biography*. Another affiliate, the Royal Ontario Museum, established in Toronto in 1914, has since built up some of Canada's largest and most important collections in Oriental art, natural history, and other fields.

In 1921 came the opening of a third affiliate, Hart House, a center for extracurricular activities which is one of the parts of the university best known to the Canadian public. Its construction on the Saint George's campus and many of its early activities in sport and the arts were financed by the Massey Foundation and the building, like the foundation, commemorates the manufacturing magnate Hart Massey, but its establishment was due to his son Vincent Massey. He had been a lecturer in modern history at the university from 1913 to 1915 and was later to become chancellor of the university (from 1947) and the first Canadian citizen to serve as governor-general of Canada (from 1952 to 1959). Hart House's collection of Canadian paintings, including many works by the Toronto-based Group of Seven, has become one of the largest in the country, while the string quartet, orchestra, and theater company which bear its name have achieved independent reputations.

While the press and Hart House have somewhat specialized reputations within their fields of activity, and most visitors to the museum are unaware of its connection with the university, one event which took place in Toronto in 1921 has probably done more than anything else to make the University of Toronto famous. This was the discovery and first manufacture of insulin, the hormone which regulates blood sugar levels, by Doctor Frederick Banting, a Toronto alumnus who had in fact started his research at the University of Western Ontario, and Charles H. Best, one of his students at Toronto. Their achievement has since immeasurably improved and extended the lives of people with diabetes mellitus (who are deficient in natural insulin). In 1923 Banting and John Macleod, the chairman of the physiology department, were awarded the Nobel Prize for physiology or medicine: Banting shared his prize money with Best. Banting and Best are now commemorated by a department of medical research named for them, which opened in 1930 with Banting as its first director; by two graduate institutes named for each of them during the 1960s; and, indirectly, by the continuing manufacture of insulin at the university's Connaught Laboratories.

After some disruption of its activities during World War II, as many of its teachers and students departed Toronto for civil service posts or military service, the university entered the 1950s as the largest and one of the most academically prestigious universities in Canada, alongside McGill in Montreal, Queen's in Kingston and the newer but rapidly growing universities of the western provinces. With the support of the provincial parliament as well as increasing research funds and other financial aid from the Canadian federal government it was able to begin a new phase of expansion. In 1958 it established an Institute of Business Administration, a graduate school which rapidly gained an international reputation; in 1959 York University was founded as an affiliate of the university, although it became a separate institution, awarding its own degrees, in 1965.

Greater changes came during the 1960s, as the secular university increased its student numbers and expanded its range of academic and residential provision by creating five more "constituent" colleges, in addition to University College and the extension department. New College, established in 1962, has built up a reputation of its own by specializing in Canadian literature and, more recently, in women's studies and in interdisciplinary courses, while Massey College, an all-graduate body opened in 1963, had as its founding master the distinguished Canadian novelist Robertson Davies, who also taught in the university's English faculty and its drama center up to his retirement from the university in 1981. The remaining three colleges were all established in 1964 and opened to students in 1965 and 1966: Innis College, near the main campus in Toronto, Erindale College, located in Mississauga nearby, and Scarborough College in the city of that name, 21 miles from the provincial capital.

During the 1960s two alumni of Toronto achieved prominence in Canadian life, one at the end of his career, the other at the beginning of hers. National politics came to be dominated by Lester B. Pearson, who, like Vincent Massey, had once lectured in history at the university (between 1924 and 1928) and had gone on to distinguish himself both in the diplomatic service and in the Liberal Party. Unlike Massey, whose career led him into ceremonial posts, Pearson went on to win the Nobel Peace Prize in 1957, specifically for his contribution to resolving the crisis over the Suez Canal but more generally for developing the concept of United Nations peacekeeping forces. In 1963 he became prime minister of Canada, retiring in 1968 after helping to initiate the major social and constitutional reforms which have come to be associated with his successor Pierre Trudeau. Meanwhile, during the same decade of national resurgence the novelist and poet Margaret Atwood, having graduated from Victoria University in 1961, published the first of her many books, among which *The Handmaid's Tale* is perhaps the best known.

The federal arrangements within the University of Toronto have continued to develop, becoming, if anything, even more complex. In 1969 seven theological colleges in Toronto, including, within the university federation, Knox, Wycliffe, Emmanuel, and the divinity faculties of Saint Michael's and Trinity, came together to form the Toronto School of Theology, which since 1979 has also included the university's most recent affiliate, the Jesuits' Regis College. In 1971 the board of governors and the senate were replaced by a single governing council. In 1973 the university opened the John P. Robarts Research Library, which serves as the central research and reference library in the humanities and social sciences for all the universities and colleges in Ontario. It is also the largest among the 49 sections of the university's own library system which, with total holdings of more than 7 million volumes, is the largest academic library anywhere in Canada. Finally (for now), since 1978 degrees in divinity have been awarded jointly by Victoria, Saint Michael's, or Trinity with the federal university, putting the seal on a cooperative relationship which the founders of the respective universities can hardly have imagined.

With its three federated universities, its four federated theological colleges, its six constituent colleges, and its numerous other affiliates—including, besides those already mentioned, 11 teaching hospitals, the Pontifical Institute of Medieval Studies, the David Dunlap Observatory at Richmond Hill, Ontario, and even a 20,000-acre university forest—the University of Toronto is one of the leading academic institutions in North America. Few of its students, now numbering more than 56,000 (including nearly 11,000 postgraduates), can have seen, let alone used, all of its facilities, which represent, in their bewildering variety, the accumulated legacy of nearly 60 years of sectarian and political controversy followed by more than a century of continuous growth, in response to the developing needs and wishes of Toronto, Ontario, and Canada.

Further Reading: *A History of the University of Toronto 1827–1927,* by W.S. Wallace (Toronto: University of Toronto Press, 1927) is still obtainable from larger libraries; Frederick H. Armstrong's *Toronto: The Place of Meeting* (Windsor, Ontario: Windsor Publications, 1983) is an impressive history of the city which places the development of the city's institutions of higher education in its local context.

—Monique Lamontagne

UNIVERSITY OF VALENCIA
(Valencia, Spain)

Location: On three campuses in Valencia, a port city in eastern Spain.

Description: A state university enrolling approximately 60,000 students in undergraduate, graduate, and professional studies.

Information: International Affairs Unit
University of Valencia
C/Nave 2 bojo
46003 Valencia
Spain
3864180

Plans for building a university in Valencia began in the thirteenth century, when the province was still a medieval kingdom. After capturing Spain from the Muslims in 1245, King James I, "the Conqueror," gave his consent, along with the pope, for the building of an *estudio,* or college, in the city. But the school, a municipal rather than royal foundation, never materialized; in 1374 city officials hired a teacher only to have him excommunicated by the bishop, who claimed that he presented unfair competition. Soon, however, freedom of education had been decreed, and state institutions sprang up throughout the area. Schools, unified by Vicente Ferrer and regulated by the 1412 constitutions, taught grammar, logic, and philosophy; in 1462, a surgery school was also opened, spurring progress in medical education in the region.

In the late fifteenth century, the magistrates of the city advanced the idea of building a university, or *estudi general,* that would incorporate the various schools as one institution. By 1499 statutes were drawn up and several buildings acquired. Pere Compte, the most famous Valencian architect of the day, was hired to convert the buildings into a suitable structure. In 1500 Pope Alexander VI, himself a Valencian, granted the university the necessary bull; two years later, King Ferdinand, "the Catholic," gave his approval as well.

The founding of the University of Valencia was part of a wider revolution in European education that emerged at the beginning of the sixteenth century. Political, religious, and social changes, shifts in demographics, and technological advances, such as the development of the printing press, all fueled the explosion in higher education; throughout Europe the number of universities, and university students, burgeoned. Spain created particularly vibrant cultural institutions, most of them supported by the intellectualism of the church; so great, in fact, were Spain's contributions to theology, philosophy, law, and art that the sixteenth and early seventeenth centuries have become known as the country's "golden century."

Because of Valencia's strong municipal interest in developing its university, and the university's links to other educational centers throughout Europe, it flourished throughout the sixteenth century, becoming competitive even with the great Castilian universities of Salamanca and Alcala. In fact, in areas such as medicine, the university even surpassed them, providing, in the eighteenth century, the first real break from the traditional Castilian emphasis on legal studies. By 1690 Valencia was the intellectual center of Spain; its university, situated in a port city with all the attendant cosmopolitan influences, was better exposed to modern scientific thought than most Spanish institutions. Foreign influences from the University of Montpellier, just over the French border, and from scientists in Italy were also important. Well known for its medical curriculum, the university was also respected for its studies in Latin and in the arts, though in theology, law, and canonical studies it was inferior.

In the mid-seventeenth century, the university's paranimf, or academic theater, was built. Used at first for academic debates, staff meetings, and public events, it was later used to stage plays, most notably the comedies of Roman dramatists Plautus and Terence, which were performed in their original language. Ornate and grandly proportioned, the trapezoidal ground floor is surrounded by a projecting gallery and wide vault decorated with trompe l'oeil mouldings. Dominating it is a 1660 painting by Jeronimo Jacinto Espinosa depicting the Immaculate Conception over an idealized scene of Valencia.

Though the University of Valencia had become a leader in education, it was to fall prey to the same cultural and economic forces that, startng in the early 1600s, were pushing the rest of the country's universities into precipitous decline. Institutions throughout Spain lost substantial numbers of students, and the quality of education eroded. Having been a cultural leader in Europe, Spain increasingly found itself out of step with a more secular outside world.

Spain's universities, which like the rest of the society were steeped in tradition and, in particular, Roman Catholicism, and still practiced medieval scholasticism, favoring verbose, theoretical arguments over scientific exploration. According to the historian Ballesteros, Spanish theology students still theorized about what language the angels spoke and of what materials the heavens consisted; texts were outdated and good maps were nonexistent. Many stu-

University of Valencia

dents were convinced that higher mathematics was a hoax and that the works of major European philosophers and scientists were meaningless. University degrees increasingly became merely a means to confer status and taught students little of practical value. The ideological constraints of the Inquisition also were stifling. During this period philosopher and humanist Juan Luis Vives, a member of the faculty at Valencia, went into exile.

In 1707 the Bourbons established rule in Spain, and Philip V severed Valencia's connection with Aragon, suspending the autonomy of the province and imposing Castilian law. Anti-French attitudes in the city were reinforced by the new regime, forcing it to centralize control of the area to a greater degree than originally planned. Nevertheless, a general upturn in Spain's economy benefited the region: trade increased, the population stabilized, and Valencia itself, the fourth largest city in the country, remained an important cultural center on the eastern coast. In 1717 Philip V instituted curricular and other reforms in universities throughout the country; in 1720, he conferred official university status upon Valencia.

But more important to the university than political reforms was the Spanish Enlightenment, which, though far more muted than the movement in Europe, introduced scientific thought and processes to university life. For the first time in decades, higher education began to show signs of vigor. Along with the University of Oviedo, the University of Valencia became a center of Enlightenment thought, due in part to the presence of two esteemed scholars. Andres [or Jose Antonio] Piquer, a professor of medicine and philosophy at the university, introduced modern physics to Spain and helped reform medical studies. Gregoria Mayans y Siscar was the country's first great modern polymath. Together their works promoted new ideas about medicine, jurisprudence, and ecclesiastical reform that were influential outside the province as well as within the university itself.

Such progressive thought attracted controversy, however. Piquer, writing in 1771, outlined the ideological battle raging in Spain and addressed the conservative attacks that he and other reformist thinkers increasingly were facing:

There reign among us two equally concerned factions. One cries against our nation in favor of foreign lands, praising highly the flourishing of the arts and sciences, politics and the enlightenment of the understanding in them. Others abhor whatever comes from without and reject it merely for being foreign. The concern of both factions is equal, but in number, activity and power the first prevails.

Because of Piquer, Mayans, and other university scholars such as Francisco Perez Bayer, the study of law, medicine, and the humanities assumed greater importance at the university. But while progress was being made in some areas, it was resisted in others: the religious reformation occurring elsewhere in Europe was firmly rejected by Spanish universities, and the study of theology at Valencia remained deeply conservative.

Indeed, religion was the central force behind academic life at the university. The chapel, or Capella de la Sapiencia, had, since its erection in 1498, been the site of *sabatines,* or academic discussions between professors and students, and was the center of religious and cultural events, including the conferring of degrees. In 1736 the chapel was reconstructed in classic Baroque style; the new structure featured a single nave with an oval dome at the front and a high chancel at back. In 1780 the chapel was redecorated and Valencia's leading painters, including Jose and Manuel Camaron, Luis Planes, and Jose Vergara, were commissioned to provide artwork for it. When the university building was bombed by Napoléon's troops in 1808 the ensuing fire destroyed the library but left the chapel and academic theater intact. Work to restore the building continued throughout the nineteenth century.

With the Enlightenment and advent of the French revolution, the modern sciences of economics and political theory took on new meaning at Spanish universities, and those changes combined with legislative reforms of Philip V, Fernando VI, and Carlos III resulted in the emergence of a more modern university structure. In 1836 the religious content of university studies was reduced, shifting the focus to the liberal arts. But at Valencia and elsewhere, reform also meant the loss of economic and institutional autonomy. A new law in 1842 gave the government greater control over universities and centralized educational finance. The trend toward government control continued with the creation of a new ministry of education. The building of the Universidad Central in Madrid was meant to provide a model for the University of Valencia and other schools undergoing expansion. Political and ecclesiastical reform had other, perhaps unintended, benefits for Valencia: its library was enriched by a collection of books from the San Miguel de los Reyes Monastery, when it was secularized in 1836. A museum of natural history was also created at the university, but it was destroyed by fire in 1931.

The construction of the *Claustre Major* (the Cloister) began at the university in 1840. Designed by Timoteo Calvo as a striking two-story trapezoid and completed by Joaquin Martinez, Sebastian Monleon, and Javier Goerlich, the Cloister commemorates important individuals in the university's history. It features a statue of Luis Vives, portraits of Vincente Blasco and San Vicente Ferrer, and wall medallions picturing the school's founders. Work on the Cloister continued until 1960, when the extension of Patriarca Square and the construction of a fountain was completed. As time passed various faculties began to move from this central building to nearby sites, leaving the university's historic headquarters. Today the original university building houses the rectorate, a museum, a library, and administrative and cultural services.

The Spanish civil war divided the country's universities into two opposing camps; Valencia joined Barcelona, Madrid, and Murcia under the Republican flag, while Salamanca, Seville, and the others fell under Nationalist control. The city of Valencia was bombed frequently, and after the war was so associated with the Republican cause it continued to suffer politically for years.

In 1939 General Francisco Franco ordered that universities again be governed by both church and state and that religious education once more become an important force in academic life. Student syndicates operated by the Falange, a Fascist political movement begun in 1933 and exploited by Franco, existed on all campuses, and exerted control over both students and faculty, many of whom knew that membership was the key to political advancement. After 1956, however, students were instrumental in the anti-Franco opposition; their protests resulted in the cancellation of the school year in 1965. A new law gave universities freedom from political control in 1970, but student agitation for easier entrance into universities led to riots in early 1987.

Today, under a democratic national government, the University of Valencia is attempting to modernize. In the 1980s, in order to cope with an increasing number of students, it reorganized its academic departments. It now employs approximately 2,300 faculty and staff members in 75 departments covering the social sciences, biomedicine, and the humanities, and, after the University of Barcelona and the Complutense of Madrid, is the country's third largest university.

The university is now divided into three campuses: the Campus de Burjassot; the Campus de Blasco Ibanez; and the Campus de la Avenida dels Tarongers, each of which houses a different concentration of studies. Though many of the university's buildings are modern, considerable energy is devoted to maintaining its historical structures. In 1985 restoration work on the chapel was begun. It reopened in 1990 and once again hosts both cultural and religious events. The Paranimf was also restored in 1985, and provides a venue for formal events such as the opening of the academic year.

The central library's Codex Room houses the university's many historical art works: among them are a 1546 map drawn by Majoring Jacobus Russus; a celestial sphere and terrestrial globe crafted in Holland in the seventeenth century; a silver Renaissance chalice that belonged to Pope Alexander VI; and the Valencian voluntary service flag representing students who fought in the defense of Zaragoza in 1808. The room also contains books illustrated in Italy by early Renaissance artists for King Alfonso V, "the Magnanimous."

Further Reading: Both the *Historical Dictionary of Modern Spain 1700–1988* (New York: Greenwood, 1990) and Stanley G. Payne's *A History of Spain and Portugal* (Madison: University of Wisconsin Press, 1973) are excellent sources of information about the formation and evolution of Spanish universities.

—Melanie Wilson

UNIVERSITY OF VIENNA
(Vienna, Austria)

Location: On the western edge of the old section of Vienna, in the concourse with the parliament buildings.

Description: A public university enrolling approximately 85,000 students in undergraduate and graduate schools.

Information: Administrative Office
University of Vienna
Dr. Karl Lueger Ring 1
A-1010 Vienna
Austria
(222) 431 40103

As the oldest university in the German-speaking countries of Europe, the University of Vienna is steeped in the history of Europe, dating back to its founding in 1365 by Duke Rudolf IV and his two brothers, the Archduke Albrecht III and Leopold III.

Created as an act of national policy, the University of Vienna and the universities of Prague, Cracow, and Heidelberg were intended to be centers for the intelligentsia and to entice scholars, thereby strengthening kingdoms whose histories bore the ravages of war.

During this era, Europe saw the powerful religious resurgence that led to the creation of Protestantism. This period of reformation found authorities in many cities expropriating ecclesiastical revenues used to financially support clerics at universities.

Confirmed by papal bull, the university was established as an autonomous institution. Allocated meager financial provisions by its founders, it was without a faculty of theology until 1384, at which time Albrecht III arranged for the inclusion of a theological department, a measure that gave the school full university status.

The university's founders took their administrative practices from the University of Paris and as such grouped teachers into faculties or departments and grouped students according to nations.

Student population rose once the faculty of theology was established, with enrollment numbers increasing rapidly. In 1390, some 350 students were enrolled at the University of Vienna, a number that doubled 20 years later. During this period, the university enrolled the majority of young male scholars from throughout the Holy Roman Empire. Increased enrollments also paved the way for prestigious professors to teach at the Viennese institution.

By the fifteenth century, the university's school of mathematics and astronomy boasted on its staff Regiomontanus, also known as Johann Muller, who published the first printed calendar and developed modern trigonometry, among his other accomplishments.

The period between the late fifteenth and early sixteenth centuries found the university becoming one of the most recognized in Europe. As such, it attracted celebrated scholars, including humanist Conrad Celtis and physician/poet Johannes Cuspinian. But the days of academic prosperity came to an abrupt halt when, in the early sixteenth century, all European institutions of higher learning suffered through the upheaval of the Reformation.

Additionally, growing theological differences reduced the student population at many learned institutions, including the University of Vienna. Moreover, financial deficits found some professors going without payment for their services, a predicament that led to the near extinction of the faculties of law and theology at the University of Vienna.

Not only did enrollment at the European universities decline, but the intellectual advances that had been made during the beginning of the Middle Ages were lost in large degree during the waning years of that period. Life in northern Europe during the sixteenth century was predicated on the notion that man was sinful and ruled by a capricious God. Centers of learning endured during this era of religious, social, and economic turbulence, however, and by 1554, Austrian ruler Ferdinand I and his imperial government opted to maintain the University of Vienna. That decision prompted financial support, larger endowments, and the hiring of several noted Jesuit scholars, whose control of the university's faculty of theology was complete by 1558. Jesuit dominance in both the faculties of theology and philosophy continued for nearly two centuries following the Reformation.

One price for Ferdinand I's support was increasing state control of the university; by the 1700s, the institution was completely state-directed due to educational reforms made in the eighteenth century by the Empress Maria Theresa, Emperor Joseph II, and Emperor Leopold II. The university's prior autonomy was lost and the school formerly recognized for its theological studies showed small progress, save for some advancements in the faculties of law and medicine. Among those developments was the construction in 1784 of the *Allgemeine Krankenhaus,* the largest and most up-to-date clinic in the world at that time.

While some attempts to change the existing formal curriculum were made during the 1830s, not until "the year of revolution," 1848, did those reforms actually occur. Triggered by the crop failures of 1846 and a subsequent eco-

University of Vienna

nomic depression, the revolutions of 1848 began in Paris, where a working-class insurrection was overpowered, and a national assembly controlled by the middle class and headed by a democratically elected legislature and executive body was established. After the Paris uprisings, similar demonstrations were played out in Vienna, resulting in conservative minister Klemens von Metternich's departure from office. The university had been at the heart of the uprisings in Vienna, a fact that the imperial army, which had been bested by the demonstrators, would not forgive or forget. The army occupied the university's quarters in the center of the city and forced the university to occupy scattered sites around the city.

The stage was then set for the 1849–51 reforms at the University of Vienna, changes that were effected by Minister of Education, Count Leo Thun-Hohenstein. With a portion of its original autonomy restored, the university asserted the long-thwarted objective of establishing freedom in its teaching and research facilities. Count Thun-

Hohenstein's one attempt to redesign the structure of the university came in 1849 when he tried to remove the school from the shadow of the Viennese Revolution of 1848 and restore it to sovereignty, but with strong ties to both church and state. Between 1853 and 1868, Thun-Hohenstein and his supporters tried in vain to create a new English- and Gothic-style university area in the city as a way of equating the university with the Vienna of centuries past, but the institution did not receive a new face and high place of honor on its boulevard until 1868 when a liberal-minded Vienna City Council, interested in the advancement of education, supported the concept of a new building plan for the university.

The neo-Italian Renaissance style of the university was chosen to illustrate the school's historical link between modern culture and the resurgence of secular learning in the Renaissance. To the liberals in power, the building also served as a symbol of the demise of what they perceived to be a protracted era of medieval ideology. Architect Heinrich Ferstel was commissioned to design the "new" university, an assignment that took him to Italy and the universities of Padua, Genoa, Bologna, and Rome, where he studied the design inherent in a country epitomizing the Renaissance.

The university's location in Vienna's Ringstrasse (Ring Street) places it in the heart of the city, situated within an expansive, circular area where it shares the spacious concourse with, among other structures, the Parliament building, the city park, and the Burgtheater. The "ring street" affords its occupants independence from one another, as trees running along its entire length create a sense of separation of one building from the next, a perception that is further heightened by the architectural differences of the Ringstrasse buildings.

Architectural modification was just one aspect of the reshaping of the university that came about during the latter portion of the nineteenth century. In 1873, the post of chancellor that had previously been the highest-ranking position was reduced to chancellor of the theological faculty. The school's original constitution was further dissolved when, in the same year, the faculties or departments were designated as individual teaching bodies. But that dissolution was the impetus for continued reorganization of the university's system, with a new building program activated to house the increasing number of departments. Another change came when women were allowed entry into the University of Vienna in 1897; however, they were confined to studies in the faculty of philosophy. Both genders were accepted to the faculty of medicine in 1900 and to the faculty of law in 1920.

The next decade brought war, and with it came serious ramifications for the faculty of medicine, then containing a group of leading researchers. In 1938, when Germany annexed Austria, more than 75 percent of the department's professors were forced to resign for political or ethnic reasons. While the political and fiscal turmoil that followed World War II had adverse effects on all European universities, the University of Vienna was again opened by May 29, 1945, and some nine years later its reorganization was complete. The 1960s brought a broadening of student enrollment, an increase that has been perennial, bringing present student counts to approximately 85,000, representing 121 countries.

Recent curriculum changes have affected several university faculties. The past two decades have resulted in major additions to the Protestant theology course study. Currently, course study includes canon law, Christian archaeology, and biblical art, in addition to the more traditional subjects of Old and New Testament studies and church history. In addition to religious course study, six other departments comprise the university.

The faculty of law, one of the original departments created when the university was founded, currently enrolls more than 10,000 students, a figure that represents some 46 percent of all Austrian law students. Divided into 13 departments, the faculty of law centers its study around civil, penal, constitutional, and administrative law. Research focuses not only on Austrian statutes but also on international and comparative law.

The faculty of social studies and economics, created in 1976 and once called the faculty of law and political science, enrolls 6,100 students. Courses within the department include sociology, statistics, public sector management, quantitative economics, and international business. The five departments within the faculty of social studies and economics uphold ties with institutions with similar curricula in the United States, the United Kingdom, Hungary, France, Germany, and the former Czech and Slovak Federal Republic.

The university has had a major impact on the international economic scene. Eugen Bohm-Bawerk (who three times served as Austria's minister of finance) and Friedrich von Weiser developed the Austrian theory of capital—based on the concept of final utility; the philosophy was to be important in several countries. Joseph Schumpteter, who was instrumental in bringing Austrian economic theories to the United States, became a professor at Harvard University in 1932 and served for nearly 30 years. His influential work, *Business Cycles,* was published in 1939.

The present university is a publicly maintained center of higher learning, with enrollment open to anyone who has obtained an Austrian school-leaving certificate or the equivalent. The academic head is the rector, who is elected for two years and is charged with making all significant decisions in joint collaboration with representatives of the university's faculties.

Recently celebrating its 630th anniversary, the University of Vienna, which embraces the motto "In Quest of Knowledge," can lay claim to having educated more than 1 million students since its beginnings in the fourteenth century. Luminaries of the scientific, political, and entertainment worlds are among those receiving degrees from this largest university in Austria. Among notable graduates are Sir Rudolf Bing, the former general manager and artistic director of the Metropolitan Opera, and Theodor Herzl, the founder of modern Zionism. Kurt Waldheim, president of Austria from 1986 to 1992, was graduated from the school's faculty of law.

Further Reading: A book that provides information about the university in the context of its city is *Fin-de-Siècle Vienna,* by Carl E. Schorske (New York: Knopf, 1980). Another source of information is *The Universities of Europe, 1100–1914,* by Willis Rudy (Madison, New Jersey: Fairleigh Dickinson University Press, 1984).

—Sharon Nery

UNIVERSITY OF VIRGINIA
(Charlottesville, Virginia, U.S.A.)

Location: Charlottesville, Virginia, 120 miles southwest of Washington, D.C.

Description: A state university enrolling approximately 18,000 students in undergraduate, graduate, and professional schools.

Information: Office of Admission
Box 9017
Charlottesville, VA 22906
U.S.A.
(804) 982-3200

Visiting: Guided tours of the Rotunda and the Lawn are available year-round. For more information, call the phone number above.

Although he had held such prestigious posts as governor of Virginia, secretary of state, and president of the United States, Thomas Jefferson ordered that his epitaph identify him as the author of the Declaration of American Independence and the statute of Virginia for religious freedom, and as father of the University of Virginia. Jefferson achieved this final goal at the end of his life, despite problems both physical and financial. He personally supervised every phase of the founding of the university from the physical design to the curriculum to the hiring of professors.

As early as 1800 Jefferson began corresponding with various learned friends about the design of a university, his dream being a state university for Virginia, in addition to the College of William and Mary. The "ancestor" of the University of Virginia was Albemarle Academy, which had existed on paper since the beginning of the nineteenth century. After Jefferson was appointed to its board of trustees in 1814, he recommended its transformation into an institution of higher learning, Central College.

Jefferson himself wrote the petition to the general assembly seeking a charter. In soliciting legislative support for his institution, Jefferson wrote to Colonel Charles Yancy that he envisioned "a university where might be taught, in its highest degree, every branch of science [knowledge] useful in our time and country." He continued, explaining his belief in mass education: "If a nation expects to be ignorant and free, in a state of civilization, it expects what never was and what never will be."

The body approved the creation of Central College on February 6, 1816, and in October, a board of visitors [trustees] was established, including not only Jefferson but President James Monroe and former president James Madison. The cornerstone for the first building (designed by Jefferson), Pavilion VII, was laid in 1817, with Jefferson, Madison, and Monroe in attendance. When the legislature approved plans for a state university in January 1818, it created a 24-member commission to plan the institution. Conscious of his failing health but passionate in his desire to oversee his project personally, Jefferson pressed for the university to be located at Charlottesville, a short distance from his Monticello home, arguing that Central College was already in existence there and available to be transformed into the new state university. When the commission voted, the Charlottesville site won handily. In March 1819, the board of visitors elected Jefferson rector of the university.

In his architectural plans for the university, Jefferson fused the practical and the artistic, adapting his European models to suit the American landscape. Architectural historian William H. Pierson Jr., described Jefferson's achievement:

> Thoroughly anti-British in his attitude toward architecture, and consciously seeking a mode of building symbolic of the new republic, he discovered what he considered an appropriate idiom in two non-English sources, the Neoclassical architecture of contemporary France, and the architecture of ancient Rome. From these he created an intensely personal style. . . . Rational at the same time that it was romantic, it remains one of the most brilliant creative outbursts of the entire Neoclassical movement.

The buildings designed by Jefferson—his "academical village"— remain the centerpiece of the university. The focus is the Lawn, a rectangular, terraced green flanked on each side by two rows of dormitories connected by colonnades, with ten pavilions for the professors spaced at intervals. At the center of the north side is the Rotunda, a sphere within a cylinder, 70 feet in diameter, half that of its prototype, the Pantheon in Rome. The Rotunda housed the library, lecture room, and other facilities, including a gymnasium and America's first planetarium. In keeping with Jefferson's desire to stress the intellectual aspects of education, the university's central building was a library, not a chapel.

Pierson finds Jefferson's campus especially American in that it is spacious and open. The living quarters on the

University of Virginia

central lawn and the ranges (also dormitories) behind them face outward, not inward. However, Jefferson also recognized the need for contemplation in seclusion. Thus, behind the dormitories and pavilions are walled gardens, enclosed by serpentine walls. In Jefferson's original designs, the pavilions were all alike, but after a meeting of the board of visitors, he wrote a friend that the pavilions should be "models of taste and good architecture, and of a variety of appearance, no two alike, so as to serve as specimens for the Architectural lecturer." Unique to Jefferson's design was the integration of living space for faculty and students with classrooms and libraries. Students lived on the Lawn and in two outer rows of rooms called the Ranges, while faculty were housed in the pavilions. The Rotunda held classroom space and the library.

Jefferson did not confine himself to designing the buildings of the university. He had strong views on curriculum and governance as well. He rejected both European and American models for "his" university. The European universities were ridden by "kingcraft" and the American ones by "priestcraft." Accordingly, students at the University of Virginia were free to pursue any discipline other than theology. Thus, in the early years, no clergyman was appointed to the faculty. In 1845 a Presbyterian minister, Reverend William Holmes McGuffey (who gained fame for his series of readers for children) joined the faculty as a professor of moral philosophy.

When the university received its first students—about 40 in number—in 1825, it was essentially a graduate school, with no required courses. For the first few years, students received diplomas, not degrees. To this day, the university has adhered to Jefferson's wishes by never awarding an honorary degree. In 1831, five years after Jefferson's death, the university offered the master of arts degree. Completion required a rigorous program in mathematics, natural philosophy, moral philosophy, ancient languages, and chemistry, a list to which two modern languages were added in 1833. This strict curriculum totally contravened Jefferson's elective system. The bachelor of arts degree (not, by the way, a prerequisite for the M.A.) was first awarded in 1848 and the Ph.D. in 1880.

Although Jefferson believed that Oxford, Cambridge, and the Sorbonne were "a century or two behind" his vision of the needs of nineteenth-century education, he scoured Europe in his search for faculty. Of the first eight professors, four were from England and the fifth from Germany. At the outset, faculty received a free residence in one of the pavilions and a salary of $1,500, plus a fee of $25 for each student in a class. Professors whose classes were large enjoyed a relatively substantial income, while those with smaller classes were considerably less affluent. Because this disparity caused unhappiness, the fee system was abandoned in 1850 in favor of a flat salary of $3,000 for each professor.

Until early in the twentieth century, the university did not have a president, as such, but the rotating position of chairman of the faculty. When the board of visitors first raised the issue of appointing a president in spring 1826, Jefferson resisted. Biographer Dumas Malone writes: "Although he did not say so, he was undoubtedly fearful of the concentration of power in anybody's hands and favored dispersal whenever possible." Jefferson's system continued until 1904, when Edwin A. Alderman became the first president of the University of Virginia.

One of Jefferson's other beliefs was that students could be trusted to govern themselves. That view was shattered early. Students rioted, attacking the choice of European professors. Physical assaults prompted faculty threats to resign unless strong action was taken. Accordingly, Jefferson recommended to the board of visitors a very strict code of behavior, among whose strictures were bans on smoking, drinking, and gambling. The most serious riot occurred in 1840, when Jonn A.G. Davis, chairman of the faculty and professor of law, left his pavilion residence to investigate a disturbance. He was shot to death by a masked student, who disappeared while free on bail, pending a trial. However, by 1842, student behavior had improved sufficiently that the honor system (still in effect) was introduced. The system, based on the belief that the university is "a community of trust," is unique, especially among state universities, in that judgments as to violation of the honor code are in the hands of students. At first, the code consisted in a student's pledge that he had received no assistance in an examination. Later, students also pledged that they had not offered assistance to another.

In earlier days of the code's operation, the accuser confronted the person he suspected of lying, cheating, or stealing. Today the accuser makes the charge to an advisor, who initiates an investigation, which must offer proof of the action, the intention, and the seriousness of the deed. If a student is found guilty of violating the honor code, there is a single penalty: dismissal from the university (if the student has not left voluntarily). As concepts of honor changed, guidelines were finally promulgated in 1935: "it is essential that the Honor System shall concern itself solely with those offenses which are classified as dishonorable by the public opinion of the student generation involved." With some modifications to protect the rights and the privacy of the accused, the honor system is still regarded by the university as one of its outstanding features.

Eighteen years after the honor system was introduced, the Civil War erupted, causing a major disruption at the university. Most students supported secession, and most faculty opposed it. Many students left the university to offer their services to the Confederacy. While the university stayed open during the war, the only students were those too young to serve or veterans who had been severely wounded. During the war years there were never more than 46 to 66 students and no more than 8 faculty. Not until 1900 did the university attain the number of students it had in 1850. Shortages of food and fuel were compounded by the decline in the Confederate dollar. In March 1865, Union Army General Philip Sheridan and his cavalry approached Charlottesville. Fearful that the university buildings would be burned to the ground, as those at the Virginia Military Institute had been, university authorities sent Professor John B. Minor (one of the country's foremost legal scholars, he later personally borrowed funds to keep the university open) and a contingent of faculty to meet the troops; Minor carried a walking cane with a white handkerchief attached to it. The commander of the advance guard, General George A. Custer, ordered that the university's property be given every protection.

Before the Civil War took its toll on student numbers, growing enrollment necessitated adding several buildings to the university. In 1850, architect Robert Mills, who had studied with Jefferson, was retained to design additional space. His mammoth Annex, joined to the Rotunda by a colonnade, was criticized from the first as being out of keeping with the symmetry of Jefferson's design. It was destroyed by fire in 1895.

Though the destruction of the buildings was averted during the Civil War, Jefferson's centerpiece—the Rotunda—was not spared when faulty wiring caused a fire in October 1895. Attempting to save the Rotunda, an engineering professor tried dynamiting the bridge between the Annex (where the fire had started) and the Rotunda. Unfortunately, he blew a hole in the Rotunda, and the fire spread even more rapidly. Before the fire was controlled, the annex, dome, and interior of the Rotunda had been destroyed. Fortunately, students and faculty had managed to save many of the books and the Galt bust of Jefferson.

To restore the Rotunda, the university engaged the eminent architect Stanford White. After he returned to New York from his first visit to the university, he encountered a friend, who found him in an unusually confused mood. White explained that he had seen Jefferson's plans for the university: "They're wonderful and I am scared to death. I only hope I can do it right." White convinced the board of visitors that Jefferson would surely have constructed the Rotunda as a "simple, single, and noble room," had not practical necessity required two stories. However, there are no documents suggesting that Jefferson had the "single room" plan in mind. A university document describes White's design as "an elaborate Beaux Arts interpretation in the Roman style. . . . White increased the height of the dome room . . . widened the skylight . . . and replaced Jefferson's slender double pillars with large single columns with Corinthian capitals." University authorities were so pleased with White's work that, ten years later, they asked him to design a house for the president, a dining hall, and an addition to the hospital.

In the 1960s and early 1970s, Professor Frederick H. Nichols of the School of Architecture spearheaded a project to restore the Rotunda according to Jefferson's design of a two-level interior. On the 223rd anniversary of Jefferson's birth, April 13, 1976 (also the year of the

U.S. Bicentennial), the restored Rotunda was dedicated. In that same year, the American Institute of Architects recognized the "academical village" as the most significant achievement of American architecture in the past 200 years.

Three years before the fire, in 1892, one of the major social issues with which the university would have to grapple in the twentieth century first surfaced: the admission of women. In that year, Miss Caroline Preston Davis applied for permission to take the examination for the b.a. degree in the school of mathematics. She was granted permission—on the condition that she take the exam apart from the male students. A further condition was that if she successfully completed the examination she would receive a certificate of proficiency, not a degree. She performed very well on the examination and was awarded the certificate. A debate ensued about how the university should treat applications from women. In 1894, both the faculty and the board of visitors voted against admitting women under any conditions. Faculty contended that admitting women to the university "would only serve to draw them away from those excellencies which made that sex such a power in the home." Virginia's general assembly voted to admit women to the graduate and professional schools in 1920–21, a decision which brought vociferous objections from students, faculty, and alumni. Women were finally admitted on the same basis as men in 1970. As the university nears the end of the twentieth century, enrollment is almost equally divided between male and female.

Even as it grappled with the issue of integrating the sexes, the university had to deal with the issue of integration of the races. In 1935, Alice Jackson, a black woman, applied for admission to the graduate school. The board of visitors instructed the dean of graduate studies to reject her application because "education of white and colored persons in the same school is contrary to the fixed policy of the commonwealth of Virginia" and "for other good and sufficient reasons." About 14 years later, a black graduate of Howard University Law School (who had been practicing law for two years) applied to take graduate courses at the University of Virginia Law School. Though the university rejected him, a U.S. Circuit Court of Appeals ordered him admitted. He entered the law school in September 1950, and dropped out in July 1951. In 1953, the university became the first major white southern university to award a doctorate to a black man. The first black professor joined the faculty in 1967, the same year that the first black athlete enrolled.

Through the years, the university has had to live down a reputation as a Southern country club, dominated by insularity and resistance to change. After World War II, a former student wrote: "Should the whole continent of Europe be destroyed by nuclear power, it would not surprise me to read a letter to the *Cavalier Daily* which discussed the effect of that catastrophe upon the parking problem." Apparently the university has broadened its horizons, since, as the twentieth century nears its close, the population is only 65 percent Virginian, more than 12 percent of the undergraduates are African-American, and nearly 9 percent are Asian.

As its academic reputation grew, the university attracted more and more distinguished faculty. Both Dumas Malone, the renowned biographer of Thomas Jefferson, and short-story writer Peter Taylor served on the faculty. A legacy enabled the university to institute a Writers in Residence program in the late 1950s. The first to hold that position was Nobel laureate William Faulkner, who remained a lecturer and consultant at the university until his death in 1962. Faulkner was followed by such luminaries as authors Katherine Anne Porter and John Dos Passos, as well as historian Shelby Foote.

In a 1969 speech, university president Edgar F. Shannon Jr. reflected: "If Mr. Jefferson were to return to the Grounds and walk along the Lawn under his familiar colonnades, he would find himself very much at home, for his academical village is still inhabited by honor students in the same dormitory rooms, and senior faculty occupy the same beautiful pavilions. I believe that he would be pleased at the progress that is being made toward fulfilling his dreams of a university."

Further Reading: Dumas Malone's *The Sage of Monticello* (Boston: Little Brown, 1981), the sixth volume of his authoritative biography, *Jefferson and His Time,* provides a lengthy account of the founding of the university. Another extensive account will be found in *Thomas Jefferson: Passionate Pilgrim,* by Alf J. Mapp Jr. (Lanham, Maryland and London: Madison Books, 1991). *Mr. Jefferson's University,* by Virginius Dabney (Charlottesville: University of Virginia Press, 1981), provides an extensive and detailed history of the university from its founding to the late 1970s.

—Mary Elizabeth Devine

UNIVERSITY OF WALES
(Cardiff, Wales)

Location: Constituent colleges located in Cardiff, Aberystwyth, Bangor, Swansea, and Lampeter, Wales.

Description: A federal university comprised of six constituent colleges enrolling students in undergraduate, graduate, and professional schools.

Information: University Registry
King Edward VII Avenue
Cathays Park
Cardiff CF1 3NS
Wales
(01222) 382656
Fax (01222) 396040

The development of the educational system in England and Wales during the early nineteenth century was mainly a matter of middle-class landowners and industrialists prodding Parliament to improve the educational opportunities for their children. Social and economic changes brought about by sudden industrialization made the working classes, especially in Wales, aware of the inadequacy of the county schools run by the Church of England and of the Sunday schools taught in nonconformist chapels. These schools were voluntary and not part of a national system. Neither prepared Welsh children to matriculate into any form of higher education. There were no colleges in Wales until the Anglican seminary, St. David's College, was established in Lampeter in 1822. Lampeter initially trained sons of the gentry and upper classes as ordinands who would then transfer to Oxford or Cambridge for their master's degree. The nonconformist Sunday schools provided basic education in reading the Bible (in Welsh) for younger children, and a forum for discussion for adults, strengthening the literary aspect of the Welsh language, and fostering a national identity which was separate from England yet loyal to the monarchy.

William Williams, a Welsh member of parliament, who had immigrated to England and become wealthy there, initiated an investigation into the education of his countrymen. He was convinced that the system of voluntary tutoring, the lack of training schools for teachers, and the money provided for schools by the gentry and industrialists were not enough. He pushed for a state system in which the Welsh could receive a "proper" education—in English and with English standards.

This inquiry into the educational opportunities provided to Welsh children by Anglican England and by voluntary educational societies proved to be a catalyst for a Welsh sense of pride. The commission report—the infamous "Blue Books" of 1847—noted that the children of Wales were being hindered by the Welsh language and by the deplorable conditions of the schools. The Welsh-speaking children who emigrated from the small towns to the industrial cities were not able to keep up in English-speaking schools that used books in English. The Welsh were not so outraged at the "discovery" that the Welsh language was a hindrance to intellectual, economic, and national growth as they were in the commission's declaration that Wales was a "primitive backwater, ignorant and immoral." The Welsh working-class society long remembered the "treachery of the Blue Books" and the Welsh, across all classes and political strata, were determined to make education a national priority.

From 1847 to the 1860s, children who reverted to the Welsh language in school were made to wear wooden signs around the their necks which said "Welsh not." At the same time members of the wealthy Welsh middle class in England, such as Sir Hugh Owens, began a movement for higher education in Wales. Owens had founded a normal training school for teachers at Bangor in 1858; he envisioned it as a working-class university, advancing beyond instruction in education alone. The Forster Act of 1870 had set up board schools in Wales and England, and another act of Parliament in 1889 (the Intermediate Education Act) prepared the way for a state system of secondary education confined to Wales, creating the opportunity for Welsh youth to receive the education necessary for matriculation into colleges.

In his history of modern Wales, Gareth Elwyn Jones wrote that Hugh Owens's efforts to establish a Welsh university which would provide an "intellectual and vocational education, with a scientific bias appropriate to an industrial society," resulted in a new "college by the sea" in Aberystwyth, conceived as a college for north and mid-Wales. Established in 1872 in an abandoned sea-front railway hotel, the Aberystwyth University College survived many reversals, such as fire, risk of financial failure, removal of professors, and an often unmotivated student body, some of whom left before completing their studies, choosing instead to return to the farms and coal mines. But the foundation of Aberystwyth University College attested to how far the Welsh would go to achieve educational parity with England.

Funded by a Sunday school campaign, mythically referred to as "pennies of the poor," Aberystwyth

University of Wales

received more than 100,000 contributions of under half a crown, given by the miners, quarrymen, and farm laborers throughout Wales on special "University Sundays" (*Sul y Brifygol*). The university did not receive the £4,000 government grant, the amount given to establish universities in Bangor and Cardiff; a major contributor to the new college was capitalist David Davies of Llandinam. The government eventually granted £2,500. There were always struggles, however, to keep the college financially afloat.

Despite the hardships, the University College at Aberystwyth served to link the Welsh in spirit and as a society. Tom Ellis, who would become a Welsh patriot, was a student at Aberystwyth in the late 1870s and early 1880s, as was historian John Edward Lloyd and Welsh-language educator/publisher Owen M. Edwards. The composer, Joseph Parry, was the first professor of music at the college. Parry's activities with the National Welsh Revival Movement's music and literary competition, the *Eisteddfod,* may have caused his dismissal from the college. By 1883, Tom Ellis and others would be members of the ACC, a forerunner of a nationalistic intellectual student society, similar to the later, more renowned *Dafydd ap Gwilym* for Welsh expatriate students at Oxford.

Historian Kenneth O. Morgan has expressed a popular opinion of the political implications of the university at Aberystwyth for the twentieth century, by suggesting that Aberystwyth was a "Celtic version" of the American "Wisconsin idea," a people's college having its own "passionate vision of populist culture, integrated with the society that gave it birth, steeped with the folk nationalism of 'Cymru Fydd,' the Wales that was to be."

Despite the academic progress for some of its students, Aberystwyth still provided an ungainly substitute for an English education and was considered a sublevel university by parliamentary standards. The Aberdare Committee in 1881 called for two universities in Wales, one in the north, one in the south. Affected by Welsh members of parliament in the House of Commons and by Stuart Rendel's lobbying of Prime Minister William Gladstone, the report led to the establishment of the University College of South Wales and Monmouthshire founded in Cathays

Park, Cardiff, in 1883, and the University College of North Wales, established in Bangor in 1884. They were intended to be regional colleges to prepare local students for transfer to English universities.

The first principal at Cardiff, John Viriamu Jones, was a distinguished scientist, who was associated with the liberals and nonconformists of the Welsh mid-nineteenth-century nationalism. The first principal of the college at Bangor was Sir Harry Reichel, an Ulster Tory, not popular with the local radicals; however, with his appointment of John Edward Lloyd as lecturer in Welsh history in 1892, and of John Morris-Jones as professor of Welsh in 1894, he encouraged the national traits of the Bangor region.

In January 1888, fueled with a passion to create a "National University" for Wales, the Cymmrodian Society, a group of London-based businessmen and intellectuals with Professor John Rhys as chairman, met and drafted an application to the Lord President of the council for a university charter. In November 1891, another conference was held (in the Welsh marshes at Shrewsbury). The main issue under discussion was whether this national university should be merely an examining university, or a teaching university—one that would teach and confer degrees on its own students, as advocated by education minister Arthur Acland. The issue hung in balance until Gladstone returned as prime minister in 1892. Gladstone appointed Owen M. Edwards commissioner to study the feasibility of incorporating Cardiff, Bangor, and Aberystwyth into a national university. By January 1893, the charter for the federal university—to be a teaching university, not merely an examining institution—was drafted by a committee of three, headed by Dr. Isambard Owen. The only hindrance to an early incorporation was the provision that St. David's of Lampeter be included, as had been recommended by the Aberdare report of 1881. In August 1893, the House of Lords carried a motion withholding royal assent to the charter unless Lampeter was included. However, Bishop Jayne of Chester, a former principal of Lampeter, claimed that St. David's College was becoming victim to "aggressive and intolerant denominationalism in Wales." Wary of the Liberal nonconformism of the movement for higher education in Wales, Lampeter wanted no part of inclusion.

Gladstone ignored the motion to wait for Lampeter's inclusion, as the Aberdare report provided a clause for the later inclusion of Lampeter. The University of Wales, incorporating Bangor, Aberystwyth, and Cardiff was established by royal charter, November 30, 1893. In 1896, it became a federal institution with the Prince of Wales as chancellor, after the death of Lord Aberdare, the first nominee. A government grant of £20,000 was "grudgingly" awarded in 1894 and another £50,000 was raised by public appeal. Viriamu Jones of Cardiff became the first vice-chancellor, and a plan was implemented to integrate the university with secondary school teaching and inspection. According to Morgan, the university

served as a powerful symbol of popular achievement and of national status: "In no other area of Welsh life, transcending political and sectarian barriers, was national pride more genuinely manifested."

The University of Wales incorporated changes over the years to consolidate and solidify its "Welshness." There were critics who denounced the federal university system's excessive bureaucracy. To detractors, the registry at Cardiff was considered a weak directing agency. In March 1905, Llewelyn Williams, a leader in the *Cymru Fydd,* a union for political nationalism associated with David Lloyd George, attacked the university in the *New Leader,* accusing it of being too detached from the "county schools" and run by a "narrow professional class."

A royal commission (Haldane Commission, 1916–18) granted a supplemental charter to the university which radically revised the federal machinery established under the charter of 1893. New federal bodies were created to serve the particular interests of Welsh learning and culture, including the University Council, an executive body which became responsible for financial matters and the allocation of funds to the colleges. The large senate and court of the old system gave way to the academic board which advised the University Council on academic matters. The Board of Celtic Studies, the University Extension Board, the Council of Music, and the University of Wales Press were also established to promote the work of the colleges in fields of "special importance" to Wales. Ninety percent of the student body were from Wales, making the University of Wales a more local university than any in England.

In 1920 the former Swansea Technical College became incorporated as the University of Wales's fourth constituent college, and in 1931 a supplemental charter was granted providing for the creation of the university's first constituent school; the Medical School of the College of Cardiff then affiliated with the university as the Welsh National School of Medicine.

While the teaching of theology had been previously prohibited within the university, graduates who went on to study at "associated" theological colleges were granted divinity degrees. Three schools of theology were created in the 1930s. The new provisions permitted establishment of joint institutions which combined the resources of the university colleges and of denominational theological colleges in what became nondenominational university schools of technology at Bangor, Cardiff, and a joint Aberystwyth/Lampeter School.

The University of Wales entered a period of expansion and change in the late 1950s and 1960s. An attempt was made to defederalize the university in 1964–66, with the argument that the university was too fragmented with the constituent colleges spread across the country. The Robbins Report of 1963–64 outlined the alleged need for a larger student population, especially in the applied and pure sciences. Lecturers such as Kingsley Amis (University College of Swansea) replied that "more means worse" in response to what he saw as the glut of foreign students. The principals at Cardiff, Swansea, and Bangor supported the movement to split up the university. In the end, the university stayed intact. But by 1968 only 39 percent of the student population was from Wales, and over half came from working-class England.

The university was reorganized in 1967, giving greater authority to the academic board for academic matters within the university. A supplemental charter that year also incorporated the Welsh College of Advanced Technology into the university. That institution, which had applied for its own independent university status due to its steady expansion since 1866 as a school for science, art, and technology, became the University of Wales Institute of Science and Technology (UWIST).

Four years later, in 1972, St. David's College, Lampeter, suspended its degree-granting powers, and due to lack of funding and decline of student enrollment, became a constituent school of the university, named St. David's University College, Lampeter. It entered the university as a liberal arts college, thus ending the special nature of its founding as a sectarian Anglican college in a nonconformist principality.

Important additions to the quality and status of Welsh language education were implemented: the Validation Board, 1974; Board for Welsh Medium Training, 1980; and the University Center for Welsh and Celtic Studies, a centrally funded research institute in Aberystwyth, 1985.

During a period in 1978–79, students held demonstrations and "sit-ins" at Bangor University College to protest the influx of non-Welsh students into the university, following a larger political movement (*Adfer*) which hoped to preserve the Welsh-speaking communities of rural Wales.

A new mission statement adopted in July 1993 rededicated the University of Wales to the "educational, cultural, and economic needs of Wales and to the enhancement of the international standing of the University."

Further Reading: *Modern Wales: A Concise History c. 1485–1979* (Cambridge: Cambridge University Press, 1984) by Gareth Elwyn Jones, a senior lecturer in history at University College of Swansea, examines the changes that took place over a 500-year period in Wales. The authoritative, analytical but unfootnoted work contains illustrated documents and reprints of quoted source material. Kenneth O. Morgan's *Rebirth of a Nation: Wales 1880–1980* (New York: Oxford University Press, and [Cardiff]: University of Wales Press, 1981), an academic study prepared as part of *The History of Wales* series edited by Glanmor Williams, is designed to appeal to the general reader. Despite his use of footnotes and his obvious scholarship, this Welsh native and fellow of Queens College, Oxford, has placed the University of Wales, its founding, and incorporations, into the wider perspective of the Welsh personality.

—Carol Shilakowsky

UNIVERSITY OF WASHINGTON
(Seattle, Washington, U.S.A.)

Location:

The University of Washington is located in Seattle, the largest city in the state of Washington, just north of the downtown area. The 703-acre campus borders the western shore of Lake Washington.

Description:

The University of Washington is a public research university governed by a nine-member board of regents. Enrolling approximately 35,000 students, the university is comprised of 16 major schools and colleges. These include law, medicine, business, engineering, dentistry, and education in addition to the traditional arts and sciences. Its nationally respected graduate and professional schools enroll over 9,000 students. A center for regional education and research, its schools have advanced the development of Washington's communities and industries.

Information:

University of Washington
Visitor's Information Center
Box 355502
4014 University Way, NE
Seattle, WA 98195-5502
U.S.A.
(206) 543-9198

The University of Washington, Seattle, was founded in 1861 as the University of the Territory of Washington, before Washington acquired statehood. The federal government had, in 1854, reserved acreage in each state and territory for the development of institutions of higher learning. Reverend Daniele Bagley, a Seattle minister, established the university from the sale and barter of this land, erecting three buildings—a two-story academic building, a residence building for students, and a president's house—on a ten-acre wooded site that is now downtown Seattle. In 1860, Seattle was a village of 200; the surrounding countryside was dotted with subsistence farms. Most residents had yet to provide themselves with the bare necessities, let alone with schools; the university was the first territorial school opened in Seattle. The university, which consisted of two instructors and 30 pupils during its opening term in 1861, amounted to little more than a frontier schoolhouse that closed several times during its earliest years due to lack of funding.

The university grew haltingly during the nineteenth century. A legislative appropriation of $3,000 for student scholarships in 1877 nearly tripled the student body from 43 to 126. During the next several years, enrollment ranged from 140 to 160 students, 35 to 40 in college-level courses. The university instructed students of both sexes in a variety of courses, including English, history, algebra, physiology, Latin, and Greek. By 1881, between 32 and 40 classes were offered regularly five times a week in 40-minute periods. Entrance to college-level courses did not require an exam but did require a proficiency in reading, spelling, geography, and fractions. In addition to programs in the arts and sciences, the university established a normal course for teacher training and a commercial course to prepare individuals for careers in business.

During the 1880s, the territory grew exponentially. With the completion of the Northern-Pacific Railroad, tens of thousands settled in the area of Puget Sound. By 1891, Seattle had grown to a population of 50,000. Legislative appropriations increased gradually from an initial $3,000 biennial appropriation for operational expenses in 1884 to include $10,000 for salaries in 1888. In addition, territorial scholarships were continued with an additional sum to cover student travel expenses. An enrollment of 217 in 1888 increased to 273 in 1889, with 63 in college-level courses. The declaration of statehood in November of 1889 brought about an additional land grant of 100,000 acres for the university and provided the state legislature with impetus for increased investment in education. President Thomas M. Gatch (1887–95), the first university staff member to hold a doctorate, presided over the university during this positive time of funding and growth. He advanced the university's capacity to function as an institution of higher learning, developing genuine differentiation of departments and disciplines and hiring instructors with more advanced professional training and greater diversity and experience.

In 1895, following the rapid growth of the 1880s and with further anticipated growth, the university moved from the heart of the city to a 350-acre campus along Lake Washington. Nearly 200 students attended classes in the newly constructed Administration Building (renamed Denny Hall in 1910), which boasted 20,000 square feet in floor space and included classrooms, laboratories, meeting halls, and library holdings. The state legislature appropriated $90,000 in 1895 for school operations and nearly as much for additional buildings and improvements. Increased funds allowed the appointment of new, better-qualified faculty; by 1896, 6 of 15 professors of collegiate subjects held doctorates. The promise of continued financial support, coupled with the increasing enrollment in college-level courses, prompted Presi-

University of Washington

dent Mark W. Harrington's (1895–97) decision to discontinue the preparatory program. The state elections in November 1896, however, reversed the university's fortune. The biennial appropriation for operations failed to cover the salary promised to Harrington, who resigned in protest.

The university languished during the year following Harrington's resignation but regained direction with the appointment of Frank P. Graves to the presidency in 1898. Graves (1898–1902) reestablished instruction at the preparatory level in an effort to ensure adequate preparatory education in Washington (at this time less than 12 schools provided a four-year program) and to ensure demand for the university's programs. Enrollment tripled during Graves's term, from less than 200 students in 1898 to nearly 600 in 1902. Graves strengthened upper-level instruction, hiring additional faculty and restructuring and revitalizing educational programs. Under Graves's direction and example, faculty spoke to audiences across the state promoting the university and spreading awareness of the available educational opportunities. The School of Pedagogy advanced from a normal training center for teachers to a thorough program in educational practice. A School of Mines branched out from the College of Engineering and Mines to offer five different programs to 45 students in 1899. A School of Law was established in 1899, which, by 1902, enrolled 68 students.

Rapid growth continued during the presidency of Thomas Franklin Kane (1902–14). Each year hundreds more students enrolled, increasing from 650 in 1902 to over 2,300 in 1913. The growth of the student body necessitated numerous faculty hires. Kane's appointments greatly strengthened the academic quality at the university; 30 of the men appointed held doctorates from such universities as Harvard, Yale, Columbia, Cornell, Chicago, Michigan, and Northwestern. Departments composed of one or two instructors in 1902 were transformed by 1914: English claimed 11 instructors; mathematics, 10; civil engineering, 9; political and social science, 9; and chemistry, history, philosophy, and modern language, from 6 to 8 each. The university soon experienced a space shortage, partially alleviated by the construction of three permanent structures and numerous temporary structures for the 1909 Alaska-Yukon-Pacific Exposition.

The exposition reflected the growing importance of western industry in the United States, and the selection of Seattle as site for the exposition attested to Washington's centrality in regional development. Washington developed rapidly during the early twentieth century. Total population nearly tripled in 14 years, from 518,000 in 1900 to 1,408,000 in 1914. The lumber and fishing industries became major enterprises and the output of manufacturing in Seattle alone more than doubled. Improvement of the state system of secondary education allowed the discontinuation of the university's prepara-

tory programs and a deepening commitment to research and higher education. Much of the university research directly benefited the development of the state. Geologists mapped and appraised Washington's mineral deposits. Botanists and zoologists offered suggestions for combating Canadian thistles and gypsy moths. Sanitary engineers assisted in the development of hospital sewage plants and the Cedar River system then being developed for Seattle.

Under President Henry Suzzallo (1915–26), research provisions improved with the development of a mines experiment station in 1917, a hydraulics laboratory in 1920, a mines laboratory in 1921, and the expansion of the Marine Biological Station on Puget Sound following a federal gift of 484 acres. Course and program offerings in numerous fields diversified and improved. The program in commerce became the College of Business Administration in 1917. Sociology separated into its own department, psychology separated from philosophy, and Chinese and Russian were added to the foreign language offerings. A program in aeronautical engineering began with William E. Boeing's provision for the construction of a four-foot wind tunnel and aeronautical laboratory. Although some protested the acceptance of private gifts by a publicly funded institution, private donations increasingly benefited the university during Suzzallo's presidency. Horace C. Henry donated his private collection of paintings (over 400,000) along with $100,000 for the construction of a campus art gallery. Agnes H. Anderson provided for the construction of a general purpose building in 1925 with the stipulation that it hold the School of Forestry. Private donations also provided for student scholarships, faculty chairs, and research.

Enrollment increased steadily from 2,300 in 1914 (despite a 30 percent drop during World War I) to 4,740 in 1919. Graduate studies, which had grown slowly during the twentieth century, enrolled 350 students in 1922, including 150 candidates for the master's degree and 30 candidates for the Ph.D. In 1915, the legislature authorized the erection of two buildings: a home economics building completed in 1916 and a commerce building completed the following year. The construction of Philosophy Hall was authorized in 1917, suspended during the war, and eventually completed in 1920. A building fund was established that included revenue collected from the lease of the university's forest lands and former campus in downtown Seattle as well as matching funds allocated by the legislature from tax dollars. This fund allowed the construction of new permanent structures at a rate of approximately one every 18 months. In 1926, the first unit of a new university library was completed. Promoted by Suzzallo to be the soul of the university, the library resembled a cathedral with its Tudor vaults and 36-foot high stained-glass windows. The university continued to grow with the construction of seven buildings in the next six years: a women's physical education building, a men's pavilion, three academic buildings, and an oceanography laboratory.

The financial crisis of the Great Depression resulted in serious allocation reductions, the elimination of 1 in 12 instructors, and a 32-percent wage and salary cut. The regional economy recovered in the mid-1930s, and the university redoubled its efforts toward quality as well as quantity. A department of general studies was developed that allowed an escape from established lines of study. Salaries were raised, teaching loads reduced, and fringe benefits increased, attracting more-qualified and better-respected professors. The university conducted more research of use to the state, including studies which led to the rehabilitation of salmon fisheries, assistance in the effort to restock state oyster beds, and efforts to develop the frozen foods industry.

University research and educational capacity increased greatly during the 1940s and 1950s. Enrollment, which had dropped from 10,000 to 7,000 during World War II, increased to 14,000 by September 1946, to 16,650 by 1948, and to over 18,000 by 1960. A postwar construction program included $21.5 million for civil and electrical engineering laboratories, nearly as much for laboratories in other sciences, $4 million for general classrooms and library stacks, over $2 million for administration and student union buildings, and $9 million for the newly created medical and dental schools. The university benefited from the federal government's transference of research responsibilities from the military to the state universities. During and after the war, millions of dollars became available for research in many fields. In 1946 the university expended $660,000 on special research through grants and contracts; in 1953, over $2 million; in 1956, $5.75 million; in 1960, nearly $14 million. The university acquired a cyclotron for nuclear research and purchased a nuclear reactor for teaching and research; in 1959 the administration announced a comprehensive program of graduate training in nuclear engineering.

During the 1960s, enrollment grew by 1,000 students per year until the state established 17 additional community colleges and the Evergreen State College to serve educational needs in southern Washington. The university emphasized upper-division education (junior- and senior-year courses held the designation of upper-division courses; freshman- and sophomore-year courses were lower-division) and made admissions requirements more selective. Offices of Equal Opportunity and Minority Affairs were formed to promote the education of minorities and women. Provisions for financial aid, tutoring, and academic counseling were made to ensure the ability of minorities to attend and to excel at the university. New courses and programs were created in women's studies, African-American studies, American-Indian studies, Asian-American studies, and Mexican-American studies.

Reviews of existing departments and fields led to the establishment of new departments and interdisciplinary programs in fields such as biomathematics, genetics, and ceramic materials. The School of Art added an art history curriculum. The School of Drama received support from the Rockefeller Foundation and the Seattle Repertory Theatre to initiate an intensive actor training program. The graduate school worked with college deans and department heads to further faculty research. By 1969, the university ranked among the top five institutions in the nation in receipt of federal research money.

Some students protested the acceptance of federal funds and the resulting research used to further the war in Vietnam. Student anti-war protest culminated in the fire-bombing of the Naval ROTC facilities on September 18, 1968, beginning an 18-month period of violent attacks on university property. The last in a series of campus disturbances occurred after the U.S. invasion of Cambodia in April 1970. Upon learning the news of the students killed at Kent State, thousands surged from the campus past police onto Interstate 5, blocking traffic in their march through the city to the federal courthouse.

As problems of social unrest dissipated in the early 1970s, the university faced difficulties of another sort. A faltering state economy led to reduced appropriations and the reduction of state research funds for environmental health issues, forest product development, aerospace engineering, and development of the fishing industry. President John R. Hogness (1974–79) attempted to offset these losses with money from private sources, increasing the activities of the development office to solicit private donations and to increase the alumni fund. He also attempted to raise public approval and support of the university with television and radio advertisements and by emphasizing the need for faculty to speak to civic, professional, and community organizations across the state. In 1981, the board of regents declared the first state of emergency in university history, permitting the university to remove faculty and staff due to fiscal stress. Although unstable funding continued during the 1980s, the university retained strength in its core disciplines through the streamlining of existing programs.

In 1990, the University of Washington opened two new campuses, one in Bothell and one in Tacoma, to broaden access to higher education; these campuses together opened to approximately 200 students and presently enroll 1,400. Throughout the 1990s, enrollment at the Seattle campus has averaged 32,500. With numerous state community colleges available to high school graduates of lesser academic standing, undergraduate admission to the university is highly competitive. Programs leading to advanced degrees are offered in over 100 areas. Of the 9,000 students enrolled in advanced studies, 35 percent are enrolled in programs in the college of arts and sciences; engineering, education, business administration, nursing, and medicine enroll significant percentages as well. In 1995, the university awarded over 6,000 bachelor degrees, nearly 2,000 master's degrees, 482 doctorates, and 370 professional degrees.

Further Reading: Two overviews of the university are *The First Century at the University of Washington, 1861–1961,* by Charles M. Gates (Seattle: University of Washington Press, 1961), and *Into the Second Century: The University of Washington, 1961–1986,* by Jane Sanders (Seattle: University of Washington Press, 1987).

—Beth Rillema

UNIVERSITY OF WISCONSIN
(Wisconsin, U.S.A.)

Location: On 26 campuses throughout Wisconsin.

Description: A state-wide system of universities, freshman-sophomore centers, and extension services.

Information: Office of University Relations
University of Wisconsin System
1856 Van Hise Hall
122 Linden Drive
Madison, WI 53706
U.S.A.
(608) 262-3571

The French fur traders who first explored what is now Wisconsin were only the beginning of a stream of immigrants who would travel from their homes in such countries as England, France, Norway, Finland, Germany, and Sweden to settle the Wisconsin area. Although ethnically diverse, these men and women shared some character qualities in common. Hardy, self-reliant, and adventurous, they left everything behind to travel to this new world. They also shared one critical belief. They believed that what the new world offered—self-determination and a government that existed for the people—was worth the sacrifices they had made. It was in this crucible of idealism, independence, and interdependence between the good of the people and the good of the state that the University of Wisconsin was born. And the circumstances of that birth have shaped the history of the University of Wisconsin, the state of Wisconsin, and the development of higher education in the United States as a whole.

In the years immediately following the American Revolutionary War, European nations ceded the lands which they had formerly controlled to the fledgling U.S. government. The land which is now the states of Ohio, Indiana, Illinois, Michigan, and Wisconsin became known as the Northwest Territory. In 1787 the United States, wanting to set some basic guidelines for its new properties, passed the Northwest Ordinance. The Northwest Ordinance not only reiterated the uniquely American concepts of religious freedom and justice by due process, but also established in the northwest lands the unique, developing concept of the state university, stating that "religion, morality, and knowledge being necessary to good government and the happiness of mankind, schools and the means of education shall forever be encouraged."

The first assembly of the Wisconsin territory met in 1836. Governor Dodge, in his welcoming address, urged that congress be petitioned to allow one township of land to be sold, and the proceeds of the sale be used for the establishment of an academy for the education of youth. He left the location and government of the institution to the legislature. The first order of business, however, proved to be the location of the capital. Debate raged over which existing city to name, but a popular judge, James Doty, who owned much of the land around Lake Mendota, succeeded in convincing the legislature to build a new city for the capital, at a junction of four lakes, and to name the town Madison (after James Madison, who had died that year).

The territorial legislature moved in 1838 to establish a University of Wisconsin at the newly established capital, but it was not until Wisconsin's statehood in 1848 that the means for establishing a state university were provided. The state legislature established a board of regents to administrate the new college. On February 5, 1849, the first 17 students began remedial classes in rented space at the Wisconsin Female Academy, and the Wisconsin State University was born.

The idea of the state university implied a break from the traditional European models for higher education—small, privately controlled institutions (usually by a particular religious denomination) with classical curricula and student bodies drawn from society's elite. Inherent in the idea of the state university was the belief that providing higher education was a basic responsibility of government, that education should be available to every citizen who could benefit from it, and that education should meet not only the intellectual desires of the scholar, but also the practical needs of the society, by equipping the citizenry for all sorts of trades and professional occupations. That the University of Wisconsin was founded on these principles is evident in the words of its first chancellor, John Hiram Lathrop: "The American mind has grasped the idea and will not let it go, that the whole property of the state whether in common or in severalty, is holden subject to the sacred trust of providing for the education of every child in the state."

State universities—under the direction of fledgling governments and without the benefit of established precedence, clear direction, or solid funding—had their difficulties, and the University of Wisconsin was no exception. The university had been planted in a town barely ten years old, where lodging was scarce before the construction of dormitories. When the university was founded in 1848, the area was still part of the western frontier, so a spartan existence was the norm for most students, even after dormitories were built. Rooms were

677

University of Wisconsin, Madison

heated by wood stoves. Students were responsible for gathering their own wood, a laborious, time-consuming process that the students sometimes abandoned in favor of stealing wood from other students. (A rash of wood theft in the 1850s led to one group of students filling their logs with black gunpowder. A few spectacular explosions later, the pilfering stopped.) Students slept on straw gathered from the univesity farm and survived on coffee, bread, molasses, graham mush, and an occasional roasted potato. Quail were so thick that they sometimes flew in the classroom windows. Game of all sort was plentiful, and livened up the otherwise meager diets of those first scholars. Difficulties of life on the frontier in general, however, limited enrollment in the regular college classes to only 41 students as late as 1865. In fact, in 1864 no commencement was even held, as all but one member of the senior class had joined the army.

The years after the Civil War saw the idea of the state university take hold and flourish. At the University of Wisconsin, enrollment—bolstered by leagues of returning soldiers—reached 300 students by 1870. The Morrill Land Grant Act of 1862 had committed 240,000 addi-

tional acres of land to the university with the condition that the land be used to encourage agricultural and mechanical arts. The agricultural department opened in 1868. Paul Chadbourne, chancellor of the university at that time, declared that the "objective of the state colleges is to obliterate the supposed superiority of the so-called learned professions by securing . . . the highest education for those who choose industrial pursuits, thus lifting agriculture and mechanic arts from the plane of mere routine labor to the dignity of learned professions."

The state college philosophy really came of age, however, under the tenure of the next president, John Bascom. Bascom became president of the university in 1874. One of his first acts was to abolish the separate female college and make the university truly coeducational. Bascom pushed for the establishment, by the legislature, of a system of public high schools (which, incredibly enough, had not existed), as well as for the first state millage tax support of the university. Rapid expansion of science, agriculture, and engineering facilities occurred. Blending roles in academic and state affairs, he campaigned for laws to regulate sales of liquor and played a leading role in the Prohibition Party. Intensely religious and an ardent supporter of human rights, he also gave popular lectures on workers' rights and the regulation of industrial monopolies. Bascom's administration saw the first practical tests of the lofty plan of the state university to benefit the people—agricultural short courses and farmers' institutes began being offered during his years in office.

When Bascom left office in 1887 after 13 years, enrollment at the university had only increased by 200 students. But the concept of the state university had been defined and the quality of the service rendered to the student and the state had been tested. The next 15 years saw the university grow—enrollment increased from 500 to 3,000—and its intellectual and social life began to resemble that of the university of today. Collegiate athletic teams in football, crew, and track and field were formed. College journalism and oratory made their mark on the campus. Social activities such as concerts and balls were held. The concept of the state university was also further realized. The school of education was founded, with a special appointee responsible for accreditation of state high schools. A school of commerce and a school of pharmacy were established. The school of economics, political science, and history was expanded. The first departments in the nation in the disciplines of psychology and Scandinavian studies were established. A State Laboratory of Health was founded. Agricultural support was expanded, leading to two important achievements in the field of agriculture by University of Wisconsin faculty: the invention of the round silo and the development of the Babcock butterfat test, which became the industry standard for measuring the quality of dairy milk.

During this period (1892) the university's first Ph.D. was awarded—to Charles Van Hise, who in 1904 became the president of the university. Governor Robert La Follette (who studied under Bascom) later remarked that it was Bascom's teaching that originated what has come to be called the "Wisconsin idea" in education. But it was under Van Hise that the "Wisconsin idea" became a living doctrine that carried the traditional concept of the state university a level further. The "Wisconsin idea" embraced the idea of academic government leaders advising the administration, thus helping to reform the government. The central functon of the state university was the training of the electorate and the specialists who would offer their expertise to the government, thereby influencing the entire populace. In effect, the entire state was the campus.

Van Hise once wrote: "I shall never rest content until the beneficent influences of the University are made available to every home in the state. . . . A university supported by the state . . . for all its sons and daughters . . . can place no bounds upon the liens of its endeavor." He lost no time in taking steps to further realize the objective of using the university to better the state. In his inaugural address he proposed appointing faculty members as state advisers. In the years that followed, close ties between

university faculty and the state government, led first by Governor La Follette (Van Hise's former classmate), and then by other progressives, led to a wave of progressive legislation that captured national attention. Wisconsin was called "an experiment station" in politics, and a "state-wide laboratory." Theodore Roosevelt himself wrote that "all through the Union we need to learn the Wisconsin lesson of scientific popular self-help."

University faculty were performing research in this laboratory. Members of the university faculty helped government officials draft reform legislation and served on regulatory commissions. When a board of public affairs was set up to watch over government operations, many faculty members served in that capacity as well. One writer observed: "Under the influence of university men, Wisconsin has become the recognized leader in progressive and practical legislation." Faculty members Richard Ely and John Commons crusaded for labor rights and collective bargaining. Progressive legislation passed during Van Hise's tenure included worker safety and compensation laws (the first Workmen's Compensation Act); regulation of insurance, railroads, and utilities; conservation initiatives; and corporate income tax. Wisconsin, during this period of time, also established the legislative reference bureau, the concepts of referendum and initiative, and the direct primary, in an effort to decrease the power of the party bosses.

In tandem with the Wisconsin idea of academic advice to government was the idea that the university should serve the state. The agricultural contributions of the university continued to grow; during Van Hise's rule the first U.S. departments of agricultural economics and experimental breeding were established. University researchers discovered vitamin A and vitamin B and demonstrated their importance in animal feed. Van Hise, hoping to take what worked with agriculture and apply it into every area of academic endeavor, established the UW Extension Service. College classes were offered in several satellite locations, aiming, in the words of Van Hise, to make "the boundaries of the University the boundaries of the state."

The Progressive movement fell out of the spotlight with America's entrance into World War I, but the reforms pioneered by university faculty, with the blessings of state government, were eventually adopted by much of the rest of the country, and in Wisconsin, the practice of the Wisconsin idea continued. A physics research project led to the development of a three-element power vacuum tube capable of voice radio transmission; WHA, the nation's oldest continuous radio station, began broadcasting from a laboratory at UW and eventually became a statewide educational radio network. The nation's first school of speech correction awarded the first Ph.D. in communicative disorders. The university opened Wisconsin General Hospital. An agricultural professor's discoveries with ultraviolet light and vitamin D helped to wipe out infantile rickets. The newly formed Extension

Service proved a boon when returning soldiers again swelled enrollment—the extension centers allowed the student body overflow to begin course work at home before transferring to the main campus.

The extension centers continued to prove useful throughout the Depression, allowing students who lacked the money for room and board to take their first- and second-year classes at home. University agricultural researchers maintained their reputation, discovering that a niacin supplement in the diet prevents pellegra and that iodine in salt prevents goiter.

By the time the Japanese bombed Pearl Harbor, the Wisconsin idea was ingrained, and the university and the United States entered the war together. Wisconsin physicists shipped the electrostatic generator they developed to Los Alamos for use in the development of the atomic bomb. Then-president Dykstra himself served as the federal chairman of the draft and served on the National Defense Mediation board. The university enrolled almost 2,000 military troops in Navy radio school. University officials created an Emergency Invention Development Council; university resources were involved in enlistment programs, in pilot training, in cooks' and bakers' schools, in war bond drives, and in free publications to the military forces. The Extension Center system expanded again following the influx of postwar GIs.

The years since World War II have seen the university grow into one of the nation's largest and most respected institutions of higher education. In 1971 the state legislature combined all the state colleges into one single University of Wisconsin, creating a huge public system comprised of two large research university—the University of Wisconsin–Madison and the University of Wisconsin–Milwaukee; plus 11 other universities, 13 centers for first- and second-year students, and an extension system that reaches all 72 counties and over 1 million people. In the last few decades, the university has consistently ranked among the top schools in the nation in measures of academic excellence. At the same time Wisconsin communities have relied on the university for help with taxation, traffic, pollution, school reform, law enforcement, social welfare, zoning problems, financial planning, and dissemination of new agricultural methods and technology.

While the Wisconsin idea has provided a climate in which both the university and the state of Wisconsin have flourished, this blending of the interests of government and academia has at times been a tightrope that proved difficult to traverse. Student commitment to changing social and government policy led to violence on campus during the turbulent 1960s. A riot in the spring of 1966 resulted in injuries to some students and police; a bomb detonated at the Mathematics Research Center in 1970 killed one student and injured three others.

However, the greatest test of the state university occurred nearly a century earlier, in 1894, when many state institutions were seeking to define the limits of the state's role in univesity affairs. A state official who was also a member of the university board of regents wrote a letter to the newspaper in which he accused Richard Ely—a UW professor and champion of social welfare—of stirring up worker strikes, encouraging boycotts against non-union firms, and teaching socialistic theories in his classes. National public attention eventually forced a formal hearing, in which the regents exonerated Ely. The verdict in the Ely hearing and the proclamation of the regents acquitting him became important for the cause of academic freedom throughout the country; Ely later termed the proclamation "a beacon light in higher education in this country, not only for Wisconsin, but for all similar institutions." The words of that proclamation are now permanently affixed to the front of Bascom Hall, and have been called the Magna Carta of the university. "Whatever may be the limitations which trammel inquiry elsewhere, we believe that the great state University of Wisconsin should ever encourage that continual and fearless sifting and winnowing by which alone the truth can be found."

Further Reading: Merle Curti and Victor Carstensen's *The University of Wisconsin* (Madison: University of Wisconsin Press, 1948) is a detailed, scholarly account of the history of the university from its founding until 1946. Robert Guard's *University Madison—U.S.A.* (Madison: Wisconsin House, 1970) offers vignettes of the university's history from its inception through the turbulent period of the 1960s.

—Wendy Sowder Wippel

UPPSALA UNIVERSITY
(Uppsala, Sweden)

Location: In Uppsala, a city of 160,000, approximately 40 miles north of Stockholm.

Description: A state-supported institution with over 18,000 students in undergraduate, graduate, and professional programs.

Information: Information Office
St. Olofsgatan 12, Uppsala
Box 256, S-751 05
Uppsala
Sweden
18 18 25 00

Uppsala University in the Swedish city of the same name was founded in 1477. Although that date make Uppsala the first such educational institution in Scandinavia, it was certainly not the first in Europe. In fact, Uppsala University was created so that Swedish youth could be educated in their own country rather than heading for Paris, Prague, Bologna, or Leipzig. The university was not an instant success. It was opened in 1477 by the Catholic Church, which provided its financial support and its raison d'être; like many other such institutions of the Middle Ages, it was founded as a theological school for the training of clergy and civil servants. The early years remain largely unknown lexcept for one fortunate circumstance. Textbooks were not used until the end of the nineteenth century. Classes were taught in the early years as lectures (with material often read by the professors directly, and dryly, from their notes). Students took down the lecturer's words and used the notes for study. Olaus Johannis Guthro, a student at the university from 1477 to 1486, took notes all the time and collected them, along with notes from his fellow students and his teachers, in seven volumes of notebooks that were returned to the university's library in the seventeenth century. These notes reveal a course of study that was heavily Aristotelian, and they show a view of the universe with the earth at its center. The dozen or so students did not pay tuition and were housed in church lodgings, probably without charge.

A major problem arose for church-supported institutions such as Uppsala in the form of the Protestant Reformation. As the Roman Catholic Church lost its influence with the population and especially with the government, the university also lost its supporters. Sometime around 1520, the school went into a state of decline and became moribund.

Not until the end of the century did the university reappear. In 1593 political and religious leaders meeting at Uppsala reestablished the university as a free Protestant institution, with three professors of theology and one each in astronomy, natural philosophy, mathematics, and logic. The 70 students were given free accommodations; both students and faculty enjoyed special societal privileges, including relief from taxes and from being brought before a public criminal law court. (The often unruly students were instead hauled before the University Senate, which often punished infractions more severely than did public courts.) Professors were paid with fishing rights, grains, and so on.

King Gustav II Adolf (Gustavus Adolphus), who reigned from 1611 to 1632, saw the wisdom of having a place within Sweden to educate civil servants ("Swedish men," as the Constitution read until 1923) and teachers. The king provided the financial backing for the reborn university. Teachers received salaries. Gustav II Adolphus's collection of books provided the nucleus for the university library. He appointed his old tutor, Baron Johan Skytte, as the university's chancellor, thus strengthening ties between crown and academia. His generous gift of 300 estates in 1624 formed the basis of an endowment that is still important to the university.

Students in the seventeenth century were subject to what today would be called hazing: each one was "cleansed" upon his arrival at Uppsala. In her history of Uppsala University, Karin Johannisson describes the ordeal:

> Clad in motley garments and with horns, donkey's ears and boar's tusks, [the student] was chased with an axe before the public. There he was abused and manhandled with the ceremonial tools . . . tongs, saw and plane, before the "depositor" put salt on his tongue, poured wine over his head and finally declared him to be a "free" student. The rite itself, not to mention the subsequent penal year during which the wretch was forced to "fag" for an older student, degenerated quite early on and was forbidden in 1691.

Another change that occurred in the seventeenth century came in the faculty of medicine. Medicine has been an important area of interest at Uppsala almost as long as theology. The first physician joined the faculty in 1613, and the faculty of medicine was founded in 1620, although most Swedes still preferred to study medicine in other countries, especially Holland. One famous professor of

Uppsala University

medicine was Olof Rudbeck, who in the seventeenth century was a scholar of anatomy, botany, mechanics, music, and archaeology—all the while dabbling in university politics. Through dissecting hundreds of animals, Rudbeck demonstrated the lymphatic vessels and their function in anatomy—building upon William Harvey's discovery of blood circulation. He also constructed an anatomical theater on the roof of the main building, the Gustavianum, with steep tiers of seats so that students could observe dissections. Unfortunately, it was particularly difficult at that time to obtain corpses for study, since only criminals, suicides, and illegitimate children could be dissected. Thus the theater, which still exists today, was used only a few times for its intended purpose.

Rudbeck also laid out a botanical garden for study and for the use of researchers seeking medicinal drugs and herbs. Predating Linnaeus by a century, Rudbeck oversaw the carving of 7,000 wood printing blocks to make hand-painted plates of botanical specimens. His life's work,

however, was destroyed in a great fire that consumed much of the city of Uppsala in 1702. He then turned his attention to Gothic archaeology and spent much scientific energy and skill attempting to prove that the lost continent of Atlantis was really Sweden. His son, Olof Rudbeck the Younger, succeeded him in the position of chair of medicine, but he had little interest in that discipline. He had spent much of his time exploring Lappland and documenting that northern region's flora and fauna; his work was also destroyed in the fire. Rudbeck the Younger's *Book of Birds* is considered the beginning of scientific zoology in Sweden.

Not surprisingly, with the varied interests of the major figures, the study of medicine proper faltered in the seventeenth century in Uppsala. Then the university hospital was founded by Lars Roberg in 1708. Roberg seems not to have been overly optimistic about support, since his request for funds included the purchase of only one bed and linen, plus food for only one patient. The hospital did not exceed his dreams; the university provided little support. In order to raise funds, Roberg was reduced to charging admission fees for those wishing to observe operations. He even rented part of the hospital as a tavern, but the scandal led to a wholesale defection by the hospital staff, closing that commercial venture. Roberg did manage to publish the first anatomy textbook in Swedish rather than Latin. Some of the terminology was considered so "explicit" that the censors forced Roberg to revise the text.

The hospital closed in the 1720s. Luckily, it was reopened in time for the appointment of Carl von Linné as professor of medicine in 1740. Carl von Linné, or Linnaeus, is still the most famous professor associated with Uppsala University. With his system of zoological and botanical classification of all living matter, he laid the basis for the study of zoology, and he was the first to place humans in the hominid family of the apes, naming humans Homo sapiens. He also recognized sexuality in plants as well as in animals; his master work *Species Plantarum* is still internationally recognized for its fundamental importance in the nomenclature of the plant world. Not only was Linnaeus a brilliant researcher, he was also an unusually gifted teacher. Where others of his colleagues still presented dry lectures and read from their scripts, Linnaeus drew an audience of 200 to 300 (a third of the student body at that time) to his lively demonstrations or his botanical rambles around Uppsala.

Linnaeus's followers traveled far and wide to carry on his work. One of his students, Carl Peter Thunberg, traveled to Java, to South Africa, and to Japan. He charted Japan's unknown plants in *Flora Japonica;* he also redesigned the botanical gardens near Uppsala Castle. Thunberg held the Linnean chair of natural history and pharmacy from 1784 until his death at an advanced age in 1828.

While Linnaeus and his followers were bringing a golden age to zoology and botany, the study of medicine at Uppsala was again in decline. Professor Nils Rosen (von Rosenstein), appointed in the same year as von Linné, was able to renovate and reopen the hospital, although it never had more than a handful of beds. Demonstrations in anatomy, surgery, and obstetrics were carried out, although not without controversy. (Abortion and impotence were considered shocking topics for study.) Rosen wrote a number of medical textbooks, including a classic on pediatrics that was translated into a number of languages.

The teaching of medicine continued at Uppsala for the next century in surges and declines, including an eventually successful struggle to prevent the faculty moving to Stockholm. By the beginning of the nineteenth century the hospital was still struggling financially and had only a dozen or so beds. In 1831 the university received a state grant used partially to improve and run the hospital, which grew to 40 and then nearly 100 beds when the university and county hospitals were joined in the 1850s.

Once more, disaster struck. It was the practice at that time to fumigate mattresses by smoke-treating them over burning coal strewn with juniper bushes. Since the mattresses were made of straw, it is not difficult to envision the result: an 1862 fire that burned the building to the ground and killed 30 patients. Rebuilt, literally from the ashes, the new hospital, opened in 1867, was the most modern in northern Europe.

Later advances in medicine at Uppsala included: research into ophthalmics by Allvar Gullstrand, winner of the 1911 Nobel Prize for physiology or medicine; another Nobel Prize awarded in 1914 to Robert Barany for work in otology performed primarily at Uppsala, although he later moved to Vienna; the first appendectomy in Sweden, carried out by Karl Gustaf Lennander in 1889; an operation to remove a bullet from a patient's brain by Thor Stenbeck in 1896, believed to be the first time a metal object was visualized via Roentgenphotography in the brain prior to surgery; and the research by pathologist Robin Fahraeus in the 1920s that added the normal values of erythrocyte sedimentation ("sed rate") to routine health examinations.

While medicine has been the major source of renown for Uppsala University over the centuries, it is not its only area of prestige. Anders Celsius, already a famous astronomer, received funding to support an astronomical observatory in Uppsala in the 1730s. There he studied the aurora borealis, the stars, and the constellations. Through his experimentation he developed the temperature scale that bears his name, delineating 100 degrees between the freezing and boiling points of water.

Another eighteenth-century physicist of renown was Samuel Klingenstierna, who gained fame for his theatrical and popular lecture style using Leyden jars, air pumps, and magic lanterns. Klingenstierna also helped improve the telescope. He had rejected Isaac Newton's belief that a problem with the refraction of light was insoluble. Using geometric methods, he provided a solution, which provided new sharpness in the study of heavenly bodies.

A quartet of physicists (two father-and-son pairs) brought honor to Uppsala for over 100 years. Anders Jonas Angström, after whom a length of measurement (one ten-millionth of a millimeter) was named, began spectroscopic research in the new Physicum laboratories; his interest in this research was carried on by his son Knut. From Knut the baton was passed to Manne Siegbaum and eventually to Siegbaum's son Kai; with increasingly sophisticated instruments and measurements, the structure of materials has been an important focus of research in Uppsala laboratories to the present day. The work brought Nobel Prizes in physics to Manne (1924) and Kai (1981) Siegbaum.

Scientific work at Uppsala was not always recognized at once for its brilliance. Consider the case of Svante August Arrhenius, whose research revolutionized electrochemistry but did not win him an associate professorship because his superiors did not understand his ideas. It took a visit from a brilliant and famous Riga chemist, Wilhelm Ostwald, to explain the importance of Arrhenius's work. Arrhenius won a Nobel Prize for chemistry in 1903, by which time he had left Uppsala and had worked at Stockholm for many years.

Arrhenius's groundbreaking work in physical chemistry was continued at Uppsala by Theodore "The" Svedberg, whose investigations in colloid chemistry have been of great importance in biochemistry and molecular biology. A professor from 1912 until World War II, he also developed a method of making synthetic rubber that proved vital to the war effort. In 1926 he received the Nobel Prize for chemistry. His student Arne Tiselius developed techniques in electrophoresis and chromatography that also led to a Nobel Prize in chemistry (1948).

Not all of the great minds at Uppsala belonged to physical scientists. Nathan Soderblom, humanist and theologian at Uppsala before World War I, received the Nobel Peace Prize in 1930 for his efforts to bring different religious groups around the world into closer harmony.

Those are some of the people of Uppsala. What of the buildings? The castle, built in the 1540s by King Gustav Vasa (the First), was badly damaged by fire and reconstructed in the eighteenth century. Adjacent to the university, the castle is used as an official residence and for limited scholarly pursuits. One of the famous who lived there was Dag Hammarskjold, whose father was governor of Uppsala County when the late United Nations Secretary-General was a child.

The earliest classes were held in the Chapter House, called Carolinska Academien, near the cathedral; it served until demolished in the late eighteenth century. Meanwhile, the Gustavianum, named after benefactor King Gustav II Adolph, was constructed in the 1620s and is still used today, fittingly, for the departments of archaeology, ancient history, and Egyptology, and their respective museums.

The Skytteanum, donated by early chancellor Johan Skytte, was also constructed in the 1620s and has been used continuously since that time for the teaching of political science. In 1807 the Botanicum, or Linnean Hall, was built with greenhouses adjacent to Linnaeus's restored botanical gardens. While other buildings were constructed over the next century, the most striking changes in the campus came in the 1970s when the student body had burgeoned from less than 4,500 after the end of World War II to nearly 20,000. The enormous Biomedical Center, the Teknikum for the department of engineering, and the Center for Humanities and Social Sciences were constructed at that time.

The university library, begun with a donation of books and manuscripts from King Gustavus Adolphus in the early 1600s, consists of the main library, Carolina Rediviva, and many branch and departmental libraries. Although it contains many important archival materials,

the most important item is surely the *Codex Argenteus,* or the *Silver Book.* Taken from Prague as war booty in the sixteenth century, the North Italian handwritten translation of parts of the New Testament dates from about A.D. 500 .

If it seems that all of the famous alumni and faculty of Uppsala University have been men, there is an explanation: for most of its history, women were not allowed to study or teach there. Not until 1872 was a woman admitted; and not until 1882 was a woman allowed to defend a doctoral thesis. Slowly, more and more women were admitted, but at the turn of the century still fewer than 3 percent of the students were females. The problem was that once women received a degree, there wasn't much they were allowed to do with it. Not until 1923 could they legally teach at the university.

Like many college campuses, Uppsala University has long been home to groups of socially conscious students. A century-old organization of liberals, Verdandi, was formed to offer opportunities for debate between disputing factions. Actively supporting workers' rights and adult education, Verdandi was soon known for its radicalism. Forming libraries, publishing scientific booklets for laymen, and promoting art exhibitions, Verdandi pioneered Swedish adult education. In response, the conservative students formed Heimdal; then the social-democrats began the student society Laboremus. Antagonism among the groups often spilled over into the national political arena until a calm descended in 1915.

However, the politics of the outside world once again intruded on the university in the mid-1930s, when students became concerned that the growing number of Jewish refugees would compete with them for jobs. In 1939, the Student Union took up the matter, in a meeting that was the most heated in its history. Finally, a resolution against granting permits to Jewish refugees was passed by an overwhelming majority, despite the opposition of both Verdandi and Laboremus. The result was embarrassment for the Student Union, since some of the press reported the vote as a victory for Nazi sympathizers. The Student Union responded by removing all Nazi sympathizers from any leading positions they held.

With seven faculties (theology, medicine, arts, social sciences, science, law, and pharmacy), Uppsala University has today about 18,000 students in 150 departments. Slowly, over a period of centuries, the student population has shifted from primarily ruling class to the children of the middle and laboring classes.

An unusual facet of the Uppsala life is the presence of "nations," 13 organizations with their own buildings (including some living quarters), libraries, and social halls for special cultural and leisure events and festivities. Each student is required to belong to a nation, and many of them have connections to scholarships and exchange programs abroad.

Uppsala University reaches out today to all corners of the globe, sharing knowledge and skills with the Third

World. Exchanges with students from England, Poland, the Czech Republic, Greece, and China have been conducted, and American students reach Uppsala through programs with the University of Miami, the University of Michigan, and California State University.

With its roots planted firmly in the Middle Ages, Uppsala University today is branching toward the twenty-first century.

Further Reading: Karin Johannisson's *A Life of Learning: Uppsala University during Five Centuries* (Uppsala: Upp-sala University Press, 1989) is a scholarly look at the university, illustrated with historic portraits and photographs. "Uppsala University—Younger than Ever After More than 500 Years" is a colorful booklet available from the university. A beautifully illustrated biography of Carl von Linne is Wilfrid Blunt's *The Compleat Naturalist, A Life of Linnaeus* (New York: Viking, 1971), with many references to Uppsala University.

—Jeanne Munn Bracken

VANDERBILT UNIVERSITY
(Nashville, Tennessee, U.S.A.)

Location: In Nashville, the capital of Tennessee.

Description: A private university, enrolling approximately 10,000 students in undergraduate, graduate, and professional schools.

Information: Dean of Undergraduate Admissions
Vanderbilt University
2305 West End Avenue
Nashville, TN 37203-1700
U.S.A.
(615) 322-2561

Visiting: There are regularly scheduled orientations for prospective students and guides for informal visits. To make arrangements, call the Office of Undergraduate Admissions at (615) 322-2561.

The destructive effects of the Civil War in the United States left citizens in the north and south in search of stability and unity. One person who attempted to heal the sectional wounds was Commodore Cornelius Vanderbilt. A self-made millionaire, who first built an empire in steamboat shipping and then another in railroads, he had the largest fortune in America in the 1870s. A man accustomed to uniting geographic areas through his transportation businesses, he did as much as anyone to bring together the east and west of the newly forming country. In 1873, he wished to help bridge the gap between north and south.

Vanderbilt gave 1 million to Methodist Bishop Holland McTyeire to found a university in Nashville, Tennessee. McTyeire was the leader of a movement within the Methodist Episcopal Church, South, to establish an institution of learning of the highest order. The impetus for such a project went as far back as the 1840s, but the church was stymied first by lack of funds and then by the Civil War.

The endowment of the university was Cornelius Vanderbilt's only major philanthropy. He was influenced to perform this act of generosity by his young second wife, who was from Mobile, Alabama, and was a cousin of Mrs. Holland McTyeire. She knew that her husband wanted to leave a memorial, and she was also aware that in 1872 a charter for "Central University" issued in Nashville to petitioners representing nine Methodist conferences failed for lack of financial resources.

In 1873, McTyeire went to New York for medical treatment and stayed with the Vanderbilts. During the course of that visit, he secured the Commodore's support for the projected university. Some suspect that there was a fair degree of pre-visit consultation between McTyeire and Mrs. Vanderbilt on how best to convince the Commodore of the worthiness of the project, but accounts are inconclusive. It was known, however, that Mrs. Vanderbilt would sing lovely Methodist hymns to the Commodore, who had never joined a church. He was indeed enchanted by the hymns and deemed the Methodist Church, especially the southern branch, a worthy recipient of his largesse.

Upon receiving the gift, the bishop commented, "A citizen of the North, Mr. Vanderbilt could have found there ready acceptance of his gift and built up an institution rivaling those which abound in that wealthier and more prosperous section of the country; but to the South he looked, and extended to her people what they needed as much as pecuniary aid—a token of good will."

Vanderbilt simply saw the endowment as an extension of his business practices, whereby he endeavored to unite disparate parts of a young nation. Indeed, a year before his death in 1877, he wrote to McTyeire the only recorded statement of his purpose for founding the university: "If [the university] shall, through its influence, contribute, even in the smallest degree, to strengthening the ties which should exist between all geographical sections of our common country, I shall feel that it has accomplished one of the objects that led me to take an interest in it." These words can be seen on the pedestal of Vanderbilt's statue, erected on the campus by the citizens of Nashville.

When Vanderbilt conferred his gift, he insisted upon five conditions. Two of them were crucial to the long-term character of the institution. He insisted that McTyeire run the university as the Commodore himself would run the New York Central Railroad—as an authoritarian, no-nonsense businessman. Since the bishop did not quite have the heart to abandon his ecclesiastical responsibilities to take up this task, a compromise was reached. McTyeire would receive $3,000 and live on campus in a house constructed for him, and he would assume the very heavy responsibility of exercising veto power over the actions of the self-governing board of trust. Vanderbilt's second critical condition was that the university be located in or near Nashville. Vanderbilt had been scrutinizing his railroad maps and observed that the city was a strategic center with ease of access for the whole region. Memphis and Knoxville had offered sites and even monetary incentives, but when Vanderbilt heard that the church had located its publishing house in Nashville, his mind was made up.

Bishop McTyeire set out to choose a site for the campus, in what was then a city of 40,000 people. He purchased some land about two miles from downtown, and he received other parcels as gifts; the total tract included about 75 acres. He described the site to Commodore Vanderbilt as "west of the city, beautiful for situation, easy of approach, and of the same elevation as Capital Hill, which is in full view." The first structures to go up on the site were a main building in a Victorian Gothic style (called "Old Main"), an astronomical observatory, and houses for professors.

McTyeire then looked to Landon C. Garland, a distinguished educator and prominent Methodist layman, for help in the selection of faculty, the arrangement of curriculum, and the setting of policies. Garland consulted with old friends from academia, colleagues such as the presidents of Harvard University and Columbia University, to design an academic blueprint. He was determined that the university, rising out of the ashes of a ruined South, would rival any of the fine universities in the North. Garland, whose primary interests lay in science, was convinced that his aims could be achieved by acquiring the best and most current scientific equipment and by engaging an outstanding faculty. This belief, coupled with Garland's relentless search for the best laboratory equipment money could buy, resulted in Vanderbilt's having the best scientific apparatus in the United States for the first 20 years of the university's existence. Garland also wanted to stimulate large donations from the Methodist Church to supplement the start-up money from Commodore Vanderbilt. He worked tirelessly to construct a program that would satisfy his high educational standards, the proprieties of the church, and the wish for sectional conciliation mandated by Vanderbilt.

Garland and McTyeire decided that the university would be organized into four departments: philosophy, science, and literature; biblical; law; and medical. Garland preferred the system of separate schools similar to that at the University of Virginia, so that each degree program within the four departments was organized under a different school. The faculty Garland and McTyeire assembled was distinguished: five had been college presidents. The 1872 charter was amended in 1873 to make the legal name of the corporation, The Vanderbilt University, and in October 1875, Bishop McTyeire presided over the dedication ceremonies of the new university.

The students, all of them middle-class young men from Southern Methodist families, streamed into "Old Main" in the fall of 1875. There was one exception, however, to the male-only admission requirement: Kate Lupton, daughter of a faculty member, attended classes that very first year and even managed to acquire a degree in 1879. Other women attended classes intermittently until 1895 when the university opened its doors to full-time matriculation of women, a minor miracle in those times for an institution located in the south.

The first decade was rocky. Following Vanderbilt's wishes, McTyeire ruled with an iron hand. Within the first few years, the original academic and biblical faculties warred with the bishop over several issues, including faculty salaries. By the end of the decade, many full-time faculty had left the institution, leaving McTyeire and Garland the task of once again constructing a staff. The university also had difficulty attracting qualified students, and those who came chafed at the restrictions placed upon them by McTyeire and the stern church elders on the board of trust. There were complaints about the lack of school spirit, the inconveniences of living at off-campus boarding houses, and the lack of amenities.

At the time of Vanderbilt's death in 1877, he believed that his goal of geographical unity was being achieved. He surely could not anticipate that internal dissensions caused the university to all but begin anew in 1887. The academic program was reorganized and admissions policies were changed to allow acceptance only for those who were prepared for authentic college-level work. Garland's beloved model of separate schools was repudiated and the standard class system with courses fitted to class levels was adopted. Graduate programs were established for classical and scientific degrees.

When Bishop McTyeire died in 1889, Garland, who had always been in second place, took over the presidency of Vanderbilt at the age of 79. He launched a campaign to diminish the powers that McTyeire had held, including the president's right of veto about which Commodore Vanderbilt had felt so strongly that he had made it a condition of his financial gift. However, when the board elected a new president, Bishop Hargrove, for a life tenure, it retained the power of the presidential veto.

By 1892, Vanderbilt's governance was brought into line with many other universities, by eliminating the role of president (initially created for McTyeire) and making the chancellor the chief executive officer. This act, in one sense, repudiated the Commodore's desire for the president to be analogous to a chief executive officer and for the chancellor to be in an academic policy-making role. In 1893, the board of trust elected a chancellor who was to combine these functions and become the most influential person in Vanderbilt's history, James Hampton Kirkland.

Kirkland found a thriving academic environment. Vanderbilt's Academic Department, bolstered by young faculty with the Ph.D. from German universities, ranked just below those of Johns Hopkins, Harvard, and the University of Michigan in faculty strength. In 1890, the United States Commissioner of Education listed the university as among 12 "which, together with certain of the state universities, approach more nearly the idea of true universities than any other institutions in the country." Vanderbilt's son, William Henry and his grandsons, Cornelius II and William Kissam Vanderbilt, continued to provide funds which supported the construction of new theology, engineering, and science buildings as well as new dormitories. In 1901, Phi Beta Kappa chartered a chapter at Vanderbilt.

Garland died in 1895, leaving a university growing in scope and depth. Unfortunately, things began to decline rather rapidly toward the end of the century. A wholesale flight of faculty resulted from the meager wages that the board of trust refused to increase. The caliber of graduate students was falling and fewer came from northern schools, thus disappointing those who shared Commodore Vanderbilt's dream that the university would bring together students from different sections of the country. The university was also in debt, which meant that Kirkland was struggling with budgets, leaving little time or energy for the task of consolidating the professional schools (law, medicine, dentistry, engineering, and pharmacy), which were mostly in proprietary arrangements with the university. For example, in relation to law and medicine, local physicians and lawyers were responsible, both educationally and financially, for the two schools; the Vanderbilt Board of Trust did little more than sanction the arrangements.

But the new chancellor rallied and in 1901 began to pull all the professional schools under his and the board's effective management. He explored affiliating the George Peabody Normal School with Vanderbilt, using the teacher's college at Columbia University as a model. His vision of a firm affiliation with the Peabody School was not to be realized until some 75 years later.

Only a few years later, however, tragedy struck as, on April 20, 1905, the campus's original building, "Old Main," was gutted in a fire; the casualties included the outstanding chemistry and physics laboratories and the graduate library. The next day William Kissam Vanderbilt donated $150,000, and alumni and the citizens of Nashville donated funds, toward the reconstruction. The Victorian Gothic gave way to an Italianate style; the fourteenth-century town hall of Siena, Italy, was used as a model for the new structure, to be called Kirkland Hall.

Vanderbilt faced its most difficult period during the early 1900s, when it confronted and ultimately surmounted a crisis in its identity. The university had been carrying out Commodore Vanderbilt's desires for an open institution that would serve to unite geographical areas. The student body was comprised of men and women of different religious denominations from all parts of the country. The bishops of the Methodist Episcopal Church, South, however, felt that the relatively open admissions policy had fostered an institution that had strayed too far from its Christian origins. They were insisting on tighter control of the decisions of the board, a direction which the liberal faculty and student body would not tolerate. In 1914, after years of controversy, which culminated in a lawsuit that went all the way to the U.S. Supreme Court, Vanderbilt University severed its ties with the Methodist Church. Historian P.K. Conkin summarized the reactions to the decision: "Church newspapers lamented a total defeat . . . but the campus was delirious. Kirkland led a march of a reported 1,000 students in downtown Nashville. The celebration reportedly outclassed that following any great football victory. And in educational circles the decision was generally hailed as a victory for higher education and even for academic freedom."

The decision heralded an era of growth in the university's physical plant, but it would soon have to confront the issues of women's roles in the university and the admission of black students. Women had been part of campus life since the beginning, but they really began to play a role around the time of World War I. Enrolled in increasing numbers, women were exerting more and more influence in campus life. They began to enter the professional schools in larger numbers, formed social clubs, served as teaching fellows, and even began to be hired as full-time faculty. These accomplishments were hard won and included facing a series of measures aimed at discouraging their participation in campus life, some of them instituted by Kirkland, who saw Vanderbilt as an institution for men with women only as "guests." Nonetheless by 1929, women comprised 25 percent of the student body and maintained the highest grade-point averages in the university.

There were no black students at Vanderbilt early in the century, but by the end of the 1920s there was a nucleus of faculty members committed to equal rights for blacks, still a very radical position in the south. Interracial forums were held, attracting the ire of many Vanderbilt students and faculty. White resistance to black applicants, especially from alumni, persisted throughout the civil rights era. Black students, however, were admitted beginning in 1953 but under stringent rules and only in isolated cases. The turning point came with the famous Lawson case, which turned the Vanderbilt campus upside down and ultimately opened the door to full desegregation. John Lawson, a black divinity school student during the 1958–59 term, was involved in efforts to peacefully desegregate local Nashville lunch counters. When he refused to terminate his activities upon threats from the city's mayor, then Chancellor Branscomb was pressured to remove Lawson from the university. The divinity school faculty and dean threatened to resign if the chancellor submitted to the mayor's pressure. A compromise was finally worked out, allowing Lawson to receive a degree and reinstating the divinity school staff. Within two years, Vanderbilt was open to full participation by black students.

The Vanderbilt family was still offering its help to the university. In fact, Harold Vanderbilt, three generations removed from the Commodore, had helped hammer out the agreement that settled the Lawson case. As president of the board of trust beginning in 1954, he was the first family member to take an official position with the school. After 1955, Harold Vanderbilt became the primary source of outside income for Vanderbilt.

In the 1950s, Vanderbilt, emerging as a major university, was outgrowing its provincial roots and even merging with other institutions. Oberlin's Graduate School of

Theology moved to Vanderbilt Divinity School; George Peabody School for Teachers was officially made part of the university; and the Blair School of Music joined in the early 1980s.

Additional distinction was added to Vanderbilt when one faculty member and one alumnus were made Nobel Laureates—Professor Earl W. Sutherland Jr. for physiology or medicine in 1971, and alumnus Stanford Moore, who shared the Nobel Prize for chemistry in 1972. Another alumnus, Robert Penn Warren, was awarded three Pulitzer Prizes.

As the years have passed, the university has continued to fulfill Commodore Vanderbilt's original dictum to heal sectional divisiveness by bringing together students from all parts of the country to study together. In the last year of Chancellor Alexander Heard's tenure (1963–82), students came from 50 states and 73 foreign countries. The 1994–95 freshman class was comprised of 47.4 percent women and 16.2 percent members of underrepresented racial groups.

Given its geography, its sectarian conflicts, and the expected sturm und drang of beginning and maintaining any institution, Vanderbilt University has more than ful- filled the founders' hope and expectation that it become a major southern university.

Further Reading: Vanderbilt University's *The Inauguration of Oliver C. Carmichael and a Symposium on Higher Education in the South* (Nashville, Tennessee: Vanderbilt University, 1938) provides insightful essays by academics on the place of Vanderbilt's programs in the present and the future. Robert A. McGraw's *The Vanderbilt Campus: A Pictorial History* (Knoxville, Tennessee: Vanderbilt University Press, 1978) contains archival photos of buildings and students from the university's founding to 1974. Mark Royden Winchell edits a series of essays commemorating the English department at Vanderbilt, which fostered a tradition of gifted writers (*The Vanderbilt Tradition: Essays in Honor of Thomas Daniel Young* [Baton Rouge: Louisiana State University Press, 1991]). The most extensive account of Vanderbilt is found in P.K. Conkin's *Gone with the Ivy: A Biography of Vanderbilt University* (Knoxville: The University of Tennessee Press, 1985).

—Marcia Horowitz

VASSAR COLLEGE
(Poughkeepsie, New York, U.S.A.)

Location: The college sits two miles outside of the small city of Poughkeepsie along the Hudson River, 75 miles north of New York City.

Description: A coeducational college of 2,250 students offering the B.A. and M.A. in liberal arts.

Information: Director of Admissions
Vassar College
Poughkeepsie, NY 12601
U.S.A.
(914) 437-7300

Visiting: Student led tours are available year round. Call the number above for schedule.

Born in England in 1792, Matthew Vassar and his family immigrated to upstate New York in 1796. Finding the local ales there inferior, they decided to import barley corn from England and open a brewery. The business was successful, but after the brewery was destroyed by fire in 1811, Matthew Vassar opened his own brewery. He later diversified his holdings into the whaling industry and became part owner of a whaling fleet. In 1813, he married Catherine Valentine; the marriage produced no children. With no heirs and with a great fortune, Vassar decided to leave a memorial named for himself. During a trip to London in 1845, Vassar and his wife visited the new Guy Vassar Hospital, named for a relative in England who had funded it. Matthew Vassar then determined that his own memorial would also be a hospital.

In 1854 Vassar had a historical meeting with educator Milo P. Jewett. Born in Vermont in 1808, Jewett had studied at Dartmouth College and Andover Theological Seminary, then taught at Marietta College in Ohio. In 1839 he founded a school for women, the Judson Female Institute, in Marion, Alabama. Due to his antislavery sentiments Jewett was forced to leave the south in the 1850s. Vassar's niece, Lydia Booth, who ran the Cottage Hill Seminary for Women in Poughkeepsie, died, and Jewett purchased the school. This brought together Vassar and Jewett, a relationship which led to the development of what has become one of the major colleges in the United States.

Jewett believed that "a rich man should use his property for the glory of God." When Vassar spoke of his plans to build a hospital Jewett's response was "great hospitals are for great cities" and advised Vassar he would make "better use of his money if he threw it in the Hudson River." The

two men decided a better alternative would be to "endow a college for young women which should be to them what Yale and Harvard are to young men."

The chosen site was a former racetrack and fairgrounds stretching along the Hudson River two miles east of the city of Poughkeepsie. On February 26, 1861, Vassar transferred $408,000 to the board of trustees. Plans were being made for the construction of the campus when the guns fired on Fort Sumter and the Civil War began. Amid the chaotic economy created by the war, ground was broken for the main building on June 3, 1861. At the ceremony the 69-year-old Matthew Vassar raised the first shovel of soil.

Jewett, who was the college's first president, was not present at the ceremonies. He was busy visiting other colleges to gain ideas for designing the curriculum. That year Jewett visited his alma mater Dartmouth, Amherst College, Brown University, Yale University, and the women's college Mount Holyoke. Jewett continued his curriculum research by touring the colleges, museums, and libraries of England and Europe in 1862. Vassar was left at home with the difficulties of building a college during the financial turmoil of war. Slowly, differences of opinion began to develop between the two men. The first was the question of secularization. Vassar wanted the college to be private and nondenominational, but Jewett was determined that it should have a Baptist affiliation. Another difficulty arose in 1863 when Jewett began to push for an early opening of the school. Vassar, in turn, felt the school was not ready for students.

Jewett was an educator who lacked an understanding of the building industry and the problems Vassar was facing. He became suspicious and angry. Making a fatal mistake he wrote a nasty letter about Vassar to one of the board members with five copies going to other individuals. Either on purpose or by mistake one copy fell into Vassar's hands. In it Jewett called the founder "fickle and childish," a man who is postponing the opening of the college to "amuse himself" with his "play thing." Jewett wrote of "plots and counterplots" against himself for the "nasty love of money." Vassar sent Jewett a copy of the damaging letter and closed with his remarks, "You can no longer be useful in your position. The only alternative for me is to ask for your resignation in proper hands without delay. Whatever further communication there may be between us, they must be in writing." Jewett wrote his letter of resignation on April 16, 1864. At a special meeting on April 29 of the board of trustees it was accepted. Jewett was succeeded by John H. Raymond as president of the college. Formerly president of Brooklyn Collegiate

690

Vassar College

and Polytechnic Institute, Raymond came to Vassar in April 1864 at a salary of $4,000 per year.

In June, with the completion of the observatory, the college building was structurally complete, but the plumbing and furnishings were not yet finished. The library collection had been started, consisting largely of books purchased by Jewett in London in 1862. Vassar began the Vassar College Art Gallery with the purchase of over 400 oils and watercolors by European and American artists from board member Reverend Elias Lyman Magoon for the price of $20,000.

Given a free hand with the curriculum, Raymond opted for a strong liberal arts college for women. The new president outlined three major points regarding the college. First, the school would mirror family life or domesticity, especially since the women would board at the institution. Second, the curriculum was to be entirely devoted to the liberal arts, reflecting a college, not a ladies seminary or trade school for bookkeepers. And third, it would maintain high educational standards and not be a cheap imitation of a men's college. He also did away with Jewett's idea of a free college since the high standards of the college would have to depend on paying students. The board of trustees overwhelmingly approved of President Raymond's plan and voted to open the college in September 1865.

Tuition was set at $350 per year with an additional $50 for music and another $50 for art. Nine professors were appointed, plus instructors. Vassar advanced $25,000 for the first year of operation. The original name of the school was Vassar Female College. Vassar's close friend Sarah J. Hale, the editor of *Godey's Lady's Book,* objected to this name. Hale and Vassar had corresponded frequently over the years regarding the school. At her urging the word "female" was dropped from the name of the college in 1867, and the name became simply Vassar College. The school colors were rose and gray which symbolized the dawn of women's education. The gray represented the intellectual life of women and the rose was the sunlight which was breaking through.

On September 26, 1865, the college officially opened with 353 students. Hannah W. Lyman of Montreal, Canada, who was appointed principal, received an annual salary of $1,500 plus room and board. Male teachers received a salary of $2,500 a year but had to rent apartments in the main building. Maria Mitchell, the astronomy teacher, was paid a mere $800 per year and provided with room and board for herself and her father in the observatory. The inequity of the salaries was obvious, and in 1871 Mitchell won the fight for equal pay for both male and female professors. Mitchell later became the first woman to become a member of the American Academy of Arts and Sciences.

Vassar was seen frequently walking about the grounds of the college. One student described the founder thus: "His face is a perfect sunbeam, he seems entirely happy and contented to walk over the buildings and nod at all the girls." However, since the opening of the college, Vassar's health had been declining. Now in his 70s, the founder had suffered several minor strokes. By April 1868 he had great difficulty walking or getting in and out of a carriage. He decided to retire from the board of trustees that June. The board opened its meeting at 11:00 A.M. on June 23, the morning of Vassar's second commencement ceremonies. Matthew Vassar, too weak to stand, asked to read his annual address from his chair. As he neared the completion of his speech, the board members saw the notes fall from his hand and the founder slump over in his chair. He died at 11:50 A.M. by the Vassar clock. In his will, Vassar left much of his estate to the college. He allotted $100,000 for structural repairs, $50,000 for financial aid to promising students, $50,000 to the lecture fund, and another $50,000 to the development of the library and art gallery.

Other women's institutions of higher learning concentrated on seminary teaching or prepared women for clerical employment. The Vassar College curriculum presented the women with a rigorous course of study aimed at elevating the mind. In addition to the required study of English, students took eight semesters of Latin or Greek and four semesters of a modern language. Students had to complete courses in mathematics, physics, astronomy, and natural history. Drawing, painting, music theory, and choral singing completed the education that led to the A.B. degree. Postgraduate studies were offered which led to the A.M. degree. This degree required two years of additional study plus an accepted dissertation.

In 1878 President Raymond died, and Vassar College appointed a Baptist minister, formerly a professor at Newton Theological Seminary in Newton, Massachusetts, Samuel Caldwell, who became Vassar's third president. That same year a young woman, Stematz Yamakama, enrolled as a freshman. Studying at the expense of the Japanese government, Yamakama, class of 1882, became the first Asian woman to receive a degree from an American college.

Caldwell was not a strong president. Vassar College found itself far behind in the competition with new women's colleges, such as Smith and Wellesley, both of which opened in 1875. Neither of those colleges felt it necessary to have a preparatory department, as Vassar did. Possibly they were attracting students who were better prepared for college. Women also had opportunities at coeducational schools, as Cornell University, Oberlin College, and Antioch College had opened their doors to women. Even the Massachusetts Institute of Technology was admitting women to the study of science and technology. Enrollment at Vassar dropped from 415 students in 1871 to 300 in 1883. The alumnae, concerned about the state of their alma mater, blamed the president. A famous visitor concurred in the negative view of Caldwell. In May 1885 Mark Twain visited Vassar and read two stories in honor of Founder's Day. Unhappy with the treatment he received, Twain refused dinner afterward, referring to Caldwell as "a sour old saint."

Due to the complaints from alumnae, the board of trustees terminated Caldwell's appointment in 1885. The next year James Monroe Taylor, a Baptist minister from Providence, Rhode Island, became Vassar's fourth president. His first order of the day was to rework the curriculum. He opened up more electives during the sophomore year and made the junior and senior years entirely elective. In 1887 the all-male board of trustees elected three women from the alumnae association to sit on the board.

Taylor revived construction on the campus. In 1889 the first gymnasium in a woman's college was built. In 1891 and 1892 the first faculty houses were built on Raymond Avenue. In 1893 an ugly addition was made to the main building. Called Thompson Annex, it was better known as "Uncle Fred's Nose" in "honor" of trustee Frederick Ferris Thompson, who endowed it. That same year, John D. Rockefeller donated $35,000 for Strong Hall, the college's first dormitory. It was named for his daughter, Bessie Rockefeller Strong, who attended Vassar College from 1886 to 1888. Rockefeller, then a trustee, paid for the construction of a classroom building and in 1902 donated $100,000 in memory of his mother to build Eliza Davison House.

Under Taylor's administration the college raised the level of curriculum, improved its facilities, enlarged the library, and refined its faculty. In many ways Taylor brought the college into the twentieth century, except on one issue. Taylor did not support women's suffrage. Although he supported the education of women, he did not approve of their political activity. While in public, Taylor called himself neutral on the issue of women's suffrage, he made his anti-suffrage sentiments clear in private words and later in public acts. In her biography of Henry Mac-Cracken, Elizabeth Daniels describes Taylor's 1907 exchange with Bryn Mawr president, M. Carey Thomas:

He admitted that he was against any extension of suffrage for men or women. His letter to Thomas was a response to one from her asking if Jane Addams, head of Hull House in Chicago, might come and speak at Vassar on the working woman's need of the ballot. [Note: As early as 1866 feminist Caroline Wells Healy Dall had lectured at Vassar on the subject of women's rights.] He declined, saying that such a speech would be "propaganda" rather than education, and that he could not agree to any propaganda on the campus "in regard to socialist matters . . . questionable forms of missionary effort, and extreme temperance agitators, as well as regarding this question of suffrage."

Despite Thomas's protestations that Addams had been invited to Mount Holyoke, Radcliffe, Smith, and Wellesley, Taylor would not relent.

In 1909 suffragist and Vassar senior Inez Milholland arranged a debate on the issue of suffrage in a college lecture hall. Although Taylor had approved of the debate, he was outraged to learn, after returning from an out-of-town trip, that faculty members had participated. After he disciplined them at a meeting, the faculty argued that Taylor was infringing on their right to free speech. The controversy culminated in a 1912 resolution drawn up by 13 faculty members attacking Taylor for his efforts to keep faculty out of decisions regarding campus life. Taylor, then 65, responded by announcing his plans to retire.

During the six-month search for a new president, faculty had opportunities for open discussion about the policies of the college. They were reorganized under a new committee system and their right to a role in determining educational policies was recognized. Faculty were not the only ones to benefit during this interim. Students became active in self-government, discussing issues ranging from curriculum to the abolition of required daily chapel. For the first time, students were able to see their grades; in the past students were denied knowledge of their grades unless they were in serious academic difficulty. Another first during this period was a formal graduation ceremony. At the behest of the students, graduates at the 1914 commencement wore cap and gown.

Henry Noble MacCracken, a Chaucerian scholar with a Ph.D. from Harvard and the first president who was neither a Baptist nor a minister, was inaugurated as Vassar's fifth president on October 13, 1915. A play, The Pageant of Athena, was presented on the occasion. It had been written by a junior, Edna St. Vincent Millay, who was to become a protégé of MacCracken, without whose intervention she would not have been graduated from Vassar. Arriving at Vassar at the age of 23, Millay found herself in trouble with teachers and with academic routine. Mac-Cracken, however, recognized her talents and encouraged her creativity. After disobeying an order that she was not to leave the campus—as a punishment for missing two days of school to see Enrico Caruso perform—she was caught, and the faculty voted to expel her. MacCracken overruled the decision, and Millay was graduated with her class in 1917. MacCracken later said that this occasion was the single time in his presidency that he had overridden a faculty decision.

MacCracken remained at the college for 31 years. He saw Vassar through Prohibition, the Depression, and two world wars. During his administration 11 new buildings were constructed, 170,000 new books were added to the library, and the endowment was increased to $12 million. When he retired in 1946 the new president, Sarah Gibson Blanding, became the first woman president of Vassar. During her administration the first male students studied at Vassar. Although not officially coeducational, the college opened its doors to returning World War II veterans. In 1969 Vassar would become the first of the Seven Sister colleges to admit men.

Vassar College claims many famous alumnae. Edna St. Vincent Millay was the first woman to win the Pulitzer Prize. First Lady Jacqueline Kennedy Onassis attended Vassar as did Academy Award-winners Jane Fonda and Meryl Streep. The first Vassar alumna to become a Rear Admiral in the U.S. Navy was Grace M. Hopper, who was coinventor of the COBOL computer language. Rick Lazio, class of 1980, became a New York congressman. Writers and poets who went to Vassar include Elizabeth Bishop, Muriel Rukeyser, Eleanor Clark, and Lucille Fletcher.

Vassar College became the subject of a best-selling novel and a major motion picture. In 1963 Mary McCarthy, class of 1933, published the book *The Group*. Banned in several countries for its sexual explicitness, the novel follows the lives of eight Vassar women from their graduation in 1933 to the beginning of World War II. Following the careers, loves, and political activism of a college clique, the book outraged some of McCarthy's classmates. McCarthy neglected to change some first names, and certain character attributes were so obvious to classmates that the author was threatened with legal action. The book remained on the bestseller list for two years, was made into a movie in 1966, and has sold over 5 million copies.

The Vassar College of today is no longer the Vassar of Mary McCarthy's day. Maids, waitresses, and dining rooms have been replaced by the All College Dining Center where food is served cafeteria style. The century-old commencement ceremony of the Daisy Chain—sophomore women in white dresses bearing ropes of daisies ahead of graduating seniors—is now mixed with sophomore men in blazers and white slacks.

Today the school is racially and economically mixed, with 20 percent of students representing minority groups, and 60 percent of the students receiving financial aid. No longer a wealthy girls' college, Vassar has students from diverse backgrounds, representing every corner of the United States and 30 other countries. Over 90 percent of the students accepted are from the top quarter of their high school class, and 80 percent of Vassar graduates received advanced degrees five years after graduation.

Further Reading: James Monroe Taylor, Vassar's fourth president, provides an excellent history of Matthew Vassar and Milo Jewett as they planned the college in *Before Vassar Opened* (Freeport, New York: Books for Libraries, 1972). This same period, 1845–65, is also covered in Edward Linner's *Vassar: The Remarkable Growth of a Man and His College 1855–1865* (Poughkeepsie, New York: Vassar College, 1984). A chronology of Vassar College by Dorothy Plum, called *The Magnificent Enterprise: A Chronicle of Vassar College* (Poughkeepsie, New York: Vassar College, 1961), covers the origins of the college up to 1961.

—Patrice Kane

VISVA-BHARATI UNIVERSITY
(Santiniketan, West Bengal, India)

Location: Visva-Bharati University at Santiniketan is part of Bolpur town in the state of West Bengal. One hundred sixty kilometers from Calcutta, it is located in Birbhum district which is a rural part of the state.

Description: A largely residential university, Visva-Bharati has two campuses, at Sriniketan and Santiniketan. It is also a central university, receiving funds from the federal government. It has 13 departments or institutes of study, the best-known ones being the Institute of Fine Arts (Kala Bhavan) and the Institute of Music and Performing Arts (Sangit Bhavan). Visva-Bharati also has a large collection of manuscripts in various languages, including Tibetan and Persian.

Information: Visva-Bharati University
P.O. Santiniketan
Distt. Birbhum
West Bengal 731 235
India
(03463) 52751-6

Visiting: Write to the Office of the Registrar or to the Public Relations Officer at the address mentioned above for further information. Visva-Bharati is closed on Wednesdays.

The sight of schoolchildren attending classes in the outdoors, under the shade of trees is the first clue that Visva-Bharati is not the average, conventional university. Although the buildings and infrastructure reflect the financial shortages common to all Indian universities, and though the curriculum has gradually been conventionalized over the years, the university still differs in many respects from its peers elsewhere. Visva-Bharati grew out of a school that the Indian poet and Nobel laureate, Rabindranath Tagore, established at Santiniketan in 1901. Based on the ancient Indian tradition of education, the school was Tagore's experiment in reviving an old educational tradition that stressed simple living, creativity and self-expression rather than rote learning and dull lessons. In its time, the school was a unique departure from the stultifying education that Indian children received elsewhere.

Rabindranath Tagore's influence is pervasive in Visva-Bharati University. Born into the well-known Tagore family of Calcutta, Rabindranath had a great advantage over other creative artists—family support and encouragement. His grandfather, Dwarkanath Tagore was a highly successful businessman and he also supported the Brahmo Samaj, the early nineteenth-century Hindu reform movement in Bengal. Rabindranath's father, Debendranath Tagore continued Dwarkanath's contributions to cultural activity in Calcutta. A leading activist in the Brahmo Samaj, he was also an outspoken advocate of education as a vehicle to social reform. As part of his religious activities, Debendranath founded a meditation center at Santiniketan in 1863. It was here that Rabindranath began the open-air school called the Brahmo Vidyalaya in 1901.

Rabindranath's poetic genius surfaced early in his supportive family environment. He had already produced quantities of verse, before his family sent him to England in the late 1870s for education. Tagore disliked the highly (and to his mind, narrowly) structured format of British education and returned home. In 1882, his collection of verses, *Sandhya-Sangeeta,* earned critical praise and announced the arrival of a new talent on the Bengali literary scene. In 1891, Rabindranath's father handed over charge of the family estates in East Bengal (present-day Bangladesh) to him. Tagore's creativity blossomed in the lush green countryside of Shilaidah and Shazadpur. His houseboat Padma (named after the grand river of the region) allowed him to travel extensively in both business and creative journeys. In this period, Tagore produced many short stories that drew on the Bengali countryside for themes and images. His famous collection of poems, *Sonar Tari* (*The Golden Boat*; 1894) and the play *Chitrangada* (1892) also date from this period. At the Tagore estate in Shilaidah, Tagore ensured that his children were spared the stifling influence of the prevailing education system. He arranged for live-in tutors to teach his children English, mathematics, and science. He himself instructed them in Bengali and the Indian classics. In 1892, he made his criticism of the education system public in an article in the magazine, *Sadhana*. He also stated that for education to be effective, the medium of instruction should be the native language of the students.

Once Tagore decided to translate his views on education into practical action, he busied himself with the establishment of the school at Santiniketan. He believed that nature and natural surroundings greatly aided education. Unable to find such institutions around him, Tagore found his model in the ancient Indian schools or Gurukul system where students and teachers resided together, and where education was a continuous experience rather than a separate segment of a child's life. The school opened with five students, one of whom was Tagore's son, Rathindranath. Despite the initial difficulties, the school endured. The curriculum emphasized simplicity in externals, to the point of austerity. The students—all boys initially—were required to wear simple yellow clothes, eat vegetarian meals, and sleep in a starkly bare dormitory. The cultural life of the place made up for the lack of physical comfort. Students were encouraged to participate in musical *soirées*, plays, and to express themselves through art and music. Tagore himself wrote many of the plays that the teachers and students performed at Santiniketan. This culture of participation and artistic expression distinguished Santiniketan from other schools even in its earliest days.

Despite the simplicity of life at Santiniketan, the school was a great financial burden on Tagore. The school was supported entirely out of the initial endowment and subsequently, Tagore's personal funds. Along with the crushing problems of administration, Tagore also endured a series of personal tragedies. In 1902, his wife died; nine months later, Tagore also lost a young daughter to tuberculosis, and in 1907, his youngest son to cholera. The experiment at Santiniketan continued however, as did the poet's literary output. These latter were now tinged with sadness and had a deeper, more reflective quality about them. Acting upon the advice of his doctors, Tagore retired to Shilaidah to recover his health, which he had strained greatly, nursing his wife and children in their long illnesses. In the solitude of his beloved Bengali countryside, he translated some of his poems into English. These were the poems that he took with him to England in 1912 and which took the literary world there by storm. Tagore befriended the poet W.B. Yeats and the artist William Rothenstein. *Gitanjali* (Song Offerings) became his best-known collection of poems in England. In 1913, he received the Nobel Prize for literature. The world travels generated by the post-Nobel recognition brought Tagore into contact with many different world cultures, including Japan in 1916. He also became close to the French philosopher Romain Rolland. On his return to India, Tagore set about creating a center for the study of various world cultures with the aim, in his own words, "to seek to realize in a common fellowship of study the meeting of the East and the West, and thus ultimately to strengthen the fundamental conditions of world peace through the establishment of free communication of ideas between the two hemispheres." Visva-Bharati University thus came into being at Santiniketan and registered itself as a public institution in December 1921.

In the years following, Santiniketan developed rapidly as an unconventional university and a unique center of learning. The children's school remained but it was now merely a part of many different activities on a campus that was now filled with people. Students from across the country flocked to Visva-Bharati. In 1923, Uttar Vibhaga, or the Department of Higher Studies began with the mis-

sion of generating knowledge about the different cultures of the world. Besides Bengali and Hindi, German, Latin, and Persian were part of the choices offered to students. Tagore's international reputation attracted many foreign scholars to Santiniketan. The French Indologist, Sylvain Levi came here as did the Italian scholar Carlo Formichi. Various departments and institutes sprang up as the university expanded. So, in 1937 a Sino-Indian Studies Institute or Cheena Bhavan came into being and in 1948 a Teachers' Training Center was established. Among the famous students at the university in the interwar period was the late Indian prime minister, Indira Gandhi.

The best-known feature of Visva-Bharati remained its active and rich culture of arts and music. Already before 1921, Tagore had drawn to Santiniketan a host of Bengal's most talented artists, including his cousins Abanindranath and Gaganendranath Tagore, Nandalal Bose, and Surendranath Kar. All of them contributed to the collegial atmosphere at Santiniketan in which young painters found immeasurable support and encouragement. Founded in 1922, the department of fine arts, Kala Bhavan, separated into two schools in 1934, one for fine arts and the other for music. To this day, Visva-Bharati is considered a leading center for the fine arts. Kala Bhavan offers degrees in sculpture, art history, and design among others. The department of music, dance, and drama, Sangit Bhavan, keeps alive the tradition of Rabindra-sangit, the music centered around Tagore's poetry and dance-dramas. It also offers training in the north Indian school of classical music. Visva-Bharati's rich repertoire of performance and fine arts reveals itself in the annual fair—the Pous Mela—that takes place every December to mark the foundation of the original retreat by Debendranath Tagore. Troupes of students present song and dance from all regions of the country and thus keep alive Rabindranath Tagore's dream of education through intense cultural activity rather than rote learning.

Tagore was above all a humanist and an internationalist. He was also in his own way, anti-imperialist. Gandhi's favorite song was one composed by Tagore, "If no one heeds your call, then walk alone, walk alone." In 1919, as a protest against the British army's firing on an unarmed crowd in the city of Amritsar—that left over 300 dead—Tagore resigned the knighthood that the British had conferred on him. Still, he did not always agree with the methods of nationalists. Against those who called for boycott of the foreign-made goods that had paralyzed the Indian economy, Tagore called for a simultaneous revival of rural industry and crafts. Mere boycotting of goods and services was, according to him, a negative act that contributed nothing to the alternative, noncolonial culture that India should aspire toward. Tagore's ambivalence to nationalist strategies earned him many critics in activist circles. At Santiniketan, Tagore tried to express his feelings about the idea of proactive rural work through the institution of a Rural Reconstruction Institute or Palli

Samgathana Vibhaga. Set up in 1922, the Institute achieved modest results till independence. Currently, it has an active rural outreach program, emphasizing literacy, health care, and cottage industry.

Rabindranath Tagore died in 1941. Ten years later, Visva-Bharati, to which he had contributed not only his aura but also almost all his personal finances, was declared "an institution of national importance" by the Indian parliament. Since then, it has been supported from central funds. The university curriculum now reflects far more mainstream concerns (such as degrees and formal courses of study) than during the time of Tagore. However, the emphasis on arts and music makes its campus activities unique. The university also maintains a center on Tagore, Rabindra Bhavan, which is a major research center for Tagore Studies scholars. Tagore's residences at Santiniketan—such as Udayan, Konark, and Udichi—are also part of the campus. Their beautiful gardens are a distraction from the ugliness of overdevelopment that has currently overwhelmed Bolpur and Santiniketan. Equally charming are the children of Visva-Bharati's campus schools, sitting in their yellow uniforms under shady trees, learning their lessons, presenting a reminder of simpler days when Tagore's vision of the "cooperative enthusiasm of teachers and students" had seemed more easily attainable.

Further Reading: All works on Tagore's life deal with the establishment of Visva-Bharati. A good overview of Rabindranath Tagore's life and literature by one of his contemporaries is *Rabindranath Tagore, His Life and Work,* by Edward John Thompson (New York: Haskell, 1974). A more recent work is *Rabindranath Tagore,* by Mary M. Lago (Boston: Twayne, 1976). The journal of Visva-Bharati University, *The Visva-Bharati Quarterly* (Santiniketan), is available in many university libraries and provides a good entry point into campus activities. An insight into the more personal aspects of life at Santiniketan and the personal choices of Tagore are available from the poet's son's reminiscences: see *On the Edges of Time,* by Rathindranath Tagore (Westport, Connecticut: Greenwood Press, 1958).

—Sharmishtha Ray Chowdhury

WASHINGTON AND LEE UNIVERSITY
(Lexington, Virginia, U.S.A.)

Location: In western Virginia, in the valley between the Appalachian, Allegheny, and Blue Ridge Mountains, in rural Lexington.

Description: A private university enrolling approximately 2,000 students in undergraduate and professional schools.

Information: Office of Admission
Washington and Lee University
Lexington, VA 24450
U.S.A.
(703) 463-8400

Consistently, Washington and Lee University has been ranked among America's top 25 liberal and law schools by *U.S. News and World Report*. In the category of faculty resources, the institution is considered number one nationally. With an excellent reputation and a small student/faculty ratio of 9/1, Washington and Lee has earned itself a place in the top tier of U.S. liberal arts schools.

This impressive academic reputation has evolved over a period of 250 years and has been the result of contributions made by two famous Americans. Five years before the French and Indian War of 1754–63, Washington and Lee's predecessor, Augusta Academy, had been founded near Lexington, Virginia by resolute Scotch-Irish Presbyterians in search of a classical education for their children. The ideology of the American Revolution influenced the small school which, in 1776, changed its name to Liberty Hall Academy and sought to emulate the ambitious curriculum offered at Princeton.

After independence had been achieved, however, the academy struggled. In 1796, George Washington, preparing to enter his long-delayed retirement at Mount Vernon, saved Liberty Hall Academy from extinction. At the urging of friends associated with the school, the president gave Liberty Hall a major endowment gift (the largest at that time, ever given to any American educational institution) of $50,000 in James River Canal stock. In gratitude, the trustees changed the school's name in 1798 to Washington Academy. Five years later, it moved to nearby Lexington.

The institution's history was heavily influenced by George Washington's early generosity. While physically not present on campus, Washington shielded, in a sense, the school from the fierce battles which occurred between Jefferson and Hamilton and the resulting birth of the two-party political system. Washington Academy weathered

those storms and also the War of 1812 which, despite the best efforts of American propagandists, was considerably less than a victory for the United States.

By 1813, the academy had grown sufficiently to become a college. Despite being chartered by the commonwealth of Virginia in 1782, Washington College was unique among southern colleges in that it had no official relationship with either a church (as in the case of the University of the South) or state (as with Virginia Military Institute, founded in Lexington by the state in 1839). Therefore, Washington College's first century was influenced by the stability of its namesake, a man who cautioned against entanglements—foreign and domestic.

The school's second 100 years began on a bleak note. The Civil War wrecked the valley of Virginia, stripping farmers of their crops and disillusioning a generation of southerners who had embraced the flawed tenets of the Lost Cause. The college's classrooms had emptied in 1861 when students enthusiastically rallied around the Confederacy. An 1864 raid by Union General David Hunter, and subsequent occupation of the campus by Federal troops, turned the initial enthusiasm concerning the war into a flood of despair.

In the final months of the conflict, Washington College deteriorated with regard to its physical plant (e.g., wrecked library, shattered laboratory, splintered classrooms) and its pitifully small student body. Four professors taught 40 boys who, all under military age, came to class sporadically as the south's military effort collapsed. By war's end, Washington College had become, once again, sort of a preparatory school—a far cry from what it had been only five years earlier.

Financially, the college had, amid the exhilaration of 1861, invested unwisely in the Confederacy. Upon General Robert E. Lee's surrender, the school had $2,458.20 in worthless Confederate currency and a considerable amount of equally worthless southern bonds. Once again, George Washington's 1796 endowment saved the school but, until the state legislature met in December, the college existed in somewhat of a quandary. While the 1796 gift's value had increased to $94,000, this endowment was snarled in the uncertainty associated with the death of the Confederate States of America.

The trustees were not discouraged. They sought to borrow $500 to reopen the school for the fall 1865 semester. Rejected, the trustees decided, in a peculiar display of logic, to apply for a larger loan of $4,600 based on the reasoning that amid the terrible destruction the war larger—instead of smaller—loans had better chances of gaining approval. Additionally, the board of trustees

Washington and Lee University

passed this motion: "Resolved, that a committee of three be appointed to wait upon the Commandant of the Federal forces now at Lex. and ask that the college buildings be at once vacated by the troops."

Therefore, Washington College, a school with more than 100 years of success, stood in late 1865 perilously near the edge of bankruptcy with a campus occupied by northern troops who showed no sign of desiring to vacate the premises. Additionally, the college had no president since the prewar chief executive had been driven from town because of his Union sympathies.

At a crucial trustees' meeting, the board pondered the presidential search. Several names were discussed and then, in a dramatic moment, one trustee mentioned that General Robert E. Lee's daughter, Mary, had confided that the defeated commander needed a job. The suggestion is noted in the board records thusly: "Then various members of the board said what a great thing it would be for the col-

lege if the services of General Lee could be secured, and wondered if there was any chance of doing so."

Within minutes, and without Lee's knowledge, the trustees had found a new president. Judge John Brockenbrough, board chairperson, was appointed to carry an official invitation to the general. Some board members wondered if Lee would accept the presidency of a "broken-down college."

Wearing a borrowed suit, Judge Brockenbrough, with borrowed funds, met with Lee at Lee's borrowed Richmond home. Surely, the symbolism of the moment painted a dismal portrait of the south in the months following Appomattox. A destitute judge offered a defeated commander the presidency of an all-but-closed college.

Brockenbrough's offer was a modest one. Lee would receive a house, garden, percentage of tuition, and $1,500 a year. As the general considered the proposal he thought of 1852 when he had tried earnestly to refuse the superintendency of West Point. Agriculture—not education—was the pathway he wished to follow now that the war was over.

Three words, "Duty, Honor, Country," had guided Lee since his student days at West Point. These words had caused him to reject command of the Union forces in early 1861 and accept the leadership of the Army of Northern Virginia. It had been *duty* to his native state which had motivated him for four long years. Now, it would be *duty* to Virginia, to rebuilding a small college in Virginia, which would influence Lee's decision.

One of Lee's friend, William Nelson Pendleton, and Episcopal rector and former Confederate general, wrote Lee:

> One great reason why I hope you may judge favorably of this invitation is, that the destiny of our State and Country depends so greatly upon the training of our young men. And now our Educational Institutions are so crippled that they need the very best agencies for their restoration and the revival of high aims in the breasts of Virginian and Southern youths.

After three weeks of contemplation, Lee conditionally accepted the Washington College presidency. He explained to the board that his personal situation might, unfortunately, become like that of the imprisoned Jefferson Davis. He also warned the trustees that he feared "my occupation of the position of President might draw upon the College a feeling of hostility."

Still, the board stressed in its reply, Robert E. Lee was their choice to guide Washington College. Five months after Appomattox, Lee, because of his perception of duty, became president of an institution he had never visited. Immediately, he began to call for "the healing of all dissensions."

Lee's five-year tenure at Washington College was characterized by increases in student enrollment (from 40 to 400), financial stability, teacher recruitment, a modern honor code, a revitalized curriculum, the birth of a national fraternity (Kappa Alpha Order) which considered Lee its spiritual founder, and an overpowering sense of sectional reconciliation. According to one account, Lee daily passed a Lexington home with a shattered oak tree in front, a casualty of war. The tree's owner, a woman who daily greeted Lee as he walked by the tree, criticized the Union soldiers who had splintered the oak. Finally, Lee, in his softspoken manner, advised "Ma'am, just cut the tree down."

The Lee years saw the establishment of the country's first journalism program and, in 1866, a law school began. Students from 20 states and 1 foreign country came to the school and, by Lee's death in 1870, the school had surpassed its prewar prosperity to become national in character.

A year after Lee's demise, the institution was renamed Washington and Lee College, honoring "in fit conjunction" the two generals. Both men personified a commitment to "duty, honor, and country." Despite a late nineteenth-century struggle, those potent three words guided the school into the present century. Washington and Lee's Law School became coeducational in 1972 with its graduate programs and the inclusion of women undergraduates occurred in 1985.

Since 1983, Washington and Lee University has been led by John D. Wilson, who, in the style of General Lee, presides over a school which has earned a national reputation. Rhodes Scholars have been chosen, on average, every third year since 1970. The ranking by *U.S. News and World Report* and other publications attests to the emphasis placed by Lee, Wilson, and other university leaders on providing students an educational experience deeply rooted in "duty, honor, and country."

Further Reading: For two useful treatments of the importance of George Washington in the formative years of the Republic, see Douglas Southhall Freeman's *George Washington* (New York: Scribner, 1956) and Marcus Cunliffe's *George Washington: Man and Monument* (revised, New York: Penguin, 1982). A good study of Lee's role in saving the college is Emory Thomas's *Robert E. Lee* (New York: Norton, 1995).

—Joseph Edward Lee

WASHINGTON UNIVERSITY
(Saint Louis, Missouri, U.S.A.)

Location: In the Forest Park neighborhood of northwestern St. Louis.

Description: An independent university that enrolls approximately 11,500 students in its undergraduate, graduate, and professional programs combined.

Information: Washington University
Office of Undergraduate Admissions
1 Brookings Drive
Campus Box 1089
St. Louis, MO 63130-4899
U.S.A.
(314) 935-6000

State Senator Wayman Crow of Missouri was the first great patriarch of Washington University. He drafted by himself a charter for a tax-free educational institution to be located in St. Louis, and he brought the document to his fellow legislators in the form of a bill. The charter was signed into law by Governor Sterling Price on February 22, 1853, even before Crow had informed William Greenleaf Eliot, a Unitarian minister, that the new institution was to be named "Eliot Seminary" in his honor. Indeed, it was only after the law was enacted that Eliot and 15 select members of his congregation learned that Crow had listed them as incorporators of the seminary, along with himself. The incorporators, or trustees, were somewhat daunted by the task to which Crow had magisterially assigned them, for St. Louis was at that time still a young city on the edge of America's western frontier. Years later, Eliot wrote: "It took us quite by surprise . . . for none of us had dreamed of such a thing, and an educational institution seemed quite beyond our strength."

The name of the seminary was changed three times before the trustees settled on "Washington University." Apparently too modest to accept Crow's generous homage, Eliot directed that the seminary operate under the name of the "Washington Institute of St. Louis," and in 1855 legislation was drafted to adopt that name legally. However, a charter for a Washington College in St. Louis was enacted that same year, and so the trustees withdrew their proposal. According to university records, some "unauthorized parties" then introduced legislation to change the seminary's name to Lafayette Institute, but the bill was halted at the governor's desk by a telegram asking him to veto the proposal. The trustees then agreed to the title of the O'Fallon Institute, in honor of Colonel John O'Fallon, who donated the first plot of land acquired by the seminary. However, plans for the Washington College fell through that same year, and so O'Fallon requested that his name not be used. Finally in 1858, the name Washington University was officially assumed in an amendment to the school charter.

Washington grew rapidly, despite financial strain and major setbacks suffered during its first several years of operation. The O'Fallon Polytechnic Institute opened under the auspices of the university in 1855 and was scheduled to be moved soon after into a spacious new building on the corners of Chestnut and Seventh in downtown St. Louis. However, primarily because of financial hardship brought on by the Civil War, the construction was not completed until 1866, and its total cost, combined with the expense of operating the polytechnic itself, proved too much for the young university. Both the polytechnic and the five-story building were temporarily assigned to the public school system in 1868. More favorable events during the same period included the construction in 1856 of the university's first building, Academic Hall, at the corner of St. Charles and Seventeenth Streets, and the opening of the scientific department in 1857, the forerunner to the modern school of engineering.

Washington evolved into a complex university between the time of its foundation and its move to the famously well-designed Hilltop Campus in 1905. The law school opened in 1867, having retained a highly qualified faculty including two state supreme court justices. The first woman was enrolled in the school five years later, following the decision in 1869 to make Washington the first institution in the nation to accept women into a law program. In 1891, the university acquired the formerly independent St. Louis Medical College, which was united with the Missouri Medical College eight years later, thus forming the Medical College of Washington University. In 1892, Washington incorporated the Missouri Dental College. The school of fine arts opened in 1879, the Henry Shaw School of Botany in 1885, the school of architecture, and the school of engineering in 1902.

The downtown campus was crowded and worn by the early 1890s, and the trustees began to consider a move. In an unpublished history of Washington University, the late Dean Alexander Langsdorf described the university's buildings as suffering from "dusty wooden floors, numerous partitions of tongue-and-groove lumber added as afterthoughts . . . and lighting fixtures so inadequate by modern standards as merely to punctuate the gloom of

Washington University

dark winter afternoons." Thus, in 1893 the board of directors passed a resolution floated by Henry Eliot, son of William G. Eliot, to move the university's colleges and the polytechnic to a new location. The university was financially prepared to accomplish the move thanks largely to the generosity of Robert Brookings and Samuel Cupples. Brookings retired from business and joined Washington's board of directors in 1891, having decided to devote his full energies to improvement of the university. He may be considered the second great patriarch of Washington. Not only did he lead a successful fundraising campaign, but Brookings and Cupples donated half of their holdings in Cupples Station properties to Washington, the sum valued at several million dollars.

The new campus was carefully and slowly planned. In 1894, the university purchased 103 acres of land in northwestern Forest Park, then a nearby suburb northwest of St. Louis. While the location seemed rather remote, the trustees recognized the potential for growth of the area. A preliminary site plan was drafted by the landscape

architectural firm of Olmsted, Olmsted and Eliot. The Olmsted brothers pointed out that the university would be deleteriously confined unless 50 additional acres abutting the southern border of the original site were purchased. Indeed, their plans all presumed ownership of such an extension, although no further land was actually secured until 1899. Washington then staged a limited competition for the design of the Hilltop Campus, in keeping with the plans drawn up by the Olmsteds. The university organized a building committee, the members of which drafted guidelines for a limited architectural competition. Plans for at least the first seven buildings to be raised on the new campus were to be included in the winning design.

Six of the most prestigious architectural firms in the country were invited to participate in what turned out to be a competition of some national interest. In October 1899, a jury of eight declared Cope and Stewardson of Philadelphia the winners, but unfortunately there is no record of the members' deliberations or the basis for their decision. They were likely impressed by the way that Cope's plan

(Stewardson died in 1896) abandoned the rigid classicism dominating each of the competing proposals, and by the way that Cope's block plan could gracefully accommodate future building on campus in varied architectural styles. One of the jury members later commented on the fact that Cope's design harmonized with the natural contours of the land and thoroughly considered the special needs of each building and its departments.

The first six buildings that Cope designed were under construction by 1900. They were all long, narrow Tudor Gothic works constructed of red Missouri granite and Bedford stone. None was more than three stories high, except the small towers adorning several constructions. These horizontally oriented buildings were arranged around a series of interconnected courtyards, modeled upon the layouts of Oxford and Cambridge Universities. University Hall (later renamed Brookings Hall) served as the main entrance to the new campus, as it still does today. Its great length is divided by an arched breezeway, guarded by two gargoyles, that opens upon the inner courtyards.

Robert Brookings exercised his business acumen to partially fund the construction of the new plant. The United States hosted the World's Fair in 1902, and the Louisiana Purchase Exposition was held in Forest Park. Brookings took the initiative to lease the new university buildings to the fair's management for the considerable sum of $750,000. By a happy coincidence the first Olympic Games ever held in America were staged on the university's new Francis Field that same year. Thus, the Exposition events literally ran abreast the 38 athletic competitions taking place on Washington's virgin campus. When the festive events finally came to an end, the university resumed construction, and, by 1910, there were 12 buildings on campus, all constructed in the Gothic style of Cope's original plan.

Washington's Hilltop Campus is widely considered one of the most beautiful in the country, with modern additions carefully planned to harmonize with Cope's design. Murphy and Mackey, the architects of the Olin Library, located two of the library's floors underground in order to retain visual proportions commensurate with the older buildings. When the university embarked on a $63-million expansion project in 1957, dormitories were constructed on a newly acquired site known as the South Forty, which is connected to the main campus by an underpass. All of the old dormitories were then converted to academic buildings, thus affording the university badly needed facilities, while preserving the original campus.

Washington quickly grew in size and stature following the move to Forest Park. Ten new buildings were raised between 1923 and 1927, and a record number of 7,895 students enrolled during the academic year 1926–27. The medical school was almost immediately transformed into one of the nation's finest, following its dramatic restructuring in 1910. That year, Abraham Flexner published a report on the state of medical education in America under auspices of the Carnegie Foundation for the Advancement of Teaching. Even before that report was available to the public, word reached Brookings that Flexner looked very dimly upon Washington's medical school. Brookings went to New York and brought Flexner to St. Louis, where he then observed operations at the medical school and offered advice on how it might be bettered. The creation of some of the nation's first full-time professorships of internal medicine, surgery, and pediatrics were among the changes that vastly improved the quality and reputation of the medical program.

During this same period of growth, the university suffered a rather honorable loss. In 1923, Brookings organized the Graduate School of Economics and Government, which was to award doctoral degrees. However, Brookings's plan for students to spend a year in Washington, D.C. proved unfeasible. The university's tax-exempt status had been granted by the Missouri legislature and applied only so long as the corporation operated within the state. Thus, the school splintered off from Washington to become the prestigious and still respected Brookings Institution.

Chancellor George Throop, who served from 1927 until 1944, adeptly guided the university through both the Great Depression and World War II, a period in which most of the university struggled under financial hardship. The medical school achieved an astounding record for seminal research during that otherwise difficult era, however, thanks to the changes instituted by Brookings. In 1933, Professor Evarts Graham performed the first successful lung removal on a cancer patient, and he then won the prestigious Lister Medal for surgery in 1942. In 1943, Dr. Edward Doisy, formerly on the school's faculty, received the Nobel Prize for physiology or medicine. The next year, Dr. Joseph Erlanger, then on the faculty, and his associate Dr. Herbert Gasser, formerly on the faculty, won a Nobel Prize in the same area for their research on neural transmission. In 1947, yet another Nobel Prize in physiology or medicine was shared by Carl and Gerty Cori, both on the medical school faculty, for their research on the processes by which glucose and glycogen can be transformed each into the other.

Not until after the end of World War II did the university embark on any serious improvement projects beyond the medical school. Chancellor Allen Shepley, who served from 1953 until 1961, raised professors' salaries to a competitive level, thus allowing Washington to retain a first-rate faculty. Then under Chancellor Eliot, 1962–71, the university launched a highly successful fundraising campaign. Those efforts had a considerable effect, for in 1966, the Cartter Report ranked Washington's graduate programs among the top 25 in all of the United States. However, it was during the chancellorship of Henry Danforth, who served from 1971 until 1995, that Washington took its place among America's best research institutions. In

1995, *U.S. News and World Report* magazine ranked Washington 20th in the United States, and in the same year, the National Research Council ranked eight of Washington's doctoral programs in the top ten. Just 13 years earlier, only one program was so highly rated. Mark S. Wrighton, who became Washington's chancellor in October of 1995, came to be in charge of one of the best endowed and best equipped universities in the country.

Further Reading: An interesting history of the Hilltop Campus can be found in *Washington University in St. Louis: Its Design and Architecture,* by Buford Pickens and Margaretta J. Darnell (St. Louis, Missouri: Washington University, 1978). Several brief articles outlining the history of the university can also be found in the spring 1973 issue of *Washington University Magazine.*

—Christopher Hoyt

WEIZMANN INSTITUTE OF SCIENCE
(Rehovot, Israel)

Location: Rehovot, Israel, 15 miles southeast of Tel Aviv.

Description: A research and teaching institute of approximately 2,300 researchers, engineers, technicians, and scientists-in-training. The campus is also home to the Feinberg Graduate School, with an enrollment of approximately 800 students.

Information: The Weizmann Institute
Office of Admissions
Rehovot 76100
Israel
(972) 8 343111

Founded by statesman and scientist Chaim Weizmann, the Weizmann Institute of Science stands as one of Israel's foremost interdisciplinary centers of learning, with a history directly connected to its founder and namesake. Born into a family of 15 in Czarist Russia, Chaim Weizmann was 17 years old in 1891 when he left his homeland and its anti-Semitic university quotas to pursue studies in Germany and Switzerland. Weizmann earned his Ph.D. in chemistry nine years later in Fribourg, Switzerland.

A natural leader, who, in 1916, came to head the Zionist movement, Weizmann realized his two most ambitious goals when he was named the first president of the state of Israel and the first president of the Weizmann Institute of Science. His prominence as a statesman was established when Weizmann was recognized as a key negotiator of the pact known as the Balfour Declaration, a document that officially sanctioned a national homeland for the Jewish people. In his capacity as a statesman, he headed the Zionist Commission to Palestine and as such played a major part in the 1929 establishment of the Jewish Agency for Palestine.

Weizmann's career as a scientist led to his distinction as a Zionist leader. As a research chemist living in Manchester, England, he invented a process that produced acetone from maize, and in so doing contributed to the production of the smokeless gun powder, cordite, used by the Allies during World War I. In the years preceding World War II, buoyed by the British pledge of a Jewish homeland, Weizmann moved to Palestine. No stranger to the world of academia, Weizmann, a founder in 1918 of the Hebrew University in Jerusalem, sought to combine the scholastic with the scientific in a setting connected with both the past and future of the Jewish people.

The Weizmann Institute of Science, initially named the Sieff Institute, saw its beginnings in 1933, a year when Nazism was becoming an international threat. Weizmann set his sights on founding a scientific research center in what was then still British-mandated Palestine; he did so in the small agricultural community of Rehovot. Located on Israel's Mediterranean coastal plain, the Rehovot of biblical days was the site of an ongoing war between the Hebrews and Philistines. Today it is situated a few miles from Yavne, a town considered by Israelis as a center of the high-technology industry. Weizmann determined that an independent state where refugees from the Nazi regime and other Jews could live and thrive would also require an industrial base. The scientist in him realized that technological advances and scientific achievement must become synonymous with the Zionist effort to create a Jewish homeland.

Weizmann's vision of creating such a dominion was fueled both spiritually and financially by his friends Israel and Rebecca Sieff, who, in 1934, established the Daniel Sieff Research Institute, named in memory of the couple's son. In the years prior to World War II, the Sieff Institute concentrated on research in organic chemistry and biochemistry, with a focus on yielding medical products from synthesized chemicals. When World War II broke out in 1939, the Sieff Institute turned its attentions toward ever-increasing needs created by the war. The small number of Jewish scientists making their home in the Rehovot research center developed a series of pharmaceutical supplies to aid the Allied forces in the Middle East. Subsequently, the scientific corps of the Israeli defense forces (Hemed) adopted Rehovot as its home. Working under the institute's auspices, these young scientists developed a cadre of weapons and other war materials.

While Weizmann endorsed the need for institute scientists to devote much of their attention to the war effort, his long-term focus remained the creation of a Jewish state and its subsequent need to be recognized as a force in the free world. Indeed, the Sieff Institute's motto—"Work for this Country. Work for Science. Work for Mankind"—embodied Weizmann's vision for the research center. Therefore, on the occasion of his 70th birthday in 1944, with the world still embroiled in war, Weizmann's answer was clear when his colleagues desired to pay tribute to their mentor but lacked what they considered to be a suitable gift. "I need nothing for myself, but if you wish, do something for the expansion of the Daniel Sieff Research Institute," said Weizmann. That birthday wish was the impetus for the development of the multidisciplinary research institute that today is world renowned for its scientific conferences and symposia. On June 3, 1946, two years after Dr. Chaim Weizmann announced his hope for the future, the cornerstone for the Weizmann Institute of Science was laid in Rehovot.

Completion of the Weizmann Institute was interrupted by Israel's War of Independence. Despite the outside struggles, research at the Institute continued, and in 1946, when the U.S. Army announced completion of the world's first computer, Rehovot mathematicians turned their attention toward the new technology. Eight years later, the resulting WEIZAC computer, which placed the institute on the computer science map, was recognized by Albert Einstein as a technological achievement.

On November 2, 1949, with the permission of the Sieff family, the Daniel Sieff Research Center was formally rededicated as the Weizmann Institute of Science. Under the dual leadership of Meyer W. Weisgal and Dewey D. Stone, the new institute saw swift development, as it rapidly increased its staff with both Israeli and non-Israeli scientists. The Weizmann Institute of 1949 consisted of 60 laboratories in 9 scientific fields. In its first decade as the Weizmann Institute of Science, the research center established itself both as a scientific and a political entity. The institute's first major scientific conference in 1956 generated so much interest that a campus auditorium was constructed to accommodate participants. The conference, an international symposium on macromolecular chemistry, attracted not only leaders in the scientific and research communities, but political notables such as Golda Meir and David Ben-Gurion, both of whom attended the opening dinner.

Nine years after its founding, the Weizmann Institute established the Feinberg Graduate School, and in so doing rivaled the Hebrew University of Jerusalem and the Technion in Haifa as a graduate training center. The school's master of science and doctor of philosophy degrees in the life sciences, chemistry, mathematics, physics, science teaching, and computer science are accredited by both the State of Israel and the Board of Regents of the State of New York. Its first Ph.D. was conferred in 1964. The current student/teacher ratio at the graduate school is two to one. In addition to taking courses, students enrolled in the graduate program must show active involvement in one of the 800 ongoing research projects at the institute.

In an effort to draw upon industrial sponsorship for processes developed at the institute, the Yeda Research and Development Company was founded in 1959. Yeda, Hebrew for "know-how," holds title to all inventions and scientific advances made at the institute and acts as a liaison between scientists and industrial investors. The company, the first of its kind in Israel, also apprises institute scientists of projects for which industrial sponsorship is available.

When the department of science teaching was established on campus in 1968, the institute began paving the road for educational reform in Israel. A youth activities division was added to encourage youngsters considering careers in science. The program attracts some 15,000 students annually.

Since the death of Chaim Weizmann in 1952, the institute has more than doubled in size. A faculty and staff numbering more than 2,300 is divided among 19 departments; in addition, 19 interdisciplinary centers have been established on grounds that cover 300 acres. Campus growth is ongoing, and in the late 1900s some nine major buildings and areas were inaugurated, including the Brain Research Building, the Helen and Martin Kimmel Campus Area, the Dolfi and Lola Ebner Auditorium, and the Weizmann Archives. More than 40 buildings and research facilities grace the campus, in addition to residential housing, recreational areas, historic and memorial sites, and numerous gardens.

A campus architectural focal point is the Weizmann Institute's Canadian Institute for the Energies and Applied Research. Touted as one of the foremost advanced solar research facilities in the world, the structure features 64 large motor-driven mirrors, all tracking the sun onto a 2,100-foot-high central receiving tower.

The Weizmann Institute of today owes much of its prominence to the financial support of the American Committee, a group of leaders in the worlds of science and art that originated in 1944 and has contributed more than $300 million over the past five decades for the institute's projects and operating needs. Financial contributors to the institute include Walter Annenberg, publisher of *TV Guide;* philanthropists Helen and Norman Asher; Edgar M. Bronfman, president of the World Jewish Congress; and Sara Lee Schupf of Sara Lee pastry fame.

Although it has been little more than 60 years since the institute was founded, its prominence in the spheres of technology and academia are documented. Identified by Nobel Prize-winner Christian B. Anfinsen of Johns Hopkins University as "one of the world's preeminent centers of research in the service of mankind," the institute's contributions to the understanding of cancer and immunological diseases, genetics, computer science, and solar energy have had global impact. According to an institute publication, major advancements in the fight for disease control over recent years include the discovery of antibodies to nerve tissue protein, a development that has improved the diagnosis of a childhood malignancy known as neuroblastoma. Medications for the treatment of epilepsy, stroke, and Alzheimer's disease are also among the institute's contributions, and research into finding the gene responsible for causing several types of acute childhood leukemia has been successfully conducted by Professor Eli Canaani. Recent Weizmann Institute contributions to the study of the earth's environment include the development of solar-powered laser systems used to monitor the atmosphere from space and an unprecedented turbine that generates electricity from concentrated sunlight.

Noted for its international scientific conferences and its department of visiting scientists, the institute has welcomed researchers from institutions throughout the world, and in 1993 received 105 visitors from former Soviet bloc countries. The restructuring of Eastern Europe has also made available to the Weizmann Institute many premiere researchers heretofore inaccessible; Eastern Europeans now constitute a large contingent of visiting scientists. Current staff members include Shlomo Alexander, who was awarded the 1993 Israel Prize in Physics; Varda Rotter and Moshe Oren, joint recipients of the 1993 Feher Prize in Medicine; and Professor Mati Fridkin, winner of the Teva Pharmaceutical Industries Prize.

The shifting political environment in the Middle East is identified by institute president Haim Harari as impetus for the institute to confer a master's degree and post-doctoral designation upon students from Egypt. In a 1994 message, Harari maintains that while the Middle East is "on the threshold of change," certain elements of the research center will remain uncompromised, including its "commitment to recruiting the finest minds and providing them with optimum conditions, and our determination to hold fast to the ideals of our founder, Chaim Weizmann."

Further Reading: Insights into Chaim Weizmann, his career, and the Weizmann Institute will be found in the following: Harold M. Blumberg's *Weizmann: His Life and Times* (New York: St. Martin's Press, 1977); Barnet Litvinoff's *Weizmann: Last of the Patriarchs* (New York: Putnam, 1976); the memoirs of Weizmann and his wife: *Chaim Weizmann, Trial and Error* (New York: Harper, 1949; reprint, 1977); and Vera Weizmann's *Impossible Takes Longer: The Memoir of Vera Weizmann, Wife of Israel's First President, as told to David Tutaen* (New York: Harper and Row, 1967).

—Sharon Nery

WELLESLEY COLLEGE
(Wellesley, Massachusetts, U.S.A.)

Location: Wellesley, Massachusetts, 12 miles west of Boston.

Description: A private four-year women's college with 2,300 students from 42 countries and 49 states.

Information: Board of Admission
                    Wellesley College
                    106 Central Street
                    Wellesley, MA 02181-8292
                    U.S.A.
                    (617) 283-2270

Visiting: Students lead tours of the campus throughout the year. Call the telephone number above for specific details.

Wellesley College is the only major private women's college in the United States that has appointed only female presidents. Each of the 12 presidents has contributed toward moving the college forward, given the issues, priorities, and twists of fate of the time. The continuity of vision and direction is evident. Wellesley remains committed to educating women for leadership roles in the community and society, a goal sought by the founders Henry and Pauline Durant.

The Wellesley College story begins with the marriage of Henry Fowle Durant and Pauline Cazenove on May 23, 1854. They bought a rambling brown farm cottage (now known as Homestead) as a summer retreat 12 miles west of Boston. Their son Harry was born in 1855 and daughter Pauline Cazenove in 1857. When Pauline died at six weeks, their grief turned to total absorption with two-year-old Harry. They purchased 300 acres on Lake Waban, built barns, greenhouses, and gardens, and planned to give it all to Harry as his country estate.

Those dreams were abruptly halted when eight-year-old Harry died of diphtheria on July 3, 1863. The Durants sold the cottage, purchased the nearby Webber residence, and moved to New York City. They saw clearly the need for improved educational opportunities for women and the scarcity of teachers after the Civil War.

In 1867 they made a key decision: they would use their 300-acre estate to educate young women. They began planning every aspect of the college—grounds, buildings, curriculum, faculty. Believing that beauty of surroundings were important in the shaping of character, they began providing for it.

On March 17, 1870, the commonwealth of Massachusetts chartered and authorized the Wellesley Female Seminary to provide a program of education beyond high school. The board of trustees' initial meeting on April 16, 1870, was the beginning of the governing body which expanded to include alumnae representation in 1889 and student non-voting presence in the present day. On March 7, 1873, the name of the institution was changed to Wellesley College.

On August 13, 1871, Pauline Durant laid the first foundation stone for College Hall and gave each worker a copy of the Bible. The architect Hammatt Billings of Boston designed the building in the French Second Empire style, developed in France in the reign of Napoléon III. Henry Durant supervised the day-to-day construction. Following the single building concept for a college, College Hall was to contain classrooms, library, residences, laboratories, assembly hall, and administrative offices. It stretched for over one-eighth mile on the hill overlooking Lake Waban and resembled a cathedral more than a college.

On September 8, 1875, 314 students arrived, primarily via the Boston-Albany Railway, stopping at West Needham. Horse-drawn buses with signs saying WELLESLEY COLLEGE created a caravan for the one mile between the station and campus. President Ada L. Howard greeted the students; school representatives assigned rooms in the nearly completed College Hall and reassured parents. One student, Louise McCoy, recalled, "We were pioneers in the adventure—voyagers in the crusade for the higher education of women, that perilous experiment of the 70's, which all the world was breathlessly watching and which the prophets were declaring to be so inevitably fatal to the American girl."

The Durants stated that Wellesley College was opened for the "purpose of giving to young women a collegiate education, opportunities fully equivalent to those usually provided for young men." This pioneering spirit contrasted with the thoughts of a Boston physician who said that "woman's brain was too delicate and fragile a thing to attempt the mastery of Greek and Latin."

The first president, Ada L. Howard, an 1849 graduate of Mount Holyoke Seminary, was strongly influenced and directed by the Durants' presence during her tenure (1875–81). Woven into the ideals of the college were the Durants' strong Christian beliefs. With his son's death, Henry had taken on an evangelical fervor.

The curriculum grew with Henry Durant's ability to attract strong teachers in varying subject areas. His love of literature, music, and the sciences influenced the initial

Wellesley College

departments: philosophy, history, art, music, German, English literature, mathematics, Greek, Latin, French, and the sciences. The first faculty consisted of 7 professors as heads of departments and 11 teachers of academic subjects. With the exception of Charles H. Morse, professor of music, all were women living in College Hall, and all were members of evangelical churches.

The Durants initiated several lasting traditions. The first Flower Sunday was held in September 1876 to welcome students back and exchange flowers. In 1877 the students planted a tree marking the first Tree Day, a tradition which the first-year students continue to this day. An embedded stone in front of each tree indicates the class year. In 1878 Pauline Durant was instrumental in establishing the Students' Aid Society to assist with expenses and to encourage a diverse community. In 1879 the Durants imported and planned for the planting of 1,000 rhododendrons and azaleas, and over 7,000 crocus and snowdrop bulbs. The parklike grounds included fields of wildflowers for students and faculty to pick.

On February 16, 1877, the commonwealth of Massachusetts authorized Wellesley College to grant degrees; two years later 18 students were graduated in the first commencement. The Alumnae Association began in 1888, a clear indication that graduates wished to retain ties with Wellesley.

Two graduates of the class of 1880 had significant influence on the curriculum of the young college. Charlotte Fitch Roberts earned her Ph.D. in chemistry at Yale University in 1894 and taught chemistry at Wellesley for 37 years (1880–1917). Katherine Lee Bates, poet, author, and teacher, wrote "America the Beautiful" in 1873, in an inspired moment on Pike's Peak, Colorado. She helped build a distinguished department of English literature as a faculty member from 1885 to 1925.

In October 1881 Henry Durant died, drawing to a close his attentive, strong presence. President Howard's physical health had been failing, and she submitted her resignation that same year.

The second president, Alice Freeman Palmer, came to Wellesley in 1879 as professor of history and was appointed president in 1881 at the age of 26. During her six years as president (1881–87), this spirited, visionary woman was credited with transforming Wellesley into a modern collegiate institution. It became clear that many students were not adequately prepared for the academic rigors of college life. As an example of working with "feeder schools," President Freeman arranged with secondary schools to prepare students well for Wellesley. Dana Hall School in Wellesley was the first such school. Freeman is credited with "inspiring the principals of 15 schools with the idea of definite training for entrance into Wellesley." Her work was instrumental in the increased numbers of qualified applicants, which led to higher standards of admission, which evolved into higher standards for academic work. When Freeman arrived, Wellesley

had 375 students; when she left there were 628 students. She continued the Durants' tradition of appointing women scholars to teach and conduct research.

The desire for a tightly knit community brought other developments: Simpson Cottage offered a quieter environment than College Hall; two dormitories opened; and Eliot House became the first cooperative house where students could assume more housekeeping responsibilities in exchange for lower fees.

The third president, Helen A. Shafer, came to Wellesley in 1887 as professor of mathematics and head of the department of mathematics. Her intense interest in scholarship was coupled with organizational ability and patience. She began her presidency (1887–94) with curriculum revision that significantly expanded the number of electives. Student involvement was evidenced with the publication of the first student newspaper, *The Courant* (1888), and the first yearbook, *Legenda* (1889). In 1889 the first foreign student arrived, Kin Kato, from Japan.

In 1891, Mary Whiton Calkins established the first psychological laboratory in a college for women. Her experimental studies included work with memory, association, and a method of investigation. She was a faculty member from 1887 to 1929 and head of the psychology and philosophy department from 1898 to 1929. She was elected president of the American Psychological Association in 1905 and of the American Philosophical Association in 1918.

Annie Jump Cannon, class of 1884 was an acclaimed alumna and considered the foremost woman astronomer in the country. She was a member of the staff of Harvard Observatory. She was the first woman awarded the Henry Draper gold medal from the National Academy of Sciences. In 1933 she developed the classification system still used to identify the spectre of more than 300,000 stars.

Upon President Shafer's death in 1894, Julia Josephine Irvine became the fourth president (1894–99). She was an inspiring professor of Greek at Wellesley. As a commitment to the expansive, undulating grounds, a committee on buildings and grounds was established. Irvine is best known for her extensive revision of the curriculum, from one that largely prescribed courses to one with many electives.

Responding to the need for more informal fellowship among students and faculty, the development of Society Houses resumed. Since 1877 Shakespeare House had been a gathering place for faculty and students interested in Shakespearean drama. In 1889 the Art Society (which became Tau Zeta Epsilon in 1894) was granted a charter to provide opportunities for additional study of art, to encourage scholarly work, and to promote fellowship among undergraduates. The limited membership in the societies has been controversial. Two additional societies are currently on campus: Zeta Alpha House (literature) and Phi Sigma Lecture Forum (cultural and public affairs).

In honor of their father and the college's spiritual needs, the children of former trustee William Houghton gave a gift for the construction of the Houghton Memorial Chapel. Controversy arose about its placement and relationship to the landscape and to the college's other architectural styles. Decades later, Dr. Owen H. Jander, professor emeritus of music, spearheaded the project to build a seventeenth-century mean-tone organ in the chapel. Jander taught at the college from 1960 to 1993 and was a lecturer and scholar of seventeenth-century Italian music and the instrumental music of Ludwig van Beethoven.

Caroline Hazard, the fifth president (1899–1910), was a highly cultivated woman from Rhode Island with experience in business, philanthropic affairs, and long-range planning. Hazard personally financed the building of Oakwoods, the president's house at that time. Campus expansion included five dormitories, the Whitin Observatory, Billings Hall, and Mary Hemenway Hall (a gymnasium). The Wellesley College Library opened in 1910, the result of a challenge gift by Andrew Carnegie.

In 1901 following an initiative by students and faculty, the Student Government Association was formally established. Currently all students belong to the college government, and the senate is composed of elected representatives from each residence hall as well as from off-campus students. College government officers are elected each spring, campus-wide. A student-run judicial system handles violations of the honor code.

Another initiative by faculty and alumnae recommended the adoption of a plan for the college grounds. Frederick Law Olmsted Jr. prepared recommendations for the board of trustees in 1902, including the desirability of buildings which honor the landscape and the benefits of comprehensive planning.

After Hazard's resignation in 1910, the sixth president, Ellen Fitz Pendleton (class of 1896), who was dean of the college, was appointed president. The first alumna to become president, she served for 25 years (1911–36), the longest tenure of any president of Wellesley. Early in her tenure Wellesley College experienced four hours that irrevocably changed its face and direction. The night was March 17, 1914. At 4:30 A.M. fire broke out on the fourth floor of College Hall; by morning, the entire building was destroyed. No injuries occurred, due to early warnings and diligent fire drill training. Faulty equipment in the zoology laboratory was suspected.

Overnight, Pendleton's primary focus became the rebuilding of the campus. A makeshift wooden structure between the library and the chapel provided classroom and office space. Tower Court, the first dormitory on College Hall Hill, was built within a year; two others followed within a decade. Five dormitories became cooperative houses.

The board of trustees accepted the plan to design a block of buildings and construct sections when funds were available. Wellesley's use of the Collegiate Gothic style began with Founders Hall in 1919 and continued with Alumnae Hall, a library addition, Green Hall, and

Pendleton Hall. Science facilities were also improved and a greenhouse was built. Pauline Durant lived in what is now the president's house and remained actively involved with the college until her death in 1917.

Following the retirement and death of Pendleton in 1936, Mildred McAfee, formerly dean of the college of women at Oberlin, became the seventh president of Wellesley College and served from 1936 to 1949. Physical development slowed with World War II: the recreation building was the last major construction after the fire. The college granted McAfee a leave of absence to be the first director of the WAVES in Washington, D.C.; for her work she received the Distinguished Service Medal.

In 1940 Harriet B. Creighton (class of 1929) joined the faculty as associate professor of botany and retired as professor emerita. During her tenure of over 30 years, she was a meticulous curator of the botanical garden and internationally known for her horticultural concerns and her scholarship.

Lucretia Mowry came to the college faculty as professor of religion and biblical studies in 1942, specializing in New Testament literature. She was the first woman on the committee to revise the Revised Standard Version of the Bible.

Following McAfee's resignation in 1949, Margaret Clapp, class of 1930 and Pulitzer Prize-winning biographer, became the eighth president (1949–66) and the second alumna to be elected president. Expansion began again with three dormitories, another library expansion, and the Jewett Arts Center, the latter providing facilities for students for art, music, and theater. During President Clapp's tenure, several well-known faculty came to Wellesley: Carolyn Shaw Bell held the Catherine Coman Chair in Economics and taught at Wellesley from 1950 to 1989. Her research interests were human capital, income details, and quality of economic data.

Eleanor Rudd Webster (class of 1942) taught at Wellesley for 33 years with specialization in the history of science and physical organic chemistry. She helped in the design and direction of the National Science Foundation-supported Wellesley College Institute in Chemistry. This program enabled women whose undergraduate training had been completed 5 to 25 years earlier to return to school to pursue an M.A. in chemistry. She also served as the first director of Wellesley Continuing Education, a program for women of nontraditional college age.

Clapp expanded curriculum offerings in innovative directions. In 1949 the college first offered interdepartmental majors, including natural resources and conservation, Latin American studies, and medieval studies. The new biological department combined all life science courses.

During Clapp's tenure, many students who worked in very visible fields were graduated. In the class of 1959 were Madeline Albright, foreign policy analyst and U.S. ambassador to the United Nations, and Amalaya L. Kearse, judge in the U.S. Court of Appeals. Four graduates have excelled in broadcast journalism: Lynn Sherr (1963), Cokie Roberts (1964), Linda Wertheimer (1965), and Diane Sawyer (1967). Authors include Nora Ephron (1962), Nancy Friday (1955), and Susan Sheehan (1958), winner of the Pulitzer Prize. Actresses include Ali McGraw (1960) and Barbara Babcock (1960). President Clapp resigned, effective June 1966.

Ruth M. Adams, a specialist in Victorian literature, served from 1966 to 1972 as Wellesley's ninth president. Wellesley College experienced significant expansion of educational experiences for students. New curriculum included Afro-American studies, Asian studies, classical civilization, molecular biology, American studies, and urban studies. Cross registration with the Massachusetts Institute of Technology (MIT) began in 1968. Students may study at both institutions and be eligible for a double degree program with MIT.

Hillary Rodham Clinton (1969), First Lady of the United States in the administration of her husband, Bill Clinton, majored in political science and was graduated with high honors. She served as president of the college government in her senior year and received her law degree in 1973 from Yale Law School. Her professional work has included work as an advocate for children's health, for quality education, and for the changing roles of women in American society.

In 1971, the board of trustees decided that Wellesley should remain a women's college, reaffirming its mission to educate women for roles of leadership. This response followed a report from the elected Commission on the Future of the College, made up of students, faculty, alumnae, trustees, and administrators. The majority of the commission had recommended that Wellesley begin offering a limited coeducational program in 1972–73. The commission's reasons were the expressed preference of high school seniors for coeducational colleges and universities, student questionnaires, and the sense that male student would improve the cultural, educational, and social life at Wellesley.

The trustees' primary reason for not accepting the commission's recommendation was the lack of hard data or research to support or oppose the change. The proposed cost was questioned, as were the consequences of losing the identity of the all-women's college. Reaction to this decision varied; most faculty members strongly urged that women's programs be emphasized. When the question arose regarding the search for the next president, the majority of the college community believed it should be a woman.

This strong restatement of purpose was crucial to the charge given Barbara Warne Newell as the tenth president (1972–80). She was a well-known advocate of women's rights in the academic world. The college experienced renewed conviction around the single-sex decision with Newell as an articulate, visible spokesperson. During Newell's term, significant expansion of existing facilities took place, including the 1974 opening of the Center for Research on Women. Currently more than 100 men and women work there on public policy and family issues. In 1975, the expansions were completed of the Margaret Clapp Library and Sage Hall (renamed the Science Center).

In Wellesley's centennial year of 1975, Newell wrote, "Wellesley College entered its second century at a critical juncture in American higher education and American Society. We have opportunities to pioneer new directions in the education of women." Wellesley later granted Newell a leave of absence, during which she was ambassador to UNESCO in Paris.

In 1981, Nannerl Overholser Keohane (class of 1961), became the 11th president and 3rd alumna to lead the college. With her 12 years of leadership (1981–93), Wellesley's reputation was enhanced through expansion of research and special programs. In 1981 the Stone Center for Developmental Services and Studies opened in the former Simpson Cottage. The center focuses on women's psychological development and the prevention of psychological problems. The college reinstated the required writing program and began an interdisciplinary cluster program for first-year students. The latter was replaced in 1995–96 by INCIPIT: Introduction to Collaboration: Interdisciplinary Problems and Intellectual Tools.

In 1982 Anna and Samuel Pinanski established the Pinanski Prize for Excellence in Teaching, an annual award given to up to three members of the Wellesley faculty. Nominations come from within the college community, and the selections are made by the president in consultation with the Pinanski Prize Committee. In the first year's awards, the Pinanski Prize was given to David R. Ferry, Sophie Chantal Hart Professor of English Emeritus, for his notable poetic achievement. His areas of concentration have been Shakespeare, romantic, and modern poetry. In 1994 he was awarded the Academy of American Poets Fellowship.

Keohane's fundraising efforts resulted in a record-breaking capital campaign which raised $168 million and strengthened the financial status of the college. The campaign brought alumnae groups throughout the country together in support of the college's needs for increased financial aid, endowment, faculty resources, and building projects. Koehane left Wellesley College in 1993 to become the first woman president of Duke University.

The Davis Museum and Cultural Center, designed by Rafael Moneo of Madrid, was dedicated in October 1993. It houses ten galleries for exhibition of the permanent collection of 5,000 pieces, a gallery for special exhibitions, a cinema, and a cafe.

Diana Chapman Walsh, class of 1966, became the 12th president in August 1993. As the fourth alumna president, she brought extensive experience in public health policy and works as an advocate for medical research and preventative health issues.

In 1993, Marjory Stoneman Douglas (class of 1912) received the Freedom Medal, America's highest civilian award, from President Bill Clinton. Her life had been dedicated to preserving the Everglades. Her book *The Everglades: River of Grass,* published in 1947 and her founding of the Friends of the Everglades in 1970 are expressions of her intense environmental concern and activism. In March 1995, she gave the Freedom Medal to President Walsh, saying "I have no living relatives so Wellesley is like my family. It will be there long after I am gone."

Thus, the pioneering vision of the Durants has passed through the hands and talents of 12 female leaders. Wellesley College's 120-year history continues with 2,300 students knowing that they are there, in the words of the college motto, "not to be ministered unto but to minister."

Further Reading: At the time of Wellesley College's centennial, Jean Glasscock, general editor, compiled writings about many aspects of the college's history in *Wellesley College, 1875–1975: A Century of Women* (Wellesley, Massachusetts: Wellesley College, 1975). In *Adamless Eden, The Community of Women Faculty at Wellesley* (New Haven, Connecticut: Yale University Press, 1995), Patricia Ann Palmieri provides a narrative history of the founding and first generation of Wellesley faculty. *The Survey of Buildings and Grounds* includes a section "Development of the Wellesley College Campus," which documents the history and development of the campus (Wellesley, Massachusetts: Wellesley College, 1989).

—Chris Farrow

WILLAMETTE UNIVERSITY
(Salem, Oregon, U.S.A.)

Location:
Adjacent to the state capitol building in Salem, Oregon.

Description:
The first institution of higher learning in the Pacific Northwest, Willamette is now a private liberal arts university enrolling over 2,200 students in undergraduate, graduate, and professional schools.

Information:
Office of Admission
Willamette University
900 State Street
Salem, OR 97301
U.S.A.
(503) 370-6303

The origins of Willamette University are intertwined with the missionary activities of the Methodist Episcopal Church (now the United Methodist Church) in the 1830s. One of the institution's eventual founders, Reverend Jason Lee, was chosen by the Missionary Society of the Methodist Episcopal Church in New York to establish a mission among the American Indian population of the Oregon territory. Lee and a small group of missionaries traveled across the country with members of a trading expedition and arrived at the Willamette River in northern Oregon in September 1834. Soon afterward, a mission school for Indian children was opened. In 1838 Lee made the return trip east to report to the mission board. His accounts of the mission stirred support, and the board agreed to provide nearly $40,000 in supplies and personnel for the purpose of further establishing the mission. Those chosen to assist Lee at the mission, referred to in the annals of Willamette history as the "Great Reinforcement," traveled by boat to the Oregon coast, sailing around the southern tip of the South American continent in 1839.

In the year that followed, a small community began to form in Chemeketa (present-day Salem), and a debate arose among community members as to whether a separate school for the children of missionary settlers was necessary. A meeting to discuss the issue was held in the home of Jason Lee in January 1842, where members decided that immediate action should be taken to establish the school. Two weeks later a board of trustees was appointed, the constitution and bylaws were adopted, and the school was given the name Oregon Institute. These acts constitute the founding of Willamette University.

Lee traveled east again in 1843 and 1844 to solicit more funds from the mission board but was told upon arrival that he had been replaced. When he arrived at Chemeketa in the spring of 1844, George Gary, Lee's replacement, found enrollment at the Indian Mission School (now called the Indian Manual Labor School) to be virtually nonexistent, due to an epidemic of scrofula. Gary closed the India Mission School and sold its principal building (a newly constructed three-story building that was considered to be the largest on the Oregon coast and valued at $10,000) to the trustees of the Oregon Institute for $4,000.

Having acquired at minimal cost a building constructed expressly for academic purposes, the board of trustees formally opened the Oregon Institute in the fall of 1844. The faculty consisted of one teacher; enrollment for the first term was five students. Enrollment grew steadily until community leaders decided that the growing population at Salem and the resources available to the school warranted the establishment of a postsecondary institution at the Oregon Institute. Specifically, plans called for the institute to remain a preparatory school; however, the institute would now comprise a department within the larger institution. The board of trustees petitioned for and received a charter from the Oregon Territorial Legislature on January 2, 1853. The first degree was awarded to Emily York in 1859.

In its early years, the school maintained a strong affiliation with the Methodist Episcopal Church, as the church continued to give financial support to the fledgling institution. Moreover, nearly all faculty and administrative staff were members of the Methodist Episcopal Church and presumably were committed to the church's missionary efforts. Thus, the school's activities were connected in a religious atmosphere and governed by a strict moral code that applied to all individuals associated with Willamette: the university's third president, Joseph Henry Wythe, although acknowledged as a brilliant scholar, was dismissed from his duties as president on grounds that he refused to curtail his use of tobacco products in public.

Construction began on University Hall, the first permanent building on the Willamette campus, in 1864. To construct the building, 500,000 bricks were made out of clay taken from a nearby location. The building, which took three years to complete, was later named Waller Hall in honor of the trustee who had raised the monies to build it. The decision on the part of the university trustees to commence by raising a large, permanent structure would prove fortuitous, for in 1872 a fire

Willamette University

destroyed the Oregon Institute building, formerly the Indian Mission School. (This was the first of many fires that would seriously damage the university.) Fortunately, however, alternative classroom space was available; otherwise the preparatory school's very existence would have been jeopardized.

The university witnessed considerable growth over the next two decades. By the early 1870s it had a commercial department, a medical department, and a music department, the latter awarding its own degrees by 1872. Average annual enrollment through the 1870s was 280 students, although only 30 percent of these students studies at the postsecondary level. After much fervent debate,

a women's college was established at Willamette in 1880. Fittingly, then-president Thomas Van Scoy purchased the home of Chloe Clarke Willson, first instructor at the Oregon Institute, intending to convert the home into an academic building for the Women's College. Additions to Willson's house were made and the building was then named Lausanne Hall, after the boat that carried the "Great Reinforcement." Also established was the College of Law in 1883, which is still in operation today.

The 1890s, however, was a troublesome decade for the Willamette community. In 1890, Van Scoy appointed Charles Carroll Stratton to the office of chancellor. Stratton, realizing the institution was heavily in debt and that it was, to some extent, still mobile (having only one permanent building), campaigned to transplant the school from Salem to Portland, a more urban location. There ensued a competition between the two communities, both of which offered substantial gifts of property to the school. The board of trustees eventually voted to remain in Salem. Stratton, leaving behind his responsibilities at Willamette, helped establish the University of Portland in 1891. Much to the dismay of the Willamette community, Van Scoy followed Stratton to Portland to become dean of the newly established school.

The Methodist Conference apparently agreed with Stratton and Van Scoy that Portland would make a better base for a university than Salem, for they withdrew significant financial support from Willamette and gave it to the University of Portland. A bitter competition for students followed, and rumors circulated in Salem that Van Scoy and his cohorts were infiltrating the Willamette campus to lure students to Portland. This state of affairs continued until 1899, by which time the University of Portland folded and subsequently was "reunited" with Willamette University in Salem by the Methodist Conference.

In the fall of 1891 fire again struck the campus; the roof and tower of University Hall was consumed by flames. Adding to the growing list of difficulties was an increasing debt. In the years 1892 and 1893, trustees secured loans totaling $24,000 to cover expenses and previous debts, but many trustees feared the institution could not be saved.

It was not until the turn of the century that the school's fortunes rose. Under the direction of John Coleman, university president from 1902 to 1907, construction began on four new academic buildings. On of the new structures was built to house the medical school, a department that had been in a state of transition since its inception in 1867. In 1880 the department had moved to Portland to take advantage of better medical facilities, but in 1895 doctors in the department lost their privileges at a Portland hospital to their counterparts at the University of Oregon. Classes were held in Waller Hall and in vacant rooms around Salem until the new building was completed in 1906. Ironically, Willamette's medical school would close seven years later, merging with the University of Oregon College of Medicine.

Willamette's fortunes improved markedly during the administration of Carl Gregg Doney, which lasted from 1915 to 1934. Overall enrollment nearly doubled during Doney's tenure as president, and total endowment and number of faculty members tripled. Willamette not only survived the era of World War I and the Great Depression, but it began to flourish. The school also withstood two more major fires on campus.

At the same time that Willamette began to establish itself more firmly, certain aspects of its character began to fade. Notably, the Kimball School of Theology—a school for which trustees had not charged tuition, revealing the high priority they placed on training ministerial candidates—closed its door in 1930. Its closing seems to have coincided with Willamette's general shift in focus, wherein strict adherence to the teachings of the Methodist Episcopal Church was no longer expected of students and faculty. Corresponding to this change was the gradual adoption and promotion of a liberal arts curriculum. In fact, the Methodist Church no longer substantially supports Willamette University: by 1987 the church accounted for only three-tenths of one percent of the school's annual donations.

On December 7, 1941, a group of Willamette athletes witnessed firsthand the immediate aftermath of the bombing of Pearl Harbor and, effectively, the beginning of the United States' involvement in World War II. The Willamette football team had traveled to the Hawaii Islands to play the University of Hawaii the day before and were still there when the bombing took place. They returned home on a ship that carried wounded back to the mainland for further medical attention. Willamette again became involved in the events of World War II, if only peripherally, when the new Lausanne Hall was made a base for a College Navy Training Program from July 1943 to November 1945. The program trained individuals as medical personnel and deck officers.

In 1965 Willamette University established what is termed a "sister-college relationship" with the International College of Commerce and Economics, now known as Tokyo International University. This arrangement allowed students from both schools to travel overseas as part of their curriculum, and to attend classes specifically designed for visiting students. In 1989 Tokyo International took this relationship a step further by establishing a satellite school (Named Tokyo International University of America) in close proximity to Willamette University, with the intention of establishing similar satellite campuses around the world. Students from the parent institution in Tokyo initially are required to take accelerated English-language courses, after which they may enroll in courses designed by Willamette professors that explore elements of U.S. history, culture, and society, as well as U.S. commerce and trade. For Willamette students the curriculum is much the same. In recent years Willamette also has established sister-college relationships with Xiamen University of the People's Republic of China, Kookmin University in Seoul, South Korea, and Simferopol State University in the Ukraine.

Today, Willamette University enjoys a position of geographic prominence—adjacent to the grounds of the state capitol of Salem—far removed from its humble beginnings in the frontier wilderness of the Oregon Territory.

Further Reading: Accounts of Willamette's founding may be gleaned from various volumes dealing with the history of

Oregon and the Oregon Territory. A more detailed discussion of Willamette's history is included in *Chronicles of Willamette,* by Robert M. Gatke (Portland, Oregon: Binsford and Mort, 1943), and *Chronicles of Willamette Volume Two,* by Robert D. Gregg (Portland, Oregon: Durham and Downey, 1970). A briefer history published by the university is *The First Hundred Years: 1834–1934,* by Wright Cowger (Salem, Oregon: Willamette University, 1981).

—Christopher Hudson

WILLIAMS COLLEGE
(Williamstown, Massachusetts, U.S.A.)

Location: Williamstown, Massachusetts, 135 miles northwest of Boston.

Description: A private college enrolling approximately 2,000 students in undergraduate and graduate programs.

Information: Office of Admissions
Williams College
P.O. Box 487
Williamstown, MA 01267
U.S.A.
(413) 507-2211

Visiting: Tours are conducted daily for prospective students and their families. Phone the number above for the schedule.

The contents of Colonel Ephraim Williams's army chest testified to his regard for religion, education, and the western frontier of Massachusetts. Killed in September 1755, on a reconnaissance mission during the French and Indian War (sometimes known as the Seven Years' War), he left in his army chest 11 books, including a *New Testament* and a series of essays on social, political, theological, and academic issues. Also in the chest was his will, which left his "residuary estate" for the "support and maintenance of a free school (in a township commonly called the west township) for ever." Williams's will stipulated that the township in which the school was to be located be named Williamstown and that it must be "within the jurisdiction of Massachusetts Bay."

Though the colony of Massachusetts very early demonstrated a commitment to education by decreeing in 1647 that every township of 100 families should have a public grammar school to prepare youths for university study, the initial reaction of the people of West Township to Williams's bequest was cool to indifferent. Not until 1765 did a meeting of the citizenry choose a committee to obtain a copy of the colonel's will. Several time the proprietors (governing persons) of the town dismissed an article calling for a committee to pursue the idea of a free school. However, by 1770, minds had changed, and the idea of a free school had become so appealing that the town brought the executors before the state legislature, accusing them of neglecting their duties, which neglect meant that the town could not "reap the intended of so noble and worthy donation."

Executors blamed the delay on a border dispute between Massachusetts and New York for the area in which Williamstown was located. At the time Williams wrote his will, they replied, New York claimed jurisdiction of the territory. Not until 1784 did the executors raise the issue again with the legislature. They asked that the legislature pass an act creating a corporation of "Meet Persons" to carry out "the pious and Charitable Intention of the Testator." In March 1785, the legislature incorporated "The Trustees of the donation of Ephraim Williams, Esq., for maintaining a Free School in Williamstown."

Williams's bequest of $9,297 was not sufficient to establish a free school. Local subscriptions brought in another $1,000, and a lottery—a common practice at that time—brought in another $3,500. Construction was begun in 1790 on the school's first building, which later became known as West College. The Free School opened in 1791 with two departments—a grammar school (or academy), which charged a tuition of 35 shillings yearly, and an English free school. When the Free School, transformed into Williams College, opened its doors on October 9, 1793, it had an enrollment of 18 undergraduates: 11 freshmen, 3 sophomores, and 4 juniors.

The school was open scarcely a year when the ambitious trustees focused on creating a college for "young men from every part of the Union," a goal that violated the intentions of Williams's will. What the colonel had wanted was a free school for the children of military families in the township west of Fort Massachusetts. His legacy instead is the second oldest college in Massachusetts.

One constant in the history of Williams College had been the issue of its location in the topmost northwest corner of Massachusetts. Before the founding of the college, Colonel Williams's father, Ephraim Williams, Senior, who had been involved in surveying the land in 1739, found it suitable for settlement. Others, however, found it remote and were distressed at the frequently harsh winters. There was no post office until 1797. Though attempts were made to establish regular tri-weekly stage runs, not until 1826 did regular stage runs begin between Bennington, Vermont, and Pittsfield, Massachusetts. The route included Williamstown.

The issue of moving the college was raised early in its existence. In 1815 an article in the Hampshire *Gazette* asked, "What does Williamstown have that can . . . render a term of four years' residence agreeable or pleasant? . . . Many scholars . . . having entered the institution . . . soon became sick of the place and obtained dismissions." In November 1818, the trustees reversed a previous vote in August; they would favor a move to Amherst if the legis-

Williams College

lature would fund it. In explaining their support of the move, the trustees cited the inaccessibility of the town, the declining enrollment, the dwindling income, and the competing academic institutions that had sprung up in Vermont and New York.

The day after Williams's commencement in 1821, the college's second president, Zephaniah Moore and 15 stu-

dents left Williams for Amherst Collegiate Institute (now Amherst College), where Moore assumed the presidency; the students also remained at Amherst. Moore, who had favored moving the college, left because he lacked confidence in the college's future. Though Williams began to prosper in its location, when enrollment increased from 84 in 1822 to 118 in 1823, the following year the

Amherst Collegiate Institute, about 50 miles east of Williams College, petitioned the state legislature for a college charter. Williams's trustees protested that a second college in western Massachusetts would destroy the first. (Western Massachusetts currently holds over half a dozen institutions of higher education.) Despite its protests, the charter was granted, and Williams's enrollment did indeed drop, from 120 to 80. The college's president (Edward Door Griffin, Moore's successor) said, "The heavens were covered with blackness; . . . we often looked up and inquired, 'Is this death?'" After Moore's departure, Griffin assumed the presidency of the college. He attempted to squelch discussion of a move by raising $25,000, of which the trustees earmarked $15,000 to endow a professorship of rhetoric and moral philosophy. He also secured the building of a chapel. Griffin credited a religious revival, during which 70 of the 80 enrolled students were converted, with providing the motivation for raising the $25,000.

A major watershed in Williams's history occurred with the accession of Mark Hopkins to the presidency. His influence was attested to when, in 1940, the U.S. government issued a series of stamps to honor American education, and Hopkins was chosen to represent the small liberal arts college. Probably the most famous encomium to Hopkins came from a Williams alumnus, President James A. Garfield, who said in 1871, "The ideal college is Mark Hopkins on one end of the log and a student on the other." Hopkins spent 58 years at Williams—as student, tutor, professor, president, and again professor. He was a country boy who had trained as a physician before he returned to his alma mater to teach moral and intellectual philosophy.

In his biography of Hopkins, Frederick Rudolph summarized the trustees' arduous search for a successor to Griffin:

In 1836 Williams College was looking for a president again. The little college in the northwestern corner of Massachusetts was in a characteristic fix: for the third time since the election of the first president in 1793 the board of trustees was being called upon to make the management of a wilderness institution sound attractive, and once more it was failing.

When their first choice turned down the position, the trustees responded to the senior class's advocacy of Hopkins as a suitable candidate by electing him to the post on August 17, 1836. In his inaugural address, Hopkins revealed his priorities in how the students would be influenced:

opportunities and inducements for physical exercise, a healthy situation, fine scenery, proper books, a suitable example on the part of instructors, companions of correct and studious habits, and above all,

a good religious influence. . . . The true and permanent interests of man can be promoted only in connection with religion.

Solidly puritan in character, Hopkins operated on the principle that, according to Rudolph, "he had already found all the truth that was necessary, both for himself and for the Williams student."

Commenting on Williams students after attending commencement exercises in 1838, Nathaniel Hawthorne wrote that the students were "country graduates—rough, brown-features, schoolmaster-looking . . . A rough hewn, heavy set of fellows from the hills and woods in this neighborhood; great unpolished bumpkins, who had grown up as farmer-boys." However, some 14 years later, Williams students apparently aspired to be gentlemen. Hopkins's future son-in-law, John H. Denison, described the Williams student as considerably different from Hawthorne's vision, at a class day exercise in 1862:

He is neither a sneak, nor a hermit, not a bigot . . . nor a bootlick to the Faculty, nor a seeker after the valedictory. He is genial, generous, humane, social. He knows how to behave in company, to get out of a bad space and into a good one; can adapt himself to the world, to circumstances, and the ladies. He does not care so much for college rank as for general information.

By most accounts, academic standards were rot rigorous during the Hopkins years. During his student years at Williams, Hopkins himself wrote in a letter, "I find myself able to get my lessons without difficulty in study hours so I go to bed when I please." The letter of another student read, "I never study more than an hour and a half a day, and plenty of time is left for reading, writing, hunting, and skinning and stuffing." Apparently it was not until the 1860s that a Williams professor took roll in class and paid strict attention to class attendance. While Hopkins was out of town in 1868, the faculty instituted a rule that student absences be counted as failing grades. Students voted to secede from the college. When Hopkins returned, he mediated the dispute, and the rule was amended to allow students to make up unavoidable or excused absences. An area in which Hopkins didn't succeed was in his attempt to abolish fraternities. He regarded "the general spirit of secret societies as opposed to that of our Republican institutions and Christianity." Sometime before 1845 the board of trustees overruled Hopkins; after that year he felt the fraternities were too deeply rooted to be removed. Over 100 years later, in the 1960s, Williams College banned fraternities.

When Hopkins resigned in 1872, the college was concerned about its future in the face of low enrollment and inflation. Enrollment was down from 233 to 169 in 1862, a decline not entirely attributable to the Civil War. Only

29 students had withdrawn to go into military service, while enrollment had been declining since 1853. This decline posed a serious problem for a school whose finances depended primarily on student fees. From 1793 through 1870 the commonwealth of Massachusetts appropriated for Williams College over $150,000. The state then ended its financial support, although in 1888 the state declared the college's cows tax exempt. Fortunately, private benefactors stepped in to alleviate some of the financial difficulties. First of these benefactors was merchant Amos Lawrence, whose 1844 donation of $5,000 was the first installment of the $40,000 he donated to the college, making him the largest private donor to the school until 1875.

Unlike most colleges founded in the American colonies, Williams did not have roots in religion. Ephraim Williams had a purely secular purpose when he left his money for the education of sons of the military. In addition, the period when the college was chartered was one of indifference to religion. Thus the college was not required to include clergy on its board of trustees. Only 4 of the original 12 trustees were ministers. During the early days of its existence, when the issue of moving the college arose, the members of the board of trustees who pressed for moving to the Connecticut Valley were clergymen, since they believed that it would be a better location from which to battle the Unitarian influences emanating from Harvard. Mark Hopkins was a strong advocate of religion as an important component of the college's influence on young men. During a religious revival at the college in 1847, he wrote "How much better to be a ploughboy & a Christian, than to be a vicious, sensual, conceited collegian!" Even before Hopkins brought his religious fervor to the presidency, students were concerned with combating "pagan" influences in foreign lands. Five students met in the summer of 1806 for an outdoor prayer meeting; when an electrical storm threatened, the students moved to the cover of a haystack, and there they proposed to send the Gospel to the "pagans" of Asia. The Haystack Prayer Meeting led to the formation of the American Board of Commissioners for Foreign Missionaries.

As early as 1854, the issue of the absence of women from the college was raised in a letter by (later president) James A. Garfield: "the absence of females from table and society takes away a very wholesome restraint and leaves roughness in its stead." In 1871, though no women had applied for admission, an alumni-trustee committee investigated admitting women on equal terms with men. In 1872 and 1873, the Society of Alumni overwhelmingly accepted the majority report of the committee, recommending that the college not adopt coeducation, Not until 1970 were women accepted on equal terms with men. Today, approximately half of Williams students are women.

For a small college, Williams boasts a number of pioneering efforts in education. In 1821 a group of alumni organized the Society of Alumni, the first college alumni society in history. The oldest astronomical observatory in the United States was erected in 1838 by Professor Albert Hopkins (brother of Mark Hopkins) with funds raised by the Society of Alumni. In 1925 Williams was the only major American college without any absolutely required courses and without any wide-option electives. In the fall semester of 1988 Williams introduced in each department at least one course taught as a tutorial, in which, typically, pairs of students meet weekly with the professor to discuss a paper, problem set, or work of art produced by one of the students.

Despite its remote location and its problems with funding, Williams College has, from the first, produced an impressive roster of graduates. Of the 455 students who received degrees during the administration of the college's first president, Ebenezer Fitch (1793–1815), 2 became U.S. senators, 13 became U.S. congressmen, 6 served as justices of the supreme court in their respective states, and 10 went on to teach in a college or a seminary. The twentieth century has included such renowned figures a lawyer Telford Taylor (chief U.S. prosecutor at the Nuremberg war crimes trials after World War II), Fred Wiseman (documentary filmmaker), William Bennett, former U.S. "drug czar" and editor of the best-selling *The Book of Virtues*), George Steinbrenner (owner of the New York Yankees), Fay Vincent (former baseball commissioner), Stephen Sondheim (lyricist for *West Side Story,* composer-lyricist for winning musicals, and 1984 Pulitzer Prize-winner for *Sunday in the Park with George*), and Elia Kazan (director of such Broadway classics as *A Streetcar Named Desire, Death of a Salesman,* and *Cat on a Hot Tin Roof,* and Academy Award-winning films *Gentleman's Agreement* and *On the Waterfront*).

Further Reading: Leverett Wilson Spring's *The History of Williams College* (Cambridge, Massachusetts: Houghton Mifflin, 1917) is a comprehensive treatment of the college's early history by an emeritus professor of English from Williams. Frederick Rudolph's *Perspectives: A Williams Anthology* (Williamstown, Massachusetts: Williams College, 1983) is a compilation of original documents relating to the history, growth, and character of the college by a 1942 graduate, who introduces each document and follows it with an editorial commentary. Frederick Rudolph's *Mark Hopkins and the Log* (New Haven, Connecticut: Yale University Press, 1956) is a biography of the college's third president, who held that position for 36 years.

—Diana d'India and Mary Elizabeth Devine

YALE UNIVERSITY
(New Haven, Connecticut, U.S.A.)

Location: New Haven, Connecticut, 80 miles northeast of New York City, 155 miles southwest of Boston.

Description: A private university enrolling approximately 10,760 students in undergraduate, graduate, and professional schools.

Information: Yale University
Office of Undergraduate Admissions
P.O. Box 1502A Yale Station
New Haven, CT 06520
U.S.A.
(203) 432-1900

Visiting: The university maintains a guide service for visitors to the campus. Tours are one hour and begin at Phelps Gate on College Street, between Chapel and Elm Streets. Call the Information Office at Phelps Gate at (203) 432-2300.

In March 1638, David Yale, the father of Elihu Yale for whom Yale University was named, was 23 years old and unmarried when he landed on the bank of the Quinnipiac River on Long Island Sound. Yale was in the company of people seeking a "new haven," the Founders of the New Haven Colony and trading post in New England. Among others, he was accompanied by his stepfather, Theophilus Eaton; his mother, Anne Lloyd Yale Eaton (daughter of Bishop Lloyd of Chester, England); his brother Thomas; and his sister Anne.

Theophilus Eaton, a staunch Puritan, had been a prosperous merchant in London, England, and was chosen the first governor of the New Haven Colony. Accompanying Eaton to New England was another eminent London merchant, Edward Hopkins (who married Anne Yale, Elihu Yale's aunt). Hopkins chose not to settle in New Haven, but rather in Hartford where he was repeatedly elected governor of the Connecticut Colony.

The leading spirit of the New Haven Colony was a graduate of Oxford, the celebrated Puritan and nonconformist, the Reverend John Davenport, vicar of St. Stephen's Church in London. As a nonconformist, Davenport challenged the rites and practices of the established Church of England (and the Crown) and was forced to seek safety in Holland, where he remained for three years. It was there that he worked out his theory for an independent Christian state, a plan which he shared with his devoted friend, Theophilus Eaton.

Davenport's plan for a Christian state led to the founding of New Haven with a group of followers, his former parishioners of St. Stephen's. His plan included a comprehensive system of education, to establish "schools for all, where the rudiments of knowledge might be gained; schools where the learned languages could be taught; a public library; *and to crown all, a College in which youth might be fitted for public service in Church and State.*" Ten years after the founding of the colony, the General Court in New Haven appointed a committee to find suitable grounds to set apart for a college.

Integral to the Davenport scheme was that "the worship of God should be the only rule for ordering the affairs of government in the commonwealth." This led to the General Court of New Haven establishing the mosaic law as the basis for its legal system. The vote, or franchise, as well as the right to hold office was restricted to church members referred to as "freemen."

David Yale was not chosen as a member of the church at New Haven. Indeed, the tension in the Eaton household under the uncompromising rule of the Puritan Theophilus, had caused his mother to break down. Her strange behavior led to public trials and she was excommunicated from the church. Dissatisfied with the condition of life in New Haven, David Yale moved to Boston, married, and was appointed attorney for the Earl of Varwick. Here, Elihu was born April 5, 1649, shortly after news arrived of the trial and execution of King Charles I of England.

While in Boston, David Yale joined with Dr. Robert Child, Samuel Maverick, and others in challenging the theocracy of Massachusetts law and policy which was as rigid and intolerant as that in New Haven. They presented a Remonstrance, or petition, to the General Court in May 1646 which declared that "the Colony had no 'setled forme of government according to the lawes of England'; that no 'body of lawes' secures them enjoyment of their lives, liberties and estates, and no settled rules of judicature provide due process; for which many are in fear of arbitrary government."

The Court felt that David Yale had been misled by the other rebels. He was fined £30. The leaders had stiffer fines and were imprisoned. In 1652, when Elihu was three years old, his family sailed for England and soon after David Yale established himself in London.

Meanwhile, the serious intention of the New Haven colonists to establish a college had suffered a setback. The colony was going through hard times. Samuel Maverick wrote of New Haven in his "Description of New England (1660):"

Yale University

This Towne is the Metropolis of that Government, and the Government took its name from this Towne; which was the first built in those parts, many stately and costly houses were erected the Streete layd out in a Gallant forme, a very stately Church; but ye Harbour not proveing Comodious, the land very barren, the Merchants either dead or come away, the rest gotten to their Farmes. The Towne is not so glorious as once it was.

In 1652, a college at New Haven was brought up and voted on at a meeting of the General Court for the Colony. It was thought "to be too great a charge" for the "jurisdiction to undergo alone; especially considering the unsettled state of New Haven Town; . . . But if Connecticut do join, the planters are generally willing to bear their just proportions for erecting and maintaining a College there." Three years later, the Reverend Davenport encouraged the town to pass a vote appropriating £60 a year for the proposed institution.

Davenport also wrote to his old friend, Edward Hopkins, the governor of Connecticut, to request his aid in carrying out the work. Hopkins had gone to England to settle the estate of his brother, but died in London in 1657. In his will he provided a large bequest, "for the breeding up of hopeful youths, both at the Grammar School and College, for the public service of the country for future times." His wife, Anne, who suffered a "mental distress" as her mother did, was put in the care of her brother David Yale, and survived her husband by 40 years.

By 1660, public documents of the time spoke of the foundations begun for the institution as the "college already begun." But further difficulties kept the Hopkins College in New Haven from ever rising above the level of a grammar school.

Davenport's hope for establishing a church state, with a college "where youth's might be fitted for public service," was further eroded in 1665, when the colonies of Connecticut and New Haven were united. Davenport opposed this union on the grounds that "all government should be in the church and all freemen must be members in full communion."

But in the Connecticut Colony, the church had less of a stronghold, because voting in town affairs was open to orderly persons who owned property and were "admitted inhabitants." So with all hopes of establishing a church-state removed, in 1668 Davenport accepted an invitation to take charge of the First Church in Boston. Two years later, he died from a stroke.

At the close of the seventeenth century, an attempt was made by Connecticut Congregationalists to preserve orthodoxy and a high standard of education in the ministry, by devising a plan for the establishment of a college by a general synod of the churches. The college would be called "the school of the church" and the churches would contribute to its support.

According to Charles Henry Smith, in his *History of Yale University,* the project failed. "But the following year," he wrote, "ten of the principal ministers of the Colony were nominated and agreed upon by common consent, both of the clergy and the laity, to be Trustees, to found, erect and govern a college. . . . Seven of these men were identified with towns of the old New Haven jurisdiction."

Smith further explained that "the most active man among the promoters of the new scheme," the one he refers to as the founder of Yale, was Reverend James Pierpont (Harvard 1681), upon whom "Mr. Davenport's mantle had fallen." Not only was he following in Davenport's footsteps as the pastor of the First Church in New Haven, his wife was Davenport's granddaughter.

A meeting of the ten clergymen, held in Branford in 1701, is regarded as the beginning of Yale College. Tradition states that each laid on the table a few volumes, saying, "I give these books for founding a college in this colony." In deference to three clergymen of the original Connecticut Colony, the New Haven men agreed "for the present" to locate the college at Saybrook, so that "all parts of Connecticut Colony with the neighboring colony may be best accommodated."

In October 1701, the legislature met in New Haven and granted a charter "to certain Learned & Orthodox men upholding & Propagating the Christian Protestant Religion . . . for the founding, *suitably endowing* & ordering a Collegiate School within his Magisties Colony of Connecticut wherein Youth may be instructed in the Arts and Sciences who through the blessing of Almighty God may be fitted for public employment both in Church and Civil State."

It should be noted that up until 1745, a majority of the graduates became clergymen. And until the twentieth century, an unbroken chain of rectors (later presidents) of the college, as well as trustees (later fellows) at Yale, were ministers of the "orthodox" church, namely, Congregational ministers from Connecticut.

The college depended on an annual grant from the colony's legislature and tuition fees from the few students. This was insufficient to pay the rector's salary, and so the rector was authorized to continue work as pastor in Killingsworth. In 1702, the first student, Jacob Heminway of New Haven, began studies at the rector's house in Killingworth. The commencement was held at Saybrook, where many of the college books were stored. Later students also studied at Killingsworth and a tutor was added to the staff.

By 1717, sufficient funds were raised for erecting the college building. Some trustees and patrons wanted the school to remain in Saybrook, and others wanted the building in Hartford, but the site chosen was New Haven. Following this decision, one tutor "established himself at once in New Haven, in charge of about a dozen pupils; the other, influenced by the Hartford Trustees, opened a rival school, with as many or more pupils in Wethersfield; . . . three or four pupils remained at Saybrook, under the care of a village pastor, a former tutor."

The college building was completed in 1718 in time for the commencement (torn down in 1782) and was built of wood. It was 170 feet long, 122 feet wide, and 3 stories high and stood facing College Street, near Chapel. It contained a library, kitchen, and 50 "studies," or rooms; in addition a dining hall extended across the building and was also used for prayers and public meetings. It cost about £1,000 sterling.

At the first public commencement in New Haven, the Collegiate School and building were named Yale College, to honor the primary benefactor, Elihu Yale. Meanwhile a rival commencement was held in Wethersfield. But the next year brought a reconciliation, with New Haven winning out.

Yale had made a fortune in private trade while serving as the governor of the East India Company's settlement at Madras. (His uncle, Governor Hopkins, had been a merchant with the East India Company.) Upon his return to London in 1699, he developed a reputation as a generous philanthropist, and later became active in the Anglican-dominated Society for the Propagation of the Gospel which was helping to fund American missionaries, particularly those to the Indians.

Shortly before commencement in 1718, new that Elihu Yale had donated books, paintings, and trunks of textiles reached the trustees. The estimated value was £800, and there were promises of more to come. This donation prompted the trustees to change the name of the Collegiate School to Yale College in time for the commencement.

Though Elihu Yale was reportedly elated, the people of Saybrook objected to the removal of the valuable collection of college books from their town. Over 800 volumes had been collected, largely though the efforts of Reverend Pierpont and Jeremy Dummer. The catalog of books included donations from Elihu Yale, and Sir Isaac Newton, who donated the second edition of his *Principia,* a copy of his book on optics, plus some Greek books. Additional donations were from the poet laureate Sir Richard Blackmore; Sir Richard Steele, the English essayist and playwright; Sir Francis Nicholson, the governor of Virginia; the British governor of the American Colonies, Sir Edmund Andros; as well as from the Society for the Propagation of the Gospel in Foreign Parts.

Disappointed at losing the college, the people of Saybrook were determined to hold onto the library. In the *History of Yale University,* Professor Charles Henry Smith reports on a demonstration in Saybrook:

The Governor and Council repaired to the scene of the disturbance, and ordered the Sheriff to take possession of the books. This he did, though not without encountering much resistance from the populace. To move the books to New Haven, it was found necessary to impress unwilling men, together with oxen and carts. During the night which followed this

exciting day, wheels were taken off the carts, and bridges were broken down on the way to New Haven, and worse than all, about a quarter of the books with many valuable papers disappeared and were never recovered.

An additional £100 in goods for the college was shipped out by Elihu Yale in February 1721 with assurances that an annual provision would take place after his death. However, when Yale died in July 1721, his will was contested, and his bequest to the college lost.

Along with endowing a foundation for one of America' great universities, many books Yale and the Society for the Propagation of the Gospel donated were of Anglican ideology which quickly bore fruit. The year following his death, the trustees of Yale College excused the rector of Yale, Reverend Cutler from further service following his declaration that he had converted to the Episcopal faith. The "dark cloud drawn over" their collegiate affairs was blamed on the library that been sent over. The next rector, Reverend Elisha Williams was inducted after giving "Satisfaction of the Soundness of his Faith in Opposition to Armenian and prelatical Corruptions."

The course of studies at Yale College in the eighteenth century was similar to the course followed at Harvard. Latin was the language of ordinary conversation. Greek, Hebrew, logic, physics, metaphysics, and mathematics were staples in a scholar's instructional program. Rhetoric, ethics, and theology were also mandatory.

Shortly before the American Revolution, while serving as a tutor at Yale, John Trumbull wrote a satirical poem entitled *The Progress of Dullness:* "And yet, how oft the studious gain, The dullness of a lettered brain; . . . And plodding on in one dull tone, Gain ancient tongues and lose their own."

Unfortunately, policies at the college under president Thomas Clap (1740–66) were also narrowly sectarian. During his tenure, men were trained for orthodox ministry, to the exclusion of other professions and callings. This led to an attempt by the Connecticut legislature to assert visitorial power over the college.

To keep the state out of Yale, the trustees appointed Ezra Stiles as president ; he placated the state by drafting a plan in July 1778 which would, according to John Whitehead in his *Separation of College and State,* "turn Yale from the narrow sectarian mold Clap advocated into a broadly useful institution." His plan was to move Yale from a college into a university, and he suggested that the state endow professorships of law and physics.

During the Revolutionary War, freshmen were moved to Farmington, and the sophomores and juniors to Glastonbury. The seniors remained in New Haven where a company of them were drilled on the green at New Haven by General George Washington. They escorted him "as far as Mill River" while he was on his way to take command of the American forces in Cambridge. Noah Webster (Yale 1778) led the company "with music." Yale men were also at Bunker Hill, and Captain Nathan Hale (Yale 1773) was chosen by Washington to spy within the British camp on Long Island. In July 1779 New Haven and Yale's college buildings were taken by the British.

At the beginning of the nineteenth century, Benjamin Silliman was appointed professor of chemistry and natural history at Yale College and served from 1802 to 1853. Silliman assured trustees of his loyalty to Congregational tenets. Studies of rocks, soil, water, wildlife, as presented by Silliman, stayed within the prescribed bounds of religious dogma, yet inspired scores of students to consider careers in botany, zoology, geology, and chemistry.

Silliman's students included Amos Eaton, the founder of the Rensselaer Polytechnic Institute, and inventor Eli Whitney. Another student, Othniel Marsh became the first professor of paleontology at Yale. His uncle, George Peabody, funded the Peabody Museum of Natural History which, completed in 1876, houses March's greatest memorial, the Dinosaur Hall.

In 1818, Silliman founded and became the first editor of the *American Journal of Sciences and Arts*. Ironically, scientific theories advanced by this publication challenged the rigid thinking of Christian orthodoxy, which held to the creationist theory. The scientific age was dawning and Silliman helped its advance.

The nineteenth century also brought fund drives and expansion to the college. Between 1701 and 1830 the college had received only about $145,000 in total gifts and grants. Yale launched its first major fund drive in 1832. Deficits were wiped out and more than $100,000 was brought into the treasury. That same year, the Trumbull Gallery was opened; it is considered the first art museum connected with an educational institution in America.

Money raised in 1835 was used to build a dormitory for theology students, and by 1846 a library building was completed at the cost of $34,000. The Old Library was in use from 1889 to 1931, now called Dwight Memorial Chapel in commemoration of two presidents named Dwight. 1856 brought a deed of property from Joseph E. Sheffield, for the use of the scientific school. His gifts, bequests for equipment, and endowments exceeded $1 million.

The bachelor of law degree was first conferred at Yale in 1843. By 1852, authorization was given to confer the degree of bachelor of philosophy, and the same year, a school of engineering was organized. In addition, the corporation voted in 1860 to establish the degree of doctor of philosophy as recommended by the faculty of the scientific school, "to retain in this country many young men, and especially students of Science who now resort to German Universities for advantages of study no greater than we are able to afford." In 1864 a professorship of modern languages was established, and the school of fine arts was opened to students in 1869. Yale became a university in 1872.

Meanwhile, growth continued: a master of arts degree was first conferred in 1876. And by 1892, the courses of the graduate department with the degree of Ph.D. was open to women; however it was not until 1969, that women were admitted as undergraduates.

As the nineteenth century drew to a close, many Yale alumni were among the entrepreneurs of the northeast, the rising industrial aristocracy of America. These alumni made it clear they wanted to see Yale move toward greater secular control, despite the belief that the Charter mandated that the president and fellows be Congregational ministers living in Connecticut.

Through a careful review of the revised charter of 1745, Simeon E. Baldwin, a professor of law at Yale discovered that the current charter made no reference to ministers, though the charters of 1701 and 1723 had. In 1881, he read a paper before the New Haven Colonial Historical Society, claiming that he "could find no necessity for either the President or another member of Yale Corporation being a clergyman." By 1910, the clergy lost their majority.

As Yale moved into the twentieth century, it experienced a brief decline in scholarship and a rise in extracurricular activities. Football, baseball, crew, and track were now rigorously disciplined. From 1872 to 1909 in soccer, rugby, and American football, the Yale teams ran up a record of 324 victories, 17 losses, and 18 ties.

The early 1930s brought the College Plan to Yale, a building boom which provided housing and dining facilities for all upper-classmen (freshmen live on the Old Campus), together with faculty offices, a master's house, and a library. The undergraduate residential college system was financed initially through a gift of Edward S. Harkness. Modeled after medieval English universities, primarily Oxford and Cambridge, today 12 residential colleges enable Yale to offer the intimacy of a small college environment as well as the vast resources of a major university.

Many other buildings constructed during this period were financed by John W. Sterling whose death in 1918 brought a bequest of $15 million for new buildings, new professorships, and other worthwhile causes. Through his generosity the Sterling Chemistry Laboratory, Sterling Hall of Medicine, Sterling Power House, Sterling Memorial Library, Sterling Law Building, Sterling Divinity Quadrangle, Sterling Tower, Sterling Quadrangle, and the Hall of Graduate Studies were built.

During Yale's 250th celebration, in 1951, *Newsweek* noted that Yale had "a world reputation for excellence." *Time* magazine was enthusiastic about "Yale's whole interlocking curriculum, where psychiatrists teach in the law school, physicists rub elbows with philosophers, engineers teach in the medical school. At 250 years, Yale is more than ever what it has taken pride in being—a teaching institution."

From 1950 to 1963, Yale's endowment jumped from $121 million to $375 million under the leadership of

President A. Whitney Griswold, and 26 buildings worth over $75 million were in process or completed when he died. The Yale of today, despite financial belt tightening, maintains its world-class reputation for excellence, while upholding (some would say "revelling in") tradition.

Further Reading: Hiram Bingham's *Elihu Yale, The American Nabob of Queen Square* (New York: Dodd Mead, 1939) is an authoritative biography that includes an outline of the Yale family involvement in New Haven and the college. *Yale, A Pictorial History,* by Ruben A. Holden (New Haven, Connecticut: Yale University Press, 1967) traces Yale from its beginnings in a small Connecticut farmhouse to the university of the late 1960s. A publication of the American Revolution Bicentennial Commission of Connecticut, *Connecticut's Seminary of Sedition: Yale College,* by Louis Leonard Tucker (Chester, Connecticut: Pequot Press, 1974) explores Yale's involvement in the Revolutionary era of 1763 to 1787. *Yale: A History,* by Brooks Mather Kelly (New Haven, Connecticut: Yale University Press, 1974) studies the survival of the college as a center for intellectual life. *School of the Prophets, Yale College, 1701–1740,* by Richard Warch (New Haven, Connecticut: Yale University Press, 1973) deals primarily with the religious dimensions of the school and the society surrounding it.

—Genevieve C. Fraser

INDEX

INDEX

Entries in **boldface** indicate article titles.

NOTES ON
CONTRIBUTORS

Adams, Bob. Freelance writer. **Essay:** University of Pennsylvania.

Bachin, Robin F. Assistant Professor of History, University of Miami, Coral Gables, Florida. Contributor to *American Cities and Suburbs,* edited by Neil Larry Shumsky (1977). Essay: University of Chicago.

Bernasconi, Andrés. Freelance writer. **Essay:** (with Daniel C. Levy) University of Chile.

Bonnigal, Dorothée M. Allocataire Moniteur Normalien, University of Burgundy, Dijon. Contributor to *Interfaces* and the edited collection of essays *The Southernness of Eudora Welty* (1995). **Essay:** École Normale Supérieure.

Bosworth, Marla G. Freelance editor and writer. **Essays:** Oregon State University; University of Melbourne.

Bracken, Jeanne Munn. Reference Librarian, Lincoln Public Library, Lincoln, Massachusetts. Author of *Children with Cancer* (1986), *The Shot Heard Round the World* (1994), and *Iron Horses across America* (1995). **Essays:** Boston University; Philipps University of Marburg; Uppsala University.

Brandano, Phyllis. Freelance writer. **Essay:** Northeastern University.

Carson, Justine H. Partner, Carson and Associates. Editorial Director, Institute for Scientific Information (1987–92). **Essay:** Barnard College.

Chapman, Richard Allen. Freelance writer. Contributor to *American Political Science Review.* **Essays:** Reed College; United States Military Academy at West Point.

Chepesiuk, Ron Joseph. Associate Professor, Head of Special Collections, Winthrop University, Rock Hill, South Carolina. Author of *The Palmetto State: Stories from the Making of South Carolina* (1992) and *Sixties Radicals, Then and Now: Candid Conversations with Those Who Moved an Era* (1995). **Essays:** Atlanta University Center; Chinese University of Hong Kong; (with Mary Elizabeth Devine) Emory University.

Chowdhury, Sharmishtha Roy. Graduate student in modern French history, Northwestern University, Evanston, Illinois. **Essays:** Aligarh Muslim University; Jawaharlal Nehru University; Tata Institute of Fundamental Research; Visa-Bharati University.

Conley, Kathleen M. Assistant Professor, Reference Librarian, Illinois State University, Normal. **Essays:** Cornell College; Tulane University; University of Illinois.

Coyle, Bill. Staff Assistant, English Department, Salem State College, Salem, Massachusetts. **Essays:** Massachusetts Institute of Technology.

Devine, Mary Elizabeth. Professor of English, Salem State College, Salem, Massachusetts. **Essays:** (with Ron Chepesiuk) Emory University; (with Frank M. Jossi) University of Minnesota; University of Virginia; (with Diana D'India) Williams College.

D'India, Diana. Graduate student, Weston Jesuit School of Theology, Cambridge, Massachusetts, and teacher of basic writing skills, Boston Center for Adult Education, Massachusetts. **Essays:** Amherst College; (with Mary Elizabeth Devine) Williams College.

Dubovoy, Sina. Freelance writer. **Essay:** Al-Azhar University.

Dupee, Junelle. Freelance writer, consultant, and photographer. **Essays:** University of Arizona.

Ellingson, Stephen. Freelance writer. **Essay:** Hebrew University.

Emery, Theodore A. Freelance writer. **Essay:** University of Rochester.

Farrow, Christine. Freelance writer and photographer. Author of *The Coordinator's Handbook: A Guide for High School-Based Community Service Programs* (1991). Contributor to *Friends Journal.* **Essays:** University of Canterbury; Wellesley College.

Fraser, Genevieve Cora. Playwright and writer. **Essay:** Yale University.

Garduno, José María García. Freelance writer. **Essay:** (with Daniel C. Levy) National Autonomous University of Mexico.

Gerber, Judith B. Business and technical writer. Contributor to *Global Industry Profiles* (1996) and *American National Biography* (1998). **Essays:** Bryn Mawr College; University of Southern California.

Gladfelter, Sandra. Freelance writer. Contributor to *Back Home in Kentucky* and *Bluegrass.* **Essays:** University of Bordeaux; (with Susan R. Stone) University of Paris.

Goodin, Vera-Jane. Freelance writer. **Essay:** University of Missouri.

Heenan, Patrick. Independent researcher and writer. Contributor to *International Dictionary of Company His-*

tories (1993) and *International Dictionary of Historic Places* (1995–96). **Essays:** Doshisha University; Harvard University; Keio University; Laval University; University of Cambridge; University of Durham; University of Leiden; University of London; University of Tokyo; University of Toronto.

Hollister, Pam. Freelance writer. **Essays:** Georgetown University; Oberlin College; Princeton University.

Holtkamp, Wolfgang. Assistant Professor of American Literature, University of Stuttgart. **Essays:** Albert Ludwigs University; Free University of Berlin; Ruprecht Karls University.

Horowitz, Marcia R. Editorial Associate, Center for Creative Leadership. Associate Editor, *Issues and Observations*. **Essays:** Duke University; Vanderbilt University.

Hoyt, Christopher. Freelance writer. **Essays:** Columbia University; Dartmouth College; Gallaudet University; Howard University; Northwestern University; United States Naval Academy; Washington University.

Hudson, Christopher. Editor, Fitzroy Dearborn Publishers. Editor of *The China Handbook* (1997). **Essays:** Cooper Union for the Advancement of Science and Art; University of the South; Willamette University.

Isles, Mary Jane. Graduate student in English, Slippery Rock University, Slippery Rock, Pennsylvania. Contributor to *Poet Magazine*. Editor-in-Chief of *Ginger Hill* (1988–90). **Essay:** Rice University.

Jack, Sybil. Freelance writer. **Essay:** University of Sydney.

Jossi, Frank M. Freelance writer. Contributor to *Los Angeles Times, Chicago Tribune, Newsday,* and *Minneapolis Star Tribune.* **Essay:** (with Mary Elizabeth Devine) University of Minnesota.

Kane, Patrice M. Head of Reference and Special Collections, Fordham University, Bronx, New York. **Essays:** City University of New York; Mount Holyoke College; University of Mumbai (Bombay); Vassar College.

Lamontagne, Manon. Assistant Director, National Film Board of Canada. **Essays:** École National d'Administration; École Polytechnique; Federal Institute of Technology; University of Orléans.

Lamontagne, Monique. Independent researcher and writer. Contributor to *International Dictionary of Company Histories* (1991) and *International Dictionary of Historic Places* (1995–96). **Essays:** McGill University; University of Toronto.

LaRue, Sherry Crane. Assistant Dean of Students, Humanities Division, University of Chicago. Contributor to *International Dictionary of Historic Places* (1995). **Essay:** University of Louvain.

Lee, Joseph Edward. Professor of History, Winthrop College, Rock Hill, South Carolina. Author of *An Oral History of Investigative Journalism in America* (1996). **Essay:** Washington and Lee University.

Levi, A.H.T. Freelance writer and independent scholar. Buchanan Professor of French Language and Literature, University of St. Andrews, Fife. Author of *French Moralists: The Theory of the Passions 1585–1649* (1964), *Religion in Practice* (1966), and *Guide to French Literature 1789 to the Present* (1992). Editor of *Erasmus: Satires* (1986). **Essays:** Prefatory Essay; Jagiellonian University; University of Pisa.

Levi, Claudia. Freelance writer. **Essays:** Georgia Augustus University of Göttingen; Ludwig Maximilians University of Munich; University of Cologne.

Levy, Daniel C. Freelance writer. **Essays:** College of Mexico; (with José María García Garduno) National Autonomous University of Mexico; (with Marcela Mollis) University of Buenos Aires; (with Andrés Bernasconi) University of Chile.

Maciuba-Koppel, Darlene. Freelance writer and marketing consultant. Author of *Telemarketer's Handbook* (1992)**. Essays:** Rutgers: The State University of New Jersey; State University of New York.

Margerum, Christine. Freelance writer. **Essay:** University of Granada.

Margerum, Edward S. Freelance writer. **Essay:** University of Aberdeen; University of Edinburgh.

McNulty, Mary. Freelance writer and editor. Editor, American Association of Law Libraries newsletter, 1988–93. **Essays:** Johns Hopkins University; St. John's College; University of Barcelona.

Mertz, Cindy. Research assistant, Wayne State University, Detroit, Michigan. **Essays:** Michigan State University; University of Salamanca; University of Seville.

Mollis, Marcela. Freelance writer. **Essay:** (with Daniel C. Levy) University of Buenos Aires.

Mundt, Michael. Freelance writer and editor. **Essays:** (with Fran Sherman) Brandeis University; Federal University of Rio de Janeiro; National University of San Marcos.

Nery, Sharon Messinger. Freelance journalist. **Essays:** University of St. Andrews; University of Vienna; Weizmann Institute of Science.

Newman, Robert S. Retired professor of anthropology. Author of *Grassroots Education in India: A Challenge for Policy Makers* (1989). Contributor to *Canadian and International Education.* **Essay:** Indian Agricultural Research Institute.

Noble, Bette. Freelance writer. **Essay:** Kyushu University.

Ogorek, Cynthia L. Historian, Washington and Jane Smith Home, Chicago, Illinois. Contributor to *Historical Encyclopedia of Chicago Women* (forthcoming). Managing Editor, *Creative Woman* (1989–91). **Essays:** Aarhus University; Loránd Eötvös University.

Olson, Antonella D. Senior Lecturer, Department of French and Italian, University of Texas, Austin. **Essay:** University of Florence.

Oswald, April A. Freelance editor and writer. English teacher, Hangzhou University, China, 1992–93. **Essay:** Beijing University.

Paterson, Anne C. Senior Editor, Ferguson Publishing, Chicago, Illinois. **Essays:** Illinois Institute of Technology; Purdue University; University of Oxford.

Phillips, Michael D. Freelance writer. **Essay:** University of Alcalá de Henares.

Picozzi, Michele. Principal, MP Creative Services. **Essays:** Smith College; University of Witerwatersrand.

Pittman, Ruth. Freelance writer. Author of *Roadside History of California* (1995). **Essays:** Antioch University; Case Western Reserve University; Ohio State University.

Price, Karen. Freelance editor and writer. **Essays:** College of William and Mary; University of Manchester.

Rees, Warren D. Freelance writer. **Essay:** University of Michigan.

Rillema, Beth A. Freelance writer. **Essays:** Brigham Young University; University of Notre Dame; University of Washington.

Rogoziński, Jan. Freelance writer. Author of *Pirates! Brigands, Buccaneers, and Privateers in Fact, Fiction, and Legend* (1995) and *A Brief History of the Caribbean: From the Arawak and the Carib to the Present* (1992). **Essay:** University of Iowa.

Sautter, Udo. Professor of History, University of Windsor, Ontario. Author of *Three Cheers for the Unemployed: Government and Unemployment before the New Deal* (1991). **Essay:** Eberhard Karls University of Tübingen.

Schoenberg, Robert P. Writing Instructor, Buffalo State College, New York, and Niagara University, New York; freelance translator and writer. Co-translator of *Moscow Racetrack,* by Anatoly Gladilin (1991). **Essays:** M.V. Lomonosov Moscow State University; New School for Social Research; University of Copenhagen.

Sherman, Fran Shonfeld. Freelance writer. Contributor to *Britannica Book of the Year* and other general reference works. **Essay:** (with Michael Mundt) Brandeis University; Technion—Israel Institute of Technology; Tufts University; University of Glasgow.

Shilakowsky, Carol. Freelance journalist. **Essays:** Charles University; Humboldt University; Leipzig University; Martin Luther University of Halle-Wittenberg; Strasbourg University; University of Wales.

Steffensen, Jan Bitsch. Freelance writer. **Essay:** Aalborg University.

Stone, Susan R. Freelance writer. **Essay:** University of Montpellier; (with Sandy Gladfelter) University of Paris.

Strickland, Charlene. Technical Editor, Science Applications International Corporation, Albuquerque, New Mexico. **Essay:** Claremont Colleges.

Sullivan, James. Freelance writer. **Essays:** Stanford University; University of California.

Sultan, Rosemarie Cardillicchio. Freelance writer. **Essays:** National University of Ireland; Radcliffe College; University of Cape Town.

Sutliff, Laura. Managing Editor, *Voice.* **Essay:** California Institute of Technology.

Taggart, Elizabeth. Writer, editor, graphic designer, and owner, Spark Communications. **Essays:** Seoul National University; University of Texas System.

Tegge, Jeffrey M. Associate Editor, *New Standard Encyclopedia.* Contributor to *International Dictionary of Historic Places* (1995), **Essay:** University of Coimbra.

Tew, J. Cameron. Freelance writer and journalist. **Essays:** Complutense University of Madrid; Guilford College; University of North Carolina at Chapel Hill.

Urbiel, Alexander. Freelance writer. **Essay:** Indiana University.

Voyer, Celeste A. Owner, M and J Marketing Services. **Essay:** Brown University.

Watts, Tim J. Humanities Bibliographer, Kansas State University, Manhattan. **Essays:** University of Aix-Marseille; University of Poitiers.

White, Lawrence William. Postgraduate researcher and writer, University of Dublin Trinity College, School of English. **Essay:** University of Dublin Trinity College.

Whitney, Carol. Lecturer in English, Tufts University. **Essay:** India Institutes of Technology.

Wilder, Joan. Freelance journalist and copywriter. **Essay:** New York University

Wilson, Melanie. Freelance writer. **Essays:** University of Siena; University of Valencia.

Wippel, Wendy Sowder. Research Biologist. Contributor to *Lancet* and *Journal of Bone and Joint Surgery.* **Essays:** The Citadel; Cornell University; University of Wisconsin.

PHOTOGRAPH ACKNOWLEDGMENTS

Aarhus University, 7
Al-Azhar University, 11
Albert Ludwigs University, 15
Amherst College, photo Amherst College Public Affairs Office, 22
Antioch University, 26
Barnard College, photo Barnard College Office of Public Relations, 35
Beijing University, 39
Boston University, photo Boston University Photo Service, 43
Brandeis University, 47
Brigham Young University, 52
Brown University, photo John Foraste, 57
Bryn Mawr College, 61
California Institute of Technology, photo Bob Paz, 65
Case Western Reserve University, photo Daniel M. Milner, 70
Charles University, 75
Chinese University of Hong Kong, 79
The Citadel: The Military College of South Carolina, 82
Claremont Colleges, photo Public Affairs, Pomona College, 95
College of William and Mary, 102
Columbia University, photo Joe Pineiro, 106
Cooper Union for the Advancement of Science and Art, photo Joel Greenberg, 113
Cornell College, photo Bob Campagna, 118
Cornell University, 122
Dartmouth College, photo Dartmouth News Service, 127
Duke University, 136
Eberhard Karls University of Tübingen, 141
École Nationale d'Administration, 145
École Normale Supérieure, 149
Emory University, 157
Federal University of Rio de Janeiro, 165
Gallaudet University, 170
Georgetown University, 174
Georgia Augustus University of Göttingen, 178
Guilford College, 182
Harvard University, 186
Hebrew University, 191
Howard University, 196
Humboldt University, photo Waltraud Harre, 201
Hunter College, City University of New York, 89
Illinois Institute of Technology, 206

Indiana University, photo Jerry Mitchell, 214
Jagiellonian University, photo Konrad K. Pollesch, 221
Jawaharlal Nehru University, 225
Johns Hopkins University, photo Office of News and Information, 229
Keio University, 234
Kyushu University, 239
Laval University, photo Renée Méthot, 242
Loránd Eötvös University, 250
Martin Luther University of Halle-Wittenberg, 257
Massachusetts Institute of Technology, photo MIT News Office, Donna Coveney, 261
McGill University, photo University Relations Office, 266
Michigan State University, 271
Morris Brown College, Atlanta University Center, 31
Mount Holyoke College, photo Office of Communications, 276
M.V. Lomonosov Moscow State University, 281
National Autonomous University of Mexico, 286
National University of Ireland, 289
New School for Social Research, photo Bob Adelman, 296
New York University, 301
Northeastern University, photo J.D. Levine, 305
Northwestern University, 309
Oberlin College, photo Rick Sherlock, 314
Ohio State University, 319
Oregon State University, 323
Philipps University of Marburg, 328
Princeton University, 331
Purdue University, photo Vincent P. Walter, 336
Radcliffe College, 340
Reed College, 345
Rice University, 350
Ruprecht Karls University, 354
Rutgers: The State University of New Jersey, 357
St. John's College, 361
Seoul National University, 365
Smith College, 369
Stanford University, 374
State University of New York, 380
Strasbourg University, 384
Tata Institute of Fundamental Research, 389
Technion—Israel Institute of Technology, 392

Tufts University, 396
Tulane University, 399
United States Military Academy at West Point, 404
United States Naval Academy, 409
University of Aberdeen, photo Sean Hudson, 413
University of Arizona, 424
University of Barcelona, 427
University of California, Berkeley, 437
University of California, Los Angeles, photo Terry O'Donnell, 440
University of Cambridge, 446
University of Canterbury, 453
University of Cape Town, 457
University of Chicago, photo P. Kàar, 461
University of Coimbra, 469
University of Cologne, 473
University of Copenhagen, 476
University of Dublin Trinity College, 481
University of Durham, 487
University of Edinburgh, 491
University of Glasgow, 499
University of Granada, 503
University of Illinois, 507
University of Iowa, 512
University of Leiden, 517
University of London, 523
University of Manchester, 534
University of Michigan, photo Bob Kalmbach, 540
University of Minnesota, 545
University of Missouri, 550
University of Montpellier, 554
University of Mumbai (Bombay), 559
University of North Carolina, 564
University of Notre Dame, 568
University of Orléans, 573
University of Oxford, 577
University of Paris, 581
University of Pennsylvania, 589
University of Pisa, 593
University of Rochester, 600
University of St. Andrews, 605
University of Salamanca, 608
University of Siena, photo Lensini Fabio, 616
University of Southern California, 620
University of Sydney, photo R. de Berquelle, 624
University of Texas at Austin, 633
University of the South, 637
University of the Witwatersrand, 643
University of Valencia, 657